PHOTO CREDITS

p. 2 © Gatewood, The Image Works; **p. 19,** © P. Vandermark, Stock Boston; **p. 25,** © E. Crews, Stock Boston; **p. 30,** © S. Takatsuno, The Picture Cube; **p. 38,** B. Schultz, Richmond Public Schools; **p. 38,** © D. Abramson, Stock Boston; **p. 41,** M. Rouke, Comm. Rel. Dept., Cleveland Public Schools; **p. 42,** © H. Frost, Frost Publishing Group, Ltd.; **p. 53,** © Y. DeBraine, Black Star; **p. 62,** © H. Hankin, Stock Boston; **p. 68,** © S. Goldblatt, Photo Researchers; **p. 77,** © M. Siluk; **p. 80,** © M. Heron; **p. 82,** © G. Portnow; **p. 90,** Wide World Photos; **p. 96,** J. Isaac, U.N.; **p. 104,** © B. Rios, Photo Researchers; **p. 118,** © M. Granitsas, The Image Works; **p. 134,** Wyoming Travel Comm.; **p. 140,** M. Rouke, Comm. Rel. Dept., Cleveland Public Schools; **p. 159,** Frost Publishing Group, Ltd.; **p. 170,** U.N.; **p. 178,** M. Rouke, Comm. Rel. Dept., Cleveland Public Schools; **p. 194,** © E. Crews, Stock Boston; **p. 220,** © V. Fish, Photo Researchers; **p. 238,** S. Skloot, Photo Researchers; **p. 244,** © R. Friedman, The Picture Cube; **p. 250, p. 257,** © E. Crews, Stock Boston; **p. 282,** © J-C. Lejeune, Stock Boston; **p. 301,** B. Schultz, Richmond Public Schools; **p. 313,** © G. Belleron, Stock Boston; **p. 330,** © S. Takatsuno, The Picture Cube; **p. 341,** © B. Barnes, Stock Boston; **p. 356,** M. Rouke, Comm. Rel. Dept., Cleveland Public Schools; **p. 375,** © D. Strickler, Monkmeyer Press Photo; **p. 384,** Wide World Photos; **p. 388,** © B. Powers, Frost Publishing Group; **p. 400,** © E. Crews, Stock Boston; **p. 402,** M. Rouke, Comm. Rel. Dept., Cleveland Public Schools; **p. 408,** © D. Strickler, The Picture Cube; **p. 447,** B. Schultz, Richmond Public Schools; **p. 449,** © F. Siteman, Stock Boston; **p. 472,** © B. Hrynewych, Stock Boston; **p. 479,** B. Schultz, Richmond Public Schools; **p. 484,** © M. Siluk; **p. 488,** © M. Siluk; **p. 495,** Girl Scouts of the USA; **p. 498,** © B. Rios, Photo Researchers; **p. 508,** © R. Sidney, Stock Boston; **p. 519,** B. Schultz, Richmond Public Schools; **p. 536,** © G. Portnow; **p. 548,** © U. Sjostedt, FPG; **p. 560,** © C. Fleischmann, FPG; **p. 580,** © G. Zucker, Stock Boston; **p. 585,** © G. Bellerose, Stock Boston; **p. 601,** © J. Myers, FPG; **p. 622,** Vt. Travel Div.; **p. 634,** © B. Daemmrich, Stock Boston; **p. 669,** S. Dimartini, U.N.; **p. 680,** © M. Reinhart, Photo Researchers; **p. 695,** © E. Crews, Stock Boston; **p. 703,** © M. Siluk; **p. 740,** © F. Siteman, Stock Boston; **p. 750,** © P. Jensen, Stock Boston; **p. 759,** © Phillips Photo Illustrators.

CONTENTS

PREFACE

Appropriate instruction makes a difference in the efficiency of learning in all types of educational settings. The purpose of this book is to improve instruction by helping teachers understand the realities of teaching, understand and organize relevant psychological theory, and become competent at tasks instructors perform.

The *Fourth Edition* has been thoroughly revised and updated to provide a comprehensive, current description of educational psychology and its application to teaching. We have edited with an eye toward providing a scholarly, authoritative knowledge base in a concise, readable, and *useful* text. In particular, we have revised and systematically reorganized the sections on classroom management and student motivation and on learning and instruction, and we have rewritten and considerably expanded the section on mainstreaming and special students. Our focus remains on the applications of educational psychology to K-12 *teaching*, but we also acknowledge the increasing importance of student variables.

Most educational psychology textbooks emphasize theories or topics isolated from one another and from the tasks of teaching. While teachers need to master psychological concepts and principles, the key to successful teaching is the *integration* of concepts into *teaching strategies* that are responsive to the learning needs of particular students. Effective teaching requires a fundamental understanding of how students learn and develop, and the ability to use this information to coordinate knowledge and skills in a specific context. To that end, this book is organized around applications designed to enable readers to become decision makers who can stimulate student learning. It is research-oriented, but with an eclectic attitude toward theory. No single approach can solve all problems teachers confront; an integration of ideas from a variety of viewpoints can provide the basis for successful instruction.

Our aim is to prepare future teachers for their jobs. Our approach to both learning and teaching is optimistic and humanistic, but we want our readers to recognize realistically the problems, constraints, and limitations in students, in classes, and in themselves. Through this realistic approach, students are prepared to face the challenges and rewards of teaching others.

Teaching Features

As in previous editions, this book includes features designed to enhance student learning:

Chapter Outlines allow students to familiarize themselves with upcoming content and to organize material for examinations.

Chapter Objectives describe what the reader will be able to do after mastering the material in each chapter.

Marginal Notes highlight information and make it easy for the reader to locate and go back to material.

Chapter Summaries provide concise reviews of material covered.

Questions and Problems can be used for class discussions, assignments, or independent study.

Case Studies end each chapter by describing provocative, true classroom dilemmas or problems in other settings relevant to each chapter.

Ancillaries

Standard ancillaries include a *Study Guide*, which contains questions (and answers) for reviewing each chapter and independent projects involving observation and experimentation; and an *Instructor's Manual*, which will help instructors in planning curricula and contains over a thousand test items arranged in test sets and unit exams, ideas for lectures and demonstrations, Study Guide Feedback Sheets, a film guide, and general resources.

In addition, the test items in the *Instructor's Manual* are available to users of the *Fourth Edition* in a *Computerized Test Bank*, which may be requested from the publisher.

Acknowledgments

We gratefully acknowledge the support provided by the Center for Research in Social Behavior, University of Missouri at Columbia, and the Institute for Research on Teaching, Michigan State University, as well as that of several individuals who helped us prepare the manuscript: Gail Hinkel, June Smith, and Teresa Hjellming. Many staff members at Longman also provided capable professional assistance, and we are particularly grateful to Naomi Silverman and Camilla Palmer.

FOURTH EDITION

EDUCATIONAL PSYCHOLOGY

A REALISTIC APPROACH

PART 1
INTRODUCTION

Jane Lawton, a junior at State University majoring in secondary education, had wanted to be a teacher since she was a junior high school student. Finally she had the opportunity to take teaching methods courses. Until now she had taken a range of arts and sciences courses—courses that she generally found interesting and important. She was excited that now she had the chance to combine her knowledge of content and teaching processes. She was worried, however, because she had received a phone call from her mother earlier that day informing her that both she and Jane's father were very ill with the flu and it was important for Jane to come home. Jane wondered how she could approach Harry Shelton, the professor who taught her Foundations of Education course, and how she could tell him she needed to miss the first course examination that was scheduled that day. Would he think she was conning him? She had a good grade now, and she didn't want to jeopardize that. However, she wondered what she would do if she were in that situation as a teacher. She thought, "Is it fair to extend extra time to some students but not to all; how does a teacher go about making exceptions?"

Bill Bowers was a twelfth-grade chemistry teacher at Newton High School. As he listened to Hank Sherman discuss an experiment, he wondered why Joe Rogers had difficulty in answering the question that he had just asked him. A few days ago Joe knew the material and Bill was puzzled as to why Joe did not retain the information. As he continued listening to Hank, he noticed that two students in the back of the room had started a conversation. He wondered if he should say anything to them to bring them back to the class discussion, but he decided not to do so because the conversation "appeared" as if it would be a short one, and Bill did not want to disrupt the entire class. As he continued to listen to Hank's response, Bill wondered what follow-up question he should ask, whether or not he had spent too much time in the lecture/discussion phase of the lesson, and if the class should begin laboratory work.

Ruth Mentor, a fifth-grade teacher at Casis Elementary School, noticed that Robbie Baker was extremely inattentive and doing poorly on her assignments since she had moved to the back of the room a couple of weeks ago. Ruth wondered if Robbie's poor performance was due to the fact that she had been moved away from her best friend for excessive talking, or perhaps because she was having trouble attending that far away from the teacher. Did Robbie need the extra structure and contact with the teacher that she had gotten when she was in the front of the room? Perhaps Robbie couldn't see the board or hear well from the back of the room. Ruth started to think about what she would do next in order to determine which of these possibilities was most likely. She was concerned about Robbie and wanted to get her back on track.

Tim Coleman was a seventh-grade math teacher at Jennings Junior High. He was teaching one of his favorite topics—converting base 10 to other number systems. This week he had been showing students how to convert a base 10 number system to base 2 and then to base 8. However, he was disturbed by the fact that most of the students seemed to be extremely bored with the material and assignments. He kept getting questions like, "Why do we have to study this stuff? We'll never use this in a million years." He lamented the fact that he had not been able to convey to the students the importance of the work that he was presenting.

Carolyn Lanier listened as Alice and Dick, two of her star pupils, complained after class about the exam that she had handed back that day. Alice said irritably, "That test was totally unfair. We spent 80 percent of our time the past three weeks on topics that were not covered on the exam. The material on which we spent only 20 percent of class time made up virtually the entire test! That's not a test, that's a guessing game!"

As we state in this chapter, teaching involves making many decisions and making them quickly. Some contend that teachers make more decisions, under worse conditions, than any other managers in society. Teaching is complex because it demands the ability to analyze carefully rapidly changing social and instructional interactions and to respond to a variety of issues simultaneously. Furthermore, successful teaching requires that teachers have a thorough understanding of human development, learning theory, instructional theory, motivational theory, and classroom management theory, as well as knowledge of how to assess student learning.

The vignettes here present dilemmas that teachers have to deal with in the classroom. For example, instructors must determine the extent to which social factors affecting students should be taken into consideration when making decisions about course requirements. Teachers must be fair to all students while at the same time being especially responsible to unique needs of individual students. For instance, the issue that Harry Shelton faces involves a type of decision teachers have to make every day.

To reiterate, as the Bill Bowers example shows, teachers must make many rapid decisions if they are going to be effective in the classroom. Teachers who are well organized, who know their subject matter, and who plan ahead (proactively understand what they are trying to do in the classroom) are more likely to be successful than teachers who lack the prerequisites for effective decision making.

As the example

involving Ruth Mentor and her student Robbie indicates, teachers often have to make subtle inferences about whether student difficulties are caused by developmental factors, motivational factors, or instructional factors. The first step in solving a problem is understanding the cause of a student's difficulty. Teachers who have better subject-matter backgrounds and who know how students learn and develop will have a fuller range of tools with which to assess student problems.

The Tim Coleman and Carolyn Lanier examples illustrate two enduring problems of classroom teaching. If teachers are to be successful they have to motivate students so that students are involved in and actively trying to learn assigned material. Teachers must develop evaluation systems that accurately and objectively measure student ability. These vignettes represent only a few of the issues that successful classroom teachers will have to deal with.

We believe that teachers can have a major, positive influence on the way students learn and develop. Some teachers are vital forces; others have only minor impact on their students. Teachers who have an impact on students' lives have a genuine interest in students and the ability to express that interest, know their subject matter, and possess detailed information about instructional processes and the ways students learn and develop. In this chapter, we will explore the knowledge and conceptual skills that are emphasized in this textbook. You will see that educational psychology can provide an important framework for looking at learners, the learning process, and the learning situation. The content of educational psychology—including an understanding of students' development and personality, the learning process, the psychology of teaching methods, classroom management, classroom motivation, and evaluation—offers important tools that can be utilized to become an effective classroom teacher.

CHAPTER

Classrooms, Teachers, Instruction, and Educational Psychology

CHAPTER OUTLINE

TEACHERS MAKE DECISIONS
Educational Psychology and Instructional Decision Making
Why Emphasize Decision Making?
Teacher Planning—The First Step in Decision Making
A Model for Decision Making
Decision Making: An Example

DECISION MAKING IS A CONTINUING PROCESS
Teachers Constantly Make Hypotheses
Appropriate Expectations

IMPEDIMENTS TO EFFECTIVE DECISION MAKING
Schools Are Busy Places
Schools Are Familiar, Stable Places
Pressure on Students to "Look Good"

EXTERNAL PRESSURES ON DECISION MAKING

INITIAL TEACHING EXPERIENCES
Student Teaching
The First Year

OBJECTIVES

When you have mastered the material in this chapter, you will be able to

1. List the component skills of teaching and explain how the study of educational psychology can help one become a successful instructor
2. Describe the relationship between theories and hypotheses and between teaching and decision making
3. Describe Good and Brophy's general model of teacher decision making, using a practical example
4. Explain how the common features of classrooms, noted by Doyle (1986a) and Jackson (1968), shape the task of teaching
5. Describe Shavelson's (1978) model of teachers' preinstructional decisions
6. Distinguish successful from less successful teachers on the basis of their expectations and attitudes toward students
7. Describe how the classroom environment, its routines, and the role expectations for teachers and students constrain teacher decision making
8. Describe ways that group pressure affects individual student performance

TEACHERS MAKE DECISIONS

Jan Reisch was irritated because class discussion wasn't going well, and she thought that few of the students had read the material. She was also upset and distracted by the minor but constant misbehavior of a few students. Finally, she responded: "Ralph Jordan, give Terri her pencil back and get in your seat now! You've been fooling around for two weeks! I've had it! For the next two afternoons, I want you to report to detention period." After class, Ralph came to her desk and said, "I'm sorry about being out of my seat playing with Terri. I know I've been a pain recently. I've had problems at home and . . . well, I don't want to talk about it." He hesitated a moment and then said, "Look, I'm genuinely sorry and I'll shape up, but I just started to work at a grocery store and I need to be there after school. I really need the job. Can we work something else out?"

Should Jan stick with her statement so as not to undermine her credibility with students? Should she compromise? (She could give Ralph a couple of days to rearrange his schedule with his employer.) If she cancels the punishment or provides a substitute, should she say anything to the class?

Bill Bower looked at fifth graders' test results on the math unit. Half of the class had less than 60 percent correct—a miserable performance. He asked himself, "Should I reteach this unit? It's an important one, but it's getting late in the year and I've only covered half the text. At this rate they won't be ready to do sixth-grade work. Maybe I should go on but assign some type of homework review."

Should Bill Bower reteach the unit? Are students having difficulty because the work is too hard for them or because of lack of effort? If he assigns homework but students still do relatively poorly, what then? Is the "sixth-grade curriculum" a relevant restriction on a fifth-grade teacher?

John Dalton paused and tried to think of a way to rephrase a question to help Helen answer. He believed that she really knew the material. However, Helen and two other students, Rick and Jeannie, were so shy that it was difficult to determine whether they didn't respond because they didn't know the answer or because they lacked confidence.

Should John ask Helen, Rick, and Jeannie easier questions than he asks other students? Or will this just increase their embarrassment? If they don't answer his first question, should he ask additional questions until they give a response? Or would such persistence only deepen their insecurity in public response situations?

As these vignettes indicate, teaching requires countless decisions, some of which need to be made on the spot. Teachers need to decide what to teach, how to present the material, and how to determine whether students understand and can apply it. Successful teachers use principles of educational psychology to make such decisions.

Educational Psychology and Instructional Decision Making

What is educational psychology?

Anyone who attempts to instruct others (e.g., not only classroom teachers but parents teaching children or instructors teaching managerial trainees) can benefit from knowledge of educational psychology and decision-making models. For example, a nutrition educator needs to determine the amount of information to present in one training session and the sequence in which to present it as well as what material students can master through self-study and how to design self-study units that will motivate learners to complete them successfully. Nutrition educators, like all educators, need to define their goals, determine criteria for meeting those goals, and assess conditions that will enhance learners' motivation to master the material. In this chapter the examples of decision making focus on classroom teaching; keep in mind, however, that the decision-making model is applicable to all instructional settings and teaching roles. Educational psychology provides a framework for looking at the student, the learning process, and the learning situation. The study of educational psychology includes the following areas:

- Educational objectives and instructional design
- Student development, personality, and aptitude
- The learning process
- The psychology of teaching methods (selecting, organizing, motivating, and presenting)
- Classroom management (preventing and responding to behavior problems, obtaining student cooperation, allowing students to assume appropriate responsibility for managing their own learning)
- Evaluation of results

Dembo and Hillman (1976) believe that good teaching requires mastery of three areas: (1) knowledge and conceptual skills (the content of educational psychology), (2) teaching skills, and (3) decision-making skills. Our goal in this book is to provide a format for integrating these three areas. Good teaching involves the integration of knowledge of teaching with knowledge of content and of students (Biddle & Anderson, 1986; Shulman, 1986) and, more broadly, the enactment of curriculum (Doyle, 1988).

Why Emphasize Decision Making?

Importance of decision making

Effective instructors know that the method of instruction used affects learning, so they apply principles drawn from the study of learning, motivation, development, and teaching to tailor their approach to the situation. We stress a decision-making approach to teaching because there is no simple formula for classroom success. Research yields valuable concepts and ways of looking at classrooms, not "answers."

Action-zone concept

For example, consider Adams and Biddle's (1970) finding that students who sit in the *action zone* (the middle front-row seats and the seats extending directly up the middle aisle) receive more opportunities to participate in class than do other students. The action-zone concept is important for analyzing classroom participation patterns. If Adams and Biddle's study were interpreted too literally, however, one might conclude that the action zone is always centered on the front row and the middle aisle. More recently, Alhajri (1981) studied thirty-two classrooms and found only one with an action zone that matched the pattern Adams and Biddle described. Alhajri found many classrooms in which a different kind of action zone was present. If observers had been monitoring these classes for only one type of action zone, they might not have perceived the action zones that were present but took a different form.

Structural elaboration versus personal elaboration

It is important to distinguish between two possible uses of research findings. Fenstermacher (1983) noted that sometimes research is used to generate answers or specific guidelines for how to teach, and he referred to this use as *structural elaboration*. A school district, for example, might urge teachers to teach in a specific way because of findings obtained in another school district. This approach often leads to the misapplication of research findings: What makes good sense in a rural district may not work as well in a suburban district. Similarly, what works well in seventh-grade math may be less effective or even counterproductive in second-grade math or seventh-grade history. Thus research findings should not be used for structural elaboration but instead for *personal elaboration*, to stimulate informed and thoughtful action. Good and Power (1976) also argued that the role of research in the social sciences is to make practice more reflective.

In this book we stress that theoretical principles and research findings provide a basis for planning and implementing instruction. Teachers, however, must act as independent decision makers when applying these general concepts and principles, keeping their particular students and goals in mind. The text provides information and introduces concepts that teachers can use to develop solutions to problems such as those that Jan Reisch, Bill Bower, and John Dalton faced. We see this text and the field of educational psychology generally as the systematization of information and concepts that help teachers to become more aware of classroom behavior, to interpret its significance (e.g., to understand the motivation that is associated with it), and to bring about desired changes in students.

Subject-matter knowledge versus action-system knowledge

Unfortunately, some teachers never become active decision makers or effective instructors. Some fail because they do not have adequate knowledge of the content they teach. Others, especially in elementary schools, know the subject matter but fail because they do not understand students or classrooms. Leinhardt and Smith (1984) distinguished between action-system knowledge and subject-matter knowledge. *Subject-matter knowledge* includes the specific information necessary to present content. *Action-system knowledge* refers to skills for planning the lesson, making decisions about lesson pace, explaining material clearly, and responding to individual differences in how students learn.

Teaching is combination of processes

Doyle (1988) argued that pedagogical processes are deeply embedded in issues of curriculum. For example, in most acts of teaching there are both general processes (providing explanations, asking questions) and domain-specific content knowledge (i.e., teachers ask questions about particular content). Doyle suggested that teaching is best viewed as ''curriculum enactment'' or the synthesis of curriculum content (materials, assigned task), pedagogical processes (teachers' presentational style), and classroom management (accountability, grading system). We, too, believe that teaching involves the orchestration of various types of knowledge and skills; to reiterate, however, the focus of this book is on action-system knowledge, and this knowledge needs to be combined with subject-matter knowledge and subject-matter pedagogy if teaching is to be successful.

This book presents knowledge that will help you to understand how students learn and develop, how classrooms can be managed, and how to present information, general concepts, and learning assignments effectively. This information will complement the subject-matter knowledge you gain in other courses by providing you with a knowledge of educational psychology—action-system knowledge that will help you to become a successful teacher.

The study of educational psychology and, more specifically, the material presented in this book will help you turn content knowledge (gained in other courses) into what Shulman and Sykes (1986) referred to as content pedagogical knowledge, or knowledge for teaching; that is, principles of educational psychology are useful for transforming subject-matter knowledge (e.g., concepts like gravity and density) into forms that students can comprehend.

Even with both action-system knowledge and subject-matter knowledge, however, some teachers may fail because they do not apply the knowledge they possess. Such teachers may have inappropriately low expectations for students' ability to learn or for their own ability to teach. Or they may not be active decision makers. Lacking an integrated set of theories and belief systems to provide a personal framework for informed decision making, they do not have effective strategies for organizing information gleaned from numerous, rapidly occurring classroom events.

In this chapter we introduce a model of classroom decision making that illustrates that teachers who make good decisions (and who are willing to correct poor ones) are most likely to foster student motivation and learning. After presenting a decision-making model, we discuss a few problems that almost all teachers must solve if they are to make good decisions. Finally, we discuss some of the special problems that beginning teachers face.

Teacher Planning—The First Step in Decision Making

Teaching plans and theories

Teachers must be able to develop a variety of plans (for daily lessons, weeks, units, and semesters) (Clark & Peterson, 1986). McDonald (1965) stated that any teaching plan is (1) a guide for action, (2) a set of decisions, and (3) a small theory about how to produce learning. We all use personal theories (systematic sets of beliefs) to make decisions. For example, we have theories about how to maximize our chances of making a good impression in a conversation. Some of us believe that listening is the best strategy; others prefer to take the initiative. Our theories, whether or not we make them explicit to ourselves, guide our behavior in conversations with new acquaintances.

Gage (1963, pp. 94–95) presented the view that all persons are theorists this way: "They differ not in whether they use theory, but in the degree to which they are aware of the theory they use. The choice facing the man in the street and the research worker alike is not whether to theorize but whether to articulate his theory, to make it explicit, to get it out in the open where he can examine it. Implicit theories . . . are used by all of us in our everyday affairs."

Common beliefs and assumptions

Many beliefs that are common among teachers turn out to be myths when subjected to systematic study. For example, the view that frequent teacher praise of student performance facilitates achievement has been shown to be false. Selective praise is useful, but excessive praise may interfere with learning. Also, the timing and quality of praise are generally more important than its frequency (see Brophy, 1981). Such complexities, even about seemingly obvious matters, illustrate why teachers must continually think and make decisions. Research does not yield simple answers like "praise is always good."

Educational psychologists develop explicit assumptions about the conditions that facilitate learning and then collect data to verify or refute these assumptions. Some readers probably raised a puzzled eyebrow upon reading the previous sentence. They prefer the facts—"Just tell me what works; that's all I want to know." Unfortunately, if we were to restrict ourselves to a discussion of what *always* works, we would end the book here. No teaching strategy will work for all students, goals, or settings. However, some teaching behaviors have high probabilities of bringing about desired responses. For example, correcting a minor disturbance nonverbally (with perhaps a shake of the head) is usually, but not always, more efficient and less disruptive than a verbal strategy. Similarly, preventing behavioral problems is more effective than correcting students after misbehavior has occurred (Doyle, 1986b). The study of educational psychology provides a way of formulating hypotheses about effective classroom strategies.

Hypotheses

Strategy decisions are based on hypotheses about what will work. *Hypotheses* are simply intelligent guesses based on all available information. The more information we have, the more confident we can be. The less information we have, the greater the risk that our strategy will fail. One may hypothesize, for example, that an attractive stranger is "dateable" because there is no ring on the "key" finger. However, many married people do not wear wedding rings because the ring is lost, is too small, or irritates the skin.

Teaching decisions and goals

Decisions about teaching strategies operate in the same way. Often one must make a decision ("Will my students integrate ideas better if I require them to prepare for a formal exam or if I assign a take-home exam on this new topic that I am teaching for the first time?") using only minimal knowledge. Other decisions can be based on considerable knowledge—research, past experience with students—but still with the risk that the strategy will not work. If we are explicit about our teaching goals and about what we will accept as evidence that students are making satisfactory progress, we can identify poor hypotheses and change teaching plans. Some decisions can be made through better use of our own time and resources (e.g., talk to students who are having difficulty and attempt to see the problem from their perspective), but others can be made only after obtaining information from other teachers or parents (Rosenholtz, 1989).

A Model for Decision Making

Instructional goals

Figure 1.1 presents a model for decision making. It suggests that intelligent decision making begins with a clear statement of instructional goals. Teachers need clear goals, ordered according to their relative importance, if they are to make optimal use of classroom time and resources. However, it is impossible for teachers, especially beginning teachers, to be explicit about all decisions. For example, a new third-grade teacher who observed in a first-grade classroom during an early field-experience course and then student taught in a sixth-grade classroom must make decisions about how much structure nine-year-olds need and identify key third-grade mathematics objectives and how they can be presented in an interesting fashion.

Thus, as Figure 1.1 suggests, teachers must form hypotheses and make many decisions about how best to arrange learning tasks so that students will make good progress. First, given all of the possible content (e.g., understand how a bill becomes a law) and general learning goals (e.g.,

Figure 1.1 Good and Brophy's General Decision Model

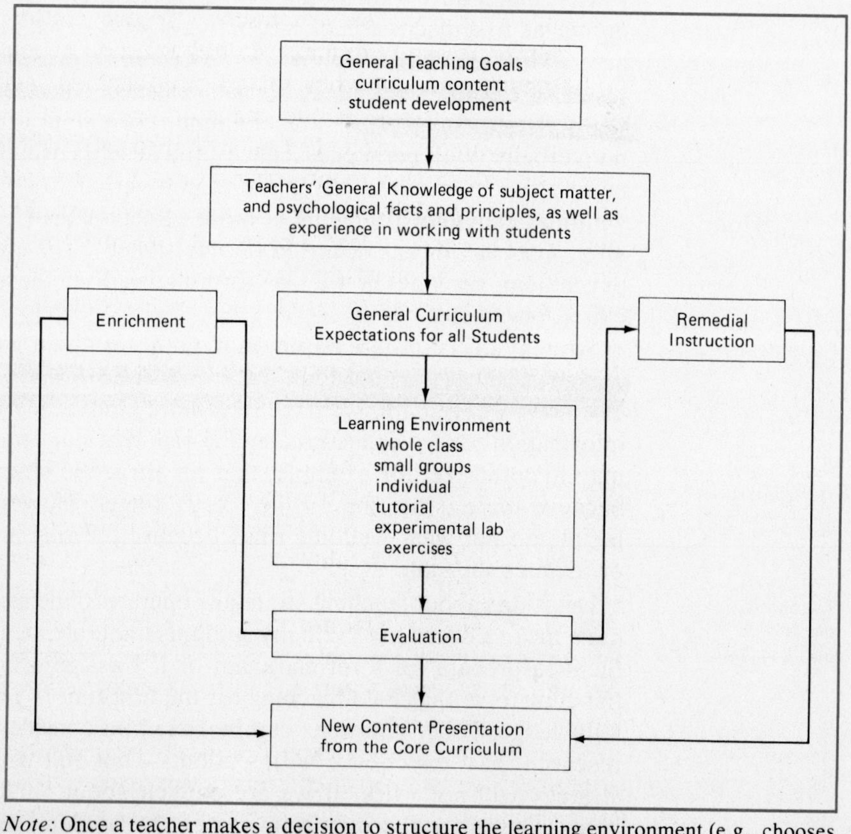

General Teaching Goals
curriculum content
student development

Teachers' General Knowledge of subject matter, and psychological facts and principles, as well as experience in working with students

Enrichment

General Curriculum
Expectations for all Students

Remedial
Instruction

Learning Environment
whole class
small groups
individual
tutorial
experimental lab
exercises

Evaluation

New Content Presentation
from the Core Curriculum

Note: Once a teacher makes a decision to structure the learning environment (e.g., chooses to use a whole-class or small-group format), it is possible to produce more explicit models of decision making.

Source: T. Good and J. Brophy, "Teaching the Lesson," in R. Slavin, *School and Classroom Organization* (Hillsdale, NJ: Lawrence Erlbaum, 1988). Reprinted by permission.

help the student to learn skills for self-evaluation), teachers must use their knowledge about curriculum goals and student development and performance to select goals that are reasonable for students in particular classes. Then teachers must determine to what extent students need to master core curriculum content (and at what level—80 percent, 95 percent) and develop procedures for dealing with students who fail to meet these goals initially (i.e., remedial programs) as well as have viable plans for students who quickly master core material (enrichment).

Teaching is sufficiently complex that teachers can never gather all of the information they would like to have and then make decisions in a leisurely fashion. Because of lack of time, teachers must depend on routines, heuristics, and other strategies to simplify information processing (Bromme & Brophy, 1986). For example, they often have time to ask only three or four students to respond and thus must make inferences about whether other students have mastered material. Later in the chapter we illustrate other factors that hinder teachers' ability to make decisions. However, despite these problems, successful teachers behave in a deliberate, reflective way whenever possible.

Decision Making: An Example

Assume that Ted Wilson, a high school speech teacher, wants his students to develop the ability to make skillful extemporaneous speeches. This is his ultimate goal. But when should Ted teach this skill—early or late in the year? How can he decide (make a hypothesis)?

Goals and goal statements

To make this decision, Ted must first specify the other goals he has in mind (e.g., the ability to introduce a speaker; to deliver a formal, informative speech; to deliver a formal, persuasive speech; to make an extemporaneous speech; to lead a committee discussion; and to conduct interviews). Next, he must define his goals more explicitly. What does he mean by "the ability to introduce a speaker"? That the student will be able to deliver with ease a brief introduction that someone else has written, or that the student will be able to write and deliver appropriate introductions for different types of audiences (such as audiences who are hostile, neutral, or supportive toward the speaker)?

Scheduling class work

After defining what he wants to accomplish, Ted will be in a better position to estimate the time it will take to fulfill each goal. If he determines that the ability to deliver a formal, informative speech is his most important goal, he probably should introduce informative speeches early in the year. This will enable each student to present several such speeches and to improve in response to Ted's feedback. In contrast, if interview technique is relatively unimportant, he may want to schedule it toward the end of the year, where it can be eliminated if some units take more time than anticipated.

Pretesting

After becoming more explicit about their goals, teachers may want to evaluate their students' entering achievement through pretesting. For Ted, this might mean having everyone make a one-minute, ungraded presentation to the class. Even from brief performances, Ted can gain valuable information about the general ability of the class and predict how fast he can proceed in the course. Furthermore, he can identify students who are likely to make excellent presentations and use this information profitably when he arranges the order of speakers for the first assignment.

DECISION MAKING IS A CONTINUING PROCESS

Student feedback

Even without such preliminary evaluation information, teachers can start making instructional decisions based on their understanding of general learning principles, instructional methods, and knowledge acquired from past experience with students. However, they must evaluate the wisdom of their initial decisions regularly by using the feedback (student comments, observation of student behavior) from day-to-day teaching activities and from formal evaluation (classroom tests, themes). Hence goals or strategies may change in a class as new information is gathered. For example, teachers may see that some students have already mastered certain objectives, so they can replace these objectives with new ones. Conversely, teachers may realize that they cannot reach some of their instructional objectives. Thus, as suggested by Figure 1.1, evaluation is an important and continuous aspect of teaching.

Plans and objectives

The system we describe here is active and dynamic. Teachers make *plans* based on their professional judgment, the policies of the schools in which they teach, and their students' characteristics. Once *objectives* are set, effective teachers monitor student progress and alter instruction as necessary. It is important to monitor student progress closely, not only because some tasks may be learned more quickly than others but because students may interpret teacher behaviors and class assignments in different ways (Wittrock, 1986), and some will develop misunderstandings that will need to be corrected. Good teachers are open to the possibility that lessons or units that have worked in the past may be less successful generally or with certain students in the present class.

Logical sequencing

Teachers' plans are influenced not only by the relative importance of various instructional objectives but also by their *logical sequencing*. Some objectives involve skills that must be mastered first as prerequisites (e.g., students need to learn subtraction before tackling division).

In Ted's speech class, the simplest task is the introduction of a speaker. This task contains key elements common to all other tasks (assumption of leadership role, public utterances, and so on), but it is more structured, is briefer, and requires few memory or timing skills. The limited scope of this task, its minimal anxiety-arousal properties, and the high probability that students can complete it successfully combine to make it a good first presentation.

Task analysis

Task analysis, the attempt to find logical starting and connecting points in sequencing instruction, is an important activity. In this particular example, with relatively mature high school students, Ted could probably start with any of the goals. There is no critical starting point, as there often is with more sequentially organized subject matter. Still, some arrangements would be more efficient than others.

In addition to goal and task analysis, *information about students*—their general aptitudes, their interests, and other learner characteristics such as achievement motivation or anxiety—is essential for making effective instructional decisions. Concepts of intelligence (e.g., Sternberg, 1984; Sternberg & Wanger, 1986a, 1986b) and motivation (e.g., Ames & Ames, 1984, 1985) are useful in making instructional decisions. For example, if most of Ted's students are highly capable, he may decide to start the course with challenging assignments and move along at a rapid pace. If his students are less capable, he may initially decide to cover fewer skills and move at a slower pace so that students can review key skills frequently. He may also spend some time in gamelike activities to maintain student interest and to allow him to build student interest to the point where he can increase the pace and level of difficulty of assigned work. If the class has a wide range of abilities, he may choose other strategies. Motivation can be conceptualized in various ways, and it is important to adjust the motivational focus to the students and the task (Brophy, 1987). Teachers who see student ability as fixed (compared to teachers who see it as flexible) are less likely to assign novel and challenging tasks to students perceived as low in ability and are less likely to teach these students active metacognitive strategies for controlling their own learning (Weinstein & Mayer, 1986).

It is possible to develop more specific models depicting different types of teacher decisions. Figure 1.2, based on Shavelson's (1978, 1983) work, illustrates how teachers make preinstructional decisions and shows some of the factors involved in planning instruction.

Teachers possess much information about students from observations of previous class performance, standardized test scores, and reports from

Figure 1.2 Some Factors Contributing to Teachers' Preinstructional Decisions

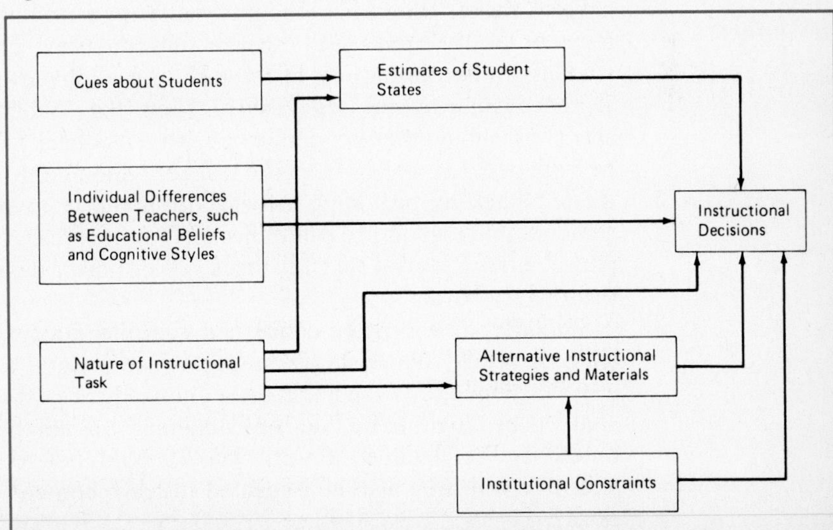

Source: Adapted from a paper presented at the 1978 American Educational Research Association meeting, Toronto, March, by Richard J. Shavelson and reprinted with his permission.

other teachers. Teachers make judgments about what students can do, what they are interested in, and so forth. Such information can improve instructional planning *if teachers use it appropriately*. Sometimes teachers—especially when dealing with special education students—focus too much on students' reputations or backgrounds rather than on *what these students can do* (Brantlinger & Guskin, 1987).

Teaching goals

Teachers also have personal beliefs about the purposes and nature of instruction that vary widely and affect instructional decisions in many ways (Clark & Peterson, 1986). Teachers interested in affective goals (how students *feel* about content, themselves, and others), for example, are likely to consider different instructional strategies than teachers who are more interested in cognitive goals (subject-matter knowledge). Teachers who emphasize affective goals may group students frequently and allow them to work cooperatively (Slavin, 1984; Slavin et al., 1985). In contrast, teachers who want to maximize cognitive growth may individualize the curriculum and encourage students to learn at a rapid pace.

Shavelson's model (see Figure 1.2) suggests that the nature of instructional tasks is another source of influence on instructional decisions. At present there is a great deal of research interest in the possibility that different types of teaching may be needed in different subjects (Doyle, 1988; Shulman, 1986). Particular texts or curricula will orient the teacher toward certain instructional strategies, activities, assignments, or cues to student progress and away from others. Again, teachers who are aware of how they make decisions and who monitor progress toward their goals will be more effective than teachers who operate with vague theories.

Teachers Constantly Make Hypotheses

Analyses indicate that teachers have to make complex decisions rapidly and under adverse conditions. Consider a few of the decisions Ted will have to make. When his students make their presentations, should the focus be on the entire skill (speaker introduction), or is it better for the students to do only a part of the task (e.g., deliver an effective opening sentence that avoids triteness)? When the students complete their speeches, should they get public or private feedback? Should the feedback be from peers as well as from the teacher? Should the teacher systematize the feedback by providing a form, or should it be spontaneous? When students make good presentations early in the year, should they receive praise, just matter-of-fact feedback, or criticism designed to encourage them to try harder?

Similarly, Ted must be concerned with the student audience and their learning needs. When should students read about a topic before hearing a speech about it? When might prior knowledge be a disadvantage? Should students be taught to be "active listeners"? Should they be taught to take notes (see Weinstein & Mayer, 1986)? Should they focus only on critique skills, or will they also be expected to learn content from the presentations?

Day-to-day decision making

The decisions discussed so far are ones that teachers can make before instruction and student performance. Many decisions, however, have to be made on a day-to-day basis. Suppose that five students are talking quietly but persistently in the middle of the room as George shakily delivers his first extemporaneous speech. Should Ted stop the disturbance, reassure George, and then allow him to continue? Or should Ted wait until the speech is over? What if several students do not participate in the feedback discussions that follow each presentation? Should Ted ask these students to outline speeches as they listen to them? Should he call on reluctant students directly rather than allow participation in the discussion to be voluntary? Now assume that students are performing a new speech skill and that the first two students do poorly. Ted suspects that the students have misunderstood the assignment. Should he continue with the next three presentations planned that day? What other options does he have? Another day, Ted decides to allow students, for variety, to analyze presentations in small groups. However, the groups engage in little substantive exchange. Should he continue with the small groups, perhaps after giving more guidance about what he expects? What information does he need to make the decision?

The psychological concepts presented in this text are useful tools for assessing classroom behavior and making on-the-spot decisions. If teachers can see and analyze problems as they occur, they can make appropriate modifications immediately or the next day rather than delaying until they can collect formal evaluative information (perhaps a week or two later). Teaching experience and insight into the teaching-learning process provide a base for making intelligent decisions about the design of instruction, but it is equally important that the teacher examine day-to-day instructional processes to be sure that learners are making progress. Research on teacher planning has shown that most teachers do not monitor their day-to-day activities in terms of general instructional goals (Clark & Yinger, 1979).

Examination of assumptions

Effective teachers must be aware of the implicit assumptions they hold with regard to how learners make progress and must periodically reexamine these assumptions. To accept a strategy as "the truth" regardless of its effect on learning is blind faith, not careful thinking and creative adaptation. Indeed, a procedure that has worked for five consecutive classes may prove to be ineffective for the sixth class.

Appropriate Expectations

To function as decision makers, teachers must believe that they can make a difference—that they can be effective in the classroom. Teaching skills and knowledge are important, but if a teacher is not motivated to use them consistently, little will be accomplished.

Effective Teachers

Brophy and Evertson (1976) provided an interesting description of how relatively effective and ineffective teachers see themselves. They reported that the most pervasive differences between teachers who enabled students to make good learning gains and less effective teachers were in the teachers' basic role definitions. Successful teachers saw teaching as an interesting and worthwhile challenge that they approached by assuming personal responsibility for the learning of their students. These teachers saw problems but believed that the problems could be overcome and were therefore motivated to search for solutions. Less successful teachers saw teaching as merely a dull job. They were likely to respond to problems by giving up because they did not assume personal responsibility for students' learning. Such teachers discussed problems as if they were too serious to be solved, and their behavior often guaranteed that the problems would remain unsolved. They did not believe that they could make a difference, and therefore they did not. Positive expectations alone are not sufficient to ensure teaching success, but without them no teacher will be effective in the classroom.

Brophy and Evertson also observed that teachers who reported a sense of inner control and personal responsibility clearly reflected this in their classroom behavior. More successful teachers were prepared to work with slow students, helping them to overcome failure by reteaching and providing extra practice.

Realistic attitudes

Successful teachers held realistic attitudes toward students. They liked them and enjoyed interpersonal interaction with them but mostly within teaching-learning contexts. Less successful teachers tended to fall into one of two groups, both of which represented extreme responses to students. One group romanticized students as warm and wonderful. These teachers concentrated on their personal relationships with students, often to the point of failing to manage the classroom effectively or to meet the students' instructional needs. Such teachers' expectations were unrealistic, and their behavior, despite its warmth, was inappropriate because it met their own needs rather than the needs of their students. The second group of unsuccessful teachers was disillusioned and bitter, looking upon their students as enemies.

Successful teachers see themselves as instructors and problem solvers rather than as parent substitutes or disciplinarians. Their goal is to design educational environments that work—to help students learn and not to accept classroom problems and student limitations as unchangeable. This requires facing problems and working toward their resolution. Researchers have also found that teachers' efficacy perceptions (Can I teach? Can I make a difference?) as well as their attitudes toward students' learning capacities can affect classroom learning (Ashton & Webb, 1986; Gibson & Dembo, 1984; Rosenholtz, 1989).

IMPEDIMENTS TO EFFECTIVE DECISION MAKING

We have stated that teachers who have teaching skill, knowledge of the learning process, and a "can do" attitude can make a major impact on learners. Teachers do not always make decisions independently, however. Many decisions are influenced by the behavior of previous teachers or by parents, students' peers, and school policies. For example, Schwille and associates (1983) showed that teachers' views of what to teach in an elementary school mathematics course are influenced not only by what they believe to be important but also by what is required by district or school policies.

Assumptions about students

Some instructional decisions are not made in a conscious, deliberate way, often because teachers simply do not see a problem. One teacher may view a pupil as pleasant, capable, and hard working, whereas another teacher might realize that this student is anxious and excessively dependent on teachers, performing capably because he or she is a compulsive worker and socially withdrawn, seldom engaging in conversations with peers. If teachers are unaware of such problems, the decisions they make about handling the students will be less than optimal. Careful monitoring of one's teaching behavior and periodic reexamination of assumptions about individual students or instructional strategies help to reduce errors and to minimize their effects.

Unexamined ideas

Teachers frequently make decisions on the basis of enthusiastic allegiance to an idea that has never been carefully examined. The open school, for instance, where students presumably have more opportunity to select and evaluate learning tasks, became an all-embracing answer to some educators who did not see that such an environment might be more compatible with the needs of some students than others. To other teachers, the self-contained classroom featuring instruction from one teacher and an emphasis on basic skills is the universal solution. These teachers do not see that some students can be stifled by too much structure. However, there is growing awareness that the quality of classroom organizational structure—the way it is implemented—is much more important than the form (Cuban, 1983; Good & Biddle, 1988; Marshall & Weinstein, 1984).

We now turn to some of the factors that make it hard for teachers to be active decision makers. These factors operate in most classrooms, although the form of a problem may differ from classroom to classroom.

Schools Are Busy Places

Limited time

Classroom settings impose constraints on what can and cannot be accomplished. Whether teachers instruct the whole class, divide the class into three or four groups, or allow students to work individually, they have limited time for one-to-one contact with students. Teachers must therefore decide which students to interact with and under what circumstances.

Teachers are best viewed as managers making executive decisions in a fast-paced environment (Berliner, 1983). As managers, teachers have a

Interaction among teachers creates a better learning environment.

"doable" but difficult job. Philip Jackson, in his book, *Life in Classrooms* (1968), provided a view of what school is like in the following passage:

> School is a place where tests are failed and passed, where amusing things happen, where new insights are stumbled upon, and skills acquired. But it is also a place in which people sit, and listen, and wait, and raise their hands, and pass out paper, and stand in line, and sharpen pencils. School is where we encounter both friends and foes, where imagination is unleashed and misunderstanding brought to ground. But it is also a place in which yawns are stifled and initials scratched on desktops, where milk money is collected and recess lines are formed. Both aspects of school life, the celebrated and the unnoticed, are familiar to all of us, but the latter, if only because of its characteristic neglect, seems to deserve more attention than it has received to date from those who are interested in education. (pp. 4–5)

Limited resources

Jackson reminded us that classrooms guarantee that there are crowds, as well as frequent and pervasive evaluations. Large groups of students are under one teacher's direction and share limited resources, so the life of an individual student is filled with interruption, delay, denial, distraction, and boredom. No matter how teachers behave or what characteristics they possess, they have to deal with these inherent characteristics of classrooms that will affect their decisions.

Jackson (1968) reported that teachers commonly engage in as many as a thousand interpersonal exchanges each day. When teachers talk with individual students they must do so with only partial attention, because they must also monitor the class and respond to general problems at the same time. They get to know some students much better than others. When they respond to students' questions and behavior, they do so partly on the basis of what they have just witnessed and partly on the basis of their previous interactions with these students and the general expectations they hold for them.

Thus teachers may interpret an ambiguous expression such as a puzzled look as evidence of thinking when it appears on the face of a high achiever but as evidence of confusion on the face of a low achiever. The decision is rapid and has immediate consequences—the teacher pauses and waits for the "thinking" student to answer but asks another student to help the "confused" peer. Teachers may misinterpret an expression or give up too soon on a student because they must make almost instantaneous decisions. It is impossible to interpret correctly everything that occurs in a short time, so they must learn to observe selectively and to monitor key aspects of their interaction with students.

Teachers not only have to explain concepts and demonstrate skills, they also have to monitor students for apparent understanding and provide feedback to students' responses. Furthermore, they must do this within a classroom context where they must maintain pupil attention, respond to interruptions, and move through activities at an appropriate pace. Consequently, teachers' interactive decision making usually cannot involve much deliberation about alternative courses of action. Instead, like other skilled individuals required to make expert decisions in complex situations, teachers build up systematic routines and rely on heuristics (implicit rules that people use, without conscious awareness) to reduce the complexity of the classroom (e.g., Shavelson & Stern, 1981).

Heuristics

Routines are standardized methods for proactively organizing and delivering instruction and for responding to common problems. In subsequent chapters we provide detailed information about developing routines for classroom management, classroom planning, and evaluating student performance. In addition to relying on routines, teachers also use *heuristics*—rules of thumb for making sense of their environment and making decisions in complex situations (Bromme & Brophy, 1983; Tversky & Kahneman, 1974). To the extent that you develop routines and heuristics that are consistent with the principles discussed in this book, you are likely to make effective decisions in the classroom.

Schools Are Familiar, Stable Places

Despite the complexity of classrooms, some enduring aspects of schools allow stable predictions and thus make it possible to develop routines and shared assumptions that allow teachers to act as decision makers. Doyle (1986) argued that classrooms have the following stable features:

Classroom features

1. *Multidimensionality:* Many different tasks and events occur in the classroom. Records and schedules must be kept, and work must be monitored, collected, and evaluated. A single event can have multiple consequences. Waiting a few seconds for one student to answer a question may support that student's motivation but reduce the interest of another student who would like to respond, and it slows the pace of the lesson for the rest of the class.
2. *Simultaneity:* Many things happen at the same time in classrooms. During a discussion a teacher not only listens and helps improve students' answers but also monitors students who do not respond for signs of comprehension and tries to keep the lesson moving at a good pace.
3. *Immediacy:* The pace of classroom events is rapid. Sieber (1979) found that teachers evaluated pupil conduct an average of 15.89 times per hour, or 87 times a day, or an estimated 16,000 times a year.
4. *Unpredictable and public classroom climate:* Things often happen in ways that are unanticipated. Furthermore, much of what happens to a student is seen by many other students. Clearly, students can infer how the teacher feels about certain students by the way the teacher interacts with them in class.
5. *History:* Classes meet for several weeks or months, so common norms and understandings develop. Emmer, Evertson, and Anderson (1980) showed how events that happen early in the year sometimes influence how classrooms function the rest of the year. To a student teacher or observer, some classes appear easy to manage; events that took place earlier in the school year, however, may explain why things run smoothly at the time of observation.

Although many classrooms now have nontraditional physical arrangements such as group-discussion corners, independent-study cubicles, learning stations, and microcomputer and word processing corners, even such open or individualized classrooms remain stable for a variety of reasons. The same students use the committee table together, individual study comes at the same time each day, class routines remain the same, and so on.

Predictability

To the extent that students have shared experiences in the past, expectations for the forthcoming year become narrower and more predictable. Suzi and Arlene, for instance, represented the homeroom on student council last year, and it is likely that one or both of them will be nominated again this year. Bob is expected to complain about homework, and Terri will probably push the teacher for information about what will be covered on tests. Bill and Alice will have their hands up 90 percent of the time, but Mary and Jim will rarely raise their hands and will seldom respond if the teacher calls on them.

Student expectations

Similarly, if teachers have taught long enough in a particular school, students will bring expectations about them to the class. "She'll read mystery stories to the students who don't go to music." "Chemistry lab exercises don't mean anything." "Don't sweat it; he only grades on tests, and they're straight from the book." Such preconceptions no doubt make it either easier or more difficult to start the year. Students may overreact or respond inappropriately to the ambiguous expressions or statements of teachers who have poor reputations.

Thus students who have spent thousands of hours sitting in classrooms will have expectations about what should take place in the room. Many also know how well they perform various classroom activities and whether they enjoy doing them. By middle childhood (ages nine through twelve), most students have developed relatively stable views of themselves and often reject information that presents or describes them as better or worse than they believe themselves to be. Such expectations about school life and personal performance can be changed only by systematic effort.

Students' rigid expectations (e.g., that they don't like and/or can't do math well) may lead students not to apply themselves to new mathematical assignments (e.g., problem-solving tasks) at which they might succeed if they applied themselves. Both teacher and student can become "lulled" to accept as normal that a student is uninterested in math; hence the teacher stops trying new ways to make math understandable. Thus expectations and routines can become so entrenched or rigid that teachers (and students) begin to do things without thinking about them at all or realizing that they are in effect making decisions by choosing certain options over others that would be possible in the situation and failing to assess the wisdom of those decisions.

Pressure on Students to "Look Good"

Group life affects the performance of individual students. Groups exert pressure on an individual to play a role (attentive participant, class clown, class rebel), and group pressure makes it difficult for teachers to have sustained, open dialogues with individual students. The presence of others, whether strangers or friends, is sufficient to alter behavior.

Holt (1964) and Covington (1984) both described a number of self-defeating strategies that students engage in to prevent them from looking bad in the classroom. In particular, Holt suggested that many dependent students read the teacher like a traffic light. They begin their answers slowly and softly. If the teacher smiles, nods, or in any way indicates approval, the answers become more animated (louder, quicker) and more relaxed. If the teacher nonverbally signals dissatisfaction, the student shifts into a "thinking act" and the game begins—a furrowed brow and a remark such as "let me think about that" followed by "no, what I meant to say . . . ," resulting in a beaming teacher.

Student strategies

Students learn to use countless games and strategies, and no doubt you can recall many of them from your own experience. We suspect that most of you who took a language course in high school or college occasionally did not do all of the required translation. At such times you may have tried to be called on to read one of the first five or so paragraphs that you did translate by tactics such as waving your hand energetically, feigning sleep, or staring out the window, depending on the teacher. Your desire to look good to peers and the teacher and possibly your wish for good grades motivated such behavior (along with your wish not to look bad by saying, "I don't know, I didn't do the translation").

Such strategies for camouflaging lack of knowledge often work, largely because the interactions occur in a group setting. Pressure to "perform for the group" leads many students to adopt strategies that are ultimately self-defeating or at least ineffective. The strategies work temporarily because the teacher either feels the pressure to move on or is embarrassed by the student's failure to respond. In the long run, however, students profit little from such activities because they are not learning the material.

Goffman (1959) provided a classic description of the pressure to look good in social settings in his book, *The Presentation of Self in Everyday Life*. Other research has focused on *attributional egotism*—the motive to take credit for success and to deny blame for failure in order to enhance self-esteem (Snyder, Stephan, & Rosenfield, 1978). Social pressure such as being compared with peers may encourage students to spend considerable time in impression management—trying to look good by projecting the image of listening to the teacher or perhaps developing self-defeating behavior patterns such as learned helplessness. There is growing evidence that students' beliefs about *why* they do well or poorly on a task are important because they influence how much time students spend on similar tasks in the future (see Stipek, 1988 for a discussion of related work).

Impression management

In an interesting ethnographic study, Spencer-Hall (1976) found that some students are better impression managers than others. She contended that students' different rates of misbehavior are not as important in cuing teachers' evaluations of students as are their styles of misbehavior. Many students are able to maintain favorable evaluations from teachers and peers alike by being careful to misbehave in ways that escape teacher attention.

Hence the actions of some students may "encourage" teachers to monitor their behavior closely and over time make it more likely that these students' misbehavior will be detected and that teachers will blame them in ambiguous situations. More generally, students' responses to pressure to look good (not to ask for information when needed) sometimes cause them to mislead teachers, thus making teachers' interpretations of student behavior more difficult.

EXTERNAL PRESSURES ON DECISION MAKING

External influences also affect teachers' decisions and thus what happens in classrooms. Hall and Spencer-Hall (1980) studied the effects of school administrations, community groups, and government agencies on expectations for schools. They reported an instance in which the media affected a community's expectations for its schools. Because of newspaper coverage of low student performance on basic skills tests, local administrators and school board members were subjected to community pressures that reflected a concern that students were not performing as well as they should. As a result, the administration went through a series of negotiations that included reinterpretation of the meaning of test scores and resulted in a curriculum that placed greater emphasis on basic skills. Hence public expectations can and do influence classroom functioning.

School environment

The school environment is also an important determinant of what teachers are able to accomplish. Some schools produce higher achievement than other schools with comparable student populations and resources (Purkey & Smith, 1985; Rutter, 1983). Some principals are more supportive and active leaders than others (McDonnell, 1985), and it is easier to teach in some schools than in others. If most teachers in a school support its curriculum standards, for example, it is easier for beginning teachers to maintain standards of excellence than it would be in a school where most teachers simply kept students busy.

Teacher's role in academic achievement

Because so many factors (e.g., parents, administrators, students' experiences in earlier grades, crowding) affect what teachers can accomplish, one may wonder if teachers can substantially affect students' learning. Even responsible scholars have seriously questioned whether teachers affect student performance (see Coleman et al., 1966; Heath & Nielson, 1974). Research in the past fifteen years (reviewed by Brophy & Good, 1986), however, clearly shows that teachers at all levels do have significant effects, either positive or negative, on student achievement. Although there are constraints on what teachers can accomplish, teachers are not simply implementors of bureaucratic or administrative policies; they are active agents—thinking professionals who can have important effects on student learning (Feiman-Nemser & Floden, 1986).

Much evidence supports the conclusion that how teachers teach affects what and how much students learn. It is because of such data that we, like many other educators and researchers (e.g., Shavelson, 1983; Shulman, 1986; Shulman & Sykes, 1983), emphasize that good teaching makes a major difference in classroom learning and recommend an active, decision-making approach to teaching.

INITIAL TEACHING EXPERIENCES

Student Teaching

Student teachers and cooperating teachers

Student teachers' classroom behavior is influenced by their cooperating teachers (Good & Brophy, 1984). Even though student teachers may not approve of the styles their cooperating teachers use, they may practice the cooperating teachers' styles in hopes of getting a good grade. This may become second nature to them and resurface later when they have their own classrooms. Many cooperating teachers encourage student teachers to develop their own styles, so the pressure to conform is not a problem. Some cooperating teachers believe that their role is to help student teachers teach as they do. Furthermore, during the first year of teaching, a new teacher may encounter peer teachers with strong preferences.

Unfortunately, many student teachers are not encouraged to think analytically and to discuss why they make certain decisions (Stout, 1989). Furthermore, action-system knowledge is seldom part of discussions between cooperating and student teachers. Griffin and associates (1983) found that during such discussions little attention was paid to developing a knowledge base that would help student teachers later when they had their own classrooms. Interactions focused on immediate, specific issues and a "let's see if this works" approach without explanation of rationales or references to learning theory, child development, or instructional models. Interaction was dominated by the cooperating teacher, who selected the topics and controlled how they were discussed. Conversations usually focused on a particular classroom at a specific time; they rarely concerned alternate ways to understand and respond to classroom events.

Some cooperating teachers enjoy discussing why they make decisions and how they evaluate them. Others function differently. As a student teacher, however, you can be analytical even if your cooperating teacher is not. Think about each instructional day. Consider, for example, the motivational structures that the teacher used, such as how lessons were introduced or ended and the types of feedback that were given, and spec-

Student teachers need to establish their own style and relationship with students.

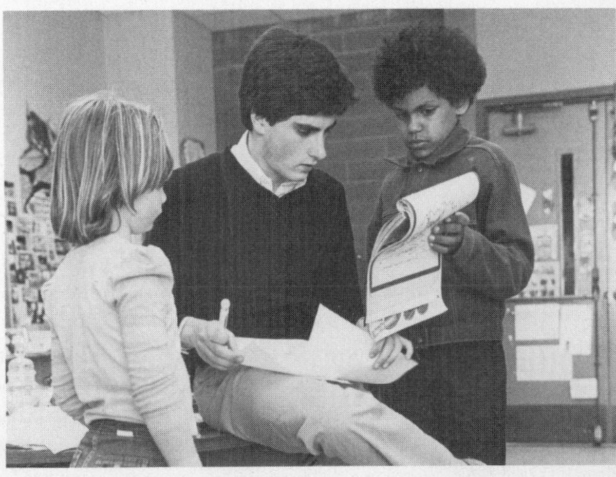

ulate about their effects on various students. On another day, think about the management system in the classroom—what types of alerting and accountability systems were used? Was the structure too rigid or too loose for specific students? By using the vocabulary and concepts in this text, you can become a more educated observer of classroom events—the first step in becoming an active classroom decision maker.

Peer teacher exchanges also exhibit some of the same characteristics as cooperating teacher-student teacher exchanges. Rosenholtz (1989) noted that teachers often avoid discussing instructional problems and hence deny themselves potentially useful information. If teachers are to be active decision makers they must seek useful information from peers.

The First Year

Beginning teachers

Beginning teachers have an especially difficult task because in addition to facing the enduring demands of teaching, they worry about things such as whether students will like them and follow their directions or whether they will enjoy teaching. New teachers must also prepare lessons and develop tests while trying to apply action-system knowledge.

Because of increased awareness that the first years of teaching can be difficult even for talented college graduates, many states now have induction programs to assist beginning teachers. These programs vary from state to state; however, most offer beginning teachers more assistance than newcomers have traditionally received (e.g., a mentor teacher, observation and feedback). Although the objective of induction programs is to ease adjustment to teaching, they also bring special pressures (e.g., the need to demonstrate selected action-knowledge teaching skills in the classroom) and may even mandate that a teacher teach in a certain way. Various educators discuss induction (see for example Carter & Richardson-Koehler, 1989; Howey & Zimpher, 1989; Medley & Vance, 1989).

Secondary teachers must get to know as many as 180 students quickly, and elementary teachers have to prepare daily lessons in several subjects. Teachers must also implement different teaching formats and plan activities. Yinger (1977) reported on one teacher who used fifty-three activities during a twelve-week period, including tasks such as book reports, creative writing, cooking, newspaper assignments, spelling bees, field trips, and reading groups.

Whatever help may or may not be available to you in the form of induction programs and assistance from principals or peers when you begin working as an inservice teacher, you can prepare now to make the decisions you will need to make by articulating and organizing your own theory of teaching that will allow you to operate as a proactive teacher.

Summary

Teachers can have a major, positive influence on the way students learn and develop. Some teachers are vital forces; others have only minor effects. Teachers who significantly affect students' lives communicate a genuine interest in students, know subject matter, and possess detailed information about instructional processes and the way students learn and develop.

In this chapter we have presented a decision-making model because we believe that there are no simple answers to successful teaching. We stress that theoretical principles and research findings provide a basis for planning and implementing instruction. Teachers, however, have to act as independent decision makers and apply these general concepts and principles in relation to their students and educational objectives. The model illustrates that teachers who make good decisions and are willing to correct poor ones foster student motivation and learning.

Effective teachers see their roles as positive and worthwhile, whereas ineffective teachers see teaching as a dull job. Effective teachers exhibit inner control, personal responsibility, realistic attitudes, and a problem-solving orientation. They are successful in developing positive relations with both students and peers.

Factors that restrict a teacher's decision-making ability are lack of awareness of students' problems, allegiance to unworkable ideas, limited resources, and a lack of feedback about the effects of instruction. Also, both student and teacher expectations, coupled with the self-defeating strategies that some students adopt, can interfere with learning.

We believe it is difficult for new teachers to be active decision makers unless they want to be and are willing to work to develop the necessary skills. It is easy for them to be overwhelmed by the rapid pace of classrooms and simply to *react* to classroom events. To be *proactive*, it will be important for you to consider how to apply the ideas presented in this book as you read them, as you observe classes, and when you student teach.

The best way to become a proactive teacher is to develop an explicit theory of teaching. You must also master subject-matter content, understand and apply the concepts presented in this text, and develop an explicit approach to teaching (e.g., know when you will group pupils for instruction and when you will teach the entire class, know the bases for your decisions and how to collect evidence to determine their appropriateness).

Educational psychology provides a framework for looking at the learner, the learning process, and the learning situation. It includes an understanding of educational objectives, student development and personality, the learning process, the psychology of teaching methods, classroom management, and evaluation procedures. Students who apply educational psychology in their preservice and inservice teaching will understand students better and design more appropriate instruction. Successful teaching requires subject-matter knowledge and knowledge of educational psychology as well as teaching and decision-making skills. Our goal in this book is to provide basic knowledge of psychological concepts that can be combined with subject-matter knowledge and teaching experience to allow you to become an effective teacher.

QUESTIONS AND PROBLEMS

1. How did you decide to become a teacher (or nurse or whatever your vocational aspiration may be)? What explicit assumptions did you hold? In retrospect, what implicit assumptions and hypotheses did you make?
2. What are your own theories of teaching? On what are they based? Be explicit. Think about a particular lesson for a certain group of students. What five things would you need to do to be successful? Why?
3. How do instructional goals influence planning? What does it mean to say that some classroom decisions "aren't made"? What is the difference between explicit and implicit decisions? What sorts of things happen in classrooms without teacher intent or awareness?
4. Considering the complexities of teaching, shouldn't we provide you with a few clear, prescriptive guidelines rather than urge you to master a broad range of concepts and skills to draw on later when you are teaching and making decisions under pressure?
5. Think about the teachers you have had. Which were the most effective? Why? Were they equally effective for all students?
6. What sort of "front" have you presented to your teachers in the past?
7. How does classroom teaching differ from teaching patients about the effects of a pending operation and how they can help their own recovery by performing certain exercises?
8. As a beginning teacher, how might pressures to "look good" interfere with your ability to learn from experienced peers?

CASE STUDIES

DISTURBING FIRST ENCOUNTER. Tim is apprehensive because he knows that Mr. Wilson, his cooperating teacher, had given his previous semester's student teacher a "D" and was an abrasive man. Tim anxiously knocks on the door and shivers as Mr. Wilson says loudly, "Come in!" As Tim hesitantly enters, Mr. Wilson says, "Oh! You must be my new aide from the university! I thought you'd have been here 15 minutes ago!" What would you do if you were Tim?

RICK STRIKES OUT. Rick felt like a fool. "Why didn't I read the assignment more carefully?" he asked himself. Last night, to get ready to teach his first class, he spent considerable time preparing a ten-minute introduction and even more time working on discussion questions. But the lesson hadn't gone as planned. His ninth graders didn't seem to want to talk. And so, foolishly, he later thought, he asked for questions. He fielded the first three or four questions poorly. Finally, one student said with irritation, "I still can't understand the point of the experiment." Rick simply couldn't think; his mind went blank. After a full minute of awkward silence he threw the question back to the class. Weakly, he asked, "Can anybody help . . . (pause) . . . I'm sorry, I forgot your name." What should Rick do now? What should he do the next day?

JIM BEGINS. Jim Miller, a recent college graduate, will teach chemistry for the first time at a large high school that serves a full range of student abilities. However, only college-bound students take chemistry. What are some of the decisions that Jim must make immediately? List 10 to 15.

A CHALLENGE FOR NANCY. Nancy Litton has never taught reading before. She is both excited and frightened by the prospect of teaching first graders because she did her student teaching in a third-grade classroom. She has never observed first-grade reading instruction, nor has she seen a teacher start the school year. It's a week before the year begins. If you were Nancy what information would you try to obtain and what are the major decisions that must be made?

PART 2
DEVELOPMENT

Tommy was the shortest third grader in class. Although his mother and father said that he was going to get bigger and the doctor told him that he was going to be a tall adult, Tommy wanted to be tall right now. He felt bad about how short he was, and peers sometimes made fun of him because of his height.

Ruth, a fifth grader, was the first girl in her class to show signs of physical maturity. In one sense she was pleased, but in another sense she was frightened and felt alone. She wished that she had someone to talk to about her changing body.

Alan was a tenth grader beginning to feel uneasy about his academic progress. His grades were acceptable, but he didn't know what he wanted to do after high school. His friends were beginning to talk about colleges and careers.

Jane was disturbed because many of her classmates in an advanced senior chemistry course were cheating on assignments and exams. She felt that their behavior was outrageous, yet she did not want to "rat" on them. She wished that more students had concerns about academic standards and honesty.

Karla, a sophomore in college, enjoyed courses in which she could develop her own learning assignments and do independent research, particularly on social issues. She found her emerging interest in independent thinking and scholarship surprising, because as recently as her junior year in high school, she still looked to others to define what she should think about. In the past three years, however, she had developed a strong preference for independent work and the skills for pursuing it.

This unit is about human development. As we grow and mature, our development creates new opportunities and skills but also creates new conflicts, as these brief vignettes illustrate.

Teachers are in a unique position to help their students to deal successfully with these developmental issues. Several types of development are covered in the unit: Chapter 2 covers physical development; Chapter 3 presents principles and theories of cognitive development; Chapter 4 places these principles and theories in the context of education; and Chapter 5 deals with social and moral development. These chapters are intended to help you understand and respond to developmental issues that affect classroom life. To make this point more clearly, let's consider a particular experience that occurs regularly in schools.

I pledge allegiance to the flag of the United States of America, and to the republic for which it stands, one nation, under God, indivisible, with liberty and justice for all.

The pledge of allegiance is familiar because it is basic to American culture. In fact, you may have skimmed over it once you realized what it was. If so, go back and look again as you think about these questions: Do you understand what all the words and phrases mean? Do you understand the connotations—all of the other things implied in these brief statements? As you think about these questions, do you now notice anything in the pledge that you never noticed before, even though you probably know it by heart and have recited it many times? If so, what does this mean?

For example, you may be aware that the pledge is not a statement to the flag as such but a loyalty oath to the nation. If you think about it, you can see that a loyalty oath to the United States does not require mention of its flag. Furthermore, the meaning of the pledge would remain the same even if the design of the flag should change, as it did when new states entered the Union.

From the point of view of developmental psychologists, you are in the stage of formal operations. This means that you are capable of understanding the abstract aspects of knowledge. Fourth graders, on the other hand, would have difficulty with some of the vocabulary of the pledge, would not interpret these statements as you did, and would not be able to follow this discussion. Their understanding of it is limited to familiar, concrete experiences, although within these limits their interpretation is logical.

Saying the pledge is a relatively meaningless experience for first graders. It is associated with standing and holding the right hand over the heart while reciting the words in the presence of the flag. First graders have a general idea that the words relate to the flag (not the country) but not much understanding of what the words mean.

This example illustrates some of the insights that developmental psychologists offer. By identifying systematic changes that occur as children get older and limitations that apply when they have not yet acquired insights associated with higher stages of development, psychologists help us to understand children of different ages by enabling us to see things from their perspectives. This ability is essential if we are to interact with children meaningfully and interpret their difficulties when they do not understand something that an adult would understand with ease. It also enables us to correct children's ideas that are logical, given their point of view, but incorrect because they do not take into account other things that make a difference.

In the four chapters in this section we will elaborate on children's stages of development in relation to their ability to learn and to be taught.

CHAPTER

Physical Development

CHAPTER OUTLINE

OBJECTIVES

When you have mastered the material in this chapter, you will be able to

1. Differentiate the terms *growth* and *development* in the context of physical changes during childhood and adolescence
2. Describe Epstein's (1978) work on brain growth stages
3. Describe work by Lenneberg (1967) and others on cerebral lateralization and the controversy that surrounds its educational implications
4. Describe the universal sequence of human growth and the importance of nutrition and exercise for physical growth and development
5. Define Sheldon's (1942) body types and explain the research relating body types to personality and development
6. List the important preadolescent growth and development characteristics and tell how schools can accommodate these characteristics

7. Explain how boys and girls differ in physical development during preadolescence
8. Explain the physical causes of the preadolescent growth spurt and discuss environmental factors that affect it
9. Discuss adolescent sexual maturation and the differential effects of early versus late maturation on both boys and girls

Developmental perspective

To deal with students effectively, it is helpful to know where they have been and where they are likely to be going, not just where they are now. This requires a *developmental perspective*, a concern with changes occuring over time. Psychologists discuss three aspects of such changes: *sequence*, the order in which changes occur; *rate*, the speed with which changes occur; and *form*, the shape or appearance of the developing entity at any point in time.

True developmental sequences are fixed and universal. Stage A always precedes B, which always precedes C, and so on. One cannot get from stage A to C without first going through B. Many of these sequences involve physical growth and development under the control of genetics and maturation. However, universal sequences have been proposed for aspects of psychological development as well.

Growth versus development

It is useful to distinguish "growth" from "development" when discussing physical changes. *Growth* refers to increases in height, weight, or physical size. *Development*, a term that can refer to the mind and the emotions as well as the body, is an orderly progression to increasingly higher levels of differentiation or organization.

Development can occur when no growth is taking place. For example, children of similar age and size differ in ability to ride a tricycle or use a pencil. One reason is that differences in rates of maturation of the nervous system produce differences in the ability to control and coordinate various parts of the body. Children lacking the physical maturation needed to succeed at such tasks are unlikely to master them until this maturation takes place, even if they have lots of instruction and time to practice. Persistent developmental immaturities plague certain students throughout childhood and even into adolescence. For example, hyperactive students may have difficulty concentrating or inhibiting physical movement, and students with poor coordination may embarrass themselves in the gym or on the playground.

Differentiation

Most physical development involving differentiation of new parts occurs in the early weeks following conception, as the fertilized egg continually reproduces itself and at the same time differentiates into the nervous system and sense organs, the digestive system, and so on. At birth, almost all parts are differentiated, except for the myelin sheaths that cover nerve cells in the brain. These sheaths, which apparently help speed up neural transmission and thus make the brain more efficient, continue to develop for at least the first few years after birth. By the time children start school, though, they are essentially fully differentiated. Consequently, their further physical development consists of simple growth and progress toward higher levels of organization and coordination of existing body parts.

BRAIN-DEVELOPMENT THEORIES

Epstein and Brain-Growth Stages

Brain-growth stages

Even though brain development seems to be complete by early childhood, some have theorized that brain growth or changes in brain functioning affect children's intellectual development and performance at school. Epstein (1978), for example, pointed out that the brain increases about 35 percent in weight after age two due to (a) extension and branching of the axons and dendrites that extend outward from brain cells and connect them with other cells, (b) extension of the myelin sheaths along axons, and (c) increases in arterial blood supply to the brain. He suggested that these forms of brain growth affect intellectual functioning, and that such growth takes place in well-defined spurts rather than occurring continuously throughout childhood. Epstein believes that brain-growth spurts occur between the ages of three to ten months, two to four years, six to eight years, ten to twelve or thirteen years, and fourteen to sixteen or seventeen years.

These ages correspond closely to the stages in intellectual development that have been identified by Piaget (1983), so Epstein drew educational implications by suggesting that children should be presented with greater intellectual challenges and stimulated to develop their thinking to higher levels during periods of rapid brain growth but should be allowed to consolidate their gains and be presented with less demanding challenges between these growth periods. Thus a great deal of new and demanding information would be included in the first- and second-grade curricula (corresponding to the growth-spurt period spanning ages six to eight), but less demanding curricula would be developed for grades three and four (corresponding to the in-between period spanning ages eight to ten).

Epstein's ideas are intriguing, but three major obstacles would have to be overcome before educators would feel compelled to act on them. First, his theories are not accepted among biological scientists. There is little relationship between brain weight and brain functioning and little biological evidence to support Epstein's notions about spurts in brain growth (Marsh, 1985). Second, the growth-spurt ages are approximate, so many children could be ahead or behind a year or more. Thus, even if Epstein's notions about brain-growth spurts should turn out to be correct, changing the school curriculum along the lines he suggested might yield no significant improvement in the matching of curriculum demands to student readiness. Third, brain growth could just as well be an effect as a cause of advances in intellectual functioning—perhaps the increased range and sophistication of intellectual activities that occur with development stimulate brain growth rather than vice versa. If so, changes in rates of brain growth would have no educational implications.

Despite these problems, some educators are developing teacher-training programs and an approach to curriculum called *cognitive-level matching* based on Epstein's ideas. The best known of these programs is the one sponsored by the Shoreham-Wading River School District in Shoreham, New York (Brooks, Fusco, & Grennon, 1983).

Lenneberg and Cerebral Lateralization

Brain-lateralization theories

The cerebrum of the brain (the "gray matter" that controls higher-level intellectual functioning) is divided into left and right hemispheres. The hemispheres appear to have equal potential; if one hemisphere is severely injured, the other hemisphere usually takes over its functions. However, the hemispheres develop specialized functioning in most people. The left hemisphere controls verbal functioning and the linear, logical thinking associated with verbalization, and the right hemisphere controls visual or spatial imagery and the intuitive, holistic thinking associated with perception or discovery rather than logical reasoning. This hemispheric specialization is called *cerebral lateralization* and is evident from infancy (Kinsbourne & Hiscock, 1978).

Some writers have theorized that delayed or incomplete lateralization causes learning disabilities. Thus periodically there are claims that learning disabilities are more likely among left-handed children or children with mixed patterns (such as those who prefer the right hand and right foot but use the left eye for sighting). Lenneberg (1967) argued that language is progressively lateralized to the left hemisphere as the child develops and that language disabilities are associated with disturbances in these brain-lateralization tendencies. Lenneberg's ideas about brain lateralization are interesting but not well supported by biological data (Carter, Hohenegger, & Satz, 1982; Kinsbourne & Hiscock, 1978). Furthermore, it is not clear what, if any, educational implications would follow from them.

Other writers, however, have drawn implications for education based on brain-lateralization theories. Wittrock (1978), for example, believes that reading instruction that includes encouraging students to visualize and use imagery should be more effective than instruction restricted to purely verbal approaches because it will allow children to use processes controlled by both brain hemispheres rather than only the left one.

Others, noting that children from higher socioeconomic status homes tend to have more efficient left-hemisphere functioning (Waber et al., 1984), have suggested that "right-brain" approaches to instruction are especially important for teaching lower socioeconomic status children. Still others, equating right-brain functioning with creativity and problem solving, suggest that schools need to emphasize creativity and problem solving to develop the functioning efficiency of the right hemisphere (Bogen, 1977).

These theories go far beyond the available biological data and essentially amount to speculation. However, the suggested educational implications may be sound even if the ideas about stimulating brain lateralization do not turn out to be correct. That is, whether or not there are meaningful linkages between classroom teaching and brain lateralization, there are many reasons for advocating that students be taught with multiple methods and receive opportunities to develop their problem-solving and creative-thinking abilities. In summary, although there has been interesting speculation about brain-growth spurts and hemispheric lateralization of brain functioning, clear linkages between these hypothesized brain activities and implications for classroom instruction remain to be demonstrated.

GENERAL DEVELOPMENTAL TRENDS

Growth spurts

Humans exhibit rapid growth in the first two years of life, slower but noticeable growth over the next eight to twelve years, a second period of rapid growth during adolescence, and a tapering off thereafter. Within these larger sequences, growth typically occurs in spurts. There may be noticeable growth for a few months, followed by no noticeable growth for another six months to a year (Tanner, 1970).

Much development, however, occurs between growth spurts, especially consolidation of previously learned skills through practice with the newer, larger body, as well as exploration of activities possible for the first time. Growth spurts often create awkwardness, since children and adolescents must learn to adjust to new arm lengths, leg lengths, and so on when performing activities requiring physical coordination. They may temporarily become clumsy at doing things that had been easy for them earlier.

The timing of growth spurts and the general course of physical growth are controlled by secretions of growth hormone from the pituitary gland, which ultimately are controlled by genes inherited at conception. Thus rate of growth and ultimate size are not influenced significantly by consuming health foods or large quantities of vitamins or by doing calisthenics or stretching exercises. These activities may affect physical appearance or muscle tone, but they do not stimulate actual growth.

NUTRITION AND EXERCISE

Most children get plenty of exercise in their normal daily activities, so this factor ordinarily should not be of concern to elementary teachers. As the years go by, however, certain students develop sedentary habits, some to the point that the only real exercise they get is in physical education classes. Teachers can help by encouraging these students to become more active, especially in activities (e.g., hiking, cycling, swimming) that they can sustain on their own as lifelong sports or hobbies.

Nutrition is likely to be a problem for some students in all grades and in all schools. Perhaps as many of 30 percent of the children growing up in the United States today do not receive adequate nutrition. Most are from lower-income families, but many are from economically advantaged

Diet—good or bad—can affect performance at school.

homes where parents lack the knowledge or interest to ensure adequate nutrition by monitoring their children's food intake. Children with unbalanced diets absorb too many carbohydrates and fats and not enough protein, vitamins, and essential minerals (Brozek, 1978).

Inadequate nutrition can adversely affect physical growth and development (Bogin & MacVean, 1983) and, by lowering energy and alertness, can interfere with progress at school (McKay et al., 1978). Listlessness in the classroom can be the result of poor nutrition rather than motivational problems (Barrett, Radke-Yarrow, & Klein, 1982). This underscores the value of school breakfast and lunch programs and of teaching students about health and nutrition.

BODY TYPES

Increases in height and general size follow cycles or *growth curves* (Tanner, 1970) that are genetically programmed for each individual. Assuming adequate nutrition and exercise, these inherited growth patterns will determine the timing and duration of increases in body size. Some individ-

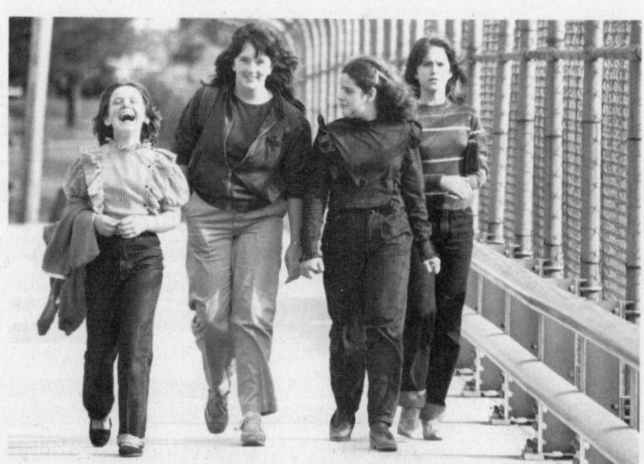

All the same age, these classmates have matured physically at significantly different rates.

uals will be very close to average for their gender and ethnic group throughout development; others will be taller than average for much of childhood but end up shorter than average as adults. Some will show relatively even growth throughout childhood, and others will shoot up every couple of years with little observable growth in between. The variety of growth curves makes it impossible to predict future growth patterns or ultimate adult stature for specific individuals without collecting detailed information about rates of bone ossification (the gradual calcification of living bone tissue, which hardens the bone but also slows and eventually stops its growth). One can make an educated guess if information about parental growth patterns is available, especially when a child seems to be modeling after a parent of the same gender, but even here there are plenty of exceptions. Thus one cannot assume that relative stature in childhood will be maintained into adulthood.

Personality stereotypes

Height is only one aspect of body type and perhaps not even the most important one for determining self-image and self-satisfaction. Following Sheldon (1942), psychologists often differentiate between *ectomorphs* (lean, elongated), *mesomorphs* (muscular, athletic), and *endomorphs* (heavy-set, fleshy); see Figure 2.1. Sheldon held that these body types are inherited and thus stable, although they can be temporarily masked by growth spurts and either minimized or exaggerated by exercise and nutrition. He also believed that these body types are associated with predictable personality features: ectomorphs are preoccupied with their brains and nervous systems and thus are intellectual, artistic, and sensitive; mesomorphs are preoccupied with bone and muscle and thus are athletic and action oriented, as well as sociable, outgoing, and popular; and endomorphs are preoccupied with their digestive systems and thus are oriented toward food and drink rather than thought or action, and are slothful and phlegmatic. These stereotypes did not originate with Sheldon; they go back a long time in folklore and fiction. Sheldon merely added the biologically based theory that body types were inherited and that they determined the personality characteristics (McCandless & Coop, 1979).

Sheldon's theory has face validity because we all know individuals who fit the stereotypes. Systematic research has not supported his notions of inherited predispositions toward distinct body types or causal relationships between body types and personality characteristics. His ideas fit certain individuals but do not hold up as general rules (Hall & Lindzey, 1970).

Developmental tasks

Yet body types can influence development (Clausen, 1975). Directly, physical development determines what a child can or cannot do. Those who cannot compete on equal terms with their peers may be excluded from games and sports or be discriminated against in other ways. Indirectly, physical development influences attitudes toward self and others. In extreme cases the result can be a vicious cycle of self-fulfilling prophecy effects, in which failures produce defeatist attitudes that in turn produce more failures. This is especially likely when a child has difficulty with what Havighurst (1972) calls *developmental tasks*—tasks that arise at a certain period of development and if mastered lead to success on later tasks but if failed lead to unhappiness in the individual, disapproval

Figure 2.1 Three Body Types

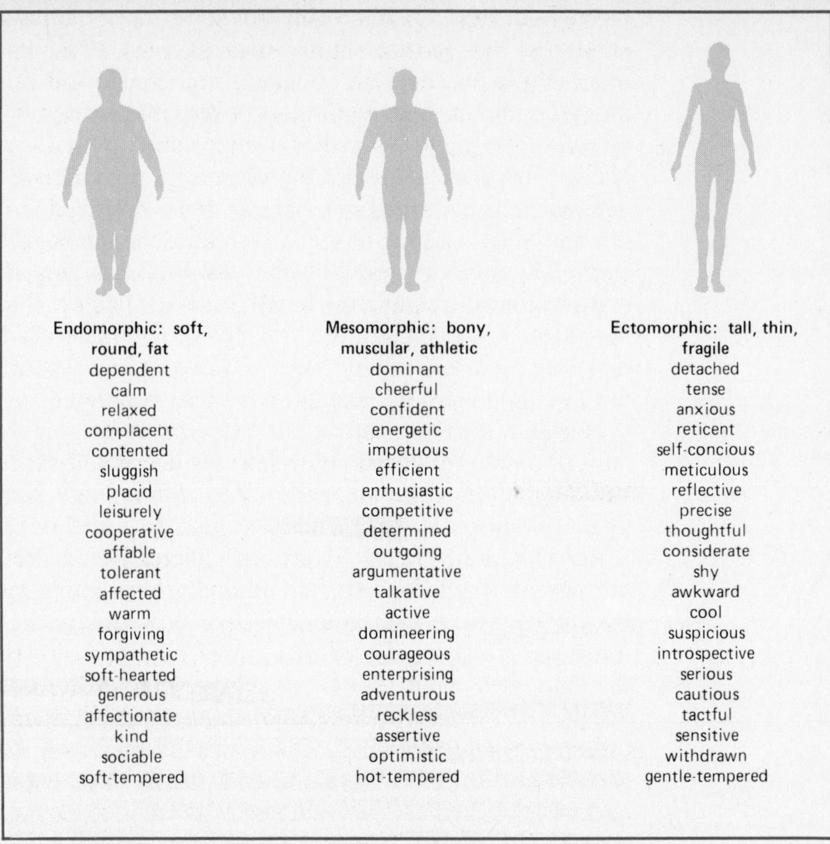

Endomorphic: soft, round, fat
dependent
calm
relaxed
complacent
contented
sluggish
placid
leisurely
cooperative
affable
tolerant
affected
warm
forgiving
sympathetic
soft-hearted
generous
affectionate
kind
sociable
soft-tempered
Mesomorphic: bony, muscular, athletic
dominant
cheerful
confident
energetic
impetuous
efficient
enthusiastic
competitive
determined
outgoing
argumentative
talkative
active
domineering
courageous
enterprising
adventurous
reckless
assertive
optimistic
hot-tempered
Ectomorphic: tall, thin, fragile
detached
tense
anxious
reticent
self-concious
meticulous
reflective
precise
thoughtful
considerate
shy
awkward
cool
suspicious
introspective
serious
cautious
tactful
sensitive
withdrawn
gentle-tempered

Source: J. Cortes and F. Gatti, "Physique and Self-Description of Temperment," *Journal of Consulting Psychology* 29 (1965): 434. Copyright 1965 by the American Psychological Association. Reprinted by permission of the publisher and author.

by others, and difficulty with later tasks. For students at school, developmental tasks that can be affected by physical factors include not only the physical demands of games and sports but demands for concentrated attention, inhibition of physical movement, grasping/controlling writing instruments, manipulating laboratory equipment, and producing the sustained motor control required to cut an intricate design pattern or dissect a frog.

Factors influencing self-concept

Failures in such activities may lead not only to temporary and specific failure perceptions (I can't do this task now) but also to generalized self-concepts of inadequacy (I can't do this kind of task, and I never will be able to). Once formed, such perceptions are likely to hamper performance on similar tasks in the future. Task concentration will be interrupted by defeatist feelings (I can't do this; I'm going to fail; I look foolish), often to the point that giving up becomes easier than prolonging the anxiety and pain. Chances for mastering a task also may be reduced by teachers or peers who believe that the person cannot handle it and thus do not even give him or her the opportunity to try. This can occur out of indifference (he can't do it, so why bother) or humanitarian concern (I don't want to put her on the spot or embarrass her). Either way, such exclusion will enhance the problem unless it is accompanied by other methods of providing the student with opportunities to practice the task.

Physical development effects on general self-concept are most often felt by mesomorphs (especially those who are attractive as well as athletic) and endomorphs (especially those whose body type is exaggerated by too little exercise and too many calories). Students who are attractive and athletic tend to be more popular with both adults and peers, better adjusted psychologically, and social leaders (Hartup, 1970; Lerner & Lerner, 1977; McCandless & Coop, 1979; Staffieri, 1967). They are likely to receive preferential treatment because others favor them (often unconsciously) and because their well-developed social skills make them adept at getting what they want.

Unattractive students, especially if they are obese, are often rejected by adults and peers and ultimately by themselves. Some may compound this by withdrawing from social interaction and overeating (Krogman, 1953). Even when this does not occur, the rejection they suffer from peers may deprive them of important social experience and thus place them at a disadvantage in dealing with others. Such students need not only sympathy from their teachers but also encouragement to help them sustain the will to try to overcome the problem and help in the form of specific suggestions about developing good eating habits, coping with taunts, and initiating friendships.

PHYSICAL DEVELOPMENT IN PREADOLESCENT CHILDREN

Physical development factors are important primarily to teachers working with preschool or early primary children or with adolescents. Some young children have difficulty using writing instruments because of slow maturation or lack of practice in holding and using tools for printing, writing,

Some children need to practice doing assignments that involve the use of writing instruments.

or drawing. Sometimes the problem is easy to see, such as when the child grasps a pencil by enclosing an entire fist around it or holds it more toward the top than the bottom. However, pencil work is laborious for some children even when they hold the pencil correctly. These children will need practice over a considerable time. So will children who have difficulty with certain gym activities because they lack coordination or are too short or otherwise physically unsuited to the equipment.

Unique characteristics of young children

Young children also have unique characteristics that schools need to take into account. They need more activity than older children, yet also require more sleep (sometimes even a midday nap), and they require more frequent but smaller meals. It should be kept in mind that our sleeping and eating customs are arbitrary and that school is an artificial environment in which certain rules exist because they are needed for group living but are unnatural for young children with limited attention spans and lots of energy for physical activity.

The implications of physical development seem obvious; yet problems such as the following are often observed:

- Seats that are too small or large
- Failure to provide for the needs of left-handed students
- Adult-sized furniture or storage facilities that force children to depend on the teacher for things that they could handle themselves if materials were within reach
- Poor seating patterns or other physical layout problems (traffic patterns that cause unnecessary jostling)
- Chalkboards and drinking fountains too high for young children to use, and wall decorations or bulletin boards too high for them to read

Individual differences in growth

Besides arranging the classroom to meet students' physical needs, teachers can help meet students' emotional needs by maintaining awareness of their individual differences in rates and forms of physical growth. This will help teachers to accept the individuality of all students and enable them to provide information and reassurance to those who feel inferior because they are different from their classmates.

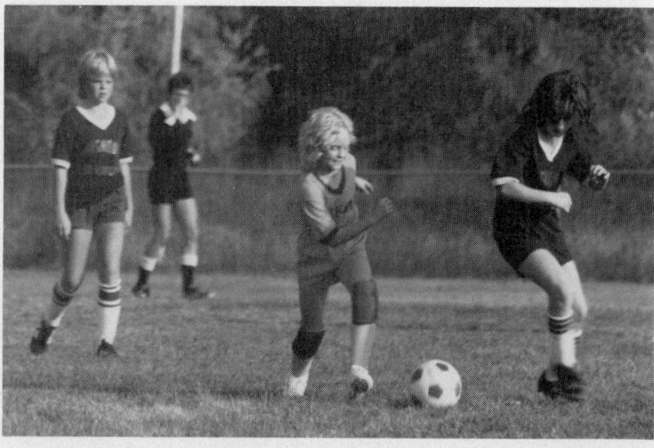

Talent and interest, not gender, are the appropriate factors in selecting sports activities for children.

Preadolescent Growth

Once past the first few grades, most students settle into a slow, stable growth pattern. Except for fundamental considerations such as provision of appropriately sized desks or chairs, physical growth and development factors recede in importance until preadolescence, when the growth spurt and the development of sexual characteristics introduce new dimensions into students' lives.

Gender Differences in Physical Development

In general, physical maturation occurs earlier in girls than in boys, and girls mature earlier at adolescence (see Figures 2.2 and 2.3). Thus throughout childhood, girls are slightly ahead of boys in progression toward ultimate adult characteristics and in ability to control and inhibit physical activity. However, most boys are developing toward an ultimately larger

Figure 2.2 Typical Individual Growth Curve Rates for Height in Boys and Girls

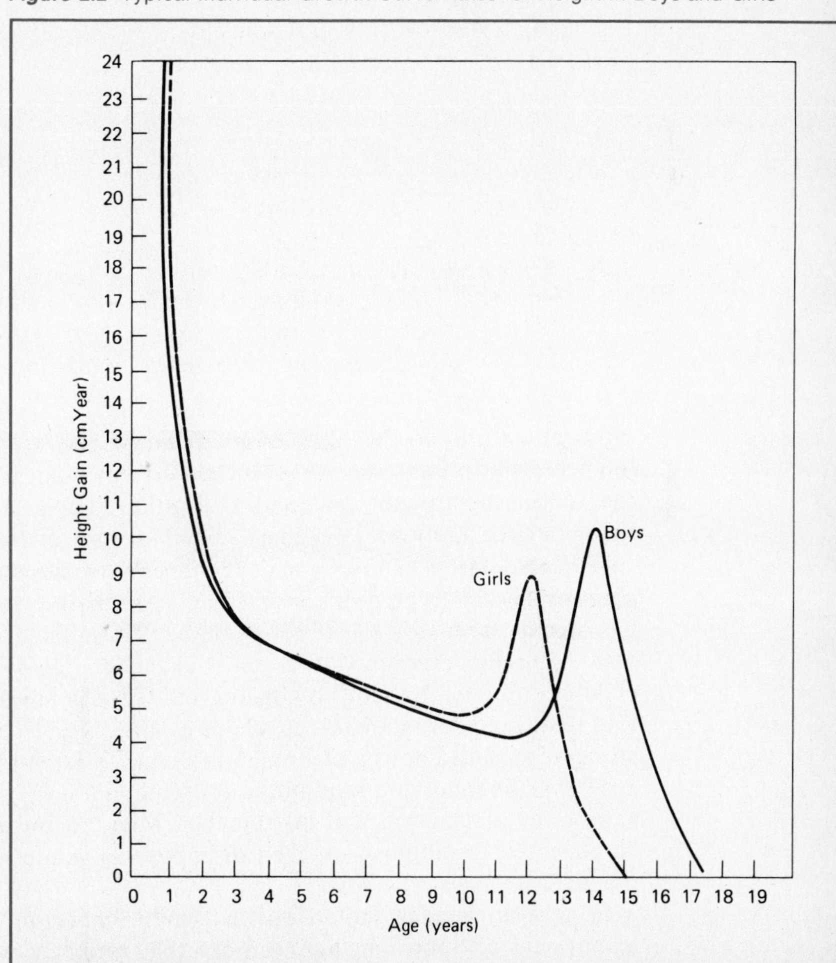

Source: From *Adolescents: Behavior and Development*, Second Edition, by Boyd R. McCandless and Richard Coop, copyright © 1979 by Holt, Rinehart and Winston, Inc., reprinted with permissions of the publisher.

Figure 2.3 Typical Individual Height-Attained Curves For Boys and Girls

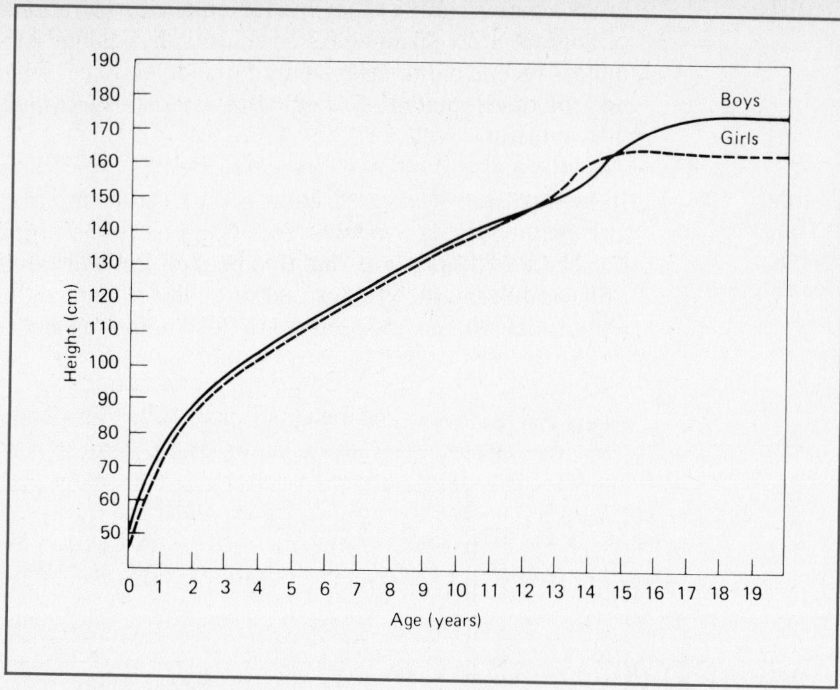

Source: From *Adolescents: Behavior and Development*, Second Edition, by Boyd R. McCandless and Richard Coop, copyright © 1979 by Holt, Rinehart and Winston, Inc., reprinted with permissions of the publisher.

physical stature, so that differences in height and weight tend to favor boys from birth until age ten or eleven. At this point girls begin to enter the adolescent growth spurt and as a group become taller and heavier than boys for a few years (Faust, 1977; Maccoby & Jacklin, 1974).

Sex-role socialization

Gender differences in motor development are minimal, although boys generally attain greater size and strength and girls better fine motor development, especially finger coordination. These factors, in combination with culturally determined differences in gender-role socialization—what children are taught about how males and females are expected to act—lead to differences in ability. Boys are usually superior in skills requiring strength or speed/power combinations such as large-muscle sports and girls in skills involving fine motor coordination such as arts and crafts, sewing, or playing musical instruments. Many of these differences can be expected to diminish or even disappear as gender-role socialization practices change.

In general, gender should not determine opportunities for exposure to physical activities, including those that formerly were restricted to the opposite gender. Development that occurs subsequent to initial exposure should depend on individual talents and interests rather than on gender.

PREADOLESCENCE: THE GROWTH SPURT

Transition from childhood to mature physical status occurs over several years. During preadolescence (the year or two before maturation of the sex organs), the pituitary gland begins increasing its production of growth hormones, causing a period of rapid growth that is noticeable for a year or two and continues at a reduced pace for several years thereafter (Faust, 1977; Tanner, 1970).

The timing and duration of the preadolescent growth spurt are ultimately controlled by the genes. However, they also are affected by nutrition, climate, and other environmental factors. Healthy, well-nourished children mature earlier than less advantaged children, urban children earlier than rural children, and children living in the temperate climates earlier than those living in tropic or arctic zones (Tanner, 1970). Children with endomorphic and mesomorphic builds are likely to mature earlier than ectomorphs, so that in the junior high school years the former types may be not only bigger but also much more developed in the trunk areas, whereas the latter may seem to be all arms and legs. Late-maturing children often grow at a rapid rate once they begin their growth spurt and can show gains of four inches and 30 pounds in just a few months.

ADOLESCENCE: SEXUAL MATURATION

While the pituitary gland begins secreting increased amounts of growth hormone, the gonads (ovaries in females and testes in males), which were relatively inactive until puberty, begin to secrete hormones that stimulate the development of the sex organs. The result is growth of the primary sex characteristics and development of the secondary characteristics.

Primary and secondary sex characteristics

Growth of the primary sex characteristics occurs externally in males but internally in females. The testes not only secrete hormones but show a growth spurt, and soon afterwards the penis begins to grow, first in length and then in circumference (Ford & Beach, 1951). The growth spurt of the ovaries in females is followed by *menarche*, the onset of menstruation, and by growth of the uterus and the rest of the female reproductive system. These events are soon accompanied by development of secondary sex characteristics: growth of hair on the face and body, change to a lower voice pitch, development of breasts in the female, and general changes from a childish to an adult body contour.

Children mature a year or two earlier now than they used to, because of industrialization, improvements in health and nutrition, and other environmental factors (Bullough, 1981; Tanner, 1970). Biologists refer to this as a *secular trend*, a worldwide change in a genetically based phenomenon that occurs without changes in the genes themselves. The trend may be continuing, although there is little evidence of change in the past forty years (Eichhorn, 1980).

The average age of puberty for girls is now about twelve, with ten to sixteen as the normal range. For boys the average age is fourteen, with twelve to eighteen as the normal range (Tanner, 1973). Physical maturation is a major life event that brings not only physical changes but also emotional consequences that may affect self-concept and social relationships (Petersen & Taylor, 1980).

Early Maturation

Social adjustment

Students who mature early are likely to become socially dominant within their peer groups (Savin-Williams, 1979), although they also may begin to have more problems than their peers have with adults. Conflicts with parents increase early in the pubertal cycle (Steinberg, 1987), and teachers may see early maturers as bad influences on classmates if they begin to show resistance to authority.

In general, though, early maturation is an advantage to boys. The early-maturing boy is more likely to be treated as a mature individual, to be popular and a leader among his peers (Jones, 1957), and to have higher academic achievement and educational and occupational aspirations (Duke et al., 1982).

Research by Mussen and Jones (1957) on stories made up in response to projective test stimuli illustrates some of the psychological differences between early- and late-maturing teenage boys. The stories of the early-maturing boys revealed independence, self-confidence, and the ability to take an adult-like role in interpersonal relationships. In contrast, the stories of the late-maturing boys revealed frequent feelings of inadequacy, dependency, and low status with respect to parents and peers. Thus during the junior high and especially the high school years, early-maturing boys will have many advantages in social adjustment and peer-group relationships.

Early maturation is more of a mixed blessing for girls (Brooks-Gunn, Petersen, & Eichorn, 1985). The girls who mature the earliest usually are the earliest-maturing students of either sex in the school. This may cause them confusion or concern, especially if they have negative expectations (Clarke & Ruble, 1978). They may need reassurance and support and perhaps specific suggestions about matters such as bras, feminine hygiene, and coping with the questions and comments of classmates.

Early-maturing girls are more likely than other girls to react negatively to menarche, which may stimulate ambivalent or confused emotions and associated pain or distress, especially in girls who are unprepared or who have been led to develop negative expectations (Ruble & Brooks-Gunn, 1982). Many girls become self-conscious, embarrassed, or secretive at first, although these negative reactions are usually mild and temporary, and menarche also has positive connotations associated with maturity and deepening of female identity (Brooks-Gunn & Petersen, 1983; Greif & Ulman, 1982).

In high school, early maturers, especially boys whose growth spurts ended early, may become upset to find their friends passing them in height, weight, and general physical development. Many who were star athletes in early adolescence, partly because of early maturation, find three years later that they are now smaller than average. For those who are deeply ego involved in athletics, this can be a serious blow requiring some informal counseling. Similarly, some girls who realize that they have stopped growing may be dissatisfied with their height or body proportions and need help in learning to accept themselves as they are.

Late Maturation

Negative forms of adjustment

Notably late maturers are likely to suffer anxiety and embarrassment. They need reassurance that there are wide individual differences in the onset and duration of maturation and that they will eventually catch up with their classmates. In a typical ninth-grade class, for example, all of the girls and most of the boys will have at least begun the maturation process. The few late-maturing boys who look like "little kids" are likely to suffer teasing or rejection. They will need information and support to keep them from becoming deeply depressed by their temporary status or from turning to undesirable forms of adjustment such as becoming the class clown. Late-maturing girls are less likely to suffer intense peer problems, but they may have troubling doubts about their normality and also may need reassurance.

Summary

A developmental perspective involves concern with changes occurring over time in sequence, rate, or form. True developmental sequences are fixed and universal. In physical development, the sequence involves rapid growth in the first two years, slower but noticeable growth for the next eight to twelve years, a second period of rapid growth in adolescence, and a tapering off thereafter. Growth spurts of a few months' duration occur within larger growth curves, controlled by pituitary growth hormones and ultimately by the genes. Normal nutrition and exercise are also important, however. Listlessness and poor school achievement can result from poor nutrition, along with adverse influences on growth and development.

Body types do not directly cause psychological variables but can influence developmental task achievement, self-concept, and social acceptance. Young children may have difficulties at school because of lack of size, strength, coordination, or familiarity with tasks or equipment. They also need more sleep, more frequent meals, and more opportunity for exercise than older children or adults.

Physical maturation occurs earlier in girls than in boys, so that girls tend to be taller and heavier between the ages of ten or eleven and thirteen or fourteen. Unusually early or late maturation may cause adjustment problems requiring reassurance and support from adults.

Questions and Problems

1. Summarize research on body types and growth curves. What are the implications of this work, if any, for teachers?
2. Summarize what is known about differential rates of physical devel-

opment of boys and girls. What implications does this knowledge have for teachers?

3. Describe these aspects of development: sequence, rate, and form.
4. What is the difference between growth and development?
5. What does Epstein's work on brain growth imply about children's intellectual development in general and performance in school specifically? How much research supports these contentions?
6. Discuss in your own terms the meaning of cerebral lateralization. Specifically, what activities are controlled by the left and right hemispheres?
7. Discuss the potential implications of brain lateralization for classroom instruction. Why do the authors argue that any such implications remain to be demonstrated?
8. To what extent does body type (ectomorph, mesomorph, and endomorph) influence students' intellectual or social adaptations in school?
9. What are the differential benefits and costs for boys and girls of late or early maturation?
10. Suppose that peers begin to call one of your less physically attractive students "Pruneface" or "Frankenstein." Should you do anything about this? If so, what?
11. In gym class, two of your students are poorly coordinated and thus repeatedly fail to "make the play" during volleyball games. Embarrassed, they ask to be excused from further participation. What should you tell them?
12. Should schools try to control what or how much students eat at lunch? If so, how? If not, why not?
13. What is a reasonable length of time to expect first graders to sustain concentrated attention to a lesson? Fourth graders? Tenth graders?
14. Suppose that sex education is one of your homeroom teaching duties. How would you handle it in an inner-city school? In a suburban school? What would you do if you disagreed with part of the mandated sex-education curriculum?

Case Studies

SHARON THE OUTSIDER. (Sharon is a reasonably bright but obese high school sophomore who comes from a lower-class home.) "Sharon, you have weird ideas and you're incredibly fat," said Jane (with finality). "Yeah," Mary added. "Your dumb ideas just waste our time. We have to finish the group lab project this period. You just sit there and keep your fat lip closed." Ms. Fillmore, the biology teacher, overheard these remarks, as well as similar ones made by other students in recent weeks. What, if anything, should she say to Jane, Mary, or Sharon about this particular instance? What, if anything, should she do for Sharon generally?

JIM THE UMPIRE. Jim Moore is a third grader at Benton School. Although he is poorly coordinated, he loves sports, especially softball. However, he has poorly developed skills and peers often laugh at him or blame him for the team's failure to win. Eventually, Mr. Wilson, Jim's teacher, decides to let Jim umpire during games so that he can participate and yet be spared from criticism of his poor play. He also plans to work with Jim after school a couple of times a week to help him develop his softball skills. How adequate is this plan for responding to Jim's physical problems? Are there other things that the teacher should do in addition or instead?

TOO GOOD TO BE TRUE. Ruth is an attractive fifth grader who also is a top student in mathematics. Her peers look up to her and voted her to be the class president. For the last two months, though, Ruth has been unhappy at school despite all her obvious "successes." Ms. Kline, her teacher, has noticed that Ruth was the first student in the class to show signs of sexual maturity and that she has also seen that Ruth has been uncomfortable with the way she looks and feels. What should Ms. Kline do at this point, if anything?

CHAPTER

Basics of Cognitive Development

CHAPTER OUTLINE

OBJECTIVES

When you have mastered the material in this chapter, you will be able to

1. Define and distinguish the concepts of *maturation* and *readiness*
2. Explain how Jean Piaget's view of learning differs from the behaviorist view
3. Define *scheme* and discuss the adaptation-equilibration process of cognitive growth
4. Explain how thought and behavior differ in the four major developmental periods
5. Define *operational thought* and the key characteristics of concrete versus formal operational thinking
6. Contrast Piaget's versus American psychologists' views on teaching readiness and on the extent to which cognitive development can be speeded up
7. Explain the implications of Piaget's theory for deciding what should be taught in school and how it should be taught

Stage theorists

A century ago, intellectual development was treated primarily as a growth process: Children's minds were considered to be the same as those of adults, only smaller, and they were thought to expand gradually as knowledge and experience accumulated. The Swiss psychologist Jean Piaget and other *stage theorists* rejected this notion that intellectual development is a smooth, gradual process in which each new concept is just another brick added to a pile. Instead, they argued that children develop through a series of qualitatively distinct stages, where each new stage represents a new level of organization of knowledge and brings a different kind of knowledge, not just more of the same kind as before. This stage concept is illustrated graphically in Figure 3.1.

The stage concept of development includes the concepts of maturation and readiness. In physical development, for example, infants cannot learn to walk until the maturation of biological structures takes place. Gesell and Thompson (1929) demonstrated this by studying a variety of physical skills in identical twins. One twin was given special training and practice in acquiring a skill such as climbing stairs, while the other was not, to see if the special treatment would speed up development. In most cases, it did not. The special help would not have much effect until almost the time that the ability being taught was expected to develop naturally, and once this point was reached, the twin who had not been given special help would soon catch up with the other. Thus development of most physical skills in infants and toddlers depends heavily on maturation.

Readiness

One implication drawn from these studies was that one should not try to teach a skill until children develop *readiness*—the capability of learning it with relative ease. The concept of readiness was later expanded to include cognition and interest as well as physical ability: If children lack the prerequisite knowledge to learn a skill, or are not interested, do not try to teach it until later when both knowledge and interest have developed.

Cognitive readiness

Piaget's theory encompasses the notion of readiness, but it refers to *cognitive readiness*. Unlike readiness to develop physical skills, cognitive

Figure 3.1 Schematic Representation of Stages in Physical and Psychological Development

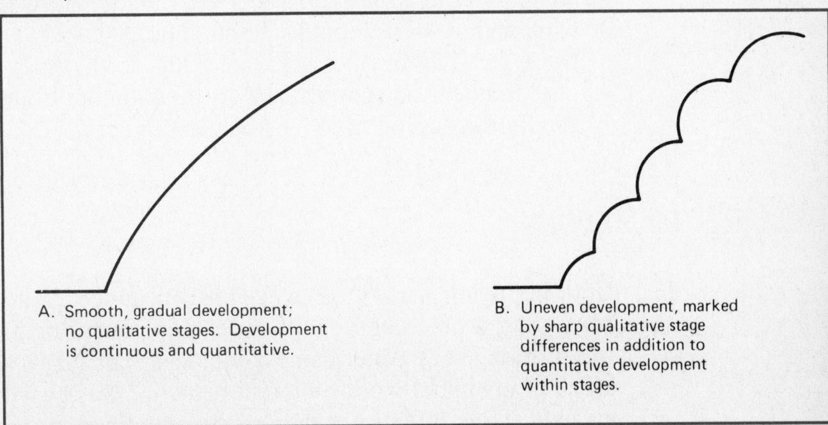
A. Smooth, gradual development; no qualitative stages. Development is continuous and quantitative.
B. Uneven development, marked by sharp qualitative stage differences in addition to quantitative development within stages.

readiness is not seen as determined primarily by biological maturation, except very early in development. Piaget viewed the mind of the child as a structure that evolves through successively higher levels of organization and integration. At any particular stage children will be oriented toward information that is *moderately novel*—new enough to be interesting but familiar enough to be comprehensible (Ginsburg & Opper, 1988). They will lack interest (at least for now) in further exploration of overly familiar topics, and they will lack both interest in and readiness for topics that are beyond their present ability to comprehend.

Qualitative versus quantitative development

Not everyone agrees with Piaget on these points. Most American behavioral and cognitive theorists, for example, reject the notion of qualitative stages in intellectual development and construe learning as a step-by-step, quantitative process. If readiness does not exist, it can be created by moving learners through successive approximations from where they are now to where one wants them to go. Even Jerome Bruner (1966), an American psychologist who otherwise is similar to Piaget in his general ideas about development, believes that any subject matter can be taught to a child of any age to at least some degree, if the instructor presents it in a form suited to the child's level of cognitive development.

We will return to these issues after considering Piaget's ideas at length. In the meantime, check your beliefs about maturation and readiness by answering the following questions:

1. At what age should children begin formal academic schooling?
2. Should children who seem cognitively "ready" be allowed to start school early or to skip grades?
3. Should children who appear "unready" be held back from school or retained in the same grade for another year?
4. Should schooling be organized to allow students to learn mostly by exploring and making discoveries on their own, even though they appear to learn more efficiently in teacher-structured lessons?
5. Children become more differentiated with age. By adolescence it is clear that some should easily succeed at college, but others will have to work hard just to graduate from high school. Also, the college-bound students tend to socialize together, as do the working-class students (Coleman, 1961). Should schools simply adapt to these differences and track the students into separate paths so that they do not see much of one another, or should they try to promote contact through heterogeneous grouping in at least some subjects?

PIAGET'S THEORY

Until his death in 1980, Piaget (1983) produced a staggering number of books and articles on cognitive development. For a long time his work was disparaged by American psychologists because it seemed unscientific. Much of his initial work on infant behavior was based on observations of his own three children in natural surroundings, done using sketchily reported, homemade methods rather than established laboratory procedures (Voyat, 1982). Nevertheless, most of his findings were later supported by other investigators, including many who set out to disprove them.

As a result, Piaget eventually achieved enormous respect and prestige, being ranked with Freud and Skinner among the most influential psychologists of all time. By the 1960s and 1970s his ideas about developmental changes in the nature and structuring of children's knowledge became the framework within which most discussions of cognitive development took place (including debates about curriculum and instruction in the schools). In the 1980s attention has turned away from the general cognitive restructuring and stage phenomena studied by Piaget toward the study of children's learning within particular knowledge domains (Flavell, 1985), although Piaget's ideas remain very influential and useful for conceptualizing the larger developmental trends within which more specific kinds of learning are occurring.

PHYSICAL ACTION AS THE BASIS FOR COGNITIVE DEVELOPMENT

Learning and physical actions

Piaget was one of the first psychologists to recognize in his theorizing that humans are born as active, exploratory, information-processing organisms. He saw people as constantly striving to adapt to the environment, which requires learning to comprehend and control it through adaptive mechanisms.

Piaget viewed the acquisition of concepts and skills as internally motivated and actively directed, not merely "elicited" by external cues. For Piaget, learning is rooted in physical actions. We observe and conceptualize our own behavior, so that *what we learn is what we do*. Through activity we learn what stimuli we can use to do certain things and what the outcomes will be if we do those things. It is not so much that stimuli elicit responses as that our own activity engenders a search for relevant stimuli. Thus consequences are important not for the motivational or re-

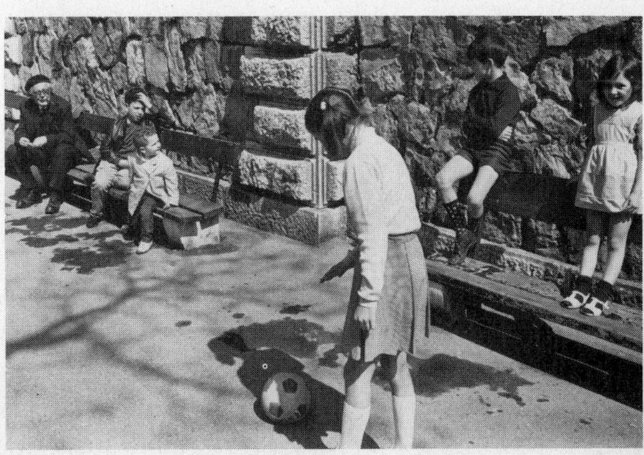

For Piaget, learning is rooted in developing and perfecting physical skills.

inforcement reasons stressed by behaviorists but because they provide feedback about the effects of our activity.

Manipulation of stimuli

Consider children learning to ride bicycles. Behaviorists would stress both the bicycle itself and the input it provides when one tries to ride it as cues that elicit responses. Responses that are successful lead to reinforcement (successful riding) and thus are retained and perfected. Responses that are unsuccessful are not reinforced (the child has difficulty maintaining balance and forward motion) and are extinguished. As practice continues, the child learns to recognize meaningful stimulus events, respond accordingly, and achieve increasing efficiency. The ability to ride a bike, then, is elicited in raw form and shaped into smooth efficiency through cues and reinforcement.

Piaget thought that the child's present interests focus attention on certain aspects of the stimulus situation (the bicycle as opposed to other things in the environment and, specifically, those aspects that are relevant to learning to ride it, rather than just looking at it or turning it upside down and spinning the wheels). Having selected these stimuli, the child manipulates them by pumping the pedals, moving the handlebars, and so on and uses the feedback from these actions to make corrections to increase efficiency. The child actively controls this learning rather than passively responding to cues and reinforcement. The bike is a prop for the child to use in perfecting skills, not a stimulus that somehow "elicits" responses. Consequences are important because they provide feedback relevant for adaptive responding rather than because they function as rewards or punishments. In short, whereas behaviorists would see the child as learning how to respond to a bike, Piaget believed that the child is learning what to do with a bike.

SCHEMES

Piaget's basic unit of cognition, speech, and behavior is the *scheme*. The term is similar to behavioristic concepts like "habit" or "response," but it also includes purely cognitive concepts, and it implies more active information processing. It is useful to distinguish different kinds of schemes. *Sensorimotor (or behavioral) schemes* refer to skills such as walking, turning doorknobs, or opening bottles; *cognitive schemes* refer to concepts, images, and thinking and reasoning abilities such as understanding the differences between plants and animals, being able to envision a triangle, or reasoning from causes to effects; and *verbal schemes* refer to word meanings and communication skills such as associating names with their referents or mastering grammar and syntax. Piaget used the term *scheme* flexibly. He spoke of specific schemes such as an infant's grasping scheme—coordination of the sensorimotor abilities required to grasp an object—but also used the term to refer to complex bodies of knowledge or skills.

Organization versus acquisition of schemes

The newborn infant's schemes are mostly simple reflexes, but new schemes begin to appear quickly, and *existing schemes become coordi-*

nated into larger schemes. For example, although the grasping scheme is an isolated and specific sensorimotor scheme in one sense, it also reflects the coordination of several previously acquired schemes such as the abilities to fix visual attention on a single object, distinguish objects that can be grasped from those that cannot, and coordinate eye and hand to reach out and grasp an object smoothly. Piaget stressed the coordination of existing schemes into more complex ones at least as much as the acquisition of new schemes.

ADAPTATION

Adaptation is part of the human condition—a continuous process of interacting with the environment and learning to predict and control it. Adaptation experiences lead to the development of new schemes, initially through trial and error exploration but then more through systematic experimentation as schemes begin to accumulate. Each new discovery is a revelation to the child who makes it, even if it is commonplace to adults (automobile tires have "nothing" but air in them; hamburgers come from cattle). Knowledge literally is *constructed* as the child gains experience, resolves apparent contradictions (all daddies are men, but all men are not daddies), and coordinates isolated schemes into clusters and ultimately into a stable, internally consistent cognitive structure.

Accommodation

Piaget identified two fundamental adaptational mechanisms involved in every action: accommodation and assimilation. *Accommodation* is change in response to environmental demands. It includes both development of entirely new schemes and adaptation of existing schemes to fit new situations. Extensive accommodation is necessary when we encounter adaptational demands that we cannot meet with existing schemes, such as when an appliance stops working for no apparent reason and we must accommodate by inventing new schemes through troubleshooting efforts.

Assimilation

Assimilation, roughly equivalent to the behavioristic term *transfer*, is the process of responding to a stimulus situation using already-established schemes. Familiar everyday activities mostly involve assimilation, although some minor accommodation is also demanded—we walk "automatically" but make accommodations when we encounter obstacles, corners, or slippery surfaces.

All behavior includes both assimilation and accommodation. Theoretically, situations that were entirely foreign to previous experience would produce panic or behavioral paralysis, since we would have no adaptation mechanisms (existing schemes) to call on. Such situations rarely if ever occur, however, because virtually any situation is *partially assimilable* to existing schemes, so we can make some systematic response to it (consider people on the "Candid Camera" show confronted with talking mailboxes and other "impossible" situations). Conversely, even the most overlearned responses require at least some accommodation, because no two situations are ever exactly the same.

Functional variants

Consider your signature, for example. In Piaget's terms, you respond to situations calling for your signature by assimilating them into your "signature-signing" scheme, which probably is the most automatic of all your writing schemes. Nevertheless, no two signatures are ever exactly the same because each signing differs from others in small ways (space available; presence or absence of a line; placement on the page; distance from the shoulder) that demand minor accommodations. This is why Piaget referred to assimilation and accommodation as universals, or *functional invariants*. They exist in every behavior, large or small, new or familiar.

Scheme-development differences

Piaget saw scheme development as universal in sequence, somewhat variable in rate, and considerably variable in form. Differences in rate and form are attributed to four factors (Ginsburg & Opper, 1988): (1) *maturation*; (2) *individual experience* (in the specific environment that one grows up in, including the stimulation that one encounters "accidentally" rather than because of the other three factors); (3) *social transmission* (formal and informal socialization and education); and (4) *equilibration* (internal self-direction and regulation).

Disequilibrium

The *equilibration principle* demonstrates Piaget's emphasis on humans as intrinsically active and exploratory in trying to impose order, stability, and meaning on experience. It postulates that we periodically sense disequilibrium such as boredom, curiosity, or the need to resolve some problem and that this sense of disequilibrium motivates us to engage in adaptational behavior. At any point in development, one's schemes are related (assimilated) to one another to form one's unique cognitive structure. This existing cognitive structure interacts with the specific possibilities and demands presented by the current environment in order to determine one's actions.

Certain aspects of a situation will be completely foreign to one's existing schemes and thus not even partially assimilable. Other aspects will be familiar and almost completely assimilable into existing schemes. Finally, some aspects will be *partially assimilable*, and they will induce disequilibrium. These *moderately novel* aspects will motivate adaptational or exploratory actions that involve accommodation.

The resulting accommodation will require development of new schemes or extension of existing ones and will continue until the originally motivating sense of disequilibrium has dissipated and has been replaced either by boredom or by a shift of attention to some other aspect of the situation that now produces sufficient disequilibrium to motivate adaptational activity. If nothing in the situation has this potential, one will be motivated to leave and find a situation that does.

Motivation to explore

This pattern is easy to observe in infants and toddlers. Placed next to a variety of toys, a toddler will inspect them and then select one for play. Different toddlers will select different toys, according to their unique interests defined by the match between the toys and their current cognitive structures. The toy that induces the most disequilibrium will be the one selected. Then the toddler will play with the toy for some time, perhaps repeating the same operations but becoming more skillful. This may continue long past the point where adults would have shifted to something else, because the activity is still new and interesting to the child. Eventually, though, the child will either start a new activity with the same toy or put the toy aside.

As another example, consider your own self-guided exploration. If you develop interest in a new kind of music or form of recreation, it probably will be familiar enough for you to relate to but different enough to make it interesting and enjoyable. For a time you may indulge your new interest during every spare moment, but eventually the novelty wears off and other interests emerge. Piaget would say that you reached a state of equilibrium with regard to the new interest and are now ready to explore something else that induces a greater sense of disequilibrium.

Equilibration principle

The equilibration principle is used not only to explain short-term relationships between motivation and behavior but also to explain trends occurring over longer periods. In particular, it predicts that, as people develop, their attention will focus on progressively more complex aspects of their environment. Rather than repeatedly returning to the same place in their efforts to maintain a state of equilibrium with their environments, people continue to develop new and more sophisticated schemes and thus operate from continually more complex cognitive structures. Therefore, since the principle of equilibration refers to the cognitive structure as a whole and not just to individual schemes, much more and better integrated knowledge is needed to maintain a ten-year-old at equilibrium than is required to maintain a five-year-old at equilibrium. Furthermore, the equilibration principle implies that people are always interested in extending the knowledge they presently possess, so they will prefer learning new things or new responses to familiar things over continued application of familiar schemes (Block, 1982; Moessinger, 1978).

PIAGET'S FOUR DEVELOPMENTAL PERIODS

We have discussed Piaget's four primary concepts for describing how humans adapt to their environments by approaching situations with cognitive structures composed of interrelated *schemes*, *assimilating* certain aspects into existing schemes but also *accommodating* these schemes to take into account unique situational factors, all under the control of the *equilibration* principle. The sequence of scheme acquisition is universal, but the rates at which schemes develop and the forms they take depend on individual differences in maturation, environmental experiences, social transmission, and unique equilibration factors. Scheme development proceeds through four qualitatively distinct periods (stages); see Table 3.1.

The Sensorimotor Period

During the first eighteen months of life, scheme development is concentrated heavily in the sensorimotor area. The infant develops and coordinates a great variety of behavioral skills, but development of verbal and cognitive schemes is minimal and poorly coordinated.

TABLE 3.1 PIAGET'S STAGES OF COGNITIVE DEVELOPMENT

Stages	Approximate Age	Characteristics and Accomplishments
Sensorimotor	0–1½ years	Formation of concept of "object permanence"—i.e., objects continue to exist when they are no longer in view. Gradual move from reflexive behavior to goal-directed activity.
Preoperational	1½–7 years	Development of language and the ability to think and solve problems through the use of symbols. Thinking is egocentric, making it difficult to see another person's point of view.
Concrete operational	7–12 years	Improved ability to think logically due to the attainments of reversible thinking, conservation, classification, serialization, negation, identity, and compensation. Able to solve concrete (hands-on) problems logically. Notion of intentionality in moral reasoning is constructed.
Formal operational	12 years to adulthood (if attained)	Hypothetical and purely symbolic thinking become possible (e.g., complex verbal). Thinking becomes more scientific as the person develops the ability to generate and test all of the logical combinations pertinent to a problem. Concerns about identity and social issues emerge.

The Preoperational Period

From about eighteen months until about age seven, children internalize their sensorimotor schemes (behavioral skills) in the form of cognitive schemes (imagery, thought). Instead of relying on laborious trial and error, for example, when working a picture puzzle or trying to construct something from blocks, children begin to guide their actions with imagery based on memories of previous experiences in the same situation.

As the development of imagery and the ability to retain images in memory progress, learning becomes more cumulative and less dependent on immediate perception and concrete experience. This makes possible more systematic reasoning and problem solving in which children relate current situational factors to previously developed schemes retained in memory by visualizing activities without carrying them out. Preoperational children, for example, can "think ahead" during a sequential task like block building or copying letters, whereas previously they had to act everything out behaviorally and thus make many errors.

Despite its strengths, preoperational logic is notably egocentric and unstable. It is *egocentric* because children of this age have not yet learned to consider things from other people's perspectives. They act as if everyone else thinks exactly as they do, knows exactly what they mean, and so on. Furthermore, they often seem not to notice or be bothered by indications that these assumptions are incorrect (Flavell et al., 1968; Miller, Brownell, & Zukier, 1977; Vygotsky, 1962).

Scheme instability

Schemes are unstable during the preoperational period because children have not yet learned to distinguish invariant aspects of the environment from aspects that are specific to particular situations. They are easily confused by *conservation problems* that require them to "conserve" invariant aspects of objects in their minds and avoid becoming confused by manipulations of other aspects. For example, many children will say that a ball of clay contains more or less clay after it has been rolled up into a "hot dog" shape even though no clay has been added or taken away, and most will assume that a taller container holds more water than a shorter one, even though the tall one may be a test tube and the shorter one may be a drinking glass or even a pitcher.

The Concrete Operations Period

Starting about age seven and continuing to about age twelve, children *become operational*. Their cognitive schemes, especially their thinking and problem-solving skills, become organized into *concrete operations*—mental representations of potential actions.

Classification skills

One set of concrete operations involves *classification skills*. Consider class-inclusion questions about how objects can be classified (McCabe et al., 1982). A collection of toy chairs, tables, cars, and trucks, for example, can be divided into these four groups but also into two larger groups of furniture and vehicles. Preoperational children have difficulty distinguishing between these two levels of classification, especially if asked questions such as "Are there more trucks or more vehicles?" that require them to consider both classes simultaneously (Piaget & Inhelder, 1964).

Children whose classification skills have become operational can handle such questions, because *concrete operations are reversible*. Thus these children can reverse combinations of smaller classes into larger ones (they can redivide the vehicles into separate groups of cars and trucks), as well as divisions of larger classes into smaller ones (they can reassemble the vehicles into a single group). Furthermore, they can perform these operations mentally, without having to move the objects around.

Conservation concepts

As children move through the concrete operational years, they gradually attain *conservation concepts*. Around ages six to seven, they attain conservation of *substance* (realizing that the amount of substance does not change if you divide it into subparts), *length* (the length of a piece of string does not change if you cut it into parts or bend it into a curved shape), and *continuous quantity* (pouring liquid from one container to another does not change the amount of liquid). About seven years of age, children attain conservation of *number* (the number of objects does not change if they are placed close together or spread far apart) and *area* (the total area covered by a piece of paper will not change if the paper is cut into pieces or the pieces are rearranged into new shapes). Between ages nine and twelve children attain conservation of *weight* (a piece of clay weighs the same regardless of the shape one forms it into). Finally, at ages eleven or twelve they attain conservation of *volume* (a piece of clay reformed into various shapes will always occupy the same volume when immersed in a liquid).

Seriation

Among the concrete operations that develop is *seriation*—the ability to place objects in order from least to most in length, weight, or some other common property. Younger children tend to proceed laboriously on seriation tasks because they have to make paired comparisons. Concrete operational children are more able to "see the big picture" and place ten or twelve objects in order without having to compare each of them with each of the others. Also, preoperational children are more easily confused by misleading cues. For example, if asked to order objects from lightest to heaviest, they may confuse size and weight so that they misplace objects that are large but light or small but heavy.

Negation

Another concrete operation is *negation*—the recognition that an action can be negated or reversed to restore the original situation. In a liquid volume conservation task, for example, preoperational children recognize that identical pitchers contain the same amounts of water when equally filled, but they become confused if the contents of one pitcher are poured into several glasses ("Is there more water in the remaining pitcher, or in all these glasses?"). Children who have mastered the concrete operation of negation immediately recognize that the amounts must be the same, because if you pour the contents of the glasses back into the pitcher, you will have its original contents.

Identity

Other concrete operations can also be illustrated with the same example. One is *identity*—recognition that physical substances retain their volume or quantity even if moved around, divided into parts, or otherwise transformed in appearance, as long as nothing is added or taken away. Children using the operation of identity will say that the amounts are the same because it's the same quantity of water—it was moved but none was added or taken away.

Compensation

Another concrete operation that helps children comprehend this problem is *compensation* or *reciprocity*—recognition that a change in one dimension is balanced by a compensating or reciprocal change in another dimension. Operational children will note that the pitcher holds more water than a single glass but that there are several glasses.

Higher levels of equilibrium

Concrete operations not only allow children to solve specific problems, but also constitute learning-to-learn skills and logical reasoning abilities that help them make sense of their general experience. Consequently, concrete operations are important components of school readiness (Arlin, 1981). Once children become operational in their thinking, they become more systematic in moving toward higher levels of equilibrium. Their schemes, especially cognitive schemes concerning which aspects of the world are invariant and which are subject to situational changes, become more stable, dependable, and integrated into a single comprehensive cognitive structure. The schemes within this structure become coordinated and mutually supportive, so they become available for systematic and consistently logical application to problem solving (*accommodation*).

Upon reaching this point, children think logically in the same way that adults do, although they cannot yet handle purely abstract content. Thus this is called the period of concrete operations because although children now are capable of logical reasoning, they still depend on direct, concrete experiences (or at least the ability to imagine such experiences vividly) to provide "props" for their thinking. They cannot yet learn abstract content that does not lend itself to concrete examples, except to memorize verbal statements that they do not really understand.

The Formal Operations Period

The period of formal operation begins at about age twelve and gradually consolidates over the next several years (Inhelder & Piaget, 1958). Much is involved in this transformation, but the hallmark is the development of the ability to think in symbolic terms and comprehend content meaningfully without requiring physical objects or even imagery based on past experience with such objects. Formal operations are the logical and mathematical concepts and rules of inference used in advanced conceptualization and reasoning, including reasoning about abstract ideas or about events that are theoretically possible but have never occurred in reality.

Binary operations

In describing formal operations, Piaget made reference to the binary operations used in propositional logic and the "INRC group" used in algebra. *Binary operations* are logical operations that apply to problems involving two propositions that each may be either true or false. People who possess well-functioning formal operations can generate all of the logical combinations that could apply to the relationship between the two propositions. These combinations yield a total of sixteen possible outcomes, which can yield statements of affirmation, negation, denial, equivalence, conjunction, implication, reciprocal implication, conclusion, and so on.

INRC operations

The *INRC group* includes more formal and algebraic versions of the reversibility schemes previously attained in concrete form. In thinking about transformations such as those that occur during a conservation task, for example, a person with well-functioning INRC operations can follow all of the changes that occur without becoming confused about the qualitative and quantitative properties of the material and can mentally reverse the entire process if necessary. To accomplish this, the person must understand the structural possibilities of *identity* (I), *negation* (N), *reciprocity* (R), and *correlativity* (C). In a conservation of matter task, for example, a person would realize that the material is the same material regardless of changes in its shape (identity), that increases in length are compensated for by decreases in width (reciprocity), that thinness is related to length and fatness to height (correlativity), and that the whole process can be reversed to undo any of the changes made (Bybee & Sund, 1982). Furthermore, in contrast to the concrete operational child who could deal with only one or two of these relationships at a time and only in connection with observation or vivid memory of demonstrations involving actual objects, formal operational people have a more abstract and better integrated understanding of these logical and algebraic relationships that enables them to think rapidly yet comprehensively and without dependence on concrete props.

Development of well-functioning formal operations apparently occurs only among individuals whose cognitive structures have been well developed and integrated at the level of concrete operational thought. Evidence of formal operations is lacking altogether in certain societies, especially those without formal education systems (Dasen, 1972; Luria, 1976; Riegel, 1973), at least when measured with the usual Piagetian methods that involve probing understanding of the actions of a pendulum (What factors affect its frequency of oscillation?) or the bending of rods (Does the degree to which a rod will bend when a weight is placed on it depend on its composition, length, thickness, cross-sectional form, or some combination of these factors?). Critics of these experiments point out that they assume knowledge of Western classical sciences and suggest that evidence of formal operational thinking might appear if individuals in undeveloped societies were questioned about things that were familiar to them (Brislin, 1983; Laboratory of Comparative Human Cognition, 1983; Modgil & Modgil, 1982). This is possible but so far has not been demonstrated convincingly.

Within-society comparisons of individuals who have experienced formal schooling with individuals who have not suggest that schooled groups not only attain literacy but also learn to deal with abstractions, to organize objects into logically based categories that differ from the organizations encountered in natural experience, and to manipulate concepts logically without having to carry out physical actions or refer to prior experience (Laboratory of Comparative Human Cognition, 1986; Rogoff, 1981). This suggests that a certain amount of formal schooling may be necessary, if not sufficient, to ensure the development of well-functioning formal operations.

In any case, it is clear that even within our society only certain individuals, perhaps a minority, develop well-functioning formal operations in which schemes are coordinated to the point that they can be expressed in purely symbolic form as abstract logical or mathematical principles that can be used without reference to concrete objects or imagery (Capon & Kuhn, 1979; Crain, 1980; Killian, 1979; Neimark, 1979; Towler & Wheatley, 1971). This level of cognitive development is necessary to understand advanced concepts in philosophy, mathematics, and science, as well as many of the concepts taught in college courses in any subject. Among college students, formal operations are more developed with reference to

In the formal operations stage, learners acquire the ability to think in symbolic terms.

one's major subject than to other content (DeLisi & Staudt, 1980). Also, students with more developed formal operations tend to take more math and science courses and do better in them than students with equal ACT scores but less developed formal operations (Commons, Miller, & Kuhn, 1982). There are small but statistically significant differences favoring males over females in formal operations (Meehan, 1984), possibly due to gender differences in course enrollments in science and mathematics (Peskin, 1980).

Problem-finding stage of cognitive development

Some psychologists have argued that the concept of formal operations needs to be elaborated to take into account cognitive development that occurs beyond the adolescent years (Commons, Richards, & Armon, 1984; Commons, Richards, & Kuhn, 1982). For example, Arlin (1975) argued that a fifth stage of cognitive development occurs in adulthood. She described this as a problem-finding stage that builds on the problem-solving abilities that come with Piaget's formal operations. People who attain this fifth stage not only can solve problems but also can infer implications and think creatively and divergently about the objects of their thought. Riegel (1973) has made a similar proposal.

Others have argued the need to distinguish preadolescents who are just developing the ability to think abstractly about concrete experiences from older students who are capable of sustained logical reasoning on abstract or hypothetical issues. We agree and prefer to divide the period of formal operations into two substages or at least to refer to preadolescents just entering the stage as *transitional* students rather than as students who have attained formal operations. Table 3.2 shows the typical ages and stages at which certain mathematical concepts develop.

IMPLICATIONS FOR EDUCATION

Piaget made few specific statements about the implications of his work for teachers, so that any curriculum or teaching method labeled as "Piagetian" is an interpretation based on his work and not a direct statement from Piaget himself (Ginsburg & Opper, 1988). For what he did say, see Piaget (1970) and Hooper and DeFrain (1980).

Piaget's work has inspired varied and sometimes even contradictory approaches to schooling that are claimed to be "Piagetian" or "based on Piaget" by their designers (Hooper & DeFrain, 1980; Kuhn, 1979; Sigel, Brodzinsky, & Golinkoff, 1981). Some early interpreters, stressing Piaget's research on learning through natural interaction with the environment and his emphasis on self-regulated learning governed by the equilibration principle, seemed almost hostile to the notion of instructing children (rather than allowing them to learn on their own). This extremism has faded, but among Piagetians who stress self-regulated learning as a key concept, there is still an emphasis on *discovery learning* as the preferred approach to education. In this view, teachers should minimize direct instruction in a set curriculum taught in a prescribed sequence and instead should emphasize discovery of schemes accomplished through

Discovery learning

TABLE 3.2 AVERAGE AGES WHEN SELECTED MATHEMATICAL CONCEPTS DEVELOP

Concept	Late Preoperational Period (4–7) ages	Concrete Operational Period (7–9) ages	Concrete Operational Period (9–11) ages	Period of Formal Operations (11–15) ages
Topological space	×			
Classification	××			
Seriation	××			
Number conservation	××			
Length conservation	××			
Area conservation	××			
Closure	××			
Addition of classes	××	×		
Multiplication of numbers	××	×		
Euclidean space	××	×		
Multiple classification	××	××		
Identity	××	××		
Commutativity	××	××		
Associativity	××	××	×	
Distributivity	××	××	××	
Space	××	××	××	××
Time	××	××	××	××
Movement, velocity	××	××	××	××
Volume	××	××	××	××
Measurement	××	××	××	××
Functions	××	××	××	××
Proportion	××	××	××	××
Deduction/induction				××
Formal logic				××
Probability				××
Proofs				××

Note: The initial steps in the construction of many of these concepts can be traced to the sensorimotor period.
Source: *Wadsworth, 1978.*

active manipulation of concrete materials. The teacher would be oriented more toward instructing individuals than groups and more toward responding to students' initiatives or evidence of readiness for learning experiences than toward teacher-initiated instruction (Ginsburg & Opper, 1988; Wadsworth, 1978).

Piagetian research and theorizing about how children learn in natural play situations are compatible with these ideas but silent about how they might be applied at school. Perhaps they can be applied in preschool classes with low student-teacher ratios, but they do not appear feasible for elementary and secondary classes. Also, there are limits as to how seriously teachers can take concepts such as readiness or developmental stages. Duckworth (1979), a writer generally sympathetic to Piagetian notions, noted that overemphasis on self-regulated learning in "applying Piaget" creates a dilemma for teachers, who may be led to think that "either we're too early and they can't learn or we're too late and they know it already."

Application of Piagetian theories to the classroom

Some would-be appliers of Piaget took the opposite approach and built Piagetian tasks into the curriculum by teaching students to conserve, to solve class-inclusion problems, and so on. This was contrary to the spirit of Piaget's work, although it was based on the notion that if conservation and the other key concepts and operations that he discovered were truly basic to intellectual functioning, direct instruction in them might enhance or at least accelerate cognitive development. Unfortunately, such instruction did not have generalized effects.

Most attempts to apply Piaget's work to education have emphasized his ideas about how children learn rather than his stages of development. Hooper and DeFrain (1980), after reviewing several "Piagetian" programs, suggested the following principles: (1) Attend to the processes and not just the products of students' thinking. Don't concentrate just on getting correct answers; make sure that the students really understand the concepts or operations being taught. (2) Appreciate the value of play and exploration/manipulation opportunities for developing cognitive schemes, especially in the early grades. (3) Be aware that children learn a great deal from interacting with one another and in particular from debating conflicting views. (4) Remember that learning that occurs through active exploration and discovery is more likely to be retained and to be meaningful than learning that occurs through more passive response to teachers' initiatives.

Matching Input to Student Readiness

The problem of the match

Unless teachers are willing to rely completely on discovery learning, they will have to find ways to keep the level and variety of input matched to students' schemes so as to maximize disequilibrium (and thus motivation to learn). Material that is too easy or familiar will be boring, material that is too difficult will be frustrating, and material that lacks interest will not be explored actively.

Underestimation of children's knowledge

These notions appear sound as general principles but difficult to apply to particular situations. For one thing, it appears that Piaget systematically underestimated both the extent of knowledge that children at particular ages possess and the degree to which their existing knowledge can be extended with relative ease (Flavell, 1985). His findings concerning conservation of number, for example, seemed to imply that preoperational children do not have useful quantitative knowledge. Later research on children's understanding of number, however, showed that two- and three-year-olds possess notions of quantity and the ability to compare quantities even before they can count and that older preoperational children not only can count but possess a variety of accurate and useful number concepts even before they can qualify as conservers on conservation-of-number tasks (Briars & Siegler, 1984; Gelman & Gallistel, 1986). Furthermore, counting and related number concepts and operations may be more basic to development of knowledge about numbers than ability to succeed on Piagetian tasks (Fuson, 1988).

Horizontal versus vertical decalage

Another problem is that Piagetian stage notions are very general, and students' thinking can be inconsistent even when they are clearly within a particular overall stage. Piaget referred to such inconsistency as decalage and acknowledged the frequency of both *horizontal decalage* (the child shows mastery of a concept in one task or situation but not another, such as being able to conserve length but not weight) and *vertical decalage* (the child appears to be at a higher stage in certain respects but at a lower stage in other respects). Scholars concerned with school curriculum and instruction issues are increasingly focusing on studies of children's restructuring of ideas in particular knowledge domains rather than on studies of the more general types of restructuring stressed by Piaget in seeking guidance about matching input to students' readiness (Carey, 1985; Siegler, 1986; Vosniadou & Brewer, 1987). In addition to these ambiguities about when children are ready for instruction in particular concepts, there are ambiguities about what is meant by matching input to students' readiness. Early Piagetian interpreters assumed that such matching meant presenting students with tasks that called for application of schemes and operations learned during their current stage of cognitive development.

Plus-one matching

Later, other interpreters began to call for *plus-one matching*—presenting students with tasks that require application of schemes or operations associated with the stage of development one level higher than their current stage. Their rationale is that matching input to existing development will merely provide for additional exercise of already well-developed schemes and operations, whereas plus-one matching will stimulate the development of schemes and operations that are just now emerging. Vygotsky (1962, 1978) advanced a similar notion in arguing that instruction should concentrate on the *zone of proximal development*—on teaching knowledge and skills that the student will not master spontaneously but could master with relative ease if given instructions and assistance.

Critics of Piagetian ideas reject what they see as overemphasis on the need for spontaneous and self-regulated learning. They note, for example, that motivation to learn a particular thing may not exist at the moment but might be stimulated easily by the teacher. Similarly, they note that *readiness* is simply a term for particular prerequisite knowledge and interests that may be possible to stimulate easily through systematic intervention. In other words, such critics stress *teaching readiness* rather than waiting for it to occur spontaneously.

Teaching Readiness

The issues just discussed led to a controversy between the Piagetians and a group of psychologists, mainly American, who were interested in training nonconservers to conserve (Kuhn, 1974). The "conservation trainers" used brief treatments designed to bring about conceptual advances that Piaget believed would require years of broad-based natural experience.

Their data seemed to show that children could learn such concepts much earlier than Piaget had claimed.

Piaget was not impressed with these findings. He believed that educational efforts should attempt to develop logical structures that would transfer to a great many tasks rather than to train students to perform particular tasks correctly. In effect, he viewed attempts to stimulate general cognitive development by teaching students particular Piagetian tasks as akin to attempting to increase children's intelligence by teaching them to respond correctly to the particular items on IQ tests.

Criteria for concept acquisition

In addition, Piaget and his colleagues (Inhelder, Sinclair, & Bovet, 1974) were dissatisfied with the conservation training findings because they believed that the criteria for concept acquisition were not strict enough. Also, they doubted that the new learning would generalize to natural situations. The American studies usually were restricted to verbal questioning of children, and correct answers were accepted as evidence that the child had acquired the concept being taught (such as the ability to conserve number). The Piagetians required not merely initially correct answers but the ability to withstand challenges designed to confuse children who did not have a firm grasp of the new concept. They believed that true conservers not only know what is true but know that it is *necessarily* true—that it could not be otherwise. In support of their position, the Piagetians showed that many newly "acquired" concepts could not withstand this kind of probing. When children were required not only to produce correct verbal responses but also to indicate understanding with corresponding physical actions, and especially when they were confronted with counterarguments, many became confused, backed down, or reverted to lower-level concepts. Typically, these were the children who showed the least evidence of readiness to achieve the concept before training began.

More recent work by Miller (1986) also supports Piagetian claims that true conservers view conservation as *necessarily* true. Even so, work by other investigators indicates that apparently genuine, generalizable gains can be induced by methods such as confronting conservers and nonconservers with each other's beliefs and requiring them to come to agreement (Botvin & Murray, 1975; Russell, 1982) or asking children to pretend that their beliefs are opposite to the real ones (Murray, Ames, & Botvin, 1977). Others have also succeeded with more traditional approaches involving instruction in rules, provision of feedback, or exposure to models (Brainerd, 1977).

Research on attempts to teach preadolescents to use formal operations has produced the same pattern of mixed and controversial findings as the "conservation training" studies (Greenbowe et al., 1981; Nagy & Griffiths, 1982). Taken together, the data suggest that cognitive development is more open to meaningful stimulation through instruction than Piaget thought but that Piaget was correct in stating that there are limits on what can be accomplished with a given child and on whether it will be worth the effort involved (Murray, 1978; White & Tisher, 1986).

Figurative versus operative knowledge

Piaget drew on a distinction between figurative and operative knowledge in describing much of the "learning" produced in the American experiments as superficial and "merely verbal." *Operative knowledge* comes from actions, specifically those used to respond to (operate on) the environment. These actions can be either overt (physical) or internal (mental). For Piaget, operative knowledge is the most basic kind of knowledge—knowledge about what we can do and how to do it. *Figurative knowledge* involves taking in some representation or reproduction of the environment without actually changing it or operating on it. Mainly this involves perceptions or mental images of things observed in the environment, although it also includes imitations of the actions of other persons or things (simply copying without operating on the input, such as by memorizing a multiplication fact or a definition). Figurative knowledge is subject to egocentrism and all of the other distortions of perception and comprehension that children show, and it may or may not be meaningful to them. It is meaningful only to the extent that the children can link it to relevant operative knowledge.(See Figure 3.2.)

Readiness

These developmental considerations lead to the issue of *readiness*. To a cognitive development specialist who describes changes that occur with age, readiness emerges slowly over time. However, to a teacher trying to induce change through systematic intervention, readiness is something to teach if it is not already present. Within the limits of learner capacity, a learner who is not ready to master a given concept or skill can be made ready to master it through successive approximations involving intermediate objectives. But is this worth doing in the first place? Often it is, because teaching both the intervening readiness skills and the ultimate learning objective is relatively easy. However, if readiness can be taught only with continuous and highly concentrated effort that requires maximal learner motivation and application, it may be best to teach other things and wait for the learner to develop greater readiness naturally.

According to Piaget, concrete objects, diagrams, charts, maps, and other visual aids facilitate learning.

Figure 3.2 Figurative Knowledge without Operative Knowledge

Dr. Judith Lanier of Michigan State University composed the following exercise on "traxoline" to illustrate what happens when we present (and require application of) knowledge only at the figurative level.

TRAXOLINE

It is very important that you learn about traxoline. Traxoline is a new form of zionter. It is montilled in Ceristanna. The Ceristannians gristerlate large amounts of fevon and then bracter it to quasel traxoline. Traxoline may well be one of our most lukized snezlaus in the future because of our zionter lescelidge.

Please answer the following questions in complete sentences and in your best handwriting.

1. What is traxoline?
2. Where is traxoline montilled?
3. How is traxoline quaselled?
4. Why is it important to know about traxoline?

If this example seems too farfetched, consider the next one, putting yourself in the place of a 10-year-old from Luckenbach, Texas.

Pittsburgh, "Heart of the Nation," is known for its steel production. It is located in southwestern Pennsylvania, where the Allegheny and Monongahela rivers join to form the Ohio. Iron ore, especially hematite, magnetite, and taconite, is first concentrated and then purified, using limestone as a flux to combine with impurities and float the resulting slag to the top of the melted iron in the blast furnace. Then, pig iron from the blast furnace is combined with scrap iron and various additives, annealed or tempered through heat treatment, and formed into steel ingots ready for shipment to finishing mills.

Questions

1. What is Pittsburgh's nickname and what is the reason for it?
2. In steel production, what is the function of a flux?
3. What types of iron ore are commonly used in Pittsburgh's steel industry?
4. What happens to the ingots of annealed or tempered steel?

This second example *should* look familiar, because it is representative of the kinds of exercises included all too frequently in the social studies curricula used in elementary schools. Note that students can answer each question correctly without learning anything at all, at least not anything beyond isolated and relatively meaningless figurative knowledge.

Providing Concrete Props for Learning

Piaget's work shows why *concrete objects, diagrams, charts, and other visual aids facilitate learning* and why *learning requires active response*. If what we learn is what we do, we must actually practice the doing, acting it out in behavior or at least formulating a plan in our own words. Just watching and listening alone will result in "merely verbal" learning rather than meaningful learning of a network of related schemes.

Piaget's work suggests that everything is learned most easily and thoroughly if mastered in *the order in which discovery learning would occur naturally*. Sensorimotor schemes would precede cognitive schemes, and concrete experience would precede formal analysis and abstraction.

Concrete props help students to bridge the gap between the known and the unknown, thus increasing the degree to which new material is relatively assimilable. In science classes, for example, laboratory demonstrations illustrate literally the abstract principles being taught.

Other implications concern what can be taught at different developmental levels. Some students may have difficulty with certain new learning if they have not yet developed the schemes to comprehend the new information, even though most of their peers have developed these schemes. Instruction is unlikely to be successful until the schemes develop, either spontaneously or in response to instruction (Renner et al., 1976). Successful teachers present material in a variety of ways, so that it becomes meaningful to students who differ in cognitive development.

School Curricula and Methods

Briefly, Piaget's developmental work suggests the following about matching school experiences to existing cognitive development. First, toddlers in the sensorimotor period and early in the preoperational period learn primarily through play and exploration, and their learning is concentrated on sensorimotor schemes. The way to optimize cognitive development in these early years is to provide a rich, stimulating environment that encourages learning through exploration. Attempts to teach concepts that call on schemes that would not appear naturally for several years are not likely to succeed, except in producing "merely verbal" learning (few environmentalists accept this last implication).

Matching presentation to schemes

In the late preoperational and early concrete operational stages, children can benefit increasingly from more systematic and even formal instruction, although the content and modes of presentation must be matched to their existing schemes. They can learn a great deal about many things, particularly about familiar experiences or about concrete objects that they can manipulate and explore for themselves. They also learn words and memorize things easily, although they will not understand the meanings of the memorized statements if they are too abstract or if they refer to events that are beyond the children's experience and imagination (i.e., if figurative knowledge is not integrated with operative knowledge).

Instruction versus discovery

We believe that these implications do not necessarily contradict the school practices, traditional in the early grades, that Piagetians have criticized. Certain things are learned much more easily from instruction than by discovery. The list is debatable, but it includes the fundamentals of reading, writing, and arithmetic taught in the early grades. Piaget's work reminds us, however, that instruction in these fundamentals should focus on meaningful learning, not just rote practice of isolated skills. Thus students should read meaningful text for information and enjoyment (not just practice decoding), write to communicate ideas (not just practice penmanship), and learn computation skills in the context of meaningful problem solving (not just do computation worksheets).

Abstract subject matter

In general, the traditional school curriculum is fairly well matched to natural levels of cognitive development. Typically, the middle grades that correspond to the period of concrete operations call for more conceptual learning than do the first few grades, but they avoid highly abstract subject matter and emphasize concrete objects, specific examples, or other aids to promote meaningful understanding. Beginning in junior high school the curriculum concentrates increasingly on more abstract subject matter. Elementary school history, for example, stresses names, dates, places, and events and usually is simplified and personalized around central characters. In contrast, history courses in high school, and particularly in college, dispense with most of these "childish" personalizations and concentrate on more conceptual matters such as the political, social, and economic reasons for historical events.

Logical reasoning of students

Remember, *all students operate with some type of logic, although their logic may differ from that used by most adults*. Teachers must be able to recognize the general developmental levels and particular logical reasoning used by their students if they are to diagnose learning difficulties accurately and communicate meaningfully. All teachers, but especially those in grades two and three (when children start to become operational) and those in the junior high school grades (when some students begin to acquire formal operations), must be prepared for a great range in developmental levels as well as in IQ. Many third graders will be preoperational in their logic, with all of the egocentrism and other childish limitations that this implies. Others will be well into the concrete operational stage, capable of reasoning logically as long as they do not have to deal with purely abstract concepts. All students in junior high classes will be logical in their thinking, but only some will be able to deal with abstract material meaningfully (Cox & Matz, 1982).

Even students who do show formal operational thinking in certain tasks may not do so in other, less familiar tasks. Martorano (1977) measured formal operations in middle-class girls who had IQs between 100 and 120, using ten tasks. Even in this above-average group, only about 20 percent of the eighth graders and 60 percent of the tenth graders were scored for formal operations on Piaget's "pendulum" and "rods" problems. Across the ten tasks, the percentages of students scored for formal operations ranged from zero to 60 percent in sixth graders, zero to 85 percent in eighth graders, 5 to 95 percent in tenth graders, and 15 to 90 percent in twelfth graders. Thus ability to think abstractly depends not only on age and general cognitive development but also on specific knowledge and experience with particular intellectual content.

Use of ability to think abstractly

Finally, it should be noted that *possession of the ability to think abstractly does not mean that one always or even often uses that ability. Nor does attaining the period of formal operations imply that previous modes of thinking are lost. On the contrary, they persist and in fact constitute most of the cognitive structure*. Even professors routinely use formal operational thinking only in certain situations, most obviously when theorizing in their areas of specialization. When trying to comprehend politics or the stock market, and especially when trying to fix an appliance or automobile, they may have to make do with primarily concrete operational or even sensorimotor schemes.

Summary

Piaget and other *stage theorists* believe that children develop through qualitatively distinct stages in acquiring and organizing knowledge. Both maturation and readiness are involved in this process, which contrasts with the step-by-step quantitative process of acquiring knowledge described by learning theorists. Piaget stressed physical action and experience with the environment in learning but differed from behaviorists in his emphasis on learner purposes. He believed that the scheme is the basic unit of cognition, speech, and behavior. The constant process of adaptation, accomplished via the mechanisms of assimilation and accommodation and guided by the principle of equilibration, modifies existing schemes.

Piaget divided development into four basic periods: (1) *sensorimotor* (birth to eighteen months), (2) *preoperational* (eighteen months to seven years), *concrete operations* (seven to twelve years), and (4) *formal operations* (twelve years and beyond). Scheme development in the sensorimotor stage is concentrated heavily on sensorimotor skills, whereas the preoperational stage brings expansion into the areas of thought and imagery. During the period of concrete operations, children add classification skills, reversibility of operations, negation, identity, and reciprocity. Finally, the ability to use symbols, abstractions, and propositions contrary to fact develops during the period of formal operations.

Questions and Problems

1. Can one teach readiness? What are the issues associated with this question?
2. If Piagetians are correct in their belief that children go through a series of qualitatively distinct stages in cognitive development, what implications does this have for the types of learning activities and content that students can be assigned?
3. What is a scheme? Differentiate, in your own words, the following types of schemes: sensorimotor, cognitive, and verbal.
4. Explain the equilibration principle and its role in Piaget's theory.
5. How does problem finding differ from problem solving? Why do some writers contend that problem finding represents a fifth stage of cognitive development?
6. According to Hooper and DeFrain (1980), what important general principles can be derived from Piaget's work?
7. Define the terms *plus-one matching* and *zone of proximal development*. What are the implications of these concepts for classroom practice?
8. Notice that we have accepted differences in learner capacity (both

Piagetian stage differences and general IQ differences among those at the same Piagetian stage) as real. Do you? What does this imply with respect to nature-nurture issues such as tracking, special education, and IQ testing?

9. Piagetian theory and research suggest that natural learning proceeds according to the equilibration principle rather than following logical and hierarchically arranged sequences. What (if anything) does this imply about the structuring of curricula?
10. What aspects of poetry and science can be taught meaningfully to first graders? Fourth graders? Tenth graders? Which of these aspects should be taught?

CASE STUDIES

MS. HERBERT AND A HEAT WAVE. Ms. Herbert worked with her slowest second-grade reading group. She and the children perspired because it was a hot day and the inner-city school did not have air conditioning. Everyone had to strain to focus attention on the reading task, as opposed to personal discomfort. During the lesson two students raised questions that were touched off by the story but not directly related to it. Jim asked, "Does anybody's father in this room work on a farm like the guy in the story?" Tim asked, "What do they eat?" Ms. Herbert made minimal responses to these questions in order to keep the children "on task." What principles of human development did she ignore? Specifically, how could she improve the situation?

SUCCESSFUL PRACTICE. Millie Mohatt was an enthusiastic seventh-grade general math teacher. She believed that most students could learn and that she could teach them. She went through the curriculum slowly so that students would repeatedly experience success on assignments. Characteristically, all students worked all or almost all problems correctly, and they seemed to enjoy the opportunity to continue to practice things that they could do well. To what extent do you agree with Millie's teaching techniques? What suggestions might you make about improving her approach? How do the concepts of plus-one matching and zone of proximal development apply to her teaching?

MR. FLAKER AND BOOK SCIENCE. Jim Flaker was a second-grade teacher who enjoyed presenting science to his students and spent considerable time at it (forty-five minutes per day instead of only fifteen minutes two or three times a week). He often described famous scientists and told how and why they did experiments. Jim also liked to talk about great discoveries, about the general processes of science, and about the things we might have in the year 2050 that presently are not available. However, he did not like to actually *do* experiments with the students, because the class was hard to control and things would break. What principles of human development was Jim Flaker ignoring? What advice might you have for him?

SUPERVISOR ON THE SPOT. Marge Guffy, the English coordinator for the school district, had just observed an eighth-grade lesson taught by Kim Anderson. After the lesson, Marge said, "Kim, that was generally a very good English lesson, but you taught as though the students were second graders!" Kim thoughtfully replied, "Well, I'm not sure I agree with you. What would I need to do differently?" Based on your knowledge of developmental theory, what are the differences between teaching second graders and eighth graders that should lead to differences in teaching and learning activities in the classroom?

CHAPTER

Cognitive Development and Education

CHAPTER OUTLINE

OBJECTIVES

When you have mastered the material in this chapter, you will be able to

1. Specify what and how teachers should teach to ensure meaningful learning in grades one through three versus grades four through six versus the secondary grades
2. Explain what occurs when a child "becomes operational"
3. Distinguish the thinking characteristics of concrete versus formal operational students and the types of instruction appropriate to these two periods
4. Explain what the structural aspect of language is and how it develops via the language-acquisition device (LAD)

5. Explain how one's functional use of language develops
6. Contrast the views of Vygotsky (1962) and Piaget on the interaction of language and thinking
7. Explain methods of adapting teaching to the needs of students who use nonstandard English

Piaget's theories are basic to understanding how the human mind develops by gradually constructing knowledge about the world from the feedback received during interactions with it. These theories underlie much of what will be presented in this chapter on the implications of developmental phenomena for schools and teachers. However, the chapter is based on developmental psychology in general, not just Piaget. It represents a consensus across almost all theorists except extreme environmentalists or nativists.

THE PREOPERATIONAL YEARS

Children show the capacity for operational thinking at five or six, but they usually do not become functionally operational (use operational thinking most of the time) until at least a year or two later. Thus in effect, the preoperational period extends until about third grade for most children and beyond this for some.

Three general kinds of learning seem most appropriate for preoperational students: (a) development of knowledge about familiar experiences and observable phenomena, (b) exploration and manipulation of concrete objects, and (c) learning and practice of the Three Rs and other basic knowledge and skills. Ideally, tool skills will be taught in an integrated way that stresses explanations for meaningful understanding and opportunities for realistic application (Anderson et al., 1985; Hooper & DeFrain, 1980). It must be recognized, however, that younger students have only limited abilities to transfer and generalize their learning and that basic knowledge and skills must be mastered to the point of automaticity. This will mean considerable time spent in drill and practice activities.

Children at these ages depend on the teacher for direct instruction. They can learn from verbal presentations, but the teacher cannot just lecture and assume that they will understand everything they hear. They require demonstration, instruction, elicitation of responses to check understanding, correction as necessary, and continued practice to the point of mastery once they grasp the basic concept (Brophy & Good, 1986).

Difficulty with Purely Verbal Instruction

Importance of good worksheets

Good demonstrations and visual aids provide children with concrete models to watch or imitate, so that they do not have to struggle to follow purely verbal instruction. If tasks are complex, they should be divided into subtasks that children can master in sequences that gradually connect until the ultimate task is learned. Follow-up assignments also should contain models for imitation and other aids to learning that can help overcome short attention spans and difficulty in following purely verbal instruction. Good work sheets, for example, include features such as spacing and lines to help keep separate things separate; arrows, boxes, and lines to indicate where responses should be placed or where to go next; and division of assignments into modular units that can be presented, corrected, and discussed separately.

Eliciting and Monitoring Responses

It is vital to elicit and monitor responses to check children's understanding. Once they understand, they can practice successfully on their own. If they are confused, however, their practice will involve the repetition of errors.

Mastery of fundamentals

Practice to mastery is necessary to ensure that skills are learned to the point that they can be used in solving higher-order problems. It is essential to students' future school success for teachers in the early grades to make sure that they master the fundamentals of reading, writing, and arithmetic, even if this requires extra instruction and practice.

Demonstration of mastery of a concept

Teachers cannot reliably evaluate students' understanding through questions that can be answered yes or no or that merely ask the child to indicate which of two or three alternatives is correct. It is too easy for children to come up with the right answers to such questions by guessing. To find out whether they really understand, the teacher needs to ask questions that require them to demonstrate mastery of the concept or skill (Nagy & Griffiths, 1982). For skills, this means having them perform the skill, observing to see if they use the proper process and achieve the desired outcomes, and correcting them if they do not. For verbal learning, fact questions (who, what, when, where, or how many) and explanation questions (how or why) will require the children to produce answers from memory or to figure them out. Correct responses to such questions are much more likely to demonstrate true understanding of the concept than correct answers to yes-no or either-or questions, because the former offer much lower odds of success through sheer guesswork (Blank, 1973).

In the early grades, it is important to elicit responses from each student, even during lessons. Young children have only limited ability to learn from watching and listening to others without making overt responses themselves, so it is important to elicit responses and provide corrective feedback to each student (Anderson, Evertson, & Brophy, 1979; Brophy & Evertson, 1976).

Grounding the Content in Operative Knowledge

Teaching in subject areas other than basic skills should emphasize familiar content or else make the strange familiar by using concrete props or other media. Actual objects are best, but substitutes such as films or pictures also are useful. Because young children have major gaps in their vocab-

Familiar models and events help children grasp more complex concepts.

ularies and difficulties in following purely verbal presentations, such props literally help ensure that the students understand what the teacher is talking about (Renner et al., 1976).

Mastery of the Three Rs

The difficulty that preoperational children have in understanding complex or abstract content makes it unwise to place too much emphasis on such content, even though this may seem to be an attractive alternative to those who view drilling in the Three Rs as drudgery (most children do not mind it). Certain curricula, such as the "new math" of the 1960s and 1970s in general and math systems meant for individual use in particular, have encountered difficulties in the early grades (American Institute for Research, 1976) for this reason.

These curricula were organized logically from the adult perspective but were ill-suited to children's learning needs. Children tend to learn specifics first and to build up abstract generalizations only gradually as they accumulate experience; they have trouble following the logical pattern (flowing from general rules to specific examples) that adults find helpful. Also, too many of these curricula assumed the presence of independent, self-guided learning abilities that few young children have developed yet. Because these fundamental assumptions were incorrect, the programs did not work very well. Only the brightest children tended to profit from them; others did better when taught more directly by their teachers.

Teaching at appropriate developmental levels

Even when teachers instruct their students directly, it is important to focus on familiar and observable events or at least events that are easily assimilated into the students' existing schemes. Attempts to discuss things totally outside their experience will fail. So will attempts to present content at too-sophisticated levels. Concerning social studies content, for example, Fair (1977) suggested the following generalizations about difficulty level: (a) the sheer quantity of things to be dealt with simultaneously leads to increased difficulty (it is harder to compare or interpret three things than two things); (b) more abstract content is more difficult than less abstract content; (c) fine distinctions are more difficult than gross ones; (d) relying solely on print as the source for input makes for greater difficulty than relying on a multimedia approach; (e) it is easier to develop skills in thinking about matters that students see as closely related to their own lives than about other matters; and (f) providing structure, cues, and props makes thinking easier. Fair went on to suggest that children in the primary grades need opportunities to manipulate concrete objects and need experience in comparing and contrasting, ordering before and after, identifying cause and effect, distinguishing true from false, and distinguishing main ideas and important points from supportive material.

The idea that social studies involves abstractions that are not well grasped until about the fourth grade has caused some to argue that social studies instruction should not begin until that time and many to argue that history should not be taught until the secondary grades. However, McKenzie (1986) argued that these pessimistic notions are based on early Piagetian claims that since have been disproven. Modern information-processing and schema theories indicate that children must learn stories, information, and ideas of precisely the sort that are included in history and the social sciences in order to comprehend the sketchy statements that they hear or read each day and to solve problems through logical reasoning. The key is to convey this information in concrete terms that the students can understand. For example, the phrase "the separatists faced many difficulties" may be relatively meaningless to young children, but it takes on meaning when the term *pilgrims* is substituted for *separatists*. Similarly, a problem such as "How can you determine the volume of an irregularly shaped object like a statue?" would stump most people who are able to think about volume only in geometric terms, but it could be solved by those who know that volume is related to displacement and especially by those who have heard the story of Archimedes in the bathtub.

Similarly, Elkind (1981) pointed out that even Piaget spoke of "anticipations"—intuitive ideas and interests that children develop that will become fully elaborated only at a later stage. Regarding history, for example, children have an intuitive sense of the past and a spontaneous interest in it that can provide a basis for instruction. Such instruction, however, is likely to be effective only if it gets to the operative level based in students' concrete experiences, such as by having them investigate their own family histories, explore the geography of the neighborhood, or examine cultural artifacts. If the information stays at a purely figurative level (Indians wear headbands, Mexicans wear sombreros, etc.), it will not have much meaning or much likelihood of being included in permanent and powerful networks of social studies principles and concepts.

Marshall (1985) also argued that even in the primary grades children can benefit from instruction in history if the material is presented primarily in the form of vivid narratives about real people rather than abstractions and if it is organized around concepts such as courage, cowardice, oppression, resentment, victory, and defeat that children experience in their own lives. Levstik (1986) elaborated on this point, noting that children's literary interests include the distant and fantastic of adventures, fairy tales, and so on and that they can understand content that is placed into a narrative framework and that deals with motives or thoughts that they have experienced or can identify with. Egan (1979) similarly argued that history, science, literature, and other subjects that include abstract elements can be made both very interesting and easily comprehensible to children if presented to them in the form of narratives built around the intentions and actions of central figures. Thus there is no need to avoid content drawn from the academic disciplines in the early grades as long as this content is grounded in children's operative knowledge and thus made meaningful to them.

Nor should teachers in the early grades ignore learning-to-learn skills, independent work skills, integrative concepts, or conceptual understanding (how to read for understanding; how to evaluate information and integrate it with information from elsewhere; how to budget study time and plan work on complex tasks). These concepts and skills develop slowly as children become operational and more responsive to the student role. As they master tool skills, they begin to read for pleasure and knowledge (not just to practice reading) and to use math skills for solving problems of personal interest (such as computing batting averages or money transactions). When children reach this point, they are ready for instruction in new content using methods that rely on the tool skills.

Building readiness

Although it does little good to try to teach children at conceptual levels far beyond their present grasp, teachers can develop readiness through modeling—making integrative or abstract statements about material being taught mostly at lower levels of analysis. Not all children will understand these statements, but some will, and the effect on the others will be to build readiness for more conceptual instruction later.

The Central Importance of Reading Ability

The best way to compensate for a home environment that has not prepared a child for success in school is to make the child a functional reader. Children who learn to read for understanding can always learn on their own by reading in other content areas, but children who never learn to read functionally will have to struggle in reading and most other subjects for the rest of their school years. A great deal of information about effective reading instruction is now available (Anderson et al., 1985).

Reading is the most important skill students can acquire.

BECOMING OPERATIONAL

Children make the transition to regular, functional use of concrete operational thinking during the early grades—the brightest at age six but most not until age eight and many later. Piaget stessed three aspects of becoming operational: (1) developing the ability to discriminate between invariant and variant aspects of the environment, (2) coordinating separate schemes into larger ones and, ultimately, into concrete operations and a unified cognitive structure, and (3) achieving the ability to reason forward from causes to effects and backward from effects to causes (reversibility).

Equilibration needs cause children to become more active in seeking information by asking questions and (when able) by reading. Much of this information seeking involves attempts to fill gaps and resolve discrepancies so as to render the existing cognitive structure comprehensive and internally consistent. For the first time, children become notably aware of such gaps and inconsistencies. They want to clear up confusion between concepts such as husband and father or states and nations, and they want more information about matters such as what parents do at work or what differentiates humans, animals, plants, and inanimate objects.

Transposition problems

Researchers have noted distinct changes in children's responses to certain experimental situations as they become operational. We have already mentioned the changes in responses to conservation problems and other tasks used by Piaget. Another example occurs in responses to *transposition problems*. In a typical example, children are taught to discriminate between a smaller and a larger circle by rewarding them for choosing the larger circle. This is usually learned easily when the correct choice is rewarded each time.

Then a new set is introduced, in which the smaller circle is identical to the one that was larger before (see Figure 4.1). Animals and children in the sensorimotor or preoperational stages respond to this new pair by picking the circle that is now the smaller one (but is identical to the one that was rewarded in the previous trials). Concrete operational children, as well as older children and adults, typically respond by picking the larger circle, even though they have not seen it before (Stevenson, 1970).

These and other results indicate that preoperational children tend to respond to the specific, concrete features of stimuli and to retain what they learn in isolation without much assimilation to other schemes. In-

Figure 4.1 Typical Stimuli Used in Transposition Experiments

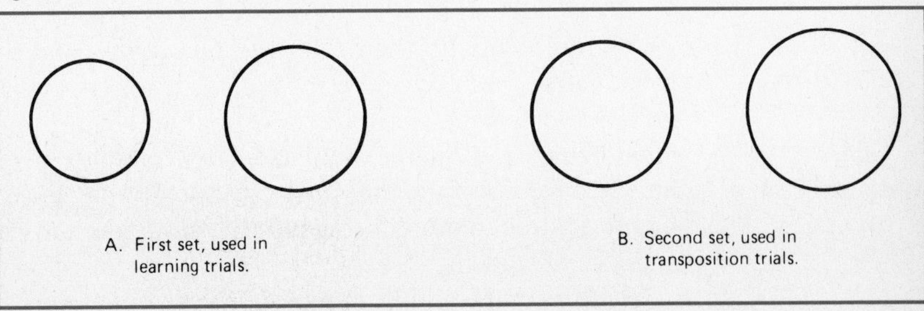
A. First set, used in learning trials.
B. Second set, used in transposition trials.

Teachers should encourage students to express themselves verbally.

dividuals at higher levels of cognitive development are less "stimulus bound" by concrete observables and more likely to attend to their more formal, conceptual, and invariant properties and thus to approach problems with concrete or formal operational logic. They assimilate the input by relating it to existing schemes rather than accommodating to it as if it were completely new. In contrast to younger children who respond to the circle task as if the problem is to "find the one exactly like the other one," operational children generate hypotheses such as "the relevant principle here is to find the larger one." This leads to a different definition of the task and, consequently, a different mode of responding.

Task identification

In the process of becoming operational, children usually begin to ask many and varied questions. It is helpful if teachers recognize what is happening, are patient in allowing children time to express themselves clearly enough to indicate what they want to know, and avoid embarrassing them by laughing at childish mistakes. Without being so insistent as to put children on the spot, teachers should foster verbal communication of concerns and questions and should patiently encourage rephrasing of questions that are too cryptic or ambiguous. This will socialize children to express their needs verbally and at the same time give them practice in doing so. The process of learning to use words for thinking is facilitated by question sequences that require students to express themselves verbally.

THE PERIOD OF CONCRETE OPERATIONS

Understanding and integrating concepts

As children solidify their concrete operations and their ability to engage in inductive and deductive reasoning, teachers can place more emphasis on abstract and integrative concepts and require more verbalizing, self-monitoring, and independent work on complex projects. However, this must be kept within the concrete operational level. Attempts to teach highly abstract content using purely verbal methods still will produce only superficial learning.

Children in the middle grades can work out elaborate mathematics problems or science experiments if they can carry out the operations physically or at least sketch them or visualize them in their minds. They also can respond meaningfully to questions about the reasons for historical events, if these reasons were presented clearly, or about the reasons for events occurring in stories, if the stories involve situations that children can understand by putting themselves in place of the characters.

Personalization of material

When learning about Columbus's discovery of America, for example, children can relate to the crew's fear of sailing away from the known world, to the concept of mutiny, and, with the help of a globe, to the reasons why the men thought they had reached India. Similarly, they can relate to lessons on modern space exploration or adventures into the unknown, such as the explorations of the North and South Poles. They will get more out of such lessons, however, if teachers personalize them with objects and pictures, stimulate the imagination by having them put themselves in the places of people they are talking about, and relate the material to familiar and observable events.

Events involving masses of people are more easily understood if personalized around the actions of specific people working from motivational systems that children can comprehend. For example, complex political and economic rivalries may be best presented as contests between individuals or countries, because children can relate to the motivations involved in trying to win a contest. The same events would be incomprehensible to them if presented at an abstract level using terms such as *hegemony*, *import-export ratio*, and *expansionist doctrine*. These terms are abstractions that require formal operations to be understood in a meaningful way.

THE PERIOD OF FORMAL OPERATIONS

Beginning around the eighth grade, some students will be entering the formal operations stage and will be able to handle largely abstract material. Some indications of readiness for formal operations are:

- Strong enjoyment in reading science fiction or mysteries
- Ability to write a good mystery, science fiction, or utopian story
- Ability to write a good essay in which each paragraph builds another point moving toward the thesis
- Possession of an identity in the Eriksonian sense (an abstract notion of who they are and where they're going), for example, can they state who/where they want to be in five years and how, specifically, they will get there?
- Certain types of responses to Kohlbergian dilemmas
- Answering hypothetical questions such as "What would the U.S. have been like if Kennedy had not been assassinated?"
- Ability to see and point out symbolism and figures of speech
- Ability to solve a mental problem with several variables
- Ability to apply formulas to different situations, for example, being

able to solve a class of math problems that are variations of the same type of problem

Several cautions should be noted, however. First, many students (a majority in some schools) will never develop formal operations to the point that they can be used with efficiency in thinking and problem solving. They may memorize the formulas in algebra, for example, but will never really understand them or be able to use them to solve nonroutine problems. Second, even students with very efficient formal operations will learn more easily if aided by imagery, diagrams, examples, or concrete presentations. Even high school students who can use formal operations should not have to rely on them exclusively, and in any case, only a small percentage will be capable of doing so. It is more accurate to assume that college students can handle purely abstract material, particularly in courses such as advanced mathematics or philosophy, but even at this level it is unwise to make the material any more difficult than necessary if the goal is to promote the most learning by the most students.

Assessing degree of formal operations

Teachers can assess formal operational thinking in their students by asking them to induce general principles from the results of scientific experiments (such as determining why pendulums oscillate at different rates) or by asking them to define concepts such as independence or justice. Certain students will be able to produce formal responses ("length is inversely related to rate of oscillation," "justice is a condition in which all parties get the treatment they deserve"), but others will only be able to respond at a concrete level ("the short ones move the most," "justice is when a crook goes to jail and an innocent person is set free").

The Use of Integrative Concepts

To the extent that students do possess formal operations, it becomes possible to present bodies of knowledge in sequences involving articulation of general principles followed by logically deduced specifics. In other words, learning can be structured around integrative concepts that promote conceptual understanding, and curricula can be organized more according to the structures of the underlying disciplines and less according to the order in which students tend to learn things on their own.

In earlier stages, conceptually integrated levels of knowledge were the last to develop, occurring only after students had mastered a great many facts and skills and gradually had assimilated them into increasingly larger schemes. This process can be reversed for students who have developed truly efficient formal operations. Instead of having to start with specifics and end up with general principles, it becomes possible to instruct by presenting the general principles first, promoting learning by using organizational concepts to structure the content. In fact, this is how highly abstract bodies of knowledge, particularly those such as mathematics or science that are inherently organized in a logical way, are taught (see Chapter 8).

Formal knowledge versus concrete experience

Formal knowledge, however, is no substitute for concrete experience. Just as a physicist who can explain why a paper airplane can fly cannot necessarily construct a good paper airplane, a student who passes a pencil-

and-paper chemistry test cannot necessarily conduct laboratory demonstrations or do worthwhile chemical research. Teachers who expect their students to be able to apply what they are learning will have to provide application opportunities. Typically, confusion about abstract principles is only one problem encountered during such applications. Students will often have problems because they know the principle but do not understand how to apply it in a specific instance (such as how to apply a theorem to an algebra problem) or because they lack concrete knowledge or experience (such as how to use a protractor to measure angles).

Ability to integrate knowledge

In fact, a challenge facing teachers at any level, but especially as instruction begins to rely on formal operations, is finding ways to get students to "put it all together." It is much more difficult to teach students to integrate knowledge and skills and apply them to problem solving than it is to communicate the essence of a single concept, even a very abstract one. Thus even at the high school level and beyond, we must remember Piaget's discovery that what we learn is what we do. Opportunities for concrete experience and for practice of skills to mastery remain important for learning at any age and essential for skillful application. Knowledge must be operative, not just figurative.

It is helpful to bear in mind that school curricula are tools, not ends in themselves. The larger goal is to empower students by equipping them with useful knowledge that they can access and apply whenever it would be appropriate for them to do so, in or out of school. Most curricula do not appear to be meeting this goal particularly well at present. To do so, they would have to adjust by addressing fewer topics but in greater depth, with emphasis on teaching for conceptual understanding (not mere memorization) of content and on applying the content in the context of critical thinking, problem solving, decision making, and other higher-order applications.

THOUGHT AND LANGUAGE

Piaget stressed thought (cognitive schemes) over language (verbal schemes), which he viewed as little more than a means for communicating thought. Others, however, place much more stress on language and its importance relative to thought (Piatelli-Palmarini, 1980; Zivin, 1979). This issue is important for education, which depends heavily on language to communicate concepts and skills. Clarity about the differences between thought and language can help teachers distinguish between students who "have the concept" and those who have "merely verbal" learning.

Structural and Functional Aspects of Language

Language development can be separated into structural and functional aspects. *Structural aspects* subsume the elements of sentences (grammar) and how these elements are combined to form meaningful communications that conform to the language's structural requirements (syntax). *Functional aspects* concern the ability to use language to communicate, think, and solve problems. Different factors are involved in determining the development of these two aspects of language.

Innate Language-Acquisition Device

Traditionally, learning theorists explained language development with concepts such as exposure (modeling), repetition, and reinforcement. Children were believed to learn to speak a particular language using particular vocabularies and idioms because they were reinforced by imitating what they heard in their homes and neighborhoods.

Chomsky on language

Chomsky (1965) rejected this explanation. He argued that reinforcement cannot explain why or how children regularly generate new sentences they have never spoken or even heard before and that the structural aspects of language are learned spontaneously. He postulated an innate language-acquisition device (LAD), unique to and present in all humans, that enables us to learn language simply by being exposed to it. By "learning" a language, he meant learning not only its vocabulary words but also its structure. Like Piaget, Chomsky is a nativist; he believes that the ability to generate language according to grammatical rules is inherent in the human brain and functions without requiring systematic instruction or reinforcement. Although language can be learned through systematic instruction, Chomsky's point is that typically it is not.

Linguistic conventions

This is illustrated in the errors that children make as they learn language. Except for errors caused by common pronunciation difficulties ("aminal," "aksed"), most of their linguistic errors are "logical." That is, they conform to the structural rules implicit in the language and are errors only because certain expressions do not follow the typical rule. For example, it is common for children to say "they goed" instead of "they went." This error indicates that although they are using it inappropriately in this case, the children have mastered the general rule that past-tense verbs are formed by adding a "d" sound to the present-tense verb (*open-opened*, *lift-lifted*).

Syntax

Analysis of errors that rarely occur is also instructive. In contrast to common errors that involve using rules that do not happen to apply in a specific instance, errors that involve violations of syntax—violations of the basic structure of grammatical sentences—hardly ever occur. Thus children might say "they goed to the store," or "they gone to the store," but not "store to the they went" or "went they the store to." English sentence structure has an implicit "subject-then verb-then object" rule that children know and use intuitively, even though they cannot express it verbally. Such data illustrate what Chomsky meant in stating that language is learned spontaneously via an innate language-acquisition device.

Chomsky appears correct in his assertions, but only for the structural aspects of language. By itself, even complete language structure is not sufficient to ensure good language functioning—the ability to use language to communicate and solve problems efficiently (Neimark & Santa, 1975; Pozner & Saltz, 1974). Language development is affected by environmental input, not just the operation of an innate LAD (Nelson, 1977; Whitehurst, 1977).

Mediational Deficiencies in the Functional Use of Language

People differ considerably in the degree to which they can use language to communicate, think, and solve problems. Difficulties often reflect poor language development, but sometimes individuals who possess relevant language do not use it when it would be helpful to them. For example, Kendler and Kendler (1962) have shown that some children between five and seven years old possess all of the verbal and cognitive schemes needed to respond to transposition problems in the more developmentally sophisticated way but nevertheless do not do so.

Mediational deficiencies

The Kendlers used the term *mediational deficiency* to refer to situations in which children verbalize concerning a problem, but their verbalizations do not result in the higher-level response (e.g., they do not pick the larger circle in a transposition problem). Since thoughts can be mediated by language at this age (children can think by literally talking to themselves, if they have the relevant cognitive and verbal schemes), and since the children are known to possess and use the necessary language, those who use it but fail to respond to the problem at the higher level of development are considered to have a mediational deficiency. For some reason, their language does not succeed in "carrying" (mediating) their thought processes. They verbalize the problem correctly but then respond incorrectly, contrary to their own verbalizations. This phenomenon is rare, but it happens.

Production Deficiencies in the Functional Use of Language

Other investigators have noted a similar but more frequent problem termed *production deficiency* (Flavell, Beach, & Chinsky, 1966). The phenomenon was originally noted in studies of memory in children. Like transposition problems, the memory problem studied by these investigators could be approached with either a lower-level or a higher-level solution strategy. A typical problem involved memorizing a list of words such as *apple*, *cow*, *lamp*, *peach*, *horse*, *table*, *pear*, *chair*, *pig*. Preoperational children typically try to learn such lists by rote, memorizing words in order without regrouping them. Operational children and adults tend to recognize that there are three fruits, three items of furniture, and three animals, and they use this information to aid them in memorizing. In fact, if it is not necessary for them to repeat the words in order, they usually reorder them according to these conceptual clusters. In any case, individuals who use these conceptual clusters master the task much more quickly than those who do not.

Production deficiency

Some individuals who possess all of the necessary concepts and language and understand the relationships among the subsets nevertheless do not use this information and instead approach the problem with rote memorizing methods like those used by young children. In contrast to the *mediational deficiency* problem, in which the person verbalizes relevant language but this language does not mediate thought processes, the *production deficiency* problem occurs when relevant language and thought processes are available but nevertheless are not produced in the situation and thus are not used to mediate it.

The educational implications of both mediational and production deficiency problems are the same: It is important to see that children not only master fundamental verbal and cognitive schemes but also learn to use them as tool skills or learning-to-learn skills. Production deficiency apparently occurs because the relevant schemes, while learned to some degree, are either not mastered enough individually or not coordinated enough with other schemes to allow the person to use them for solving problems. Consider algebra, for example. If you know it thoroughly, you can use it to solve everyday problems that lend themselves to algebraic formulation. If you studied algebra but did not learn it thoroughly, however, you cannot apply it except to problems presented routinely in class.

The Interaction between Language and Thought

Whorfian hypothesis

These considerations return us to the general problem of thought and language and to the distinction between structural and functional aspects of language. Piaget represents one extreme in theorizing about the relationship between thought and language. He deemphasized language by subordinating it to thought. He saw language primarily as a vehicle for expressing thoughts, not as a precursor or cause of thought. At the other extreme are certain linguists and psycholinguists who believe that language is at least as important as thought. Some still endorse the so-called *Whorfian hypothesis*, named after Benjamin Whorf (1956). In its most extreme form, the Whorfian hypothesis states that language structures thought. Ironically, Whorf himself never stated or accepted the hypothesis in this extreme form, although many others propound it even today.

It is true that language and thought interact, although it does not seem to be true that language structures thought. Instead, it appears, as Ferguson (1956) stated, that cultures focus attention on certain aspects of the environment because of their importance for adaptation or cultural traditions. This focus leads both to a relatively rich conceptual understanding of these salient aspects of the environment and to a proliferation of vocabulary for discussing them. For example, Eskimos have many different words referring to different kinds of snow, whereas people living in warmer climates have only the single noun, *snow*, perhaps modified by adjectives such as *soft* or *fluffy*. Skiers and others, however, who have interest in more specific aspects of snow have developed specialized vocabularies that facilitate communication about those aspects. Any such proliferation of discriminations about a topic is likely to be associated with vocabulary development about the topic, although in our opinion it is going too far to state that language causes thought.

Independence of thought and language development

The relationships between thought and language probably have been expressed best by Vygotsky (1962), a Russian psychologist interested in many of the same topics that interested Piaget. Vygotsky noted that in the sensorimotor and early preoperational stages, thought and language develop independently. Thought mostly involves nonverbal sensorimotor and cognitive schemes. Children think but do so in intuitive ways that do not involve much use of language. They do have language, however; it develops all along, parallel to but not in direct conjunction with thought. *Language develops primarily as a way to express personal needs, emotions, and feelings.* It functions as a method of communication rather than as a means of thinking during these early years.

However, *as children become operational, thought and language become related*. Children become increasingly able to express thoughts in language, to use language to communicate concepts, and to think and solve problems verbally. Apparently, because of this, they also shift from lower to higher forms of response to transposition problems and overcome mediational and production deficiencies. In short, as children become operational, a confluence of developments occurs that creates qualitative changes in their cognitive structures and in the ways that these structures function, especially in new situations that require accommodation or problem solving.

Egocentric speech

Kohlberg, Yeager, and Hjertholm (1967) produced data that support Vygotsky's contentions. Their findings concern what Piaget called *egocentric speech*—overt utterances that children make in the presence of listeners that at first resemble ordinary social speech but do not require response from the listeners. Piaget minimized the importance of egocentric speech, seeing it as just more evidence that young children are egocentric. Vygotsky, however, noted developmental changes in the rates and types of egocentric speech that occur as children develop. Among children who are clearly preoperational, egocentric speech is mostly social (verbalizations about feelings and emotions, important life events, or the child's family or possessions). Usually, it has little direct bearing on what the child is doing at the moment. As children become operational, their egocentric speech shifts from such primarily social speech to what Vygotsky called "inner speech." *Inner speech* is verbalized thought, the self-talk that occurs when we are thinking. Thus children playing in a sandbox, who when younger might have chattered about other matters, will begin to talk more about the sand castles they are building. Their egocentric speech becomes less social and more like inner speech and also more focused on the task at hand. Increasingly, they seem to be talking to themselves. They literally think out loud about how to solve problems in building the castle. Still later, their inner speech becomes virtually unintelligible, because most of the thinking is done silently. The child may utter only a few phrases aloud or perhaps mutter unintelligibly.

Inner speech

Berk (1986) reported similar patterns in her study of the private speech uttered by first and third graders observed during math seatwork times. Changes in individual students over time showed developmental trends toward increasingly task-relevant and less audible private speech. Individual difference comparisons showed that the brighter students moved into and through this private speech cycle earlier than the lower-achieving students. The brighter first graders were using mature forms of private (but audible) speech to help them think about the math problems. Later, when other students had begun to use overt private speech to guide their thinking more consistently, the private speech of the brighter students had already become mostly internalized and thus was no longer as observable.

Taken together, the results of many studies suggest that egocentric speech is *functional* and that the changes that occur in it as the child becomes operational are part of the process of linking thought and language (Frauenglass & Diaz, 1985; Wertsch, 1985; Zivin, 1979). Apparently, children think out loud for the same reason that they count on their fingers: It is a temporary learning aid that helps them make the transition to a new mode of functioning (e.g., thinking in words). When they no longer need to verbalize out loud, they begin to mutter and eventually to think silently. Actually, the process never completely ends. Most adults find it helpful to think out loud occasionally when wrestling with a complex problem. Thus egocentric speech is functional throughout life.

In summary, thought and language mostly develop separately until children begin to become operational around age six or seven. Verbal and cognitive schemes then become assimilated to one another and coordinated into more powerful and differentiated schemes that ultimately become learning-to-learn strategies, concrete operational logic, and other information-processing and problem-solving skills.

LANGUAGE AND THE SCHOOL

Because children acquire structural aspects of spoken language spontaneously merely by being exposed to it, there is little that teachers can or should do to promote mastery of the local idiom. However, teachers can foster the ability to use language functionally for communication and problem solving by encouraging students to verbalize their thoughts and patiently assisting them as they struggle to do so. Teachers can also help students to master written forms of expression and, when necessary, to learn to communicate in standard English.

Use of Local Dialect

Many children learn so-called black English or other variations on the standard English that forms the basis for school curricula. These dialects are structurally complete languages with their own grammatical rules, not immature forms of standard English such as those spoken by young children (Burling, 1973; Labov, 1972). Even so, dialect speakers may have difficulty with certain lessons that assume standard English. For example,

Lyndon Johnson's performance as a speaker was often criticized because of his heavy Texas accent.

children who pronounce words *pour*, *more*, and *sew* as if they all rhymed with one another may have difficulty with rhyming lessons, and children who tend to drop the "t" sound in past tense verbs (saying "pass" instead of "passed") may have trouble with verb-tense lessons.

Experts disagree about how teachers should handle nonstandard dialects. Advice ranges from insisting on standard English to teaching in the local dialect. Experiments in which students were taught in nonstandard dialects suggest that this is not a good idea, although it appears that teachers should *accept* local dialects rather than punish students or make them feel inferior for using them. The ideal seems to be acceptance of whatever dialect the student uses to communicate, with emphasis on helping the student to succeed in communicating (Harber & Bryen, 1976).

Developmental errors versus specialized errors

Teachers need to distinguish common errors that arise in normal development and later disappear from specialized errors that are associated with subcultural dialects or unique problems in language learning. Developmental errors that come and go on their own should be ignored, although the teacher should model correct language when speaking to the child in ways that do not interrupt the natural flow of conversation or make the child feel inadequate. Thus the teacher should respond to "He goed out" with "Yes, he went out, and then what did he do?"

Use of dialect in the classroom

Teachers familiar with local dialect or expressions might want to use them occasionally in the classroom. This can promote solidarity with the group but only when the teacher is credible in using the local language. Attempts that come off as forced or phony are likely to undermine rather than reinforce credibility. Thus teachers should use local language only when they feel comfortable with it. Students expect teachers to use "teacher language," so failure to use local language will not create problems.

Summary

During the preoperational years, children learn best through exploration and manipulation of concrete objects, although they also can learn letters, numbers, sounds, words, computation, and writing skills. They have difficulty with purely verbal instruction and require demonstrations, visual aids, or concrete examples. Practice with feedback is essential at this stage.

Piaget stressed three central aspects of becoming operational: (1) discrimination of variant from invariant environmental features; (2) coordination and integration of separate schemes into a unified cognitive structure; and (3) achieving the ability to reverse operations. Teachers dealing with students in the stage of concrete operations should emphasize understanding and integrative concepts. Children also thrive on "personalized" material. Beginning about the eighth grade, some students will be able to cope with abstract material using formal operations. Many never reach that point, however, and even those who do will profit from imagery, diagrams, and concrete examples.

Piaget placed great stress on thought and relatively little on language, but the functional aspects of language require attention because of their importance in dealing with school tasks. Chomsky believes that a language-acquisition device provides for spontaneous learning of language. Whorf advanced the hypothesis that language structures thought, which is the opposite of Piaget's view. Vygotsky noted that in early stages language and thought develop independently, but later, egocentric speech gives way to inner speech that mediates thought processes.

Questions and Problems

1. Assume that you teach in an inner-city high school where many students speak with foreign accents. You fear that their accents will reduce their chances for employment, but you don't want to embarrass them by calling unnecessary attention to their speech. What would you do, if anything? What if you were a first-grade teacher in the same district?
2. Why are simple choice questions less useful than fact or explanation questions as ways to assess student comprehension?
3. Why can teachers who work with older students monitor learning by questioning just a few of them, whereas teachers of younger children have to question all students?
4. Why does it do little good to try to teach children at conceptual levels beyond their present ones? What distinctive materials and teaching methods do preoperational children need that older children do not?
5. What three central aspects of becoming operational in thinking did Piaget stress?
6. What does it mean to state that young children primarily accommodate to the situation, but older individuals primarily assimilate the situation into existing cognitive structures? How might this affect the teaching of second-grade versus eighth-grade students?
7. Differentiate the structural and functional aspects of language.
8. What is egocentric speech, and what is its function? How did Piaget and Vygotsky differ in their beliefs about it?
9. Why is it important, especially with younger students, frequently to elicit overt response or performance? How can this be done effectively when teaching humanities or social studies?
10. Suppose that you teach an elementary class in which some students have well-functioning concrete operations, but many do not (or a secondary class in which some have well-functioning formal operations, but most do not). What organizational and instructional strategies could you use to make sure that most instruction is meaningful to *all* of your students?

Case Studies

APPROPRIATE TEACHING? Jim Roberts is working with a group of fifth graders assigned to read a selection from James Michener's *Centennial*. Responding to a student's answer, Jim says, "Yes, Jane, that is an important point. His willingness to stake himself to the ground and fight to the death is a revealing dimension. Well, now, we've noted 12 important events on the board. How can we use these to generalize about his basic character traits? What kind of man was he?'' Describe the type of teaching that Jim is engaging in. If he were teaching the same material to tenth graders, how might he approach the task differently?

SAM NOT TURNED ON. Sam Baker, a tenth grader, achieves at an average level, but his teachers suspect that he can do better, for two reasons. First, his measured IQ has regularly exceeded 120 on a variety of tests taken over the years. Second, his performance on classroom exams is uneven. He absorbs topics he is interested in but does not take the time to read carefully in other areas. Sam is in the college-preparatory program but has no vocational plans and only a vague commitment to college. His father manages a grocery store and his mother is a first-grade teacher. An only child without close friends, Sam's only interests are hunting with his dad on occasional weekends and reading about hunting in general and guns in particular. How could Sam's existing interests be used and eventually broadened in the following subjects: history, Spanish, physics, and geometry?

HARD TO TELL. Jane Prawat is a first-grade teacher who especially enjoys teaching reading. She tries to involve students in thinking about what they are reading, not just looking at words and using learning strategies to decode meaning. She spends considerable time talking to students about the words that they see in the stories, and after reading the stories with the children, she asks them a number of questions. The following activity is typical. With great interest and enthusiasm, she asks, ''Did you believe that Mr. Martin would ever let the cats go back to Timmy?'' All students nod their heads approvingly. One or two say ''yes'' audibly. With continuing interest Ms. Prawat asks, ''Do you think Tim was glad to see the kittens when they got home?'' Again, students nod affirmatively. Then she asks, ''Do you think the kittens were glad to see him?'' The students nod their heads yes. Based on principles of development, what suggestions do you have for improving Ms. Prawat's teaching?

GOING BEYOND THE INFORMATION GIVEN. Jan Brooke is in her third year of teaching at Astoria Middle School. She enjoys working with the eighth graders and tries to get them to think about the social studies that they are studying. She especially enjoys having students challenge the conclusions authors reached and think of alternative ways to explain key historical figures' behavior. She also likes to have her students examine economic motivation as well as individual and social motivation. She constantly reminds them that most accounts of history were written from an individual framework that did not take into consideration general economic and social factors. Some students enjoy this course but others find it vague and boring. Based upon your knowledge of development, how might you account for these differences in students' responses? How could the teacher alter some aspects of the class in order to help *all* students to think more fully about the material they are reading?

CHAPTER

Social and Personal Development

CHAPTER OUTLINE

OBJECTIVES

When you have mastered the material in this chapter, you will be able to

1. Contrast the relative importance of social learning (environmental) factors versus inherited (biological) factors in social development
2. Explain Erikson's (1968) eight stages of the human life cycle
3. Describe principles for effective childrearing
4. Explain how teachers can help students to cope successfully with developmental crises
5. Describe strategies for helping students build positive self-concepts
6. Explain how children reason about moral issues at each of Kohlberg's (1984) six stages of moral judgment
7. Critically evaluate the usefulness of Kohlberg's theory for teachers who want to teach moral reasoning and moral behavior in school

Arousal level

Most personal qualities and social traits are developed in response to conditioning via social expectations and reinforcement or modeling by significant others, especially one's parents. Certain stable traits exist at birth, however. One of them is *arousal level.* Some infants usually are alert and active, exploring the environment and reacting to stimulation. Others sleep much of the time and even when awake are mostly quiet and relatively unresponsive. These individual differences tend to persist and correlate with differences in arousal level and behavior observed later (Buss & Plomin, 1984).

Gender differences

Certain *gender differences* also are observable from birth. Boys tend to be relatively more active, initiatory, aggressive, and oriented toward physical manipulation of objects. Girls are more apt to observe environmental events than to manipulate objects, and they do more watching, listening, and verbalizing. They also tend to be more physically mature—their body parts and especially their neurophysiological control mechanisms tend to be more advanced and to function more efficiently. These differences also tend to persist throughout childhood.

Early predispositions and environmental influences

Early predispositions interact with environmental influences, however. For example, one active child who has siblings or peers available may spend much time in rough-and-tumble play, but another who lacks playmates may spend a lot of time exploring the physical environment. Active children raised in an atmosphere of violence are likely to become predisposed to fighting and bullying (Huesmann et al., 1984; Patterson & Stouthamer-Loeber, 1984; Steinmetz, 1977), but similar children raised in warmer, more humanistic environments tend to become assertive, but nonaggressive, peer leaders (Maccoby & Martin, 1983; Rohner & Nielsen, 1978; Staub, 1979). Thus although biological predispositions toward certain personal and social traits exist, environmental influences interact with these predispositions to affect behavior.

modeling—esp behavior

Also, despite tendencies toward family resemblances in everything from food preferences (Rozin, Fallon, & Mandell, 1984) to political philosophies (Boshier & Thom, 1973), most personal and social traits develop in response to environmental rather than genetic influences (Ahern et al., 1982). They include cooperative, competitive, or individualistic motives and activity preferences; personal interests; status as a peer leader, follower, or isolate; and a great variety of personal traits such as optimism versus pessimism, sociability, or styles of solving problems and coping with frustrations. Such traits are developed in response to the influences of *significant others*, initially parents and family members but later teachers and peers encountered at school and the real or fictional people portrayed on television and in other media. All of these *socializing influences* involve modeling of behavior that can be imitated and projection of social expectations that tell developing children how they are supposed to act and what they are supposed to value, strive for, and even feel.

Age and gender roles

Certain broad influences affect all children in a given society, at least to some degree. Prominent among them are *age and gender roles*—the norms for personal qualities and behavior for boys or girls and for children at particular ages. Children stress both age and gender in defining them-

As children become aware of gender differences, they tend to develop a preference for playmates of their own sex.

selves and their peers, and most are highly motivated to learn about and try to fulfill the role expectations that they believe apply to themselves (Bradbard & Endsley, 1983; Kohlberg, 1966; Masters et al., 1979). Once a child comes to understand that she is a girl (this usually occurs between ages two and three), for example, she is likely to begin observing intensely and asking questions about what being a girl means (implications for clothing and grooming, toy and game preferences, and personal mannerisms and interests). The same thing happens to boys. For several years, this leads to preoccupation with gender differences and preference for playmates of one's own gender. This builds to a peak sometime in midchildhood, typically around age eight in brighter and more socially mature children but later in other children (Kohlberg & Zigler, 1967); then it recedes.

Heredity and behavioral differences

The role of heredity in producing gender differences in cognitive functioning and social behavior is still debated (Brooks-Gunn & Matthews, 1979; Parsons, 1980; Wittig & Peterson, 1979). After an exhaustive review, Maccoby and Jacklin (1974) concluded that all behavioral differences other than those involving aggression probably result from socialization rather than heredity. Others argue for a greater genetic role. Like other nature-nurture controversies, this one is unlikely to be resolved with available data, because findings are inconsistent and open to conflicting interpretations.

Several writers caution against exaggerating gender differences, noting that they tend to be small, both in absolute terms and in comparison with the range of individual differences (Hyde & Linn, 1986; Plomin & Foch, 1981). This point is well taken, especially because these already small differences have become even smaller in recent years due to changes in gender role socialization (Feingold, 1988).

Socialization influences

Regardless of how much heredity contributes to gender differences, it is clear that socialization factors do contribute. People treat male and female infants differently from birth, regardless of their behavior. Such differential treatment continues throughout life and tells people how males and females (including themselves) are expected to act. Most people conform, for the most part, to these expectations. Individuals also can shape their environments, however, and even children may condition their parents to treat them in particular ways (Bell, 1971; Osofsky, 1976; Schaffer, 1977). Many girls, for example, resist the restrictions built into the traditional female role and succeed in defeating most pressures to conform to it.

Stages of socialization

Personal and social development in other areas follows a similar process. That is, behavioral predispositions and notions about oneself are acquired through socialization influences. These influences tend to be consistent at first because they are confined to the immediate family. However, as children encounter peers, the media, and other sources of influence, they become aware of new possibilities and of conflicting ideas. Those who have adapted easily to reasonably consistent socialization pressures that are mostly reinforced by the major sources of influence that they encounter are likely to become well adjusted in that their personal traits and behavior are satisfactory to them and to significant others in their lives (Kagan & Moss, 1962). Those, however, who have been unable or unwilling to adapt to consistent pressures or who have been confused by inconsistent pressures are likely to have adjustment problems.

Several distinct stages can be identified in the development from a relatively undifferentiated infant without much "personality" to a well-defined individual with characteristic personal qualities and behaviors. Freud was the first to delineate such stages in his writings about the oral, anal, phallic, Oedipal, latency, and genital stages of psychosexual development. These stages are not discussed much here because they are subsumed within the more broadly accepted psychoanalytic stage theory of Erikson (1968).

ERIKSON'S STAGE THEORY

Erikson identified eight stages in the life cycle (see Table 5.1), of which six occur before or during schooling (including college). Each stage involves a central developmental crisis, and one's success in coping with the crisis is seen as affecting one's more general development during and after the stage.

Trust versus Mistrust

Erikson's first stage (corresponding to Freud's oral stage) concerns the crisis of *trust versus mistrust*. It is a *universal human experience* to spend the first year or so of life totally dependent on others for food and general care. Erikson believes that fundamental dispositions toward others are formed during this dependent stage. *If the infant's needs are met reasonably well, a positive orientation toward and trust in others are likely to develop*. If caretakers are inadequate or inconsistent in meeting basic needs, infants may develop insecurity and a fundamental mistrust of others, laying the groundwork for a paranoid attitude of "the world is a jungle; you have to get yours and keep others from taking it away from you." In general, people who trust others are happier, better adjusted, and better liked than those who lack trust in others (Rotter, 1980).

TABLE 5.1 ERIKSON'S EIGHT STAGES OF THE HUMAN LIFE CYCLE

Stage	Ages	Central Conflict	Primary Implications for Optimal Development
1	Infancy	Trust vs. mistrust	Developing general security, optimism, and trust in others (based on consistent experiences involving satisfaction of basic needs)
2	Toddlerhood	Autonomy vs. shame and doubt	Developing a sense of autonomy and confident self-reliance, taking setbacks in stride (based on consistent experiences involving encouragement and limit setting without rejection or blame)
3	Early childhood	Initiative vs. guilt	Developing initiative in exploring and manipulating the environment (based on consistent experiences of tolerance, encouragement, and reinforcement)
4	Middle childhood	Industry vs. inferiority	Enjoyment and mastery of the developmental tasks of childhood, in and out of school (based on consistent experiences of success and recognition of progress)
5	Adolescence	Identity vs. identity confusion	Achievement of a stable and satisfying sense of identity and direction (based on consistent personal experiences involving success and satisfaction combined with social acceptance and recognition)
6	Young adulthood	Intimacy vs. isolation	Development of the ability to maintain intimate personal relationships (based on personal openness and confidence complemented by consistently rewarding experiences with intimate others)
7	Adulthood	Generativity vs. stagnation	Satisfaction of personal and familial needs supplemented by development of interest in the welfare of others and of the world in general (based on achievement of a secure and rewarding personal life and a freedom from pressures that limit one to self-preoccupation)
8	Aging	Integrity vs. despair	Recognizing and adjusting to aging and the prospect of death with a sense of satisfaction about the past and readiness about the future (based on consistent success in prior stages, which provides a real basis for satisfaction in having led a full and good life and for accepting death without morbid fears or feelings of failure)

Source: *Constructed from the information contained in Erikson, 1968.*

Whether or not the first year of life has special importance, it seems clear that children whose needs are met by loving and reliable adults are likely to be secure, happy, trustful, and sociable toward others, and that children who suffer because apathetic or unreliable adults do not meet their basic needs consistently are likely to be insecure and mistrustful.

A common misconception regarding Eriksonian stages is that one pole (e.g., trust) is totally positive and the other (in this case, mistrust) is totally bad. Actually, optimal development involves attaining a favorable ratio of the two poles. One can be naively or overly trusting.

Autonomy versus Shame and Doubt

Erikson's next stage (roughly paralleling Freud's anal stage) centers on the crisis of *autonomy versus shame and doubt*. The universal human experience involved here is the transition from being treated as a helpless infant to being treated as a child capable of exercising self-control and therefore expected to conform to rules of conduct. Freud termed this the anal stage because conflict often appears when parents try to toilet train their children. However, toilet training is just one example of the more general crisis: *For the first time, adults are imposing rules and expectations for self-control and self-denial.*

Parental demands

If such socialization is carried out with proper timing and appropriate methods, toddlers are likely to adjust to it smoothly and without losing their sense of personal autonomy. If parents make too many demands, make them too early, or emphasize threats and punishment in enforcing them, the children may lose their sense of personal autonomy and begin to feel completely dependent on and controlled by adults. To the extent that the children want to please the adults by meeting their expectations, failure to do so may result in feelings of shame and development of doubt about their own capabilities. This sets the stage for later difficulties in areas such as self-concept and impulse control.

Initiative versus Guilt

Erikson's next stage involves the crisis of *initiative versus guilt*. Freud called this the phallic stage, believing that boys aged four or five tend to show off their bodies generally and their penises in particular. The broader universal human experience here is the *development of interest in one's self and one's capabilities*, including an interest in showing off these things to others.

Inhibition

Children treated with warmth and support during this stage are likely to develop the confidence and sense of well being needed to take the initiative in trying out new things and "showing off." If these activities are rejected, however, the children may develop feelings of inhibition or guilt, initially about the specific behaviors but perhaps ultimately about initiatives in general. They may become inhibited by fear of failure or rejection rather than feeling free to set and pursue challenging goals.

Industry versus Inferiority

Erikson's next stage involves the crisis of *industry versus inferiority*. It corresponds roughly to Freud's latency stage and to Piaget's concrete operational period. Freud stressed reduction of sexual curiosity and exploration after resolution of the Oedipus complex as the hallmark of the latency stage, but Erikson stressed the universal experience of *moving out from the home into the neighborhood, the peer group, and the school.*

These changes present new roles and related expectations that children usually are motivated to try to fulfill (Havighurst, 1972). In the peer group this means learning to cooperate, share, and generally get along with others, as well as to master the skills involved in childhood play. In school it means mastering school tasks and the role of pupil. Students who have had a good start at home attack these tasks and role expectations with a sense of industry. Success results in more success and more motivation, setting off a chain of positive self-fulfilling prophecy effects. Conversely, if children should fail in meeting these expectations (or even just feel that they failed because they did not do as well as their friends), they may develop a sense of inferiority and low self-esteem.

Development of personal relationship

Sullivan (1953), Thornburg (1982), and others have suggested that *the transitional years between childhood and adolescence* (roughly ages eleven through thirteen) also constitute a stage, at least with respect to social development. Sullivan stressed the transition from playing in large groups, where the emphasis is on the activity, toward forming close "chumships" with individuals, where the emphasis is on developing more intimate personal relationships. He believed that such chumships are important facilitators of social and personal development. Research suggests that friendships tend to be intimate during these years, especially among girls, and that early adolescents are likely to act prosocially toward their friends and to try to achieve mutually satisfying outcomes in situations in which younger or older people might go their own way or compete (Berndt, 1982). Also, preadolescents who are involved in chumship relationships display higher levels of altruism and greater ability to assume another's perspective (McGuire & Weisz, 1982).

Thornburg (1982) noted that ages eleven through fourteen signal shifts from same gender to both genders to opposite genders in peer relationships and from socializing primarily in *natural environments* in the home or neighborhood to socializing in *contrived environments* (shopping centers, movie theaters). At school, these years signal a shift from identification with teachers to identification with peers, often accompanied by a degree of resentment of or even resistance to teachers' exercise of authority.

Identity versus Identity Confusion

Concerning adolescence, Erikson wrote about the crisis of *identity versus identity confusion.* Whereas Freud confined himself primarily to sexual considerations in referring to the genital stage, Erikson considered the *identity crisis* that most adolescents experience as they begin to question beliefs, attitudes, and value systems that they had internalized previously without much thought. As adolescents attain formal operations and greater understanding of people and ideas, they begin to see that some of the beliefs and values to which they have been exposed conflict with one another and also that preaching and practice do not always coincide in the words and actions of parents, teachers, or other socialization agents.

Belief conflicts

Many young persons become either depressed or romantically idealistic about the fact that values often are honored more in theory than in practice, so they not only seek values they can accept but go out of their way to practice them conscientiously. Included in this assessment of values are questions of personal identity (Who am I? What kind of person should I be? What kind of occupational, social, and gender roles should I play?).

Adolescents who solve these dilemmas with reasonable ease tend to adjust smoothly to changes in role and status and to move into adult occupational, spousal, and parental roles without much difficulty. However, many become confused about who they are and where they are going, so it may be years before they "find themselves." They may have a continual undercurrent of dissatisfaction with their lives, a feeling of confusion that can cause difficulties in motivation, an inability to concentrate on studies, or personal adjustment problems in and out of school.

Identity status categories

Marcia and Schiedel (Marcia, 1980; Schiedel & Marcia, 1985) have developed ways to measure progress in coping with the identity crisis. They studied the degree to which adolescents experienced crises and made commitments in five areas: occupation, religion, political philosophy, gender role attitudes, and beliefs about personal sexuality. Based on responses to interview questions, they classified young people into four *identity status categories: identity achievement* (has passed through a period of exploration and made self-chosen commitments); *moratorium* (currently in crisis, has not yet made firm commitments); *foreclosure* (commitments generally mirror parental positions, has not yet experienced a crisis involving serious questioning of those positions); and *identity diffusion* (may or may not have experienced crises, currently lacks commitments and is not especially concerned about lack of direction).

Another way of conceptualizing the four identity statuses described by Marcia (Figure 5.1) is to place them in the four quadrants resulting from perpendicular axes based on commitment and crisis, respectively. In this understanding, the person with *achieved identity* has faced a crisis—that is, has examined or tried various alternatives and has made a commitment. The person with a *foreclosed identity* has made a commitment but has never wrestled with the alternatives. The person with a *diffused identity* has not made a commitment or (usually) faced a crisis, although sometimes there may be an unresolved nonpressing crisis. The *moratorium identity* results when a person is facing a crisis but has yet to make a commitment to any of the pressing alternatives. A fifth identity status, mentioned by Erikson but not by Marcia, is the *negative identity*. Here the person has faced a crisis and made a commitment to a socially hostile identity such as a drug pusher or gang member. This type of choice is often as much or more a choice against something as it is a choice of a role or identity that truly fits the individual.

These four identity-status categories are not always related to other variables in ways that would be predicted by Erikson's theory (Coté & Levine, 1983), but they have proven useful in assessing progress in achieving identity. Archer (1982) studied sixth, eighth, tenth, and twelfth graders and found that identity status increased significantly at each grade level.

Figure 5.1

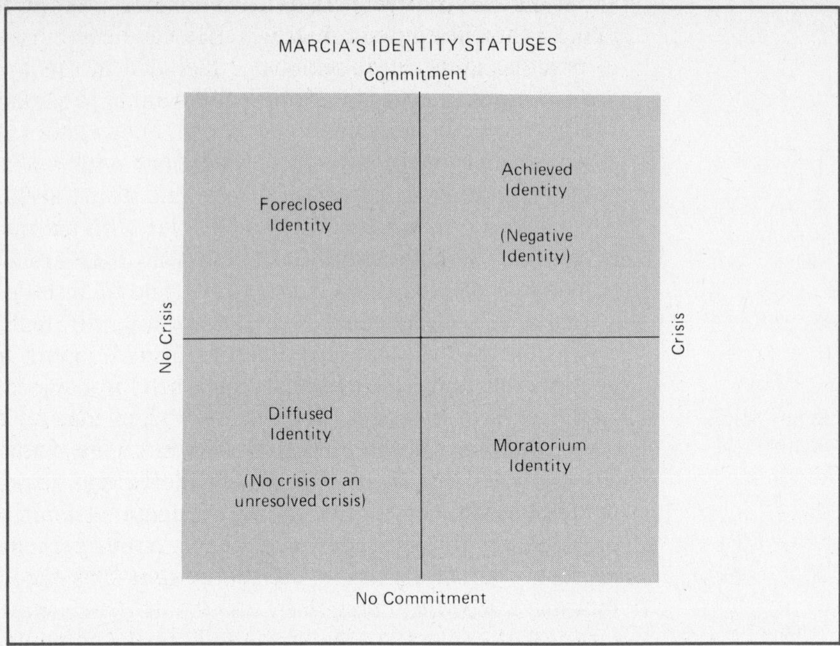

Source: This chart was created by Philip Powel, University of Texas, Austin. Reprinted by permission of the author.

Still, the diffusion and foreclosure statuses were most evident at all grades, so even by the twelfth grade, only a minority of students had reached the identity achievement level. Furthermore, when identity achievement status was attained, it usually was only in the vocational choice or religious beliefs areas. The moratorium status was seen most frequently with vocational choice, whereas the foreclosure status was most frequent with gender-role preferences, and the identity diffusion status was most frequent with political philosophies. In general, the most extensive advances in identity formation occur during the college years rather than the high school years (Waterman, 1982).

Adolescents' identity status predicts their patterns of interaction with family and friends. Compared to diffused peers, identity-achieved adolescents are less self-conscious and more comfortable in revealing themselves to others (Adams, Abraham, & Markstrom, 1987). Also, the identity-achieved adolescents tend to engage in more extended dialogue with their parents and, in the process, to articulate and defend their own points of view more assertively (Bosma & Gerrits, 1985). Thus identity-achieved adolescents not only have better articulated concepts of personal identity but also tend to be more comfortable in being themselves and asserting themselves with others.

Intimacy versus Isolation

Erikson's next stage, *intimacy versus isolation*, focuses on the crisis faced in late adolescence or young adulthood when intimate relationships, particularly one with a single member of the opposite gender, become viable and desirable. Individuals who have weathered previous stages successfully will enter this one trusting others, feeling a sense of autonomy, being willing to take initiatives, having healthy self-esteem and confidence, and being reasonably sure about who they are and what they want. These strengths will prepare them to enter truly intimate relationships, sharing everything about themselves with their partners. In contrast, individuals who show mistrust of others, low self-esteem, or fear of taking initiatives will be less prepared to establish intimate relationships, even if good opportunities should appear. They may want such relationships but lack the confidence and skills needed to establish them and thus may feel frustrated and lonely.

Intimacy statuses

Marcia and his colleagues (Orlofsky, Marcia, & Lesser, 1973) have elaborated and operationalized Erikson's intimacy stage. They assigned individuals to *intimacy statuses* based on three criteria: (1) presence of close relationships with male and female friends; (2) presence of an enduring, committed sexual relationship; and (3) depth of peer relationships. The five intimacy statuses are: *isolate* (lives in an interpersonal void with only casual acquaintances); *stereotyped* (is pleasant but shallow and conventional in personal relationships); *pseudointimate* (similar to the stereotyped but is involved in a relatively permanent sexual relationship that is defined more by conventional roles than by sharing of self or feelings); *preintimate* (has close, open relationships with others based on mutuality and understanding, yet is ambivalent about commitment to an enduring sexual relationship); and *intimate* (similar to the preintimate except is committed to a long-term sexual relationship).

People whose interview responses place them in higher intimacy categories know their friends better and can predict their partners' response to personality inventories better (Orlofsky, 1976) and are more self-disclosing with other people and better able to articulate their emotional experiences (Orlofsky & Ginsburg, 1981). Furthermore, as predicted by Erikson's stage notions, people typically attain high status on identity measures before they attain high status on intimacy measures (Fitch & Adams, 1983; Kacerguis & Adams, 1980; Schiedel & Marcia, 1985). These findings are clearer for males than for females, however; many women deal successfully with intimacy issues before resolving identity issues (because of differences in gender role socialization that orient females toward interpersonal relationships and thus toward dealing with both identity and intimacy issues throughout the adolescent and early adult years). In contrast, males are oriented more toward intrapersonal soul searching and thus toward preoccupation with identity issues during the adolescent years, followed by attention to intimacy issues in the young adult years.

Generativity versus Stagnation and Integrity versus Despair

Erikson's final two stages deal with development in adulthood. The crisis of *generativity versus stagnation* refers to the degree to which adults feel capable to have and raise children and the advantages and disadvantages that result if the crisis is or is not met successfully. The final stage, *integrity versus despair*, refers to the degree to which aging persons adjust to the impending reality of death. Those who do so positively become resigned to death and can look back on their lives with satisfaction, feeling that they have been generally successful, happy, and useful. Individuals who do not resolve this crisis develop morbid fear or unrealistic denial of death or at least feel that their lives have been failures because they never amounted to anything.

SOCIALIZATION

Universal human experiences define stages and present crises, but readiness to respond to these crises depends on the quality of the socialization that children receive, particularly the quality of parenting in the home. Good information about parental behavior and its effects on children is available, much of it collected during the past twenty years (Baumrind, 1971; Brophy, 1977; Henderson, 1981; Hess, 1970; Hoffman, 1970; Maccoby, 1980; Maccoby & Martin, 1983; Martin, 1975). The following adult attributes are mentioned consistently as vital for fostering optimal development in children.

1. Basic acceptance of the child as an individual
2. Communicate acceptance through warm, affectionate interactions
3. An approach to socialization that emphasizes instruction, not just "discipline"
4. Clear rules and limits but with input from the child and with flexibility in response to changing needs
5. Present expectations in ways that communicate respect for and concern about the child as opposed to arbitrarily "laying down the law"
6. Explain the rationales underlying demands and expectations
7. Stress Golden Rule morality and regard for the effects of one's actions on oneself and others rather than appealing to fear of punishment or essentially empty logic such as "good children don't do that"
8. Practicing as well as preaching well-articulated value systems

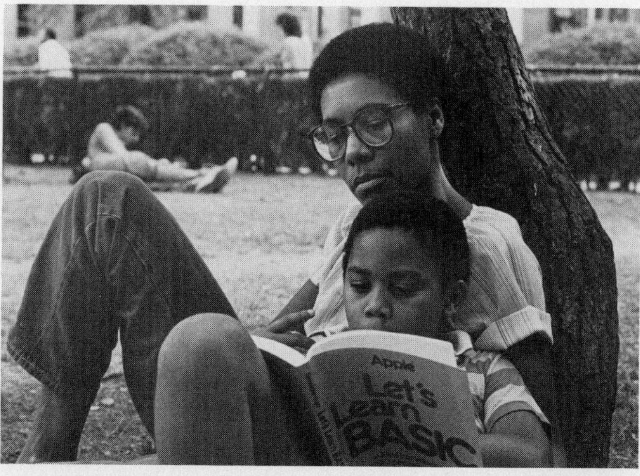

Children benefit from parents who accept them as individuals and communicate this with warmth and affection.

9. Continually projecting positive expectations and attitudes; treating children as if they already are, or at least are in the process of becoming, the kind of people that the parents value
10. Understanding and accommodating individual differences so that children are encouraged to capitalize on their strengths and follow their interests rather than feeling pressured into becoming something else
11. Preaching (and practicing) humanistic values but doing so in ways that leave the children emotionally free to think about and question values during the adolescent identity crisis

Socialization in the Classroom

Erikson's stage theory helps alert teachers to major sources of conflict for students at varying levels of development. Students in the early grades are likely to be struggling with the crises of initiative versus guilt and industry versus inferiority. Teachers can help inhibited and guilt-ridden children by encouraging them to explore, satisfy their curiosity, ask questions, make suggestions, and take initiatives. Furthermore, they can reassure such children that mistakes and ventures that work out poorly are normal and expected, not causes for shame or guilt.

Encouraging emerging abilities

Children obsessed with their competitive standing can be helped to attend more to their own cumulative gains and emerging abilities than to comparisons with classmates. Others who do well in such competition but who are becoming egotistical about it might also profit from such socialization. In any case, many children need to learn the satisfactions of doing a job well through care and persistence. Children also need to learn that individuals possess unique patterns of strengths and weaknesses and that everyone has something to offer everyone else, so an atmosphere of friendliness and cooperation is desired.

Dealing with reality

In dealing with feelings of inferiority or shame, teachers need to be realistic rather than well meaning but condescending. Students know how they are doing relative to their classmates, so there is no point in trying to deny reality or distract them from failures that concern them by switching the conversation to something else. To a child, this is like saying, "So what if you are stupid; I like you anyway." *Poor performance needs to be faced realistically but in a supportive way.* If the problem is the student's own fault (e.g., not listening or doing the work), point this out firmly but gently. If the problem is one of relative ability, stress absolute progress; that is, compare the student's current and past performance. When students become depressed to the point of insisting that they cannot learn, vigorously reject this claim but in ways that provide support and realistic reasons for expecting improvement in the future. Instead of just offering empty reassurances, schedule individual goal-setting conferences geared to produce specific plans (such as assigning remedial work or arranging to see that the student gets tutorial help).

Teachers working with adolescents will need to help them cope with identity and intimacy crises. Teachers who relish a socialization role and foster close relationships with students will have opportunities to deal with identity crises in depth, perhaps for a time becoming the primary source of realistic information and feedback for some students. Teachers can be of enormous help by making good career suggestions to students, because most adolescents are confused about career options.

Developing Positive Self-Concepts

Importance of positive feedback

Teachers can help students build high self-esteem and positive self-concepts by communicating positive expectations and offering positive feedback, especially about students' perceptions of their own academic skills and progress rates. Positive self-concepts also can be developed in other areas not directly related to instruction. Helping students cope with developmental crises has already been discussed. Other opportunities include helping them to become aware of and develop their strong points (Hauserman, Miller, & Bond, 1976), to gain confidence and improve in areas of weakness, and to accept limitations that cannot be changed. Some students may also need guidance in accepting their gender or their physical attributes or in developing empathy toward others ("How do you think Jenny feels when you say that to her?"), social awareness ("What do the other girls think about you when you put Jenny down?"), role-taking skills ("Let's act it out. I'm Jenny, and I say, 'What are you doing?' Now, what should you say?"), or insights into self and others ("Why do you think you treat Jenny this way, when you're pleasant and friendly with everyone else?") (Eisenberg, Lennon, & Roth, 1983; Rushton & Sorrentino, 1981; Smith, 1982).

Dealing with frustration

Students must also learn to cope with frustrations by striving to overcome them rather than trying to deny them or responding with hostility or childish regression. Teachers can promote good group relations by helping isolates to become accepted group members and by teaching hostile students to value friendships and learn to cope with their frustrations in positive ways rather than by taking them out on others.

Unaccustomed roles

Well-established self-concepts based on long-standing status in peer groups are not easily changed, and attempts to help by thrusting individuals into unaccustomed roles may cause discomfort, even if the roles are attractive. This was shown by Klinger and McNelly (1976), who studied Boy Scout troops with established leaders and followers. The boys were asked to compete in teams of four against teams from other troops, under circumstances in which the role of captain of the team involved considerable power and responsibility. If each team had been allowed to select its own captain, the boy with the highest existing leadership status in the troop probably would have been picked. However, captains were assigned so that some were the same boys who would have been elected anyway, but others were boys accustomed to follower status. Observation and interviews showed that boys who already were leaders functioned effectively as team captains and enjoyed the game, but boys accustomed to follower status who were thrust into the role of captain did not. Some even became withdrawn or anxious. These findings show that self-concepts are powerful and resistant to change through short-term or artificial interventions. Teachers can stimulate real change in students' self-concepts, but this will usually require producing *gradual* changes not only in self-perceptions but also in the personal characteristics and behavior on which they are based.

Changing self-concepts

Consider students who have developed stable but undesirable concepts of themselves as tough or evil. Certain children are labeled this way consistently enough by significant others to lead them to accept and even try to live up to the label. Altering such a self-concept takes time, but it can be done through consistent projection of positive expectations leading to self-fulfilling prophecy effects, in which teachers reject the students' negative self-images and instead project images of them as persons who are basically well meaning and who will do the right thing when they understand the situation fully. Students treated this way consistently can be expected to acquire and begin to try to live up to more positive self-concepts (Grusec et al., 1978; Lepper, 1973; Miller, Brickman, & Bolen, 1975).

Altering undesirable self-concepts

To help rejected or isolated students, teachers may have to work with the peer group as well as the students themselves. Self-concept is influenced heavily by the response of one's immediate peers and reference groups (Coopersmith, 1967; Rogers, Smith, & Coleman, 1978). Private conferences with peers might lead to better treatment of rejected students, especially those who are not being rejected because of their own antisocial behavior. Peer relationships may also be improved by introducing cooperative activities, especially activities in which each participant has a necessary role to play and thus cannot be ignored (Lucker et al., 1976).

Aiding rejected and isolated students

Teachers do not have as many opportunities as parents to influence students because they see them for only a limited time and because their interactions are structured by the teacher and student roles. Even so, teachers who work at it can have significant socialization effects on their classes and on individual students with whom they form special relationships. Felker (1974) suggested the following principles for teachers who want to foster healthy self-concepts in their students: (1) praise yourselves to model self-reinforcement for accomplishments, (2) help students to evaluate themselves realistically, (3) teach them to set reasonable goals, (4) teach them to praise themselves, and (5) teach them to praise others.

Working with adolescents

Such treatment will help students learn to recognize, value, and take pride in realistic accomplishments. Felker offered additional suggestions for teachers working with adolescents: (1) Allow them to make choices and learn to accept the consequences, but within a supportive relationship; (2) help them cope with adolescence by explaining what is happening to them in terms of physical, social, and emotional development; (3) help them see and accept the fact that few decisions involve easy choices or perfect solutions, so compromise is often appropriate. For more about self-concept development, see Harter (1983), Damon and Hart (1982), or Lynch, Norem-Hebeisen, and Gergen (1981).

MORAL DEVELOPMENT

Children do not become truly moral individuals, capable of using a set of stable ethical principles to guide behavior, until they enter the concrete operational period. Sometime during the early elementary grades, they attain what theologians used to call the "age of reason," indicating an intuitive recognition of the cognitive development that occurs at this time.

Piaget (1932) was one of the first to study the changes in moral reasoning that accompany changes in cognitive development. He noted that as children overcome egocentrism and develop the cognitive abilities needed to assume the perspective of another person, they begin to understand moral concepts such as fairness and reciprocity.

Kohlberg's Stage Theory

Kohlberg (1969, 1984) elaborated on Piaget's ideas in his stage theory of the development of moral judgment. Over the years he used different terms and even spoke of varying numbers of stages, but typically he discussed three general levels of moral thinking, with two stages at each level (see Table 5.2).

Preconventional morality

Individuals at the *preconventional* level do not yet possess an organized system of moral concepts. *Stage 1* individuals (mostly young children) are egocentric, concerned about their own interests but not the interests of others. If they do not do whatever they feel like doing, it is because they fear punishment rather than because they feel a sense of duty or a desire to live up to some ideal. *Stage 2* individuals also lack generalized moral notions and are primarily concerned with themselves, but they will enter into limited reciprocity agreements of a "you scratch my back and I'll scratch yours" nature. Most Stage 2 persons also are developing children, but some older children and adults (particularly criminals) never get beyond this stage.

Conventional morality

Persons who reveal *conventional* moral thinking internalize the socialization they receive. Children at *Stage 3* identify with their parents and other adult authority figures and strive to please them by being a "good boy" or "good girl." Older persons display more adult forms of Stage 3 thinking when, rather than using more abstract moral concepts, they think in terms of doing their duty, living up to expectations, and displaying virtues. Individuals who develop from Stage 3 to *Stage 4* change from a focus on pleasing others to a more generalized orientation that considers laws and social expectations as means toward the end of maintaining the social system as a whole. Stage 4 persons stress the need for social order and for fulfillment of individuals' obligations. However, they often carry their emphasis on the need to uphold the law to extremes, such as by viewing exceeding the speed limit as wrong, even in emergencies, "because it is against the law." Stage 4 conventional morality is seen in adults who display a "law and order" mentality when thinking about social issues.

Most middle- and many high school students are predominantly conventional (Stages 3 or 4) in their moral reasoning. In fact, their responses to moral issues do not involve much actual reasoning at all in the sense of thinking through an issue and arriving at their own considered judgments. Instead, they merely repeat moral norms that they acquired as children and learned to verbalize when appropriate (It's wrong to steal. We should all share.). Typically, young children commit these moral norms to memory with little thought about their implications, even though

TABLE 5.2 KOHLBERG'S SIX STAGES IN THE DEVELOPMENT OF MORAL JUDGMENT

Level I: Preconventional Morality

Stage 1. Heteronomous morality. Obedience based on fear of punishment. Egocentric point of view, difficulty in appreciating the viewpoints or interests of others. No real conscience or sense of morality yet, but behavior can be controlled through reinforcement, especially fear of punishment.

Stage 2. Individualism, instrumental purpose, and exchange. Still primarily egocentric and concerned with own interests, but aware that others have their interests that they try to pursue. Generally concentrates on meeting own needs and letting others do the same, but when necessary will help meet others' needs in order to get one's own needs met. In this case, what is right is what is seen as fair or what amounts to an equal exchange.

Level II: Conventional Morality

Stage 3. Mutual interpersonal expectations, relationships, and interpersonal conformity. Good boy-good girl orientation: Try to please authority figures and live up to expectations for one's role as son, daughter, sibling, friend, etc. Concern about being good by practicing the "golden rule," showing concern about others, and displaying virtues such as trust and loyalty.

Stage 4. Social system and conscience. Moral ideals become more generalized, and motivation to live up to them shifts from concern about the reactions of immediate others to a sense of duty to respect authority and maintain the social order. Awareness of the individual's responsibility to keep the system as a whole going by following its rules and meeting its defined obligations. Belief that laws are to be upheld except in extreme cases where they conflict with other fixed social duties.

Level III. Postconventional (or Principled) Morality

Stage 5. Social contract or utility and individual rights. A sense of duty and obligation to fulfill the social contract still prevails, but with recognition that laws are means to ends rather than ends in themselves, and that laws should be written to obtain the greatest good for the great number. Awareness that certain values and rights should take precedence over social arrangements and contracts. Recognition that the moral and the legal points of view are different and sometimes conflict; confusion about what is right when such conflict occurs.

Stage 6. Universal ethical principles. Belief in and sense of personal commitment to universal moral principles (justice, equality of human rights, respect for the dignity of humans as individual persons). Particular laws or social agreements are usually considered valid and followed because they rest on these principles, but the principles take precedence when there is conflict between what is legal and what is right.

they repeat them many times. The norms function not so much as principles for guiding behavior but as "merely verbal learning" that is displayed on cue and then forgotten until a similar situation arises.

Satellization and desatellization

Ausubel and Sullivan (1970) have described children who identify closely with their parents as satellites of the parents. They discuss the consequences of different forms of the *desatellization* that occurs as the children move away from parental influence. Children who desatellize gradually from generally facilitative homes tend not only to verbalize the value systems that they have been taught but to use them to guide their own behavior. Ultimately, these value systems are internalized and become the basis for self-control. Children who have problems in desatellization processes may learn to verbalize the value systems they are taught, but they are less likely to develop truly internal controls or use these value systems to guide behavior.

Value systems

This process is compounded when adolescents begin to think about the meanings of their value systems and to evaluate them objectively. Those who either have limited intellectual capacities or have what Ausubel called desatellization problems do relatively little serious thinking about value systems. As a result, they remain fixated at the conventional or even the preconventional level, so their moral judgments stay developmentally immature and their value systems remain mostly empty verbalizations that do not control behavior. In contrast, children who develop formal operations and spend time evaluating their value systems make important advances in moral reasoning. They switch from merely verbalizing values to deliberating and adopting them consciously (sometimes the same ones they were taught, sometimes not). *To the extent that children adopt values consciously, they are likely to use the values to guide behavior.*

Postconventional morality

Persons who attain the *postconventional* level develop more abstract and better integrated moral concepts. Moving beyond the emphasis on social conventions and law and order seen at Stage 4, *Stage 5* individuals begin to view laws more flexibly, seeing them as devices that the community agrees on to enable people to live in harmony. They realize that laws can be changed if they are not meeting the needs of society and that basic values such as liberty or justice might take precedence over the law itself. However, they would only try to change laws through orderly democratic activities, stopping short of advocating civil disobedience.

Individuals who reach *Stage 6* have clear conceptions of abstract universal principles like fairness, justice, and individual human dignity that transcend the law. Kohlberg had difficulty defining this stage in ways that differentiate it clearly from Stage 5. He believed that few persons ever reach this stage. The examples he gave tended to be persons known not only for moral teaching but for being willing to stand up and if necessary suffer for their beliefs (e.g., Socrates, Jesus, Gandhi, Martin Luther King, Jr.).

Criticism of Kohlberg's Theory

Rest (1974), Hoffman (1977), and others have criticized the methods Kohlberg used to measure moral judgment. Yet Kuhn (1976) reported reasonably good stability across a period of a year for moral judgment levels in children aged five through eight. Of fifty children interviewed, thirty-two showed an increase in moral judgment levels across the year, thirteen did not change, and only five declined. These figures are comparable to those for conservation and other aspects of Piagetian stages. Other studies also support Kohlberg's stages (Colby et al., 1983; Davison, Robbins, & Swanson, 1978; Nisan & Kohlberg, 1982; Page, 1981; Parikh, 1980; Rest, Davison, & Robbins, 1978; Snarey, Reimer, & Kohlberg, 1985; Walker, 1980; White, Bushnell, & Regnemer, 1978).

Kohlberg's theory has also been critiqued from a feminist perspective. Gilligan (1982) noted that all of the subjects whose responses to moral dilemmas were used to develop the original theory were male. She further asserted that men and women speak different but equally valid moral languages: Men speak more of rights and women speak more of responsibilities. Gilligan argued that men are more likely to view moral dilemmas as bargaining games or conflicts of rights between players who rationally pursue their own self-interests, whereas women tend to stress resolutions that involve concern, continued attachment, responsibility, sacrifice, and avoiding hurting others. Men are seen as searching for general principles that can be applied to any moral dilemma and women as concentrating on particular situations, relationships, and people.

Gender differences in moral thinking

Gilligan's ideas about gender differences in moral thinking reflect traditional differences in gender-role socialization in our society, and they are valid for most people. Furthermore, to the extent that such differences appear in people's responses to moral dilemmas, they would tend to cause conventional women to be scored at Stage 3 but conventional men to be scored at Stage 4 and to make men more likely than women to score at Stage 5. Thus there is reason for concern that Kohlberg's scoring scheme is biased against women (Pratt, Golding, & Hunter, 1984). However, research shows that Kohlberg's measurement methods and scoring schemes do not yield reliable gender differences in moral judgment scores (Walker, De Vries, & Trevethan, 1987). Gilligan's ideas about gender differences in general orientation toward moral dilemmas appear to have some validity, but these differences apparently do not lead to gender differences in moral judgment as measured by Kohlberg's methods. Thus Kohlberg's ideas and methods appear to be valid but limited to the cognitive or logical aspects of moral thinking, without addressing the emotional or social/interpersonal aspects (Hoffman, 1983).

Increasing Students' Moral Judgment Levels

Most people find Kohlberg's theory sensible and helpful, and it has considerable empirical support. His ideas have been applied successfully in educational programs designed to increase children's moral judgment levels (Damon & Killen, 1982). Typically, these programs involve presenting students with moral dilemmas like those that Kohlberg used to measure moral reasoning:

Application of Kohlberg's theory

> Joe's father promised he could go to camp if he earned $50 to pay for it, but then he changed his mind and asked Joe to give him the money he had earned. Joe lied and said that he had only earned $10 and went to camp using the other $40 he had made. Before he went, he told his

younger brother Alex about the money and about lying to his father. Should Alex tell their father?

These moral dilemmas produce a variety of responses, and similar solutions can be reached via many different chains of moral reasoning that can be scored according to Kohlberg's six stages. For example, a Stage 1 response might state that Alex should tell the father because if the father finds out that Alex knew and did not tell, he might punish Alex as well as Joe. A Stage 3 response might stress that fathers and sons should be good to each other, so Alex should tell because this is what a good son would do. A Stage 5 response might note that Alex has no legal obligation but does have a moral obligation to be truthful in his dealing with others, including his father, even though the father did not keep his earlier promise to Joe. Failure to tell the father here would constitute sharing in Joe's lie and thus would violate one of the implicit social contracts that underlie an orderly and effective society. Note that all three responses involve the same conclusion about what Alex should do but differ in the level of moral reasoning that underlies the decision.

Plus-one matching principle

Teachers who want to use discussion of moral dilemmas to promote development of moral reasoning are usually encouraged to use the *plus-one matching principle* by confronting students with moral reasoning that is one level above their own. The discrepancy between the plus-one level and their present reasoning will introduce cognitive conflict that should cause them to think more about the problem than they might otherwise and thereby to develop higher levels of moral reasoning. Programs based on the plus-one matching principle are usually effective (Enright et al., 1983; Mosher, 1980; Norcini & Snyder, 1983; Walker, 1983), although one study (Walker, 1982) found that plus-two reasoning was equally effective. Whether or not the plus-one matching principle really is the key, it is clear that some moral development programs successfully raise children's levels of moral judgment, especially when discussion of moral dilemmas is supplemented by exercises in empathy training, peer counseling, role playing, listening, and communication. Even so, most changes have occurred at Stages 2 and 3, with less positive results at the higher levels (Lockwood, 1978).

Synthesizing research on moral discussion in the classroom, Nucci (1987) suggested that such discussions be focused on issues of justice and human welfare, integrated within the curriculum rather than treated separately as a special program or unit and structured to promote debate among the students themselves rather than so as to depend on the teacher to confront students with levels of moral thinking that contrast with their own. Such discussions appear to be most effective when students who differ from each other by about one-half of a stage level are drawn into argumentative yet respectful debate in which they listen carefully to each speaker and then attempt logically to refute the arguments made or the assumptions on which they are based.

Values clarification approach

The *values clarification approach* developed by Raths, Harmin, and

Simon (1966) is somewhat more affective and less cognitive than the *moral reasoning approach* to moral education in the classroom. These authors believe that values must be recognized and chosen freely if we are to expect people to act on them consistently, so their approach concentrates on encouraging children to identify and clarify their own values rather than on trying to promote particular values as preferable to others. This approach has been less successful than the moral reasoning approach in documenting significant changes in children (Lockwood, 1978), but it is appealing to many people. For more details about moral education approaches, see Berkowitz and Oser (1985), Chazan (1985), Purpel and Ryan (1976), Schulman and Mekler (1985), or the various issues of the *Journal of Moral Education*.

Moral Judgment, Moral Affect, and Moral Behavior

Moral reasoning and behavior

Most teachers will not be satisfied with concentrating only on moral judgment, because moral reasoning does not always control behavior. In fact, research generally reveals low correlations between (1) *levels of moral reasoning* as measured by the methods of Piaget, Kohlberg, or Rest (1974); (2) *quality and intensity of moral affect* (feelings of satisfaction following good deeds or guilt following misdeeds); and (3) *moral behavior* (prosocial, cooperative versus antisocial or otherwise objectionable behavior).

Early studies suggested almost no correlation between moral judgment and moral behavior, but more recent studies have revealed moderate relationships, at least at the extremes of the moral judgment scale; that is, students who score particularly low in moral judgment are likely to be disruptive at school (Bear & Richards, 1981; Geiger & Turiel, 1983) and delinquent outside of school (Fleetwood & Parish, 1976; Hains & Miller, 1980; Wright, 1978). In contrast, those who score at Stage 5 are especially likely to engage in principled moral behavior, such as helping a stranger having a bad trip on drugs (McNamee, 1978) or working actively to bring about social justice (Blasi, 1980).

The parents of students who score at Stage 5 tend to use inductive socialization techniques, stressing the harmful consequences of inappropriate behavior on others, whereas the parents of those who score at Stages 1 and 2 tend to use power assertive techniques, displaying frequent threats and punishment (Eisikovits & Sagi, 1982; Hoffman, 1979; Olejnik, 1980). Thus there is reason to believe that programs that increase moral judgment will also increase moral behavior, although comprehensive programs aimed at all facets of moral development likely will be more effective than programs restricted to just one of them.

Aiding in moral development

In general, *teachers can promote moral development by both modeling and articulating humanistic Golden Rule behavior*. The socialization strategies that will be most successful in the classroom are providing guidelines and limits, offering explanations of why they are appropriate, and minimizing threats and punishment. It is also helpful to discuss idealized conduct and the reasons why it is valued. Degeneration of the discussion into a listing of punishments threatened for specific violations will

TABLE 5.3 DEVELOPMENTAL THEORISTS

Theorist Domain	Piaget Cognitive	Kohlberg Moral judgment	Erikson Psychosocial
Some key assumptions	1. Each person has needs to act out and to know. 2. Knowing depends on acting.	1. Moral judgment and moral action are different. 2. Moral judgment depends, in part, on cognitive development. 3. Moral judgment consists of two aspects: *content* (the what) and *structure* (the why).	1. Freudian theory (e.g., drives to maximize pleasure and minimize pain). 2. The quality of social relationships is vital.
Notion of stage	Structured whole, hierarchical, invariant, universal.	Structured whole, hierarchical, invariant, universal.	Nonstructured whole. 1. Loosely integrated into next stage. 2. Never given up entirely.
Mechanisms of development	1. Maturation of central nervous system. 2. Experience with physical objects and processes. 3. Experience with social objects. 4. Equilibration.	Same as Piaget, with a specific emphasis on moral dilemmas and discussions.	1. Physical maturation determines the general timetable. 2. Cultural/social experiences.
Nature vs. nurture	Interactionist.	Interactionist.	Interactionist but also heavily maturational.
Strengths	1. Recognizes the central role of cognition. 2. Value as an integrative and heuristic theory. 3. Discovery of surprising features of children's thinking.	1. Extensive empirical research, including in varied cultures. 2. Recognition of the importance of structure. 3. Willingness to modify theory to fit the data.	1. Expansion of the psychoanalytic theory. 2. Broad perspective, including social and historical variables.
Weaknesses	1. Vagueness of crucial terms such as *assimilation, accommodation, equilibration,* and *stage*. 2. Need for a theory of performance—i.e., a detailed account of exactly *how* cognitive structures are translated into behavior (making it difficult to apply in the classroom at times). 3. Methodological weaknesses.	1. Incompleteness—moral judgment is only part of moral development. 2. Possible gender bias. 3. Framework does presuppose certain philosophical roots (e.g., Kant, Rawls)—it is not value free.	1. Lack of systematicity, making it difficult to test empirically. 2. Lack of specific mechanisms of development.

Source: *Adapted from P. Miller,* Theories of Developmental Psychology (*New York: W. H. Freeman, 1983*).

only reinforce students' tendencies to persist in an authority-maintaining level of morality (Kohlberg's Stage 4), without advancing to higher stages.

Table 5.3 provides a summary of leading developmental theories.

SUMMARY

Although most personal and social traits are learned, biological givens such as arousal level, gender-linked traits, and physical characteristics interact with environmental influences to determine behavior. The influences of biology and environment are topics of great interest to developmental theorists. Erikson, for example, built on Freud's theory to develop a theory of psychosocial development that integrates stages of development and social experiences to describe conflicts and adaptations that are likely to occur at given points in the developmental sequence. Successful accommodations lead to optimal progression toward mature functioning, whereas failure leads to fixation or distortion.

Self-concept theorists emphasize the importance of positive expectations in promoting success and satisfaction in life. They note the stability of both positive and negative self-concepts, their resistance to artificial change, and their influences on behavior.

Kohlberg has identified six stages of moral judgment nested within three levels corresponding to Piaget's preoperational, concrete operational, and formal operational stages. Teachers can help their students progress to higher moral judgment levels by discussing moral issues with them, placing emphasis not just on what ought to be done but on the moral concepts and principles that provide the rationales for such conclusions.

QUESTIONS AND PROBLEMS

1. If children are born with certain biological predispositions (e.g., high arousal levels), do environmental influences make much difference in determining how they will develop? Why or why not?
2. Discuss Erikson's stages of industry versus inferiority and identity versus identity confusion. How can teachers help students adjust to these stages?
3. The authors present eleven adult attributes that are associated with optimal development in children. Reexamine them and identify the three or four most important ones. Why do you feel this way? Compare your list with the list of another student and discuss the differences between them.
4. How can teachers deal with students' feelings of inferiority, shame, guilt, or low self-esteem?
5. Why did some Boy Scouts in the study by Klinger and McNelly not want to be leaders?
6. Discuss the difference between conventional and postconventional moral judgment as defined by Kohlberg. If you were dealing with a student who was not obeying classroom rules, would the student's

level of moral judgment make any difference in how you responded? Explain.

7. School success is basic to the industry versus inferiority stage and to self-concept generally. What can you do to help students who overreact to school failures by becoming depressed or withdrawn? What about students who are becoming insufferable egotists due to constant success?
8. Almost everyone scoffs at psychoanalytic stage theories; yet they are regularly drawn upon for "explanations." Why?
9. Should teachers respond differently to the same misbehavior if the culprits differ significantly in level of moral development? What effect might this have on other students in the room?
10. Gender roles often hinder successful instruction. What might you do when certain boys are unresponsive to literature or poetry lessons or when certain girls are unresponsive to math or science lessons?
11. In general, there are orderly relationships between the modeling and socialization that children are exposed to and the personal traits that they develop. Yet siblings from the same families are sometimes very different. Also, some individuals manage to emerge well adjusted from poor backgrounds, and others emerge poorly adjusted from apparently loving and advantaged backgrounds. How can these exceptions be explained?

CASE STUDIES

ACTIVE ALICE. Alice Plice is a very active sixth grader—to put it nicely. She is always first in line due to her speed and willingness to shove, she has something to say about everything, and hers is the only voice that distinguishes itself from the playground hubbub. Despite her "gusto" for living, though, she drives people away from her and is lonely. Her teacher plans to try to improve her peer relationships. One way is to involve Alice frequently in cooperative group work with the same four peers. What other strategies might be used?

DEPENDENT DAN. Dan behaves anxiously in Mrs. Connor's seventh-grade English class. He watches her intently and constantly nods his head in agreement as she talks. He double-checks every assignment with her, asking if he is proceeding correctly. Dan is an attractive boy with an IQ of 130. Mrs. Connor knows of no reason for his anxiety, dependency, or desperate need for her approval. In what ways could Mrs. Connor approach the problem? What types of tasks should she assign him, and how should she interact with him?

QUICK HANDS JAN. Jan, a third grader from an affluent home, has started to "borrow" classroom supplies like scissors and jars of paste. Mrs. Murphy notices one of her rulers sticking out of Jan's open bag. Looking more closely, she sees other classroom supplies in the bag. During recess, she asks Jan to stay in to discuss the problem. What should she say or ask Jan? Write three or four responses that Jan might make, reflecting different stages of development. How should Mrs. Murphy respond to Jan if she determines that Jan is at a preoperational stage of development versus a concrete operational stage?

STICKY HANDS LUKE. Luke, a tenth grader from an affluent home, has started to "borrow" various supplies, including school property as well as items belonging to other students. During recess he pilfers supplies from the chemistry room or the industrial education room if they are left unattended. One day Mr. Thornton, who teaches industrial education, catches Luke putting several cans of enamel into his gym bag. This is the first time he has proof that Luke has been taking materials. What should he say to Luke? How should Luke be treated in comparison to Jan, the third grader?

INVIDIOUS SOCIAL COMPARISONS: LIFE IN THE FAST LANE. Jim Slink is a sophomore at Eastside High School. Jim has always been a talented student who progressed rapidly in every school subject, but this year he is doing poorly in an honors physics class composed mostly of seniors. Partly because of his concern about his poor progress in physics, his grades in other subjects are beginning to suffer as well. One day he stays after school to discuss his problems with his physics teacher. Jim whines, "I've never been in a class like this before. Everybody else picks up the material much more quickly than I can. The other day three-fourths of them had finished the experiment before I even figured out what to do." If you were the teacher, what could you do to help Jim view himself realistically but positively?

PART 3
LEARNING

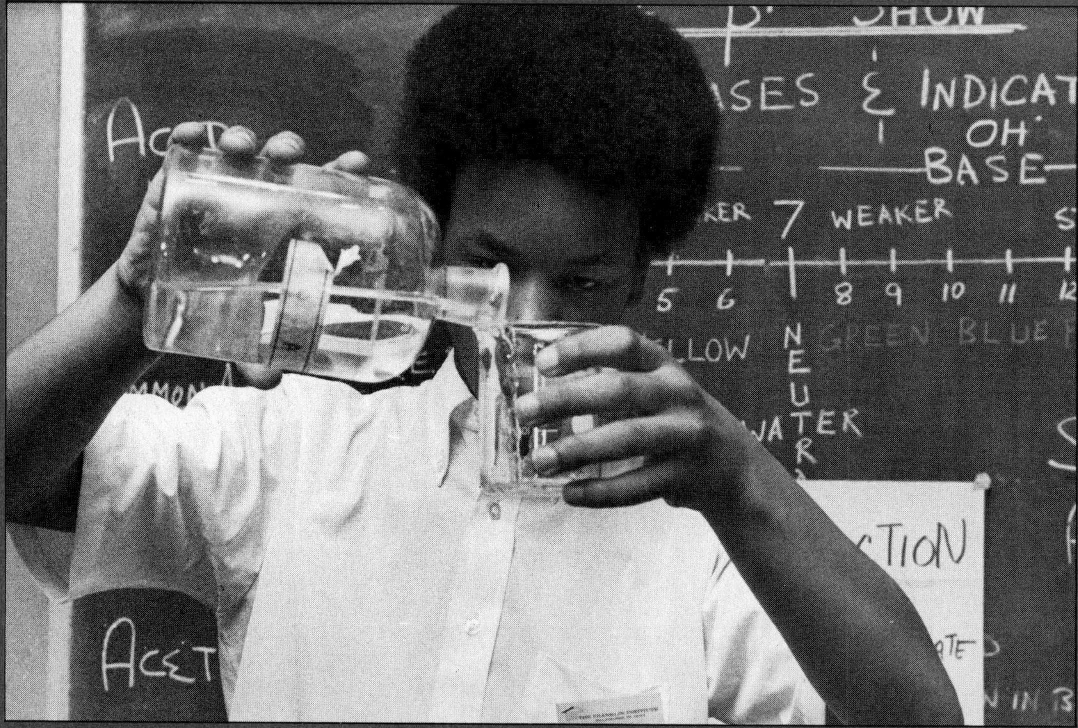

Mr. Simpson makes sure that his algebra students know their equations. He introduces each new equation with clear and detailed explanations, demonstrates their application by working out computation problems using the overhead projector, and assigns many more computation problems as seatwork or homework. As a result, most of his students learn to solve equations with speed and accuracy. Yet Mr. Simpson finds that as soon as he gives his students word problems that can be solved using the equations they are learning, their performance breaks down. Many students act completely confused, and most of the rest solve problems only by guessing at possible formula applications. Very few of them think about the problem, formulate it in algebraic terms, and then solve it using appropriate equations. Why might this be?

Mrs. Abbott and Mrs. Costello both teach American history. They use the same texts and similar brief assignments to cover the same material with similar students. However, Mrs. Abbott grades according to weekly quizzes, a midterm covering the first half of the course, and a final covering the second half, whereas Mrs. Costello grades according to a single final exam that covers the entire course and a term paper based on research about an important historical figure. Given these differences in grading, what differences would you expect in (a) amount and distribution of student study time, (b) attitudes toward history and interest in taking more history courses, and (c) how much students will remember about American history several years later?

Ms. Brinks was pleased with her science unit on force, gravity, and vectors. She felt comfortable teaching it, the students seemed to enjoy and understand the material, and the class did well on the unit test. Therefore, she was jolted to discover how poorly they performed on a seemingly easy final exam item several weeks later. She had asked, "If you released a 2,000 pound safe and a canteloupe at the same time from the top of the Leaning Tower of Pisa, which would hit the ground first, if either would hit first?" She had expected that nearly everyone would remember the basic principles they seemingly had learned so well, and therefore would say that the two objects would hit the ground at the same time. What had happened to that clear understanding seemingly displayed on the unit test?

Mrs. McGuffy is patient and encouraging with her low reading group but discouraged with the progress of most students in it. They have basic word-attack skills, but their ability to "put it all together" and read is poor. Some are "word callers" who handle most individual words correctly but don't keep track of meaning as they read, so they don't get the meaning unless they repeat their reading several times. Others are still struggling to blend sounds into words, let alone words into sentences. Yet they all understand letter-sound relationships (phonics) and are familiar with the basic processes of sounding out syllables, blending syllables into words, and combining words into sentences in order to get the meaning. So why don't they read with more efficiency and better comprehension?

Mr. Anderson is unhappy with the new social studies text. It's more visually attractive than the old one, and readability formulas suggest that it should be easier to understand. Yet student performance on early assignments and tests has been poor, and students are complaining about the text, saying that, "It doesn't explain clearly—you can read it again and again and still not know what it is trying to say," and "It's hard to take notes—you can't find out what the main points are." What do you think that Mr. Anderson will find when he compares the two texts to identify the reason for the problems with the new text? Given that the new text may be used for some time, what can he do to counter its deficiencies and help the students learn more successfully?

These vignettes illustrate just a few of the many principles of human learning discussed in the next four chapters. Mr. Simpson's problem illustrates the need for curriculum alignment: Logical relationships between the objectives of instruction, the content taught, the teaching methods and assignments, and the methods used to assess mastery. Mr. Simpson's instructional objectives implicitly included not only the ability to solve equations in computation exercises but the ability to apply learning about equations to the solution of practical problems. However, he failed to teach for application. He gave good explanations and demonstrations of how to solve computation exercises but never modeled the process of applying knowledge about equations to solution of practical problems or provided his students with sufficient opportunities for such applications.

Mrs. Abbott and Mrs. Costello illustrate that differences in assignments and assessment procedures will produce differences in study patterns and thus in what students learn. Mrs. Abbott's students are likely to retain most of the main ideas taught in the course, because they will both study small subsets of the material for weekly quizzes and review larger subsets for the two major exams. In contrast, many of Mrs. Costello's students probably will do little studying early in the term, cram for the final, and then forget most of the material. However, Mrs. Costello's students will learn a great deal about the individual they select as the focus of their term papers and will gain practice in research skills and the ability to integrate information from various sources, skills that won't be developed in Mrs. Abbott's class.

Ms. Brinks is discovering that instruction usually involves conceptual change rather than infusion of information into a vacuum. Students often bring to a learning situation a great deal of prior knowledge that establishes a framework within which new input is interpreted. When the prior knowledge is accurate, the results are desirable and produce more efficient learning. However, when the prior knowledge includes misconceptions, the result may be distortion or even rejection of the new learning, especially if the misconceptions are well anchored in experience and thus stubbornly resistant to change (such as the belief that heavy objects fall faster than lighter objects). In those situations, teachers must not only teach the new information clearly but also make their students aware of and willing to part with their misconceptions.

Mrs. McGuffy's low-group readers illustrate the fact that there are severe limitations on short-term working-memory capacity. If a set of tasks takes up all of the available capacity, there will be none left for additional tasks. Her beginning readers needed most of their working-memory capacity for processing syllables and blending them into words, so they had little left over for making sense of the meaning at the sentence level. As basic word processing becomes more automatic and thus less demanding on working memory, more of this limited capacity will become available for sentence-level processing.

Mr. Anderson's students' problems with the new textbook illustrate how learning efficiency is affected not only by the difficulty of the content but by the clarity and organization of the presentation. ''Considerate'' texts make learning easier by organizing and sequencing the content in a logical way, presenting it in clear language, highlighting structural features, signaling transitions between sections, calling attention to main ideas, and so on. The same is true of ''considerate'' lectures and demonstrations. Since the new text is not considerate in this sense, Mr. Anderson will need to supplement it by distributing content outlines, lists of key terms, and other study aids that will help students to organize and retain the material.

Even good curricula only provide materials and suggestions for teachers to use. Teachers must be prepared to instruct their students personally rather than depend only on texts to do so, especially younger students and slower students of any age. Such preparation begins with understanding of student learning processes, which are the focus of the next four chapters. Chapter 6 provides an overview. It defines learning, differentiates it from related concepts, identifies different types of learning and the forms of instruction that are associated with them, and illustrates how this information is needed for establishing objectives and planning instruction.

The next three chapters review theory and research on human learning, organized according to three major paradigms. Chapter 7 covers the behavioristic tradition, beginning with early research on the conditioning of animal behavior, continuing through Skinner's operant conditioning and Bandura's social learning theory, and culminating with contemporary applications such as programmed instruction, computerized instruction, and cognitive behavior modification.

Chapter 8 discusses the cognitive structuralist approach, which stresses helping learners to understand input as an organized body of meaningful concepts and information rather than as a seemingly random list of things to memorize. Bruner's ideas about encouraging learners to discover key concepts and relationships for themselves are covered in this chapter, as are Ausubel's ideas about organizing and sequencing expository instruction to maximize meaningful reception learning.

Chapter 9 describes information contributed by theorists interested in how humans attend to only limited input at any particular time, process it in short-term memory, encode it for storage in long-term memory, and retrieve it for use later. These information-processing theorists stress that learning involves actively making sense of new input by interpreting it within previously developed schemes, and they stress the need to teach learners to process information in active ways by making rote learning more meaningful and meaningful learning more systematic.

CHAPTER

Psychology of Learning

CHAPTER OUTLINE

OBJECTIVES

When you have mastered the material in this chapter you will be able to

1. Define learning accurately and distinguish it from related concepts
2. Distinguish figurative knowledge from operative knowledge, intentional learning from incidental learning, rote learning from meaningful learning, and reception learning from discovery learning
3. Classify different learning objectives according to the Bloom taxonomy
4. Classify various levels of learning according to the Gagné hierarchy and different types of learning according to the Gagné and Briggs typology
5. State the different learning conditions required to accomplish various types of learning objectives
6. Formulate learning objectives that operationalize curricular roles accurately and function as effective guides to the planning of instruction, practice, and evaluation

DEFINITION OF LEARNING

This is the first of four chapters on the psychology of learning. In this chapter we will define *learning*, identify different types of learning, and show how this information is used to establish learning objectives.

Learning must be differentiated from related concepts such as thinking, behavior, development, or change. Wittrock (1977) defined it this way: "Learning is the term we use to describe the processes involved in changing through experience. It is the process of acquiring relatively permanent change in understanding, attitude, knowledge, information, ability, and skill through experience" (p. ix).

Defined this way, learning is an internal, cognitive event that cannot be equated with observable performance. It is true that learning increases capacity for performance, that we must observe changes in performance to infer that learning has occurred, and that certain kinds of learning, especially motor learning, are refined through practice. Nevertheless, the performance potential acquired through learning is not the same as its application during any particular performance. Furthermore, relationships between prior learning and subsequent performance are imperfect. The absence of a particular behavior does not mean that the person does not know anything about it, and the disappearance of a behavior observed in the past does not mean that the ability to perform it has been lost.

Learning and change

Learning involves change, but only some kinds of changes qualify as learning. Because learning implies relatively permanent change, it does not include temporary phenomena such as random situational behavior or the effects of drugs or fatigue. Also, because learning refers to change produced by experience, it does not include change produced by physical growth, maturation, or senility.

Development versus learning

Learning is more difficult to differentiate from development. Traditionally, learning psychologists emphasized manipulation of the environment (particularly reinforcement contingencies), and developmental psychologists emphasized internal maturation and tried to identify progressive age differences that were universal across individuals and cultures. However, these differences have become blurred in recent years. Learning psychologists (Anderson, 1984; Corno & Rohrkemper, 1985; Weinstein & Mayer, 1986) have begun to emphasize information processing and other activities that occur within learners in addition to events that occur in the environment, and developmental psychologists (Palincsar & Brown, 1984) have begun to study environmentally induced changes that involve little or no biological maturation. Thus at present, the differences are more in emphasis and methods of study than in substance. We have presented information generated by these two major approaches to psychology in separate sections to make it easier to learn, but the two kinds of information are complementary, and you will need to draw on both in thinking about students and their instructional needs.

Thinking versus learning

Finally, learning is not the same as thinking, although these two processes are closely linked and mutually supportive. *Thinking* refers to the exercise or application of cognitive skills (posing and attempting to answer questions, searching memory, processing information, and evaluating potential solutions to problems). When applied in routine fashion to familiar content, thinking is the mere exercise of already learned cognitive skills, analogous to the exercise of physical skills. However, thinking can produce learning. This occurs routinely when cognitive skills are used to process new input, and it also occurs when reflection on prior experience yields new insights. Both kinds of learning are important, which is why we define *learning* as change induced through experience (including inner reflection) rather than defining it more restrictively as change induced through encounters with the external environment. Although all learning is ultimately traceable at least in part to environmental events, only a portion of it involves adapting to events occurring in the external environment. Other portions, which grow in importance with age, involve either reflecting on past experiences or manipulating abstract concepts that we have never encountered in concrete form in the external environment.

In summary, learning is a relatively permanent change in capacity for performance, acquired through experience. The experience may involve overt interaction with the external environment, but it will also involve (and sometimes will be confined to) covert cognitive processes.

QUALITATIVE DISTINCTIONS

No single theory or brief list of principles fits all learning situations equally well. Thus you will need to recognize different kinds of learning that are called for by different instructional objectives so that you can plan appropriate strategies for accomplishing them. We will present several qualitative distinctions and then cover typologies that have proven useful for conceptualizing learning and instruction.

Developmental Stages

We have already noted that different types of learning can be classified according to the various information processing skills or cognitive operations that develop with age. Thus Piaget (1983) wrote about sensorimotor, preoperational, concrete, and formal operational thinking, and Bruner (1964) considered learning as involving enactive, iconic, or symbolic knowledge (see Chapter 8). Klausmeier (1976) and others have also developed classification schemes that reflect developmental phenomena. These schemes help us to appreciate the *qualitative changes* that can occur in knowledge about particular topics (movement from concrete toward increasingly abstract knowledge and from isolated toward increasingly integrated knowledge). They also remind us that learning is likely to be most meaningful when it is anchored in concrete experience.

Knowledge That versus Knowledge How

In Chapter 3 we discussed Piaget's concepts of figurative and operative knowledge. *Figurative knowledge* (also called declarative, propositional, or theoretical knowledge) is "knowledge that." It is intellectual knowledge of facts and principles. *Operative knowledge* (also called procedural

Figurative versus operative knowledge

or practical knowledge) is "knowledge how." It is the ability to perform tasks and solve problems. Ideally, one possesses both forms of knowledge and can use them in integrated, mutually supportive ways to solve problems. Often, however, just one form predominates. For example, most baseball pitchers who can throw a curve ball do not have well-articulated figurative knowledge of the principles that explain why a curve ball curves, and most physicists who possess this figurative knowledge are nevertheless unable to throw a good curve ball. One frequent criticism of schooling is that too much of what is taught is confined to figurative knowledge that never becomes very useful because students do not get enough opportunities to link it to operative knowledge developed through application exercises. Such criticisms have led, for example, to the inclusion of laboratory experiences in science and foreign language classes.

Intentional versus Incidental Learning

Intentional learning is consciously goal directed: the person intends to learn certain things and sets out to do so. *Incidental learning* occurs without deliberate intention. Much incidental learning occurs when the person is relatively passive, responding to the environment but not actively pursuing specific goals. For example, you probably have watched hundreds of television dramas dealing with law enforcement, primarily to be entertained rather than to develop knowledge. Yet in the process you have learned specialized terms used in police stations and courtrooms, and you probably could "read" prisoners their rights or swear in witnesses using what you remember from seeing these activities modeled by actors. When people are actively seeking to learn, their attention focuses on the material to be learned intentionally. Nevertheless, some incidental learning occurs even here. In classrooms, for example, students incidentally learn a great deal about the mannerisms and personal attributes of teachers, even while concentrating on intentional learning of course content.

Rote versus Meaningful Learning

Discussions of the rote/meaningful dimension and the reception/discovery dimension are among the contributions of David Ausubel to the psychology of learning (Ausubel & Robinson, 1969). Both dimensions refer to situations in which learners are attempting to learn meaningful information. The rote/meaningful dimension refers to the learners' approach to the task. To the extent that they merely try to memorize the new information without relating it to their existing knowledge, they are engaging in *rote learning*. To the extent that they try to relate the idea to what they already know and thereby make sense of it, they are engaging in *meaningful learning*. Meaningful learning is retained longer than rote learning (material memorized for a test through "cramming" is soon forgotten), and it is much more efficient since a few general principles can accommodate a great many specific applications. Consequently, it is important for teachers to make information meaningful to their students and to teach them strategies for engaging in meaningful learning.

Reception versus Discovery Learning

The reception/discovery dimension refers to the means by which the knowledge is made available to learners. In *reception learning*, knowledge is presented in its final form, typically through expository instruction that states the information and then elaborates and provides examples. In *discovery learning*, learners are exposed to experiences and guidance designed to lead them to discover the target concept or principle. Discovery learning involves instruction in that a planned series of questions or experiences is used to guide the learners toward the target discovery, but the instructor does not present the target information in its final form, except perhaps to summarize and elaborate on it after the learners have discovered it for themselves. Like the rote versus meaningful distinction, the reception versus discovery distinction refers to a continuous dimension. Combination forms involving varying degrees of reception and discovery learning occur in between the extremes of pure reception learning and pure discovery learning.

Ausubel has shown that these two dimensions (rote/meaningful and reception/discovery) are separate and that although meaningful learning is generally superior to rote learning, discovery learning is not necessarily superior to reception learning. It is true that discovery learning is active by definition and is likely to produce long-lasting, meaningful knowledge when successful. It is also true, however, that discovery learning is time consuming and can become confusing or frustrating if not handled carefully. Thus discovery learning is more appropriate for some objectives than others, and it requires moving students through well-planned series of structured experiences rather than merely exposing them to content in some haphazard way and hoping that they will discover the target learning.

Expository instruction

Just as discovery learning is not necessarily effective, reception learning is not necessarily ineffective. Expository instruction (lecture, demonstration) is often stereotyped as producing only parrotlike repetition or rote memorization of isolated facts. If designed to produce meaningful reception learning, however, expository teaching can be an efficient method of instruction. It is especially useful for conveying well-organized bodies of knowledge, so it is the primary method of instruction (partly through teacher lectures but mostly through texts) used in schools once students master basic tool skills. Expository instruction and reception learning can be ineffective, however, if addressed to inappropriate content (isolated facts without general organizing principles) or if overused to the point that instruction is restricted to figurative knowledge.

LEARNING TYPOLOGIES

In addition to these qualitative distinctions, learning theorists have proposed typologies that distinguish types of learning according to differences in what is being learned. These typologies are also helpful as organizers for instructional planning. Two of the best known of these typologies are the taxonomy of cognitive objectives published by Bloom and associates (1956) and the classifications and learning hierarchies published by Gagné (1977) and Gagné and Briggs (1979).

Bloom's Taxonomy

Recognizing the potential value of a classification scheme that would identify different learning objectives with standardized terminology, a group of experts surveyed taxonomies in the early 1950s and sought to develop a common scheme. The most influential result of their work was a taxonomy of educational objectives in the cognitive domain (Bloom et al., 1956), which is often called "Bloom's taxonomy" for short. Other taxonomies were published later for objectives in the affective (Krathwohl, Bloom, & Masia, 1964) and psychomotor (Harrow, 1972) domains.

Major categories in Bloom's taxonomy

The six major categories in Bloom's taxonomy are shown in Table 6.1 (Bloom et al., 1956, also list numerous subcategories). Educators find this taxonomy useful because it includes most of the goals stressed by schools and describes them in commonly used language, although those in mathematics and science may prefer the term *problem solving* to the term *analysis*, which is used more in the humanities.

Imperfections in theory

Like most taxonomies, this one can be criticized on several grounds. First, the boundary between comprehension and application is fuzzy (Ausubel & Robinson, 1969). Second, the sequencing of categories from low to high in cognitive level has been questioned on the basis of both logical considerations (Furst, 1981) and empirical data (Kunen, Cohen, & Solman, 1981; Seddon, 1978). In particular, many believe that synthesis, rather than evaluation, should be placed at the highest level. Third, the notion of cognitive level is sometimes confused with the notion of difficulty level of a task or question. In fact, these concepts are independent. A "low-level" knowledge item (name Henry the Eighth's fourth wife) is extremely difficult if you don't know the answer, and yet you may be able to respond to "high-level" tasks (evaluate the theory that all wars ultimately result from economic causes) with some success even if you have little organized knowledge about the topic.

Another concern is that Bloom's taxonomy (and any other taxonomy that features levels arranged into a hierarchy) misleadingly implies a clear separation of lower-level from higher-level content and suggests that one must proceed linearly from lower to higher levels when teaching content. Cognitive researchers have found that presumably lower-level skills such as arithmetic computation actually involve abstracting, making inferences, and engaging in other forms of higher-level thinking. Similarly, higher-level thinking and problem solving require the use of lower-level knowledge and skills. Finally, other research suggests that, rather than have students practice low-level skills in isolation and only gradually begin to combine them and apply them to higher-level tasks, teachers should embed skills instruction and practice within a context of meaningful problem solving (or other higher-order applications such as critical thinking or decision making) right from the beginning. That is, students should learn to read, not just discriminate letters (Anderson et al., 1985); should learn to use mathematics to solve problems, not just to compute (Fennema, Carpenter, & Peterson, 1989); and so on.

Despite these imperfections, Bloom's taxonomy is a useful tool for planning or assessing instruction. Implicitly, at least, we as a society want the school curriculum taught so that effective learning occurs at all levels in the taxonomy. Yet critical analyses typically reveal that very high percentages of textbook content, practice exercises, and classroom activities focus on the knowledge and comprehension levels, with little attention to higher levels (Freeman et al., 1983; Gall, 1970; Trachtenberg, 1974). The same is true of the tests used to assess learning. The lesson here is obvious: To the extent that we expect students to master learning objectives that go beyond the knowledge and comprehension levels, we will need to provide instruction and application opportunities geared to these higher cognitive levels and to assess learning accordingly.

Bloom's taxonomy is also a useful tool for constructing good tests. This application of the taxonomy is discussed in Chapter 28.

Gagné's Learning Varieties and Hierarchies

Other well-known systems for classifying types of learning have been developed by Robert Gagné and published either on his own (Gagné, 1977, 1984) or in collaboration with Leslie Briggs (Gagné & Briggs, 1979).

Learning hierarchies

The Gagné (1977) Learning Hierarchy Gagné began with a behavioristic orientation but with interests in the different types of learning and their relationships. This led him to develop typologies called *learning hierarchies*, in which learning tasks were arranged in sequence from the simplest to the most complex. For example, the following learning hierarchy contains seven categories (Gagné, 1977):

1. *Signal learning*. Learning a general response to a signal (stop socializing and prepare for class when the bell rings; respond with fear when overtaken by a police car with flashing lights).
2. *Stimulus-response learning*. Learning a precise response to a discriminated stimulus (pronounce words on sight, call people by their names, produce and use the key needed to open a particular lock).
3. *Chaining*. Learning to link two or more previously learned stimulus-response connections (sounding out the individual letters in a word and then blending these sounds to form the word itself; combining letters to form words when writing).
4. *Verbal association*. Learning to link combinations of words as stimuli with other words as responses (recognizing whole words on sight when reading; translating other languages into English).
5. *Discrimination learning*. Distinguishing among members of a set of similar stimuli so as to respond to each individually (identify different breeds of dog; rely on context to identify the intended usage of words that have several meanings when listening to an oral presentation; use the proper versions of homonyms when writing).

TABLE 6.1 OUTLINE OF BLOOM'S TAXONOMY OF EDUCATIONAL OBJECTIVES IN THE COGNITIVE DOMAIN

Category	General Description of Category	Illustrative Items
I. Knowledge (a) of *Specifics* (terminology, facts) (b) of *Ways and Means of Dealing with Specifics* (conventions, classifications, criteria, methodology) (c) of *Universals and Abstractions* (principles, generalizations, theories)	*Recall* of specifics and universals, methods, and processes, pattern, structure of setting. Knowledge objectives emphasize most of the psychological processes of *remembering*.	About what proportion of the population of Canada is living in cities? 1. 10% 2. 20% 3. 40% 4. 50% 5. 60% (knowledge of specific fact) The volume of a given mass of gas varies directly as the ________ and inversely as the ________ . 1. Pressure and temperature 2. Temperature and pressure 3. Atomic weight and pressure 4. Temperature and atomic weight (knowledge of principles and generalizations)
II. Comprehension (a) Translation (b) Interpretation (c) Extrapolation	Lowest level of understanding of what is communicated. Can use idea being communicated without necessarily being able to relate it to other ideas or see all its implications.	Four less than three times a certain number equals eight. In algebra this may be expressed as: 1. $4 - 3X = 8$ 3. $3X - 4 = 8$ 2. $4X - 3 = 8$ 4. $4 + 3X = 8$ (Translation)*
III. Application	The use of abstractions in particular and concrete situations.	Two basic laws governing an electrical circuit are: Voltage = (Current) × (Resistance) Power = (Voltage) × (Current) if an electric iron develops greater resistance (rust, etc.) its power will: 1. increase 2. remain the same 3. decrease

IV. Analysis (a) of *Elements* (b) of *Relationships* (c) of *Organizational Principles*	Breakdown of a communication into its constituent parts, such that relative hierarchy of ideas is made clearer and/or the relations between the ideas expressed are made clear.	The given figure represents a hoop of 28 in. diameter. If the hoop is rolling without slipping in the indicated direction, how many inches has point *A* moved horizontally when the hoop has finished half a turn? ($\pi = 22/7$) (Analysis of Relationships)*
V. Synthesis (a) Production of a unique communication (b) Production of a plan (c) Derivation of a set of abstract relations	Putting together of parts to form a whole; analyzing and combining pieces in such a way as to constitute a pattern or structure not clearly there before.	Without adding all items, find the sum of: $\frac{1}{1 \times 2} + \frac{1}{2 \times 3} + \frac{1}{3 \times 4} + \frac{1}{4 \times 5} \cdots \frac{1}{98 \times 99} + \frac{1}{99 \times 100}$*
VI. Evaluation (a) *Judgments in terms of internal criteria* (b) *Judgments in terms of external evidence*	Making judgments about the value of material and methods for given purposes. Judging extent to which material and methods satisfy given criteria.	The ability to indicate logical fallacies in arguments (Internal Evidence) Ability to compare a work with highest known standards in its field. (External Criteria)

* *Illustrative items from Avital and Shettleworth, 1968.*

Source: *Adapted from B. S. Bloom (ed.),* Taxonomy of Educational Objectives: The Classification of Educational Goals, Book 1: Cognitive Domain. *White Plains, N.Y.: Longman, 1985. Reprinted by permission of Longman Inc.*

6. *Concept learning*. Learning to identify individual objects, events, or ideas as members of a common general class (identify the subjects and predicates of sentences; identify instances of concepts such as "peninsula," or "prime number," or "solvent").
7. *Rule learning*. Learning general rules or principles with sufficient understanding to recognize their applications or use them to solve problems (use the rules of English grammar and composition when writing prose; use mathematical principles to reduce or enlarge recipes or determine how much paint or fertilizer to purchase).

Gagné's learning hierarchy uses more specialized terms and makes finer distinctions among types of learning placed at the low and middle levels of the Bloom taxonomy. On the other hand, it makes fewer distinctions at the higher levels. Consequently, Gagné's scheme is more suited to the skills taught in the primary grades than to the knowledge taught in higher grades.

Learning capabilities

The Gagné and Briggs (1979) Typology As Gagné's interests shifted toward the educational applications of the psychology of learning, his approach to classification became broader and more concentrated on higher levels of learning. In addition, he shifted from a focus on what is learned toward a focus on the *capabilities* that learners acquire. Gagné and Briggs (1979) identified five types of learning:

1. *Attitudes:* Internal states that influence personal action choices.
2. *Motor skills:* Organized muscle movements used to accomplish purposeful actions.
3. *Information:* Facts and organized knowledge about the world stored in memory.
4. *Intellectual skills:* Skills that permit learners to carry out symbol-based procedures (these skills are subdivided into discriminations, concrete concepts, defined concepts, rules, and higher-order rules).
5. *Cognitive strategies:* Strategies that learners bring to bear on their own cognitive processing in order to control their learning or develop solutions to problems.

Table 6.2 shows examples of these five capabilities as well as action verbs that apply when they are translated into performance.

Like the Bloom taxonomy, the Gagné and Briggs scheme defines several categories of learning, identifies them with common terms, and is useful in planning or assessing instruction. Although there is some overlap, the two systems are largely complementary. The Gagné and Briggs system distinguishes among several types of learning that are included within the comprehension and application levels of the Bloom system, but the highest levels of the Bloom system are not addressed by Gagné and Briggs. Consequently, analyses of instruction that draw on both systems are likely to be more complex than analyses that use only one.

Conditions of Learning Gagné and Briggs (1979) also offered guidelines about the different types of instruction that each type of learning requires.

TABLE 6.2 STANDARD VERBS TO DESCRIBE HUMAN CAPABILITIES, WITH EXAMPLES OF PHRASES INCORPORATING ACTION VERBS

Capability	Capability Verb	Example (Action Verb in Italics)
Intellectual skill Discrimination	DISCRIMINATES	Discriminates, by *matching* French sounds of "*u*" and "*ou*"
Concrete concept	IDENTIFIES	Identifies, by *naming,* the root, leaf, and stem of representative plants
Defined concept	CLASSIFIES	Classifies, by using a *definition,* the concept "family"
Rule	DEMONSTRATES	Demonstrates, by *solving* verbally stated examples, the addition of positive and negative numbers
Higher-order rule (problem solving)	GENERATES	Generates, by *synthesizing* applicable rules, a paragraph describing a person's actions in a situation of fear
Cognitive strategy	ORIGINATES	Originates a solution to the reduction of air pollution, by *applying model* of gaseous diffusion
Information	STATES	States orally the major issues in the presidential campaign of 1932
Motor skill	EXECUTES	Executes *backing* a car into driveway
Attitude	CHOOSES	Chooses *playing golf* as a leisure activity

Source: *From* Principles of Instructional Design, *second edition, by Robert M. Gagné and Leslie J. Briggs. Copyright © 1970 by Holt, Rinehart and Winston Inc., reprinted by permission of the publisher.*

Internal and external conditions

They discussed internal and external *conditions of learning* that must be established for each type of learning to occur. *Internal conditions* refer to events occurring within the learner, especially recall and activation of previous learning that the new learning must build on. *External conditions* refer to events in the environment, particularly instructional events that activate and support learning processes. Conditions of learning differ for each type of learning.

Attitude Learning Gagné and Briggs believe that attitudes are acquired primarily through exposure to respected *models* that exhibit the attitudes, rather than through more typical instruction. However, they also note that attitudes can be stimulated through *persuasive communication* (if the learner accepts the message) and can be *conditioned through experience* with rewarding or punishing events (people who enjoyed early success at activities such as playing musical instruments or solving mathematical problems may believe that they have talent for these activities and come to enjoy them, but others who encounter early frustration may conclude that they lack talent and come to dislike them).

Clearly, we cannot teach an attitude the way we would teach the concept of a triangle. We can try to stimulate attitudes indirectly through modeling, persuasion, or manipulation of incentives, but we cannot produce them directly through instruction because they involve elements of emotional involvement and personal commitment that can come only from the learners themselves. Because of these important qualitative differences between attitude learning and other forms of learning, most of what we have to say about shaping students' attitudes will appear in sections on classroom management and student motivation rather than in sections on learning and instruction.

Motor Learning Motor skills are a primary focus of some classes (art, music, physical education, machine shop), and they play a role in certain academic activities (handwriting, illustrating, handling laboratory equipment). Learners develop some motor skills intuitively through experience and sustain them in the form of what Piaget (1983) called sensorimotor schemes. However, motor learning is more efficient if learners are provided with *modeling* that they can imitate and with *verbal instructions* and *visual imagery* that they can use to guide their performance in addition to opportunities for practice with corrective feedback.

Importance of practice

Practice is critical to the development and maintenance of motor skills. Although it is true that a skill (such as roller skating) that is practiced until it is thoroughly mastered will be retained indefinitely and can be recovered to some degree with relative ease when it has not been used in years, it is also true that continuous practice is needed to maintain motor skills at high levels of proficiency. That is why professional musicians, dancers, and athletes practice continuously, with attention to fundamentals as well as to higher-level accomplishments.

To be useful to learners, practice must provide *feedback*. Some motor-skill feedback is internal (Adams, 1977). Learners can learn to recognize and benefit from physical sensations, body images, and other forms of psychomotor feedback. Tennis players, for example, can learn to recognize when they are executing a stroke successfully so as to meet the ball with the "sweet spot" of the racquet. Sometimes they even utter sounds of satisfaction as they do so. In addition to this internal feedback,

Developing and maintaining highly proficient motor skills, for most children, takes practice.

motor-skill performance may produce external feedback conveyed through environmental events. Learners can observe for themselves the results of their actions (the flight of the ball as it leaves the racquet). External feedback can also be supplied through opportunities to observe videotapes of performance, to get feedback from an instructor, or to compare products with ideal examples (i.e., to compare a page of printing or a product produced in the wood shop with the model being emulated).

Verbal instructions

Verbal instruction can assist motor performance, as the popularity and usefulness of "how-to" books attest. However, verbal instructions do not always communicate the desired motor image. You may know that you are supposed to "bend your knees and shift weight as you swing," and yet you bend your knees too far or shift weight too soon. Thus opportunities to observe models perform motor skills properly are valuable, especially if the models verbalize their thinking as they perform the skill so that one can monitor the self-talk that guides behavior in addition to observing the behavior itself.

Feedback is likely to be more helpful if presented in the *same form* (enactive, iconic, or symbolic) that the learner is using (Bruner, 1966). In teaching a golf swing, for example, instructors should not merely model and prescribe proper form but should also position the learners' bodies properly and physically guide them through proper executions of the swing.

Bad-habit prevention

In teaching motor skills, it is important to *prevent bad habits from developing*. Unless they are taught basic principles and good form, learners may develop skills that are functional to an extent but inefficient or potentially counterproductive. For example, one of the authors learned to skate "the hard way" as a child and did not find out until adulthood (upon receiving instruction) that he could achieve better balance and more speed, and yet use less effort, by capitalizing on principles of good skating form. Many injuries sustained from running or participation in vigorous activities occur because the person unnecessarily stresses some part of the body. Instruction in good form with attention to eliminating bad habits could minimize this problem.

Information Learning Superficially, the learning of verbally encoded information is straightforward: If a message is clearly formulated, learners can understand it by relating it to the network of concepts, vocabulary, and verbally articulated experience they have accumulated. In practice, however, things are more complicated. First, the message may not be noted when first encountered. Second, if registered at that time, the message may not be understood exactly as it was intended by the communicator. Third, its meaning may become transformed over time.

People pick up information every day with relative ease, especially in this age of modern communications and in information-rich environments such as schools. Teachers, however, need to direct students' attention to the particular information included in the formal school curriculum and help them to assimilate and retain it.

Importance of good presentation

This process begins by *cuing students' attention* to relevant information, preferably by stimulating their interest or curiosity. It is also important to see that the students can *understand the information in meaningful fashion* by relating it to their existing knowledge. If the message contains undefined terms or refers to concepts or events unknown to the students, they will not be able to understand and retain it as meaningful information (although they may memorize it long enough to regurgitate it on a test). Finally, even if everything is clear and meaningful, there are limits on how much information learners can retain. More information will be remembered when it is *presented in an organized fashion* (in a sensible sequence, with each segment containing main ideas followed by elaboration or supportive material) and in ways that *stimulate students to process it actively and encode it in their own words*.

Intellectual Skill Learning Gagné and Briggs believe that intellectual skills fall into the following five categories (ordered from simple to complex): discriminations, concrete concepts, defined concepts, rules, and higher-order rules.

Discriminations

Discriminations are capabilities for detecting and responding to differences in physical stimuli. Discrimination learning is especially important in early reading and writing, when students must learn to respond differently to various letters that have similar components (*b, d, p, q*) and to the capital and small versions of the same letter (*P, p*). Discrimination learning also assumes importance occasionally at higher grade levels (hearing subtle sound discriminations in foreign languages that are not made in English, noting subtle but important differences in similar algebraic equations or chemical formulas).

Discriminations are typically taught using the principles of *contiguity, feedback,* and *repetition*. That is, the stimuli to be compared are presented either simultaneously (two objects, side by side) or, when that is not possible, in rapid succession (one sound followed closely by another). This close contiguity between two stimuli facilitates comparison of them. Following presentation of the stimuli, learners are asked to state whether they are the same or different, and their responses are given immediate feedback. Such practice is repeated until the discrimination is mastered.

Concrete concepts

Concrete concepts are capabilities for recognizing that stimuli belong to a class that shares one or more common attributes (red color, round shape, etc.). Once learners "have the concept" of red, for example, they can correctly identify objects as red even though they may differ in size, shape, or function.

Gagné and Briggs suggest teaching concrete concepts by *presenting a variety of stimuli that all share the defining attributes of the concepts and by pointing out these attributes to learners*. In teaching the concept of "apple," for example, one would present apples or pictures of apples that differed in size, shape, and color, noting that all of them were apples. Then learners would be asked to discriminate apples from nonapples, beginning with easy discriminations (nonexamples that have nothing in common with apples) and moving gradually toward the most difficult nonexamples (cherries, pears).

Defined concepts

Defined concepts are capabilities for demonstrating the meanings of classes of objects, events, or relations. Unlike concrete concepts, which are based on physical attributes that one can point to directly, defined concepts are based on formal definitions (examples: prime number, iambic pentameter, potential energy, adverb). Learners who "have the concept" not only can state the definition but can show that they understand it by using the terms in appropriate contexts with the appropriate meaning (e.g., they can identify iambic pentameter when they see it and can explain why a poem is or is not written in this meter).

The terms used to identify defined concepts are often used informally to refer to concrete objects or events. The use of the term in everyday language may make it easier to learn the defined concept (hearing various three-sided objects called "triangles" facilitates understanding of the geometrical definition of a triangle as a three-sided plane figure), but it also can be confusing (in geometry, a *point* is a specified location in an abstractly defined space, not a dot made with a pencil or the sharpened end of some object that "comes to a point"). When acquiring defined concepts, students must learn to use them with precision and to avoid connotations that apply to their colloquial use but not to their formal use.

Gagné and Briggs suggested teaching defined concepts by first *stating their definitions* and then (as with concrete concepts) *presenting examples and nonexamples*. The examples and nonexamples usually must be described verbally rather than shown, however, so that the meaningfulness of the instruction will depend on learners' familiarity with the vocabulary and concepts used. When a term is commonly used with colloquial meanings that differ from what is implied by the defined concept, it will be important to make the learners aware of this fact.

Rules

Rules have been learned when individuals can respond with regularity in dealing with classes of relationship among classes of objects or events. Much human activity is rule-governed behavior in which general principles are applied to specific situations. We follow the rules of English grammar, for example, when speaking or writing. This is true, for the most part, even of people who have not received formal instruction in English grammar and could not verbalize the rules that they follow when they speak or write.

We can receive formal instruction in rules and learn to apply them in specific situations. In fact, this is the rationale for instructing students in principles of science, mathematics, literary composition, historical analysis, and other academic disciplines. The ability to use defined concepts is one example of rule learning (in this case, the ability to follow a classifying rule). Other rules deal with such relationships as equal to, similar to, greater or less than, or sequential position. As with defined concepts, the ability to state a rule accurately does not necessarily mean that it is understood. Evidence of rule mastery must include demonstrated ability to apply the rule correctly in appropriate contexts.

Rules are usually taught through verbal instruction. Ordinarily this would include a *statement of the rule followed by guided practice*. Gagné and Briggs (1979) illustrated rule teaching using as an example the rule for pronouncing words that end in a single consonant followed by a final "e." "The teacher may say, 'Notice that the letter *a* has a long sound when followed by a consonant, in a word that ends in *e*. This is true in words that you know like *made, pale, fate*. When the word does not end in *e*, the letter *a* has a short sound, as in *mad, pal, fat*. Now tell me how to pronounce these words which you may not have seen before: *Dade, pate, kale*'" (pp. 68–69). The information given before asking students to pronounce these words helps them to remember concepts related to the rule (consonant, short and long sounds) and to arrange these related concepts in appropriate order (consonants followed by a final "e" versus consonants not followed by the final "e").

Higher-order rules

Higher-order rules are invented by learners to solve problems that are new to them. Once they invent a rule, they can store it in memory and use it again to solve other problems. Higher-order rules are constructed by combining two or more simpler rules that the learner has available to bring to bear on the problem. Gagné and Briggs (1979) illustrated this process with the following example:

> Suppose that a small car has been parked near a low brick fence, and is discovered to have a flat tire on one of its front wheels. No jack is available, but there is a ten-foot two-by-four, and a piece of sturdy rope. Can the front of the car be raised? In this situation, a possible solution might be found by using the two-by-four as a lever, the wall as a fulcrum, and the rope to secure the end of the lever when the car is in a raised position. (p. 69)

Such a solution would involve "putting together" rules that the learner knows but has never applied to such a problem before: application of force (to lift the car), use of a fulcrum (including recognition that the wall is capable of bearing the estimated weight), and using leverage to lift weights that cannot be lifted by hand (including recognition that the two-by-four could be used as a lever).

In contrast to the previously described intellectual skills that can be taught directly through expository instruction (as well as through less direct means), the *discovery of higher-order rules must be stimulated indirectly by presenting learners with problem-solving situations*. The instructor designs the problem-solving situation so that it is suited to the learners (i.e., it presents a problem that the learners cannot solve directly using any of the rules they have been taught already but that they can solve by combining some of these rules into a higher-order rule). The instructor may want to guide discovery by posing questions that will help learners to formulate the problem clearly or to realize that certain familiar rules are applicable to it. The instructor does not, however, "put it all together" for the learners by articulating the higher-order rule directly or teaching it in expository fashion. Thus higher-order rule learning is discovery learning or problem solving.

Cognitive Strategy Learning *Cognitive strategies* refer to the internal control processes by which learners monitor and regulate their thinking and problem solving. When learners have mastered cognitive strategies, they can approach problem solving in self-consciously deliberate and systematic ways that include what have been described as "metacognitive awareness skills" and "cognitive strategies." These strategies (when present) are most evident when learners are confronted with novel problems that they must first formulate and then try to solve in some systematic way. To the extent that they employ cognitive strategies, learners will guide their problem solving with verbally articulated "self-talk" that includes generating relevant questions about the problem, formulating answers, and organizing the information into a systematic plan for working out a solution. This activity may also include "internal dialogues" in which learners describe, comment on, review, and criticize their own problem-solving efforts in order to assess the appropriateness of their strategies and formulate plans for what to do next. This subjective monitoring and evaluation is directed toward learners' own thinking and problem-solving efforts, which is what makes cognitive strategies different from the intellectual skills described above that are directed toward manipulation of input from the environment.

Creation of favorable conditions

Gagné and Briggs believe that cognitive strategies cannot be taught directly or even stimulated in direct ways through guided discovery methods. Instead, they believe that, other than arming learners with prerequisite information and skills, teachers can only create "favorable conditions" for allowing learners to develop cognitive strategies by frequently providing them with *opportunities to think creatively or solve novel problems*. Other writers, however, believe that cognitive strategy development can be stimulated more directly through *modeling*, especially modeling in which the model "thinks out loud" to allow learners to see how he or she generates and uses cognitive strategies in a particular situation (Palincsar & Brown, 1984; Weinstein & Mayer, 1986).

Learning Hierarchies and Task Analyses In developing his classification systems, Gagné identified not only different types of learning but also hierarchical relationships that exist between types. When a true learning hierarchy exists, types can be ordered from simple to complex in such a way that each new type combines or in some way builds on similar types. The Gagné (1977) typology discussed earlier is considered to be a hierarchy in this sense, and so is the intellectual skills section of the Gagné and Briggs (1979) typology shown in Table 6.2.

Note that *Gagné and Briggs postulate hierarchical relationships only among the subtypes of intellectual skills*. That is, their five major categories (attitudes, motor skills, information, intellectual skills, and cognitive strategies) are considered qualitatively different from one another, representing separate domains. However, the five subcategories in the domain of intellectual skills are seen as forming a hierarchy with higher-order rules at the top, followed next by rules and defined concepts (considered equivalent in the hierarchy), then by concrete concepts, and finally by discriminations. This is because in order to discover a higher-order rule, learners must know various prerequisite rules and defined concepts. Similarly, rules specify relationships between concepts, so knowledge of these concepts is prerequisite to rule learning. Similarly, defined concepts often have concrete concepts as referents. Finally, before a concept can be learned, one must be able to make discriminations between critical attributes.

Dunn (1984) characterized the Gagné hierarchies as incomplete (some intellectual skills are probably left out) but as correct as far as they go (the hypothesized hierarchical relationships between the different skills are apparently correct). He went on to show that although these hierarchies are used mostly for developing instruction in science and mathematics, they are also applicable to other school subjects such as social studies or driver education and even to conceptualization of skills such as "knowing when to hold 'em, and knowing when to fold 'em" in poker.

Task-analysis procedures

Gagné has shown how information about learning hierarchies can be used for *task analysis*, which is his term for identifying component parts and deciding what needs to be taught and in what order. Curriculum designers routinely rely on task analysis in their work, and teachers find it useful not only for designing their own lessons but also for preparing to teach lessons using published materials. Lessons often fail because they assume that students have certain prerequisite knowledge or skills that they do not actually have. Preparation that includes task analysis designed to identify these potential problems and formulate ways to deal with them by providing on-the-spot instruction can transform potential lesson failures into mere rough spots. It also leaves the teacher in good position to plan remedial instruction for students who need it.

Figure 6.1 shows a learning hierarchy produced by analyzing the prerequisite subtasks involved in oral reading (decoding) of printed text. This scheme is useful for diagnosing the errors that students make in oral reading. For example, one student might mispronounce certain syllables, and another might pronounce individual syllables correctly but fail to blend them properly. The first student needs remedial instruction in one set of subskills, and the second needs instruction in a different set.

In a laboratory class, students learn both laboratory procedures and the skills necessary to perform experiments and analyze results.

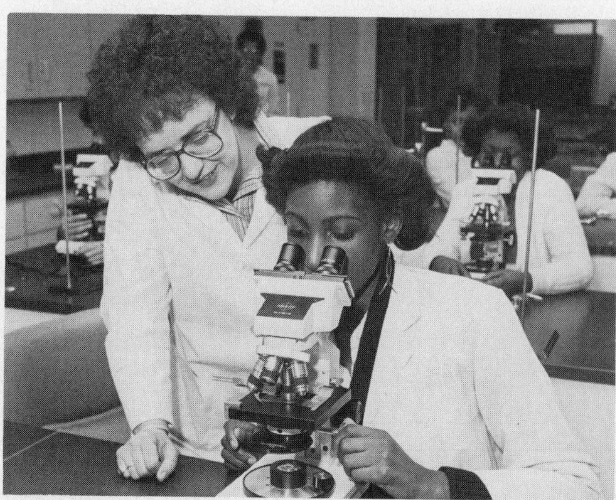

Figure 6.1 A Learning Hierarchy for a Basic Reading Skill ("Decoding")

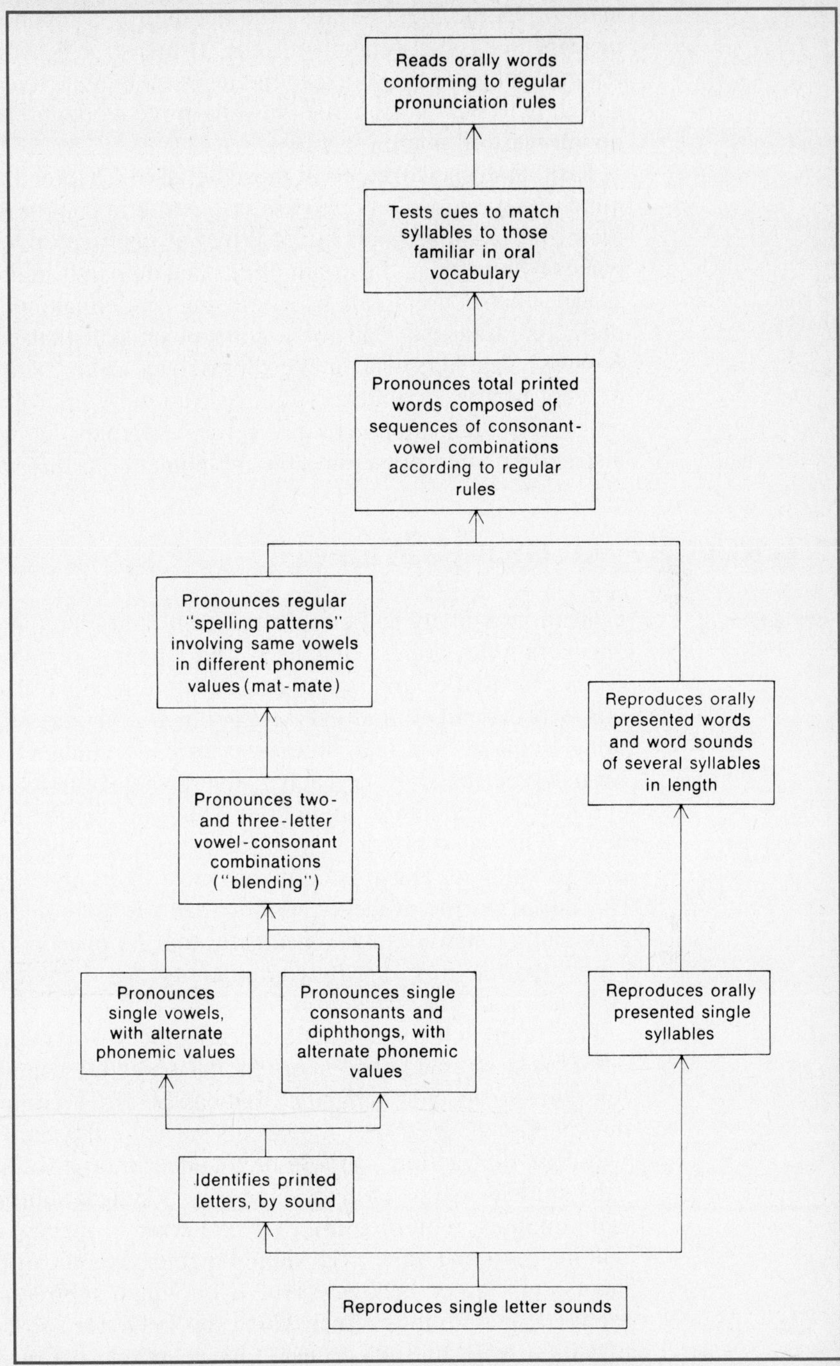

Source: From *The Conditions of Learning*, second edition, by Robert M. Gagné, copyright © 1970 by Holt, Rinehart and Winston, Inc., reprinted by permission of the publisher.

There is no single correct way to conduct task analyses and identify learning hierarchies, because the number of component parts that could be identified is theoretically infinite. However, it is usually easy to identify component parts that correspond to learning objectives taught previously and thus to plan systematic ways to move students from where they are now toward ultimate objectives.

Preparation for instruction

Task analysis is treated in more detail in Chapter 11. For now, bear in mind that wise teachers prepare for instruction not only by thinking about their own teaching goals but also by putting themselves in their students' places by analyzing the assumptions and demands built into the tasks they assign. Instructions can be confusing or ambiguous, examples can be poor, or tasks may call for a concept or skill that the students do not possess. Teachers who make themselves aware of these problems can prevent needless confusion and frustration by improving on assignments or by providing more clarity, better examples, or needed preparatory instruction when presenting the assignments to the students.

INSTRUCTIONAL OBJECTIVES

Formulation of objectives

Education is likely to be more coherent and effective to the extent that curriculum developers, teachers, and students remain aware of the purposes of activities and how they fit within the big picture. One way to do this is to formulate and use *instructional objectives* in planning instructional sequences. Clear objectives provide guidance to teachers about what to teach and how to teach it, about what students should have learned and how to evaluate it, and about what kinds of feedback to give to students. They also provide guidance to students about what to study and how to study it. These benefits are most likely to accrue when attention is focused on the students, rather than on the content to be taught, in formulating instructional objectives; that is, *instructional objectives are best formulated by stating what students should be able to do following completion of the instruction*.

This approach to instructional objectives was popularized by Mager (1962). He stressed that instructional objectives should be stated with reference to specific behaviors that can be observed and measured. Thus he argued that objectives statements such as "the student will understand two-digit subtraction" should be avoided in favor of statements such as "the student will be able to solve fifty two-digit subtraction problems in eight minutes, with no more than one error." Specifically, Mager argued that instructional objectives should include specification of three key elements: (1) target behavior (solve two-digit subtraction problems correctly), (2) conditions under which this behavior will be demonstrated (a fifty-item test), and (3) criteria for acceptable performance (completion of the fifty problems within eight minutes with no more than one error).

Even though Mager used the term *instructional objectives* in the title of his book, his emphasis on stating objectives in precise behavioral terms led to the popularizing of the term *behavioral objectives*, which became

Behavioral objectives and approaches

associated not only with Mager but also with a particular approach to curriculum planning and control. In its most extreme form, the behavioral objectives approach involved expressing the entire curriculum as behavioral objectives, sequencing these objectives in some sensible way, and developing materials and methods for both instruction and evaluation of each objective. The worst versions were unwieldy and overly rigid, confronting teachers with hundreds of objectives to be taught in a given order using particular materials and following prescribed practices. In other versions, teachers continued to use the curricula they were using but were pressured to justify all of their instructional activities by stating behavioral objectives for them, even when the objectives were more cognitive or affective (enjoyment, appreciation) than behavioral. Sometimes teachers were required to drop activities that could not be so "justified." Consequently, the term *behavioral objectives* carries negative connotations for many educators. For this reason, and also because we do not believe that all instructional objectives can or should be stated strictly according to Mager's criteria, we will not use the term *behavioral objectives*. We will, however, refer to "instructional objectives" or simply "objectives."

Specific statements of learning outcome

Gronlund (1985) distinguished between general instructional objectives and more specific statements of intended learning outcomes. He recommended that general objectives be stated using verb forms that (a) communicate what students should be able to do on completion of instruction but (b) are general enough to encompass a domain of student performance that would include many more specific activities. He recommended eight to twelve general instructional objectives for an entire course and perhaps two to four general objectives for a brief unit. General objectives for a science course, for example, might include the following (Gronlund, 1985, p. 13): (1) knows the meaning of terms, (2) knows specific facts, (3) knows laboratory procedures, (4) understands concepts and principles, (5) applies concepts and principles to new situations, (6) demonstrates abilities needed to conduct an experiment, (7) interprets data in scientific reports, and (8) displays a scientific attitude.

In planning particular activities, more specific objectives would be developed within these general ones. "Knows laboratory procedures," for example, might be broken into subobjectives such as selecting appropriate equipment for a given experiment, assembling it correctly, manipulating it appropriately, measuring accurately with measuring devices, following safety rules, and cleaning and returning the equipment properly. Similarly, a general language-arts objective such as "writes effective compositions" might be broken into subobjectives such as expressing ideas clearly, relating ideas to the main thesis, developing the thesis in an organized way, writing well-structured paragraphs, using correct grammar, and minimizing spelling errors.

We believe that attention to such objectives should be an important part of instructional planning. As long as it is not carried to extremes, the process of formulating instructional objectives and using them to guide the development and evaluation of instruction is likely to have the beneficial effects mentioned above. This is shown in the following example.

Using Instructional Objectives: An Example

Mrs. Wolfe is a junior high physical education teacher who plans to teach a six-week unit on basketball. How can she use this time most effectively? Which knowledge and skill objectives should she concentrate on as the "core curriculum," and which should be touched on only briefly or not at all? There are no simple "right answers" to these questions. A range of objectives and associated activities might be appropriate, depending on the students' current knowledge and skill levels and on how basketball instruction fits into the school's larger physical education program (as seen by Mrs. Wolfe and the other physical education teachers).

Given these considerations and her knowledge about what can be accomplished in a six-week unit, Mrs. Wolfe will have to formulate instructional objectives that address one or more of the three major domains of learning: (1) *affective objectives* (stimulate appreciation for the game by emphasizing teamwork, sharing, coordinated body movement, and general aspects of play); (2) *cognitive objectives* (develop knowledge of rules, infractions and concepts underlying strategies for offensive and defensive play); (3) *psychomotor objectives* (teach the students to dribble, pass, shoot, and rebound). Mrs. Wolfe's selection of objectives for her unit will determine what activities will be included, how much time will be allocated to each, and what she will stress in evaluating the effectiveness of her instruction.

Attention to instructional objectives

To the extent that Mrs. Wolfe decides to emphasize cognitive objectives, for example, she will need to provide the students with topic outlines and textual material, to deliver lectures and present slides or films, to conduct recitation and discussion lessons, and to administer written tests. In contrast, to the extent that she wishes to emphasize psychomotor objectives, she will need to explain and demonstrate skills, observe and provide feedback to students as they practice these skills in the gym, provide opportunities for students to blend and apply these skills during drills and controlled scrimmages, and (possibly) evaluate skill development using performance checklists or other methods of rating the quality of physical performance.

Mrs. Wolfe probably will want to include both cognitive and psychomotor objectives in her basketball unit, integrating them as much as possible. In teaching a jump shot, for example, she would provide information about when and how to use the shot, verbal description of procedures to follow in executing the shot, and modeling accompanied by verbalization of the self-talk, visual-motor imagery, or kinesthetic feedback that can be used to guide the shot during its execution. If she wants her students to become skilled jump shooters, however, she will have to go beyond this figurative knowledge and give them opportunities to develop operative knowledge by practicing jump shooting in skill drills and game situations. Furthermore, if she wants to assess whether her objective has been met, she will need to assess actual jump shooting under specified conditions and not merely assess whether students can label a picture of a jump shot correctly or answer essay questions about jump-shooting technique.

In the process of expressing her general goal (teaching basketball) in terms of specific instructional objectives, Mrs. Wolfe will develop *clarity about her own values and priorities* (what she thinks these students should learn about basketball). They may differ from the priorities of another teacher assigned to the same course, even one who is ostensibly teaching the same things. Two teachers, for example, may agree to concentrate on psychomotor skills, but one may stress general body skills (running, jumping, pivoting), whereas the other may stress ball skills (passing, dribbling, shooting). Thus attention to instructional objectives helps teachers to become aware of similarities and differences in "the same" course as it is taught in different sections. Such information is important for *curriculum control* (making sure that objectives considered essential are covered adequately in each section), and discussion of differences helps to broaden teachers' perspectives on how instruction can be approached.

Once a list of instructional objectives is drawn up, the teacher can assess it for feasibility and consider its implications for the nature and sequencing of instructional activities to be included within the unit. Often it will be necessary to compromise by reducing the number of objectives to be addressed or by addressing certain objectives in less depth than one had planned to originally. Mrs. Wolfe, for example, may decide that her students need to know about basic rule infractions so that they can avoid them in playing the game, but that they will not need to know the referees' signals associated with various infractions. Similarly, she may decide that she has time to cover both jump shots and hook shots but only if she sticks to the basic forms and only teaches the students to shoot directly at the basket. Another teacher might decide to ignore hook shots and concentrate on jump shots but to teach several variations on basic jump-shooting form and to teach the students to use the backboard in addition to shooting directly for the basket. Each teacher's choices can be supported with a sensible rationale, but each involves trade-offs (some things are learned at the expense of others). However, because both teachers are clear about their respective objectives, both are likely to achieve them. The same could not be said of teachers who teach haphazardly or who try to cram so much in that nothing is covered in sufficient depth.

Guidelines for Using Instructional Objectives

Learning situations are likely to be most effective when most of the learning is intentional—when you as the teacher know what you want to accomplish and how you intend to accomplish it and your students know what is expected of them. This is especially true when *planning includes attention to the steps that students must go through* in the process of moving toward the ultimate objectives (i.e., not merely attention to what the teacher will do). It is useful to formulate instructional objectives and use them to plan both instruction and evaluation. In doing so, keep in mind three general principles.

General principles

1. *State a few major objectives rather than a great many trivial ones for a given unit.* Concentrate on the objectives that represent new advances over previous learning or terminal objectives that come at the ends of curricular strands. When appropriate, perform task analyses, identify learning hierarchies, and provide instruction and practice on

whatever subskills need work before smooth performance of the ultimate target skill will become possible. Keep in mind, however, that you are building toward the ultimate target skill, which will need to be taught, practiced, and evaluated in its final form. Don't lose the forest for the trees.

2. *Don't be unnecessarily behavioral or precise* in formulating objectives. For psychomotor objectives and for many of the cognitive objectives taught in the early grades, it is possible and usually desirable to express objectives in specific behavioral terms as advocated by Mager (1962). For affective objectives, however, and for higher-level cognitive objectives that do not translate directly into behavioral skills, it may be appropriate to formulate instructional objectives in less behavioral terms. Even so, try to be specific and formulate objectives in terms of changes in the students that will occur as a result of instruction (rather than in terms of content coverage or other teacher behavior). The objectives should be stated specifically enough so that both you and the students can easily determine whether or not they have been reached.

3. *Don't be overly rigid in using objectives to guide instruction*. Research on teacher planning (Clark & Peterson, 1986) suggested that most teachers do not pay nearly enough attention to instructional objectives when planning instruction (they tend to read the teacher's manual that comes with the curriculum to learn how the lesson is to be conducted, giving little thought to the purpose of the lesson or how it might be adapted if it doesn't succeed). This same research also shows, however, that among teachers who do pay attention to objectives, some respond to them in an overly rigid manner. These teachers develop lesson plans that are admirably specific and detailed, but then they implement these plans so rigidly that they are unable or unwilling to adapt them when events dictate or to respond to unanticipated student questions or comments. Wise teachers formulate and use instructional objectives to guide instruction, but they are flexible enough to deviate from their plans when unanticipated problems occur or when they have a chance to take advantage of a "teachable moment" by following up on a relevant student question or comment.

According to Mager (1962), instructional objectives should:

	CLEARLY SPECIFY	ANSWER QUESTION
1.	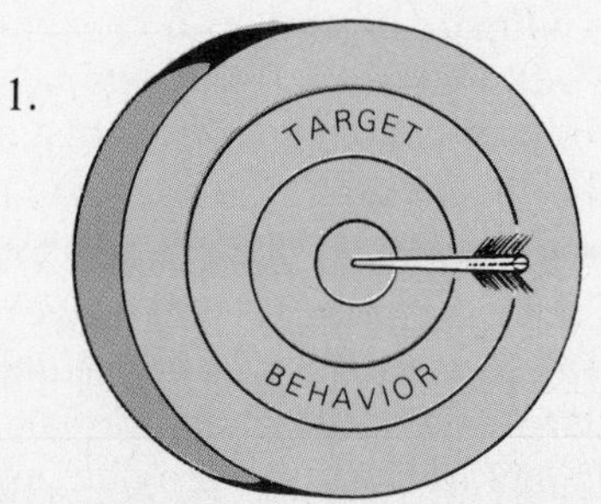	What?

2. Conditions under which behavior will be demonstrated   How?
3. Criteria for acceptable performance   How well?

As noted in the guidelines for affective and higher-level objectives, however, it may be appropriate to formulate them less behaviorally.

SUMMARY

Learning is the process of acquiring relatively permanent change in understanding, attitude, knowledge, or skill through experience. It is a change in capacity for performance that must be distinguished from performance itself and from development, thinking, and various situational phenomena. There are different kinds of learning. Common qualitative distinctions include the developmental stages suggested by Piaget and others, "knowledge that" versus "knowledge how," intentional versus incidental learning, rote versus meaningful learning, and reception versus discovery learning.

The Bloom taxonomy distinguishes between knowledge, comprehension, application, analysis, synthesis, and evaluation objectives. Gagné's learning hierarchy distinguishes between signal learning, stimulus-response learning, chaining, verbal association, discrimination learning, concept learning, and rule learning. Gagné and Briggs distinguished between five major types of learning—attitudes, motor skills, information, intellectual skills, and cognitive strategies—and further divided intellectual skills into discriminations, concrete concepts, defined concepts, rules, and higher-order rules.

Gagné and Briggs also presented guidelines concerning the different conditions of learning required for each of the types of learning that they distinguished. Attitudes are learned primarily through exposure to models, persuasive communication, or conditioning. Motor learning is stimulated through modeling, verbal instructions combined with visual imagery, and practice with feedback. Information learning is stimulated by presenting the input in organized fashion and helping students to relate it to their existing knowledge, process it actively, and encode in their own words.

Discriminations are taught using the principles of contiguity, feedback, and repetition. Concrete concepts are taught by presenting a variety of stimuli that all share the defining attributes of the concept and pointing out these attributes to the learners, and then having them discriminate examples from nonexamples of the concept. Defined concepts are taught by stating their definitions and then presenting examples and nonexamples. Rules are taught through rule statements followed by guided practice in applying the rule to specific examples. Higher-order rules cannot be taught directly, but their discovery can be stimulated by presenting learners with problem-solving situations that require them to invent such higher-order rules. Gagné and Briggs do not believe that cognitive strategies can be either taught or stimulated directly, although they believe that teachers can encourage students to develop such strategies by giving them frequent opportunities to think creatively and solve novel problems. Other writers believe that cognitive strategy development can be stimulated more directly through modeling of the self-talk that occurs when cognitive strategies are applied to particular situations.

Gagné and Briggs hold that the five categories of intellectual skills form a hierarchy with higher-order rules at the top, followed by rules and defined concepts, then by concrete concepts, and finally by discriminations. They suggested using information about such learning hierarchies for conducting task analyses to identify the component parts of tasks and decide what needs to be taught and in what order.

Instructional planning begins with formulation of clear instructional objectives. Objectives are best formulated by stating what students should be able to do following completion of the instruction. By formulating objectives in terms of student performance rather than merely in terms of what is to be taught, instructional planners not only provide guidance to teachers about what to teach and how to teach it but also provide guidance to teachers about how to evaluate the effects of instruction and guidance to students about where to focus their learning efforts. The authors believe that teachers should formulate instructional objectives to guide their planning and teaching, although they suggest that teachers state only a few major objectives rather than a great many trivial ones, that they do not attempt to be unnecessarily behavioral or precise in stating those objectives, and that they not be overly rigid in confining their instructional activities to those that are related directly to the objectives. Planning should allow for enough flexibility to take advantage of unanticipated teachable moments.

Questions and Problems

1. In your own terms, differentiate between *learning, development,* and *thinking*. Why are these distinctions and terms important? How might they influence the decisions you make as a teacher?
2. Distinguish between *figurative* and *operative* knowledge. Which is more difficult to achieve? Why? Which is more important? Why? Think about the courses that you took as a college freshman. Were most of the outcomes of instruction in those courses figurative or operative? How do you account for this?
3. What are the important differences between the Bloom and the Gagné taxonomies? Think about the teaching situation that you want to be in. Which of these two taxonomies would be more useful to you? Why?
4. Examine a test that you have taken at some point during your college career. Try to determine, for each question, the level it represents in the Bloom and the Gagné taxonomies. How difficult is it to classify the question? How useful does the classification appear to be in summarizing the knowledge emphasis of the test?

5. Read the questions that appeared at the end of Chapters 2, 3, 4, and 5 in this text. How would you characterize these questions?
6. In some classrooms, teachers emphasize a great deal of drill. In mathematics classes, for example, students may spend 60 to 70 percent of the period practicing number facts. However, this material often has to be retaught the following year. How can you account for this? What is the role of practice in retaining information? What are the conditions for successful practice?
7. How would you apply the material presented on motor learning in this chapter if you were teaching someone the basics of ice skating? How would you apply it if you were teaching free-style skating?
8. What is the appropriate role of instructional objectives in effective instruction? Reread the objectives that we presented at the beginning of this chapter. How effective were these objectives for conveying the important content that was presented in the chapter? If you were writing objectives for the chapter, what changes would you make in those that were presented?
9. Why is there a need for distinction between covert learning and overt performance?

Case Studies

WHAT'S THE BIG IDEA? Miss Ditto and Miss Freehand both devote considerable attention to the topic of main idea in language-arts instruction. Each introduced it in a lesson that described the process of organizing lengthy texts into sections and paragraphs and suggested that each paragraph should have a single main idea. The two teachers differed considerably, however, in the nature of the follow-up activities they assigned. Miss Ditto emphasized seatwork assignments calling for students to identify the main-idea sentence in a paragraph. She began by passing out pages full of short, disconnected paragraphs and having students underline the main-idea sentence. Later, she assigned them increasingly longer sections of connected text to read and had them copy the main-idea sentence or state the main idea of a paragraph in their own words if they believed that no single sentence captured it adequately. For variety, she occasionally distributed several pages of uninterrupted connected text and assigned the students to mark the places where new paragraphs should begin. In contrast, Miss Freehand followed up on the main-idea lesson mostly in her writing assignments. She assigned several compositions each week, and in addition to giving guidelines for the type of composition, the desired length, and so on, she reminded the students that the compositions should be divided into paragraphs such that each paragraph is built around a main idea. Sometimes she had the students underline the main idea in each of their paragraphs.

Given these differences in approach, how would you characterize what Miss Ditto's and Miss Freehand's students are learning about main idea using concepts presented in this chapter? In particular, how would their learning compare in terms of figurative versus operative knowledge, and how would it be classified according to the Bloom taxonomy and to the Gagné and Briggs typology? What does this suggest about the relative effectiveness of these two approaches?

EVERYTHING YOU ALWAYS WANTED TO KNOW ABOUT APPLE PIE. Merry Cook is a home economics teacher who offers a ''carbo cooking'' course as a high school elective. The course involves baking treats and desserts, but Merry wants to make sure that it includes appropriate cognitive content (chemical composition and nutritional value of foods, changes induced by cooking and in various cooking methods, trade-offs involved in serving at various temperatures, etc.). In one activity, the students will work in small groups preparing apple pies. What might she teach about this topic if she were to set out to include at least one worthwhile objective at each of the six levels of the Bloom taxonomy and each of the nine types of learning described in the Gagné and Briggs typology (counting each of the five types of intellectual skill as separate types)? If she were to ask your help in drawing up such a list of objectives, what would you suggest? Keep in mind that each objective should be worthwhile in its own right and should fit together with the other objectives to form a coherent sequence of instruction.

CHAPTER

The Behavioral Approach to Learning

CHAPTER OUTLINE

OBJECTIVES

When you have mastered the material in this chapter, you will be able to

1. Describe the behaviorist approach to learning and differentiate it from other approaches
2. Define key concepts in the classical conditioning paradigm (unconditioned stimulus, unconditioned response, conditioned stimulus, conditioned response) and describe the role of contiguity and repetition in the classical conditioning process
3. Describe Edward L. Thorndike's work on instrumental conditioning and explain how it differs from classical conditioning
4. Explain the law of exercise and the law of effect
5. Describe the key findings of the functionalists concerning learning curves, overlearning, and massed versus distributed practice
6. Define the key concepts associated with B. F. Skinner's operant conditioning (positive reinforcement, negative reinforcement, extinction, punishment, behavioral shaping, re-

inforcement schedules) and explain how operant conditioning differs from classical conditioning and instrumental conditioning

7. State the similarities and differences between Skinnerian approaches to operant conditioning of animals in the laboratory and Skinnerian approaches to instructing students in the classroom
8. Define the key concepts associated with the work of Albert Bandura and other social learning theorists (modeling, imitation, vicarious learning)
9. Describe the similarities and differences between modeling as used in traditional behavioristic approaches to instruction and the combination of modeling with verbalized self-instruction as used in cognitive behavior-modification approaches
10. Define the key concepts used in programmed instruction (modules, frames, linear versus branched programming, self-pacing, learner control) and explain the basic principles of instruction used in Fred Keller's Personalized System of Instruction (PSI) and in Mastery Learning
11. Describe the potential advantages that computerized instruction offers over traditional instruction, as well as its current limitations
12. Identify the key weaknesses in proposed instructional innovations that attempt to work around, rather than through, teachers.

Behaviorists versus other learning theorists

In this chapter, we describe the contributions of learning theorists known as behaviorists. Behaviorists approach the study of learning by concentrating on overt behaviors that can be observed and measured. They seek general laws that apply across species and can be used to predict and control behavior. Behavior itself is seen as determined by events external to the learner—by stimuli that elicit or cue particular behavior and by reinforcement that maintains these stimulus-response relationships. Behaviorists recognize that learning is mediated by perceptions, thoughts, and other covert processes, and some of them refer to such processes in their theorizing. However, even these cognitively oriented behaviorists prefer to minimize their reliance on hypothetical constructs that must be inferred rather than observed directly. This is a major difference between behaviorists and other learning theorists (discussed in the next two chapters) who stress cognitive structures or information processing.

Behaviorism was the first major approach to the study of learning to become well established. It developed and spread early in the twentieth century in Europe and especially the United States, where it became the dominant approach to psychology in general and remained so until the 1950s. Behaviorism is still a highly respected and influential tradition, although it no longer is predominant and most modern behaviorists are much more cognitive in orientation than their forebears were. The tradition retains its emphasis on developing theory, using the theory to predict behavior and then conducting experiments to test these predictions.

Over the years, behaviorists have developed many theoretical principles and instructional techniques designed to *induce learning* (i.e., to cause learners to develop new stimulus-response associations or to add to their behavioral repertoires). These instructional applications of behaviorism are discussed in this chapter. Behaviorism has also produced principles and techniques designed to *control behavior* (i.e., to increase or decrease the frequencies of already-learned behaviors). These applications of behaviorism are more relevant to the topic of classroom management than to the topic of learning and so are discussed in Chapter 21.

PAVLOV AND CLASSICAL CONDITIONING

Contingiuty

Since at least the time of Aristotle, it has been observed that much learning involves recognizing *associations* between stimuli or events (i.e., the sight of lightning is regularly followed by the sound of thunder). The key to such recognition is *contiguity*—the associated items regularly occur together, either simultaneously or in rapid succession. If encounters with associated events are salient (i.e., a brilliant flash of lightning followed by a loud clap of thunder) or if we happen to be paying attention for some reason, we may learn the association in one trial. Usually, however, associations develop gradually through a combination of contiguity and *repetition*—repeated encounters with the associated items make us more aware of their association. We become *conditioned* to expect the associated stimuli to occur together.

When stimulus events regularly occur in close temporal contiguity, the appearance of the first event in the sequence eventually becomes a signal that the other event(s) will follow. When one event always precedes the other(s), it may be perceived as the cause of, and not merely a signal for the appearance of, the other(s). This is sometimes misleading, because the first in a series of associations does not necessarily cause what follows. Also, some genuine cause-and-effect relationships are hard to see because the contiguity principle is not operating. It was easy for people to associate pain and skin swelling with bee stings, for example, because the pain follows immediately after the sting, and the swelling sets in shortly thereafter. In contrast, the linkage between mosquito bites and malaria had to be discovered without contiguity clues. Only a fraction of people bitten by mosquitoes develop malaria, the process takes time, and there is no obvious link between the bite and the later symptoms.

Experiments on learning through conditioning

Despite these complexities, contiguity and repetition are basic to the learning of associations through conditioning. Early in the twentieth century, Russian psychologist Ivan Pavlov (1927) conducted experiments on learning through conditioning. He had been studying the salivation response (the automatic increase in salivation that occurs during feeding and promotes digestion) by presenting dogs with food under controlled conditions. The salivation response is a reflex action in which an *unconditioned stimulus* (the taste of food in the mouth) automatically elicits an *unconditioned response* (salivation). Other reflex actions such as blinking in response to a puff of air or the "startle response" to an unexpected loud noise also involve unconditioned responses to unconditioned stimuli.

Unconditioned stimuli and unconditioned response

In each case, the stimulus automatically elicits the response; no process of conditioning or learning is involved.

Pavlov noticed, however, that his dogs sometimes salivated in anticipation of feeding. The mere sight of food or even the arrival of a laboratory assistant (signaling that feeding was about to occur) could elicit salivation, well before the presentation of the food itself.

In a series of experiments, Pavlov showed that any *neutral stimulus* (one that produced no particular response from the dog) could become a *conditioned stimulus* for the salivation response if it were routinely presented immediately before the unconditioned stimulus (food). For example, if Pavlov routinely sounded a bell right before presenting food, the dog would soon begin to salivate at the sound of that bell. The bell had become a *conditioned stimulus* capable of producing salivation as a *conditioned response*. Further experimentation identified the following principles:

- *Extinction*. A conditioned response built up by repeatedly presenting the conditioned stimulus (bell) followed by the unconditioned stimulus (food) could be extinguished by continuing to present the conditioned stimulus but no longer following it with the unconditioned stimulus. If Pavlov stopped presenting food after sounding the bell, the dog would gradually stop salivating in response to the bell.
- *Spontaneous Recovery*. Conditioned responses that are extinguished are not lost permanently. They recover, at least to some degree, over time. Thus if Pavlov first established salivation as a conditioned response to a bell, then extinguished this response, then allowed several days to elapse, and then sounded the bell again, the dog would salivate. This "spontaneously recovered" conditioned response would soon extinguish again, however, unless Pavlov resumed presenting the food following the sound of the bell.
- *Generalization*. Once conditioned responses are established, they can be elicited by a range of stimuli that are similar to the original conditioned stimulus. Thus dogs trained with a particular bell would salivate in response to other bells with similar tones. The conditioned response generalized to a range of conditioned stimuli.
- *Discrimination*. The dogs could also learn to discriminate between similar stimuli if these were paired with different outcomes. Thus if Pavlov regularly presented food following one bell tone but did not present food following a second bell tone, the dog would learn to salivate in response to the first tone but not the second.
- *Higher-Order Conditioning*. Conditioned responses could be chained together. Once a particular bell tone was well established as a conditioned stimulus, one could establish something else (such as a flash of light) as a conditioned stimulus by routinely presenting the light followed by the bell. Soon the dog would begin to salivate at the sight of the light flash, without waiting for the bell (let alone the food).

Classical conditioning

The type of conditioning studied by Pavlov is known as *classical conditioning* (because it was first described in a series of classic experiments). Narrowly defined, *Pavlovian conditioning* refers only to situations in which reflex actions become elicited by conditioned stimuli in addition to the unconditioned stimuli that normally elicit them. Rescorla (1988), however, has argued that the term should be given a cognitive reinterpretation that would broaden it to include an organism's learning of relationships among events that enable it to develop a cognitive representation of its environment. Similarly, the term *classical conditioning* is sometimes used more broadly to refer to *stimulus substitution learning*, *signal learning*, and any other learning in which contiguity and repetition in presentation of stimuli are used to induce learners to generalize an existing stimulus-response connection to some new stimulus. This kind of conditioning can be used in teaching vocabulary, for example, by showing pictures paired with the printed names of the things pictured or by showing Spanish words followed by their English equivalents.

JOHN B. WATSON

The term *behaviorism* was coined by John B. Watson (1914), who argued that psychologists should focus on overt, measurable behaviors and avoid "unscientific" theorizing about thoughts, intentions, or other subjective experiences. Watson also viewed the scientific study of behavior as a method for perfecting the human condition. He saw the potential child-rearing applications of Pavlov's demonstration that initially neutral stimuli can acquire the power to elicit conditioned responses. This led to his famous boast that:

> Give me a dozen healthy infants, well formed, and my own special world to bring them up in, and I'll guarantee to take any one at random and train him to become any type of specialist I might select—doctor, lawyer, artist, merchant-chief and yes, even beggarman and thief, regardless of his talents, penchants, tendencies, abilities, vocations, or race of his ancestry. (Watson, 1925, p. 82)

Classical conditioning processes in human emotional development

Neither Watson nor anyone else has ever demonstrated such power, although Watson demonstrated the importance of classical conditioning processes in human emotional development by conditioning the responses of an infant named Albert to a white rat (Watson & Rayner, 1920). Watson knew that Albert feared sudden loud noises, so he created a loud noise (by banging a steel bar with a hammer) whenever Albert touched a white rat. Soon Albert began to fear and avoid the rat, even though he had shown no such fear previously. This fear response also generalized to other small animals (a rabbit and a dog) and to a sealskin coat and a bearded Santa Claus, although not for long.

Watson's work with Albert was more like a pilot study with mixed results than a definite experiment. It has been widely publicized, however, and accounts of it often suggest that the conditioned fear was more permanent and powerful than it really was or that Watson went on to extinguish the fear with delivery of rewards. Watson himself was responsible for some of these distortions, because he overstated his findings in his own subsequent writings (Harris, 1979; Samelson, 1980).

From today's perspective, Watson can be pictured as an extremist given to unsubstantiated boasting and ethically questionable research on infants. However, he deserves credit for his theoretical contributions to behaviorism and for demonstrating the role of conditioning processes in the development of generalized emotional responses (fears, phobias, prejudices). Within the school setting, conditioning acquired during traumatic experiences is usually the reason why certain students dread making public speeches or attending gym class.

EDWARD L. THORNDIKE

Although early behaviorists studied animals rather than humans, they supplemented classical conditioning research by studying adaptive behavior (not just instinctive reflexes) under more natural (although still controlled) conditions. E. L. Thorndike (1913) studied what came to be called *instrumental conditioning* by placing animals in problem-solving situations. A hungry cat, for example, might be put in a cage where it could see food but could not reach it without escaping from the cage. The cat could escape by working a latch, but it would have to discover this for itself. Typically, the first few escapes would be accidental—the cat would happen to make the right response in the process of clawing at the cage. However, the principle of contiguity was in effect: The cage would open immediately after the "correct" response was made. After several repetitions, essentially random clawing evolved into "scientific" search behavior. The cat had learned that there was a "trick" to getting out of the cage, concentrated on performing this "trick" properly, and became more efficient at doing so.

Instrumental conditioning

Such experiments were said to involve "instrumental" conditioning because the animals learned behavior that was instrumental in helping them to reach their goals. These studies extended Pavlov's work on classical conditioning by showing that environmental manipulations could produce entirely new conditioned responses. Cats that learned to escape their cages were not acting reflexively by making unconditioned responses; instead, they were discovering and refining new responses adapted to novel stimulus situations.

Laws of exercise and effect

Thorndike postulated "laws" of learning, most notably the laws of exercise and effect. According to the *law of exercise*, repetition of a conditioned response would strengthen the stimulus-response bond. This was Thorndike's version of "practice makes perfect." The *law of effect* was his version of the pleasure-pain principle. It held that responses followed by pleasure or reward would be strengthened, and responses followed by pain or punishment would be weakened.

Although both of these principles were largely correct, each had to be modified in view of later findings. The law of exercise had to be modified to take into account the need for variation in responding and for feedback about the effects of responses. Exercise alone, without feedback and without systematic testing of alternative forms of response, does not necessarily improve performance. However, when practice includes systematic response variation that yields knowledge of results, performance tends to improve until peak efficiency is reached. The law of effect had to be modified to allow for certain exceptions. Sometimes consequences that would usually be considered pleasurable do not motivate performance, or consequences that usually would be considered painful do not suppress it.

Thorndike was influential for his attacks on "faculty psychology" and the "mental discipline" approach to education. Influenced by philosophers and classical scholars, educators believed that courses in science, mathematics, languages, and classical literature not only were of value in their own right but also had a more generalized value for "training the mind." Exposure to these subjects presumably provided "mental discipline" that made people more perceptive and incisive in their thinking, whereas practical subjects such as business, agriculture, or home economics presumably did not have these effects. Thorndike (1924) disproved this theory by showing that there was no evidence that there were special mental faculties that could be "disciplined" or that classical subjects were any more valuable than practical subjects for stimulating intellectual development. After Thorndike's attack, the school curriculum began to include more practical subjects. His conclusions hold up as well today as when he stated them: There still is no evidence that particular subject matter has generalized "mind-broadening" effects. However, there is some reason to believe that training in study skills and information-processing strategies will improve students' abilities to learn efficiently (see Chapters 9 and 10).

Mental discipline

FUNCTIONALISM

While Thorndike was developing general laws, other behaviorally oriented investigators were developing information about factors that influence learning in particular situations. These investigators were known as *functionalists* because their experiments were designed to show that performance in particular situations "is a function" of some determining factor (i.e., to show that specified changes in the determining factor will produce predictable changes in performance).

Functionalists preferred to describe performance in quantitative terms (number of seconds required to run a maze or escape from a cage) and to express improvements in performance over repeated trials by using graphic depictions. These graphs typically resembled "flattened" S-shaped curves such as the one shown in Figure 7.1, and eventually became known as *learning curves*. Learning curves typically revealed: (1) little progress in early trials (because the animal was exploring the problem

Learning curves

Figure 7.1 Learning Curves

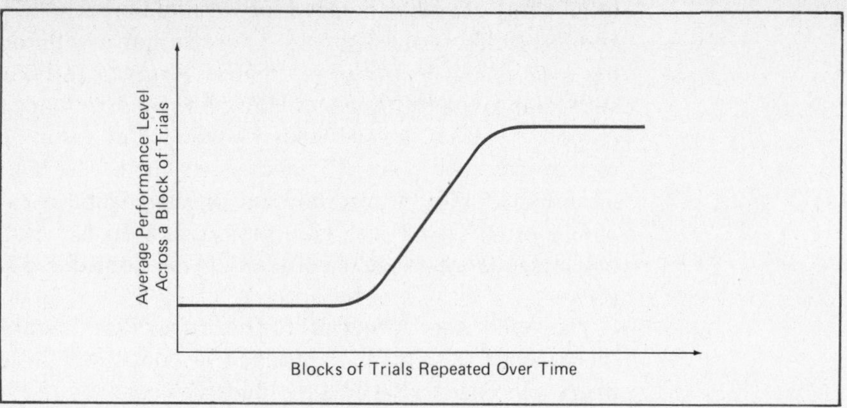

through trial and error and had not yet discovered the "trick" to solving it); then (2) a sharp rise in the curve indicating rapid improvement in performance as the animal discovered the "trick" and became efficient; and (3) an eventual leveling off as the animal reached its performance peak. Most of the learning studied by early behaviorists produced such learning curves when depicted graphically, although some curves rose steeply (because the animal made rapid progress in moving toward peak performance once it discovered the "trick"), whereas others rose more slowly and were spread over many more trials (because the animal made only slow, gradual progress).

Overlearning

Once the peak level of performance is attained, further trials no longer produce improvement (the curve levels off and becomes a horizontal line). The point at which continued practice no longer produces improvement is known as the *point of overlearning*, and skills practiced beyond this point are said to be *practiced to overlearning*. Functionalists discovered that skills practiced to overlearning tend to be retained indefinitely and to be recovered with relative ease, whereas skills that are mastered only partially tend to deteriorate. If you did a lot of skating or cycling as a child, you could perform these skills competently now with little or no practice, even though you may not have done so in years. However, if you were exposed to these skills only briefly and never really mastered them, you would have to start over virtually from scratch.

Massed versus distributed practice

Functionalists discovered that progress in learning depended not merely on number of practice trials but also on how practice was distributed. *Massed practice* is concentrated into one or just a few lengthy sessions spaced close together. In contrast, *distributed practice* involves a larger number of shorter sessions, spaced further apart. Massed practice is more efficient for simple skills that can be mastered to overlearning with relative ease. Distributed practice is more efficient for most learning, however, including most of what is taught in school. This is why curricula are divided into brief lessons and assignments that address limited content and frequently involve review. It is also why frequent drills and quizzes are important and why a progressive series of tests spaced throughout the term usually produces more learning than a single final exam at the end. The benefit of distributed practice (or "the spacing effect" as it is now sometimes called) has been reaffirmed recently by cognitive psychologists interested in the mechanisms that may explain it (Glover & Corkill, 1987; Smith & Rothkopf, 1984).

The Role of Practice in the Classroom

Practice is one of the most important yet least appreciated aspects of learning in classrooms. Little or no practice may be needed for simple behaviors like verbalizing the names of objects, but practice becomes more important as learning becomes more complex. Prolonged practice is needed for polishing skills such as reading or performing computations, as well as for learning to apply general or abstract principles (such as applying scientific principles in the laboratory or using mathematical principles to solve problems).

Need for immediate feedback

To be useful, practice must involve not only opportunities to exercise skills but opportunities to receive feedback, preferably *immediate feedback*. So-called self-teaching or self-correcting curriculum materials make use of this principle by presenting learners with tasks that can be completed successfully in only one way. Here, correct response leads to immediate feedback and reinforcement in the form of success, and incorrect responses are extinguished. Much of the equipment used in Montessori schools is designed this way, as are educational toys such as "shape sorters" that require children to place blocks into holes that correspond to their shapes. Each block will fit into only one hole. The same general principles are used in form boards, puzzles, and tasks involving matching and discrimination. Programmed instructional materials also use these principles, but the learning and performance involved are more cognitive.

Usually, though, teachers will assign seatwork and other practice activities that do not have immediate feedback and self-correction features built in. Here, teachers need to provide feedback to the students person-

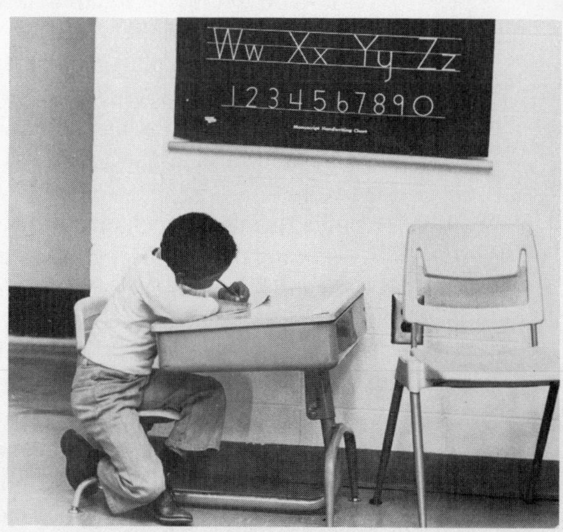

Practice is one of the most important aspects of learning, especially in polishing skills such as reading, writing, and computing.

ally or arrange for them to get it by consulting answer keys, comparing their work with ideal models, or providing feedback to one another. Ideally, students will be monitored during their practice and provided with immediate feedback. If feedback is delayed several days and limited to a grade and a few remarks, it may be too little and too late to do much good. In fact, for students who are confused about what to do and how to do it, practice may be counterproductive. If they are operating from misconceptions or using erroneous response patterns, repetition of this level of functioning without correction will only deepen the misconceptions and reinforce the erroneous response patterns. Thus successful practice involves making smoother, more efficient, and more automatic skills that are already established at rudimentary levels, not trying to establish such skills through trial and error.

SKINNER AND OPERANT CONDITIONING

We have described how behaviorism evolved from Pavlov's classical conditioning of salivation responses through Watson's emphasis on conditioning as a mechanism for socializing human development, Thorndike's study of instrumental behavior, and the functionalists' graphic depictions of performance change and demonstration of how external factors influence learning. As these trends took root, it became clear that behaviorism offered not merely a method of studying learning, but a method of developing principles for producing learning and controlling behavior by manipulating the environment. The work of B. F. Skinner on operant conditioning was the most influential of these developments.

Skinner used the term *operant conditioning* because he preferred to study *operant behaviors*: voluntary behaviors used in operating on the environment. This distinguished his work from classical conditioning research on what he called *respondent behaviors* (involuntary reflex actions). Skinner's operant conditioning is closer to instrumental conditioning, except that Skinner was not content merely to record animals' behavior when placed in particular environments and allowed to discover "tricks" for responding to them. Instead, Skinner assumed a more active role by manipulating the environment to shape the animal's behavior in desired directions. See Table 7.1.

Contingent Reinforcement

The primary mechanism for accomplishing such behavioral shaping was *contingent reinforcement*: One could increase the frequency of any operant behavior by rewarding the animal for performing it. Delivery of reinforcement was contingent on such performance, so the animal had to perform the behavior to get the reward.

Skinner's work on contingent reinforcement reformulated and applied Thorndike's law of effect but with two important differences. First, Skinner used contingent reinforcement in an active way to shape behavior and speed up the learning process; he did not wait for animals to learn through exploration and discovery. Second, Skinner defined reinforcers

TABLE 7.1 TWO BASIC FORMS OF STIMULUS-RESPONSE CONDITIONING

	Classical Conditioning (Pavlov)	Instrumental Conditioning (Skinner)
Order of stimulus and response	S-R conditioning	R-S conditioning
Nature of the process	Stimulus substitution	Response modification
Psychological principle involved	Contiguity (no reinforcement) Adhesive principle	Reinforcement Feedback principle
The basic paradigm	$S_1 \rightarrow R$; $S_2 \dashrightarrow R$	R←S

Source: From *Learning Theories for Teachers* by Morris L. Bigge. Copyright © 1982 by Harper & Row, Inc. Reprinted by permission of the publisher.

in terms of their situational effects on behavior (thus avoiding the problem that consequences generally thought of as rewarding are not experienced as rewarding by everyone in every situation). Skinner defined a *reinforcer* as any consequence that increases the frequency of some operant behavior when made contingent on performance of that behavior. This definition is circular, but it has proven extremely useful.

Conditioning Mechanisms

Operant conditioning is accomplished through four basic mechanisms:

- *Positive reinforcement* or reward: Responses that are rewarded are likely to be repeated (good grades as reinforcement for careful study).
- *Negative reinforcement*: Responses that allow escape from painful or undesirable situations are likely to be repeated (exemption from a major test as reinforcement for good performance on quizzes).
- *Extinction* or nonreinforcement: Responses that are not reinforced are unlikely to be repeated (ignoring students who call out answers without first raising their hands and being recognized should extinguish this tendency to call out).
- *Punishment*: Responses that bring painful or undesirable consequences will be suppressed, although the behavioral potential will remain and the responses may reappear if reinforcement contingencies should change (penalizing students who call out answers by withdrawing privileges should cause the students to suppress their calling out).

Behavioral Shaping

Skinner captured the public imagination by showing that operant conditioning principles could be used to teach animals to do things that they would never learn through natural experience (such as teaching pigeons to dance or play pingpong). He accomplished this through *behavioral shaping* in which *successive approximations* of the ultimate target behavior were reinforced until the animal learned to produce the target behavior itself.

Teaching a pigeon to "dance," for example, might begin with reinforcement (delivery of a food pellet) following any lifting of the left leg. Once the pigeon learned to lift the left leg to earn a food pellet, the reinforcement contingency would be changed so that, for example, the pigeon now first had to lift the left leg and then replace it on the floor again before being reinforced. When this sequence was learned, reinforcement contingencies would change again, so that the pigeon would first have to go through the sequence with the left leg and then repeat it with the right leg. At this point, the pigeon would have developed a hopping sequence that resembled dancing, and this "dancing" could be extended into a "routine" through additional shaping.

Behavioral chaining

A great range of behaviors could be shaped in this manner. If a target behavior was in the animal's present or potential repertoire, it could be produced by initially reinforcing a partial or primitive version and then systematically reinforcing successive approximations of the final form. If some combination or sequence of behaviors were desired, one could teach the first step, then the second, and so on. This process is called behavioral chaining, or simply *chaining*.

Discrimination Training

Stimulus control

Contingent reinforcement can be used not only to shape behavior but also to bring the behavior under *stimulus control* by applying the principles of contiguity and repetition. Just as Pavlov had shown that a conditioned stimulus could become a signal for the appearance of an unconditioned stimulus, Skinner showed that a conditioned stimulus could become a signal for the availability of contingent reinforcement. For example, if he reinforced a pigeon's dancing behavior only when a particular light was on, the pigeon would learn to dance when the light was on but not when the light was off. "The light had become a *discriminative stimulus* (or *cue*) for the dancing behavior, which was now under stimulus control (it would occur only when the light was present).

Stimulus discrimination

Contingent reinforcement principles could also be used to develop *stimulus discrimination*: The pigeon could learn to dance only in the presence of a particular light. Here, only the "right" light would function as a discriminative stimulus to cue the dancing behavior. Other light sources would be neutral stimuli without special significance.

Response discrimination

Contingent reinforcement principles could also be used to produce *response discrimination*: A pigeon could learn to dance when cued by one light source but to press a lever when cued by a different light source. The pigeon could learn that a particular situation (in this case, being placed in a specially designed experimental cage that came to be called a "Skinner box") offered a range of stimuli. Some were neutral and of no special significance, but others functioned as cues indicating the chance to produce particular responses in order to earn expected reinforcements.

Much of what is taught in school involves discrimination training. Students must learn not only to distinguish between relevant stimuli but also to respond appropriately to each one: A plus sign cues addition operations, but a "times" sign cues multiplication operations.

In the classroom, cuing can be accomplished through direct statements ("Watch what happens when I add acid to the test tube"), as well as remarks such as "I wonder what will happen when I push this button. Oh, look!" Cuing can also be accomplished through pointing, holding objects up for viewing, telling students where to look, or asking questions that will cause them to process information and find the appropriate stimulus. Attention should be directed through cuing whenever students may be confused about where to look or what to listen to.

Partial Reinforcement Schedules

Operant responses are established most rapidly when the target behavior is reinforced immediately each time it occurs (not just some of the time). Before Skinner's work on *schedules of reinforcement* (Ferster & Skinner, 1957), it was assumed that a 100 percent reinforcement schedule (reinforcing the target response every time it occurs in the presence of the controlling cue stimulus) also would maximize the strength and persistence of the response. This assumption had to be changed when Skinner showed that once responses were established, they could be maintained better through *partial reinforcement schedules* than through 100 percent reinforcement schedules.

Interval schedules

Partial reinforcement schedules include interval schedules and ratio schedules, and each of them can be either fixed or variable. In *fixed interval schedules*, the target response is reinforced only after a fixed interval of time (such as sixty seconds) has elapsed since the last reinforcement. In *variable interval schedules*, opportunities to earn reinforcement are also scheduled according to the time elapsed since the previous reinforcement, but the time intervals vary (randomly or according to some predetermined scheme) within set limits.

Ratio schedules

Ratio schedules are based on the number of target responses that have occurred, rather than the time that has elapsed, since the previous reinforcement. In *fixed ratio schedules*, a fixed percentage of the target responses made is reinforced. In *variable ratio schedules*, the number of response repetitions required varies within set limits. For example, opportunity for reinforcement may recur following anywhere from two through fifty repetitions of the target response.

Response rates

Different schedules of partial reinforcement have different effects on response rate. Under fixed schedules, where reinforcement delivery is predictable, learners adjust their behavior accordingly. When they know that a fixed time interval must elapse before the next reinforcement opportunity, they will simply wait (or do something else) while the time elapses and then begin producing the target response around the time that the next reinforcement is due. Under fixed ratio schedules they learn that a fixed amount of work is required to earn reinforcement, so they tend to repeat the target behavior rapidly and forcefully at times when they particularly desire the reinforcement but with less frequency and vigor when they are satiated. Variable interval and (especially) variable ratio schedules produce steadier and more persistent rates of response, because learners know that their effects will pay off eventually even though they cannot predict when. For example, you may have noticed that you tend to "keep up" by maintaining a steady study schedule in courses in which unannounced quizzes are expected (variable schedule) but to concentrate your studying in days before exams in courses in which a fixed exam schedule is followed.

Maintaining responses

Skinner showed that an established response persists longer in the absence of reinforcement when it has been maintained by partial reinforcement than by 100 percent reinforcement. This finding suggested that operant conditioning methods for maintaining established behaviors might be more feasible and cost effective than previously suspected (one would only have to reinforce the target behavior occasionally, not every time it occurred). The power of partial reinforcement schedules to maintain responses is quite remarkable. A response that would extinguish quickly following termination of a 100 percent reinforcement schedule can be sustained through thousands of unreinforced repetitions using a variable ratio schedule. These findings hold up for humans as well as animals. For example, if you often purchase snacks from a particular vending machine, you are on a 100 percent reinforcement schedule because each time you put in money and pull a lever, you get reinforced with the desired snack. Yet this behavior would extinguish quickly (probably in just one trial) if the machine retained your money but did not deliver the snack, and it would not reappear until the machine had been fixed or replaced. Contrast this with responses to slot machines. Most people will continue to put money into slot machines even though pulling the lever yields no payoff most of the time, because they know that the machine will pay off eventually. Response persistence is sustained through a variable ratio schedule of reinforcement. State lotteries and most other gambling devices operate on the same principle.

Fading

Skinner discovered that responses maintained through 100 percent reinforcement could be switched to partial reinforcement schedules through *fading*. Like shaping, fading is accomplished through successive approximations. To introduce an interval schedule, one would initially delay just a second or two before delivering reinforcement and then gradually extend this interval as the learner became accustomed to waiting. To introduce a ratio schedule, one would occasionally skip a response or two before reinforcing and then gradually reduce the reinforcement rate as the learner became more accustomed to repeating the response several times before being reinforced. Once begun in this manner, fading would continue until the desired schedule of reinforcement was established (typically, the lowest rate of reinforcement that would still maintain the response at the desired rate).

Skinner and Education

Like Watson in earlier times, Skinner has become famous not only for advocating behaviorism as an approach to psychology (Skinner, 1974) but also for advocating it as a way to perfect the human condition. Along with the Skinner Box for research on animals, he designed a special "air crib" that allowed him to keep one of his daughters in a controlled environment (soundproof, with constant temperature and humidity) frequently during her infancy. He also wrote *Walden Two* (Skinner, 1948), a fictional depiction of a Utopian community in which reinforcement principles were used to maintain cooperation and labor in the service of the common good. In this vision, credits accumulated through work were exchanged for reinforcement (basic necessities of living, opportunities for recreation or pleasure). Those willing to undertake the least desirable jobs could accumulate credits more quickly.

Reinforcement principles

Skinner believed that we are controlled by our reinforcement histories to the extent that our notions of self-determination are mere illusions (Skinner, 1971). His ideas about using operant conditioning to perfect the human condition are essentially humanistic in that they are designed to minimize suffering, meet basic needs, and maximize quality of life for all, but many find his approach too cold and impersonal, and some fear that its manipulative aspects would lead to the sort of totalitarian "Big Brotherism" depicted by George Orwell in *1984*.

Operant conditioning

Skinner (1968) argued that operant conditioning principles should be used in developing technologies for classroom management and instruction. Teaching machines, programmed instruction, and computer-assisted instruction are among the technologies developed at least in part on the basis of his ideas. His principles for teaching students are the same ones he uses in the laboratory for teaching animals: Elicit desirable responses in the presence of discriminative stimuli or cues and reinforce these responses immediately, continue cuing and reinforcing until the responses become well established, shape the ultimate target behavior through successive approximations, and fade reinforcement once the established stimulus-response connection can be maintained without it. There are two major differences, however, between conditioning animals and instructing students. First, students can understand and respond to language, so one can cue responses directly by calling for them, without having to shape them gradually. Thus classroom instruction is more efficient than animal conditioning, and it emphasizes eliciting responses through cuing at least as much as reinforcing them after they are elicited. Second, responses are reinforced primarily through feedback; there is no need to rely on food or other material rewards.

Conditioning animals versus instructing students

Skinnerian approach to instruction

In summary, the Skinnerian approach to instruction involves building stimulus-response associations by cuing learners as to the nature of the response desired and then providing immediate feedback about the correctness of the response elicited, so that correct responses are reinforced and incorrect responses are extinguished. Where necessary, programs are sequenced to move learners through successive approximations toward the ultimate target responses. If applied properly, these principles should produce learning that is not only efficient according to "cold" criteria such as number of trials required to reach criterion but also desirable according to humanistic criteria. Learning should be more enjoyable to the learners because they get to respond actively, their responses yield immediate feedback, they can move along at their own pace, and the emphasis is on producing success experiences through reward. Examples of how these principles are used in programmed instruction approaches are given near the end of the chapter.

SOCIAL LEARNING THEORY

Although Skinner and other purists continue to believe that behaviorism can get along without reference to cognitive information processing or subjective experience, most behaviorists have integrated at least some of these covert processes into their theorizing. This is especially true of behaviorists who study human learning that occurs in social situations, much of which does not seem explainable without reference to covert mental activities.

Imitation of Models

Humans learn to speak their native language, to use tools, and to behave appropriately in various social situations, among other things, mostly by imitating others. Sometimes complex sequences of behavior are displayed following just a single observation of a model, even without any deliberate cuing or behavioral shaping. Similarly, the situational specificity of various social behaviors usually is learned without systematic discrimination training. Seemingly effortlessly, we learn to act one way in a library, another at a party, and yet another at a formal meeting. Such phenomena underscore the distinction between learning and performance and appear to require theorizing about learning that is qualitatively different from operant conditioning—learning that occurs before learners even begin to make overt behavioral responses, let alone to have those responses reinforced.

Delayed imitation

Sometimes, behavioral capacities acquired through observation of models are not acted out for considerable periods (even years) following their acquisition. When teaching a particular topic, for example, teachers may use the same general approach and content emphasis that were used with them when they were students at the grade level they now teach. Such delayed imitation phenomena suggest that human behavior is mediated by cognitive processes, not merely learned as isolated stimulus-response associations.

Vicarious learning

We can learn not only by imitating the overt behavior of others but also by observing how others are affected by events that occur in their lives. By putting ourselves in their place (i.e., by identifying with them), we experience their thoughts and emotions vicariously. For example, much of what we know about interpersonal relationships and the emotions that accompany them has been learned from books, movies, or television programs about real or fictional people.

To accommodate phenomena such as observational learning, delayed imitation, and vicarious learning, social learning theorists have broadened behaviorism to include cognition and emotion in addition to behavior. Learning is seen as a cognitively mediated capacity for performance rather than identified with performance itself. It can be acquired merely through observation of models, and it includes stimulus-response-reinforcement linkages, not just information about behavioral possibilities. That is, we learn not only about potential responses but about the situations in which those responses may be relevant, the stimuli that may cue them, and the consequences that they are likely to bring about. Such learning is *mediated* through cognitive processes such as focusing of attention, encoding of input, and retention in long-term memory.

Bandura and Modeling

Learner mediation of stimulus input

Albert Bandura (1977, 1986) is a leading social learning theorist whose ideas are important for thinking not only about classroom learning and instruction but also about classroom motivation and management (as will be explained in later chapters). Bandura believes that human behavior must be described in terms of reciprocal interaction between cognitive, behavioral, and environmental determinants and not just shaping through reinforcement. Reinforcement remains important, but human mediation capacities make it unnecessary to wait for responses to occur before being able to use it. Instead, one can use modeling or verbal explanation to inform learners about the consequences of producing desired behavior and thus cause them to begin to produce the behavior. Here, reinforcement has effects even before it occurs, because learners anticipate its delivery and adjust their behavior accordingly. Such reinforcement effects initially occur through learner mediation of cognitive input rather than through delivery of consequences to learner behavior.

Social learning theorists also leave room for learner mediation of stimulus input, because different people will respond differently to the same situation. If you and two friends were to visit a classroom together, for example, and then discuss the teacher's effectiveness, you might disagree because of differences in what each of you paid attention to. One might have concentrated on the efficiency of classroom management, another on the teacher's rapport with students, and the third on the clarity of the teacher's explanations.

Nominal versus functional stimulus

Such phenomena have led social learning theorists to distinguish between the *nominal stimulus* (the stimulus situation described in terms of observable and measurable characteristics) and the *functional stimulus* (the stimulus situation as observed and interpreted by the learner). To understand learning in complex environments, and especially to understand why different individuals learn different things from "the same" experience, one must identify the functional stimulus that cues each learner's response. When teaching, one needs to see that students attend to the right things (i.e., to see that each student's functional stimulus is the one that the student should focus on). Modeling and verbal explanation can be used to enhance the salience and distinctiveness of cues and thus to focus students' attention.

Bandura has done a great deal of research on learning induced through modeling. At first, this form of learning was called *imitation* because learners were exposed to filmed models who acted out a series of discrete behaviors in exaggerated fashion and then were observed to see how much they imitated these models when placed in the same situation. Children, for example, would watch a model "take out" frustration against an inflated rubber Bobo doll and then would be observed to see if they responded to the same frustration in the same way. The results showed that learners seldom imitated models in the sense of duplicating their behavior precisely. Instead, cued by the models' behavior, they developed general notions about how to respond in the situation but then acted on these notions in their own ways. In the Bobo doll example, the children observing the model did not learn a specific sequence of behaviors (first punch the doll with the right hand and then kick the doll with the right foot, etc.). Instead, they learned a general principle (take out frustration by attacking the Bobo doll) that could be implemented in a variety of ways (various combinations of the aggressive responses that had been modeled, along with other forms of aggression that were not shown in the film).

Learning through modeling

Because the term *imitation* is somewhat misleading, Bandura proposed that the term *modeling* be used to refer to learning that occurs as a result of observing models. Much human learning occurs through modeling, including much of what we learn about coping with everyday situations. For example, most adults typically behave much as their parents did when they respond to frustration (calm and analytical versus hysterical or resigned), discipline their own children (forgiving versus punitive), or perform household repairs (skillful versus inept).

Modeling in classroom learning

Modeling is responsible for much classroom learning as well. Three general types of such modeling can be identified. First, teachers are role models for students. They continuously supply students with information about how to think not only about the academic curriculum but about social, political, and personal issues. To the extent that this modeling is done systematically, it can be a significant factor in *socializing* students' attitudes, beliefs, and behavior. The other two types of classroom modeling are more specifically instructional. One involves *modeling of cognitive skills* (creative thinking, problem solving). These skills cannot be taught directly in step-by-step fashion, but teachers can stimulate their development indirectly through modeling. The third type of modeling does involve step-by-step *demonstrating of procedures*, which is often the most efficient way to teach motor skills and low-level cognitive skills.

COGNITIVE BEHAVIOR MODIFICATION

Behavioral modification is a general term for the use of techniques based on behavioristic principles to shape and control behavior. Just as behavioristic theorizing ranges from the pure behaviorism of Skinner to the cognitive approach represented by Bandura, so do the approaches taken to behavior modification. The most "conservative" approach is called *applied behavior analysis*, which is based on Skinner's ideas and concentrates on using reinforcement principles to bring behavior under stimulus control. More "liberal" approaches that combine reinforcement techniques with techniques drawn from pedagogy, instructional psychology, and psychotherapy are called cognitive behavior modification.

Controlling one's own behavior

As described by Meichenbaum (1977), *cognitive behavior modification* techniques are designed to develop in learners the capacity for controlling their own behavior through goal setting, planning, self-instruction, self-monitoring, and self-reinforcement. These techniques feature modeling combined with verbalized self-instruction in which models not only perform tasks but also "think out loud" as they do so, enabling learners to see how to use self-talk to guide one's behavior in searching for relevant cues, developing ideas about how to respond, monitoring the effectiveness of responses, and so on.

Meichenbaum and Goodman (1971) used these techniques to train a group of boys to respond analytically, rather than impulsively, to matching-to-sample tasks that required them to inspect a sample stimulus and then identify its duplicate among a set of alternative choices (the alternatives were all similar to the sample, but only one was identical to it). The boys had been doing poorly on such tasks because they impulsively selected the first choice that looked right, rather than taking time to study all of the choices and make sure that they had selected the correct one. In this experiment, the models used exaggerated gestures and motions to make it clear that they were comparing each alternative choice to the stimulus before reaching a final decision. As they did so, they maintained a running monologue by verbalizing thoughts such as "Let's see, I'm going to have to compare each of these to make sure I don't get the wrong one by mistake. How about this one? Is this ear the same? How about the other ear? No, this one has a round ear, and that one has a long ear. . . ." This approach was effective in improving the boys' performance on such tasks, even though other approaches (such as urging the boys to slow down and take their time) were not effective.

Modeling combined with verbalized self-instructions

The combination of modeling with verbalized self-instructions is a powerful instructional technique, especially when teaching complex processes that are guided by covert self-talk that remains hidden from learners unless the teacher shares it with them (Fox & Kendall, 1983; Meichenbaum & Asarnow, 1979; Sarason & Sarason, 1981). Students will not learn much from watching a teacher identify the main ideas in a series of paragraphs, solve mathematics problems on the board, or perform experiments in the laboratory if these "demonstrations" do not include verbalization of the thinking that guides the observable actions. When teachers do share this thinking, however, students not only can understand what the teachers are doing and why but also can learn the general approach used in solving the problem and apply it later in working on their own. The latter advantage makes modeling combined with verbalized self-instruction more effective than traditional lecture/demonstration methods for most instructional purposes. Such modeling in first-person language provides students with an integrated, within-context demonstration of how to approach and solve the problem. This is easier for them to retain and use than general information presented in third-person language or even instructions presented in second-person language (''First you do this, then do this . . .'') that must first be internalized and then translated into first-person language that can be used to guide behavior.

EDUCATIONAL TECHNOLOGIES

In addition to generating principles that teachers can use during lectures, discussions, and other traditional forms of instruction, educational psychologists have developed technologies designed to enhance teacher-delivered instruction or replace it with instruction from some other source. Most of the early innovations in educational technology were based on behavioristic principles.

Teaching Machines

Pressey (1932) invented *teaching machines*, which were simple self-teaching devices that presented learners with questions, required them to respond in some way, and then allowed them to get feedback by turning a knob or opening a slot to reveal the answer. Nothing much came of Pressey's ideas, however, until Skinner (1954, 1958) and others began to tout teaching machines as practical alternatives to traditional schooling. By then it had become clear that the ''machine'' aspects of such instruction (knobs, viewing windows, etc.) were not essential and that the key elements were design principles such as sequencing the instruction, providing corrective feedback, and programming for consistent success. Consequently, interest in mechanization and gimmicks waned (except as motivational devices), and educational technologists began to focus on *programmed instruction* (Skinner, 1986).

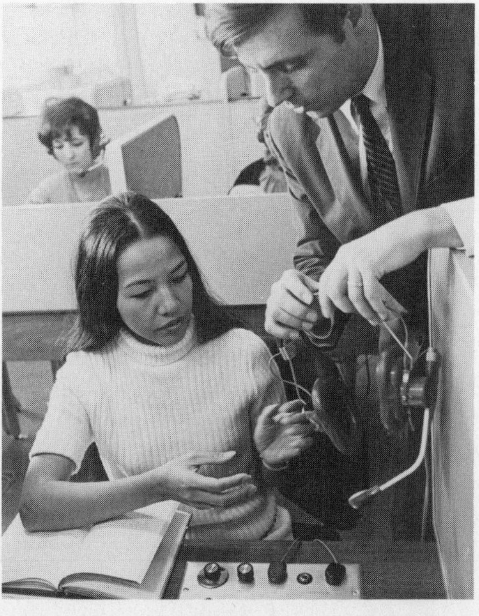

Teachers use a variety of specialized machines to aid student learning.

Programmed Instruction

Instructional programming involves designing instruction to move learners in small steps from "entry level" performance to the target objective. Typically, programs are designed to be self-contained and ready for independent use by learners who have the appropriate entry characteristics (i.e., their knowledge of the topic is such that the program will be neither too easy nor too difficult for them). Programs are divided into segments called *modules* that can be mastered easily in a short time. Modules are divided into small steps called *frames* that build knowledge step-by-step. Examples are shown in Figures 7.2 and 7.3.

Frames

Programs reflect careful task analysis. Frames are sequenced so that material is presented in a logical order and prerequisite knowledge is taught before higher-level objectives. After a review if considered necessary, the frame introduces the next step. This may be a new concept, a check on mastery of previously introduced concepts (use of discrimination or inference), or a change in focus from teaching information to requiring the learner to apply it. The frame requires that the learner make some active response such as answering a question by filling in a blank.

Fading of cues

Correct responses lead to reinforcement in the form of positive feedback. Extended praise statements may be frequent early in the program, but they soon evolve into simple feedback statements with just occasional praise (i.e., reinforcement is faded). There is also *fading of cues* (also called *vanishing of prompts*): Early frames provide the information needed to answer questions correctly, but later frames provide less information and require learners to draw inferences from information presented earlier. For example, a module may begin with questions about a fully labeled map, then ask about a version of the map that has some parts missing, and then ask questions without showing any map at all.

Figure 7.2 A Set of Frames Designed to Teach a Third- or Fourth-Grade Pupil to Spell the Word Manufacture

1. Manufacture means to make or build. *Chair factories manufacture chairs.* Copy the word here:

   □□□□□□□□□□□

2. Part of the word is like part of the word **factory**. Both parts come from an old word meaning *make* or *build.*

   manu□□□□ure

3. Part of the word is like part of the word **manual**. Both parts come from an old word for *hand.* Many things used to be made by hand.

   □□□□facture

4. The same letter goes in both spaces:

   m□nuf□cture

5. The same letter goes in both spaces:

   man□fact□re

6. **Chair factories** □□□□□□□□□□□ **chairs**.

Figure 7.3 Part of a Program in High School Physics

Sentence to be completed	Word to be supplied
1. The important parts of a flashlight are the battery and the bulb. When we "turn on" a flashlight, we close a switch that connects the battery with the ______.	bulb
2. When we turn on a flashlight, an electric current flows through the fine wire in the ______ and causes it to grow hot.	bulb
3. When the hot wire glows brightly, we say that it gives off or sends out heat and ______.	light
4. The fine wire in the bulb is called a filament. The bulb "lights up" when the filament is heated by the passage of a(n) ______ current.	electric
5. When a weak battery produces little current, the fine wire, or ______, does not get very hot.	filament
6. A filament which is *less* hot sends out or gives off ______ light.	less
7. "Emit" means "send out." The amount of light sent out, or "emitted," by a filament depends on how ______ the filament is.	hot
8. The higher the temperature of the filament the ______ the light emitted by it.	brighter, stronger

Note: The machine presents one item at a time. The student completes the item and then uncovers the corresponding word or phrase shown at the right.

Linear and branched programming

Program sequencing may be linear or branched. *Linear programming* is designed to move learners through a single fixed sequence of objectives. It is used when there is reason to believe that the same program will enable different learners to achieve the objective with few if any errors and no need for individualized remediation. If errors should occur, learners are recycled through earlier points in the program. *Branched programs* are designed to meet individual needs. Learners are instructed to skip certain modules when performance on pretest frames indicates that they have already mastered the material. Also, when learners fail to master certain modules even after being recycled through them, they are first "branched" into special modules that provide remedial instruction and then returned to the main program.

Self-pacing

Programmed instruction is said to be *self-paced* or under *learner control*. Students progress quickly through material that they already know or can master easily, but they spend more time on material that they find difficult. Errors are private, and feedback is immediate and constructive. In branched programs, persistent errors lead to different or more thorough remedial instruction, not just repetition of the instruction that has not worked so far. Programmed instruction requires learners to attend actively to the information presented and respond thoughtfully to the questions asked, but it also reinforces these learning efforts by allowing learners to respond overtly, receive immediate feedback, achieve consistent success, and progress at their own pace.

Variations in programmed instruction

Most programmed instruction is designed for use by learners working privately. However, some variations allow for teacher-student interaction while retaining the advantages of programmed instruction. Others are designed to emphasize particular learning modalities (visual, auditory) for students who need special stimulation. Still other adaptations are meant for students who lack independent work skills or functional reading ability. Reading is minimized by using tape-recorded information and instructions, but active responding is retained by using worksheets. After presenting information and a question, the recorded message will tell students to respond, give them time to do so, and then provide feedback.

Limitations

These programs typically are not as successful as reading-based programs because they lack self-pacing and flexibility in providing individualized instruction. If students keep making too many errors, they keep repeating the same program. This can cause them to memorize correct responses without really understanding the material. Even if branched remedial programs are available, they cannot be brought to bear immediately except through expensive computerized methods. Usually, the best that teachers can do is to identify the problems that particular students are having and then channel them into individualized remedial work.

Research on Programmed Instruction Much programmed instruction has been successful, yet research on it has produced confusing findings that call into question some of its underlying ideas that seem most intuitively obvious. For example, comparisons of learning by students using carefully sequenced programs with learning by students using the same programs presented in randomly mixed or even reversed order often show no group differences. The learners in these studies usually are relatively sophisticated (college students), and the programs are brief and easy to learn. Under these circumstances, poor sequencing does not make enough of a difference to impair learning. However, when learners are less sophisticated or the material is sufficiently lengthy and difficult, carefully sequenced instruction produces more learning than instruction presented randomly or in some nonoptimal sequence.

Puzzling results have also been obtained in studies comparing programs that require learners to respond actively and repeat frames on which they make mistakes with programs that require learners merely to read the material without making overt responses. These studies often show no differences or even differences favoring the group that merely reads the material. The most common interpretation for such findings is that the value of active responses and remedial subprograms depends on the length and difficulty of the material for the learners (Tobias & Ingber, 1976; Abramson & Kagen, 1975). Sophisticated students working on a brief program that they can learn easily may get as much information from reading alone as from responding overtly (in fact, having to respond overtly following each frame may be more time consuming and irritating than helpful).

Some cognitively oriented theorists have used these puzzling findings to question the very assumptions underlying programmed instruction. They interpret the findings involving scrambled sequences as evidence that incongruity stimulates discovery learning, and interpret findings favoring reading over active responding as evidence of the futility of trying to make learners conform to logic imposed by someone else rather than letting them encode and organize material in their own ways. These interpretations may be correct for students who are able to learn efficiently through reading and do not require immediate feedback. However, students in the early grades appear to benefit from step-by-step sequencing and frequent opportunities to make overt responses and get immediate feedback.

Comparisons between programmed instruction and conventional instruction are about evenly split, and the differences tend to be small in any case (Bangert, Kulik, & Kulik, 1983; Jamison, Suppes, & Wells, 1974). Consequently, interest in programmed instruction has waned in recent years.

Keller and PSI

Working from principles of operant conditioning, Fred Keller (1968) developed a method of individualizing instruction that he called the *Personalized System of Instruction* (PSI) and that since has become known as the *Keller Plan*. The Keller Plan was developed originally for use in a college psychology course and is presently used in a variety of college courses. Its main features are self-pacing (within limits, students can go as fast or as slow as they choose), mastery orientation (students move on to a new unit only after mastering the preceding unit to criterion), and student control of the examination schedule (students take tests when they decide that they are ready, and may repeat tests until they reach criterion). Following an initial orientation to the course, there are few if any class meetings. Instead, students work individually or with one another to learn from textbooks or programmed materials and consult with the teacher or with assistants called *proctors* to get help (Keller & Sherman, 1982).

The PSI is popular with college students or at least with those who enroll in PSI courses (Robin, 1976). These students enjoy the self-pacing, individualized tutoring, and contract options that guarantee particular grades for particular levels of performance. Also, the PSI students typically achieve as well as or better than students in conventional sections, partly because they tend to put in more time and effort.

Need for self-discipline

The PSI works best for students who have the self-discipline and inclination to learn independently (Johnson & Ruskin, 1977). Procrastination and high withdrawal rates are commonly reported in PSI courses, although stiff mastery requirements may minimize this problem for some students. Robin (1976) reported that students with low grade-point averages began studying earlier and studied more often in PSI courses with 100 percent mastery criteria than in PSI courses using 50 percent criteria. Many students were not willing to make this effort, though, and withdrew from the PSI sections. Thus the PSI courses demand more self-discipline than many students are willing or able to exert.

Bloom and Mastery Learning

Another systematic approach to teaching that is based in part on principles of operant conditioning is learning for mastery, or *mastery learning*. Benjamin Bloom (1968) first developed mastery learning as a form of indi-

Mastery learning

vidualized instruction, but the concept has since been expanded to include group-based methods.

Bloom's ideas were a reaction against the notion that individual differences in general aptitudes and abilities necessarily make for individual differences in levels of curriculum mastery. Bloom was influenced by John Carroll (1963) who had argued that differences in mastery levels are produced not by inherent differences in students' learning potential but by differences in the time needed to learn (some students may take longer, but they will master the material if given enough time). He expressed the argument in the following equation:

$$\text{degree of learning} = \frac{\text{time actually spent}}{\text{time needed}}$$

Carroll suggested that five elements determine students' rates of learning: aptitude, ability to understand instruction, task perseverance, opportunity to learn, and quality of instruction. Bloom (1968, 1976, 1980) elaborated on Carroll's model to develop the concept of mastery learning. Bloom's model includes student-entry characteristics (both cognitive and affective), the learning task itself, the quality of the instruction provided, and a variety of learning outcomes (level and type of achievement, rate of learning, affective outcomes). Bloom suggested that the outcome of a student's encounter with a learning task will be determined not only by the time available for learning but also by the appropriateness of the task for the learner (in terms of both its cognitive level and its affective appeal) and by the quality of the instruction provided. Learning will proceed most smoothly when students are taught effectively on tasks that they are motivated to engage in and able to master with relative ease. In suggesting guidelines for quality of instruction, Bloom stressed four aspects: (1) *cues* or directions about what to do, (2) *active learner participation* in the task, (3) *reinforcement* that is derived from participating in the task and experiencing success on it, and (4) *feedback/correction* from the instructor.

Bloom's guidelines for quality instruction

Bloom argued that an effective combination of these elements should enable 80 percent of students to reach mastery levels that only the top 20 percent reach in traditional classrooms. He also argued that the extra time and instruction provided to slow learners when they are working on tasks that come early in a hierarchical sequence not only will allow these students to master these tasks but also will reduce the time they need to learn tasks that appear later in the sequence. Taken together, these assumptions imply that mastery learning should (1) increase the percentage of students who master a given objective from about 20 to 80 percent, (2) reduce the variance (individual differences) in mastery of any particular objective and the curriculum as a whole, and (3) over time, reduce the variance in time needed to learn (because as slower students master more and more prerequisites, they will become able to master higher-level tasks with relative ease).

Initial applications of these ideas were at the high school and college levels where students were experienced at learning primarily on their own from instructional materials. Instruction from the teacher took the form of individualized tutoring. Later, Block and Anderson (1975) adapted the approach for use by elementary and secondary teachers in tandem with, rather than instead of, traditional instruction. At present, most mastery learning programs in the schools feature group rather than individualized instruction (Levine, 1985). Anderson (1985) suggested that the following six features will be found in any true mastery learning program: (1) clearly specified learning objectives; (2) short, highly valid assessment procedures; (3) preset mastery performance standards; (4) a sequence of learning units, each composed of integral sets of facts, contents, principles, and skills; (5) provision of feedback about learning progress to students; and (6) provision of additional time and help to correct misunderstandings of students who fail to achieve mastery on their first try.

Cycle of mastery learning

The heart of mastery learning is the cycle of teaching, testing, reteaching, and retesting. Students are informed of the objectives of a unit and then receive instruction designed to enable them to master those objectives. After completing the instruction and related practice activities, the students receive formative evaluation tests designed to assess their mastery levels. Those who achieve preset performance standards (usually calling for passing 80 percent of the items on the test, although sometimes requiring 90 percent or more) are certified as having mastered the unit and are not required to do further work on it. These students will move on to the next unit or, more typically, will work on enrichment activities or activities of their own choosing until the rest of the class is ready to move on. Meanwhile, the students who did not meet mastery criteria will receive corrective instruction and additional practice, and then their mastery levels will be assessed again.

Theoretically, these cycles of assessment and reteaching would go on indefinitely until all students reached mastery, but in practice, attempts to bring students to mastery usually cease after the second test administration, and the class then moves on to the next unit. Thus typical group-based mastery learning programs are a compromise between traditional programs that allow little if any extra time to slow learners and ideal mastery programs that would allow all learners as much time as they needed. Even so, half or more of the total time devoted to a unit in a typical group-based mastery program is spent on corrective instruction with students who fail to reach mastery criteria on the formative test following initial instruction (Slavin & Karweit, 1984).

The mastery learning philosophy is very appealing at first glance, but critics have suggested that individual differences in student learning ability are too stable and powerful to be compensated for by relatively minor adjustments in time allocation for teaching and learning and that, in any case, it is inappropriate to pursue the goal of reducing individual differences in student achievement levels because this can be accomplished only by holding back high achievers in addition to providing extra time and instruction to low achievers. Research on mastery learning has not resolved these issues clearly.

Comparisons of mastery learning with traditional instruction usually show both better attitudes and higher achievement in mastery classes and, in particular, show that a much higher percentage of mastery students master the content believed to be basic (Block & Burns, 1976; Guskey & Gates, 1986). However, these highly favorable findings are misleading in several respects. First, a great deal of additional learning time is required to achieve the reported gains in mastery of the material. Arrangements must be made to provide corrective instruction before or after school or, more typically, to do so during class time and thus hold back the faster learners while the teacher works with the slower ones. If these extra time needs are taken into account, there is little or no advantage to mastery learning at all.

Another problem is that research does not support the key assumption that taking time to ensure mastery of early objectives will reduce the time that students need to learn later ones (Arlin, 1984). In practice, then, it appears that mastery learning does not really solve the dilemma of having to choose between fixing time allotments and accepting individual differences in mastery levels or fixing mastery levels and accepting individual differences in time to learn. Instead, they merely substitute the second choice for the first.

A third problem is that the findings from comparative studies tend to be more impressive for brief studies (lasting a week or less) involving instruction in content not normally taught at school than they are for studies of instruction in basic school subjects assessed over significant periods (Guskey & Gates, 1986). Slavin and Karweit (1984), for example, found no advantage to mastery learning over traditional instruction in ninth-grade general mathematics classes in inner-city Philadelphia schools studied over the course of an entire semester. Similarly, the Chicago schools initiated a large-scale mastery learning program with a great deal of enthusiasm in the early 1980s (Jones et al., 1985) but dropped it just a few years later after teacher complaints about the curriculum materials and about difficulties in implementing the program.

Finally, even though mastery learning was developed with low achievers in mind, it appears to be especially difficult to implement in inner-city schools populated largely by low achievers. This is partly because such schools tend to have higher student-to-teacher ratios, higher rates of absenteeism and transiency, high enrollments in pull-out instructional programs, fewer instructional materials, and less time for groups of teachers to coordinate planning (Jones & Spady, 1985). Also, however, the corrective sequence of mastery learning is designed to correct relatively minor errors or misunderstandings, whereas students in inner-city schools may have a great many serious and idiosyncratic problems that need individualized attention (Slavin & Karweit, 1984). Thus group-based mastery learning approaches may be difficult to implement in inner-city schools.

In conclusion, it appears that some attempt to implement the mastery learning philosophy would be desirable because of the achievement and motivation benefits it is likely to bring to low achievers. We believe, however, that the emphasis should be on maximizing each student's achievement progress, rather than on reducing the variance in achievement levels as an end in itself. It appears that mastery learning will not succeed in reducing the time that slow learners need to learn (relative to the time that faster learners need), so one can reduce individual differences in achievement progress only by deliberately holding back the faster learners. This is not to state that faster learners should be continually pushed to higher curriculum levels instead of being allowed to engage in enrichment activities or other alternatives to acceleration through the curriculum. Activities planned for faster learners, however, should be selected for sound pedagogical reasons and not as mere time fillers designed to slow their progress in order to give slower learners more time to catch up. A sensible compromise here would seem to be to identify those learning objectives that seem most essential and see that all students master them while tolerating more variable performance on objectives considered less essential.

Computerized Instruction

The ultimate in educational technology is computerized instruction, which offers the computer's information storage and retrieval capacity to enhance the possibilities for offering students varied and individualized instruction. At least potentially, computerized instruction offers several advantages. First, it brings novelty and variety to schooling and thus may be experienced as more enjoyable than conventional seatwork. Second, if combined with videodisc technology, it can incorporate animation, time-lapsed photography, and other audiovisual techniques for communicating information and demonstrating processes in ways that are not possible through conventional print materials. Third, it can allow students to respond more actively and in more varied ways than they can respond to conventional seatwork, and it can provide them with immediate feedback following their responses. Fourth, computers can be programmed to keep track of students' responses and thus accumulate records for teachers to use in monitoring progress and planning remedial instruction. Fifth, it is possible to build diagnosis and prescription capacities into the program itself, so that students are automatically routed to skip parts that they do not need and to work through remedial sequences when they have not achieved mastery on the regular program. Sixth, many programs provide

Computers are becoming more and more familiar tools in the instructional environment.

not only feedback but tutorial instruction and friendly encouragement similar to what the student might receive from a tutor (Lepper & Chabay, 1985). Finally, computerized instruction can provide opportunities for higher-level problem solving and simulation activities of the kind seldom seen in conventional seatwork or programmed instruction. To the extent that these potential advantages can be achieved at reasonable cost, transferring significant instructional functions from the teacher to the computer might be a feasible way of implementing individualized instruction or adaptive education principles in typical school settings (Lesgold, 1986; Lipson & Fisher, 1983; Taylor, 1980).

Computer-assisted instruction

The earliest forms of computerized instruction were called *computer-assisted instruction* (CAI) and involved presenting learners with opportunities to work through programmed packages by interacting with a computer rather than using workbooks or programmed learning modules. Much early CAI involved nothing more than computerized workbooks, and even today this remains true of most of the drill and practice programs developed for mass distribution. From the standpoint of instructional theory, these CAI programs offer no advantages over traditional programmed instruction, and the need for learners to type in answers and conform to other computer-use requirements actually makes CAI less efficient than traditional programmed instruction in many cases. However, the novelty and other motivational features (flashy graphics, gamelike elements) associated with computerized drill and practice make it worth the trouble for certain learners. Also, because computers are perceived as impersonal and thus more "fair," students may learn to take more responsibility for their own performance under CAI than under teacher-led instruction (Griswold, 1984).

Computer-managed instruction

Computer-managed instruction (CMI) becomes possible when a powerful computer system is available that can keep track of each student's performance on learning modules and associated tests. The computer can be programmed to direct learners through sequences of modules when they are progressing smoothly, to recycle or branch them through remedial modules when they are having difficulties, and to provide the teacher with records of responses and test results to use in diagnosing the probable source of the problem when special help is needed. The CMI eliminates much of the record keeping that is a major burden on teachers attempting to implement individualized learning systems.

Contemporary innovations in computerized instruction are going well beyond electronic workbooks for drill and practice. Early language-arts instruction is being enhanced through programs such as *Write to Read* and *Bank Street Writer* and programs designed to teach students to plan, write, and edit stories or poetry (Lawlor, 1982). Early mathematics education is being supplemented with applications of LOGO (Papert, 1980), *Turtle Geometry* (Abelson & diSessa, 1981) and other imaginative forms of computerized instruction (Davis, 1984). Social studies instruction can be enhanced with programs such as *Oregon Trail*, a simulation of a family's journey to the west in a covered wagon in 1847, or *Community Search*, a game in which student teams act as leaders of a primitive agricultural society trying to decide where and how to relocate their community to a better natural environment. Interesting tutorial programs and simulation activities have been developed for science as well (Arons, 1984). New developments occur daily, and a research and development center has been established (at Harvard University) to generate and synthesize information about applications of technology to the classroom.

It remains to be seen whether computerized instruction's theoretical potential can become a practical reality. To date, reviewers interested in computer applications to ordinary classroom settings have identified several important limitations (Becker, 1982; Brophy & Hannon, 1985; Educational Products Information Exchange, 1986; Sloan, 1985). One is the limited availability of good software. Most programs available even today are nothing more than electronic workbooks providing drill and practice on low-level skills. Once the novelty of using the computer wears off, a steady diet of these programs is likely to be just as boring as a steady diet of comparable workbook exercises and even less efficient. Also, most programs are short modules (requiring only an hour or two at most to complete) on limited topics, not full curricula designed for a semester or year of instruction in conventionally taught courses. Thus teachers may be unclear about how to use good software even when they find it. At present, most teachers use computerized instruction only for enrichment with faster students or remedial practice with slower students.

Limited access to computers creates additional feasibility problems. Even in classrooms containing eight computers, students spend as much as three-fourths of their time waiting for a turn at the computer (Center for Social Organization of Schools, 1984). This problem can be alleviated somewhat by having students work together in small groups on a single computer (Clements & Nastasi, 1988; Fish & Feldman, 1987), although most currently available software is designed for use by individuals rather than groups.

A related problem is the trade-off between computer cost and capacity. Many of the most interesting instructional possibilities in computerized instruction require videodisc technology in addition to microcomputers, and the kinds of programs that make possible the most desirable and sophisticated advances over ordinary programmed instruction (interactive simulation exercises and games; tutorial programs that provide diagnosis and corrective instruction in addition to drill and practice with feedback; provision for automatic record keeping and preparation of diagnostic performance summaries) require mainframe computers that are vastly more powerful and expensive than microcomputers.

Still, it is clear that even microcomputers can be useful classroom tools. In science, mathematics, and economics courses, for example, computerized simulation exercises allow students to apply what they are learning by testing predictions or trying to solve problems under realistic conditions (Arons, 1984). The text-editing capabilities of microcomputers are being used in writing classes, where students can edit and revise their compositions by computer and thus bypass the drudgery involved in doing so by hand (Lawlor, 1982). The graphics capabilities of computers have considerable potential for application in courses in design, art, and architecture. In general, computerized instruction has potential application to just about any grade level or subject matter. What remains to be seen is whether the advantages that it brings to a particular situation will be sufficient to justify the trouble and expense involved.

It is too early to draw strong conclusions from available research on microcomputer use in schools. Becker (1988) noted that such research is just beginning to appear. Survey data indicate that teachers report positive experiences with microcomputers in four respects: (1) Students enjoy working with them, (2) they provide good opportunities to engage pairs or groups of students in cooperative learning, (3) they provide opportunities for high-ability students to engage in computer-programming activities and other higher-order thinking and writing tasks, and (4) they provide low-ability students with remedial instruction and practice in basic math and language-arts skills. Early studies of the effects of microcomputer use on academic achievement are extremely variable in quality of research design and nature of findings. The overall trend is positive, but better controlled studies are needed that would produce guidelines for when and how microcomputers can be used cost effectively for instructional purposes.

Concluding Comments on Educational Technology

From teaching machines through programmed instruction and educational television to computerized instruction, new educational technologies have been introduced with great enthusiasm and predictions that they will revolutionize education. So far none has, although most technological innovations have proven useful to some degree. Instead of replacing teachers, they have been assimilated into the traditional teacher-led group instruction model.

Limitations

We expect that the same will be true of computerized instruction and all other innovations that depend on the independent learning efforts of the individual student for two reasons. First, under these individualized learning systems, students must be willing and able to maintain concentration, understand and follow directions, and correct and learn from their mistakes while working independently for sustained periods. Most students in the early grades and many other students lack the reading comprehension and other independent learning skills required, and many students who do have the necessary skills lack the motivation to work on their own in this way for very long. Second, even students who have both the skills and the motivation to learn independently tend to run into trouble if left on their own too long, even when they seem to be progressing nicely. For example, Erlwanger (1975) interviewed bright students who consistently met mastery criteria on unit tests from their individualized mathematics curricula. Many students had misunderstood the material and developed mathematical misconceptions. They had invented rules of thumb that were useful for solving particular assigned problems but would not work (and would leave them confused) later when they encountered different applications of the concepts they were supposed to be learning.

Technological innovations can improve schooling, but as tools that enhance the effectiveness of teachers rather than as replacements for them. So far, it remains to be demonstrated that media and technology provide significant educational benefits in their own right, independent of the quality of the instruction with which they are being used (Clark, 1983b; Gillingham & Guthrie, 1987).

Summary

Behaviorists concentrate on overt, measurable behaviors and seek to discover general laws that can be used to predict and control such behaviors. They locate causality in external events that cue behavior and reinforce stimulus-response relationships.

Early behaviorists studied the conditioning that occurs as associations become established through contiguity and repetition. Pavlov developed the classical conditioning paradigm in which repeated presentation of the conditioned stimulus before the unconditioned stimulus develops associations between them so that learners begin to produce a conditioned response to the conditioned stimulus. Conditioned responses can be extinguished by continuing to present the conditioned stimulus but no longer following it with the unconditioned stimulus. Extinguished responses show spontaneous recovery for a time, but evenually disappear unless the conditioning paradigm is reinstated. Once established, conditioned responses can be expanded through generalization or refined through discrimination.

Watson popularized the term *behaviorism* and showed the application of classical conditioning processes to human emotional development. Thorndike developed the instrumental conditioning paradigm and formulated the laws of exercise and effect. Functionalists studied factors that affected the rate or extent of learning, especially the effects of massed versus distributed practice and of continuing practice to overlearning. They popularized learning curves as visual depictions of progress in learning.

Skinner developed the operant conditioning paradigm for shaping behavior through contingent reinforcement. The paradigm can be used to bring behavior under stimulus control by reinforcing responses only when they occur in the presence of the cue stimulus, to develop stimulus and response discrimination, and to maintain established stimulus-response connections by fading the original 100 percent reinforcement schedule to some partial schedule. Learners adjust to fixed schedules because they allow prediction of reinforcement delivery, so variable schedules, especially variable ratio schedules, produce steadier and more persistent rates of response.

Operant conditioning principles have been incorporated into behavior modification programs, teaching machines, programmed instruction, mastery learning, and computerized instruction. Over time, however, the emphasis has shifted from reinforcement to programming for continuous progress through small successive approximations.

Social learning theorists include the covert mental activities of the learner in their theorizing, and they study learning that occurs through imitation of models or vicariously experiencing what is happening to models being observed. In the classroom, modeling is an important mechanism for demonstrating skills and for influencing students' attitudes, beliefs, and behavior.

Meichenbaum and others have developed cognitive behavior modification techniques to develop in learners the capacity for controlling their own behavior through goal setting, planning, self-instruction, self-monitoring, and self-reinforcement. Modeling combined with verbalized self-instruction is a powerful method of teaching thinking and problem solving.

Behaviorists have been prominent in developing technology for use in classrooms. Early work on teaching machines evolved into the science and technology of programmed instruction. Programs are designed to move learners in small steps with high rates of success from their initial entry level of skill to the target objective. Linear programs move all learners through a fixed sequence believed to be effective for everyone, and branched programs include options for skipping certain modules or providing remedial instruction as learner needs dictate.

The Keller Plan (also known as the Personalized System of Instruction, or PSI) features self-pacing, a mastery orientation, and student control of the examination schedule, typically coupled with a contract system for determining grades. Students learn from textbooks or programmed materials, get assistance from proctors when they need help, and take examinations when they are ready. The Keller Plan is popular with students who enjoy learning individually and effective with those students who have the self-discipline to maintain the necessary study schedule.

The mastery learning approach focuses on the needs of low achievers by providing them with additional time and corrective instruction designed to enable them to master material that high achievers master more quickly and with less help. Research on mastery learning indicates that the approach does significantly increase the percentage of students in a class who evenually meet mastery criteria, but that it does not enable low achievers to catch up with high achievers when the high achievers are not held back. This and various feasibility of implementation problems make mastery learning impractical as a basic model of classroom teaching, but parts of its philosophy and some of its methods appear useful for teachers who wish to adapt typical instructional methods to meet the needs of low achievers more successfully.

Computerized instruction offers several significant potential advantages over traditional classroom teaching, although most currently available programs are little more than computerized workbooks, and even most of the better programs are not well articulated with regular school curricula. To the extent that these and other problems can be addressed cost effectively, classroom use of computerized instruction may increase. Computerized approaches are likely to be most effective, however, when planned as supplements in teacher-guided instruction rather than as replacements for teachers. No approach that requires students to learn through extensive independent interaction with curriculum materials or computers in the absence of frequent input, guidance, and supervision from teachers is likely to be successful.

Questions and Problems

1. Without rereading the text, differentiate among the following terms: *extinction*, *spontaneous recovery*, *generalization*, and *discrimination*. Most students will have a difficult time defining these terms after reading the text just one time. Why is this? What are the implications for how key terms need to be taught?
2. Without rereading the text, define Thorndike's law of exercise and law of effect. We suspect that you found it easier to remember and differentiate these terms than the terms mentioned in Question 1. Why is this? What makes one set of terms more difficult to learn than the other?
3. Why is massed practice usually less efficient than distributed practice? Cite examples where massed practice would be *more* efficient.
4. What is partial reinforcement? What are its unique and powerful advantages in a classroom setting?
5. How might teacher self-talk that is modeled verbally help students to become more reflective and analytical in the classroom?
6. Might you use mastery learning principles in your own teaching? Why or why not?
7. Visit a school and determine how microcomputers are being used. Do some students have more frequent or different computer experiences than others?
8. What are the advantages and disadvantages of microcomputers in the modern classroom? Will you use the technology in your own classroom? If so, how?
9. Supporters of programmed instruction and related individualized learning systems tout them as solutions to the boredom and frustration problems of lock-step curricula. Critics attack them as ineffective, asocial/mechanistic/dehumanizing, and based on false assumptions about learning. Where do you stand? Why?
10. Would you rather be called a teacher or an instructional manager? Why?

Case Studies

LUMP IN THE THROAT. Cindy Clutch, an otherwise successful student, is having a terrible time in her high school speech class. Each of her first two speeches, although short and involving familiar content, was a disaster. She started out nervously and became increasingly so as she went on, turning red, losing her train of thought, stammering uncharacteristically, and, in general, showing every sign of acute anxiety. Her speech teacher arranges a private conference to discuss the problem, and after some hemming and hawing, Cindy explains that she has dreaded making speeches ever since a traumatic experience occurred in the eighth grade. As an attractive early maturer, Cindy had been the object of a great deal of attention, both desired and undesired, from the boys. She had handled this well enough during informal contacts, but once while making a presentation to the class, she suddenly became acutely aware that she was wearing a tight sweater and several boys were staring at her breasts. She blushed, lost her train of thought, and had difficulty finishing the presentation. She has been anxious in public speaking situations ever since. How does the theory and research on conditioning apply to Cindy's problem? What steps might Cindy take to overcome it? How might her speech teacher help?

CONDITIONING SHANK. Karen hurled the frisbee and shouted, "Go get it, Shank!" Shank, a young German shepherd, arched his eyebrows and turned over on his back. Karen grumbled to herself, tramped to get the frisbee, and returned to find Shank asleep. She shook Shank gently, but said with irritation, "Look at the frisbee." Shank pawed it and, then turned over. Karen reached into her jeans and pulled a handful of dog pellets. As Shank devoured them, Karen said, "Shank, look at the frisbee." Then she hurled the frisbee, yelling, "Go get it, Shank!" Shank ignored her. What is Karen's training problem? Taking into account the principles of operant conditioning, how would you advise her to change her approach? What would you do if you were a teacher experiencing problems training a messy and forgetful student to put things away and keep his desk in order?

PRACTICE MAKES BOREDOM. Jim Butkus, a second-grade teacher, walks to Terry Stone's desk. Terry nervously stashes a comic book as Jim asks with concern, "Terry, why aren't you practicing your spelling words?" Terry's face reddens as he shuffles through the book trying to find today's assignment. "It's okay," Mr. Butkus continues reassuringly, "Tell me why you aren't studying." Terry remains silent for a moment and then blurts out, "I'm tired of spending fifteen minutes every day studying spelling words. Practice, practice, practice . . . it's boring!" Assuming that Terry and his classmates need this spelling practice, how might Mr. Butkus provide more interesting (or at least varied) ways for the students to get it? List several examples.

CHAPTER

The Cognitive Structural View of Learning

CHAPTER OUTLINE

GESTALT PSYCHOLOGY
Learning through Insight

BRUNER AND DISCOVERY LEARNING
Modes of Representation of Knowledge
The Spiral Curriculum
Discovery Learning

OTHER APPROACHES TO DISCOVERY LEARNING
Open Education
Inquiry Training
Simulation Games
When to Use Discovery Learning

AUSUBEL AND MEANINGFUL RECEPTION LEARNING
Advance Organizers
Linking the New to the Familiar
Teaching for Transfer

OBJECTIVES

When you have mastered the material in this chapter, you will be able to

1. Describe the cognitive structural approach to learning and differentiate it from the behaviorist approach
2. Define the key concepts of gestalt psychology (gestalt, holistic perception, figure-ground relationships, good form, learning through insight) and explain the implications of this approach for classroom instruction
3. Define Jerome Bruner's three modes of knowledge representation (enactive, iconic, symbolic) and his concept of the spiral curriculum and explain his ideas about how teachers can stimulate students' cognitive development
4. Describe the principles of discovery learning built into *Man: A Course of Study* (MACOS)
5. Explain the key ideas underlying three other well-known approaches to stimulating learning by discovery (the open education movement, inquiry training, and simulation games)
6. Identify the strengths and weaknesses of discovery learning and the circumstances under which it can and cannot be used effectively
7. Define meaningful reception learning as described by Ausubel
8. Define advance organizers and state their instructional functions
9. Define Ausubel's ideas about structuring and sequencing instruction so as to ease learning and enhance transfer

In the previous chapter, we described how behaviorists view learning as response to external stimulation controlled through reinforcement. In this and the next chapter, we describe the approaches taken by cognitive theorists who stress the conceptual aspects of learning over its behavioral aspects. Cognitive theorists concentrate on human learning, especially the meaningful learning of information and intellectual skills that occurs in schools and is mediated through language.

Cognitive theorists recognize that much learning involves associations established through contiguity and repetition. They also acknowledge the importance of reinforcement, although they stress its role in providing feedback about the correctness of responses over its role as a motivator. However, even while accepting such behavioristic concepts, cognitive theorists view learning as involving the acquisition or reorganization of the cognitive structures through which humans process and store information. According to cognitive theorists, intake of information from the environment is active and purposeful rather than passive and controlled by cue stimuli, learning involves cognitive processing of information rather than mere stimulus-response association, and items of information acquired through learning are "sorted," "filed," and "cross-indexed" rather than stored in isolation from one another.

Cognitive structural approach

In this chapter, we discuss the ideas of theorists who stress the *cognitive structural approach* to learning. This approach holds that meaningful learning involves understanding of not only individual facts and principles but also the relationships between them, thus building up cognitive structures for retaining this information in an organized way. These theorists approach instruction by developing ways to teach or guide learners to discover the key ideas that can be used to organize bodies of information. In the next chapter, we will describe the ideas of cognitive theorists who approach instruction by developing ways to stimulate learners to use their own *information-processing* capabilities to process the information to be learned.

The present chapter begins with gestalt psychology, which provided the theoretical roots for the cognitive structural approach that eventually developed. It then discusses the two best-known cognitive structural approaches: discovery learning and meaningful reception learning. Discovery learning is stimulated by arranging for students to engage in activities that will guide them toward discovery of key ideas. Meaningful reception learning is stimulated by presenting the key ideas directly so that they can be used as organizers around which to structure related information.

GESTALT PSYCHOLOGY

In the first third of the twentieth century, when behaviorism dominated American psychology, a variety of approaches thrived in Europe (Freud in Vienna, Piaget in Geneva, mental measurement work in France and England). *Gestalt psychology* was developed in Germany by Max Wertheimer and his associates Kurt Koffka and Wolfgang Kohler, all of whom later emigrated to the United States to escape the Nazis. The gestalt psychologists were interested in the fact that perception tends to be organized into meaningful patterns that include relationships between elements in addition to the elements themselves. *Gestalt* is a German word that means "pattern" or "configuration." A *gestalt* is an integrated whole that has identity and meaning in its own right, not merely as the sum of its parts. Individual parts can be identified as elements, but they are related in *Gestalten*, or configurational patterns, to form larger parts and ultimately the whole.

Gestalt psychologists developed visual illusions and other demonstrations that *perception is both subjective and organized in gestalt fashion*. For example, what do you see when you look at the following?

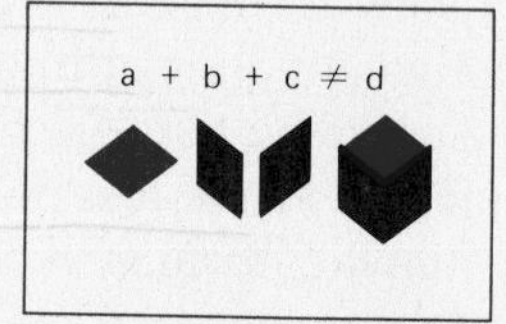

Individually, you see three two-dimensional figures with four sides each. But when these figures are fitted together, they form the image of a three-dimensional cube. This illustrates that human perception tends to be *holistic*. Typically, we do not take in isolated bits of information and impose meaning on them gradually. Instead, the very act of perception includes the organization of incoming stimuli within meaningful patterns that are recognized instantly (if they are familiar).

Figure-ground discrimination

Perception also includes instantaneous *figure-ground discrimination*: We select certain meaningful patterns of input to focus on as figures that stand out from the rest of the input that acts as background. As illustrated in Figure 8.1, these figure-ground relationships often shift, especially when we process complex input. Gestalt psychologists used such illustrations to show that we actively impose meaning on input—different people see the same input differently.

Contrast effects

Gestalt psychologists also developed demonstrations that figures can be perceived differently depending on how they contrast with other figures or with the background. A gray dot looks lighter against a dark background but looks darker against a light background. Similarly, identical lines can be made to look either longer or shorter by adding other lines near or in connection with them. Such *contrast effects* occur with more complex perceptions as well. For example, teachers grading compositions will tend to grade an average essay higher if it follows several poor ones but to grade it lower if it follows several well-written essays.

Explanation for factors governing perception

Gestalt psychologists proposed "laws" to explain the factors governing perception and to allow predictions about how stimuli would be perceived and remembered. The general principle underlying these laws is that people tend to impose *good form* on stimulus input: to perceive and remember objects and events as conforming to familiar or expected patterns. Even when the input is not simple, regular, or complete enough to justify such

Figure 8.1 Do you see a stylish younger woman or a sad-eyed older woman?

perception, we tend to see and remember it as if it were. Elements present in the objective stimulus that conflict with our perceptions are likely to be ignored during the initial perception and forgotten when the perception is remembered later.

Although gestalt psychology dealt more with perception than learning, Wertheimer drew on it to formulate guidelines for instruction. He noted, for example, that just as highlighting, framing, contrasting, and other illustration techniques can be used to make visual stimuli stand out as a figure against the background, parallel techniques for information presentation can be used to make key ideas stand out. More generally, he stressed the importance of making learners aware of the structure of the content to be learned and the relationships among its elements, so that it could be retained as an organized body of knowledge.

Clarity

If they are to be heard without difficulty, lectures need to have a high signal-to-noise ratio—a relatively quiet background without distracting noises and with the speaker talking loudly enough for everyone to hear without straining. Attention to key words can be stimulated by enunciating them more loudly, more slowly, or with exaggerated emphasis. Similar principles hold for reading materials, where space, contrast, letter size and spacing, and other figure-ground considerations can be used to make materials easier to read and to minimize confusion or fatigue. Key words can be stressed using underlines, boxes, italics, or capital letters.

Some students have difficulty separating figure from ground even when actively trying to do so. It may be necessary to aid such students by pointing out distinctive features, tracing, showing several examples, or using visual aids. Similarly, it may be necessary to draw some students' attention to contrasts that they might not notice otherwise.

Learning through Insight

Some gestalt psychologists conducted research demonstrating that complex learning sometimes occurs rapidly through insight. In a typical experiment, chimpanzees were placed in a situation where food was in sight but could not be reached. After giving up trying to reach it by stretching or jumping, the chimps sometimes appeared to engage in thinking that culminated in an "aha" experience followed by rapid solution of the problem. For example, if the food had been suspended from the ceiling so as to be too high to reach, and if the cage contained a box, the chimp might realize that the food could be reached if the box was moved under it and used as a platform. In another situation the food was placed outside the cage, but a stick was available that could be used to push the food close enough to be grabbed. In a more complex variation, a short stick could be used to gather in a longer stick, and the longer stick could be used to gather the food (Kohler, 1959).

Learning by discovery

The chimps did not always solve such problems, and sometimes they solved them only when the experimenter arranged conditions to favor discovery of the solution. For example, the problem involving the short stick, the long stick, and the food was more likely to be solved if the items were lined up in order outside of the cage (first the short stick, then the longer stick, and then the food). In any case, these experiments proved that instrumental learning could occur without trial and error or shaping of successive approximations. Instead, the chimps "figured out" the solution and then demonstrated it in a single trial. If placed in the same situation again, they solved the problem immediately without the need to hesitate for thought, indicating that the learning was retained. This was *learning by discovery* achieved through cognition culminating in *insight*. It is the same kind of learning that students demonstrate when they intuitively "see" a way to prove a complex geometry theorem. Many educational psychologists believe that discovery learning should occur regularly in classrooms and approach instructional questions by asking how conditions can be arranged to guide students toward such discoveries.

BRUNER AND DISCOVERY LEARNING

Jerome Bruner (1966, 1971) is a leading cognitive structural theorist who has suggested ways that teachers can guide students to discover principles and relationships. Bruner's ideas begin with his assumptions about human perception and information processing. He noted that we are constantly bombarded with much more stimulation than we can consciously attend to and process, so we attend selectively—we focus on that portion of the input that is most important or interesting. The input that we attend to is actively perceived and interpreted in organized fashion, using expectations developed through prior experience. Input processed in this manner is stored in the form of imagery, concepts, and other representational structures, and they are ultimately organized into a grand structure that constitutes the person's model of reality.

In Bruner's view, *knowledge is organized into categories* that simplify the task of processing and retaining information by allowing us to interpret the new with reference to the familiar. We can recognize instances as examples of more general categories of knowledge or events.

Modes of Representation of Knowledge

Enactive mode

Bruner identified three general modes of representation of knowledge, similar to the developmental stages postulated by Jean Piaget. The first, predominant in early childhood but continuing throughout life, is the enactive mode. Similar to Piaget's sensorimotor schemas and reflecting his notion that we know what we do, *enactive mode* knowledge is knowledge about how to manipulate the environment through overt behavior. Images, words, and symbols are not involved to any significant degree. Because both Piaget and Bruner see this kind of knowledge as primary in normal development, many educational theorists assume that all learning will be most efficient if it begins with an experience designed to provide a base of enactive mode knowledge on which to build.

Iconic mode

With development, thinking becomes less stimulus bound and dependent on active manipulation of concrete objects. Children become capable of understanding knowledge presented in the *iconic mode* via pictures, images, or memories of previously experienced objects or events. They can begin to think about the properties of objects rather than only about what can be done with these objects, perform arithmetic computations without having to count actual objects or use their fingers, discuss objects or events based on pictures or stimulated memories, and conserve the constant properties of objects after they have been transformed (a square is still a square if you change its color or size).

Symbolic mode

Around adolescence, students become able to represent knowledge in the *symbolic mode* and thus to understand and manipulate purely abstract concepts. They must be able to do this in order to profit from extended verbal instruction in the more formal aspects of subject-matter knowledge (higher-order rules and principles expressing relationships among defined concepts).

Importance of variety of experiences

Although Bruner recognized that students with well-developed abilities to represent knowledge in the symbolic mode are able to understand extended expository instruction, he did not recommend this as a way to teach. Only some students become highly skilled in symbolic mode representation, and even these students will not profit much from extended lecture about abstract content because this will tend to produce figurative knowledge without corresponding operative knowledge—students will memorize definitions, formulas, or scientific principles without truly understanding them or being able to apply them. Consequently, Bruner advocated offering students a variety of educational experiences and instructional methods. They include active "hands-on" experiences in addition to verbal explanations, as well as examples presented in the enactive and iconic modes in addition to explanations in the symbolic mode. He also urged teachers to help students integrate their knowledge by presenting them with organizing principles, cause-effect explanations, and other aids to help them see how things relate to one another.

The Spiral Curriculum

Bruner is famous for his statement that any subject can be taught in some intellectually honest way to any learner. This was not a claim that anyone can learn anything; note the qualifier "in some intellectually honest way." Bruner believes that at least some aspects of any subject can be presented so as to be both (a) true to the spirit of the discipline from which the information is drawn (i.e., accurate, organized around important concepts, and complete in some sense, even though a subject-matter specialist might see it as just part of a much larger picture); and (b) meaningful (i.e., the learner can relate it to his or her existing cognitive categories).

In applying this idea, Bruner recommended the *spiral curriculum*—instead of sequencing objectives so that learners move in lock-step fashion through successive steps of increasing difficulty or complexity, learners are brought back to given topics periodically but encouraged to address them at different levels of knowledge representation and analysis. The idea is that each time the "spiral" comes around to a particular topic, learners will have broadened and deepened their knowledge about this and related topics and therefore will be both able and motivated to undertake a deeper exploration of it. For example, the ability to recognize and label different animals might be an appropriate initial objective. Then students could learn classifications for animals and the similarities and differences among animal types. Later they could learn about the natural habitats and behavior of various animals, and still later they could study animal anatomy or physiology.

Useful errors

Thus Bruner is interested in sequencing, but not the step-by-step sequencing that behaviorists prefer. He has little interest in minimizing errors, a principle that is basic to Skinner's approach. Bruner believes errors are useful for maintaining interest and stimulating hypotheses, if students are not made to feel ashamed of their mistakes or taught with methods that emphasize speed in covering material rather than success in developing a deep understanding of it. Also, even though he acknowledged the value of organizing the content to be taught, he noted that often there is no one best way to structure it and that there are limits to what can be accomplished by imposing structure externally. He believes that learners will retain more if allowed to organize material according to their own interests.

Discovery Learning

Bruner believes that much of the learning that is most meaningful to learners is developed through discoveries that occur during exploration motivated by curiosity. He would like schools to provide learners with more opportunities to expand their knowledge by developing and testing hypotheses rather than merely reading or listening to the teacher. Consequently, he advocates instructional methods that encourage students to learn by discovery. Opportunities to manipulate objects actively and transform them through direct action are valuable for inducing curiosity, as are activities that encourage students to search, explore, analyze, or otherwise process input rather than merely respond to it. In theory, such opportunities not only will increase students' knowledge about the topic at hand but also will help them to develop generalized learning-to-learn strategies useful for discovering knowledge in other situations.

Man: A Course of Study (MACOS) Bruner's ideas about discovery learning are illustrated in *Man: A Course of Study*, a social studies program for the middle grades. MACOS deals with the varieties of human beings and their habitats, cultures, and behaviors. It relies on novelty, incongruity, and contrast to stimulate students' curiosity and cause them to address the content in an inquiry-oriented mode. Rather than routinely presenting information and then moving to application, MACOS frequently introduces topics by presenting application problems and inviting students to formulate guiding principles and generate possible solutions on their own before reading further. Thus the students might be invited to explore questions such as "How does one get through territory where there are strong predators?" before reading information on this topic. Perhaps the classic example is the "fill-in-the-map" exercise in which students are given maps indicating the physical features of an area (temperatures, rainfall, elevations, and locations of natural resources and waterways) and are invited to speculate about the locations of the capital city and the major seaport, the economic emphases likely to develop in particular regions or the placement and functions of the major highways or railroads. Later, the students are given more detailed maps indicating the development that actually occurred. This feedback generally confirms the usefulness of the principles of geography being learned but also introduces complexity by showing that exceptions can occur due to unique local factors (capitals are not always the largest or most centrally located cities).

Use of novelty

MACOS uses novelty to stimulate curiosity by exposing students to unfamiliar people, places, and practices. It also helps students to structure the content by repeatedly calling attention to four kinds of contrast: humans versus animals, humans versus prehistorical evolutionary precursors, contemporary humans versus primitive humans, and adults versus children. In general, the program tries to provide students with models to use in analyzing the social world, to impart respect for the capacities of humans as a continually evolving species, and to develop students' confidence in their own thinking and problem-solving abilities.

Evaluation of program

MACOS is difficult to evaluate because little research is available on it and because attention to its pedagogical features and effects has been obscured by political controversy over its emphasis on evolution and its depictions of cultural practices that some consider immoral or unsuitable for presentation to children. MACOS has produced mixed responses among psychologists and educators. Supporters believe that it is one of the best programs available. Others see it as just another social studies curriculum, and still others criticize it for depending too much on student initiative and discovery or, conversely, for not going far enough in this direction. Many social studies educators like its use of novelty and emphasis on discovery, but dislike its content, wanting more emphasis on contemporary societies and issues.

Evaluation data on MACOS suggest that students enjoy it and achieve at levels comparable to those of students using more traditional curricula (Cole & Lacefield, 1980; Cort & Peskowitz, 1977). Since it is a classical example of the discovery learning approach, you might examine MACOS if this approach appeals to you. If you are interested more in the primary grades, you might read *Young Children Reinvent Arithmetic* (Kamii & DeClark, 1985). This volume describes a discovery learning approach to early mathematics instruction, although the approach is based more on the theorizing of Piaget than of Bruner.

OTHER APPROACHES TO DISCOVERY LEARNING

Many other approaches to education have been developed at least in part as efforts to foster learning by discovery (Shulman & Keislar, 1966). Unlike MACOS, they tend to be general approaches rather than curriculum packages designed for specific courses.

Open Education

During the 1960s, ideas about how children learn drawn from Piaget, Bruner, and other psychologists were combined with ideas about design and management of schools drawn from the British "infant" (elementary) schools to form what became known as the open education movement. In contrast to the traditional model of whole-class instruction featuring expository lecturing, recitation, and individual seatwork, *open education* calls for (1) more flexible use of space (replacing anchored desks with light chairs and small tables that can be rearranged easily to create a variety of settings and using bookcases, area rugs, movable room dividers, and special equipment to create learning centers), (2) planning for a range

The open classroom allows small-group and individual activities to occur simultaneously.

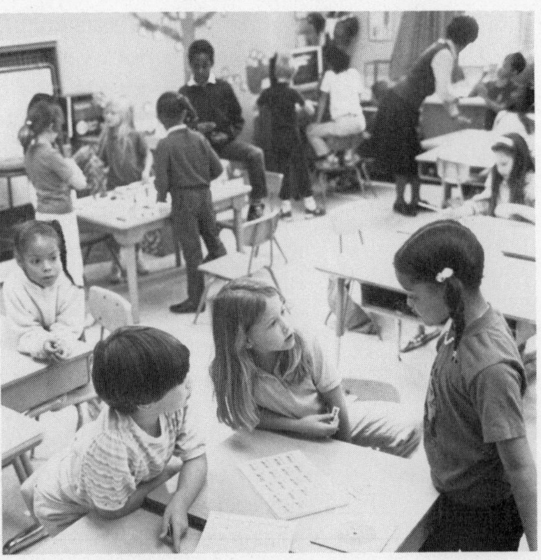

of activities to occur simultaneously as students learn through exploration and discovery on their own or with peers, and (3) readiness to respond to students' initiatives and help them to pursue their individual interests.

Open-space architecture

Open education philosophy and teaching methods should not be confused with *open-space architecture* (construction of schools without stationary internal walls so that the space can be used flexibly). The two concepts are distinct: Open educational practices can be implemented in self-contained classrooms, and traditional group-based instruction can be conducted in open-space settings (Gump, 1980).

Partially as a result of strong advocacy (see Barth, 1972), the open education philosophy achieved considerable popularity among teacher–educators in the 1960s and 1970s and was implemented to some degree in many elementary schools. Many contemporary elementary classrooms are equipped with learning centers offering hands-on experiences, although these centers are usually intended to supplement rather than replace traditional group instruction.

The effects of open education are difficult to evaluate. Most studies have been small and poorly controlled, so that any effects observed could have been due to preexisting teacher differences rather than to the introduction of open education principles, or they could have been short-term novelty effects rather than more permanent changes due to the principles themselves. Also, "open education" means different things to different people, and it is difficult to know which dimensions of the philosophy were being implemented in particular studies (Marshall, 1981).

Consequently, there has been a great deal of disagreement about the effects of open education. Some reviewers (Horwitz, 1979; Walberg, Schiller, & Haertel, 1979) have concluded that there are no differences between open and traditional education in effects on student achievement but that open education improves affective outcomes (students' attitudes, self-concepts, curiosity, etc.). Others reported no trend at all (Lukasevich & Gray, 1978) or minor differences favoring traditional classes on achievement measures but open classes on affective measures (Gage, 1985; Giaconia & Hedges, 1982; Peterson, 1979). The largest study completed to date (Hayes & Day, 1980), which covered ninety-six third-grade classrooms in eighteen schools, found no relationship between degree of "openness" and measures of student achievement, self-perceptions, and school attendance. Our impression is that the smaller and less well controlled studies tend to favor open education (especially on affective measures) but that the larger and better controlled studies tend to favor traditional education (especially on achievement measures).

Combining open with traditional approaches

In any case, it appears that well-planned and coordinated combinations of traditional approaches with open approaches work better than extreme versions of either philosophy. Within such balanced approaches, students receive both expository instruction and opportunities to explore and discover, but most discovery learning occurs during planned activities designed to guide them toward particular discoveries. To implement open education, see Brown and Precious (1973) or Silberman (1973).

Inquiry Training

Suchman (1966) has developed principles for teaching the information-processing, thinking, and analytic skills associated with scientific inquiry. He believes that students will not engage in inquiry, especially when it is new to them, unless they are both motivated to do so and taught how. He suggested stimulating curiosity by presenting puzzles or discrepancies, helping students to realize that they can pose and attempt to answer questions for themselves, and arming them with the skills for doing so. Such skills include verification (checking facts), experimentation (isolating particular aspects of the problem to be pursued one at a time), and constructive hypothesis generation (working systematically from the information given rather than guessing randomly).

Phases of inquiry training

Weil and Joyce (1978) identified five phases in inquiry training: (1) presentation of puzzling stimuli, (2) data gathering, (3) experimentation, (4) explaining the problem, and (5) consolidation. The students learn first to establish the facts, then determine relevant questions, and then develop ways to pursue those questions and build explanations for the results they discover. The teacher structures the learning context and supervises the social system, but allows students' ideas to control the intellectual development of work on the problem. Weil and Joyce (1978) suggested the following principles: (1) encourage students to ask questions that can be answered yes or no (more general questions are harder to verify); (2) when students raise open questions, ask them to rephrase the questions in terms that can be verified; (3) help students to recognize when they make statements that have not been verified; (4) use and encourage the use of inquiry language (i.e., call informed guesses hypotheses, describe students' explanations as theories); (5) do not approve or reject students' theories; (6) encourage them to state their theories and assumptions clearly and to make specific plans for testing them; (7) encourage interaction among students.

Results from research on inquiry teaching are mixed. The approach appears to be beneficial when implemented properly, especially for cognitively mature students who are pursuing complex content. It is one way to prepare students to explore and discover on their own as opposed to merely encouraging them to do so.

Simulation Games

Bruner's *Toward a Theory of Instruction* (1966) was influential in encouraging educators to use simulation activities as vehicles for promoting discovery learning (Boocock & Schild, 1968; Groff & Render, 1983). Some of them are role-play activities based on actual events, such as when social studies students are divided into groups representing various special interests in a state legislature and invited to propose and seek support for budget-allocation recommendations, or science students are assigned to groups to work on problems such as figuring out how to use X-rays to kill cancerous growths without killing the patient.

Students generally respond enthusiastically to simulation games, although they do not always generalize the principles they use in the games to other circumstances. The most helpful simulations appear to be those that include information-processing opportunities—chances for students to develop concepts or strategies that can be used in solving a range of problems (Coleman et al., 1973).

Cohen and Bradley (1978) found that the benefits claimed for simulation games were not supported by convincing data. Most studies were brief and confined to just a small part of the school day, so that positive results might have been due to novelty effects. Students who spent most of the day in simulation activities might eventually welcome something else.

Cohen and Bradley assessed the impact in eight fifth- and sixth-grade classes of a simulation game that included both information-processing opportunities and experiential learning. Control teachers taught the regular lesson on map skills from the textbook, using normal procedures over four consecutive sixty-minute periods. Experimental teachers played the game "Phantom Submarine." The game assumes that a submarine has been sunk off the coast of Florida and lies 200 feet below the surface but not on the floor of the ocean. The ship carries 200 tons of mercury and is believed to contain a self-triggering device that will cause it to explode if it is entered or brought to the surface. The ship is floating, however, so it may strike an object and self-destruct even if left alone. John L. Greedy, a treasure hunter, wants to salvage the submarine because the mercury is worth two million dollars. However, if the mercury should be set loose, great damage will be done to fish and plant life. The game builds toward a simulated meeting of the World Pollution Control Committee where students play assigned roles to discuss the problem and try to agree on a solution.

The class is divided into several five-person groups that begin by compiling knowledge about currents, the route of the Gulf Stream, mountain ranges on the ocean floor, and so on. Individuals gather this information, share it with the group, and fill in verbal and graphic material on their own map cards, so eventually, all students in each group have the same information. The group decides what to do with the submarine. Finally, the students role play the conference and try to reach a conclusion.

In this study, teachers learned to play the game and then used it as a vehicle for teaching map skills in four sixty-minute periods. Both groups were tested immediately following the unit and again two weeks later. There were no significant differences on the tests administered immediately following the unit, but two weeks later, the map skills of the control students had declined whereas those of the experimental students had improved. Cohen and Bradley suggested that the experience with using information from maps to solve the problem of the submarine may have caused the experimental students to develop a theory about map symbols and usage that enabled them to recognize previous errors more easily and thus to improve their performance over time.

Evaluation

Despite these positive findings, Cohen and Bradley suggested that simulation should not be the only method used in social studies courses but should be combined with more traditional methods. For more information about simulation methods, see issues of the journal *Simulations and Games*. For ideas about how to evaluate the potential value and application of proposed simulation activities, see Orbach (1977).

When to Use Discovery Learning

Discovery learning approaches were developed from the premise that learning that occurs through self-motivated, active exploration of areas of personal interest is especially likely to be retained in long-term memory and integrated with previous learning. Despite widespread acceptance of this premise, however, there has not been widespread acceptance of discovery learning principles as the primary approach to instruction in classrooms. Ausubel (1963), Skinner (1968), and others have noted important limitations on the discovery approach: (1) true discoveries are rare, and most of them are made by the brightest and most motivated students, (2) discovery learning is uncertain and inefficient compared to more direct instruction, (3) it places the teacher in the unnatural role of withholding information from students who are experiencing frustration or "discovering" mistaken notions that will have to be "unlearned" later, and (4) it needs careful planning and structuring—providing the students with clear goals and with needed information or skills, guiding their exploration with cues or questions, and finishing with a review to make sure that what they learn is complete and accurate.

Limitations of discovery learning

Another problem is that many discovery activities appear to be more trouble than they are worth. Inquiry-oriented science curricula, for example, often include an experiment calling for comparison of plants grown in sunlight with plants grown in the dark. This experiment often does not work because the plants raised in the light fail to thrive for some reason or because the other plants are not sufficiently protected from light or are not left in the dark long enough. Furthermore, even if it does work and the expected differences in plant growth appear, the results are anticlimactic because they are so predictable and because they must be related to concepts taught several weeks earlier (Anderson & Smith, 1987).

Expository instruction

Even direct comparisons with expository instruction do not always favor discovery learning. First, expository instruction is more efficient, especially if the material is well organized and geared to the students' levels of development. Second, skilled teachers usually can create student motivation to learn about academic topics, even where none existed before. Third, because discovery learning approaches assume a great deal about student motivation, background knowledge, and learning-to-learn skills, they are difficult to implement. Thus total reliance on discovery learning approaches is rarely if ever feasible.

Uses for discovery learning

On the other hand, although data on the matter are spotty and provide only mixed support (Ausubel & Robinson, 1969; Breaux, 1975; Hermann, 1969; Strike, 1975), discovery learning does appear to be useful, and perhaps optimal, when students have the necessary motivation and skills.

Thus it is wise to build in exploration and discovery opportunities whenever it is important that students be able to apply and not just understand the principles they are learning. In addition, discovery learning is essential for objectives involving problem solving or creativity.

Wise teachers will supplement expository instruction and practice exercises with frequent opportunities for students to discuss what they are learning, apply it in ways that reveal the linkages between abstract principles and concrete experience, and engage in various simulations and inquiry activities. Such teachers will also capitalize on the "teachable moments" that arise when students ask a question or make a comment about a lesson topic. By incorporating such comments into the lesson and by answering such questions, redirecting them to the class, or arranging to follow up on them later, teachers can provide students with information that the students want, when they want it. These brief departures from lesson plans encourage active inquiry and are greatly appreciated by students (Evertson et al., 1980; Flanders, 1970).

AUSUBEL AND MEANINGFUL RECEPTION LEARNING

For efficiency reasons, most knowledge and comprehension-level learning is accomplished through expository instruction rather than discovery methods. In David Ausubel's terms, it involves *meaningful reception learning*, in which the entire content is presented to the learner in final form. The teacher's task is to present the material in ways that encourage learners to "make sense" of it by relating it to what they already know (not just memorizing it in rote fashion). Compared to rote learning, such meaningful reception learning will be retained longer, be better integrated with other knowledge, and be more readily available for application.

Ausubel's affinity with Bruner and other cognitive structuralists is seen in his famous statement that "the most important factor influencing the meaningful learning of any new idea is the state of the individual's existing cognitive structure at the time of learning" (Ausubel & Robinson, 1969, p. 143). Like Bruner, Ausubel emphasized that school learning should involve organized bodies of knowledge structured around key concepts. In contrast to Bruner's emphasis on guiding students to structure the content themselves, however, Ausubel stressed ways that teachers can structure the content for the students (Ausubel, 1963; Ausubel & Robinson, 1969; Ausubel, Novak, & Hanesian, 1978).

Subordinate and superordinate concepts

Ausubel started with the notion that knowledge is organized into *hierarchical structures* in which *subordinate concepts* are not only related to one another but subsumed under higher-level *superordinate concepts*. Even if we gradually forget details, we tend to remember key ideas associated with a particular cognitive structure and to retain the structure itself. The structure provides scaffolding that supports retention of the information as an organized body of knowledge and functions as a frame within which to interpret related new knowledge or efficiently relearned forgotten knowledge. Even if you do not remember the details of Bloom's taxonomy, for example, or Gagné's learning hierarchies, you are likely to remember that there are many types and levels of learning that need to be considered in planning instruction.

Signaling

Mayer (1984) has elaborated on Ausubel's ideas by developing signaling techniques for calling learners' attention to the structural features of presentations. Specifically, *signaling techniques* refer to the placement within a passage of noncontent words that serve to emphasize the passage's conceptual structure or organization. Four major types of signals are (1) *Specifications of the structure of relations* (cues such as "first," "second," "third," or "the problem is . . . and the solution is"); (2) *premature presentations* of abstracted or paraphrased statements of key information that will follow ("the main ideas to be discussed are . . ."); (3) *summary statements* (similar to premature presentations except that they occur at the ends of passages); and (4) *point words* that indicate the author's perspective or emphasize important information ("more importantly," "unfortunately").

Such signaling helps make the structure of a passage more clear and provides a conceptual framework for learners to use in identifying important information and organizing it coherently. Experiments have shown that passages that include such signaling elements are learned better than the same passages without such signaling (Loman & Mayer, 1983; Mayer, Dyck, & Cook, 1984).

Advance Organizers

Ausubel stressed organizing content in logical ways and helping learners to recognize this organization by presenting outlines, noting transitions between parts, and including summaries at the end. In addition, he advocated presenting *advance organizers*, superordinate concepts within which learners can subsume the new material and relate it to what they already know. Advance organizers are not conventional previews or summaries that briefly state the main points in a presentation. Instead, advance organizers characterize the material to be learned at a higher level of abstraction, generality, or inclusiveness. For example, Ausubel (1960) had college students read a 500-word advance organizer before reading a 2,500-word text on the metallurgical properties of carbon steel. The organizer discussed similarities and differences between metals and alloys and their respective advantages and weaknesses. It presented ideas relevant for understanding the longer passage but did not include material given in the passage itself. Students who read the advance organizer retained more of the passage than students who read a 500-word passage on the historical development of methods used for processing iron and steel. Although both passages were relevant to the general topic of steel, only the advance organizer presented superordinate concepts within which students could subsume the longer material (the advance organizer reminded them that alloys exist in addition to pure metals and that different properties affect their usefulness for various purposes; then, the longer passage described the properties of a partciular alloy—carbon steel).

Advance organizers versus previews or summaries

Instead of merely summarizing the content in briefer form, advance organizers characterize the general nature of the text (such as by describing its purpose and the line of argument taken to accomplish it) and provide superordinate concepts within which the text can be subsumed. This does not mean that advance organizers should be highly abstract or difficult to understand, however. To be useful, they must be stated in terms already familiar to the learners (Anderson, 1984a).

Ausubel believes that advance organizers are especially useful when the material to be learned is not well organized and learners lack the knowledge needed to be able to organize it well for themselves. Research has supported these predictions (Ausubel, 1978; Luiten, Ames, & Ackerson, 1980; Mayer, 1979a, 1979b; Tudor, 1986).

Other varieties of organizers

Other research indicates that organizers can facilitate learning when placed either before or after the text (Alexander, Frankiewicz, & Williams, 1979) and that other types of organizers besides those described by Ausubel can be effective. They include organizers presented in oral rather than written form (Alexander, Frankiewicz, & Williams, 1979), organizers that present key terms or principles rather than characterizing the material to be learned with reference to previous knowledge (Mayer, 1984), and organizers that present models or illustrations rather than expository explanations (Abel & Kulhavy, 1986; Mayer, 1984). In general, concrete models, analogies, or examples; sets of higher-order rules; or discussions of main themes in familiar terms are more effective organizers than specific factual prequestions, outlines, summaries, or directions to pay attention to specific key facts or terms (Mayer, 1979b).

Postlesson summaries and review questions

Besides advance organizers, Ausubel has studied postlesson summaries and review questions as devices to help students integrate what they learn. His work has provided much support for the advice "Tell them what you are going to tell them; then tell them; then tell them what you told them." For teachers, this would mean the following: (1) Start lessons with advance organizers or at least with previews that include general principles, outlines, or questions that establish a learning set; (2) briefly describe learning objectives and alert students to key concepts; (3) present new material in small steps organized and sequenced logically; (4) elicit student responses regularly in order to stimulate active learning and ensure that each step is mastered before moving to the next; (5) finish with a review of the main points, stressing general integrative concepts; and (6) follow up the lesson with questions or assignments that require students to encode material in their own words and apply or extend it to new contexts.

Linking the New to the Familiar

Various investigators who share Ausubel's concern with structuring content to encourage meaningful reception learning have studied other factors besides advance organizers and signaling of the organizational structure. These include analogies, metaphors, examples, and concrete models that help learners to link new concepts to familiar ones or to develop concrete referents for abstract concepts.

Analogies

Analogies help link the new to the familiar. Mayer (1984) explained the principles of radar by drawing analogies between the reflection of radio waves and the reflection of sound waves that underlies familiar echo phenomena. Royer and Cable (1975) taught the crystalline structure of molecules by drawing analogies to a *model* constructed from tinker toys. *Diagrams* or *flow charts* showing simplified models of biological systems or the working of machines can make it easier to learn such information than it is when the presentation is restricted to verbal information. In general, analogies that help learners link the new to the familiar can be expected to facilitate learning (Hayes & Tierney, 1982; Mayer, 1979a), although care must be taken to ensure that any potentially misleading aspects of the analogy do not lead to misconceptions in the learners.

Teaching for Transfer

Ausubel stressed that learning should be available for transfer to new contexts. That is, besides being able to remember and apply it within the context in which it was originally learned, students should be able to generalize the learning to other relevant contexts and to activate and build on it when extending their learning to new areas. Transfer of existing knowledge to new situations simplifies the task of learning in such new situations.

Vertical transfer

Transfer may be vertical or lateral. *Vertical transfer* is desired when teaching hierarchically organized skills in which new levels are built on lower levels. To promote vertical transfer, Ausubel recommended following a sequential organization if this applies to the material, making sure that learners have whatever knowledge they need at each step, consolidating learning and ensuring mastery before going on to higher steps, stressing general and integrative principles, and following a pattern of progressive differentiation in presenting the content. When new material may appear to conflict with what has already been taught, it will be important to reconcile the apparent conflicts so that the new material can be integrated within the cognitive structures already developed.

Lateral transfer

Lateral transfer occurs when knowledge is used to speed up or simplify learning in some other domain. Although Ausubel recognized limits on how much lateral transfer can be expected, he believes that teachers can promote lateral transfer by concentrating on underlying principles and generalizations and by giving students opportunities to apply material in realistic situations. He also suggested emphasizing aspects of subject matter that have the most potential for lateral transfer such as Latin-language roots of modern English words or general logic and problem-solving applications of mathematics.

Research has confirmed many of these ideas. Bromage and Mayer (1981) found that organizing a technical passage around general principles produced better transfer to problem solving than organizing it by topic. Similarly, Mayer (1975) found that organizing a mathematics lesson to move from familiar prerequisite concepts toward formal definitions and algorithms produced better transfer to problem solving than organizing it to move from the formal to the familiar. In general, the text-structuring factors stressed by Ausubel appear to be especially important for ensuring that learners grasp the main ideas in a presentation and are able to transfer and apply them later (Mayer, 1979a).

Summary

Cognitive structuralists hold that meaningful learning involves not only understanding individual facts and principles but noting the relationships between them and building cognitive structures to retain information in an organized way. These theorists approach instruction by developing ways to teach or guide learners to discover key ideas that can be used to organize bodies of information.

The roots of the cognitive structuralist approach lie in gestalt psychology. Gestalt psychologists noted that perception is organized into meaningful patterns structured holistically. They conducted experiments on topics such as figure-ground discrimination and contrast effects, showed that people impose good form on stimulus input, and demonstrated that learning can occur by discovery achieved through sudden insight.

Jerome Bruner combined ideas from gestalt psychology with ideas from the study of cognitive development in his approach to education. He noted that humans attend to input selectively and organize it into categories that become increasingly better integrated, differentiated, and mediated by language with development. Early knowledge is mostly in the enactive mode, but children later become capable of understanding and manipulating knowledge in the iconic mode via pictures, images, or memories of previously experienced objects or events, and beginning around adolescence, they become able to represent knowledge in the symbolic mode and thus to understand and manipulate abstract concepts.

Bruner believes that any subject matter can be taught to any learners in some intellectually honest way. He advocated the spiral curriculum, in which students are exposed to the same topic several times but in more abstract and sophisticated ways each time. He suggested that teachers instruct by stimulating students' curiosity and guiding them to explore and discover on their own. His approach is illustrated in the social studies program *Man: A Course of Study*.

Discovery learning approaches have also been featured in the open education movement, in Suchman's Inquiry Training approach, and in the simulation games approach to instruction. Discovery learning approaches tend to be enjoyable to students and useful for promoting certain higher level objectives and thus should be used to some degree in most classrooms. However, they are time consuming and involve other practical limitations, so few teachers will be able to use them as their primary approach to instruction.

David Ausubel and others have developed cognitive structuralist approaches to promoting efficient meaningful reception learning through well-structured presentations. Such presentations begin with advance organizers or at least previews that include general principles, outlines, or questions that establish the desired learning set in the students; describe learning objectives and alert the students to key concepts; present new material in small steps organized logically and sequenced in ways that are easy to follow; elicit student responses regularly to stimulate active learning and ensure that each step is mastered before moving to the next; finish with a review of the main points, stressing general integrative concepts; and follow up with questions or assignments that require learners to encode the material in their own words and apply it to new contexts. Analogies, metaphors, examples, or concrete models are used to help learners link the new to the familiar, and the instruction plan includes provision for vertical and lateral transfer when this is part of the overall objective.

Questions and Problems

1. Describe in your own words the differences between behavioral and cognitive approaches to learning. In contrast to the first two chapters in this unit, what new emphasis is placed on learning in the present chapter?
2. Define the term *gestalt psychology*. What is a gestalt? How is the gestalt psychology viewpoint useful to teachers?
3. Reexamine the beliefs of Thorndike, Skinner, and Bruner. Given their beliefs, what would typical homework assignments look like from each point of view? In particular, what might the length and type of these assignments be?
4. Assume that you are going to teach the following: Pledge of Allegiance, Bill of Rights, and free-form ice skating. For which of these learning outcomes would a cognitive model be preferable? Could the same learning model be equally appropriate for each outcome? Why or why not? Specifically, if you were teaching the Bill of Rights from a Skinnerian point of view, how would you proceed? What if you were teaching it from the viewpoint of Bruner?
5. Define *inquiry training* in your own terms. If you were going to teach about the presidential election in American politics and Boyle's law in physics, would it be equally important to use inquiry procedures? Why or why not?
6. Think about teaching your children to play either soccer or monopoly and then write an advance organizer that would convey the structure of what you would teach.
7. Can students really be taught, or must they learn on their own? Just how much can teachers realistically expect to accomplish?
8. Many behaviorists are offended by the tendency of discovery-learning theorists to view themselves as humane rather than mechanistic, so they counter by claiming that it is cruel to force students to discover things on their own when you could save them trouble by telling or showing them. Do you agree? Why or why not?
9. Are there times when it is better for teachers to prevent errors and other times when it is better to allow students to make them? What are some specific examples?

Case Studies

AN ACT OF DISCOVERY. Mr. Wilson believes that his American government students passively accept and take notes about whatever he says but do not carefully evaluate this input or integrate it with their prior knowledge. He wants to get them to think more actively and make discoveries on their own. One of the points to be made in the next unit is that most elected officials holding national office are lawyers. How might he arrange for students to discover this fact and the reasons for it on their own?

JUST A GAME? In his government class, Mr. Johnson uses a simulation game in which students are assigned to act as state legislators working out the compromises needed to pass the annual budget. There are five groups, each representing a different area with unique political interests (the big city, the tourist-oriented counties along the lake, etc.). Each group is assigned goals that would involve capturing more than its share of the budget for purposes favored in its geographical region. The budget cannot accommodate all of each group's target goals, so it will be necessary to make compromises and to form coalitions to get as much as possible for one's own group.

The game takes place over the course of a week. By Wednesday, Mr. Johnson is pleased in most respects. The students find the game absorbing and challenging, to the point that they are getting together at lunch time to plot strategy and calling up members of other teams after school in an attempt to cut deals. Mr. Johnson is bothered, though, about the personal competitiveness that has crept into the game. The more assertive students have emerged as group leaders and are working hard to outsmart one another. Despite his efforts to keep students aware that they are role playing state legislators representing constituencies, most interaction takes place at the level of whether Mary Barnett and her group will outfox Greg Richards and his group, rather than whether the farming interests will be able to pursue their agenda at the expense of the big city interests. In short, although the game clearly has great motivational value, Mr. Johnson wonders if it has enough pedagogical value to justify the time spent on it.

What would you tell Mr. Johnson if he explained this to you as a fellow teacher? Should he use the game again next year? Should he do anything right now to try to influence what occurs during the rest of the week?

CHAPTER

The Information-Processing View of Learning

CHAPTER OUTLINE

OBJECTIVES

When you have mastered the material in this chapter, you will be able to

1. Describe the information-processing approach to learning and explain how it differs from the behaviorist approach and the cognitive structuralist approach
2. Identify similarities and differences between associationist theories and constructivist theories
3. Differentiate semantic memory from episodic memory
4. Define the key concepts in the three-stage information-processing model—sensory reg-

ister, short-term or working memory, rehearsal, chunking, long-term memory, levels of processing—and explain how it depicts information processing, storage, and retrieval
5. Define the schema concept and explain how schema activation facilitates comprehension
6. Describe the factors known to affect rote learning and explain the nature of their effects: degree of meaningfulness, serial position (primacy and recency effects), stimulus distinctiveness, practice, transfer (positive versus negative, specific versus general), interference (proactive versus reactive), organization of input, levels of processing, state- or context-dependency, and use of mnemonics
7. Describe and give examples of commonly used mnemonics—place method, link method, peg method, keyword method, elaboration method, pictorial mnemonics, rhymes, acronyms, and visual imagery
8. Describe the factors known to affect meaningful verbal learning—abstraction of the gist of the passage, levels of organization of the passage, activation of schemas and prior knowledge, drawing of inferences, filtering of input through preexisting misconceptions, responding to structuring and organizational factors built into the text, and generating mathemagenic activities—and explain the nature of their effects
9. Define adjunct questions and state the relative advantages and disadvantages of prequestions and postquestions
10. Describe the major findings of information-processing theorists' research on reading, on the behavior of novices and experts, and on cognitive simulation and artificial intelligence

The *cognitive structuralists,* described in the previous chapter, emphasize that school learning involves acquiring organized bodies of knowledge, and teaching involves expository instruction or guided discovery designed to call the learners' attention to key ideas and structural features around which the information is organized. Other cognitively oriented theorists place more emphasis on the learner than on the content to be learned. For these *information-processing theorists,* learning involves actively processing, storing, and retrieving information, and teaching involves helping learners to develop their information-processing skills and apply them systematically when mastering the curriculum. In short, cognitive structuralists emphasize the ways that subject matter has been structured in the underlying academic disciplines, whereas information-processing theorists emphasize cognitive structures built up by the learners themselves. For the most part, the two groups of theorists deal with different issues and are complementary rather than competing as contributors to a cognitive account of learning and instruction.

INFORMATION-PROCESSING THEORIES: OVERVIEW

Organization of knowledge

Following the theories of Jean Piaget and others, information-processing theorists assume that humans develop increasingly differentiated and integrated cognitive structures that represent and organize their knowledge.

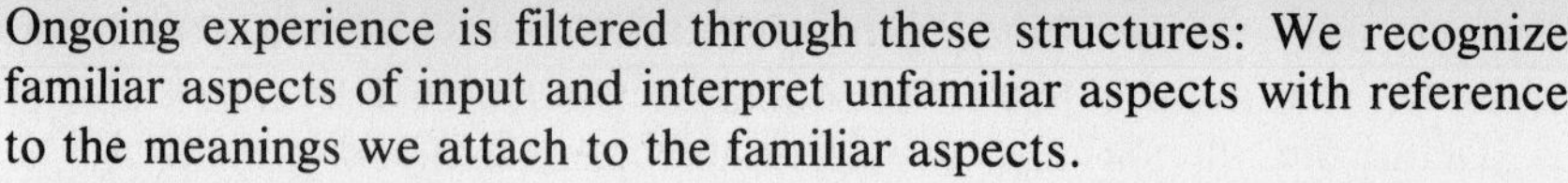

Ongoing experience is filtered through these structures: We recognize familiar aspects of input and interpret unfamiliar aspects with reference to the meanings we attach to the familiar aspects.

Interaction between learner and input

Information-processing theorists have shown that relationships between particular items of input and the learner's larger cognitive structures are surprisingly active and continuous. Because perception of new experience is filtered through existing cognitive structures, and because new input is often open to multiple interpretations, the process of making sense of experience can be seen as an interaction between the learner and the input rather than as a one-way effect of the input on the learner. Thus in reading this textbook you do not merely take in fully specified information that has only one meaning. Instead, you interact with the material by filling in bits of meaning that are inferred but not spelled out explicitly, interpreting the probable meanings when you come across unfamiliar terms, relating the content to your prior experience and knowledge, and making decisions about what content is especially important to remember either for a test or for future application. You and your classmates are all using the same book; yet each of you will attend to a unique subset of the content as being of focal importance, and even when several of you focus on the same content, each will have a unique interpretation of that content and will associate it with a unique set of prior experiences and related concepts.

Furthermore, your memory of the content itself or your ideas about its meanings may change over time if you undergo significant development in key cognitive structures such as your general self-concept, your ideas about what schools should accomplish with students, or your notions about what makes a good teacher. For example, if you have not yet taught, you may think that classroom management is the most important topic in this book, and you may find some of what is said about it to be surprising, such as the notion that skills for keeping students engaged in well-paced lessons and well-chosen assignments are more important than skills for handling defiance. As you gain experience and progress through the developmental stages that new teachers typically go through, however, your ideas probably will change. If you should review this text a few years from now, much of the material on classroom management will seem "obvious" and old hat, and much of the material on learning and instruction will seem more relevant and important.

Theory and research about information processing as it affects learning are presented in this chapter and the next. The present chapter discusses methods of promoting rote learning (when necessary) and meaningful learning (whenever possible). Information about more general methods of teaching students to read with comprehension, to study systematically, and to solve problems is presented in the following chapter.

ASSOCIATIONIST AND CONSTRUCTIVIST VIEWS OF MEMORY

Most research on human memory has been guided by one of two influential types of theory. *Associationist theories* were the first to become

Associationist theories

well established. These theories assume that the retention of new learning depends on the nature and strength of associations between that new learning and previous learning stored in memory and that forgetting is caused by interference from competing associations. Much of the research supporting associationist theories has involved rote learning of relatively meaningless and disconnected input.

Constructivist theories

More recent research has led to the development of *constructivist theories,* in which learners are seen as constructing meaning from input by processing it through existing cognitive structures and then retaining it in long-term memory where it remains open to further processing and possible reconstruction. Constructivists assume that retention of new learning depends on the degree to which learners can activate existing cognitive structures or construct new ones to subsume the new input, and they assume that material stored in memory can be distorted as well as forgotten. Most research supporting constructivist theories has involved meaningful learning of connected discourse, typically written prose. The classical work of Ebbinghaus and of Bartlett illustrates the associationist and the constructivist approaches.

Ebbinghaus

Ebbinghaus (1885) pioneered what became the associationist approach. He published one of the first treatises on learning and memory that was based on empirical data (records of his own attempts to memorize various types of input under various conditions). He wanted to study "pure" memory uncontaminated by previous learning, so he avoided connected discourse and instead used nonsense syllables (such as *dev* or *lup* in English) that are relatively free of associations to prior knowledge. His experiments showed that learning improved when material was rehearsed overtly rather than merely read silently and when practice was distributed over several shorter trials rather than massed into a few lengthy trials.

Serial-position effects

He also discovered *serial-position effects:* Material at the beginning and end is memorized more quickly than material in the middle. You may have noticed these effects yourself in memorizing poems, literary passages, or even lecture notes.

Forgetting curves

Ebbinghaus also was among the first to note the relationship between time and learning. He showed that increases in practice time led to increases in performance, although less so as practice time increased and he neared his peak performance level. Graphs illustrating these relationships were among the first *learning curves.* Ebbinghaus also illustrated *forgetting curves:* forgetting is rapid in the early minutes and hours following learning but much slower thereafter (Figure 9.1).

Interference theory

Ebbinghaus adopted the *decay theory* of forgetting, meaning he assumed that memory traces simply fade with time. However, later work caused the decay theory to be replaced by the *interference theory,* which holds that forgetting is caused by new learning that interferes with the ability to remember prior learning. For example, people who memorized a word list before going to bed at night could remember more after sleeping for eight hours than could people who first learned the original list, then

Figure 9.1 Curve of Forgetting, after Ebbinghaus

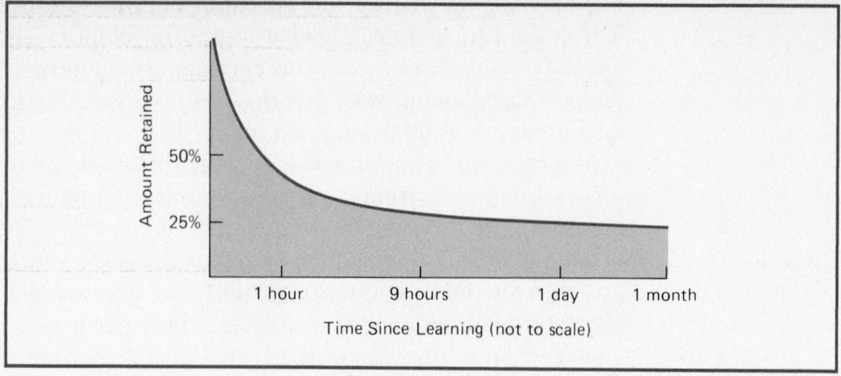

Source: From *The Brain Book* by Peter Russell. Copyright © 1979 by Peter Russell. Reprinted by permission of the publisher, E.P. Dutton, a division of Penguin Books USA, Inc.

learned several similar lists, and then were tested on the original list only an hour later (McGeoch & McDonald, 1931).

Interference theory still holds up well for rote learning of disconnected material. Here, subsequent learning of similar material interferes with memory for the original material. For the meaningful learning of connected discourse, however, subsequent learning of similar material is likely to facilitate memory for both sets of material (i.e., transfer effects rather than interference effects occur), if the previous learning is sufficiently clear, stable, and discriminable from the new learning (Ausubel & Robinson, 1969). The semantic network theory and the schema theory described in the following sections apply better to such meaningful learning than the interference theory does.

Bartlett

Constructivist approach

Bartlett (1932) pioneered what became the constructivist approach. He rejected Ebbinghaus's attempts to study "pure" memory in favor of studying memory as it occurs in ordinary living, and he rejected nonsense syllables in favor of more natural stimuli such as human faces, pictures, and connected discourse. In his best-known experiments, subjects read brief stories and then produced written versions from memory, first after a delay of fifteen minutes and then later at intervals of several weeks or months.

Bartlett's subjects read relatively long (200- to 500-word) stories and had relatively short practice times (they read each story twice). Consequently, decay theorists such as Ebbinghaus and associationists such as Thorndike would have predicted a great deal of forgetting due to the decay of associative memory traces that were weak to begin with. They would not have predicted significant distortion, however, because no other stories that might have produced interference effects were interpolated between the original reading and the subsequent attempt to reproduce the story from memory.

Bartlett's results did not confirm these associationist predictions. First, compared to the retention expected for relatively meaningless material of equal length, memory for these stories was good, especially for material related to the gist or main idea. Second, to the extent that story reconstructions were less than perfect, they often involved actual distortions and not just omissions or substitutions of equivalent phrases. For example, in one study, British subjects read about the cultural practices of certain North American Indians. In recounting the story, they tended to "normalize" it by substituting thematically similar but culturally more familiar content. Thus a seal hunt became a fishing trip, and a canoe became a boat.

"Effort after meaning"

On the basis of such evidence, Bartlett argued that subjects engaged in an "effort after meaning" when they read stories, seeking to understand them by connecting them to existing cognitive structures that he called *schemas*. They use this process to construct a meaning that is plausible and consistent, although it might not be the same meaning intended by the author. Thus there may be some distortion even in the original learning, especially if the story contains unfamiliar elements that can be understood only partially (by filtering them through familiar schemas). Furthermore, the stories as originally constructed can undergo *reconstruction* later if changes occur in the schemas to which the stories have been connected. Thus just as immediate memory measures may show distortion from the original story read only fifteen minutes earlier, measures taken weeks or months later may show additional distortion from the version produced on the immediate memory test. Subsequent research has supported and elaborated most of Bartlett's ideas (Spiro, 1977), although there is much more evidence that activation of relevant schemas affects how material is interpreted and encoded in the first place than there is that later schema change produces significant reconstruction of the originally encoded material (diSibio, 1982).

Story reconstruction

INFORMATION-PROCESSING MODELS OF LEARNING AND MEMORY

The contrasts between Ebbinghaus and Bartlett illustrate some of the diversity that exists in theory and research on human information processing and memory. A great deal of progress has been made since Ebbinghaus began his work; yet some questions have not received much attention, and some that have been studied heavily have yielded a range of theory and data that defy integration.

Most research has focused on the intentional learning of material communicated through oral or written language, partly because so much of formal education involves intentional verbal learning. Tulving (1985) suggested that memory for such language-based information, which he called *semantic memory,* is accomplished through systems of encoding, storage, and retrieval that differ from those used in accomplishing memory for personal experiences, which he calls *episodic memory*. He argued, for example, that episodic memory tends to be rich in concrete detail and stored in the form of sequences of events occurring at particular places

Episodic versus semantic memory

and times, whereas semantic memory is more abstract and stored in terms of logically related concepts and principles. This distinction is useful, although evidence for the larger theory behind it is mixed (Horton & Mills, 1984). Most of what is said in this chapter concerns semantic memory.

Intentional versus incidental learning

The chapter also concentrates on intentional rather than incidental learning. A great deal of incidental learning occurs in and out of school, but the factors that determine it are not well understood. Some aspects of experience, such as the timing, frequency, and spatial location of commonly experienced events, appear to be encoded automatically, without intention or apparent effort (Hasher & Zacks, 1984). Consequently, most people can tell about how many movies they have seen in the past year, where they sat when they last visited a favorite restaurant, or whether there are more lawyers or more tailors in the United States. Other things, such as the fact that attending to the structure of a text is useful for learning it, are learned incidentally by some people but not others, although the latter people can be taught this information and can use it intentionally thereafter.

What Is Encoded?

Dormant memories

Many people think of memory as a continuous, sequenced record of previous experience, akin to a videotape that begins with the earliest memory and proceeds linearly through the present. In this view, certain segments have become faded or forgotten, and some may be temporarily unavailable but potentially recoverable through hypnosis, psychotherapy, or encounters with cues such as old photos that stimulate long-dormant memories. This view fits many of the known facts about memory. Some people, for example, have eidetic imagery (popularly known as photographic memory) that allows them to visualize and retrieve previous experience in extreme detail. It is commonsensical to believe that everyone else's memory works the same way but not as efficiently. Furthermore, even people with ordinary memories can remember many details about important events in their lives or about what they were doing when they heard the news about the death of John Kennedy or John Lennon or about the Challenger disaster (Brown & Kulick, 1977).

Despite its face validity, this commonsense view of memory is not correct (Wickelgren, 1981). First, it applies only to episodic memory, not semantic memory. Even if the episodes in our personal lives were routinely encoded and stored as the equivalent of a running videotape, it would remain true that semantic memory for concepts and principles does not work this way. When we remember a principle, we remember it as a verbally phrased abstraction, not as an image of ourselves reliving the events that occurred when we originally learned the principle. Second, the model is not accurate even for episodic memory. Only certain experiences are encoded as "videotape segments" in the first place, and our memories for even these segments can be distorted (not just weakened) by the effects of later experiences (Loftus & Loftus, 1980). Also, our memories typically work with more speed and less evidence of sequential processing than the videotape model predicts.

Semantic memory is apparently encoded and stored in the form of ver-

Verbal abstractions

bal abstractions (concept definitions and statements of rules and principles), although with associated imagery or linkages to particular prior experiences. You know that 2 + 2 = 4, for example, and although you can apply this information in concrete situations and can visualize examples of it, it is stored and retrieved primarily as a verbal abstraction—a semantically encoded number fact. Information-processing theorists are concerned with how such input is encoded into semantic memory and what happens to it after it gets there.

Three-Stage Information-Processing Model

Most learning theorists, however much they disagree on other matters, accept a general three-stage model of human information processing that was developed using concepts borrowed from computer science (Table 9.1). Versions of the model have been offered by Atkinson and Shiffrin (1971), Kintsch (1977), Klatzky (1980), and Loftus and Loftus (1976). The model proposes that input first enters a *sensory register,* then is processed in *short-term memory,* and then is transferred to *long-term memory* for storage and potential retrieval. The three stages are seen as integrated subparts of a larger system for coding and transforming raw sensory information into forms that are more appropriate for integration with previously stored information. All of this is seen as occurring under the *executive control* of the person, whose *allocation of attention* determines which aspects of the great range of input available at any moment will be processed through the *limited capacity* of the system.

Sensory Register The sensory register receives input from the sensory receivers, primarily the eyes and ears. The neurological processing of this input is very brief, ranging from less than a second for visual sensations to about four seconds for auditory sensations, and then disappears through

TABLE 9.1 DIFFERENCES AMONG THE THREE STAGES OF MEMORY

Feature	Sensory Register	Short-Term	Long-Term
Inputting of information	Preattentive	Requires attention but very fast	Rehearsal, relatively slow
Maintenance of information	Not possible	Very brief (c. 15–20 sec.) unless continually rehearsed	Virtually unlimited
Capacity	Large	Small (7 ± 2 chunks)	Virtually unlimited
Loss of information	Decay	Displacement, possibly decay	Possibly no loss but loss of accessibility
Retrieval	Readout	Immediate	Varies depending on retrieval cues, organization, etc.

Source: F. Craik, and R. Lockhart, "Levels of Processing: A Framework for Memory Research." *Journal of Verbal Learning and Verbal Behavior II*, 1972. Reprinted with permission.

decay or replacement by new input. Consequently, input that enters the sensory register must be transferred to short-term memory if it is to receive focal attention and further processing. Information entering the sensory register is monitored at some level so that we can respond to it more actively if necessary. For example, drivers attending primarily to conversations with passengers nevertheless monitor and respond to traffic signals and road conditions. Most of this visual input never enters their short-term memories, however, so it decays quickly and is lost permanently.

Short-Term Memory and Rehearsal Sensory input that the person recognizes as important or interesting is transferred in the form of meaningful perceptions from the sensory register to short-term memory, where it can be retained longer (up to fifteen to twenty seconds without active *rehearsal* and indefinitely longer if the person keeps repeating it). However, short-term memory has a very limited capacity. Most people can remember about seven items (numbers, words, phrases) on a list without making errors or omissions if the items are unrelated to one another. Thus even a single phone number may be difficult to remember for even twenty seconds unless it is repeated continually or written down.

Chunking

Short-term memory capacity can be increased, however, by *chunking* the input into subsets. For example, the sequence 149210661984 is difficult to memorize as a string of twelve separate digits but easy to remember if divided into three chunks corresponding to three famous years (1492, 1066, 1984). Similarly, the words truck, cow, red, train, horse, green, plane, pig, and yellow are remembered much more easily if reorganized into chunks of three vehicles, three animals, and three colors than if memorized in serial order.

George Miller (1956) showed that the chunk, and not the individual term, is the real unit determining short-term memory capacity and that this capacity is remarkably stable. Whatever the stimuli, short-term memory capacity averages about seven chunks of information (plus or minus two, allowing for individual differences). This "7 ± 2" rule holds up well: Any particular chunk of information can be retained indefinitely in short-term memory through active rehearsal, but interference effects will cause memory failures once the limited capacity (7 ± 2 chunks) of short-term memory is exceeded.

Working memory

Short-term memory is called *working memory* by theorists interested in goal-directed thinking and problem solving (Baddeley, 1986). When engaged in such mental work, our ability to attend to a combination of input from the external environment and information retrieved from long-term memory is subject to the limit of 7 ± 2 chunks. Therefore, we cannot cope with complex cognitive tasks unless we can simplify them. Chunking is one way to simplify by reducing the load on working memory. Another is to break the task into subparts and take on one at a time. Another is to practice certain skills until they become automatic (i.e., they can be used with little conscious effort, thus freeing working memory for concentration on other aspects of the larger task). Most of us have learned to walk, eat, and drive automatically, so that we can think or carry on conversations while engaged in these activities.

Basic academic skills have become automatic for successful students. For example, skilled readers can use most of their working memory capacity for making sense out of what they are reading, because basic skills such as decoding words and instantly recognizing the meanings of familiar words have become automatic for them (Chall, 1983; Frederiksen, 1984). Most of the working-memory capacity of less skilled readers is needed just to decode and understand individual words, so that little is left for "putting it all together." As a result, their comprehension is poor unless they review the passage several times.

Case (1978) has stressed the importance of minimizing the load placed on students' working memory, especially when teaching young children or teaching complex new material. He suggested limiting the number of things that students must attend to at the same time, using familiar terms where possible (familiar input can be processed automatically and thus does not take up limited working memory capacity), and making cues as salient as possible (so that students will not have to devote much working memory capacity to the search for cues).

Long-Term Memory and Storage Information needed for future reference is stored in long-term memory, which theoretically has unlimited capacity and duration, barring senility or other physical malfunction. Some additions to long-term semantic memory are acquired through incidental learning, but many are the results of intentional efforts. If necessary, you can commit material to long-term memory through "brute force" by actively rehearsing it to the point of overlearning. This approach is inefficient and requires considerable effort and concentration, but it may be needed for memorizing such things as phone numbers or lock combinations.

Deeper levels of processing

The more efficient way to store material intentionally in long-term memory is to go beyond mere rehearsal by processing the information at deeper levels (Craik & Lockhart, 1972). Such *deeper levels of processing* may involve identifying or generating linkages between the new material and other material that is already retained in organized fashion, developing images to supplement the semantic form of the content, thinking about applications of the material, or answering questions about it.

Most theories about how material gets stored in long-term memory and what happens to it after it gets there fit within one of two families: semantic network theories and schema theories. Semantic network theories (Anderson & Bower, 1973; Collins & Loftus, 1975; Kintsch, 1974; Rumelhart, Lindsey, & Norman, 1972) are the modern counterparts of early associationist theories. They assume that concepts are stored in long-term memory within hierarchically organized networks of meaningful association. Some concepts have superordinate-subordinate relationships (animal–dog–collie). Concepts that are part of the same network share some degree of linkage, varying from direct and immediate associations (black–white) to more distant relationships (black–powder, black–blacksmith).

Within a network, the common attributes of the superordinate concept are stored with that concept, whereas only the particular attributes of each member of the class are stored with the member concept. Thus the attribute "has wings" is stored with the superordinate concept "bird," but only the attribute "red breast" is stored with the subordinate concept "robin." Because the proximity of concepts stored within the same network is assumed to depend on their degree of meaningful relatedness, semantic network theories predict that the time needed to retrieve information about relationships between two concepts will depend on the distance between them in the network. Thus it should take less time to decide whether robins are birds than to decide whether robins are animals. Similarly, it should be easier to answer the question "Does a robin have a red breast?" than "Does a robin fly?" because memory searches that begin with "robin" move quickly to "red breast." One must move up the hierarchy before encountering "able to fly," because this concept is attached to "bird" rather than "robin."

Most predictions based on semantic network theories have been borne out, and these theories provide useful models for the storage of information in semantic memory. Furthermore, because they can be built into computer programs, they have been useful in cognitive simulation research involving construction of models of human information processing followed by study of how such models respond to new input.

Semantic network theories, however, portray long-term memory as a relatively static storage system that supports routine, predictable access and retrieval. Consequently, they have been supplemented in recent years by schema theories that help explain the constructive encoding of input and the reconstruction of stored memories reported by Bartlett and others.

Since Bartlett's groundbreaking work, many investigators have shown that new input is not first understood in some abstract way and only then related to existing knowledge; instead, it is interpreted from the beginning within contexts supplied by that existing knowledge. These collections of related information that provide context for meaningful interpretation of new input are usually called *schemas* (Anderson, 1984a; diSibio, 1982; Rumelhart & Norman, 1978), *scripts* (Schank & Abelson, 1977), or *frames* (Minsky, 1975; Winograd, 1975).

Even seemingly familiar material may not have much meaning unless we can interpret it within relevant schemas. Consider the following sentence: "The notes were sour because the seam split" (Bransford & McCarrell, 1974). This sentence contains familiar words arranged according to the English syntax rules, and you can even recognize it as a causal explanation for an observed event. Yet it probably will have little meaning for you until you are given the clue "bagpipe," and can interpret it within your "bagpipe playing" schema. For a more extended example, consider the following paragraph from Dooling and Lachman (1971):

> With hocked gems financing him, our hero bravely defied all scornful laughter that tried to prevent his scheme. "Your eyes deceive," he had said, "an egg not a table correctly typifies this unexplored planet." Now

> three sturdy sisters sought proof, forging along sometimes through calm vastness, yet more often over turbulent peaks and valleys. Days became weeks as many doubters spread fearful rumors about the edge. At last from nowhere welcome-winged creatures appeared signifying momentous success. (p. 217)

In Dooling and Lachman's experiment, most subjects who read this paragraph without an accompanying title found it relatively meaningless and could not remember much of it later. However, subjects who read it under the title "Christopher Columbus discovering America" found it entirely meaningful and were able to remember much more of it.

Lest you think that schema activation always leads to a single interpretation, consider the following paragraph from Anderson, Reynolds, Schallert, and Goetz (1977):

> Tony slowly got up from the mat, planning his escape. He hesitated a moment and thought. Things were not going well. What bothered him most was being held, especially since the charge against him had been weak. He considered his present situation. The lock that held him was strong but he thought he could break it. He knew, however, that his timing would have to be perfect. Tony was aware that it was because of his early roughness that he had been penalized so severely—much too severely from his point of view. The situation was becoming frustrating; the pressure had been grinding on him for too long. He was being ridden unmercifully. Tony was getting angry now. He felt he was ready to make his move. He knew that his success or failure would depend on what he did in the next few seconds. (Anderson, 1984a, pp. 244–245)

If you are like most people, you thought that this paragraph was about a convict planning to escape from prison, and you interpreted it by relating it to schemas concerning the thinking of convicts, prison life, and prison escapes. However, if you are familiar with the sport of wrestling, you may have interpreted the paragraph as being about a wrestler trying to escape the hold of an opponent. These two interpretations are equally valid, and either yields meaningful understanding and good memory for the passage.

Although these specially constructed demonstrations call attention to the role of schemas in facilitating and determining the nature of text comprehension, the larger point here is that such schema effects occur routinely, whether or not we are aware of them. How input is encoded and stored in memory will depend on what relevant schemas are activated when interpreting it in the first place, and reconstruction of the input may occur later if changes occur in these schemas. These and other factors affecting long-term memory for connected discourse will be discussed later, following discussion of factors affecting rote learning.

FACTORS AFFECTING ROTE LEARNING

Although most school learning involves meaningful learning of connected discourse, some of it involves primarily rote learning of disconnected

Serial, paired associate, and free-recall list learning

material. There are school learning parallels for each of the three major types of learning studied in verbal learning experiments (Mayer, 1982). In *serial learning,* students are given lists of items to be memorized in order, such as the alphabet or the roster of U.S. presidents. In *paired associate learning,* students must learn stimulus-response pairs so that they can supply the response item when given the stimulus item, such as with states and their capitals or foreign language synonyms for English words. Finally, in *free-recall list learning,* students are given lists of items that may be recalled in any order, such as naming the countries in Europe or listing the thirteen original colonies. Rote learning of such verbal material is subject to meaningfulness effects, serial position effects, practice effects, transfer effects, interference effects, organization effects, levels of processing effects, state dependent effects, and mnemonic effects (Mayer, 1982).

Meaningfulness Effects

Highly meaningful words are easier to learn and remember than less meaningful words (Cofer, 1971). Retention will be improved to the extent that learners are able to make relatively meaningless material more meaningful by associating it with more familiar material (see the section on mnemonic effects below) or by substituting familiar, concrete words for unfamiliar, abstract words (Wittrock, Marks, & Doctorow, 1975).

Serial Position Effects

Serial position effects result from the particular placement of an item within a list. Memory is better for items at the beginnings (*primacy effects*) or ends (*recency effects*) of lists than for items in the middle. An exception to these serial position effects is the *distinctiveness effect*—an item that is distinctively different from the others, such as a male name among a list of female names, will be remembered better regardless of its serial position.

Serial position effects may occur because the items at the beginnings and ends of lists serve as "cognitive landmarks" that provide anchors to which the other items may be attached in memory (Mayer, 1982). Other explanations are also possible, however. For example, if the memory test follows immediately after the practice time, recency effects may occur simply because learners are able to hold the last few items of the list in short-term memory long enough to be able to reproduce them first on the test. Also, primacy effects may occur because the first few items enter an empty short-term memory register, so more time is available and less interference is encountered in transferring them to long-term memory, compared to what happens with later items. Research in support of this theory shows that the recency effect disappears when the recall test is delayed, but the primacy effect is still evident (Craik, 1979). An implication here is that students may remember the beginnings of lessons better than the parts that come afterwards, suggesting the importance of advance organizers and early presentation of key ideas and structuring concepts. See Figure 9.2.

Figure 9.2 Recall during Lecture. Memory for the beginning and end of lecture is almost perfect, but it tails off increasingly rapidly in the middle.

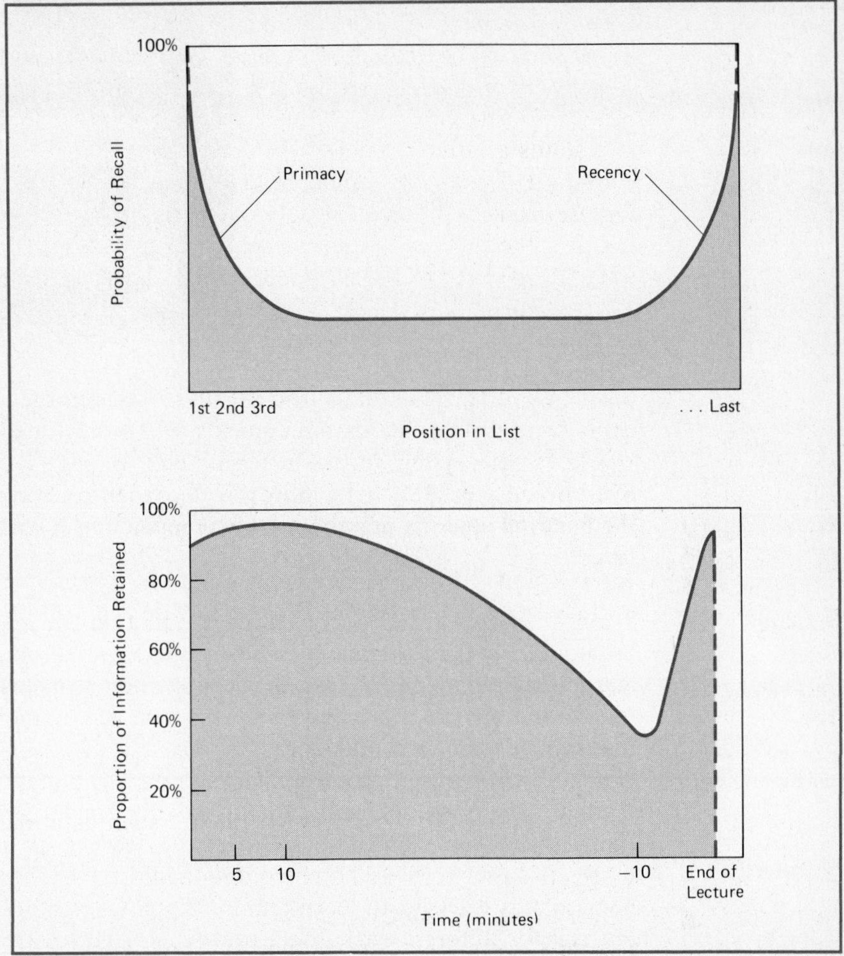

Source: Adapted from P. Russell, *The Brain Book* (New York: E.P. Dutton, 1979). Information from E.J. Thomas, *Studies in Adult Education*, April 1972.

Practice Effects

Active *practice* or *rehearsal* improves retention, and *distributed practice* is usually more effective than *massed practice*. The advantage of distributed practice is especially noticeable for long lists, fast presentation rates, or unfamiliar stimulus material (Underwood, 1961; Underwood, Kapelak, & Malmi, 1976). It apparently occurs because massed practice allows the learner to associate a word with only one context, but distributed practice allows association with many different contexts (Glenberg, 1976).

An implication here is that practice in memorizing poems, spelling words, arithmetic tables, or foreign-language vocabulary is most efficient when distributed over many short sessions. If the material is intended to be learned permanently or applied later, there should be practice to the

Active practice and recitation is a proven aid to memory.

point of overlearning and sufficient review thereafter to ensure that students can retrieve the learning quickly when they need it.

When memorizing verbal material such as poetry or dramatic lines, overt practice is likely to be more effective than silent reading. Rehearsing the material aloud is helpful, as is accompanying it with appropriate gestures.

Transfer Effects

Transfer effects are effects of prior learning on the learning of new material. *Positive transfer* occurs when previous learning makes the new learning easier; *negative transfer* occurs when it makes the new learning more difficult. The more that two tasks have in common, the more likely that transfer effects will occur.

Specific transfer

Specific transfer occurs when tasks share components. When the tasks involve similar stimuli and call for making similar responses, positive transfer may be expected. Thus having learned two-column addition makes it easier to learn three-column addition, and having learned ping pong makes it easier to learn tennis. When tasks involve similar stimuli but call for different responses, however, negative transfer may occur. Thus knowledge about adding suffixes to regular words may interfere with handling of irregular words (a child says "runned" instead of "ran"), knowledge about dividing whole numbers may interfere with learning to divide fractions, and knowledge of Spanish may interfere with the learning of Portuguese.

Unfortunately, the majority of specific transfer effects that occur in rote learning are likely to be negative (the opposite is true with meaningful learning). The danger is greatest when the two sets of similar items are being learned at the same time and neither set is well anchored. Less confusion is likely when one set has been mastered to overlearning before the second set is encountered (see Chapter 11).

General transfer

General transfer is transfer that cannot be attributed to shared components among tasks. An example would be general study skills learned in one course and then applied later in other courses on different topics. Such general transfer is discussed later in this chapter and in the next chapter. Unfortunately, rote learning of specific material offers little potential for positive general transfer, which is why schools should not place much emphasis on it.

Interference Effects

Proactive and retroactive interference

Interference effects occur when memory for particular material is hurt by previous or subsequent learning (Underwood, 1983). Whereas transfer effects occur when learning the new material in the first place, interference effects occur later when trying to remember it. Interference effects are always negative. *Proactive interference* occurs when previously learned material impedes ability to remember more recently learned material. Americans accustomed to the traditional system of weights and measures, for example, tend to have difficulty remembering the Metric system. *Retroactive interference* occurs when something learned recently interferes with ability to remember something learned previously. Students who first study Latin and then one of the romance languages derived from Latin are likely to forget more Latin than students who first study Latin and then study some unrelated language.

Interference effects are the major causes for forgetting of material learned by rote. You can minimize such forgetting by varying the contexts within which practice takes place, seeing that practice continues to overlearning, and, most importantly, encouraging students to process the material in ways that make it meaningful rather than rote learning.

Organization Effects

Organization effects occur when learners categorize the input. Free recall of lists is better when learners organize the items into categories rather than memorizing them in serial order (Bower, 1970). Learning is likely to be most efficient when teachers organize lists in logical ways and call students' attention to this organization (Bower, Clark, Lesgold, & Winzenz, 1969).

Levels-of-Processing Effects

Craik and Lockhart (1972) argued that words may be processed at several levels ranging from low-level sensory analysis of their physical characteristics to high-level semantic analysis of their meaning. They reviewed literature indicating *levels-of-processing effects*—the more deeply a word list is processed, the better it will be remembered. In particular, semantic encoding of the content leads to better memory than nonsemantic encoding. Thus subjects instructed to note whether or not each word belonged in a certain category remembered more words than subjects instructed to circle every vowel (Jenkins, 1974).

The levels-of-processing notion has held up well as a general principle, although it applies better to some contexts than others and different investigators do not always agree in classifying types of processing as high or low level (Craik, 1979; Horton & Mills, 1984). Consequently, other investigators prefer terms such as *distinctiveness* of encoding, *elaboration* of encoding, or *effort expended* during encoding. The common element in these ideas is that memory will be better when learners actively process the information and develop meaningful associations to it (*elaborative encoding*) than when they merely try to memorize it rotely (*maintenance rehearsal*).

Elaborative encoding

Stein and Bransford (1979) showed the value of *elaborative encoding*. Subjects were presented with lists of sentences such as "the bald man read the newspaper" or "the funny man liked the ring" and then were asked memory questions such as "which man read the newspaper?" Memory was improved when learners were supplied with, or encouraged to generate, elaborations that made the sentences more meaningful by placing the described behaviors within cause-effect contexts (The bald man read the newspaper to look for a hat sale; the funny man liked the ring that squirted water). These elaborations made the described actions meaningful given the nature of the man (bald, funny, etc.). Other elaborations that did not provide such cause-effect information were not successful in improving memory (the bald man read the newspaper while eating breakfast; the funny man liked the ring that he received as a present).

Transfer appropriate processing

Bransford (1979) also referred to *transfer appropriate processing*—what constitutes proper processing will depend on what information the learners need and what they will be expected to do with it. In studying word lists, for example, semantic processing usually is appropriate because learning is usually measured with recall tests. Processing of the physical characteristics of the words, however, is appropriate if the test focuses on these physical characteristics. Tversky (1973) has shown that learners can adjust their information processing and study strategies according to the kind of test they expect. Teachers can help their students remember what they learn by encouraging them to think about the contexts in which they will need the information and what they will do with it when they apply it.

State-Dependent Effects

State- or *context-dependent effects* occur because learning takes place within a specific context and may be most accessible later, at least initially, within that same context. For example, lists are more easily remembered when the test situation is similar to the learning situation, apparently because this maximizes the contextual cues available to aid retrieval (Mayer, 1982). Baddeley (1976) has reviewed some unusual state-dependent effects, such as that lists learned under water are recalled better under water and lists learned while under the influence of alcohol are recalled best while in the same state. Of more direct relevance to schooling are the *encoding specificity effects* demonstrated by Tulving and Thomson (1973): If the word *light* is associated with *head* during learning, it will be easier to remember *light* if the test gives the cue *head* than if the test gives the cue *dark*.

Encoding specificity effects

At first glance, these state-dependent effects may seem to imply that testing conditions should be kept as similar as possible to learning conditions. This would be true if learning goals were narrowly defined in terms of scores on tests of memory for specific information. However, we usually desire transfer and application rather than mere retention of specific knowledge. Therefore, the contexts of learning should be varied so that learners can retrieve the information in response to a variety of cues rather than remaining dependent on particular cues embedded in particular contexts.

Mnemonic Effects

Learners can increase the effectiveness of their rote learning by using *mnemonics*—strategies for elaborating on relatively meaningless input by associating it with more meaningful images or semantic contexts. Four well-known mnemonics methods are the place method, the link method, the peg method, and the keyword method.

The Place Method The *place method* (also called the *method of loci,* after the Latin word for places) involves associating each item on a list with a particular place within a familiar location. For example, you might think of walking through your house and encountering items on the list as you move from one room to the next. The familiar sequence involved in ''walking'' through the house would help you to remember the items on the list in the proper sequence, and the visual imagery involved in ''seeing'' the items in the rooms would help you remember each one individually. The place method has received considerable support in research on human memory (Bower, 1970), and it is usually stressed in popular memory improvement books (Lorayne & Lucas, 1974).

The Link Method The *link method* involves forming an image for each item and then linking them together into an interactive chain. For example, if you need to pick up butter, celery, flour, ground beef, and ice cream at the food store, you might remember these items by imagining preparing a meal in which you first used the flour to make bread, stirring the mixture with celery as you did so, and used the ground beef to make a meat loaf and then enjoyed a meal of bread and butter and the meat loaf, with ice cream for dessert. Like the place method, the link method aids memory for specific items by tying the items to images and linking the images into a continuous ''story.'' If necessary, the sequence of the items can be built into a story as well.

It often is easier to make a written list than to use mnemonic devices. However, such devices are useful for memorizing lists when writing is not possible or permissible or when preparing for a speech that must be given without notes.

The Peg Method The *peg method* (also called the *hook method*) involves using a familiar series of items as ''pegs'' on which newly learned items can be ''hung'' as they are learned. In the most common example, the pegs are easy to visualize and their names rhyme with the number names (one is a bun, two is a shoe, three is a tree, etc.). The items to be learned are linked to the items on this peg list through imagery (Glover, et al., 1987). Thus the first item might be pictured between the halves of a bun, the second linked to the image of a shoe, and so on. Whereas the link method involves linking the items to be learned to one another, the peg method involves linking them to peg items that are easily visualized and already sequenced.

The Keyword Method The *keyword method* is a useful mnemonic device for paired associate learning. Originated as a technique for teaching foreign language vocabulary (Atkinson, 1975), the method is also useful for aiding memory for definitions of unfamiliar English words (Pressley, Levin, & Miller, 1982) and technical terms (Jones & Hall, 1982), as well as for linking cities to their products (Pressley & Dennis-Rounds, 1980), states to their capitals (Levin et al., 1980), and proper names to events, accomplishments, or biographical information (Jones & Hall, 1982; McCormick & Levin, 1984; Schriberg et al., 1982).

The method involves identifying a key word that links the items to be associated. For example, the Spanish word *carta* means "letter" in English. A good key word for *carta* would be *cart*, a familiar English word that is easily visualized. The key word can then be used to link the items through either an image (of a shopping cart transporting a letter) or a sentence (The cart carries the letter). As another example, the state of Maryland (key word = *marry*) can be linked with its capitol of Annapolis (key word = *apple*) using an image of two apples getting married (Levin, 1981).

The method works best when the key word refers to something easily visualized and sounds like part of the word to be learned. Thus *car* is a good key word for *carlin,* and the image of an old woman driving a car can help one to remember that "carlin" means "old woman."

The keyword method substantially improves vocabulary learning, both in foreign language and in one's own language, across the range of grade levels (Pressley et al., 1982). Furthermore, students using the keyword method learn more than students who use semantically based methods such as writing word definitions, using words in sentences, or inferring their meanings from context (Pressley et al., 1982; McDaniel & Pressley, 1984). The keyword method is especially helpful for lower-ability students who have not developed efficient methods for learning on their own (McDaniel & Pressley, 1984).

Elaboration method

Other Methods There are many other mnemonic devices besides the place, link, peg, and keyword methods (Bellezza, 1981; Lorayne & Lucas, 1974). Bower and Clark (1969) reported success with the *elaboration method,* where learners who weaved together the words on a list into a running story retained more than learners who memorized in the usual way.

Pictorial mnemonics

Ehri, Deffner, and Wilce (1984) used *pictorial mnemonics* to help children remember the sounds that are associated with letters of the alphabet. In teaching the letter "f," for example, they showed an illustration in which the letter was drawn as the stem of a flower. This visual image helped the children to remember the shape of the letter "f" and the drawing depicted something whose name begins with the "f" sound (flower).

Rhymes are often useful mnemonic devices ("*I* before *e* except after *c*,"

Rhymes and acronyms

"30 days hath September, . . ."). So are *acronyms* (*YMCA, FBI*), especially when they are pronouncable (*NATO, UNICEF*). You can create your own acronyms for special purposes. For example, if you are to give a speech that has five major ideas, you could employ a word (e.g., *TIGER*) whose letters each stand for a key point (*T* represents the role of transportation, and so on).

Imagery and spatial visualization

Imagery and *spatial visualization* are often useful mnemonic devices, as well. Verbal learning can be assisted by picturing words in the mind, solving problems involving making change can be assisted by visualizing the coins involved, and spatial computations can be assisted by visualizing the rooms portrayed in the problems. In general, anything that helps one to process input more deeply, relate it to more familiar material, or supplement the verbal presentation with vivid imagery will help one to learn and remember the material.

FACTORS AFFECTING MEANINGFUL VERBAL LEARNING

The main problem in trying to learn disconnected material is to find ways to make it meaningful and thus not have to depend on purely rote learning strategies. Meaningfulness is not a problem in learning connected discourse, however, unless the material is so unfamiliar or difficult as to make meaningful comprehension impossible. Instead, the problem is coping with the sheer volume of the material by learning it in an organized fashion and retaining it so that it can be retrieved when needed.

Learning connected discourse

Mayer (1982) has identified the following sets of findings from research on learning connected discourse: abstraction effects, levels effects, schema effects, prior knowledge effects, interference effects, text organization effects, and mathemagenic effects. We will discuss these findings along with those on student misconception effects.

Abstraction Effects

Abstraction effects reflect the tendency of learners to remember the gist of a passage rather than its specific wording. If they read a passage and later are asked to state whether particular sentences were included in it, learners can recognize that certain sentences are irrelevant or contradictory to what they read, but they usually cannot distinguish verbatim quotations from similar sentences that carry the same meanings (Bransford & Franks, 1971; Sachs, 1967). If learners assume that the goal is understanding rather than verbatim memory, and if the material can be analyzed into main ideas and supportive detail, learners will tend to concentrate on the main ideas and to retain them in semantic forms that are more abstract and generalized than the verbatim sentences in the passage.

Levels Effects

Levels effects occur when learners believe that some parts of the passage are more important than others. If the passage is well organized or if the learners are able to provide such organization themselves, they will tend to learn parts that occupy higher levels in the organization better than parts occupying lower levels. Generalizations and key ideas associated with the main theme will be learned especially well (Bromage & Mayer, 1986; Meyer, 1977).

Schema Effects

We have already given several examples ("The notes were sour because the seam split," the paragraph on Christopher Columbus, and the ambiguous prisoner/wrestler story) illustrating how text comprehension is affected by existing schemas. Along with Bartlett's research indicating that memory for previously learned material can become reconstructed over time if the schemas to which it is attached should undergo change themselves, these are all examples of *schema effects*. Elaborating on such schema effects, Gagné and Dick (1983) suggested that (1) newly learned information is incorporated into existing schemas, (2) recall of previously learned information is influenced by these schemas, so that remembering is a constructive act, (3) schemas not only aid retention of new material by providing frameworks for storage but also alter the new information by making it "fit" the expectations built into schemas, (4) schemas allow learners to make inferences that fill in the gaps in stories or expository prose, (5) schemas are organized not only in terms of figurative verbal knowledge but also in terms of components of intellectual skills (operative knowledge), and (6) ideally, learners will become able not only to process new information efficiently but also to evaluate and modify their own schemas.

Functions of schemas

Similarly, Anderson (1984a) identified the following six functions of schemas: (1) providing ideational scaffolding for assimilation of text information, (2) facilitating selective allocation of attention (concentration on the important aspects of the text), (3) enabling inferential elaboration (inferring details that are implied but not spelled out), (4) allowing orderly memory searches (identifying the relevant information that will be needed to understand the text most efficiently), (5) facilitating editing and summarizing (abstracting the gist for storage in long-term memory), and (6) permitting inferential reconstruction (filling in the gaps in memory later by replacing lost or never-encoded details with inferences about what those details probably were).

Used in a general way, the term *schema effects* would refer not only to these effects but also to abstraction effects, levels effects, prior knowledge effects, inference effects, and student misconception effects. Mayer (1982), however, used the term *schema effects* to refer more specifically to situations in which learners recognize that the text describes an instance of a larger class of events for which they have a well-developed schema and then use that schema both to process the information (using expectations about the elements to be expected and their probable order and degree of importance) and to aid comprehension (by filling in gaps where information is implied rather than stated explicitly). Consider the following paragraph:

> When Mary arrived, the woman at the door greeted her and checked her name. A few minutes later, she was escorted to her chair and shown the day's menu. The attendant was helpful but brusque, almost to the point of being rude. Later, she paid the woman at the door and left.

Chances are that this paragraph was meaningful to you because you recognized that it took place in a restaurant, that Mary had made reservations, that she was seated by the hostess at a table (not merely in a chair), that the "attendant" was a waiter, and that the "woman at the door" was a cashier. Schank and Abelson (1977) suggested that you could infer all of this information (none of which was explicit in the text) because you possess a schema called a "restaurant script" that includes such slots as "being seated," "ordering," and "paying the check."

Story grammars

Similarly, Rumelhart (1975) and Thorndyke (1977) suggested that people use specialized schemas known as *story grammars* when reading stories. A story grammar is a set of rules that specify the hierarchical relationships among events or states in a story. Its four main slots are the setting, the theme, the plot, and the resolution. The setting involves a particular time and place and a cast of characters. The theme surrounds an event that the characters are involved in or a goal that they are working toward. The plot involves a series of episodes, each with a goal, behavior directed toward that goal, and the outcome of this behavior. The resolution occurs when the story reaches the climax toward which it has been building and offers some moral or conclusion relating to its theme. Younger children have poorly developed story grammars and thus tend to focus on actions rather than motives and to process stories as if they were relatively disconnected descriptions of events (Voss & Bisanz, 1982). Gradually, however, they bring to bear increasingly sophisticated schemas that help them to know what to look for as they read and how to organize their memory for the story. Setting, theme, plot, and resolution are remembered, perhaps along with some key phrases or quotations. Unimportant details and verbatim phrasing are not.

Preparing for story reading

Reading comprehension theorists recommend that teachers prepare students for story reading by telling them what the story is about and asking them questions to activate schemas that they will find useful in comprehending it. They include schemas relating to the content of the story in addition to story grammars concerning the forms and functions of fiction.

Prior-Knowledge Effects

Even when material does not lend itself to interpretation within a well-developed schema with ready-made slots, *prior-knowledge effects* will still occur to the extent that learners can use existing knowledge to establish a context or *construct a schema* into which the new information can be assimilated (Bransford, 1979). The convict/wrestler paragraph presented earlier is an example. Few people have specific "thinking about breaking a hold" schemas, but people knowledgeable about wrestling can use this prior knowledge to interpret the paragraph as being about a wrestler trying to escape a hold.

Providing cues

Learners can control the perspective they take in interpreting information if cued to do so (Anderson, Pichert, & Shirey, 1983). For example, Pichert and Anderson (1977) had subjects read a passage describing two boys playing in a house. Some were directed to read from the perspective of a home buyer, and others from the perspective of a burglar. These assigned perspectives affected the pattern of details that were remembered later. "Home buyers" were more likely to remember that the roof leaked, but "burglars" were more likely to remember the color television set.

Providing cues about what prior knowledge is relevant to understanding a passage is one way for teachers to make vague passages more meaningful to students. For expository passages, such cuing might involve suggesting analogies or visual imagery that would link the strange to the familiar. For poetry or fiction, it might involve providing explanations or asking questions designed to alert students to metaphors and other literary devices.

Inference Effects

Inference effects occur when learners use schemas or other prior knowledge to make inferences about intended meanings that go beyond what is explicitly stated in the text. Three kinds of inferences are case grammar presuppositions, conceptual dependency inferences, and logical deductions.

Case grammar

Fillmore (1968) used the term *case grammar* to refer to the assumptions and implications that are built into the use of language. For example, declarative sentences typically take a subject-verb-object form, and the verb implies that the subject took some action on the object. In the context of baseball, the verb *hit* implies a subject (the batter), an object (the ball), and in this case, an instrument for accomplishing an action (the bat). These logical relationships and the imagery associated with them are brought to bear in interpreting statements that are not completely explicit. Thus people familiar with baseball will infer that the ball was pitched and the batter hit a fair ball and reached base safely when they hear "It's a hit," or "He drives a single to left" (Kintsch, 1974; Meyer, 1977).

Conceptual dependency inferences

Conceptual dependency inferences occur when learners recognize cause-effect relationships or other dependencies among ideas in a passage. For example, Kintsch (1977) had students read a story containing the sentences "A burning cigarette was carelessly discarded. The fire destroyed many acres of virgin forest." Students who read this version of the story were just as likely to report that the cigarette started the fire as were students who read a version that spelled this out explicitly.

Logical deductions

Logical deductions occur when readers are given premises that compel certain conclusions. For example, if told that A is taller than B and B is taller than C, they will be able to answer the question "Is A taller than C?" correctly.

Simplification of communication

Inference effects simplify communication enormously. Instead of having to specify everything that we say in complete detail, we can convey the gist and rely on the listener or reader to infer the rest. In teaching, however, it is wise to be sure that learners get the complete picture when it is important for them to do so. Teachers ordinarily should spell out cause and effect relationships, logical deductions, and the implications of examples or experiments. They should also be alert to the failures of textbooks to be explicit. In recent years, publishers have sought to simplify texts by substituting shorter words and sentences for longer ones. Ironically, this often reduces clarity because vague terms are substituted for precise terms and because important logical connectives ("because," "therefore," etc.) are omitted when longer sentences are divided into shorter ones (Anderson & Armbruster, 1984).

Student-Misconception Effects

So far, our discussion of schema effects, including prior knowledge effects and inference effects, has emphasized the positive by showing how schemas allow us to embed input within meaningful contexts and fill in gaps whenever the message is not complete. However, there is a negative side to this process. Schema activation also makes possible the *student-misconception effects* that occur when input is filtered through schemas that are oversimplified, distorted, or just plain incorrect. This happens routinely with young children whose thinking is still in the process of becoming operational, and it happens more often than you might think with older students and adults, especially when dealing with abstract scientific concepts that contrast with naive ideas about the world built up through concrete experiences.

For example, Anderson and Smith (1987) studied the teaching of a fifth-grade science unit on light. One point made repeatedly in the unit is that sunlight reflects off objects to our eyes and that it is this reflected sunlight that we are processing when we see. This scientific conception of vision differs from the naive conception that most people develop, namely, that the sun brightens the objects themselves. A test item shows the sun, a tree, and a boy and asks the students to show how sunlight enables the boy to see the tree. The correct answer is to draw rays coming from the sun to the tree and then reflecting off the tree to the boy's eyes. On pretests, only about 5 percent of the students answered this item correctly. Of the remaining students who responded at all, the majority drew rays from the sun to the tree but did not show these rays being reflected to the boy's eyes.

So far, this was unremarkable. However, the students then spent several weeks on the unit, which covered light reflection and vision several times in different contexts. Yet on the posttest only 24 percent of the students showed light rays reflecting off the tree to the boy's eyes, and the majority still thought that we see objects because the sun "brightens them up." Replications of this work have yielded similar results, even in classrooms taught by teachers considered to be generally effective who were using widely adopted curriculum materials.

Inadequate curriculum material

How could this happen? In part, the authors believe, it happened because the curriculum materials were not as explicit as they need to be. Also, however, many students never became aware of the conflict between their current beliefs and what the text was saying. They read the words, but they did not appreciate their full implications. Consequently, they sailed right through the unit with the same misconceptions that they brought into it.

Mathematics misconceptions

These findings are not unusual. A variety of common misconceptions has been discovered in both mathematics (Davis, 1984) and science (Champagne, Klopfer, & Anderson, 1980; diSessa, 1982), and more are being discovered every day. For example, Davis and McKnight (1980) found that few third or fourth graders solved the following subtraction problem correctly the first time they saw it: 7,002 − 25. Furthermore, because of a common misconception about the process of borrowing, one particular incorrect answer was common: 5,087. Nor are such misconceptions confined to young children. Matz (1980) included the following in a list of thirty-three algebra errors commonly made by high school and college students:

- Evaluating $4X$ when X equals 6 as 46 or $46X$.
- Evaluating XY when X equals -3 and Y equals -5 as -8.
- Computing $2X$ divided by $2X$ to be 0.
- Claiming that one can't multiply by X because "you don't know what X is."

Such misconceptions can be difficult to remove even with tutoring, and they often reassert themselves after learners seemingly have mastered the correct concepts. Anderson and Smith (1987) made adjustments in the way that the fifth-grade light unit was taught and managed to raise scores on the sun/tree/boy item from 24 to 79 percent correct. However, this took both special teacher training (alerting the teachers to probable student misconceptions and ways to confront them) and special curriculum materials (a revised text that was clearer and more explicit about the difference between the scientific concept and the naive concept, supplemented by illustrations shown on the overhead projector).

Conceptual change

Such findings regarding student misconception effects have led to better appreciation of the fact that teaching involves *conceptual change* rather than infusion of knowledge into a vacuum. Students usually have at least some background knowledge to bring to bear in processing new input, and often they have considerable knowledge organized into powerful schemas. Consequently, they may process the new input primarily by assimilating it, or a distorted version of it, into old schemas, rather than by accommodating the old schemas to take into account the new input. This may be desirable when existing schemas are accurate, but if they are not, it will lead to student misconception effects. Therefore, in addition merely to explaining material, teachers need to confront common misconceptions by making students aware of them and helping them to see how and why they are incorrect.

Text-Organization Effects

Text-organization effects refer to the effects that the degree and type of organization built into a passage have on the degree and type of information that learners encode and remember. We described in the previous chapter the value of structuring elements such as advance organizers, previews, logical sequencing, outline formats, highlighting of main ideas, and summaries. These structuring elements make it possible for learners to retain more of the material by facilitating chunking, subsumption of material into existing schemas, and encoding of it as an organized body of knowledge rather than a list of unrelated items.

In addition, text organization elements determine what is learned by cuing the learners to important aspects of the material. Kintsch and Yarbrough (1982), for example, had subjects read essays written in either good or poor rhetorical form. Later tests showed that the two groups were equally good at supplying specific facts but that the group that had read the well-organized essays were better at answering open-ended questions about main points. Thus a well-organized text or lecture sequences material in a sensible way and helps learners to encode it as a series of major ideas supported by elaborative details.

Mathemagenic Effects

Rothkopf (1970) coined the term *mathemagenic activities* to refer to the things that learners do to assist their own learning (get ready to concentrate, approach the material with the intention of studying and remembering it, etc.). Wittrock (1974) has discussed learning as a *generative process* in which learners actively build the to-be-learned material in memory. *Mathemagenic effects* are effects of such active information processing by learners. Mathemagenic activities such as answering adjunct questions or taking notes can enhance intentional learning of meaningful material.

Increasing intentional learning

Adjunct Questions *Adjunct questions* are questions included with prose passages: *prequestions* at the beginning, *inserted questions* within the passage itself, or *postquestions* at the end. Students who learn from passages that include such adjunct questions retain more than students who read the same material without them (Andre, 1987; Rickards, 1979; Reynolds & Anderson, 1982). More specifically, adjunct questions tend to increase intentional learning of material directly related to the questions; they do not improve and may even reduce incidental learning.

Prequestions

Much research on adjunct questions has focused on where such questions should be inserted. Most investigators have concluded that postquestions are more valuable than prequestions. *Prequestions* are effective in alerting learners to important issues, but they interfere with the learning of material not addressed in the questions (McConkie, 1977; Sagaria & DiVesta, 1978; Klauer, 1984). Prequestions tend to be most effective when they deal with the most general or important ideas, and they are most helpful to low-ability learners (Wilhite, 1983).

Postquestions

Postquestions are less likely to reduce incidental learning by constricting attention to the material addressed in the questions. In addition, they allow learners to assess whether or not they understand the material and they aid retention by encouraging them to encode the material in their own words (Sagaria & DiVesta, 1978). Postquestions that direct attention to points that are often misunderstood or missed altogether because of student misconception effects are especially valuable (McConkie, 1977). In general, postquestions facilitate learning by causing learners to review the material systematically (Sagerman & Mayer, 1987; Wixson, 1984).

Note taking

Other Mathemagenic Activities Besides responding to adjunct questions, learners can engage in *self-initiated mathemagenic activities* that will enhance learning. One of these is *note taking*. Note taking is not helpful when students must learn from a rapidly presented lecture or when they are not given opportunities to review their notes, but it is an effective way to enhance learning from reading text or listening to lectures presented at a slow enough rate to allow both monitoring of the input and writing of notes (Faw & Waller, 1976; Weinstein & Mayer, 1986). Note taking is especially effective when students use outline formats and concentrate on main ideas (Carrier & Titus, 1981; Mayer, 1984).

Underlining and shadowing

Another useful mathemagenic activity when reading text is *underlining*, apparently because it helps students to remember key terms and ideas (Rickards & August, 1975). A parallel technique for aiding memory of orally presented material is *shadowing:* After presenting a key word or phrase, the teacher pauses to let the students repeat it aloud (Mayer & Cook, 1981). Shadowing should be particularly useful in early reading instruction and foreign-language instruction.

Mathemagenic activities are discussed in detail in the following chapter.

CURRENT RESEARCH ON HUMAN INFORMATION PROCESSING

Many exciting advances in contemporary educational psychology are being contributed by investigators studying the information-processing aspects of human learning and memory. Many of them involve applications of schema theory (broadly conceived), especially in the areas of reading comprehension, comparisons of novices with experts, and cognitive simulation and artificial intelligence.

Reading-Comprehension Research

Reading comprehension (which includes all learning from text, not just what goes on during reading lessons) used to be thought of as information processing that proceeded from the bottom up. That is, readers processed letters and associated them with their sounds, then formed sounds into words, and then strung words together to infer meaning from sentences. Beginning readers do process information this way for a time, as do poor readers who never become efficient at decoding. Skilled readers, however, process text much more rapidly and use top-down methods in which the text is filtered through well-formed schemas.

Interaction with text

In effect, skilled readers interact with the text to construct meaning. Comprehension occurs when expectations associated with relevant schemas are fulfilled by specific information in the text. Information that neatly satisfies these expectations is easily encoded into memory so as to "instantiate" the "slots" in the schema. Information that does not fit the schema may not be encoded at all or may be distorted to make the fit better. Gaps in the information are filled in by inferences that make the entire meaning gleaned from the passage consistent with expectations. Later, these same expectations that guided encoding of the information in the first place are brought into play again to guide retrieval and reconstruction (Anderson, 1984a).

When the material can be assimilated into readily available schemas, reading with comprehension is rapid and relatively effortless. Much of the material is processed in the form of already well-organized and meaningful chunks, so that attention and working memory can concentrate on unfamiliar elements that do not fit established expectations. However, when no schema is readily available for processing material, it takes much more time and effort to read with comprehension. Even if the words can be decoded with relative ease (as in the paragraph about Christopher Columbus given as an example earlier), it becomes necessary to think about them and try to imagine what the author is trying to say. If decoding is a problem, too, the reader will have to decode the words first and then review them to try to construct a meaning. Given limited working memory, the task of reading with comprehension is too difficult to take on all at once under these circumstances.

Importance of reading practice

This work has led to renewed appreciation of the importance of practicing reading until basic decoding processes become smooth and automatic, because proficiency in decoding is necessary if readers are to have most of their working memory capacity available for comprehending and keeping track of the meaning of the text. At the same time, however, this work has also increased understanding and appreciation of the strategies that skilled readers use for comprehending text, along with related mathemagenic activities and study skills (see next chapter).

Expert-Novice Comparisons

By asking people to think out loud as they solve problems, information processing theorists have been studying how people use their knowledge for thinking about specialized areas such as physics, radiology, or chess (Chi & Glaser, 1982; Chi, Glaser, & Rees, 1981; Larkin, 1981; Newell & Simon, 1972). Often this research involves comparing skilled and experienced experts with novices in the same field, both to describe "how experts do it" and to identify the problems that novices experience. Such knowledge can become the basis for instruction designed to move novices toward expert status by teaching them to think as experts do (Greeno, 1980a).

DeGroot (1965) compared expert and novice chess players and found that if twenty to twenty-five pieces were arranged randomly on a chess board, experts were no better than novices at reconstructing the arrangement from memory. Both groups averaged about seven pieces correct, as Miller (1956) predicted. However, when the arrangements were recreations of actual chess games, the experts could reconstruct the positions of most or even all of the pieces, whereas the novices could do little better than before.

How can expert chess players reconstruct twenty-five pieces after seeing them in place for only five to ten seconds? Apparently, they do it by relying on chunking strategies and by activating familiar chess strategy schemas (Simon, 1979). Instead of trying to keep track of twenty-five individual pieces, the experts chunk by conceptualizing the progress of the game in terms of the placement of several *groups* of pieces (perhaps five or six groups with three to five pieces each). Given what they know about chess strategy, they recognize relationships among the pieces within groups and relationships of groups to one another. Besides enabling them to reconstruct games accurately from memory, this kind of chunking and schema activation enables chess experts to play, and usually defeat, a large number of novices at the same time by circulating continuously and taking only a few seconds to decide on a move (Chase & Chi, 1980).

Novice and expert category groupings

Closer to the classroom, Chi, Feltovich, and Glaser (1981) asked expert physicists and novice physics students to sort a variety of mechanics problems into categories and explain their reasoning. Novices sorted problems into the same category because they mentioned the same objects (such as pulleys or inclined planes) or the same physics concepts (such as friction). Experts, however, grouped problems because they involved the same general principle (such as conservation of energy), even though such principles usually were not mentioned explicitly. Similar findings were reported in mathematics by Schoenfeld and Hermann (1982) and Silver (1979). See Figures 9.3 and 9.4.

These differences in perception and organization of knowledge are paralleled by differences in thinking and problem solving (Newell & Simon, 1972; Shulman & Elstein, 1975). Here again, novices tend to focus on specific features of problems and try to link them to specific information stored in memory, whereas experts tend to "get the big picture" by identifying problems as particular instances of the application of general principles and then solving them by activating associated schemas. Confronted with a mathematics or physics problem, for example, novice students will try to relate it to a memorized theorem, equation, or formula. This approach often leads to errors, and even when it leads to the correct answer, the novices may not really understand what they have done or why. In contrast, experts first read and think about the problem as a whole to identify its general nature and the principles that apply to it and only then begin to make calculations.

Domain-specific knowledge

Experts can bring to bear much more *domain-specific knowledge* about the domains in which they specialize, and their knowledge is much better organized to allow smooth movement between levels ranging from concrete particulars to abstract generalities. In addition, experts are more efficient in using their knowledge. They do not have to work through all logical possibilities when classifying problems or identifying likely solution strategies. Instead, they create a workable *problem space* (cut the problem down to size) by identifying one or a small number of schemas that probably apply to the problem. There may be some initial checking to make sure that the right schema has been chosen (this is why experts analyze the problem first before trying to solve it), but once the problem is properly categorized, they solve it rapidly.

Research applied to teachers

Expert-novice comparisons have been used in studying how experienced teachers know when to use specific strategies with specific students and how novice teachers can develop this knowledge (Fogarty, Wang, & Creek, 1983; Peterson & Comeaux, 1987). Like experts in other fields, expert teachers use chunking strategies and schema activation to keep track of more things, to recognize (diagnose) student needs more quickly and accurately, and to bring to bear more strategies with better articulated understanding of why the strategies are appropriate to the situation.

Figure 9.3 Two Pairs of Problems Grouped Together by Novice Physics Students and Their Explanations for the Grouping.

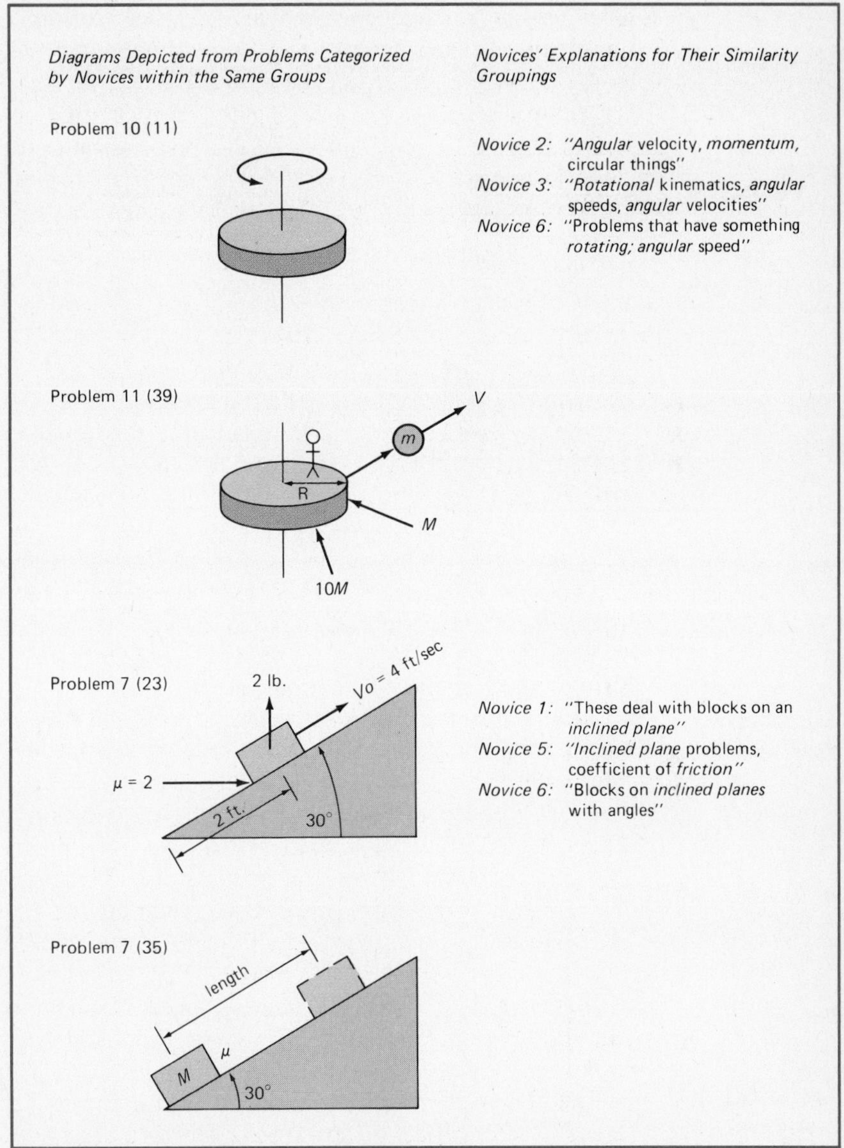

Diagrams Depicted from Problems Categorized by Novices within the Same Groups
Novices' Explanations for Their Similarity Groupings
Problem 10 (11)
Novice 2: "*Angular* velocity, *momentum,* circular things"
Novice 3: "*Rotational* kinematics, *angular* speeds, *angular* velocities"
Novice 6: "Problems that have something *rotating; angular* speed"
Problem 11 (39)
V
m
R
M
10M
Problem 7 (23)
2 lb.
Vo = 4 ft/sec
μ = 2
2 ft.
30°
Novice 1: "These deal with blocks on an *inclined plane*"
Novice 5: "*Inclined plane* problems, coefficient of *friction*"
Novice 6: "Blocks on *inclined planes* with angles"
Problem 7 (35)
length
M
μ
30°

Source: Chi, M.T.H., Feltovitch, P.J., and Glaser, R. (1981). "Categorization and representation of physics problems by experts and novices." *Cognitive Science* 5(2): 126–127. Reprinted by permission of the Ablex Publishing Corporation.

Figure 9.4 Two Pairs of Problems Grouped Together by Expert Physicists and Their Explanations for Why They Grouped Them (from Chi, Feltovich, & Glaser, 1981).

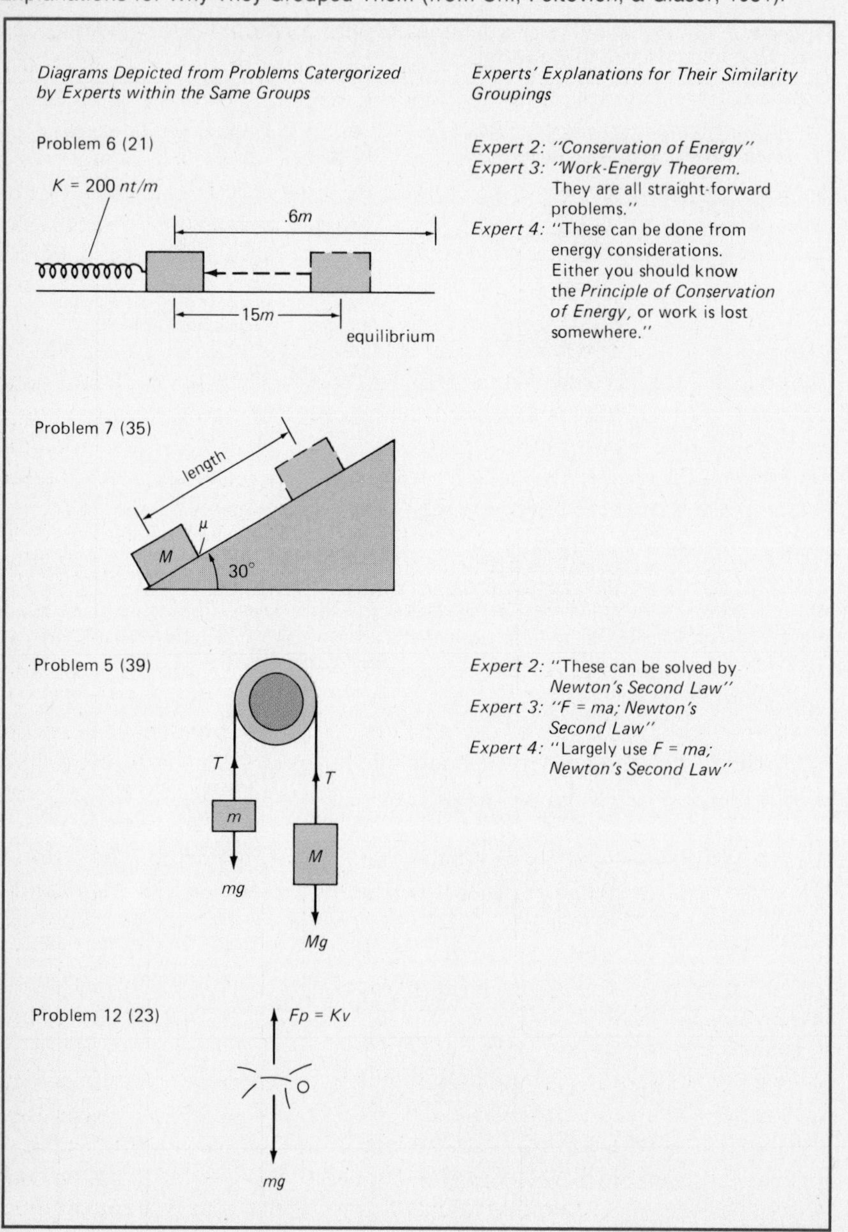

Diagrams Depicted from Problems Catergorized by Experts within the Same Groups
Experts' Explanations for Their Similarity Groupings
Problem 6 (21)
K = 200 nt/m
.6m
15m
equilibrium
Expert 2: "*Conservation of Energy*"
Expert 3: "*Work-Energy Theorem.* They are all straight-forward problems."
Expert 4: "These can be done from energy considerations. Either you should know the *Principle of Conservation of Energy,* or work is lost somewhere."
Problem 7 (35)
length
μ
M
30°
Problem 5 (39)
T
T
m
M
mg
Mg
Expert 2: "These can be solved by *Newton's Second Law*"
Expert 3: "*F = ma; Newton's Second Law*"
Expert 4: "Largely use *F = ma; Newton's Second Law*"
Problem 12 (23)
Fp = Kv
mg

Source: Chi, M.T.H., Feltovitch, P.J., and Glaser, R. (1981). "Categorization and representation of physics problems by experts and novices." *Cognitive Science* 5(2): 126–127. Reprinted by permission of Ablex Publishing Corporation.

Leinhardt and Greeno (1986) showed this in their comparison of an expert versus a novice teacher opening elementary mathematics lessons with homework review. Although the goals and the nature of what had to be accomplished in the homework review activities were similar in the two classrooms, the expert was able to use established routines for taking attendance, signaling the beginnings and endings of lesson segments, and regulating when students would respond chorally and when they would need to raise their hands and be called on. This teacher efficiently recorded information about attendance and about who did and did not do the homework, elicited mostly correct answers throughout the activity, managed to get all of the homework corrected, and noted who would need individualized help later. Interviews showed that most of her behavior during the activity was systematically adapted to the time constraints, the goals of the lesson, and its place within the larger mathematics curriculum strand. In contrast, the novice teacher was less clear about the purposes of the activity and how they could be best accomplished, and she lacked established routines for proceeding efficiently. Consequently, she had problems with taking attendance, was not clear about who did or did not do the homework, asked ambiguous questions that caused her to misunderstand the difficulty of the homework for the students, had trouble controlling the pace of the activity, and failed to identify the students who would need individualized follow-up. As more is learned about how expert teachers cut through the complexities of the classroom in order to function efficiently as instructors, it should become possible to move novices toward such expert levels of functioning more quickly and systematically.

"Counting all" method

Interesting research is also being done on the development of expertise in novices, including novice academic learners (Bereiter & Scardamalia, 1986). Children's mathematics learning provides several examples. Groen and Parkman (1972) have shown that preschool children typically use a "counting all" method for solving simple addition problems. For 3 + 4, for example, these children will recite "1, 2, 3, 4, 5, 6, 7." By first grade, however, most children use a "choice plus counting on" procedure in which they first choose the larger of the two numbers to be added and then "count on" the additional numbers. Thus for 3 + 4, they would recite "5, 6, 7." Most children discover this more sophisticated strategy on their own, without having to be taught explicitly.

Shortcuts

They also discover various shortcuts. Fuson (1982) has shown that first graders are fast at adding "doubles" (2 + 2, 3 + 3, etc.) because they have memorized the answers and do not need to count at all. They also use their "doubles" knowledge for solving other problems (i.e., they can recognize 5 + 7 as the equivalent of 6 + 6 and thus solve it without needing the "counting on" procedure). Expert algebra students can use estimates of what answers are likely to be to check their work as they go along. In combining the expression $a/b + c/d$, for example, they may substitute numbers for the letters (1/2 + 3/4) and work out the numerical version as a way to make sure that they have combined properly (in this case, by first dividing and then adding), something that is not so obvious when just the letters are used (Davis, 1984).

These data suggest several implications for teachers. First, there appear to be no shortcuts to expert knowledge. Detailed domain-specific knowledge is needed, not just a few general principles. Second, learners not only need to acquire knowledge and master strategies, they also need to know when the knowledge is relevant and how to use the strategies in various situations. This implies emphasis on the processes involved in formulating problems and working through solutions, not just on using the right formula or getting the right answer. Third, linkages between the abstract and the concrete need to be made explicit. Students should understand why they are working through a geometric proof or conducting a scientific experiment, so that they appreciate the larger meanings of the exercise and come away from it with more than just the notion that they got it right. Finally, students need opportunities to apply and synthesize their knowledge. Lectures and demonstrations is not enough.

Cognitive Simulation and Artificial Intelligence

Program strategies

Many cognitive scientists develop and test models of human information processing using computers. One approach is known as *artificial intelligence*—applying what is known about knowledge, logic, and communication to the development of computer programs designed to process information and solve problems (Simon, 1981). Computers have been programmed to translate text from one language to another, to interpret pictures, and to "learn" or solve problems by operating on input (using decision-making programs). The programs involve such strategies as *means-end analysis* (comparing the present state to the desired end state to identify the difference and develop ideas about how it might be reduced), *hypothesize and test* (using available information to develop and test hypotheses), and *best-first search* (evaluating hypotheses to identify the one most likely to be correct and beginning with this "best" one).

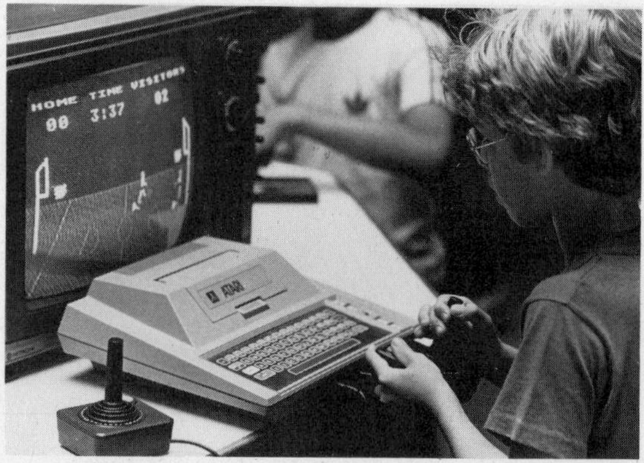

Although computers with specialized software can challenge and often defeat young learners at various games, they cannot play as creatively or efficiently as their human opponents.

Limitations in strategic thinking

Artificial intelligence work has produced impressive practical demonstrations, such as chess programs that defeat all but the most expert chess players. Yet these programs are successful only because of the huge memory capacities and rapid information-processing capabilities of computers. They approach strategic thinking in thorough and logical but inefficient ways, more like novices than experts, and they are not good at certain things that human experts do routinely, such as distinguishing relevant from irrelevant information, responding to situational particulars, and, in general, using "common sense." For example, Waldrop (1984) noted Minsky's "dead duck" example: Using rules of logic, computers would be programmed to conclude that Charlie can fly given information that ducks can fly and Charlie is a duck. If Charlie is dead, however, he cannot fly. Humans easily accommodate this information, but artificial intelligence programs can do so only with enormous increases in programming complexity and memory capacity.

Simulation of human cognition

Cognitive scientists also have worked on the *simulation of human cognition*. Here, programs are developed on the basis of actual thinking of humans engaged in problem solving rather than on the basis of purely logical considerations. Many of these are "expert systems" programs that model the behavior of experts in various fields, although programs have also been developed to model the learning of young children (Klahr & Wallace, 1976) and even the *buggy algorithms* (systematic but erroneous methods) were developed by learners for solving mathematics problems (Brown & Burton, 1978).

Cognitive simulation procedure

Cognition simulation proceeds according to a bootstrapping procedure in which scientists first identify the essential elements of the behavior to be modeled, then develop a model that includes these elements and build it into a computer program, then test and improve the model's ability to "predict" the originally observed behavior in similar situations, and then use the model to process new input. One program of research, for example, began with analysis of the behavior of reading specialists trying to diagnose and prescribe for students encountering reading difficulties. What sorts of information did the experts request? Which of this information did they actually use in developing a diagnosis? Which specific diagnoses were used, and what were their critical indicators? What treatments were prescribed for remediating the diagnosed reading skill deficiencies? No two reading experts handled a given case in exactly the same way, but commonalities observed across experts and cases could be built into a computer program designed to diagnose reading difficulties. The researchers were able to construct a simulated "consensus expert" that diagnoses and prescribes for reading difficulties more reliably than individual experts do. Furthermore, computer-assisted instruction involving application of this program to actual cases of reading difficulty has been used to train teachers to diagnose such cases (Vinsonhaler et al., 1983). Heller and Reif (1984) followed similar procedures in developing a model of expert problem solving in physics that has proven useful for teaching students to represent mechanics problems accurately and thus to solve them more efficiently.

Summary

Information-processing theorists study information processing, storage, and retrieval in human learning. In contrast to the relatively passive and static version of human learning and memory presented by associationist theorists, information-processing theorists adopt a constructivist view. They construe learning as a cognitive representation constructed actively by a learner attempting to make sense out of experiences and see this cognitive representation as subject to change over time as it interacts with previously stored memories and is affected by newer experiences. The rote memory experiments of Ebbinghaus and the story reconstruction studies by Bartlett are examples of the associationist and constructivist approaches, respectively.

Experiences are encoded and stored in memory in different ways. Episodes in our personal lives are stored in episodic memory, which features images of ourselves reliving those events. However, intentional learning of material communicated through language is encoded in semantic memory, which features concept definitions, statements, principles, and other verbal abstractions.

Most information-processing theorists accept the three-stage information-processing model, in which input first enters the sensory register, then short-term or working memory, and then long-term memory. The sensory register has a capacity of 7 ± 2 items of information, so rehearsal and chunking strategies must be used when this limited capacity is strained by the need to consider many items of input at once. Chunking can greatly increase the capacity of working memory to accommodate individual items. Information about concepts and relationships appears to be stored in long-term memory in the form of semantic networks organized hierarchically.

Learning is an active process of sense making in which the learner activates prior knowledge to generate frameworks within which to interpret new input. The learner "goes beyond the information given" by filling in gaps and assuming meanings and implications that are implied but not directly stated.

Learners must rely on rote processes when input is not very meaningful or organized. Besides the level of meaningfulness of the input, rote learning is affected by serial position effects (primacy and recency effects), item distinctiveness, amount and distribution of practice, and the effects of transfer, interference, organization, levels of processing, state- or context-dependency, and mnemonics. The place, link, peg, and keyword methods, along with other mnemonics such as the elaboration method and the use of pictures, images, rhymes, and acronyms, assist learning of relatively meaningless material by associating it with meaningful and organized material.

The meaningful verbal learning of connected discourse shows abstraction effects, level effects, schema effects, prior knowledge effects, inference effects, student-misconception effects, text-organization effects, and mathemagenic effects. Adjunct questions (prequestions, inserted questions, and postquestions) help to elicit mathemagenic effects.

Contemporary contributions can be seen in recent research on reading comprehension, comparisons between novices and experts, and cognitive simulation and artificial intelligence. These lines of research not only advance our understanding of sophisticated human cognition in various domains but also suggest potential methods for moving novices efficiently toward expert status.

Questions and Problems

1. Without reexamining the text or looking at notes, outline what you remember from what was presented about human development in Chapters 2 through 5. Why have you remembered some things and forgotten others? How do the models presented in this chapter for how memory works account for your learning?
2. Describe the conditions under which students are most likely to retain information for future use. How can teachers help students to retain information meaningfully?
3. Can teachers present too much as well as too little information? List conditions under which detailed information may be inappropriate. If you took a behavioral view instead of a cognitive view of learning, would you answer this question differently? Why or why not?
4. In your own words, explain the "7 ± 2" rule and its implications for designing instruction.
5. Reexamine the guidelines that Case (1978) has presented for minimizing the load placed on students' working memory. If you were teaching seventh graders the differences between red and white blood cells and their role in body functioning, how would you proceed?
6. How might encouraging students to ask questions about material facilitate or inhibit their learning?
7. Differentiate between transfer effects and interference effects. How do they differ from organization and levels-of-processing effects?
8. Explain how *distinctiveness* of encoding, *elaboration* of encoding, and *effort* expended during encoding influence how much information is retained in long-term memory.
9. To what extent should teachers cue students to the sorts of questions that they will ask on tests? What are the advantages and disadvantages of sharing this information?
10. Should we as authors raise questions with you before or after you read a chapter? If so, what kind? What are the relative advantages of different types of prequestions and postquestions?
11. What are useful mathemagenic activities for students to engage in? How can teachers encourage them to do so?
12. Using the concepts discussed in this chapter, explain why you could not do as well on a high school history test today as you did when

you took it. In particular, what was the long-term effect of studying for the test?

13. As a teacher, how can you help students to learn material so that they will retain it in long-term memory?

CASE STUDIES

CAN'T PUT IT ALL TOGETHER. Mrs. Washington is unhappy with her mathematics students' performance on word problems. They solve equations quickly, and most can complete a page of forty problems with no errors. Yet with word problems, it's as if they had never heard of algebra. Some can't even begin, others guess answers without showing any work, and still others represent the problem incorrectly and end up solving the wrong equation. Even the students who get the right answer seem unsure of themselves when questioned.

Even more puzzling and frustrating, the students usually can respond correctly when she guides them through these problems by asking a series of questions. Thus it is not that they lack knowledge; it's that they don't get the point or are unable to put it all together when asked to apply this knowledge to problems that are not already formulated algebraically. Using concepts such as information storage and retrieval, limited capacity of working memory, or novice versus expert problem solving, develop an explanation for the production deficiency problems that Mrs. Washington's students are experiencing. What can she do to help them overcome these problems?

TWO DIFFERENT WORLDS. Mrs. Karo and Mrs. Tapper both use the Raleigh Company's second-grade science curriculum. They are teaching a unit on trees and leaves, and today's lesson focuses on maple trees and the process of collecting sap to use in making maple syrup. Mrs. Tapper teaches in a small town in Michigan. Most of her students are familiar with maple trees because they are surrounded by them. Furthermore, many have had firsthand experience with the sap-collecting process, either through their own relatives or through attending demonstrations and tasting experiences offered to the public by commercial sap collectors.

Mrs. Karo teaches in inner-city Phoenix. Few of her students have ever been outside of the city, let alone traveled the country, so most of them have never even seen a maple tree. In fact, most of the local vegetation has needles rather than leaves, and none of it looks much like maple trees.

Given what was said about how learners activate prior knowledge when responding to input, what will be the similarities and differences in the responses of Mrs. Tapper's students and Mrs. Karo's students to the science lesson? How meaningful will the information be, and how are they likely to process and store it? How might the two teachers adapt this lesson to their students? How can Mrs. Tapper work around her students' belief that they "already know that" and get them to learn something? How can Mrs. Karo make the material meaningful and interesting to her students? Which teacher should do more demonstrating and explaining, and which should allocate more time to discussion?

PART 4
INSTRUCTIONAL APPLICATIONS

Charlie Curvesetter and Frank Frustrated are in the same history class. They are similar in ability and time spent studying history, but Charlie consistently outperforms Frank on tests and assignments. How can this be?

Mrs. Fitzgerald finds that some students learn division of decimals easily, some divide correctly but often misplace the decimal point, and a few don't even divide correctly. Those few students appear to need remedial instruction in the division skills and associated number facts taught in earlier grades. How can Mrs. Fitzgerald determine what needs to be included in this instruction, and how might she identify appropriate materials and activities?

Mr. Becker and Mr. Rowe both emphasize teacher-led group instruction featuring presentations to the class, recitation activities, and independent seatwork. Both are successful. However, Mr. Becker's presentations tend to last only a few minutes, and an hour in his classroom usually includes several short but fast-paced activities. In contrast, Mr. Rowe frequently lectures for twenty to thirty minutes, and an hour in his class usually includes only two or three slower-paced activities. What might explain these differences between two teachers who use the same general approach to instruction and achieve similar success?

After completing a lecture–demonstration, teacher Susan Melnick moves into a recitation phase of her lesson and begins questioning her students. After calling on volunteers and receiving correct responses to several questions, she decides to call on Terry Tense, an anxious and reticent student. Susan was willing to risk putting Terry on the spot in this situation because she was confident that he would be able to answer her question. However, in the seeming eternity since she called his name, actually only about two seconds, he hasn't taken his eyes off the floor and he has begun to turn red. What should Susan do now?

In Part Four of our text (Chapters 10–13), we discuss some of the instructional applications of the theories, concepts, and research discussed in Part Three on learning. We begin in Chapter 10 with information about developing students' skills for strategic reading, systematic studying, problem solving, and critical thinking. Chapter 10 will explain how differences between Charlie Curvesetter's and Frank Frustrated's note-taking and study skills may explain the differences in their performance. Charlie takes organized notes that outline the presentation and paraphrase its gist, but Frank's notes are a haphazard selection from the presentation rather than an organized synopsis of it. Also, when studying, Charlie underlines sparingly and uses chunking strategies keyed to the structuring and sequencing devices the author has used in organizing the text, whereas Frank underlines three-fourths of the material and tries to memorize as much of it as possible. Chapter 10 explains how students like Frank can learn to take notes and study more effectively.

Chapter 11 presents concepts and procedures for conceptualizing curricula, establishing sequences of objectives, and designing instruction. It explains how Mrs. Fitzgerald could do a task analysis of the hierarchy of skills required for successful division of decimals and then work backward from the target objective to her students' present skill levels to establish a starting point for remedial instruction. More generally, the chapter explains how to design instruction that moves students efficiently from the simple/familiar to the complex/unfamiliar, drawing examples from research on the teaching of concepts.

Chapters 12 and 13 present findings from process-outcome research linking teacher behavior to student-achievement gain. Chapter 12 explains the value of active teaching in which the teacher provides instruction and guides learning personally rather than relying exclusively on the curriculum materials to do so. The chapter also notes, however, that the particulars of active teaching must be adapted to the grade level, the subject matter, and the students. Given the descriptions of their classes, it is likely that Mr. Becker teaches in the primary grades and spends most of this time working on basic skills but that Mr. Rowe teaches at the secondary level in a subject matter (such as history) that emphasizes knowledge more than skills.

Chapter 13 focuses on two sets of instructional skills—making presentations and conducting activities that involve questioning and responding to students. It also offers guidelines for handling seatwork and homework assignments. One principle for effective questioning and responding is that teachers should train their students to respond overtly to questions and not allow them simply to remain silent and wait for the teacher to give the answer or call on someone else. Thus Ms. Melnick usually should simply wait for Terry Tense to respond or perhaps help him by rephrasing the question or giving a clue. However, this situation may be an exception to the general rule, especially if continued waiting yields only further evidence of tension and embarrassment.

CHAPTER

Skills for Learning: Strategic Reading, Systematic Studying, Problem Solving, and Critical Thinking

CHAPTER OUTLINE

OBJECTIVES

When you have mastered the material in this chapter, you will be able to

1. Define the five general types of learning strategies identified by Weinstein and Mayer (1986)—rehearsal, elaboration, organizational, comprehension monitoring, and affective
2. Define the term *metacognition* and explain why teachers should strive to stimulate students to develop metacognitive awareness of their learning in addition to stimulating the learning itself
3. Describe the strategies used by expert readers that are not used by novice or poor readers
4. Describe the strategy training approach to improving reading skills and identify the strategies that have been included in successful training experiments
5. Explain and use the SQ3R method for effective studying
6. Describe the deep-level processing and elaboration strategies used by successful studiers
7. Explain and use principles for effective note taking
8. Describe commonly encountered text patterns that can be used as bases for organizing notes

9. State methods of helping students become strategic learners by reading and studying effectively
10. Define key concepts associated with the information-processing approach to human problem solving (well- versus ill-structured problems, algorithms, heuristics, task environment, problem space) and describe the findings of this research indicating that most human problem solving relies on heuristics rather than on the more systematic and logical-deductive mechanisms postulated by classical models
11. Describe the heuristics typically used by expert problem solvers for representing and solving problems and explain the implications of this information for teaching students to solve problems effectively
12. Explain Ohlsson's (1983) enaction theory of human thinking and its implication for teaching thinking skills to students
13. Describe the approaches taken in contemporary programs designed to teach general thinking skills (Philosophy for Children, the CoRT Program, and the Instrumental Enrichment Program)

In previous chapters we noted that the transfer value of particular learning tends to be limited, and that a great deal of domain-specific knowledge must be accumulated before a novice can become an expert. Thus there appear to be no easy shortcuts to expert functioning.

However, certain relatively generic skills facilitate learning in a broad range of situations—reading with speed, accuracy, and comprehension; critical thinking; general principles of problem solving; and various mathemagenic behaviors, "learning to learn" skills, and study skills. As part of the recent emphasis on cognition and human information processing, a great deal of research has been done on the development of effective strategies for learning, and on how these strategies may be taught to individuals who do not develop them spontaneously.

Types of learning strategies

In a review of this work, Weinstein and Mayer (1986) identified the following five general types of learning strategies.

- *Rehearsal strategies* involve actively repeating (saying, writing) material or focusing on key parts of it. For brief rote learning tasks, rehearsal may involve nothing more than repeating the material aloud. For more complex learning from lectures or from studying, rehearsal may involve repeating key terms aloud (shadowing), copying the material, taking verbatim notes, or underlining important parts.
- *Elaboration strategies* involve making connections between the new and the familiar. For rote learning, elaboration strategies include forming mental images to associate with the material, generating sentences that relate the items to be learned to more familiar items, or using mnemonic devices like the keyword method. For more

complex meaningful learning, elaboration strategies include paraphrasing, summarizing, creating analogies, taking notes that go beyond verbatim repetition to extend or comment on the material, answering questions (either adjunct questions already included with the text or self-generated questions), and describing how the new information relates to existing knowledge.

- *Organizational strategies* involve imposing structure on the material by dividing it into parts and identifying superordinate-subordinate relationships. In simple rote learning, organizational strategies involve breaking lists into chunks. Organizational strategies for complex meaningful learning include outlining the text, creating a hierarchy or network of concepts, or creating diagrams showing their relationships.
- *Comprehension monitoring strategies* involve remaining aware of what one is trying to accomplish, keeping track of the strategies one uses and the success achieved with them, and adjusting behavior accordingly. Comprehension monitoring strategies include self-questioning to check understanding, taking action when one does not understand, using prequestions or statements of objectives to guide study, establishing subgoals and assessing progress in meeting them, and modifying strategies if necessary.
- *Affective strategies* include establishing and maintaining motivation, focusing attention, maintaining concentration, managing performance anxiety, and managing time effectively.

These relatively generic learning strategies and related cognitive skills are not only worth teaching to elementary and secondary students; you, the reader, should find them helpful in your own learning. We discuss skills involved in reading for comprehension, studying for retention, problem solving, and thinking.

STRATEGIES FOR READING WITH COMPREHENSION

Production deficiency

In discussing *production deficiency* in Chapter 4, we noted that some children use rote learning methods when memorizing lists of meaningful words, even though they possess superordinate concepts that could be used to chunk the words into categories (Flavell, Beach, & Chinsky, 1966). Later work showed that such production deficiencies in use of clustering strategies for free recall of word lists were special cases of a more general phenomenon: Children's awareness of and ability to use strategies for remembering what they learn emerge gradually and uncertainly, so they often use an inefficient strategy when they possess knowledge that should enable them to use a more efficient strategy. Their knowledge about strategies (rehearsal, chunking, etc.) for learning and remembering is spotty and poorly integrated.

Metamemory

Work on this topic eventually became known as the study of *metamemory:* knowledge about how memory works and how to memorize

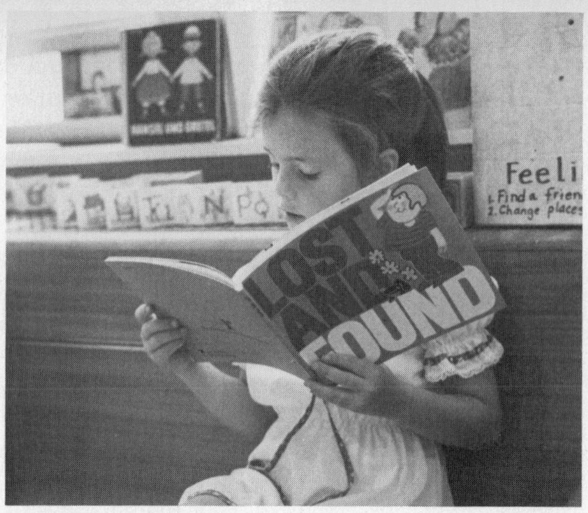

Children who are taught to use efficient reading strategies are better learners.

effectively (Flavell & Wellman, 1977; Kail & Hagen, 1982). This work revealed that children only gradually come to learn that some kinds of material (meaningful, organized, interesting) are easier to learn than others, that recognition tests are easier than recall tests, that paraphrased recall is easier than verbatim recall, or that active rehearsal will produce better results than silent reading. Training studies showed that children given metamemory strategies usually learned more than control children but often reverted to their pretraining behavior unless continually reminded to use the strategies (Kail & Hagen, 1982).

Metacognition

Other research revealed developmental differences in children's knowledge about cognitive operations other than memory (comprehension, problem solving, etc.). The term *metacognition* refers to the general topic of knowledge about cognitive processes and how they function, and the term *metacognitive awareness* refers to a person's conscious monitoring of his or her own cognitive strategies during the process of applying them.

Metacomprehension

A particularly interesting subtopic in research on metacognition is the study of *metacomprehension:* the strategies that readers use in monitoring, evaluating, and repairing their comprehension during the act of reading (Baker & Brown, 1984; Paris, Lipson, & Wixson, 1983). Children can be taught comprehension monitoring strategies that help them understand what they read and remember it in an organized way. These strategies include identifying relevant background knowledge, generating and responding to questions about the material, making connections between its parts, drawing inferences from it, and summarizing and organizing it (Pearson & Gallagher, 1983; Tierney & Cunningham, 1984). Unfortunately, students rarely receive instruction in these comprehension monitoring strategies in typical classrooms (Durkin, 1978–79; Duffy & Roehler, 1982). Thus it is important for teachers at all grade levels to be aware of these strategies and prepared to teach them to students who do not use them spontaneously.

Novice versus Expert Readers

Much has been learned about comprehension strategies by tracing developmental changes in reading skills. At first, novice readers focus on word recognition and verbatim recall of text, rather than on trying to make sense of what they are reading (Wixson et al., 1984). Only gradually do they learn that studying requires deliberate effort and strategies to understand and remember what is being read. Young children presented with memory tasks often fail to generate plans or allocate effort to studying (Kail & Hagen, 1982), and poor readers instructed to study a passage may read it only once, fail to check their understanding, and say they are ready for the test without selective studying (Brown, Campione, & Barclay, 1979).

In general, poor readers do not skim, scan, reread, integrate information, plan ahead, take notes, or make inferences as often as skilled readers (Anderson & Armbruster, 1982; Golinkoff, 1976; Ryan, 1981). They are less planful and metacognitively aware when they read, and they have difficulty evaluating a text for its clarity, internal consistency, and compatibility with what they already know (Markman, 1981). They are often unaware that they are experiencing problems in comprehension, and they often fail to take corrective action even when they recognize problems (Brown & Smiley, 1978; Paris & Myers, 1981).

Strategies used by skilled readers

In contrast, skilled readers use strategies appropriate for the purpose of reading, monitor their comprehension as they read, and take corrective actions (*repair strategies*) in response to ambiguities and comprehension failures. In particular, they use strategies for (1) clarifying task demands, (2) reading for meaning, (3) focusing on important content rather than minor details (reading for remembering), (4) monitoring their comprehension as they read, (5) checking and reviewing to make sure that goals are being met, (6) taking corrective action when comprehension fails, and (7) recovering from disruptions so that text processing can continue (Brown, 1980).

Strategy Training

Strategy training experiments in which younger or poorer readers are trained to use the strategies employed by more skilled readers usually yield at least some success and sometimes remarkable results. Trained students usually do not function as effectively as students who develop the strategies spontaneously, but they do learn to read with better comprehension. Often the training needs to be explicit; simply giving students a little general information is not enough. Many will need training that includes both *procedural knowledge* (how to use the strategies) and *conditional knowledge* (when and why to use them) (Paris et al., 1983). We now sample recent training studies, arranged roughly in order of the grade levels of the students for whom the strategies were designed.

Informed strategies for learning

Strategy Training in the Primary Grades Paris, Cross, and Lipson (1984) developed a training program entitled Informed Strategies for Learning (ISL) designed to increase third and fifth graders' use of effective reading strategies. The program is a set of fourteen weekly modules that illustrate strategies and show students the effort required and the benefits to be expected from their use. For example, one lesson describes skimming, shows how to skim, and tells when skimming is useful (as a preview or review technique) and when it is not (during reading for full understanding of the meaning). Students first observe models use the strategies and then practice doing so themselves (with guidance from the teacher). Strategies are explained using metaphors. For example, the lesson on evaluating to discover clues to the topic, length, and difficulty of a passage uses the metaphor "be a reading detective." Comprehension monitoring strategies are made comprehensible by using analogies to traffic signs ("Stop—say the meaning in your own words." "Dead end—go back and reread the parts you don't understand").

The program includes modules on purposes of reading (Reading is Like a Puzzle), comprehension strategies (A Bag Full of Tricks for Reading), task evaluation (Be a Reading Detective), forming plans (Plan Your Reading Trip), reading goals and kinds of meaning (What's in the Meaning?), abstracting critical information (Tracking Down the Main Idea), ambiguity and inference (Infer the Hidden Meaning), summarizing main points (Round Up Your Ideas), critical evaluation (Judge Your Reading), comprehension monitoring (The Road to Reading Disaster), resolving comprehension failures (Road Repairs), speed versus accuracy (Skimming Along), and abstracting and highlighting (Focus and Develop the Big Picture). Evaluation data revealed that ISL students made greater gains on cloze tests (requiring them to supply missing words) and error-detection tests than control students taught with conventional methods and materials. There were no significant differences on standardized reading comprehension tests, possibly because these tests involve answering multiple-choice questions about short paragraphs under time constraints rather than comprehending longer and more integrated text studied under normal conditions (Johnston, 1984).

Practice in answering questions

Strategy Training in the Intermediate Grades Hansen and Pearson (1983) improved fourth graders' reading comprehension using strategy training and practice in answering questions. The strategy training involved story introductions in which students were asked to (1) relate what they knew from prior knowledge about what to do in circumstances like those facing the upcoming story characters, (2) predict what the protagonist would do, (3) record their prior knowledge answers on one sheet of paper and their predictions on another and then weave the two together (to establish the metaphor that reading involves weaving together what one knows and what is in a text).

The other part of the treatment involved the questions asked following story reading. Typically, students are asked about 80 percent literal memory questions and only 20 percent inferential questions. In this study, the students were asked only inference questions. Evaluation data showed that this combination of strategy training with practice in responding to inference questions improved reading comprehension, especially among poor readers.

Text-explicit, text-implicit, and script-implicit questions

Raphael (1984) trained intermediate grade students in strategies for answering questions about text. Following Pearson and Johnson (1978), she distinguished three types of questions: *text explicit,* in which the answer is stated explicitly in a sentence in the text; *text implicit,* in which the information is located in the text but requires integration of material found in separate sentences; and *script implicit,* in which the information must be supplied by the reader through activating relevant scripts (schemas). Raphael taught the students to identify and respond to these three types of questions, respectively, by noting whether the information was "right there," whether they had to "think and find it," or whether they had to supply it "on my own." The training was effective in improving students' ability to answer such questions, especially for low-ability students.

Strategies for low reading group students

Duffy, Roehler, and their colleagues (Duffy et al., 1987; Duffy & Roehler, 1989) have trained intermediate grade teachers to provide explicit, detailed instruction in comprehension strategies to their low reading group students. Teachers are trained to explain the nature of each strategy (identifying the main idea, using the dictionary, etc.), tell when and why it is used, model by verbalizing the mental processes that occur when using it, and then provide students with opportunities to use the strategy and see its effectiveness for themselves. Following instruction, the students are interviewed to see if they can state in their own words what they learned, how one does it, and why it is important to know how to do it. Evaluation data reveal improvements in reading comprehension test scores and in student awareness of how the reading process works and how to use the strategies taught.

Strategies for generating self-questions

Wong and Jones (1982) trained normally achieving sixth graders and learning-disabled eighth and ninth graders in a five-step procedure for generating self-questions designed to help them monitor their understanding of important information in texts. This training substantially improved the learning disabled students' awareness of the important ideas, ability to formulate good questions about those ideas, and performance on comprehension tests. The training was less helpful to the normally achieving sixth graders, however, apparently because they had developed their own comprehension monitoring strategies.

Strategy Training in the Secondary Grades André and Anderson (1978–79) studied three groups of high school students—one trained to generate questions about main points in a text, one directed to ask such main idea questions but not trained in strategies for doing so, and one that simply read and reread the material. They found that the trained group outperformed the other groups, and the self-questioning treatment was especially effective with low- and medium-ability students.

Singer and Donlan (1982) taught high school students to read fiction analytically using a problem-solving frame based on story grammers. Students learned to note what the lead character was trying to accomplish, what stood in the way, and so on. Students eventually learned to apply the strategy consistently, with corresponding benefits to their comprehension and appreciation of short stories.

Cognitive behavior modification

Meichenbaum and Asarnow (1979) and Fox and Kendall (1983) reviewed research on cognitive behavior-modification approaches to strategy training that feature modeling combined with verbalized self-instruction. Learners first observe the model, then practice the strategy while verbalizing self-instructions overtly, and then fade overt verbalizations and transform them into silent self-talk. Skills addressed include identifying the problem (What is it I have to do?), focusing attention and guiding response (Now, carefully stop and repeat the instructions), self-evaluation and reinforcement (Good, I'm doing fine), and coping with and correcting mistakes (That's okay; I can take my time until I get it right).

Using reciprocal teaching

Palincsar and Brown (1984) taught four comprehension fostering and comprehension monitoring strategies to seventh-grade poor comprehenders: summarizing (self-review), questioning, clarifying, and predicting. They used a *reciprocal teaching* method, in which the teacher initially did most of the modeling and explaining but then gradually turned over the instructional responsibilities to the students themselves, until eventually they took turns acting as the teacher and leading small group discussions of the texts being read.

When beginning a passage, the teacher would note the title and ask for predictions about its content. Then the group would read the first segment silently, and the "student teacher" would ask a question about it, summarize it, and then offer a prediction or ask for clarification if appropriate. If necessary, the adult teacher would prompt ("What questions do you think a teacher might ask here?"), instruct ("Remember, a summary is a shortened version; it doesn't include detail"), or modify the activity ("If you are having a hard time thinking of a question, why don't you summarize first?"). The adult teacher also provided feedback and praise concerning the quality and specificity of questions and the logic used in making predictions.

Reciprocal teaching produced sizable gains in comprehension, maintenance of these gains over time, generalization to other comprehension tests, and transfer to novel tasks. Positive results were also obtained in a follow-up study in which ordinary classroom teachers, rather than the experimenters, functioned as instructors and also in a recent adaptation of the method for use with first graders (Palincsar & Brown, 1989).

Goal frame

Armbruster and Anderson (1984) identified *frames* (organizing structures or schemas) that are frequently used in social studies texts. In history texts, for example, the goal frame is common. This frame has four slots: Goal, plan, action, and outcome. The slots correspond to the main ideas in psychological explanations of historical events. The goal is the desired state sought by the group; the plan is their strategy for attaining the goal; the action is the behavior taken in response to the plan, and the outcome is the consequence of this action. Armbruster and Anderson suggested that students who are made aware of this goal frame should be able to read with better comprehension and to take more organized notes about historical events to which the frame is applicable (accounts of voyages of discovery, for example). They also identify a problem/solution frame (a variation of the goal frame that applies to accounts of situations in which problems arose during attempts to meet the goal), a compromise frame, and a war frame (both of which apply to accounts of situations in which the goals or plans of two groups are incompatible).

Conclusions about Strategic Reading

Efficient reading with comprehension is strategic: It involves allocation of attention and use of strategies to understand the meaning of what is being read and to remember it for future reference (Paris, Lipson, & Wixson, 1983). Specifically, strategic reading involves attending to the purposes of the reading, activating relevant schemas and background knowledge, concentrating on major points, evaluating the content for internal consistency and compatibility with prior knowledge, monitoring ongoing comprehension through periodic review and self-questioning, and drawing and testing of inferences by making interpretations, predictions, and conclusions (Palincsar & Brown, 1984). There is great variability in the degree to which individuals develop such strategies and thus in the efficiency with which they read and study. Students who do not develop such strategies spontaneously will need instruction in them. Consequently, in addition to becoming a strategic reader yourself, it will be important for you to teach your students to do so, using methods appropriate to their ages and developmental levels (Pearson & Dole, 1987).

LEARNING STRATEGIES AND STUDY SKILLS

To learn efficiently from texts, students must be able not only to comprehend what they read but also to retain and use the information. This requires use of effective strategies for independent learning. Even college students differ considerably in the nature and outcomes of their studying strategies.

Surface-level versus deep-level processors

Van Rossum and Schenk (1984) had students take a pretest, then read a 400-line historical passage while having the opportunity to study it and take notes, and then take a posttest and answer questions about how they studied. About half of the students used a surface-level study approach—they tried to memorize the content. The other half processed the material at deeper levels. For example, one student first skimmed the text to get an overview of the content, then read more slowly with attention to the connections within and between paragraphs, then tried to repeat the main lines of information and argument himself without looking at the text. *Surface-level* processors tried to memorize the material so as to be able to reproduce it, whereas the *deep-level* processors tried to understand the material, develop insights, and think about how it would be used.

When questioned about their conception of the learning process, thirty-three of the fifty-five surface-level studiers emphasized memorizing the content, trying to increase their knowledge, or trying to acquire facts to be retained or used in practice. Only two described learning as the abstraction of meaning or as an interpretive process aimed at understanding reality. In contrast, twenty-three of the thirty-four deep-level studiers emphasized the latter definitions of learning, and only eleven emphasized the former. The surface-level studiers were less likely to report enjoying reading the text and were more nervous in testing situations (Benjamin and associates [1981] also found that highly anxious students tend to rely excessively on repetition and rote memorization rather than more effective study strategies).

Evaluation data revealed no difference in responses to factual knowledge questions but a superior performance by the deep-level studiers on "insight" questions. The free-response answers of the surface-level studiers were merely lists of facts with few connections between them, but those of the deep-level processors usually were more coherent, containing main ideas linked to supportive material presented in logical lines of argument toward conclusions.

A great deal has been learned about effective strategies for studying and learning independently and about how to teach these strategies to students who have not developed them spontaneously. Most of this work has been done recently, although it has roots in Robinson's SQ3R method (Robinson, 1970).

SQ3R Method

The five steps of SQ3R method

SQ3R stands for the five steps in the SQ3R method: survey, question, read, recite, and review. First, skim or *survey* the passage: Read the title and any introductory material to get a general idea of what the passage is about, note its length and organization to identify the author's general approach, and preview any pictures, charts, or illustrations. Second, *question* yourself by identifying information that you want or are likely to get from reading the passage. The headings are useful in identifying such questions. On encountering the previous heading, for example, you might have asked yourself, "What are the steps in the SQ3R method?" Third, *read* the material, paying attention to introductory paragraphs and main ideas, rereading difficult passages and looking up unfamiliar words if necessary, and keeping in mind that you are trying to understand and respond to the author's main purpose. Fourth, *recite* (or *recall*) the material. Close the book and try to answer in your own words the questions you raised earlier and to state the author's purpose and main ideas. Fifth, *review:* Concentrate on passages that you find difficult or have not yet fixed in your mind, and on remembering the main ideas and the linkages between them.

The SQ3R method fits well with the information processing view of human learning (Tadlock, 1978), and it appears to be worth adopting as a systematic "deep-level processing" approach to studying (Darch, Carnine, & Kameenui, 1986). See Robinson (1970) for more information about SQ3R, and Devine (1981) for information about related methods.

Elaboration Strategies

Weinstein (1982) trained ninth graders in *elaboration strategies* to use during study: generating verbal or imaginal elaborators to make material more meaningful, creating analogies to express new material in more familiar terms, drawing implications, and creating relationships through elaborative paraphrasing (relating the material to what is already known while also restating it in one's own words). Five hours of training in application of these strategies to school tasks produced better test performance than was produced by a control group that practiced the same tasks but did not receive the training in elaboration strategies. Subsequent work by Weinstein has involved training college students to use these strategies in their studies.

Note Taking

To retain material for future use, it usually is necessary not only to study it in an active, systematic way but also to take notes or in some other way preserve key ideas in a form that makes them easy to refer to later (Kiewra & Benton, 1988). Devine (1981) discussed underlining, marginal notes, summarizing, and outlining as common forms of note taking.

Underlining

Underlining and related forms of highlighting important material are among the study techniques used most by college students (Policastro, 1975). Underlining appears to be less effective than other note-taking techniques, however, because it is comparatively passive, and it psychologically defers the active learning process to some future time. Also, many students use it ineffectively because they underline too much or underline before they have absorbed enough of the material to know which parts are most important. Thus underlining may be most useful if done only after reading through the material the first time.

Marginal comments and coding systems

Devine (1981) suggested supplementing underlining with marginal comments or coding systems. *Marginal comments* include questions, rephrasings of difficult sentences, and definitions of unfamiliar words. *Coding systems* include color coding (using markers) to indicate main ideas and separate them from supporting evidence, circles around new terms, arrows indicating relationships between ideas, boxes to contain related ideas, marginal numbers to indicate sequential patterns, stars to indicate important ideas, or question marks to indicate disagreement with the author. Marginal comments or coding systems involve the reader more actively in the author's presentation than mere underlining does.

These methods can be used, however, only by students who own the books and are willing to write in them. Other students will have to rely on outlining, summarizing, and other forms of note taking. Students who learn to take notes systematically will be more successful than those who

Taking notes efficiently is an essential part of the learning process.

take notes haphazardly (Carrier & Titus, 1981; Kiewra, 1987; Ladas, 1980).

Summaries

Note taking in the form of written *summaries* is likely to facilitate learning (Brown, Campione, & Day, 1981; Doctorow, Wittrock, & Marks, 1978; Taylor, 1982). Good summaries condense the material and focus on the important ideas. Brown and Day (1980, cited in Armbruster & Brown, 1984) identified six rules essential to effective summarizing: (1) delete trivial material, (2) delete redundant material, (3) substitute a superordinate term for a list of subordinate items when possible, (4) substitute a superordinate event for a list of subordinate actions when possible, (5) select a topic sentence if the author has provided one, and (6) write your own topic sentence if necessary.

Simply telling students these rules was sufficient to improve performance for some. Others needed training in strategies: delete redundant information with red pencil, delete trivial information with blue pencil, write in superordinates for any lists, underline topic sentences if provided, write topic sentences where needed. Students who practiced these strategies and also checked their performance using a checklist gained the most.

Note-taking principles

In addition to summarizing, guidelines have been developed for other forms of *note taking*. Carrier and Titus (1981), for example, suggested the following general principles for taking notes during lectures: (1) distinguish between superordinate and subordinate information, (2) abbreviate words, (3) paraphrase in your own words, and (4) use an outline format. Kiewra (1987) suggested that notes that both condense the material and represent a conceptual gathering of main ideas or an integration of new with old information are likely to be more effective than verbatim notes or simple paraphrased lists of information. Notes that elaborate or process information at a deeper level are more likely to be effective than simple recording (Shimmerlick & Nolan, 1976), although verbatim copying and rote studying may be more effective for students who are so anxious as to be unable to use elaborative or deep-level processing strategies efficiently (Biggs, 1978).

Using Text Patterns to Organize Notes In taking notes from well-organized text, the author's own structuring (headings, subheads, etc.) can often be used effectively to organize notes in *outline* form. It also helps to be aware of *text structures* (organizing schemas) used in expository writing. Devine (1981), for example, identified six such structures: (1) *generalization supported by examples;* (2) *enumeration* (of lists of items); (3) *time pattern* (items or events are placed in chronological order); (4) *climax pattern* (items are arranged from least to most important, worst to best, or smallest to largest); (5) *compare and contrast pattern;* and (6) *cause and effect pattern.*

Similarly, Meyer (1981) identified the following structures in a passage about supertankers: (1) *covariance* (lack of power and steering in supertankers leads to oil spills); *comparison* (ground stations for supertankers are like control towers for aircraft); (3) *collection* (three ways to improve supertanker safety are training of officers, building safer ships, and installing ground control systems); (4) *description* (oil spills kill wildlife, as indicated by 200,000 sea birds being killed); and (5) *response* (a solution to the spill problem is to improve supertanker safety).

Using these text structures when taking notes and studying can improve comprehension (Armbruster, Anderson, & Ostertag, 1987; Mayer, 1984; Weinstein & Mayer, 1986). Cook (1982), for example, trained college students to recognize the following five types of structures in science texts: (1) *generalization* (explains, clarifies, or extends a main idea); (2) *enumeration* (lists); (3) *sequence* (describes a connected series of events or steps in a process); (4) *classification* (groups material into categories or classes); and (5) *compare/contrast* (examines relationship between two or more things). Students taught to recognize these text structures and outline their notes accordingly outperformed control students who were not given this training.

Comprehensive Training Programs

Recently, several investigators developed comprehensive programs for training students (especially college students) in learning strategies and study skills (Dansereau, 1983; McCombs, 1984; Novak & Gowin, 1984; O'Neil, 1978; O'Neil & Spielberger, 1979; Weinstein & Underwood, 1983). For example, Dansereau and his colleagues (Dansereau, 1983; Dansereau et al., 1979) have developed a program that features two primary strategies elaborated by several substrategies and backed by several support strategies. The primary strategy designed to help learners comprehend and retain material is known as first-degree MURDER: Set the *m*ood to study; read for *u*nderstanding (mark important and difficult ideas); *r*ecall the material without referring to the text; correct the recall by amplifying and storing the material in order to *d*igest it; *e*xpand knowledge through self-inquiry (asking and answering questions); and *r*eview mistakes (by learning from tests). Once basic comprehension and retention have been accomplished using first-degree MURDER, learners prepare to recall and use the information when it will be needed (when taking a test or on the job) by invoking the second primary strategy known as second-degree MURDER: set the *m*ood, *u*nderstand the requirements of the task; *r*ecall the main ideas relevant to task requirements (using means-ends analysis and planning); *d*etail the main ideas with specific information; *e*xpand the information into an outline; and *r*eview the adequacy of the final response.

Networking

Training in these primary strategies is backed by training in support strategies such as goal setting and scheduling, managing concentration, combating anxiety, monitoring comprehension, and responding to confusion or mistakes. In addition, the first-degree MURDER strategies are elaborated through substrategies. Students are taught to paraphrase material in their own words and generate imagery to help them retain it, to identify key ideas, and to note the linkages between these ideas using a note-taking strategy known as *networking*. Networking involves using codes and symbols to underscore the following six types of linkages: (1) *part link* (the process of wound healing has three parts: the lag phase, the fibroplasia phase, and the construction phase; (2) *type link* (two types of wounds are open and closed); (3) *leads-to link* (the growth of a scab leads to a scar); (4) *analogy link* (a scab is like a protective bandage); (5) *characteristic link* (an open wound involves a break in the skin); and (6) *evidence link* (an X-ray test can reveal that a bone is broken). Students trained in these learning strategies tend to outperform other students, especially on essay questions. The strategies are especially effective with low achievers and highly anxious students. McCombs (1984) also emphasized these motivational aspects of learning (in addition to the cognitive aspects) in her program.

Helping Students Become Strategic Learners

Besides teaching your students about learning strategies and study skills, you can stimulate their use by building them into activities. In preparing students for a seatwork assignment, you can instruct them to skim the material to get an overview and note questions they want to get answered before reading the material word for word, provide advance organizers or study guides that call attention to key ideas and structural elements, list key terms and provide definitions or instruct the students to look them up, and encourage students to pay attention to the author's apparent purpose and degree of success in achieving it (Devine, 1981).

Partial outlines

Providing students with partial outlines or skeletal notes to fill in while listening to a presentation or reading an assignment is particularly helpful (Kiewra, 1987). It is also helpful to see that students know how to use a textbook: Help them to appreciate the information contained in the title page and preface, the index, the table of contents, the glossary, and the various structuring elements (headings, highlighting, marginal notes) and illustrations (graphs, charts, picture captions). In general, help them to appreciate that learning involves actively making sense of material and organizing it for retention and future use and that this can be accomplished using strategies that are usually more effective than the rote learning strategies that many of them rely on.

PROBLEM-SOLVING STRATEGIES

Besides being able to read with comprehension and study efficiently, students need to learn to solve problems effectively—not just in mathematics, but in any subject area. A *problem* exists when a person perceives a need to achieve some goal but does not immediately know how to achieve it.

Algorithms

Problems differ in degree of structure (Fredericksen, 1984; Simon, 1979). *Well-structured problems* present both a clearly defined goal and all of the information needed to solve the problem using appropriate *algorithms* (fixed rules or procedures that guarantee correct answers if followed precisely, such as the rules for whole-number addition). In contrast, *ill-structured problems* are more difficult to define, let alone solve. The person is aware that a problem exists but may not be clear about what information will be needed to solve it, where this information can be obtained, or how to apply it. There may not even be a single correct answer.

Heuristics

Ill-structured problems must be attacked using *heuristics*—general rules of thumb and procedural guidelines for processing information and solving problems, such as identifying what information is given and what is needed. Heuristics do not guarantee solutions the way algorithms do, but they are applicable to a broader range of problems and allow people to discover solutions for themselves. Thus well-structured homework problems in mathematics or science are solved using algorithms based on algebraic operations or Ohm's Law, but ill-structured problems such as predicting changes in market conditions or discovering cures for diseases require heuristics.

Educational psychologists have long been interested in identifying ways to teach people to solve problems effectively. Pessimists, impressed by limitations on transfer effects and the need for broad experience and development of a deep fund of domain-specific knowledge in the process of moving from novice to expert status, believe that problem solving cannot be taught directly (although students will benefit from frequent opportunities to develop their problem solving skills through practice). Optimists, on the other hand, believe that problem-solving skills can be developed directly by teaching students effective problem-solving heuristics. So far, data appear to support the optimists by showing the teachability of specific skills for use in specific situations but to support the pessimists by showing only limited transfer effects.

Early Views of Problem Solving

Early learning theorists developed contrasting theories about problem solving. Behaviorists such as Thorndike viewed it as an incremental process of trial and error (recall his experiments on cats discovering how to escape cages by working latches), whereas gestalt psychologists such as Kohler saw it as a matter of achieving sudden insight following reflection (recall his experiments with chimpanzees induced to discover that props could be used as tools to reach food). Their debates illuminated interesting issues but did not lead to programs for teaching problem solving.

Wallas (1921) described four stages in the discovery process, reminiscent of Kohler's earlier descriptions of the discovery behavior of chimpanzees: (1) *preparation* (learning about the problem and about information that might be useful in solving it); (2) *incubation* (reflection, analysis, generation of hypotheses, and other thinking about the problem (some of which may be unconscious or may occur during sleep); (3) *illumination* (the "Aha!" experience when one suddenly becomes aware of a likely solution); and (4) *verification* (testing the proposed solution).

The discovery stages were merely descriptive, but they formed the basis for later prescriptive writings. For example, Polya (1957) offered the following guidelines for problem solving in a famous book entitled *How to Solve It:*

1. *Understand the problem*. Identify what information is given or known, and what is required.

2. *Devise a plan.* Look for connections between the given information and the unknown. Does the information fit a general principle or a familiar algorithm? Is the problem analogous to a more familiar problem that might provide guidelines for solving it?
3. *Carry out the plan.* Once a plan has been formulated, carry it out, checking to make sure that each step is included and done correctly.
4. *Look back.* Make sure that the obtained result solves the problem and squares with all of the information given. If so, review the result itself and your method of obtaining it for information that may be useful in solving future problems.

John Dewey (1910) was among the first to suggest steps for effective problem solving:

1. *Presentation of the problem:* Become aware of the problem or be made aware of it.
2. *Definition of the problem:* Define the problem by identifying the present state and the desired goal state and consider the implications for solution. Sometimes a problem can be defined in different ways, with various solution implications.
3. *Development of hypotheses:* Given the problem definition, generate hypotheses for solving it.
4. *Testing of hypotheses:* Identify the advantages and disadvantages associated with each proposed solution.
5. *Selection of the best hypothesis:* Identify the solution that offers the most advantages and the fewest disadvantages.

These early approaches contain good advice and are still influential today. Many modern programs for teaching people to solve problems in everyday living follow the steps first proposed by Dewey (Heppner, 1978). So do many authors' suggestions to students. Clifford (1981), for example, suggested teaching students the following rules for problem solving: (1) Clearly define the problem and state the goal, (2) formulate possible solutions, (3) order the proposed solutions in terms of their potential, (4) try each one in turn until the solution is found, (5) critically evaluate the results of each solution tried, and (6) decide how the process and the product might be used to work out other problems.

Similarly, Bransford and Stein (1985) describe the IDEAL method of problem solving: *i*dentify the problem, *d*efine it, *e*xplore possible strategies for solving it, *a*ct on those strategies, and *l*ook at the effects of your efforts.

Contemporary Cognitive Views of Problem Solving

Contemporary views of problem solving reflect the ideas about human information processing described in the previous chapter, especially the research comparing novice with expert problem solvers (Tuma & Reif, 1980; Mayer, 1983). This work shows that expert problem solvers do not proceed in the manner implied by Dewey's stages (in particular, they do not generate a large number of hypotheses and then test each one). Instead, they conceptualize the problem by identifying key features and

Limiting hypotheses

relating them to background knowledge and then identify only one or just a few promising hypotheses for testing. Physicians diagnosing medical problems, for example, do not begin by listing every conceivable source of the symptoms. Instead, they ask questions designed to quickly narrow the search to a few probable diagnoses and then pursue them (Elstein, Shulman, Sprafka, 1978). When used by experts with sufficient experience and domain-specific knowledge, this approach is much quicker than the classical approach, because it minimizes the time spent (and usually wasted) checking out low-probability hypotheses.

Task environment versus problem space

Newell and Simon (1972) described such expert problem solvers as relying on heuristics to cut down complex problems to workable size. They differentiated between the task environment and the problem space. The *task environment* is the large structure of facts, concepts, and their interrelationships within which the problem is embedded. The *problem space* is the problem solver's mental representation of that task environment. The problem space must simplify the task environment enough to allow the person to address the problem within the limits of working memory and yet be an accurate enough representation to foster effective problem-solving efforts.

Accurate problem representation

Accurate *representation of the problem* in the first place is the key to the success of this method. If key features of the problem are recognized accurately and related to appropriate background knowledge or problem-solving schemas, the result is likely to be a quick and successful solution. However, if the problem is represented inappropriately, the resulting solution efforts will fail, and the person will have to begin all over again. In well-structured problems, accurate representation may be followed by activation of algorithms that lead directly to a solution. In ill-structured problems, the person may have to rely on heuristics such as reasoning by analogy from more familiar problems, working on subparts before dealing with the whole, working backwards from proposed solutions, or testing the most promising hypotheses first (Newell & Simon, 1972; Polya, 1957; Simon, 1980).

Cyert (1980) suggested the following heuristics (drawn from the work of Rubenstein, 1975): (1) Keep the big picture in mind without getting lost in details; (2) avoid committing yourself too early to a single hypothesis; (3) create models to simplify the problem using words, images, symbols, or equations; (4) try to change the representation of the problem if the present one is not working; (5) use the information to generate questions to task yourself; (6) be willing to question the credibility of your premises; (7) try working backwards from possible solutions; (8) keep track of partial solutions that you may eventually be able to combine; (9) use analogies and metaphors; and (10) talk about the problem.

Books and courses on problem solving (Bransford & Stein, 1985; Hayes, 1981; Newell & Simon, 1972; Polyna, 1957; Rubenstein, 1975) provide instruction in such heuristics and opportunities to practice them on ''brain teasers'' as well as on academic problems. Such books and courses can increase your effectiveness as a problem solver by teaching you to use heuristic strategies systematically and with metacognitive awareness, although they cannot short-circuit your need for experience and domain-specific knowledge.

Pattern recognition

One approach that may help accelerate development from novice to expert status, however, is training in *pattern recognition* as it applies to problem solving within particular domains. In algebra, for example, Mayer (1981) has identified more than 100 basic problem types. Each category of problem (such as "motion problem") is represented by different subtypes (such as "overtake," "closure," "round trip," and "speed change"). Similarly, Greeno and his colleagues (Greeno, 1980a; Riley, Greeno, & Heller, 1982) have identified three types of algebra word problems: *cause/change problems* (Joe has three marbles, Tom gives him five more. How many marbles does Joe have now?); *combination problems* (Joe has three marbles. Tom has five marbles. How many do they have altogether?); and *comparison problems* (Joe has three marbles. Tom has five more marbles than Joe. How many marbles does Tom have?). Teaching students to recognize such *problem types* increases their ability to represent problems correctly and link them to appropriate schemas and algorithms (Fennema, Carpenter, & Peterson, 1989; Mayer, 1985).

Numberless problems

Other work in mathematics is designed to reduce novicelike reliance on formulas without genuine understanding and to increase expertlike concentration on representing the problem accurately before proceeding. One method is to give students *numberless problems* requiring them to conceptualize the problems and state the strategies that would be used to solve them but without performing any actual calculations (Good & Grouws, 1979). For example, students might be asked, "You know the dimensions of a room that you want to paint, the cost of paint per gallon, and the square feet a gallon of paint will cover. How would you calculate the approximate cost of the paint needed for the job?"

Strategy training

Bloom and Broder (1950) reported success with *strategy training* in mathematics problem solving for college students who were scoring poorly on examinations. The students were asked to think aloud and pay attention to their own problem-solving processes as they worked through problems and then to compare them with the processes revealed in transcripts taken from students who solved the problems more effectively, stating in their own words the differences between the models' strategies and their own. This training increased the students' problem-solving confidence and performance. Schoenfeld (1979) reported similar success from training students in strategies for responding to algebra problems (draw a diagram, try to establish subgoals, consider similar problems with fewer variables, etc.).

Conclusions about Teaching Problem-Solving Strategies

To the extent that you expect your students to be able to apply what they are learning, you will need to provide them not only with frequent opportunities to solve problems but also with instruction in problem-solving processes. This instruction should include heuristics such as reading the problem carefully and paraphrasing it into one's own words, identifying the information given and desired as well as the linkages between these problem elements, separating relevant from irrelevant information, representing the problem clearly and sketching a general plan of attack before trying to apply formulas or perform calculations, and developing a workable problem space by dividing the problem into subproblems, reasoning by analogy from more familiar problems, working backwards from possible solutions, or substituting specific examples for abstract symbols. Such instruction should include first-person modeling with thinking aloud in addition to typical lecturing and should proceed to coaching, guided practice, student reflection on and assessment of their strategies, and other activities designed to increase students' metacognitive awareness of the processes involved in solving problems successfully.

TEACHING THINKING SKILLS

Instruction in reading comprehension, study skills, or problem-solving strategies will tend to develop students' thinking skills (or at least to stimulate a more thoughtful approach to learning). The most direct approach, however, is to teach students key elements of the thinking process itself. The classical approach to training the mind to think called for curricular emphasis on subjects such as Latin, philosophy, mathematics, and science. Thorndike (1924) showed long ago that this approach does not yield generalized improvements in mental functioning, but it continues to be emphasized even today. A more focused variation of this same general approach is to emphasize instruction in *thinking skills* and *tools for developing knowledge*.

Logic classes

One approach to the teaching of thinking skills is course work in *logic*—the use of formal rules of inference to develop conclusions from established premises. Courses in logic teach students to deduce implications and evaluate whether conclusions follow from the premises. For example, given the premises that animals require food and that dogs are animals, it is logical to deduce that dogs require food, but not to deduce that all animals are dogs.

Critical thinking skills

A related form of instruction is training in *critical thinking skills* for evaluating the credibility of information. Critical thinking skills include assessing the validity of authors' premises and the soundness of their logic in developing conclusions, as well as identifying their purposes in writing the material (distinguishing attempts to be objective from attempts to sway the reader toward particular conclusions), distinguishing relevant from irrelevant information, recognizing bias and slanted language, rhetorical devices that appeal to emotion rather than to evidence, and distinguishing fact from opinion (Beyer, 1985).

Tools for developing knowledge

Instruction in *tools for developing knowledge* usually emphasizes training in scientific methods. The emphasis here is on scientific rules of inference, and especially on the logic involved in stating questions as formal hypotheses that can be tested experimentally.

Deduction theory versus enaction theory

Ohlsson (1983) criticized these approaches as being limited to what he called the *deduction theory* of human thinking: They view thinking as systematic application of logical rules of inference. Ohlsson argued that human thinking is better represented by the *enaction theory:* the notion that thinking involves mental simulations of real world actions. Instead of using purely verbal methods to draw verbally phrased conclusions from verbally phrased premises, Ohlsson argued, we work with multisensory models of what we think about and with mental representations of concrete actions that could be performed. For example, liquids could be poured, subdivided, or boiled, and algebraic expressions could be rearranged, simplified, or substituted into other expressions. Ohlsson believes that our conceptions of the world are more similar to pictures, sculptures, holograms, toy trains, chemical formulas, muscial scores, diagrams, or paintings than they are to verbal texts and that thinking proceeds by application of operators to these mental models under the guidance of heuristics.

This implies that traditional approaches to teaching thinking skills will not generalize well because they do not include sufficient attention to the procedural knowledge and heuristics involved in deciding when and why to use a particular procedure. Even if one understands what a theorem says and why it is true, this knowledge is not sufficient to enable one to know when and how to use the theorem. To teach students to think, Ohlsson argued, teachers should emphasize the processes involved in acquiring and applying disciplinary knowledge. Each field would be thought of as being about the kinds of *change* that apply to its subject matter, rather than as a static collection of information. For example, instead of just teaching geographical facts about mountains, continents, forests, and climates, social studies teachers might emphasize mountain formation and erosion, continental drift, deforestation, and changes in average world temperature and might frequently ask students to predict future situations from current trends or to speculate about what would happen to the ecosystem as a whole if an important change were introduced into one part of it.

Programs for Teaching Thinking Skills

Instead of designing ways to build more emphasis on thinking into instruction in traditional subject-matter areas, some authors have developed programs designed to develop students' generic thinking skills. Some of these programs teach cognitive skills such as Piagetian conservation or the skills stressed by IQ tests (Detterman & Sternberg, 1982), and others teach students to think creatively (see Chapter 24). Three of the most comprehensive "thinking" curricula are described below.

Philosophy for Children Lipman and his colleagues (Lipman, 1985; Lipman, Sharp, & Oscanyan, 1980) have developed a "philosophy for children" program that introduces preschool and elementary school children to principles of logic and formal inquiry. Using fictional passages and questions about philosophical issues as the bases for initiating group discussion, teachers induce their students to exchange views, debate, reason, and function as a "community of inquiry" concerning concepts such as fairness, friendship, and truth. The children learn to use language to reason—to assume, suppose, compare, infer, contrast or judge, induce or deduce, classify, describe, explain, define, and inquire. In the process, they learn to recognize and assess chains of logic, deal with syllogisms, recognize fallacies, and develop logical reasoning and critical thinking skills. Information about this program can be found in issues of the journal *Thinking: The Journal of Philosophy for Children.*

The CoRT Program DeBono (1985) developed the CoRT program (CoRT stands for Cognitive Research Trust, an organization located in Cambridge, England). The CoRT program consists of sixty lessons on thinking intended for ages nine to eleven, although it has been used with younger and older students. It focuses on thinking skills that will help students to function better in their lives outside of school. Consequently, its content avoids both specific school subjects and relatively impractical puzzles and games to concentrate on life events such as deciding on a career, how to spend a vacation, moving to a new house, or changing jobs. Instruction focuses on the processes of thinking and decision making.

PMI exercises

The first lesson, for example, teaches a scanning tool known as PMI. The teacher invites the students to consider the merits of some idea (e.g., basic foods should be supplied free to everyone) by thinking about its implications and categorizing them into three sets labeled: *P*lus (desirable implications); *M*inus (undesirable implications); and *I*nteresting (neither good nor bad but interesting and worth noting). PMI helps students to clarify their thinking about the issue and to state the reasons underlying the decisions they make.

The PMI exercise is the first of the sixty CoRT lessons. As the program progresses, additional tools for thinking and decision making are added, and students are encouraged to use them for thinking about real life decisions rather than merely fanciful ones. They learn to consider multiple aspects of issues before settling on solutions, and to get input from others through brainstorming and related mechanisms.

The Instrumental Enrichment Program Feuerstein and his colleagues (Feuerstein et al., 1980; Feuerstein et al., 1985) have developed the Instrumental Enrichment program for students aged nine or older. The program was originally developed as a special education tool for use with disadvantaged students or students suffering from cognitive deficiencies or learning disabilities. Its goal was to change the cognitive structures of these students and transform them into autonomous independent thinkers capable of initiating and elaborating ideas. As the program became further developed and better known, it began to be used with normal students as well.

The program encourages cognitive activities such as perceptual organization of information, problem representation, planning, goal analysis, and restructuring of problems when existing plans are not working. It uses a series of progressively more demanding paper and pencil exercises that encourage learners to discover relationships, rules, principles, operations, and strategies. The tasks were designed on the basis of analyses of the processes involved in mental activities. Many resemble tasks used in psychometric tests and laboratory learning experiments. There are some puzzles and brainteasers as well, but in general the program is seen as a bridge between approaches based on thinking within curriculum content domains and approaches that try to develop thinking through content-free exercises.

The exercises range from simple recognition tasks to complex activities involving classification, seeing analogies, and seriation, and they make use of a variety of modalities including numerical, spatial, pictorial, and verbal. Each operation is considered to have input, elaboration, and output phases, and assessment focuses on identifying the phase that is responsible for failure when failure occurs.

Conclusions on Teaching Thinking Skills

Thinking skills programs are one response to the criticism that schooling concentrates too much on specific information and not enough on higher-level processes and applications. You may wish to investigate them and incorporate them into your teaching. Bear in mind, however, that despite the enthusiasm with which these programs have been received by some educators, their efficacy remains to be demonstrated. Enthusiastic testimonials abound, but few systematic data exist, and they suggest only limited effects (Chance, 1986; Nickerson, Perkins, & Smith, 1985; Sternberg & Bhana, 1986). Also, bear in mind that even when programs are successful in developing general thinking skills, they will not eliminate the need for broad experience and domain-specific knowledge for functioning as an expert in any particular area of application (Glaser, 1984; Sternberg, 1987).

Summary

This chapter concerns relatively generic learning skills—strategic reading, systematic studying, problem solving, and critical thinking. Weinstein and Mayer (1986) identified five general types of learning strategies: rehearsal strategies, elaboration strategies, organizational strategies, comprehension monitoring strategies, and affective strategies.

Reading comprehension researchers have developed methods of teaching students to read with metacognitive awareness and active strategies for metacomprehension (monitoring, evaluating, and repairing comprehension of text during the act of reading it). Strategy training experiments conducted at various grade levels have taught a variety of strategies with mostly positive results. Palincsar and Brown (1984) improved reading comprehension by using the reciprocal teaching method to instruct students in the strategies of summarizing, self-questioning, clarifying, and predicting.

Researchers studying learning strategies and study skills have found that some students are surface-level processors who rely primarily on rote learning, whereas more successful students are deeper-level processors who try to understand what they are learning, develop insights, and think about how to use it. Methods have been developed for teaching students to use deeper-level strategies. Many of these are variations of

SQ3R (survey, question, read, recite, review). Others are built around elaboration strategies through which learners generate analogies, imagery, or other linkages relating the new to the familiar.

Teaching students to take better notes is another common strategy. Notes that use an outline format, retain key structuring elements, and summarize or paraphrase main ideas in the learner's own words tend to be more effective than merely underlining or taking less complete and organized notes. Calling students' attention to the structuring patterns used to organize presentations will help them to take organized notes.

Comprehensive training programs such as Dansereau's MURDER provide students with systematic training in learning strategies and study skills. The chapter suggests ways that teachers can help their students to study effectively by providing them with information and guidance.

Classical models viewed human problem solving as proceeding systematically from goals through the formation and testing of hypotheses to the development of conclusions. More recently, human information processing research has shown that many problems are ill-structured and thus not well suited to the classical approach and that these problems are attacked with heuristics rather than systematic logic and algorithms. Experts cut a complex task environment down to a convenient problem space by bringing to bear relevant schemas and prior knowledge to develop an accurate problem representation, and when this occurs, solution typically follows quickly. In the absence of such expert knowledge, individuals must rely on heuristics such as working backward from proposed solutions, reasoning by analogy, or dividing the problem into subparts. Programs designed to develop problem-solving skills include instruction in such heuristics and in recognition of various commonly encountered patterns of problems.

Traditional approaches to development of thinking skills featured units in logic and critical thinking. Ohlsson criticized these approaches as being limited to the deduction theory of human thinking, and he argued for approaches representing the enaction theory—emphasis on procedural knowledge and heuristics in addition to figurative knowledge and subject-matter teaching that emphasizes producing and studying change rather than learning static collections of information. Others have developed comprehensive "thinking" curricula such as the Philosophy for Children program, the CoRT program, and the Instrumental Enrichment Program.

Questions and Problems

1. Are you a strategic learner? Do you routinely use the five types of learning strategies described by Weinstein and Mayer (1986)? If not, what should you be doing that you are not doing now? Draw up a plan for change and use it to guide your studying in the future.
2. Think about the subject matter and grade level that you intend to teach. What strategies will you use to help students to learn strategically and with metacognitive awareness of what they are doing and why they are doing it?

3. Many teachers of social studies, mathematics, or science take the attitude that they will teach their subject matter and leave reading to the reading teachers. Many students in their classes, however, have difficulty mainly because their skills for learning from texts are not well developed. What, if anything, should such teachers do about this? Discuss this issue with your friends.
4. The Palincsar and Brown (1984) study produced unusually large reading comprehension gains, presumably because of the reciprocal teaching method. What do you think made this method so effective?
5. We discussed the value of noting the structures used to organize texts when reading or taking notes, and we gave examples of text structures commonly used in history and science texts. What structures are commonly used in the texts written for the grade level and subject matter that you intend to teach?
6. What kinds of notes do you take (underlining, outlining, summarizing)? Do you see ways to improve your note-taking abilities?
7. Given the grade level and subject matter that you intend to teach, do you expect your students to take notes when you make presentations to the class? If so, what instructions should you give them?
8. Do you believe that thinking and problem solving can be taught? Why or why not? Do you plan to teach thinking and problem solving yourself? If so, how?
9. Teaching has been described as an unusually complex task environment that requires the teacher to rely on heuristics to create a workable problem space for decision making. What does this mean, and how does it apply to the statement that teaching is partly an art and partly an applied science?
10. If you were to apply Ohlsson's suggestion that instruction concentrates on the kinds of change that apply to a subject matter, how would you teach your subject matter differently from the way it was taught to you?

Case Studies

PREPARING FOR A TEST Sue complained to her roommate Suzi, "I've got to do well on this test or I'm in trouble in the course. I really blew the first test." Suzi said in a questioning fashion, "Yeah, I wonder why that course gives you so much trouble. You get A's in your other courses, even though you typically do nothing but go to class and then stay up all night before the exam to put it all together." Sue stated with resignation, "All I know is that next week I had better do well or it's curtains." Then she added with excitement, "You know, there is one thing about that course; we have to cover twice as much material as we do in any other course, and the instructor is really interested in the facts." How would you suggest that Sue prepare for the exam?

NOBODY EVER EXPLAINED IT TO ME LIKE THAT! Gregg is a bright teenager taking demanding advance placement courses. He handles most assignments with ease but has occasional difficulty with math problems. At these times, he goes to his father, an engineer, for help. In the past, the problem always involved mathematics that the father was familiar with, so he was able to help Gregg after studying the problem for a few minutes. Today, though, Gregg asks for help with a problem of a type that his father has never seen before. After realizing that he can't figure it out simply by studying it briefly, Gregg's father draws on his own problem-solving heuristics and begins to fire questions at Gregg. Is this the first time that this kind of problem has come up, or has Gregg done similar problems earlier? What does this term mean, and where is it explained in the book? Are there parts of the problem that Gregg recognizes and knows how to handle, and if so, which are the "extra" parts that are causing the difficulty? Has Gregg tried backtracking to the place in the book where this type of problem is introduced so as to review simpler versions?

Gregg is initially surprised and displeased. He expected an explanation of the problem, not suggestions about how he might solve it himself. Gregg's father is surprised and displeased, too, because Gregg's responses to his questions don't go much beyond "I don't know," or "I never thought of that." Further questioning makes it clear that Gregg has been going through the book problem by problem without getting the big picture. He has never thought about the sequencing of the material, paid attention to the table of contents or the chapter outlines, or used the index. Nor has he fully appreciated the fact that curriculum strands are organized hierarchically and that exercises occur in an easy-to-difficult sequence, so reviewing is wise when one is stuck on a problem.

As the reality of this sinks in, Gregg's father realizes that Gregg needs more than help with a particular problem—he needs to learn how to use a textbook and heuristics for problem solving in mathematics. If you were Gregg's father, how would you handle this situation in such a way as to widen Gregg's overly narrow concentration on getting an answer to this particular problem and help him to see that he could be using much more powerful and effective methods of studying?

CHAPTER

Instructional Design

CHAPTER OUTLINE

OBJECTIVES

When you have mastered the material in this chapter, you will be able to

1. Define instructional design and list the steps in Robert Gagné and Leslie Briggs's approach
2. Define a curriculum scope and sequence statement and describe the preparation and decision making involved in developing one
3. Describe how curriculum-sequencing decisions are made with the assistance of information-processing analysis, task classification, and learning task analysis
4. List the instructional events that Gagné and Briggs believe must be planned for each instructional objective
5. Describe the practical considerations involved in developing or selecting materials and media
6. Describe Gropper's (1983) ideas for designing an easy-to-difficult sequencing into instruction by manipulating the treatment tools used in teaching tasks
7. Contrast B. F. Skinner's behavioral approach, Gagné's task-analysis approach, and Case and Bereiter's (1984) cognitive development approach to instructional design
8. Define concepts and concept learning tasks
9. Describe Owen, Blount, and Moscow's (1978) model for teaching concepts

10. Distinguish the role of positive examples from the role of negative examples in teaching concepts and explain how to use rational sets of examples to teach concepts efficiently
11. Define Engelmann and Carnine's (1982) key concepts (faultless communication, juxtaposition of examples, stipulation, interpolation, extrapolation) and explain their procedures for teaching object concepts, comparative concepts, and transformation sequences.

In Chapters 6–8 we discussed Gagné's learning hierarchies and his concept of task analysis, work on programmed instruction with its emphasis on careful sequencing of frames, and ideas about structuring and sequencing information around key concepts. In Chapters 9 and 10 we described findings indicating that certain texts are more "considerate" than others because they are organized around structuring devices that provide coherence and flow. All of these ideas suggest that, *for a given set of instructional objectives, certain approaches to instruction are likely to be more effective than others.*

In particular, they imply that instruction will be more efficient when the content to be learned is divided into units and ultimately individual lessons that are structured and sequenced in ways that maximize clarity and ease of learning and minimize potential for confusion. *Instructional design* is the art (and applied science) of creating such efficient methods of attaining educational objectives. It includes attention to the materials and activities as well as the methods of instruction, and includes testing and revision cycles in addition to creation of original versions (Gagné, Briggs, & Wager, 1988; Posner & Rudnitsky, 1986).

THE GAGNÉ AND BRIGGS SYSTEMS APPROACH

Gagné and Briggs (1979) stated that instructional design is most effective when conducted by means of a *systems approach* that begins with analysis of needs and goals and proceeds through a series of fourteen stages toward eventual demonstration that a developed system of instruction succeeds in meeting established goals (see Table 11.1).

Instructional system

Gagné and Briggs view an *instructional system* as an overarching framework that supplies the means for achieving the outcomes called for in a curriculum being considered. The systems approach to instructional design accepts whatever goals may have been adopted (by the designers themselves or by others empowered to establish instructional objectives) and then draws on teaching models, learning theories, and other relevant sources of information. The various components included in an instructional system should be mutually reinforcing, but they need not be identical in format or derived from a single theory. Thus, for example, instructional designers might use some approaches to accomplish certain

TABLE 11.1 STAGES IN DESIGNING INSTRUCTIONAL SYSTEMS

System Level	1. Analysis of needs, goals, and priorities
	2. Analysis of resources, constraints, and alternate delivery systems
	3. Determination of scope and sequence of curriculum and courses; Delivery system design
Course Level	4. Determining course structure and sequence
	5. Analysis of course objectives
Lesson Level	6. Definition of performance objectives
	7. Preparing lesson plans for modules
	8. Developing, selecting materials, media
	9. Assessing student performance (performance measures)
Final System Level	10. Teacher preparation
	11. Formative evaluation
	12. Field testing, revision
	13. Summative evaluation
	14. Installation and diffusion

Source: From *Principles of Instructional Design*, Second Edition, by Robert M. Gagné and Leslie J. Briggs, copyright © 1970 by Holt, Rinehart and Winston, Inc. Reprinted by permission of the publisher.

objectives (lecturing and modeling to develop knowledge and comprehension) but use other approaches to accomplish other objectives (questioning and discussion followed by exercises to promote application).

Commercial publishers of curriculum materials should routinely go through all fourteen of the stages shown in Table 11.1, continuing to recycle through them until the learning system as a whole and each of its parts have proven their effectiveness in attaining their goals. They seldom do so, however, so the curricula (including the materials, associated activities, and recommended teaching strategies) that teachers must work with are typically less than ideal and sometimes seriously flawed. Thus even though most teachers will not design learning systems that extend across several grade levels, they nevertheless will need to know basic principles of instructional design to identify the flaws in the curricula they are given to work with and to be able to adapt or substitute for ineffective components. Furthermore, most teachers will be expected to adapt curricula to the needs of their particular classes and to develop remedial programs for students who need them. These activities require the ability to execute the first nine stages in Table 11.1.

System-, course-, and lesson-level stages

Gagné and Briggs identified system-level stages, course-level stages, and lesson-level stages. *System-level stages* concern the development of the system as a whole, including all courses or other subdivisions within it. In developing an elementary mathematics curriculum, for example, system-level work would include deciding what should be taught, sequencing these objectives, and then assigning a portion of the sequence to each grade level. Provision would be made for review at the beginning of each year and when introducing new topics that build on content taught earlier, but in general, overlearned material would be phased out and new or more difficult material phased in. Some system level stages (1–3) concern initial planning before development of lessons and materials, but others (10–14) involve the testing, revision, and dissemination that should follow such development. *Course-level stages* concern the development of separate courses within the larger system, and *lesson-level stages* concern the development of individual lessons within these courses.

Initial System-Level Stages

Stage 1: Analysis of Needs, Goals, and Priorities Instructional systems are designed to meet perceived needs, so planning begins with establishing consensus on these needs, setting priorities among them, and stating their instructional implications. In military, industrial, or other specialized educational settings, it is possible and often necessary to be precise in specifying and prioritizing needs. There is more leeway for decision making in designing instruction for the schools, however, at least in the United States (some nations with highly centralized educational systems control curricula to the extent that all students in a given grade work on the same assignments from the same book on any given day). Each state has its own guidelines and requirements, but they tend to be general references to the numbers of courses required in various subject-matter areas, without details about what will be taught in these courses or how it will be taught. Commercial publishers use these legal guidelines, the pronouncements of national councils representing the subject-matter specialities, and the content included on standardized tests for guidance in setting curriculum objectives. Local developers (individual teachers or school curriculum committees) may also be guided by standards adopted by their local school boards, although they usually exercise considerable autonomy in making curriculum decisions (Schwille et al., 1983).

In any case, instructional designers need to make decisions about what content to teach, to what levels of depth and mastery, to what students, and in what sequence. Once consensus is reached on these decisions, the designers develop a *curriculum scope and sequence statement* that provides a detailed listing of the objectives to be included and the order in which they will be taught.

Stage 2: Analysis of Resources, Constraints, and Alternative Delivery Systems Given the intended curriculum scope and sequence, the designers now need to consider how each objective can be accomplished efficiently. What methods are known or believed to be effective for this purpose? What materials will be needed, and what activities will the students engage in?

These questions must be addressed within the context of whatever financial or other constraints apply. Some activities or equipment are too expensive, bulky, noisy, or dangerous for use in typical schools. Similarly, some activities do not lend themselves to implementation within the physical setting of the typical classroom, and some are not feasible for use by a single teacher who must work with twenty-five to thirty students. Consequently, compromises will have to be made, and certain objectives may even have to be dropped or reduced in priority. Ultimately, the work of Stage 2 should culminate in feasible plans for teaching identified objectives to certain types of students within anticipated constraints.

Stage 3: Determination of Scope and Sequence of Curriculum and Courses: Delivery System Design At this stage, the designers elaborate the scope and sequence statement by assigning sequences of objectives to courses, stating objectives in terms of learner performance and clarifying the details of the delivery system to be developed. Objectives are stated in terms of learner performance (rather than in terms of what the materials present or what the teacher does) so that measures of performance can be developed and used later for evaluating the system. Clarifying the details of the delivery system involves identifying the materials, equipment, and media forms that will have to be purchased or developed, the activities that will be involved, and the manuals and procedures that will be required for training teachers. Once this stage of system-level planning has been completed, the focus shifts to course and lesson-level work.

Course-Level Stages

Target and enabling objectives

State 4: Determining Course Structure and Sequence Gagné and Briggs distinguished between *target objectives* (major objectives to be reached only by the end of the course) and *enabling objectives* (smaller objectives that represent steps toward attainment of the target objectives). At this stage, the target objectives of each course are clustered into units of instruction that will require perhaps one to three weeks to complete. Sequencing of instruction is then considered, first for units themselves and then for the sequencing of objectives within units.

Sequencing

Sequencing may or may not be crucial. In designing a course to teach a hierarchically ordered series of mathematics skills, it is essential to begin with the simplest skills and proceed in orderly fashion up the hierarchy. In designing a social studies course on Western Europe, however, units on Germany, France, and Great Britain can be presented in any order. Sometimes the content lends itself to presentation in different sequences that offer trade-offs depending on the specific objectives to be pursued or the personal preferences of the instructor. Courses in history or in developmental psychology, for example, can be organized either *chronologically* (taking up the developmental or historical periods in order and embedding coverage of each major topic within the presentations on each of the periods) or *topically* (treating each topic separately and embedding discussion of change over time within these topical units). The chronological approach highlights "the big picture" and shows how it changes over time, but it results in fragmented discussion of particular topics. The topical approach has the opposite characteristics.

Preparing units as modules

When there are no hierarchical relationships or logical dependencies to dictate that objectives be taken up in a particular sequence, instructional designers may want to *modularize* their units (make them self-contained and usable in any order) so as to provide instructors with flexibility. This strategy has been followed in preparing the present text. The present unit on instructional application assumes mastery of the previous unit on learning, but otherwise, the units have been prepared as modules that can stand on their own without depending on mastery of prior units. The book has been prepared this way because (1) some instructors will not have enough time to cover everything; (2) some will want to omit certain material (child development, measurement, and evaluation) because their students take an entire course on that topic in addition to a course in educational psychology; and (3) instructors differ in what they want to emphasize in teaching educational psychology and in their preferences for sequencing that material. The modular organization of the present text allows for instructors to omit certain units or to reorder them into the sequence they prefer.

Stage 5: Analysis of Course Objectives At this stage, the instructional designer performs detailed analyses of the target objectives of the course. Gagné and Briggs recommended three kinds of analysis: information-processing analysis to reveal the sequence of the mental operations required to perform the objectives, task classification to categorize learning outcomes and identify the conditions of learning that will have to be established, and learning task analysis to identify the enabling objectives that will need to be taught prior to teaching target objectives.

Use of flow charts

Information-processing analysis identifies the sequence of steps involved in a target performance. Gagné and Briggs advocated using *flow charts* to depict these steps. Figure 11.1 shows a flow chart of the information processing involved in subtracting two-place numbers, using

Figure 11.1 An Information-Processing Analysis of the Subtraction of Two-Place Numbers

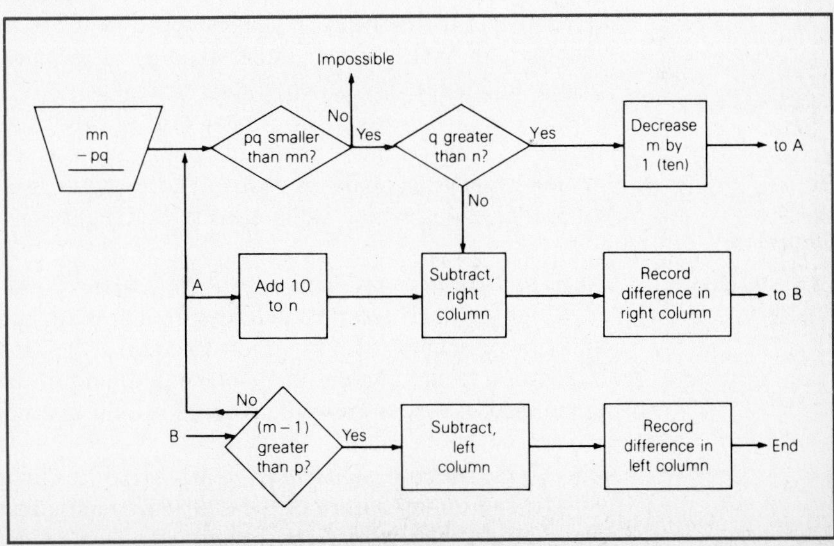

Source: R. Gagné (1977). "Analysis of Objectives," in L. J. Briggs (Ed.), *Instructional Design*. Englewood Cliffs, N.J.: Educational Technology Publications. Copyright © 1977. Reproduced by permission of the copyright owner.

trapezoids to represent inputs, rectangles to represent actions, and diamonds to represent decisions.

Uses for information-processing analysis

Such information-processing analyses provide clear descriptions of a target objective and thus help sharpen one's planning for both instruction and measurement of the objective. Also, they often reveal steps in the process that might not have been recognized otherwise. Figure 11.1, for example, clarifies that learners must be able to distinguish the larger from the smaller of the two numbers before carrying out the process of subtraction. If they do not already possess this capability, it will have to be taught as an enabling objective that supports progress toward the target objective of subtracting two-place numbers.

Task classification

Task classification involves categorizing course objectives into task categories that imply different conditions of learning. In the Gagné and Briggs system, tasks are categorized as involving intellectual skills, cognitive strategies, information, attitudes, or motor skills, and intellectual skills are further categorized into discriminations, concrete concepts, defined concepts, rules, and higher-order rules. Different conditions of learning are associated with each of these categories (see Chapter 6), so awareness of task type is helpful in planning instruction.

Learning task analysis

Learning task analysis involves identifying the prerequisites for learning both target and enabling objectives. In the case of intellectual skills, this analysis will produce a formal *learning hierarchy* that begins with discriminations and proceeds through concrete concepts, defined concepts, rules, and higher-order rules. Other categories of learning objectives (verbal information, cognitive strategies, motor skills, attitudes) are not embedded within formal learning hierarchies, but it is often possible to identify certain ideas or skills that are logically prerequisite to other ones and to use this information in sequencing instruction. In teaching a mnemonic device (i.e., a cognitive strategy), for example, to help learners remember a list of rules, it makes sense to teach the rules first so that the learners have a better understanding of the meaning and usefulness of the mnemonic device when they learn it.

A *learning hierarchy* for subtraction of whole numbers is shown in Figure 11.2. Such hierarchies, in combination with more detailed information-processing analyses such as those shown in Figure 11.1, are helpful in identifying which skills need to be taught and in what order.

Lesson-Level Stages

Stage 6: Definition of Performance Objectives At this stage, specific objectives are written for each lesson. These objectives will be used to guide development of instruction (including the materials and activities in addition to the content to be presented) and of the evaluation devices to be used to assess the effectiveness of that instruction.

Stage 7: Preparing Lesson Plans (or Modules) The nature of these plans will depend on the nature of the instruction anticipated. For teacher-led, group-based instruction, the lesson plan is a guide for the teacher. If individualized, self-paced learning modules are to be developed, the plan will be addressed to the learner and will include a statement of objectives,

Figure 11.2 A Learning Hierarchy for Subtracting Whole Numbers

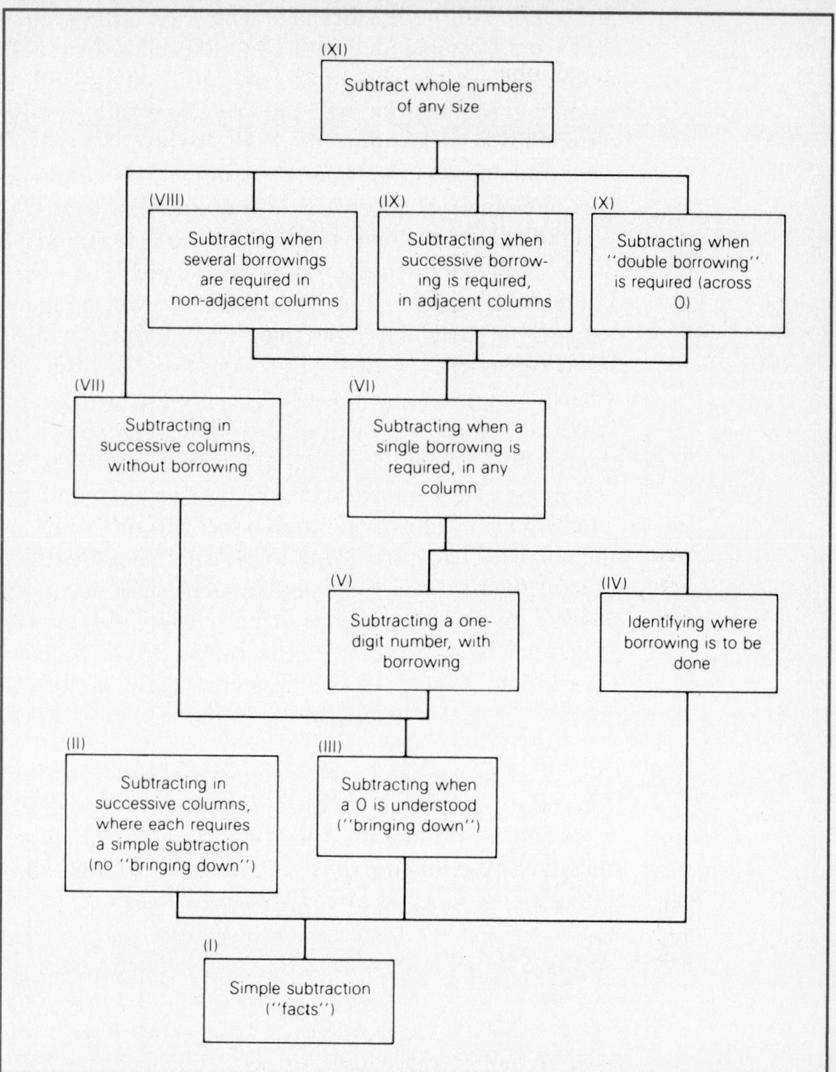

Source: The Conditions of Learning (3rd ed.), by Robert M. Gagné. Copyright © 1977 by Holt, Rinehart and Winston. Reprinted by permission of CBS College Publishing.

a list of materials to be read, a guide to activities to be performed, a self-check test, and instructions about presenting completed work and arranging to be tested (Gagné & Briggs, 1979). In this text, we concentrate on planning for teacher-led group instruction.

For each lesson objective, a plan needs to be developed that (1) lists the instructional events to occur; (2) determines the materials, media, or agents needed to implement these instructional events; (3) designs or plans learning activities, including plans for how media and materials are to be used; and (4) previews the selected media and materials to plan the roles or events that the teacher needs to accomplish for the lesson.

The *instructional events* mentioned by Gagné and Briggs are the words and actions of the teacher. They have identified nine instructional events that would be included in a complete plan for teaching a particular objective. These are shown in Table 11.2, along with the information processing activities that they are supposed to engender in learners. In addition, Table 11.3 shows the different forms that instructional events take depending on whether one is teaching intellectual skills, cognitive strategies, information, attitudes, or motor skills.

It is here and in the next stage that the instructional designer's creativity and knowledge of subject matter, pedagogy, and the learners' needs and interests come into play. Usually, there will be many ways to approach teaching a particular objective. The designer will have to decide what information to present (and at what level of difficulty and redundancy), what examples or demonstrations to use, what media or materials are important enough to justify the trouble and expense involved in including them, and what practice and application activities will be needed.

Gaining attention

Gaining attention, for example, can be accomplished simply by saying, "Look here." However, the lesson will probably be more successful if the teacher begins by trying to arouse the students' curiosity or interest. This might be done by posing an interesting question that the lesson will answer, by showing a prop or performing a demonstration, or by telling students why they will need the knowledge or skills to be taught or where they will use them. Depending on the learning objective and the students,

TABLE 11.2 EVENTS OF INSTRUCTION AND THEIR RELATIONS TO PROCESSES OF LEARNING

Instructional Event	Relation to Learning Process
1. Gaining attention	*Reception* of patterns of neural impulses
2. Informing the learner of the objective	Activating a process of *executive control*
3. Stimulating recall of prerequisite learnings	*Retrieval* to working memory
4. Presenting the stimulus material	Emphasizing features for *selective perception*
5. Providing "learning guidance"	*Semantic encoding*
6. Eliciting the performance	Activating a *response organization*
7. Providing feedback about performance correctness	Establishing *reinforcement*
8. Assessing the performance	Activating *retrieval*; making *reinforcement* possible
9. Enhancing retention and transfer	Providing cues and strategies for *retrieval*

Source: From *Principles of Instructional Design*, Second Edition, by Robert M. Gagné and Leslie J. Briggs, copyright © 1970 by Holt, Rinehart and Winston, Inc. Reprinted by permission of the publisher.

TABLE 11.3 INSTRUCTIONAL EVENTS AND THE CONDITIONS OF LEARNING THEY IMPLY FOR FIVE TYPES OF LEARNED CAPABILITIES

	Type of Capability				
Instructional Event	**Intellectual Skill**	**Cognitive Strategy**	**Information**	**Attitude**	**Motor Skill**
1. Gaining attention	Introduce stimulus change: variations in sensory mode				
2. Informing learner of objective	Provide description and example of the performance to be expected	Clarify the general nature of the solution expected	Indicate the kind of verbal question to be answered	Provide example of the kind of action choice aimed for	Provide a demonstration of the performance to be expected
3. Stimulating recall of prerequisites	Stimulate recall of subordinate concepts and rules	Stimulate recall of task strategies and associated intellectual skills	Stimulate recall of context of organized information	Stimulate recall of relevant information skills and human model identification	Stimulate recall of executive subroutine and part skills
4. Presenting the stimulus material	Present examples of concept or rule	Present novel problems	Present information in propositional form	Present human model demonstrating choice of personal action	Provide external stimuli for performance including tools or implements
5. Providing learning guidance	Provide verbal cues to proper combining sequence	Provide prompts and hints to novel solution	Provide verbal links to a larger meaningful context	Provide for observation of model's choice of action, and of reinforcement received by model	Provide practice with feedback of performance achievement
6. Eliciting the performance	Ask learner to apply rule or concept to new examples	Ask for problem solution	Ask for information in paraphrase, or in learner's own words	Ask learner to indicate choices of action in real or simulated situations	Ask for execution of the performance
7. Providing feedback	Confirm correctness of rule or concept application	Confirm originality of problem solution	Confirm correctness of statement of information	Provide direct or vicarious reinforcement of action choice	Provide feedback on degree of accuracy and timing of performance
8. Assessing performance	Learner demonstrates application of concept or rule	Learner originates a novel solution	Learner restates information in paraphrased form	Learner makes desired choice of personal action in real or simulated situation	Learner executes performance of total skill
9. Enhancing retention and transfer	Provide spaced reviews, including a variety of examples	Provide occasions for a variety of novel problem solutions	Provide verbal links to additional complexes of information	Provide additional varied situations for selected choice of action	Learner continues skill practice

Source: From *Principles of Instructional Design*, Second Edition, by Robert M. Gagné and Leslie J. Briggs, copyright © 1970 by Holt, Rinehart and Winston, Inc. Reprinted by permission of the publisher.

some methods of gaining attention will be more effective than others. The same is true of other instructional events such as stimulating recall of prerequisite capabilities (Can they merely be mentioned or elicited through questioning, or will it be necessary to lead the students through a series of review exercises?), presenting the stimulus material (Which examples would be helpful and which might be misleading?), or providing learning guidance (When and how should the teacher instruct didactically? Attempt to elicit insights through questioning? Assign activities designed to stimulate discovery learning?).

Stage 8: Developing or Selecting Materials and Media Some instructional events will require media or materials. It may be possible to select or adapt them from existing sources, although if this is done it will be important to preview them to make sure that they are appropriate. When materials cannot be obtained elsewhere, it will be necessary to design them. Besides effectiveness in helping students to accomplish lesson objectives, materials and media need to be assessed with an eye toward practical factors such as the size of the group with whom the activity can be used, how easily the medium can be interrupted for discussion or response to questions, its probable affective impact on the learners, the need for special training in its use, the time and trouble required to set it up, and the costs involved in purchasing, storing, and maintaining it (Briggs, 1970). Many of the special materials and media proposed for use in schools have proven to be overly time consuming, difficult to use, or otherwise impractical (Clark, 1983b), which is why relatively inexpensive and convenient print materials continue to be relied on heavily despite developments in audiovisual technology and computers.

Stage 9: Assessing Student Performance (Performance Measures) Lesson design includes not only preparation of instructional materials and methods but also preparation of performance measures for determining whether students achieve the lesson's objective. Instructional planning is not complete without preparation for assessment, and instructional development is not complete until the instruction succeeds in achieving its objective.

Final System-Level Stages

Stages 10–14 in the Gagné and Briggs scheme apply only to the designers of comprehensive learning systems and are not considered in detail here. They involve designing methods for training teachers to use the new system, conducting *formative evaluation* by pilot testing courses or individual lessons in a few classes to identify revision needs (Dick, 1977), *field testing* the system as a whole in a few sites and making further revisions, conducting *summative evaluation* in which the revised system is implemented in enough sites to allow statistical analysis of its effectiveness, and developing methods for diffusing information about the (presumably proven) system and installing it in new sites.

OTHER GENERAL APPROACHES TO INSTRUCTIONAL DESIGN

The Gagné and Briggs (1979) treatment is perhaps the best-known approach to instructional design, but it is just one of many such approaches (for reviews and information, see Andrews & Goodson, 1980; Braden & Sachs, 1983; Dick & Carey, 1978; Gagné & Dick, 1983; Reigeluth, 1983; and the various issues of the *Journal of Instructional Development*). Many of these other approaches are similar to that of Gagné and Briggs, differing only in terminology and degree of elaboration of particular points. A few differ considerably, however, because they envision a different kind of instruction from the didactic approach stressed by Gagné and Briggs.

Gropper

Treatment tools

Gropper (1983) outlined a behavioral approach that uses Skinnerian terminology and focuses on skills instruction but otherwise is similar in most respects to the Gagné and Briggs approach. Gropper went into detail in discussing what he called *treatment tools* for designing practice tasks: the degree of cuing provided, the size of the unit of behavior to be practiced, the mode of stimulus and response required, the variety built into tasks, the content built into tasks, and the frequency with which the task is practiced. He provided guidelines for variations in the use of these treatment tools at different stages in the instructional sequence.

Cuing

Cuing, for example, would be frequent and specific early in a unit but would fade gradually as mastery develops. In learning penmanship, students might first trace over model script, then copy (but not trace over) model script, and then write on their own without visual cues available. In learning French, students might first imitate French spoken on tape, then read French from printed text, and then speak it in conversation.

Size and complexity of task

The *size of the unit of behavior to be practiced* would also vary across the sequence of instruction. Practice might begin with isolated subskills (punctuating sentences), proceed to intermediate combinations of steps (writing sentences or paragraphs), and then move to final practice (writing essays). In addition to varying the sheer *size* of a task, the designer can vary its *complexity* (driving in empty parking lots versus driving on the streets in traffic) or the *standards* for acceptable performance (gradual decrease in the numbers of errors acceptable in typing).

Response and stimulus modes

Variations in *response mode* can also be used to increase the level of demand gradually. Initial practice might require only recognition of the correct answer (by selecting it from several alternatives), whereas intermediate practice might call for editing (correcting the answer if it is incorrect) and final practice for production (supplying the answer in the absence of cues). Similarly, the *stimulus mode* of presentations can be varied by beginning with concrete examples and moving toward more technical or abstract definitions or beginning with procedures before introducing general principles.

Variety

A variety of examples would be planned to promote generalization and transfer. They would be sequenced from easy to difficult according to the degree to which they were familiar to the students, similar to previously encountered examples, and salient in their defining characteristics. Thus students would practice forming plurals for regular nouns before taking on irregular nouns and would design experiments involving only one variable before moving to designs involving multiple interacting variables.

Varying content

The *content* of practice tasks can also be varied. Early in a sequence, for example, critical features of examples can be exaggerated to call attention to them and help prepare students to note more subtle variations to be presented later. Also, for certain objectives it may be helpful to promote the practice of errors (usually one wants to minimize this, but sometimes it is helpful to call students' attention to common errors and help them discriminate correct from incorrect performance) or to alter the typical sequence of behaviors (to disassemble something or work backward from a goal before attempting to assemble or work forward toward the goal).

Varying frequency

Finally, the *frequency* of practice can be varied. Typically, a great deal of distributed practice (however much it takes to produce mastery) is programmed following introduction of a new skill, with fading to a maintenance level thereafter.

Gropper's ideas show how an easy-to-difficult sequencing can be designed into instruction not only by sequencing objectives in an appropriate order but also by manipulating the treatment tools used to teach each objective.

Case and Bereiter

Limitations of Gagné's approach

Case and Bereiter (1984) credited Gagné for moving instructional design from behaviorism to cognitive behaviorism but argued that the field needs to develop further toward "cognitive development." Following Skinner (1954), they argued that the behavioral approach to instructional design includes the following steps:

1. Identify potential reinforcers that are available and effective.
2. Identify and objectively describe the desired behavior.
3. Describe the initial or "entering" behavior of the learner.
4. Define a series of behaviors, starting with the entering behavior and leading to the desired behavior, such that each successive behavior represents a small modification of the previous one.
5. Move students through the sequence using demonstrations and instructions coupled with reinforcement.
6. Ensure, through reinforced practice, that each behavior is thoroughly learned before advancing to the next step.

Case and Bereiter credited Gagné with correcting three important weaknesses in Skinner's approach. First, Skinner emphasized reinforcement and the issue of *how* to change behavior, but Gagné showed that the more typical problem is identifying in sufficient detail *what* needs to be taught. Gagné shifted the focus of attention from reinforcement to the nature of the behaviors themselves. Second, behavioral theory dealt exclusively with observable behaviors and thus was difficult to apply to school learning. Gagné recognized different types of learning, emphasizing the intellectual skills taught in school. Third, behaviorists had failed to specify how to carry out Step 3. Gagné's learning hierarchies and tasks analyses provided such guidance.

Case and Bereiter suggested that the following steps characterize Gagné's approach:

1. Identify the intellectual skill to be taught and develop a measure to assess its presence.
2. Using hierarchical task analysis, identify successively lower-level skills until reaching a level that all students are expected to possess on entry.
3. Develop assessment devices for each skill and use them to determine entering competence.
4. Present instruction that progresses from existing skills to successively higher levels.
5. Before beginning to teach any new skill, make sure that the student has mastered all the lower-level skills that it depends on.

Case and Bereiter argued that the Gagné approach works well for many but not all instructional situations and that its failures are typically due to one of two common problems. First, with highly difficult tasks, it sometimes yields instruction that is too difficult because students have to consider so many components in progressing through the hierarchy that the task exceeds the limits of their working memories. Second, the hierarchies yielded by purely logical analyses of tasks do not always correspond to the developmental order in which task components are mastered naturally, and this natural order may be more appropriate for instruction. Furthermore, students at particular levels of cognitive development will have particular concepts and preconceptions about the task, and instruction may have to begin with these familiar concepts and take into account these preconceptions. If the preconceptions happen to be incorrect, it will be necessary to show their inadequacies in order to enable the students to appreciate fully the instruction and make the necessary changes in their present thinking. Combining these considerations, Case and Bereiter (1984) suggested that a "cognitive development" approach to instructional design should include the following steps:

1. Identify the task to be taught and develop a measure for assessing mastery of it.
2. Develop a procedure for assessing the strategies that students employ in responding to the task.
3. Use this procedure to assess the strategies students use at a variety of ages, including ages when success is not achieved by current methods.

4a. Devise an instructional sequence for "recapitulating development" (i.e., for moving through the same sequence of steps that students would eventually move through on their own).

4b. Keep the working memory load at each step within reasonable limits.

5. Once performance at one level becomes relatively automatic, move on to the next.

Collins and Stevens

Questioning and inquiry teaching strategies

Collins and Stevens (1983) presented an approach to instructional design that differs from most others because it uses questioning and inquiry strategies to stimulate discovery learning. They described ten instructional strategies: (1) selecting positive and negative examples, (2) varying case studies systematically, (3) selecting counterexamples, (4) generating hypothetical cases, (5) forming hypotheses, (6) testing hypotheses, (7) considering alternative predictions, (8) entrapping students, (9) tracing consequences to a contradiction, and (10) questioning authority.

Creating dissonance or curiosity

The first three strategies are similar to those appearing in didactic approaches, except that Collins and Stevens focused on *selecting and sequencing examples so as to create dissonance or curiosity* and thus to set the stage for inquiry-oriented discussion, rather than on using examples to illustrate didactic explanations. The strategy of generating hypothetical cases is used to challenge students' reasoning or force them to take into account factors that they are presently ignoring.

In this inquiry approach, students are challenged to form and evaluate hypotheses rather than give rules or principles and are prodded to consider alternative predictions whenever they tend to jump to conclusions without adequate consideration of alternatives. The strategy of entrapping students is used to reveal the inadequacies of erroneous preconceptions by showing how the students' own thinking leads to incorrect predictions or conclusions. Tracing consequences to a contradiction is a similar strategy. Finally, the strategy of questioning authority involves training students to think for themselves rather than rely on the teacher or the book for correct answers.

In addition to discussing these instructional strategies, Collins and Stevens (1983) presented rules for structuring and sequencing dialogue with students designed to achieve particular objectives. We mention their work briefly here not to explain it in detail but to underscore the point that thoughtful instructional design is just as important for discovery and inquiry-oriented approaches as it is for other approaches to teaching.

Power and Limits of Systematic Instructional Design

The principles articulated by instructional design theorists can be helpful in planning effective instruction. They underscore the need to clarify objectives and to keep these in mind when designing and evaluating instruction, and they remind us that certain sequences, methods, examples, or activities may be more helpful than others for accomplishing those objectives. On the other hand, these theories have yet to be tested or supported with much scientific research (Mayer, 1985). Furthermore, despite the progress noted by Case and Bereiter (1984), instructional design theories are still of limited value for developing ideas about how particular objectives can be taught most effectively. Task analysis and related procedures are helpful, but instructional developers still have to rely primarily on their own knowledge of content and pedagogy and especially on their knowledge of what students of particular cognitive development levels know about the topic and how this knowledge can be profitably expanded. To illustrate some of the complexities involved, we will review research on the learning and teaching of concepts.

CONCEPT LEARNING

Concept learning

Educational psychologists have accumulated a great deal of information about concept learning to inform the design of methods for teaching concepts. Following Tennyson and Park (1980), we define a *concept* as a set of objects, symbols, or events that share common characteristics (defining attributes) and thus can be referenced by a particular name or symbol. *Concept learning* involves identifying the defining attributes of concepts that can be generalized to new examples and used to discriminate valid examples of the concept from nonexamples.

Early work on concept learning presented experimental subjects with a series of stimuli and asked them to state whether each stimulus was or was not an example of the concept. For example, Bruner, Goodnow, and Austin (1956) used a series of eighty-one cards that presented stimulus combinations varying along four dimensions: shape (squares, circles, or crosses); color (red, green, or black); number of objects shown (one, two, or three); and number of borders around these objects (one, two, or three). In a typical experiment, subjects were shown a chart illustrating all of the cards and asked to select one that they thought might illustrate the concept to be learned (such as that any card showing at least one red object was an instance of the concept and all other cards were not). The subject given feedback and then allowed to select another example. This continued until the subject verbalized the concept correctly.

Cue salience

Such experiments revealed several factors that influence concept learning. One is *cue salience:* Certain cues are noticed and used to discriminate stimuli more easily than others. Trabasso and Bower (1968), for example, used flower designs that varied in color of flower, number and shape of leaves, and angle of branches. They found that students learned concepts based on color more quickly than concepts based on angle of branch.

Task variables that influence learning

There are also several *task variables* that influence learning (Bourne, Ekstrand, & Dominowski, 1971; Mayer, 1982). One of them is *the nature of the rule* defining the concept. Rules involving only one attribute (choose the red object) are easier than rules involving more than one (such as color and shape). Furthermore, among rules involving more than one attribute, conjunctive rules (choose red squares) are easier to learn than disjunctive rules (choose any card that contains either a red object or a square or both). Also, when rules involve more than one attribute, increasing *the number of relevant dimensions* leads to quicker solution, but increasing *the number of irrelevant dimensions* makes learning more difficult. Finally, subjects usually learn faster from *positive instances* than from negative instances.

Limitations

Such findings were interesting but not very useful for developing guidelines for instruction. For one thing, the "instruction" was restricted to presentation of examples, so learners had to rely on guesswork and reasoning to learn by discovery. Other research suggests that concept learning is more efficient when accomplished through didactic instruction that includes direct statements of rules and definitions in addition to presentation of examples (Clark, 1971; Francis, 1975; Klausmeier, Ghatala, & Frayer, 1974; Woodson, 1974).

Models for teaching concepts

The latter research suggests the following model for teaching concepts (Owen, Blount, & Moscow, 1978):

1. Present a concept definition that includes the concept's label and defining attributes.
2. Present positive examples, emphasizing the defining attributes.
3. Present negative examples that help distinguish defining attributes from irrelevant attributes.
4. Present positive and negative examples and ask the student to identify the positive examples. Then ask why the negative examples are not examples of the concept.
5. Provide feedback, giving specific reasons for errors.

A second limitation of the early work on concept learning was that many of the concepts were arbitrary or artificial, and the stimuli were limited to examples that clearly were or were not instances of these concepts. For example, squares, circles, and crosses are obviously different from one another, as are red, green, and black colors. Under more normal learning conditions, however, stimuli often differ less starkly, and concepts sometimes are difficult to define and discriminate clearly.

Fuzziness of natural categories

Rosch (1978), for example, has shown that *natural categories* learned through experience (bird, furniture, student) are *fuzzy* in that the boundaries between them are not firm. Unlike conjunctive concepts defined by specific critical attributes that are all present in any example of the concept, natural categories merely share a *family resemblance* based on a basic core of features (Rosch & Mervis, 1975). Any example of the category contains some of these features but usually not all. For example, "singing," "flying," and "smallness" are all attributes that help define the natural category "birds." *Prototype* examples (e.g., robins) possess all of these attributes. However, many birds do not have all of these attributes, and some, like the ostrich, have none. People can rate the degree to which examples show "goodness of fit" to natural categories ("pillow" is a poor example of "furniture," "lamp" is better, and "chair" is excellent). They also can answer questions about typical examples ("Is a chair furniture?") more quickly than questions about atypical examples ("Is a pillow furniture?").

Children's use of basic-level categories

Children first learn to classify and label objects using *basic-level categories* (chair, table) rather than *superordinate-level categories* (furniture) or *subordinate-level categories* (easy chair, kitchen table), and adults are better able to use basic-level categories for thinking and reasoning purposes than they are able to use superordinate- or subordinate-level categories (Rosch et al., 1976; Rosch & Lloyd, 1978). Such data suggest that concept teaching might proceed most efficiently by starting with basic-level categories rather than with seemingly simpler or more specific concepts. Basic-level categories are not yet well understood, but it appears that the basic level is the most abstract level at which instances of a concept still have roughly the same shapes or parts. Thus "chair" is basic because all chairs share certain structural features, whereas "furniture" is not basic because it subsumes subtypes that look entirely different.

TEACHING CONCEPTS

We have seen that instructional designers typically call for sequencing material from the simple to the complex and that research on concept learning suggests first stating the concept definition and identifying its defining attributes, next presenting positive examples, and then presenting negative examples. These are useful general principles, but there are exceptions. Case and Bereiter (1984) noted the value of starting with learners' current concepts and preconceptions (and in the case of misconceptions, to confront them directly), and Rosch's work suggests beginning with basic-level categories and then working both upwards and downwards from there, rather than starting with simpler concepts that represent subordinate-level categories. Other investigators also have suggested qualifications and elaborations of general instructional design principles (Van Patten, Chao & Reigelith, 1986).

Positive introductory examples

Clark (1971) reviewed the concept of teaching literature and concluded that instruction should begin with positive introductory examples, next move to positive confirmatory examples, and then move to negative examples. *Positive introductory examples* illustrate the defining attributes and are as free as possible of irrelevant attributes. They call attention to the defining attributes with minimal confusion or distraction. Defining attributes for the concept of "square," for example, would include (a) four sides, (b) all sides of equal length, and (c) all corners right angles. Irrelevant attributes would include (a) how square is oriented in space and (b) its size. Squares shown as positive introductory examples would all be the same size and constructed from horizontal and vertical lines.

Positive confirmatory examples

Positive confirmatory examples also contain all of the defining attributes but in addition display irrelevant attributes. Thus positive confirmatory examples for "square" would include squares of varying sizes and spatial rotations. These examples would show learners that squares can come in any size or spatial rotation as long as they are constructed of four equal sides joined at right angles.

Negative examples

Finally, *negative examples* lack one or more of the defining attributes. They range from stimuli that are not even on the same dimensions as the concept (a picture of an elephant) through those that share certain similarities but none of the defining attributes (geometric figures with more or fewer than four sides) to those that share defining attributes but are still negative examples (rectangles that are almost square). Ordinarily, negative examples would be confined to those sharing the same conceptual class with positive examples (in this case, geometric figures). Within this restriction, however, an increasing variety of both positive and negative examples would be displayed as instruction progressed. This would make learners aware of both the degree to which the concept generalizes (illustrated by the range of positive examples) and the limits beyond which it cannot be stretched (illustrated by negative examples, especially the "near misses").

Merrill and Tennyson

Merrill and Tennyson (1977; see also Tennyson & Park, 1980) suggested similar guidelines. Their model includes (1) definition of the concept expressed in terms of its defining attributes, (2) expository presentation using *rational sets* of examples, and (3) practice in which students differentiate examples from nonexamples and justify their choices with reference to the defining attributes.

Rational sets

Rational sets of examples are assembled to call students' attention to defining attributes and minimize errors due to overgeneralization, undergeneralization, or misconception. Rational sets include examples that are diverse in form, ordered from easy to difficult, and selected for their value in illustrating particular points. Undergeneralization errors (identifying examples as nonexamples), for example, can be minimized by making sure that the set of examples includes the full range of variation in the defining attributes (squares come in many sizes and spatial rotations). Overgeneralization errors (identifying nonexamples as examples) can be minimized by making sure that the nonexample set includes typical "near misses" (rectangles that are almost square).

Matched pairs

To focus learners on the defining attributes, it is often helpful to use *matched pairs* of examples and nonexamples that differ on a defining attribute but not on irrelevant attributes. The presence or absence of irrelevant attributes must be varied from one set of examples to the next, however, to avoid inducing misconceptions. If all examples shown are constructed of horizontal and vertical lines, for example, learners might develop the misconception that this spatial orientation is essential to the definition of a square. Petty and Jansson (1987) found that rationally sequenced sets of examples (including matched pairs) were more effective than randomly ordered presentations of the same examples for teaching the concept of parallelogram to sixth graders.

Engelmann and Carnine

Engelmann and Carnine (1982) provided suggestions about the selection and juxtaposition of examples when teaching different kinds of concepts. They believe that instruction should be designed to accomplish *faultless communication*—instruction that communicates exactly what is intended and nothing else. A faultless communication admits of only one interpretation. If tryout produces unexpected responses, the instruction is faulted and needs revision (different selection or sequencing of examples or better accompanying explanation).

Faultless communication

Communications are judged faultless if they (1) present a set of examples that are "the same" with respect to only one distinguishing quality (the one that is the basis for generalization), (2) provide two signals—one to identify every example that possesses the quality to be generalized ("square") and a second to identify every example that does not ("not square"), (3) demonstrate a range of variation among positive examples that will encourage learners to induce a rule for classifying new examples on the basis of "sameness" (the defining attributes), (4) show the limits of permissible variation by presenting negative examples, and (5) provide a test of generalization (new examples within the range of variation in defining attributes demonstrated earlier). Sameness is demonstrated through positive examples, selected and juxtaposed to show not merely the most typical or easily observed examples but the entire range of examples to which the concept applies (or if this would be too much, to show that portion of the range that the instructor expects the learner to be able to master).

Juxtaposition rules

The basic *juxtaposition rules* are as follows: To show sameness, juxtapose examples that are greatly different and treat each example in the same way; to show difference, juxtapose examples that are only minimally different and treat them differently. In teaching "truck," for example, one would include pictures of a variety of trucks (panel trucks, tankers, moving vans) to make sure that the examples do not inadvertently *stipulate* that the term *truck* applies only to a particular type of truck. Furthermore, to help clarify the limits of the concept, negative examples would concentrate on objects that are just minimally different from trucks (cars, trains, pushcarts), rather than objects that are drastically different (apples, roses).

Including the full range of variation among the positive examples allows the learner to *interpolate*—to recognize that the concept applies to all examples that fall in between these extremes. Concentrating the negative examples on objects that are just minimally different from the target concept allows the learner to *extrapolate*—to recognize that the target concept does not apply to objects that are even more different than the negative examples shown.

Different concepts call for different sequencing of examples. Object concepts (nouns) are usually taught best by beginning with positive examples, but noncomparative single-dimension concepts (between, over, curved, running, pointed) are usually taught most efficiently by beginning with negative examples. Ultimately, the most effective way to teach a particular concept must be determined empirically through systematic tryout and revision based on formative evaluation data.

Object Concepts (Nouns) In teaching "vehicle" (a noun standing for a class of objects), for example, Engelmann and Carnine recommended the following sequence using pictures to illustrate the examples:

EXAMPLE	TEACHER WORDING
1. Rowboat	This is a vehicle.
2. Train	This is a vehicle.
3. Car	This is a vehicle.
4. Truck	This is a vehicle.
5. Swing set	This is not a vehicle.
6. Power lawn mower	This is not a vehicle.
7. Tractor	Is this a vehicle?
8. Rowboat with motor	Is this a vehicle?
9. Electric drill	Is this a vehicle?
10. Treadmill	Is this a vehicle?
11. Car	Is this a vehicle?

The first four examples establish that a vehicle is something that one gets into for the purposes of transportation. The diversity of positive examples includes transportation on water as well as on land, and muscle-powered as well as motor-powered transportation. The two negative examples are selected to rule out likely misinterpretations. The swing rules out the notion that sitting and moving is sufficient for something to be called a vehicle, and the lawn mower rules out the idea that moving and being motor powered makes something a vehicle. Presumably, learners will extrapolate from these minimally different negative examples to conclude that other things that are even less like vehicles (such as the electric drill and the treadmill in the test segment) are not vehicles, either. Note also that the test segment contains positive examples not encountered previously (tractor, rowboat with motor) that will fall within the range illustrated in the first four positive examples. By interpolating the information given in those first examples, learners should realize that the later positive examples are also vehicles.

If the presentation had been confined to positive examples, learners might have overgeneralized the concept of vehicles to include anything that moves or accommodates a person in a sitting position. The negative examples illustrate that these features by themselves are not sufficient to define a vehicle. They are especially well chosen because they each have not one but two features that might be confused in identifying vehicles (the power mower has both a motor and movement; the swing has both movement and the capacity to accommodate a person in a sitting position). The same information could have been conveyed using other examples but less efficiently (more examples would have been needed).

Comparative Concepts In contrast to the positive examples–first sequence in teaching nouns, Engelmann and Carnine suggested that instruction in comparative single-dimension concepts begin with negative examples. The sequence below would be used for teaching the concept "getting heavier." The student's hand would be placed palm up on a table or flat surface, and the teacher would exert downward pressure to create the sensation of the finger getting heavier or not heavier.

EXAMPLE	TEACHER WORDING
Starting point: Pressure 3	Feel this.
1. Pressure 2	It didn't get heavier.
2. Pressure 2	It didn't get heavier.
3. Pressure 3	It got heavier.
4. Pressure 7	It got heavier.
5. Pressure 9	Did it get heavier?
6. Pressure 9	Did it get heavier?
7. Pressure 5	Did it get heavier?
8. Pressure 6	Did it get heavier?
9. Pressure 3	Did it get heavier?
10. Pressure 4	Did it get heavier?
11. Pressure 2	Did it get heavier?

EXAMPLE	TEACHER WORDING
12. Pressure 5	Did it get heavier?
13. Pressure 1	Did it get heavier?

Since "getting heavier" is a comparative concept, the sequence begins with a starting point that establishes the dimension (the teacher exerts pressure and says, "Feel this"). Then come two negative examples that are minimally different from the concepts to be taught. One involves a slight decrease in pressure, and the other involves no change at all. The learner is now alerted to attend to the "pressure on the palm" dimension and to anticipate a change that does involve "getting heavier." Then come two positive examples, a small change and a larger one. The examples illustrate that any increase in pressure, and not an identical increase each time or a progressively greater increase each time, is "getting heavier." This sequence should have established the concept: Examples 5 through 13 are test items to ensure that it did. They include another "no change" item as well as a variety of positive and negative changes, including some that the learner has not seen yet. The sequence as a whole and certain examples in particular are designed to focus the learner on change (getting heavier), rather than on a particular state (lightness or heaviness). At Example 6, for example, the teacher exerts heavy pressure; yet this is not an example of "getting heavier" because it represents no change from Example 5.

Transformation Sequences The previous examples involving juxtaposition of positive and negative instances are used when teaching simple concepts. *Transformation sequences* are more complicated because they require learners to produce different responses to different examples. There are no negative examples. Much of what is learned in school involves transformation sequences. Consider teaching students to recognize the subject of a sentence. Engelmann and Carnine suggested beginning with typical examples that differ in only minor ways (A runner went to the park; five runners went to the park; that runner sat in the park). Then introduce examples that illustrate the range of the concept while minimizing potential confusion due to variation on other factors (Henry's dog ran in the park; those pigeons flew over the park; he wanted to go to the park). Finally, introduce examples that include variation in both the concept to be taught (the subject of the sentence) and other elements (A dog and five men sat on the hill; the yellow pencil and the white pencil are on the desk; telephone books are very useful).

Although recognizing the advantages of presenting examples in an easy-to-hard sequence, Engelmann and Carnine argued the need for a variety of examples chosen to prevent undesirable stipulations by learners. If given nothing but examples in which the subject is a noun modified by an adjective (fast runners, a runner, five runners, etc.), for instance, students might infer that all sentence subjects took this form and might be confused by other forms (pronouns, unmodified nouns, compound subjects, etc.).

In addition to providing more information about the concepts discussed briefly here, Englemann and Carnine (1982) discussed strategies (including example selection and juxtaposition) for teaching more complex concepts, cognitive operations, and behavioral skills. Their book is especially useful for those interested in designing instruction for the elementary grades.

CONCLUSION

Instruction is likely to be most effective when designed systematically, although so far there has been more theory development than research on this topic, and there are exceptions to even seemingly obvious principles (sometimes it is more efficient to start with the most typical or familiar concepts in a hierarchy rather than with the simplest ones; to avoid undesirable stipulations, one must introduce a broad range of positive examples early in a sequence, rather than proceeding from easy-to-hard examples or from regular-to-atypical examples). The principles described in this chapter will be helpful, but ultimately there is no substitute for systematic tryouts followed by revision based on evaluation data.

Assessing curricula

In assessing curricula being considered for potential adoption, consider the degree to which the developers have conducted such evaluation and revision before publishing. Are claims based on substantial field testing with impressive results or merely on unsupported assertions and testimonials? Is the content sequenced in appropriate ways? Are the clarity of exposition and the selection and juxtaposition of examples effective in creating faultless communication? Curricula that fail to meet these and other criteria implied in this chapter should be avoided if better alternatives are available.

SUMMARY

Instructional design is the art (and applied science) of creating efficient methods for attaining educational objectives. Gagné and Briggs recommended a systems approach containing system-level stages, course-level stages, and lesson-level stages. The initial system-level stages involve analyzing needs, goals, and priorities and then considering resources, constraints, and potential delivery systems to develop a curriculum scope and sequence statement that specifies objectives, sequences them in a sensible order, and identifies the delivery system to be used for instruction.

Course-level stages involve dividing and sequencing the content into courses organized around target objectives and their respective enabling objectives. To accomplish this, one performs information-processing analyses (perhaps using flow charts to depict the results visually), task classifications (with attention to the conditions of learning associated with each task), and learning task analyses (including identification of relevant learning hierarchies for instruction in intellectual skills).

Lesson-level stages involve identifying the objectives for each lesson and planning the instructional events (including media, materials, and evaluation) to be used. It is here that instructional designers bring to bear their creativity, knowledge of subject matter, and knowledge of students to decide what information to present and what examples or demonstrations, media or materials, and practice and application activities to use. Final system-level stages involve evaluating, field testing, and diffusing information about the developed learning system.

Gropper presented ideas on how to structure practice activities in an easy-to-difficult sequence by manipulating the treatment tools or degree of cuing provided, size of unit of behavior practiced, mode of stimulus and response required, and variety, content, and frequency of practice. Case and Bereiter argued the need to take into account limitations on learners' working memories and to teach steps in the order in which they tend to be learned naturally rather than necessarily teaching in the subordinate-to-superordinate order suggested by logical analysis. Collins and Stevens presented ideas for designing guided discovery and inquiry approaches. Their emphasis was on selecting and sequencing examples so as to create dissonance or curiosity, to stimulate students to make predictions and consider alternative possibilities, and eventually to arrive at the target objective through exploration and discovery.

The systems approach to instructional design is useful but limited by the fact that the best ways to teach something are rarely obvious and must be established through experimentation. Some of these complexities are illustrated in research on concept learning. Early work viewed concept learning as a matter of logical deduction from clear-cut positive and negative instances. However, Rosch has shown that the natural categories involved in most concept learning are fuzzy sets based on family resemblances. Frequently, such learning begins with basic-level categories (chair) before it proceeds to either superordinate-level categories (furniture) or subordinate-level categories (easy chair).

Most advice concerning concept teaching stresses beginning with clear definitions that state defining attributes, next display positive examples, and then move to negative examples and discrimination exercises. Merrill and Tennyson, for example, discussed presenting rational sets of examples selected to call attention to the defining attributes and minimize errors due to overgeneralization, undergeneralization, or misconception. They recommended sequencing examples from easy to difficult and making sure that the positive examples include the full range of variation that occurs in the defining attributes and that the negative examples include "near misses."

Engelmann and Carnine argued the importance of designing instruction to achieve faultless communication and noted that this is not always achieved by beginning with positive examples or by proceeding in an easy-to-difficult sequence. Unlike object concepts, comparative concepts are usually taught more efficiently by beginning with negative examples. Also, instructional designers need to select and juxtapose examples in ways that will not only communicate the range of variation and limits of application of the concept but also will prevent inappropriate stipulations—

beliefs that the concept applies only to a particular subset of its actual range.

QUESTIONS AND PROBLEMS

1. Compare the scope and sequence statements for curricula designed to teach the same subject at the same grade level. Each curriculum will include objectives not included in the other, and the objectives shared in common will not always be taught in the same order. Are these differences merely matters of taste, or is one curriculum better than the other in its selection or sequencing of objectives?
2. Study a curriculum developed for the grade level and subject matter you intend to teach. Would you use it as is, or would you omit certain objectives and associated activities or supplement by bringing in or developing additional ones? If possible, compare notes with experienced teachers who have used this curriculum.
3. Would you prefer to select objectives and develop curriculum materials and activities yourself or have this done for you by policy makers and commercial publishers? If the former, how will you respond to administrative and parental pressures to emphasize certain objectives, and how will you evaluate and perfect the materials and activities you develop? If the latter, what will you do if you find that the adopted curriculum package is not well suited to your students or if some students need remedial work that the package does not provide?
4. Select an objective commonly taught in the grade level and subject matter you intend to teach. Perform an information-processing analysis to identify the sequence of steps leading to the target performance and construct a flow chart to depict this visually. What does this tell you about where instruction should begin, what steps should be included, and in what order?
5. The list of instructional events shown in Table 11.2 was composed with didactic instruction in mind. How might this list be changed for lessons designed to achieve higher-level cognitive objectives? For lessons that relied on inquiry procedures or discovery learning?
6. Given that special materials or media may add important dimensions to teaching but also may not be practical, what special materials and media do you foresee using in your own teaching? What advantages do they bring that make them worth the trouble?
7. For a given objective that you are likely to teach, describe how an easy-to-difficult sequence can be designed into a series of practice tasks by manipulating the treatment tools described by Gropper.
8. Gagné advocated using learning hierarchies and other tools for sequencing tasks on a logical basis, whereas Case and Bereiter advocated sequencing tasks according to the order in which their components are typically developed through ordinary experience. What students and tasks do Gagné's ideas fit best, and what students and tasks do Case and Bereiter's ideas fit best? Why?

9. Select two concepts from subject matter you are likely to teach and design instruction for each that includes a clear definition that specifies the defining attributes of the concept and a rational set of examples that illustrates both the range and limits of its application. Make sure that you do not inadvertently confine your positive examples to a subset that would cause learners to stipulate inappropriately. Also, be sure that your positive examples are not all confounded with an irrelevant attribute that learners could mistake for a defining attribute.
10. Engelmann and Carnine found that object concepts are generally taught most easily by beginning with positive examples, but comparative concepts are generally taught most easily by beginning with negative examples. Why should this be? Can you formulate a more general rule about when to begin with positive examples and when to begin with negative examples? Compare notes with your friends.

Case Studies

TINKERING. Jim Anderson is not pleased with the new science curriculum adopted by this district. The general objectives make sense—he likes what is taught and the order in which lessons are sequenced. Many of the lessons, however, just don't work very well. Sometimes the materials are inadequate or overly cumbersome, and some of the suggested activities and exercises seem pointless. Therefore, Jim decides to stick with the objectives but to find or develop better ways to accomplish them in the case of about half of the lessons. Should teachers make wholesale changes like this? Why or why not? What steps could Jim take to ensure that the new materials and activities succeed in meeting the objectives and really are improvements over the old ones?

BETTER SEQUENCING AND EXAMPLES? Ed Sikes is generally pleased with his course in educational psychology, but he is aware of certain repeated failures. It always seems that many students confuse Piaget's terms assimilation and accommodation, confuse negative reinforcement with punishment, confuse cognitive level with difficulty level, and have trouble describing the differences in mental functioning between a bright six-year-old and a dull fourteen-year old. What may be causing these problems, and what might Dr. Sikes do to eliminate them? In particular, what changes might he make in the sequencing of his instruction and in the number and kinds of examples he uses to illustrate concepts?

CHAPTER

Approaches to Classroom Instruction

CHAPTER OUTLINE

OBJECTIVES

When you have mastered the material in this chapter, you will be able to

1. Define process-outcome research and describe the relationships with achievement gain established for opportunity to learn/content covered, role definition/expectations/time allocation, classroom management/student engaged time, consistent success/academic learning time, and active teaching
2. Identify teacher behaviors associated with positive student attitudes
3. Define ethnographic research and identify the classroom process variables found associated with achievement gain in the ethnographic study reported by Tikunoff, Berliner, and Rist (1975)
4. Describe the models of active teaching used in experiments by Good and Grouws (1979) and by Anderson, Evertson, and Brophy (1979)
5. Describe the uses and limits of teacher-led, group-based instruction
6. Explain and give examples of the concept of functionally equivalent paths to the same achievement outcomes
7. Describe how effective active teaching differs between the early grades and the upper grades and between low socioeconomic status (SES) and high SES settings

8. Describe how to adapt teaching to students' individual characteristics (aptitude, developmental stage, reading level, personality, work mode preference, and general work habits)
9. Explain Good and Power's (1976) guidelines for adapting instruction to the needs of successful, social, dependent, alienated, and phantom students

Teachers have to process a great deal of information to make intelligent decisions about how to instruct their students. We noted in Chapter 6 that different types of learning (cognitive strategies, intellectual skills, information, motor skills, attitudes) require different types of instruction, and in Chapters 7–9 we reviewed three major lines of theory and research on learning (behaviorist, cognitive structuralist, and information processing) and the approaches to instruction that each has spawned.

Models of teaching

Other approaches could have been presented as well. Joyce and Weil (1980) have described twenty-three *models of teaching*, classified into four types (information processing, social interaction, focus on the individual person, and behavior modification). *Information-processing models* concentrate on presenting material in ways that learners can process and retain most easily and on fostering information-processing skills. *Social interaction models* seek to foster good group relations and arrange instruction so that students interact with and learn from one another as well as the teacher. *Personal models* apply humanistic principles to promote both intellectual and emotional development in individuals (self-actualization, mental health, creativity). Finally, *behavior-modification models* sequence activities to promote efficient learning and the shaping and control of behavior through reinforcement.

Each model has something worthwhile to offer and stresses certain things at the expense of others. Even if we ignore personal and social development for the moment and confine attention to instruction in the academic curriculum, it is obvious that teachers face choices about what to teach and how to teach it. Furthermore, the decisions facing teachers are more complex than those facing curriculum designers. Teachers cannot take time to devise and perfect instruction intended for individual learners. Instead, they must find ways to both manage and instruct classes of twenty to forty students, while working almost continuously in public and responding to the multidimensionality, simultaneity, immediacy, and unpredictability of classrooms as described in Chapter 1. Consequently, teachers are seldom able to sustain instruction that is ideal according to some theoretical model. Instead, they must accept compromises that enable them to accomplish the most progress possible with the most students possible under the prevailing circumstances.

Theories of learning and models of teaching provide useful input to teachers facing these complexities. So does research on teaching, especially research that establishes linkages between classroom processes (teacher behaviors, teacher-student interaction) and the outcomes of instruction (gains in achievement, changes in students' attitudes or self-concepts). Research designed to develop information about these linkages is known as *process-outcome* (or *process-product*) *research*.

PROCESS-OUTCOME RESEARCH

In a typical process-outcome study, teachers are observed under specified conditions (subject matter, time of day, etc.) by observers trained to use systematic data-collection methods. Some of them are *high-inference* methods that require observer judgment (rate the clarity of the teacher's explanations on a five-point scale: 1 = very low, 2 = low, 3 = medium, 4 = high, 5 = very high). Others are *low-inference* checklists or category systems used to record the presence/absence of prespecified events (each time the teacher asks a question, the observer notes whether the student answered it correctly and, if so, whether the teacher praised the answer). Once observations are completed, the data are aggregated to develop averages or other scores representing each teacher's behavior (average clarity rating; average number of student answers praised per hour; percentage of correct answers that were praised). These process measures are then correlated with measures (typically standardized tests) of student achievement (adjusted for class differences at entry) or measures of affective outcomes.

Teacher Behavior and Student Achievement

Several large field studies have been conducted using these methods (Bourke, 1985; Brophy & Evertson, 1976; Evertson et al., 1980; Fisher et al., 1980; Flanders, 1970; Good & Grouws, 1977; McDonald, 1977; Soar & Soar, 1979; Stallings, 1975; Stallings et al., 1977, 1978; Tikunoff, Berliner, & Rist, 1975). Along with several smaller ones by other investigators, these studies have established a well-replicated body of knowledge about the relationships between teacher behavior and student achievement. Furthermore, some of these correlational relationships have been established as causal through experimental studies (Anderson, Evertson, & Brophy, 1979; Clark et al., 1979; Good & Grouws, 1979; Good, Grouws, & Ebmeier, 1983; Stallings, 1980). Common elements in these studies point to certain classroom events and teacher behaviors as consistent correlates of student achievement gain. The evidence is strongest for the following five sets of variables (Brophy & Good, 1986).

Opportunity to Learn; Content Covered Amount learned is related to opportunity to learn, whether this is measured in terms of the number of pages of curriculum covered (Good, Grouws, & Beckerman, 1978; Borg, 1979) or the percentage of test items that were taught through lecture or recitation activities in class (Arehart, 1979; Armento, 1977; Cooley & Leinhardt, 1980; Dunkin & Doenau, 1980; Nuthall & Church, 1973; Smith, 1979). Student opportunity to learn is determined in part by length of school day and school year and in part by the following four variables.

Role Definition; Expectations; Time Allocation Achievement is maximized when teachers: (1) define instructing students in the academic curriculum as basic to their roles as teachers, (2) expect their students to master this curriculum, and (3) allocate most of the available time to activities designed to promote such mastery (Brophy & Evertson, 1976; Fisher et al., 1980; Stallings, 1975). Observers describe such teachers as businesslike and task oriented and report that most classroom time is allocated to activities with academic objectives rather than to activities with other objectives (personal adjustment, group dynamics) or no clear objectives at all (''free time,'' games, or pastimes).

Classroom Management; Student Engaged Time Not all time allocated to academic activities is actually spent in these activities. Students' engagement rates depend on the teacher's ability to organize and manage the classroom as an efficient learning environment in which academic activities run smoothly, transitions are brief and orderly, and little time is spent getting organized or dealing with inattention or resistance. High task-engagement rates attained through such successful classroom management are among the most frequent and powerful correlates of student achievement (Brophy & Good, 1986). These classroom-management strategies are discussed in Chapter 20.

Consistent Success; Academic Learning Time To learn efficiently, students must be engaged in activities that are appropriate in difficulty level. Thus it is important not only to maximize content coverage by pacing students briskly through the curriculum but also to see that they make continuous progress all along the way by moving through small steps with high or at least moderate rates of success and minimal confusion or frustration (Brophy & Evertson, 1976; Fisher et al., 1980). High (90–100 percent) success rates are especially desirable when students must work independently without teacher supervision or the opportunity to get help immediately if they become confused. Lower success rates are acceptable (and sometimes desirable) when the teacher is present to provide guidance and immediate corrective feedback.

Timing and quality of errors

Three additional points should be made about success rates. First, we need to consider not only the frequency of errors but their timing and quality. Relatively frequent errors may be expected early in a unit when new learning occurs, but errors should be minimal later when mastery levels are achieved. Also, some errors should occur because students have the right idea but make a minor miscalculation or because they rely on sound logic that is based on plausible but faulty assumptions. Such ''high-quality'' errors are understandable and may even generate useful ''teachable moments,'' but errors suggesting inattention, hopeless confusion, or alienation from the content are undesirable.

High success rate

Second, in speaking of the desirability of high rates of success, we do not mean to imply that such success is always attained easily. High success rates are construed to result from effort and thought, not mere ''automatic'' application of already overlearned algorithms.

Preparation of students for task

Third, bear in mind that success rates will depend not only on the inherent difficulty level of a task but also on the degree to which the teacher has effectively prepared the students for the task by explaining key concepts, reviewing the directions, and working through examples. A task that might be too difficult if presented with little preparation might be just right if introduced with sufficient structure and implemented with sufficient provision for guidance and feedback. Thus, nothing in these findings contradicts Vygotsky's notion (Rogoff & Wertsch, 1984; Vygotsky, 1978) that instruction should focus on the student's zone of proximal development (i.e., on what the student is able to learn with help rather than on what the student is already able to do independently). The findings do, however, caution against creating undue frustration or confusion by trying to move too far too fast.

Active Teaching Students achieve more in classes when they spend most of their time being taught or supervised by their teachers rather than working on their own or not working at all (Arehart, 1979; Brophy & Evertson, 1976; Good & Grouws, 1977; Stallings, 1975; Stallings et al., 1977, 1978). Such classes include frequent lessons in which the teacher presents information and develops concepts through lecture and demonstration, asks recitation questions or conducts discussions, prepares the students for follow-up assignments by giving instructions and going through practice examples, monitors progress on those assignments after releasing the students to work independently, and provides correction or reteaching when necessary. The teachers carry the content to the students personally rather than relying solely on the curriculum materials to do so, although they usually convey information in brief presentations followed by recitation, discussion, or application opportunities. Much teacher talk involves asking questions and giving feedback rather than extended lecturing.

Research findings

Taken together, these findings indicate that teachers who systematically pursue academic objectives elicit higher achievement than teachers who fail to pursue any clear objectives at all, who try to pursue academic

Student achievement increases when teachers actively supervise work and provide feedback.

objectives but are unable to do so for lack of effective classroom-management skills, or who concentrate on affective objectives more than on teaching the academic curriculum. Also, teachers who use group-based instructional methods and carry the content to their students personally through active instruction get better results than teachers who rely on individualized learning modules or other materials-based approaches. As noted in Chapter 7, most students are not prepared to learn efficiently through independent reading and direction following: They need explanation, guidance, and supervision from the teacher. Thus despite its limitations, traditional teacher-led group instruction may be the optimal solution to the challenge of maximizing the achievement of the class as a whole while working within the constraints imposed by the typical classroom (in particular, the high student:teacher ratio).

Teacher Behavior and Student Affect

Teacher warmth

Studies that have related classroom processes to affective outcomes (Evertson et al., 1980; Flanders, 1970; Stallings, 1975) indicate that student attitudes are linked most closely to measures of teacher warmth and student orientation: praise, use of student ideas, and willingness to listen to students, respect their contributions, and socialize with them. These teacher behaviors are mostly different from those that are associated with achievement. The two sets of behaviors are compatible to an extent, but beyond some point, further efforts devoted toward pursuit of achievement gain will come at the expense of opportunities to pursue other objectives. Thus even the best teaching will involve trade-offs rather than optimizing in an absolute sense (Clark, 1982; Peterson, 1979; Schofield, 1981).

Relationship between emotional climate indicators and achievement gain indicators

Soar and Soar (1979) clarified the relationships between the cognitive and the affective aspects of teacher-student interaction by showing that there is a disordinal relationship between emotional climate indicators and achievement gain indicators. That is, negative emotional climate indicators (teacher criticism of students, negative affect displayed by teacher or students, student resistance to the teacher) usually correlate negatively with achievement, whereas positive emotional climate indicators (teacher praise, positive affect displayed by teacher or students) usually do *not* show significant positive correlations. Thus it appears that efficient learning in classrooms does not require a notably warm emotional climate. It is true that negative climates are disfunctional, but neutral or mildly warm climates appear to be at least as supportive of achievement as more clearly warm climates. In short, student-achievement gain depends primarily on the amount and quality of instruction received from the teacher. Teacher warmth will make for a good classroom climate and for student liking of the teacher but by itself will not produce achievement.

Some Examples from Research

To develop a more concrete picture of the kind of instruction that is associated with high achievement gain, we will provide three examples. Tikunoff, Berliner, and Rist (1975) studied second- and fifth-grade reading and mathematics instruction. The 40 teachers selected for observation (from a larger sample of 200 teachers who earlier had taught specially prepared two-week units) included the 10 at each grade who had elicited the largest adjusted achievement gains and the 10 who had elicited the smallest. These 40 teachers were observed during reading and mathematics lessons by observers trained in the *ethnographic methods* of data collection developed by anthropologists. These ethnographers took detailed *field notes* describing and attempting to make sense of events as they unfolded. Later, transcripts of these field notes were rated on sixty-one dimensions. For twenty-one of these dimensions (shown in Table 12.1), significant differences were observed between the more effective and less effective classes at both grade levels and in both subjects.

Effective teaching and structure

Note that these differences do not support simple statements about effective and ineffective teaching. The more effective teachers encouraged their students to work on their own but also monitored the work and provided a great deal of structure. Similarly, they showed more spontaneity about their teaching, even though their lessons were structured (frequent reviews, clear objectives). To allow more focused examination of the processes seen in more effective classrooms in their study, Tikunoff, Berliner, and Rist arranged the list into the following clusters:

Classroom Climate	
Conviviality	more
Engagement	more
Defiance	less
Cooperation	more
Promoting self-sufficiency	more
Adult involvement	more
Teacher Instructional Moves	
Attending	more
Monitoring learning	more
Structuring	more
Spontaneity	more
Pacing	sensitive to students' individual differences
Abruptness	less
Filling time	less
Illogical statements	less
Teacher Behavior-Control Moves	
Consistency of message	more
Belittling	less
Oneness	less
Teacher Characteristics	
Accepting	more
Optimistic	more
Knowledge of subject	more
Recognition seeking	less

The following two examples come from experimental studies in which teachers were trained to use instructional principles that had been linked to student achievement in earlier correlational work. Then classrooms

TABLE 12.1 BEHAVIORS THAT SEPARATED MORE AND LESS EFFECTIVE MATHEMATICS AND READING TEACHERS AT BOTH SECOND AND FIFTH GRADE

Teacher (T) or Student (S)	More (+) or Less (−) Frequently a Descriptor of Effectiveness	Behavioral Variable and Definition
T	−	*abruptness:* unanticipated switching by teacher, e.g., from instruction to classroom management, to behavior management, to instruction, to behavior management.
T	+	*accepting:* teacher reacts constructively (overt, verbal, nonverbal) to students' feelings and attitudes.
T	+	*adult involvement:* adults other than the teacher are allowed to instruct.
T	+	*attending:* teacher listens actively to what a student is saying, reading, reciting.
T	−	*belittling:* teacher berates child in front of others.
T	+	*consistency of message* (control): teacher gives a direction or a threat and follows through with it.
T & S	+	*conviviality:* warmth, familylike quality to classroom interaction; good feelings between teacher–students, students–students.
S	+	*cooperation:* students cooperate with other students, teacher; willingness on part of students to help each other.
S	−	*defiance:* a student's open resistance to teacher's direction; refuses to comply.
S	+	*engagement:* students express eagerness to participate, appear actively, productively involved in learning activities.
T	−	*filling time:* teacher fills "empty" time periods with busy work.
T	−	*illogical statements:* teacher makes a statement whose consequences would be ridiculous if carried out.
T	+	*knowledge of subject:* teacher seems confident in teaching a given subject, and demonstrates a grasp of it.
T	+	*monitoring of learning:* teacher checks on student's progress regularly and adjusts instruction accordingly.
T	−	*oneness:* teacher treats whole group as "one" in order to maintain peer climate.
T	+	*optimism:* teacher expresses positive, pleasant, optimistic attitudes and feelings.
T	+	*pacing:* teacher appears to perceive learning rate of students and adjusts teaching pace accordingly.
T	+	*promoting self-sufficiency:* teacher encourages students to take responsibility for their own classwork.
T	−	*recognition seeking:* teacher calls attention to self for no apparent instructional purpose.
T	+	*spontaneity:* teacher capitalizes instructionally on unexpected incidents that arise during class time.
T	+	*structuring:* teacher prepares students for lesson by reviewing, outlining, explaining objectives, summarizing.

Source: *Drawn (with slight alteration) from Tikunoff, Berliner, & Rist, 1975, p. xvii.*

were observed to assess implementation of the principles, and students were tested to assess learning outcomes. Each study found that the experimental teachers (1) implemented the principles more systematically than control teachers who used whatever methods they had developed on their own and (2) produced significantly greater achievement gain.

Good and Grouws (1979) developed the instructional model shown in Table 12.2 for fourth-grade mathematics. The model includes guidelines for time allocation to ensure that mathematics is taught for about forty-five mintues each day, and calls for supplementing this instruction with homework assignments. Students work primarily individually on assignments, but there is a great deal of active instruction by the teacher. New concepts are presented in detail during the development portion of the lesson, and the teacher both makes sure that students know how to do the assignment before releasing them to work individually and reviews the assignment with them the next day.

TABLE 12.2 SUMMARY OF KEY INSTRUCTIONAL BEHAVIORS

Daily Review (First 8 minutes except Mondays)
1. Review the concepts and skills associated with the homework
2. Collect and deal with homework assignments
3. Ask several mental computation exercises

Development (About 20 minutes)
1. Briefly focus on prerequisite skills and concepts
2. Focus on meaning and promoting student understanding by using lively explanations, demonstrations, process explanations, illustrations, and so on.
3. Assess student comprehension by
   a. Using process/product questions (active interaction)
   b. Using controlled practice
4. Repeat and elaborate on the meaning portion as necessary

Seatwork (About 15 minutes)
1. Provide uninterrupted successful practice
2. Momentum—keep the ball rolling—get everyone involved, then sustain involvement
3. Alerting—let students know their work will be checked at the end of the period
4. Accountability—check the students' work

Homework Assignment
1. Assign on a regular basis at the end of each math class except Fridays
2. Should involve about 15 minutes of work to be done at home
3. Should include one or two review problems

Special Reviews
1. Weekly Review/Maintenance
   a. Conduct during the first 20 minutes each Monday
   b. Focus on skills and concepts covered during the previous week
2. Monthly Review/Maintenance
   a. Conduct every fourth Monday
   b. Focus on skills and concepts covered since last monthly review

Source: *Good, T., Grouws, D., and Ebmeier, H.,* Active Mathematics Teaching. *Copyright © 1983 Longman Inc.*

Anderson, Evertson, and Brophy (1979) developed a more lengthy set of guidelines for first-grade teachers to use during small-group reading instruction. Most of them were supported by their findings, although the data indicated that a few principles should be dropped and that others should be revised. The revised set of principles (Anderson, Evertson, & Brophy, 1982) is shown in Table 12.3.

The model is similar to that of Good and Grouws in that it includes time-allocation guidelines and an emphasis on active instruction followed by practice with feedback. However, there are important differences due to subject matter and grade level. First, first-grade reading is typically taught in small groups (to accommodate the slow pacing associated with taking turns reading aloud), so the model was developed with the small-group format in mind. Second, because first graders are still learning the student role and teachers must be concerned about maintaining their attention and controlling the timing and nature of their contributions to lessons, the principles cover group organization and management, not just instruction in the content. Third, the principles focus on the teacher's interactions with individual students, even though the instruction takes place in a group context, because much of first-grade reading instruction involves interactions with individual students rather than instruction to the group as such. In contrast, whole-class mathematics instruction in the fourth grade is directed mostly at the group.

Adapting instruction to each situation

These examples illustrate how even within the domain of basic skills instruction in the elementary grades, *instruction must be adapted to the subject matter, the students, and other context factors*. Classroom research continues to develop support for instructional principles of varying generality, but there appear to be no specific instructional behaviors that are ideal for all students and situations. Different cognitive objectives (e.g., mastering skills versus applying them to complex problem solving or creativity) require different instructional methods, and other kinds of objectives (promoting the personal development of the students or the social development of the class as a whole) require still other methods. Research can inform teachers about the relationships between teacher behavior and student outcomes, but teachers must decide for themselves what outcomes they wish to promote and in what order of priority.

Uses and Limits of Group-Based Instruction

Teachers make a difference

Process-outcome research has reaffirmed what should have been obvious all along—*teachers make a difference*. Some teachers elicit more achievement than others, and researchers have begun to identify the classroom management and instructional behaviors associated with such success. This helps to move the field beyond testimonials and unsupported claims toward scientific statements based on credible data. Also, the findings are gratifying to most teachers because they validate many of the principles of practice that they have developed intuitively or through their own experimentation.

Effective lessons

For example, Madeline Hunter (1984) has developed "templates" for describing, interpreting, and evaluating the quality of teaching. One such template suggests that effective lessons contain the following elements:

TABLE 12.3 GUIDELINES FOR FIRST-GRADE TEACHERS

General Principles

1. Reading groups should be organized for efficient, sustained focus on the content.
2. All students should be not merely attentive but actively involved in the lesson.
3. The difficulty level of questions and tasks should be easy enough to allow the lesson to move along at a brisk pace and the students to experience consistent success.
4. Students should receive frequent opportunities to read and respond to questions and should get clear feedback about the correctness of their performance.
5. Skills should be mastered to overlearning, with new ones gradually phased in while old ones are being mastered.
6. Although instruction takes place in the group setting, monitor each individual and provide whatever instruction, feedback, or opportunities to practice that he or she requires.

Specific Principles

Programming for Continuous Progress

1. *Time.* Across the year, reading groups should average 25–30 minutes each. The length will depend on student attention level, which varies with time of year, student ability level, and the skills being taught.
2. *Academic focus.* Successful reading instruction includes not only organization and management of the reading group itself (discussed below), but also effective management of the students who are working independently. Provide these students with: appropriate assignments; rules and routines to follow when they need help or information (to minimize their needs to interrupt you as you work with your reading group); and activity options available when they finish their work (so they have something else to do).
3. *Pace.* Both progress through the curriculum and pacing within specific activities should be brisk, producing continuous progress achieved with relative ease (small steps, high success rate).
4. *Error rate.* Expect to get correct answers to about 80 percent of your questions in reading groups. More errors can be expected when students are working on new skills (perhaps 20–30 percent). Continue with practice and review until smooth, rapid, correct performance is achieved. Review responses should be almost completely (perhaps 95 percent) correct.

Organizing the Group

1. *Seating.* Arranging seating so that you can both work with the reading group and monitor the rest of the class at the same time.
2. *Transitions.* Teach the students to respond immediately to a signal to move into the reading group (bringing their books or other materials) and to make quick, orderly transitions between activities.
3. *Getting started.* Start lessons quickly once the students are in the group (have your materials prepared beforehand).

Introducing Lessons and Activities

1. *Overviews.* Begin with an overview to provide students with a mental set and help them anticipate what they will be learning.
2. *New words.* When presenting new words, do not merely say the word and move on. Usually, you should show the word and offer phonetic clues to help students learn to decode.
3. *Work assignments.* Be sure that students know what to do and how to do it. Before releasing them to work on activities independently, have them demonstrate how they will accomplish these activities.

Insuring Everyone's Participation

1. *Ask questions.* In addition to having the students read, ask them questions about the words and materials. This helps keep students attentive during classmates' reading turns and allows you to call their attention to key concepts or meanings.
2. *Ordered turns.* Use a system, such as going in order around the group, to select students for reading or answering questions. This insures that all students have opportunities to

participate and it simplifies group management by eliminating handwaving and other attempts by students to get you to call on them.

3. *Minimize call-outs.* In general, minimize student call-outs and emphasize that students must wait their turns and respect the turns of others. Occasionally, you may want to allow call-outs, to pick up the pace or encourage interest, especially with low-achievers or students who do not normally volunteer. If so, give clear instructions or devise a signal to indicate that you intend to allow call-outs at these times.
4. *Monitor individuals.* Be sure that everyone, but especially slow students, is checked, receives feedback, and achieves mastery. Ordinarily this will require questioning each individual student and not relying on choral responses.

Teacher Questions and Student Answers

1. *Academic focus.* Concentrate your questions on the academic content; do not overdo questions about personal experiences. Most questions should be about word recognition or sentence or story comprehension.
2. *Word attack questions.* Include word attack questions that require students to decode words or identify sounds within words.
3. *Wait for answers.* In general, wait for an answer if the student is still thinking about the question and may be able to respond. However, do not continue waiting if the student seems lost or is becoming embarrassed, or if you are losing the other students' attention.
4. *Give needed help.* If you think the student cannot respond without help but may be able to reason out the correct answer if you do help, provide help by simplifying the question, rephrasing the question, or giving clues.
5. *Give the answer when necessary.* When the student is unable to respond, give the answer or call on someone else. In general, focus the attention of the group on the answer and not on the failure to respond.
6. *Explain the answer when necessary.* If the question requires one to develop a response by applying a chain of reasoning or step-by-step problem solving, explain the steps one goes through to arrive at the answer in addition to giving the answer itself.

When the Student Responds Correctly

1. *Acknowledge correctness (unless it is obvious).* Briefly acknowledge the correctness of responses (nod positively, repeat the answer, say "right," etc.), unless it is obvious to the students that their answers are correct (such as during fast-paced drills reviewing old material).
2. *Explain the answer when necessary.* Even after correct answers, feedback that emphasizes the methods used to get answers will often be appropriate. Onlookers may need this information to understand why the answer is correct.
3. *Follow-up questions.* Occasionally, you may want to address one or more follow-up questions to the same student. Such series of related questions can help the student to integrate relevant information. Or you may want to extend a line of questioning to its logical conclusion.

Praise and Criticism

1. *Praise in moderation.* Praise only occasionally (no more than perhaps 10 percent of correct responses). Frequent praise, especially if nonspecific, is probably less useful than more informative feedback.
2. *Specify what is praised.* When you do praise, specify what is being praised, if this is not obvious to the student and the onlookers.
3. *Correction, not criticism.* Routinely inform students whenever they respond incorrectly, but in ways that focus on the academic content and include corrective feedback. When it is necessary to criticize (typically only about 1 percent of the time when students fail to respond correctly), be specific about what is being criticized and about desired alternative behaviors.

Source: *Anderson, Evertson, & Brophy, 1982, pp. 2–10.*

(1) anticipatory set (something said or done generally to prepare the students to learn and to focus them on key stimuli), (2) objective and purpose (tell students the purpose of the lesson), (3) input (new information), (4) modeling (demonstrations of skills or procedures), (5) checking for understanding (through questions or requests for performance), (6) guided practice (under direct teacher supervision), and (7) independent practice (once students know what to do and how to do it). The process-outcome findings reviewed in this and the next chapter fit well with Hunter's notions about effective teaching.

Effectiveness of teacher-led group-based instruction

Along with points made earlier about what is reasonable to expect teachers to accomplish while working within typical constraints, these findings suggest that *most teachers will use the traditional method of teacher-led, group-based instruction as their basic approach*. This is especially true when they focus on instruction in basic skills or on knowledge, comprehension, or (most) application objectives in almost any subject matter. Compared to the feasible alternatives, *teacher-led, group-based instruction appears to be effective for classroom teaching of any body of knowledge or set of skills that has been sufficiently well analyzed and organized so that it can be presented (explained, modeled) systematically and then practiced or applied during activities that call for student performance that can be evaluated for quality and (where incorrect or imperfect) given corrective feedback.*

Limitations of use

This covers much of what teachers try to accomplish, but it also excludes a lot: activities with analysis, synthesis, or evaluation objectives (creative writing; conducting research or creating a product of considerable complexity that requires diverse skills) that are accomplished more effectively using inquiry or guided discovery methods. It also excludes activities designed primarily to develop attitudes rather than knowledge or skills (art or music appreciation and many activities in English, social studies, and physical education). Thus teacher-led, group-based instruction may not be the primary approach used in certain courses, and even when it is the primary approach, it ordinarily is a base to work from rather than the only method used.

Active instruction

We prefer the term *active instruction* to the term *teacher-led, group-based instruction* and its synonyms. This is because, even though we expect most lessons to be structured and led by the teacher and most instruction to be delivered to groups rather than individuals, we also expect teachers to depart from these general tendencies as instructional objectives or situational circumstances dictate. Even during these departures, however, we expect teachers to engage in planned activities designed to accomplish particular objectives and thus to actively interact with students while monitoring their performance on assignments.

DIFFERENT PATHS TO SUCCESS

We have cautioned that the common forms of active teaching that are associated with success in producing achievement gains on standardized tests are not necessarily appropriate for teaching to objectives that are not well measured by such tests. We now want to add a second caution: Even if established as successful, particular methods are not necessarily the only or even the best way to achieve knowledge, comprehension, or application objectives. *There may be different but functionally equivalent paths to the same achievement outcomes*. It may make no significant difference, for example, whether the three main points of a presentation are summarized at the beginning or the end, as long as they are summarized, or whether a mathematics computation review is done with flash cards during a lesson or through a seatwork assignment afterwards.

Checking for student understanding

Rosenshine (1983) elaborated on this point in arguing that certain teaching functions must be accomplished in some way, but a variety of methods may be available for accomplishing them. One such function, for example, is checking for student understanding after presenting new information. This might be accomplished through (1) a recitation activity in which the teacher asks a great many questions on the material, (2) having students write answers to written questions while the teacher circulates, (3) having students write answers and then check them with a neighbor, or (4) assigning students to discuss the information in small groups and prepare a summary for presentation to the class.

Good and Power (1976) also have discussed common teaching tasks that can be accomplished through different approaches. Five such tasks and some alternative methods of accomplishing them are shown in Table 12.4.

Two Successful Classrooms

Comparable success using different approaches

Given that particular teaching functions can be accomplished using different methods that can be combined in different configurations, we can expect different teachers to achieve comparable success using different approaches, even if they work at the same grade level and teach to the same objectives. Ralph Kinderstone and Judith Blondell are two such teachers.

Ralph has taught fourth grade at Grandview School for the past three years. He graduated from the state university and completed the first year of law school, but while working part time for a law firm, he realized he would not enjoy the day-to-day roles that lawyers perform. So he went back to school, obtained his teaching certificate, and became a teacher, which he has found to be demanding but satisfying work. Judith has taught fourth grade for three years at Golden West School. She had always wanted to be a teacher, so she majored in education and then moved directly into the profession. Although it is more demanding than she expected, she likes her job and plans to continue teaching indefinitely.

Ralph and Judith have at least three things in common: (1) they teach fourth grade, (2) they enjoy teaching, and (3) they are successful. The fifth-grade teachers at their schools are happy to get their students because they have good study habits and have mastered basic knowledge and skills. Their students do better on standardized achievement tests than students of similar aptitude and background, and both students and parents speak favorably of them. There are both similarities and differences

TABLE 12.4 MULTIPLE WAYS TO ACCOMPLISH COMMON TEACHING TASKS

Teaching Task	Behavioral Resolution
1. Task differentiation	A. material assigned or made available in the classroom B. grouping students C. teacher questions that vary in cognitive demand
2. Maintaining task involvement	A. highly interesting tasks B. tasks that lead to student mastery C. insulation from interruption of fellow students
3. Review	A. distribution of printed teacher summary B. students prepare their own written summary C. teacher or student oral summary D. supervised board work
4. Accountability	A. oral questions B. call for show of hands during group work followed by random check of hand raisers C. group discussions followed by student written responses to discussion questions
5. Making time for teacher to work with individual students	A. peer tutoring B. learning centers C. independent work

Source: *Good & Power, 1976, pp. 45–60.*

in the ways that they achieve this success. Consider how they teach mathematics.

Ralph Kinderstone Ralph basically teaches the class as a whole group (although a few faster students work a couple of units ahead of the class). His presentations and demonstrations are well done. After he gives a demonstration, he may request students to repeat it (but he seldom calls on more than two). He expects students to listen, and they do. He listens carefully to them and demonstrates respect for their responses.

After his presentations (development work on a concept or a review of skills), he will ask several questions. He does not let students call out answers without permission, and he insists that they listen carefully to one another's responses. When students answer incorrectly (as they do about 30 percent of the time), he tends to ask another student or else explain why the answer was wrong, but this is done briefly. The activity is rapidly paced.

Before releasing students to do seatwork, he has them work a couple of problems and he inspects the work of some to ensure that they understand the task that they will do independently. If students do poorly, he repeats the demonstration and explains more fully.

Typically, about half of a forty-five-minute period is spent reviewing homework and introducing new assignments. After the initial presentation, students work individually or in small teams (whichever they choose) on assigned problems. The work is sufficiently difficult that no more than 20 percent will finish it before the period ends. Students who finish may choose from a series of interesting mathematics tasks that vary widely in difficulty. Those who do not finish the assignment complete it as homework. If students apply themselves in class, they seldom have more than 15–20 minutes of homework.

After Ralph assigns seatwork, he stands at the front of the class, scanning the room for a minute or so, and then goes to those few students who seem confused or have difficulty in settling down. Once he engages these students in the task, he retires to his desk and, depending on the circumstances, either visits with individual students (reviewing their work, helping them to set goals) or works demandingly (but genuinely) with the students who are ahead of the class. However, he is available at all times for students who encounter difficulty (early in the year he consistently encouraged students to seek him out when they had difficulty). When students come to him, they receive immediate, brief, and task-relevant feedback. He rarely circles the room looking at students' work. When students want help, they seek him out.

Things move quickly in this classroom. Students drill a couple of minutes each day on important skills, and occasionally Ralph will conduct a general review. However, the students regularly learn new material and proceed through the text rapidly. He gives brief (fifteen-minute) tests once or twice a week. Test scores are graphed and students see their own graphs privately each month. Students whose work reaches a specified high plateau and students who show sufficient improvement over the year have been promised a gift of a math game that everybody enjoys playing.

Once every two weeks or so, a math period will be devoted to games in which matched teams compete against one another. The tournaments are always unannounced but are "alleged" to be contingent on good student performance on tests and homework (students believe that good work leads to tournament play).

Teachers should be available to help students who have difficulty with an assignment.

When minor misbehavior occurs, Ralph ignores it or corrects it with a nod of his head. If it is impossible to use such techniques, or if they go unheeded, he is quick to stop the behavior by reminding students of the rules and the effect of their conduct on classmates. He is more likely to warn students than to punish them, but if he does promise a punishment, he invariably carries it through.

Judith Blondell Judith's mathematics program is different from Ralph's. She teaches math twice a day (twenty to twenty-five minutes in the morning and twenty to twenty-five minutes in the afternoon) rather than once a day in a long block. Also, the pace in her class is slower. The same types of problems are worked on for several consecutive days. However, math periods often end with a few minutes of drill time accomplished within the context of games. Judith supervises this activity by watching certain students closely and by having all students keep written records of the errors they make in these games.

Judith is very active in the classroom. Much of her time is spent demonstrating skills and watching students perform them in front of the class. She works hard to get participation and will accept (respond to the answer, praise effort, and so on) virtually any academically relevant response that a student makes, whether or not the student has permission to speak. Her students respond with wrong answers less frequently (15–20 percent of the time) than Ralph's students do. When a student responds inappropriately, she typically waits for the student to correct the response, provides a clue, or repeats the question. She actively encourages student responses.

Judith's students spend only 15–20 percent of their time in individual seatwork (up from only 10 percent early in the year). In contrast, Ralph's students spend 50 percent of their time working independently.

Early in the year, Judith rarely used nonverbal techniques to control students. Now she uses eye contact and will ignore minor misbehavior. She still responds quickly, consistently, and firmly to more serious misbehavior, but she is not loud or punitive.

TEACHING EFFECTIVELY IN DIFFERENT CONTEXTS

Some of the differences between Ralph and Judith occur simply because of differences in personal preference and merely provide additional illustrations that particular teaching functions can be accomplished in a variety of ways. However, several differences occur because these teachers work with very different types of student. Ralph's school is located in the nicest part of a university town. The parents of his students tend to be professors, lawyers, physicians, business executives, and others of high socioeconomic status (SES). For fourth graders, his students have very well developed skills for reading, following directions, and working independently. In contrast, Judith's school is located in an inner-city neighborhood and serves students from low-SES families in which most parents are either unemployed or working in low-paying, unskilled occupations. Her students do not have very well developed independent study skills.

Matching teaching style with SES background

Both teachers are effective because each has molded an instructional system that meets the needs of the students. In other words, they are successful *because* they teach differently. If they were to exchange classrooms, they would not be nearly as successful unless they changed their teaching styles.

Both teachers are effective classroom managers who maximize the time that their students spend engaged in appropriate academic activities, and both are active teachers who carry the content to their students rather than depend solely on curriculum materials to do so. However, they differ in several ways that illustrate additional findings from process-outcome research (reviewed in Brophy & Good, 1986) concerning teacher behaviors associated with achievement gain in low-SES versus high-SES classrooms.

Teachers in high-SES elementary schools have to be concerned with overcompetitiveness among their students, whereas teachers in low-SES schools have to be more concerned about fear of failure and general anxiety. Consequently, Ralph works to make sure that his students do not overcompete for public response opportunities (he does not allow them to call out answers, and he encourages them to listen to one another). He does use competitive games, but he does not announce them in advance, and he rotates the teams regularly to minimize possible negative consequences of such competition.

In contrast, Judith encourages her students to participate actively in academic activities, because most of them tend to be reticent (at least in public response settings). She asks simpler questions (her students answer about 83 percent of her questions correctly, whereas his answer only about 70 percent correctly). Furthermore, if her students do not respond or respond incorrectly, she will usually stay with them and try to elicit an improved response by giving them more time, rephrasing the question, or giving clues. Ralph does not need to provide such support or assistance nearly as often, because his students are usually eager to respond and will speak up if they know the answer or have a likely guess.

Most of Ralph's students achieve well above grade level. Because they can read assignments, have mastered basic math concepts, and are motivated to perform, it makes sense to allow them to spend time in independent work or small-group activities and to allow them to come to him and seek feedback when they need it. In contrast, Judith's students need much more direct instruction in the content and more teacher structuring and supervision when working on assignments. Consequently, it makes more sense for her to divide mathematics instruction into two shorter segments and to circulate during seatwork time rather than wait for students to come to her for help.

There are some similarities in the two teaching styles. Both teachers are very consistent and follow through on what they say (both in managerial and in instructional situations). Also, both are nonevaluative. That

is, rather than responding with personal praise or criticism, they give feedback that focuses on the content of the students' answers or the correctness of their work (although Judith's students are more in need of encouragement than Ralph's, so it is useful for her to provide more praise than he does). Both teachers basically teach the class as a whole group and regularly present structured lessons followed by assignments with clear expectations about the mathematics goals to be accomplished. Ralph allows his students to work in groups as a social outlet, but he expects that time to be spent on the work, and he holds individual students accountable for mastery via his frequent quizzes.

Context variables

Student SES is just one of many variables to take into account in adapting instruction to the context. Other *context variables* include grade level; subject matter; time (of year, week, or day); the specific objectives of the activity and its place within the curriculum as a whole; the status characteristics of the students (gender, race, ethnicity, language dominance); and the heterogeneity of the group. Information is available regarding some of these context variables. We discuss some of it here and some in a later section on individual differences.

Brophy and Good (1986) reviewed several sets of interaction effects that appear repeatedly in process-outcome research and suggested that different kinds of treatment are needed to maximize achievement for different kinds of students.

Grade Level In the early grades, students need a great deal of instruction in and opportunity to practice classroom-management routines and procedures in addition to instruction in the curriculum. Less instruction in routines and procedures is needed in the intermediate and secondary grades, but here it becomes especially important to be clear about expectations and to follow up on accountability demands. Also, in the early grades, lessons focus on basic skills and are often conducted in small groups, and it is important that each student participate overtly and often. In the later grades, lessons typically are with the whole class and involve applications of basic skills or consideration of more abstract content. Here, the overt participation of each student is less important than factors such as teachers' structuring of the content, clarity of statements and questions, and enthusiasm. Finally, praise and symbolic rewards are common in the early grades but give way to more impersonal and academically centered instruction in the later grades. Older students do not respond as positively to praise (especially public praise) as younger ones, although it is important that teachers treat their contributions with interest and respect.

Student SES; Ability; Affect SES is a "proxy" for a complex of correlated cognitive and affective differences between subgroups of students. The cognitive differences involve IQ, ability, and achievement levels. Process-outcome data indicate that, compared to high-SES/high-achieving students, *low-SES/low-achieving students need more structuring from their teachers:* more active instruction and feedback, more redundancy, and smaller steps with higher success rates. Across the school year, this will mean exposure to less material (the material that is considered most basic and important).

Three additional points need to be made here to ensure that these implications of SES difference findings are not misunderstood. First, although low-SES/low-achieving students would be exposed to less material, this would be done with emphasis on mastery of the material that is taught and on moving the students through the curriculum as briskly as they are able to progress. This means serious, thorough instruction in a reduced curriculum, not abandonment of serious attempts to teach. Second, the notion of reducing the curriculum to concentrate on the most basic and important objectives should not be operationalized by abandoning varied and integrated instruction in favor of heavy concentration on worksheets or overly repetitious practice of relatively isolated skills. Instead, there should be active instruction by the teacher and meaningful (i.e., not rote) learning by the students, in the context of integration and application of skills (i.e., not just practice). Third, to the extent that the students make good progress and become more like high-SES/high-achieving students, the instructional methods used with them should evolve accordingly (e.g., less structuring, more challenge, etc.).

Affective correlates of SES include the degree to which students feel secure and confident versus anxious or alienated in the classroom. High-SES students are likely to be confident, eager to participate, and responsive to challenge. They typically want respect and require feedback but do not require a great deal of encouragement or praise. They tend to thrive in an atmosphere that is academically stimulating and somewhat demanding. In contrast, low-SES students are more likely to require warmth and support in addition to good instruction from their teachers and to need more encouragement for their efforts and (possibly) more praise for their successes. It is especially important to teach them to respond overtly rather than to remain passive when asked questions and to be accepting of their relevant call-outs and other academic initiations when they do occur. This combination of demandingness and supportiveness is part of what is involved in adopting positive but realistic expectations and a teacher role definition that includes assuming responsibility for making sure that students learn.

Teacher's Intentions/Objectives To the extent that lesson objectives imply that students must acquire new information, the students are likely to need group lessons featuring information presentation by the teacher followed by recitation or discussion opportunities. The appropriateness of follow-up practice or application opportunities also depends on the objectives. When it is sufficient that students be able to reproduce knowledge on cue, routine seatwork assignments and tests might suffice. However, if students are expected to integrate broad patterns of learning or apply them to their everyday lives, it will be necessary to schedule activities that involve problem solving, decision making, essay composition, preparation of research reports, or construction of some product.

ADAPTING INSTRUCTION TO STUDENTS' INDIVIDUAL CHARACTERISTICS

Even when working from teacher-led group instruction as a base, teachers can introduce some degree of differential treatment of students to accommodate individual differences in aptitude, developmental level, reading ability, personality, work-mode preferences, or work habits.

Aptitude

Aptitude makes a difference. Brighter students can process information quickly; less capable students need more time to assimilate and integrate material. The former can watch a demonstration and perform, but the latter may need to manipulate objects themselves or see several examples. Also, bright students often enjoy difficult assignments, but less capable students like easy assignments.

Development stage

Developmental stage also has important instructional implications. Younger children's attention spans are short, so they generally need relatively short lessons and frequent review. Older students can benefit from longer lessons, more complex choices, and more independent work. Preoperational students need numerous concrete examples; students beyond this stage can work with abstractions and learn propositionally. Young students generally want to please adults; subsequently, peer influences rival adult influences.

Reading level

Reading level may seem to be an obvious consideration; yet many teachers assign reading that is too demanding for some students and too easy for others. Teachers who employ many individualized assignments (where students have to read material, directions, and so forth on their own) need to be especially alert to the need for materials that vary in reading difficulty.

Student's individual personality

Student personality affects levels of success achieved in a given learning environment. Dependent students seek teacher structuring and support; independent students want little of either. Extroverted students want to be with peers; others prefer more solitude. A student's personality influences the frequency and type of feedback that is needed or preferred.

Preference for work mode

Preference for work mode can be accommodated when objectives can be met in different ways. Some students enjoy writing reports and stories, for example, but dislike answering questions; other students have the opposite preference. Some prefer open-ended writing assignments, but others prefer typical workbook exercises.

Work habits

Work habits are also important considerations. Some students are careless and poorly organized. Others are enthusiastic bookkeepers but somehow cannot put together all of the data they collect. Teachers may want to design learning activities so as to either work around or begin to change such problematic work habits.

Five Student Types and Their Instructional Needs

Good and Power (1976) discussed the instructional needs of five student types found in most classrooms:

1. *Successful students* are task oriented and academically successful. They participate in lessons, turn in assignments on time (almost always complete and correct), and create few if any discipline problems.

Teachers are likely to direct difficult questions to them, because they get most of them right. Successful students like school and tend to be liked by both teachers and peers.

2. *Social students* are more person than task oriented. They may be able to achieve but value socializing with friends more than working on assignments. Teachers tend to call on them fairly often, both to keep them involved in lessons and because they are able to answer easy questions. Social students tend to have many friends and be popular in the peer group but are usually not well liked by teachers (because their frequent socializing creates management problems).
3. *Dependent students* look to the teacher for support and encouragement and often ask for additional directions or help. They are frequent hand raisers. In secondary schools, most dependent students achieve at a low level. Teachers generally express concern about their academic progress and do what they can to assist them. Peers often reject them because they tend to be socially immature.
4. *Alienated students* are reluctant learners and potential dropouts. In the extreme, they reject the school and everything that it stands for. This rejection may take one of two forms: open hostility or withdrawal into cynicism and passivity. Hostile alienated students create serious disruptions through aggression and defiance, whereas passive alienated students withdraw to the fringes of the classroom and may be ignored by teachers and most peers. Teacher attitudes toward alienated students typically range between indifference and rejection.
5. *Phantom students* seem to fade into the background because they are rarely noticed or heard from. They tend to be average in everything but involvement in public settings. Some are shy or nervous, and others are quiet, independent workers of average ability. They work steadily on assignments but are rarely involved actively in group activities because they never volunteer and are rarely involved in managerial interchanges because they never create disruption. Typically, neither teachers nor peers know these students very well.

Accommodating to students' preferences

Good and Power (1976) surveyed the literature on these five student types and developed suggestions about how teachers might accommodate their contrasting preferences and needs. Some of their suggestions are shown in Table 12.5. Although based partly on research, the suggestions given in Table 12.5 should be considered speculative hypotheses rather than proven guidelines for two reasons. First, accommodating students' preferences may not be the same as meeting their needs. Several studies have shown that allowing students to choose their own learning methods or teaching them in ways that they prefer will produce *less* achievement gain than teaching them in some other way (Clark, 1982; Schofield, 1981; Solomon & Kendall, 1979). Second, accommodating students' personal qualities will tend to reinforce those qualities, and sometimes they are qualities that the teacher wants to change if possible. It would be easy, for example, to respond reciprocally to phantom students and passive-withdrawn alienated students by minimizing interaction with them and

TABLE 12.5 LEVELS OF INSTRUCTIONAL NEEDS OF FIVE TYPES OF STUDENTS

	Success	Social	Dependent	Alienated	Phantom
I. Type of Teacher Input					
A. Substantive Explanation of Content	very high	very high	high	high	high
B. Procedural Directions	low	low	high	moderate-high	moderate-low
C. Socializing, Emotional Support, Humor	very low	low-moderate	moderate	moderate (establish private rapport)	low
II. Type of Task					
A. Reading Skills Required	high	high	low	low	moderate
B. Task Difficulty Level	very high	high	low-moderate	low-moderate	moderate
C. Abstractness Level	high	moderate	low initially	low initially	moderate
D. Cognitive Level	high	moderate	low-moderate	low-moderate	moderate
E. Degree of Structure (Specificity about what to do and how to do it)	low	moderate	high	high	moderate
F. Opportunity to Make Active, Overt Responses	not important	high	high	high	moderate
G. Opportunity to Make Choices	moderate (stress on enrichment)	moderate (stress on choices to work with others)	low	moderate (stress on relevance)	low
H. Interest Value of Task to Student	not important	moderate	low	high	low
I. Length of Task	long	short	moderate	moderate	long

III. Type of Response Demanded					
A. Written	high	low	high	moderate	high
B. Oral	low	high	low	low	low
C. Physical	low	moderate	moderate	high	low
IV. Individual vs. Group Settings					
A. Individual	high	low	high	high	high
B. Group	low	moderate	low	low-moderate	low
V. Emphasis on Competition	high	moderate	low initially	low	moderate
VI. Type of Feedback from Teacher					
A. Personal Praise	low	low	moderate	moderate (private)	low
B. Personal Criticism	low	low	low	very low	low
C. Praise of Good Work	low	moderate	moderate	moderate (private)	low-moderate
D. Criticism of Poor Work	moderate	moderate	low	low (but communicate demand)	low-moderate

Source: *Condensed and adapted from Good and Power, 1976, pp. 45–60.*

never calling on them unless they raise their hands. This might even maximize the comfort of both the teacher and the students involved. However, it probably would not be in the students' best interests.

Individualizing instruction

Even though these complexities must be kept in mind, Table 12.5 offers ideas about how teachers can introduce a degree of individualization into their instruction even while basically teaching the class as a group. Some suggestions can be incorporated with relative ease (those that merely involve interacting more often or more affectively with certain students). Others are more difficult and time consuming to implement (those that call for preparing different activities or assignments for different subgroups). Even when it is not possible to introduce such variation into the activities and assignments planned for a particular day, however, these guidelines are useful for judging the degree of variety built into a week or a unit. *There should be enough balance to deliver "something for everyone,"* rather than restriction to activities and assignments that match the needs of one or two subgroups but not the others.

The suggestions are also useful for identifying the basic approach that is most likely to be successful for particular classrooms. Ralph Kinderstone's approach, for example, was well suited to his classroom because of its high percentage of successful students, whereas Judith Blondell's approach was well suited to her classroom because of its high percentages of dependent and alienated students. Most classes are less homogeneous in student composition, but these two examples are useful for illustrating how teachers can tailor active whole-class instruction to the needs of their students.

Summary

Process-outcome research links classroom processes to their cognitive (achievement) or affective (attitudes) outcomes. Such research has shown that achievement gains are associated with opportunity to learn and content covered; role definition, expectations, and time allocation; classroom management and student-engaged time; consistent success and academic-learning time; and active teaching. Positive attitudes are associated with measures of teacher warmth and student orientation. Negative classroom climates are associated with poor achievement gain, but good achievement gain is at least as likely in neutral or mildly warm climates as in more clearly warm climates.

The correlational findings from the ethnographic data collected by Tikunoff, Berliner, and Rist (1975) and the teacher-behavior guidelines developed from earlier correlation work and used in experimental studies by Good and Grouws (1979) and by Anderson, Evertson, and Brophy (1979) were reviewed as examples of the kinds of active teaching that process-outcome research has shown to be associated with achievement gain. Most teachers will use active teaching as their basic method of instruction, because compared to the feasible alternatives, it is effective for teaching any body of knowledge or set of skills that has been sufficiently well analyzed and organized so that it can be presented (explained, modeled) systematically and then practiced or applied during activities that call for student performance that can be evaluated for quality and (where incorrect or imperfect) given corrective feedback. Instructional objectives that do not fit this characterization will require different methods.

Few if any specific instructional behaviors are appropriate in all teaching contexts, and there may be different but functionally equivalent paths to the same achievement outcome. Thus it makes more sense to think in terms of instructional functions that need to be accomplished than in terms of specific behaviors to be labeled as appropriate or inappropriate. Even within the general method of active teaching that appears to be an appropriate base for most teachers, the specifics of application will vary with grade level, subject matter, and other context variables. Ralph Kinderstone and Judith Blondell provide examples of such variation.

Guidelines are given for how instruction can be expected to vary with grade level; student SES, ability, and affect; and teachers' intentions or objectives, as well as for how teachers can adapt instruction to students' individual characteristics. In particular, Good and Power (1976) presented suggestions for adapting whole-class instruction to the needs of successful students, social students, dependent students, alienated students, and phantom students.

Questions and Problems

1. Were you under the impression that effective teaching is simply a matter of mastering a few "crucial" behaviors? What is wrong with that statement? What would be a more accurate description of effective teaching?
2. Do the suggestions made for teaching different student types make sense to you? If so, can you see ways to do all of these things simultaneously (remember, most if not all of these student types will exist in any classroom)? List some of the ways.
3. Most process-outcome research has used standardized tests for measuring achievement gain. In what ways might this make the results of such research limited or misleading? Compare notes with your friends.
4. Suppose a process-outcome study were to eliminate differences in quantity of instruction by limiting the sample to experienced teachers who were effective classroom managers committed to active teaching toward the same set of objectives. Under these conditions, any differences in success would be due to quality rather than quantity of teaching. What qualitative factors do you think would lead to differences in student learning? How could you measure these quality indicators?
5. As a teacher, you will have considerable autonomy in allocating classroom time to particular objectives. What would you see as your re-

sponsibilities and options in the following three situations? (1) The adopted curriculum contains a unit on a topic that you do not consider very important, and there is no particular pressure on you to teach it; (2) you do not consider the unit important, but it is part of the official curriculum mandated by your school district; (3) you recognize that the unit is important but do not feel competent to teach it effectively or do not enjoy teaching it. Would you omit the unit or reduce the time allocated to it under these circumstances? Why or why not?

6. How can you both move students through the curriculum at a brisk pace and program for consistent success and minimal frustration? Write down some specific strategies for responding to this dilemma. In particular, what should you do when 80 percent of the students have clearly mastered the objectives of a lesson but 20 percent have not?
7. Should school districts evaluate teachers according to whether or not they display behaviors that process-outcome research has shown are correlated with student achievement gain? Why or why not?
8. If Ralph Kinderstone and Judith Blondell were to trade places, which of their present teaching strategies could they retain and which would they have to change?
9. What does it mean to state that SES is a "proxy" standing for a complex of correlated cognitive and affective differences between subgroups of students? What are the advantages and disadvantages of using such "proxy" variables? How can we use them in ways that help teachers to meet different student needs effectively but do not create undesirable biases and stereotyped expectations in teachers?
10. What does it mean to state that accommodating students' preferences is not the same as meeting their needs? How should teachers define "meeting their students' needs," and how can they evaluate their degree of success in doing so?

Case Studies

Read each of the following descriptions of how a teacher conducts his or her class, and using the material presented in this chapter, critique the teacher's approach.

A MIXED CLASS. Laura Stemard teaches fourth-grade mathematics. Her students are distributed fairly equally among the top, middle, and lower ranges of social class background. She has two students who are being mainstreamed.

Laura works with the entire class for twenty to thirty minutes a day (only the two students being mainstreamed work on individual assignments). In general, she spends fifteen minutes reviewing homework and discussing the assignment. Questions she asks are very easy (90 percent are answered correctly), and if students miss a question she simply goes on. The last fifteen minutes of each day are spent completing assigned seatwork. She circles the room, providing detailed feedback to students who are not finished. When students finish, they are expected to find something to do (although nothing explicit is provided) and not to bother others.

AN ELITE GROUP. "Pack" Wilson runs his algebra class as smoothly as he ran the high school football team fifteen years earlier. All of his students are college bound, but, as he puts it, he likes to "let the good horses run." The top five to eight students in each class are taught as a separate group and receive special assignments.

Classroom discussion involves application of concepts and infrequent review. He tests twice a week, and students have one hour of homework daily. He spends roughly half of each period with each of the two groups.

When he works with one group, the other group works on assigned seatwork individually. The assignments are clear but difficult. Students rarely misbehave in his class. The small group of top students in each class is moving through curriculum material 25 percent faster than other students. He almost never talks to individual students during class about their work and actively discourages average students from approaching him unless they are totally stuck.

AN INNER-CITY SPEECH CLASS. Toni Frick teaches a high school speech course in an inner-city school. Although the course is an elective, most students take it. Each day in the class is different, although there is a general sense of purposefulness. On the average, three days a week are spent in oral speech (teacher demonstrating technique, student practice, and so on). Toni has two goals for the students: (1) to be able to write and deliver an interesting and informative speech and (2) to be able to talk extemporaneously.

During most oral presentations she divides the class into outliners (these students attempt to chart the flow of the speech), critics (students who attempt to note the weakest part of the speech), and helpers (who focus upon the especially good parts of the speech). Sometimes the criticism and support are aimed at particular parts of the speech; at other times—especially later in the year—students can choose from any part of the speech.

In addition to writing down comments relevant to their roles, students fill out general evaluations (how interesting, how clear, and so on) and may be called upon by the teacher to present and defend their critiques. After presenting a speech students listen to the public evaluations carefully, because each speech is typically repeated once and major criticism must be accommodated.

The remaining two days of each week are reserved for an analysis of written speeches (Who would have written this speech? What content is avoided? Is it too emotional? How would a black audience respond? Why?) and to practicing speech writing. In such activities the teacher attempts to match the complexity of the task to the students' level of mastery, although most of this work is done individually.

CHAPTER

Basic Instructional Skills

CHAPTER OUTLINE

OBJECTIVES

When you have mastered the material in this chapter, you will be able to

1. List the strengths and weaknesses of the lecture method and identify situations in which the method is appropriate
2. Describe the steps to be taken and the decisions to be made in planning effective lectures
3. List factors that enhance and detract from the clarity and organization of presentations
4. List factors that enhance and detract from the effectiveness of presentations in gaining students' interest and holding their attention
5. Describe the purposes and uses of different types of activity that involve questioning and responding to students (drills, reviews, recitations, discussions)
6. List the strengths and weaknesses of recitation activities as instructional devices
7. State the findings of process-outcome research on difficulty level of question and cognitive level of question as they relate to student-achievement gain
8. List criteria for judging the quality of teachers' questions
9. State the findings of research on the length of time that teachers wait before calling on a student to answer a question

10. Explain how pacing and wait time should vary with the objectives of recitation activities
11. Describe the factors to be considered in deciding which student to call on to respond to a question
12. State guidelines for reacting when students fail to respond, respond incorrectly, give an incomplete or only partly correct response, or give a correct response
13. State guidelines for responding to relevant and irrelevant student questions and comments
14. Describe the differences between the teacher's role in drill and recitation activities and the teacher's role in discussions
15. State criteria for identifying effective discussions
16. Describe alternatives to questioning that teachers can use for producing lengthy and insightful student responses during discussions
17. State criteria for judging the effectiveness of seatwork and homework assignments and guidelines for handling seatwork and homework effectively

Whatever their grade level, subject matter, or approach to instruction, most teachers often rely on two basic sets of instructional skills: (1) those involved in *making presentations* (lecturing on content, demonstrating skills or procedures, elaborating on the text); and (2) those involved in *questioning and responding to students* (conducting drills, recitations, and discussions). These skills are basic to the concept of active teaching as described in Chapter 12, as well as to common notions of what it means to teach. We consider these skills in detail in this chapter, along with the skills involved in managing seatwork and homework assignments.

MAKING PRESENTATIONS: LECTURING

In this chapter, we use the terms *lecture* to refer to extended presentations, *explanation* to refer to brief explications of a particular concept, and *demonstration* to refer to the modeling of skills or procedures. Explanations and demonstrations may be embedded within lectures or delivered in isolation. *Presentation* is used as a general term that includes lectures, explanations, and demonstrations.

Teachers frequently make presentations in the form of lectures, explanations, or demonstrations to the whole class or to small groups. Sometimes, especially in advanced subjects at the secondary level, they are lengthy lectures or lecture–discussions. More typically, however, presentations by elementary and secondary teachers are short (five to twenty minutes) and followed by some practice or application activity or, if longer, are broken into segments with periods of questioning or discussion in between (Arehart, 1979; Good & Grouws, 1977).

Lecturing

Popularity and criticism of the lecture method

Lecturing is a commonly used teaching technique because it is efficient (in a brief time, the teacher can expose students to content that might take them much longer to locate on their own), it can be used with groups or entire classes rather than just with individuals, it gives the teacher control over the content, and it is easily combined with other methods and adjustable to fit the available time, the physical setting, and other situational constraints. Also, it gives teachers the opportunity to display their knowledge and "perform" for their students. For these reasons, the lecture method has retained popularity even though it has been criticized as limiting students to a passive learner role, denying them the opportunity to learn socially, relying on the usually false assumption that they all need the same information, wasting their time by telling them things that they could read for themselves, focusing on the lowest level of cognition, or going on too long to the point of boredom or confusion (Henson, 1988; McLeish, 1976). Note that most of these criticisms reflect overuse or inappropriate use of the lecture method, not problems inherent in the method itself (McMann, 1979).

Nor do empirical data suggest that lecturing is inappropriate in any general sense. Reviewers of studies comparing lecture versus discussion or other methods typically conclude that about half of the studies favor the lecture approach and half do not (Dubin & Taveggia, 1968; Voth, 1975). Such "no difference" findings are to be expected when data are aggregated without taking into account factors such as the quality of the instruction or the objectives to which it is directed. Thus the real question is not "Is the lecture method better than other alternatives?" but "For what purposes is the lecture method appropriate?" McKeachie and Kulik (1975), for example, separated studies according to whether they focused on facts, higher-level thinking, or attitudes and motivation. They found lecture to be superior to discussion for promoting factual learning, but discussion to be superior to lecture for promoting higher-level thinking and attitudes and motivation.

Appropriate use

Various authors (Davis & Alexander, 1977; Gage & Berliner, 1984; Henson, 1988; McMann, 1979) have suggested that *the lecture method is appropriate in the following situations:*

1. When the objective is to present information
2. When the information is not available in a readily accessible source
3. When the material must be organized and presented in a particular way
4. When it is necessary to arouse interest in the subject
5. When it is necessary to introduce a topic before the students read about it on their own or to provide instructions about a task
6. When the information is original or must be integrated from different sources
7. When material needs to be summarized or synthesized (following discussion or inquiry)

8. When the curriculum materials need updating or elaborating
9. When the teacher wants to present alternate points of view or to clarify issues in preparation for discussion
10. When the teacher wants to provide supplementary explanations of material that students may have difficulty learning on their own

Lecturing is probably *appropriate* if used for these purposes. How *effective* it will be will depends on the care and skill with which the lecture is prepared and delivered. The following guidelines for preparing effective lectures are based on the advice of experts and the findings of process-outcome research.

Elements of effective lessons

Preparing the Lecture In Chapter 8 we suggested that effective lessons would (1) start with advance organizers or previews that include general principles, outlines, or questions that establish a learning set; (2) briefly describe the objectives and alert the students to new or key concepts; (3) present new material in small steps sequenced in ways that are easy to follow; (4) elicit student responses regularly to stimulate active learning and ensure that each step is mastered before moving to the next; (5) finish with a review of the main points, stressing general integrative concepts; and (6) follow up with questions or assignments that require students to encode the material in their own words and apply or extend it to new concepts.

Davis and Alexander (1977) note the importance of motivating students at the beginning of a presentation, stimulating attention periodically, and following principles of effective delivery (maintain eye contact, avoid distracting behaviors, modulate voice pitch and volume, use appropriate gestures). They also suggest limiting one-way communication to twenty to thirty minutes (this norm was intended for lectures to adults; correspondingly shorter norms would apply to younger students).

Process-outcome research supports these guidelines. Achievement is maximized when teachers not only actively present material but also structure it by beginning with overviews, advance organizers, or review of objectives; outlining the content and signaling transitions between lesson parts; calling attention to main ideas; summarizing subparts of the lesson as it proceeds; and reviewing main ideas at the end (Alexander, Frankiewicz, & Williams, 1979; Armento, 1977; Clark et al., 1979; Fisher et al., 1980; Smith & Sanders, 1981; Wright & Nuthall, 1970). Also, achievement is higher when presentations are clear (Good & Grouws, 1977; Smith & Land, 1981) and delivered with enthusiasm (Armento, 1977) and with appropriate gestures and movements (Rosenshine, 1968).

Instructional objectives

Planning begins with the instructional objectives: What information is to be conveyed, and what will students be expected to do with it? Effective lectures are presented with specific objectives in mind; they are not rambling, "off the top of the head" discourses. Lectures should supplement, not merely overlap, the input that students get from other sources.

Given appropriate objectives, planning begins with practical matters. Do the students possess needed knowledge and skills? Does the teacher possess needed information and have needed materials and equipment

Teachers who lecture effectively begin with specific objectives in mind and supplement the information that students get from reading textbooks.

available? Can these objectives be accomplished within the available time?

Comprehensive instruction plan

Once these practical matters are worked out, Davis and Alexander (1977) suggest preparing an outline: List two or three key points to be made, order them logically, and identify interesting examples, illustrations, anecdotes, or experiments that will help make them. Then develop a comprehensive plan. Outline the presentation of content, list questions to ask during or after the presentation, plan any demonstrations that will be needed, prepare overhead transparencies or other audiovisual aids, prepare handouts to distribute to students, and prepare follow-up activities or assignments. Handouts might include diagrams or illustrations, definitions of key terms, outlines of the presentation (including partial outlines to be used as guides to note taking), or study guides.

Motivational elements

Planning should include attention to motivational elements as well. Unless the students are known to be already highly motivated to learn the information, it is wise to begin the presentation by posing a provocative question, presenting a powerful epigram or quotation, telling an interesting related anecdote, or mentioning puzzling or paradoxical facts to arouse interest and curiosity.

Delivering the Lecture Successful lectures typically begin with establishment of a learning set, proceed to presentation of information structured and sequenced for clarity and delivered with enthusiasm and appropriate gestures, and end with review or integration of the material.

Establishing a learning set. Besides stimulating interest or curiosity, teachers should begin lectures by establishing an appropriate learning set in their students. Thus the introduction should include advance organizers or previews that cue students as to the nature of the content and the schemas or prior knowledge to bring to bear in understanding it. Teachers should also mention the objectives to be accomplished and give instructions if the students are supposed to pay particular attention to certain content or to take particular kinds of notes. If the information is going to be used in some way following the lecture, alert the students to this so that they can listen with the subsequent application in mind. In general, a good introduction leaves the students not only motivated to attend actively to the lecture but also well informed about its contents and about how they are expected to respond to or use the information.

Vagueness terms

Clarity of presentation. Good lectures are clear and easy to follow. What makes for clarity? At minimum, clear presentations are free of what Hiller, Fisher, and Kaess (1969) called *vagueness terms:*

1. Ambiguous designation (somehow, somewhere, conditions, other)
2. Approximation (about, almost, kind of, pretty much, sort of)
3. "Bluffing" and recovery (actually, and so forth, anyway, as you know)
4. Error admission (excuse me, I'm sorry, I guess, I'm not sure)
5. Indeterminate quantification (a bunch, a couple, a few, a lot, a little, some, several)
6. Multiplicity (aspects, kinds of, sort of, type of)
7. Possibility (chances are, could be, maybe, perhaps)
8. Probability (frequently, generally, often, probably, sometimes, usually)
9. Negated intensifiers (not many, not very)

Smith and Land (1981) reviewed studies indicating that such vagueness terms detract from clarity of presentations. In the following example, the vagueness terms are italicized.

> This mathematics lesson *might* enable you to understand *a little more* about *some things* we *usually* call number patterns. *Maybe* before we get to *probably* the main idea of the lesson, you should review *a few* prerequisite concepts. *Actually,* the first concept you need to review is positive integers. *As you know,* a positive integer is any whole number greater than zero. (Smith & Land, 1981, p. 38)

Mazes

Smith and Land also noted that clarity can be reduced by *mazes,* which are false starts or halts in speech, redundantly spoken words, or tangles of words. Mazes are italicized in the following example.

> This mathematics lesson will *enab . . .* will get you to understand *number, uh,* number patterns. Before we get to the *main idea of the,* main idea of the lesson, you need to review *four conc . . .* four prerequisite concepts. The first *idea, I mean, uh,* concept you need to review is positive integers. A positive *number . . .* integer is any whole *integer, uh,* number greater than zero. (Smith & Land, 1981, p. 38)

Discontinuity

A third element that can detract from clarity is discontinuity, in which the teacher interrupts the flow of the lecture by interjecting irrelevant content or mentioning relevant content at inappropriate times. Repeatedly saying "uh" is another detractor from clarity.

Clarity of presentation

Other research has specified indicators of clarity in more positive terms. Smith and Sanders (1981) showed that presentations were easier to follow when highly structured in terms of linear redundancy in the appearance of key concepts. In well-structured presentations, key concepts tend to be repeated from one sentence to the next, although new ones are gradually phased in and old ones phased out. This structure is typical of prose that moves systematically through a series of related statements. In poorly structured presentations, the content is more jumbled. Key concepts are repeated just as often but not in contiguous sentences. As a result, even if the same sentences are included in each version, the well-structured presentations are recognized as organized sequences of related facts, but the poorly structured presentations seem more like lists of unrelated facts.

Rule-example-rule pattern

Rosenshine (1968) reviewed research indicating that clarity of presentation is associated with appropriate gestures and movements, rule-example-rule patterns of discourse, and frequent use of explaining links. In the *rule-example-rule pattern,* the teacher first presents a general rule, then a series of examples, and finally a restatement of the rule. This contrasts with patterns in which the rule is never stated or is stated only once rather than given both before and after the examples. *Explaining links* are words that denote cause, means, or purpose: *because, in order to, if . . . then, therefore, consequently,* and so on. They make causal linkages explicit. For example, consider the following sentences:

Explaining links

1. Chicago became the major city in the Midwest and the hub of the nation's railroad system.
2. Because of its central location, Chicago became the hub of the nation's railroad system.

The first example presents relevant facts but does not make explicit the linkage between them, as the second example does. If asked, "Why did Chicago become the hub of the railroad system," most students taught with the second example would respond "because of its central location." However, many students taught with the first example would respond "because it is a big city" or would answer in some other way that indicated failure to appreciate the linkage between the city's geographical location and the role that it played in the nation's railroad system.

Other guidelines about clarity can be inferred from the work on text structuring described in Chapters 9 and 10 and the work on selection and juxtaposition of examples described in Chapter 11. Students are likely to find a presentation easier to follow to the extent that a logical organizing structure has been used and made explicit to them and to the extent that concepts are taught using rational sets of examples.

Judging clarity factors

Perrott (1982) suggested that clear presentations feature continuity, simplicity, and explicitness. She suggested the following criteria for judging these clarity factors:

CONTINUITY

1. Sequence of discourse: Follow a planned sequence that is made obvious to students. Keep diversions to a minimum, and when they do occur (usually in response to student questions or comments), make it clear that they are diversions.
2. Fluency: Speak in easily intelligible grammatical sentences, seldom leaving sentences unfinished or interrupting to reformulate a statement.

SIMPLICITY

1. Avoid grammatical complexity: Keep sentences short, minimize multiple qualifying clauses, and use visual means (diagrams, tables, models) to communicate complex relationships that are difficult to understand from a verbal presentation.
2. Vocabulary: Use simple language that is within the students' normal vocabulary. Introduce only those technical terms needed for adequate comprehension of the material, and define or explain them adequately.

EXPLICITNESS

1. Include all of the elements of an explanation, both (1) identification of the components (objects, events, processes, etc.) to be related and (2) specific description of their relationships (causal, justifying, interpreting, etc.).
2. Explicit explanation statements: Include explaining links that clarify causal or logical relationships.

Use of chunking strategies

If the lecture is lengthy, the teacher can help students use chunking strategies by explicitly noting its subparts and the transitions between them, and by including internal summaries at the end of each subpart (Duffy et al., 1986). If continuity has been broken by student questions or discussion, the teacher can reestablish the desired learning set by reminding the students of the overall structure of the presentation and of the place at which it is being resumed.

Pacing, gestures, and enthusiasm. There is no substitute for appropriately selected and well-structured content, but the success of a lecture will also depend on the lecturer's communication skills.

Pacing

Pacing is one crucial component. An overly slow pace will induce boredom and cause many students to tune out, and an overly rapid pace will leave many students frustrated and confused. Pacing is often too slow, and experiments involving increasing the tempo of presentations have sometimes increased student achievement (Rippey, 1975; Carnine, 1976). Thus at least for material that is relatively familiar and easy, brisk pacing may be ideal. On the other hand, experiments in science classes involving presentations of abstract or complex content have shown increased achievement after teachers were taught to slow their pacing by waiting three to five seconds following each statement (Tobin, 1980; Tobin & Capie, 1982). Thus relatively familiar, easy, or low-level content may be taught best with brisk pacing, but relatively unfamiliar, difficult, or high-level content requires slower pacing, possibly considerably slower than normal in some situations.

Gestures and movements

Gestures and movements can also enhance the effectiveness of a lecture. Gestures, facial expressions, pointing, and appropriate movements can increase comprehension if they supplement the oral communication and are not overly theatrical or otherwise distracting. The stimulus variations introduced through such gestures and movements are especially likely to enhance the comprehension of secondary students (Wyckoff, 1973).

Enthusiasm

Finally, teacher *enthusiasm* during lecturing is likely to affect both achievement and attitudes (Rosenshine, 1970; Abrami, Leventhal, & Perry, 1982). There is no need for histrionics, especially by teachers who are not comfortable "performing" for their students, but it should be clear from the presentation that the teacher finds the content meaningful and interesting and expects the students to do so too.

Concluding the lecture. Rather than simply coming to a stop, lectures should end with planned conclusions designed to accomplish particular objectives. Usually, the conclusion will involve review of main points, with emphasis on the structuring elements that tie them together. Following this review, the teacher usually would shift from lecture to some other mode of interaction with students (inviting questions, initiating discussion, or shifting to a follow-up activity or assignment).

QUESTIONING AND RESPONDING TO STUDENTS

Besides being able to make effective presentations, teachers must be able to structure effective reviews, recitations, and discussions by planning good sequences of questions and responding effectively to the answers that these questions elicit from students. Such questioning provides teachers with feedback about the effectiveness of their instruction and provides students with opportunities to practice and receive feedback about their progress in meeting knowledge and comprehension objectives and with opportunities to pursue higher-level objectives by applying, analyzing, synthesizing, or evaluating what they are learning. Process-outcome research (reviewed in Brophy & Good, 1986) indicates that, along with frequent presentation of academic content, frequent questioning and responding to students during public lessons is part of the pattern of active teaching that is associated with success in eliciting student-achievement gain.

Drills, recitations, and discussions

Activities involving questioning and responding to students range from *drills* or fast-paced *reviews* designed to test or reinforce knowledge of specific facts, when the emphasis is on obtaining "right answers" and moving at a brisk pace, to *discussions* designed to stimulate students to respond diversely and at higher cognitive levels to what they have been learning. Here, the pace is slower and the emphasis is on developing insights and implications (there may be many acceptable answers to a question and no single "right answer"). In between are *recitation* activities that vary in pace and cognitive level of question. They include the questioning and response segments that occur between presentation segments of extended lessons, as well as most activities that teachers refer to as "going over the material" or "elaborating on the text." Board work in mathematics and the questioning that occurs in the process of preparing students for assignments are included here too.

Recitation method

Educational critics often speak warmly of discussion but criticize drill and most forms of recitation as boring, unnecessarily teacher dominant, restricted to low-level objectives, or tending to make students passive and oriented toward producing right answers rather than thinking. Yet like the criticisms of the lecture method, these criticisms are directed mostly to the overuse or inappropriate use of the recitation method rather than to weaknesses inherent in the method itself. Like the lecture method, the recitation method persists as a common approach to instruction (Dillon, 1982; Durkin, 1978–79; Gall, 1970; Hoetker & Ahlbrand, 1969; Sirotnik, 1983; Stodolsky, Ferguson, & Wimpelberg, 1981), apparently because it is well suited to the classroom context (Farrar, 1986). It allows the teacher to work with the whole class or a significant subgroup rather than with individuals; it provides students with opportunities to learn from one another as well as from the teacher; it is an efficient way to enable students to practice and receive immediate feedback on their learning of new content; it is a convenient way for teachers to check on the effectiveness of their instruction before moving on; and it is much easier to manage than individualized instruction. Thus for most teachers the question is not whether to use recitation but when and how to use it effectively.

We will review expert advice and research findings concerning the nature and sequencing of questions to ask and the processes of calling on students, eliciting responses, and responding with feedback or additional questioning.

Preparing Sequences of Questions

Much advice to teachers about questioning, as well as much research on the topic, concerns level of question. This issue subsumes two separate topics: difficulty level and cognitive level.

Difficulty Level of Question The difficulty level of a question is determined by whether or not the students can answer it. Whatever the cognitive level of the response that a question demands, it is easy if most students can answer it correctly and difficult if most students cannot.

Accuracy of response

Process-outcome data indicate that the highest achievement gains are seen in classes in which most (perhaps 75 percent) of the teachers' questions are answered correctly, and most of the rest yield partially correct or incorrect answers rather than no responses at all. Brophy and Evertson (1976) found that the optimal percentage varied according to the socioeconomic status of the students. Achievement gain was maximized in high-socioeconomic-status (SES) classes when about 70 percent of questions were answered correctly, but achievement gain was maximized in low-SES classes when about 80 percent of questions were answered correctly. Thus students appear to learn efficiently when they can answer most recitation questions correctly, although high-SES students profit from a somewhat greater level of challenge than the level that is optimal for low-SES students.

The 75 percent norm is a useful rule of thumb, but is is just an average calculated by aggregating data from various question-and-answer settings. Success rates might often be lower than 70 percent when teachers begin to question students about new material but closer to 100 percent for drills on familiar material that is supposed to have been mastered. Furthermore, the 75 percent norm applies only when answers can be characterized as either right or wrong; it is irrelevant to discussions on matters of taste, value, or opinion.

Cognitive Level of Question Cognitive level of question is determined by scoring the nature of the response that the question demands according to the Bloom taxonomy (knowledge, comprehension, application, analysis, synthesis, evaluation) or related typologies (fact versus thought question; product versus process versus opinion question). Most (usually 80 percent or more) of teachers' questions are low-level knowledge or comprehension questions (Dunkin & Biddle, 1974; Gall, 1970; Winne, 1979). Educational critics typically take this as evidence that teachers ask too many low-level questions and not enough high-level questions, but the empirical research on this issue is mixed.

High-level questions

Higher-order questions do tend to elicit higher-order responses (Klinzing, Klinzing-Eurich, & Tisher, 1985; Lamb, 1976; Martin, 1979), although many students often respond at a lower cognitive level than the question called for (Dillon, 1982; Mills et al., 1980). Many process-outcome studies revealed positive relationships between the number or percentage of higher-level questions asked by teachers and student achievement, especially achievement of higher-level objectives (Redfield & Rousseau, 1981). However, several studies revealed positive relationships between achievement gain and lower-level questions, coupled with negative relationships or absence of significant relationships for higher-level questions. Most of them were correlational studies done in the primary grades in schools serving primarily low-SES populations (Brophy & Evertson, 1976; Good & Grouws, 1977; Soar & Soar, 1979; Stallings, 1975), but some involved middle-class students at higher grade levels (Clark et al., 1979; Clasen, 1983). Also, some experimental studies seem to show that lower-level questions are at least as effective as higher-level questions for promoting achievement of both lower-level and higher-level objectives (Clark et al., 1979; Dillon, 1981a; Gall et al., 1978; Ryan, 1973, 1974). Given such conflicting findings, it is not surprising that even reviewers draw conflicting conclusions (Redfield & Rousseau, 1981; Samson et al., 1987; Winne, 1979).

What conclusions can be drawn? First, the data refute the simplistic (but frequently assumed) notion that higher-level questions are categorically better than lower-level questions. Several studies indicate that lower-level questions can facilitate learning, even learning of higher-level objectives. Second, even when the percentage of higher-level questions correlates positively with achievement gain, the numbers on which these correlations are based typically show that only about 25 percent of the questions asked were classified as higher level. Thus as a rule of thumb, we should expect teachers to ask more lower-level than higher-level questions, even when dealing with higher-level content and seeking to promote higher-level objectives.

Question sequence

These are just frequency norms, however. They do not take into account teachers' goals (it seems obvious that different kinds of questions will be needed for different goals), the quality of the questions (clarity, relevance, etc.), or their timing and appropriateness given the flow of the lesson. Also, they refer to individual questions rather than to *question sequences*. Teachers do not plan in terms of asking certain percentages of lower-level and higher-level questions. Instead, they plan sequences of questions designed to accomplish particular objectives. For some purposes (such as asking students to suggest a possible application of an idea and then probing for details about how this application might work), sequences that begin with a higher-level question and then proceed through several lower-level follow-up questions would be appropriate. A different purpose (such as trying to call students' attention to relevant facts and then stimulate them to integrate these facts and draw a conclusion) would call for a series of lower-level questions followed by a higher-level question.

If question sequences are carefully planned to accomplish particular objectives that in turn are integral parts of a well-designed unit of instruction, issues surrounding the cognitive level of questions will tend to take care of themselves; that is, if the objectives of an activity make sense and the planned sequence of questions is suited to those objectives, the sequence should make sense. On the other hand, if the activity is supposed to stimulate students to analyze or synthesize what they have been learning but the questions are all at the knowledge level, the plans will need to be revised. The same is true if the questions appear to be random selections of test items rather than planned sequences designed to accomplish clear objectives.

Quality of Questions

Aside from difficulty level and cognitive level, research does not have much to say about the quality of teachers' questions. Wright and Nuthall (1970) found that teachers who asked one question at a time elicited higher achievement gain than teachers who tended to ask two or more questions consecutively before stopping to give students a chance to respond. Presumably, the latter teachers were not well prepared, so many of their initial questions were poorly formulated and had to be rephrased.

Groisser (1964) suggested that good questions are clear, purposeful, brief, natural, and thought provoking. *Clear* questions precisely describe the specific points to which students are to respond. In contrast, *vague* questions can be responded to in many ways (too many), and their ambiguous nature confuses students. Thus, "What tense is used in this clause?" (written on the board) is better than "What do you see here?" and "Should eighteen-year-olds be allowed to buy beer?" is better than "What about beer?"

Purposeful questions are planned and sequenced with particular objectives in mind. *Brief* questions tend to be preferable to longer ones because they usually are more clear and to the point. If several points have to be made to set up a final question, this is usually best done through a series of questions that move one step at a time rather than by asking a single long, involved question.

Thought-provoking questions

Questions ordinarily should be phrased in *natural* language adapted to the level of the class. If students do not understand the question, they cannot respond as desired. Finally, good questions are *thought provoking,* especially in discussions. They arouse curiosity and interest and help students to clarify their ideas and to analyze or synthesize facts in addition to merely listing them.

Yes-no questions

Groisser (1964) also cautions against frequent use of four types of *questions that often lead to unproductive student responses:* yes-no questions, tugging questions, guessing questions, and leading questions. *Yes-no questions* are often used merely as warm-ups to other questions. The teacher, for example, first asks "Was Grant a good general?" and only then asks "Why?" Groisser believes that these yes-no questions break lesson continuity and waste time, so it is better to ask the real question in the first place. We see two additional problems with yes-no questions and all other questions that involve a simple choice between two alternatives ("When water freezes, does it expand or contract?"). First, such questions encourage guessing, because students will be right 50 percent of the time even if they have no idea of the correct answer. Second, such questions have low diagnostic power. Questioning should give the teacher feedback about whether students know the material and about the nature of any confusion they may be experiencing. However, because of the guesswork and the lack of elaboration involved in responding to yes-no and simple choice questions, such responses do not carry as much useful information as responses to more substantive questions do.

Tugging questions

Tugging questions typically follow halting or incomplete student responses ("Well . . . ?" "Yes . . . ?"). Essentially, tugging questions say, "Tell me more." They provide no help to students who are stuck for a response, and they may be perceived as nagging or bullying. Teachers are usually better off to remain silent or else provide help by rephrasing the question or giving clues.

Guessing questions

Guessing questions require students to guess because they lack information that would allow them to deduce the answer systematically. Guessing questions can be useful for arousing interest in a topic, and they may have instructional value if they are designed to stimulate students to think logically rather than merely guess randomly (e.g., estimation exercises in mathematics and inquiry approaches to science). However, guessing questions asked for no particular purpose usually just waste time and may encourage students to respond to questions thoughtlessly rather than rationally.

Rhetorical questions

Leading or *rhetorical* questions ("Don't you agree?") reinforce student dependence on the teacher and undercut attempts to condition students to expect that teacher questions call for serious thought and formulation of responses.

Addressing entire class

Other suggestions about good questioning procedure, drawn from Loughlin (1961), Groisser (1964), Good and Brophy (1987), and Wilen and Clegg (1986) are as follows: First, *most questions should be addressed to the entire class* rather than to individuals. That is, the teacher would first ask the question, next give the class time to think, and then call on someone to respond. This way, everyone is responsible for the answer. If the teacher were to name a student to respond before asking the question, only that student would be held responsible and the other students would be less likely to try to answer it in their own minds. However, there are purposes for calling on a student before asking a question: (1) to draw an inattentive student back into the lesson, (2) to ask a follow-up question of a student who has just answered, or (3) to prepare a shy student who may be "shocked" if called on without warning.

Questions ordinarily should be distributed widely among the students rather than addressed primarily to the same few students who provide most of the answers. This keeps most students attentive and accountable and provides everyone with opportunities to respond and get feedback.

Questions should be asked in a normal conversational tone rather than in a formal tone that connotes testing. *Typically, they should be asked one at a time and should not be repeated,* to condition students to the notion that each question calls for an answer. Multiple or continually revised questions are signs of poor preparation, and repeating questions merely distracts students.

In summary, a good question (1) is clear in identifying the issue on which the students are to focus and the nature of the response desired; (2) demands a substantive, thoughtful response; and (3) is followed by a pause during which students are given time to formulate such a response.

Waiting for a Response

Rowe (1974) reported data that at first seem remarkable, even hard to believe: After asking questions, teachers tend to wait less than one second before calling on someone and even then they tend to wait only about a second for the student to give the answer before supplying it themselves, calling on someone else, or providing help by rephrasing or giving clues. Such findings do not seem to make sense, because they suggest that teachers undercut the value of their questions by failing to give them time to have the desired effect on student thinking.

Results of increasing wait time

Rowe followed up these observations by training teachers to extend their wait times from less than one second to three to five seconds. Surprisingly, most of the teachers found this difficult to do, and some never did succeed. However, in the classrooms in which the teachers did extend their wait times to three to five seconds, several desirable changes occurred: (1) increase in average length of response, (2) increase in the frequency of unsolicited but appropriate responses, (3) decrease in failures to respond, (4) increase in incidence of speculative responses, (5) increase in incidence of student-to-student comparisons of data, (6) increase in incidence of statements that involved drawing inferences from evidence, (7) increase in frequency of student-initiated questions, and (8) increase in variety of students' contributions to lessons.

In short, longer wait times led to more active participation in lessons by more students, coupled with an increase in the quality of this participation. Subsequent research (reviewed in Rowe, 1986 and Tobin, 1987) has verified that increasing wait time leads to longer and higher-quality responses and to participation by a greater percentage of the students

(Fagan, Hassler, & Szabo, 1981; Rice, 1977; Swift & Gooding, 1983; Tobin, 1980; Tobin & Capie, 1982). These effects are most notable on the less able students.

Subsequent research has also verified Rowe's findings that many teachers have difficulty extending their wait times. In DeTure's (1979) study, for example, even after training, no teacher attained an average wait time longer than 1.8 seconds. Why should this be? The answer probably lies in the pressures on teachers to maintain lesson pacing and student attention. Teachers may be reluctant to extend their wait times because they fear (with justification in some cases) that they may lose attention or even control of the class if they do. This is one of many illustrations of how good classroom management and good instruction are supportive of each other, and it also represents one of the continuing dilemmas that require teacher decision making and adjustment to immediate situations. Wait times of 3.0 to 5.0 seconds are preferable to shorter wait times because they allow more thinking by more students, but a teacher may have to move to shorter wait times when the class is restive or when time is running out and it is necessary to finish the lesson quickly.

Problems of extending wait time

In general, interactions featuring mostly lower-level questions will move at a quicker pace with shorter wait times than interactions featuring higher-level questions. The appropriateness of these pacing and wait-time factors will depend on the objectives of the activity. Most studies in which teachers were trained to slow the pace and extend wait time have produced positive outcomes, but most of these studies were done in intermediate and upper-grade levels and in the context of teaching abstract or difficult material. Anshutz (1975) reported no science-achievement differences between short and long wait times for students in grades three and four, and Riley (1980) reported interaction effects on science achievement in grades one to five. A decrease in achievement occurred when wait time was extended for low-level questions, whereas an increase was noted when wait time was extended for high- and mixed-cognitive-level questions.

Matching pacing and wait time to questions

The basic principle here is that *pacing and wait time should be suited to the questions being asked* (*and, ultimately, to the objectives that these questions are designed to accomplish*). A fast pace and short wait time are appropriate for drill or review activities covering specific facts. However, to the extent that questions are intended to stimulate students to think about the material and formulate original responses (rather than merely retrieve responses from memory), it will be important to allow time for these effects to occur. This is especially true for complex or involved questions, for which students may need several seconds merely to process the question before they can even begin to formulate a response. When a slow pace and thoughtful responding are desired, teachers should not only adjust their wait times but should make their objectives clear to students. Unless cued, some students may not realize that they are supposed to formulate an original response rather than remember something taught to them explicitly, and some may think that the teacher is looking for speed rather than quality of response.

Selecting a Respondent

It is usually best to address a question to the whole class, pause to give the students time to think, and then call on one of them to respond rather than to identify the respondent before even asking the question. Once the question has been asked, however, whom should the teacher call on? A student likely to know the answer? A volunteer? A student who has not participated lately? Little research is available on this issue.

Teachers are often advised to be random or at least unpredictable in calling on students, because this will make all students accountable for being prepared to answer and thus will help maintain their attention. Research does suggest that attention is better when teachers are unpredictable in their patterns of calling on students (Kounin, 1970; Smith, 1980). Thus it probably is wise to *distribute questions so that students know that they may be called on at any time.*

Brophy and Evertson (1976) and Anderson, Evertson, and Brophy (1979) observed an exception to the "unpredictable" guideline in their studies of small-group reading instruction in the primary grades. In these studies, teachers who elicited the most achievement used a predictable, patterned method of allocating reading turns and response opportunities. Rather than skip around unpredictably, they would start with one student and then proceed systematically around the group, moving from one student to the next. There appear to be several reasons why the patterned-turns method was appropriate in this setting. For one, it insured that all students participated often and roughly equally. This is important in the early grades, when students need opportunities for overt practice with feedback. Unless teachers use patterned turns or some other method of making sure that response opportunities are distributed equally, they will tend to call on the brighter and more assertive students more often than the other students. Also, given the age levels of the students, the structure and predictability of the patterned turns probably was supportive of their learning. In low-SES settings, such structure probably helped anxious and alienated students to concentrate on the lessons, and in high-SES settings, it cut down on the students' tendencies to compete for response opportunities (because they knew that everyone would get a turn).

Patterned-turns method

The patterned-turns method ordinarily is inappropriate in whole-class settings, however, because it slows pacing in unhelpful ways, and its lack

Teachers usually should be unpredictable in their selection of students to respond to questions.

of flexibility creates mismatches between the nature of a question and the readiness of a particular student to respond. Furthermore, it is not advisable even in small-group settings with older students who are prone to look ahead and try to predict and practice material that they expect to be questioned about later (and to tune out most of the discussion that occurs in the meantime). Thus the suggestion that teachers be unpredictable in distributing response opportunities is good advice for most teaching situations.

Need for involvement of everyone

This leaves the issue of whom to call on. A good rule of thumb is to *try to keep everyone involved and, within that, to accommodate individual needs and preferences*. As students move through the grades, they become progressively more able to learn from monitoring classroom interaction and consequently less in need of responding overtly at frequent intervals. Thus calling more often on "phantom" students who pay attention but seldom volunteer will not necessarily increase their achievement (Hughes, 1973; Good & Brophy, 1974). Even so, it is probably a good idea to call on these students (and on any students who seldom volunteer) when opportunities arise, both to develop their confidence and willingness to participate and to reinforce the perception that questions are meant for all students, not just the subset who volunteer routinely.

Nonvolunteers

Thus *students who do not volunteer often probably should be called on whenever they do volunteer and, in addition, should sometimes be called on as nonvolunteers*. Calling on nonvolunteers is not harmful, and sometimes is advisable, as long as the students are able to respond correctly most of the time. Thus it is a good idea to call on nonvolunteers when one is confident that they will be able to respond correctly but not to embarrass them with questions that they cannot handle. Even when calling on nonvolunteers, teachers should maintain a conversational tone suggestive of interest in exploration of the subject matter rather than in finding out who knows the answers and who doesn't.

Setting guidelines

Sometimes teachers may wish to invite or at least allow students to call out answers without first getting permission to respond, especially if the students are typically anxious or reticent. *Even so, it is important that teachers retain control over response opportunities by socializing their students to follow desired guidelines*. If teachers fail to do this and instead allow themselves to be conditioned by the students, a small subgroup of assertive students will coopt most response opportunities for themselves, and an alientated subgroup will cease active attention to lessons.

Reacting to Students' Responses

Teachers' reactions to student responses will depend partly on the nature of the question and the characteristics of the student but mostly on the nature of the student's response. Possibilities include failure to respond at all, responding incorrectly, giving a response that is partly correct or incomplete, and responding correctly.

When the Student Fails to Respond Sometimes, students make no overt response. They remain silent, possibly formulating a response or possibly simply waiting for the teacher to do something. Teachers who *sustain* the interaction in these situations by waiting for a response or eliciting one through additional questioning elicit higher achievement than teachers who *terminate* the interaction by giving the answer or calling on someone else. This is another situation where it is important for teachers to socialize their students rather than allow themselves to be conditioned by the students. Teachers should train their students to respond overtly to questions, even if only to say "I don't know."

Waiting for the response

Thus the initial strategy is simply to wait for the student either to begin to answer the question or to say that he or she does not know how to respond. The teacher should wait patiently and see that the other students remain quiet and give the designated respondent a chance to answer, rather than waving their hands or calling out answers. When teachers do this routinely, their students are likely to respect one another's response opportunities and the designated respondent is likely to say something before long. *If waiting does not elicit a response, the teacher should probe* ("Do you have an idea?").

Simplifying the question

If there is still no response, the teacher should simplify by rephrasing the question or giving clues. This should continue until the teacher elicits a substantive response (correct, partly correct, or incorrect), at which point the feedback responses described in the following sections can be used. If it is necessary to give the answer, it may be advisable to have the student repeat it, to give the student practice in responding overtly and to end the interaction on a positive note. Failure to respond at all is likely to be a problem only with very young students. See Blank (1973) for suggestions about methods of simplifying response demand to levels that will allow such students to respond overtly.

When the Student Responds Incorrectly When students make a substantive response that happens to be incorrect, teachers usually should *begin by indicating that the response was not correct*. Almost all (perhaps 99 percent) of the time, this negative feedback should be confined to simple negation of the correctness of the response and should not include personal criticism of the student. However, such criticism may occasionally be appropriate for students who have been persistently inattentive.

Acknowledging the correct answer

The teacher should note explicitly, but in a matter-of-fact way, that the response was incorrect, because the respondent and some of the onlookers may not realize this unless told. Thus one should not leave the matter ambiguous, or worse, treat the answer as if it had been correct. This will only confuse the students who do not know what is going on and communicate a low opinion of the respondent's intelligence to those who do. It may sometimes be appropriate to try to encourage the respondent by praising the effort or good thinking involved in deriving an answer, but this should be done in a way that leaves both the respondent and the onlookers clearly aware that the answer was incorrect.

Eliciting an improved response

Following initial negative feedback, teachers usually should try to elicit an improved response by rephrasing the question or giving clues, especially when the question is a complex one that lends itself to simplification.

Again, the idea is to sustain the interaction with the original respondent and try to elicit an improved response and thus end the interaction on a positive note. If the question, however, calls for a specific fact that one either knows or does not know, if sustained questioning appears to be creating significant anxiety or embarrassment in the respondent, or if the teacher believes that further questioning would amount to "pointless pumping," it may be preferable to terminate the interaction by giving the answer or calling on someone else.

Giving extended explanations

If it becomes necessary to give the answer, it may be advisable to elaborate by explaining why the answer is correct or how it can be determined from the information given. Such explanation should be included in the feedback whenever the respondent (or some of the onlookers) might not "get the point" from hearing the answer alone.

When the Response Is Incomplete or Only Partly Correct Frequently, especially in response to complex questions, students offer responses that are partly correct and partly incorrect or are correct as far as they go but less complete than the teacher desires. The teacher's response should *begin with affirmation of the correctness of that part of the response that is correct*. For *incomplete responses,* this would be followed by additional questioning designed to elicit the part that the student left out. For *partly correct and partly incorrect responses,* the initial affirmative feedback would be followed by negative feedback or additional questioning designed to call attention to the error and help the respondent to correct it.

When a response is too vague or ambiguous to allow the teacher to be sure whether or not it is correct, or when the teacher wants the respondent to elaborate for the benefit of the rest of the class, the teacher's initial response might be a *call for clarification or elaboration* ("Tell me more about that").

If the answer is correct but not desired because it will move the discussion away from the topic, the teacher can acknowledge its correctness but then refocus the discussion by asking a follow-up question ("Okay, but how does that relate to . . . ?").

When the Student Responds Correctly *Correct answers should be acknowledged as such, unless this is obvious without an explicit statement* from the teacher (as it is, for example, when students understand that an answer is correct whenever the teacher simply moves on without commenting on it). Perhaps 90 percent of the time, such acknowledgment should be limited to brief head nods or short affirmation statements and thus should not include more intense or personal praise of the respondent. Such praise is often intrusive and distracting, and it may even embarrass the recipient, especially if the accomplishment was not especially praiseworthy in the first place.

Student achievement and teacher praise

These guidelines are suggested by research indicating that *teachers who maximize achievement gains are sparing rather than effusive in praising correct answers*. They keep attention focused on the academic content of the lesson rather than on the success or failure of individuals in responding to their questions. When such teachers do praise, the praise tends to be spontaneous admiration of genuinely noteworthy accomplishment rather than premeditated application of "praise technique."

Although it is not especially important to praise students' answers frequently, it is important, especially in the upper grades, to *treat students' contributions with interest and respect*. Older students feel especially encouraged and reinforced when teachers *use their ideas by incorporating them into the lesson* (Edwards & Surma, 1980; Evertson et al., 1980; Flanders, 1970).

Another useful response, both for encouraging the respondent and for moving the activity in desired directions, is to *ask follow-up questions or invite the respondent to elaborate* on the original correct answer.

Finally, in the case of questions that do not have correct answers or have many potentially correct answers, the teacher can accept a response by writing it on the board and then *redirect* the question to the class to elicit additional answers. Questions about the possible motives for a fictional character's actions or about factors that led to World War I, for example, could be redirected to the class repeatedly.

Responding to Students' Questions and Comments

Besides reacting to students' responses to questions, teachers must react to their comments and questions. Teachers who elicit high achievement gain ignore or reject irrelevant student questions and comments that intrude into an activity or suggest failure to pay attention or take it seriously but *are receptive to relevant questions and comments*. Relevant questions indicate a need for clarification or a desire to know more about the subject, and relevant comments suggest that students are actively thinking about the material and relating it to their experiences. Thus such questions and comments present "teachable moments" that teachers would be foolish not to take advantage of.

Relevant student questions

Teacher receptiveness

Yet some teachers cut off such questions and comments with irritation or respond in a manner that makes the students sorry that they asked the question or made the comment in the first place. Embarrassment or humiliation due to a teacher's response to one's question or comment is a frequent experience among students, and many students stop asking questions because of it (Dillon, 1981a). Thus although response to questions or comments occasionally may have to be kept very brief or delayed until after class because time is short or because a more complete response would move the lesson too far off topic, teachers should make clear to their students that they welcome relevant questions and comments and, when possible, should respond to them fully or incorporate them into the ongoing lesson.

CONDUCTING DISCUSSIONS

Although drill and recitation are frequent in classrooms, true group discussion is rare (Dillon, 1984). Even activities that teachers call "discussion" tend to be recitations in which teachers ask questions and students respond by reciting what they already know or are presently learning. Relatively few such activities are actual discussions in which the teacher and students, working as a group, share opinions in order to clarify issues, relate new input to their prior knowledge or experience, or try to resolve some question or problem.

Discussion leader role

To structure and conduct such discussions, teachers must adopt a different role from the one they play in drill and recitation activities. Instead of acting as the primary source of information and the authority figure who determines whether answers are correct, the teacher acts as a discussion leader who establishes the activity's focus, sets boundaries, and facilitates interaction but otherwise assumes a less dominant and less judgmental role. The discussion may begin in a question-and-answer format, but it should gradually evolve into an exchange of views in which students respond to one another as well as to the teacher and respond to statements as well as to questions.

Discussion pace

If ideas are being collected, the teacher should record them (on the board or the overhead projector) but should not evaluate them as good or bad. Once the discussion is going, the teacher may wish to intrude into it periodically to make connections between ideas, point out similarities or contrasts, request clarification or elaboration, invite students to respond to one another, summarize progress achieved so far, or suggest and test for possible consensus as it develops. However, the teacher should not push the group toward some previously determined conclusion (if the teacher were to do this, the activity would be a guided discovery lesson rather than a discussion).

Compared to recitation activities, the pace of discussions will be notably slower, with longer periods of silence between bursts of speech. These periods will provide the participants with opportunities to process what has been said and to formulate responses to it.

Alternatives to questions

Dillon (1981b) has shown that *teacher statements can be just as effective as questions for producing lengthy and insightful responses* during discussions. Questions may even impede discussions at times, especially if they are closed-ended questions that call for brief responses or are perceived as attempts to test the students rather than to solicit their ideas. To avoid this problem, Dillon (1979) listed *six alternatives to questioning* that teachers can use to sustain discussions:

1. *Declarative statements.* In discussing the effects of war on the domestic economy, the teacher might respond to a statement by thinking, "When the war broke out, unemployment dropped." The teacher could introduce this thought into the discussion by stating it directly rather than asking a question such as, "What happens to the unemployment rate in wartime?" The statement provides information that the student will have to accommodate and respond to, but compared to a question, it invites longer and more varied responses.
2. *Declarative restatements.* Teachers can show that they have attended to and understood what students have said by occasionally summarizing. This may be useful to the class as a whole, and in addition,

psychotherapists have found that reflecting people's statements to them tends to stimulate additional and deeper responding.

3. *Indirect questions*. When a direct question might sound challenging or rejecting, the teacher can make a statement like "I wonder what makes you think that" or "I was just thinking about whether or not that would make any difference." Such indirect questions might stimulate further thinking without generating anxiety.
4. *Imperatives*. Similarly, statements such as "Tell us more about that" or "perhaps you could give some examples" are less threatening than direct requests for the same information.
5. *Student questions*. Rather than do all of the questioning themselves, teachers can encourage students to ask questions in response to statements made by their classmates.
6. *Deliberate silence*. Sometimes the best response to a statement is to remain silent for several seconds, to allow time to absorb the content and formulate follow-up questions or comments.

In general, if teachers expect an activity to involve genuine discussion and not merely recitation, they will have to make this clear to the students and alter their own role accordingly.

MANAGING SEATWORK AND HOMEWORK ASSIGNMENTS

Not much research is available on seatwork assignments, even though students typically spend half or more of their time in school working independently (Fisher et al., 1980). Similarly, although homework can provide a useful supplement to classroom instruction and may increase student achievement, at least in the secondary grades (Cooper, 1989; Rickards, 1982; Strother, 1984), little is known about how much or what kind of homework to assign.

Process-outcome research suggests that *independent seatwork is probably overused and is not an adequate substitute either for active teacher instruction or for drill-recitation/discussion opportunities*. However, seatwork and homework assignments provide needed practice and application opportunities, and thus should be used to some degree. Ideally, such assignments should be varied and interesting enough to motivate student engagement, new or challenging enough to constitute meaningful learning experiences rather than pointless busywork, and yet easy enough to allow high rates of success with reasonable effort.

Effective seatwork guidelines

Student success rates, and the effectiveness of seatwork assignments generally, are enhanced when teachers *explain the work and go over practice examples with the students before releasing them to work independently*. Furthermore, once the students are released, the work goes more smoothly if the teachers *circulate to monitor progress and provide help when needed*. If the work has been well chosen and explained, most of these "helping" interactions will be brief, and at any given time, most students will be progressing smoothly through an assignment rather than waiting for help.

Performance should be monitored for completion and accuracy, and students should receive timely and specific feedback. When the whole class or group has the same assignment, review of the assignment can be part of the next day's lesson. Other assignments will require more individualized feedback. When performance is poor, teachers should provide not only feedback but reteaching and follow-up assignments designed to ensure that the material is mastered.

Need for stating objectives

Anderson (1984) showed that students often did not understand the purpose of assignments and tended to think about them primarily in terms of finishing them rather than in terms of learning what they were supposed to be learning. Observations of the teachers in these classrooms suggested why this was so. When presenting the assignments in the first place, these teachers concentrated on what to do and how to do it but seldom included statements about the objectives. When they circulated to monitor work on the assignments, the teachers tended to comment more on keeping busy and finishing the work than on the level of understanding displayed. They seldom talked about cognitive strategies for doing the work (checking for accuracy and meaningfulness, identifying difficulty areas, applying general strategies to particular tasks). Instead, most of their explanations were procedural (''Read the sentence and circle the word that goes in the blank,'' without explanation of how to select the appropriate word). Anderson's work suggests that if teachers want their students to view assignments as learning experiences rather than merely as routine chores that have to be done for no particular purpose, they will have to provide appropriate modeling and instructions.

Unsuccessful seatwork tasks

Most seatwork appears to be intended to extend or deepen knowledge rather than merely to keep students busy, but critical analyses suggest that much seatwork is defective and unlikely to succeed in meeting its intended objectives. This is just as true of the workbooks and other assignments provided with published curricula as it is of seatwork that teachers design themselves (Osborn, 1984). These tasks are frequently either too easy or too difficult for most students, poorly coordinated with what is being taught at the time, or more likely to confuse or mislead the students than to teach them the target concepts. Osborn suggested the following guidelines for seatwork and workbook tasks.

1. A sufficient portion of these tasks should be related to the instruction going on in the rest of the unit or lesson.
2. Another portion should provide for systematic and cumulative review of what has already been taught.
3. Tasks should reflect the most important (and seatwork-appropriate) aspects of what is being taught in the larger curriculum. Less important tasks should be used only as voluntary activities.
4. Extra tasks should be available for students who need extra practice.
5. The vocabulary and concept level of a task should relate to that used in the rest of the program and used by the students.
6. The language used in a task should be consistent with that used in the rest of the lesson and in similar seatwork tasks.

7. Instructions should be clear, unambiguous, and easy to follow; brevity is a virtue.
8. The layout of pages should combine attractiveness with utility.
9. Tasks should contain enough content to enable students to *learn* something, not just merely be *exposed* to something.
10. Tasks that require discriminations should be preceded by sufficient practice on the components of these discriminations.
11. The content should be accurate and precise; tasks should not present wrong information or perpetuate misrules.
12. At least some tasks should be fun and have an obvious benefit to the students.
13. Most response modes called for should be consistent from task to task.
14. Response modes should be as close as possible to actual reading and writing (as opposed to circling, underlining, drawing arrows from one word to another, etc.).
15. The instructional design of individual tasks and of task sequences should be carefully planned.
16. There should be a finite number of task types and forms.
17. Artwork should be consistent with the prose of the task.
18. Cute, nonfunctional, space- time-consuming tasks should be avoided.
19. Tasks should be accompanied by brief explanations of purpose.
20. English-major humor should be avoided.

Workbooks accompanying published curricula

These notions may seem basic and obvious, but inspection of the workbooks that accompany most published curricula will reveal that many tasks violate one or more (usually several) of these guidelines. Frequently, the directions are so long and complex (or so brief and ambiguous) that they cannot be understood by most students, so that guesswork or copying result. Sometimes the response procedures called for are so complex as to obscure the ostensible academic purpose of the assignment (draw a red circle around present-tense verbs, draw a black line under past-tense verbs, and draw green parentheses around future-tense verbs). Many tasks do not develop skills but instead require students to exercise some skill for no useful purpose (count the prime numbers in a number series or the pronouns in a paragraph). In summary, teachers should keep Osborn's guidelines in mind not only when creating their own assignments but when inspecting workbooks that come with published curricula and deciding which assignments to use. *Wise teachers will inspect such assignments to see if they have pedagogical value in the first place, and even if they do, will follow up by working the assignments themselves to identify inadequate or misleading instructions, erroneous examples, printing errors, and other complications that students should be made aware of.*

Homework assignments

The same general guidelines apply to *homework* but with the additional constraint that the assignment should be realistic in length and difficulty given the students' abilities to work independently. Thus five to ten minutes per subject might be appropriate for fourth graders, whereas thirty

30-60 min

to sixty minutes might be appropriate for college-bound high school students.

Need for monitoring homework assignments

Another important point is that homework performance must be monitored. Voluntary homework might be of some use to those students who do it conscientiously, but if homework is to have systematic instructional value for the class as a whole, it will be necessary to set up accountability systems to make sure that homework is completed on time, to review the work the next day, and to take corrective action (such as by requiring students to correct all mistakes and then turn in the work again, and by providing reteaching and follow-up remedial work for students when necessary).

Summary

All teachers are likely to rely regularly on two basic sets of instructional skills—those involved in making presentations (lecturing, demonstrating, explaining) and those involved in questioning and responding to students (conducting drills, recitations, and discussions).

Presentations tend to be short and sandwiched between other activities in the early grades, but extended lectures become more frequent in the upper grades. Even at the secondary level, however, lectures should not ordinarily extend beyond twenty to thirty minutes. Although it has limitations, the lecture method also has important strengths and versatility and can be used appropriately when the objective is to present information, especially information that is not found in readily accessible sources.

Preparation for lectures begins with consideration of the objectives and of the constraints and practical considerations that may apply. This is followed by development of an outline listing key points and then a comprehensive plan that includes attention to questions that might be asked during or after the lecture, demonstrations and visual aids to be used, handouts to be distributed, and follow-up activities or assignments. There should be a beginning that will attract student attention and interest and induce the appropriate learning set and an ending that will review key points, tie things together, and bring the presentation to closure.

The lecture should be clear and easy to follow. This will be accomplished if the teacher avoids vague terms, mazes, and discontinuity problems that detract from clarity, as well as enhances clarity by structuring and sequencing the material appropriately, beginning with advance organizers, using rule-example-rule patterns and including explaining links that make explicit the causal or logical connections between elements. Comprehension will also be enhanced if the lecture is delivered with appropriate pacing, gestures, and communication of enthusiasm about the content.

Like lecturing, activities involving questioning and responding to students have both strengths and limitations that make them more useful for some purposes than for others. Such activities provide opportunities for the teacher to assess student understanding of what has been presented and for the students to process and respond more actively to the material than they are likely to do when merely listening to a presentation. Such activities have greater pedagogical value when more emphasis is on providing the students with opportunities to process and respond to input than on finding out who knows the answers and who does not.

Questioning activities range from fast-paced drills and reviews to slow-paced discussions designed to stimulate students to respond diversely and at high cognitive levels. Either of these extremes, as well as the range of recitation activities that lie in between, may be appropriate for accomplishing particular objectives. Teachers have been criticized for conducting too much drill and recitation and not enough discussion, and this may be true in many classrooms. However, in such cases the problem is a lack of balance between different instructional objectives and their associated activities and not something inherently inappropriate with drill or recitation. Achievement gains are maximized when teachers elicit correct responses to about 75 percent of their questions and elicit substantive (partially correct or incorrect) answers, rather than no responses at all, to the rest of their questions. High-SES classes appear to respond to a somewhat greater level of challenge than low-SES classes, but even here, perhaps 70 percent of the questions should be answered correctly. Within these general rules of thumb, we should expect lower success rates on questions about material just being introduced and considerably higher success rates on review questions covering material that has supposedly been mastered.

Research on the cognitive level of teachers' questions has produced confusing and contradictory results. There is no support for the simplistic conclusion that higher-level questions are good and lower-level questions are bad, but it is difficult to develop more specific guidelines from this body of research that has used the individual question rather than the sequence of questions as the unit of analysis. Assuming the appropriateness of the instructional objective in the first place, the real issue is the degree to which a planned sequence of questions makes sense as a way to accomplish that objective.

Research and expert opinion suggest that good questions are clear, purposeful, brief, adapted to the level of the class, thought-provoking, addressed initially to the entire class rather than to an individual, distributed widely, asked one at a time, and asked in a conversational tone of voice. After asking a question, the teacher should wait long enough for students to process it and formulate responses. This wait time may be very brief, perhaps a second or less, following factual questions during fast-paced reviews, but it should be three to five seconds or longer during slow-paced discussions or during activities designed to get students to analyze or synthesize their knowledge. Longer wait times produce more active participation by a larger percentage of the students, coupled with an increase in the quality and length of responses.

For accountability reasons, it is usually wise to distribute questions in such a way that students know that they may be called on at any time. Although research on primary-grade reading groups has shown that the patterned-turns method is effective in this particular setting, it seems advisable that teachers try to be unpredictable in their selection of respondents when teaching in whole-class settings or at higher grade levels. To provide all students with opportunities to respond in public and to avoid having classroom recitations evolve into interchanges between the teacher and just a few assertive students, it is wise to keep everyone involved and call on nonvolunteers as well as volunteers. The nonvolunteers should be able to answer most of the questions they are asked, however.

Guidelines are given for reacting to students in four situations: when the students fail to respond at all, when they respond incorrectly, when they give an incomplete or partially correct response, and when they give a correct response. In general, it is best for teachers to sustain the interaction with the original respondent and attempt to elicit an improved response rather than terminate the interaction by giving the answer or calling on someone else. Teachers should train their students to respond overtly, even if to say "I don't know," rather than to remain silent when called on. If the student needs help, the teacher can simplify or rephrase the question or give clues.

Students who answer correctly need to know that their answer has been correct, as do the onlookers, but this is usually best accomplished with simple affirmative feedback rather than more extended or intense praise. Except for spontaneous expressions of admiration of outstanding answers, teacher praise of correct responses in public situations tends to be intrusive and distracting and may even embarrass certain students. On the other hand, it is important to treat students' contributions with interest and respect, to use their ideas by incorporating them into the lesson whenever possible, and to be receptive to their relevant questions and comments.

To conduct effective discussions, teachers must adopt a discussion-leader role that differs from the role that they play in drill and recitation activities. Although they structure the discussion and keep it on track, they act more as a collector and clarifier of opinions than as a judge of their correctness. A good discussion will proceed at a slower pace than a typical recitation activity, and although it may begin with questions and answers, it should evolve into an exchange of views in which students respond to one another as well as to the teacher and respond to statements as well as questions. Dillon suggested six alternatives to questioning that teachers can use to elicit thoughtful student responses.

Independent seatwork and homework assignments are desirable elements of a balanced instructional approach, although some teachers overuse seatwork. Ideally, assignments will be interesting enough to engage student interest, new or challenging enough to constitute worthwhile learning experiences or practice/application opportunities, and yet easy enough to allow success with reasonable effort. Their effectiveness is likely to depend on the degree to which teachers go over the assignments with the students before releasing them to work independently, monitor performance for completion and accuracy, supply timely and specific feedback, and follow up with appropriate remedial instruction when necessary.

Questions and Problems

1. In your judgment, what makes for differences in interest value, clarity, and all-around usefulness of the presentations made by instructors in your various classes? Can you identify criteria beyond those included in this chapter?
2. What types of presentation are used most typically in the grade level and subject matter you expect to teach? Given that your students will have textbooks, films, and other sources of input, what do you foresee as the role of your presentations? How will these presentations complement or supplement these other sources?
3. How can you check on the effectiveness of a presentation during or immediately following it? Is it enough to ask, "Any questions?" If not, what should you do?
4. Using the guidelines presented in this chapter, develop a comprehensive plan for a presentation at the grade level and in the subject matter you intend to teach. Include attention to the selection and organization of content. If possible, get your plan critiqued, revise it, and then try out the presentation in a classroom setting and revise it once more if necessary.
5. If possible, audiotape or, preferably, videotape yourself making a presentation and then analyze the content for organization, sequencing, and clarity and the delivery for pacing, gestures, and enthusiasm.
6. What types of drill/review, recitation, and discussion activities do you expect to use in your own teaching? Are these expectations realistic given the grade level and subject matter?
7. Why is it that, even when pursuing higher level cognitive objectives, teachers are likely to ask more lower-level questions than higher-level questions?
8. Why is it more profitable to plan in terms of question sequences rather than individual questions?
9. If you expect your questions to generate cognitive activity in your students rather than merely to provide an opportunity to test their knowledge, what does this imply about pacing, wait time, and distribution of response opportunities?
10. Might you be one of those teachers whose wait times are too short? If so, why? What steps could you take to inhibit your impulsiveness and increase your tolerance for the periods of silence associated with longer wait times?
11. Some students understand what they are learning, turn in assignments correctly, and earn high grades. Yet they seldom volunteer, preferring

to watch and listen rather than to contribute to classroom activities. Should you accommodate them by mostly leaving them alone, or should you frequently call on them as nonvolunteers? Why?

12. How should you handle students who feel pressured and embarrassed in public response situations when they cannot supply the correct answer immediately? Should these students be considered exceptions to the rule that teachers should sustain the interaction and try to elicit an improved response in these situations?
13. How should you respond if a student asks a question that from one point of view is an excellent question that sets up a "teachable moment" that may have value in extending the content for the class but that you suspect has been asked as a ploy to put off an unexpected quiz until tomorrow?
14. If you really want students to ask questions when they feel the need for information, what are some dos and don'ts concerning your response to those questions?
15. Are you prepared to adopt the change in role that is required to stimulate genuine discussion? How should you respond when students express opinions that differ from yours? How should you respond when a student offers a sincere but naive opinion that produces snickering by classmates?
16. What seatwork assignments do you expect to use, and for what purposes? What accountability procedures and mechanisms for providing assessment and feedback will you use?
17. Will you assign homework? If so, for what purposes? How will you assess whether these purposes are being met?

Case Studies

TOO MANY QUESTIONS. Ms. Kane has been teaching for two weeks at Bayside Jr. High. This is her first teaching job. She had been looking forward to it, but now she is discouraged and beginning to feel that she has made a poor choice of career. In particular, she is bothered by the fact that after about five minutes of lecturing, she often notices a number of confused student faces, inevitably followed by what to her are irritating questions (Why are you telling us this? Do we have to remember all of this? Didn't we do this yesterday?). If Ms. Kane asked you for advice about how she might improve the introductory aspects of her lesson presentations, what would you suggest?

OH, SHUT UP! Mr. Moderator likes to include a lot of discussion in his social studies classes. He particularly likes to pose some problem, invite student opinions on how it might be solved, and then assess these suggestions in discussions in which students respond to one another as well as to him. This approach has worked successfully in the past. Even though some students participated more than others, there was wide participation and students found the discussions stimulating and educational.

This year, though, the discussions have increasingly been dominated by two students who enjoy hearing themselves talk and arguing with each other. This makes for useful interchange at times, but often the two of them seem to be arguing just for the sake of arguing, and both Mr. Moderator and the rest of the class are getting tired of listening to them day after day. What can Mr. Moderator do about this? List possible options and order them in terms of their probable effectiveness in solving the problem.

PART 5
MOTIVATION

Sandra noticed her heart beating rapidly while she listened to a classmate make an extemporaneous speech. "Four more speakers, and then it's my turn," she moaned to herself. "Why do I get so nervous when I have to speak? I hate this class and this pressure!"

Sam flung the box against the wall. "Helen!" he screamed. "This space cruiser kit is driving me crazy! The directions say a child can assemble it in fifteen minutes, but I've been working on it for over an hour. Don't buy any more toys that need to be assembled on Christmas Eve!"

Jane confidently walked into the professor's office and sat down. "Jane," the professor said, "I've been pleased with your writing in this course. Your themes are interesting and you support your beliefs quite well." Jane smiled and said, "I'm glad to hear this. I've really worked on my writing until I was satisfied with my work. I'm glad your evaluation matched my own."

Mr. Robbins told his tenth-grade chemistry class, "This is a critical experiment. The procedures will be used often in the next three weeks. If there are any questions, ask them now." Although no student was certain of the process demonstrated and many were confused, none sought additional clarification.

"Look, Sally, I know that Rick is going to raise hell with you, but we can make it worth your while to take the overseas job. After all, it's just two or three years. When you come back, you can expect a big promotion." Sally listed several personal objections, but after forty-five minutes of conversation, her supervisor said, "Sally, there's one thing I haven't told you: Your salary would jump from $25,000 to $36,000." Within a few minutes, Sally agreed to the assignment.

These vignettes illustrate important themes in motivation. The first shows how anxiety can interfere with performance. Minor stress associated with wanting to do well is probably helpful, but too much stress undermines performance.

The second vignette is central to classroom motivation. Many students learn to blame themselves when things go wrong, even though they may not be at fault. Frustration and failure in school can lead to self-castigation and eventually erode performance.

The third vignette depicts a student who is responding capably and with intrinsic motivation. She has defined the task and evaluated her performance. She is interested in feedback from others but is not overly dependent on their evaluation. One goal for classroom teachers is to help students to develop such initiative and confidence.

The fourth vignette depicts a common but unfortunate situation. In too many classrooms, students have learned that it is better to "look good" than to get academic information when they need it. The fifth vignette shows that external rewards can influence people to do things that they might not do otherwise.

In the chapters that follow, we discuss theories of motivation and illustrate how they apply to classroom practice. Enhancing student motivation is not an easy task because students bring different levels of interest, energy, and ability to the classroom and thus vary widely in their responses to learning opportunities.

Chapter 14 presents some major distinctions and concepts and shows the evolution of motivational theory. Chapter 15 provides extensive coverage of modern cognitive theories and some of the research evidence on which they are based.

Chapter 16 focuses on application of motivational principles. It stresses the need for teachers to function as decision makers and tailor their motivational strategies to the students and the situation.

Chapter 17 discusses the relationship between teachers' performance expectations and the ways that teachers interact with students, especially low achievers. It summarizes research on teacher expectation effects and presents guidelines for communicating positive, appropriate expectations.

Chapter 18 discusses the humanistic perspective on teaching and its suggestions about ways to make classrooms more pleasant and supportive for students and to foster students' affective development (self-esteem, prosocial behavior, etc.).

CHAPTER

Basic Concepts of Motivation

CHAPTER OUTLINE

OBJECTIVES

When you have mastered the material in this chapter, you will be able to

1. Explain the expectancy *x* value model of motivation
2. Define motivation from both the behavioristic and cognitive perspectives
3. Explain how needs and drives develop and how their satisfaction affects students' motivation to learn
4. Explain the practical application of Abraham Maslow's need hierarchy to the motivation of classroom learning
5. Explain the concept of intrinsic motivation and its relationship to student effort and performance
6. Explain how cognitive dissonance is created and can be used to motivate belief changes
7. Explain how contrasting levels of achievement motivation develop and manifest themselves, and their implications for teaching

Definition of motivation

Motivation is a hypothetical construct used to explain the initiation, direction, intensity, and persistence of goal-directed behavior. It subsumes concepts such as *need for achievement* ("I want to do well on the final"), *need for affiliation* ("I want to work with my friends"), *incentives* (reward or punishment), *habit* ("I never take a study break until 11 p.m."), *discrepancy* ("How could I, a moral person, have lied to my friend?"), and *curiosity* ("That seems to work, but I wonder why?").

Each of these concepts is useful as a way to look at behavior, but none by itself provides an adequate explanation for motivation. Habit, for example, is a powerful concept for predicting behavior but only when there are established patterns. Furthermore, the concept does not help explain why habits sometimes change or even disappear.

Models of understanding and predicting behavior

Compared to individual concepts such as those listed above, general models and theoretical frameworks provide more comprehensive ways to understand and predict behavior. One general model that most theoretical frameworks can be subsumed within is *the expectancy x value model* (Feather, 1982). This model postulates that the effort that people are willing to expend on a task is a product of (a) the degree to which they *expect* to be able to perform the task successfully if they apply themselves (and thus the degree to which they expect to get the rewards that successful task performance will bring) and (b) the degree to which they *value* those rewards. Effort investment is viewed as the product rather than the sum of the expectancy and value factors because it is assumed that no effort at all will be invested in a task if one factor is missing entirely, no matter how much of the other factor may be present. People are not willing to invest effort on tasks that do not lead to valued outcomes even if they know that they can perform the tasks successfully, and they do not invest effort on even highly valued tasks if they believe that they cannot succeed on these tasks no matter how hard they try. Thus the expectancy *x* value model implies that teachers need to both help their students appreciate the value of school activities and make sure that they can achieve success in these activities if they apply reasonable effort.

Factors that influence behavior

Most theory and research on human motivation have been developed by psychologists working within one of three major theoretical frameworks: behaviorism, cognitive psychology, and humanism. *Behaviorists* believe that behavior is determined by reinforcement contingencies, so they seek to explain motivation by identifying the cues that elicit behavior and the reinforcement that sustains it. *Cognitive psychologists* believe that thought processes control behavior, so they focus on how people process information and interpret personal meanings in particular situations. *Humanists* also believe that people act on their environments and make choices about what to do, but they are more concerned with the general course of personal development, the actualization of potential, and the removal of obstacles to personal growth. In this chapter we will stress the cognitive approach. Most aspects of the behavioral approach have already been outlined in Chapter 7, and the humanistic perspective will be presented in Chapter 18.

BEHAVIORISTIC THEORY

The behavioristic point of view begins with the fact that infants are born with primary biological drives such as hunger that motivate behavior. Certain behavior patterns become established through basic conditioning processes because they are associated with the satisfaction of primary drives. Through this association these behavior patterns eventually acquire motivating powers of their own and begin to function as secondary drives (such as dependence, social affiliation, or aggression), so that behavior that satisfies these secondary drives is reinforced and thus repeated. A history of consistent reinforcement produces strong response tendencies. Children who get attention and social rewards for clowning, for example, are likely to become "class clowns," even though better alternatives may be available to them. Different reinforcement histories will lead to different interests and ultimately to different abilities. A person who is consistently rewarded for playing the piano, for example, and develops a strong interest in doing so will, in time, outperform others with similar talent that is not comparably reinforced.

Behavioristic versus cognitive approach

Distinctions between the behavioristic and the cognitive approaches to motivation gradually have become blurred as behaviorists have expanded the list of potential secondary drives (e.g., curiosity, competence) and reinforcers (e.g., symbolic behavior in the form of internal statements such as "I was right! It works!' may be the only reinforcement in some situations). In general, however, behaviorists place more emphasis on *external* rewards and the systematic arrangement of reinforcement contingencies, whereas cognitive theorists place more emphasis on *internal* rewards and related cognitive processes.

Bandura: A Contemporary Behaviorist

Bandura's (1977) social learning theory is behavioristic in that it focuses on the consequences of specific behavior, yet cognitive because it also considers how students interpret past events and set goals for themselves. According to Bandura, there are two major sources of motivation. One source involves *predicting outcomes* of behavior: If I study hard, will I pass? Can I make the team? Will my speech be well received? Based on consequences of past actions, the person tries to predict the consequences of contemplated actions. A second source of motivation is actively *setting goals* that become personal standards for evaluating performance. While working toward a goal, we imagine the positive things that will occur if we succeed and the negative things that will occur if we fail. We tend to continue our efforts until we meet the standards we have set. Upon reaching a goal, we are satisfied for a time but then begin to identify new goals or to set new (higher) standards for ourselves.

Predicting outcomes

Setting goals

Efficacy expectations

Bandura believes that *efficacy expectations,* beliefs about one's ability to reach a goal, determine how much effort one will expend and how long one will persist in the face of obstacles. The nature of the goal itself will also influence behavior. Goals that are specific, moderately difficult, and seen as reachable in the not-too-distant future are most likely to stimulate persistent effort and to lead to increased efficacy expectations if reached successfully. Specific goals provide unambiguous standards for judging performance, and goals of moderate difficulty provide realistic challenges so that success in reaching them reinforces confidence in one's own abilities and thus increases efficacy perceptions.

Applying Bandura's Theory

If goals are to be specific and obtainable for all students, different students will need different goals. What is moderately difficult for one student may be very difficult for another. Research indicates that getting students to set goals and make a commitment to try to reach those goals increases their performance (Bandura & Schunk, 1981; Tollefson et al., 1984). Goal setting is especially effective when the goals are (a) *proximal rather than distal (they refer to performance on a task to be attempted here and now rather than to attainment of some ultimate goal in the distant future),* (b) *specific* (complete a page of math problems with no more than one error) rather than global (do a good job), and (c) *challenging* (difficult but reachable) rather than too easy or too hard. Students may need help in formulating challenging but reachable goals that represent what they can expect to achieve if they consistently put forth reasonable effort. In the case of a long series of activities that ultimately leads to some distal goal, they will need help in establishing specific goals for each of these activities and in understanding the connection between achieving intermediate goals and achieving the ultimate goal (Bandura & Schunk, 1981; Morgan, 1985).

Besides assistance in learning to set goals, students may need help in learning to evaluate performance and to reinforce themselves for success. Teachers can provide such help through modeling, cueing, and reinforcing ("That's a good list of goals to accomplish during study hall. Last week you were still trying to do too much. You should be able to complete all of these things today. Good planning").

NEED THEORIES

Many of the earliest approaches to explaining human motivation were based on the concept of need. Need theories emphasize conditioning mechanisms similar to those stressed in behavioral theories, but they also include cognitive elements. Henry Murray and Abraham Maslow are two prominent need theorists.

Murray

Murray (1938) defined need as a hypothetical construct that stands for a force that influences one's perception and behavior in the attempt to change an unsatisfying situation. A *need* is a tension that leads one to pursue a goal (which if achieved will release the felt tension).

Effective press

Table 14.1 contains a list of twenty social needs that Murray identified based on an exhaustive study of a small number of "normal" people. These needs are learned through cultural experience and typically triggered by an effective *press* (external determinant of behavior), so that need and press combine to form a *theme,* or pattern, of behavior. Murray

TABLE 14.1 MURRAY'S PSYCHOGENIC NEED SYSTEM

1. Abasement—to surrender . . .	11. Harmavoidance—to avoid pain, physical injury . . .
2. Achievement—to overcome obstacles . . .	12. Infavoidance—to avoid failure, shame, humiliation . . .
3. Affiliation—to form friendships and associations . . .	13. Nurturance—to nourish, aid or protect . . .
4. Aggression—to assault or injure . . .	14. Order—to arrange, organize . . .
5. Autonomy—to resist influence on coercion . . .	15. Play—to relax, amuse oneself . . .
6. Counteraction—proudly to refuse admission of defeat . . .	16. Rejection—to snub, ignore or exclude . . .
7. Deference—to admire and willingly follow . . .	17. Sentience—to seek and enjoy sensuous impressions . . .
8. Defendance—to defend oneself against blame or belittlement . . .	18. Sex—to form and further an erotic relationship . . .
9. Dominance—to influence or control others . . .	19. Succorance—to seek aid, protection or sympathy . . .
10. Exhibition—to attract attention to one's person . . .	20. Understanding—to analyze experience . . .

Source: *Excerpted from* Explorations in Personality, *edited by Henry A. Murray.*

suggested that needs become established by the frequent occurrence of a specific press. Children, for example, may develop the need to achieve if their parents begin to challenge them at an early age, expect them to meet these challenges, and reinforce their achievements. Conversely, children whose parents frown on competition are unlikely to develop a driving need to achieve. More generally, children who are reared in different cultures or in constrasting social-class settings within the same culture will be exposed to different presses and thus will come to school with different felt needs.

Murray's view suggests that most behavior is motivated by the desire to avoid or release unpleasant tensions. Early experiences are seen as especially important because once a need is established, it tends to perpetuate itself. A child who is taught to compete, for example, may demonstrate competitiveness even in situations that do not call for it. Furthermore, behavior that reduces needs within a given context is likely to become habitual, so that it will be easier to teach people new behavior in a new context than in a familiar one.

These views suggest that teachers can have some effect on students' motivation, but that change gets more difficult as students get older. Unless the school effort is systematic and sustained, it is likely to have little permanent effect (as we shall see, other viewpoints are more hopeful).

Few psychologists today believe that all human behavior is motivated by a need to avoid unpleasant tensions. Still, Murray was correct in noting that our needs often compel us to act in certain ways. We all know people who *must* achieve, compete, or dominate.

Applying Murray's Theory

Needs vary, so that no one classroom activity can satisfy the needs of all students simultaneously. However, teachers familiar with their students' needs can use this knowledge to motivate learning efforts. A student may be unmotivated to learn matrix arithmetic for several weeks, for example, but then develop a *need* for this skill in physics class and thus learn the necessary operations in a single week.

Teachers need to think about ways to help students fulfill achievement needs, affiliation needs, and power needs. Some students may need more cognitively stimulating assignments, others may need more opportunities to work cooperatively with peers, and still others may need more opportunities to compete or to exercise autonomy. This implies that effective instruction requires varied organizational structures, lesson approaches, and incentives.

Maslow

Maslow (1962) conceptualized a hierarchy of needs arranged in the following order of priority (Figure 14.1):

Hierarchy of needs

1. Physiological needs (sleep, thirst)
2. Safety needs (freedom from danger, anxiety, or psychological threat)
3. Love needs (acceptance from parents, teachers, peers)
4. Esteem needs (mastery experiences, confidence in one's ability)
5. Needs for self-actualization (creative self-expression, attempt to satisfy one's curiosity).

Maslow theorized that unless lower needs are satisfied, higher needs may not even be appreciated, let alone motivate behavior. The well-rested, psychologically secure student may seek to master academic skills and even generate questions to pursue independently, but the exhausted student will have little energy for such activity.

Physiological needs

Physiological needs are basic to survival, but once they are met, higher needs can take over. If both physiological and safety needs are satisfied, people will be able to appreciate warm, interpersonal relationships, and love needs will begin to motivate their behavior. Subsequently, they will seek a stable and usually high evaluation of themselves and perhaps begin to pursue self-actualization needs.

Resolution of lower needs

There may be temporary exceptions to the order in which needs are fulfilled. People occasionally deprive themselves of a prepotent need like sleep, for example, in order to prepare for an exam, in the hope of mastering the material (an esteem need). However, Maslow believes that people generally respond first to the more basic of two needs.

Applying Maslow's Theory

Several implications of Maslow's theory are obvious. A student who comes to class hungry or tired is unlikely to become engrossed in academic activities. Similarly, students who have suffered humiliating failure will not become autonomous learners until they are convinced that the teacher will support their efforts and that they can make errors without being blamed or punished. Anxious students are likely to seek precise instruction and resist attempts to get them to take risks or make independent decisions.

Figure 14.1 Abraham Maslow's Hierarchy of Needs

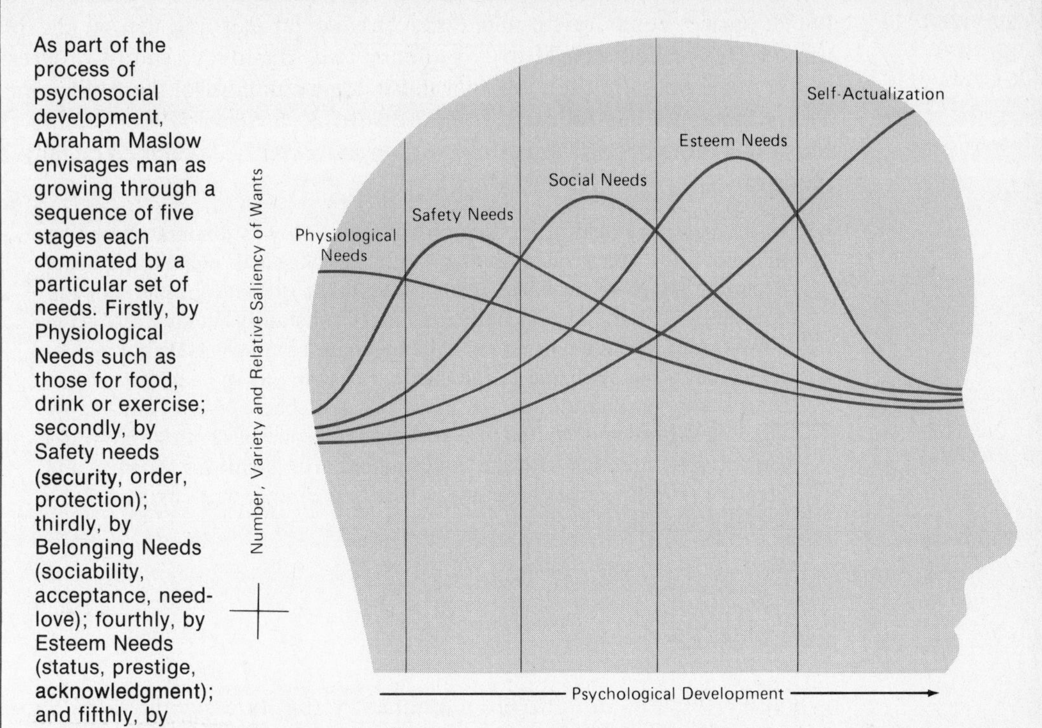

As part of the process of psychosocial development, Abraham Maslow envisages man as growing through a sequence of five stages each dominated by a particular set of needs. Firstly, by Physiological Needs such as those for food, drink or exercise; secondly, by Safety needs (security, order, protection); thirdly, by Belonging Needs (sociability, acceptance, need-love); fourthly, by Esteem Needs (status, prestige, acknowledgment); and fifthly, by Self-actualization Needs (personal fulfilment and growth). The peak of the earlier stage must be passed before the next and "higher" need emerges to dominate the organism. This sequence characterizes not only growth from childhood to maturity, but the growth of cultures from subsistence to free self-expression. For this reason an individual's stage cannot be used as an automatic value judgment on personal worth, but is rather indicative of a benign social environment.

It is important to note that all needs are simultaneously present (or latent) in all persons at all times. The sequence refers to the strength of the need within the conscious purposes of the mind. Sudden emotional or physical deprivation will cause "lower" needs to reawaken. Maslow's approach can include many psychologies, from behaviourism, which has anchored itself in physiological drives, to the more humanistic approaches concerned with creativity and self-fulfilment.

Source: C. Hampden-Turner, *Maps of the Mind* (London: Mitchell Beazley Ltd., 1982). Reprinted by permission of the publisher.

Addressing higher levels prematurely

Sometimes teachers try to address higher needs too soon. Students may need to feel secure in the classroom, achieve limited but real mastery, and learn to work with other students before they address higher needs. Most young children are not ready for completely autonomous functioning; to force them to shoulder such responsibility prematurely is to ask for poor progress (this was a common problem in open education classes, and one of the reasons why the open education model never caught on).

Building a base

Building a base for future growth takes time. How can adults help students look at their actions, think about them, and plan for (rather than fear) evaluation? Maslow (1954) stated that the most stable and healthy self-esteem is based on deserved respect rather than unwarranted adulation. To allow for growth, students need to experience mastery.

From Behavioral to Cognitive Theories

The evolution of motivational theory, illustrated by the difference between earlier behaviorism and Bandura's social learning theory and by the difference between Murray's theory and Maslow's, shows progressively more belief in the view that individuals can control their behavior. The statement that follows, from Edward J. Murray (1964), connects Maslow's thoughts on motivation with more recently developed cognitive theories:

> In the past, the field of motivation and emotion was dominated by two theories—the classical Freudian and the classical behaviorist. The Freudian image of man was that of a creature driven by inherited, unconscious sexual and destructive instincts constantly seeking release in a frustrating social environment. The behaviorist view was that of a creature quietly metabolizing in the shade, occasionally goaded into action by the hot sun and the lure of a cold glass of beer. Man is not simply warding off noxious stimuli and seeking the peace of death or Nirvana. He actively interacts with the environment. He is curious, playful, and creative. He conceives great ideas, seeks meaning, and envisions new social goals. (p. 119)

COGNITIVE THEORIES

Cognitive theories of motivation emphasize that how people *think* about what is happening to them is as important a determinant of subsequent behavior as the objective reality of what takes place. Our reaction to a test score, for example, is based in part on what we have come to expect due to our past performance and on our perceptions of how hard we worked, how fair the test was, and so on.

Cognitive perceptions influencing behavior

Weiner (1966) conducted a study that illustrates how cognition influences behavior. He began with the finding that students with high anxiety levels do better on certain tasks when they initially experience success. If they do not do well on the first task, their performance on the second task declines. Conversely, with low-anxiety students, failure facilitates and success depresses subsequent performance. Behaviorists interpret such results to mean that some students need more drive than others, depending on the difficulty of the task.

In the original research done from a behavioristic perspective, experimenters initially assigned subjects to either easy tasks to ensure success or difficult tasks to ensure failure and then had all subjects work on tasks of comparable difficulty. In contrast, Weiner (1966) manipulated the naturally occurring relations between easy tasks and success and between difficult tasks and failure. Subjects working on difficult tasks were led to believe that they were doing well, and subjects working on easy tasks were led to believe that they were doing poorly. Under these conditions, low-anxiety students did better (learned after fewer attempts) on the easy tasks, but high-anxiety students did better on the difficult tasks, presumably because they thought that they were succeeding. These findings, showing that motivational consequences stem from *perceived success or failure,* rather than from the individual's drive level, are difficult to explain from a behavioristic stance. They illustrate a critical difference between the behavioral and the cognitive frameworks: the extent to which *perception* of events is seen as a determinant of behavior.

Weiner's theory of motivation will be presented in detail in the next chapter. We now turn attention to three other cognitive theories—intrinsic-motivation theory, cognitive-dissonance theory, and achievement-motivation theory.

Intrinsic-Motivation Theory

Jean Piaget and many other theorists hold that activity is intrinsic to human nature—that besides meeting basic survival needs and responding to external presses, humans will display curiosity, explore their environments, amuse themselves, and seek to fulfill their potential. Even when in a state of need satisfaction, humans will engage in certain activities because they find them rewarding. Intrinsic-motivation theorists have tried to conceptualize such intrinsic motivation and to identify what it is about the activities that causes them to be experienced as intrinscially rewarding.

According to Edward Deci (1975), intrinsically motivated behaviors are those in which one engages in order to feel competent and self-determining. He hypothesized that intrinsic motivation depends on the perception that one's behavior results from internal causes rather than external pressures and that intrinsic motivation will decrease if one's feelings of competence and self-determination are reduced.

Deci contended that consequences of actions, including feedback and rewards, have two parts—a controlling element and an informational element. If the *controlling element* is salient, the actor is likely to perceive the locus of causality of his or her behavior as external. If the *informational element* dominates, the actor will tend to attribute his or her behavior to internal causes—to be intrinsically motivated. This implies that rewards may control behavior but erode intrinsic motivation unless they are used in informational as opposed to controlling ways. Evidence produced by several investigators confirms the value of distinguishing between control and information elements (Lepper & Greene, 1978).

Deci: Types of intrinsically motivated behavior

Deci (1975) identified two types of intrinsically motivated behavior. One occurs when the person is comfortable but bored and thus motivated to find stimulation. The other involves mastering challenges or reducing incongruity (or dissonance). Deci argued that people feel competence and self-determination when they are able to master challenges that are optimal for them (novel enough to be interesting, difficult enough to be challenging).

Applying Intrinsic-Motivation Theory

It is desirable but difficult for teachers to sustain intrinsic motivation to engage in academic tasks in their students. First, a task that is interesting for one student may be uninteresting to the others. Furthermore, even if two students are initially interested in the same task, one may reach saturation much earlier than the other.

Still, teachers can at least create conditions favorable to development of intrinsic motivation by allowing students choices of activity and encouraging them to exercise autonomy in regulating their own learning efforts. Also, teachers who use extrinsic rewards can strive to make them informational (helping students to see themselves as fulfilling their own goals) rather than controlling (causing students to see themselves as responding to teacher demands) by stressing the effort and accomplishment that the rewards represent.

Corno and Rohrkemper: Self-Regulation Theory

Corno and Rohrkemper (1985) extended the notion of intrinsic motivation and linked it to ideas about teaching for strategic learning (see Chapter 10) in their discussion of self-regulated learning. *Self-regulated learning* is defined as the highest form of cognitive engagement that students can use to learn in classrooms: It is systematic effort put forth by students to develop meaningful understanding of academic content by deepening and manipulating the associative network of ideas they possess in relation to that content and by monitoring their progress in doing so.

Applying Self-Regulation Theory

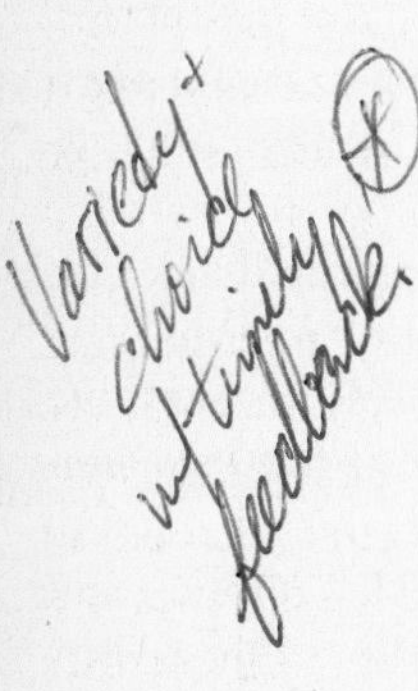

Corno and Rohrkemper suggested that teachers can set the stage for development of self-regulated learning by emphasizing classroom features that foster intrinsic motivation to learn: use of a variety of activities and teaching methods and frequent provision of student choice to accommodate individual differences in preferences and interests, classroom discourse that includes both teacher-student and student-student discussion of the content, pursuance of topics in depth through related activities that build toward understanding and application of significant networks of knowledge, and provision of feedback that is timely, informative, encouraging, and oriented toward private support of learning rather than public comparison of performance. Within this context, teachers then can promote self-regulated learning more directly by (a) clarifying goals, modeling strategies, and otherwise working to ensure that students' learning is meaningful and strategic and (b) withdrawing these learning supports when they are no longer needed and providing opportunities for students to work with increasing autonomy on tasks that challenge them to integrate and apply what they are learning. Corno and Rohrkemper's ideas about self-regulated learning are useful extensions of intrinsic-motivation theory because they suggest that, in addition to finding ways to capitalize on students' existing intrinsic motivation to engage in other activities, teachers can model and encourage the development in students of intrinsic motivation to engage in *academic* activities (and in the process, increase the degree to which the students engage in self-regulated learning).

Festinger: Cognitive Dissonance Theory

Cognitive dissonance is tension that arises when one becomes aware of inconsistency between two or more cognitions (such as perceptions, attitudes, or beliefs). Festinger (1957) hypothesized that cognitive dissonance is especially acute when one becomes aware of perceptions (such as recognition that one has behaved immorally) that are contrary to one's beliefs about oneself (e.g., as a good person). Presumably, the two inconsistent cognitions create an unpleasant tension or dissonance that motivates one to take action to reduce it.

People as rationalizing agents

As Aronson (1972) pointed out, cognitive dissonance theory sees humans as rationalizing rather than as rational: People are more motivated to believe that they are right than to be right and often use defense mechanisms to justify their behavior rather than take corrective action. Deci (1975) argued that dissonance may lead to positive (e.g., curiosity) motivation in some individuals, but most experts characterize dissonance as an unpleasant state that motivates defensive behavior.

Cognitive dissonance theory, for example, predicts that people will "cover their tracks" after making a decision. Before buying a new television, they seek comparative information about different brands. After the purchase is made, however, they may begin to read advertisements selectively (only reading ads about the television they purchased), to guarantee that they will be reassured about the wisdom of their choice and spared the dissonance of nagging second thoughts.

External justification

Often we can rationalize our behavior and thus ignore dissonance. Fred wants to know if you liked his presentation in speech class. Your response, "It was good; I enjoyed it," may conflict with your covert evaluation, "It was dull," and your perception of yourself as an honest person. The dissonance here might be minimal, though, if you could justify your behavior on "obvious" grounds (I didn't want to hurt his feelings and I had no constructive suggestions). You would not be motivated to change your opinion of Fred's speech or to examine your motives for saying what you said.

Threat to self-concept

To account for such phenomena, Aronson (1972) stated that dissonance is most powerful in situations in which the self-concept is threatened. He argued that people like to think of themselves as decent individuals who would not mislead someone else unless there was good reason to do so and especially not if doing so would mean harmful consequences for the person. If people believe that their statements will have serious consequences, they are more likely to experience powerful dissonance because their self-concept is directly threatened (How can I, a good person, behave this way?).

Applying Cognitive-Dissonance Theory

Through the careful use of materials and assignments, students can be taught that first impulses (such as "I can't do this") are often erroneous. Systematic teaching of the need to check and improve work on assignments and to form our own opinions rather than to accept input uncritically would be valuable.

Role playing

Students who have rigid and inappropriate role definitions or attitudes toward self or others can be helped to change those beliefs by role playing more appropriate behaviors. Dissonance theory suggests that if people can be induced to behave contrary to their current beliefs, they may try to reduce dissonance by changing those beliefs if they cannot find an easy way to justify their behavior. Placing students who do not get along on the same team, for example, so that they must depend on each other and cooperate, may cause them to develop more favorable opinions of each other.

Atkinson: Achievement-Motivation Theory

Another type of cognitive theory that has been used to explain behavior is achievement-motivation theory. Why do persons of similar aptitude often achieve in dramatically different ways? Some psychologists argue that this occurs because some individuals have a more powerful need to achieve than others. Achievement becomes a dominant part of their lives, and they organize their time and talents to pursue achievement goals rather than affiliative or other goals.

Achievement versus avoidance

Atkinson (1964) formulated a comprehensive theory of achievement motivation and behavior. He postulated that the tendency to approach an achievement goal (T_s) is a product of three factors: the need for achievement or the motive for success (M_s), the probability of success (P_s), and the incentive value of success (I_s). However, fear of failure can also be aroused in an achievement-related situation. Thus there is also a tendency to avoid failure (T_{af}), which is the product of three factors: the motive to avoid failure (M_{af}), the probability of failure (P_{af}), and the incentive value of failure (I_{af}). M_s is conceptualized as the capacity to experience pride in achievement, and M_{af} is the capacity to experience embarrassment or shame in the face of failure.

Jane Walker, for example, has been practicing law for three years as a junior partner in an established firm. She has some regular clients but not enough to guarantee that she could maintain her present standard of living if she went into private practice. She wants to be her own boss and to decide which cases to accept, but financial security is important too. In Atkinson's framework, Jane's decision to stay with the firm or go off on her own involves the following basic question: How much does she want to be her own boss and how probable is her success versus how much does she fear failing to make it on her own and what is the probability of such failure?

According to Atkinson's theory, the strength of a person's motivation to strive for a particular goal is determined by the relative strengths of the tendency to approach the task and the tendency to avoid failure. Thus a person is high in *resultant achievement motivation* when M_s exceeds M_{af}. As Weiner (1972) pointed out, for subjects *low* in resultant achievement motivation, all achievement tasks are somewhat aversive and elicit fear. However, tasks that are very easy or very difficult are comparatively less aversive for these people than are tasks of intermediate difficulty.

Incentive values of success and failure

Atkinson and Litwin (1960) showed that people *high* in resultant achievement motivation are much more likely to choose tasks of intermediate difficulty than are subjects low in resultant achievement motivation. The subjects in this experiment played a ring-toss game. They were free to stand wherever they wished within a range of one to fifteen feet from the target peg. Presumably, the subjective probability of success was high at one foot and low at fifteen feet. As subjects stood farther from the peg, the incentive value of success was assumed to increase and the incentive value of failure was assumed to decrease, so that a successful toss from fifteen feet would be perceived as a demonstration of competence, but failure from this distance would be "no big deal." Conversely, a successful toss from two feet would be only a minor accomplishment, and a miss from two feet would be disappointing and perhaps embarrassing. As predicted, subjects with high achievement motivation (a high tendency to approach success and a low tendency to avoid failure) tended to toss their rings much more frequently from the moderate-risk distance (nine to eleven feet). Subjects low in achievement motivation generally made close tosses of between one and six feet or distant tosses of between twelve and fifteen feet, avoiding the intermediate distances.

An interesting test of Atkinson's theory of achievement motivation involves task choice following success or failure. In the theory, M_s (I want to achieve) and M_{af} (I don't want to fail) are viewed as relatively stable personality factors, and the incentive values of a goal depend on the person's perception of the probability of success (P_s). Weiner (1972) summarized general trends in the literature on the effects of success and failure on motivation to continue with a given activity:

1. Motivation is enhanced following failure among individuals high in resultant achievement motivation (they want to do better).
2. Motivation is inhibited following failure among individuals low in resultant achievement motivation (they are "turned off").
3. Motivation is decreased following success among individuals high in resultant achievement motivation (they have proven their skills and have no need to continue to do so).
4. Motivation is enhanced following success among individuals low in resultant achievement motivation (they are relieved to find that they are successful and want to continue with this safe, rewarding activity).

Applying Achievement-Motivation Theory

Teachers can maximize their students' achievement motivation by keeping criticism constructive and minimizing reasons for fearing failure, by helping the students to set challenging but realistic goals and to take pleasure in reaching those goals, and by offering incentives for good effort and performance.

Realism in vocational aspiration

Two additional findings from achievement-motivation research are worth noting. First, there is evidence that more realism in vocational aspiration is exhibited by students who are high in resultant achievement motivation than by students who are low in it. Individuals low in achievement motivation do not appear to have adequate self-knowledge to make realistic vocational choices and may need assistance from teachers and counselors.

Second, the difficulty of assignments affects student motivation and effort. Too often task difficulty is fixed for the entire class at a level that only stimulates average students maximally. If students are told that they will get an A if they do 90 percent of a set of math problems correctly, for example, this may be comparable to tossing a ring from two feet for some students but more like tossing from twenty feet for others.

Programs for increasing achievement motivation involve teaching the relationship between risk-taking behavior and accomplishment and helping students to understand the advantages of setting moderately difficult goals. Alschuler, Tabor, and McIntyre (1971) suggested beginning by giving students assignments that are both "doable" and linked to personal involvement, so that success or failure will have real meaning. Task definitions such as "finish my history project" that suggest a dull, "have to do it" orientation should be replaced with goal statements that reflect personal interest and commitment ("I want to give a better class presentation that I did last time—to hold everyone's attention and even teach the teacher something new"). Related objectives include helping students to identify problems that prevent them from completing tasks successfully and helping them to translate long-range assignments into smaller, more manageable units.

Examples of games in achievement motivation

One application of Alschuler, Tabor, and McIntyre's (1971) principles involved a math game that called for each student to establish a contract with the teacher that involved earning play money through performance on chapter tests. Each student begins the game with two thousand dollars but must pay an initial fee directly related to the percentage of correct answers that he or she contracts for as the target goal. All students must meet two contractual obligations: getting the predicted percentage of problems correct and doing so before a specified deadline.

Students earn the most play money by contracting for performance levels that represent their best efforts. They are penalized for underbidding or overbidding (for example, they lose 1 percent of their gross earnings for each wrong answer below the percentage contracted for). Students can revise their contracts at any time before one week before the due date, at a cost of ten dollars, if performance on practice assignments indicates that their predictions have been unrealistically high or low. Thus students who anticipate their best ultimate performance levels earlier are rewarded more fully, but the cost for an early mistake is minor if corrected. Penalties are heavier for failure to fulfill the contract by the due date (10 percent of gross earnings for each day the contract goes unfulfilled).

The use of this game has striking effects in one fifth-grade classroom. All fourteen students gained over a year in mathematics (as measured by the Stanford Achievement Test) during the fifth grade, whereas only two of them had gained more than a year in mathematics during the previous school year. The teacher believed that early in the year enthusiasm was produced by the game rather than by any intrinsic interest in mathematics but that by the end of the year, the students had become intrinsically interested in mathematics.

These data indicate that stress on helping students to set realistic goals, rewarding them for doing so and penalizing them for failure to do so, providing feedback, and implementation of a game approach to learning raised student achievement. Which of these factors was most important is impossible to determine. We suspect that the goal-setting aspects were most central to the development of students' achievement motivation.

The gamelike aspects were probably of more value for lower-ability students than for other students.

Games appear to be especially useful in situations that call for practice of basic facts and skills. Games can be overused, however, and they can be used inappropriately if the activity does not have a sufficient curricular purpose in the first place, if the gamelike aspects overwhelm the academic aspects, if the game intensifies the competitiveness of the classroom reward structure, or if it publicly embarrasses some of the students.

One can also ask how far the process of achievement-motivation training should go. An emphasis on self-reliance and on the taking of calculated risks probably is appropriate, but commitment to achievement, especially to its competitive aspects, can be overemphasized (we all know people who are driven to achieve and whose identities are too closely related to their achievement). The key for teachers is probably to help students of all ability levels learn to set realistic achievement goals in the context of also helping them to achieve social goals and other developmental goals.

Stipek: The Development of Achievement Motivation

Stipek (1984a) analyzed the antecedent conditions of achievement motivation. She emphasized developmental issues, with particular attention to changes in *cognitions related to achievement* (such as performance expectations, self-perceptions of ability, or perceptions of causes of achievement outcomes). She also stressed the development of several related *emotions*—how children value achievement outcomes, their attitudes toward school, and their emotional responses to achievement outcomes.

Failure-avoidance behavior

Stipek's own observations indicate that younger students focus on tasks rather than outcomes. They are egocentric, concerned about their own work rather than the progress of peers. However, as they mature and become more responsive to social comparisons and competition, they start to become defensive and may seek to avoid difficult tasks or even begin to demonstrate behaviors such as learned helplessness.

Performance expectancy

Developmental changes in children's cognitions appear to account for these changes in students' achievement behavior. *Performance expectancy,* for example, is generally high until second or third grade but then decreases through sixth grade (Stipek, 1984b). *Self-perceptions of competence* also generally decrease during the elementary grades. Initially, overly optimistic ability perceptions drop and begin to correlate increasingly with objective performance measures (Eshel & Klein, 1981). A further, and often substantial, drop in self-perceptions occurs after students enter junior high schools (Eccles, 1987). Attitudes toward school also drop as grade level increases (Eccles, 1987), with an especially steep decrease in junior high (Haladyna & Thomas, 1979).

There is little research on students' emotional responses in achievement contexts. One study showed that fourth and fifth graders generally described their classroom-related emotions negatively (Weiner, Anderson, & Prawat, 1982). Younger students are more likely to say that they engage in achievement behavior to master tasks (intrinsic motivation), whereas older ones more often report extrinsic reasons such as grades (Blumenfeld & Pintrich, 1982; deCharms, 1980).

Teacher Feedback and Student Response

Performance evaluations

In seeking explanations for these changes in achievement motivation, Stipek focused on teachers' *performance evaluations,* which also change with grade level, and on students' responses to teacher feedback. Young children focus on *social* (praise or criticism) rather than *objective* (I got all problems correct), *symbolic* (I got an A), or *normative* (I did better than everyone else) feedback about their performance. Older students tend to consider both objective and social feedback in developing expectations for future performance.

Social feedback

Stipek believes that young children focus on *social feedback* because they perceive their teacher's role as being similar to that of their parents and because they view adults as moral authorities and are eager to please them. She also observed that kindergarten and first-grade teachers frequently praise and rarely criticize the results of students' efforts. Brophy (1981) pointed out that teachers in early elementary grades sometimes praise students even after they make mistakes and that students view this praise as a positive reflection of their ability. Older students, however, interpret praise following failure as an indication of teacher sympathy toward students of low ability.

Symbolic feedback

Symbolic feedback includes such things as grades, smiling faces, and stars. Kindergarten and first-grade students often associate these symbols with social approval. Grades begin to affect self-concept of ability and students begin to value grades for their own sake at about third grade (Eshel & Klein, 1981). Older students also come to value grades because grades allow them to compare their performance with that of their peers.

Objective feedback

Objective feedback conveys information only about the correctness of a student's response. It becomes a more important influence on students' achievement-related cognitions over time, due to changes in their cognitive processing. Younger students generally expect to succeed and retain high self-perceptions of ability even after failures, suggesting that they do not accurately process and integrate information about repeated failure. Even if they were able to do so, they tend not to view ability as a stable attribute, and instead equate ability with effort until age 10 or 11 (Dweck, 1986).

Recent research suggests that young children between the ages of four and eight can process objective information about past failures and make accurate predictions about future performance but more so when speaking about peers than about themselves (Stipek, 1984a). Another study (Stipek & Hoffman, 1980) showed that pupils' predictions about their own future performance were more accurate when they were rewarded for accuracy of prediction.

Normative feedback

Most students do not compare their performance to that of others until about second grade, so that their self-evaluations are largely unaffected by *normative feedback* about the performance of others (Boggiano & Ruble, 1979). Stipek and Tannatt (1984) found that second and third grad-

Comparing work can help students understand and learn.

ers were more likely to explain competency ratings of self and others in terms of relative performance and task difficulty than were younger students. Stipek believes that these developmental differences are due largely to changes in classroom organization. Classrooms become more formal in the upper grades, with more whole-class instruction, public recitation, formal testing, use of letter grades, and other factors that encourage normative comparisons of one's performance with that of peers.

Once students begin to define academic success in relation to the performance of others, many will begin to view themselves as failures. By sixth grade, most will view ability as stable and may see increased effort as being of little use. This may account for the negative feelings that many junior-high students have toward school and for the sharp decrease in students' self-perceptions of ability that occurs at this age. A major challenge facing junior high and high school teachers is sustaining their students' interest in achieving for the sake of mastering content or skills and not just for symbolic rewards such as grades.

Summary

Concepts such as needs, incentives, habits, or cognitive dissonance are useful, but no single concept adequately explains student motivation. The expectancy *x* value model and various theoretical frameworks are needed to link concepts and improve predictions about behaviors. Behaviorists focus on past reinforcement and present contingencies, whereas cognitive psychologists believe that people decide what they want to achieve and that perception, understanding, information processing, and curiosity are important.

Behaviorists begin with the assumption that the drive to fulfill biological needs motivates behavior. Through attempts to satisfy biological drives, secondary drives such as dependence or aggression are learned. If reinforced, behavior associated with them is repeated; if not, it disappears. Murray postulated that needs interact with environmental pressure to form a pattern of behavior, or theme. Once created, needs tend to perpetuate themselves, so early experiences are especially important. Murray's theory can be used to identify student needs and to predict how students might respond to given circumstances. Maslow also used the concept of needs and arranged them into a hierarchy. He believed that unfulfilled basic needs interfere with learning.

Cognitive explanations emphasize individuals' perceptions of events and their influences on behavior. Murray and Maslow, for example, both stressed individuals' control of their own behavior. Deci argued that intrinsic motivation is a goal that teachers can promote. Aronson proposed that cognitive dissonance serves to motivate and can be used to bring about constructive changes in student behavior. Atkinson has formulated a comprehensive theory of achievement behavior involving both individual and situational variables. Stipek has reviewed extant work about how students' need for achievement develops and how various classroom conditions influence students' motivation.

Questions and Problems

1. Human motivation has been debated for centuries. Pessimists believe that people must be pushed by external pressures, including threats of punishment for noncompliance. Optimists believe that the same degree of motivation can be accomplished through the pull of positive incentives. Those who are still more optimistic believe that no incentives at all are necessary, because positive and prosocial motives are basic to human nature. Where do you stand on these issues? Why? What does your stance imply concerning your approach to classroom motivation?
2. Maslow implies that students will not be very motivated to learn in school unless their basic needs are met. However, teachers rarely are in a position to meet basic needs that are not being met at home. Does this mean that teachers cannot motivate such students to learn? Why or why not?
3. Individual differences in students' motivational needs are problematic because the same teacher behavior that might motivate certain students might not motivate others. What can be done about this?
4. If you have selected teaching as your vocation, you probably are favorably disposed toward education and find learning rewarding. However, you will teach some students who are apathetic toward learning, anxious when placed in testlike situations, or even completely negative toward school. What can you do to prepare yourself to deal with these students effectively?
5. Given that students require different types of assignments because of

their varying abilities, how could you make differential assignments without implying that one student is less capable than another?

Case Studies

JUDY'S DILEMMA. Judy enjoys mathematics and works hard at it. Her mathematics class is individualized, and within limits, she can proceed at her own pace. Sometimes she has to wait until a few other students reach her level so that the teacher can begin another unit. Even when she has to wait to begin a new topic, however, she still enjoys the class. The teacher offers options that students can select during "delay" times. Some involve straightforward review, but others involve "tricky" problems or novel applications of concepts. Other choice units deal with people who have discovered mathematical principles or with illustrations of ways that mathematics is used in the "real world."

Judy, however, hates history. Every week is the same: Monday and Tuesday the teacher lectures (BORING!). Wednesday, Thursday, and Friday are devoted to small-group work, but a few students always talk even though they have little to say, and Judy dislikes answering the questions assigned each day. She often thinks, "How can one person keep asking such boring questions about an interesting subject?"

Using a motivational framework, how would you explain Judy's responses to the two subjects? Is it the content, the way the teacher presents the content, or Judy's individual needs that are most important? If you were her history teacher, how could you make the course more interesting to Judy? Are there students with needs/interests different from Judy's who might be "hurt" by these changes? If so, what types?

DESPONDENT DICK. Dick's face flushed. He desperately tried to recall what he was going to say next. His knees became weak and he was embarrassed. Finally, he said, "Ms. Townsend, I can't remember what I was going to say. I'd better stop." She said, "That's okay, Dick, but look at your notes, and after Jean answers the next proof I want you to explain yours." Later Dick gave an acceptable explanation. After the class Dick approached Ms. Townsend and said, "It's getting tougher and tougher for me in geometry. Everybody's so much better than I am. I feel like an idiot." If you were Ms. Townsend what would you say and do?

CHAPTER

Cognitive Viewpoints

CHAPTER OUTLINE

OBJECTIVES

When you have mastered the material in this chapter, you will be able to

1. Explain how attribution theory explains achievement motivation and the motivational tasks of teachers
2. Define *task-endogenous motivation* and explain its role in the classroom
3. Differentiate task-involvement from ego involvement and explain their roles in the classroom

4. Define *learned helplessness* and describe how teachers can cope with this problem
5. Explain deCharms' (1976) theory of personal causation and its applications
6. Discuss motivation from the standpoint of direction, persistence, continuing motivation, activity, and performance

This chapter on recent cognitive views of motivation begins with a discussion of attribution theory, currently one of the most popular theories for explaining classroom motivation. It then discusses recent motivational work that distinguishes between task and ego involvement in activities and between teacher- and student-controlled learning environments. Finally, the chapter discusses the relationship between students' perceptions of self-worth and their classroom motivation and describes a general theory that suggests ways to enhance students' perceptions of personal causation.

ATTRIBUTION THEORY

Attribution theory deals with perceived causes of success or failure in achievement situations, such as ability, effort, task difficulty, luck, or failure to use the right strategy for solving the problem. This is not an exhaustive list, but it does include the reasons typically offered to explain success and failure (Frieze, Francis, & Hanusa, 1983; Weiner, 1984).

The cognitive and behavioral aspects of task engagement as described within attribution theory are shown in Figure 15.1. In Stage 1 the student assesses the task and makes causal attributions (How difficult does the task appear? Will my performance on it depend on ability, effort, or luck?). Then the student estimates his or her probable level of success at the task and develops an affective anticipation: hope of success or fear of failure.

Causal factors

Causal factors vary in *stability*. Perception of one's own general ability tends to be stable over time, as do perceptions of the difficulty of tasks. However, there is more variation in the amount of effort put out and in the role of luck as a determinant of performance. Causal factors also vary in *controllability*. We cannot control luck, but we can control effort. Finally, causal factors vary in *internal versus external locus*. Ability and effort are internal to a person, whereas the task and its difficulty are external factors. A person brings to a task a given level of ability and may or may not put forth effort, but the nature of the task and luck (or the lack of it) are beyond the person's immediate control. Hence in addition to looking at these four possible determinants of performance, it

Figure 15.1 Cognitive and Behavioral Sequence in an Attributional Model of Achievement Behavior

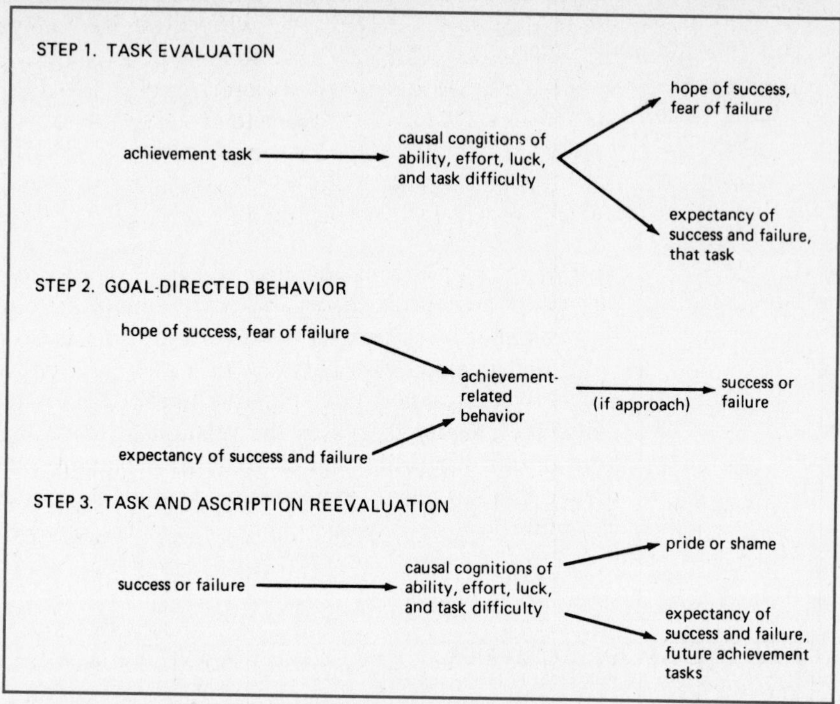

Source: From B. Weiner. *Theories of Motivation* (Boston: Houghton Mifflin Company, 1972), p. 355. Copyright © 1972 by Houghton Mifflin Company and reprinted by permission.

is possible to classify them on the basis of stability and locus of control as shown in Table 15.1.

Locus of control

The term *locus of control* refers to how individuals tend to explain their successes and failures. Those who perceive an external locus of control see their performance as caused by external factors (I succeeded because I was lucky; I failed because the teacher doesn't like me). Individuals with an internal locus of control feel that they are responsible for their successes and failures (I was successful because I'm bright; I succeeded because I worked hard; I failed because I didn't try).

Internality versus externality

Rotter (1966) and others have shown that changes in expectations for future success or failure are more frequent and pronounced in skill (in-

TABLE 15.1 DETERMINANTS OF ACHIEVEMENT BEHAVIOR

	Stability	
Locus of Control	**Stable**	**Unstable**
Internal	Ability	Effort
External	Task difficulty	Luck

ternal locus of control) than in chance (external locus of control) situations. Individuals with an internal locus of control prefer conditions where skill determines the outcome, whereas those with an external locus of control prefer chance conditions (Lefcourt, 1966). Because school achievement depends on development of knowledge and skill, students with an internal locus of control tend to get higher grades and achievement test scores (Crandall, Katkovsky, & Crandall, 1965), even when matched on IQ with external students (Messer, 1972), apparently because they spend more time in intellectual activity (Crandall, Katkovsky, & Preston, 1962).

It is important to stress that locus of control is a learned perception that can be altered, although change, especially in naturalistic settings, may not occur rapidly. Success or failure on one task usually will not produce major changes in perception of ability. In general, though, performance on a task affects one's beliefs about one's ability on that task and others like it. To the exent that performance is attributed to internal and stable characteristics (e.g., ability), similar performance will be expected in the future. To the extent that performance is attributed to external or unstable characteristics (e.g., level of effort or choice of strategy), one might expect a different outcome in the future.

Weiner: An Attribution Theory of Student Motivation

Weiner (1984, 1986), an influential theoriest in the attribution tradition, summarizes the salient characteristics of students high in achievement motivation as follows: (a) they prefer situations in which performance outcomes can be ascribed to their own actions, (b) they have learned to attribute outcome to effort, and (c) they notice and react to cues indicating the importance of effort expenditure.

Weiner's general framework of motivational influences is shown in Figure 15.2. He believes that a theory of student motivation that accurately reflects the complexity of classroom life must include three general principles (Weiner, 1984). First, it should incorporate the full range of *cog-*

Figure 15.2 Partial Representation of an Attributional Theory of Motivation

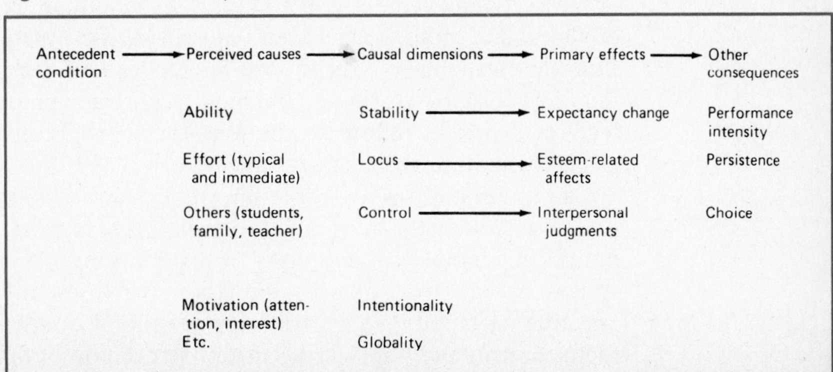

Source: B. Weiner (1979). "A theory of motivation for some classroom experiences." *Journal of Educational Psychology, 71,* p. 18. Copyright © 1979 by American Psychological Association.

nitive processes, including information search and retrieval, attention, memory, categorization, judgment, and decision making. The theory must emphasize the conscious thoughts that accompany mental events and behavior, particularly students' concern with self. Second, the theory should include the full range of *emotions.* Previous theories have tended only to involve the broad pleasure-pain principle and not to distinguish among emotions within these two categories. Third, the theory must use the same concepts to explain both *rational actions* (such as when students use strategies to deal with anxiety) and *nonrational actions* (such as when students attribute failure to bad luck when poor effort was the real cause).

Weiner (1984) asserted that the basic principle of attribution theory is that persons attempt to understand *why* events occur and to search for *causes.* He presented the following classification of causes.

Causal Dimensions of Weiner's Attribution Theory

Locus

The first dimension, *locus* of causality, distinguishes between causes located within a person, such as intelligence, effort, or physical attractiveness, and *external* causes like task difficulty or luck.

Constancy, stability, and globality

A second dimension, *constancy,* includes temporal stability and globality. Causes differ in their *stability* over time. Ability, for example, is perceived as relatively lasting, as opposed to effort, which can vary considerably within a short time. Thus outcomes perceived as due to ability predict performance in the future more accurately than outcomes ascribed to effort. *Globality* refers to the cross-situational generality of causes, which may be specific (failing a math test due to low math aptitude) or general (failing because of low intelligence).

Responsibility

A third dimension, *responsibility,* consists of *controllability* and *intentionality* and is strongly related to evaluative consequences of behavior. Controllability refers to how much control the actor has over his or her behavior. A person is assumed to have more control over effort than over ability, for example. Similarly, failure due to lack of effort is perceived as more intentional than failure due to improper choice of strategy.

Attributions and Affect

There are affective consequences to success or failure. Studies show that success at achievement-related activities results in happiness, regardless of the cause of success. Other, more specific attribution-emotion relationships are ability–sense of competence, long-term effort–relaxation, help from others–gratitude, and luck–surprise/happiness. Contrasting affective responses follow attributions for failure (e.g., low ability–humiliation; hindrance from others–anger).

Causal dimensions as determinants of emotions

Causal dimensions also are important determinants of emotions: pride or self-esteem stem from attribution of success to self, anger from attribution of failure to the actions of others, gratitude from attribution of success to help from others, guilt from attribution of failure to one's own negative traits, pity from attribution of others' troubles to factors beyond their control, and hopelessness from attribution of failure to stable, negative, internal factors.

Studies support an attribution–emotion–action sequence. For example, people are more likely to pity and subsequently to offer help to an indi-

Affect as a motivator of action

vidual who is in need because of factors they perceive to be beyond his or her control than a person they perceive as in need due to controllable factors. Research further shows that emotions rather than causal perceptions seem to be the immediate motivators of action.

Applying Attribution Theory

Attribution theory underscores the need for tasks that are of appropriate difficulty and for helping students to perceive the relationship between effort investment and performance outcome. Many students explain their successes or failures on the basis of habitual ways that they have learned to view their behavior, without noting the actual causal factors. They may say, "I failed because I am dumb," rather than "I failed because I got frustrated and gave up too easily." From an attribution-theory perspective, the teacher's role is to help such students develop the capacity to use feedback appropriately. We elaborate on this in Chapter 16.

Attribution retraining programs have been developed to improve discouraged students' achievement-related behavior by reducing their tendency to attribute failures to uncontrollable causes. Students who attribute their academic failures to low ability, for example, would be trained to attribute failure to internal, controllable causes such as insufficient effort or use of the wrong strategy.

TASK-INVOLVEMENT THEORY: NICHOLLS

Nicholls (1984) contrasted two psychological states associated with mastering a task. *Task involvement* is the desire to master a task primarily in order to develop one's ability. *Ego involvement* is the desire to demonstrate successful performance to oneself or others, preferably by achieving success without having to expend too much effort.

Ego involvement

Generally, the tendency to become ego involved in task performance increases in the presence of cues that heighten concerns about evaluation of one's ability. Thus when a teacher announces a test of important skills, students are likely to view their performance as reflecting their abilities, and ego involvement should be high. Nicholls cited several studies that support these predictions. Testlike or competitive conditions and public performance settings heighten ego involvement (Ames, Ames, & Felker, 1977). Furthermore, these same conditions increase external attributions and reduce intrinsic interest in the task (Deci et al., 1981; Ryan, 1982).

Nicholls (1984) predicted that *task-involved persons,* regardless of their self-perceptions of ability, will view tasks that appear to require moderate to high effort as offering them the best chance to perform well and demonstrate their ability. Consequently, they will prefer such tasks over tasks on which either success or failure seems certain, and they also will show higher effort on such moderately challenging tasks. In contrast, the task preferences and performance patterns of ego-involved persons will depend on how well they expect to perform in comparison with others. *Ego-involved persons who believe that their ability is low* (those who have given up the attempt to demonstrate high ability) will avoid moderately difficult tasks offering realistic challenges and will not perform well when required to work on such tasks because they believe that their best efforts will not be good enough. Instead, such individuals will tend to choose easy tasks, where effort will result in success. Those who have a low self-concept of ability but still desire to demonstrate high ability to others will choose extremely difficult tasks on which failure does not necessarily indicate lack of ability.

Ego-involved persons who believe that they have high ability are not threatened by ego-involving situations. They expect reasonable effort to result in success and thus expect to perform best on moderately difficult tasks. These persons also expect to do relatively well on difficult tasks, but they may relax their efforts on tasks that they perceive as easy and thus perform less well than they could. For these high-ability, ego-involved persons, easy tasks are not motivating because they do not offer the opportunity for them to demonstrate their abilities.

Applying Task-Involvement Theory

Butler (1987) applied task-involvement theory in an experiment on the effects of different teacher responses to the task performance of fifth and sixth graders. One group was given comments that related specifically to each student's performance and included both a reinforcing and a goal-setting component (''You thought of quite a few ideas; maybe it is possible to think of more different ideas''). A second group was given numerical grades without comments, a third group was given global praise (''very good''), and a fourth group received no evaluation or feedback. Data collected after three repetitions of this treatment indicated that the students who received individualized comments showed the most interest in the task, the highest levels of performance, and the most tendency to attribute their levels of effort, the quality of their performance, and the effect of the feedback to task-involved causes (interest, enjoyment, desire to improve). In contrast, students who had received either numerical grades or global praise without specific comments on their performance

Students should learn to use teacher feedback in assessing their efforts to complete a task successfully.

were more likely to make attributions to ego-involved causes (desire to do better than others, concern about proving one's ability). Such findings underscore the importance of teaching students to evaluate their performance in terms of personal effort and improvement over previous levels, including the use of individualized qualitative feedback that orients them toward task involvement. If left to follow their own inclinations, most students, and, ironically, low achievers in particular, concentrate on social comparison feedback and ego involvement rather than task involvement (Ruble & Flett, 1988).

Nicholls (1984) argued that the idea that task involvement is superior to ego involvement is supported not only by theory and research but also by a values position that holds that the purpose of education is to develop students' intellectual potential to the fullest extent. Thus if teachers can promote motivation for intellectual development in all students, they can achieve educational equity (Nicholls, 1979). In contrast, teachers who unnecessarily increase ego involvement will hinder the learning of students who are low in perceived ability.

One could, however, view the major purpose of education as preparing students for work in our capitalistic economic system, where self-worth and income depend on status, and thus could view ego-involving competitive classrooms more favorably. But even those who hold this view would not want lower-ability students to become too ego involved, and thus to give up on learning, until they had mastered basic skills.

PERSONAL CAUSATION THEORY: DECHARMS

DeCharms (1984) believes that the key to enhancing motivation involves adopting the view that the learner is an active *agent* who interacts with the environment. He defined *personal causation* as "doing something intentionally to produce a change" and *agency* as "the reasonable use of knowledge and habits (learned responses) to produce desirable changes" (p. 276). When agency is successful, a person causes a desired change and believes that he or she was the *origin* of it. When agency fails, the person does not cause the change (some other person or object has inhibited change), and the agent believes that he or she is a *pawn*. The result of a successful change is reinforcement and, in particular, enhancement of the person's sense of being able to act as an *origin* capable of effecting change through personal causation.

The concept of origin includes *choice,* which implies a degree of freedom but also responsibility that encourages the actor to feel *ownership* of behavior. However, an "origin-enhancing" classroom is *not* one in which students are allowed to do as they please; the terms *origin* and *pawn* are relative. DeCharms (1984) described a curvilinear relationship between classroom structure and pupil motivation; that is, an optimal level of structure is ideal, and both overstructured and understructured classrooms are likely to inhibit origin enhancement.

Two key aspects of classroom structure are number of *choices* students have and degree of *teacher dominance*. DeCharms noted that dominance and choice are negatively related and that two of these often have curvilinear relationships to a third variable (in this case, motivation).

Hidden cost of rewards

DeCharms (1968) referred to the negative effects of extrinsic rewards on intrinsic motivation as "the hidden costs of rewards." Thus if a person independently decides to behave in a specific manner but later finds that someone else values the behavior enough to reward it, the person may not continue to feel freedom, ownership, and choice. Instead, the person may begin to produce the behavior only to get the reward and to cease to do so when the reward is not being offered.

Research Evidence: The Carnegie Project

DeCharms and his colleagues tested these ideas in a large research program (the Carnegie Project) that began in 1967 with a four-year study in grades four through eight of low-income students whose sixth- and seventh-grade teachers were trained to use motivation-enhancing exercises focused on self-concept, achievement motivation, realistic goal setting, and the origin-pawn concept (deCharms, 1976). Activities related to each concept were emphasized for about 100 minutes per week for ten weeks.

Results on the origin-pawn variable were measured through coding of stories written by the students. Analyses showed that, compared to those of control students, the experimental groups's story characters more frequently set their own goals, determined their own activity, were more realistic, took more personal responsibility for their actions, and were more self-confident. The training significantly improved experimental students' achievement test scores in grades six and seven, reduced their absences and tardinesses, and increased their willingness to take moderate risks in a spelling game.

Characteristics of an Origin Classroom Observation showed that origin classrooms were neither laissez-faire (do anything you want) nor democratic (they required individual choices, not voting on common actions). Questionnaire data showed that the experimental students perceived their teachers as more encouraging of the origin behaviors mentioned previously.

Teacher Influence Cohen (1979) distinguished between two types of teacher influence attempts—*inviting* influence from pupils and *imposing* influence on pupils. After spending many hours on classroom training, a group of seventeen teachers used more inviting than imposing influence attempts compared to control teachers. Pupils of trained teachers showed significant changes in their influence attempts, with fewer "noise" attempts (disruptive attempts) and an increase in "expressive" (constructive) attempts.

Long-term Effects of Origin Training Jackson (1976) studied eleventh graders who had received origin training in the seventh grade. Using the origin–thought–sample measure and interviewing students about personal life goals and responsibility, he found that trained students still had significantly higher origin scores and also showed more career planning and responsible behaviors. Another follow-up study showed that more trained than untrained boys graduated from high school.

The Right Amount of Structure It is difficult to judge the correct amount of structure according to a generalized concept such as origin–pawn. Milak (1980) found that beginning brass-instrument players performed better under a teacher-structured approach than under an unstructured approach that offered them more autonomy. DeCharms speculated that the students who were exposed to the unstructured approach did not feel successful and thus did not feel personal causation because their behavior was not effective. The other students had enough structure to enhance success but not so much as to reduce their feelings of ownership.

Applying Personal Causation Theory

DeCharms stated that the most important way that teachers can enhance motivation is to believe that they themselves are origins and that all of their students can be origins too. Teachers can also establish the right amount of structure for the class and for individuals within it by allowing students some choices and by encouraging constructive influence attempts and independent activity.

Students should not be allowed too many or too few choices. They must understand the alternatives they can choose from, beginning with choices that are simple and short range. The choices also should be personal, if possible, and moderately challenging.

Anderson and associates (1988) provided evidence in support of these ideas in their study of the relationship between classroom task environments established by teachers and the task-related beliefs of their students. In this research, students were forced to feel more competent, to have a greater sense of control over outcomes, and to perceive more intrinsic value in academic tasks in classrooms in which the teachers both (a) structured expectations by providing information that made academic activities predictable and comprehensible and (b) provided frequent opportunities for students to regulate their own task activity.

SELF-WORTH THEORY: COVINGTON

Self-worth motive

Covington (1984) referred to a person's tendency to present a positive self-image as the *self-worth motive*. Research on the self-worth motive in achievement situations indicates that individuals tend to attribute their successes to themselves and their failures to external conditions.

In the classroom, the self-worth motive is reflected primarily in *self-perceptions of competence*. Students want to appear competent, so they want others to attribute their success to ability rather than effort (Nicholls, 1976). However, the competition that typifies most classrooms makes it possible for only a few students to achieve noteworthy success. Furthermore, this competition overemphasizes the role of ability in determining achievement (Ames & Ames, 1981), causing students who fail to feel inadequate. Thus most students are likely to develop strategies designed to avoid failure and save face.

Strategies to Avoid Failure

The most direct way to avoid failure is *not to participate*. Some students, for example, may avoid volunteering to answer questions in class or even "hide" from the teacher in an attempt to avoid being called on. When they are forced to participate, yet expect to fail, students may attempt to *blame failure on factors other than ability,* such as by setting unrealistically high goals, delaying work until the last minute, or expending little effort on a task. A third strategy to avoid failure involves *setting low goals* or selecting (when possible) simple tasks that are well below one's abilities. A student, for example, may announce that he or she will be satisfied with a grade of C. This strategy ensures "success," but because it is both empty and routinely experienced, such "success" loses its value as a reinforcer.

Failure-avoidance strategies

Ironically, all of these failure-avoidance strategies ultimately lead to failure, and students who use them are *failure prone*. According to Covington, the problem is not low ability but basing one's self-concept on achievement and setting unrealistically high standards for oneself. Some students develop failure-avoidance strategies early as a result of home experiences (Coopersmith, 1967), whereas others do so later as a result of competitive classroom environments.

The Role of Effort and Excuses

Failure dynamics

Student manipulation of effort expenditure is important in avoiding the threat of failure, because failure despite high effort implies low ability and results in shame. Covington and Beery (1976), for example, found that self-estimates of effort expenditure were low following failure. Furthermore, describing a task as very difficult improves the performance of persons who frequently worry about failure. This reduces the threat to self-esteem, because failure can be attributed to external causes rather than to one's skill deficiencies. Thus expending little effort in failure situations may preserve one's self-perceptions of ability. However, Covington, Spratt, and Omelich (1980) found that this failure-avoidance strat-

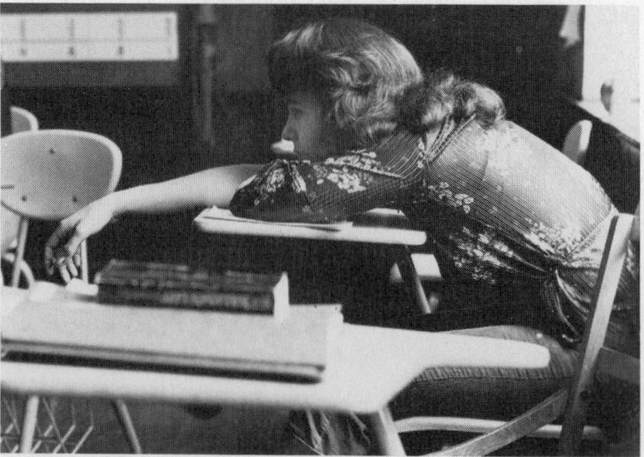

For some students, nonparticipation is a way to avoid embarrassment and failure.

egy also causes students to label themselves negatively (e.g., as unmotivated or lazy).

Success dynamics

Covington and Omelich (1979b) demonstrated that, at least under hypothetical conditions, increases in college students' perceived effort enhanced their pride in success and offset the negative effects of perceptions of low ability. Because successful performance increases self-perceptions of ability, there is little need for the self-protective reports of reduced effort that people often give in failure situations. Most students are willing to accept public acknowledgment of effort that leads to success, though some try to minimize the role of effort even when they are successful.

The desire to learn probably depends as much on the *certainty* of an individual's self-concept of ability and the degree of *discrepancy* between a positive, publicly projected image and a negative, privately held image, as it does on the *level* of self-concept. Thus as long as students are not convinced that they lack ability, they may respond well to praise and to achieving successes even if they tend to mask their efforts by using defensive tactics.

Reward and Punishment from Teachers

Although the primary determinant of teacher rewards is high achievement, teachers also reward effort (Blumenfeld et al., 1983; Eswara, 1972). Students whom teachers see as having tried hard are rewarded more for success and punished less for failure. This presents struggling students with a dilemma: high effort suggests low ability if they fail, but obvious lack of effort leads to punishment from the teacher. Covington and Omelich (1979b) thus characterized effort as a *double-edged sword* and studied the role of excuses as strategies for managing effort perceptions.

Covington and Omelich asked college students to state how teachers and they as students would respond to test failure that followed high effort, low effort with an excuse, or low effort without an excuse. Results showed that the students believed that teachers would punish those who failed without making an effort more than those who tried. Students and teachers had conflicting responses to effort. Teachers were least likely to punish in the failure under high-effort condition, for example, but students in this condition would feel the most incompetent and experience the most personal dissatisfaction and shame. Low effort would reduce these negative feelings but result in more punishment by the teacher, unless the student had a plausible excuse for the low effort. In the case of success, there was little conflict between teacher and student values.

Attributional Factors

Successful students tend to attribute their successes to skill and effort and their failures to lack of effort. Students who accept failure, however, attribute their successes to external factors such as luck and their failures to lack of ability (Ames, 1978). In its extremes, failure-acceptance results in *learned helplessness,* a condition in which people do not even try to reach a goal because they believe that their efforts cannot succeed (Abramson, Seligman, & Teasdale, 1978).

Learned helplessness

Demoralization

Little is known about the process by which frequent failure leads to demoralization, except that self-perceptions of low ability, effort, and the availability of excuses are critical factors. Covington and Omelich (1981) showed the role of these three factors in a study of repeated test-taking failures that occurred naturally among college students in a mastery-based psychology course. Students could take several similar forms of the same test and could study between tests to obtain what they considered an acceptable grade. However, many students never achieved a grade that was even minimally acceptable to them and thus experienced repeated failure. Such repeated failure lowered self-perceptions of ability, increased the tendency to attribute failure to lack of ability, and produced feelings of grief and hopelessness. This process occurred more rapidly for students who initially had low self-concepts; self-confident students tended to attribute their failures to external causes. Thus one factor mitigating against development of low self-perceptions of ability in response to failure is the availability of plausible external explanations. However, as failure becomes routine, it is harder to find plausible self-serving explanations, and one's public image becomes more like one's negative private one.

Applying Self-Worth Theory

Research points to the need for teachers to reduce competition and make it possible for all students to succeed, so that some do not have to concentrate on avoiding failure. Techniques such as absolute standards for excellence, self-competition, and cooperative learning are helpful in this regard.

Teachers should demonstrate to students that effort and outcome are strongly related. Students should be taught to divide a complex task into more manageable parts, for example, a process that may allow success without requiring them to set lower goals. It also helps if teachers emphasize reasons for failure that students can control: incorrect task analysis, overly high expectations, and low effort.

Effort-affect linkage

Teachers can promote positive effort-affect linkages by emphasizing the quality of effort and improvement over prior accomplishments when they evaluate student performance. If tasks are appropriate in difficulty, students will be able to achieve success by applying reasonable effort and to experience pride in their accomplishments.

Covington concluded that teachers must design curricula to promote both *self-validation* and *self-accuracy* in their students. Without devaluing the role of ability in achievement, teachers must ensure that students do not equate personal worth with ability or performance. Also, students must come to view ability not as a stable trait but as a repertoire of skills that increases continuously throughout their lives.

TOWARD A THEORY OF PERSONAL INVESTMENT: MAEHR

Maehr (1984) pointed out that teachers and students have other goals besides academic achievement. Some students, for example, may complete their homework only because their parents will not let them play until they do so, and some who are not motivated to achieve in school may practice very hard to make the basketball team. Maehr proposed a theory of personal investment designed to take a broader view of motivation by addressing other social motives besides the need for achievement.

According to Maehr (1984), past study of motivation has been concerned largely with internal processes such as attribution or competence. However, we make inferences about motivation on the basis of *observed behavior*. Most discussions of motivation in academic settings involve five overlapping aspects of behavior: direction, persistence, continuing motivation, activity, and performance.

Direction refers to the choices that individuals make between alternative behaviors when options are available. A student may decide to play tennis rather than study. *Persistence* is the attention given to a task over a period of time. *Continuing motivation* is the voluntary, self-initiated return (after an interruption) to a task that one has worked on previously. Teachers usually are eager to develop continuing motivation to engage in academic learning in their students. *Activity level* refers to the fact that some persons do more things than others. It is generally a less reliable indicator of motivation than direction, persistence, and continuing motivation. Finally, *performance* refers to the level of task success achieved. It is not a direct measure of motivation, but it is often the basis for inferences about motivation.

Using personal resources

To integrate these five aspects of behavior, Maehr used the concept of *personal investment,* the idea that one can observe the five aspects of behavior to determine how a person is investing his or her personal resources of time, talent, and energy. Maehr emphasized the distribution of these personal resources rather than their availability, so that his model stresses qualitative differences in motivation rather than its presence or absence.

Sources of Personal Investment

The Role of Meaning Maehr believes that the *meaning* of a situation to a person is the primary determinant of personal investment. Although a person may appear to an observer to have succeeded on a task, for example, the person may not feel that he or she has succeeded. People perceive success levels differently because they have varied standards for performance. Also, they may judge the value of a task differently (this may explain many cross-cultural differences in achievement motivation). People are more likely to feel successful when they achieve goals that they value than when they achieve other goals. One's social-cultural group(s) cause certain behaviors to be more acceptable or valued than others. Culture affects achievement by defining what success and failure mean (Maehr & Nicholls, 1980) and by specifying how one should seek success (Fyans et al., 1983).

Three basic, interrelated aspects of meaning determine personal investment in a particular situation: (1) beliefs about self, (2) perceived goals of behavior, and (3) action possibilities (perceived alternatives for pursuing these goals). Action possibilities are determined not only by what the person perceives as possible but also by what he or she views as appropriate in terms of sociocultural norms. Thus one may have recognized talent for learning to play the violin but may not be interested in doing so if this behavior is not encouraged by one's reference groups.

Beliefs about self

Subjective judgments of competence or ability to perform a task effectively are among the determinants of task choice. People tend to prefer tasks that enhance the development of their recognized talents and abilities (Kukla, 1978; Maehr, 1983; Nicholls, 1983).

Types of goals

Maehr focused on four goal possiblities: task, ego, social solidarity, and extrinsic rewards. *Task goals* involve attempts to master a task simply because one has become absorbed in the task or because one is trying to demonstrate competence to onseself. *Ego goals* involve trying to surpass a socially defined standard, especially relative to the performance of others. *Social solidarity goals* involve attempts to gain social approval (often by demonstrating good intentions rather than by showing competence). *Extrinsic rewards* refer to goals such as money, prizes, or grades that are not intrinsically related to the performance of a task.

Goals and behavior

Goals Affect Behavior Extrinsic rewards can control behavior in particular situations, but a task-goal orientation must be encouraged to develop the independent, self-initiated learning pattern that is the goal of many educators. If a student is interested primarily in performing a task rather than in how others evaluate that performance, he or she is likely to choose to perform it even when no one will evaluate the performance. In many classrooms, however, ego goals prevail.

Applying Personal Investment Theory

Challenge-seeking behavior

On the basis of Atkinson's theory and research, Maehr hypothesized how the four goal conditions might affect challenge-seeking behavior. Under task-goal conditions, all persons will show challenge-seeking patterns similar to those of persons with high achievement motivation. Under ego-goal conditions, however, self-perceptions of competence will mediate challenge seeking. Persons confident of their ability will seek challenge; those who lack confidence will avoid it. Motivation will be fairly high in the social solidarity condition and will not vary according to subjective probabilities of success or levels of challenge. In the extrinsic rewards condition, people will strive to maximize their rewards. Given a choice between an assured means of obtaining the reward and a less certain one, they will choose the certain one.

Antecedents of Meaning Maehr identified four antecedent factors that determine the meanings of activities: personal experience, the teaching-learning situation, information, and sociocultural factors. Individuals usually bring a set of meanings based on their past experiences to each new situation. Maehr used *meaning* to refer to an enduring personality characteristic (I can't do math). A student's sense of competence in a particular subject is affected by past successes and failures in that area.

Teaching-learning situations

Two important aspects of the teaching-learning situation that affect its meaning to the person are *social expectations* and *task design*. In the classroom, social expectations frequently take the form of peer expectations that pressure students to attempt certain goals and to behave in certain ways. People who are designated as leaders, for example, often show more achievement motivation than those who are given the role of followers.

Several features of a task can affect its meaning to a student. First, some tasks elicit intrinsic motivation because they offer ideal levels of uncertainty and unpredictability (Deci, 1975). The manner in which performance is evaluated can also affect motivation. External evaluation tends to reduce intrinsic interest, making students less likely to continue working on a task on their own. Another task feature is the amount of choice students are allowed. Choice promotes task goals, whereas external control promotes extrinsic goals.

Information

Information affects all aspects of meaning that determine personal investment but especially behavioral options. Vocational information, for example, can affect the choices that students make concerning career goals.

THE CONTRIBUTIONS OF DIFFERENT COGNITIVE VIEWS

The various cognitive views of motivation reviewed in this chapter may seem very similar, perhaps to the point of appearing to express the same theory in different terms. In one sense, this is true. All of these theories are concerned with the effects of subjective experience (beliefs about why one is engaging in a task in the first place, perceptions of the difficulty of the task, expectations concerning one's probable performance and the factors that will determine it, and expectations concerning the probable consequences of such performance) on task preference, goal setting, effort investment, and other aspects of task engagement. The theories all agree that motivation is optimized when people believe that they are engaging in tasks for their own reasons rather than in response to external pressure, when they see the task as moderately challenging but feel capable of succeeding on it if they invest reasonable effort, and when they engage in it with concentration on the task itself rather than concern about the quality of their performance or how it will be evaluated by others.

While sharing these and other common elements, each of the theories reviewed in the chapter has spawned uniquely useful concepts and research. Attribution theory focuses on students' posttask performance assessments and attributions, along with the effects of them on their emotions and on their motivation to engage in similar tasks in the future. Attribution theory underscores the importance of providing students with feedback in ways that help build or preserve their confidence that they can succeed on such tasks if they invest reasonable effort. Task-involvement theory focuses on students' subjective experience during task engagement. It underscores the need to present tasks to students as opportunities for them to develop knowledge or skills rather than as occasions for performance evaluation. Personal causation theory complements these themes by reminding us that student motivation is affected not only by the handling of individual tasks but also by the characteristics of the more general learning environment that the teacher establishes in the classroom. Self-worth theory focuses on the defense mechanisms that ego-involved students are likely to engage in when they do not achieve enough success. This theory helps teachers to understand the failure-avoidance strategies of such students and to respond to them in ways that communicate genuine encouragement and praise rather than misplaced sympathy or pity. Finally, personal investment theory reminds us that motives are socially learned constructs that can be developed or changed through systematic socialization and that it is important to understand students' existing motives as a starting place.

Summary

Cognitive explanations of motivation emphasize individuals' perceptions of events and the influences of these perceptions on behavior. Weiner discussed attribution theory and four perceived causes of success and failure—ability, effort, task difficulty, and luck—as explanations for achievement behavior. Weiner also discussed the role of affect in the motivational process.

Nicholls distinguished between mastering a task in order to acquire knowledge or skill (*task involvement*) and mastering a task to demonstrate ability in comparison to another person (*ego involvement*). He suggested that how students define tasks influences whether they select high- or low-risk tasks and how they interpret success or failure on those tasks.

DeCharms argued that teachers can enhance their students' motivation if they believe that those students can be origins who act on the environment and who plan and assume responsibility for success. "Origin-enhancing" classrooms do *not* allow students to do whatever they please but they do offer *choice,* which implies a degree of both freedom and responsibility and encourages students to feel *ownership* of behavior.

Cognitive theorists believe that individuals are motivated to present a positive self-image; Covington referred to this as the self-worth motive, which in the classroom is seen primarily in self-perceptions of academic competency. Some students develop strategies to avoid failure, such as nonparticipation, blaming failure on others, or ensuring success by attempting easy tasks that are ultimately self-defeating. Covington concluded that teachers must design curricula so as to promote both self-validation and self-accuracy in their students.

Maehr noted that students and teachers have other important goals besides academic achievement. Also, although recent motivational discussions emphasize internal processes such as attribution, Maehr contended that we make inferences about motivation on the basis of five aspects of behavior: direction, persistence, continuing motivation, activity, and performance. He stressed the need to structure classrooms so that students develop interest in academic activities during class and continuing motivation to learn more outside of class.

Questions and Problems

1. What difference does it make if students believe that their grades depend more on luck than on hard work? How might such a perception influence the way that they prepare for exams?
2. What are the major differences between achievement motivation theory (Chapter 14) and attribution theory (Chapter 15)?
3. Define *task involvement* and *ego involvement* in your own words. If you were introducing a new curriculum unit, what could you do to make it more likely that students would respond to it with task involvement?
4. Think about the course that you are now taking from the perspective of task and ego involvement. What percentage of the assignments creates task involvement in you? Why is this the case?
5. How would you characterize your coursework in college with regard to origin and pawn characteristics? Can a classroom involve too much decision making and too little teacher structure? What is the difference between a laissez-faire environment and one that is appropriately open ended?
6. Given that too much structure for one student may be too little structure for another, how can teachers apply theories of personal causation in the classroom?
7. What do you see as implications of research on strategies to avoid failure? How can a teacher reduce the likelihood that students will feel the need to employ such strategies?
8. How might you begin and end lessons to improve their motivational value?

Case Studies

MIDDLE OF THE ROAD. Clara Green is a tenth-grade speech teacher at a high school serving an upper-middle-class population in a small but affluent community that includes a state university. Clara's class is distinguished by infrequent disturbances but minimum student involvement. Students pay attention but do not seem interested in activities. Class periods usually involve three or four students presenting speeches, with each speech followed by a couple of minutes of critique. Types of speeches vary from month to month (e.g., a prepared sales speech, an expository speech).

The course is well organized, and Clara distributes examples of model speeches, reading lists, and evaluation sheets adapted to the different types of speeches that students give. The evaluation sheets emphasize speech format rather than content (e.g., Are all parts of the expository speech there? Is too much time spent on any one part? Is the delivery acceptable?). Few students in Clara's class dread giving their speeches or feel embarrassed about the feedback they get from other students, because she emphasizes that students should be positive and gracious in their responses. Accordingly, students often gush when they give feedback to classmates. In general, they view the course as easy and mildly interesting.

What types of students are most likely to benefit from this class? Why? How might Clara make the class more meaningful to other types of students?

PLAYING IT SAFE. Although Frank spends an hour and a half each night studying for Spanish class, he tells his friends that he never studies. Furthermore, he tries to get the teacher's attention early in the lesson because he wants to answer easy questions. When he takes part in the conversational part of the lesson (which he does only when called on), he is careful to use words that are easy to pronounce. How would you characterize Frank's problem? What, if anything, should his teacher do about it?

CHAPTER

Guidelines for Motivating Students

CHAPTER OUTLINE

OBJECTIVES

When you have mastered the material in this chapter, you will able to

1. List four motivational tasks teachers must perform and explain how they can accomplish these tasks by manipulating four classroom conditions
2. Explain the value that accommodating student interest and allowing choice in learning activities has for classroom motivation

3. Describe three ways to individualize instruction and motivate learning that do not require hiring additional teachers or aides
4. Discuss Keller's (1983) motivational model in terms of interest, relevance, expectancy, and satisfaction
5. Discuss Brophy's (1987) list of motivational strategies, especially those for increasing students' motivation to learn

Chapters 14 and 15 reviewed several prominent theories developed to explain why people initiate and maintain behavior. These theories provide rich input for teacher decision making concerning student motivation, but they do not translate directly into guidelines for practice. One reason is that students differ in their motivational systems, so what is ideal treatment for any particular student will not be optimal for the others. Also, much of the research on applications of motivational theories has involved studying single individuals for brief periods under tightly controlled laboratory conditions, whereas classrooms are crowded social settings in which groups who share a past history interact under much less controlled conditions.

MOTIVATIONAL TASKS FOR THE TEACHER

These differences do not mean that motivational theories lack classroom application, but they do mean that the theories cannot be interpreted literally and applied in oversimplified ways. Intrinsic-motivation theories, for example, are meant to predict behavior in free-choice situations, but students are required to attend school and learn a curriculum prescribed for them by someone else. Similarly, most students would take more risks takers in a casual ring-toss game where nothing much is at stake than in ego-involving classroom situations where their reputations for intellectual competence may be on the line.

The motivational challenge facing teachers involves going beyond eliciting student cooperation with requirements. If students are motivated solely by grades or other extrinsic rewards or punishments, they will concentrate merely on meeting minimal requirements. They will do what is necessary to prepare for tests but then will forget most of what they have learned. To get better results, teachers will need to use motivational strategies capable of eliciting a higher quality of student engagement in classroom activities—ideally, the self-regulated learning described by Corno and Rohrkemper (1985). Four important subtasks involved in the larger motivational task facing teachers are (a) structuring assignments, (b) maintaining task involvement, (c) maintaining motivation over the school year, and (d) building or enhancing students' capacity for self-evaluation.

Structuring Assignments

Although students spend a great deal of their time in classrooms working on academic tasks, such tasks have not received much research attention until recently, and the findings produced so far are not encouraging. A virtually universal finding of surveys on educational practices, for example, is that students appear to be spending too much time on isolated skills practice in the form of workbooks or worksheets emphasizing dull repetitions of primarily low-level activities. Students with low achievement motivation due to strong fear of failure may value such activities to the extent that they are both predictable and easy, but no students are likely to be genuinely enthusiastic about them. Most assignments could be much more interesting, varied in both format and cognitive level, and enjoyable than they are.

Even though assignments tend to be generally low in the cognitive level of response required of students, they vary in difficulty level and often are poorly matched to students' current needs. This will almost necessarily be true whenever teachers give everyone the same assignment. It may also be true to some extent even when teachers attempt to individualize by varying assignment difficulty levels, because teachers tend to underestimate the capabilities of their highest achievers and overestimate those of their lowest achievers (Bennett & Desforges, 1988).

Doyle's four parts of academic tasks

Doyle (1986b) defined academic tasks as consisting of four parts: (a) a product to be produced by the student (answers to questions, an essay, and so on); (b) operations to produce the product (remembering facts from previous instruction, looking up facts in a text, generating and organizing ideas, and so on); (c) resources (lecture notes, the text, and so on); and (d) the significance or weight of the task in the accountability system (how much it counts toward the final grades). Doyle believes that students tend to be highly concerned about their grades and thus motivated to ask questions and negotiate with teachers to minimize the degree of ambiguity (about exactly what must be done) and the degree of risk (of failure) that a task entails. This can lead to both a proliferation of guidelines about the form that responses should take (the composition should conclude at least 300 words, at least four paragraphs, a clear topic sentence for each paragraph, at least three reference sources, and so on), often with an accompanying reduction in the cognitive level of the task (what was supposed to be an opportunity for creative synthesis becomes a routinized exercise in fact telling), sometimes to the point that both teacher and students lose sight of the original academic purpose of the task and it becomes just one more thing to get done.

Task content and form in relation to involvement and achievement

Blumenfeld, Mergendoller, and Swarthout (1987) described other ways in which task form can submerge or defeat the academic purposes that tasks were designed to accomplish. They note that task form and content are independent, so that tasks can have simple forms while being cognitively complex (workbook pages featuring very difficult problems) and also can be cognitively simple but complex in form (scientific experiments that demand that many materials be used by several students but require the students only to record a simple observation and not to make any inferences or draw conclusions). Their research indicates that students often become confused when new or ambiguous tasks are introduced or when tasks are procedurally complex even though they may be cognitively simple. Unless teachers provide sufficient guidance in these situations, students may become overly focused on the procedural aspects of tasks so that they do not get the proper academic benefit from them (e.g., they may spend so much time gathering and preparing materials for a science experiment that they do not spend sufficient time actually carrying it out or thinking about the results). Blumenfeld and Meece (1988) found that students' cognitive engagement in tasks was low when tasks were procedurally complex, so it was important for teachers to counteract this by structuring and guiding the students' work, monitoring their task engagement, and making it clear that they expected the students to master the academic content that the task was designed to teach (not merely to participate in the procedural activities). Thus it is clear that student motivation and learning will be affected both by the nature of the assignments they are given and by the ways in which these assignments are structured by their teachers.

Students need tasks that are challenging but only moderately difficult given their ability levels. The context in which the students will work and their interest in the task can affect its difficulty level. Tasks need to be somewhat easier, for example, when students are to work independently than when they have access to immediate feedback.

Second, assignments should capture students' attention. Teachers should either choose topics that relate to students' interests or else try to create interest in the topic. Task interest can be ensured by allowing students to choose topics whenever possible. In this regard, teachers might have students provide a brief written explanation of the reasons for their choices. Such feedback might help the teacher and student, in time, to understand personal preferences and interests. Unfortunately, because of time restrictions, limited resources, or importance of content, it often is not feasible to provide choice.

Recess and relaxation are particularly welcome after a challenging assignment.

Another aspect of structuring assignments well is to be sure that their goals are clear. Otherwise, students may work hard but perform poorly on tests because they concentrate on the wrong material.

Maintaining Task Involvement during Seatwork

For some students, the hardest aspect of doing seatwork is getting started. Hence after releasing the students to begin work, teachers should monitor the class to see that everyone gets off to a good start.

Demanding attention to the task

Teachers can create conditions for maintaining involvement in several ways. They can demand attention to the task. If students are going to work for fifteen minutes on an assignment, the teacher might remind them that their work will be checked at the end of that period. Why should students begin work immediately if their work will not be checked until the next day or not at all?

Anderson (1984) examined what first graders do during seatwork and how they try to understand and complete assignments. Results showed that the students spent from 30 to 60 percent of the time allocated to reading instruction working on seatwork. Furthermore, an average of 50 percent, but in some classes virtually 100 percent, of seatwork assignments used commerical products such as workbooks, dittos, and reading materials, often all from the same basal series.

Within a given class, assignments were very similar across time, with the same forms often used two to five times a week (e.g., Read a sentence and then choose which of four pictures represents its meaning). In six of the eight classes, over half of the assignments were given to the whole class. Thus despite the fact that the students were assigned to different reading groups, they often had the same seatwork assignments.

Teacher Directions and Explanations Anderson found that teacher instruction related to seatwork assignments seldom included statements about what would be learned. When teachers monitored seatwork progress, they focused on students' behavior rather than their understanding of the content. For instance, teachers seldom discussed cognitive strategies for responding to the task when providing feedback; rather, their comments were usually procedural or focused on correctness of answers or neatness of work.

Classrooms require management, so these strategies are sometimes appropriate. Also, if students are working on familiar tasks and already possess the needed cognitive strategies (e.g., the purpose is to work on speed and fluency), the teacher does not need to say much about task purposes and strategies. Still, it seems likely that most students would benefit from more specific content-related explanations and feedback than the students in these classes received.

Seatwork for Low Achievers Anderson (1984) reported that low achievers often received overly difficult assignments and responded by using strategies that allowed them to derive answers and complete tasks without ever understanding what they were supposed to be learning. Such poor seatwork habits developed in first grade may contribute to development of a passive learning style. If they often work on assignments they do not understand, low achievers may come to belive that school work does not have to make sense and that they do not need to get help when it does not make sense.

Maintaining Motivation throughout the Year

Creating special events

All of us grow tired of doing the same thing day after day. One way to maintain interest is to schedule something occasionally that is both unexpected and pleasurable. Such special events can be related to academic goals. Students might prepare a classroom newspaper, for example, or construct a new learning center, or they might be assigned responsibilities that are fun and suited to their individual abilities and interests (e.g., writing a creative essay, interviewing peers, reporting sports results).

There are good reasons for making special events relevant to previous academic assignments. Once students complete a unit they often do not encounter the material again, so the use of previous learning in novel ways can encourage student motivation on daily assignments by helping students to see that the material they study will benefit them in the future. Knowing that the material will be used later encourages retention and integration.

If progress is to be made, much classroom work must involve hard work and persistence. Teachers need to expect this and to teach students how to mobilize their time and energy for extended periods. However, teachers also need to incorporate variety and occasional pauses into the classroom routine to reinvigorate student motivation throughout the entire school year. Athough the value of an instructional technique depends on its curriculum content and learning goals, *variety* in learning modes and assignments is useful for motivational purposes.

Building Student Self-Evaluation

Teachers can help students to develop their own academic interests and to evaluate their academic progress. However, younger students have limited capacity for such self-direction, and certain students of all ages have little interest in planning and evaluating their own learning, so teachers need to be aware of these limitations and try not to go too far too quickly.

Special events that allow students to demonstrate particular interests and abilities can often enhance motivation.

Benefits of feedback

Feedback can be used to help students set realistic goals and evaluate their performance objectively. Many students may find it difficult to evaluate their performance at first, but with training and specific focus, they can become better critics of their own work. Teachers can provide criteria for making evaluations (e.g., does each paragraph have a clear topic sentence?) and can help students to estimate how long it will take them to complete assignments and to identify the types of work that interest them.

TEACHER STRATEGIES OF INFLUENCE

Teachers can manipulate four major conditions in the classroom: the *tasks* students are assigned, *students' perceptions of these tasks*, their *rapport* with students, and the *reward structures* they introduce.

Teachers can manipulate task design features (content, difficulty, abstractness, length) as well as the settings in which tasks occur (whole class, small groups, individual) and the time allowed for completion. They also can alter the frequency of feedback, the type of feedback (conference, written), and the percentage of time students work on assigned or self-selected tasks. Many combinations are possible. Teachers can use student-selected assignments, for example, that are not related to student interests and teacher-assigned tasks that are or vice versa. The point is that teachers who match learning tasks to students' cognitive abilities and interest levels have taken a major step in establishing the conditions necessary for learning.

Matching tasks to cognitive abilities and interest levels

Teachers can also manipulate students' perceptions of tasks. Here the task remains constant, but the teacher shapes the students' attitudes toward it through modeling of attitudes and communication of expectations.

Teacher's relationship to students

Teachers also motivate through their rapport with students. It helps if teachers develop personal relationships with students, especially those who are suspicious of adults, so as to position themselves to motivate through encouragement and reinforcement. In the long run, teachers' informal evaluations probably affect student behavior as much as formal grades.

Reward mechanism

A fourth major way of viewing the teacher's motivational role is through the reward mechanisms established in the classroom. Can all students be successful, or does the way in which assignments are structured and evaluated guarantee that some students will succeed at the expense of others? Teachers who set high standards and individual goals are mainly helping those students who are ready to compete and are maximizing student mastery of cognitive material. Teachers who place students in groups, grade group performance, and reward effort are mainly helping students who are less able to compete and are maximizing prosocial and general affective growth.

In practice, it is difficult to separate these sources of influence. The teacher who manipulates task design by allowing students to work together, for example, may affect the reward structure as well. However, it is helpful for teachers to consider all types of influence, because this may help them to plan a variety of motivational strategies (not just, for example, curriculum changes or talks with students).

In the remainder of this chapter we discuss several specific recommendations made by educators and psychologists as ways teachers can enhance motivation. Potential problems in applying these methods are also discussed.

STUDENT CHOICE IN ASSIGNMENTS

Many instructional goals involve the acquisition and use of processes, rather than the learning of specific content. Usually, there is no single way to learn the processes most efficiently, so the teacher has the opportunity to provide students with equally appropriate options. The value of providing students with such choices depends on the developmental levels of the students, the reward structure associated with the task, the general climate of cooperation-competition in the classroom, the extent to which students have been prepared to make choices, and the nature of the task itself.

Relationship of student choice to learning

If used appropriately, choice allows students a chance to satisfy personal interests while completing learning tasks. In addition, there is reason to believe that students in classrooms that allow opportunity for choice are more likely to believe that they, not the teacher or other external forces, are responsible for their own learning (Ames & Ames, 1984; deCharms, 1984).

Providing choices is also a way for teachers to express their trust in students and the positive expectation that students can design and control many aspects of their educational lives. However, even this process can go too far. Some high schools, for example, have allowed students to drop a course any day before taking the final exam. We think that such a policy communicates the attitude that the school staff does not care about student learning. Student choice should be combined with real commitments to learning.

Also, some students will need help in making choices. Those who see themselves as pawns and have external attributions concerning success or failure, for example, may not make good choices unless guided to accept levels of challenge matched to their current abilities. Such students need attention to their underlying motivational dispositions at least as much as they need opportunities for choice.

OPPORTUNITIES FOR INDIVIDUALIZATION AND TEACHER-STUDENT CONTACT

Teachers need to interact individually with students to assess their interests and needs and help them adjust their expectations appropriately. How can teachers find the time to do this? We now discuss instructional techniques that not only motivate students but also provide teachers with time for conferences with individuals.

Learning Centers

Teachers can make time to meet with individuals or small groups through the effective use of independent learning assignments—work done at a special place in the room, such as a learning center. Such assignments provide for student choices and interests and for individualizing certain aspects of instruction. They also function as a backup system when students finish their work. Teachers might set up one or two activity centers where students complete assigned tasks on a predetermined schedule or to which students can go when they finish other assignments.

Many types of assignments might be used at a learning center. Some involve elaborate equipment, whereas other equally useful assignments do not need concrete materials. Older students can even help prepare their own learning stations. Figures 16.1 and 16.2 illustrate different activities that could be used.

Use of the classroom as a laboratory for active involvement of students in "hands-on" experience has become a popular technique. Students actually measure and construct rather than deal only with paper-and-pencil problems at learning stations equipped with sufficient manipulable equipment to accommodate a few students and allow them to perform or experiment directly. Relatively complex assignments can be set up at such learning stations that would be impossible to set up at each student's desk. If not overused, such activities add variety and may spark student interest. At the high school level, work stations allow students who need to perform manipulations at the level of concrete operations to learn the abstract concepts being taught.

Microcomputer Use

Assignments to be done using microcomputers provide another way to structure more time for teachers to interact with individuals or small groups. Everything just mentioned about learning stations can be accomplished with microcomputers. Also, besides facilitating the cognitive learning of individual students, microcomputers can be used to facilitate social interactions in small-group assignments on topics such as learning computer programming (Webb, 1984) or writing a story or working on classroom newsletters, polls, and so on (Rubin, 1982).

Peer Tutoring

Peer tutoring can be a useful strategy for helping the teacher individualize instruction, motivating student behavior, and allowing students to become responsible for assisting other students. Both the student who receives help and the student who provides it can benefit (see Good & Brophy, 1987).

Added gains for tutors

Tutors often gain as much as the students being tutored. The extra review of material they teach and the additional practice they get while tutoring are likely to increase their own knowledge or skills. Furthermore, when students are trained for their roles, they are more likely to be effective. Thus if the tutoring focuses on cognitive skills that are important rather than on exercises that just kill time, and if the tutor and the one

Figure 16.1 A Card from *Project Mathematics Activity Kit, K-3*

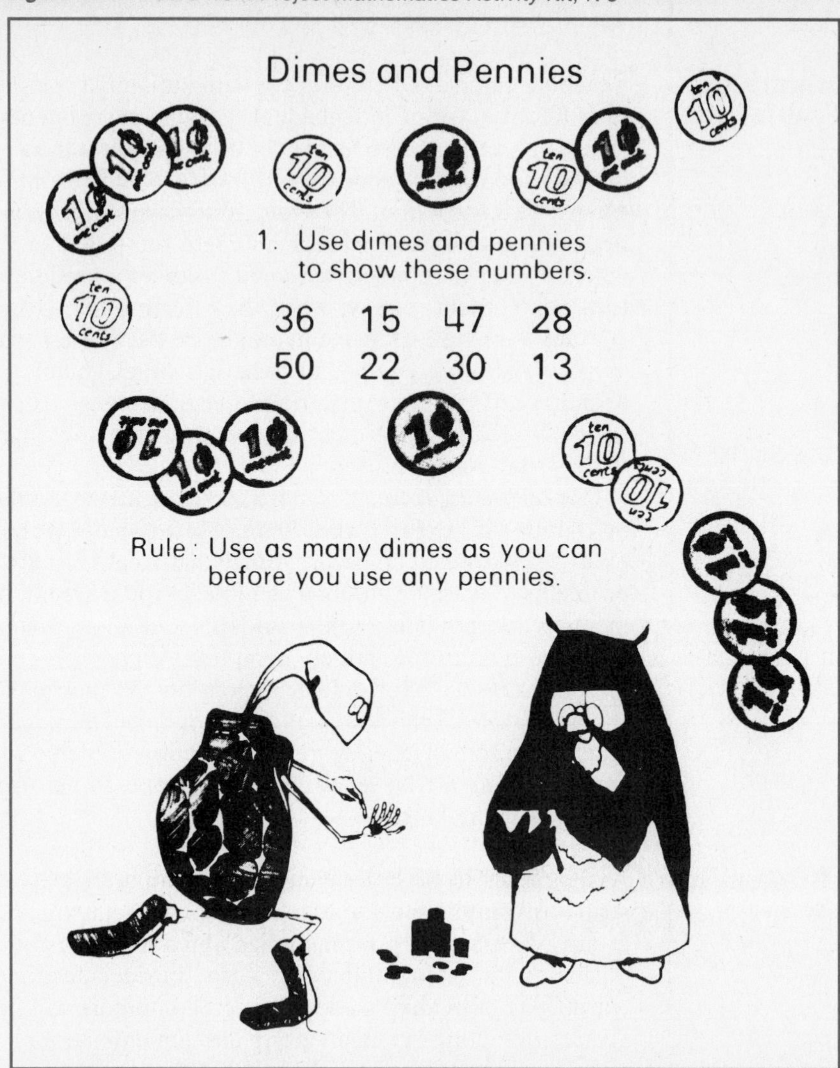

Dimes and Pennies
1. Use dimes and pennies
to show these numbers.
36 15 47 28
50 22 30 13
Rule: Use as many dimes as you can
before you use any pennies.

Source: Project Mathematics Activity Kit, K-3. Copyright © by Holt, Rinehart and Winston of Canada, Ltd.

being tutored know and understand their roles (e.g., if the teacher has role played tutoring techniques in the classroom), tutoring can be a valuable instructional and motivational aid.

Tutoring styles

Under certain conditions, student tutors may even be more effective than an actual teacher or adult aide: when direct instruction is called for, when a simple vocabulary is sufficient, and when students remember their own difficulties and can use those experiences in the teaching situation. Thomas (1970) examined the behavior of fifth- and sixth-grade tutors and college tutors who were all tutoring second graders in reading. The elementary age tutors were generally direct and businesslike. They accepted

Figure 16.2 Examples of Series and Parallel Activities

Mathematical Topic—Multiplication

Progressive Interpretations of Multiplication

I Union of Equivalent Disjoint Sets

II Cartesian Product

III Algorithmic

Series and Parallel arrangements within the above interpretations.

I. Ia Join 3 sets of 2 buttons each

Ib Equal jumps on number line i.e. 0 2 4 6

Ic Rectangular arrays i.e. 3 by 2 array depicted as
$$\begin{cases} 0 & 0 \\ 0 & 0 \\ 0 & 0 \end{cases}$$

Id If 3 persons each have 2 shoes, how many shoes in all?

II. IIa Problem: I have 3 kinds of ice cream (vanilla, chocolate, strawberry) and 2 kinds of topping (Pistachio and Blueberry). If a sundae is made of 1 kind of ice cream and 1 kind of topping, how many different kinds of sundaes can I make?

IIb If Nicole has 3 blouses and 2 skirts how many blouse-skirt combinations can she make?

IIc How many ways can I pair a letter with a number using the following sets: Set A = (a,b,c); Set B = (1,2).

IId If Set A has 3 members and Set B has 2 members, how many elements are there in AXB? (AXB is the symbol used to denote the Cartesian Product of Set A and Set B.)

III. IIIa $3 \cdot 17$ interpreted as
$$\begin{array}{r} 10 + 7 \\ 3 \\ \hline 30 + 21 \end{array} = 51$$

IIIb* $3 \cdot 7$ interpreted as $3(10 + 7) = 3 \cdot 10 + 3 \cdot 7 = 30 + 21 = 51$

IIIc $3 \cdot 17$ interpreted as
$$\begin{array}{r} 17 \\ 3 \\ \hline 21 \\ 30 \\ \hline 51 \end{array}$$

IIId $3 \cdot 17$ interpreted as
$$\begin{array}{r} 17 \\ 3 \\ \hline 51 \end{array}$$

Source: R. Reys and T. Post. *The Mathematics Laboratory: Theory to Practice* (Boston: Prindle, Weber, and Schmidt, 1973). Reprinted by permission of the authors.

Peer tutoring increases motivation and provides benefits for students giving and receiving help.

the fact that the younger students were having problems and used the time to help them. The college students were much less direct. They felt that it was necessary to get children to like them and the story.

Strategies such as peer tutoring and learning stations are helpful in part because they bring variety and the opportunity to meet different needs to the classroom. However, they are also useful because they free the teacher to talk to students. If teachers are to create task involvement rather than ego involvement (Nicholls, 1984), they will need time to talk to students and to understand their perspectives.

KELLER'S PRINCIPLES FOR MOTIVATIONAL DESIGN OF INSTRUCTION

Keller (1983) synthesized many theories of motivation to form a model for application that features four major dimensions: (1) *interest*, or the extent to which the learner's curiosity is aroused and sustained over time; (2) *relevance*, or the learner's perception that instruction is related to personal needs or goals; (3) *expectancy*, or the learner's perceived likelihood of achieving success through personal control; and (4) *satisfaction*, which refers to the learner's intrinsic motivations and responses to extrinsic rewards. Keller's model is a valuable heuristic for thinking about the design of instruction in classrooms.

Interest

Keller presented the following five strategies for stimulating and maintaining student interest and curiosity in lessons:

1. Use novel, incongruous, conflictual, or paradoxical events. Attention is aroused when there is an abrupt change in the status quo.
2. Use anecdotes and other devices to inject a personal, emotional element into otherwise purely intellectual or procedural material.

3. Give students the opportunity to learn more about things they already know about, but also give them moderate doses of the unfamiliar.
4. Use analogies to make the strange familiar and the familiar strange.
5. Guide students into a process of question generation and inquiry.

Conflict in strategies

On the surface, some of these strategies seem to conflict. For example, Strategy 1 encourages teachers to use novel situations, but Strategy 3 encourages them to give individuals the opportunity to learn about things that they are already interested in. Obviously, people want to learn more about things that they are already interested in; this is why they join clubs, attend dinners with friends more than strangers, and so forth. As Keller noted, however, the inclusion of unusual or exotic material from time to time can help initiate or maintain curiosity. If a student is already interested in a topic, the teacher's attempts to create such interest may be counterproductive. In general, though, Keller assumed that students are more likely to be understimulated than overstimulated.

Relevance

Keller argued that personal motivation will increase when individuals perceive that an instructional task will satisfy basic motives such as needs for achievement, power, or affiliation. Keller's strategies for increasing personal motivation call for (1) enhancing achievement striving by providing opportunities to achieve standards of exellence under conditions of moderate risk; (2) making instruction responsive to the power motive by providing opportunities for choice, responsibility, and interpersonal influence; and (3) satisfying the need for affiliation by establishing trust and providing opportunities for no-risk, cooperative interaction.

Strategies

It is important to realize that these three objectives cannot be met simultaneously. Keller's first set of strategies responds to the need for achievement, where moderate levels of competition and individual contracting may be most appropriate. The second set of strategies is related to helping individuals fulfill power needs. It is important to give students positions of genuine authority and assign activities that allow them to satisfy power needs, such as debates or argumentative essays. The third set of strategies would help students to initiate and maintain close working relationships with peers during cooperative activities (see Chapter 18 for an extended discussion of cooperative learning).

Expectancy

Keller offered four strategies for increasing expectancy for success: (1) increase experiences with success (on meaningful tasks—not on trivial or easy tasks), (2) be clear about requirements for success, (3) use techniques that offer personal control over success, and (4) use attributional feedback and other devices that help students relate success to personal effort and ability. We will say more about teacher expectations for student performance in Chapter 17.

Outcomes

Outcomes refer to the satisfaction of goal accomplishment and its effects on motivation for performing similar tasks in the future. Keller suggested several strategies for increasing the appropriateness of outcomes for maintaining intrinsic satisfaction with instruction. His chief recommendations are to use task-endogenous rather than task-exogenous rewards and to use verbal praise and informative feedback rather than threats, surveillance, or external performance evaluation.

BROPHY'S LIST OF MOTIVATION STRATEGIES

Preconditions and motivational strategies

Brophy (1987) reviewed the literature on motivation in the classroom and synthesized its implications for teachers by identifying four essential preconditions and compiling a list of motivational strategies organized into a framework suggested by the expectancy *x* value model of motivation (see Table 16.1). The framework was developed in part as a learning aid that structures the list of strategies by categorizing them according to their intended effects on students. Another purpose, however, was to call attention to the need for teachers to stimulate their students' *motivation to learn*, which is defined as student engagement in an activity that is guided by the intention of acquiring the knowledge or mastering the skill that the activity is designed to teach.

The framework serves as a reminder that even if the four essential preconditions are met and even if students believe that they can achieve success on a task if they invest reasonable effort, they probably will not be motivated to learn the knowledge or skill that the task is designed to teach unless the teacher uses one or more of the strategies designed to stimulate such motivation to learn. Strategies for capitalizing on students' existing intrinsic motivation may cause the students to enjoy the activity, and strategies for controlling their behavior by supplying extrinsic motivation may cause the students to do what they see as necessary to meet minimal demands, but more will be required to stimulate student motivation to learn.

Essential Preconditions

The framework begins with identification of basic assumptions and preconditions that underlie the effective use of any motivational strategies in the classroom. *No motivational strategies can work effectively if these assumptions and preconditions are not in effect.*

Supportive environment

Supportive Environment Anxious or alienated students are unlikely to develop motivation to learn academic content. Nor is such motivation likely to develop in a chaotic classroom. Thus we assume the teacher (a) is a patient, encouraging person who makes students feel comfortable during academic activities and supports their learning efforts and (b) uses classroom organization and management skills to establish the classroom as an effective learning environment. The classroom atmosphere is businesslike but relaxed and supportive. Students feel comfortable taking intellectual risks because they know that the teacher will not embarrass or criticize them if they make a mistake.

TABLE 16.1 BROPHY'S FRAMEWORK FOR CLASSIFYING MOTIVATIONAL STRATEGIES

A. Essential Preconditions
   1. Supportive environment
   2. Appropriate level of challenge/difficulty
   3. Meaningful learning objectives
   4. Moderation/optimal use of strategies

B. Motivating by Maintaining Success Expectations
   5. Program for success
   6. Teach goal setting, performance appraisal, and self-reinforcement
   7. Provide remedial socialization for discouraged students
      a. Portray effort as investment rather than risk
      b. Portray skill development as incremental and domain specific
      c. Focus on mastery
      d. Provide attribution retraining
      e. Minimize test anxiety

C. Motivating by Supplying Extrinsic Incentives
   8. Offer rewards as incentives for good (or improved) performance
   9. Structure appropriate competition
   10. Call attention to the instrumental value of academic activities

D. Motivating by Capitalizing on Students' Existing Intrinsic Motivation
   11. Adapt tasks to students' interests
      a. Incorporate content that students find interesting or activities that they find enjoyable
      b. Offer choices of alternative tasks or opportunities to exercise autonomy in selecting among alternative ways to meet requirements
      c. Encourage student comments and questions
      d. Include divergent questions and opportunities for students to express opinions or make other responses to the content
   12. Plan for novelty and variety
   13. Provide opportunities to respond actively
   14. Provide immediate feedback to student responses
   15. Allow students to create finished products
   16. Incorporate "fun features" into academic activities
      a. Fantasy or imagination elements
      b. Simulation exercises
      c. Gamelike features
      d. Peer interaction opportunities

E. Strategies for Stimulating Student Motivation to Learn
   17. Model interest in learning and motivation to learn
   18. Communicate desirable expectations and attributions about students' motivation to learn
   19. Minimize students' performance anxiety during learning activities
   20. Project intensity
   21. Project enthusiasm
   22. Induce task interest or appreciation
   23. Induce curiosity or suspense
   24. Induce dissonance or cognitive conflict
   25. Make abstract content more personal, concrete, or familiar
   26. Induce students to generate their own motivation to learn
   27. State learning objectives and provide advance organizers
   28. Model task-related thinking and problem solving

Appropriate Level of Challenge/ Difficulty

Activities must be of an appropriate difficulty level for the students. If the task is so familiar or easy that it constitutes nothing more than busy work, and especially if it is so unfamiliar or difficult that the students cannot succeed in it even if they apply reasonable effort, no strategies to induce student motivation to learn are likely to succeed. Tasks are of appropriate difficulty level when students are clear enough about what to do and how to do it so that they can achieve high levels of success if they apply reasonable effort.

Meaningful learning objectives

Meaningful Learning Objectives We cannot expect students to be motivated to learn if we present them with pointless or meaningless activities. Therefore, we assume that activities have been selected with worthwhile academic objectives in mind; that is, they *teach some knowledge or skill that is worth learning*, either in its own right or as a step toward some larger objective. The following activities will *not* meet this criterion: continued practice on skills already mastered thoroughly, memorizing lists for no good reason, looking up and copying definitions of terms that are never used meaningfully in readings or assignments, reading material that is too vague or sketchy to allow the students to develop a concrete and visualizable understanding of its content, reading about things that are described in such technical or abstract language as to make the material essentially meaningless, and working on tasks assigned merely to fill time.

Moderation/Optimal Use Strategies used too often or too routinely may lose their effectiveness, and any particular use of a strategy can become counterproductive if it goes on too long or gets carried to extremes. Also, different activities will call for different motivational strategies. When content is relatively unfamiliar and its value or meaningfulness is not obvious to students, significant motivational effort involving several of the strategies described here may be needed. In contrast, little or no special motivational effort may be needed when the task involves something that students are already eager to learn.

Motivating by Maintaining Success Expectations

Achievement motivation

Efficacy perceptions and causal attributions

Much of the best known research on motivation has focused on the role of success expectations in determining performance. Research on *achievement motivation* (Dweck & Elliott, 1983) has established that effort and persistence are greater in individuals who set goals of moderate difficulty level (neither too hard nor too easy), who seriously commit themselves to pursuing these goals rather than treating them as mere pie-in-the-sky hopes, and who concentrate on trying to achieve success rather than on trying to avoid failure. Research on *efficacy perceptions* (Bandura, 1982; Bandura & Schunk, 1981; Schunk, 1985; Schunk & Hanson, 1985; Weisz & Cameron, 1985) has shown that effort and persistence are greater in individuals who perceive that they are capable of performing the task successfully. Research on *causal attributions* for performance suggests that effort and persistence are greater in individuals who attribute their performance to internal and controllable causes rather than to external and uncontrollable causes (Weiner, 1984, 1986). In particular, better performance is associated with a tendency to attribute success to a combination of sufficient ability with reasonable effort and a tendency to attribute failure either to insufficient effort (if this has been the case) or to confusion about what to do or reliance on an inappropriate strategy for trying to do it (Butkowsky & Willows, 1980; Frieze, Francis & Hanusa, 1983; Whitley & Frieze, 1985).

Several strategies have been suggested for helping students to maintain expectations for success and the desirable goal-setting behaviors, efficacy perceptions, and causal attributions that are associated with such success expectations. All of these strategies assume that students are given tasks of appropriate difficulty level and receive timely and informative feedback that is specific about the correctness of their responses and about the progress they are making toward ultimate objectives. In short, these strategies involve helping students to make and recognize genuine progress, rather than misleading them or offering them only empty reassurances.

Program for Success The simplest way to ensure that students expect success is to make sure that they achieve success consistently by beginning at their level, moving in small steps and preparing them sufficiently for each new step so that they can adjust to it without much confusion or frustration. Two points need to be made about this strategy to ensure that it is not understood as suggesting that teachers should mostly assign unchallenging busy work.

Success through mastery learning

First, we speak here of success achieved through reasonable effort that leads to gradual mastery of appropriately challenging objectives, not to quick, easy success achieved through ''automatic'' application of overlearned skills to overly familiar tasks. It is true that certain basic knowledge and skills must be practiced until mastered to a level of smooth, errorless performance, but it is also true that students should be paced through the curriculum as briskly as they can progress without undue frustration. Thus programming for success must be seen as a means toward the end of maximizing students' achievement and not as an end in itself.

Role of teacher in student success

Second, keep in mind the role of the teacher. Levels of success that students can achieve on a particular task depend not only on the difficulty of the task itself but also on the degree to which the teacher prepares them for the task through advance instruction and assists their learning efforts through guidance and feedback. Help in making sure that students know what to do and how to do it is an important factor in determining whether they will succeed.

It can be difficult to program low achievers for success, especially in heterogeneous classrooms. You can help by providing extra instruction and assistance and by monitoring their progress more frequently. Give them briefer or easier assignments if they cannot succeed even with extra help and support, but continue to demand that they put forth reasonable effort and progress as briskly as their abilities will allow. If necessary, divide the class into subgroups that receive differentiated instruction and assignments, and grade according to mastery learning procedures that do not penalize slower students for the extra time that they take to achieve mastery (Levine, 1985) or according to criteria specified in individualized performance contracts.

When grades must be assigned according to fixed common standards, you may need to help low achievers learn to take satisfaction in receiving B's or even C's when such grades represent successful performance based on reasonable effort. For some lower achievers, achieving a grade of C is an occasion for taking pride in a job well done. When this is the case, teachers should express to these students (and to their parents as well) their recognition of the accomplishment and their appreciation of the effort that it represents.

Regardless of the range of achievement levels in a class, conditions should be arranged so that every student who consistently puts forth reasonable effort can earn at least a grade of C. When this is not the case, neither motivation nor achievement will be fostered effectively.

Teach Goal Setting, Performance Appraisal, and Self-Reinforcement Help your students to identify and use appropriate standards to judge their progress. This begins with *goal setting*, which is especially effective when the goals are *proximal*, *specific*, and *challenging*.

Goal setting is not enough by itself; there must also be *goal commitment*. Students must take goals seriously and commit themselves to trying to reach them. It may be necessary to negotiate appropriate goals with some students, or at least to provide them with guidance and to stimulate them to think about their performance potential. When an ultimate or cumulative level of performance that would earn a grade of A is not a realistic goal, help students to identify and commit themselves to realistic goals that, if reached, would yield grades of B or C (rather than to verbalize unrealistically high goals that they are not really committed to). One way to do this is to provide a menu of potential goals (graduated in terms of the levels of effort that would be required to meet them and the grades that would be earned if success was achieved) and then ask students to commit themselves to particular goals and associated levels of effort.

Setting appropriate standards for goals

Finally, students may need help in assessing progress toward established goals by using *appropriate standards for judging levels of success*. In particular, they may need to learn to compare their work with absolute standards (progress toward achieving an objectively specified level of success) or with their own previous performance levels (improvement over time) rather than to judge only by comparing their work with that of peers. You can help by providing accurate but encouraging feedback. That is, your feedback about specific responses must be accurate (errors must be labeled as such if they are to be recognized and corrected), but your more general evaluative comments should provide encouragement by noting levels of success achieved in meeting established goals or by judging accomplishments with reference to what is reasonable to expect (rather than with reference to absolute perfection or to the performance of peers). When performance is unsatisfactory, provide remedial instruction and additional opportunities for improvement, along with continued encouragement that realistic goals will be achieved if the student continues to put forth reasonable effort.

Some students will need *specific, detailed feedback* concerning both the strengths and the weaknesses of their performance (Elawar & Corno, 1985). These students may have only vague appreciation of when and why they have done well or poorly, so they may need not only general evaluative feedback but also concepts and terms that they can use to describe their performance and evaluate it with precision. This is especially true for compositions, research projects, laboratory experiments, and other complex activities that are evaluated using general qualitative criteria rather than by scoring answers to specific questions as correct or incorrect. Rather than just assigning letter grades, provide your students with detailed feedback about their performance in such activities (concerning compositions, for example, comment on the relevance, accuracy, and completeness of the content; the general organization and structuring of the content into a composition with a coherent, beginning, middle, and end; the sequencing of the content and subdivision into appropriate paragraphs; the structuring of paragraphs to feature main ideas; the variety and appropriateness of sentence structures and vocabulary for communicating the content; and the mechanics of grammar, spelling, and punctuation).

Students who have been working toward specific proximal goals and who have the necessary concepts and language with which to evaluate their performance accurately will be in positions to *reinforce themselves* for the success that they achieve. Many students will do this habitually, but others will need encouragement to check their work and take credit for their successes (that is, to attribute their successes to the fact that they had the ability and were willing to make the effort required to attain success). If necessary, you can focus students' attention on their progress more directly by comparing their current accomplishments with performance samples from earlier points in time or by having the students keep scrapbooks, graphs, or other records to document their progress.

Provide Remedial Socialization for Discouraged Students Some students with long histories of failure will tend to give up at the first sign of difficulty and will need more intensive and individualized motivational encouragement than the rest of the class. These students are likely to benefit from the strategies used in mastery learning approaches: Program for success by giving them tasks that they should be able to handle, provide them not only with the usual group instruction but also with individualized tutoring as needed, and allow them to contract for particular levels of performance and to continue to study, practice, and take tests until that level of performance is achieved. By virtually guaranteeing success, this approach builds confidence and increases discouraged students' willingness to take the risks involved in committing themselves seriously to challenging goals (Grabe, 1985).

Effort as investment

You can also help by working to improve these students' beliefs, attitudes, and expectations about learning. One way is to *portray effort as investment rather than risk*. Help discouraged students to appreciate that learning may take time and involve confusion or mistakes but that persistence and careful work should eventually yield knowledge or skill mastery. Furthermore, such mastery not only represents success on the particular task involved but also "empowers" the students by arming them with knowledge or skills that will make them that much more capable of handling higher-level tasks in the future. If they give up on tasks that they could master if they persisted, they cheat themselves out of such growth potential.

Skill development is incremental and domain-specific

It also helps to *portray skill development as incremental and domain-specific*. Make sure that your students realize that their intellectual abilities are open to improvement, rather than fixed and limited, that they possess many such abilities rather than just a few, and that their success depends not only on general ability but also on possession and use of a great range of specific knowledge and strategies built up gradually through many experiences in each domain. Difficulty in learning mathematics does not necessarily imply difficulty in learning other subject-matter areas, and even within mathematics, difficulty in learning to graph coordinates does not necessarily mean difficulty in learning to solve differential equations or understand geometric relationships. Even within a problem area (such as graphing coordinates), knowledge and skills can be built up gradually through mastery of each successive step toward the ultimate objectives, if the student persists in putting forth reasonable effort, accepts teacher help, and does not lose patience or give up whenever success is not achieved easily.

In this connection, it is helpful if you *focus on mastery* when monitoring the performance of discouraged students and giving them feedback. Stress the quality of students' task enagement and the degree to which they are making continuous progress rather than compare them with peers (McColskey & Leary, 1985). Treat errors as learning opportunities rather than as test failures: Errors should lead to remedial or additional instruction followed by additional practice opportunities. Make-up exams, credit for effort, or extra credit assignments should be used to provide struggling students with opportunities to overcome initial failures through persistent effort.

Attribution retraining

Discouraged students may also benefit from *attribution retraining* (Craske, 1985; Dweck & Elliott, 1983; Fowler & Peterson, 1981; Medway & Venino, 1982). Attribution retraining involves modeling, socialization, and practice exercises designed to help students learn (a) to concentrate on doing the task at hand rather than to become distracted by fear of failure, (b) to cope with frustrations by retracing their steps to find their mistakes or by analyzing the problems to find other ways to approach them (rather than to give up), and (c) to attribute their failures to insufficient effort, lack of information, or reliance on ineffective strategies rather than to lack of ability. Rather than merely telling students about these things using third-person (lecture) language or even instructing or coaching them using second-person (direction-giving) language, you are likely to communicate these cognitive strategies for coping with academic tasks most successfully if you model them for students using first-person (thinking out loud) language—demonstrating how to do the task yourself while verbalizing the thinking ("self-talk") that guides your actions. Discouraged students are especially likely to benefit from modeling that includes verbalization of the self-talk involved in maintaining composure and focusing on developing solutions to the problem when confronted with frustration or failure (as opposed to modeling of smooth, successful performance that unfolds without confusion or difficulty). In other words, your modeling should not only convince discouraged students that *you* can do the task (they already know that, anyway), but also should convince these students that *they* can do the task (because they already possess, or can reasonably expect to learn, the necessary knowledge and skills). Such modeling demystifies the task for the students and arms them with coping strategies that they can use instead of giving up when they become confused or frustrated.

Finally, some students may suffer from severe *test anxiety*. These students may perform well enough in informal, pressure-free situations but become highly anxious and perform considerably below their potential on tests or during any testlike situation in which they are aware of being monitored and evaluated. You can minimize such problems by avoiding time pressures unless they are truly central to the skill being taught, stressing the feedback functions rather than the evaluation or grading function of tests when discussing tests with students; portraying tests as opportunities to assess progress in developing knowledge or skills rather than as measures of ability; when appropriate, telling students that some problems are beyond their present achievement level so they should not be concerned about missing them; giving pretests to accustom the students to "failure" and to provide base rates for comparison later when posttests are administered; and teaching stress-management skills and effective test-taking skills and attitudes (Hill & Wigfield, 1984; McCombs, 1984; Plass & Hill, 1986).

How to Maintain Students' Success Expectations Bear in mind that the expectancy aspects of student motivation depend less on the degree of objective success that students achieve than on how they view their performance: what they see as possible for them to achieve with reasonable effort, whether they define this level of achievement as successful or not, and whether they attribute their performance to controllable factors (effort, learning effective strategies) or to uncontrollable factors (fixed general ability, luck). Therefore, whatever their ability levels, the motivation levels of all students, even the most discouraged, are open to reshaping by their teachers. Empty reassurances or a few words of encouragement will not do the job, but a combination of appropriately challenging demands with systematic socialization designed to make the student see that success can be achieved with reasonable effort should be effective.

In this regard, it is worth noting that teachers (not just students) need to learn to view academic frustrations and failures realistically and respond to them adaptively. As Rohrkemper and Corno (1988) pointed out, a manageable degree of student failure is not only inevitable but desirable—when students are challenged at optimal levels of difficulty, they will make mistakes. The important thing about these mistakes is not that they occur but that learning conditions be arranged so that students get and use feedback from the mistakes and respond to them with renewed motivation rather than discouragement. Learners cannot avoid mistakes, but they can learn to respond adaptively to them.

Strategies for Inducing Students to Value Academic Activities

The previous section focused on the expectancy factor within the expectancy x value approach to motivation, suggesting strategies for helping students to develop and maintain the expectation that they can achieve success on school activities if they put forth reasonable effort. The remaining sections concern the value factor. They describe strategies for helping students to see good reasons for engaging in the activities in the first place—good enough reasons to motivate them to take the activities seriously and put forth the necessary efforts. They include strategies for supplying extrinsic motivation, strategies for capitalizing on existing intrinsic motivation, and strategies for stimulating student motivation to learn.

Strategies for Supplying Extrinsic Motivation

Strategies for supplying extrinsic motivation do not attempt to increase the value that students place on the task itself. Instead, they link successful task performance with delivery of consequences that the students do value. These consequences typically include grades, but they may also include (a) material rewards (money, prizes, trinkets, consumables); (b) activity rewards and special privileges (opportunity to play games, use special equipment, or engage in self-selected activities); (c) symbolic rewards (honor rolls, hanging up good papers on the wall); (d) praise and social rewards; and (e) teacher rewards (opportunities to go places or do things with the teacher).

Offer Rewards as Incentives Rewards will motivate students to put forth effort, especially if they are offered in advance as incentives for striving to reach specified levels of performance. However, rewards are more effective for stimulating intensity of effort than thoughtfulness or quality of performance, and they guide behavior more effectively when students must follow a familiar path to a clear goal than when they must discover or invent strategies for responding to a novel task. Therefore, rewards are better used with routine tasks than with novel ones, better with tasks intended to produce mastery of specific skills than with tasks designed to encourage incidental learning or discovery, and better with tasks for which speed of performance or quantity of output is of more concern than creativity, artistry, or craftsmanship. It is more appropriate, for example, to offer rewards as incentives for meeting performance standards on skills that require a great deal of drill and practice (arithmetic computation, typing, spelling) than it is for work on a major research or demonstration project.

It is helpful if rewards are delivered in ways that support attempts to develop student motivation to learn, so that students are encouraged to appreciate their developing knowledge and skills rather than just to think about the rewards. Guidelines for accomplishing this are given in Table 16.2. The guidelines are phrased in terms of verbal praise, but they apply to other types of rewards as well.

Rewards will be effective as motivators only for those students who believe that they have a chance to receive the rewards if they put forth reasonable effort. With students who lack such self-efficacy perceptions, rewards will not be effective and may even backfire by causing depression

TABLE 16.2 GUIDELINES FOR EFFECTIVE PRAISE

Effective Praise	Ineffective Praise
1. is delivered contingently	1. is delivered randomly or unsystematically
2. specifies the particulars of the accomplishment	2. is restricted to global positive reactions
3. shows spontaneity, variety, and other signs of credibility, suggests attention to the student's accomplishment	3. shows a bland uniformity that suggests a conditioned response made with minimal attention
4. rewards attainment of specified performance criteria (which can include effort criteria, however)	4. rewards mere participation, without consideration of performance processes or outcomes
5. provides information to students about their competence and the value of their accomplishments	5. provides no information at all or gives students information about their status
6. orients students toward better appreciation of their own task-related behavior and thinking about problem solving	6. orients students toward comparing themselves with others and thinking about competing
7. uses own prior accomplishments as the context for describing present accomplishments	7. uses the accomplishments of peers as the context for describing students' present accomplishments
8. is given in recognition of noteworthy effort or success at difficult tasks (for *this* student)	8. is given without regard to the effort expended or the meaning of the accomplishment
9. attributes success to effort and ability, implying that similar successes can be expected in the future	9. attributes success to ability alone or to external factors such as luck or task difficulty
10. fosters endogenous attributions (students believe that they expend effort on the task because they enjoy the task and/or want to develop task-relevant skills)	10. fosters exogenous attributions—students believe that they expend effort on the task for external reasons like pleasing the teacher or winning a competition or reward
11. focuses students' attention on their own task-relevant behavior	11. focuses students' attention on the teacher as an external authority figure who is manipulating them
12. fosters appreciation of and desirable attributions about task-relevant behavior after the process is completed	12. intrudes into the ongoing process, distracting attention from task-relevant behavior

Source: Jere E. Brophy, *"Teacher praise: A functional analysis,"* Review of Educational Research, (Spring 1981): 5–32. Copyright 1981, American Educational Research Association, Washington, D.C.

or resentment. Therefore, to ensure that rewards act as incentives for everyone and not just the high-ability students, it will be necessary to ensure that everyone has equal (or at least reasonable) access to the rewards.

Structure Appropriate Competition The opportunity to compete for prizes or recognition can add incentive and excitement to classroom activities. Such competition may be either individual (students compete against everyone else) or group (students are divided into teams that compete with one another). In addition to structuring competition based on test scores or other performance measures, it is possible to build competitive elements into ordinary instruction by including activities such as argumentative essays, debates, or simulation games that involve competition (Keller, 1983).

Two important qualifications need to be kept in mind by teachers who consider using competition as a motivational strategy. First, competition is even more salient and distracting than rewards for many students, so it will be important to depersonalize the competition and emphasize the content being learned rather than who won or lost. Second, competition will be motivating only to students who have a good (or at least equal) chance of winning. To ensure this, it will be necessary to use team competition in which teams are balanced by ability profiles or individual competition in which a handicapping system has been developed to equalize everyone's opportunity to win. Team approaches are more desirable because they can be structured so that students cooperate in addition to competing (members of the same team help one another learn in preparation for competing against members of other teams). See Slavin (1983) for more information about such team learning approaches.

Call Attention to the Instrumental Value of Academic Activities Call students' attention to applications of the knowledge and skills taught in school to their lives outside of school (especially applications that will help them cope with the demands of living in our society). When possible, note that the knowledge or skills developed by a task will be useful in enabling students to meet their own current needs, in providing them with a "ticket" to social advancement, or in preparing them for occupational success or success in life generally. Better yet, cite concrete examples by relating personal experiences or telling anecdotes about individuals with whom the students can identify (famous people that they look up to, former students from the same school, or individuals with whom they are already familiar).

This strategy is probably not used as often as it could be, and when it is used, it is often used in self-defeating ways. Rather than stress the positive by identifying the present or future application value of what is being learned, many teachers stress personal embarrassment ("You don't want people to think that you are ignorant") or future educational or occupational disasters ("You'll never get through sixth grade"; "How are you going to get a job if you can't do basic math?"). Other teachers use variations that cast the student in a more positive light but portray society as a hostile environment (''Learn to count so that merchants don't cheat you''; ''Learn to read so that you don't get taken when signing a contract.'')

Therefore, besides forewarning your students that certain knowledge and skills will be needed in the future at school and making them aware that most desirable occupations require at lest a high school diploma, help them to appreciate the more specific applications of what they are learning at school. Basic language arts and mathematics skills are used daily when shopping, banking, driving, reading instructions for using some product, paying bills and carrying on business correspondence, and planning home maintenance projects or family vacations. General knowledge is useful for everything from coping effectively with minor everyday challenges to making good decisions in emergency situations. Knowledge of history and related social studies topics is useful for everything from voting on local issues to determining national policy (as several U.S. presidents have acknowledged). In general, a good working knowledge of the information, principles, and skills taught in school prepares people to make well-informed decisions that result in saving time, trouble, expense, or even lives, and it empowers people by preparing them to recognize and take advantage of the opportunities that society offers. These benefits of schooling are well recognized and highly prized in societies in which education is still a privilege rather than a right, but they tend to go unrecognized or be taken for granted in societies like ours in which education for the masses is not only available but required. Do what you can to rekindle this appreciation in your students by helping them to see academic activities as enabling opportunities to be valued rather than as imposed demands to be resisted.

Concluding Comments about Extrinsic Motivational Strategies Extrinsic motivational strategies can be effective under certain circumstances, but teachers should not rely on them too heavily. If students are preoccupied with rewards or competition, they may not pay as much attention as they should to what they are suppposed to be learning and may not appreciate its value. The quality of task engagement, and ultimately the quality of achievement, is higher when students perceive themselves to be engaged in tasks for their own reasons (intrinsic motivation) than when they perceive themselves to be engaged in order to please an authority figure, obtain a reward, escape punishment, or respond to some other extrinsic pressure (Deci & Ryan, 1985; Lepper, 1983). More specifically, if students perceive themselves as performing tasks solely to obtain a reward, they will tend to adopt a ''piecework mentality'' or ''minimax strategy'' in which they concentrate on maximizing rewards by meeting minimum standards for performance (and then moving on to something else) rather than doing a high-quality job (Condry & Chambers, 1978; Kruglanski, 1978). As a result, they may write 300-word essays containing exactly 300 words or read only those parts of a text that they need to read to answer the questions on an assignment. You can minimize the risk of encouraging students to develop such undesirable attitudes by following the guidelines in Table 16.2, but even so, bear in mind that even effective use of extrinsic motivational strategies will not help students to value academic activities. The latter will require strategies that capitalize on existing intrinsic motivation or that stimulate students' motivation to learn.

Strategies for Capitalizing on Existing Intrinsic Motivation

The intrinsic motivation approach calls for teachers to select or design academic activities that students will engage in willingly because they enjoy them or because the activities incorporate content that the students are already interested in. Teachers' opportunities to capitalize on students' existing intrinsic motivation are limited by several features inherent to the nature of schooling (attendance is compulsory, the curriculum is prescribed externally rather than chosen by the student, mistakes may lead to public embarrassment, and teachers must assign grades and enforce school rules in addition to assisting students' learning efforts). Furthermore, students differ from one another in the topics they find interesting and the activities they find enjoyable. Even so, teachers can sometimes take advantage of students' existing intrinsic motivation by selecting or designing classroom activities that incorporate elements that most, if not all, students will find rewarding. Several such elements are discussed in the following sections.

Adapt Tasks to Students' Interests Whenever particular curriculum objectives can be accomplished using a variety of examples or activities, take advantage of the opportunity to *incorporate content that the students find interesting or activities that they find enjoyable.* People, fads, or events that are currently prominent in the news or the youth culture, for example, can be worked into everyday lessons when giving examples or applications of the concepts being learned. We observed a history teacher doing this by pointing out that the Ark of the Covenant mentioned in the ancient history text was the same ark featured in the movie *Raiders of the Lost Ark.* Similarly, a geography teacher sparked student interest in studying the coordinates (latitude and longitude) by pointing out that the sunken remains of the *Titanic* can easily be located again, even though they lie on the ocean floor hundreds of miles out to sea, because the discoverers fixed the location precisely using the coordinates.

Autonomy and choice in the classroom

Another way to adapt school activities to student interest is to *offer the students choices of alternative tasks or opportunities to exercise autonomy in selecting among alternative ways to meet requirements.* Most written composition assignments and many research projects, for example, can be adapted to student interests by allowing students to choose topics or at least by taking their known interests into account when assigning topics. If the students might make undesirable choices if left completely on their own, provide them with a menu of choices to select from or require them to get your approval of their choices before going ahead.

Finally, you can incorporate students' interests into your activities by making it clear that you *encourage student comments and questions* about

Encourage student comments and questions

the topic and by asking questions or making assignments that invite the students to state opinions, make evaluations, or in some other way respond personally to the content. Relevant student-initiated questions and comments provide "teachable moments" that wise teachers take advantage of by temporarily suspending the planned sequence of events to pursue the issue raised by the student. The fact that the question was asked or the comment was made guarantees interest on the part of the student who voiced it, and the chances are that this interest will be shared by many of the other students as well.

Expression of student opinion

It is also helpful, from both instructional and motivational points of view, to see that your questions and assignments cover both basic factual knowledge and *include divergent questions and opportunities for students to express opinions or make other personal responses to the content*. After reviewing the basic facts about the Christians and the lions, the gladiators, and other excesses of the Roman circuses, for example, a history teacher who we observed began asking the students why they thought such practices had developed in Roman society, how otherwise cultured people could take pleasure in such cruelty, and other similar questions. This led to a very productive discussion in which the students made contributions and developed insights about issues such as violence in sports and in contemporary society generally, the role of peer pressure in escalating aggression once a conflict flares up, and the difference between desirable enjoyment of pleasures and undesirable indulgence in excesses. The same teacher, after reviewing the facts of life in Athens and Sparta, asked the students which city they would rather live in and why. Again, this led to a lively discussion that included parallels among modern nations and contrasted societies that place heavy priority on building up military strength (at a cost in quality of civilian life) with societies that have more balanced sets of priorities.

Plan for Novelty and Variety Students faced with the same routines and the same types of tasks each day will soon become bored. Therefore, try to make sure that something about each task (its form, its content, the media involved, or the nature of the responses that it demands) is new to the students or at least different from what they have been doing recently. When introducing a novel activity, call attention to its new or different elements and take the opportunity to state that you expect the students to find the activity particularly interesting, challenging, or enjoyable.

Provide More Opportunities for Students to Respond and to Receive Feedback Most students prefer activities that allow them to respond actively—to interact with the teacher or with one another, to manipulate materials, or in some other way to respond more actively than by merely listening or reading. This is one function of drill, recitation, discussion, board work, and seatwork activities. Ideally, however, students will often receive *active response opportunities* that go beyond the simple question-answer formats seen in typical recitation and seatwork activities in order to include projects, experiments, role play, simulations, educational games, or creative applications of what they have been learning. Language-arts instruction, for example, should include dramatic readings and prose and poetry composition, mathematics instruction should include problem-solving exercises and realistic application opportunities, science instruction should include experiments and other applications or laboratory work, and social studies instruction should include debates, research projects, and simulation exercises. Such activities allow students to feel that school learning involves *doing* something, not just having something done to them.

Activities that call for students to apply skills or processes they are learning to particular academic content (whether in the same or in a different subject-matter area) often can be used not only to provide students with opportunities for active response and feedback but also to allow them to integrate their learning. Students learning statistics, for example, typically work on assignments calling for them to find the mean, median, and mode for numerical distributions. Instead of confining such assignments to skill practice involving making computations using provided sets of numbers, teachers could include ''hands-on'' applications based on measurements that the students would take themselves (of the physical characteristics of the people or objects in the classroom) or on information gathered during social studies or science activities (statistics on states or nations, findings from probability experiments). The statistical computations might be just part of a larger integrative assignment calling for students to collect and analyze data and prepare a written report of their findings about some issue concerning social studies or science content.

Students particularly enjoy tasks that allow them to respond actively and to receive *immediate feedback* that can be used to guide subsequent reponses. Such feedback features are among the reasons for the popularity of computer games and other pastimes featured in arcades (Malone & Lepper, 1987). Automatic feedback features are built into many educational toys and Montessori materials used in preschools and kindergartens and into programmed learning materials and other ''self-correcting'' materials used in elementary and secondary classrooms. The same is true for computerized learning programs that allow students to respond actively and then receive immediate feedback.

You can also build feedback features into more typical classroom activities. You can provide such feedback yourself when leading the class or a small group through an activity or when circulating to supervise progress during seatwork times. At times when you are less available for immediate response (such as when you are teaching a small group and the rest of the students are working at their seats), you can still arrange for students to receive feedback by consulting answer keys, following instructions about how to check their work, consulting with an adult volunteer or appointed student helper, or reviewing the work in pairs or small groups.

Among activities that allow for active response with immediate feedback, students are especially likely to enjoy activities that allow them to *create a finished product*. Industrial psychologists have shown that workers enjoy jobs that allow them to create a product they can point to and identify with more than they enjoy jobs that do not yield tangible evidence of the results of their labor. It seems likely that students will respond similarly to academic tasks; that is, they are likely to prefer tasks that have meaning or integrity in their own right over tasks that are mere subparts of some larger entity and are more likely to experience a satisfying sense of completion or accomplishment when they finish such tasks. Ideally, task completion will yield a finished product that the students can use or display (a map, diagram, or some other illustration, an essay or report, a scale model, a completed puzzle, or something other than another ditto or workbook page).

Incorporate "Fun Features" Most academic activities can be planned to incorporate certain features that most students find enjoyable. Three of them are fantasy or simulation features, gamelike features, and opportunities to interact with peers.

When more direct applications of what is being learned are not feasible, you can *introduce fantasy or imagination elements that will engage students' emotions or allow them to experience events vicariously*. In studying poems or stories, you can tell students about the authors' motives in writing the poems or stories or about formative experiences in the authors' lives that led to these writings. In studying scientific or mathematical principles and methods, you can tell students about the practical problems that needed to be solved or the personal motives of the discoverers that led to the development of the knowledge or skills being taught. Or you can set up role play or simulation activities that allow students to identify with real or fictional characters or to deal with academic content in direct, personal ways. Rather than simply assigning the students to read history, for example, you can make history come alive by arranging for students to role play Columbus and his crew debating what to do after thirty days at sea or have them take the roles of the American, British, and Russian leaders meeting at Yalta.

Simulation exercises

Simulation exercises include, but are not confined to, full-scale drama, role play, simulation games, and other "major productions." Other, more modest simulation exercises can be incorporated into everyday instruction. They include brief simulation exercises or invitations for students to use fantasy or imagination to expand their thinking about the content they are learning. In teaching a particular mathematical procedure, for example, you might ask students to name problems that come up in everyday living that the procedure might be useful to help solve (and then list them on the board). We observed a history teacher bring ancient history alive by having students describe what facilities they would expect to find in a visit to an ancient Roman bath, and we saw a geography teacher "bring home" material about the Soviet Union by asking students to imagine and talk about what it would be like to seek housing in a country in which the goverment owned all of the property and to acquire accurate information about world events in a country in which the government controlled all of the media. Such brief fantasy or simulation exercises do not take much time or require special preparations, but they can be useful for stimulating students to relate to the content more personally and to take greater interest in it.

Practice and application activities for almost any kind of content can be presented as games or structured to include *features typically associated with games or recreational pastimes* (Keller, 1983; Malone & Lepper, 1987). With a bit of imagination, ordinary seatwork assignments can be transformed into "test-yourself" challenges, puzzles, or brainteasers. Some of these kinds of activities involve clear goals but require the students to solve problems, avoid traps, or overcome obstacles to reach the goals (e.g., exercises that call for students to suggest possible solutions to science or engineering problems or to find a shortcut that will substitute for a tedious mathematical procedure). Other such activities challenge the students to "find the problem" by identifying the goal itself in addition to developing a method for reaching the goal (many "explore-and-discover" activities follow this model). Some gamelike activities involve elements of suspense or hidden information that emerge as the activity is completed (puzzles that convey some message or provide the answer to some questions once they are filled in). Other such activities involve a degree of randomness or some method of inducing uncertainty about what the outcome of one's performance is likely to be on any given trial (knowledge games that cover a variety of topic areas at a variety of difficulty levels that are assigned according to card draws or dice rolls—Trivial Pursuit is an example).

Note that most of these gamelike features involve presenting intellectual challenges appropriate for use by individual students or groups of students working cooperatively. This is mentioned to call attention to the fact that the term *gamelike features* is intended to have a much broader meaning than the typical meaning of the term *games*, which most teachers associate specifically with team competitions. There is reason to believe that the gamelike features described above are likely to be less distracting from curriculum objectives and more effective than competitive games in promoting student motivation to learn, especially when competitive games emphasize speed and memorized facts rather than integration or application of knowledge.

Most students enjoy activities that allow them to interact with their peers. You can easily build *peer interaction opportunities* into whole-class activities such as discussion, debate, role play, or simulation. In addition, you can plan follow-up activities that allow students to work together in pairs or small groups to tutor one another, discuss issues, develop suggested solutions to problems, or work as a team preparing for a competition, participating in a simulation game, or producing some group product (a report or a display, for example).

Peer interactive activities are likely to be most effective if (a) they are sufficiently structured around curriculum objectives to make them worthwhile learning experiences rather than mere occasions for socializing and (b) conditions are arranged so that every student has a substantive role to play and must participate actively in carrying out the group's mission, rather than so that one or two assertive students can dominate the interaction and do all the work while others watch (see Slavin, 1983 and Slavin et al., 1985 for more information about peer interactive and cooperative learning activities).

Concluding Comments about Intrinsic Motivational Strategies Schooling should be as enjoyable as possible for both teachers and students. Therefore, whenever curriculum objectives can be met through a variety of activities, wise teachers will emphasize activities that students find rewarding and avoid activities that they find boring or aversive. However, two important limitations on what can be accomplished through intrinsic motivational strategies should be kept in mind.

Limitations

First, your opportunities to use intrinsic motivational strategies in the classroom are limited. You must teach the whole curriculum, not just the parts that appeal to the students, and you must teach factual knowledge and basic skills in addition to higher-level objectives. Opportunities to provide choice or gamelike features are limited. Thus even if you make optimal use of these intrinsic motivational strategies, your students will still be in school rather than in a recreational setting, and all of the constraints that are built into the teacher and student roles will still be in place. Learning will often be enjoyable, but it will still require concentration and effort. It will not be "fun" of the sort implied by a visit to an arcade or an amusement park.

Second, although intrinsic motivational strategies should increase students' enjoyment of classroom activities, they will not in any direct way increase the students' motivation to learn the content or skills being taught. Therefore, as is the case with extrinsic motivational strategies, intrinsic motivational strategies will need to be supplemented with strategies for stimulating motivation to learn (described in the next section). Otherwise, the students may enjoy classroom activities but fail to derive the intended knowledge or skills from them.

In this connection, it is worth noting that our colloquial language for discussing intrinsic motivation is misleading. We commonly describe certain topics or tasks as "intrinsically interesting" and speak of engaging in activities "for their own sake." Taken literally, such language implies that motivation resides in activities rather than in people. In reality, *people generate intrinsic motivation*; it is not somehow built into topics or tasks. We study or do something, not for *its* sake, but for *our* sake—because it brings us pleasure, meets our needs, or in some other way provides desirable stimulation or satisfaction.

We all have our own amounts and patterns of intrinsic motivation, developed in response to our experiences and to the socialization we received from significant others in our lives. In the case of motivation to learn academic knowledge and skills, teachers are important "significant others." Therefore, rather than confining themselves to accommodating classroom activities to students' existing motivational patterns, teachers can think in terms of shaping those motivational patterns through systematic socialization efforts designed to stimulate student motivation to learn the curriculum.

Strategies for Stimulating Student Motivation to Learn

The following strategies are recommended methods for going beyond manipulating student performance through extrinsic reward and punishment and beyond using intrinsic motivational strategies to encourage students to engage in classroom activities because they enjoy them in order to stimulate students' motivation to learn (e.g., to stimulate the students to take academic activities seriously and attempt to acquire the knowledge or skills that these activities were designed to develop). The first three strategies are general ones that describe pervasive features of the learning environment that should be established in the classroom. They involve socializing students to understand that the classroom is primarily a place for learning and that acquiring and applying knowledge and skills are important contributors to quality of life (not just to report card grades).

General Modeling of Motivation to Learn Throughout all of your interactions with your students, routinely model interest in learning: *Let the students see that you value learning as a rewarding, self-actualizing activity that produces personal satisfaction and enriches your life*. In addition to teaching what is in the textbooks, share your interests in current events and items of general knowledge (especially as they relate to aspects of the subject matter that you teach). Call attention to current books, articles, television programs, or movies on the subject. Also, call attention to examples or applications of subject-matter knowledge in everyday living, in the local environment, or in current events.

Teacher as classroom model

"Modeling" here means more than just calling students' attention to examples or applications of concepts taught in school. In addition, it means acting as a model—sharing your thinking about such examples or applications so that your students can see how educated people use information and concepts learned in school to understand and respond to everyday experiences in their lives and to news about current events occurring elsewhere. Without being preachy about it, you can relate personal experiences illustrating how language-arts knowledge enables you to communicate or express yourself effectively in important life situations, how mathematical and scientific knowledge enables you to solve everyday household engineering or repair problems, or how social studies knowledge helps you to appreciate things you see in your travels or to understand the significance of events occurring in other parts of the world. You can also share insights or opinions about current events or questions that you are raising or predictions you are making about how current crises will be resolved. In general, let the students see that it is both stimulating and satisfying to understand (or even just to think or wonder about) what is happening in the world around us.

One teacher that we observed used modeling effectively in connection with an assignment involving reading about current events in the newspaper. He began by noting that he reads the editorial page of this newspaper regularly, finding that he sometimes agrees and sometimes disagrees with the editorials, but in either case, the material is always informative and thought provoking. He went on to discuss the newspaper's position and his own position concerning a forthcoming summit meeting of international leaders, noting that he was initially relatively uninformed about, uninterested in, and pessimistic about the likely outcome of this summit meeting but that he had become more interested and more optimistic about it as he became better informed through reading the newspaper and watching news programs on television. This led to a stimulating discussion that clarified for the students and provoked many questions about the positions of the United States and the Soviet Union on major issues to be discussed at the summit meeting, the positions of the editorial writer, and the positions of the teacher. In addition, the teacher provoked further interest and curiosity from the students by noting that, although he was sharing his own positions on the issues being discussed that day, he often deliberately withheld his positions on issues discussed in class to encourage the students to think for themselves and avoid inhibiting students who might disagree with him. Throughout the discussion he made references to aspects of the history and geography of the United States and the Soviet Union that helped shape their present rivalry as world leaders and their positions on issues to be discussed at the summit meeting. In addition, he communicated the pride and satisfaction he took in "feeling like an expert in world affairs" when he read articles or watched televsion programs on the summit meeting and realized that he had a good understanding of the issues and events involved. It is likely that this modeling increased his students' interest in and appreciation of the importance and usefulness of social studies concepts and information. In addition, it probably increased their interest in newspaper articles and television programs about current events, as well as providing them with a model to follow in reading those articles or responding to those programs in active, thoughtful ways.

Communicate Desirable Expectations and Attributions Throughout all of your interactions with students, routinely project attitudes, beliefs, expectations, and attributions (statements about the reasons for students' behavior) that imply that your students share your own enthusiasm for learning. To the extent that you *treat your students as if they already are eager learners*, they will be more likely to become eager learners. Let your students know that you expect them to be curious, to want to learn facts and understand principles clearly, to master skills, and to see what they are learning as meaningful and applicable to their everyday lives (Marshall, 1987).

Minimally, this means avoiding suggestions that students will dislike working on academic activities or will work on them only in order to get good grades. Preferably, it means treating students as active, motivated learners who care about their learning and are trying to understand (Blumenfeld & Meece, 1988). One teacher we observed communicated positive expectations routinely by announcing at the beginning of the year that her class was intended to make the students into "social scientists" and by referring back to this idea frequently throughout the year through comments such as, "Since you are social scientists, you will recognize that the description of this area as a tropical rain forest has implications about what kinds of crops will grow there," or "Thinking as social scientists, what conclusions might we draw from this information?" Another teacher frequently encouraged his students to

> read the material carefully and put it into your own words as you go along so that you will make sure that you understand it. Then answer the questions that follow. Remember, if you really understand the material, you should not only be able to answer the questions correctly but also be able to explain why your answers are correct.

Minimize Students' Performance Anxiety Motivation is likely to develop most fully in classrooms in which the students are goal oriented but relaxed enough to be able to concentrate on the task at hand without worrying about whether or not they can meet performance expectations. You can accomplish this by making clear separations between instruction or practice activities designed to promote learning and tests designed to evaluate performance. *Most classroom activities should be structured as learning experiences rather than tests.*

When instruction or practice activities include testlike items (recitation questions, practice exercises), treat them as opportunities for the students to work with and apply the material rather than as attempts to see who knows the material and who does not. If you expect students to engage in academic activities with motivation to learn (which implies a willingness to take risks and make mistakes), you will need to protect them from anxiety or premature concern about performance adequacy.

It is necessary, however, to evaluate student performance and assign grades using tests or other assessment devices. Until that point in the unit, though, the emphasis should be on teaching and learning rather than on evaluation, and students should be encouraged to respond to questions and performance demands in terms of "let's assess our progress and learn from our mistakes" rather than "let's see who knows it and who doesn't." When possible, give students opportunities to correct their mistakes or improve their responses by rephrasing the question or giving a clue (i.e., do not give the answer or move on to someone else). If it is necessary to give the answer or elicit it from another student, be sure to include any explanation that may be needed to make sure that the first student gets the point and understands why the answer is correct. Have students correct their mistakes in seatwork and homework assignments. In general, encourage your students to treat each question and performance demand as an opportunity to check their own understanding or apply what they are learning rather than as an opportunity to gain or lose points toward their grades. When necessary, you may also want to make statements such as, "We're here to learn, and you can't do that without making mistakes," to caution students against laughing at the mistakes made by their peers or to use the strategies for minimizing students' text anxiety, described in an earlier section.

If you consistently implement these three general strategies, you will establish a learning environment in which student motivation to learn can flourish, and you will subtly encourage students to develop such motivation to learn as a general trait. Then when implementing particular academic activities, you can supplement these general strategies by using one or more of the following specific strategies for motivating students to learn the content or skills that a particular activity is designed to develop.

Project Intensity Whenever you instruct, but especially when you present key explanations, you can use timing, nonverbal expressions and gestures, and cueing and other verbal techniques to project a level of intensity that tells the students that the material is important and deserves close attention. An intense presentation might begin with a direct statement of the importance of the message ("I'm going to show you how to invert fractions—now pay close attention and make sure that you understand these procedures"). Then, you would present the message using verbal and nonverbal public speaking techniques that convey intensity and cue attention: a slow paced, step-by-step presentation during which you emphasize or underline key words, unusual voice modulations, or exaggerated gestures to focus attention on key terms or procedural steps, scanning the group intensely following each step to look for signs of understanding or confusion (and allow anyone with a question to be able to ask it immediately). In addition to the words you speak, everything about *your tone and manner should communicate to the students that what you say is important* and that they should give it full attention and be prepared to ask questions about anything that they do not understand.

Tone and manner in communications

Projecting intensity through slower pacing, exaggerated cueing, and related rhetorical techniques is an especially useful strategy when demonstrating procedures or problem-solving strategies (as opposed to giving or reviewing information only). Such demonstrations have built-in step-by-step structures that lend themselves to slow pacing punctuated by exaggerated cueing, and the first- or second-person language that is used in modeling or demonstrating procedures lends itself more naturally to a high-intensity communication style than the third-person language typically used to communicate information.

You will have to pick your spots for deliberately using an intensive style, however, because you cannot be intense all of the time, and even if you could, students would adjust to it so that it would lose much of its effectiveness. Therefore, reserve special intensity for times when you want to communicate that "this is important: Pay especially close attention."

Teacher attitudes and beliefs as cues to students' enthusiasm

Project Enthusiasm Unless they are already familiar with the topic or assignment, students will look to you as the teacher for cues about how to respond to academic activities. Consciously or not, you model attitudes and beliefs about topics and assignments, and students pick up on these cues. If you present a topic or assignment with enthusiasm, suggesting that it is interesting, important, or worthwhile, your students are likely to adopt this same attitude (Bettencourt et al., 1983). In suggesting that you project enthusiasm, we do not mean pep talks or unnecessary theatrics. Instead, we mean that you would identify your own reasons for being interested in a topic or for finding it meaningful or important, and you would project these reasons to the students when teaching about the topic. Use dramatics or forceful salesmanship if you are comfortable with these techniques, but if not, low-key but sincere statements of the value that you place on a topic or activity will be just as effective to communicate your enthusiasm for it. Thus a brief comment showing that a topic is food for thought or illustrating why it is interesting, unique, or different from previously studied topics may be sufficient. In short, the primary objective of projecting enthusiasm as a strategy for motivating students to learn is to induce the students to value the topic or activity rather than to amuse, entertain, or excite them.

One history teacher who we observed generated a great deal of enthusiasm (and also pulled together a great many concepts) by enthusiastically explaining to his students that during the Middle Ages, the Mediterranean was the center of the world, Mediterranean seaports were major trade centers, and places like England were outposts of civilization. All of this changed drastically with the discovery of the New World and the emergence of new centers of trade and culture. He demonstrated these issues with references to maps, reminders about the primary modes of transportation at the time, and characterizations of the attitudes of the people and their knowledge about other countries and trade possibilities. Similarly, another teacher brought ancient Israel alive by elaborating enthusiastically on the textbook to tell his students about David as the slayer of Goliath and ancestor of Jesus, Abraham leading his people to the Promised Land, Solomon as a wise man and builder of the temple, and Moses as the man who presented the Ten Commandments and led the people out of the wilderness. This included locating of Jerusalem, Israel, and the Sinai Peninsula on a map and speculation about whether the temple might be rebuilt in modern Jerusalem (noting that a major Moslem temple is located immediately next to the spot occupied by Solomon's Temple). In each of these cases, the teacher was able to parlay personal interest in the topic with detailed knowledge about the topic into an effective presentation that sparked interest and elicited many questions and comments from the students.

Connections between new tasks and previous knowledge

Induce Task Interest or Appreciation Besides projecting intensity or your own personal enthusiasm, you can induce students' interest in or appreciation for a topic or activity by verbalizing reasons that the students should value it. If the topic or activity has connections with something that the students already recognize as interesting or important, these connections should be noted (such as the earlier mentioned connection between the Ark of the Covenant and *Raiders of the Lost Ark*). When the knowledge or skills to be taught have applications for everyday living, these applications should be mentioned (especially applications that will allow the students to solve problems or accomplish goals that are important to them). You can also mention new or challenging aspects of the activities that the students can anticipate, especially interesting or exotic aspects.

We observed a history teacher, for example, who motivated students to read about the ancient Greek legal system by noting that it was similar to our system in many ways except that it called for 501 jurors. A geography teacher motivated his students to study the map of Greece with interest and appreciation by explaining that no place in Greece was more than forty miles from the sea and that the country's jagged contours gave it far more coastline than most other countries, including much larger ones.

Induce Curiosity or Suspense You can stimulate curiosity or suspense in your students by posing questions or constructing "setups" that make them feel the need to resolve some ambiguity or obtain more information about a topic. To prepare them to read about the Soviet Union, for example, you could ask your students if they know that Russia is just a part of the Soviet Union, what the term *Iron Curtain* means, how many time zones there are in the Soviet Union, or how the United States acquired Alaska. Such questions help transform "just one more reading assignment" into an interesting learning experience by encouraging students to make connections between the information they will acquire and the information they already know (or think they know). Furthermore, by inducing curiosity or suspense, such questions make the new information food for thought rather than merely more material to be memorized. Most students will think that Russia is another name for the Soviet Union, and will be curious to find out the difference once they have been alerted to the fact that a difference exists. Most students will have heard the term *Iron Curtain* but will not have thought actively about it, and they will become curious to learn more about it when stimulated to think about it in interesting ways (Is there an actual curatin? Is it made from iron? If not, why is the term used?). Similarly, most students will be amazed to discover that the Soviet Union encompasses eleven time zones and that the United States purchased Alaska from Russia. These are just four basic facts found in most treatments of the history or geography of the Soviet Union. Whether or not students find these facts (a great many others that could have been mentioned) interesting and will think actively about them rather than merely trying to memorize them will depend largely on the degree to which their teachers stimulate curiosity and provide a context for thinking about associations between these facts and existing knowledge or beliefs. This is another illustratation of the point made earlier that interest value does not reside in topics or activities—interest resides in people.

You can encourage your students to generate such interest by (a) asking them to speculate or make predictions about what they will be learning; (b) raising questions that successful completion of the activity will enable them to answer; (c) when relevant, showing them that their existing knowledge is not complete enough to enable them to accomplish some valued objective, that their knowledge is internally inconsistent or inconsistent with new information, or that their present knowledge exists in scattered form but could be organized around certain general principles or powerful ideas (Malone & Lepper, 1987). More generally, you can put your students into an active information-processing or problem-solving mode by posing interesting questions or problems that the activity will address (Keller, 1983).

Stimulate questioning in students

Induce Dissonance or Cognitive Conflict When the topic of a text is already familiar, students may think they already know everything that there is to know about it and thus may read the material with little conscious attention or thought. You can counter this tendency by pointing out unexpected, incongruous, or paradoxical aspects of the content, by calling attention to unusual or exotic elements, by noting exceptions to general rules, or by challenging students to solve the "mystery" that underlies a paradox.

We have observed several teachers using this strategy effectively. One teacher introduced a unit on the Middle Ages by telling students that they would learn about "our ancestors" who chose to remain illiterate and ignorant and who persecuted people who did not share their religion. Later he noted the Moslem advances in mathematics, medicine, and the construction of libraries and then contrasted them with the illiteracy of most Christian kings and lords during the Middle Ages. Another teacher stimulated curiosity about the Persian Empire by noting that Darius was popular with the people he conquered and by asking students to anticipate reasons why this might be so. Another teacher introduced a selection on the Trojan War by telling the students they would read about "how just one horse enabled the Greeks to win a major battle against the Trojans." Another teacher introduced a movie on the fall of the Roman Empire by saying, "Some say that the factors that led to the decay of the Roman Empire are presently at work in the United States—as you watch the film, see if you notice parallels."

Make Abstract Content More Personal, Concrete, or Familiar Definitions, principles, and other general or abstract input may have little meaning for students unless you make them more concrete or visual. One way to accomplish this is to promote personal identification with the content by relating experiences or telling anecdotes illustrating how the content applies to the lives of particular individuals (especially individuals whom the students are interested in and likely to identify with). We observed a history teacher read to the students a brief selection about Spartacus in order to personalize a selection that they were to read about slavery in ancient times. When covering the crusades, this teacher gave particular emphasis to the Children's Crusade, noting that the children involved were "your age and younger" and that most of them died before this crusade eventually ended in failure. He also made poignant connections

Relate studies to students' lives

to contemporary Iran, where religion-based zeal is also causing preadolescents to volunteer to go to war. Another teacher brought the medieval guilds alive for her students by describing them in detail and soliciting the students' reactions to the fact that if they had lived during the Middle Ages, to become a journeyman they would have had to leave their homes as children and spend seven years apprenticed to a master craftsman.

You can make abstractions concrete by showing objects or pictures or by conducting demonstrations. You can also help students to relate new or strange content to their existing knowledge by using examples or analogies that refer to familiar concepts, objects, or events. We have observed teachers make the following connections: (a) the Nile River flooding and its effects on Egyptian customs compared to spring flooding in Michigan rivers and its effect on local customs; (b) the Washington Monument as a modern example of an obelisk; (c) three times the size of the Pontiac Silverdome as an example of the size of the largest Roman circus colosseums; (d) identifications of students in the class (or failing that, famous personalities) descended from the ancient peoples or the geographical areas studied; (e) linking of students' family names to the guilds (Smith, Tanner, Miller, Baker); (f) similarities in climate and potential for flower raising and dairy farming as reasons why the Dutch were drawn to the Holland, Michigan area; (g) similarities in the customs associated with the Roman Saturn Festival compared to those associated with modern Christmas festivities; and (h) explanation of how the medieval social and political systems worked by describing the local (rural central Michigan) area as part of the outlying lands surrounding a manor based in Lansing, which in turn would be under the protection of and would pay taxes to "the King of Detroit."

Sometimes the problem is not so much that the content would be too abstract or unfamiliar for the students to understand if it were explained sufficiently, but that the text simply does not provide enough explanation. It is not enough, for example, to state that Russia stopped participating in World War I because "the revolution came and a new government was established." This brief statement does not supply enough details to enable students to understand and visualize the events surrounding the Russian revolution. To make these events more understandable to the students, you would have to elaborate on the text by explaining why and (especially) how the Communists and others organized political and, eventually, military resistance to the czar's regime, killed or expelled the czar's family and key officials, and established a new government. Such elaboration on the text transforms the relatively meaningless statement that "the revolution came and a new government was established" into a meaningful statement that the students can explain in their own words because they can relate it to their prior knowledge and can visualize the events to which it refers. This will enable them to process the content actively instead of simply trying to memorize it.

As a teacher recently explained in an interview, good teachers look on texts as outlines to be elaborated on, not as the entire curriculum.

Induce Students to Generate Their Own Motivation to Learn You can induce your students to generate their own motivation to learn by asking them to think about topics or activities in relation to their own interests or preconceptions. You can ask the students to identify questions about the topic that they would like to get answered, for example, to list their particular interests in the topic, or to note things that they find to be surprising as they read. Besides generating motivation in a particular situation, such exercises are useful for helping students to understand that motivation to learn must come from within themselves—that it is a property of the learner rather than the task to be learned.

State Learning Objectives and Provide Advance Organizers You can prepare your students to gain more from lectures, films, or reading assignments by clarifying what you want them to concentrate on or think about as they process the information. You may want to distribute a partially filled-in outline or study guide, for example, or to give specific guidelines about note taking. If particular structuring devices have been built into the content (lists, generalizations followed by elaborations, comparison or contrast structures, historical narratives or other sequential descriptions, or presentations of rules followed by examples, questions followed by answers, or concept definitions followed by examples and nonexamples of the concept) you could call the students' attention to these structural elements to increase the likelihood that the students would be able to use them as bases for organizing and remembering what they learn (Armbruster & Anderson, 1984). In general, to the extent that you can be clear about exactly how you want your students to approach an activity (to memorize verbatim versus to get the gist and be able to explain it in their own words, degree of emphasis on specific facts versus more general principles or applications, use of particular main ideas for organizing or interpreting the larger body of information), your students will be more likely to adopt the appropriate learning set and gain what you want them to gain from the activity.

Model Task-Related Thinking and Problem Solving The information-processing and problem-solving strategies that you use when thinking about curricular content and responding to academic tasks will be invisible to your students unless you make them overt and observable by modeling them. Therefore, when teaching particular content, and especially when demonstrating skills or problem-solving strategies, do not tell the students what to do using the typical second- or third-person language of instruction. In addition, model the process by showing the students what to do and by thinking out loud as you demonstrate. Include the thinking that goes into selecting the general approach to use, deciding on options to take at choice points, checking progress as you go along, and satisfying yourself that you are on the right track. Also, model recovery from false starts and from use of inappropriate strategies on occasion so that students can see how one can develop a successful strategy even when one is not sure about what to do at first (Diener & Dweck, 1978).

Cognitive modeling

This kind of *cognitive modeling* is a way to show students what it means to approach a task with motivation to learn by modeling some of the general beliefs and attitudes associated with motivation (patience, confidence, persistence in seeking solutions through information processing and rational decision making, benefiting from the information supplied by mistakes rather than giving up in frustration).

Modeling opportunities occur whenever an academic activity calls for use of some cognitive process or strategy. Among other things, this includes demonstrations on how to conduct scientific experiments, understand and develop ways to solve mathematics problems, identify the main ideas in paragraphs, develop a plan for conducting a research project or an outline for writing a composition, identify the moral of a story, induce general principles from collections of facts, deduce applications of general principles to specific situations, check your own understanding of content by trying to answer questions about it or paraphrase it into your own words, or find and correct your own errors.

Strategies for Motivating Students to Learn Contemporary learning theorists have shown that learning, and most especially the kind of cognitive learning emphasized at school, is not mere response to stimulation. Nor is teaching mere infusion of knowledge into a vacuum. Learning involves actively processing input and making sense of it by relating it to existing knowledge, ideally in ways that involve transformation of the input into the student's own terms and retention in a form that makes it easily accessible for retrieval or application. Similarly, ideal teaching involves not only presenting input to students but helping them to be able to process the input actively using *generative learning strategies* (Weinstein & Mayer, 1986), relating it to their existing knowledge, putting it into their own words, and making sure that they understand it. In the classroom context, motivating students to learn means first stimulating them to take an interest in and see the value of what they are learning and then providing them with guidance about how to go about learning it. Although strategies can be separated for purposes of analysis, in practice, strategies for effectively motivating students to learn are closely intertwined with strategies for planning and implementing effective instruction generally (see Chapters 10–13).

SUMMARY

Motivation, the process of arousing, directing, and maintaining behavior, is heavily influenced by group context and multiple stimuli. Classroom teachers must adjust research findings and theoretical positions to specific individuals in given settings.

In the area of structuring assignments, teachers can foster motivation by providing stimulating and appropriate tasks, capturing student attention, allowing student choices, and setting clear learning goals. They can maintain task involvement during seatwork by allowing students to work without interruption, demanding attention to the tasks, and providing knowledge of results. Maintaining motivation over the year involves scheduling a change of pace occasionally, making special events relevant, breaking up the day with special brief assignments that are enjoyable, and providing feedback about academic performance.

Teachers can manipulate four major motivation-related conditions in the classroom: tasks students are assigned, student perceptions of tasks, teacher rapport with students, and the reward structure. They can employ techniques such as using student preferences, student choices, individualization, learning centers, "hands-on" experience, peer tutoring, games or simulations, and other variations of "standard" practices. These techniques should be used with due regard for students' needs and motives, as outlined by Murray and others.

Keller (1983) provided four categories that can be used to think about classroom motivation: (1) *interest* (learner's curiosity), (2) *relevance* (learner's perception that task relates to personal need), (3) *expectancy* (learner's perceived likelihood of success), and (4) *satisfaction* (learner's intrinsic motivation or reaction to external rewards).

Brophy provided a comprehensive list of motivational strategies that teachers can use to stimulate students to engage productively in academic activities, and in particular, to do so with motivation to learn the academic content skills that the activities were designed to teach.

Questions and Problems

1. Summarize in your own words Keller's motivational model. Think about your own experience as a student and describe the classrooms that most and least approximated this model. What do these experiences suggest about the value of Keller's model and about strategies for motivating students?
2. Before listing motivational strategies, Brophy presented four major assumptions about necessary preconditions. In your opinion, why does he make these assumptions? Have you been in classrooms where these assumptions did not pertain? If so, describe one such class.
3. Do you include student motivation in your definition of teaching success? That is, are you satisfied as long as students learn the material, or do you believe that they also must become enthusiastic about you and the subject matter? What difference does it make? Can one goal get in the way of the other goal? How?
4. Think about your own teachers. Which ones stand out in your mind as especially good or bad? How did they attempt to motivate students in general and you in particular? What does this imply about how you define motivation?
5. Do you find it intuitively obvious or perhaps seriously confusing that students with notably poor motivation may be won over by teachers who concentrate mostly on instruction and only secondarily on motivation? Can you see why teachers who try to improve students' self-

concepts without making demands or providing success experiences could be perceived as patronizing bleeding hearts by such students? Explain.

6. What is your position on intrinsic versus extrinsic motivation? Both research and simple observation reveal that intrinsic motivation is not observable in certain students and that extrinsic methods seem to work under most circumstances. What does this suggest about human nature? About motivation? About your views on teaching and learning?
7. Once you have led a horse to water, can you make it drink, or not? Why? Are there students whom no teacher can motivate? If so, what does motivate these students?
8. As an exercise in inducing your own motivation to learn, pick a chapter in this text that you have not read yet and generate a list of questions relating to its topic. Given your current knowledge and beliefs about the topic, what more would you like to know about the topic simply because the questions interest you? What would you like to know because you think you will need the information to apply in the classroom when working with students? Compare your list with the questions prepared by two or three of your classmates.

Case Studies

TEST REVIEW. The bell rings, students dash for their seats, and conversations are left dangling in midsentence. The excited buzz of informal exchange becomes a formal, passive, heavy silence. Marge Hiebert audibly sighs and starts the class. "Last Friday we had an exam, so I guess I should give back your papers and tell you what you did wrong. The geography proofs were poorly done. Let me show you the really bad, silly mistakes on the test. Pay attention because you have to learn this stuff. . . . it's going to be on the midterm exam and I don't want to see these same mistakes." How effective is this teacher feedback going to be in motivating student behavior? Why? What would be a more effective strategy?

A POOR FOLLOW-UP. Helen finished the experiment and walked around the class with the beaker so that all of the students could see the chemical reaction. Then she placed the beaker on a lab table and turned to the front of the room. She smiled and confidently asked, "Now, are there any questions?" She paused and waited fifteen seconds and said, "Okay, then go to your lab table and do the follow-up experiment." At first, the tables buzzed with talk and activity; however, after a couple of minutes, Helen noticed that purposeful activity was occurring at only one of the five tables. She was puzzled because she knew that the students had seen her example and that the follow-up experiment was simple. How could she find out what the problem was? What should she say?

HOSTILE BILL? Mr. Baker hesitated to call on Bill Maddi, a large boy who sat with a sullen look on his face in the rear of the sixth-grade classroom, because Bill acted in a distant, hostile way all day, even though nothing had transpired between him and Bill on this, the opening day of school. Finally, he decided that he had to interact with Bill, and he said, with some uncertainty, "Bill, would you read the directions for the next set of exercises?" Bill retorted loudly and quickly, "No, I'm not interested in this stupid stuff." After quieting the class, Mr. Baker called on another student to respond, and the period continued.

During the rest of the week several similar incidents occurred. In each case, when Bill was asked to read he refused to do so, sometimes gracefully or humorously but generally with belligerence or hostility; when Bill was asked to make an oral response, however, he usually did so. Finally, Mr. Baker put two and two together and concluded that Bill could not read well and was embarrassed to do so in front of the class. How could Mr. Baker verify his hypotheses during an interview with Bill? What should he say and do? If he is correct that Bill cannot read well, what should he do about it? Specifically, what instructional tasks should Bill be assigned? What would a typical school day be like for Bill?

CHAPTER

Communicating Appropriate Expectations to Low Achievers

CHAPTER OUTLINE

OBJECTIVES

When you have mastered the material in this chapter, you will be able to

1. Explain, with examples, the process by which teacher expectations can become self-fulfilling prophecies
2. Identify ways in which teachers communicate self-defeating expectations to low achievers
3. Describe the effects of ability grouping on students' expectations and performance
4. Differentiate among proactive, reactive, and overreactive teachers, and explain how and why the latter two types may produce undesirable self-fulfilling prophecy effects
5. List and explain what a teacher can do to develop more accurate expectations of students and to help low-achieving students develop more realistic expectations for themselves

Motivational strategies that teachers might use with all students were discussed in the previous chapter. In this chapter, we focus on low achievers, the students who typically present the most serious motivational problems. In particular, we stress ways in which teachers might inadvertently undermine the efforts of low achievers and how these problems can be avoided. We begin with an experiment conducted by Rosenthal and Jacobson (1968), which proved to be one of the most exciting and controversial reports to appear in the history of educational research. These investigators presented data suggesting that teachers' experimentally induced expectations for student performance influenced the students' actual performance.

A test of general ability was given at the beginning of the year, and then randomly selected students were described to their teachers as "late bloomers" who would probably make large gains that year. This information was not actually based on student test performance, so except for expectations that the experimenters created in the teachers, there was no reason to predict improved performance by the "late bloomers." Yet when the same test was readministered at the end of the year, the data indicated that the experimental students did outgain their classmates, at least in grades one and two (grades three to six showed no significant differences). Experimental students in grades one and two also outperformed their classmates in reading achievement, and teachers described them as more likely to succeed in the future, more interesting, happier, and more intellectually curious than students who were not labeled as late bloomers.

This study captured the imagination of the general public, but unfortunately, secondary sources describing the findings made exaggerated claims that went far beyond those made by Rosenthal and Jacobson. An ad in the *Reader's Digest*, for example, was titled "Self-Fulfilling Prophecy—A Key to Success." The ad itself read: "Actual experiments prove this mysterious force can heighten your intelligence, your competitive ability, and your will to succeed. The secret: Just make a prediction! Read how it works."

Attempts to replicate Rosenthal and Jacobson's findings using their exact methodology have been unsuccessful, and the study remains controversial (Wineburg, 1988). A larger body of work, however, by many different investigators using a variety of methods has established that teachers' expectations can and do affect classroom behavior and student achievement. (For reviews see Brophy, 1983; Brophy & Good, 1974; Cooper & Good, 1983; and Dusek, 1985.)

TEACHER EXPECTATIONS

Teacher expectations are inferences that teachers make about present and future academic achievement and general classroom behavior of students (either the entire class or specific individuals). General expectations include teachers' beliefs about the changeability versus the rigidity of students' abilities, the students' potential to benefit from instruction, the appropriate difficulty of material for the class or for a subgroup, and whether the class should be taught as a group or individually. Expectations for individual students may be based on student record information (test data, past grades, comments by previous teachers), knowledge about the family, or initial contact with the student in the classroom (apparent motivation, attentiveness and contributions to lessons, general work habits). Willis (1972) has shown that contact with students leads to the formation of stable (and largely accurate) differential expectations within a few days after the school year begins. Her study (described in detail in Brophy & Good, 1974) illustrates that the formation of expectations is normal and is inherently neither good nor bad. The critical issues are the *accuracy* of the expectations and the *flexibility* with which they are held. Inaccurate expectations will do damage if teachers not only do not correct them but begin to base instructional decisions on them.

Inaccurate expectations

Expectations affect perception and interpretation

Expectations tend to be self-sustaining. They affect both *perception*, by causing teachers to be alert for what they expect and less likely to notice what they do not expect, and *interpretation*, by causing teachers to interpret (and perhaps distort) what they see so that it is consistent with their expectations. Some expectations persist even though they do not coincide with the facts.

Self-Fulfilling Prophecy Effects of Teacher Expectations

Teachers' expectations can function as *self-fulfilling prophecies* if they influence teachers to behave in ways that confirm the teachers' original expectations. When a teacher's initial perceptions of students' ability or motivation are inaccurate, the teacher may treat the students as if they were different from how they really are. In time, such teacher behavior may move students in the direction of the originally erroneous perceptions, thus confirming the teacher's expectations, at least in part.

The following is an example of a self-fulfilling prophecy. Jan Getty, an average first grader, is the daughter of a well-known artist. Her teacher knows that the artist is bright and creative, and she attributes these same qualities to Jan even though Jan rarely exhibits behavior that others would call creative. Jan's day-to-day behavior is actually routine and marked by a dependency on others for direction. Yet the teacher consistently encourages Jan "to do her own thing." She accepts Jan's work but demands that Jan express her own thoughts. By the end of the year, Jan is among the most original thinkers in the room. She can project five or six plausible but creative alternative endings for the stories in the reader.

Expectations are expressed through behavior

The process described in this example is not magical; nor do teacher expectations influence student behavior directly. If student behavior is influenced, it is because the expectations are expressed through teacher behavior or classroom arrangements (the types of assignments the student receives, the level of group he or she is placed in, and so on).

Consider another example. Bill Burt, the son of a former All-American basketball player, is six feet, five inches, tall and weighs 225 pounds as a sophomore in high school. Quin Chase, his coach, expects him to be a star. During practice, Coach Chase works Bill as hard as any other player. He acknowledges Bill's success on the floor but also points out his mistakes, just as he does for the other players. Bill earns a starting position, wins All-State honors as a sophomore, and leads the team to a second-place finish in the state tournament. Despite the fact that Bill developed as a star, as Coach Chase had originally expected, this is not an example of a self-fulfilling prophecy. Coach Chase did not treat Bill differently from the other players.

Let us consider a variation on this example that *would* reflect a self-fulfilling prophecy. Early in the year, Coach Chase realizes that Bill is going to be outstanding but he doesn't think that Bill can make All-State unless he puts considerable pressure on him and focuses publicity on him. So, he demands that Bill practice on Saturdays and part of Sundays (to the possible neglect of his studies), asks him to engage in conditioning exercises beyond normal procedures prescribed for all team members, and arranges for Bill to work on weaknesses in his game by scrimmaging against college players. He also emphasizes Bill and his talents rather than the team during discussions with the press, allows Bill to guard the weakest opposing player so that he can concentrate on his offense, and leaves Bill in games that the team has won so that he can build up his scoring statistics.

Factors for a self-fulfilling prophecy

True instances of self-fulfilling prophecies include these three factors: (1) *an originally unjustified expectation*, (2) *behaviors that consistently communicate that expectation*, and (3) *evidence that the original expectation has been confirmed*. In the case of Jan Getty's teacher we saw the expectation work subconsciously; in the case of Bill Burt's coach, it worked as an explicit strategy. Self-fulfilling prophecies may occur with or without teachers' awareness that their behavior is being systematically influenced by their expectations.

Sustaining Effects of Teacher Expectations

Self-fulfilling prophecies are the most dramatic teacher-expectation effects because they involve *changes* in student behavior. Cooper and Good (1983) used the term *sustaining expectations* to refer to situations in which teachers fail to see student potential and hence do not respond in ways that encourage the students to fulfill their potential. If a teacher, for example, automatically places all students who were in a low group last year into a low group this year (i.e., without assessing their current abilities), the teacher will fail to capitalize on new potential that may have developed in some of these students.

In general, self-fulfilling expectations bring about change in student performance, whereas sustaining expectations prevent change. Sustaining expectation effects are subtle but occur frequently, whereas self-fulfilling prophecy effects are more dramatic but occur less frequently. In this chapter, we organize information around the concept of self-fulfilling prophecies, but both types of expectation effects are important.

TEACHER-EXPECTATION EFFECTS: A MODEL

Below is a model that we developed (Brophy & Good, 1974) to describe how teachers' expectations can become self-fulfilling prophecies:

1. The teacher expects specific behavior and achievement from particular students.
2. Because of these expectations, the teacher behaves differently toward different students.
3. This treatment by the teacher tells each student what behavior and achievement the teacher expects, and it affects the student's self-concept, achievement motivation, and level of aspiration.
4. If this teacher treatment is consistent over time, and if the student does not actively resist or change it in some way, it will shape the student's achievement and behavior. High-expectation students will be led to achieve at high levels, but the achievement of low-expectation students will decline.
5. With time, the student's achievement and behavior will conform more and more closely to that expected by the teacher.

Teacher expectations are not automatically self-fulfilling. Students may prevent such expectations from becoming fulfilled by resisting them in ways that force teachers to change them.

Communication of Low Expectations

The following are some of the more common ways in which low teacher expectations can be expressed through teacher behavior (Good & Brophy, 1987):

1. Waiting less time for lows to answer questions (compared to how long the teacher typically waits for other students to answer).
2. Giving lows the answer or calling on someone else (instead of trying to elicit the answer by giving clues or rephrasing the question).
3. Rewarding inappropriate behavior of lows: In some studies teachers have been found to inappropriately praise marginal or inaccurate student responses. Praising incorrect responses when peers know the answer may only emphasize the academic weakness of low achievers.
4. Criticizing lows more frequently for failure: In contrast, in some studies teachers have been found to criticize lows proportionately more frequently than highs when they provide wrong answers. This is likely to reduce the risk-taking behavior and general initiative of lows. (The contrast between variables 3 and 4 probably reflects different teacher personalities. Teachers who praise inappropriate answers from lows may be overly sympathetic toward these students, whereas overly

critical teachers may be irritated at them for delaying the class or providing evidence that instruction has not been completely successful.)

5. Praising lows less frequently for success: Some research has shown that when lows provide correct answers they are less likely to be praised than highs, even though they provide fewer correct responses.
6. Not giving feedback to public responses of lows: Teachers in some studies were found simply to move on to the next question following lows' answers (especially correct answers), instead of first taking a moment to confirm those answers. This is particularly undesirable in that these students, more than others, may be unsure of the adequacy of their responses.
7. Paying less attention to lows or interacting with them less frequently.
8. Calling on lows less often (this is especially likely in the higher grades).
9. Different interaction patterns with highs and lows: In elementary classrooms, highs dominate public response opportunities, although highs and lows receive about the same number of private teacher contacts. In secondary classrooms, highs become even more dominant in public settings, but lows receive more private conferences. Here, frequent private conferences with teachers may be a sign of inadequacy and a source of embarrassment, especially if the teacher does not initiate many such conferences with highs.
10. Demanding less from lows: This is an extension of the more focused "giving-up" variable discussed in 2 above, and refers to activities such as giving lows easier tests (and letting them know it) or simply not asking them to do academic work.
11. Other forms of differential treatment include (a) seating lows farther from the teacher; (b) interacting with lows more privately than publicly and monitoring and structuring their activities more closely; (c) differential grading of tests and assignments in which highs but not lows are given the benefit of the doubt in borderline cases; (d) less friendly interactions with lows, including less smiling and less informative feedback to their questions; (f) less eye contact and other nonverbal communication of attention and responsiveness; (g) less use of effective but time-consuming methods with lows when time is limited; (h) less acceptance and use of lows' ideas.

Assignment to groups

Group-Level Effects Expectation effects at the group level are possible whenever teachers use within-class grouping, especially if the groups have been formed according to ability or achievement level. Weinstein (1976), for example, showed in a study of first-grade classrooms that reading-group membership added 25 percent to the variance in midyear reading achievement that could be predicted beyond what was predictable from readiness scores taken at the beginning of the year. Placement in high groups accelerated achievement and placement into low groups slowed it, relative to the differences that would have been expected due to variation in initial readiness.

Weinstein did not identify differences in teaching behavior that might have accounted for these differential effects of group assignment. However, other research comparing instruction in different reading groups (reviewed by Hiebert, 1983) suggests some possible explanations. Teachers tend to give longer reading assignments and to provide more time for discussion of stories with high groups than with low groups. They are quicker to interrupt low-group students when they make reading mistakes (Allington, 1983) and more likely just to give them the word or prompt them with graphemic (phonetic) cues rather than to offer semantic or syntactic cues that might help them to recognize the word from its context (Allington, 1983; Pflaum et al., 1980). In general, low-group students spend most of their time decoding words and providing short answers to low-level questions from the teacher, whereas high-group students spend most of the time on more extended reading for meaning and providing longer answers to more diverse questions focusing on story interpretation (Borko & Eisenhart, 1986; Hart, 1982).

Reading groups

Eder (1981) provided evidence indicating that some of these differences are due to the development in low groups of social contexts that are not conducive to learning. Eder studied first-grade reading groups in a school serving a relatively homogeneous middle-class population. Considering this and the fact that none of the students could read before entering first grade, it is not clear that the teacher needed to group these students according to ability. However, the teacher did use "ability grouping," based on kindergarten teachers' recommendations, which in turn were based on the maturity of the students in addition to their perceived ability. Consequently, the low group contained a high percentage of immature, inattentive students whose disruptive behavior frequently interrupted lesson continuity. Compared to the high group, the low group spent almost twice as much time off task, and when they were paying attention, they were more likely to read out of turn or call out words or answers that were supposed to be supplied by other students. Thus the achievement of low-group members can be slowed not only by limitations in their own ability and by low teacher expectations but also by the undesirable social

Some teachers think that dividing classes into smaller groups allows them to meet differing learning needs more effectively.

contexts that develop when groups contain too few academic peer leaders and too many attention and conduct problems.

Class-Level Effects Teachers differ in their expectations for entire classes of students, just as they do in their expectations for individuals or for within-class groups. Brophy and Evertson (1976) found that a "can-do" attitude was associated with teachers' relative success in eliciting achievement from students. The most successful teachers believed that their students were capable of mastering curriculum objectives and that they (the teachers) could meet the students' instructional needs. These expectations were associated with behaviors such as augmenting or even replacing the curriculum materials or evaluation instruments if they did not appear suited to the needs of the students.

Sense of efficacy

Ashton and Webb (1986) reported similar findings for teachers who differed in *sense of efficacy*. Compared to teachers with a low sense of efficacy, teachers who believed that they could motivate and instruct their students successfully were more confident and at ease in their classrooms, more positive (praising, smiling) and less negative (criticizing, punishing) in interactions with students, more successful in managing their classrooms as efficient learning environments, less defensive, more accepting of student disagreement and challenges, and more effective in producing student achievement. Low-efficacy teachers concentrated on rule enforcement and behavior management, whereas high-efficacy teachers focused on instructing students in the curriculum and interacting with them about academic content.

Cooper and Good (1983) found that teachers who held lower expectations for their classes tended to teach easier lessons, to spend less time on rigorous academic activities, and to accept less-than-perfect performance from their students before moving on to new material. Sedlak et al. (1985) found that many teachers, especially at the high school level, make implicit "bargains" with students; that is, the teachers minimize their work demands (i.e., assign easy, routine, and predictable tasks) in exchange for student cooperation and goodwill.

Effects in tracking systems

Teacher-expectation effects at the class level are especially likely to appear in schools that use tracking systems. Evertson (1982) studied the same teachers in their high- and low-track classes and found that these teachers were less clear about their objectives, introduced content less clearly or completely, made fewer attempts to relate the content to the students' interests or backgrounds, were less reasonable in their work standards, were less consistent in their discipline, and were less receptive to student input in low-track classes. Other research suggests that most teachers prefer to teach high-track classes (Finley, 1984) and that they tend to assign more independent projects and to introduce more high-level and integrative concepts in these classes (Heathers, 1969) but to stress more structured assignments dealing with basic facts and skills in low-track classes (Borko, Shavelson, & Stern, 1981). In addition, teachers appear to plan more thoroughly for high-track classes but to spend more time allowing low-track students to do activities of their own choosing rather than spending the time teaching them academic content (Brookover et al., 1979; Keddie, 1971; Leacock, 1969; Rosenbaum, 1976).

School-Level Effects Studies of school-effectiveness and school-improvement programs (reviewed by Good and Brophy, 1986) indicate that high expectations and commitment to bringing about student achievement are part of a pattern of attitudes, beliefs, and behaviors that characterizes schools that are successful in maximizing students' learning. Brookover and associates (1979), for example, found that teachers in more effective schools held higher expectations for students and acted on them by setting goals expressed as minimally acceptable levels of achievement rather than using prior achievement data to establish ceiling levels beyond which students would not be expected to progress. Such teachers responded to failures as challenges, requiring students to redo failed work (with individualized help as needed) rather than giving up on students or referring them to remedial classes. They responded to mistakes during class with appropriate feedback and reinstruction rather than with lowering of standards or inappropriate praise. Similar findings have been reported by Rutter (1983).

Desirable Individualization versus Undesirable Expectation Effects

There is a general tendency *in some classrooms* for low students to be treated in ways that differ from how students believed to be more capable are treated. Good and Weinstein (1986) defined these general differences in Table 17.1.

Facts about differential student treatment

We need to make several points about the differential student treatment that has been documented in various studies. First, it does not occur in all classrooms. Teachers differ considerably in how much they differentiate their treatment of students for whom they hold different expectations (more on this later).

Second, sometimes the differences are due primarily to the students rather than to the teacher. If lows seldom raise their hands, for example,

Teachers can reduce the sometimes debilitating effect of concentrated special attention to low achievers by maintaining periodic individual contact with all students.

TABLE 17.1 CENTRAL DIMENSIONS OF TEACHERS' COMMUNICATION OF DIFFERENTIAL EXPECTATIONS

Students Believed to Be More Capable Have	Students Believed to Be Less Capable Have
more opportunity to perform publically on meaningful tasks	less opportunity to perform publicly, especially on meaningful tasks
more autonomy (e.g., more choice in assignment, fewer interruptions)	less autonomy (frequent teacher monitoring of work, frequent interruption)
more assignments that deal with comprehension, understanding	less choice of curriculum assignments but more opportunity to work on drill-like assignments
more opportunity to think	less opportunity to think and analyze since much work is aimed at practice
more opportunity for self-evaluation	less opportunity for self-evaluation
more honest/contingent feedback	less honest/more gratuitous feedback
more respect for the learner as an individual with unique interests and needs	less respect for the learner as an individual with unique interests and needs

Source: *T. Good and R. Weinstein (1986), "Classroom expectations: One framework for exploring classrooms." In K. Kepler-Zumwalt (ed.),* Theory into Practice: 1986 ASCD Yearbook. *Reprinted by permission of Association for Supervision and Curriculum Development, and T. Good and R. Weinstein.*

it is difficult for the teacher to ensure that they get as many response opportunities as highs, and if their contributions are of lower quality, it is difficult for the teacher to use their ideas just as frequently.

Third, some forms of differential treatment may be appropriate at times and may even represent good individualized instruction rather than inappropriate projection of negative expectations. Lows appear to require closer monitoring of their work and more structuring of their activities, for example, so one could argue that it makes sense to interact with them more privately than publicly or to ask them easier questions. Similarly, it is difficult to distinguish seatwork monitoring that includes just the right degree of extra structuring and assistance from seatwork monitoring that amounts to giving students the answers without requiring them to think and learn. Thus one should not automatically assume that all forms of differential treatment are inappropriate.

Dangers

On the other hand, there are danger signals, especially if the differentiation is obvious and encompasses many of these variables rather than just one or two. Such a clear pattern of differentiation suggests that the teacher is merely going through the motions of instructing low-expectation students without genuinely trying to encourage their academic progress. The danger of this is especially great where ability grouping is used within the classroom or tracking is used within the school. A "low-group psychology" often develops when teachers work with low groups or classes, so that these students get taught at a slower pace and get exposed to less interesting and varied activities than they are capable of handling.

Note that some of these forms of differential treatment would have direct effects on students' opportunity to learn and thus could have self-fulfilling prophecy effects on student achievement, even if other forms of differentiation did not occur. To the extent that teachers provide lows with less information and less feedback than they provide to highs, for example, the lows are almost certain to make less progress than the highs. This will occur regardless of whether or not the lows are aware of the differential treatment and its implications about their teacher's expectations for them.

Thus although differential treatment of high and low achievers does not automatically indicate inappropriate teacher expectations or undesirable teacher-expectation effects, it is wise to keep these possibilities in mind when making instructional decisions and monitoring one's teaching. Research has shown that undesirable differentiation in treatment of students can be avoided and also that it can be ameliorated if it already exists. The latter findings were shown in a three-year "Equal Opportunity in the Classroom" inservice education project sponsored by the Los Angeles County School System (Martin, 1973). The goals of the project were to sensitize teachers to the possible damaging effects of inappropriate behavior toward low achievers and to present teachers with a variety of skills to use with these students. The data showed that the teachers did change their behavior toward low achievers (such as starting to call on them more frequently) and that the low achievers in the classrooms of teachers who participated in the project showed a marked increase in achievement relative to low achievers in comparison classes. Furthermore, these benefits to low achievers were accomplished without any reduction in the achievement of other students. Thus it is possible to improve the achievement progress of low achievers by changing teacher behavior and to do so without adversely affecting their classmates.

INDIVIDUAL DIFFERENCES AMONG TEACHERS

We have noted that teachers differ in the degree to which they treat low achievers in what appear to be inappropriate ways. Based on a series of observational studies, Brophy and Good (1974) suggested that teachers can be thought of as being on a continuum from proactive through reactive to overreactive.

Proactive teachers

Proactive teachers are guided by their own beliefs about what is reasonable and appropriate in setting goals for the class as a whole and for individual students. If they set realistic goals and have the needed skills, they are likely to move students toward these goals. Proactive teachers are the most likely to have positive expectation effects on students.

Overreactive teachers

At the other extreme, *overreactive* teachers develop rigid, stereotyped perceptions of students based on prior records or on first impressions in the classroom. Overreactive teachers treat students as stereotypes rather than as individuals, and they are the teachers most likely to have negative expectation effects.

Reactive teachers

Most teachers fall in between these extremes and are classified as *reactive* teachers who hold their expectations lightly and adjust them in response to new feedback and emerging trends. Reactive teachers have minimal expectation effects on students, tending merely to sustain existing differences between high and low achievers (actually, these differences tend to increase slightly because of contrasts in the behavior of the students themselves that reactive teachers do not compensate for).

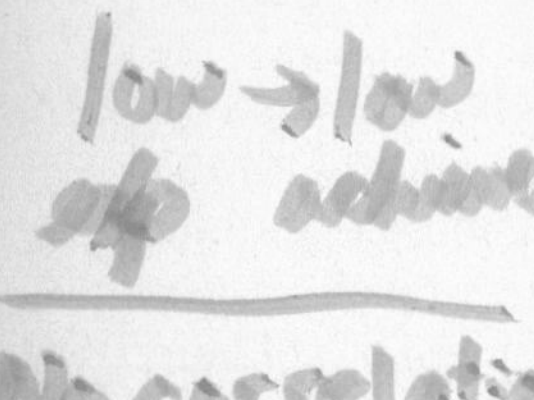

Research supports these distinctions, but unfortunately it also indicates that the most sizeable teacher-expectation effects on student achievement are negative ones in which low expectations lead to lower achievement than might have been attained otherwise (Brophy, 1983). There is little evidence that even proactive teachers significantly augment the achievement of individual students by projecting positive expectations but much evidence that overreactive teachers minimize student progress by projecting low expectations.

Reasons for inappropriate behavior

Given that most teachers want to be effective in the classroom, why do some behave in obviously inappropriate ways toward low achievers? There are several possible explanations. The most basic is that teachers simply are not aware of much of their classroom behavior. As we noted in Chapter 1, the complexities of teaching make it difficult for teachers to monitor their classroom decisions and actions continuously, so it is easy for them to develop habitual patterns without realizing that they have done so. Teachers are often unaware of their differential treatment of students (Good & Brophy, 1987).

A second reason why teachers might behave differently toward different students is that the students condition them to do so. Teachers may wait longer for answers, for example, and work harder to improve answers when dealing with high achievers than when dealing with low achievers because the high achievers respond more positively to such challenges and reward the teachers more often with improved responses. Also, as Cooper (1979) has noted, teachers may be less willing to stay with low achievers in public response situations because the behavior of these students is less predictable than that of high achievers, and there is always the danger that they will say something that will disrupt the lesson or even threaten the teacher's control of the class (e.g., complain about being badgered for answers or make an unwelcome humorous remark).

Teacher personality characteristics provide a third explanation for differential treatment of students, especially the extreme kind shown by overreactive teachers. Several studies indicate that these teachers tend toward conventionalism, rigidity, intolerance of ambiguity, and other aspects of authoritarianism or dogmatism (Babad, 1985; Tom, Cooper & McGraw, 1984).

Teachers' beliefs about intelligence

A fourth explanaton concerns teachers' beliefs about the nature of intelligence. Dweck and Elliott (1983) have shown that some teachers view intelligence as an *entity* and thus see it as relatively stable and singular in nature. In contrast other teachers view intelligence as *incremental*, as a repertoire of skills and knowledge that can be increased continuously. Marshall and Weinstein (1984) suggested that teachers who hold an entity view of intelligence are more likely to place students in stable hierarchies according to performance expectations and to treat these students differently on the basis of such expectations. They go on to suggest that low achievers in the classrooms of these teachers may perceive that they are being treated differently according to their ability and may use this information to compare themselves with other students in ways that cause them to lower their self-concepts and begin to expect less of themselves. In contrast, in classrooms where teachers hold an incremental view of intelligence, teachers' statements and curriculum assignments communicate the belief that each student has the ability to improve regardless of current status, that individual differences in rates and modes of learning are normal, and that students can learn from those who have already acquired certain skills.

The data presented by Ames and Ames do not necessarily indicate a more wholesome teacher perspective. Teachers who attribute success and failure exclusively to student characteristics may also be unwilling to examine their own behavior as a possible factor that may interfere in the learning process. We suspect that student, environmental, and teacher-school factors are all involved and must be examined when failure occurs.

More reasons for inappropriate differential treatment of students

Good (1983) identified several additional reasons for inappropriate differential treatment of students. One stems from the fact that most classroom behavior is ambiguous and subject to multiple interpretations. Some teachers develop ways to monitor classroom behavior more systematically and accurately than others and are more willing to examine classroom behavior from multiple viewpoints. These teachers may be more likely to communicate appropriate expectations to all students.

Another reason stems from teachers' efficacy beliefs. Teachers who believe that they can and will influence student learning may interpret student failure as a need for more instruction, more clarification, and eventually increased opportunity to learn. Other teachers, because they assign blame rather than assume partial responsibility for student failure, may interpret such failure as indicating a need to provide less challenge and fewer opportunities to learn.

Another explanation involves the ways in which students present themselves to the teacher. Because they use nonstandard language or lack familiarity with certain social cues, some students may have difficulty convincing teachers that they know the material. Finally, some expectation effects occur because teachers and students are culturally conditioned to expect certain behavor from girls or boys or from minority students.

APPROPRIATE EXPECTATIONS AND TREATMENT OF LOW ACHIEVERS

Appropriate versus inappropriate expectations

We have described the invidious effects of low expectations and the reasons why some teachers communicate them to certain students. We now consider what are *appropriate* expectations and related treatment of low achievers. We begin by noting two expectations that are sometimes recommended but that we see as *inappropriate*: equal expectations for all or high expectations for all.

Need for realistic expectations

First, we do *not* suggest that all students should receive equal (in the sense of identical) classroom treatment. Some students will learn more quickly than others. Some will be reticent but able to learn by actively listening and covertly responding to what they hear. Thus *sameness* is inappropriate as an expectation and self-defeating as a strategy. Nor are high expectations realistic for all students. In hopes of motivating student performance, a teacher might announce: "This story is interesting and easy to read, so all of you should finish it in ten minutes." If some students need twenty minutes to read the story, they are left with two choices: They can pretend to finish it and hope they are not "found out," or they can continue to read while the teacher or their peers make remarks about their slowness. These students will feel bad either way, and if such events are repeated regularly, they will tend either to accept their inferior status or to blame the teacher. Thus overly high performance expectations that are consistently impossible for students to reach will eventually erode their efforts.

Awareness of classroom behavior

Teachers are human and will make errors in assessing students' needs. The way to reduce errors is to obtain information about classroom behavior. Teachers need to become more aware of their classroom behavior in general and their interactions with low achievers in particular. As a starting point, teachers could review their behavior with an eye toward the following questions:

- Do I praise or encourage lows when they initiate questions or comments?
- Do I stay with lows in failure situations?
- Do I stay with lows in success situations?
- Do I avoid calling on lows in public situations?
- How often do lows experience success in public situations?
- Are lows needlessly criticized for wrong answers or failure to respond?
- Are lows placed in a "low group" and treated as group members rather than as individuals?
- How often do lows get to select a study topic?
- How frequently do lows have a chance to evaluate their own work and to make important decisions?

Skill Development through Meaningful Practice

Skill work and task motivation

Teachers sometimes overrespond to low achievers' skill deficiencies. At first glance, this seems to be reasonable. If students are weak in word-attack skills, they need to develop such skills if they are to become independent readers. However, if they work constantly on skills without reading for meaning, their motivation to learn may be eroded. Thus teachers who constantly interrupt poor readers when they are reading may compound their problems by reducing the time they spend directly practicing reading. If students are to derive personal satisfaction from any task, they must have the opportunity for meaningful and successful practice. Students who have low reading ability need the chance to practice *the act of reading*. It is amazing to see how little time low achievers have for reading in some classrooms. Too often they are drowned in a sea of drill work and constant reminders of inadequate performance. Teachers need to balance their demands for drill with opportunity for students to read for meaning and pleasure (in content area books and works of fiction, not just basal readers).

Need for practicing skills

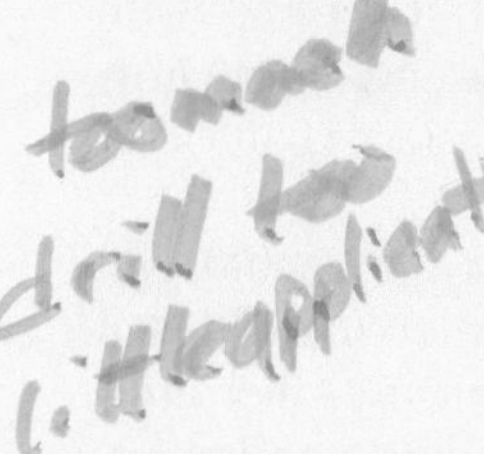

Similar problems are seen in other curriculum areas. Low-group students sometimes spend too much mathematics time on drill and too little on learning mathematical concepts and how they can be used.

Erosion of student motivation

Variation of assignments

Student motivation can be eroded in other ways. How would you feel if everything that you did was done better and faster by someone else? This is the situation that poor readers often face. They hear the teacher discuss a story with other students long before they have a chance to read it. If this experience is repeated daily, it is apt to lower their interest in the reading material because they have already heard others discuss the story. Furthermore, it is hard for teachers to bring the same degree of enthusiasm to each new discussion of the same story. Teacher motivation may thus influence student response. Teachers may inadvertently focus more on the mechanics of reading than on general comprehension by the time they read the story with low achievers. One way to break out of this joint trap for teachers and poor readers would be to assign different stories periodically to the low reading group. New stories would provide a chance for these students to reach their own conclusions and insights.

Challenge high achievers

Another way that teachers can address the motivational problem of low achievers is to challenge high achievers appropriately. If teachers are exposing high achievers to material of appropriate difficulty, then they, too, will make mistakes from time to time. Teachers will have to review word-attack and interpretive skills with these students as well. The fact that all students have to exert effort will not be lost on the low achievers.

Unequal opportunities

The low-ability student frequently gets to do an activity only *after* more capable students have performed the task. In elementary schools, teachers often allow students free work time *after* assigned tasks are completed. In high school chemistry classrooms, more complex experiments are performed only after simpler experiments have been completed successfully. Opportunities for independent study are often available only after certain work has been completed.

There are times when a fixed sequence has to be followed (for example, all students need to master safety procedures in the lab). If teachers analyze the situation carefully, however, it is often possible to assign tasks so that students who move through the curriculum more slowly do not always just repeat the same experience as the others. These students could be asked to perform relatively simple but different experiments. Indeed, when slower students are doing such work, more advanced students might be referred to them to learn about the outcomes of experiments that they themselves did not perform.

Treating Low Achievers as Individuals

Teachers too often group and treat all low achievers as though they were one student. It is especially vital to learn about the unique needs and interests of students who may view school as irrelevant or aversive. Unfortunately, when teachers visit informally with students, it is rarely with lows. Most of these students want teacher contact but do not know how to obtain it, and they may think that teachers like them less than other students and do not want to be bothered with them.

Many lows initially played the academic game as best they could, but teacher or peer feedback proved so disheartening that they learned that an academic question avoided is an academic battle won. Teacher criticism of any serious response attempt is inappropriate in any situation but especially for passive, low-achieving students. Students who respond with passivity have been rewarded for such behavior and have learned that making no response is better than taking a chance. Teachers need to convince such students that their responses will not be evaluated harshly and that responding is the best way to get teacher attention and help.

Other students will respond to threatening situations with different strategies. Some play the class clown and supply clever but irrelevant responses. This protects their self-esteem and punishes the teacher for calling on them. Other students may respond to teachers with open hostility. Such behavior may bring teacher criticism for rudeness and poor attitude, but it avoids negative teacher evaluation of the student's ability and sometimes even elicits indirect compliments ("If you read and improved your attitude, you'd be one of the best students in the class!").

Recognizing coping strategy

Student behaviors that have been institutionalized through practice and reward are difficult to change. The first step is to recognize the coping strategy that the student uses and then systematically reward competing responses (e.g., answering versus not answering). But to be able to do this, it is necessary for teachers to know individual students.

Students who are victimized by low expectations and inappropriate classroom treatment may be entirely correct when they attribute their task success to external factors. If teachers do not make it possible for such students to achieve success with reasonable effort and reward such effort, it is unlikely that the students will perceive a dependable relationship between personal effort and task success.

CHANGING STUDENTS' LOW EXPECTATIONS

Many students do poorly in school because they are hesitant and fear failure. Students with poor self-concepts may give up hope and expect mediocrity or worse as inevitable. The precise way in which a teacher can help students to improve their self-views will vary with the individual and the teaching situation. The difficulty of changing self-views increases as the age of the student increases. However, two general strategies are noncontingent acceptance and honest feedback.

McCandless and Evans (1973) stressed the importance of noncontingent acceptance (of sincere effort) and provision of sensitive but realistic and

Noncontingent acceptance and honest feedback

honest feedback. Too often, teachers overlook low achievers' problems or provide them with unrealistic feedback. Despite the good intentions behind it, such behavior is counterproductive. The maladaptive effects of inappropriate praise are aptly summarized in the following:

> First, the child who realizes that his product or performance is lacking may become confused by the discrepancy between his own judgment and the feedback he is receiving. He may then alter his own judgment and standards to coincide with the feedback he has received, or he may become distrustful of the adult and discount his future pronouncements. . . . Another possible consequence of excessive praise is the establishment of the child's image of himself as infallible. The child who is lavishly approved or rewarded for any performance may have difficulty at a later time accepting the harsh reality that he, too, sometimes fails. Faced with failure, the child may become defensive and refuse to admit that his performance is lacking. He may possibly be overwhelmed by the failure and magnify it out of proportion so that it becomes incapacitating. In either event, this child will have difficulty coping with failure and turning it to his advantage as a learning experience. (Nardine, 1971, pp. 342–343)

If teachers are to provide students with more appropriate feedback, they must understand how low achievers are apt to respond to teacher feedback. In general, success leads to high but realistic aspirations, whereas failure leads either to unrealistically low expectations or unrealistically high aspirations that students do not genuinely expect to fulfill.

Repeated failure experiences will cause students to develop an inability or unwillingness to use task feedback appropriately. If they begin to experience success, their past history of failure may still lead them to continue to make unrealistic predictions for subsequent task performance. They may need time to get accustomed to success, and this success will have to be in *realistic* tasks. Sometimes teachers with the best intentions can inadvertently undermine student initiative by making assignments obviously easy or by using too much praise. Teachers who can help students to achieve success on tasks that they perceive as challenging will have taken a major step in helping students to develop appropriate, positive expectations for learning.

Linking Outcomes to Effort

Assessing students' predictive ability

A key teacher task in increasing student motivation is to help students perceive the relationship between success and personal effort. As a starting point, teachers might ask students to discuss tasks on which they have done poorly and to explain why their performances were poor. Teachers also need to assess students' ability to determine the time and effort necessary to complete tasks successfully. Teachers might ask students to estimate the time necessary to complete a particular task, for example, collect follow-up information, and provide this information to students during conferences. Teachers could also help students to distinguish between tasks they can and cannot do. Similarly, teachers could check the accuracy of students' perceptions by asking them to indicate the extent to which they thought they had correctly answered various examination questions.

Helping students make realistic predictions

Such assessment should be followed by attempts to help learners distinguish between tasks that they can do and those that are really too difficult. The critical factor is that some practical benefit will follow. Students need to see what happens when they apply themselves to an academic tasks. Thus the next step is to create a series of tasks that are clearly tied to work effort so that greater effort produces greater success. Task feedback should focus on the process, that is, the relationship between effort and success.

Assisting students in pursuit of academic goals

After demonstrating that performance outcome is related to effort expenditure, it would be useful to let students know through individual conferences that the teacher regularly assigns tasks that they can do and that anytime they cannot find information or do not know how to proceed, they should ask for help. It is also useful to stress that tasks are assigned to facilitate learning and thus designed to benefit the student, not just to fill time. The teacher also should create the expectation that assigned tasks, although appropriately difficult and challenging, can be completed if the students want to do so. From dissonance theory we know that once students see that their personal efforts are related to task success, it is difficult for them to explain away failure. The incongruity between poor performance and knowledge that they can accomplish the task may exert subtle pressure on them to expend more time and effort trying to succeed.

Emphasizing Instructional Help, Not Sympathy

Sympathy alone is misplaced and self-defeating. Teachers who give easier tests to lows, who always ask them elementary questions, or who give up on them in public-response situations do not help, and often worsen, their plight.

Kleinfeld (1975) showed this in a penetrating ethnographic analysis of teacher behavior with Indian and Eskimo students who were experiencing culture shock on moving from their native, rural schools to urban, integrated schools. She found that the most effective teachers were those who took a personal interest in students, engaged in informal conversations with them, adapted instruction to their different backgrounds and achievement levels, were highly supportive of their attempts to learn, and avoided use of criticism. In addition, these highly effective teachers elicited high intellectual performance from the village Indian and Eskimo students by creating warm personal relationships and demanding a level of academic work "that the student does not suspect he can attain." Village students interpreted the teacher's demandingness not as bossiness or hostility but rather as another expression of personal concern, so meeting the teacher's academic standards became their reciprocal obligation in an intensely personal relationship.

Creating an Appropriate Classroom Climate

Teachers have to justify any special help that they provide to lows, or else the lows (and other students as well) will interpret the increased teacher attention as a sign that they are inferior. Teachers can help lows gain more self-respect and respect from classmates if they allow them to

Individual contact with students

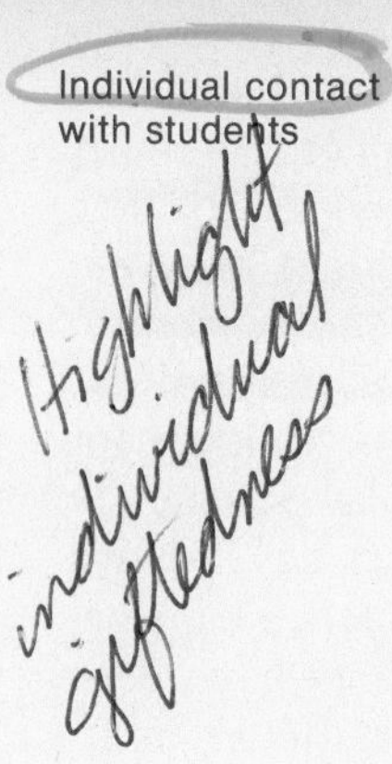

achieve notable *public success* from time to time. This involves careful planning, because trivial or unsuccessful exposure of lows may deepen the problem. However, public success is important and worth planning for, because most of the successes of lows are private, although many of their failures occur in public.

Often teachers can use unique talents that students already possess or can capitalize on their life-styles. Kleinfeld (1975), for example, reported that some teachers were able to increase the prestige of village students and reduce hostility toward them by making their skills, such as "surviving in the wilderness," public knowledge. At other times, teachers need to work with students to help them learn skills (such as teaching a fifth-grade student how to run a projector or allowing the student to make a movie) that they can demonstrate publicly. Repeated public successes, especially those involving skills deemed important by the peer group, will do much to raise the esteem with which lows are regarded by their classmates.

A Comprehensive and Collaborative Intervention

Weinstein (1988), Soule (1988), and their colleagues have reported promising findings from a comprehensive intervention program that involves collaboration between university researchers and the staff of an urban high school. The project focused on incoming ninth graders who were assigned to low-track classes based on low achievement test scores and recommendations by junior high school counselors and teachers. The participating teachers attended university classes on the motivation problems of low achievers and then worked in collaboration with the researchers to develop a systematic program for preventing or remediating these problems with the low-achieving (largely minority) students who enter their school each year.

Eight components of a comprehensive intervention

The program included deliberate interventions in eight areas: (1) task and curriculum (minimize tasks that heighten ability comparisons; give low achievers frequent opportunities to work on higher-order thinking and application aspects of what they are learning); (2) grouping (minimize ability grouping; make use of heterogeneous grouping and cooperative learning activities); (3) evaluation (emphasize qualitative evaluation; provide private feedback that stresses continuous progress achieved through a combination of ability and effort); (4) motivational climate (minimize competition; stress intrinsic rewards in addition to extrinsic rewards); (5) student role in learning (provide opportunities for students to make choices and gradually assume increasing responsibility for managing their own learning); (6) class relationships (develop a sense of community among the students that includes valuing of diversity and fostering of cooperation in learning); (7) parent-teacher communication (establish positive relationships with parents; emphasize students' positive attributes and progress rather than their deficiencies or problems); and (8) school-level supports (with cooperation from school administrators, establish increased and varied opportunities for low achievers to participate in school activities and get recognition for their achievements in and out of the classroom).

Early results suggest that the program has had positive effects, even though it has been implemented within a tracking system that minimizes contact between the target students and students in the upper two-thirds of the distribution of student achievement at the school. Teachers have reported significantly greater use of tasks relevant to student lives and less use of tasks requiring sequential mastery, and they have begun to feel less constrained by existing materials in designing student activities. They also report more use of mixed-ability groups and less tendency for students to acquire reputations based on ability, as well as a generally more positive and cohesive learning community. Students have shown better grades compared to the grades earned by comparable students before the initiation of the program, and small improvements have been seen in absence, transfer, and disciplinary referral rates. Better information on the effects of the program will become available as additional cohorts enter and as students are followed into subsequent grades to assess longitudinal effects. The early data are promising, however, and the program illustrates ways in which collaboration by school staff can improve the learning climates for low achievers in ways that go beyond the confines of an individual classroom.

SUMMARY

Teacher expectations—the inferences that teachers make about present and future achievements and behaviors of students—can undermine the efforts of low-achieving students by acting as self-fulfilling prophecies. Three factors are involved in self-fulfilling prophecies: (1) an originally unjustified expectation, (2) behaviors that communicate that expectation, and (3) evidence confirming that the original expectation has been fulfilled. There is evidence of a wide variety of ways in which low expectations are expressed to low-achieving students, including verbal feedback, grouping, wait-time, attention, seating, and various subtle teacher communications.

Attempts to reduce the negative effect of low expectatons include sensitizing teachers to the potentially damaging effects of such expectations, increasing their awareness of their own classroom behavior, and providing better feedback and support to teachers dealing with low achievers. It has been found that proactive teachers are less likely to allow low expectations to influence their interactions with students than are reactive or overreactive teachers. Also, teachers who have realistic expectations of all of their students and base differential treatment on such expectations are likely to elicit greater achievement than those whose expectations are unrealistic.

In general, dealing with students as individuals and giving them challenges and opportunities appropriate to their development will provide the kind of setting in which healthy self-concepts, levels of aspiration, and motivation will thrive. To be successful, however, teachers have to find time for individual contacts with low achievers and become sensitive to the way these students perceive classroom tasks.

Questions and Problems

1. In your own words, explain the difference between sustaining and self-fulfilling expectations.
2. One can view intelligence as *entity* or *incremental.* What is the importance of this distinction?
3. Consider the concepts of origin and pawn that were presented in Chapter 15 and discuss them in terms of teacher expectations.
4. Consider the concepts task involvement and ego involvement (Chapter 15) and explain their relationship to expectation effects.
5. What types of tasks are most likely to be assigned to students who are viewed as more or less capable? Why is this the case?
6. In this chapter stress has been placed on inappropriate expectations. Think of some positive and appropriate expectations that teachers could express to the entire class. For example, what could teachers say at the beginning or end of a lesson to encourage the best efforts of all, or at least most, of the students?
7. There probably are certain topics or broad subject-matter areas that you will be required to teach even though you find them uninteresting or distasteful. What are some of them? What can you do to reduce the danger that you will create the same kinds of negative attitudes in your students?
8. Students need success experiences, but they also need to be corrected when they make mistakes and guided when they are confused. How can this be accomplished in ways that will not damage motivation?
9. Differentiate between teachers' appropriate and inappropriate use of praise in the classroom. Can praise be harmful?

Case Studies

A STUDENT CONFERENCE. Mr. Morgan has graded the first set of history papers and sees that Jim Kline has done a terrible job. In a vague way he remembers Jim, a student in the third period who sits in the back of the room and has never spoken in class. He appears well dressed but uninterested. Mr. Morgan decides that he wants to have a conference with Jim, to let him know that his performance was poor, but also that he accepts Jim and wants to work out a way for Jim to improve. What would you do in this conference? Write out a few lines of dialogue to show how you would begin.

AN INSTRUCTIONAL DILEMMA. Jane Stoverink teaches with two other teachers in a unit composed of sixty-two students (in terms of traditional organization, most are fifth and sixth graders, although a few very bright fourth graders are in the room). Unfortunately, the weakest students in the unit are mostly minority students. How can Jane and the other two teachers group students for regular instruction and special activities in ways that will motivate them and yet provide a good chance for high and low achievers to interact regularly? Describe and defend your plan in detail.

AVOIDING CONFRONTATION. Tom, a first-year science teacher, left the fall teacher orientation wondering how he was going to survive attendance registers, purchasing, what to do with the Baker boys who evidently cause trouble, and many other things. In his first week of teaching he concentrated on organizing the classroom, learning his students' names, preparing lesson plans, and so on. One afternoon he asked one of his students, Mark, to collect the matches they had been using in a Bunsen burner experiment. Mark was larger than the rest of his classmates and had showed that he enjoyed this slight responsibility. Later, Tom was matching first and last names of his students when the name Mark Baker clicked in his mind. "Is he one of those Baker boys the principal warned us about?" he wondered. A chat with the school counselor verified that this was so. Soon Tom could hear himself finding fault with Mark and demanding behavior he had not required previously. A confrontaton occurred, Mark said some words that Tom felt were uncalled for, and Mark was sent to the principal for discipline. What role did teacher expectations have in Mark's involvement in a disciplinary situation? How could Tom have prevented this confrontation?

READING DRILL. Mary teaches first grade in a neighborhood school in an affluent section of town. Earlier in the year, she had divided the class into five equal-sized reading groups. By May, the top reading group, the Cardinals, was discussing stories they read on their own and were tape recording their own stories and listening to stories recorded by other students in their group. Mary has worked hard with the lowest group, the Cubs, because she wants them to make progress. She spends a little more time with the Cubs each day than the other groups, and she carefully examines their oral reading and emphasizes correct pronunciation and reading expression. She discourages word substitution because she wants students to learn to pay attention to detail—to be careful readers. How many of these differences in group treatment do you believe to be appropriate and necessary? Should a teacher teach the low group the same way as the high group? Defend your answer.

CHAPTER

The Humanistic Perspective

CHAPTER OUTLINE

OBJECTIVES

When you have mastered the material in this chapter, you will be able to

1. Contrast humanistic goals for learning and motivation with more cognitive goals
2. List the parent and teacher behaviors associated with high self-esteem and affective growth
3. Explain how the affective taxonomy can be used in planning ways to integrate affective goals into the curriculum
4. Explain the relationship of class scheduling and structuring to students' personal development
5. Define *individualized* and *open education* and explain their effects on student affect
6. Define *prosocial behavior* and tell how teachers can promote it through cooperative-learning activities
7. Describe research on cooperative and affective programs
8. Explain the three important characteristics of humanistic teachers and the value decisions involved in teaching for humanistic goals

Humanistic psychologists, like cognitive psychologists, emphasize the importance of perception and awareness as forces that determine behavior. However, humanistic psychologists are interested in the effects of schooling on the affective development of students as well as on their cognitive growth. In brief, humanists are somewhat more interested in how people feel about their perceptions, whereas cognitive psychologists are somewhat more interested in how individuals conceptualize or think about an event. Combs et al. (1974) summarized one humanistic perspective in the following statement:

> To understand humans . . . it is necessary to understand the behaver's perceptual world, how things seem from his point of view. This calls for a different understanding of what the "facts" are that we need in order to deal with human behavior; it is not the external facts that are important in understanding behavior, but the meaning of the facts to the behaver. (p. 15)

Self-perception and potential

This concern for an individual's feelings and self-perceptions has much in common with cognitive theories of motivation. However, humanists' interest in self-perceptions is not limited to improving attitudes toward school and achievement. Humanists emphasize the importance of understanding a student's perceptual world in order to help the student fulfill his or her basic potential (Rogers, 1983). The following quote captures some of the spirit of becoming "more human."

> If I had my life to live over, I'd try to make more mistakes next time. I would relax, I would limber up, I would be crazier than I've been on this trip, I know very few things I'd take seriously any more. I'd certainly be less hygienic. I would take more chances, I would take more trips, I would scale more mountains, I would swim more rivers, I would watch more sunsets. I would eat more ice cream and fewer beans. I would have more actual troubles and fewer imaginary ones. You see . . . I was one of those people who lives prophylactically and sensibly and sanely, hour after hour and day after day. Oh, I've had my moments and if I had it to do all over again, I'd have many more of them. In fact, I'd try not to have anything else, just moments, one after another instead of living so many years ahead of my day. I've been one of those people who never went anywhere without a thermometer, a hot water bottle, a gargle, a raincoat, and a parachute. If I had it to do all over again, I'd travel lighter, much lighter than I have. I would start barefoot earlier in the spring, and I'd stay that way later in the fall. And I would ride more merry-go-rounds, and catch more gold rings, and greet more people, and pick more flowers, and dance more often. If I had it to do all over again—But you see, I don't.

Although the concern for developing human potential is present in the writing of all humanists, the importance attached to particular outcomes varies widely. Some argue that humanistic approaches enhance cognitive performance and mastery of school subjects. Others state that they do not know if humanistic teaching improves general school performance. Yet others state that they do not care if humanistic teaching relates to academic achievement because personal development is an important objective of schooling in its own right.

THE PROBLEM OF SCHOOLING FROM A HUMANISTIC PERSPECTIVE

Carl Rogers (1983) was one of the most prolific and widely read proponents of humanistic education. Describing many of the aspects of schooling that bother humanists, he claimed that too many students have learned that there is no place for restless energy in class; one conforms or else suffers unpleasant consequences; submission to rules is expected; making a mistake is bad; punishment for a mistake is humiliating; spontaneous interest does not belong in school; teacher and disciplinarian are synonymous; school on the whole is unpleasant; most textbooks are boring; it is not safe to differ with the teacher; there are many ways to get by without studying; it is okay to cheat; daydreams and fantasy can make the day pass more quickly; studying hard to get good grades is frowned on by one's peers; most of the learning relevant to life occurs outside of school; original ideas have no place in school; exams and grades are the most important aspects of education; and most teachers, at least in class, are impersonal and boring.

This list provides one basis for considering school reform. However, school climate conditions vary; some schools are much more attractive, from both an affective and a cognitive viewpoint, than others (see Purkey & Smith, 1985). The problems on the list do not exist in all schools or classrooms.

Humanistic learning principles

Rogers (1983) also listed ten humanistic principles concerning general motivational processes that underlie meaningful growth: (1) Humans have a natural potential for learning; (2) significant learning takes place when students perceive the subject matter as relevant to their own purposes; (3) learning that would require a change in self-organization—in one's perception of oneself—is threatening and tends to be resisted; (4) learnings that are threatening to the self are more easily perceived and assimilated when external threats are at a minimum; (5) when threat to the self is low, experience can be perceived in differentiated fashion and learning can proceed; (6) much significant learning is acquired through doing; (7) learning is facilitated when the student participates responsibly in the learning process; (8) self-initiated learning that involves the whole person—feelings as well as intellect—is the most lasting and pervasive; (9) independence, creativity, and self-reliance are all facilitated when self-criticism and self-evaluation are basic and evaluation by others is of secondary importance; and (10) the most socially useful learning is the learning of the process of learning, a continuing openness to experience and incorporation into oneself of the process of change.

The meaning of most of these principles appears obvious at first, but applying them in the classroom can be difficult (for example, what are the best ways to encourage constructive self-criticism, and are some things impossible to learn by doing?). In any event, these ten principles suggest that students are best motivated on an intrinsic basis and that much individualization of the curriculum is needed if basic needs are to be fulfilled.

Teachers can accept these ten principles and still be either very interested or only moderately interested in fostering academic achievement, depending on their beliefs about what is important in teaching and about how to motivate students. The classroom strategies of teachers who primarily want to promote cognitive gain will differ from those of teachers who are more concerned about helping students to learn about themselves and others. In this chapter a variety of ways for integrating humanistic perspectives into the curriculum will be explored.

AFFECTIVE DEVELOPMENT

If one wants students to develop more differentiated views of self and others at school, one must present content that will allow students to feel and think about themselves and others in more complex and systematic ways. Initially, we learn about ourselves through concrete experiences and feedback from others. Gradually, we form concepts of who we are, what we can and cannot do, and, ultimately, our general worth. Initial self-views are shaped by the quality of early life experiences.

Parent behaviors

Research on the home conditions that produce children who feel good about themselves and others suggests that the following parent behaviors appear important: (1) completely accepting the child as a person, although not accepting all of the child's behavior, (2) setting clear standards and expectations for the child, and (3) offering respect and giving latitude for child initiative within defined limits (Coopersmith, 1967; White & Watts, 1973).

A reasonable hypothesis, at least for the preschool and early elementary school years, is that behaviors similiar to those observed in parents of high self-esteem children will be most conducive to growth in school. In addition, affective growth, like cognitive growth, depends on a sensible match between an individual's ability and assigned learning tasks. Few teachers would assign a story demanding seventh-grade reading ability to a child reading at the second-grade level. However, teachers often provide students with too much or too little structure in learning assignments.

Interchangeable teacher comments

An example of a variable that appears central to both positive self-concept development and achievement is the interchangeable teacher comment (Aspy, 1977; Rogers, 1983). An *interchangeable teacher comment* is a statement following a student's comment (especially an expression of feeling) that paraphrases the student's comment or in some other way lets the student know that he or she has been heard and understood. Such comments tell students that they are accepted, and acceptance by others appears to be a fundamental prerequisite to self-acceptance. Furthermore, interchangeable teacher comments have been found to have favorable effects on student achievement.

More is known about how teachers can assist students' cognitive growth than about how they can facilitate affective development. There is evidence, however, that teachers can make a difference in affective development, and promising programs for doing so have been developed.

A TAXONOMY FOR AFFECTIVE EDUCATION

Figure 18.1 presents a taxonomy for classifying affective goals. Ringness (1975) suggested that this taxonomy might help teachers to clarify their understanding of how to teach in ways that promote students' affective development. If a teacher were conducting a unit on pollution, for example, it would be useful to realize that merely making students aware of pollution as a problem will not necessarily make them willing to take action.

Student response

Higher levels of the taxonomy suggest ways to develop students' commitment to values or beliefs. Initially, the students may only verbalize the teacher's position (acquiescence), but in time they may become willing to state and defend their own positions publicly. At the third level of the taxonomy, students begin to internalize their own beliefs (e.g., accept the need to manage the environment), so they are no longer controlled by the opinions of others. Students subsequently may integrate their beliefs about the environment with other beliefs and might even generalize further by becoming involved in a related concern or by voluntarily devoting time to environmental issues.

Key questions concern the extent to which classroom experiences should help students to build a cohesive value structure, what topics should be subjected to such value examination, and how much curriculum time should be used in this way. Relatively little time is needed to accomplish receiving or responding goals; considerably more time may be needed to reach higher levels of the taxonomy.

Limitations of taxonomy

This taxonomy provides a useful conceptual reference that suggests how various levels of student affect might be associated with curriculum content, and it includes many of the principles that Rogers (1983) listed, such as helping students to generate more internal beliefs. However, Patterson (1973) has criticized the taxonomy because it deals with only a small part of affective development:

> Affective education is concerned with the development of self-awareness. This development requires first that the individual be permitted and be able to express and disclose himself, so that he can see or perceive himself as he is. This requires that he feel free to be himself, to be open and honest, in his expression of himself. Second, the individual must be able to explore, look at, and evaluate himself. Part of this process includes feedback from others on how he is perceived by them.

The taxonomy does not include some of the more dynamic aspects of

Figure 18.1 The Range of Meaning Typical of Commonly Used Affective Terms Measured against the Taxonomy Continuum

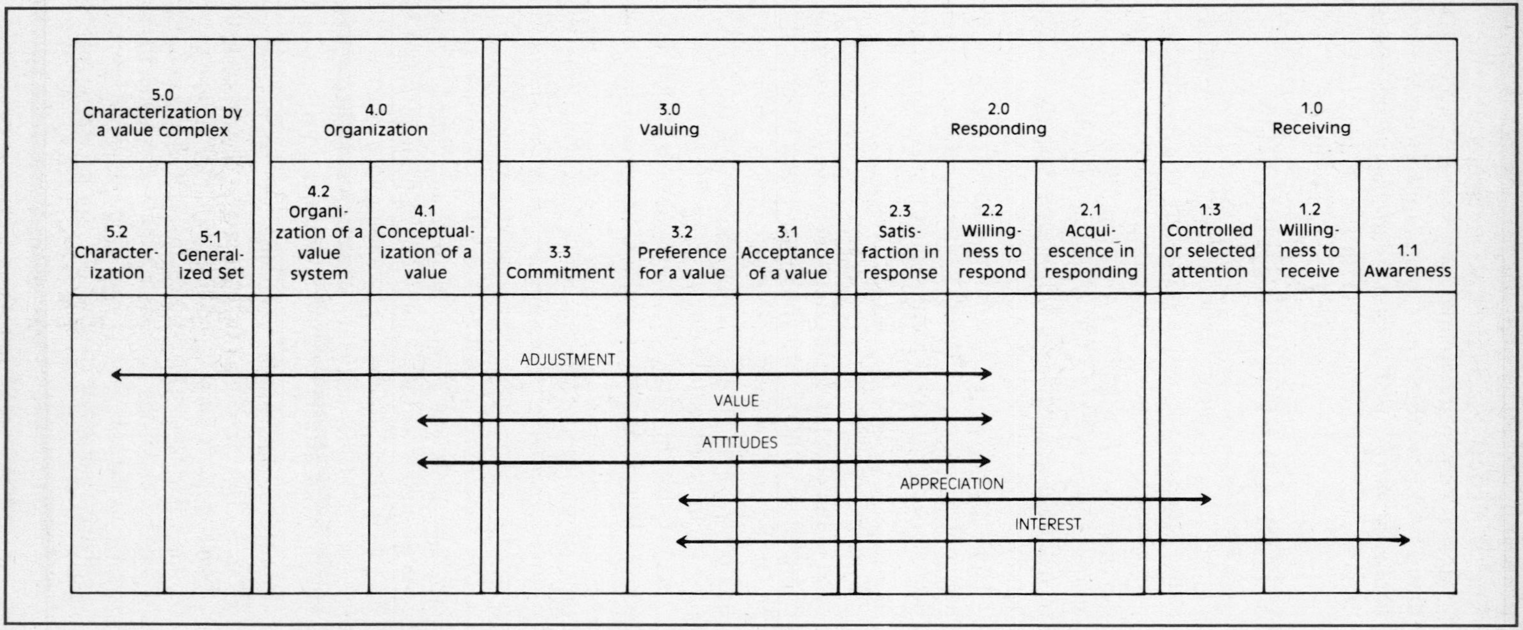

5.0 Characterization by a value complex		4.0 Organization		3.0 Valuing			2.0 Responding			1.0 Receiving		
5.2 Character-ization	5.1 General-ized Set	4.2 Organi-zation of a value system	4.1 Conceptual-ization of a value	3.3 Commitment	3.2 Preference for a value	3.1 Acceptance of a value	2.3 Satis-faction in response	2.2 Willing-ness to respond	2.1 Acqui-escence in responding	1.3 Controlled or selected attention	1.2 Willing-ness to receive	1.1 Awareness

ADJUSTMENT

VALUE

ATTITUDES

APPRECIATION

INTEREST

Source: D. Krathwohl, B. Bloom, and B. Masia. *Taxonomy of Educational Objectives: Book 2 Affective Domain*, p. 37. Copyright © 1964 Longman Inc.

personal development that might be pursued in affective education. Still, it provides a useful way to consider affective goals and thus allows teachers to select methods, procedures, and content to help students to achieve them. Teachers who are trying to help students to internalize beliefs, for example, might want to use role-playing methods (see Weil & Joyce, 1978).

THE APPLICATION OF HUMANISTIC PRINCIPLES

Patterson (1973) believes that schools stifle self-expression, causing feelings of alienation and leading to passive conformity that is inconsistent with self-actualization or responsible citizenship. Teachers who encourage students to state their own learning objectives, to evaluate their own learning, and to challenge the evidence on which texts or the teachers themselves base their conclusions will help students to respond more openly and effectively.

How can education enhance students's self-insight and personal development? Patterson suggested that the following changes need to be made in schools if more humanistic goals are to be pursued: (1) more open scheduling, (2) more active learning, (3) more student independence, (4) more stress on creativity, (5) more cooperative learning, (6) more opportunity for self-evaluation, and (7) greater emphasis on personal integrity, nonacademic potential, and an intrinsic curriculum.

Open Scheduling

Too often classroom learning is restricted by arbitrary time limits. Humanists would like to see more open schedules that relate better to students' needs. Many high school students, for example, have part-time jobs and would appreciate more flexible class schedules or course credit for work experience. Schools might well consider this, because even though many high school students work primarily to pay for cars and recreational activities, working does not have a detrimental effect on commitment to education, time spent on homework, or attachment to school (Gottfredson, 1985). Thus sensible accommodation here would call for flexibility but with continued encouragement of students' academic growth—not replacement of educational values by youth culture values.

It is easy to identify ways in which routine time schedules interfere with learning. To illustrate certain chemical reactions, for example, it would be useful to have students for a two-hour block of time if the schedule could be modified so that students could occasionally spend extended time in particular subjects when the nature of the learning experience suggests that more time is desirable.

Student Independence

How far should teachers go in reducing structure or letting students set goals? DeCharms (1984) noted that he modified some of his early thoughts about how to help students function as "origins" after working in classrooms. He wrote:

> A romantic view of an Origin as a free spirit untrammeled by pressure from others and society is popular with many college students in the United States. In this view, the person bears no responsibility to established authorities. We have become more and more skeptical of such a view. . . . Not to push people around is a beginning in treating people as Origins, but we soon found that letting them do anything they wanted to do was *not* treating them as Origins either. (p. 83)

DeCharms stressed the need for teachers to encourage students to assume responsibility *within manageable limits*. Teachers who want to help students to function as origins can do so by helping them to set realistic goals, recognize their strengths and weaknesses, make concrete plans for reaching goals, and monitor their efforts (see Chapter 15).

Individualized and Open Education

Most humanists are not satisfied with the traditional self-contained classroom or the idea of providing the same instruction at the same time to students with diverse abilities and interests. Consequently, they argue that schooling should be made more adaptive to students' individual needs, such as by allowing them to proceed at their own pace, to choose some of their learning activities, and so on. Two commonly advocated adaptations are individualization and open education.

Suiting learning to individual needs

Walberg (1985) described a range of accommodations that schools can make to students' individual differences. A minor one is to allow for differences in learning time while still using essentially the same methods and materials to move all students toward mastery of the same objectives (i.e., the Mastery Learning approach). A more substantial accommodation is to retain the same achievement goals for all students but to introduce variation not only in time to learn but in the methods and materials used to accomplish this learning. The individualized instruction/adaptive education methods described below take this approach, at least in theory. A still more extreme form of accommodation is to allow students to pursue different achievement goals, as well as to allow them a great deal of autonomy in deciding not only what to learn but how to learn it. The open education approach represents this extreme level of accommodation.

Attempts to make schooling more effective by fitting instruction to students' individual needs have traditionally been described as *individualized instruction* approaches, although the terms *adaptive instruction* or *adaptive education* have been popularized in recent years (Glaser, 1977; Wang & Walberg, 1985). Wang and Lindvall (1984) listed the following as distinctive features of adaptive education: (1) instruction based on the assessed capabilities of each student; (2) materials and procedures permit each student to progress at a pace suited to his or her abilities and interests; (3) periodic evaluations inform the student concerning mastery; (4) student assumption of responsibility for identifying present needs and abilities, planning learning activities, and evaluating mastery; (5) alternative activities for aiding student acquisition of essential academic skills and content; (6) student choice in selecting educational goals, outcomes, and activities; and (7) peer assistance in pursuing individual goals and cooperation in achieving group goals.

Features of adaptive education

Limitations

Most individualized instruction programs were developed by instructional designers concerned primarily with academic achievement rather than with students' personal or affective development, although affective benefits are frequently claimed for them. With the exception of programs that include cooperative learning elements (Slavin, 1983), however, individualized programs have not been notably successful in promoting students' personal or affective development. A major reason for this is that such programs have had to rely heavily on requiring students to work through individualized curriculum modules, a form of instruction that is well suited to drill and practice in basic facts, concepts, and skills but not to instruction in higher cognitive processes (problem solving, thinking, creativity) or to developing general dispositional states such as interests, attitudes, or values (Jackson, 1985). Consequently, most of these programs included only the first few features on the Wang and Lindvall (1984) list. Oral reading was often sacrificed in favor of worksheet activities concentrating on phonics subskills, creative writing sacrificed for practice in spelling and punctuation, work with concrete manipulatives in mathematics sacrificed for computational exercises, and science and social studies virtually eliminated (Kepler & Randall, 1977). Despite a degree of individualization, such instruction was often boring, repetitive, and in other ways less satisfying than traditional instruction (Carlson, 1982; Everhart, 1983).

Criticisms by humanists concerned with the lock-step curriculum and related aspects of traditional instruction led during the 1960s to the open education movement (Barth, 1972). *Open education* means different things to different people and has been implemented in many different forms (Marshall, 1981), but common elements include flexible use of space and time, increased variety in topics addressed and types of activities (linked to students' interests), and an emphasis on working responsively with individual students rather than teaching the whole class as a group.

Student anxiety

Research on the effects of open education has produced mixed results, but most reviewers agree that practices reflecting its principles, at least when implemented in moderate rather than extreme forms, are associated with improvements in students' attitudes, self-concepts, creativity, curiosity, independence, peer cooperation, and group atmosphere (Giaconia & Hedges, 1982; Good & Brophy, 1987; Hayes & Day, 1980; Horwitz, 1979; Peterson, 1979). Differences tend to be small, however, and are not always positive. Several studies, for example, found that student anxiety was higher in open classrooms than in traditional classrooms, perhaps because the open classrooms provided students with too little structure and too many demands for decisions that they were not prepared to make.

Legacy of open education

Although it was ushered in on a tremendous wave of enthusiasm created by committed advocates during the 1960s and was implemented (primarily in the elementary grades) in a great many schools during the 1970s, open education had virtually disappeared as a significant movement by the 1980s. But it left legacies that have become assimilated into traditional mainstream schooling: more flexible furnishings and use of classroom space, more diversity in curriculum activities, more activities calling for

Educators continue to debate the value of open classrooms.

students to work together in pairs or small groups, and learning centers that allow students to work independently or in cooperation with peers on "hands on" projects. It appears that these elements of open education, if implemented appropriately and in moderation, can enhance students' progress toward affective goals without harming their progress toward cognitive goals.

Tasks and Social Relationships

Activity structures

Bossert (1977) studied the effects on teacher and student behavior in elementary classrooms of various *activity structures* such as teacher-led recitations, class tasks (assigned to the whole class), and multitasks (done independently or in small groups). Different activity structures are associated with different forms of management by teachers. In the recitation format, all participants are highly visible and all interactions are public, so teachers must rely more on commands than on personal influence in controlling the activity. In the other formats, teachers can use more private control techniques.

Benefits of multitask activity structures

Bossert described two ways in which activity structures influence social relationships in classrooms. He argued that teachers who use multitask activity structures are better able than teachers who rely primarily on recitation structures to provide individualized instruction and assistance to students. The multitask structure frees the teacher from the need to control ongoing instructional activities continuously and thus allows the teacher time to interact with individuals. In the recitation structure, in contrast, teachers have fewer opportunities to interact at length with individuals, and when they do, it is usually with the highest achieving students.

A second consideration is the fact that heavy reliance on recitation structures requires teachers to exercise their formal authority frequently and publicly. This is likely to impede teachers' progress in developing affective bonds with students, bonds that promote willing cooperation and interest in learning. In contrast, multitask structures allow a teacher to become involved in activities as a participant with a small group, to assist individuals, or in other ways to interact with students more as a resource person and helper than as an authority figure. Also, by functioning less continually in the role of classroom authority figure who regulates student participation in common activities, teachers can provide students with more opportunities to develop self-regulation and to work socially with peers.

Classroom Environment

Marshall and Weinstein (1984) provided a model specifying how classroom environment factors may reflect different teacher-performance expectations that in turn influence students' own expectations and performance. Two of these factors are locus of responsibility for learning and evaluation and motivational variables.

Responsibility and choice

Teachers control the locus of responsibility for learning and evaluation in the classroom, and they can share that responsibility to varying degrees with individual students. Marshall and Weinstein argued that the amount of responsibility students have may affect their susceptibility to teachers' expectations. Research has shown that students perceive that teachers offer more choices to high achievers but give more directions to low achievers. It may be that when teachers allow high-achieving students to plan their own goals and projects, the goals that these students select and the procedures that they follow may show more variety and thus diminish the comparability of the products that they are working on (Rosenholtz & Rosenholtz, 1981). In any case, high achievers benefit from having more choices because their work is less open to comparison with others in their group and because the freedom to pursue to some extent their own chosen learning activities may motivate them to work harder than they would if they had to follow fixed directions, as low achievers usually must do.

Responsibility and evaluation

Shared responsibility for evaluation is not a part of many classrooms. Teachers generally do most of the evaluation, and when students do check answers, it is usually against an answer sheet that the teacher has prepared. When the teacher is the evaluator, students are dependent on the teacher for judgments about their ability, and their performance is more susceptible to teacher expectations. In contrast, when the teacher encourages students to evaluate their own performance and to develop their own standards and criteria, evaluation may be more private and may be based on criteria that are more understandable to students. Thus students may be less vulnerable to external evaluation pressures. Being called on as frequently as other students to make public responses, for example, may be less important in a classroom in which students spend considerable time setting their own goals and engaging in self-evaluation. Clearly, the locus of responsibility for learning and evaluation will mediate grouping effects and the individual response opportunities that students receive.

Self-evaluation

It is ironic that in some high school classrooms, students get fewer opportunities to make choices and to evaluate their own work than in most first-grade classrooms. We suspect that if teachers placed more emphasis on helping learners to develop the capacity for self-direction and self-evaluation, many of the students' invidious comparisons of their work to the work of others would disappear.

One important outcome of schooling should be to help students develop greater capacity for self-direction and independent learning. Although students should be able to do as their teachers request and feel some pride when they accomplish externally set goals, in time they should learn to determine when and how well they have completed a task without feedback from others.

AFFECTIVE CURRICULA

There are many ways to build affective education into the curriculum. Issues of modern science and medicine can be topics for affective instruction, as can virtually any social studies topic, if one considers feelings, values, or personal decision making in relation to these topics along with their more cognitive aspects. Lessons on explorers might touch on what they thought about when exploring new frontiers, for example, and students could be encouraged to relate these feelings to their own experiences.

Confluent education

Brown (1971) used the term *confluent education* to reflect the integration of affect into subject matter. He suggested numerous exercises for doing this when teaching English and social studies. However, there is no reason for affect to be limited to responses to text material. Students could be requested to keep a personal log, for example, to note how they feel about topics such as life in school or a presidential campaign. Similarly, they could be encouraged to interview other students about their feelings or interview productive elderly people or social activists.

Some humanists urge that affect be studied directly, not just in relation to traditional school topics. It is beyond the scope of this chapter to review such curricula in detail (for this, see Simpson & Gray, 1976); however, we provide a few examples of how affect can become a part of the curriculum.

Magic Circle exercises

As an example of an exercise for use in elementary schools, Simpson and Gray cited the *Magic Circle* (based on the Human Development Program developed by Harold Bessell and Uvaldo Palomares). During Magic Circle group meetings, students have a chance to exchange perceptions and opinions with their peers about topics such as "something I like about you," "something I like about myself," or "if I could do anything I wanted it would be ______."

"Something I like about you" exercise

The "something I like about you" exercise allows students to hear positive comments about themselves from other students. They have a chance to experience the feeling of someone's saying something nice about them and the chance to verbalize that feeling. Through such activities students can begin to consider the events that keep them from doing as they wish and to look at their behavior as it affects other people.

Trumpet March exercise

At the secondary level, one activity Simpson and Gray described is the *Trumpet March* (developed at the Center for Humanistic Education at the University of Massachusetts). In this activity students gather and evaluate data about their own behavior and that of others. Table 18.1 illustrates some of the questions on which students are asked to reflect.

TABLE 18.1 EXAMPLES OF QUESTIONS ASSOCIATED WITH THE TRUMPET MARCH

Step One: Experience Confrontations
I interact with a situation that generates data; and

Step Two: Inventory Responses
How did I respond? What was unique? What common?
a. What did you just do? Describe your behavior.
b. What were you aware of?
c. At what points did you feel comfortable or uncomfortable?
d. At point X, how did you think or feel?
e. Where in your body did you feel something?
f. What sentences did you say to yourself? Were these *should, can't,* or *won't* sentences?

Step Three: Recognize Patterns
What is typical of me?
a. Did you do anything that surprised you?
b. Did you do anything different from what you usually do?
c. How do you usually respond in similar situations? Can you think of a similar situation where you've responded the same?
d. How often have you thought, felt, or acted like this? In what circumstances?

Step Four: Own Patterns
What function does this pattern serve for me?
a. How does it serve you?
b. How does your pattern make you feel good?
c. What does it protect you from?
d. What kinds of freedom does it give you?

Step Five: Consider Consequences
What does happen or could happen in my life because of this pattern?
a. What price do you have to pay?
b. How much does it cost you?

Step Six: Allow Alternatives
Will I allow myself any additional patterns of response?
a. What are the first steps you could take to change?
b. What are the options you have?
c. Using each alternative, go through the trumpet again.

Step Seven: Choose

Source: *From Simpson and Grey,* Humanistic Education and Interpretation. *Copyright © 1976 by The Ford Foundation. Reprinted with permission from Ballinger Publishing Company.*

Values-clarification activities

Another way in which affect has become part of the school curriculum in some classrooms is through values clarification activities. Simon, Howe, and Kirschenbaum (1972) argued that many persons do not clearly understand their values. To facilitate self-insight, these authors prepared seventy-nine values-clarification activities. One asks the participants to list ten to fifteen things that provide them pleasure or joy and to write after each item the date that they last experienced it. Then they place a dollar sign by each item that costs money, a *P* by those items that require planning, an *S* by those items done with someone else, and an *A* by those things done alone. Finally, they study the list and contemplate what it reflects about their values.

Children's attitudes toward the elderly

Jantz and associates (1976), at the Center on Aging at the University of Maryland, have produced a curriculum guide on children's attitudes toward the elderly. Included are films and books to which children might react, as well as experiences to share with elderly individuals. This curriculum offers children accurate information about the elderly, a chance to see the behaviors of different elderly people in a variety of roles, and the opportunity to develop positive feelings about growing old.

Womens' role in society

Many curriculum materials describe the nature and importance of women's roles in society. Teachers could use such information profitably in discussions about gender discrimination and related issues. One particularly good set of materials is a series of pamphlets entitled *Cracking the Glass Slipper: PEER's Guide to Ending Sex Bias in Your Schools.* PEER is a project of the National Organization for Women's Legal Defense and Education Fund. Its goals are to monitor enforcement progress under federal law forbidding sex discrimination in education and to assist groups working for sexual equality in education in their local schools.

Aesthetic education

Yet another way in which more affective material might be taught to students is through aesthetic education. In the past few years some have argued that students should become sensitive to the aesthetic aspects of experience (see the report *Coming to Our Senses: The Significance of the Arts for American Education*). The interest here is not necessarily in improving students' ability to perform but in making them more aware of aesthetic issues. How does one respond to art, music, and objects of beauty? How does one evaluate a theatrical performance? By direct involvement and teaching, aesthetic education programs help students to develop and understand criteria for responding to aesthetic experiences. In short, the goal of such training is to make students better consumers of such experiences.

Evaluation of Affective Programs

Baskin and Hess (1980) evaluated the following programs, selected because they used affective curricula to achieve affective goals, were implemented at a specific time during the school day, and had produced acceptable evaluation data: (a) A Cognitive Approach to Solving Real Life Problems; (b) Developing Understanding of Self and Others (DUSO); (c) Human Development Program (HDP); (d) interpersonal skills training project; (e) AWARE; (f) Schools without Failure (SWF); and (g) Teacher Effectiveness Training (TET).

Baskin and Hess classified these seven programs in three areas: internal–emotional, cognitive, and overt–behavioral. The internal–emotional dimension includes feelings, emotions, self-perceptions, and attitudes toward school. The cognitive dimension refers to students' understanding of principles of social causation and their ability to generate alternative solutions to hypothetical social situations. The behavioral dimension involves observable interpersonal behavior such as effective interactions with peers or adults. The goals are summarized in Table 18.2. Baskin and Hess indicated that although the effectiveness of the programs varied with

TABLE 18.2 CURRICULUM OBJECTIVES OF SEVEN AFFECTIVE EDUCATION PROGRAMS

	Affective Education Programs						
Goals	**CA[a]**	**DUSO**	**HDP**	**IST[b]**	**PA[c]**	**SWI**	**T.E.T.**
Internal Emotional Area							
Raising student self-esteem		X[d]	X	X	X	X	
Accepting self-responsibility	X	X				X	
Encouraging positive attitudes toward school						X	
Developing a success identity						X	
Cognitive Area							
Understanding social causation	X		X		X		
Generating alternative solutions	X				X		
Generating alternative consequences	X				X		
Developing self-knowledge	X	X	X	X[e]	X		
Gaining ability to talk about emotions	X	X	X		X		
Overt Behavioral Area							
Developing better interpersonal relationships	X						
Developing respect for others				X[e]	X		X[e]
Increasing communication skills	X			X[e]			X[e]
Increasing interpersonal effectiveness	X	X	X	X[e]	X		X[e]
Decreasing discipline problems	X					X	X
Developing role taking skills					X		
Using "I messages"							X[e]
Using active listening							X[e]
Using "Method III" problem solving							X[e]
Increasing academic achievement		X		X			

[a] *A Cognitive Approach to Solving Real Life Problems.*
[b] *Interpersonal Skills Training.*
[c] *Project AWARE.*
[d] *An "X" indicates that the affective program states the mediating outcome as one of the objectives of the program. This objective was not necessarily assessed in the evaluations reviewed.*
[e] *These objectives apply to teachers rather than to students.*
Source: *Excerpted from E. Baskin and R. Hess, "Does affective education work: A review of seven programs."* Journal of School Psychology *18(1), 1980. Reprinted by permission of Human Sciences Press, 72 Fifth Avenue, New York, N.Y., 10011. Copyright © 1980, Human Sciences Press, Inc.*

objectives, the data show that affective programs can positively influence both cognitive outcomes and overt behavior.

Focusing on outcomes other than cognitive ability

Elardo and Elardo (1976) summarized information about programs dealing with social development and criticized four programs that have been implemented in elementary schools: Ojemann's Causal Approach to

Human Behavior, the Human Development Program, Reality Therapy/Schools without Failure, and Developing Understanding of Self and Others. They concluded that these four programs are major attempts to humanize education during the early and middle childhood years and provide examples of ways in which traditional school curriculum can be expanded but that the programs were disappointing in several respects. First, the program descriptions did not contain clear statements regarding the mechanisms by which human understanding develops, making it difficult to determine on what basis the planners sequenced curriculum materials. Also, the four programs were not well integrated into current child-development research and theory. Each program expressed much concern for developing self-esteem, but there was little focus on students' relations with others. The authors argued the need to move beyond individualism, to look at the group and the classroom needs of students, and to consider prosocial behavior.

TAD program

Hudgins (1979) presented data from a test of the effects of the Toward Affective Development (TAD) program. He pointed out that there were no significant effects of this program on students' self-concepts or social adjustment. He noted that there is considerable anecdotal praise of such affective programs in the literature but few data to support such advocacy. Furthermore, he stated that the strong intuitive appeal of affective education for some people may cause them to support a program without even considering research on its effectiveness.

ACCOMPLISHING AFFECTIVE OUTCOMES THROUGH COOPERATIVE LEARNING

Affective objectives and cooperative learning

Besides addressing affective objectives directly through inclusion of affective curricula in school programs, it is possible to accomplish these objectives indirectly by changing the conditions under which students participate in academic activities. In traditional classrooms, students typically have responsibility only for themselves, are not allowed to help one another, and must compete for grades. Cooperative learning approaches to instruction have altered these conditions, often with positive effects on affective outcomes. Cooperative learning approaches replace independent seatwork with cooperative learning activities in which small groups (typically four to six students) work together on practice or application exercises. Some of the best known and widely researched cooperative learning programs are described below. For additional information about these and other cooperative programs, see Sharan et al. (1984), Slavin (1983), or Slavin et al. (1985).

Cooperative-Learning Programs

Learning Together The Learning Together model of cooperative learning was developed by David and Roger Johnson (Johnson & Johnson, 1975; Johnson et al., 1984). It has four basic elements: (a) positive interdependence (tasks are structured so that group members depend on one another to contribute to the success of the group's effort—each member

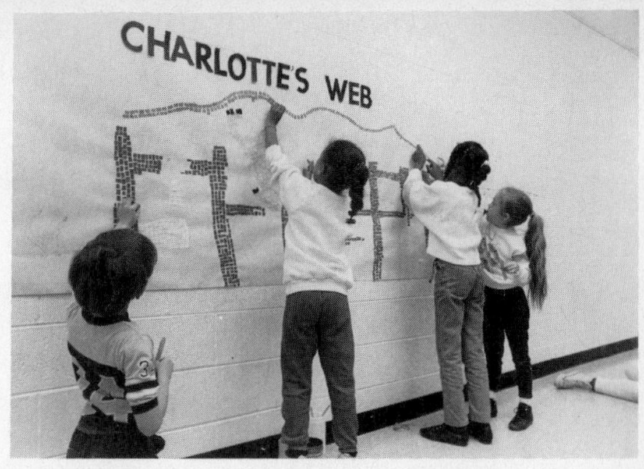

Students can often learn cognitive subject matter through group study, sharing, and group projects.

brings unique materials, resources, or information to the group task or performs a unique role); (b) face-to-face interaction among group members (the tasks require group members to interact rather than to work on their own); (c) individual accountability for mastering assigned material (each member has clear objectives for which he or she will be held accountable, so it is not possible for brighter or harder-working members to "cover" for other members who are ignored or who fail to do what they are supposed to do); and (d) instruction of students in appropriate interpersonal and small-group skills (such as asking and answering questions, ensuring that everyone participates actively and is treated with respect, and assigning tasks and organizing cooperative efforts).

Group Investigation Schlomo Sharan and his colleagues (1984) have developed what they call Group Investigation methods in Israel that are similar to the Learning Together methods developed in the United States by the Johnsons. Group Investigation students form two- to six-member groups to work together using cooperative inquiry, group discussion, and cooperative planning and projects. They choose subtopics from a unit studied by the whole class, break them into individual tasks, and carry out activities needed to prepare a group report on the subtopic. Eventually, the group makes a presentation or display to communicate its findings to the class and is evaluated based on the quality of its report.

Jigsaw The Jigsaw method (Aronson et al., 1978) ensures active individual participation and group cooperation by arranging tasks so that each group member possesses unique information and thus has a unique role to play. The group product cannot be completed unless each member does his or her part, just as a jigsaw puzzle cannot be completed unless each piece is included. Information needed to compose a biography, for example, might be broken into early life, first accomplishments, major setbacks, later life, and world events occurring during the person's lifetime. A different group member would be given the needed information and assigned responsibility for each of these five sections. Members from different groups who were working on the same section would meet together in "expert groups" to discuss their section. Then they would return to their regular groups and take turns teaching their group mates about their section. Since the only way that students can learn about sections other than their own is to listen carefully to their group mates, they are motivated to support and show interest in one another's work. The students then prepare biographies or take quizzes on the material individually.

Several cooperative-learning methods have been developed by Robert Slavin and others at the Johns Hopkins University. Collectively these methods are known as *Student Team Learning*. The four Student Team Learning methods are TGT, STAD, Jigsaw II, and TAI.

Teams-Games-Tournament (TGT) TGT calls for students to work together in four- to five-member heterogeneously grouped teams to help one another master content and prepare for competitions against other teams (Slavin, 1983). After the teacher presents the material to be learned, team members work together to study from worksheets by discussing the material and tutoring and quizzing one another. Cooperative practice in this form continues throughout the week in preparation for tournaments held on Fridays. For the tournaments, students are assigned to three-person tables composed of students from different teams who are similar in achievement. The three students at each table compete at academic games covering the content taught and practiced that week. Students can earn points by answering questions correctly or by successfully challenging and correcting the answers of the other two students at the table. Since they are competing against peers of similar achievement, low achievers have just as much opportunity to earn points for their teams as high achievers do. Points are summed to determine each team's score, and the teacher prepares a newsletter to recognize successful teams and unusually high scores attained by individuals.

Student Teams-Achievement Divisions (STAD) STAD is a simplification of TGT (Slavin, 1983). It uses the same heterogeneous grouping and cooperative learning procedures but replaces the tournament with a quiz. Quiz scores are translated into team competition points based on how individual students' scores compare with the scores of other students in their "achievement division" (composed of students of similar achievement), and individuals' points are combined to yield team totals. Both TGT and STAD combine cooperative-learning task structures with team competition and group rewards for cumulative individual performance. However, STAD depersonalizes the competitive elements. Rather than compete face to face against classmates at tournament tables, students in STAD classrooms try to do their best on quizzes that they take individually. They know that points will be awarded depending on how they do in comparison with peers in the same achievement division, but they do not know who these students are (teachers do not disclose achievement division membership). Slavin and his colleagues have gradually placed more emphasis on STAD and less on TGT, because STAD is simpler to implement and because it reduces the salience of competition.

Jigsaw II Jigsaw II is a simplification and adaptation of the original Jigsaw (Slavin, 1983). It is simplified in that the teacher does not need to provide each student with unique materials. Instead, all students begin by reading a common narrative but then each student in the group is given a separate topic on which to become an expert. Also, whereas the original Jigsaw called for assignment of individual grades based on quiz scores, Jigsaw II incorporates the additional element of computing team scores and recognizing team accomplishments through a class newsletter.

Team-Assisted Individualization (TAI) TAI is an adaptation of individualized mathematics instruction that introduces cooperative-learning methods and team competition with group reward, as in STAD (Slavin, 1985). TAI students work cooperatively in pairs or triads within their teams by tutoring, quizzing, and otherwise helping one another to master individually assigned content. At the end of the week, the students take individualized criterion-referenced tests, and their scores are used both for individual accountability purposes and for assigning team points for competitions.

Research on Cooperative-Learning Methods

Benefits of cooperative learning

Slavin (1983) has summarized most of the research on cooperative-learning methods. Effects on achievement are generally positive, although they tend to be associated more with the use of group rewards based on summing individual members' performance scores than with the use of cooperative-task structures. Thus the Student Team Learning methods that include team rewards (TGT, STAD, Jigsaw II, TAI) tend to have consistently positive effects on student achievement, whereas the more purely cooperative methods (Learning Together, Group Investigation, and the original Jigsaw) are less likely to produce significant achievement advantages over traditional teaching (Moskowitz et al., 1985; Okebukola, 1985; Slavin, 1983).

Effects on affective outcomes are more impressive. Cooperative-learning arrangements have been found to promote friendship choices and prosocial patterns of interaction among students who differ in achievement, gender, race, or ethnicity and to promote the acceptance of mainstreamed handicapped students by their nonhandicapped classmates. Cooperative methods also frequently have positive effects on affective outcomes such as self-esteem, academic self-confidence, liking for the class, liking and feeling liked by classmates, empathy, and social cooperation (Slavin, 1983).

Cooperative-learning methods are not wholesale replacements for traditional approaches but adaptations in which teachers introduce and develop concepts in the usual ways but then assign practice and application activities to be done cooperatively rather than individually. The student-team learning methods seem best suited to practice of basic skills, whereas the more purely cooperative methods seem best suited to research activities and other project work in science or social studies. Such cooperative-learning activities can be effective ways to structure learning experiences so that both cognitive and affective outcomes are pursued, especially if the activities are designed so that each student must play an active role (i.e., groups cannot be dominated by one or two brighter or more assertive students) and if the students are properly prepared in group skills such as planning, sharing, listening, integrating the ideas of others, and resolving disagreements through negotiation.

PROSOCIAL BEHAVIOR

Many people who are concerned about the increasing dependence on others dictated by modern society or about what they see as moral deterioration argue that schools must encourage prosocial behavior (i.e., becoming more considerate, helping, and altruistic toward others). Mussen and Eisenberg-Berg (1977) defined *prosocial behavior* as "actions that are intended to aid or benefit another person or group of people without the actor's anticipation of external rewards. Such actions often entail some cost, self-sacrifice, or risk on the part of the actor" (pp. 3–4). Little is known about the day-to-day experiences that motivate people to express generosity, sympathy, or help to others, although individuals who write about prosocial behavior often suggest that *self-rewards* (increased feelings of self-satisfaction that follow a helping act) or internalized needs or motives influence prosocial behavior.

Benefits of prosocial behavior

Parents of notably prosocial children assign *manageable* responsibility to the chilren at an early age, encourage them to reflect on their feelings and those of others, and explain the reasons behind their conduct rules. Teachers can praise prosocial behavior when it occurs and model prosocial behavior themselves(for example, by behaving in kind ways toward teacher aides, student teachers, fellow teachers, and, most importantly, toward students).

Degree of emphasis

Teachers must decide how much emphasis to place on prosocial learning. Students, for example, can be assigned to work together on a committee report in such a way that the report is the major goal of the activity and cooperation is an indirect benefit. Teachers can also explore prosocial topics directly by scheduling discussion of moral dilemmas, role play or simulation of social situations, or other activities designed to develop prosocial, cooperative attitudes and dispositions in their students.

THE HUMANISTIC TEACHER

The question "Who is the humanistic teacher?" is apt to provoke a wide range of responses. Patterson (1973) cited three dimensions that are commonly mentioned by writers who attempt to define the humanistic teacher.

Expression of feelings

He noted that humanistic teachers are *genuine*. They do not fear the students they teach or hide behind a facade. They are willing to share their views openly. Patterson wrote: "He doesn't feel one thing and say another. He isn't likely to be able to conceal his real feelings completely or consistently, but in his expression of his feelings he recognizes and accepts them as *his* feelings. He does not project blame for his feelings and reactions onto the students. He accepts responsibility for his own behavior. He says, 'I'm irritated,' 'I'm angry'" (pp. 103–104).

Patterson did not condone the frequent expression of anger or other personal feelings that might harm students, but he did note that teachers who are aware of their feelings and those of their students can prevent disruption by acknowledging such anger openly. Speaking to the issue of anger, Patterson wrote: "He recognizes it as his feelings and accepts responsibility for his behavior. If a child's behavior angers him, he makes it clear that it is the behavior, not the child, which does so."

Respect for children

A second characteristic is *respect for the child as a person*, which is shown by accepting the student for what he or she is and caring actively about the student's opinions and feelings. In Patterson's words, "There is an acceptance of imperfections, mistakes, and errors, changes in mood and motivation, etc., as aspects of being human. There is confidence in the basic goodness of each individual, in the capacity of the individual to grow and to develop, to actualize his potential in an appropriate environment" (p. 107).

Empathic understanding

Empathic understanding is a third characteristic of the humanistic teacher. This involves an active attempt by teachers to place themselves in their students' positions and to understand their perceptions and feelings. Humanistic writers believe that empathic understanding is rare and that if teachers could express, even occasionally, that they see, understand, and accept students, much potential would be unlocked. The call is for more *nonevaluative feedback* that illustrates to students that teachers understand the feelings that students verbalize.

Nonevaluative feedback

Characteristics of high-empathy teachers and classrooms

Rogers (1983) reviewed research on teachers who are high in expression of empathy and of positive regard toward their students. These teachers exhibited the following behaviors: (1) more response to student feeling; (2) more use of student ideas in ongoing instructional interactions; (3) more discussion with students; (4) more praise of students; (5) more congruent teacher talk (more authentic, less ritualistic); and (6) more tailoring of content to individual students. In addition, the activities in high-empathy classrooms exhibited more of the following characteristics: (1) the learning goals are derived from cooperative planning between teacher and student; (2) the classroom is individualized; (3) there are more projects and displays created by students—more active involvement of students; (4) more freedom from time limits—fewer deadlines, more flexibility; and (5) more emphasis on productivity and creativity than on evaluation.

Rogers (1983) also reviewed research on instructing teachers in how to become more empathetic and presented summaries of several important programs that have attempted to implement these ideas. He included a thorough discussion of the politics of education and outlined some of the

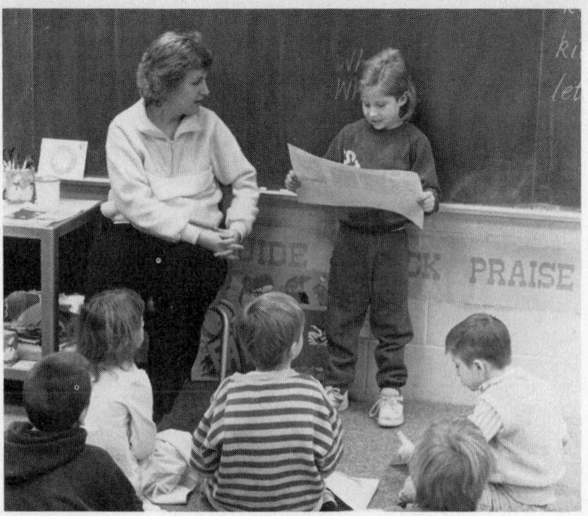

In high-empathy classrooms, students are encouraged to create special projects and reports.

problems that teachers who try to implement a humanistic philosophy will encounter.

Affective student outcomes

In an attempt to define the way teachers perceive student affect, Prawat and Nickerson (1985) asked teachers to describe the affective behavior of students by writing about five events that had actually occurred in their classrooms. The task was relatively open ended to allow teachers to express their own meanings. They found that teachers reported incidents of *interpersonal* affect most frequently, incidents involving students' *attitudes toward self* less frequently, and incidents that reflected *affect toward subject matter* only rarely.

Prawat and Nickerson found that positive student affect was *not* more evident in the classrooms of teachers who placed higher priority on affective outcomes than on cognitive outcomes. Indeed, high-affective teachers were *less* successful in promoting affective outcomes than were teachers with more balanced goals. They argued that valuing affect to the exclusion of cognition may be counterproductive for both affective and cognitive progress.

These data, although based on a small sample, are consistent with the viewpoint that we have expressed previously in this chapter—that there can be either too much or too little emphasis on most instructional goals.

Balance of goals

Prawat and Nickerson's findings suggest that a balance of goals may be associated with more optimal levels of student motivation and more progress toward cognitive and affective goals.

SUMMARY

Because humanists are interested in emotional and affective development as well as cognitive goals, their theories stress self-perceptions and potential. In the area of motivation, humanists focus on intrinsic variables, as exemplified by the theories of Abraham Maslow and Carl Rogers.

Good attitudes toward self and others appear to develop in homes where there are complete acceptance of the child, clear standards and expectations, and respect and latitude for the child within defined limits. Either too much or too little structure seems to inhibit affective growth, but teacher recognition and acceptance appear central to positive self-concept development and achievement. Patterson and others argued that humanistic goals require the following changes in schools: (1) more open scheduling, (2) more emphasis on active learning, (3) more stress on student independence, (4) more stress on creativity, (5) more opportunity for cooperative-learning activities, (6) more opportunity for internal evaluation, and (7) greater emphasis on personal integrity, nonacademic potential, and an intrinsic curriculum.

Questions and Problems

1. To what extent should teachers be responsible for helping students develop increased understanding of individuals who differ from them, such as the elderly?
2. What does the term *humanistic teaching* mean to you? Have some of your teachers fulfilled this definition? How successful were they in presenting subject matter?
3. What is an "interchangeable" teacher comment? Write a one-page dialogue that provides specific and appropriate uses of interchangeable comments.
4. How would humanistic elementary teachers differ from humanistic college teachers? How would they be the same?
5. If teachers emphasize cooperative learning, will students have to suppress their individual academic interests so that group goals can be fulfilled?
6. Assume that you want to emphasize affective goals in the class you teach. What are the implications of the Prawat and Nickerson study for your planning?
7. Summarize in your own words the role and value of cooperative learning programs.

Case Studies

THE YEAR BEGINS. Sally Jones opens the door and walks confidently into Room 203 at Bayside Junior High. She smiles and says, "I'm Ms. Jones, your English teacher. There are five important things we are going to do in the first two months of school. First, everyone is going write critical reports on a movie and a book."

Ted, with a slight whine: "A book *and* a movie?" Sally, with warmth but finality: "Yes, both. In a few minutes I'll tell you the form for your report, but now I want to give you a general feel for what will happen so that you can begin to plan your work. The important thing in writing two critical reports is to present your genuine reactions in such a way that others can understand them. There also will be two group assignments due during the first two months. You'll be assigned one, and the other you can select yourself on the basis of the stories that interest you. These assignments will involve writing the last few pages of stories that we read. On a sheet that I'll pass out in a few minutes you'll see a list of 300 books grouped into thirty smaller divisions of topical interest. For example, sports, cars, classics, and romance are all topics included in the list."

What expectations does Sally communicate to the class? What strengths or weaknesses does her introduction have with regard to motivational variables? What other things might she have done? Rewrite "The Year Begins" from the perspective of a teacher who wants to introduce affective topics into the curriculum.

CLASSROOM DAYDREAM. Tim Blanton is a third year biology teacher at Rockhurst High School. Jane Myer is a sophomore at Rockhurst and a reluctant biology student. The class period seems endless to Jane, who stares out the window and wonders whether she will make the "cut" on the basketball team this afternoon. Mr. Blanton kindly but directly says, "Jane, what can we see about cell structure on the slide?" Jane says, "Oh, ah, I'm sorry but I wasn't paying attention. I'm preoccupied and my mind was wandering." Several kids snicker. Helen blurts out, "Yeah the subject is so boring I can see why you are falling asleep." Jane turns red and Mr. Blanton turns pale. Seeing the effect of her comments on Mr. Blanton, Helen looks apprehensively at the floor. What should Mr. Blanton say or do now?

PART 6
CLASSROOM MANAGEMENT

As Mr. Floden turns his back and heads to his desk, Huey launches a massive wad of paper that rises majestically in the air and then hits Mr. Floden squarely in the back. The class breaks out with loud, spontaneous laughter.

Judy Griffin explains the assignment carefully; as soon as she finishes several hands are waving frantically in the air. Before Judy can call on any of the students, Tim blurts out, "Do we have to do this by next Monday? Why not next Friday? This is a lot of work." The class buzzes with excitement and there is constant haggling with the teacher for the next ten minutes over the number of pages they have to do as well as the format in which the paper must be written.

Bill Roundtree curtly announces to his sales staff, "I want biweekly reports on your sales progress; we need to get sales up by 12 percent. This is important and I expect to have good progress immediately. Some of you are going to get big rewards out of this; however, others may be in trouble and you may be looking for other jobs if you don't get that sales performance up."

Helen answers the phone and at the same time nods toward the empty chair in the corner as a visitor sits down. As she continues to listen on the phone, she hands an application form to the visitor to fill out. She glances at her appointment calendar and buzzes Mr. Wilson on the office intercom to let him know that it is time for him to leave for his 10 o'clock meeting in the board room.

These vignettes involve different aspects of classroom and societal management that teachers and students must deal with. The first vignette deals with public misbehavior, a significant aspect of classroom life that teachers must address. However, although the episode in Mr. Floden's class would be a significant, threatening event for any teacher, most classroom-management issues are less dramatic than this. Still, teachers do need to develop strategies for handling direct threats to their authority.

The second vignette illustrates another difficulty that teachers face in managing classrooms. Not only do teachers have to have careful, well-laid out plans, they need to be able to convince students to become engaged in learning activities. Although rules and procedures are an important part of classroom management, there is growing evidence that a major part of success as a classroom manager is the ability to elicit student cooperation in pursuing classroom learning goals (Doyle, 1986a).

The third example illustrates two principles that often are part of management systems—alerting and accountability. Teachers need to alert students that certain performances are important and will be examined. Teachers also need to hold students accountable—actually to check their work to determine the extent to which students have mastered important skills and concepts. Unlike managers in some businesses, teachers do not have the authority, except under extraordinary circumstances, to "fire" students or assign them to other teachers. Thus the incentives and motivational systems that teachers can use depend more on logic and the ability to solicit student cooperation than they do on external rewards and incentives. As will be seen in the material that follows, teachers can engage in too much alerting as well as too little and can overstructure or understructure their classrooms.

The fourth vignette describes the essence of a successful teacher. Teachers have to do many things at the same time and do each of those things well. The executive secretary in this story is able to perform three tasks simultaneously. Successful teachers, especially in elementary schools, must be able to initiate, maintain, and supervise several different learning activities at the same time.

Successful classrooms do not just happen. They are created, maintained, and restored (when necessary) by teachers who exhibit certain personal qualities, spend time planning and preparing, and use effective techniques. Because they are effective managers, they will avoid most serious problems, but they know how to handle such problems when necessary. They also know how to structure and use the physical space and equipment in ways that work for their students.

Classroom management is usually the major concern of beginning teachers (Doyle, 1986a; Fuller, 1969), and for good reason. It is basic to success in meeting both cognitive and affective objectives, and principals and supervisors stress it in rating teachers. Teachers who have serious management problems cannot do much teaching because they spend so much time reacting to these problems. In addition, students apparently have little respect or liking for such teachers.

Despite differences in number, type, and severity of problems, the basic principles for sound classroom management are the same for all teachers. Differences are mostly in the time and energy that teachers must devote to management. In ideal situations, management is a minimal concern that primarily involves preventing problems by individualizing instruction to meet students' needs. At the opposite extreme, a teacher faced with five separate classes of unruly preadolescents may have to spend more time and energy on management than on all other aspects of teaching combined.

Prospective teachers therefore need to consider how their personal qualities and preferences affect their teaching roles, both in general and in regard to specific grade levels and classroom settings. Our treatment of classroom management will begin in Chapter 19 with a discussion of some personal characteristics that are desirable in all teachers and the factors that individual teachers must take into account in deciding on the particular teaching roles they will play.

In Chapter 20 we discuss the basic skills involved in creating and maintaining an effective learning environment. In Chapters 21 and 22 we turn our attention to techniques for dealing with students who require more individualized instruction. Chapter 21 reviews behavioristic approaches to coping with students' behavior problems, and Chapter 22 presents humanistic approaches.

Several basic ideas underlie this entire section on classroom management. First, successful classroom managers must have certain personal qualities. Without them, teachers are unlikely to succeed, no matter what specific techniques they use. Second, the keys to success lie in good planning and effective prevention of problems rather than in being able to handle problems after they occur. Third, no single approach will equip a teacher to handle all classroom management tasks successfully. As Doyle (1986a) noted, maintaining a good management system requires some attention each day. However, it is possible to build an effective, comprehensive, and internally consistent system by combining elements from different approaches that complement one another. Finally, each teacher must discover what approaches work best for him or her; teachers are not likely to use approaches successfully that conflict with their beliefs or personal predispositions.

CHAPTER

Overview of Classroom Management

CHAPTER OUTLINE

OBJECTIVES

When you have mastered the material in this chapter, you will be able to

1. Explain the implications of group and individual student differences for classroom management
2. Explain how key aspects of classroom management and student socialization change across four developmental stages
3. Identify the problems and rewards of choosing a socialization orientation to teaching
4. List and explain the expectations and responsibilities of teachers as authority figures
5. Describe five characteristics of teachers who are successful as socialization agents
6. Describe six characteristics of successful parents, showing the relevance of each for teaching
7. Explain principles for adapting to large or heterogeneous classes
8. Explain principles for adapting the physical space to functional needs
9. Diagram and explain the optimal design for a classroom at the grade level and for the subject matter you intend to teach

Problem prevention

Our discussion of classroom management stresses *problem prevention*, but we also suggest strategies for dealing with misbehavior when it does occur. We approach the topic using a cost/benefit analysis, considering strategies with an eye toward (1) what they are claimed to accomplish, (2) what they actually do accomplish, and (3) what side effects they may have.

Certain practices are deemed inappropriate because they are not essential to any worthwhile goal (requiring students to remain absolutely silent at all times unless addressed by the teacher) or because their positive effects are outweighed by negative ones (persistent authoritarian and punitive techniques). In general, *the optimal approach establishes the desired learning environment while simultaneously imposing the fewest restrictions* (Brophy & Putnam, 1979).

Expectations and knowledge

To manage classrooms effectively, teachers need both clear *expectations* about students' behavior and *knowledge* about what to do when their expectations are not being met. Expectations define classroom-management goals and guide decisions about creating, maintaining, and restoring desirable student behavior. Teachers who have clear expectations can organize the classroom accordingly, articulate these expectations to students, and recognize when discrepancies between expectations and actual student behavior are unacceptably large. Such discrepancies indicate a need for action, at which point the teacher must call on knowledge of general principles and of the characteristics of the particular students involved, to decide what to do.

Student role

Taken together, teachers' expectations about appropriate student behavior can be called the *student role*. Elements that make up the student role include: (1) mastery of basic skills, (2) development of interest in and knowledge about the topics included in the formal curriculum, and (3) participation, usually as a member of a group, in extracurricular experiences that are considered necessary for efficient institutional functioning (assemblies, fire drills) or are designed to support the program of instruction (field trips, music programs) or to develop qualities believed important for all citizens (physical education, the pledge of allegiance).

As Jackson (1968) and Doyle (1986a) have noted, the following are also identified with the student role: regimentation of activity, restriction of movement, and subordination of individual desires to the personal authority of the teacher and the less personal but often restrictive school and classroom rules.

The rules help provide for an orderly and reasonably satisfactory group living experience within an institutional setting, but they do so at a price. Much behavior considered natural and appropriate elsewhere is forbidden at school (boisterous talk and play), and many other things can be done only at certain times and in certain ways (food and refreshment, use of the toilet). Sustained attention to academic activities involves inhibition of behavior appropriate in other contexts. Finally, all this takes place in a continually public setting.

INDIVIDUAL AND GROUP DIFFERENCES IN STUDENTS

Individual and group differences among students have implications for classroom management. Differences in age, gender, and ethnicity come readily to mind, along with variables such as maturity and responsibility. Many of these variables can be overstressed, leading to overly polarized differential prescriptions for boys versus girls or black students versus white students. Actually, except for developmental differences, there is little evidence that various types of students require diverse techniques (Good & Stipek, 1984; Kounin & Obradovic, 1968). Most recommendations for differential treatment involve minor qualifications on major themes rather than clear-cut contrasts. Even so, certain group and individual differences among students do merit consideration.

Gender differences

Well-established gender differences (Maccoby & Jacklin, 1974), for example, indicate that boys are more physically active than girls, at least during childhood, so that tight restrictions on movement are more difficult for them. The combination of sustained attention and physical immobility is especially difficult for younger students, regardless of gender. This does not imply that physical restrictions should be abandoned; all students can adjust to some degree. To identify what is required, we would ask: (1) Is the instructional model being used appropriate for the students? (2) If so, what physical restrictions are really necessary? (3) Are there multiple ways to accomplish objectives (so that students can use the methods most preferred by them)?

Adjusting to restrictions

Besides minimizing restrictions, teachers can ease students' adjustment to them. Activities can be scheduled so that sustained concentration is required when students seem most able to handle it. Students who need more physical activity can be given opportunities to obtain it in ways that do not conflict with instructional goals.

Cultural characteristics

Characteristics that vary across groups or cultures also may have implications for classroom management. Many adolescents resent being touched in any way. Teachers also may anger students by taking away or otherwise overreacting to articles of clothing, combs, or other valued possessions.

Eye contact

Middle-class teachers typically expect students to maintain eye contact with them during disciplinary contacts, to indicate both attention and respect. However, students from certain minority groups will avert their eyes in such situations because they have been taught that maintaining eye contact connotes defiance. It is important for teachers to be aware of such cultural differences and, more generally, to be open minded and tolerant in dealing with students from different cultural backgrounds (Casanova, 1987).

Need for tolerance

This does not necessarily mean catering to students' preferences or reinforcing their expectations. Students accustomed to authoritarian treatment or brutality need acceptance and warmth from their teachers. Students who behave like pawns need to learn to function more as origins (assume responsibility for their own learning, make appropriate demands on the teachers). Minority-group students who are alienated from school

With students from different cultural backgrounds, teachers must be open-minded and tolerant.

learning and discriminated against by majority students require a combination of warmth and determination from the teacher in demanding achievement efforts and enforcing conduct limits (Kleinfeld, 1975). In general, the overall goals of classroom management will be similar for all students, but different methods may be used to accomplish them. Distractible students may need study carrels or other quiet places to work; slow students may need special tutoring; poor workers may need contracts or division of tasks into smaller segments (Hewett & Watson, 1979).

Most of the "problems" that teachers deal with are essentially trivial. Loud talking, noisy movements, and similar disruptions are considered normal and appropriate outside the classroom. However, some students present more enduring and serious problems. About 15 percent of boys and 5 percent of girls show moderate to severe adjustment problems. Many of them are related to specific external stress factors and will show significant improvement within a year or two, even without professional treatment (Clarizio & McCoy, 1976).

Few disturbed students carry specific psychiatric diagnoses, and in any case such labels are not very helpful to teachers. In deciding how to respond, teachers should consider variables such as their own relationship with the student, whether the problem seems to be petering out or escalating, the student's emotional state (which varies daily), whether the student's disruptive activities seem to be intentional, and the probable consequences of contemplated actions.

Dealing with offenders

Many teachers strike tacit bargains with persistent offenders, minimizing educational demands and even interactions with them in return for a degree of compliance (Hargreaves, Hester, & Mellor, 1975). This tactic can backfire, however. Teachers often will not intervene with such students when their misbehavior is relatively mild but then will overreact when they do intervene, thus reinforcing the students' perceptions that the teacher is picking on them. In general, indirect methods that try to avoid dealing with problems or pretend that they do not exist are more likely to reinforce than to extinguish the problem behavior. Although it is true that teachers may have to spend a great deal of time working with them individually, *the general principles of classroom management to be discussed here hold for disturbed students just as for other students* (Hewett & Watson, 1979; Kounin & Obradovic, 1968).

CHOOSING YOUR ROLE

As students progress through the grades they undergo personal and social development that affects the role of the teacher and the goals and techniques of classroom management. Brophy and Evertson (1978) identified four stages:

1. *Kindergarten and the early elementary grades.* Here students are being socialized into the role of student and instructed in basic skills. Most still view adults as authority figures, are predisposed to do what they are told, and are likely to feel gratified when they please teachers and upset when they do not. They turn to teachers for direction, encouragement, solace, assistance, and personalized attention. Serious disturbances usually are not yet present. Consequently, teachers function primarily as instructors and socializers who emphasize teaching students what to do rather than getting them to comply with familiar rules. These instruction and socialization aspects of classroom management are basic to the teacher's job in the early grades; indeed, it is not possible to teach young children effectively without spending considerable time on these tasks.

2. *The middle elementary grades.* This stage starts when basic socialization to the student role is completed and continues as long as most students remain adult-oriented and relatively compliant. Students are familiar with most school routines, and the serious disturbances seen frequently in later years have not yet become common. Maintaining an appropriate learning environment remains central to teaching success, but doing so takes less teacher time, and teachers concentrate on instructing students in the formal curriculum.

3. *The upper elementary and lower high school grades.* As more and more students switch orientation from pleasing teachers to pleasing the peer group, teachers begin to be resented when they act as authority figures. Certain students become more disturbed and harder to control than they used to be. As a result, classroom management again becomes a prominent part of the teacher role. In contrast to the first stage, however, the teacher's primary problem now is motivating students to behave as they know they are supposed to, not instructing them how to do it.

4. *The upper high school grades.* As many of the most alienated students drop out of school and as students become more mature, schooling once again assumes an academic focus, and teaching becomes mostly a matter of instructing students in the formal curriculum. Classroom management remains important but requires little time (except in the first few class meetings), and group socialization almost disappears. Individual socialization occurs mostly in informal, out-of-class contacts with students.

Grade-level choice

These developmental aspects of classroom management should be considered when deciding to teach at particular grade levels. Teachers who like to provide nurturant socialization as well as instruction and have the patience and skills needed for socializing young children into the student role are well placed in the primary grades. Elementary teachers who want to concentrate mostly on instruction are better placed in the middle grades. Grades seven to ten are best for teachers who enjoy (or at least are not bothered by) the provocative behavior of adolescents and who see themselves as socialization agents and models at least as much as instructors. The upper high school grades are best for teachers who want to function mostly as subject-matter specialists.

Teachers who want to minimize socialization activities can do so, although they cannot eliminate them entirely. They can get by with management strategies that are effective for maintaining an orderly classroom but not for changing severely disturbed students. They can (legitimately) take the position that responsibility for changing such students resides with school counselors or other treatment experts and can confine their own efforts with such students to instructional activities.

Handling serious problems

There has been much debate, but little research and no ironclad findings, about how to handle the most serious problems: racial and other group tensions; severe withdrawal and refusal to communicate; hostile, antisocial acting out; truancy; refusal to work or obey; vandalism; and severe behavioral disorders or criminality problems that neither psychotherapists nor correctional institutions have achieved much success in dealing with. Yet teachers typically are asked to cope with such problems, while also coping with the needs of twenty or more other students (five times as many in junior high and high school).

Recognizing limitations

Some teachers respond to this with determination to solve whatever problems come along; others conclude that it is better to concentrate on a few tasks and perform them well than to try to do everything. We prefer the former position but find the latter position understandable. A teacher who does not enjoy student socialization and chooses to teach at grades where socialization is minimized and to concentrate on becoming highly skilled at teaching subject matter probably is making a wise decision. The same is true of teachers who choose to teach at the junior high grades and concentrate on socialization. Such teachers will have different effects on students than teachers who deal with the entire spectrum of responsibilities, but their effects will tend to be positive and probably greater in the long run than they would have been if they had tried to do everything and ended up doing nothing very well.

THE TEACHER AS A SOCIALIZATION AGENT

Teacher commitment

Teachers who want to have important socialization effects on students can do so, but they will need to understand the commitment involved in this decision and the frustrations to be encountered because of rules and regulations, uncooperative school officials or parents, and students who do not respond to their best efforts. A teacher who makes a commitment to deal with students' problems in addition to instructing them in the

A teacher who is committed to helping problem students must be willing to spend time with parents.

formal curriculum also may be agreeing to invest the time and energy needed to cultivate deeper personal relationships with students than are necessary for purely instructional purposes; spend considerable time outside regular school hours dealing with students and their families, perhaps even to be "on call" as a counselor to students who have no one else to turn to; receive no extra pay for such efforts and perhaps even some opposition from school officials; in many cases, draw the wrath of parents or others involved in the situation; and try to deal with complex problems that have developed over a period of years.

Difficulties of Socialization

Teachers typically do not have special training in dealing with serious personality or behavior disorders. Nor do they have the luxury of being able to interact with students by taking a friendly, nonauthoritative therapist's role. Instead, they must find ways to reach disturbed students while still acting as an authority figure and dealing with them every day in class in addition to contacting them individually. As a result, even the most energetic, determined, and skilled teachers will have only limited success. This is not bad in itself because the success rates even of professional therapists are not impressive. It does mean, however, that teachers who commit themselves to socialization must simultaneously expect the best and yet be prepared for the worst. Teachers who expect to succeed consistently or to be rewarded with expressions of love and gratitude will be disappointed. Rewarding experiences occur, but so do frustrations. Many students do not respond to continued and appropriate attempts to reach them. Others respond and make initial progress only to regress and end up worse than they started. Among "success cases," only some respond with overt gratitude or other direct reinforcement of the teacher.

Limited success rate

If you think that you can persist in trying to reach students despite constant frustrations, you probably have a good chance to be a successful socialization agent. In fact, if you find the prospect exciting and challenging, you might consider planning to work in grades five to ten (approximately), where student socialization needs are most frequent and intense.

Teachers' Advantages as Socializers

Teachers have some advantages over therapists or other specialists. First, they see students every day and under a variety of conditions, so they have more and better information (therapists usually must rely on what clients choose to tell them). The authority-figure role has advantages too. Teachers can interact with students in a variety of realistic situations, and they can provide consequences (both rewards and punishments) to selected student behavior. The bottom line is that teachers who want to be socialization agents can achieve reasonable success and satisfaction if they approach the task with realistic expectations and attitudes in addition to the ability to identify problems and respond to them effectively.

THE TEACHER AS AUTHORITY FIGURE

Student attitudes and expectations

Students expect teachers to manage their classrooms effectively. Nash (1976) found six main themes in elementary students' attitudes and expectations concerning teachers: (1) keep order (strict rather than lenient, punishes if necessary); (2) teaches you (keeps you busy); (3) explains (can be understood, gives help if you need it); (4) interesting (provides variety, not boring); (5) fair (consistent, does not play favorites or pick on anyone); and (6) friendly (kind or nice, talks gently rather than shouts, can laugh when appropriate).

Metz (1978) found similar attitudes among high school students. Students in high tracks expected content mastery and continuous intellectual challenge from their teachers. They seldom rebelled but often challenged teachers on academic grounds. Students in low tracks were more concerned about teachers' personal qualities: is not mean, does not shout, does not play favorites, accuses only when justified, explains material so you can understand it. These students often tested teachers by disobeying rules and causing disruptions. They did not question the teacher's right to exert authority, even though they sometimes resisted that authority.

In general, *students expect teachers to act as authority figures* and desire a predictable structure in each classroom. They will accept a variety of leadership styles, as long as each teacher is consistent. They have little sympathy, however, for teachers who cannot or will not control their classrooms, taking the attitude that such teachers deserve all the grief they get.

Suppression of unacceptable behavior

Regardless of the teacher role you see as ideal, some suppression of unacceptable behavior will be necessary. Behavior that is disruptive to instruction or harmonious group living must be stopped. Violence, weapons, and destruction, among other things, cannot be allowed (Feldhusen, 1979). These "nonnegotiables" will have to be presented to students (when necessary) as absolutely forbidden. Violence will be punished, weapons will be confiscated, and property destruction will require restitution. Students (or parents) who refuse to accept this will be politely referred to the police. We speak here of situations in which serious unacceptable behavior is widespread and out of control. Such problems should not even be mentioned when they do not exist. When they exist in mild and limited forms, they should be approached in positive ways designed not only to eliminate the undesirable behavior but also to solve underlying problems and channel the students into more appropriate activities.

A basic principle should be that individuals are responsible for their own behavior; students who cause trouble despite repeated warnings will have to take the consequences (Glaser, 1977). It is self-defeating to try to "protect" such students by insulating them from the consequences of their own behavior or to minimize the seriousness of crimes such as assault and battery or mugging on the grounds that they occurred at school between students rather than on the street between strangers. The result usually is an escalation of problems, as antisocial students see that they can get away with more and other students realize that they cannot rely on school authorities to accept responsibility for controlling the situation.

Thus no matter where you stand on the issue of the degree to which the teacher has a responsibility to help students to solve their personal problems, you must be prepared to suppress misbehavior by students who leave no alternative. This fact must be absorbed emotionally by those of you who care deeply about students as individuals and not merely as learners. It is understandable that you would prefer to create situations in which everyone cooperates humanistically and shuns hostility and violence. However, such a resolution is unlikely. Almost every school exhibits continuing and inescapable problems with which every teacher must be prepared to deal at some level.

RESEARCH ON TEACHER-ROLE ORIENTATIONS

Responsibility for student outcomes

Teachers' classroom behavior is affected by the way they perceive their role and abilities as teachers (Ashton & Webb, 1986). Ames (1983) contended that teachers arrive at attributions about their teaching effectiveness through a belief system organized around personal values and that their causal attributions for student performance affect whether or not they see a need to change their teaching behavior. In an empirical study, he found that teachers who believed that teaching was important and valued their competence as teachers were more likely to consider their own behavior as a possible source of influence on students than were teachers who did not believe that teachers were responsible for student learning.

Teachers' perceptions

There is also evidence that teachers' perceptions of the reasons for students' misbehavior influence the ways that teachers respond when behavior problems occur (Rohrkemper & Brophy, 1983). In this study, teachers who had been identified by their principals as either outstanding or average in ability to handle problem students were asked to read vignettes depicting various problems and to describe what they would say and do if these problems occurred in their own classrooms. Some of the problems are shown in Table 19.1.

Based on distinctions made by Gordon (1974), these researchers in-

Vignette Instrument

1. (*Failure syndrome student, shared problem*)
Joe could be a capable student, but his self-concept is so poor that he actually describes himself as stupid. He makes no serious effort to learn, shrugging off responsibility by saying that "that stuff" is too hard for him. Right now he is dawdling instead of getting started on an assignment that you know he can do. You know that if you approach him he will begin to complain that the assignment is too hard and that he can't do it.

2. (*Hostile-aggressive student, teacher-owned problem*)
This morning, several students excitedly tell you that on the way to school they saw Tom beating up Sam and taking his lunch money. Tom is the class bully and has done things like this many times.

3. (*Hyperactive student, shared problem*)
Bill is an extremely active child. He seems to burst with energy, and today he is barely "keeping the lid on." This morning, the class is working on their art projects, and Bill has been in and out of his seat frequently. Suddenly, Roger lets out a yell and you look up to see that Bill has knocked Roger's sculpture off his desk. Bill says he didn't mean to do it; he was just returning to his seat.

4. (*Student rejected by peers, student-owned problem*)
Mark is not well accepted by his classmates. Today he has been trying to get some of the other boys to play a particular game with him. After much pleading the boys decide to play the game but exclude Mark. Mark argues, saying that he should get to play because it was his idea in the first place, but the boys start without him. Finally, Mark gives up and slinks off, rejected again.

5. (*Perfectionist student, student-owned problem*)
Beth has average ability for school work, but she is so anxious about the quality of her work that she seldom finishes an assignment because of all her "startovers." This morning you have asked the children to make pictures to decorate the room. The time allocated to art has almost run out, and Beth is far from finished with her picture. You ask her about it and find out she has "made mistakes" on the other ones and this is her third attempt at a "good picture."

6. (*Passive-aggressive student, teacher-owned problem*)
The class is about to begin a test. The room is quiet. Just as you are about to begin speaking, Audrey opens her desk. Her notebook slides off the desk, spilling loose papers on the floor. Audrey begins gathering up the papers, slowly and deliberately. All eyes are upon her. Audrey stops, grins, and then slowly resumes gathering papers. Someone laughs. Others start talking.

7. (*Distractible student, shared problem*)
George's attention wanders easily. Today it has been divided between the discussion and various distractions. You ask him a question, but he is distracted and doesn't hear you.

8. (*Shy/withdrawn student, shared problem*)
Linda is bright enough, but she is shy and withdrawn. She doesn't volunteer to participate in class, and when you call on her directly, she often does not respond. When she does, she usually whispers. Today, you are checking the seatwork progress. When you question her, Linda keeps her eyes lowered and says nothing.

continued

9. (*Underachieving student, teacher-owned problem*)
Carl can do good work, but he seldom does. He will try to get out of work. When you speak to him about this, he makes a show of looking serious and pledging reform, but his behavior doesn't change. Just now, you see a typical scene: Carl is making paper airplanes when he is supposed to be working.

10. (*Defiant student, teacher-owned problem*)
Roger has been fooling around instead of working on his seatwork for several days now. Finally, you tell him that he has to finish or stay in during recess and work on it then. He says, "I won't stay in!" and spends the rest of the period sulking. As the class begins to line up for recess, he quickly jumps up and heads for the door. You tell him that he has to stay inside and finish his assignment, but he just says "No, I don't!" and continues out the door to recess.

11. (*Immature student, shared problem*)
Betty seems younger than the other students in your class. She has difficulty getting along with them and is quick to tattle. She has just told you that she heard some of the boys use "bad words" during recess today.

12. (*Low-achieving student, student-owned problem*)
Jeff tries hard but is the lowest achiever in the class. This week you taught an important sequence of lessons. You spent a lot of extra time with Jeff and thought he understood the material. Today you are reviewing. All of the other students answer your questions with ease, but when you call on Jeff, he is obviously lost.

Brophy & Rohrkemper, 1988, pp. 32–35.

cluded in the vignettes (1) teacher-owned problems (student behavior interferes with the teacher's meeting his or her own needs), (2) teacher-student shared problems (the teacher and student interfere with each other's need satisfaction), and (3) student-owned problems (not caused by the teacher). Their results indicate that teachers' attributions of students' problems to causes, as well as their beliefs about their own potential effects on students, varied across the three levels of problem ownership. Student-owned problems yielded teacher statements of sympathy and desire to help via encouragement, support, and instruction in better coping strategies, but teacher-owned problems yielded responses that were mostly restricted to attempts to exert situational control through criticism and threats of punishment. The latter responses appear to be self-defeating and unlikely to change the problem behavior. They were associated with tendencies to attribute the problems to internal and unchangeable causes and thus to assume that the chances for long-term change were poor. Lacking confidence in their abilities to bring about long-term improvements in students who presented teacher-owned problems, many teachers did not even try.

It is natural for teachers to develop attributional interpretations and related emotional responses to student behavior. However, teachers are professionals and must be prepared to control their emotions and give students what they need. Students who present student-owned problems need to learn to cope effectively—teacher sympathy is not enough. Students who present teacher-owned problems could use a little sympathy or at least concern, as well as information about how to behave differently—teacher anger and punitive responses do not help the situation in any fundamental way.

Teacher responses as typical human responses

These teacher responses are typical human responses: We tend to respond with sympathy to people we see as victims but to respond with anger to people we see as *intentionally* causing us problems. Effective professionals, however, get beyond such immediate emotional responses in two ways: (1) controlling their emotions and suppressing the typical response to those emotions; (2) trying to help the person gain insight and develop more effective coping mechanisms. 

GENERAL ATTRIBUTES OF EFFECTIVE SOCIALIZERS

Importance of liking one's teacher

Inferences about relationships between teachers' general attributes and their success in classroom management can be drawn from studies of student attitudes and from information on attributes of individuals who are effective models (Bandura, 1977) or effective parents (Brophy, 1977). First, teachers should be liked by their students. Characteristics important here are the same ones for making anyone *well liked*: a cheerful disposition, friendliness, emotional maturity, sincerity, and other qualities indicating good mental health and personal adjustment. Certain additional qualities are essential when teachers function in the role of classroom authority figure. Many of them involve *ego strength*, an underlying self-confidence that enables teachers to remain calm in a crisis, listen actively without becoming defensive, avoid win-lose conflicts, and maintain a problem-solving orientation rather than resort to withdrawal, blaming, hysteria, or other emotional overreactions. Teachers with serious problems in these areas will not be successful classroom managers no matter what techniques they use.

Characteristics of Good Student Socializers

Teachers who are good student socializers tend to have the following characteristics (Brophy & Putnam, 1979).

Realistic Perceptions of Themselves and of Students This means seeing themselves and their students for what they are, without letting their perceptions become clouded by romanticism, guilt, hostility, anxiety, or other emotional reactions that can reduce contact with reality.

Enjoyment of Students, but within a Teacher-Student Relationship This means enjoying spending time interacting with students and getting to know them as individuals while maintaining an identity as an adult, a teacher, and an occasional authority figure. The teacher is friendly without being overfamiliar, comfortable with the group without being a group member.

Clarity concerning Roles and Comfort in the Roles Played To be consistent in their interactions with students, teachers need to be clear about their own roles and relationship to students and about the behaviors that they value or will not tolerate. Once they achieve this clarity, teachers will know exactly what they want, will be able to explain it coherently to students, and will be comfortable with it in their own minds.

Positive Attitudes toward Being Challenged and Tested Teachers who are comfortable in these situations can approach them as games of one-upmanship. This can be enjoyable, as well as useful, for impressing students, providing that the teacher ''wins'' in ways that inspire admiration rather than resentment. Students who try to get away with something, for example, by finding loopholes in the rules can be complimented for their cleverness (but firmly refused). This will soften the effect of refusal. In contrast, getting angry or punishing such students ''because you think you are so smart'' would only make things worse.

Patience and Determination Some students will persist in testing limits because they are accustomed to getting their way eventually if they keep at it long enough. Such behavior is difficult to extinguish, but it can be done if the teacher convinces the students that there will be no giving up and no such thing as getting away with misbehavior without paying a price.

Effective Parental Behavior Other qualities that probably affect teachers' socialization of students can be inferred from what is known about effective parental behavior. The following traits characterize parents who are successful in getting their children to adopt their ideals and internalize their standards for behavior (Brophy, 1977; Hoffman, 1977; Martin, 1975).

Acceptance Children who are accepted for what they are tend to develop a sense of security, a positive self-concept, and a prosocial attitude toward other people (Coopersmith, 1967). In contrast, children who are rejected because of characteristics their parents find unacceptable, and children who are accepted only conditionally (when they do things that please the parents), may feel threatened by others and hostile toward them, may have low self-esteem and other self-concept problems, or may be generally antisocial. Teacher acceptance or rejection presumably will have similar effects on students, so it is important for teachers to project acceptance and unconditional positive regard (Rogers, 1983) to each individual.

Firm but Flexible Limits Successful parents state clear limits and enforce them firmly, but they keep limits flexible and negotiable. Rules are liberalized as children assume more independence and responsibility. Parents who have too few limits tend to end up with children lacking in self-discipline and self-control, whereas the children of parents whose limits are too numerous and rigid tend to be either overconforming, dependent, and uncreative or rebellious and resentful (Baumrind, 1971). Successful classroom managers will impose clear rules and enforce them consistently but keep them to a minimum and flexible enough to allow for individual differences and changes over time.

Self-fulfilling prophecy

Positive Expectations Children tend to acquire their parents' expectations and attitudes and to use them both for defining what is "normal" and for deciding what expectations and attitudes apply to themselves. One result is the self-fulfilling prophecy effect: Regardless of whether expectations were accurate originally, children are likely to fulfill them if adults consistently expect them to have certain qualities and treat them accordingly. In school, self-fulfilling prophecy effects are not confined to student achievement; they also apply to student conduct. Students treated as basically good people who want to do the right things, whose lapses are treated as due to ignorance or forgetfulness, are likely to become the prosocial people they are expected to become (Grusec et al., 1978; Miller, Brickman, & Bolen, 1975). Students treated as if they are inherently evil or under the control of powerful antisocial impulses, whose lapses are taken as evidence of immorality rather than as isolated mistakes, are likely to become antisocial.

Thus it is important for teachers to project positive expectations by treating students as if they already are, or at least are trying to be, the kind of people that the teachers want them to be. Admonitions such as "John, be careful with that microscope—we wouldn't want to break it," or "Mary, I was surprised to hear you ridiculing Jean when you were talking to Mary Ann today—how about trying to understand her better rather than just running her down?" (said in private) illustrate these principles. The teacher treats the student as a responsible person (or at least as someone who will be responsible in this regard in the future) and provides prescriptive information rather than personal criticism. In contrast, consider responses such as "I don't know why you can't sit still," "Do you think it's funny to make noises like that?" or "You are going to have to find some other way to take out your frustrations—we'll have no hitting in the classroom." These criticisms not only fail to provide positive guidance but also imply that no change in the behavior is really expected.

Supplementing demands with explanations

Ability to see implications

Moral development

Rationales and Expectations Successful parents supplement their socialization demands with explanations. They not only tell children what to do but also tell them why it is important to do it. This helps children see that rules and demands are imposed for good reasons rather than as arbitrary exercises of adult power and to be aware of the implications of behavior for themselves and others (Hess, 1970; Hoffman, 1977). This ability to see implications or "take the role of the other" is necessary for the development of a prosocial moral orientation, a tendency to live by the Golden Rule (treating others the way one would like to be treated oneself). Furthermore, if people do not understand the reasons underlying a demand, they are unlikely to adopt it in guiding their own behavior. Although the situations producing good inner self-control and a highly developed moral sense are complex and not completely understood, at least two things appear to be important: (1) Children must see ideal behavior patterns modeled by the adults around them, and (2) they must come to see that rules are supported by rationales based on logic and consideration of the general welfare. Rules should not be seen as arbitrary demands to be followed only because they may be enforced by a powerful authority figure.

Consistency in Rule Enforcement Inconsistency is confusing. Even if they are willing, it is difficult for people to learn rules if rules are unclear or keep changing. It is also frustrating if behaviors that were all acceptable yesterday are punished today. This produces resentment and the feeling that the authority figure is arbitrary and undependable, and it encourages deliberate disobedience (usually called ''testing'') designed to see if a rule will really be enforced.

Inconsistency in the ways that different individuals are treated produces resentful feelings of favoritism and being picked on. This is perfectly understandable. If we see authority figures allow others to do something that we were punished for doing ourselves, we resent it.

Modeling Authority figures must practice what they teach. Usually, they cannot have a double standard, one for themselves and one for others. Unless they can explain any exceptions satisfactorily, they will have to live up to their own ideals and rules if they expect others to do so. Anything short of this is hypocrisy. Teachers must model and generally live up to ideals that they verbalize if they expect their students to follow suit. In areas such as politeness and good manners, friendliness and helpfulness, and consideration for the rights and feelings of others, teachers who do not practice what they preach by modeling it in their own behavior will be perceived as hypocrites or worse and will not be respected or obeyed (Bryan & Walbek, 1970; Lickona, 1975).

PHYSICAL DESIGN OF CLASSROOMS

Desk arrangement

Good management involves the *prevention* of problems; a carefully laid out physical environment is the first step. Classroom arrangements influence student involvement and participation, and the physical arrangement should be congruent with intended objectives (Gump & Good, 1976). Physical settings can influence student behavior either directly or indirectly through teacher behavior (Arlin, 1979) or different types of task structures (Doyle, 1986a).

Rosenfield, Lambert, and Black (1985), for example, showed that students asked to brainstorm about ideas for writing assignments did better when seated in circles than when seated in rows or clusters. Presumably, the enhanced visibility made it easier for students to participate and to be monitored during these interactions (see Figure 19.1).

Class Size and Heterogeneity

In general, smaller classes are easier to manage than larger classes. Teachers do not always adjust their management systems accordingly, however, Cahen et al. (1983), for example, reduced the class sizes of primary-grade classrooms either from twenty to thirteen or from thirty-five to twenty-two. They found that after the change, students (a) were more involved in work, (b) spent less time waiting for teacher help when they had a problem, (c) were off-task less frequently, and (d) spent less time waiting because they had no assignment. Thus changes did occur. However, the overall pattern of classroom instruction remained the same. Teachers did the same things but with fewer students; they did not alter the instructional activities.

Setting up smaller units

Teachers typically cannot directly affect the size of their classes, but they can divide the classes into smaller units for some instruction. By using parent volunteers and teacher aides, teachers can increase the time they spend supervising individual and group work. They also can use different organizational strategies (learning centers, peer tutoring, small groups) to reduce the size of their instructional groups.

Students and teachers may benefit from working in small groups because: (1) instruction can be geared to the specific needs of the students in the group, (2) the teacher can monitor work directly and provide corrective feedback immediately, (3) shy or slow students may feel more comfortable asking questions in small groups, (4) students may stay on task and apply themselves more consistently when they are under direct supervision, and (5) students may feel more responsible for the completion of the task in small groups.

Management and achievement of heterogeneous classes

Just as small classes are easier to manage than larger classes, homogeneous classes are easier to manage than heterogeneous classes. Evertson, Sanford, and Emmer (1981) studied the ways that junior high English teachers adapted instruction to heterogeneous classes compared to the ways that they taught more homogeneous classes. The heterogeneous

Figure 19.1 Desk Arrangements

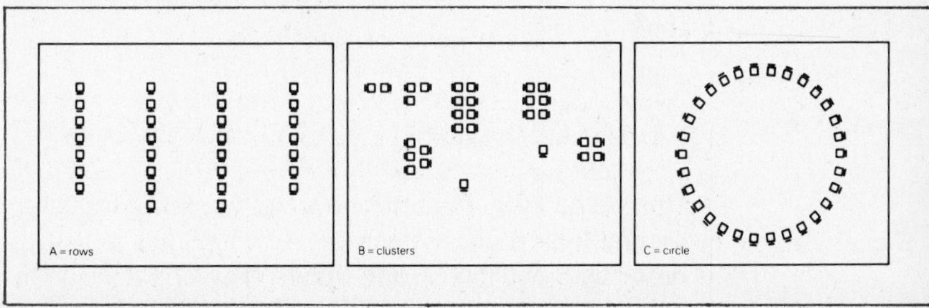

Source: P. Rosenfield, N. Lambert, and A. Black (1985). "Desk arrangement effects on pupil classroom behavior." *Journal of Educational Psychology, 77*(1), 101–108. Copyright 1985 by the American Psychological Association. Reprinted by permission of the publisher and authors.

Research demonstrates that, on average, smaller classes are easier to manage than larger classes.

classes had eight- to ten-year spreads in grade-level equivalent units between the low achievers and the high achievers. All of the heterogeneous classes got off to a poor start because the methods and materials were poorly adapted to the students' interests and abilities, and success rates in terms of completeness and correctness of assignments were poor. This pattern continued or deteriorated further in the classes in which the teachers lacked the managerial skills needed to respond effectively to heterogeneity, but the more effective managers were able to overcome these problems to an extent after about three weeks by using the following strategies: (1) special attention and help for lower-ability students, (2) limited use of within-class grouping and differentiated materials or assignments, (3) limited differential grading based on individualized effort and continuous-progress criteria, (4) limited use of peer tutoring, and (5) frequent monitoring and provision of academic feedback to all students, coupled with mechanisms to ensure student accountabilty for participating in lessons and completing assignments.

These adjustments were successful enough that there was no difference in achievement gain between the homogeneous and the heterogeneous classes. Still, there were limits on what could be accomplished. The pressures of meeting the greater range of instructional needs in the heterogeneous classes left the teachers with little time for personalized interaction with students, especially interaction concerning nonacademic topics.

IMPROVING CLASSROOM PHYSICAL ENVIRONMENTS

One of the authors observed an enthusiastic fourth-grade teacher present a creative-writing assignment. The teacher began by asking students to describe what interesting things they could do with a gigantic box that stood in the front of the room. Students were on the edges of their seats, waving their arms with excitement as their ideas were solicited and written on the board. Then the teacher said, "Now I want you to write your own original story. Tell me the fun things you could do with a giant frog that is bigger than you are! Think and be creative. Take your time. We have half an hour." Five minutes later, only two or three students had started to work on their stories. The transition from public discussion to private composition was difficult, largely because of the way the teacher had arranged the room. Individual desks had been placed together in groups of six to form rectangular tables. If students looked up, they were almost guaranteed eye contact with someone sitting close to them.

Students continued to exchange ideas for two or three minutes about what they could do with a big frog. Finally, the teacher announced with frustration, "Look, when you finish the paper, you can climb up on the chair and put it in the big box!" The race was on. The room was completely quiet except for the sound of pencils moving rapidly and the occasional ripping of paper from a pad. Within seven minutes all students had finished and climbed the magic chair to drop their stories in the big box. They had been motivated to produce quickly but not to think or use their imaginations. A seating arrangement conducive to small-group work was inappropriate for private composition.

Physical setting variables

Besides illustrating the power of motivation, this story shows how physical setting variables can exert important effects on a learning situation. The teacher's comment inviting students to put their finished papers in the big box had a powerful, negative influence on student behavior, but the seating arrangement was partly responsible for the lack of task involvement that led to the teacher's frustration and thoughtless statement.

Match between Physical Design and Program Activity

Some ecological psychologists (e.g., Ross, 1984) use the term *synomorphy* to refer to the compatibility between the action required by an activity and the physical aspects of the setting. From the perspective of order, one can easily see how the nature and arrangement of furniture can affect the density of students, their opportunities for interaction, and the extent to which teachers can observe ongoing behavior.

Figure 19.2 A Classroom Arrangement for Delivery of Student Reports

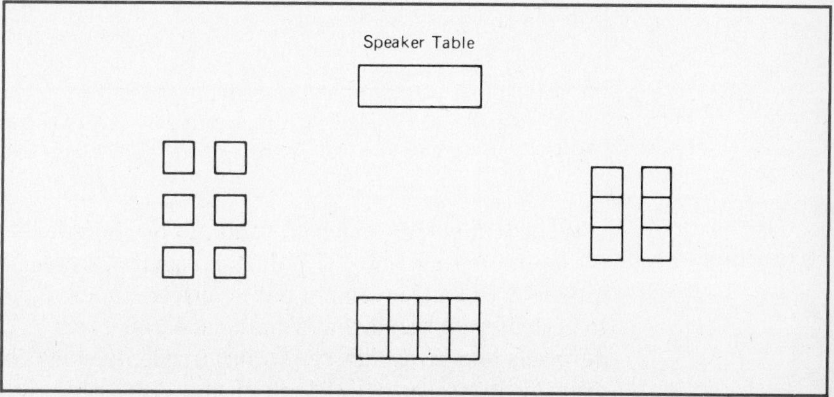

Figure 19.3 Several Classroom Seating Arrangements

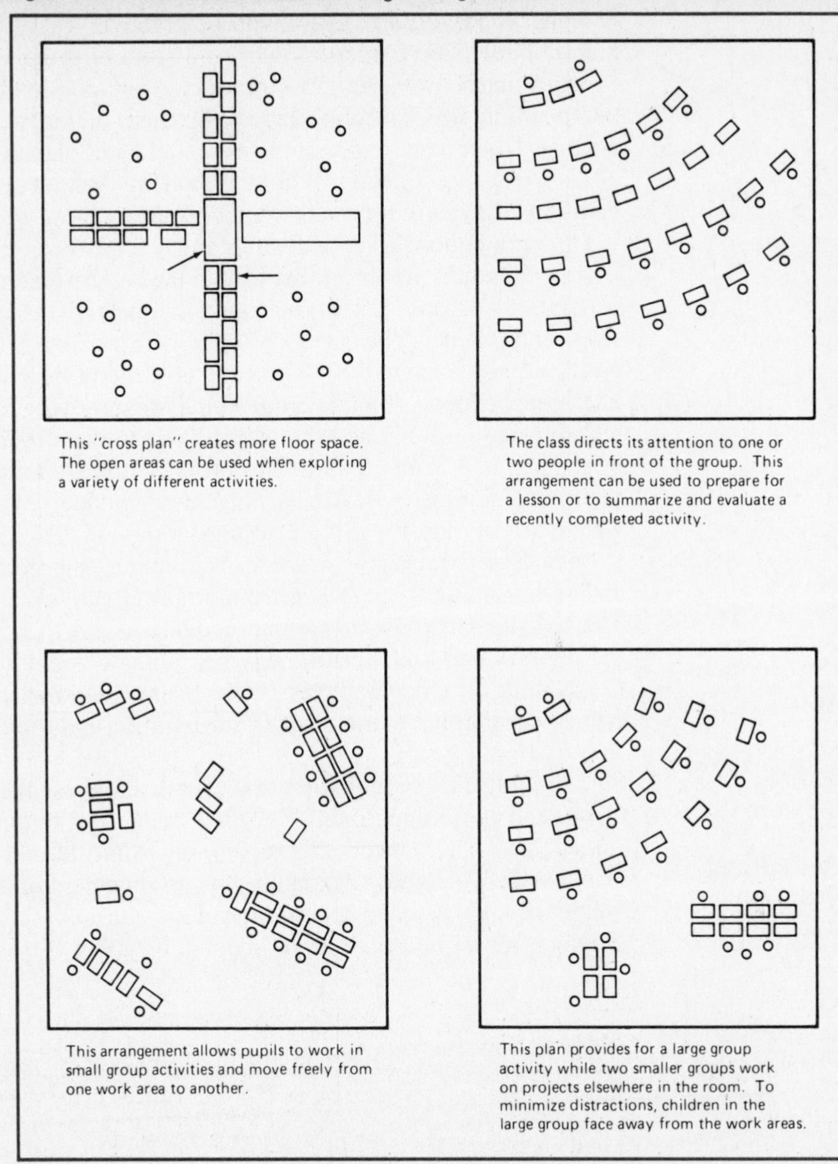

This "cross plan" creates more floor space. The open areas can be used when exploring a variety of different activities.
The class directs its attention to one or two people in front of the group. This arrangement can be used to prepare for a lesson or to summarize and evaluate a recently completed activity.
This arrangement allows pupils to work in small group activities and move freely from one work area to another.
This plan provides for a large group activity while two smaller groups work on projects elsewhere in the room. To minimize distractions, children in the large group face away from the work areas.

Source: Reproduced by permission from R. Reys, and T. Post (1973), *The Mathematics Laboratory: Theory to Practice*. Boston: Prindle, Weber, and Schmidt.

Synomorphy

Weinstein (1979) reviewed research on the effects of physical features of classrooms and noted that different spatial arrangements appear to have little effect on achievement but do affect students' attitudes and conduct. In particular, it seems important to separate clearly areas serving different purposes and to design classroom traffic avenues carefully. Density appears to increase dissatisfaction and aggression and to decrease attentiveness and involvement in assigned activities.

Figure 19.4 An Experimental Floor Plan before the Intervention

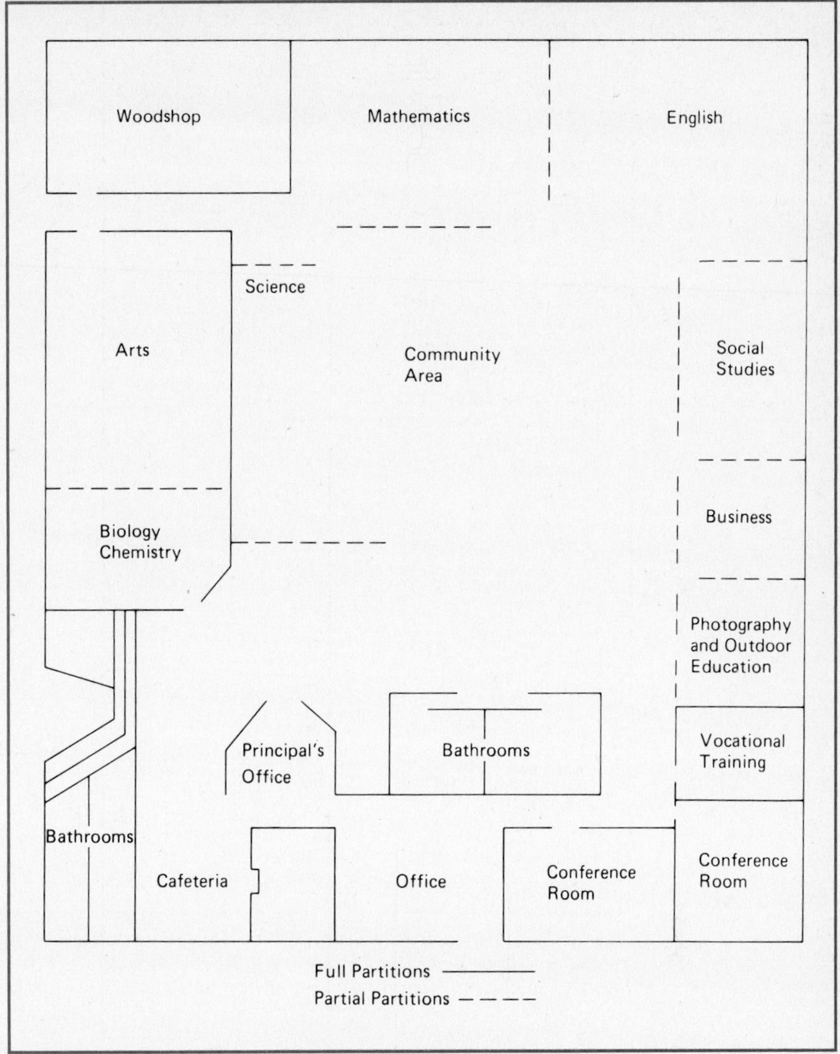

Source: G. Evans and B. Lovell (1979). "Design modification in an open-plan school," *Journal of Educational Psychology 71*(1), 41–49. Copyright 1979 by the American Psychological Association. Reprinted by permission of the publisher and authors.

As classroom functions change, seating patterns should be altered. Even though many classrooms are equipped with movable desks, some teachers use one seating arrangement exclusively. Others alter the physical arrangement too frequently. Most teachers are better off with two or three basic room arrangements that they use for reasons that students understand. Students should be able to move easily from one arrangement to another.

Altering room arrangements

The room in Figure 19.2 is arranged for students to listen to individual reports given by three students. This arrangement is acceptable for this purpose but not ideal. Most students can see the speaker (if the speaker

Figure 19.5 An Experimental Floor Plan after the Intervention

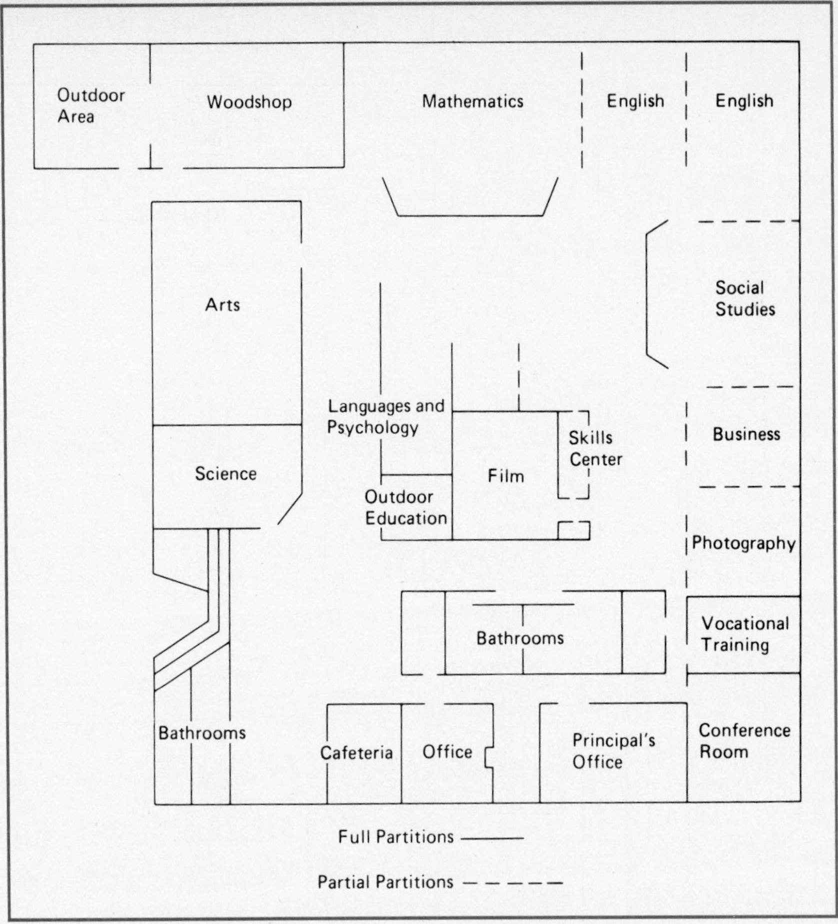

Source: G. Evans and B. Lovell (1979). "Design modification in an open-plan school," *Journal of Educational Psychology 71*(1), 41–49. Copyright 1979 by the American Psychological Association. Reprinted by permission of the publisher and authors.

stands), although pupils who have inside seats will face away from their desks and may have difficulty taking notes. If students need to pass out material or demonstrate a procedure, the clustering of students and the open space will facilitate these needs.

What makes this plan effective is the fact that the teacher plans to follow the three five-minute presentations with a half hour of related small-group work. The arrangement is fine for small-group activity, and students can begin to work as soon as the presentations end. Furthermore, the groups are arranged so that the teacher, by selecting an appropriate position while working with one group, can also monitor the other groups easily. Figure 19.3 illustrates several different seating arrangements. Some support certain types of behavior and activities better than others.

Figure 19.6 A Recommended First-Grade Classroom

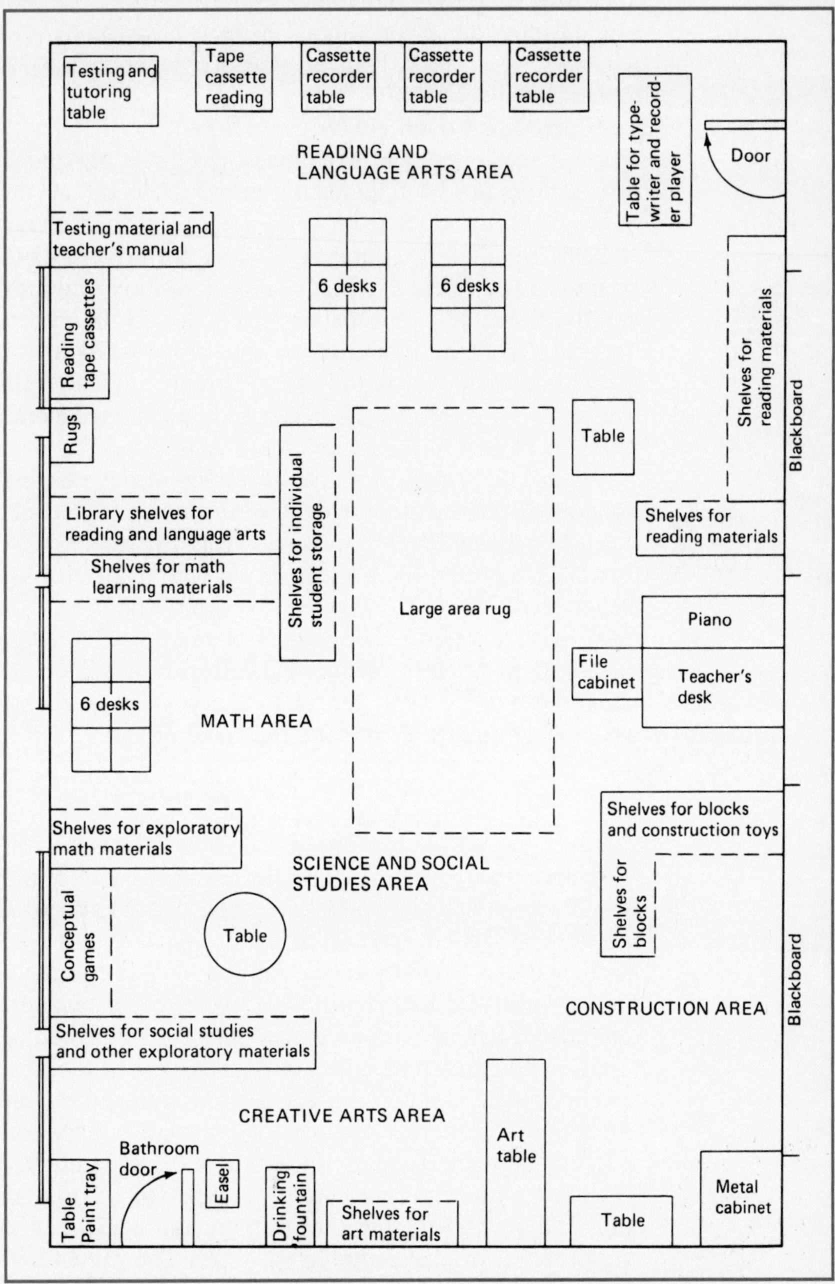

Source: Adapted from M. Wang (1973). *Teacher's manual for the exploratory learning component of the LRDC individualized instructional program for the early learning grades.* Pittsburgh: University of Pittsburgh, Learning Research and Development Center. Reprinted by permission of Mafex Associates, Inc., Johnston, PA.

Space Utilization

Physical environment and behavior

Minor changes in the physical environment can lead to important changes in behavior. Weinstein (1977), for example, found that additional shelving, increased space for individual work, and more partitions encouraged the use of individual work areas in open classrooms. After these physical changes were made, management problems decreased and task-relevant behaviors increased.

Evans and Lovell (1979) also altered the physical environment of an open-space school and examined the effects on student behavior. These researchers used sound-absorbent partitions of varying heights placed to redirect traffic away from certain areas, to make area boundaries more salient, and to add several small areas for private work. Both the control and the experimental schools were alternative high schools with similar philosophies. The physical arrangements in the experimental school before and after the modification are shown in Figures 19.4 and 19.5. Observations made in both schools before and after the design changes showed that interruptions decreased and the frequency of content questions increased in the experimental school.

Wang (1973) provided useful advice about designing classrooms for individualized instruction in the early elementary school years. Her design for a first-grade classroom is shown in Figure 19.6. Note its several features: (1) rows of desks are replaced with places for individual and small-group work, (2) each work area is clearly defined, (3) there is storage in each space so that needed material can be obtained easily, (4) areas are arranged in order to encourage integration of activities and sharing of equipment (e.g., math and science areas are adjacent), and (5) the open space encourages movement and flexibility.

Summary

Effective classroom management requires both clear expectations about student behavior and knowledge about what to do when expectations are not met. Teachers who are friendly, mature, and sincere and who have sufficient ego strength to deal fairly and constructively with students can use a variety of techniques effectively. Such teachers will consider the characteristics of various developmental stages along with gender, ethnicity, and past experiences in dealing with students.

The role of socialization agent is difficult, but teachers have some advantages over therapists and other specialists because of their frequency of contact with students and students' expectations that teachers will maintain authority over classroom behavior. To be successful, teachers must be consistent, positive in their approach, and determined in their suppression of unacceptable behavior. They must have realistic perceptions of themselves and of students, enjoy students within the confines of a professional relationship, be clear and comfortable in role portrayal, exhibit positive attitudes toward tests and challenges, and display patience and determination in dealing with persistent misbehavior.

Like parents, teachers must project acceptance and unconditional positive regard for students, set clear but flexible limits, project positive expectations for responsible behavior, provide explanations for socialization demands, be consistent in rule enforcement, and model desired behaviors that they expect students to exhibit.

Larger or more heterogeneous classes are more difficult to manage than smaller or more homogeneous ones, but teachers can adapt through grouping and other organizational strategies, limited use of peer tutoring, and differentiation of instruction, assignments, and grading standards.

Classroom environments generally can be improved by carefully considering stimuli affecting student behavior, including those originating from space, furniture, and displays. Physical design should support the psychological requirements for learning.

Questions and Problems

1. Do you fit Fuller's (1969) interpretation of developmental stages in the process of becoming a teacher? Are you concerned primarily about "survival" and classroom management right now?
2. A prospective teacher from a white, middle-class, suburban home is faced with the prospect of teaching in an inner-city school with lower-class urban, minority students. What should this person do to prepare? What should a new teacher from an inner-city background do to prepare for teaching in a "silk'stocking" district?
3. What is your preferred balance between instructional and managerial/counseling activities with students?
4. How can teachers be "overly" sympathetic to disturbed students?
5. What kinds of students are especially appealing to you (and thus likely to receive favoritism if you are not careful)? What kinds turn you off and will be especially hard for you to treat impartially and with positive attitudes and expectations?
6. Do you have strong preferences concerning seating arrangements or classroom groupings? What implications do these preferences have for your teaching (remember that as a teacher you will need to discover what things work best with your students and that these things may not correspond with your own preferences)?
7. How might you manipulate seat assignments for particular purposes? What if different goals conflict, such as minimizing social chatting among friends versus placing reticent students in action zones where they are more likely to participate?

Case Studies

PRANKSTERS. Jim Knipp, an algebra teacher at Willow High School, sits down at his desk and immediately springs to his feet. A quick glance confirms his guess that he had sat on a melted candy bar. The class howls with laughter. What should Jim do now?

TALKATIVE MARGERY. Jim Heald, a first-year high school teacher, watched with interest as three attractive girls burst into the room, glanced at him, and headed for the back of the class. As the period wore on, he became progressively more irritated because the girls talked incessantly during his presentation. Finally, in frustration he called on Margery, the loudest of the three. "Margery, I've been trying to explain the goals of our physics class. You've been talking for the past twenty minutes. Apparently, you know what our goals are here. Would you please summarize them for me?" She looked at him and half laughed as she said, "No, I think I'd better listen."

Would you have responded to Margery in the same way that Jim Heald did? If not, why not? In general, should students be allowed to choose their seats in high school classes? Why or why not? Do elementary school students need more or less choice than secondary students?

CHAPTER

Establishing and Maintaining a Good Learning Environment

CHAPTER OUTLINE

OBJECTIVES

When you have mastered the material in this chapter, you will be able to

1. Describe what a teacher can do to create a classroom environment that promotes learning, independence, and responsibility
2. Differentiate authoritarian, democratic, and laissez-faire leadership styles
3. Describe authoritative leadership and its effects and differentiate it from democratic leadership
4. Describe things a teacher can do to build personal trust and credibility with students
5. List and explain at least four characteristics of classroom rules that assist classroom management.

6. Explain these group-management skills of successful teachers: preparedness, maintaining student involvement, "withitness," overlapping, group alerting
7. Explain at least three techniques to engage and maintain students' attention during lessons or seatwork.

In this chapter we first discuss the advance preparation that contributes to effective classroom management, especially the need to arrange the physical environment for efficient functioning and to develop a workable set of classroom rules. This discussion builds on the material in the preceding chapter on the importance of a match between the teacher's goals and the physical arrangement of the classroom. Later, we review research on group leadership styles and effective strategies for maintaining attention to lessons and engagement in seatwork.

PREPARING THE PHYSICAL ENVIRONMENT

Effective management begins with preparation of the classroom itself. What can be done to make it an attractive and efficient learning environment? Regardless of how good or bad the available space and equipment may be, some arrangements will be better than others. Several may be needed if the teacher will deal with different classes that vary in size or if the students will engage in diverse activities.

Seating Arrangements

High priority should be given to arranging the room so that the teacher can monitor all areas at all times. Teachers should plan to sit or stand so that they are facing the class and should keep this in mind when identifying areas to be used for special purposes.

Seats should be located in ways that will facilitate attention and minimize disruption. Usually, this will mean keeping desks or tables in reasonably neat arrangements, with students seated facing the teacher. When students are assigned to work in groups, however, the groups can be arranged in small circles or ovals to facilitate communication among members. If several groups are meeting simultaneously, they should be spread out to minimize interference. Perhaps some can be allowed to meet outside the classroom, assuming that they act responsibly without supervision.

Traffic, Bottlenecks, and Lines

Heavily traveled traffic routes should be free of obstacles and wide enough to accommodate smooth, efficient movement around the classroom. This will minimize the problems that occur when students bump into furniture or one another.

Minimize waiting time

Problems are likely to develop when students are standing in lines, whether they are deliberately formed by the teacher or are the result of bottlenecks. Teachers can do many things to minimize the time students spend standing and waiting. One is to delegate authority or use monitors to handle time-consuming housekeeping tasks such as passing out supplies, taking attendance, and making collections. Use of the pencil sharpener or drinking fountain can be left to individual initiative within whatever limits are necessary, instead of requiring groups to go at specific times or requiring students to ask permission.

Supplies like scissors or paste should be dispensed from several places around the room, so that students do not have to line up and wait their turn at a single source. Checking of worksheets can be accomplished as a group activity by asking students to indicate when they are ready for checking or when they need help or by the teacher circulating around the room. Necessarily repetitive activities like "show and tell" or student speeches can be staggered across several days rather than massed into a single long session.

Student Independence and Responsibility

Helping students handle routine tasks

Too much time is often spent supervising students in relation to personal needs and everyday housekeeping tasks, and interruptions for this purpose are a major source of discontinuity in academic activities. Teachers can minimize these problems by preparing the classroom and the students to enable them to handle most routine tasks on their own. This is especially important in the early grades, when students' abilities to accomplish everyday tasks may depend on the degree to which the teacher has anticipated their needs. Young students can handle their belongings with the help of coat hooks and cubbyholes or lockers, but they should be within easy reach (not too high) and assigned individually. Color codes, pictures, and labels can be affixed to storage areas to help students remember where items belong. Everyday equipment should be stored where it can be reached and removed easily, and small items should be stored in easily opened containers that will not break. Notices giving instructions or rule reminders can be displayed prominently in activity centers, so that students wil not always have to come to the teacher for help.

Sometimes a private talk is the best way to resolve a question or problem.

Backup Activities and Supplies

Options for individual choice

Effective classroom managers have contingency plans for when scheduled activities are canceled or bad weather precludes outdoor recess. They prepare for these times as they would for lessons. Any needed props are handy, and the teacher is ready to conduct the activity smoothly. Even more important is the development of a system of backup activities, preferably including options to allow for individual choice, to make available to students when they finish assignments. These options should include a number of attractive individual and small-group learning activities and pastimes. The students should know what their options are and be able to exercise them without having to get directions from the teacher.

GENERAL PRINCIPLES OF GROUP LEADERSHIP

In addition to organizing the physical environment, teachers must organize the class into a cohesive group that functions effectively under their leadership. Several general principles are involved here, as well as numerous techniques for specific situations.

Group Structure

Promoting group cohesiveness

Effective groups show cohesiveness and positive attitudes. Less effective groups are divided into conflicting subgroups or into a dominant ingroup and a collection of isolates. Teachers can promote group cohesiveness by arranging for cooperative experiences, minimizing competition, promoting prosocial behaviors, and helping each student to identify with the class as a whole. They should avoid playing favorites, picking on scapegoats, fostering inappropriate competition, or refusing to allow students to work cooperatively (Johnson & Johnson, 1975; Slavin et al., 1985; Stanford, 1977).

Gaining confidence of peer leaders

When students constitute an intact group with well-established peer leadership, teachers will need to gain the cooperation of the peer leaders and avoid coming into direct conflict with them or causing them to lose face before the group. This is especially important when teachers work with students from a different social class or ethnic background or students whose attitudes and values contrast with those of the teacher.

Leadership Style

Authoritarian, democratic, and laissez-faire leadership

Lewin, Lippitt, and White (1939) conducted a classic experiment in which adults working with groups of ten-year-old boys were trained to act consistently authoritarian, democratic, or laissez-faire. Authoritarian leaders gave orders without much explanation, telling everyone what to do, and with whom. Democratic leaders took time to solicit opinions and achieve consensus about what to do and how to do it and allowed some choice of work companions. Laissez-faire leaders did not really lead at all, giving only vague directions and sketchy answers to questions. The three leadership styles were evaluated for effects on group productivity (efficiency in carrying out tasks) and affect (enjoyment of the experience).

Boys in democratic-led groups developed warm feelings for one another and the leader and enjoyed the experience. These affective benefits were achieved with only slight cost in efficiency (the productivity of democratic-led groups was not quite as good as that of authoritarian-led groups). The authoritarian-led groups were the most efficient because the leaders kept everyone working at a good pace, but group members showed tension and negative feelings toward one another and the leader. Laissez-faire leadership did not succeed by either criterion. The ostensible freedom experienced in these groups did not make up for the lack of leadership, so they spent much time working at cross-purposes, produced very little, and had negative reactions to the experience.

Later studies of group leadership have produced similar results: laissez-faire leadership is generally ineffective, authoritarian leadership is efficient but otherwise unattractive, and democratic leadership produces positive attitudes and good group relations, although at some cost in efficiency. This implies that democratic leadership is best as an overall style, although more structured leadership may be required when efficiency is important.

Authoritative leadership

Baumrind's (1971) research on childrearing provides some perspective for these findings. Baumrind classified parents as authoritarian, authoritative, or laissez-faire. She used "authoritative" instead of "democratic" because "democratic" leadership is not really democratic at all (decisons are not made by majority vote). It is "authoritative" in that the leader has a position of responsibility, speaks as an experienced and mature adult, and retains ultimate decision-making authority. Rather than act in an authoritarian manner, however, authoritative leaders solicit input, seek consensus, and make sure that everyone understands the rationales for decisions as well as the decisions themselves. Baumrind reported that children of authoritative parents show the most advanced levels of autonomy and independence for their ages and have greater confidence and healthier self-concepts.

There are two reasons for stressing Baumrind's work in discussing classroom management. First, the term *authoritative* is preferable to *democratic* because it retains the notion that the teacher has the ultimate responsibility for classroom leadership. The idea that decisions should be made by majority vote was not tested or supported by Lewin et al. (1939), despite their use of *democratic*. Nor does other research support the notion of truly democratic classroom leadership, although this style is often recommended on a philosophical basis (e.g., Glasser, 1969; Gordon, 1974).

Second, Baumrind's work provides a more convincing and data-based argument to support authoritative over authoritarian and laissez-faire methods. Authoritative methods are not merely *better perceived*; they are *more effective* in building the cognitive structures and behavioral control mechanisms within children that enable them to become both independent and responsible in managing their affairs. Authoritative teacher behavior should help students to see and internalize the rationales that underlie classroom rules and to choose to operate within the rules on their own initiative. Authoritarian approaches do not encourage the development of such internal control mechanisms. Instead, they generate conflict and tension even when they succeed in controlling behavior.

Reasonable Rules and Limits

Setting rules

Supply distribution

Teachers must decide what are reasonable rules and limits given their own role definition and values, the ages and number of students involved, the length of interaction with students (keeping the same ones all day versus changing classes each period), students' general levels of conformity versus rebelliousness, and the expectation of the principal and school district. Different teachers will need different sets of rules. A kindergarten or first-grade teacher, for example, usually will have to take personal charge of tasks such as passing out supplies, although some children can help in monitor roles. Fifth- or sixth-grade teachers will not need to perform this job because the students can handle it on their own if guided by a few supply-distribution rules. Such rules may not even be needed in high school.

Student response

Similarly, in the early grades teachers may have to insist that no one respond to questions or make comments without first being called on. As students mature, however, teachers can be more flexible, especially in group discussions. Flat prohibitions against calling out can be abandoned in favor of rules such as "feel free to contribute your ideas, but wait until the person who is speaking has finished."

Minimal and Flexible Rules

5-10

Rules should be minimal in number, should refer to general qualitative aspects of behavior rather than to specific do's and don'ts, and should be flexible and open to change as situations dictate. Minimizing the number of rules helps students to remember them and makes accepting them easier than if a long and demoralizing list were involved.

Rules such as "we will treat one another with courtesy and respect" or "we will keep the classroom clean and neat" cover a great many specific behaviors and eliminate the need for long lists of specifics. Such rules are broad but still definitive enough for most of the specifics to be obvious. Furthermore, they are phrased in positive ways that make them easier to explain in a manner likely to motivate students to accept them.

Maintaining flexibility

Maintaining flexibility is important because many behaviors are appropriate under some circumstances but not others. Quiet talking, for example, might be allowed among students who have finished assignments. If this gets too loud, the teacher can simply ask the students to quiet down—there is no need to demand total silence or to revoke the talking privilege. This avoids two problems that frequently cause conflict between teachers and students: unreasonable enforcement of a rule and loss of teacher credibility resulting from inconsistency (which students perceive as teacher confusion or hypocrisy rather than reasonable adjustment to situational differences).

Some authors have suggested that rules should be extremely specific, to avoid confusion and spell out the consequences of violations. We believe, however, that any gains in avoidance of misunderstanding that might come with a large number of overly specific rules would be canceled by the needless regimentation and communication of negative expectations. Effective classroom managers usually have five to ten general rules rather than a large number of specific ones.

Getting Off to a Good Start

Getting the year off to a good start by establishing the right expectations and routines is crucial (Doyle, 1986a; Moskowitz & Hayman, 1976). This may mean that several days or even weeks must be devoted more to getting students organized and socialized than to teaching the curriculum, but time spent this way is well worth it in the long run (Emmer, Evertson, & Anderson, 1980; Evertson & Emmer, 1982). In the early grades, teachers will need to conduct actual lessons that include instruction, practice with feedback, and review to show students how to handle daily routines (such as moving from a reading group to seatwork and vice versa, using the pencil sharpener, or managing the equipment in a learning center). Older students may not need such detailed instruction, but expectations should be made explicit.

Emmer et al. (1980) observed in twenty-seven third-grade classrooms during the first three weeks of the school year and at three-week intervals thereafter to discovery why teachers who had comparable classes at the beginning of the year differed in their management effectiveness (degree of student involvement in lessons) during the year. Their data revealed that successful managers devoted much of the first day and the first few weeks to establishing classroom procedures and rules, beginning with those of most immediate interest to the students (storage, lunch, lavatory, recess, etc.). The first few academic activities introduced were enjoyable and likely to produce success. The teachers usually worked with the whole class and personally supervised the students the entire time, putting off grouping and sustained independent work until basic routines were established. They monitored students carefully so that they could move quickly when instructional help or behavioral intervention were needed. They told students precisely what they wanted them to do and then supervised them while they did it, establishing their credibility by following through on their statements so that students learned that they meant what they said.

Importance of advanced planning

The successful managers also revealed evidence of advanced planning and preparation. They had arranged their rooms to make the best of whatever resources they were given to work with, often making changes in anticipation of problems with existing arrangements. They had thought out their rules and expectations so they could describe them to students in specific terms. They handled most housekeeping and paperwork before or after school, so that most classroom time was spent instructing the class. In contrast, poor managers created problems for themselves practically from the moment students arrived, because they were unclear or inconsistent about stating what they wanted, or because they failed to follow through.

Good managers also were more careful monitors of student behavior and dealt with misbehavior more quickly than poor managers. They *alerted* students to the behaviors they expected and held students *accountable* for those behaviors. As students internalized these rules, they could monitor their own behavior more continuously (e.g., they knew when and how to get help from other students about missed assignments). Such internalization of classroom norms for conduct and procedures not only makes students more efficient learners (e.g., it minimizes the time they spend wondering about when or how to approach the teacher for feedback), it also minimizes the number of competing demands on the teacher.

Based on the results of this and related research, Evertson and associates (1984) wrote a manual summarizing management principles and guidelines for starting the school year. The manual is organized around the eleven guidelines that appear in Table 20.1. Those researchers have also written a manual for secondary teachers (Emmer et al., 1984) indicating that such teachers do not need to do as much instructing of students in basic classroom routines as elementary teachers do. However, secondary teachers do need to be very clear and consistent in stating expectations and following up accountability procedures concerning completion of assignments. Experiments in which teachers were trained to implement the principles stressed in these manuals illustrate their effec-

TABLE 20.1 CLASSROOM GUIDELINES FOR ORGANIZATION AND MANAGEMENT

1. *Readying the classroom.*—Be certain your classroom space and materials are ready for the beginning of the year.
2. *Planning rules and procedures.*—Think about what procedures students must follow to function effectively in your classroom and in the school environment; decide what behaviors are acceptable; develop a list of procedures and rules.
3. *Consequences.*—Decide ahead of time consequences for appropriate and inappropriate behavior in your classroom, and communicate them to your students; follow through consistently.
4. *Teaching rules and procedures.*—Teach students rules and procedures systematically; include in your lesson plans for the beginning of school sequences for teaching rules and procedures, when and how they will be taught, and when practice and review will occur.
5. *Beginning-of-school-activities.*—Develop activities for the first few days of school that will involve students readily and maintain a whole-group focus.
6. *Strategies for potential problems.*—Plan strategies to deal with potential problems that could upset your classroom organization and management.
7. *Monitoring.*—Monitor student behavior closely.
8. *Stopping inappropriate behavior.*—Handle inappropriate and disruptive behavior promptly and consistently.
9. *Organizing instruction.*—Organize instruction to provide learning activities at suitable levels for all students in your class.
10. *Student accountability.*—Develop procedures that keep the students responsible for their work.
11. *Instructional clarity.*—Be clear when you present information and give directions to your students.

Source: *Evertson et al., 1983, pp. 173–188.*

tiveness for maximizing student attention to lessons and engagement in assignments (Evertson et al., 1983; Evertson, 1985).

In a study that compared beginning teachers with more experienced teachers nominated as "best" teachers by their students, Moskowitz and Hayman (1976) found that experienced teachers spent more time setting expectations and establishing behavior patterns on the first day of school. Even so, the experienced teachers also were more willing to accept and use student ideas. Hence successful managers are not necessarily stern or rigid. They do appear to be skillful in stating expectations and working with students to be sure that workable rules are established and enforced. Simply put, they *teach* norms for appropriate classroom behavior.

Why Proactive Management Works: Toward a Theory

Successful managers start the year by *establishing* rules and procedures (some announce; some negotiate) and by *communicating* their expectations. Other teachers are ambiguous about their expectations and spend so much time attempting to clarify that their students often wonder (sometimes justly so) whether or not their behavior is appropriate.

Avoiding alienation

New teachers sometimes are advised to "clamp down" early in the year to show that they mean business. This advice can backfire if taken the wrong way. Consistency and follow-through are important, but teachers who set themselves up as "the enemy" by alienating students through vindictive behavior are in for year-long conflict. Thus "don't smile until Christmas" is bad advice.

Dealing with inappropriate behavior

It is important to monitor actively and deal with inappropriate behavior (especially serious misbehavior). Effective managers therefore may correct student behavior more often during the first few days of the year than other teachers do. However, because their students eventually engage in fewer off-task behaviors, it soon becomes easier for them to monitor the class (there are fewer disruptions to attend to) and to respond to misbehavior appropriately (e.g., to correct the right student). If teachers establish workable rules, expect compliance, monitor the class, and insist on appropriate behavior when necessary, students will understand their seriousness of purpose and will begin to internalize rules, expectations, and procedures.

Necessity of completing curriculum tasks

Effective managers also demand that students use their time to complete assignments and hold students accountable for work. Students also know what to do when they finish assignments. Thus effective managers construct learning environments in which expectations for student behavior are *continuous*.

Ambiguous classroom roles

Some teachers make it difficult for students to know what is expected. Following a demonstration lesson, for example, they might assign seatwork but say, "If you work now, you won't have homework." Such statements make students' role ambiguous. Presumably, students can do the work now or later. Does this mean that they can choose not to do the work now? If so, what can they do while their classmates are engaged in seatwork?

In contrast, more effective managers are likely to make a transition from demonstration to seatwork in the following way: "Now do problems fifteen to thirty at your desks. In ten minutes we will check progress and correct any problems we encounter. If you have difficulty with a problem, do the next one. I'll be around to help you. Get started now."

Total management

As Good and Hinkel (1982) emphasized, *all* aspects of good management must operate for the system to work. Even teachers who establish credibility with students during the first few days of school, for example, establish explicit learning goals daily, and build in continuous criteria so that students know what is expected of them at a given moment will soon lose students if their work is not checked on a regular basis. Doyle (1982) argued that accountability drives the task system and that students tend to take seriously only that work for which they are held accountable.

Accountability

In essence, a good management system announces clear intentions and makes it possible to monitor behavior to see whether progress is being made toward shared goals. For self-motivated students, it tells how to proceed and do well. For other students, it establishes conditions to enable them to learn self-control and engage in academic tasks. These students come to understand that rewards and privileges are associated with personal progress on assigned tasks.

SPECIFIC GROUP-MANAGEMENT TECHNIQUES

Assuming that teachers get their classes off to a good start by following the principles discussed so far, what techniques for group management should they use in everyday teaching? Kounin (1970) approached this topic by contrasting the videotaped behavior of successful classroom managers with the behavior of teachers who had continuing and severe management problems. The initial idea was to see what differentiated the two groups of teachers in their handling of student disruptions. This approach was clear and sensible, but it failed to yield a single variable that differentiated consistently between the two groups in how they responded when faced with a classroom disruption.

Problem prevention

Fortunately, the researchers did not give up in frustration. In observing the tapes, they developed hunches about variables that *would* differentiate. Systematic follow-up that involved coding these variables paid off by revealing how the successful teachers did it. Their success lay in their ability to prevent problems from occurring in the first place rather than in their ability to deal with problems once they occurred. That is, good classroom managers are *not* successful so much because of how they *react* to student misbehavior but because they use techniques that *prevent* misbehavior by eliciting student cooperation and involvement in assigned work.

Successful versus less-successful managers

Later, Kounin and Gump (1974) studied 596 videotaped lessons and found that teachers of lessons that had higher student involvement provided continuous, explicit cues for appropriate behavior and insulated students from external intrusions. These more successful teachers were well organized, both for teaching during lessons and for assigning and monitoring seatwork. They wasted little time in making transitions from one activity to another. Less successful managers frequently had long, awkward transitions that led to student restlessness. During lessons, the successful teachers maintained high involvement in lessons by arousing motivation directly and holding students accountable for remaining attentive to what was going on (asking a lot of questions or otherwise getting student response, being unpredictable in questioning patterns). They knew where they were going and how they intended to get there. Less successful teachers continually confused the students and interrupted pacing by stopping to get something that should have been prepared in advance, stopping to check something because they were not sure what to do next, repeating themselves for no good reason or because they were vague the first time, and vacillating or even contradicting themselves. The result was slow pacing, student confusion, and low involvement.

Similar differences were observed during seatwork periods. The more successful teachers had prepared assignments that provided variety in type and level of difficulty. Their assignments were challenging as well as instructive, whereas the assignments of the less successful teachers were boring or ill suited to the interests and abilities of the students. Again, the result was student boredom and restlessness, leading to disruptions and other misbehavior.

Teacher "Withitness"

Continuous monitoring of the whole classroom

A general teacher characteristic shown by Kounin (1970) to be important in both lesson and seatwork contexts is "withitness," or the degree to which the teacher is aware of and continually monitoring what is going on in all parts of the classroom (and thus able to take action to stop a developing disruption before it becomes serious). Successful classroom managers had this quality. Less successful ones became so involved in what they were doing that they were unaware of other parts of the room. This made them slower to recognize and respond to disruptions and more likely to make mistakes such as *timing errors* (waiting too long to respond, so what should have been a minor problem developed into a major one); *target errors* (not knowing the actual culprits, failing to notice all students who were involved, or blaming some who were not); and *overreactions* (shouting, becoming hysterical, or otherwise overreacting when the situation called for calm control).

Reaction errors

Each type of error led to increased problems. Timing errors allowed routine horseplay to develop into arguments and fights. Target errors minimized student accountability by allowing culprits to get away with something and harmed teacher-student relationships when teachers mistakenly blamed the wrong students. Finally, emotional overreactions produced student resentment and sometimes led to *ripple effects*—the rise in levels of tension and distraction that often occurs when teachers respond in strongly negative or punitive ways to student misbehavior (sometimes the frequency and intensity of disruptions increase as well).

Ripple effects

Experimental studies of punishment would not predict ripple effects. In theory, seeing others being punished should reduce the likelihood of misbehavior by observers, who presumably experience the punishment vicariously (Bandura, 1977). Typically, however, experiments testing this thesis involve brief experiences with strangers. In the classroom, teacher behavior is predictable after the first few days or weeks. It is likely that explosions of anger by frustrated teachers have a cathartic effect, reducing the likelihood of similar explosions in the immediate future. When this is true, alert students are likely to take advantage of it.

Thus ironically, teachers who respond severely to current problems may be setting themselves up for extra problems in the future. In combination with the many other negative results that may occur when teachers lose their tempers and become unnecessarily punitive, this factor again underscores the need for teachers to use positive approaches to classroom management.

Overlapping Activities

Another important key to successful classroom management, related both to smooth pacing and to "withitness," is what Kounin (1970) called *overlapping*—the ability to do two or more things at once, such as responding to students who come for help without having to break the pace of a small-group lesson. Overlapping appears to be a product of preparation, ability to anticipate needs, and ability to deal with more than one thing at a time. Overlapping helps keep students engaged in productive activities by minimizing the time they spend waiting for the teacher to respond to a demand or to tell them what to do.

Smooth Transitions

Another important variable noted by Kounin was smoothness of transitions between and within activities. This involves training students to follow daily routines that promote efficiency in changing activities, supplemented if necessary by brief instructions concerning matters specific to that day or activity. Poor transitions occur when teachers allow themselves to be repeatedly distracted by the questions or actions of individuals, give out too many and too specific instructions, repeat themselves unnecessarily, interrupt everyone to ask if previous instructions have been carried out yet, or confuse students who are trying to carry out previous instructions by giving new ones that may or may not be meant for them.

Transitions within activities are often lengthy and confusing because teachers are not prepared. This leads to false starts in which orders are given and then retracted or to interruption of movement into the new activity because something omitted from the previous one is now remembered.

Group Alerting

Yet another aspect of effective management noted by Kounin is *group alerting*, which refers to teacher behavior designed to maintain or reestablish attention during lessons. In the positive sense, group alerting involves doing things to keep the rest of the group attentive while one member is reciting. This includes looking around the group before calling on someone, keeping the students in suspense about who will be called on next by selecting randomly, getting around to everyone frequently, interspersing choral responses with individual responses, asking for volunteers, throwing out challenges by declaring that the next question is difficult or tricky, calling on listeners to comment on or correct a response, and presenting novel or interesting material. Negative aspects of group alerting (things to avoid) include overconcentration on the student doing the reciting to the point that the rest of the group is not monitored, directing new questions only to the reciter, picking the reciter before a question is even stated, and having reciters perform in a predetermined order.

Accountability

In addition to naming these group-alerting techniques, Kounin identified several techniques that maximize student accountability for paying attention. Teachers can hold students accountable by requiring them to hold up props, show their answers, or otherwise indicate attention to the lesson, having them recite in unison (while monitoring carefully), asking listeners to comment on recitations, asking for volunteers, circulating and checking performance, and calling on individuals. Many of the techniques that Kounin listed under "accountability" are similar to those listed under "group alerting."

Other Studies of Group Management

Random selection of students to recite

Subsequent research by others supports most of Kounin's recommendations. In a correlational study of second- and third-grade classes (Brophy & Evertson, 1976) and in an experimental study of first-grade reading groups (Anderson, Evertson, & Brophy, 1979), "withitness," overlapping, and smoothness of lesson pacing and transitions all were associated not only with better management but also with higher achievement. These studies, however, did not support some of the group-alerting and accountability techniques, especially the notion of being unpredictable in calling on students to recite. The teachers who were more successful went around the group in order, seldom calling for volunteers and not allowing students to call out answers. Good and Grouws (1975) found that group alerting was positively related to student achievement in fourth-grade mathematics, but accountability was related curvilinearly: Teachers who used a moderate amount were more successful than those who used too much or too little.

Eliciting and maintaining student attention

In general, the major management objectives during lessons involve eliciting and maintaining attention, including at times when students are supposed to "just" watch and listen. This is done primarily by making sure that lesson content is interesting and challenging and that the teacher is prepared to conduct the lesson smoothly. This should be sufficient for most students. For others, group-alerting and accountability techniques may be required periodically.

Techniques drawn from Kounin and other sources are integrated in the next sections, which present guidelines for group management in the two most typical classroom contexts: group lessons and seatwork periods.

MAINTAINING ATTENTION DURING LESSONS

Some inattention and minor misbehavior can be expected during most lessons. This routine misbehavior is dealt with most successfully through a combination of careful monitoring of students (Kounin's "withitness"), modeling expected behavior, reinforcing expected behavior, and extinguishing undesirable behavior.

Successful monitoring

One requirement for successful monitoring is being able to see each student and to make eye contact if necessary. A second is to form the habit of continuously scanning the group or class. Students who know that the teacher regularly keeps an eye on what is going on are less likely to misbehave than students who know they have a good chance of getting away with something.

It is not enough just to see that students give the appearance of paying attention and understanding, because most students can do this without actually following the lesson (Brophy & Evertson, 1976). Both to ensure accountability and to sample student comprehension as a guide to lesson pacing, it is important periodically to ask questions or require the students to make some kind of response. Such questions usually have the greatest managerial value when students have no way of knowing in advance when the teacher might ask them or whom the teacher might call on.

Hazards in maintaining accountability

Maintaining student accountability through such questions will be successful only if the teacher avoids three potential hazards. First, care should be taken not to upset or put on the spot students who regularly show anxiety and fear of failure. It is usually better to stimulate the attention of these students in more direct ways, such as by calling for it or by giving advance warning ("John, listen carefully to Ralph, because I want to ask you about his comments").

Second, teachers should concentrate on involving everyone rather than on catching the inattentive. Some teachers often call on higher-achieving students who are expected to know the answers but seldom call on low achievers or students whom they do not like.

Third, the technique of maintaining student accountability through unpredictable questioning can be overused and become obvious to students. Teachers can counteract this by occasionally explaining the rationale for calling on a variety of students (e.g., "I want to call on most of you today, so that I can find out if you know the key concepts, or if we have to work on them some more").

Demanding student attention

So far, we have focused on conditioning attention through relatively impersonal and indirect methods. When inattention is prolonged or disruptive, however, a direct call for attention may be required. The best way to demand student attention is to do so briefly and perfunctorily (O'Leary et al., 1970). If eye contact can be made with the student, a demand for attention can be accomplished nonverbally through looks, expressions, or gestures. If verbalization is required, it should be confined to a simple directive ("Pay attention, John") delivered quickly, concisely, and with the expectation that it will be followed. The teacher should pause just long enough to make sure that the student has heard and then go on with the lesson. This minimizes the interruption of the lesson and the consequent likelihood that other students will become distracted.

Other effective ways of putting a stop to minor misbehavior include humorous or other responses that tell the student to change behavior but do so in a benign and generally positive way. If a student has been teasing a fellow student, for example, making faces or noises or doing something that he or she knows is inappropriate, there is no need to pause and explain the nature of the misbehavior. The teacher needs only to indicate that it must stop, using some comment such as ''That's enough, John,'' or ''Very funny, John, but now I want you to pay attention'' (in a pleasant tone).

MAINTAINING ENGAGEMENT IN SEATWORK

Appropriate difficulty level

Each student should have a seatwork assignment that is appropriate in difficulty and as interesting as curriculum demands allow. Also, teachers should set up mechanisms that enable students to know exactly what to do if they have difficulty with assignments and what to do when they finish them. Situations in which trouble starts because a student has given up on an assignment that is too difficult or has finished an easy assignment and has nothing to do simply should not exist. Preparation here includes not only the seatwork itself but other activities for students who complete their assignments.

General techniques

Techniques for maintaining student engagement in seatwork, assuming that the seatwork is interesting and appropriate, are similar to those for maintaining attention to lessons. The major difference is that, during lessons, students tend to be seated facing the teacher, so eye contact is established more easily and monitoring is much simpler. It is easier for students to appear to be working on seatwork assignments when they are not than it is for them to appear to be following lessons when they are not. Nevertheless, the same general principles apply: Monitor as continuously as possible; set up and explain rules; communicate positive expectations; condition through a combination of modeling, reinforcement, and extinction; and intervene only when necessary and with as little disruption as possible.

Moving around the classroom

Unless they are busy elsewhere (e.g., teaching a small group), teachers should move around the room in unpredictable patterns during seatwork times, keeping a general check on progress. When they stop to give help, they should position themselves so that they can see the rest of the class.

Establishing a work system

It is especially important to monitor the whole class during the early part of the school year while students are still learning the work system. Doyle (1984) found that successful managers establish an activity system early in the year and closely supervise it, ushering it along and protecting it from intrusion or disruption. For the first three weeks, for example, contacts with individual students during seatwork were brief, and the teacher circulated around the room to maintain a whole-group perspective. In classes with many disruptive students, successful managers tended to push the curriculum and talk about work rather than misbehavior. Less successful managers tended to focus public attention on misbehavior by their frequent reprimands, so that eventually all work ceased. By November, observations indicated that if a work system had been established effectively, successful teachers often spent less time orchestrating the total group and more time with individuals. By this point, the work system itself imposed order in the class, and the teacher was free to attend more to individual needs.

Problems can often be stopped simply by moving close to students who are goofing off, particularly when the students know exactly what they should be doing and realize that they are not doing it. Under these circumstances, there usually is no need for the teacher to say anything (and good reason not to, since it will distract students who are working).

Brief interventions

Finally, interventions with students during seatwork times should involve brief help-giving rather than prolonged tutoring attempts and should be confined to students who really need assistance. Teachers who are overly intrusive and verbal when making rounds during seatwork often interrupt students needlessly and may even create anxiety or other undesirable reactions.

Summary

Effective classroom management begins with preparation of the physical environment. Classrooms should be arranged so that the teacher can monitor all areas at all times, supplies are readily accessible, and there are no obstacles to the flow of traffic. Students should be taught to complete routine tasks with minimal supervsion, and contingency plans should be prepared for times when scheduled activities cannot take place.

Students should be organized into cohesive groups with positive attitudes and constructive goals. Gaining the confidence of leaders is an important step, as is developing an authoritative leadership style.

Kounin and others have found that successful classroom managers prevent discipline problems from emerging by being well organized and prepared, maintaining student involvement, recognizing and stopping disruptions promptly, overlapping activities, and maintaining individual accountability. Such teachers establish their expectations, rules, and work routines early in the school year and combine well-chosen assignments with active monitoring and follow through on accountability systems to maintain high student involvement in learning tasks.

Questions and Problems

1. The authors have stressed the need to get off to a good start but have said that "don't smile until Christmas" is not the way to do so. What is?
2. Much of good management is simply good instruction in "what to do and how to do it," Considering the grade at which you intend to teach,

what are the routines and procedures in which you should plan to provide students with instruction and practice?

3. Why do you believe good managers have a few general rules rather than many specific ones?
4. Why do teachers who frequently use Kounin's group-accountability techniques tend to have management problems, even though these techniques do return attention to the lesson?
5. Considering the grade at which you intend to teach, can you state clearly the types and difficulty of seatwork assignments that will be needed? If not, how can you find out?
6. How might principles discussed in this chapter be modified for teachers working in the following situations: (a) team teaching, (b) open classroom, (c) individualized, self-paced instruction?

Case Studies

AN INATTENTIVE GROUP. Ruth Miller is distracted by two boys' inattentiveness in the back of the room. As she continues to present information to the whole class, she notices that a third student has joined the discussion and that another is watching the three. If you were Ruth, what would you do now? Does it make any difference if it is a second-grade or twelfth-grade class? If so, how?

START OF THE YEAR. Jed Rohrkemper, a history teacher in an affluent suburban high school, is teaching for the first time. Given that his students have been in the school for several years, what should Jed say to the students about classroom management? Be specific; outline comments for the first class for role play with friends.

CHAPTER

Principles and Techniques of Behavior Modification

CHAPTER OUTLINE

OBJECTIVES

When you have mastered the material in this chapter, you will be able to

1. Define modeling and its effects on observers, list three characteristics of good models, and explain how modeling can be used to teach thinking and self-control
2. Discuss the role of cues in controlling behavior
3. Distinguish with illustrative examples (a) direct versus vicarious reinforcement and (b) positive versus negative reinforcement
4. Explain how a teacher can teach and then maintain increasingly complex academic and social behavior using reinforcement techniques

5. Discuss the drawbacks of teacher praise and other external reinforcement systems
6. Define satiation and extinction techniques to stop undesirable behavior and explain when their use is appropriate
7. State how the effects of negative reinforcement and punishment differ and how punishment can be used most effectively

Previous chapters describe the personal qualities of teachers that are basic to successful classroom management, and they review principles for establishing an effective learning environment and for managing everyday group activities. Although we stress the role of the teacher in managing student behavior, we recognize that school policies and support are also important.

The principles stressed in the two previous chapters are sufficient for handling most management concerns. Some students, however, require special, individualized treatment. This may involve behavior modification techniques, covered in this chapter, or various humanistic approaches to counseling, covered in Chapter 22.

Behavior modification techniques are especially useful in dealing with routine problems such as persistent inattention, daydreaming or fooling around instead of working, calling out answers or unwanted comments, trying to get attention by making faces or noises, showing off items forbidden by the school, changing seats, or moving around the room without permission.

Techniques for establishing and maintaining desired behavior include modeling, cuing, and reinforcement. Methods for stopping undesirable behavior include satiation, extinction, negative reinforcement, and punishment. We now cover techniques for establishing and maintaining desired behavior.

MODELING

We acquire a great deal of learning vicariously as we observe the behavior of other people (models) and its consequences for them. Learning through modeling goes on whenever we observe others with whom we can identify, so much learning is unplanned and unsystematic.

Conscious and systematic modeling

Teachers can accomplish much in the classroom by influencing student behavior through modeling, especially if they learn to model consciously and systematically. Bandura (1977) identified three broad classes of effects that models can have on the behavior of observers:

1. *Observational learning/modeling effects*—Observers acquire new response patterns that did not previously exist in their behavioral rep-

ertoires, for example, in observing a demonstration of laboratory equipment.

2. *Inhibitory/disinhibitory effects*—Existing response patterns in observers are inhibited when models are punished for similar behavior or disinhibited when models are reinforced for similar behavior. Students' tendencies to call out cruel or obscene comments about one another, for example, are affected by whether or not peers who do this are reinforced or punished by the teacher or their classmates.
3. *Response-facilitation effects*—The behavior of the model in a particular situation cues observers to follow suit, even though they probably would have behaved differently without such modeling. Students are likely to imitate teacher behavior in response to the principal's announcements (pay respectful attention rather than ignoring).

Modeling can be a powerful instructional tool and behavior management technique for teachers. Our definition of modeling includes nonverbal behavior, verbalizations made in carrying out the behavior, and instructions and explanations given before, during, or after the behavior. These verbalizations help define the meaning of the behavior and shape observers' responses to it.

Characteristics of Models Who Are Imitated

Teachers who form personal relationships with their students and become the kinds of individuals that the students look up to and want to be like are more apt to be imitated than teachers who remain at a distance or stress the contrasts between themselves and their students. Another factor is the degree to which the model's behavior is rewarded. Teachers who are respected and who accomplish their goals are more likely to be imitated than teachers who are not successful.

High-prestige models are more likely to be imitated than low-prestige models, particularly when the prestige is based on qualities that potential imitators would like to possess. This implies that teachers must retain students' respect and perhaps also a degree of professional distance, but

Teachers can maintain professional distance from students but still create a friendly atmosphere in the classroom.

still be friendly and attractive enough to make students want to be like them.

Modeling and Classroom Management

Everyday modeling relevant to classroom management includes things such as listening attentively when students recite or answer questions, handling equipment carefully and replacing it properly, and remaining conspicuously quiet during times for concentrated thinking.

Teacher modeling

Similarly, teacher modeling is important for developing rational control of behavior by acting on well thought-out decisions, not impulses; developing respect for others by treating them as worthwhile, valued people; developing good group climate by not making hostile criticism or scapegoating, not playing favorites, and by exhibiting emotional control by being able to accept adversity or criticism without becoming upset or angry; and responding with rational attempts to diagnose and solve problems.

Teachers can often instruct students in various classroom routines most efficiently through modeling—showing how to use the pencil sharpener or how to operate audiovisual equipment, for example. They can also use modeling to teach thinking and problem solving, especially when combined with verbalized self-instructions and other techniques of cognitive behavior modification (Meichenbaum, 1977).

Building Self-Control

Cognitive behavior modification

Cognitive behavior modification stresses the development of self-control rather than the imposition of external control. It emphasizes thinking and subjective experience more than overt behavior and goal setting, planning, and self-instruction rather than reinforcement. If a teacher and a student discuss a plan of action, for example, and the student writes out the plan, student behavior, classroom conduct, and academic performance become more explicit and hence potentially more controllable by the student. Such a technique also allows teachers to individualize arrangements with students, and it places more emphasis on student self-control, self-management, and self-instruction and less on one-to-one relationships between specific behaviors and rewards. Contracts can be helpful in dealing with students who are poorly motivated, easily distracted, or resistant to schoolwork or the teacher.

Goal setting

Experience with some of the elements involved in contingency contracting, such as goal setting and self-monitoring of behavior, revealed that these elements could have positive effects of their own, independent of reinforcement. Inducing students to set goals for themselves, for example, can lead to performance increases, especially if those goals are specific and difficult rather than vague or too easy (Rosswork, 1977). Apparently, setting goals not only provides students with specific objectives to pursue, but it also leads them to concentrate their efforts and monitor their performances more closely. The process does not always work, however. Sagotsky, Patterson, and Lepper (1978) found that exposure to goal-setting procedures had no significant effect on students' study behavior or academic achievement, largely because many of the students did not follow through by actually using the goal-setting procedures they had been shown.

Self-monitoring

The same study did show the effectiveness of self-monitoring procedures, however. Students taught to monitor and maintain daily records of their study behavior did show significant improvement in both the study behavior and tested achievement. This is only one of many studies illustrating the effectiveness of procedures designed to help students monitor their classroom behavior more closely and control it more effectively (Glynn, Thomas, & Shee, 1973; McLaughlin, 1976; O'Leary & Dubey, 1979; Rosenbaum & Drabman, 1979).

These procedures designed to develop self-control in students have two potential advantages over earlier procedures that depended on external control by the teacher. First, teachers cannot continuously monitor all the students and reinforce them appropriately. When responsibility for monitoring, and perhaps reinforcing, performance is shifted from the teacher to the students, this difficulty is removed. Second, behavior modification methods that depend on the reinforcing activity of the teacher tend not to generalize to other settings or persist beyond the term or school year. If students can learn to monitor and control their own behavior, they may also be able to apply these self-control skills to other classrooms or even to nonschool settings.

Verbalized Self-Instructions

Self-control skills are typically taught using procedures that Meichenbaum (1977) called cognitive behavior modification. One technique combines modeling with verbalized self-instructions. Rather than just telling students what to do, the model (teacher) demonstrates the process. The demonstration includes not only the physical motions involved but verbalization of the thoughts and other self-talk (self-instructions, self-monitoring, self-reinforcement) that should accompany the physical motions.

Teaching self-control skills

Modeling combined with verbalized self-instructions

Modeling combined with verbalized self-instructions (as well as various related role play approaches) can be helpful with a variety of student problems. Meichenbaum (1977) described five stages of this approach: (1) An adult models a task while speaking aloud (cognitive modeling): (2) the child performs the task under the model's instruction (overt, external guidance); (3) the child performs the task while verbalizing self-instructions aloud (overt self-guidance); and (4) the child whispers self-instructions while doing the task (faded overt self-guidance); and (5) the child performs the task under self-guidance via private speech (covert self-instruction). Variations of this approach not only have been used to teach cognitively impulsive students to approach tasks more effectively but also have been used to help social isolates learn to initiate activities with their peers, to teach students to be more creative in problem solving, to help aggressive students learn to control their anger and respond more effectively to frustration, and to help frustrated and defeated students to cope with failure and respond to mistakes with problem-solving efforts rather than withdrawal or resignation.

Recent applications of this approach include the "turtle" technique of Robin, Schneider, and Dolnick (1976), in which teachers teach impulsive

"Turtle" technique and "Think Aloud" program

and aggressive students to assume the "turtle" position when upset. The students learn to place their heads on their desks, close their eyes, and clench their fists. This gives them an immediate response to use in anger-provoking situations and thus enables them to delay inappropriate behavior and to think about constructive solutions to the problem. The turtle position is actually not essential; the key is training children to delay impulsive responding while they gradually relax and think about constructive alternatives. It is a gimmick, however, that many younger students find enjoyable, and it may also serve as a crutch to children who might otherwise not be able to delay successfully. Similarly, the "Think Aloud" program of Camp and Bash (1981) is designed to teach children to use cognitive skills to guide their social behavior and to learn to cope with social problems. It is useful with students in the early grades, especially those prone to paranoid interpretations of peer behavior or aggressive acting out as a response to frustration.

Generalization of skills taught through cognitive interventions has not yet been demonstrated convincingly (Pressley, 1979). Approaches featuring modeling, verbalized self-instructions, and other aspects of self-monitoring and self-control training, however, appear to be very promising for use in classrooms, both as instructional techniques for all students and as remediation techniques for students with emotional or behavioral problems (Hughes, 1988).

CUING

Repeated problem behavior

When students have difficulty remembering to perform certain behaviors, teachers can help by cuing—providing a brief direction or reminder to cue the students' attention and behavior. To be effective, cues must occur before the action occurs (Krumboltz & Krumboltz, 1972), and they should be delivered only when needed; otherwise, they begin to resemble nagging.

Cues are especially useful for problem behavior that occurs repeatedly in specific situations, such as when students get into squabbles while sharing equipment in a learning center. If the teacher is able to analyze the situation and identify the timing and reasons for trouble, problems can be short-circuited through cuing: "Your group will be going to the learning center next period. Remember, no more than three to a learning center at one time, and everyone is to share the equipment."

Advance reminders and coaching

Cuing through advance reminders and coaching is especially useful because providing cues during the activity itself might be embarrassing or might interrupt the flow of classroom activities. Students can be prepared through discussions of how to handle the upcoming situations and by including many examples of what to do and what to avoid. Such discussions might also include modeling with verbalized self-instructions as well as more typical explanations or perhaps even role-play exercises to give students an opportunity to practice the expected behaviors. Verbal cuing can be supplemented with supports, such as posting instruction sheets or rule reminders in learning centers or on equipment, using arrows to indicate direction of movement, or labeling shelves to show where equipment belongs. Students who have special problems managing their time independently or remembering what they are supposed to do can be helped by assigning peers to remind or supervise them or by preparing checklists for them to use themselves.

Discrimination

Cuing may be particularly useful when a problem involves discrimination—certain behavior is appropriate under some circumstances but not others. Here the student needs to learn to recognize the cues indicating whether or not the behavior is appropriate rather than how to perform the behavior itself. Explanations of the rationales for the differences are important, as are multiple examples: no shouting or shrieking at any time, quiet conversational talk in designated areas is allowed among students who have completed assignments, talk during work time is confined to getting help from designated persons and within designated limits, talk is not allowed during recitations and discussions except when you have the floor, talk is not allowed during tests. Students must make similar discriminations about when and how to move around the room, approach the teacher with an individual problem, or call out comments and suggestions. Teachers working with younger students, and all teachers in the first few days or weeks of school, will have to do a lot of this kind of cuing. Cuing should be reduced, both in frequency and specificity, however, as students begin to behave appropriately on their own.

Cuing combined with other techniques

Many aspects of cognitive behavior modification combine cuing with several other features (Glynn, Thomas, & Shee, 1973; McLaughlin, 1976). Examples include self-assessment (student evaluates own performance relative to goals), self-recording (student keeps records of own relevant behaviors), self-determination of reinforcement (student establishes own contingencies between own behaviors and type or amount of reinforcement), and self-administration of reinforcement (student reinforces self upon performing contracted behaviors).

Self-reinforcement

Self-reinforcement may be helpful for students who are deficient in achievement motivation or who make inappropriate attributions about the reasons for their successes. The self-reinforcement process calls students' attention to their specific accomplishments and encourages them to verbalize statements of satisfaction and praise to themselves for having achieved goals. It may also help them to attribute their accomplishments to their own efforts rather than to external factors.

Self-monitoring and self-evaluation

Self-monitoring and self-evaluation can often be aided with checklists, scoring keys, periodic progress reports, or other devices that help students to assess systematically what they have and have not accomplished with respect to schoolwork and behavior goals. These techniques place the responsibility for monitoring and managing student behavior on the students themselves but in ways likely to be informative and attractive to them.

Academic survival skills and prosocial personal skills

Recent extensions of these techniques include training in academic survival skills such as attending, following directions, and volunteering to answer questions (Cobb & Hops, 1973), as well as training in prosocial personal skills such as initiating interactions, helping, and sharing (Cartledge & Milburn, 1978). A combination of modeling and instructions is used to teach the skill, and self-monitoring and reinforcement procedures can be added to insure that it will be maintained.

REINFORCEMENT

Behavioristic psychologists stress reinforcement as the primary mechanism for establishing and maintaining behavior. There are difficulties in defining reinforcers. Some people are not reinforced by things that most others find rewarding, and some things commonly seen as punishments are experienced as rewards by some individuals. This has led behavioristic psychologists to use a circular definition of a reinforcer as being anything that increases or maintains the frequency of behavior when it is made contingent on performances of that behavior. That is, if a particular consequence increases or maintains the frequency of a behavior, it is a reinforcer; if it does not affect the behavior, it is not a reinforcer.

Premack Principle

This basic idea has many applications in school settings, especially Premack's (1965) formulation of it. The "Premack Principle" states that opportunities to engage in behavior that is performed spontaneously at a high rate can be used as rewards for increasing the frequencies of behaviors performed spontaneously at lower rates. Students who are not completing assignments, for example, can be motivated to do so by informing them that they will not be allowed to do something they want to do until they turn in the assignments. The Premack Principle provides flexibility, allowing teachers to develop reward systems suited to each individual, and to get around the problem that no single "reward" will be motivating for everyone.

Positive Reinforcement or Reward

Reinforcers are either positive or negative. Positive reinforcers correspond roughly to what we usually call rewards. They include material rewards (food, money, prizes, or tokens that can be exchanged for something desired), social rewards (praise, grades, honors, status symbols, attention from the teacher or peers), and activity rewards (opportunities to choose and engage in desired activities, use special equipment, or play games).

Negative Reinforcement

Negative reinforcement involves increasing the rate of a desired behavior by freeing the person from some unpleasant state when the behavior is performed. Students can be allowed to escape failing grades, for example, through makeup work that allows them to master material they should have mastered earlier. Although negative reinforcement technically involves reinforcing desirable behavior, it also involves withholding reinforcement from students who do not meet performance demands. Typically, these students are behaving in some undesirable way, not merely failing to produce desired behavior. Consequently, negative reinforcement is discussed in more detail in a later section of the chapter dealing with techniques for stopping undesirable behavior.

Vicarious Reinforcement

Reinforcement may motivate not only the student who receives it but also, through modeling effects, other students who observe it. In theory, a teacher can motivate a student to work carefully not only by praising his or her careful work but also by praising careful work performed by others, especially friends or peers with whom the student identifies. Teachers cannot assume vicarious motivating effects, however, because not all students find the same consequences reinforcing. Teacher praise of a peer will vicariously motivate students who also want such praise but not those who do not value teacher praise.

USING REINFORCEMENT IN THE CLASSROOM

Teachers can strengthen desirable student behavior by reinforcing that behavior after it occurs. The behavior can be something minor such as raising one's hand and waiting to be recognized rather than calling out an answer during a lesson or something more substantial such as turning in completed and carefully done seatwork assignments for a week. The reinforcer can be anything that the student values and is willing to work for.

When conditioning the behavior of animals, it is important to reinforce immediately after performance of the behavior, so that the animal can make the connection between performance and reinforcement. This is not as essential for humans, because this connection can be explained verbally. Language can also be used to describe the particular characteristics of the desired behavior, thus eliminating guesswork as to what is being reinforced, and to link reinforcement to a series of behaviors performed over time, as in the example just mentioned concerning seatwork performance during an entire week.

Fading of reinforcement

In the early stages of trying to establish a new behavior, it may be important to reinforce often, even 100 percent of the time, and perhaps also to reinforce immediately after performance of the behavior. As the behavior becomes more established, it is possible to delay reinforcement as well as to reduce its ratio or increase the intervals between deliveries. This fading of reinforcement can continue until one reaches the minimal level needed for sustaining the behavior.

Social and symbolic rewards

In addition to reducing the frequency of reinforcement as behavior becomes established, the teacher may want to change the nature of the reinforcers, especially if they are expensive or require too much teacher time or effort. This requires substituting social and symbolic rewards for tangible reinforcers like candy or prizes. Sometimes students will not value social or symbolic rewards, so the teacher will have to take action to build the capacity of these rewards to function as reinforcers. Krumboltz and Krumboltz (1972) suggested accomplishing this by using the principle of substitution—if a person does not value a potential reward, begin presenting it immediately before presenting a reward that is valued. This should strengthen the association of the nonvalued reward with the valued reward, so that ultimately the nonvalued reward becomes valued in its own right. Students who do not turn in assignments regularly, for example, might be given a weekly report summarizing their successes and failures in this regard. Access to a valued reward such as the opportunity to go on a special outing could be made contingent on earning positive reports. Over time, the presentation of a positive report should in itself become reinforcing to such students.

To the extent that students do respond to social and symbolic rewards, they can also be weaned from dependence on teacher reinforcement by being taught to reinforce themselves. Students can be encouraged not only to note errors but also to grade themselves and perhaps reinforce themselves for success with stars, smiling faces, or positive comments. Students who have been making progress in meeting conduct goals can learn to reinforce themselves with the help of graphs or charts.

Shaping Behavior through Successive Approximations

Subgoals

For reinforcement to be effective, successful performance must be elicited often enough to be reinforced frequently. When bad habits are deeply ingrained, or when students have not yet established reliable cognitive control of their own behavior, it may take some time before the desired behavior occurs, even if the motivation to change exists. Teachers can still use reinforcement to shape behavior, however, if they analyze the total tasks facing students and divide them into subgoals that can be organized sequentially in order of difficulty. Students can then attain success and be reinforced regularly as they approach the ultimate goals one step at a time. Hyperactive students who tend to leave their seats and roam the room or bother other students when they are supposed to be doing seatwork, for example, could be reinforced in the following way. First, the teacher could concentrate on getting them to stay in their seats, perhaps beginning by reinforcing them for remaining in their seats for five minutes at a time. As success is achieved, the teacher can increase the periods gradually until they cover the entire seatwork period. When students can remain in their seats, the teacher can add prohibitions against making noises or bothering other students. Initially, reinforcement for not bothering others might be provided separately from that dealing with staying in the seat, although eventually the two sets of criteria could be combined. If problems include careless work in addition to leaving the seat and bothering others, the teacher could begin to phase in expectations for careful work. Ultimately, reinforcement is based not only on staying in the seat and not bothering others but also on careful and sustained application to the seatwork assignment itself.

Changes in specifications

Simple behaviors like staying in the seat can be measured in time units for successive shaping: first five minutes, then ten minutes, and so on. Meeting each successive subgoal requires the student only to persist longer with the same kind of behavior. With more complex tasks, such as a series of subgoals that lead to successful completion of seatwork assignments, meeting successive subgoals often involves more complex behaviors or more complex combinations of behaviors formerly reinforced separately. This means periodic changes in the specifications of what behaviors qualify for reinforcement. The teacher must handle this carefully to ensure that students do not believe that the teacher is not keeping promises. The key here is to help students recognize and appreciate the progress they have made and thus to see that higher expectations are now appropriate. Many teachers find contingency contracting systems to be effective in communicating these perceptions.

Contingency contracting combines rewarding and extinguishing methods and applies them in a formalized way. After the teacher explains the method and outlines alternatives, the teacher and student jointly draw up a contract specifying in precise terms the behavior the student will be expected to show and the contingent rewards that will be earned once the contract is fulfilled. A contract can be purely oral, although it is customary to formalize it by having the student write down the specific details of the agreement (see Figure 21.1). In instructional areas, such contracts call for students to complete a certain amount of work at a certain level of proficiency to obtain a reward. Behavior management contracts describe specific criteria of improvement that must be met.

Providing structure

The main advantage of contingency contracts is that they ensure that students see the relationship between behavior and its consequences. Furthermore, when students are required to draw up the contracts themselves, they make personal commitments that are real and meaningful to them because they express them in their own words rather than merely agree to demands that the teacher makes.

Contracts can provide needed structure for students who are distractible. Initially, contracts can be confined to short periods and a limited number of tasks and can be displayed on or near students' desks so that students can refer to them for reminders or instruction. Contracts can also be useful for students who are poorly motivated or resistant to schoolwork or the teacher. With these students, teachers can include a period

Figure 21.1 A Sample Contingency Contract

Contract for week of April 3-7

I, John Richardson, agree to work carefully on my seatwork assignments and complete them to the best of my ability before leaving my seat to go to the game center. I further agree to redo work done incorrectly after it is returned to me and after I have received any additional instructions or help that I need. I understand that I am free to go to the game center during any seatwork period as soon as I have completed my work assignments as described above.

Signed John Richardson, Student

Agreed Sidney Weaver, Teacher

of negotiation before the finalizing of contracts in which students have the opportunity to make suggestions and state whether or not they think the demands are reasonable.

Uses of contingency contracting

Teachers can use contingency contracting to control behavior during lessons and group activities, although it probably is best suited to motivating students to work carefully on seatwork assignments. Most misbehavior occurring during lessons is relatively minor; making it the object of a contingency contract tends to call too much attention to it. Contingency contracting, however, is useful for minimizing or eliminating lesson disruptions if the disruptions are serious and if they can be clearly defined (e.g., leaving one's seat or calling out insults). A contract for seatwork can state that a student must get a specific number of problems correct within a certain amount of time in order to fulfill his or her obligation.

Contingency contracting will not work if the contracts are unreasonable. Teachers must individualize contracts, requiring different things from various students according to their relative abilities to complete assignments and cope with the behavioral demands of school.

Goal Setting

Helping students to set and meet personal goals enables them to obtain reinforcement from school activities. Rosswork (1977) found that setting goals, especially specific, difficult goals, was more effective than offering monetary incentives to produce high performance. Goal setting was also more effective than nonspecific encouragement. Extrinsic incentives may be necessary when a task is not meaningful to students, but goals and goal setting probably are more relevant to meaningful tasks (Rosswork, 1977).

The high school students studied by Ware (1978) also stressed the importance of meeting personal goals. From a list of fifteen potential rewards, students were asked to rank rewards for desirability and effectiveness. They ranked the opportunity to reach a personal goal first, followed by school scholarships; compliments and encouragement from friends, being accepted as a person or having their opinions sought; trophies, certificates, medals, or ribbons; job-related physical rewards such as raises and vacations; special privileges or responsibilities; formal letters of recognition or appreciation; having their names printed in the newspaper or repeated on a loudspeaker; teacher or employer compliments and encouragement; money for specific accomplishments; parties, picnics, trips, or banquets; election to office; being chosen to be on special programs; and being the winner in a contest. Thus not only did students rank personal goal attainment first, but they valued rewards such as peer esteem and symbolic recognition more than teacher praise and several types of concrete rewards.

Ranking rewards

Teachers did not predict students' rankings of rewards. When asked to rank the same list, teachers placed reaching personal goals and winning school scholarships at the bottom while overrating getting names printed in the newspaper or repeated on a loudspeaker, obtaining special privileges or responsibilities, and winning a contest. Interestingly, teachers ranked praise from a teacher or employer even lower than students did, demonstrating awareness that their praise is not very reinforcing compared with other potential rewards.

Social Reinforcement

Teacher praise

Theorists of virtually every persuasion stress the importance of teacher praise. Functional analyses of teacher praise in the classroom, however, typically indicate that it often is not reinforcing. Many students are not motivated by it, and praise is embarrassing for some students or makes them otherwise uncomfortable so that it actually functions as punishment. Even for teachers who have the potential to use praise as reinforcement, good intentions alone are not enough. Praise is unlikely to reinforce effectively unless it is (1) sincere (ideally, spontaneous); (2) adapted in form and intensity to the specific accomplishments in question (no gushing over trivia); (3) related to the preferences of the individual (some students cringe in response to public praise but appreciate sentiments expressed privately); and (4) specifically descriptive of what the student did that was praiseworthy (Brophy, 1981; O'Leary & O'Leary, 1977).

Vicarious reinforcement principle

Much "praise" commonly given in the classroom does not satisfy these criteria (Anderson, Evertson, & Brophy, 1979; Brophy, 1981; Weinstein, 1976). Many teachers praise students who are behaving appropriately, for example, and simultaneously try to ignore others who are behaving inappropriately, thus trying to take advantage of the vicarious reinforcement principle. This teacher behavior is rarely reinforcing in practice. First, the praise involved is seldom praise at all. It is not spontaneous, and the target behaviors are not really praiseworthy—typically they involve being quiet or standing in line. Even when sincerely intended by the teacher, such praise often causes embarrassment, even humiliation, to the students singled out for attention.

Another common class of misguided reinforcement attempts involves praise of inhibited students who hesitate to contribute to discussions. It is important to make the experience rewarding when these students do contribute (e.g., by smiling and showing interest in their contribution), but it is not wise to call attention to them with comments such as, "See, you can speak up when you want to!"

Failure to be specific

Failure to be specific is a common problem in the praise attempts of teachers. Anderson, Evertson, and Brophy (1979), for example, found that fewer than 10 percent of the praise statements made by twenty first-grade teachers specified what was being praised. This low rate held even though ten of the teachers were in an experimental group that had been advised to specify the praiseworthy aspects of student behavior whenever they praised.

Student attributes

The effects of praise and criticism interact with certain student attributes. Praise and encouragement, for example, are especially reinforcing for students who are introverted, inhibited, low in self-esteem, and accustomed to failure. Students who are self-confident and accustomed to success are not as responsive to such attempts at reinforcement.

Rewards as reinforcers

These considerations serve as reminders that teachers need to perform functional analyses of their own behavior and their students' responses to make sure that assumed "rewards" actually function as such. Praise or symbolic rewards such as stars and smiling faces may be effective, but if they are not, teachers need to use other reinforcers. In addition to including the commonly mentioned material rewards, reinforcers can be things such as the opportunity to be first in the lunch line, use of the library, performance of tasks that students enjoy, the chance to make choices that students consider to be important, and a great many other things not often thought of as reinforcers for good conduct or good academic work.

Reinforcer Satiation

Even rewards that function as reinforcers may not continue to do so indefinitely. Typically, satiation sets in if students are rewarded with the same thing again and again. Even if the reward was highly prized initially, it is likely to lose some of its attraction and power as a reinforcer as students become accustomed to it. Therefore, teachers must not only make sure that the rewards they offer to particular students function as reinforcement for those students, but they must also change reinforcers periodically or, preferably, arrange for the students to select from a variety of reinforcements (Safer & Allen, 1976).

For teachers who rely heavily on reinforcement techniques applied to the class as a whole (as opposed to using them sparingly on individual students), individualizing reinforcers and combating reinforcer satiation involve extensive record keeping and other time demands.

Token Reinforcement Systems

Token reinforcement systems provide one way to handle these problems. Such systems include instructions to students about the behaviors to be reinforced, a means of making potentially reinforcing stimuli (tokens) contingent on student behavior, and rules governing the exchange of these tokens for other privileges (O'Leary & O'Leary, 1977). Students are awarded points (paid in the form of tokens, punches on a punch card, checkmarks, or some other symbol entered in a book) and then allowed to spend these points on reinforcers they select from the menu. Points are awarded for both behavioral and academic goals (individualized, at least to some degree), and the "prices" of reinforcement selections vary according to demand. Twenty minutes in the library or twenty minutes talking quietly with friends in the classroom, for instance, might cost thirty points, whereas participation in a special field trip or other special event might cost five hundred points.

Token reinforcement systems began in hospitals and other treatment institutions, but they have also been used successfully in schools (Safer & Allen, 1976; Thompson et al., 1974). Most typical classroom teachers find these systems to be more trouble than they are worth, but they are popular with teachers conducting special remedial classes or working in programs that emphasize individualized learning packages.

Reinforcement and Intrinsic Motiviation

Humanists and others who see reinforcement approaches as mechanistic and manipulative oppose them. Instead of bribing students, these critics argue, teachers should develop students' intrinsic motivation through methods such as building novelty and interest into the curriculum, modeling enjoyment of learning and achievement motivation, and helping them to appreciate their own growth in knowledge and skills. Such thinking has recently acquired some empirical support. Deci (1975) and many others have shown that the introduction of extrinsic rewards for performance of a particular behavior reduces intrinsic motivation to perform that same behavior, so sustained performance in the future becomes dependent upon extrinsic reinforcement. As Deci noted, however, behavior modifiers call for the introduction of reinforcers only if the desired behavior does not presently exist, presumably for lack of sufficient motivation, intrinsic or otherwise. Also, behavior modifiers would build fading programs into the treatment to reduce the required frequency and intensity of reinforcement and switch from concrete or immediately consumable reinforcers to more symbolic ones. Delivery of reinforcement using the principles outlined in Chapter 16 will also reduce the danger of eroding intrinsic motivation.

Eden (1975) proposed a theory of motivation that helps explain why extrinsic reinforcement may be appropriate despite the findings of Deci (1975) and others. He noted that the motivational effects of behavioral consequences depend on the relevance of those consequences to the motive operating at the time. In theory, reinforcers congruent with operating motivational systems will have a strong positive effect on net motivation, but other reinforcers will have a slightly negative effect. Thus teacher praise for careful work will motivate students who want that social reinforcement but will have a slightly negative effect on the motivation of students who find the task intrinsically motivating or who are working toward some material reward, such as a prize.

SATIATION

A simple technique for dealing with certain minor misbehaviors is to let them run their course by allowing, or requiring, if necessary, students to repeat the behaviors until fatigue and boredom set in. According to Krum-

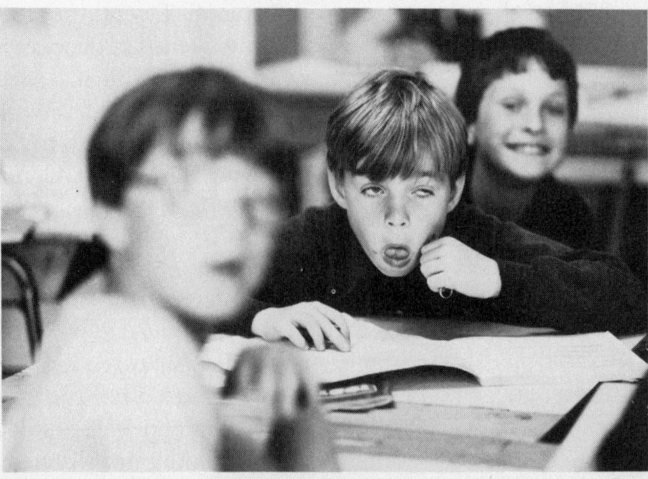

One way to deal with silly disruptive behavior is to allow students to repeat it until they become bored or tired by it.

boltz and Krumboltz (1972), satiation is effective when the behavior does not lead to powerful rewards (if it does, extinction will be necessary), the behavior is counterproductive and the student can see this, and the behavior is not harmful. Such behaviors include throwing spitballs, making faces or noises, or almost any type of classroom clowning that is silly rather than really funny. Inviting students to continue to do such things allows them to get it out of their systems and takes away the novelty and desire, at least for the present.

Limited use of satiation

Satiation is probably most effective if used sparingly and with a minimum of fanfare. If used too often, it can become an enjoyable ritual in itself, particularly if the teacher makes it an enjoyable experience, or a bone of contention between the teacher and students who feel picked on, if the teacher humiliates them.

EXTINCTION

Undesirable behavior that leads to reinforcement will not decrease through satiation unless the student becomes satiated with the reinforcement it produces. Teachers must handle such behavior with other techniques. The major means for reducing it (not merely controlling it) is extinction through nonreinforcement. To extinguish effectively, the teacher, controling the reinforcements that maintain the behavior, assures that performance of the behavior no longer leads to the expected reinforcement.

Ignoring undesirable behavior

The most common nonreinforcement technique in the classroom is simply ignoring and getting peers to ignore the behavior that appears to be motivated by a desire for attention. Some students find attention, even negative attention involving disapproval, to be reinforcing and will repeat any behavior that brings them the attention they desire.

Limits on use of extinction

Extinction is not always feasible in the classroom. Certain misbehaviors are too disruptive or dangerous to be ignored, and some students assume that anything not explicitly disapproved is acceptable. Open defiance, obscenities, hostility directed specifically at the teacher, or similarly provocative behaviors demand response. Attempts to ignore such behaviors will confuse students or leave them with the impression that the teacher is not aware of what is going on, is unable to cope with it, or doesn't care.

Reinforcement plus extinction

Even when feasible, ignoring is never effective by itself; it must be coupled with reinforcement of desired behavior (O'Leary & O'Leary, 1977). Used in combination, teacher reinforcement and extinction can be effective but only for students whose behaviors are under the control of reinforcement from the teacher in the first place. Ignoring misbehaving students will have no effect on behaviors that peers reinforce.

Tanner (1978) suggested four criteria for determining when ignoring is appropriate: when the problem is momentary, when it is not serious or dangerous, when drawing attention to it would disrupt the class, and when the student involved is usually well behaved. These criteria, along with the findings of Kounin (1970), leave little room for the systematic use of ignoring in an attempt to extinguish misbehavior that is disruptive and persistent. Kounin's work suggests that some comment or signal to the inattentive student is necessary whenever the problem seems likely to escalate.

Negative consequences

Ignoring can also have negative consequences. Students who do not realize that they are being ignored deliberately, or who do not know why they are being ignored, may increase their efforts to get attention by becoming more and more disruptive. Brief explanations to such students probably are much more effective than waiting for them to become conditioned through repeated frustration.

NEGATIVE REINFORCEMENT

Like modeling, cuing, and positive reinforcement, negative reinforcement is a technique for increasing desired behavior. It is discussed here among techniques for stopping misbehavior, however, because teachers should only use it when students have been misbehaving persistently despite more positive attempts to get them to change.

Termination of aversive experiences

Negative reinforcement occurs when improved behavior brings about the termination of an aversive experience. For ethical reasons, teachers are not advised to place students deliberately in aversive situations so that teachers can use negative reinforcement by releasing students when they behave well. The natural consequences of many forms of misbehavior are aversive, however, and teachers can often arrange to let students escape some of these consequences by improving their behavior.

Makeup exams and extra-credit assignments, for example, allow students to avoid low grades by improving their mastery of material. Unruly classes can be kept after school until they become more cooperative. Students who have not been controlling themselves can be required to take time out from classroom activities until they regain control.

Negative reinforcement is not punishment

Notice that negative reinforcement is not punishment—students do not suffer aversive consequences or lose rewards as a result of misbehavior (see Table 21.1). Instead, reinforcement is withheld pending performance of desired behavior. The aversive condition persists solely because the

TABLE 21.1 REINFORCING AND PUNISHING EFFECTS OF CONSEQUENCES OF BEHAVIOR

	Desirable Consequences	Undesirable Consequences
Application of consequences following behavior	Positive reinforcement: behavior leads to reward. Increases rate of behavior.	Punishment: behavior leads to aversive consequences. Decreases rate of behavior.
Removal of consequences following behavior	Punishment: behavior leads to loss of reward. Decreases rate of behavior.	Negative reinforcement: behavior leads to escape from aversive consequences. Increases rate of behavior.

students have not behaved appropriately, and they can terminate it at any time by changing their behavior. Negative reinforcement is most effective when the teacher warns students in advance, to underscore that the students themselves are responsible if reinforcement is not forthcoming. Ideally, such warnings stress the call for improved behavior rather than the withholding of reinforcement, for example, "Class, I know you don't like to get out late, but you're going to stay until you settle down and pay attention to this announcement."

PUNISHMENT

Punishment controls undesirable behavior by making aversive consequences contingent on such behavior.

Stopgap measure

The use of punishment should be minimized because it is a stopgap measure at best. To the extent that it is effective at all, punishment only suppresses the overt performance of undesirable behaviors, but even here the effects usually are situational and temporary. In any case, punishment does not change students' underlying desires to misbehave or the reasons why those desires exist; it does not provide guidance to students by indicating what they should do instead; and it causes problems of its own by engendering resentment.

In general, effective punishment is mild rather than severe, informative rather than merely punitive, and tailored to the specific misbehavior in ways likely to help the student see why the misbehavior is inappropriate.

Optimal moment for punishment

Redl (1966) suggested that teachers wait for the optimal moment rather than try to punish immediately, especially when students are emotionally upset. Punishing students while they are aroused and angry may only increase their alienation, while waiting until they are calm enough to listen but still concerned about the problem might be much more effective.

Ineffective Forms of Punishment

Suspension

Certain forms of punishment almost never work. Suspension from school is probably the most obvious. It does remove disruptive students from class, but many of them welcome the time off from school. Even if suspension does function as punishment, the students lose class time and fall behind in work, and most will be resentful rather than contrite. Thus except in extreme cases such as those discussed in the next chapter, school suspension is a mistake.

Extra classwork

The same is true of punishing students by forcing them to do extra classwork. By assigning schoolwork as punishment, the teacher implies that the work is unpleasant.

Physical punishment

Physical punishment is also generally ineffective. Many teachers and school administrators realize this but favor maintaining physical punishment as an option (where it is legal), intending to rely on its value as a threat without actually using it frequently. Others, including many parents, object to physical punishment on philosophical grounds. There is a simpler objection, however: Physical punishment does not work except in unusual situations. The best examples of its failure are antisocial delinquents and criminals, who almost always come from homes in which adults relied on physical punishment to socialize children. It keeps them under control to a degree while they are still young and afraid, but it builds anger and resentment that emerge as children get older (Feshbach, 1970).

Physical punishment is a direct attack on the student, and as such it almost invariably creates anger and resentment. Furthermore, these emotions usually will be much stronger than any feelings of fear or contrition, so the punishment does not reduce the tendency for the student to misbehave. It will not help to make the physical punishment as mild as possible, either. Slaps on the wrist and light paddling do not inspire much fear, especially in students accustomed to harsher treatment. Such students may even enjoy mild physical punishment because it gets them attention from peers.

Group punishment

Another technique that we do not recommend is group punishment in which contingencies are arranged so that an entire class or group is punished because of the misbehavior of an individual. Some writers recommend this technique for extreme cases, because the peer pressure generated can be very powerful. Like physical punishment, however, it is difficult to use effectively, and the undesirable side effects are likely to outweigh any advantages. For one thing, this technique forces students to choose between the teacher and one of their classmates. Many students will choose the classmate, uniting in sullen defiance of the teacher and refusing to blame the classmate if group punishment is applied. Even if students do go along with the teacher and pressure the classmate, the technique engenders unhealthy attitudes in the target student and perhaps in the other students as well.

Guidelines for Effective Punishment

When misbehavior persists despite repeated, positive attempts to stop it, mild forms of punishment may be necessary. Threat of punishment is usually even more effective than punishment itself, particularly when phrased in a way that reminds students that it will be their own fault if punishment results.

Punishment should be flexible and tailored to the specific situation. Fear of unknown consequences usually functions as a punishment, whereas expectation of known consequences frequently does not. Other guidelines are listed below:

- Punishment should be threatened before it is actually used. This should be done in a way that makes clear to students that the teacher hopes it will not have to be used and that the students will be fully responsible if it is used.
- When punishment is used, it should be a deliberate, systematic method for suppressing misbehavior, not an involuntary emotional response, a way to get revenge, or a spontaneous response to provocation.
- The punishment should be as short and mild as possible but unpleasant enough to motivate students to change their behavior.

- The punishment should be combined with positive statements of expectations and rules, focusing more on what the students should be doing than on what they should not be doing. The teacher should make clear to students why the rule exists, why their misbehavior cannot be tolerated, why they have no alternative other than punishment.
- Ideally, punishment should be combined with negative reinforcement, so that students must do something positive to show good faith and escape punishment (e.g., stating that students will lose some privilege for a specific time probably is less effective than stating that they will lose the privilege until behavior improves sufficiently to warrant removal of the punishment).

Effective punishment

Some of the most effective punishments are very mild, at least from a teacher's perspective. Merely keeping students after class for a few minutes to discuss problems, for example, can have a punishing effect, especially if it prevents them from doing something they want to do immediately. A delay of even a few minutes may cause a student to have to go to the end of the lunch line or to go home alone instead of with friends. These may be more effective punishments for most students than being sent to an isolation area, sent to the principal, or physically punished.

Overcorrection methods

Teachers do not have to present punishment explicitly as such, nor does it have to be something that we usually think of as shameful or painful. If property destruction is involved, for example, the punishment should require that the students fix or replace what they have broken. If this is not possible, punishment might involve some other kind of service such as cleaning up the school grounds or performing some similar chore that requires them to make restitution. In general, destructiveness is often handled best with overcorrection methods—the student must not only change behavior but must make restitution by fixing or replacing damaged items.

Time out

Students who are upset, angry, or out of control as a result of a particular situation, and hyperactive or aggressive students who are having bad days, may respond well to time out from regular classroom activities. Teachers can ask them to move to an isolated part of the room, a desk in the hall, or perhaps the principal's office, until they can collect themselves and behave appropriately. Time out usually works best if presented not as a punishment but as an opportunity for students to solve their own problems.

Response cost

Abuse of privileges usually is eliminated best with response cost—making it clear that costs will be attached to certain unacceptable behaviors and that students who do not heed fair warnings will have to pay those costs. Ideally, costs are logically related to the offenses; students who abuse library privileges will have them suspended, students who are persistently destructive with certain equipment will not get to use the equipment for a time, or students who start fights at recess will have to stay in or play alone.

Detention

Students who refuse to work on assignments usually are best handled by in-school or after-school detention during which they are required to work on assignments. This shows them that attempts to escape assignments by refusing to work or creating diversions will only result in their having to spend extra time in school.

Teachers can best manage provocations and attention-getting behaviors by gentle and humorous put-downs. If these behaviors persist, punishment should be designed to frustrate students' intended goals completely. Students who persist in shouting out obscenities, for example, can be required to copy them repeatedly during free time until they are satiated.

Truly effective punishment does not leave students with revengeful attitudes. Instead, it provides them with feelings of guilt, shame, frustration, or embarrassment. They realize that they have gotten into trouble because of their own failures to respond to earlier, more positive attempts to curb their misbehavior.

USING TECHNIQUES SYSTEMATICALLY

Behavior modification techniques must be used correctly and consistently with one another. Dasho (1978), for example, reported that a teacher tried the following techniques over a short period for dealing with a disobedient boy: firmly reminding the boy about the rules, moving his desk to isolate him from the class, depriving him of recess, positive reinforcement, and finally ignoring him. More generally, Dasho reported that teachers commonly vacillated among calm appeal to rationality, threatening punishment, and ignoring. Such unsystematic combining of techniques is unlikely to succeed for any length of time.

Even teachers who try to implement principles of behavior modification more systematically often have trouble at first. Harris and Kapche (1978), for example, listed twenty-six errors that such teachers commonly commit. Therefore, if you intend to use these techniques systematically, carefully study sources such as Krumboltz and Krumboltz (1972) and O'Leary and O'Leary (1977) to master concepts, and try to arrange for help in the form of observation and feedback as you work on techniques in class.

SUMMARY

A variety of minor but annoying student misbehaviors require teacher command of the principles of behavior modification in order to shape more constructive behavior. Techniques for establishing and maintaining desired behavior include modeling, cuing, and reinforcement; methods for stopping undesirable behavior include satiation, extinction, and punishment.

Modeling is a powerful influence on behavior if teachers use it systematically. Students tend to imitate most the behaviors of high-prestige models, especially when they can identify with the models and see that the models' desirable behaviors are rewarded. Modeling can foster a wide range of desired behaviors, especially when coupled with verbalized self-instruction to achieve self-control.

Cues for appropriate behavior can be of help when dealing with repeated problem behavior. Advance reminders, coaching, and similar supports are especially useful when students have trouble discriminating between appropriate and inappropriate times for talking, moving about, and the like. This technique can be combined with self-assessment, self-recording, and self-reinforcement.

Reinforcement is the primary behavioristic mechanism for establishing and maintaining behavior. When used in the form of the Premack Principle with appropriate schedules of reinforcement, it is applicable to classroom situations. Contingency contracting clarifies relationships between behavior and consequences, provides structure, and motivates students. Also, social reinforcement and various token reinforcement systems can support behavior.

Teachers can reduce undesirable behaviors through satiation, extinction, negative reinforcement, and punishment. All of these techniques require careful management to avoid undesirable side effects. It is especially important when using punishment to remain alert to the possibility of undesired and unintended consequences.

Questions and Problems

1. Does using reinforcement in the classroom amount just to bribing students to learn? Explain why or why not, and discuss your answer with friends.
2. Have you ever used modeling combined with verbalized self-instruction as a teaching device? What are its advantages and disadvantages compared to ordinary lecture/demonstration?
3. How a message is phrased is often at least as important as the content of the message itself. What principles apply to the following situations: praise that is reinforcing to students and not condescending or patronizing and cuing that involves helpful pointers or reminders and not nagging.
4. If you use contracts, tokens, or other formalized reinforcement systems in your class, you will probably want to do so only with a few students who seem to need such extra structuring/incentives. How will you explain the situation so that you do not create either self-concept problems in the few students singled out for special treatment or jealousy in the rest of the class?

Case Studies

MR. KNIGHT LOSES HIS COOL. Jim Dell, a sixth-grade student, heads for the pencil sharpener. Mr. Knight says, almost yelling, "Jim, go back to your seat! That's the fifth time I've had to tell you to get in your seat!

Stay there!'' Moments later Jim wanders out of his seat, sits on Wanda's desk, and begins a conversation with her. ''Jim,'' Mr. Knight yells, ''What's wrong with you? Can't you do anything right?'' Jim's face muscles tighten as he stares at the floor sullenly. How would you have responded to Jim's desk-sitting behavior? What should Mr. Knight do now? In general, how would you deal with Jim's out-of-seat behavior?

IN SEARCH OF SELF-MONITORING SKILLS. Jan Barnes is a tenth-grade English teacher. She bemoans the fact that when she assigns a brief research/essay paper of between four to five pages, containing twenty references, students ask endless questions. How can she develop a management system for helping students to assume more responsibility for finding their own references and making independent decisions about what to include in the paper?

CHAPTER

Humanistic Approaches to Counseling Disturbed Students

CHAPTER OUTLINE

OBJECTIVES

When you have mastered the material in this chapter, you will be able to

1. Discuss four common background experiences of students who show severe or chronic behavior problems in school
2. Explain how Rudolf Dreikurs (1968) theoretically analyzes student misbehavior and what practical advice he gives for the handling of student problems
3. Define and discuss techniques of life-space interview that deal with misbehavior problems
4. List and explain Glasser's (1977) ten-step approach to dealing with problem students and the rationale that underlies it
5. Explain the philosophy behind Gordon's Teacher Effectiveness Training (TET), his concept of problem ownership, and the TET techniques that facilitate teacher-student communication (e.g., active listening and "I" messages)
6. Discuss Gordon's (1974) six-step "no-lose" method for solving student-teacher conflict
7. Explain the two key elements of the authors' integrated eclectic approach to problem solving and identify the elements in a real-life illustration of problem solving

The classroom management principles discussed in the previous three chapters will enable teachers to establish and maintain an effective learning environment, manage the class as a group, and deal with routine school adjustment problems that students present. Certain students, however, will show chronic, severe problems that make it difficult for the teacher to reach them or that require frequent reliance on negative reinforcement or punishment to exert control. In this chapter, we shall discuss some characteristics of these students and some of the techniques for dealing with them that humanistic approaches to psychology and psychotherapy suggest.

PATHS TO DISTORTED DEVELOPMENT

Disturbed parents

The life history of each seriously distorted individual is unique, but several themes are common. First, most come from homes in which one or both parents are seriously disturbed. They need not be broken homes; many children would be better off if their parents were divorced instead of fighting continuously while remaining married. In any case, students reared in homes featuring parental strife, modeling of low frustration tolerance, verbal and physical violence, and socialization based on threats and punishment are likely to mistrust adults, particularly authority figures. They are likely to have well-developed antisocial tendencies and poor self-control.

Cycles of failure

A different type of distorted development involves cycles of failure, feelings of inadequacy, and attempts to compensate for failure or cover up by acting out. This kind of misbehavior often occurs primarily in school situations. Typically, problems start when students are in the early grades and suffer blame and rejection (usually real, but sometimes only perceived) because of school failure. Such students often develop rigid self-concepts of hopeless inadequacy in relation to school tasks. This sets in motion a series of self-fulfilling prophecy effects, since students who expect failure and rejection are likely to experience failure and rejection. By acting hopelessly inept and alienated, they condition teachers to perceive and treat them as such (Covington, 1983; Dreikurs, 1968). Teachers often give up on students who are unresponsive, impulsive, wrapped up in fantasy, or virtually certain to say or do something silly if they do respond (Brophy & Evertson, 1981).

Alienation from learning

Teachers often overlook students who are alienated from learning and who are also passive. These pupils may continue to become more withdrawn and depressed if teachers do not intervene. This means changing both students' behavior and self-perceptions by helping them to learn and to realize that they are capable of learning (Purkey, 1970; Covington, 1983).

Demands for attention

Students who do not receive enough of the right kind of attention and respect from parents, teachers, or peers may strive to obtain it through clowning or disruptive behavior. Others come to be regarded as disruptive at school because of indulgence in tobacco or marijuana, pills or other drugs, drinking, obscene language, or sexual activity. Except for involvement with hard drugs like heroin, such behavior is typical of students, especially secondary students who are relatively bright and well adjusted compared to the kinds of disturbed students described previously.

Dealing with existing conditions

Many problems, however, can be handled successfully without a full understanding of how they develop. In most cases it is more important to understand and deal with people as they are now rather than to delve into their histories. This point is worth stressing for at least two reasons. First, there is a tendency to cite poor home backgrounds both to explain disordered behavior and to justify failure to do anything about this behavior. It is true that the more disturbed individuals are, and the longer they have been disturbed, the more difficult it will be to change them. However, this is very different from saying that nothing can or should be done. Second, partly as a holdover from early psychoanalysis, teachers frequently believe that classroom misbehavior that is part of a general pattern of disorder must be handled through psychotherapy. At one level, this is true. Even when they want to, teachers probably should not attempt to solve a student's overall adjustment problems if they are serious. It is also true, however, that teachers must take action to change misbehavior in their classrooms if they expect to stop it.

COUNSELING TECHNIQUES

Personality theory and techniques of counseling and psychotherapy are natural sources for classroom teachers to draw on in developing methods for dealing with problem students, but early attempts were not very successful. Most techniques of psychoanalysis and other early forms of intensive individual psychotherapy were not suitable for use with children, and teachers, who were busy dealing with entire classes, did not have adequate time to use them.

As counseling and psychotherapy became more diversified, new techniques that were more humanistic and behavioral were developed. These techniques are more limited but also more specific in intent and more immediate in their effects. Classroom teachers can use many of these methods effectively.

Dreikurs

Importance of family dynamics

Although the writings of Rudolf Dreikurs (1968) are psychoanalytic (Adlerian), they are intended for teachers and applicable in the classroom. Predictably, Dreikurs stressed the importance of early family dynamics, tracing problems to sources such as parental overambition or overprotectiveness and sibling relationships that make certain children feel discouraged or inadequate. Dreikurs sees children as reacting to these central themes in their lives, compensating for feelings of inferiority by developing a style of life designed to protect self-esteem and avoid danger areas. He believes that children who have not worked out a satisfactory personal adjustment and place in the peer group will seek one of the following four goals (listed in increasing order of disturbance): (1) attention, (2) power, (3) revenge, or (4) display of inferiority (to get special service or attention).

Analysis of behavior

The first step for teachers is to analyze problem behavior and determine what goals students are pursuing. Attention seekers are disruptive and provocative, but will not openly defy or challenge as will power seekers, who in turn will not seek to hurt or torment, as will revenge seekers. Persistent dependency and help seeking will differ in quality and purpose, depending on whether students merely want attention or have stopped coping and have opted to display inferiority and helplessness.

Explaining the problem to students

Dreikurs advised teachers to observe problem students, diagnose the meaning of their behavior, and then explain this diagnosis to the students in private. The teacher should make the students understand the goals of their own behavior rather than speculating about presumed causes. If the teacher is not sure about these goals, it can be helpful to speculate about them to see whether or not this strikes a responsive note in students ("I wonder if you do that just to get attention").

Dreikurs opposed artificial punishment but stressed the value of allowing the natural consequences of maladaptive behavior to occur. He stressed the linkage between maladaptive behavior and unwanted consequences as part of the attempt to develop insight and be willing to abandon self-defeating goals and make productive commitments.

Life-Space Interviews

Improving life conditions

Morse (1971) described the goal of a life-space interview as fostering adjustment and obtaining a degree of behavioral compliance by providing life-space relief (improving the life conditions of the student, especially in the classroom). Incidents of defiance or serious misbehavior often provide the impetus. In this type of interview, the teacher talks to students privately, trying to obtain their perceptions of the incident and the events that led up to it. This provides an opportunity for students to experience catharsis and ventilation and for teachers to express a desire to help.

If disruptive conduct persists, stop the lesson and call a short conference with the troublemaker.

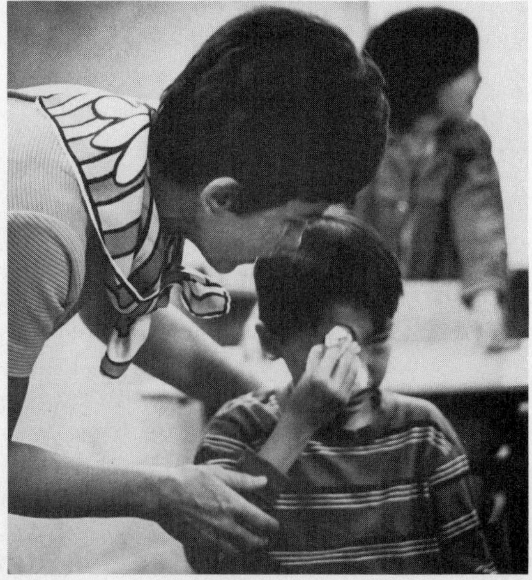

Acceptance of student's feelings

As the interview proceeds, the teacher seeks to obtain an accurate and detailed description of what happened and an indication of the meaning of the event to the student. Students may be upset by different events—one student may be concerned about being picked on by peers, and another may be upset about being blamed by the teacher. The teacher tries to communicate acceptance of the feelings the student conveys without necessarily accepting the student's actions.

Working with the student

Once this behavior is accomplished, discussion can move toward deciding what must be done. This involves analysis to identify places where relief can be provided or changes made. The teacher offers to work together with the student to find ways to prevent repetition of the problem. How can the problems that led up to the incident be eliminated or reduced? What will happen if there is a repetition of the incident? The teacher avoids moralizing and empty threats, confining discussion of consequences to those that the teacher seriously intends to use in the future if there should be a repetition of the behavior.

Within this general model, teachers should provide the following additional help that particular students need:

1. Teachers should help students see and accept reality and abandon defensive distortions.
2. Teachers should show students that inappropriate behavior is self-defeating.
3. Teachers should clarify values.
4. When necessary, teachers should suggest means that will help students deal with problems more effectively.
5. Teachers should help students think for themselves and avoid being led into trouble by others.
6. Teachers should help students release anger by expressing sympathy and understanding.
7. Teachers should help students deal with emotions like panic, rage, or guilt following emotional explosions.
8. Teachers should maintain open communication.
9. Teachers should provide friendly reminders.
10. Teachers should help clarify thinking and facilitate decision making.

Glasser and Reality Therapy

In suggesting applications of what he calls "reality therapy" to the classroom, William Glasser provided guidelines for general classroom management and for problem solving with individual students. He has a wide following among teachers, and survey data indicate that systematic implementation of his program is associated with reductions in referrals to the office, fighting, and suspensions (Glasser, 1977). More rigorous tests of his methods are not available (nor are they for other approaches described in this chapter).

Facilitative school atmosphere

The book *Schools without Failure* (1969) illustrates Glasser's interest in creating a generally facilitative atmosphere in schools, not just facilitative teacher-student relationships. He stressed that schools and classrooms be as humanistic as possible—they should be cheerful and courteous, communal, open to student input and communication generally, and staffed by people who believe that students are capable of exercising responsibility.

Jointly established rules

Glasser advocated that teachers and students jointly establish rules during classroom meetings and that they hold additional meetings to adjust the rules or develop new ones that apply to novel situations. Teachers adopt the role of discussion leaders and not authority figures during these meetings, setting limits only with respect to what is possible within the law and the rules of the school. Decisions are to be made by vote rather than negotiation. This part of Glasser's approach is not as well accepted as his problem-solving steps because many teachers oppose student self-government on principle, and others find it overly cumbersome.

Ten-step method

Glasser's ten-step method of dealing with problem students does not require use of his classroom-meetings approach to rule setting, although Glasser himself stressed the latter and, in any case, insisted that everyone must recognize rules as reasonable and beneficial if they are to be effective. Glasser described his approach to discipline as no-nonsense but also as constructive and nonpunitive. It involves making clear to students that they can and must control themselves and follow school rules if they expect to stay in school.

Glasser's first step is to select a student for concentrated attention and elicit typical teacher responses to the student's disruptive behavior. Second, analyze the list of problem-solving techniques to see which ones do and do not work, resolving not to repeat those that fail. Third, personal relations with the student should be improved. Extra encouragement should be provided by asking the student to perform special errands or by taking other initiatives to show concern and imply that things are going to improve.

This method continues indefinitely. If the problem behavior reappears, a new approach is added at the fourth step. Instead of repeating past mistakes, the teacher simply should ask students to describe what they are doing. This causes students to analyze their behavior, perhaps for the first time, and to begin to see their own responsibility for it, although they may try to rationalize. In any case, once students describe their own behavior accurately, the teacher simply should ask them to stop it.

The fifth step is used if the problem persists. The teacher should call a short conference and again ask students to describe the behavior and to state whether or not it is against the rules or recognized informal expectations. The teacher also should ask the students what they should be doing instead of what they have been doing. All this is done in a warm and supportive way but with insistence that students both express the inappropriateness of their own behavior and describe what they should be doing instead.

If this does not work, the sixth step also involves calling conferences and getting students to focus on their misbehavior but includes announcing that a plan is needed to solve the problem. The plan must be more than a simple agreement to stop misbehaving, because this has not been honored in the past.

If the sixth step does not work, Glasser's seventh step calls for isolating the students or using time-out procedures. During their periods of isolation, students should be charged with devising plans for ensuring that they follow the rules in the future. Isolation will continue until the students have devised such a plan, have had it approved, and have made a commitment to follow it.

If this doesn't work, the eighth step is in-school suspension. This should be announced to the students firmly but matter-of-factly. Suspended students will now have to deal with the principal or someone else other than the teacher, but this other person will repeat earlier steps in the sequence and press the students to come up with a plan that is acceptable.

The ninth step applies only to students who remain out of control during in-school suspension. Glasser recommended calling their parents to take them home and then starting over with them the next day. The tenth step is removal from school and referral to another agency.

Glasser's ten-step approach is attractive to a great many teachers because it clearly is applicable in the classroom and because it provides a sequence of specific steps for dealing with problems that have not responded to normal methods. It also illustrates features common to several approaches, including the behavioristic, that seem to be converging. One is insistence on minimal standards of behavior, specifically behavior in school, regardless of students' personal backgrounds. All students must follow reasonable rules of behavior.

Responsibility for behavior

A related notion is that students are responsible for their own behavior and will be held to that responsibility. Teachers will do whatever they can to help students solve their problems, but they are the students' problems and not the teacher's. This approach may seem harsh, but it assumes that rules are reasonable and fairly administered and that teachers try to be helpful, cooperate with students in making feasible adjustments, and, in general, maintain a positive, problem-solving stance. When these assumptions do not hold, Glasser's methods, like any others, can be destructive. An authoritarian teacher, for instance, can concentrate more on building a case against problem students than on trying to help them.

Gordon and Teacher Effectiveness Training

Glasser's ideas were widely disseminated and adopted in the later 1960s and early 1970s. Many teachers use them today, and interest in reality therapy workshops remains high. The same is true for workshops on behavior modification approaches. The approach being disseminated most vigorously now, however, is Thomas Gordon's (1974) Teacher Effectiveness Training (TET).

"No-lose" arrangements

Gordon's philosophy stresses freedom, responsibility, and abandonment of power and authority in favor of negotiation of "no-lose" arrangements. He advised teachers to be open and caring toward their students but also to maintain their individuality or separateness. He urged minimizing authoritative control over students, replacing this with teacher-student interdependence and mutual meeting of needs.

Problem ownership

Problem solving starts with identification of problem ownership. Some problems are owned strictly by teachers, some strictly by students, and others by both teachers and students. Solutions to problems are facilitated if all parties involved recognize problem ownership accurately and respond accordingly.

Student-owned problems

Student-owned problems include anxiety, inhibition, and poor self-concept. For these problems Gordon recommended passive listening (showing that you hear and understand what students are saying), door openers (invitations for students to talk), and, especially, active listening. Active listening goes beyond simply paying attention and showing that you understand; it includes providing feedback to students that responds to the underlying meanings of their messages.

Language of unacceptance

In short, Gordon recommended an updated form of Carl Rogers's nondirective counseling (Rogers, 1983) for such students, and he rejected as ineffective responses those that contain what he called "the language of unacceptance." This is any response to the students' expressed fears or anxieties that does not take them seriously. This obviously includes flat contradictions or scoffing but also takes in well-meaning attempts to cheer students up by praising or distracting them.

Active listening

Gordon recommended active listening as an instructional technique during class discussions as well as a management technique to use on individuals. It helps students dissipate their feelings before getting down to work when something upsetting has happened, and it helps promote smooth parent-teacher conferences. Through active listening, teachers help students not by trying to assume responsibility for their problems but by helping them to find their own solutions and become more independent, confident, and self-reliant.

Teacher-owned problems

Teacher-owned problems occur when students behave in ways that make teachers frustrated or angry. They require a different set of techniques from those used when students own the problem. In the latter case it is important for students to communicate and for the teacher to be a listener and counselor. When the teacher owns the problem, the teacher does the communicating, sending messages to students and trying to influence them to change.

"I" and "You" Messages Gordon listed a number of ineffective techniques for trying to change students. They include confrontations that backfire, "solution" messages that students resent and that induce only dependent and artificial compliance even when they do work, put-down messages that breed resentment without bringing about constructive changes, and indirect messages that may hurt the teacher's credibility. Gordon noted that most of these ineffective messages are "you" messages, used when the situation calls for "I" messages. It is the teacher in such cases who has the problem and thus the teacher who must do the communicating. "I" messages reveal feelings and vulnerabilities but in ways that pay off by fostering intimacy and describing the problem without imputing unfortunate motives to the students.

"I" messages have three major parts. The first part indicates the specific behavior that leads to the problem ("When I get interrupted. . . ."). The second specifies the effect on the teacher (". . . I have to start over and repeat things unnecessarily. . . ."). This shows students that their behavior is causing the teacher real problems, and this message alone will be sufficient to motivate most students to want to change. The third part specifies the feelings generated within the teacher because of the problem (". . . and I become frustrated"). Taken together, the three parts link specific student behavior as the cause of a specific effect on the teacher, which in turn produces undesirable feelings in the teacher.

"No-Lose" Method of Problem Solving Gordon maintained that combinations of environmental manipulation, active listening, and communication through "I" messages will solve most problems. Sometimes the needs motivating unacceptable student behavior are very strong, however, or the relationship with the teacher is very poor, and conflict will continue. Genuine conflict involves problems owned by both students and teachers. It must be approached in ways that avoid winning or losing and that meet the needs of all parties involved. Gordon's "no-lose" method is a process of searching until such a solution is found.

Conflict resolution

Prerequisites for use of the method include active listening (students must believe that their needs will be accepted if they are expected to risk serious negotiation), use of good "I" messages to state teacher needs clearly and honestly, and communication to students that this is a new and different approach (for teachers who have not been using it regularly). There are six steps to be followed in this approach: (1) define the problem, (2) generate possible solutions, (3) evaluate these solutions, (4) decide which solution is best, (5) determine how to implement the solution, and (6) assess how well the solution is solving the problem.

Defining the problem

Defining the problem properly includes accuracy about problem ownership and identification of only those people who are really part of the problem. This continues until everyone is agreed. For this purpose, it is vital that the problem be described in terms of conflicting needs, not competing solutions.

Generating solutions

When generating solutions, it is important simply to list them and not to evaluate them prematurely. Once evaluation starts, solutions that are objectionable to anyone for any reason should be eliminated. Deciding which solution is best involves a persistent search for consensus rather than a resort to voting. Proposed solutions can be tested by imagining the consequences. When agreement is reached, specific implementation plans and responsibilities are drawn up, including plans for later assessment. The result should be a "no-lose" agreement with which everyone explicitly states satisfaction and readiness to honor.

Broken agreements

Not all agreements are honored, however. Agreements may be broken when students do not perceive the conflict in the first place, seeing only the teacher's problem; do not believe that their needs are heard and understood by the teacher (this can happen even when the solution meets their needs); or agree to the solution because of peer or teacher pressure. Gordon warned teachers against using power when students break agreements. Instead, he suggested that they send strong "I" messages to communicate disappointment and indicate that now they share a new problem.

Assertion of power

Gordon clearly did not like the idea of power assertion by teachers under any circumstances, but he admitted that it may be necessary when there is danger involved, when students do not understand the logic of the teacher's position, or when there is insufficient time for more leisurely problem solving.

Value conflicts

Gordon also noted that certain conflicts involve competing value systems (dress code, use of drugs, personal grooming, language and manners, morality, patriotism, religion) for which no mutually acceptable solutions are possible. "I" messages are not effective in such cases because the teacher's logic does not make sense to the students. Value conflicts should be labeled as such and not as conflicts of personal needs. Gordon still recommended self-disclosure and "I" messages to show students where teachers stand and to open the door for possible discussion and behavior change, but that is all. He advised dropping the matter if the first "I" message does not produce any positive response from students. Teacher persistence at this point is seen as irritating preaching or nagging.

EVALUATION OF HUMANISTIC APPROACHES

There are many similarities among the recommendations of humanistic theorists. Many of their ideas are essentially identical, and most of the rest are complementary. Glasser is probably the most realistic, recognizing explicitly that power assertion sometimes will be necessary because of persistent student irresponsibility, not just because of pressures, dangers, or value conflicts. Even his approach may assume too much; some students will resist making commitments because their misbehavior is too rewarding, and some will require stronger sanctions than social encouragement (Clarizio & McCoy, 1976).

Research Evidence

Brophy and Rohrkemper (1981) examined how ninety-eight elementary teachers interpreted and stated how they would cope with twelve chronic student problem types. Problem types included failure syndrome, perfectionist, underachiever, low achiever, hostile aggressive, passive aggressive, defiant, hyperactive, distractible, immature, rejected by peers, and shy-withdrawn. The teachers who were studied had been nominated by their principals as either outstanding or average in their ability to cope with problem students.

Following Gordon (1974), Brophy and Rohrkemper (1981) classified problems as (1) teacher owned, where the students' behavior interferes with the teachers' needs or agenda, (2) student owned, where the students' needs or agenda is frustrated by people or events other than the teacher, and (3) shared problems, where the students' behavior does not directly challenge the teacher but has consequences for classroom management and control. The teachers saw students who presented teacher-owned problems as acting intentionally and thus as blameworthy for their misbehavior. Those with student-owned problems, in contrast, were seen as victims of circumstances beyond their control.

Brophy and Rohrkemper noted that teachers in this sample appeared to have limited knowledge of and skill in using the various treatment models available for these problem types and did not always believe that solving these problems was a part of their duties as classroom teachers. They were pessimistic about changing students who presented teacher-owned problems and focused on immediate control strategies rather than long-term problem-solving strategies in responding to these students. They saw students with student-owned problems as difficult to change, but they were motivated to try to do so through long-term remediation programs.

Teacher responsibility for solving problems

Teachers believed to be effective managers behaved in ways generally consistent with the principles advocated by Glasser and Gordon. Brophy and Rohrkemper found that teachers rated as effective by their principals and by classroom observers were willing to assume responsibility for solving problems. They worked with problem students themselves instead of or in addition to referring them to the principal or a counselor, and they used long-term solution-oriented approaches. In contrast, less effective teachers focused on controlling misbehavior in the immediate situation, often by using threat or punishment. Effective teachers concentrated on helping their students to understand and cope with the problems that caused their symptomatic behavior.

AN INTEGRATED APPROACH

There is so much in common among the theories of Dreikurs, Redl, Morse, Glasser, and Gordon that teachers can draw on all of them to develop an integrated, eclectic approach to problem solving. Key elements include gathering complete and accurate information and seeking genuine solutions, not just stopgap suppression measures.

Gathering Information

Unnecessary questions

Most people realize that one should not make decisions or take action without complete and accurate information. Many people, however, are not aware that undesirable outcomes can result when authority figures behave as if they were seeking information when no information is needed or obtained. If a student, for example, should call out a provocative remark or create a disturbance, there may be no need for questioning. Unless it is so serious as to require a conference, the situation should be handled with a brief or even humorous response such as, "Cool it, John." The teacher should not interrupt instruction to ask unnecessary and essentially meaningless and rhetorical questions such as "John, how many times do I have to tell you not to do that?"

Avoid student loss of face

When it is necessary to gather information, do so in ways that avoid causing any student to lose face. Investigations should be conducted in private, to minimize students' needs to save face, to refuse to back down no matter what, or to defy the teacher. It is also helpful to state that everything said during the discussion will be held in confidence unless some explicit agreement to the contrary is made. Insist that students keep quiet while classmates speak, reassure them that they will have a chance to give their versions later, and proceed toward the truth gradually by asking questions and pointing out discrepancies in different versions. Questions should concentrate on establishing exactly what happened and on trying to determine the motives behind the actions. The motives are important because students often misread one another's behavior—for example, by interpreting accidents as deliberate provocations or minor teasing as serious insults.

Recognize rationalizations

When questioning students, it is important not to be taken in by their rationalizations or attempts to project responsibility for their own behavior onto others. Students who get into regular scrapes with authority figures are usually masters of rationalization. When they cannot successfully deny or evade responsibility for their behavior, they will attempt to excuse or condone it by giving reasons such as, "He started it"; "People who leave money lying around like that *should* have it stolen"; and "He looked at me funny." For detailed and fascinating analyses of these kinds of rationalizations, see *Children Who Hate* (Redl & Wineman, 1951).

Withholding information

Investigations occasionally reach an impasse because one or more students are lying or withholding part of the truth. It usually is best to acknowledge this openly and express both disappointment that the whole truth is presently not being told and the expectation that it will be told. If persistent efforts along this line still do not succeed, the teacher must decide whether or not the discussion itself will end the matter or whether some form of punishment is required.

Finding Solutions

Positive solutions

Once all needed information is collected, the next step is to work out a solution. The solution should be perceived as positive, not punitive, in intent and effect and as acceptable to everyone, not just the majority. The teacher may have to limit the range of possible solutions by stating clearly that certain things cannot be done or are outside school rules.

At this stage, attention should focus on the future and on solving the problems that led to the conflict, not the conflict itself. Attempts to rehash points already gone over in the investigation phase should be cut short, and students should be reminded that since everyone understands the problem, it is time to work out a solution. Solutions do not have to be permanent or irrevocable; they can be explicitly tentative and subject to review at a designated future date.

Teacher suggestions

If the students are unable to come up with realistic suggestions, teachers will have to make the suggestions themselves. They should be tentative and open to comment and evaluation. If students endorse a proposed solution, the teacher should ask them to think carefully before making final agreements, again emphasizing that students must make the decision and will be responsible for abiding by it. Students should not be allowed to come away with the idea that the teacher foisted a demand on them to which they really did not agree.

Problem-Solving Vignette Many of these problem-solving principles are exemplified in the following vignette. Vera Wise is a teacher who is concerned about an increase in the frequency and seriousness of attention-getting behavior among her students over the past few weeks. The problem is worse in the last hour or so of school. Increasing numbers of students have been involved, fooling around and calling out remarks instead of working on their assignments. The primary instigators seem to be Bill, Jim, David, and Paul, four boys who sit close together and are part of a clique both in and out of school.

Vera has tried talking individually to each of these boys, as well as to other students, but the problem has worsened. The boys promise to improve their behavior, but they don't. The problem came to a head this afternoon, when one of the boys (Vera is not sure which) said something obscene and embarrassing to Mary, an attractive girl who is physically well developed and is the object of much interest and discussion among the boys. Most of the class heard the remark and passed it along to the few who didn't hear the first time. Vera responded by warning the class sharply that this kind of behavior had gone far enough and by telling, Bill, Jim, David, and Paul to stay after class to see her about it. Jim started to protest that he hadn't said it, but Vera cut him off with the statement that she wanted to see all four boys and would explain why later. During the remainder of the period, Vera decided that this particular incident was not as important as the more general problem. Consequently, she decided to concentrate on changing the behavior of all four boys rather than on trying to find out who made the remark to Mary.

At the end of the period, as classmates prepared to leave, Jim and Paul looked surly, while Bill and David looked sheepish. The others were snickering at them and making guesses about what was going to happen. A few tried to hang around to find out, but Vera made a point of getting rid of them and closing the door before beginning the meeting. The meeting went as follows:

TEACHER: As I said in class, the remark made about Mary today was out of line, and it was just the latest of a number of things like that that have been going on recently. I think the time has come to put a stop to it, and I have kept you boys here because you four seem to be responsible for most of it.	*The teacher begins by making it clear that she wants to talk about the general issue, not just what happened today, and that she considers all four boys to be responsible. Her behavior throughout the meeting is consistent with this opening statement.*
JIM: Like I said before, I didn't do it. Besides, I can't stay because I have to go to practice and coach wants us there five minutes after the bell. **PAUL:** Yeah, I didn't do it	*Jim and Paul both try to get off by making excuses. The teacher offers to call and "explain," but this offer is refused. Although the offer was genuine in the sense that the teacher would have followed through if either boy had asked her to, she knew that this was unlikely because*

either, and I have to go home and mow the lawn today.

both boys probably knew that they would only compound their troubles if the teacher called the coach or a parent. With this response, the teacher both cuts off further attempts to escape the meeting and makes it clear that she intends to keep everyone there until she is satisfied. She also makes it specifically clear to Jim again that she is not interested in finding out who insulted Mary but instead is interested in the larger problem.

TEACHER: Let's get a couple of things straight. First, I'm not especially interested in finding out which one of you embarrassed Mary today. I'm interested in discussing the larger problem of putting an end to this kind of thing. You four are here because you all do it more than anyone else. Furthermore, we're all going to stay here until we settle the problem for good. That includes everyone. Jim, if you like, I will call the coach and explain. Paul, if you want, I will call your home, but you are both going to stay here until we get finished. (Both Jim and Paul indicate that they don't want the teacher to make any calls.)

JIM: Well, David did it, not me. Besides, he does it a lot more than anyone else. When I do it, it's usually because he gets me started. (David glares but says nothing.)

Now Jim tries to blame it on David. The teacher again points out that she is interested in the larger issue and she makes it clear that Jim is both guilty of numerous instances of similar behavior recently and responsible for his own behavior regardless of what other students do. Her suggestion that David apologize is left simply as a suggestion with no attempt to follow up. This is appropriate, because a forced apology in front of the class would only further embarrass Mary and enrage David. The teacher has nothing to lose by suggesting this, and everyone might gain something if David follows through and does apologize to Mary sometime in the future. This statement also is consistent with the teacher's later statement that obscenity as such is not as important as respecting other peoples' rights and feelings. Also, by giving minimal time and attention to the information that David was responsible for today's problem, the teacher again reinforces her earlier statement that she wants to talk about the larger problem and about all four of the boys.

TEACHER: No good, Jim. David probably does do it more, but you are responsible for your own behavior, and you can't use him for an excuse. If you didn't do it yourself a lot, you wouldn't be here now. (*Jim glumly remains silent at this point.*) David, if you did do it, I think you should apologize to Mary. She was very embarrassed, and whoever is responsible owes her an apology. But, as I said, I don't want to talk about what happened today; I want to talk about what's been going on over the last several weeks, and all four of you have been heavily involved in it.

PAUL: Well, we won't do it anymore. (*Jim and David immediately nod and say "yes," while Bill nods solemnly.*)

TEACHER: Sorry, but that's not good enough, either. I've talked to all of you, sometimes more than once. Every time you said that you wouldn't do it again, but you've kept doing it. So I'm afraid I can't take your word on it and let it go at that. We're going to have to discuss this some more and come to some kind of agreement that I can accept.

Under other circumstances, it probably would have been best for the teacher to take the boys at their word, perhaps ending the discussion on a more positive note, stressing happiness that they have seen the problem and are willing to respond to it in a mature fashion. However, given that these boys have pledged to change in the past and have not done so, it is perfectly appropriate for the teacher to refuse to accept their pledges to change and to point out her reasons why. Furthermore, she now makes it clear that this discussion is going to continue until a real solution is reached.

PAUL: Well, what's the big deal anyway? Words that people think are "dirty" don't hurt anybody, and besides, everyone knows what they mean.

TEACHER: In the first place, Paul, although it is true that there is nothing really wrong with these words, they are out of place in the classroom. More importantly, though, it's not just the words. It's the other things that go with them. For example, today Mary was terribly embarrassed, and no one had the right to do that to her. Also, you are distracting the whole class from their work, and let's not forget that you're supposed to be here at school to learn, not to goof off. But you're not doing your work. You know that I allow students to talk when they finish their assignments, but you four have been fooling around and making loud remarks instead of working on your assignments and then talking quietly after you finish.

Paul now takes the tack of trying to make the teacher feel guilty for being unreasonable. She counters nicely by acknowledging that his argument is valid up to a point, but then noting that it ignores certain factors in the larger context that make it impossible for schools to allow this kind of disruptive behavior. She then goes on to make the even more important point that she is more concerned about students' mutual respect for one another than about mere obscenity. The boys are much more likely to feel guilt or shame about having embarrassed Mary than they are about having used obscene language. Finally, the teacher makes the additional point that the disruptive behavior of these students is interfering with their own work and that of their classmates. This is done in a way that points out implicitly that the teacher's rules are reasonable but that these four boys are abusing them.

JIM: Well, I can't help it. I say things without thinking, or else because David or somebody else

At this point, Jim again tries to evade responsibility. In addition to blaming others for "getting him

gets me started. I've tried to stop, but I can't. Besides, it's not natural to try to stop from saying things that pop into your head at times like that.

started," he goes on to suggest that the teacher is asking something unreasonable and unnatural. The teacher wastes no time in dismissing this specious argument, pointing out that self-control is not a problem when the student is sufficiently motivated to show it. Her choice of an example here is particularly apt—students who use obscene language, particularly boys, almost always shrink at the thought of using it in the presence of their own mothers. The teacher closes this exchange a little roughly, characterizing what the boys have been saying as "lame excuses." However, under the circumstances, she is quite justified, because this is an accurate description of what has been happening. Also, she stresses personal responsibility for actions. Ultimately, she is not responsible for controlling these boys; they are responsible for controlling themselves.

TEACHER: Really! Well, suppose I invited your mother to sit in here for a few days? Do you think you might control yourself then? (*Jim's expression changes from surly self-confidence to confusion and anxiety.*)

TEACHER: You don't have to answer the question. You all know the answer; you don't use that kind of language around your mothers, and you don't have any trouble controlling yourself, either. So why don't we drop the lame excuses and start by recognizing that you can and will stop if you make the effort to do so.

PAUL: Yeah, but what are we supposed to do then? Sit there and keep our mouths shut?

TEACHER: No. I'm not asking you to do anything special, I'm only asking you to follow the rule that applies to everyone in the class: work on your assignment until you finish it. If you have time left over, then you can talk quietly, but without disrupting others.

Paul now takes a new approach, no longer attempting to rationalize the misbehavior but attacking the reasonableness of the teacher's request. She counters this by again repeating the rule, which is clearly reasonable, and also by making a point of the fact that she is only asking these boys to keep the same rule that applies to everyone else; she is not picking on them or asking them to do anything unusual.

PAUL: But I already said I would do that.

TEACHER: Yes, and I already said that all four of you have failed to keep your word on that. So what are we going to do? I don't want to make this into a big deal. In fact, I think it's silly to have to discuss something like this with students like yourselves, who should know better.

Paul now goes back to repeating his pledge of reform and the teacher again points out that he has made this pledge and has broken it in the past. She then pulls together a few statements to make the situation clear to the boys: they have created the problem through their own misbehavior; she doesn't even want to discuss it but they have forced it on her; the problem is serious enough that it is going to be stopped one way or another; she is inviting them to make suggestions and expressing

But the problem is serious and is getting worse, and I am going to see that it stops before it gets out of hand. If I have to, I'll punish you all severely, but I don't want to do that. I asked you here to lay out the problem and to see if you had any suggestions about how it could be solved. Are there ways I could help by making some changes?

willingness to follow them if they are feasible and have a chance of improving the situation (even though she could simply make a decision on her own about what to do and present it to the boys with no opportunity for discussion).

DAVID: Like what kind of changes?

TEACHER: Well, I could change your seats and separate you from one another. I could give you extra work or other things to do so that you wouldn't have time to goof off. I could try to arrange to have some of you transferred to other classes. (*These suggestions yield negative reactions, except that Jim agrees to change seats and move away from David.*)

In suggesting changes here, the teacher knows that they are unlikely to be acceptable to the boys. This is one way of informing them of possible negative consequences that will result if the problem is not stopped, without actually threatening such consequences. The fact that Jim agrees to change his seat is mildly surprising: it probably results from his own need to try to show that he was serious in his earlier claim that David tends to get him in trouble. In any case, it gives the teacher an opportunity to agree with a suggestion, thus showing good will on her part.

TEACHER: Okay, Jim, we'll arrange that. I hope it helps. Are there any other suggestions as to how we can solve this problem? (*Long silence.*)

PAUL: All I can think of is what I said before—I won't do it anymore, and this time I mean it. (*The others nod.*)

TEACHER: Well, I have to admit that I can't think of anything else other than punishment, and as I said, I don't want that. However, let me warn you right now that if any of you breaks his word this time, I will have to punish you. At the very least, you will have to stay after school for several days, and if there's any repeat of the kind of obscenity that went on today, I may have to

When the boys offer no more suggestions, the teacher changes from refusal to accept pledges of reform to a conditional acceptance. This is the appropriate time to make this switch, because the boys now have ceased their belligerence and rationalization, realizing that they are going to have to change their behavior and begin serious discussion of what might be appropriate in the future. As a hedge against failure to keep the pledge, the teacher threatens punishment in the future. However, she does it in a way that does not suggest that she expects to have to use it. Also, the kinds of punishment she mentions help underscore her seriousness about this issue.

contact your parents. I mention this because I want you to understand just how serious this problem is, and I want you to know that your word won't be any good in the future if you break it this time.

TEACHER: What about your workbooks? I know that all of you are behind, that the work you did in the past few weeks contains a lot of sloppy errors because of your fooling around. I want those workbooks brought up to date, the errors corrected, and the books turned in to me for checking shortly. How about Friday? (*Today is Wednesday.*)

In closing the discussion, the teacher turns to the problem of incomplete and sloppy work in the workbooks. She requires the students to make this up, although she agrees to a delay when a reasonable excuse is given for it. Although this will have a punishing effect in the technical sense, it is not the kind of behavior students typically perceive as punishment. The teacher merely is requiring them to do the same things that she requires of other students. The fact that it will cost them extra time and trouble in the next few days is their fault, not hers. This aspect of the discussion also underscores the point made earlier, that failure to do work is one of her concerns, not just hearing obscene words spoken in the classroom.

JIM: (*Dejectedly*) I'm way behind, and I have practice again tomorrow and a game Friday night. I'm not sure I can get it in by Friday.

TEACHER: All right, what about Monday? That will give you all the rest of the week plus the weekend. (*All nod agreement.*) All right, then, we'll make it Monday. Remember, I want you not only to catch up, but to review your work over the last three weeks or so and correct any errors you made because you weren't paying close attention to what you were doing. Work as far as the end of page 128. Okay? (*All agree.*) Is there anything else that any of you wants to add? (*After a brief silence, all shrug or shake their heads negatively.*)

TEACHER: Well, there is still the question of what to say in class tomorrow. You four are not the only ones who have been fooling around and making remarks. To-

Finally, in closing the discussion, the teacher explicitly brings up the question of what is to be said to the class the next day. She makes it clear that she is going to make a statement, but also pledges not to

morrow I intend to tell the class that we discussed the situation and agreed that certain things need to stop, and I intend to remind everyone about the rules. I probably also will stress some of the other things I've pointed out to you, but I don't want to say anything more about our discussion. For your own good, I suggest that you say as little as possible about it yourselves. Perhaps just say that we had a talk and made some agreements.

embarrass the four boys or divulge any details of this discussion. This again underscores her intention to solve the problem rather than to punish the boys, and reiterates her earlier remarks about avoiding embarrassment of students.

TEACHER: Also, I would appreciate it if you urged some of your classmates to follow the rules, too, so that I don't have to hold any more sessions like this with anyone else. Anyway, I won't embarrass you or give any details about what we have said and done here, but I think some brief statement needs to be made, because everyone in the class is going to be wondering. Is this plan acceptable? (*All nod agreement.*) Is there anything else? (*All shake their heads negatively.*) O.K., get going, and let's have no more of this.

Note, too, that she tries to enlist the help of the boys in this endeavor, suggesting that they minimize discussion about what went on and that they encourage their classmates to follow the rules. They may or may not do this, and she makes no attempt to check up on them. However, she has nothing to lose with this request, and it emphasizes that the boys share the problem and that they are responsible for solving it.

Note that throughout the discussion Paul and Jim have been vocal and occasionally belligerent. Under other circumstances David might have been, too, but since he was guilty of the incident that led to the discussion, he apparently has chosen to remain quiet and avoid getting into further trouble. Bill said nothing throughout the discussion, except to agree on occasion when the group agreed in unison. This may be because he is very embarrassed and remorseful, or it may be that he regularly responds to such discussions with sullenness and unresponsiveness. If the latter is the case, it is important for the teacher to see that he agrees explicitly to what has transpired, so that he will not claim later that he never consented to it. In this case, the teacher judges that Bill has responded as have the other boys and has made the same commitment, even though he did not at any time speak out for himself.

Summary

Disturbed students frequently come from homes in which they have experienced cycles of failure and feelings of inadequacy, often leading them to attempt to compensate by acting out. Even if not actively aggressive, they may be alienated from learning and demand attention through clowning or disruptive behavior.

Dreikurs believes that attention, power, revenge, and displays of inadequacy (listed in increasing order of disturbance) are the four goals of student misbehavior. He advised teachers to identify the goal of misbehavior and attempt to reveal it to students in a nonthreatening, private interview. Morse recommended the life-space interview as a means for crisis intervention.

Glasser's theory, which he called "reality therapy," is based on humanistic principles involving the creation of a facilitative school atmosphere. His ten-step method is designed to be constructive and nonpunitive, with minimal but graduated responses to persistent misbehavior and self-control as the desired end result. Gordon's "Teacher Effectiveness Training" (TET) is very similar, stressing freedom and responsibility rather than authority and power. Active listening is a method he recommended for helping students find their own solutions to their behavior problems.

Since the ideas of Dreikurs, Redl, Morse, Glasser, and Gordon have much in common, teachers can draw on all of them to form an integrated eclectic approach to problem solving, which will be illustrated in the case study that appears at the end of this chapter.

Questions and Problems

1. Why do we insist that classroom problems be dealt with in the classroom when we acknowledge that they may be merely part of a much broader personality disturbance?
2. How realistic are your expectations regarding students' attitudes and behavior toward you as a teacher? Are you prepared to handle irrational hostility or defiance effectively?
3. How can teachers maintain humanistic values in harmony with their role as an authority figure? Are you prepared to punish effectively when (*when*, not *if*) you have to?
4. What should Vera Wise, the teacher in the vignette, have done if one or more of the boys blatantly failed to keep his promises? Write out your responses and analyze why certain teacher statements are desirable in dealing with blatant misbehavior.

Case Study

LAURA SIMPSON'S PROBLEMS. Laura Simpson teaches English in a junior high school that draws 85 percent of its students from five nearby elementary schools. The remaining 15 percent of the population are black students bused in from a predominantly black neighborhood in another part of town. As a group, the black students are of lower socioeconomic status (SES) than the white students, so they provide proportionately fewer high achievers and proportionately more low achievers. The students, as a group, have a wide range of ability, achievement, and attitudes toward the school.

Laura is a dedicated English teacher. She spends much of her time preparing both group and individualized activities, but the range of student abilities and interests with which she must cope creates many problems. Partly to accomplish desegregation and partly to avoid the elitism and other problems that usually accompany ability grouping by class, the school has a firm policy of heterogeneous grouping. Thus each of Laura's five classes contains students ranging from functional illiterates to bright high achievers capable of handling class activities such as drama or written assignments that involve composing poems or fiction. This makes it difficult to find activities with enough common ground to be interesting and worthwhile for everyone. Laura keeps searching for such activities and occasionally succeeds in finding them, but more often than not she must treat students differently.

She feels guilty about this sometimes, because it seems to contradict school policy and because it segregates the students by ability groups and, to a degree, by social class and race. The high achievers, however, seem to need and want the challenge of difficult and complex assignments, and they become understandably bored and restless when Laura tries to conduct general lessons on things they learned long ago. This almost always causes some problems of student disruption. These problems are occasionally fairly serious, such as the time that one of her brightest students caused a near-riot by publicly complaining that Laura was wasting everyone's time by trying to teach "those dummies who don't want to learn and couldn't learn even if they did."

On the other hand, when Laura attempts to involve everyone in a high-level activity such as a dramatic reading of a play, the activity is almost always ruined by the disruptive behavior of the low achievers in the class. The reading skills of some students are so limited that they can only be assigned the most simple parts. Thus their main role is to keep quiet and listen.

As if all this were not bad enough, the students are at "that age." Almost every day and in almost every class, Laura must deal more or less continually with adolescent behavior such as attention-getting, defiance of authority, flirting, deliberate noise making, obscene or funny gestures and sounds, and wisecracks. In addition to these merely routine problems, occasionally there are serious ones, such as fights between students or open defiance directed at her. Laura can usually handle whatever comes up, but it take a lot of energy, and it often leaves her wondering whether she is a teacher or a warden.

Laura sees about 150 students each day for about fifty-five minutes each. Ten students present serious problems that Laura has been unable to solve. Let us look at these "problem" students.

Mary is bright and comes from a high-status home. In fact, her father is on the school board, and both her parents are among the town's leading citizens. However, Mary apparently dislikes both school in general and Laura in particular. She goes out of her way to show it by affecting boredom and disdain. When Laura attempts to deal with her, she responds in a way perhaps best described as "snotty." She often states that school is a drag, strictly for squares, and has even threatened Laura with trouble, presumably through her father's position on the school board, although Mary is too smart to say this directly.

Ben and Leon are two black students bused to the school. Both are alienated from school and hostile and aggressive toward peers in general and whites in particular. They have been suspended in the past for racial incidents and have been sent to detention repeatedly for refusing to turn in work. Their mere presence, individually and especially together, puts everyone on edge. They are likely to overreact to even minor incidents, to complain loudly that they are being picked on, and to use any excuse for picking a fight.

George, Joan, and Marie have all made it clear that they do not like Laura, and frankly, Laura does not like them. Although George and Joan seem to do all right in other teachers' classes, and although Laura generally gets along quite well with most students, there is something about these three that bugs her, and apparently something about her that bugs them. As a result, they take every opportunity to embarrass or provoke her, and she finds herself responding with uncharacteristic defensiveness and anger.

Nancy provokes problems because she needs constant monitoring and protection. She has limited ability in the first place, and this problem is compounded by learning disabilities that have left her hopelessly unable to cope with the seventh-grade curriculum. She is immature, dependent, anxious, unhappy, and generally lost at school. Furthermore, unlike others in similar situations who often evoke sympathy or protectiveness from their peers, Nancy has been rejected and is often picked on or ridiculed by classmates. Laura has succeeded in stopping this for the most part, but she realizes that she has not solved the more fundamental problems involved. Students' tendencies to ridicule Nancy merely have been driven underground rather than eliminated.

Pete is both bright and attractive, maybe too attractive for his own good. He rarely causes serious problems, but he does not apply himself to his studies. Instead, he works at being "cool," trying to impress the other boys and charm the girls. He is often inattentive because he is busy "goofing off" with his friends or flirting with the girls. He is pleasant and outwardly cooperative when Laura tries to reach him, but he never really changes his behavior.

Art is commonly referred to a juvenile delinquent, and in his case this is an understatement. He has frequently been suspended from school for activities such as extorting money through threats and carrying and brandishing weapons. He is part of a gang composed primarily of boys who have been thrown out or who have dropped out of school, and the word is that they spend much of their time stealing, getting drunk, using drugs, and generally engaging in petty crimes and teenage gang activities. Art is just marking time until he can drop out or succeed in getting himself kicked out.

Finally, Jim causes little trouble, but he seems to be deeply disturbed psychologically. In fact, he shows signs of developing schizophrenia: he is withdrawn, introverted to the point where he is usually not even aware of what is going on around him, and lacks friends or apparent interests. Morbid and depressing themes are predominant in his conversation, reading, and selection of research topics for assignments. Almost all of the students say he is "weird," and they call him "Psycho" behind his back.

Laura has virtually given up serious attempts to change the fundamental problems of these ten students. She finds herself more and more often merely minimizing the disruptions they cause, even if it means excluding them from class, sending them to detention, or taking other measures that are likely to worsen their problems in the long run. At least, she reflects ruefully, this gets them out of her hair for a short time.

Laura Simpson is dedicated and generally successful, but her success requires constant energy and skill, and it is not total. There are some students she does not reach at all, and many others that she succeeds with only partially, often because of constraints beyond her control. If you were in Laura's position, how would you try to change this generally unsatisfactory situation?

PART 7
INDIVIDUAL DIFFERENCES

Helen, Jim, Ricky, and Ruth were assigned to conduct an experiment in chemistry class. They were good friends who had been in school together for several years. They worked well as a team. Jim prepared the equipment while Ricky sorted the chemicals and made the measurements so that they would be ready when Jim had the apparatus set up. Helen read the "cautions" in the instructions and made directive comments to Ricky or Jim from time to time. Ruth started to outline the group report and finished the purpose section just as Ricky and Jim finished their tasks.

This unit is about individual differences. Individuals think about what happens to them and interpret events in terms of their experiences, abilities, self-concepts, and interests, so students may perceive, interpret, and evaluate the same event (a chemistry experiment) in different ways. In our example, the students automatically started to play roles they had learned in the classroom. In this instance, the roles reflect traditional gender roles. The males are setting up and conducting the experiment, and the females are observing and writing about it. The teacher did not assign them these tasks; the students simply assumed roles they had learned.

Teachers must deal with such individual differences in learning styles and personalities that students bring to the classroom. Each student is an individual and must be treated as such. This principle is clear, even simple, in the abstract, but it involves overwhelming complexities when teachers try to put it into practice. What are the important characteristics on which students differ, and what are the implications of these differences for individualized treatment?

To deal with these complexities, educators and researchers have described and labeled students with respect to socioeconomic status, IQ, cognitive style, and creativity. Other labels describe various types of exceptional students who are deemed to require "special education." These labels and their implications for education will be considered in the present section.

There has been much opposition to such labeling in recent years, because many labels are demeaning and appear to produce undesirable self-fulfilling prophecy effects ("This child has a learning disability and can't be expected to make much progress in school."). This is a real danger, especially if the labeling of students is not accompanied by remedial instruction or other treatment designed to eliminate or compensate for their problems. When students are described with specific labels, it is helpful to ask, "So what?" If the labels are meaningful and helpful, the question should be answerable with statements such as,

"Therefore, they need treatment X," or "Therefore, they will benefit more from treatment X than from treatments Y or Z." This is clearly the case with a label like "myopic" (nearsighted): The student is fitted with corrective glasses or contact lenses. Linkages between clear-cut remedial procedures and labels such as low IQ, disadvantaged, learning disabled, or emotionally disturbed are not so clear, however. Thus the value of labels, even so-called diagnostic ones, depends not only on their accuracy but on the degree to which they provide guidance for remediating the implied problems.

In Chapter 23, we discuss socioeconomic status, IQ, and gender-role differences. In Chapter 24, we discuss students' cognitive styles and creativity, considering how teachers can foster development in these areas. Finally, in Chapter 25 we consider the instruction of students whose handicaps or special needs often caused them to be labeled as abnormal and to be segregated from the educational mainstream in the past but who now are being returned to it as a result of Public Law 94–142.

CHAPTER

Socioeconomic Status, IQ, and Gender Differences among Students

CHAPTER OUTLINE

SOCIOECONOMIC STATUS
The Disadvantaged

INTELLIGENCE QUOTIENT (IQ)
Diverse Conceptions of Intellectual Abilities
Changes in IQs
Genetic Component
Reaction Ranges

INTELLIGENCE TEST DATA AND TEACHING
Predictors of Achievement
Uses and Misuses of IQ Tests

TYPES OF INTELLECTUAL ABILITIES
Level I and Level II Skills
Increasing IQ Scores

PROCESS APPROACHES TO INTELLIGENCE
Cognitive-Components Approach
Systems of Theorizing
Social Intelligence
Future Role of Intelligence Assessment

GENDER DIFFERENCES
Subject-Matter Achievement Patterns
Improving Classrooms for Boys and Girls

OBJECTIVES

When you have mastered the material in this chapter, you will be able to

1. Describe differences between high- and low-socioeconomic-status (SES) families in the cognitive environments created for children
2. Describe the key features of the type of teaching that is most successful with disadvantaged students
3. Criticize five common but incorrect assumptions about IQ tests, showing how the theoretical concept "intelligence" differs from the term *IQ*
4. Tell how IQ test scores can be interrelated and used properly in teaching situations
5. Define Level I versus Level II skills and identify their implications for IQ improvement
6. Explain how Gardner's (1983, 1988) and Sternberg's (1985) theories differ from more traditional psychometric approaches to conceptualizing and measuring intelligence
7. Describe how males' and females' academic performance is affected by cultural expectations

8. Explain why cultural expectations and learning are relatively more important than biology in determining differences between males and females in reading and mathematics performance
9. Explain how teacher praise and criticism might differentially affect males and females and the implications for improving the classroom performance of both groups

SOCIOECONOMIC STATUS

Among individual difference variables used to describe particular students or even entire school populations, the most important may be *socioeconomic status* (SES) and *social class*. The two terms are often used interchangeably, but they are defined and measured differently. SES is a cold, impersonal statistic compiled from indices such as type of occupation, years of education, size of income, quality of housing, and desirability of neighborhood. Social class usually is defined in a more personal way that expresses local prestige and respectability. Persons are high in social class to the extent that people in their community describe them as respectable, influential, or prestigious (Mueller & Parcel, 1981).

Both SES and social class are "proxy" variables that represent a complex of intercorrelated attributes that partially describe people and are useful for making educated guesses about them but do not substitute for detailed information about the individual. We use the term *SES* in this book because SES is more objectively measured, although we usually intend it to refer to life-style variables associated more closely with the term *social class* than with variables such as income.

All of the variables mentioned above, along with race, ethnicity, and various religious, political, and social customs, tend to correlate together into clusters (Blau, 1981; Yando, Seitz, & Zigler, 1979). No single SES variable causes all of the others in any simple way, but the educational level of parents is probably the most basic because the other variables lose most of their power for predicting things such as student achievement once the educational level of the parents is statistically controlled (Hess, 1970; Stevenson et al., 1978). In any case, parental education level is especially important to teachers because it is linked to parental interest in and attitudes toward education (Laosa, 1982).

Well-educated parents

Low-SES parents

Parents who are well educated generally value education and expect their children to become well educated too. They usually show interest in their children's progress and in meeting and collaborating with teachers, and they typically volunteer, participate in PTA and fund-raising activities, and help supervise field trips. The situation is different with low-SES parents. Many quit or were expelled before finishing high school, and most of the rest ended their schooling at high school graduation. Most of them know the value of education and want their children to go as far as possible (Hess, 1970), but few are knowledgeable about schools or

Parents who value education often become active in the PTA, school board, or other school-related activities.

accustomed to dealing with them. Many are awed or even afraid when faced with the prospect of talking to teachers. Often these parents had difficult times themselves as students, so they look upon teachers with a mixture of respect for their expertise and authority (as they see it) and discomfort or even resentment based on fear, mistrust, or hostility. For these reasons, and because they often have less leisure time and less flexible schedules, they tend to have fewer interactions with teachers.

Even so, most low-SES parents value education highly, including most of those who are uncomfortable around schools and teachers. They tend to be both grateful and cooperative if teachers establish themselves as people devoted to their children's best interests (and not as authority figures threatening to expel these children).

The Disadvantaged

People at the lowest SES levels are often referred to as "the disadvantaged." In our view, there has been too much emphasis on the problems and difficulties of these people (which are clearly real and not likely to go away in the immediate future) and not enough on their *potential* (also real but relatively unfulfilled as yet). Too often, being labeled as disadvantaged causes students to be written off as lost causes rather than to receive special, effective treatment likely to enable them to succeed at school.

Identification of the disadvantaged

It is worth noting who the disadvantaged are and how they got to be that way. According to economic indicators, about 20 percent of the population is disadvantaged because they are on welfare or have inadequate incomes (see Figure 23.1). In terms of race and urban versus rural status, the majority of disadvantaged families are white and a large proportion are rural. So much attention has been focused on urban blacks that many people think terms like *disadvantaged* refer primarily to this group. It is true that a greater percentage of blacks than whites is disadvantaged, but it is also true that this percentage is a minority of the total number of disadvantaged. About 80 percent of the disadvantaged are white.

Elimination of SES differences

For a time, it was thought that SES differences could be eliminated entirely through educational enrichment, especially during the first few years of life. A few still take this position (White, 1975), but most experts do not believe that SES differences can be eliminated through any quick

Figure 23.1 The increasing minority school-age population presents both an opportunity for greater intercultural enrichment and a challenge that will demand greater sensitivity and flexibility in the years ahead.

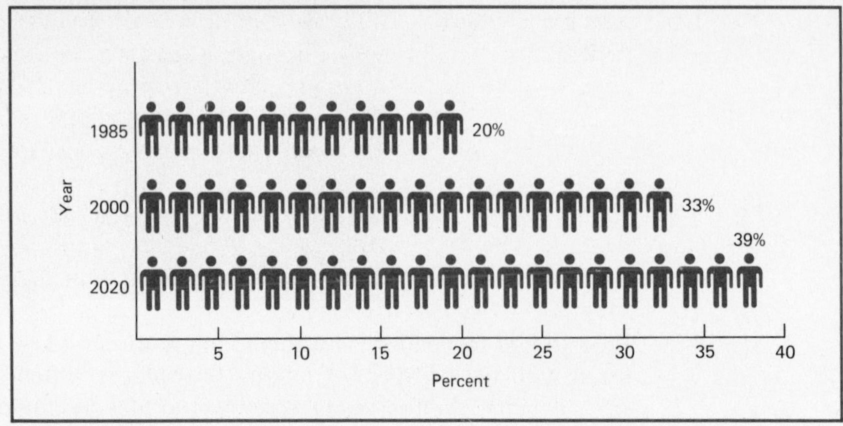

Source: American Council on Education. (1988). *One-third of a nation: A report of the commission on minority participation in education and American life*. Washington, D.C.: American Council on Education. Reprinted with permission.

and easy method. Thus Project Head Start, Project Follow Through, and other programs aimed at the disadvantaged no longer are seriously expected to eliminate SES differences in IQ, although these programs are considered helpful because of their health and nutrition benefits and because they facilitate school achievement and ultimately educational attainment (Lazar & Darlington, 1982; Miller & Bizzell, 1983; Zigler & Valentine, 1979).

The disadvantaged are often stereotyped as having values and attitudes contrary to "middle-class values," although this is not the case. To the extent that disadvantaged parents fail to nurture their children's intellectual development or mental health, this typically is not because they do not mean well or do not want the same kinds of things for their children that other parents want. The major difference between disadvantaged and advantaged parents is that the former lack the knowledge that would enable them to obtain things they want (Hess, 1970).

Cognitive environment

Furthermore, it is relevant knowledge and experience, not financial resources, that determine the quality of the "cognitive environment" that a home provides (Clark, 1983a; Gottfried, 1984; Hess, 1970; Hess, et al., 1984; Sigel, 1985). That is, children's cognitive development depends more on the modeling and intellectual stimulation they get from their parents than on the mere presence of material possessions. Parents who provide a rich cognitive environment interact with their children often (not just when they need to), frequently at length, and in ways likely to stimulate thinking (Brophy, 1977; Hess, 1970; Hess & Shipman, 1965; Hess & McDevitt, 1984). They label objects and events, explain causal relationships, discuss future activities in advance, and accompany discipline with instructions containing information as well as demands. They also answer children's questions, encourage their exploratory efforts, and, in general, provide them with a rich context of *meaning* within which to understand and assimilate new experiences. They model intellectual activity and verbal communication in everyday activities: reading newspapers and books for both information and pleasure, watching educational as well as purely entertaining television programs, and discussing their content; conversing about daily events at mealtimes; participating in social and political organizations; and visiting zoos, museums, and other educational settings.

Reaching the truly disadvantaged

Students who are truly disadvantaged do not get much of this kind of stimulation. Their parents may not even be aware of the importance of providing a stimulating cognitive environment in the home and, even if they are, may lack knowledge of what to do and how to do it. For the most part, these students need instruction that follows the same general principles outlined in the rest of this book, not something different from what is effective with other students. However, they do especially well with teachers who share warm, personal interactions with them but also hold high expectations for their academic progress, require them to perform up to their capacities, and move them along at the most rapid pace possible. In short, effective teachers break through social-class differences and other potential barriers to communication in order to form close relationships with disadvantaged students, but they use these relationships to maximize students' academic progress, not merely to provide friendship or sympathy (Brophy & Evertson, 1976; Kleinfeld, 1975; St. John, 1971).

INTELLIGENCE QUOTIENT (IQ)

Teachers form impressions, usually accurate, of their students' academic abilities very quickly, even if they do not have access to home background information and cumulative record files (Brophy & Good, 1974; Willis, 1972). They use cues such as general signs of alertness and comprehension, quality of questions and comments, and performance on academic tasks.

Origin of IQ tests

This assessment process became formalized through the use of standardized tests of intelligence and achievement, a movement that began with the work of Alfred Binet in the early 1900s in France. Binet was not trying to design a test of intelligence but to identify children likely to have difficulty in school. He analyzed the abilities that seemed necessary for school success and then worked backwards to develop tests to measure these abilities. He was looking for tests that discriminated adequately between students within each grade level. Tests that were too easy or too hard were not very useful because everyone either passed or failed, so different tests were needed for each grade. Besides the ability to discriminate, Binet's primary criterion for including a test in his battery was the degree to which the test correlated with or predicted later school success. Note that this is not the same as the degree to which a test measures some ability believed to be part of what we call "intelligence."

Binet's tests were very successful and were quickly adopted in England and America, but the psychologists who adopted them did more than just translate them into English and use them to screen children. First, they referred to the tests as "intelligence tests," abandoning Binet's detailed profiles of performance across a variety of measures in favor of a single index that came to be called the "Intelligence Quotient" or IQ. Then they elaborated the notion of intelligence testing and the concept of IQ with the following ideas about the tests and what they measure:

1. The tests are more than mere indicators of school success; they measure fundamental intellectual abilities.
2. Underlying these abilities is a generalized factor (usually called "g"). This factor is general intelligence.
3. General intelligence is transmitted genetically and thus is fixed at conception. Repeated measures may produce different scores because of situational factors or measurement errors, but theoretically, perfect measurement would yield precisely the same IQ every time for any individual.
4. Both individual and group differences are fixed and unchangeable. Differences in educational experiences or opportunities might affect the degree to which intelligence is expressed but will not affect intelligence itself.
5. Intelligence is more than simply a statistical predictor of academic achievement. It is a *cause*, usually by far the most important cause. So when students do not achieve as highly as their measured IQs lead us to expect, they are underachievers who are not working up to their abilities.

These statements combine nicely to form a consistent theory. However, *not one of them is correct*, at least in the extreme form in which each is stated. Humans possess a great many different intellectual abilities, even though many of them correlate highly with one another (Horn, 1986). Also, even though IQ tests can be constructed to yield a single score, they do not measure a single ability. There is no correspondence between an IQ score and the size or functioning efficiency of the brain or any particular part of it, and there is no single ability that we can call "intelligence" (Sternberg, 1986a, 1986b).

Diverse Conceptions of Intellectual Abilities

Diverse conceptions of intellectual abilities can be seen in the variety of tasks included on "intelligence tests." The fourth edition of the Stanford-Binet Intelligence Scale contains fifteen subtests organized into the four theoretical areas of verbal reasoning, quantitative reasoning, abstract-visual reasoning, and short-term memory (see Table 23.1), and instead of only a single IQ score, it now yields standard age scores for each of the four areas as well as a composite for the test as a whole. This emphasis on measuring abilities across a variety of areas is closer to Binet's original intention, although the utility of the four areas yielded by the new test remains to be proved by practice and research (Sandoval & Irwin, 1988).

The Wechsler Preschool and Primary Scales of Intelligence (WPPSI),

TABLE 23.1 AN OUTLINE OF THE CONTENT INCLUDED ON THE REVISED STANFORD-BINET INTELLIGENCE SCALE

- I. Crystallized Abilities
  - A. Verbal Reasoning Area Score
    1. Vocabulary: age 2–18+
    2. Comprehension: age 2–18+
    3. Absurdities: age 2–9
    4. Verbal Relations: age 9–18+
  - B. Quantitative Reasoning Area Score
    1. Quantitative: age 2–18+
    2. Number Series: age 5–18+
    3. Equation Building: age 8–18+
- II. Fluid-Analytic Abilities
  - C. Abstract/Visual Reasoning Area Score
    1. Pattern Analysis: age 2–18+
    2. Copying: age 2–9
    3. Matrices: age 5–18+
    4. Paper Folding and Cutting: age 8–18+
- III. Short-Term Memory
  - D. Short-Term Memory Area Score
    1. Bead Memory: age 2–18+
    2. Memory for Sentences: age 2–18+
    3. Memory for Digits: age 5–18+
    4. Memory for Objects: age 5–18+

Source: *This material is reprinted with permission from Thorndike, R. L., Hagen, E., & Sattler, J, (1986),* Stanford-Binet Intelligence Scale *(4th ed.). Chicago: Riverside Publishing Co.*

the Wechsler Intelligence Scale for Children, Revised (WISC-R), and the Wechsler Adult Intelligence Scale (WAIS) also contain a variety of tasks, although not as many as the Stanford-Binet. These tests are divided into subscales composed of verbal tasks (general information items, vocabulary words, series of digits to memorize both forward and backward, arithmetic word problems, items calling for statements of similarities between objects or concepts, and comprehension items asking how one should respond to problems such as finding a stamped, addressed, and sealed letter in the street or discovering a fire in a crowded theater) and performance tasks (finding the missing parts in incomplete drawings, putting scrambled cartoon panels into the right order, assembling jigsaw puzzles, and completing coding tasks in which each of ten digits is paired with a simple geometric symbol that must be written under the digit whenever it appears).

Short-form tests

The Stanford-Binet and Wechsler scales are the most reliable and best validated of the intelligence tests in wide use. There also are many short-form "IQ tests" devised for group administration that focus on just a few tasks or even only one (typically vocabulary). These group tests are notably less reliable than the individually administered batteries (Hopkins & Bracht, 1975). In any case, even when IQ is measured reliably, it does not represent a single, clear-cut ability.

Changes in IQs

IQs are not fixed at conception, either. Honzik, McFarlane, and Allen (1948) found more change than stability in a longitudinal study of middle-class children across childhood and adolescence. A majority of these children changed at least fifteen points in IQ, and a third changed twenty points or more. McCall, Appelbaum, and Hogarty (1973) reported similar findings. Changes in Stanford-Binet scores between ages two and one-half and seventeen averaged 28.5 points, and a seventh of the changes were 40.0 points or more. Furthermore, the changes were not random. High-SES children tended to maintain or gain in IQ, but low-SES children tended to drop. Gainers were described as independent and competitive in their preschool years and as independent, scholastically competitive, self-initiating, and problem-solving during elementary school. Their parents were described as providing encouragement and stimulation of cognitive activities in the home and as using rational rather than fear-oriented approaches to childrearing.

Much other research (reviewed in Willerman, 1979) confirms that high-SES children typically maintain or gain in IQ over time, and low-SES children usually lose. Also, curious, persistent children are likely to gain, but passive dependent children are likely to lose. Jensen (1969) and others interpret these data as being due to the influence of genetic IQ on personal traits as well as academic performance, but we believe that they are better interpreted as evidence of the influence of socialization (including both parental childrearing practices and education at school) on intellectual development.

Genetic Component

Human intellectual functioning clearly has a strong genetic component, but it probably is not nearly as strong as Jensen and others argue (Horn, 1986; Loehlin, Lindzey, & Spuhler, 1975; Willerman, 1979). The IQs of different social classes or racial groups can be influenced by changes in the environment (MacKenzie, 1984). Schiff and associates (1982), for example, reported that children of unskilled workers adopted as infants into high-SES families had IQs averaging fourteen points higher than those of their siblings who were reared by their natural parents. Duyme (1988) later found that adoptive children's school performance varied with the SES of their adoptive parents.

Reaction Ranges

The consensus of genetics experts is that a reaction range of about twenty-five points is to be expected for IQ scores. That is, assuming similar genes, the difference in ultimate IQs between a person growing up in a minimally stimulating environment and one growing up in a maximally stimulating environment is likely to be about twenty-five points (Scarr-Salapatek, 1975). It so happens that high-SES children typically average about 110–115 on IQ tests when they are four years old and have similar or slightly higher averages when they are adults (Tyler, 1965); urban disadvantaged children average about 95 on IQ tests when they are four years old but drop gradually to about 80 or 85 as adults. However, urban disadvantaged children in successful intervention programs maintain average IQs of about 100–105.

This difference is close to the twenty-five point difference predicted by geneticists. It is also a crucial difference, because adults with IQs in the 80–85 range are usually functionally illiterate school dropouts who tend to be unemployable or only marginally employable. Many end up on welfare or in prison. In contrast, adults with IQs in the 100–105 range are likely to at least graduate from high school, secure reasonable employment, and participate productively in society.

In addition to the enhanced understanding that IQ is not a single "entity" or fixed at birth, there is increasing argument that the genetic influence, although important, may work in multiple ways. Horn (1986), for example, suggested that intellectual abilities are derived from different genetic and environmental determinants. He argued that from an early age some individuals appear to be more uniquely prepared to bring information into their cognitive systems, whereas others are better prepared to examine and reorganize information that (less readily) enters their cognitive systems. Such individuals would be influenced differently by different environmental patterns.

INTELLIGENCE TEST DATA AND TEACHING

Intelligence testing has been controversial since its inception (Kamin, 1974). Lately, it has been under attack by those who believe that it simply labels students without doing them any good and by those who hold that intelligence tests are inherently biased in favor of white, middle-class students and against students from lower-class backgrounds and minority students (Oakland, 1977; Ogbu, 1988; Wang, Reynolds, & Walberg, 1987).

Group Differences

The latter claim does not hold up very well. Group differences in IQ are real and do not disappear when attempts are made to improve rapport with the examiner, to improve comfort in testing situations, or to use only "culture-fair" tests, although these factors may improve scores somewhat (Samuel, 1977). Still, talented minority students may be put under intense pressure when they outperform peers on intelligence tests and school assignments (Ogbu, 1988). Hence it is important to recognize that formal testing often places minority students in compromising situations and may not reliably measure the performance of some of these students.

Although intelligence tests do not measure any single, fixed general mental ability, they do measure important abilities such as understanding and following directions, reasoning and drawing conclusions, and solving problems. They also measure vocabulary, reading comprehension, arithmetic computation, and other skills taught in schools. Most people recognize these abilities as general cognitive skills important for everyone. IQ tests are not perfectly objective, however. Certain vocabulary items include words that have gone out of style or are typically used only in cities or only in rural areas, and the scoring of a few items dealing with general information or comprehension occasionally is questionable. The percentage of such items on widely used IQ tests has always been low, however, and most of them have been removed in recent revisions.

Predictors of Achievement

Despite controversy and criticism, IQ tests remain highly reliable predictors of school achievement. If used to measure students' potential and not as mechanisms to label or restrict them, IQ tests can enable teachers to make decisions that will optimize instruction. This is especially true of students who are unfamiliar with the English language, if they are tested in their native language or with nonverbal IQ tests that eliminate the need for verbal instructions and responses.

IQ tests can identify students who are bright but score poorly on typical tests due to their verbal deficiencies. Presumably, these students will achieve better if their verbal deficiencies are eliminated through effective remedial instruction on basic skills. If testing reveals poor nonverbal skills in addition to low verbal skills, poor performance is not due solely to verbal deficiency, and remediation will require more intensive and individualized treatment.

Uses and Misuses of IQ Tests

There is a real danger of misuse of IQ tests by harmfully labeling students, and in any case IQ tests have limited diagnostic usefulness because they rarely point to specific things that teachers need to do to remediate problems. They do have some uses, however, so that banning them altogether, which has been done in certain school districts, probably is a mistake.

The key is to distinguish between different kinds of IQ tests. Group-administered tests that depend heavily on reading and test-taking skills are essentially vocabulary tests that do not add anything of value to the information available from standardized achievement tests. On the other hand, individually administered omnibus IQ tests like the Stanford-Binet or the Wechsler scales provide information about a variety of abilities, and "culture-fair" tests can reveal hidden abilities among disadvantaged students or students who speak English as a second language.

TYPES OF INTELLECTUAL ABILITIES

Investigators interested in psychometric testing have searched for what Thurstone (1938) called "primary mental abilities." Some, like Cattell (1971) and Guilford (1967), developed complex models involving large numbers of specific abilities. Even such models are limited, however, because they are based on data that come only from verbal and pencil-and-paper tests and thus do not include intellectual attributes such as curiosity or social intelligence (Ford, 1986; Horn, 1986).

The distinctions between intellectual abilities that have been most useful to date are simple ones, such as the difference between associative learning and memory and higher levels of abstract thinking and reasoning. Jensen's (1969) distinction between Level I and Level II skills is perhaps the most useful formulation of this dimension.

Level I and Level II Skills

Level I skills include the association learning and rote memory that are required for tasks such as committing specific material to memory, learning to use a code that transforms the English letters into a new set of symbols, or learning to communicate in a new language. Such tasks require little reasoning or problem solving, although they do demand concentrated effort and can create cognitive strain if their demands on attention and memory are great enough. Thus tasks requiring only Level I skills are not necessarily easy, and some are beyond the abilities of most people (memorizing *Moby Dick*, typing 200 words a minute, or producing instantaneous translations for the United Nations). Level I abilities are primarily involved in mastering the basic skills taught in the early grades and in learning factual information.

Level II skills include the information-processing activities involved in perceiving stimuli and the abstract thinking and reasoning needed to solve problems, especially problems not encountered previously. They are measured in IQ test items that require one to state similarities or differences (How are an elephant and a whale alike?), supply meaningful analogies (Train is to track as automobile is to ______.), or solve abstract problems (Supply the next number: 1, 4, 9, 16, ______.). Level II skills are required to succeed in school tasks such as reading comprehension (understanding the connections between events in a story and drawing correct inferences about their implications, not just remembering the events themselves), solving most word problems in math, or understanding and applying abstract principles in any subject matter.

Although there are individual differences, there are no important social class or ethnic group differences in Level I skills. The development of Level I skills appears to be closely related to the quality and amount of schooling an individual receives. Schools are less successful in developing Level II skills, however, in part because Level II skills have a much stronger genetic component than Level I skills (Jenson & Figeueroa, 1975; Vernon, 1981).

Also, it is harder to provide direct instruction in Level II skills. We can present students with tables containing basic number facts, help students to commit these facts to memory, and immediately judge any factual answer to be right or wrong and show why it is wrong if necessary. However, the Level II skills involved in mathematical problem solving cannot be taught so directly. We can have students practice by requiring them to solve problems, and we can even instruct them in strategies such as carefully reading the problem, systematically separating the information given from the information required, and generating and testing hypotheses. These efforts, however, may not generalize to problem situations that are very different from the ones students have practiced, even if they involve the same problem-solving principles.

Part of the reason that schooling has had only marginal effects on Level II skills may be that too little instructional time is spent on higher-order goals. Elementary school mathematics instruction, for example, focuses on computational skills, without enough emphasis on conceptual understanding and problem solving (Barr, 1988; Perry, 1988; Porter et al., 1988). Teachers appear to emphasize speed and accuracy at the expense of conceptual understanding and application (Porter et al., 1988). Recent evidence, however, suggests that at least under certain conditions and for

certain tasks, speed and power (understanding) may be independent dimensions (Horn, 1986).

Increasing IQ Scores

Most educators now recognize that continuously increasing the IQs of students is not an appropriate instructional objective. Small initial increases (perhaps five to ten points across the first few grades) can be expected for disadvantaged students whose Level I skills have not been well developed at home. Few if any such gains will be seen among children whose Level I skills are already well developed before they get to school, and generalized gains in Level II abilities are not likely to occur at all. These statements refer to group averages, however; individual students may gain or lose considerably.

Lack of gain in average IQ does not mean that students are not learning or developing their cognitive abilities. Students with IQs averaging 110 are much more knowledgeable and intellectually competent at age ten than they were at age eight, even though their average IQ has not changed and even though they are in the same Piagetian stage of concrete operations. This is because IQ is a relative index of one's intellectual abilities compared to those of other individuals the same age.

Consistent IQ scores

Thus a lack of change in IQ scores over time does not mean that nothing has happened or that students possess the same skills they possessed earlier. Instead, it means that their intellectual abilities have developed at a pace that allows them to maintain the same general position, compared to other children, that they had earlier. Once children reach school age, schooling is the most important single factor affecting the rate of development of intellectual abilities (Goulet, Williams, & Hay, 1974), even though IQs do not continuously increase. Schools will be successful if they merely maintain group IQ levels (or averages on standardized achievement tests, for that matter) from year to year. The IQs of disadvantaged students, however, often slip a little from year to year. This is especially true of older elementary students who must rely more on independent reading and learning.

PROCESS APPROACHES TO INTELLIGENCE

Psychometric theorizing was the primary approach to the study of intelligence from about 1900 to 1950. Many of those working within this approach based their measures on the theory of Charles Spearman (1927), who conceived of intelligence as a single, general ability. Thurstone (1938) distinguished among primary mental abilities such as verbal comprehension, number ability, and reasoning ability.

Sternberg (1988) argued that these psychometric approaches fail to measure mental *processes*. He used the following example to make the point.

George is taller than Bill.
Bill is taller than Sam.
Who is the shortest?

Verbal and spatial approaches to problem solving

According to Sternberg, people can use different strategies to solve this problem. One person might use a *verbal* approach and decode the problem into linguistic propositions. Another might use a *spatial* approach by visualizing George, Bill, and Sam. Conventional psychometric scoring would credit both individuals with getting the right answer but would miss the differences in their mental processing.

Psychometric tests sometimes confuse different mental abilities that they purport to measure. Verbal analogies, for example, are often used to assess verbal reasoning. But if a student does not know the meaning of a word used in an analogy item, the student's failure on the item will be due to a lack of word knowledge rather than to a verbal reasoning error. Thus it appears necessary to separate the measurement of different kinds of processes (verbal versus spatial) and also to separate the measurement of mental processes from the measurement of knowledge.

Cognitive-Components Approach

Information-processing theorists have tried to separate measurements by analyzing the items and tasks that appear on tests of intelligence into their underlying cognitive components (Sternberg, 1988). Thus, by definition, this cognitive-components approach deals with a level of complexity that is at least equal to the dimensions being measured on a test. With a verbal analogy, for example, such as lawyer is to client as doctor is to (a) medicine, (b) nurse, (c) patient, and (d) kill, one would not simply score the item as correct or incorrect (as in the psychometric approach) but would attempt to look at how the individual used (or failed to use) available information and processes. An investigator, for example, might examine encoding to see what process the person used to figure out what each word meant. Another analysis might examine inference—the process used to analyze the relation between the first two terms and the third term. Finally, one might examine how the person applied this relation to the third term in order to decide among the answer options (application). Thus one can investigate the speed and accuracy with which *each* component of information processing is performed and assess how adequately the process is carried out. The cognitive-component approach offers a new means of examining information processing but does not fundamentally challenge or alter the content of conventional intelligence tests.

Systems of Theorizing

Those who propose systems viewpoints believe that intelligence is much more integrated and complicated than psychometric and information-processing theories suggest. Rather than search for static or even dynamic processes that produce relatively stable assessments of individual abilities, they attempt to understand an integrated whole consisting of various parts. Two good examples of systems theorizing are Gardner's (1983, 1988) and Sternberg's (1985, 1988) theories of human intelligence.

Gardner's Multiple Intelligences Gardner (1983, 1988) argued that intelligence is not a single entity composed of multiple abilities but, instead, that there are multiple intelligences, each important in its own right and independent of the others. Gardner defined *intelligence* as the ability to solve problems or to develop outcomes and products that are valued in one or more cultural settings. Ability to solve a verbal analogy is not sufficient reason to believe that an individual can identify and solve problems in actual social settings. In studying intelligence, Gardner argued the need to move away from tests and to look instead at more naturalistic sources of information about how individuals develop skills that are important to their way of life. What aspects, for example, define intelligent practices for surgeons, hunters, choreographers, tribal chiefs, and athletic coaches?

Gardner and his colleagues have considered diverse abilities that might be defined as intelligence and have examined what is known about the development of different skills in normal children and about what happens when various types of brain damage occur. His research group has studied special populations, such as prodigies and children with learning disabilities. They have trained individuals in certain skills to see if the training transfers to other skills (Does training in musical ability influence mathematical or verbal performance?).

Types of intelligence

Gardner's work has resulted in a list of seven intelligences, although he makes no claim that this is a final or complete list. The list includes two types of intelligence that have been stressed in the psychometric tradition: *linguistic–verbal* and *logical–mathematical*. Gardner noted that our society emphasizes linguistic and logical-mathematical intelligences because much testing is historically based on this combination of skills. A third intelligence is *spatial intelligence*—the ability to form a mental model of a spatial setting and to operate using that model. Sailors, surgeons, and painters are examples of individuals who have developed spatial intelligence. The fourth ability is *musical intelligence*, and the fifth is *bodily–kinesthetic intelligence*—the ability to solve problems or to fashion products using one's body (as dancers and craftspeople must do).

Gardner also identified two forms of personal intelligence that are important in a complex modern world. *Interpersonal intelligence* is the ability to understand what motivates other people and how to work with them. Successful salespeople, politicians, teachers, and religious leaders are all likely to possess high interpersonal intelligence. *Intrapersonal intelligence* is the capacity to form an accurate model of oneself and to use that model to function effectively in everyday living.

Gardner argued that these seven intelligences work together (as a system) to solve problems and to yield useful personal and societal outcomes. He suggested that all persons are different because we all have unique combinations of intelligences.

Gardner's ideal school

Schools Gardner questioned the meaningfulness of an education in which there is a core curriculum and a set of facts that everybody should know. He suggested that there should be more adjustment of curriculum and instruction to individuals' combinations of aptitudes. His vision of the ideal school is based on two assumptions: (1) not all people have the same interests and abilities, and we learn in somewhat different ways; (2) no one can learn everything because there is simply too much to learn.

Therefore, informed choice is necessary. Gardner called for an individual-centered school that is rich in assessment of individual abilities and proclivities and seeks to match individuals to both curriculum areas and methods of instruction. After a few years of schooling, an attempt would be made to match individuals with various kinds of jobs that are available in their cultures.

Gardner proposed new roles for educators that might make this vision a reality. Assessment specialists would try to understand the abilities and interests that students bring to school. Student curriculum brokers would match students' profiles, goals, and interests to particular curricula and styles of learning. Teachers would be free to do what they are supposed to do—teach subject matter in their preferred style of teaching. The job of master teacher would be demanding and involve supervising and guiding other teachers and making sure that the curriculum was appropriately balanced.

Sternberg's triarchic theory

Sternberg's Triarchic Theory Sternberg (1985) contended that intelligence is composed of three basic parts: *conceptual*, *creative*, and *contextual*. The conceptual part includes the information-processing components used in intelligent thought (e.g., to solve analogies or comprehend text). These conceptual processes are of three basic kinds: *executive processes* are used to plan what one is going to do, to monitor the strategy, and to evaluate it after a task is completed; *nonexecutive processes* are the performance components used to do a task; and *knowledge-acquisition components* are learning processes used to figure out how to do a task in the first place.

Sternberg (1988) argued that the components of intelligence do not operate in a vacuum; rather, they are affected by a person's experience with a task or practical situation. Thus triarchic theory suggests that good tests of intelligence should measure coping with relative novelty and automatization of information-processing components. Hence when we confront problems, we should bring a set of well-functioning skills for processing information as well as an ability to adapt to new situations.

Creative processes

In the triarchic theory, information processing is measured in ways similar to strategies used in the cognitive-components approach. Sternberg has developed new and useful techniques for measuring novelty by creating tests of a person's ability to see old problems in new ways or new problems in old ways. He proposed the following example as one way to deal with an individual's ability to respond to novel situations creatively. Rather than presenting only the analogy "Hero is to admiration as villain is to (a) treachery, (b) contempt, (c) wonder, (d) affection," one can make the analogy more a test of dealing with novelty by adding hypothetical conditions. Individuals might be asked to suppose that villains were lovable, for example; then what would the solution to this problem be?

Practical intelligence

The third aspect of the triarchic theory is contextual—the application of intelligence to everyday contexts. *Practical intelligence* is essentially what many people refer to as common sense; however, intelligence tests do not measure practical intelligence in any direct way. Sternberg and others (e.g., Peters, 1988) argued that one must distinguish between practical and academic intelligence because it is possible that individuals may be high in one area but not in the other.

Sternberg is presently developing various ways in which practical intelligence might be measured, such as recognizing a logical fallacy that is presented in a newspaper or television advertisement or assessing *tacit knowledge*—the informal knowledge one needs to get ahead in specific situations but which rarely is explicitly taught. To assess tacit knowledge one might ask a person to suppose that he or she is in the first year in a new job and has too many activities to get done in the time allocated. The question would require the person to prioritize activities and select which to pursue in the next three weeks.

Shapers

According to Sternberg, progress has been made in measuring adaptation to everyday environments, but sometimes the best answer to a problem of adjustment is to change the environment to suit oneself. He contended that really successful people—the ones who make a difference in the world—tend to be "shapers" who know what they are good at and try to influence the environment so that they can use these skills in most of their work. They either minimize the importance of their weaknesses or find someone else to compensate for them.

Sternberg argued that both the theory of multiple intelligences and the triarchic theory of intelligence are broader than standard psychometric theories. The psychometric point of view still dominates the testing of both children and adults, although we are beginning to measure intelligence in much more diversified and interesting ways.

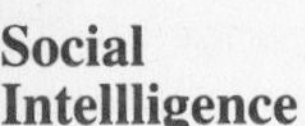

Social Intellligence

In addition to the long-standing criticism that IQ tests are unfair to certain groups because any test is more appropriate to one culture or context than to others (Ogbu, 1988), there has been the realization that such tests do not measure the practical or social aspects of intelligence or the complexities typically associated with real-life tasks (e.g., one has to define the problem in a complex setting).

Academic intelligence versus practical intelligence

Peters (1988) argued that there are important differences between what is measured by intelligence tests and practical intelligence in everyday living. First, most problems that students address in school have already been solved by someone else, and there is often a correct way to approach them. In life, however, certain problems may take days, weeks, or years to solve, and some have no solutions at all. Second, school problems often come neatly packaged, unlike life's problems. The solution to a physics problem depends on physics knowledge. To solve a real-life problem, we may have to use several types of knowledge (e.g., medical, political, mathematical). Third, practical problems often demand skills that are not normally taught in schools or measured by IQ tests. Schools do not teach sensitivity, intuition, or creativity, for example, which are necessary components of practical intelligence. Finally, practical problems often have several solutions; one must decide which ones are best or good enough, often using criteria that are complex and difficult to identify. Do we want a design that is cheap, for example, one that will last, or a combination of those criteria?

Self-assertion and integration

According to Ford (1986), self-assertion and integration are useful constructs for defining and assessing social intelligence. When people transact with their environment to assert, preserve, or expand their individuality or potency, they are seeking self-assertive social outcomes. In contrast, when they create, maintain, or strengthen interdependencies among themselves and others, they assert integrative social outcomes.

"Equifinality principle"

Many situations require a balance of self-assertive and integrative functioning, and because different goals tend to be appropriate in various situations, it is desirable for people to be socially intelligent in terms of both self-assertion and integration. In discussing the balance of self-assertion and integration, Ford noted the complexity of making assessments of social intelligence by observing that assertive behaviors can be used to accomplish integrative goals (defending a friend), and integrative behaviors can sometimes be used to accomplish self-assertive goals (e.g., being nice to others to acquire their resources). Thus he suggested the need for using the "equifinality principle" when making judgments about social intelligence. This principle asserts that depending on the person and the situation, different behaviors can lead to the same outcome. Thus one cannot search for social intelligence by looking at the superficial qualities of a person's social behavior, because that behavior must vary considerably in order for a person to maintain effective functioning in a variable environment. Rather, one must look at people's social goals to understand the meaning of their behavior and at their attainment to assess their social intelligence. Highly capable people can behave in very unintelligent ways when they are in unfamiliar social environments; conversely, people with limited capabilities may function adaptively in social contexts that are highly stable and supportive.

Compared to the arguments that were being made only a decade ago, it is clear that those who currently study intelligence view it as much more multifaceted. In particular, the notions of practical intelligence and social intelligence suggest a growing concern for adaptive behavior that is relevant in particular *contexts*. Speed of processing information may be an important aspect of intelligent behavior in some contexts, but in other social contexts the ability to share information may be more important than the ability to acquire it. Although the implications of the study of practical and social intelligence for schooling are not immediately clear, they suggest the need for greater consideration of diverse talents and skills that individuals bring to the classroom and perhaps the need for teachers to pursue more comprehensive goals (helping students to acquire both self-assertive and integrative skills).

Future Role of Intelligence Assessment

Gardner has serious reservations about intelligence tests. However, he believes that in the future, schools will make assessments of students that have curriculum implications that are more pervasive than decisions currently made on the basis of conventional IQ and standardized achievement tests. He based his view about the future of testing on a belief that tests of tomorrow will be broader (address seven or more intelligences rather than one or two) and fairer than present tests. Sternberg's work illustrates the advances that have been made and the problems that remain to be solved in the area of intelligence. Ford's conceptualization of social intelligence introduces new issues in assessment that await measurement solutions.

As we wait for these advances in testing, it is important to note that existing measures of intelligence provide only a little of the information needed to understand an individual's capacity for intellectual performance. Although intelligence tests measure students' ability to perform in school-related situations, other factors are critical to school performance (student motivation and effort, quality of instruction, match between assigned work and students' skills). Furthermore, teachers and administrators must look for talent in various forms and realize that students who have limited skills in one area may have well-developed skills in others. Too often teachers do not recognize and encourage the strengths and skills that low-status or disadvantaged students bring to the classroom. Hence we must look for various expressions of ability in classrooms (e.g., Marshall & Weinstein, 1984). Furthermore, as we attempt to define intelligence more broadly, the distinction between academic intelligence and social and practical intelligence is an important one for educators to keep in mind.

GENDER DIFFERENCES

Historically, gender differences have been the basis for pervasive differences in how children were treated at school. Until this century, formal education beyond basic skills was designed primarily for males, reflecting the cultural expectation that males, but not females, would need education in academic subjects as preparation for occupational and social-political roles that they would play in society. Schooling was often segregated by gender, and even for females whose education extended for some years, the content consisted of the fine arts and certain domestic arts believed important as preparation for household management rather than around the sciences and humanities. This changed drastically as gender segregation in occupational roles and associated cultural beliefs about gender differences waned, although there still is debate about the nature and extent of gender differences in intellectual and personal attributes and their implications for education.

Gender-role-differentiation beliefs

As a result of the women's liberation movement and a host of related social and cultural changes that have occurred since World War II, gender segregation in schooling and in society in general has for the most part disappeared, along with many of the cultural beliefs and practices that accompanied it. Gender roles are no longer as rigid and pervasive as they used to be, although most of us still expect certain differences between males and females and still view certain behavior as masculine while viewing other behavior as feminine (Deaux, 1985). Some of these gender-

Although gender discrimination still unarguably exists, progress has been made toward minimizing society's differing attitudes about and expectations for boys and girls.

role-differentiation beliefs are expressed in relatively direct ways. Beliefs that boys have more aptitude for, interest in, or future occupational need for science and mathematics than girls do, for example, appear to lead a great many parents, teachers, and school counselors to act in ways likely to encourage boys to develop positive learner self-concepts in mathematics and science and to continue to take courses in these areas but to discourage girls from doing so (Eccles, 1987). Other gender-role-differentiation beliefs are expressed much more subtly. Analyses of children's literature and of the stories included in basal readers and literature anthologies at school, for example, have shown that male characters are much more likely than female characters to play a major role in stories, to be depicted within career roles, and to be active and decisive rather than passive or ineffectual (Garrett-Schau & Scott, 1984; Marten & Matlin, 1976; Stewig & Knipfel, 1975).

Reviews of the voluminous literature on gender differences in intellectual and personal attributes reveal surprisingly little support for our still-powerful cultural tendencies to expect sizable gender differences and thus to treat boys and girls differently (Halpern, 1986; Hyde & Linn, 1986; Maccoby & Jacklin, 1974). In the intellectual sphere, males tend to score higher on tests of visual-spatial ability and mathematical ability, and females to score higher on tests of verbal ability. These differences have been consistent but very small, too small to justify the attention and emphasis that often are placed on them. Furthermore, they have become smaller still in recent years, sometimes to the point of disappearing altogether (Feingold, 1988), presumably as a result of recent cultural awareness of sexism and related reduction in gender-differentiated socialization and education.

Personality domain in the classroom

In the personality domain, males have been found to be more aggressive (across a broad range of situations and types of aggression), and females have been found to smile and laugh more (Hyde & Linn, 1986). In the classroom, boys are more active and salient than girls and have more of almost every kind of interaction with the teacher that may be measured (Brophy, 1985). In part this is because boys are more prone to misbehave in the classroom than girls, so teachers criticize or punish boys more often, and they initiate interactions with them more frequently to give them procedural instructions, check their progress on assignments, or generally monitor and control their activities. However, teachers are also more likely to call on boys than girls during lessons, and boys are more likely than girls to call out answers without first being recognized by the teacher and thus to coopt response opportunities for themselves. These patterns are just as likely to appear in classes taught by female teachers as in classes taught by male teachers, so they are due primarily to gender differences in the behavior of the students themselves rather than to gender differences between teachers in the ways that they interact with male versus female students (Brophy, 1985).

Sadker and Sadker (1986) identified gender differences in styles of participation in social conversation that they believe are pervasive in our society and thus carry over into classroom: (1) Men speak more often and frequently interrupt women; (2) listeners appear to pay more attention to male speakers, even when female speakers use similar styles and make similar points; (3) women participate less actively in conversation but do more gazing and passive listening; and (4) women often transform declarative statements into more tentative statements ("This is a good restaurant, isn't it?") that may limit their ability to influence others. The Sadkers also claimed that teachers not only accept these gender differences in social assertiveness but reinforce them in subtle ways. In one of their studies, for example, boys were eight times more likely than girls to call out answers rather than raise their hands and wait for teacher recognition. Yet the teachers were more likely to caution the girls against calling out and more likely to simply accept the boys' answers without reprimanding them for failing to raise their hands and wait for recognition.

Teacher treatment of pupils

The Sadkers also suggested that teachers tended to be bland when giving feedback to girls' responses but to be more animated and also more detailed and specific when giving feedback to boys. They also cited research suggesting that when complex tasks need to be done, teachers may simply do the tasks for girls but give boys detailed instructions and feedback that will enable them to do the tasks for themselves.

Other investigators have also reported subtle differences in teacher treatment that might reinforce assertiveness and independence in boys but dependency or inhibition in girls. Grant (1984), for example, suggested that although teachers may have more positive attitudes toward and even higher expectations for girls compared to boys, this apparent advantage can work against the girls' long-run best interests if it is associated only with teacher pressures toward conformity and responsibility but not autonomous achievement striving. Much teacher encouragement and reinforcement directed at girls focus on dress, grooming, manners, and other social role issues, whereas most of the encouragement and reinforcement that teachers direct to boys focuses on their achievement striving and accomplishments.

Differences in feedback

Similarly, Dweck and associates (1978) studied the evaluative feedback given by teachers in two fourth-grade and one fifth-grade classrooms. There were no gender differences in general frequencies of praise or criticism related to academic work, but there were qualitative differences in the degree to which such evaluative feedback referred to the intellectual aspects of the work (competence or correctness) or to nonintellectual aspects (neatness, following directions, speaking clearly). For positive evaluations of work, about 94 percent of statements directed to boys concerned the work's intellectual quality, but the corresponding figure for girls was only about 81 percent. Thus boys were almost always praised for having responded correctly or having done work competently. Girls were praised for the same reasons most of the time, but on a relative basis they were much more apt to be praised for neatness, following directions, or speaking clearly. Thus good performance on their part was less often attributed to their own personal competence. Teachers' negative evaluations of students' work showed a different pattern. Here only about 54 percent of the criticism directed to boys referred to poor intellectual quality of work, but the corresponding figure for girls was 89 percent. Thus criticism of girls' work almost always indicated that they lacked competence or did not understand the work, whereas criticism of boys' work often referred to nonintellectual aspects that did not imply lack of competence. Taken together, these patterns of evaluative feedback probably would have more favorable effects on boys than girls in developing self-confidence, sense of efficacy, and a tendency to attribute academic successes to internal factors (ability and effort) but to attribute failures to external factors (inappropriate or overly rigid teacher responses to the form rather than the substance of the work).

These subtle differences suggesting teacher tendencies to reinforce assertiveness and achievement striving in boys but to reinforce conformity and responsibility in girls do not appear in every classroom, and some may appear in the classrooms of only a minority of teachers. Still, they are useful as illustrations of pervasive yet subtle differences in ways that teachers may treat boys versus girls. Differential treatment along these lines that is likely to discourage the achievement striving and progress of girls is especially likely to appear in advanced courses in science and mathematics. Becker (1981) described the academic environment for boys in such courses as academically and emotionally supportive but described the academic environment for girls as one of benign neglect. Again, this was true whether the teachers were male or female.

Subject-Matter Achievement Patterns

Becker's study is just one of many indicating that gender differences in classroom behavior interact with gender differences in patterns of motivation and achievement in various subject-matter areas. The latter differences typically favor boys in science classes and favor girls in English classes; in mathematics, achievement-test-score patterns show no differences or even favor girls in the early grades and on tests of number computation but favor boys in the later grades and on tests of mathematical reasoning (Feingold, 1988; Hogrebe, Nist, & Newman, 1985; Hyde & Linn, 1986; Marshall & Smith, 1987).

Environmental causes of gender differences

It is tempting to link these subject-matter achievement differences to gender differences in related intellectual abilities and ascribe them all to genetic influences, but arguments for environmental causes are at least as compelling as those for genetic causes. For one thing, the gender differences in average scores are very small, whereas the individual differences within each gender are very large. Furthermore, there are exceptions to the typical patterns of average differences that would not occur if relatively straightforward genetic influences were at work. Scores on elementary school reading-comprehension tests, for example, favor girls in Canada and the United States but favor boys in England, Nigeria, and Germany (Johnson, 1976; Preston, 1962). Similarly, although gender differences in mathematics achievement typically favor boys in the continental United States, they favor girls in Hawaii (Brandon, Newton, & Hammond, 1987). Along with the previously mentioned finding that gender differences in cognitive ability and achievement-test-score patterns have been decreasing in recent years, these findings suggest that gender differences in school experiences and outcomes are due at least as much to cultural socialization of children into contrasting gender roles as to innate predispositions. To the extent that we as a society begin to expect to see equal achievement from boys and girls in different subject-matter areas, we may begin to see it.

To the extent that we expect gender differences in motivation and achievement in different subject-matter areas, however, such differences are likely to continue. Thus at least until recently, American teachers and students tended to view reading as a feminine activity and thus to expect girls to respond more positively to it than boys, despite the preponderance of males as central characters in children's literature (Bank, Biddle, & Good, 1980). There are similar tendencies to look on math and science as masculine activities (Eccles, 1987). These differential expectations can engender self-fulfilling prophecy effects, as several researchers have noted. Leinhardt, Seewald, and Engel (1979), for example, observed in second-grade classrooms during individualized reading and mathematics instruction, when teachers circulated around the room to interact with individual students. They found that the teachers had more academic contacts and spent more time discussing the subject matter with girls than with boys during reading instruction but showed the opposite pattern during math instruction. More generally, research on gender differences in classes in particular subject areas suggests that girls are relatively more active and likely to interact with the teacher in connection with the subject matter in reading and language-arts classes but that boys are relatively more active and likely to interact with the teacher concerning subject matter in math and science classes (Wilkinson & Marrett, 1985).

Teacher contact

Brophy (1985) made the following two points in discussing these findings. First, these differential patterns appear to be due mostly to gender differences in the attitudes and classroom behavior of the students themselves rather than to differences in treatment of boys versus girls by teachers. Therefore, if teachers are to counteract such gender differences effectively, it will not be enough for them merely to treat boys and girls in the same ways in the same situations. In addition, it will be necessary consciously to treat them differently, such as calling on boys more often

Counteracting gender differences

in reading and language arts and on girls more often in mathematics and science, to counteract gender differences in rates of volunteering in these subjects. Second, the findings concerning girls' progress in math and science are somewhat more serious and disturbing than those for boys in reading and language arts. Boys' problems with elementary reading seem to be primarily motivational—many boys acquire the idea that reading is primarily for girls and that they will not enjoy it. Relatively few boys, however, construe the problem as one of ability by acquiring the belief that boys lack aptitude for reading. Many girls, however, acquire the notion that they lack aptitude for mathematics and science, especially at the secondary level. When this is true, it will be necessary to motivate them not only in the sense of developing their interest in and willingness to take courses in these subjects but also in the sense of developing in them the expectation that they can achieve success if they apply reasonable effort.

The notion that motivation (as opposed to ability) is the probable cause of differential academic performance of boys and girls is strengthened by data showing that gender differences in mathematics and reading performance narrow considerably when efforts are made to increase the attractiveness of tasks (Asher & Markell, 1974; Bleakley, Westerberg, & Hopkins, 1988; Christoplos & Borden, 1978). For young males it seems especially important to use materials that are appropriately stimulating and action oriented. For young females it is important to use materials that define sex roles more broadly.

Improving Classrooms for Boys and Girls

Teachers can be helpful to girls by encouraging them to be more active in the classroom and by making systematic efforts to observe and get to know each girl as an individual. We speak of making a systematic effort because that is what will be required. If teachers merely respond passively to students, they will spend most of their time with boys. Many girls will not come to the teacher; the teacher must go to the girls. We believe that this effort is worthwhile, however, since society cannot afford to allow overrestrictive sex-role expectations to pressure girls into hiding their abilities or talents. Teachers can help by encouraging girls to speak their minds, calling on them to participate if they do not volunteer, assigning them to leadership roles for group projects, and taking similar actions to encourage them to be more assertive.

Broadening perspectives for girls

Teachers can also broaden the perspectives of young girls by helping them to realize that the full spectrum of career alternatives is open to them and by using learning experiences such as stories involving females in leadership positions or compositions or discussions about the work of female scientists. Many books detail accomplishments of women, and they should be available in classroms. Teachers can also help by encouraging girls to take advanced courses in science and mathematics.

Teachers also need to provide boys with appropriate academic encouragement and reinforcement. Teachers, for example, should expect boys as much as girls to have interest and talent in poetry, literature, and the fine arts and should treat them accordingly. To the extent that teachers treat boys ineffectively in more general ways, the problem is likely to be not so much with all of the boys as with the subset of boys who are both low achievers and hostile or alienated learners. Low-achieving girls are often dependent and conforming students who elicit teacher sympathy and concern, but many low-achieving boys are hostile and disruptive students who engender attitudes of rejection and hostility in their teachers (Brophy & Evertson, 1981; Brophy & Good, 1974). Teachers sometimes come to view these boys as lazy, immature, maladjusted, and troublesome and begin to treat them in ways that produce undesirable self-fulfilling prophecy effects. Teachers, especially those who fear loss of classroom control, need to work hard to sustain a professional manner in dealing with such hostile and potentially disruptive students (most of whom will be low-achieving boys).

Summary

The SES and social-class factors correlate with other variables such as race, ethnicity, and various religious, political, and social customs into clusters of characteristics that teachers should take into account in their planning. Well-educated parents, for example, are likely to be more interested in school activities than are low-SES parents, especially those who have had limited educations and disappointing associations with schools. Teachers must deal with the problems that disadvantaged students present but also consider these students' needs for relevant knowledge, experience, and cognitive stimulation.

Informal teacher assessments of students' academic aptitudes may be supplemented by standardized intelligence and achievement tests. Binet developed his tests to measure abilities related to school success, but American and British psychologists later established the notion of a single IQ score based on a number of questionable assumptions. The Stanford-Binet and Wechsler scales are reliable and well validated as predictors of school success, but they do not measure any single, easily definable ability. Furthermore, even though there is a strong genetic component, scores vary with time and other variables over a considerable range.

Intelligence tests have value as predictors of academic performance and may be especially useful for identifying potential that is currently masked by disadvantaged home backgrounds or difficulties with the English language. Intelligence testing can also be misused in ways that simply label students without helping them deal with their problems.

Current work in intelligence testing emphasizes the variety in human abilities and the need to consider the processes that people use in responding to problems along with the outcomes of their problem-solving efforts. Gardner identified seven forms of intelligence and believes that schools should be organized to foster the development of all seven types and to respond to individual differences in patterns. Sternberg developed the triarchic theory of intelligence and called for assessment and follow-up that would consider the conceptual, creative, and contextual aspects of intellectual functioning. Other investigators are concerned with developing measures of practical or social intelligence to complement the paper-and-pencil measures that have been emphasized to date.

The gender roles into which societies socialize their children interact with the student roles stressed in schools to create gender differences in how children respond to various school situations and how teachers respond to boys versus girls. Our society, and consequently our schooling, promotes much less extensive and rigid gender-role differentiation than in the past, which appears appropriate given data indicating that gender differences in intellectual and personal traits are few in number and very small in size and significance. Still, there are tendencies for boys to be more active and assertive in the classroom than girls and for gender differences in patterns of interest and achievement in various subject-matter areas. Teachers need to guard against drifting into self-defeating patterns of interaction with low-achieving and disruptive boys, as well as against interacting with girls in ways that encourage and reinforce obedience and conformity rather than intellectual assertiveness and achievement striving.

Questions and Problems

1. Persons promoted to supervisory positions in business and industry sometimes refuse promotion or resign their new jobs after a few weeks. They prefer to remain ordinary workers, at lower salaries and without administrative titles. Why?
2. Many Americans resist terms such as *socioeconomic status* or *social class* because they seem inconsistent with our traditional values of individualism and equality. If you feel this way, try to keep those feelings from biasing your responses when answering the following questions: (1) What is your own SES background? (2) How has it affected your development to date by influencing the experiences you have had? (3) Have you undergone changes in beliefs, attitudes, or behavior due to a change in SES? (4) How might your SES affect your interactions with students of various backgrounds?
3. How can schools and teachers simultaneously accomplish *both* of the following: (1) realistically take into account differences in SES, IQ, and other variables that can affect students' interest or readiness and (2) promote equal opportunity and quality education for all?
4. Under what circumstances, if any, would you request IQ testing for a student? Why? How would you use the results?
5. Explain how a student can achieve quite well at school, showing impressive gains on standardized achievement tests each year, and yet show no gain at all in IQ.
6. Gender-role socialization is so much a part of our society that we are all affected by it to some degree. In what ways have you been affected by it?
7. If you are male, are you reluctant to show affection or emotions or to

do things traditionally associated with a woman's role? If you are female, are you inhibited about asserting yourself, exercising leadership and authority, competing, or doing things that are traditionally associated with men?

8. How do you react to men who have characteristics traditionally labeled as feminine or to women who have characteristics traditionally labeled as masculine? What does this mean for you as a teacher?
9. As a teacher, how would you deal with a situation in which girls assume a passive role in teamwork (they take notes) while boys assume more active roles (they bisect the frog, wire the circuit, etc.)? How could you change students' attitudes and beliefs as well as their behavior?

Case Studies

LANGUAGE BARRIER. Tran Van Do is a recent Vietnamese immigrant assigned to Jo Cornell's class. He is the same age as the other students but cannot participate much or do many assignments because he knows very little English. Jo arranges to have him tested, and he is given the parts of the WISC-R that do not require language facility. His performance on these subtests would translate into an IQ of 115 if matched by equivalent performance on the verbal subtests. What, if anything, does this tell Jo about how to plan instruction for Tran?

EXPLORATION IN SEXISM. Janet Trumbower and Henry Marshall team teach at the sixth grade in an open-plan school. They have decided to examine the degree of sexism present in their social studies instruction—including curriculum content, student-student dialogue, teacher-teacher interaction, and teacher-student conversations. They intend to involve students in the process. How might they make this a valuable learning experience for everyone? How could they collect evidence (what would be looked at and by whom)? Are there things that they should be careful to avoid in this process?

CHAPTER

Cognitive Style and Creativity

CHAPTER OUTLINE

OBJECTIVES

When you have mastered the material in this chapter, you will be able to

1. Define the cognitive style called conceptual tempo, distinguishing it from simple response speed
2. Explain how differences in conceptual tempo are related to school learning and problem solving and how conceptual tempo is most effectively modified
3. Contrast the characteristics of field-dependent versus field-independent persons
4. Explain how the field-dependence/independence cognitive style affects students' preferred learning modes and teachers' preferred instructional patterns
5. Describe how creativity is measured and how it relates to IQ
6. Discuss the two general criteria of creative responses and the value of creativity measures to education
7. Describe several techniques for fostering student creativity

Most individual-difference variables relevant to education can be classified easily as either intellectual abilities or personality traits. Cognitive style and creativity, however, involve elements of both cognition and personality.

COGNITIVE STYLE

Cognitive-style variables

Cognitive style refers to the way that people process information and use strategies to respond to tasks. Several cognitive-style dimensions have been identified (Sigel & Coop, 1974), including: (1) attention to the global features of stimuli versus fine details; (2) discrimination of stimuli into a few large categories versus many small ones; (3) tendency to classify items on the basis of observable characteristics versus similarities in function, time, or space versus common possession of some abstract attribute; (4) quick, impulsive versus slow, painstaking problem-solving behavior; (5) intuitive, inductive versus logical, deductive thinking; and (6) tendency to impose one's own structure on what is perceived versus allowing perceptions to be structured by the specific features of the focal stimulus, influences from the context in which it is embedded, or other external sources.

Inspection of this list reveals why cognitive styles are called styles rather than abilities. They refer to *how* people process information and solve problems, not *how well*. Sometimes they do affect the quality of performance, however, because each style is helpful in performing certain tasks but not others. In this chapter we discuss two cognitive-style dimensions that are especially important for education: conceptual tempo (cognitive reflectivity versus cognitive impulsivity) and psychological differentiation (field independence versus field dependence).

Conceptual Tempo

Differences in conceptual tempo

Conceptual tempo is a cognitive-style dimension referring to the degree to which people are cognitively impulsive versus reflective in deciding on a response when two or more alternatives are plausible. Differences in conceptual tempo are most obvious (and are measured) in matching-to-sample tasks, in which people are shown a drawing of an object or figure and asked to indicate which of several other drawings is identical to the sample. The other drawings are all similar to the sample in varying degrees, but only one is exactly like it. *Cognitively impulsive* people inspect the alternatives briefly and then quickly select one. They have short response latencies (they respond quickly), but they may make a lot of errors because they do not take the time to compare carefully. Often they do not even inspect all of the alternatives (Kagan & Kogan, 1970), responding instead as soon as they come to one that is not obviously wrong. *Cognitively reflective* people deliberate before responding, carefully considering each alternative. They take longer to respond but make fewer errors.

When conceptual tempo was first described (Kagan et al., 1964), the emphasis was on speed of response. Since then, it has become clear that other qualitative characteristics that affect accuracy must be considered.

Characteristics of fast responders

In addition to those who are either fast and inaccurate or slow and accurate, some people are both fast and accurate or both slow and inaccurate. Thus some people respond quickly because they are efficient at a task rather than impulsive in their problem-solving behavior. Also, fast responders—even fast/inaccurate responders—are not necessarily impulsive in any general sense. Speed of response in matching-to-sample tasks does not correlate consistently with personal traits other than speed of response in other problem-solving situations in which more than one plausible alternative is available (Block, Gjerde, & Block, 1986). Specifically, fast responders are not especially likely to be hyperactive, unable to delay gratification, or otherwise impulsive in the classroom or in everyday life. Thus the term *cognitively impulsive* is misleading because it connotes general behavioral impulsivity. If anything, individuals who are both fast and inaccurate in problem solving can be described as *anxious* or *defensive* rather than impulsive (Wapner & Connor, 1986). Far from being carefree and unconcerned about making mistakes, they are anxious and vulnerable, so they respond "impulsively" in an attempt to cope with (and to escape from) stressful problem-solving situations.

Reading progress

Conceptual tempo is related to early reading progress (Kagan & Kogan, 1970) and to performance on other school tasks that require careful discrimination of similar yet different stimuli (*p* versus *q*; *if* versus *it*). Students predisposed to notice such fine differences in detail and to withhold interpretation until first impressions are verified are likely to read more accurately than other students.

Differences in conceptual tempo are believed to be shaped by modeling and socialization in the home, although Kagan, Pearson, and Welch (1966) showed that conceptual tempo can be socialized in school as well. They found that cognitively impulsive boys who spent a year in the classroom of a very reflective teacher became notably more reflective themselves. This does not have clear implications for teachers, however, because not all teachers are cognitively reflective and because a reflective conceptual tempo is not always superior to an "impulsive" one. Rollins and Genser (1977) found the reflective tempo to be superior for problem solving in simple tasks that offered only a few plausible response alternatives. In complex tasks involving many dimensions and possible response alternatives, however, "impulsive" responders who moved immediately to consideration of the most likely solutions generally solved faster and with fewer errors than extreme reflectives who tested each possible solution systematically and thus wasted a lot of time examining unlikely solutions.

Strategy use and demands of a task

The point is that *success in problem solving is determined by the match between the strategy that a person uses and the demands of a task.* This can be seen in the results of attempts to modify conceptual tempo. The earliest interventions concentrated on slowing response speed but not on changing children's information-processing or problem-solving strategies. Cognitively impulsive children were cautioned to take their time and to "pay attention" but were not directed to attend to anything specific. Typically, they learned to respond more slowly but made just as many errors as before.

Problem-solving training

Investigators who trained children to use more efficient problem-solving skills obtained much better results. Meichenbaum and Goodman (1971), for example, used a cognitive behavior-modification approach involving modeling and verbalized self-instructions to teach fast/inaccurate responders to talk to themselves to provide guidance during problem solving. First, the experimenter performed the task while talking aloud to model not only problem-solving behavior but also the self-instruction that facilitates accuracy. Then the children performed the task while the experimenter instructed them aloud, and as they achieved consistent success, verbalization of self-instructions was reduced to whispering and finally to silent (inner) speech. The experimenter's modeling stressed not only the importance of responding slowly and carefully but also the actual process:

> I have to remember to go slowly to get it right. Look carefully at this one (*the standard*). Now look at these carefully (*the response alternatives*). Is this one different? Yes, it has an extra leaf. Good, I can eliminate this one. Now, let's look at this one (*another response alternative*). I think it's this one, but let me first check the others.

The modeling also included errors and how to cope with them, a feature that probably was especially valuable for fast/inaccurate responders who tend to be anxious in problem-solving situations:

> It's OK, just be careful. I should have looked more carefully. Follow the plan to check each one. Good, I am going slowly.

Self-instructional training

Even this explicit modeling was not enough by itself, however, because children exposed only to the modeling learned to respond more slowly but did not improve their accuracy. Only the children who received self-instructional training in addition to modeling became more accurate problem solvers. This seems to have clear implications for teachers dealing with fast/inaccurate responders or any students whose information-processing or problem-solving strategies are inappropriate. Self-instructional training may be especially useful for anxious students who are unlikely to remain calm and rational when they must solve problems on their own. Teacher demonstrations or even extensive modeling may not be enough for these students, who may need opportunities to role play successful problem-solving strategies by verbalizing self-talk out loud and getting feedback.

Psychological Differentiation

Field-dependent versus field-independent people

A second cognitive-style dimension with implications for education is *psychological differentiation*, also known as *field dependence versus field independence* or as *global versus analytic perceptual style* (Witkin et al., 1977). People who are low in psychological differentiation (*field dependent*, global) have difficulty differentiating stimuli from the contexts in which they are embedded, so their perceptions are easily affected by manipulations of the surrounding contexts. People who are high in psychological differentiation (*field independent*, articulate) perceive more analytically. They can separate stimuli from context, so their perceptions are less affected when changes in contexts are introduced.

Examples of psychological differentiation

Psychological differentiation is exhibited in a remarkable variety of situations. One of the most basic is when the stimulus in question is the person's own body. Witkin et al. (1962) observed persons seated in specially constructed chairs in rooms that made use of optical illusions to confuse them about directionality and gravity. Field-dependent people were very confused by these situations and did not do well when asked to estimate the degree to which their bodily positions differed from the vertical upright. Some were off as much as 45 degrees, so that they literally did not know which way was up. Field-independent people were less affected by these manipulations.

Rod and frame tests

Similar results were obtained with the "rod and frame" test. Here, people in a darkened room are presented with a luminous rod that can be tilted in any direction and asked to adjust the rod until it is vertical. To make the task even more difficult, the rod is surrounded by a luminous frame that can also be tilted in any direction. Certain tilts produce optical illusions like those in the "tilted rooms" at amusement parks. Again, field-independent people are more successful than field-dependent people in adjusting the rod to the true vertical and resisting optical illusions.

Embedded-figures tests

Psychological differentiation also occurs in cognitive tasks such as embedded-figure tests, in which familiar stimuli are embedded in more complex configurations that mask them ("Can you find five animals in this picture?"). Field-independent people are good at such tasks, but field-dependent people have trouble with them. More generally, field-independent people are likely to impose their own organization on a perceptual field, but field-dependent people tend to adhere to the existing structure. This is true for social perceptions as well as for perceptions of the physical world. Field-dependent people's perceptions and opinions are strongly affected by those of other people, whereas field-independent people are more likely to resist social pressures and make up their minds on the basis of their own perceptions.

Social dimensions of cognitive style

The adaptive values of these cognitive styles vary with culture and with the role demands of the situation. In social situations, especially ambiguous ones, field-dependent people are more attentive to and make more use of prevailing social frames of reference, look at the faces of others more frequently for cues as to what they are thinking, attend more to verbal messages with social content, take greater account of external social referents in defining their attitudes and feelings, and get physically closer to and interact more with others. In general, they prefer to be with people in social situations (Witkin et al., 1977). As a result, field-dependent people tend to be better liked by others; to be perceived as warm, tactful, considerate, socially outgoing, and affectionate; and to know and be known to more people than are field-independent people. The latter have a more abstract, theoretical, analytical, and impersonal orientation. This makes them more able to resist external pressures toward conformity, but it also makes them more likely to be perceived as cold, distant, or insensitive. These statements apply to people at the extremes of the dimension of psychological differentiation. Most people are not nearly so extreme, although they may tend more toward one set of attributes than the other.

Note that neither cognitive style is superior in all situations. Field-independent people are better equipped to deal with situations that call for impersonal analysis, but field-dependent people are better equipped for situations that place a premium on social perceptiveness and interpersonal skills.

CLASSROOM IMPLICATIONS

Group work versus independent study

Psychological differentiation affects students' preference for, and response to, different teaching methods (Witkin et al., 1977). Field-dependent students tend to prefer to learn in groups and to interact frequently with the teacher, whereas field-independent students may respond better to more independent and more individualized learning opportunites. Field-independent students are more likely to have self-defined goals and to respond to intrinsic motivation, but field-dependent students may require more extrinsic reinforcement and more teacher structuring as to what to do and how to do it. They will work to please the teacher and be more motivated by praise and encouragement than field-independent students, who tend to pursue their own goals.

Subject-matter preferences

There are few if any overall achievement differences between students who vary in this cognitive style, but there are differences in preferences for, and achievement in, various subjects. Field-independent students prefer and generally do better in math and science, whereas field-dependent ones generally prefer and do better in the humanities and social studies. Field-independent people prefer occupations that place a premium on theoretical and analytic interests: mathematician, scientist, architect, engineer, dentist, production manager, carpenter, forest service, farmer, mechanic, artist. Field-dependent students tend to choose occupations that stress social skills: social worker, minister, counselor, probation officer, teaching, selling, advertising, administration, politics (Witkin et al., 1977).

Psychological differentiation among teachers

Within the education profession, field independence is likely among math, science, and industrial-arts teachers, but field dependence is likely among social studies, humanities, or general elementary school teachers (Frank, 1986). In addition to subject matter, however, *psychological differentiation affects the ways that teachers instruct*.

Field-independent teachers prefer impersonal teaching situations and emphasize the more cognitive or theoretical aspects of teaching, whereas field-dependent teachers prefer frequent interaction with students and class discussion. Field-independent teachers use questions mostly as instructional tools to be asked when introducing topics or inducing students to process information, whereas field-dependent teachers use questions primarily to check on student learning following instruction. Field-independent teachers tend to emphasize their own standards and to formulate principles themselves when explaining material to students, but field-dependent teachers tend to involve students more in organizing the content and sequencing the teaching-learning process and to encourage them to formulate principles themselves (Gordon & Gross, 1978; Witkin et al., 1977).

Field-independent teachers are more likely to inform students when they are incorrect, to tell them why they are incorrect, and to express displeasure with students who are performing below capacity. Field-dependent teachers are less likely to express critical feedback. More generally, field-dependent teachers are interested primarily in creating and maintaining positive attitudes and good group dynamics, and only secondarily in subject content, whereas field-independent teachers have the opposite priorities. Finally, students of field-independent teachers perceive them as emphasizing application of general principles, but field-dependent teachers are seen as teaching facts (Witkin et al., 1977); see Table 24.1.

Learning outcomes

The psychological differentiation dimension also is associated with learning outcomes. Field independence correlates with mathematics and spatial abilities even when IQ is controlled (Satterly, 1976). More generally, students tend to achieve more in subject-matter areas that they prefer, and field-independent students do better when matched in cognitive style with their teachers (Garlinger & Frank, 1986; Witkin et al., 1977).

Even so, it is not clear that students or even teachers would be better off if matched in ways likely to reinforce their preferences, especially not if they lie at the extremes of the psychological differentiation dimension. Extreme field independents have social adjustment problems, and extreme field dependents are conforming to the point that they seem to lack a mind of their own. Such individuals might be better off in the long run if they could learn to appreciate and function more frequently in their nonpreferred orientation.

Need for teacher awareness

It is important that teachers learn to recognize and respect both orientations, to build on students' strengths, and to avoid letting stylistic differences lead to discriminatory practices or personality clashes. Field-independent teachers can help meet the needs of field-dependent students by structuring their learning experiences enough to enable them to cope effectively, providing encouragement and praise, being objective and supportive when criticizing mistakes, and, in general, developing a positive personal relationship with them. Field-dependent instructors accustomed to indirect communication that depends on perception of subtle social cues will need to be more direct with field-independent students who may not recognize critical feedback unless it is presented explicitly (nor are they likely to resent or become upset by such criticism). Also, field-independent students are not likely to respond strongly or even positively to warmth or praise from the teacher (nor should the teacher feel rejected when this occurs). Finally, it is important that field-dependent teachers respect field-independent students' needs for privacy and distance and that they avoid penalizing these students unreasonably for low social participation.

The value of teacher consideration of students' cognitive styles is shown in a study by Doebler and Eicke (1979). Fifth-grade teachers in the experimental group were given information about their students' field dependence-independence, along with suggested strategies for teaching each type. Compared to students in control classes whose teachers were not

TABLE 24.1 FIELD-DEPENDENT AND FIELD-INDEPENDENT LEARNING STYLES

Learning Styles	
Field Dependent	**Field Independent**
Perceives globally	Perceives analytically
Experiences in a global fashion; adheres to structures as given	Experiences in an articulated fashion; imposes structure or restrictions
Makes broad general distinctions among concepts; sees relationships	Makes specific concept distinctions with little overlap
Social orientation	Impersonal orientation
Learns material with social content best	Learns social material only as an intentional task
Attends best to material relevant to own experience	Interested in new concepts for their own sake
Requires externally defined goals and reinforcements	Has self-defined goals and reinforcements
Needs organization provided	Can self-structure situations
More affected by criticism	Less affected by criticism
Uses spectator approach for concept attainment	Uses hypothesis-testing approach to attain concepts
Teaching Styles	
Field Dependent	**Field Independent**
Prefers teaching situations that allow interaction and discussion with students	Prefers impersonal teaching situtations such as lectures; emphasizes cognitive aspect of instruction
Uses questions to check on student learning following instruction	Uses questions to introduce topics and following student answers
Uses student-centered activities	Uses a teacher-organized learning situation
Viewed by students as one who teaches facts	Viewed by students as encouraging them to apply principles
Provides less feedback; avoids negative evaluation	Gives corrective feedback; uses negative evaluation
Strong in establishing a warm and personal learning environment	Strong in organizing and guiding student learning

TABLE 24.1 (*continued*)

How to Motivate Students	
Field Dependent	**Field Independent**
Through verbal praise	Through grades
Through helping the teacher	Through competition
Through external rewards (stars, stickers, prizes)	Through choice of activities, personal goal chart
Through showing the task's value to other people	Through showing how the task is useful to them
Through providing outlines and structure	Through freedom to design their own structure

Source: S. Garger and P. Guild. 1984. "Learning Styles: The Crusicial Differences." *Curriculum Review* 23.

given this information, the experimental students developed better self-concepts and attitudes toward school. Teachers usually do not have access to such data, but they should be able to identify students' cognitive styles by observing and interacting with them.

Frank (1984) studied field-independent and field-dependent students' learning of content from taped lectures under four conditions: (1) no notes, (2) student's notes only, (3) outline framework plus student's notes, and (4) complete outline plus student's notes. Frank found that field-independent students performed well under the student's notes only condition, because they tended to take efficient notes and to organize them within an outline format. The field-dependent students, however, seemed to need the teacher-provided outline. Frank contended that the typical classroom procedure in which the teacher lectures and students take notes may favor the performance of field-independent students. To reduce this effect, he suggested that teachers provide students with external aids (e.g., an outline on the board or a handout that organizes the presentation) that may help the field-dependent students without harming the field-independent students.

In summary, it is clear that cognitive style is one dimension on which teachers can plan for individual differences in students. Teachers, however, need to use cognitive-style information as stimulation for thinking about individuals rather than as a basis for treating students as groups (Good & Stipek, 1984; Messick, 1984).

CREATIVITY

Most of us value and can recognize creativity when we encounter it, but it is difficult to define and measure. Many writers argue that it is part of (or the same as) general intelligence but contrasts in the creative achievements of people with equal IQs dispute this (MacKinnon, 1962). Creativity is associated with IQ, but IQ tests do not measure it directly (Hattie &

Rogers, 1986; Sternberg, 1986a, 1986b). It is not a single process, so there is little point in searching for a single creativity score comparable to an IQ score.

Convergent and divergent production

Guilford (1959) provided a perspective on creativity in his model of mental abilities that he believed collectively form a map or structure of intelligence. Included in the model is a list of mental operations, of which one is basic to what many investigators mean by the creative process (see Figure 24.2). Guilford contended that information retrieval from memory storage can involve two kinds of operations—convergent production or divergent production. *Convergent production* involves searching for specific information to solve a problem that requires a single, logically necessary, correct answer (If Mary is taller than Sally and Sally is taller than Gwen, who is the tallest?). In contrast, *divergent production* is required for problems that can be answered in many different and equally acceptable ways (What can we do with a pencil besides use it for writing? How can we make ancient history meaningful to today's students?).

Figure 24.1 Examples of Types of Content in Guilford's Structure of Intellect Model.

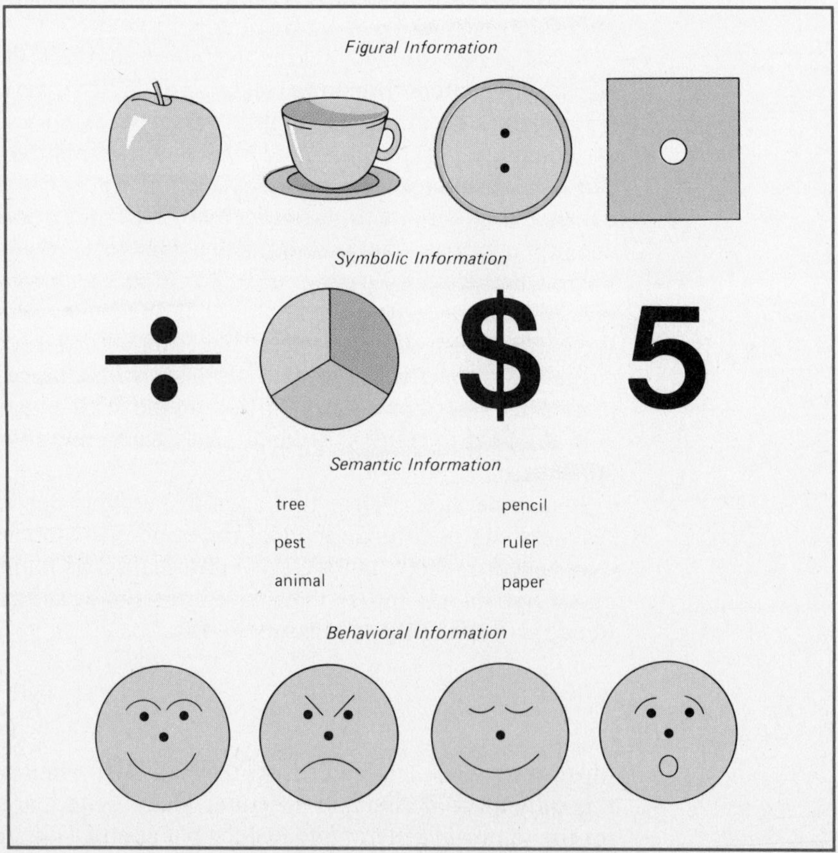

Source: C. J. Maker, *Teaching Models in Education of the Gifted* (Austin, TX: PRO-ED Inc., 1982). Reprinted by permission of the publisher.

Guilford (1959) determined that creativity involves divergent thinking, as represented by the fluency, flexibility, and originality of thought processes. Individuals high in ideational *fluency* produce a great many problem-solving ideas in a short time. Those high in *flexibility* can shift easily from the problem-solving approach they have been using if new problems or conditions call for new approaches. Individuals high in *originality* can make unusual or even unique suggestions. Thus highly creative individuals can generate ideas at a rapid pace (fluency), "break set" in order to attack problems from a new perspective (flexibility), and generate new and genuinely different ideas (originality).

Traits needed for creativity

Measures of Creativity

Torrance (1966) has developed a variety of tests for measuring divergent thinking. They include generating unusual uses for a box or a brick, completing an ambiguous partial sketch by turning it into an interesting pic-

Figure 24.2 Guilford's Model of the Structure of the Intellect. Guilford identifies five basic mental operations: cognition, memory, divergent thinking, convergent thinking, and evaluation. Each of these operations can process each of four kinds of content (behavioral, semantic, symbolic, and figural), and each of these twenty combinations of mental operations with content categories can produce any of six kinds of mental products: units, classes, relations, systems, transformations, and implications. Creativity tests call for divergent thinking, usually to produce transformation of figural or symbolic content.

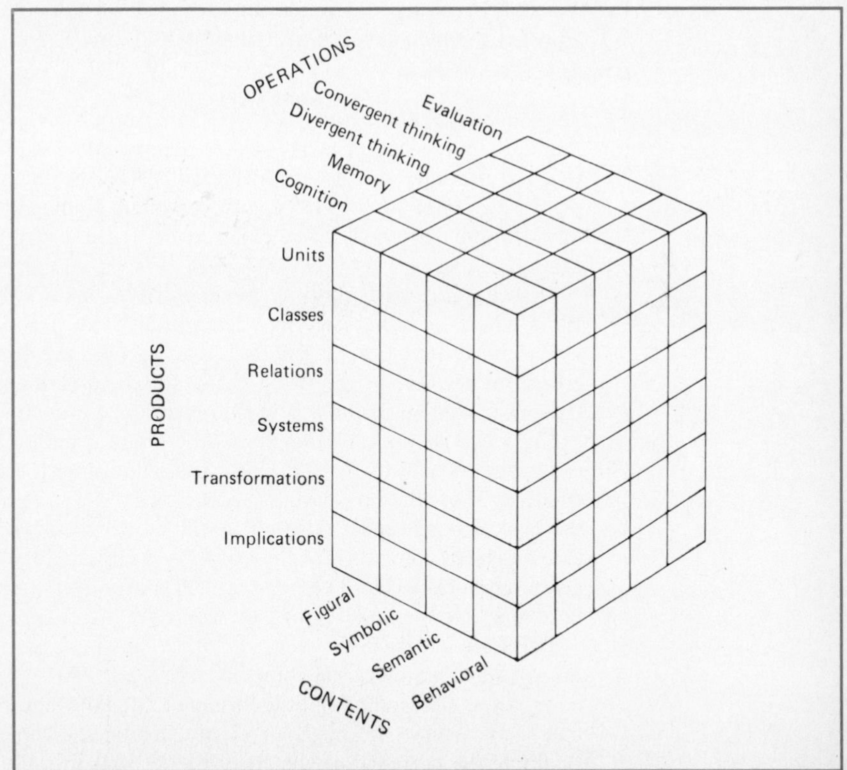

Source: From J. Guilford, "Three Faces of Intellect." *American Psychologist*, 1959, *14*, 469–479. Copyright © 1959 by the American Psychological Association.

ture, and suggesting how a stuffed animal might be improved to make it more interesting to play with. Responses to these tasks are scored for fluency, flexibility, and originality.

Relationship to IQ

These tests have low but significant correlations with IQ, averaging about 0.20 (Torrance, 1975). In general, there is a closer relationship between divergent production ability and IQ at the lower levels of the IQ range than at the higher levels; that is, individuals with low IQs generally do not score very well on divergent production tests. People who score highly on such tests usually have at least average IQs, but a high IQ does not guarantee high divergent production ability.

Wallach and Kogan (1965) discovered that the relationship between IQ and scores on so-called creativity tests varies with the tests used. Moderate or even high correlations with IQ may occur if a "creativity test" has a time limit and includes convergent production tasks in addition to divergent production tasks. On the other hand, if the "creativity test" is confined to divergent production tasks, and if testing is conducted under relaxed or playful conditions, the relationships between fluency, flexibility, and originality scores and IQs drop almost to zero.

Getzels and Jackson (1962) were early leaders in exploring the relationship between divergent thinking, intelligence, and creative performance. Within a sample composed primarily of extremely bright students, they noted some striking differences between those highest in IQ but low in divergent thinking and those highest in divergent thinking but lower in IQ. The following excerpts are responses from a stimulus card showing a man seated in an airplane and another showing a man alone in an office.

> *The low-divergent thinking student*: "Mr. Smith is on his way home from a successful business trip. He is very happy and he is thinking about his wonderful family and how glad he will be to see them again. He can picture it, about an hour from now, his plane landing at the airport and Mrs. Smith and their three children all there welcoming him home again."
>
> *The high-divergent thinking student*: "This man is flying back from Reno where he has won a divorce from his wife. He couldn't stand to live with her anymore, he told the judge, because she wore so much cold cream on her face at night that her head would skid across the pillow. He's now contemplating a new skid-proof face cream."
>
> *The low-divergent thinking student*: "There's ambitious Bob down at the office at 6:30 in the morning. Every morning it's the same. He's trying to show his boss how energetic he is. Now, thinks Bob, maybe the boss will give me a raise for all my extra work. The trouble is that Bob has been doing this for the last three years, and the boss still hasn't given him a raise. He'll come in at 9:00, not even noticing that Bob has been there so long, and poor Bob won't get his raise."
>
> *The high-divergent thinking student*: "This man has just broken into this office of a new cereal company. He is a private eye employed by a competitive firm to find out the formula that makes the cereal bend, sag, and sway. After a thorough search of the office he comes upon what he thinks is the current formula. It turns out that it is the wrong formula and the competitor's factory blows up. Poetic justice!" (Getzels & Jackson, 1962, pp. 39–40)

Getzels and Csikszentmihalyi (1975) stressed that the high-divergent students could free themselves from the stimulus, but the low-divergent students were fixated by it. "For the low-divergent students the problem was essentially one of following up on what others had given them. If the picture stimulus is of a man in an airplane, he tells a story about travel. . . . For the high-divergent thinking subject, the problem was one of constructing something that he wants to give. The picture may be of a man in an airplane, but the story he wants to tell is about a divorce" (p. 99). Such differences led Getzels and Csikszentmihalyi to view creativity as problem finding more than as problem solving.

Validation of Creativity Tests

Torrance, Tan, and Allman (1970) reported that undergraduate-teacher trainees who scored higher on situational tests of creativity demonstrated more creative teaching behavior in the classroom six years later. Predictive validity studies of Torrance's creativity tests are supportive but not decisive. They predict achievement in areas such as writing better than in fields such as business (Torrance, 1975), perhaps because the tests best measure verbal fluency.

Situational creativity

There is still little evidence that situational creativity measures can predict creative and original performance later in life. At present, it appears that such measures do *not* predict creative performance among adult professionals, although they usually correlate positively (but weakly) with indicators of creativity in nonprofessional endeavors (Mansfield, Busse, & Krepelka, 1978).

Novelty and value as creative standards

What, then, is creativity? Although there is no universally accepted definition, two criteria are widely accepted. *First, a product must be novel if it is to be called creative. The second criterion is value. A creative product must reflect value by being judged correct (a technical solution works) or good (the music is satisfying).* Additional criteria have been proposed, but novelty and value are the two most general standards.

Fostering Creativity in the Classroom

Valuing creativity in students

How can teachers foster creativity in the classroom? Probably the first step is to *learn to value it*. Nearly everyone values the concept of creativity, but student creativity in the classroom can be irritating, disruptive, or even threatening to teachers. Getzels and Jackson (1962) found that teachers preferred students low in divergent thinking to those higher in divergent thinking, even though all of the students were bright and even though the divergent thinkers produced more imaginative and original responses. This is not really surprising. Schools are inherently rule-bound and conservative institutions (necessarily, to a degree), so much student creativity contrasts or even conflicts with what is routine, expected, and "correct." If students are urged to think and act creatively, some of their responses will be both novel and valuable, but others will be silly, obscene, outrageous, or bizarre. Teachers who intend to foster creativity will have to accept this.

Importance of childhood experiences

Clues about factors that may foster creativity have been gathered in retrospective reports of the childhood experiences of creative adults, who typically report being exposed to a rich variety of experiences as children and being encouraged to ask questions and test their ideas through active experimentation. Also, they usually were encouraged to pursue their interests through collections, hobbies, development of specialized knowledge, or pursuit of talents or skills (Wallach, 1970).

Torrance (1962) included such ideas in his recommendations for developing creativity in the classroom, and added several others: encourage manipulation of objects and ideas, teach students to test their ideas systematically, teach students to value creative thinking, caution against premature or unwarranted dismissal of "wild" ideas, teach students that everyone has creative potential (creativity is not something possessed only by a few "geniuses"), and induce creative thinking by asking students to generate alternative solutions to problems, to speculate on what might have happened if historical events had been different, to suggest worthwhile inventions or improvements, or to solve other problems that call on their divergent production abilities.

Encouraging creativity

Note that most of these suggestions can be incorporated into the regular school curriculum, without special materials or the scheduling of special "creativity time." Teachers can learn to do many of these things automatically by habitually asking themselves, when planning activities and assignments, "Have I included opportunities for students to think and solve problems in connection with this topic? Have I included opportunities for them to use their divergent production abilities?" The result of this should be teacher behavior like that described above, as well as assignments involving creative writing or action projects requiring research and development of a sophisticated (for the student) product.

Special programs

Special programs designed to facilitate divergent thinking or other aspects of creativity are available. The *Productive Thinking Program* (Covington et al., 1974) is a self-instructional program for fifth and sixth graders. It attempts to develop creative problem-solving abilities and attitudes through booklets that teach problem-solving skills in a cartoon format.

Pursuing individual interests can bring children very real rewards, both emotionally and cognitively.

Many of the problems involve convergent thinking, but some involve divergent thinking as well. Evaluations indicate that the program improves student performance on tests of divergent thinking, although best results are obtained when teachers instruct students themselves rather than distribute the materials for use in self-instruction, as the developers intended (Mansfield, Busse, & Krepelka, 1978).

Brainstorming

Parnes (1967) developed a program that emphasizes a technique called *brainstorming*—generating ideas in response to some question or problem (typically in a group). Students are encouraged to volunteer whatever ideas occur to them, regardless of whether the ideas seem reasonable or correct. Ideas are recorded for later evaluation, but no criticism is permitted until after everyone's ideas have been contributed. The Parnes program is used mostly in college and high school courses, where it has been generally successful in increasing divergent thinking scores. Myers and Torrance (1966) developed sets of workbooks designed to foster creativity in elementary school children. Their approach involves teaching students to value creative thinking and provides practice in a variety of divergent production tasks. It may be useful in improving divergent thinking ability, especially when teachers guide students in the use of workbooks, although no clear data are yet available (Mansfield, Busse, & Krepelka, 1978).

Teaching creative thinking

Davis (1986) has developed a variety of methods for teaching students to think creatively. In one study, college students were asked to think of improvements for a doorknob. Three methods of encouraging creative thinking were tested, of which two proved effective. One group was given a list of seventy-three possible ways to make changes. This method was *not* very effective, apparently because students did not try to think creatively but instead simply worked their way through the list, following as many of the suggestions as they could. Most of the creative thinking had already been done for them.

A second group received lists containing only seven suggestions: add or subtract something, change color, change the material, rearrange the parts, change shapes, change size, change design or style. This short list effectively stimulated creative thinking in that the students produced about twice as many ideas as those with the long list or those who received no suggestions. The list was specific enough to stimulate a variety of ideas but not so complete as to inhibit creativity.

The group that produced the most ideas, however, used a matrix or checkerboard technique that involved analyzing the stimulus into its various dimensions and then combining the values of these dimensions into new arrangements. To generate new solutions to the energey crisis, for example, one axis of a two-dimensional checkerboard matrix could be the source of power (wind, solar, ocean tides, geothermal). Each of these power sources could be combined with ideas arranged along another axis indicating uses for the power (heating homes, transportation, cooking, manufacturing). Cross-referencing these two lists produces novel combinations that stimulate creative thinking. In this vein, ideas about changing doorknobs might be stimulated by combining consideration of where the knob is placed on the door with various lock arrangements (dead bolt versus spring lock versus no lock at all; key versus no key). Students using this method produced more ideas for the doorknob problem than students in any other group, even though they did not work as long as students using the short list of seven suggestions. Thus different approaches affected fluency (rate of idea generation), although there were no significant group differences in the originality of ideas.

Results of creativity training program

New creativity training programs and materials appear regularly. Most have at least some value in that students usually enjoy them and find them stimulating. However, it is questionable whether such programs actually produce any genuine, lasting, or generalizable improvements in creative-thinking abilities. Results are mixed, and even supportive results involve scores on tests of divergent production rather than more rigorous criteria such as evidence of increased creativity in schoolwork or in everyday life. Furthermore, higher divergent production scores can be due to increased persistence on criterion tests by students who know that they are expected to perform well, to the advantages provided by training on tasks that are very similar to the items on the tests, or even to improved attitudes or confidence.

Overcoming barriers to creativity

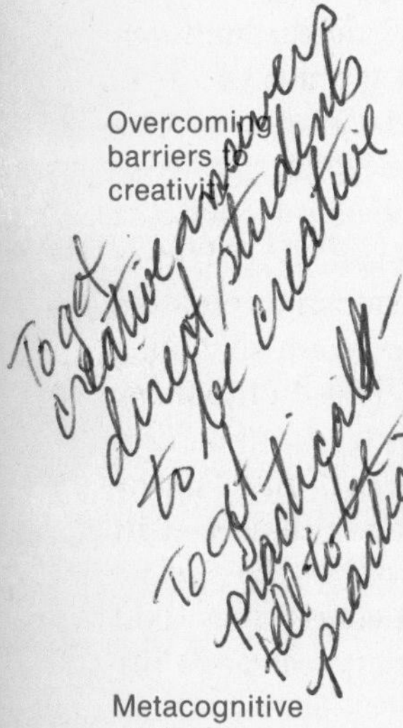

The last factor may be the most important. Manske and Davis (1968) found that students gave more original responses to problems when they were merely instructed to be original and more practical responses when they were instructed to be practical. Wallach and Kogan (1965) concluded that students who were intelligent but not highly creative were merely disinclined, rather than unable, to use their imaginations. Many students' barriers to creative thinking reside solely in their own minds: social inhibition, fear of failure, lack of confidence, or even the belief that they lack creativity (Davis, 1986). If this is true, student creativity may be fostered most effectively not by special training programs (although they may be useful) but by teachers who model and encourage creativity every day and create a classroom atmosphere that values originality and playful consideration of ideas.

Metacognitive strategies

In the past, educators focused on helping gifted students to develop their creative talents more fully. Recently, there has been increased emphasis on the need for *all* students to become more creative and independent in their classroom learning (Sigel, 1984). One area that has received special attention involves enabling students to develop metacognitive strategies for monitoring their own learning. Costa (1984) recommended twelve strategies that teachers can use to increase students' capacity for metacognition:

1. *Planning strategy*. Teachers should help students to think about the decisions they are going to make and the strategies they will follow in completing assignments. Students should be encouraged to plan ahead and to outline the task they will need to complete. If tenth graders must write term papers, for example, the teacher could have them outline their work early in the semester and provide them with

feedback about their outlines rather than giving feedback only after the papers are completed. Students should make decisions about how to allocate their time to the assignment and how to evaluate their own work.

2. *Generating questions*. It is important for students to learn to generate questions about the material they are studying and to propose some of their own learning activities. Such thinking should help them to develop self-awareness and take more control of their own learning.
3. *Choosing conscientiously*. Teachers can help students to explore the consequences of their choices and decisions before, during, and after the act of deciding. Questions that challenge students to consider the number of references that might be available on a topic, for example, are useful in getting students to think through whether or not a paper will generate new questions that should be examined or will merely summarize a topic on which considerable research has already been conducted.
4. *Evaluating multiple criteria*. Students can be encouraged to think about their responses from a variety of viewpoints and to consider how persons representing various groups might react to a report that they have prepared. Also, teachers should encourage students to think about the relative strengths and weaknesses of their work and the work of classmates.
5. *Taking credit*. The teacher should routinely describe publicly the things that students have done well and help students to identify their strengths. Students should be encouraged to identify with what they have done and to invite feedback from peers in the spirit of making their products better.
6. *Outlawing "I can't"*. Costa encourages teachers consciously to inform students that excuses such as "I don't know how to" or "I'm too slow" are unacceptable. Students should identify what information they require, what materials they need, or what skills they lack but do so as part of a problem-solving effort rather than a withdrawal attempt.
7. *Paraphrasing or reflecting ideas*. Inviting students to translate, compare, and paraphrase the teacher's ideas or those of other students stimulates them to become better listeners to others' ideas as well as their own. This helps them to think seriously about generated ideas and to become more comfortable in analyzing the relative strengths and weaknesses of potential actions.
8. *Labeling students' behaviors*. The teacher can help students to develop better awareness of their own cognitive processes by labeling their behaviors as they occur (e.g., "What you are doing is called an experiment," "That is hypothetical thinking," "I can see that you've made at least two inferences in that assumption," "What I see you doing is making a plan of action.").
9. *Clarifying students' terminology*. Teachers can help students to become more active thinkers by encouraging them to extend their think-

ing when they use vague, nonspecific terminology. Students might say, for example, "It's not fair" or "That's lousy." Teachers can help students clarify these values by asking questions such as, "What would be more fair?" or "In what sense is it lousy?"

10. *Role playing and simulations*. Costa contended that role playing can stimulate metacognition because when students assume the role of another person, they assume the thinking and attributes of the person. This can be an important step in helping them to become more hypothetical in their thinking.
11. *Journal keeping*. Writing ideas in a diary or log helps students to synthesize their thoughts and translate them into actions. Such written records also provide opportunities to revisit initial perceptions and beliefs. If teachers encourage students to look back at a process such as how they made decisions about a project, the students may gain valuable insight into how they think and learn and make these decisions more deliberately in the future.
12. *Modeling*. Teachers who demonstrate metacognition will help students to think in similar ways. Teachers can share their goals and objectives, give reasons for their actions, and explain their thinking.

Costa's recommendations are helpful for teachers who are trying to teach general higher-order thinking skills, especially when they are used to encourage students to develop original solutions and new ways to state problems. For other suggestions about teaching thinking and creativity, see Davis (1986).

Summary

Cognitive style and creativity involve elements of both cognition and personality. They refer to *how* people process information and solve problems, not *how well* they do so. Conceptual tempo is a cognitive-style dimension dealing with impulsivity versus reflectivity in choosing between two or more plausible alternatives. Psychological differentiation is a second dimension involving field dependence versus field independence or global versus analytical perceptual style. Both dimensions have implications for students' preferences for and responses to different learning situations, as well as teachers' approaches to teaching.

Creativity is difficult to define or measure. It is associated with IQ, but IQ tests do not measure it directly. Elements such as divergent production, fluency, flexibility, and originality are involved. Guilford, Torrance, and Getzels and Jackson have done extensive work in the area, but valid and reliable tests of creativity have yet to be developed.

Teachers can foster student creativity in several ways. Valuing creativity and accepting divergent thinking are critical, as is the provision of a wide variety of experiences and opportunities for students to use creative talents. Activities such as brainstorming, searching for novel solutions to problems, and dealing with several dimensions of a problem simultaneously appear to have value as well.

Questions and Problems

1. As a teacher, when should you teach to a student's strength (in a way that matches the student's cognitive style)? When should a student be required to learn in a way that forces the student to develop new skills (e.g., require a field-independent student to work in a group)?
2. Some students having problems learning to read will make many errors because of cognitive impulsivity; others will make many errors because of more serious deficiencies in perception or memory. How can teachers distinguish these two types of students?
3. Why is it not enough to teach cognitively impulsive students to slow down and take their time before responding?
4. Should participation in class discussions be taken into account in grading? Why or why not? Can you and your classmates reach a consensus on this question?
5. Although psychologists are unable to define and measure *creativity* satisfactorily, most people think they know what the word means and can recognize creativity when they see it. How do you define creativity? What are some of the things that indicate it?
6. Do you think of creativity as a genetic trait, as an ability that is learned but not teachable, or as something that is teachable? What implications does this have for your teaching?
7. Would you supplement the regular curriculum with special activities designed to foster creativity? Why or why not?
8. How might Costa's 12 principles apply to a unit you plan to teach?
9. Summarize in your own words how field-dependent students differ from field-independent students. What does this imply about your teaching?

Case Studies

DRILL. Royal Grind wants to make sure that his junior high English students know their grammar, so most class time is devoted to workbook exercises (underline the right word, cross out the wrong word, correct the misspelled words) and diagraming sentences. Students work individually, and Royal spends much of his time correcting their papers. What changes could he introduce that would (1) still allow him to stress grammar but (2) introduce elements that would be more appealing to field-dependent students and would allow all students to make more use of their creativity?

MENTAL MATHEMATICS AND ESTIMATION. Jane Keystone is a sixth-grade mathematics teacher who works in a large, departmentalized school where she teaches five math periods a day. She stresses that mathematics does not merely involve obtaining correct answers but is also a way to organize information quantitatively so that decisions can be made. Her instruction is similar to that of other teachers, except that every day she takes fifteen minutes for mental mathematics and work on estimation. Which students are most likely to benefit from Jane's teaching? Why? How can Jane adjust instruction so that more students can benefit?

CHAPTER

Educating Students with Special Needs

CHAPTER OUTLINE

OBJECTIVES

When you have mastered the material in this chapter, you will be able to

1. Explain why some students' handicapping conditions merit special classroom plans
2. Discuss three problems associated with the education of students with handicapping conditions in special settings and programs
3. Explain how Public Law (P.L.) 94-142 attempts to remedy the problems of special education through mainstreaming within the least restrictive environment
4. Explain how teachers can prepare themselves and their students to deal effectively with handicapped students
5. Explain how P.L. 99-456 and P.L. 98-199 amend and extend special services offered under P.L. 94-142
6. Understand why many educators advocate noncategorical programs and discuss the philosophy that underlies noncategorical programming
7. Define various handicapping conditions and tell how teachers can assist students with these handicaps
8. Explain what an Individual Educational Program (IEP) is, how one is written, and how it attempts to ensure due process for the handicapped
9. Define gifted education, recognize the criteria that are used for placing gifted students in special programs, and explain how teachers can teach these students effectively
10. Understand that many students who are intellectually gifted may also have handicapping conditions that merit special consideration
11. Identify expectations that may reduce the performance of intellectually gifted students and explain how teachers can counteract this problem through appropriate curriculum assignments

Theoretically, our national policy of free public education for all means that the public schools are available to any student who wants to enroll. For much of our history, however, black students either received no public education or were required to attend segregated black schools. More recently, schools in the southwestern states have attempted to disclaim responsibility for teaching the children of illegal aliens who reside within their districts. Even students initially considered appropriate for admission to public schools may be excluded from regular school programs because they are judged to disrupt normal classroom procedures.

Courts have upheld such exclusion on the basis of mental and physical deficiencies, health problems, pregnancy, flagrant or willful misbehavior, and even unconventional clothes or personal appearance. As a result, enrollment in regular public school classrooms used to be more a privilege for those who met specific criteria than a guaranteed right. More recent court decisions have struck down most of these exclusionary criteria, however, so that attendance in regular public school programs now is more clearly established as a universal right in practice as well as in theory.

Understanding of the legitimate needs of students with handicapping conditions has increased notably in the past decade, as has the willingness of educators to accommodate special students. Even so, some educators (e.g., Brantlinger & Guskin, 1987) still call for incentives for making teachers more willing to instruct mildly handicapped students in mainstreamed classrooms (i.e., not to refer most of them to resource rooms).

THE TRADITIONAL EMPHASIS ON SPECIAL PLACEMENT

Special placement within public schools

Most students affected by these changes have special educational needs because of various handicaps: impairments in vision, hearing, speech, or physical mobility; crippling diseases; mental retardation; emotional disturbances; and learning disabilities. Until recently, many of these students were placed in special institutions such as schools for the blind or deaf. Those with less extreme handicaps usually were accepted by the public schools but often were segregated from other students for part or all of the day. They attended "special education classes" or spent much of their time in "resource rooms" where instructors (who were not always properly trained) could provide them with more individual attention and specialized help.

In theory, this approach made good sense: Identify students who have special needs using screening procedures followed with diagnostic test batteries where indicated, follow diagnosis with needs assessment to identify the special services and forms of instruction that individual students require, and then place them in settings with special teachers who are prepared to provide the treatment. Unfortunately, this is not what usually happened in practice. Students who were placed in special settings often received instruction and work that was too simple or otherwise inappropriate. Disenchantment set in, and sentiment gradually switched from special placement to retaining special students in the regular classroom. Chaffin (1974) cited four major reasons for this: (1) equivocal results of research on the effectiveness of special classes for the mildly retarded, (2) recognition that many of the instruments used to identify retardation were culturally biased, (3) realization that the problems of being labeled and segregated into special settings might be greater than those involved in coping with handicaps in normal settings, and (4) court litigation that took the above problems into account and stressed the rights of all students to appropriate educational treatment over the rights of schools to choose their clients.

It is clear that all students—including those who are gifted as well as those who have handicapping conditions—have the right to an appropriate education. Both types of students may have trouble fitting into regular classrooms unless certain adaptations are made.

PROBLEMS WITH SPECIAL PLACEMENT

Data on the effectiveness of special settings and programs are unimpressive. Special programs for the deaf seem to work reasonably well; deaf students in special schools show higher achievement than comparable deaf students in regular schools. Beyond this, however, it is not clear that specialized programs and settings provide benefits that handicapped students cannot obtain in regular classrooms (Macmillan, Keogh, & Jones, 1986).

Biases in diagnosis

The data on diagnosis are equally discouraging. First, the problem of cultural bias is serious (Brantlinger & Guskin, 1987; Oakland, 1977). Although Brantlinger and Guskin noted that more students from lower-class homes are identified as handicapped, they reported that the extent of this pattern varies depending on the location and the characteristics of the sample studied and may be compounded if students are tested in English when English is not their primary language. This has led to the misclassification of a great many students of low socioeconomic status (especially if they are members of racial or ethnic minority groups) as mentally retarded (Mercer, 1973; Peterson, 1988).

Misuse of diagnostic testing

Diagnostic testing has been misused. Often the classroom teacher must request such testing, and many do so more out of a desire to get rid of students who present personality or behavior problems than out of concern about meeting these students' special educational needs. In some districts, special classrooms became dumping grounds for such students, whereas peers with similar abilities, test profiles, and achievement levels were kept in regular classrooms because they got along better with their teachers. This caused many lower-class and minority-group parents to resist placement of their children in special classes, even though at the same time many middle-class parents sought to expand special educational services (Reynolds, 1978; Reynolds & Birch, 1988).

Validity of diagnoses

In addition to problems with the instruments themselves and with the justifications for their use, there are also questions about the reliability and validity of special-education diagnoses and the presumed linkages between diagnoses and treatments. Research on the diagnostic activities of well-trained and highly regarded specialists in fields such as learning disabilities and reading problems reveals that specialists show very poor agreement with one another and even with themselves when they encounter the same case twice (Vinsonhaler et al., 1983). Also, diagnoses often are not highly related to the treatments proposed; that is, instead of recommending specific treatments for each diagnosis, specialists tend to prescribe the same general kinds of treatments regardless of the diagnosis (Weinshank, 1982). Such data indicate that although the concept of specialized diagnosis and treatment seems sensible, it does not currently function effectively in practice. Epps and Tindal (1987) noted that part of the diagnosis problem is the complexity of the task. It is important to recognize that each learner category (learning disabled, behavior disordered, etc.) represents a heterogeneous group of students who have been classified with diverse and at times ambiguous criteria.

Negative effects of labeling

There is also reason for concern about the negative effects of labeling and segregation. Psychologists and sociologists have long recognized that being labeled as different can produce social stigma, damage the self-concept, and initiate a series of negative self-fulfilling prophecy effects. The process is exaggerated if the stigma results in segregation of the "different" from the "normal" (Ianacone & Stodden, 1987).

Legal changes

Educators' recognition of these problems led to a change of attitudes in the early 1970s, and during the 1970s and 1980s many mildly handicapped students were returned from special to regular classrooms. Court litigation gradually speeded up this process, as a variety of decisions (mostly at the local and state levels) supported the rights of handicapped students (Cohen & DeYoung, 1973). This legal activity culminated on a national scale with the passage of Public Law 94-142 in 1975.

THE EFFECTS OF PUBLIC LAW 94-142

Public Law 94-142, The Education for All Handicapped Children Act, was signed by the president in 1975 and became effective in 1977. The law called for a number of sweeping changes, although its implementation was left primarily to individual states and there has been considerable variation among states. There is ambiguity, for example, about the relation of P.L. 94-142 and gifted education. Various states have differentially interpreted whether the law mandates gifted education. As will be seen later in the chapter, however, the Jacob K. Javits Gifted and Talented Students Education Act of 1988 makes clear the federal government's responsibility to talented youth. Overall, important changes in schooling have resulted from P.L. 94-142.

As various educators have noted (Ianacone & Stodden, 1987; Reynolds, 1978), the law calls for the following:

> Public schools are mandated to search out and enroll every handicapped child, no matter how profound the handicap, in an educational program that is "appropriate" to the child.
>
> Schools are required to write an individualized educational plan (IEP) for each such child. This requires forming teams of school personnel to assess a student's educational needs and specify in writing the goals, objectives, schedules, placements, and plans for evaluation and review.
>
> Schools must bring needed special services to pupils whenever this is feasible, rather than move the pupils to special sites. This procedure removes many of the barriers between regular and special education, and redefines the roles of regular and special education teachers in relation to one another and to students.
>
> Finally, the schools must seek the participation of the parents of handicapped children in making these plans and decisions. The parents must be given full access to all records on their children, and the schools must take care to observe the children's and parents' rights to due process in the event of disagreement.

Mainstreaming

In short, this law commits the nation to a policy of *mainstreaming* handicapped students by placing them in the *least restrictive environment* in which they will be able to function and still have their special needs met. The term *mainstreaming* means that these students will be kept in the mainstream of general public education by being placed as often as possible in regular classrooms rather than segregated into separate institutions or special classes. The degree to which they are labeled and treated as "different" is to be minimized, and schools are expected to see that these students not only spend as much time as possible in regular classrooms with ordinary students but also function as ordinary students by participating in essentially the same ways in the same activities.

There is increasing resistance to removing students from regular classrooms unless there is a clear need for a special program. Messick (1984) suggested that before a student is placed in a special education class, a two-phase aptitude assessment ought to occur. The first assessment should determine whether the student is able to learn under well-conceived, regular classroom instruction and whether the regular teacher has attempted adjustments designed to meet the learner's needs more effectively (e.g., trying a different approach or special curricular materials). Only after it has been established that the regular teacher has presented plausible instruction to the student should testing for placement in a special group be considered.

Least Restrictive Environment Principle

The term *least restrictive environment* implies that special students are *not* to be classified by handicap and given permanent special placement on the basis of these classifications but instead are to be moved to special settings only if necessary and only for as long as necessary. The following continuum of educational environments proceeds from most to least restrictive (Reynolds, 1978): full-time residential school, full-time special day school, full-time special class, regular classroom plus part-time special class, regular classroom plus resource room help, regular classroom with assistance by itinerant specialists, regular classroom with consultative assistance, regular classroom only.

The principle of least restrictive environment calls for students to be

Students with disabilities can often attend regular classes profitably and successfully.

placed in settings as far down this list as possible. Profoundly deaf students, for example, usually will require full-time special schools or special classes, but students with less severe hearing problems and students with a variety of vision problems can spend part or even all of their time in regular classrooms (although probably with some assistance from consultants or itinerant specialists). Emotionally disturbed students who periodically become withdrawn and uncommunicative might be able to spend most of their time in regular classrooms but receive temporary special treatment during periods of severe withdrawal.

During the 1984–85 school year, the majority of handicapped students received special education in settings with nonhandicapped students. Three settings (regular classes, 27.0 percent; resource rooms, 42.0 percent; special classes within a regular education building, 24.0 percent) accounted for almost 93.0 percent of handicapped placements. The remaining handicapped students were educated in public separate day school facilities (3.5 percent), private separate day school facilities (2.1 percent), public residential facilities (1.0 percent), private residential facilities (0.14 percent), correctional facilities (0.3 percent), and homebound-hospital environments (0.8 percent).

Most learning disabled and speech- or language-impaired students were placed in regular classes or resource rooms (77 percent and 91 percent, respectively). (See Table 25.1.) Only 5.0 percent of the mentally retarded students were assigned to regular classes, however, and 29 percent were placed in resource rooms. Nationally, 52 percent of the mentally retarded students were instructed in separate classrooms, but only 33 percent of the emotionally disturbed students were placed in separate classes.

Implementation

P.L. 94-142 did not fully spell out its implementation, so this has been determined gradually by court decisions, state laws, and local practices. The law did place six major requirements on state programs as a condition of obtaining federal support:

State program requirements

1. Handicapped students must be educated to the maximum extent appropriate, in the least restrictive environment.
2. Nondiscriminatory, culture-free testing in the native language of the student is necessary before placement into special programs.
3. Prior consultation with parents must take place before special placement.
4. An individualized educational program (IEP) must be prepared for each handicapped student.
5. Public school programs must serve nonpublic school students if they are handicapped and need services that the federal government funds.
6. Staff development programs must be conducted in every school district.

Note that these guidelines concentrate on ensuring due process, provision of services, and availability of staff development programs, but they do not mandate the content of the programs. This is determined primarily by school districts. At present, there is essentially no research-

TABLE 25.1 PERCENTAGE OF HANDICAPPED CHILDREN AND YOUTH SERVED IN NINE EDUCATIONAL ENVIRONMENTS BY HANDICAPPED CONDITION DURING SCHOOL YEAR 1984–85

Handicapping Condition	Regular Class	Resource Room	Separate Class	Public Separate Facility	Private Separate Facility	Public Residential Facility	Private Residential Facility	Correctional Facility	Homebound/ Hospital
Learning disabled	16.26	60.68	20.84	1.11	0.77	0.03	0.06	0.16	0.08
Speech or language impaired	64.80	26.33	4.90	0.97	2.46	0.03	0.03	0.03	0.46
Mentally retarded	4.80	28.83	52.37	8.29	2.10	2.52	0.40	0.19	0.50
Emotionally disturbed	11.79	34.22	33.34	8.57	4.80	1.69	2.41	1.59	1.59
Hard of hearing and deaf	21.03	23.49	31.03	7.23	4.83	10.67	1.09	0.10	0.53
Multihandicapped	2.70	13.48	42.72	17.61	9.70	6.07	2.51	0.35	4.85
Orthopedically impaired	18.27	20.62	33.42	12.99	5.50	0.80	0.72	0.03	7.65
Other health impaired	23.47	25.44	32.69	3.97	1.94	0.72	0.56	0.02	11.18
Visually handicapped	32.55	29.55	18.80	4.05	3.25	9.80	1.04	0.21	0.74
Deaf-blind	4.36	15.02	22.72	19.21	4.88	27.39	4.36	0.04	2.01
All conditions	26.73	41.61	23.76	3.47	2.08	0.95	0.39	0.25	0.75

Source: *From the Ninth Annual Report to Congress on the Implementation of the Education of the Handicapped Act of 1987.*

based knowledge about how to implement mainstreaming optimally (Macmillan, Keogh, & Jones, 1986), so local specialists will likely determine implementation in a given school district.

Current experimentation

There is currently much experimentation concerning both what kinds of special students should be placed in regular classrooms and what special arrangements (if any) their regular teachers will have to make. Teachers will get materials and help from itinerant special-education teachers or other consultants, as well as guidelines from inservice activities and from the individualized educational plan written for each student. If there is a special-education resource room in the building, mainstreamed students may spend part of the day there being taught in a group by the resource room teacher. This teacher will also be available as a consultant to regular classroom teachers.

NONCATEGORICAL INSTRUCTIONAL PROGRAMS

Although we discuss specific types of handicapping conditions in the section that follows, we have some reservations about doing so because there is a tendency to overreact to a label (e.g., behavior disordered, learning disability) as if it had some precise meaning and indicated specific instructional needs, which is not the case. Snow (1984), for example, noted that Educable Mentally Retarded (EMR) students differ from one another in as many ways as do other students. He stressed that educators need to identify these students' particular *strengths* as well as their weaknesses and to prescribe treatment accordingly.

Differing needs

According to Snow, some special-education programs simply establish generally lower expectations for students instead of adapting instruction to individual differences in order to achieve as many common goals (i.e., goals that other students achieve) as possible. He noted that such programs do not reflect special education in the best sense of the word and are actually dead-end placements with no common goals.

Ysseldyke (1987) acknowledged that many students have difficulty learning in school situations because of cognitive deficits, perception problems, emotional disorders, or language problems. However, he argued that the concepts that should drive practice have lost intended meaning, so terms such as *learning disabled* or *emotionally disturbed* do not have any clear instructional implications. Some of the issues associated with labeling are summarized in Table 25.2. Ysseldyke, along with Reynolds (1987), suggested that educators need to move from test-based classification and labeling of students toward classification systems that focus on students' instructional needs and progress.

Noncategorical programs

Reynolds (1987) noted that the term *noncategorical* refers to instructional programs that include a range of mildly handicapped students and deny that classifying labels (e.g., learning disabled, mentally retarded, etc.) are important to instruction. Few would argue for totally abandoning student classifications, and even most proponents of noncategorical programs acknowledge the need for certain broad distinctions. Such proponents try to be conservative, however, in that they believe that treat-

TABLE 25.2 ISSUES ASSOCIATED WITH LABELING

Possible Benefits of Labeling

1. Categories can relate diagnosis to specific treatment.
2. Labeling may lead to a "protective" response, in which nonlabeled children accept certain behaviors of their handicapped peers more fully than they would accept those same behaviors in "normal" children (MacMillan, 1982).
3. Labeling helps professionals to communicate with one another and to classify and assess research findings.
4. Funding of special education programs is often based on specific categories of exceptionality.
5. Labels allow special interest groups to promote specific programs and spur legislative action.
6. Labeling helps make the special needs of exceptional children more visible in the public eye.

Possible Disadvantages of Labeling

1. Labels usually focus on negative aspects of the child, causing others to think about the child only in terms of inadequacies or defects.
2. Labels may cause others to react to and hold low expectations for a child based on the label, resulting in a self-fulfilling prophecy.
3. A labeled child might develop a poor self-concept.
4. Labels might lead peers to reject or ridicule the labeled child.
5. Special education labels have a certain permanence about them. Once labeled as "retarded" or "learning disabled," it is difficult for a child ever again to achieve the status of being "just like all the other kids."
6. Labels often provide a basis by which children can be kept out of the regular classroom.
7. A disproportionate number of children from minority culture groups may be inaccurately labeled "handicapped," especially as educably mentally retarded.

Source: *W. Heward and M. Orlansky,* Exceptional Children, *Third Edition (Columbus, OH: Merrill Publishing Company, 1984). Reprinted by permission of the publisher.*

ments associated with pupil characteristics should have demonstrated validity before they are applied in schools.

We think that the caveats presented above are important and that teachers need to realize that definitions of handicaps are very general approximations and that students who share the same label may have vastly different instructional needs. However, since categories of handicaps provide general definitions of limitations and broadly outline instructional opportunities, and because legislation still ties funding to these classifications, we will discuss these categories in this chapter.

TEACHING SPECIAL STUDENTS: GENERAL CONSIDERATIONS

P.L. 94-142 has blurred the distinction between regular and special education, so most teachers now need training in methods of meeting the needs of special students in addition to the traditional preparation for teaching. These additional demands on regular classroom teachers should not be minimized, but neither should they be exaggerated.

In preparing to work with handicapped students, teachers need to shed any stereotypes they may have developed because of past labeling and segregation of these students. Their handicaps limit what they can do, but they are not different from other students in other respects. They develop and learn according to the same general principles, respond to the same kinds of incentives, develop the same kinds of motivational systems, and so on. For the most part, then, the principles described throughout this book apply as much to handicapped students as to other students (Larrivee, 1985). This is true even for students who are labeled "emotionally disturbed" (Kounin & Obradovic, 1968).

In fact, most types of students who were returned from special-education settings to regular classrooms as part of the mainstreaming effort used to be taught in regular classrooms before special-education settings proliferated. Classroom teachers known to the authors report that these students tend *not* to be defiant or threatening. Instead, they are mostly slower and more dependent than their classmates, so their special needs are more instructional than managerial (for example, they may require more structured teaching and more use of individualized programs and perhaps contract systems). Many of them are enjoyable to teach because they want to succeed and will try hard to do so.

Teachers can prepare to deal with students with special needs by reading about and taking courses in special education and consulting with specialists. They can also observe in classrooms where handicapped students are mainstreamed, both to learn about the techniques the teachers are using and about the students themselves. It is always helpful to analyze classroom events from the perspective of students (Doyle, 1982; Wittrock, 1986) but especially so from the perspective of handicapped students: What classroom tasks can they accomplish as well as other students without any special provisions or help? What additional tasks might they accomplish with assistance? When they cannot accomplish tasks even with assistance, are there other approaches that might allow them to get the same benefits?

Capitalizing on strengths

These questions illustrate a major consideration to keep in mind in dealing with special students: *Instead of concentrating on their handicaps, capitalize on their strengths* to help them compensate. Certain goals may have to be reduced, and some may have to be taught in unusual ways, but by and large these students should pursue the same objectives as other students. This principle is easy to understand when one considers blind students (since they cannot see, they are taught through other senses), but it applies to all other special students as well. Like regular students, special students need positive but realistic expectations and instruction designed to enable them to realize those goals.

Need for positive attitudes

There is evidence that some teachers hold inappropriate expectations for handicapped students. Hannah and Pilner (1983) found that although there was variation in attitudes toward particular handicapping conditions, many teachers, especially secondary teachers, had negative attitudes toward these students and were somewhat reluctant to teach them.

Guskin and Jones (1982) noted that attitudes toward handicapped persons tend to be less favorable than those toward the nonhandicapped and that the intensity of negative attitudes varies with the type and severity of handicap. These authors argued that attitudes toward handicapped persons can be improved if exposure to the handicapped is carefully structured to reduce stereotypes and if opportunities are provided to build equal status and enjoyable interactions.

Preparing the Class for Mainstreamed Students

Teachers involved in mainstreaming often structure not only their own expectations and behavior but those of other students in their classes as well. What to tell a class will depend on the nature of incoming mainstreamed students' handicaps and on what the students can and cannot do without assistance. If a handicap is not obvious, it may be best to say nothing at all about it to other students and to let the mainstreamed student enter the class as any other newcomer would.

This will not be possible in the case of obvious handicaps that require a wheelchair or a prosthetic device or that include noticeable deficiencies in vision or hearing. In such a case, other students in the class should be told what to expect and how to act. The teacher should obtain students' cooperation in welcoming new students and in helping them to participate as much as they possibly can as regular members of the class.

Handicaps should be described directly and matter-of-factly, without dramatics or attempts to generate exaggerated sympathy or pity:

> Class, tomorrow we are going to be joined by a new member named Linda Johnson. We are going to need to rearrange the room a little to get ready for Linda because she uses a wheelchair. She needs the wheelchair because several years ago she had an accident that left her paralyzed from about the waist down, so she can't walk. She hasn't let this stop her from keeping up with her studies and participating in most activities outside the classroom, however. You'll see for yourselves starting tomorrow. Meanwhile, though, I want to make sure that she can get in and out of the classroom easily. I was thinking that she could park her wheelchair right up in front of this row here. There is a nice clear path between here and the door. She won't need a regular desk but she will need some place to keep things while she is with us; we could move that bookcase up next to where her wheelchair will be parked and let her use part of it to keep her things in. . . ."

The teacher can go on to ask if there are any questions, answering any that can be answered clearly and indicating that the others will be worked out at the time Linda joins the class. A few students might be assigned as a welcoming committee to make a point of getting to know Linda and "showing her the ropes" as well as providing her with any special help she may need (peer tutoring is often valuable for meeting the needs of mainstreamed students). Beyond this, the new student can request additional forms of assistance, if needed.

Modeling and structuring of expectations

With this kind of modeling and structuring of expectations and behavior, most students adjust to new, handicapped classmates as they would adjust to any new classmates. Older students will typically take this in stride. Younger students who are unfamiliar with wheelchairs or prosthetic devices are naturally curious and ask questions, and teachers should answer these questions matter-of-factly or have the handicapped students answer and demonstrate. There is no need to protect such students from these questions; they get them all the time.

In general, then, teachers can prepare for mainstreaming by informing themselves about, observing, and talking with handicapped students, especially those being mainstreamed in other classrooms, and then by establishing appropriate expectations and behavior in their own classrooms.

DEALING WITH SPECIAL HANDICAPPING CONDITIONS

Many handicapped students have been taught successfully in regular classrooms all along (students who have allergies, asthma, arthritis, amputation, diabetes, epilepsy, cerebral palsy, or muscular dystrophy). We will not discuss health disabilities here because of their great variety; for information, see Safford (1978) or Reynolds and Birch (1988). Similarly, special situational disabilities will not be discussed here. Brantlinger and Guskin (1987) discussed various educational interventions for students who are culturally, linguistically, and or situationally unique. In particular, they analyze instructional needs of rural children, American Indian children, children of migrant workers, and limited-English-proficient children. General suggestions for dealing with students who have other types of handicaps follow.

Visual Impairment

Blind and partially seeing students

Two major distinctions are often made within the larger category of visual impairment. *Blind* students have central vision acuity of 20/200 or less in the better eye after correction. Students whose visual fields are restricted to twenty degrees (tunnel vision) are usually classified as blind as well. *Partially seeing* students have visual limitations that interfere with their learning to the extent that they require special teaching services and aids if they are to perform up to their potential.

WAYS IN WHICH THE TEACHER CAN ASSIST

1. Make referral to eye specialist for complete evaluation.
2. Acquire special learning aids (large-print texts, Braille texts, tape-recorded learning exercises).
3. Help visually impaired students to develop self-care skills (e.g., taking students on tour of playground and helping them to note potential hazards).
4. Foster conceptual development by using a variety of senses (e.g., touch, smell) to help students differentiate objects they cannot see.

5. Encourage students to express their thoughts and to communicate in the classroom (e.g., give oral book reports).
6. Encourage students to use what vision they do have.
7. Remember that reading Braille takes twice as long as reading visually.
8. Seat these students on the window side of the classroom, not facing the light, and give them desks with a dull surface.

Hearing Impairment

Deaf and partially hearing students

There are two major types of hearing impairment. *Deaf* students develop a severe hearing loss at birth or before age two or three that prevents them from learning to speak. *Partially hearing* students' hearing losses are not severe enough to prevent the development of spoken language, or they develop a hearing loss after they learn to talk.

WAYS IN WHICH THE TEACHER CAN ASSIST

1. Make referral to specialist for complete evaluation.
2. If the loss is slight (twenty to forty decibels), the student may benefit from a hearing aid and from extra help with new vocabulary. Favorable seating and lighting and speech-reading instruction may be needed as well.
3. Students with moderate (forty-one to fifty-five decibels) hearing losses can hear conversational speech at a distance of three to five feet but may miss as much as 50 percent of class discussion if they cannot see the lips of speakers or if speakers' voices are weak. Hence teachers need to make visual cues available (speak clearly, don't turn away from the student when talking, and don't stand between the student and the window).
4. If the hearing loss is marked (fifty-six to seventy decibels), teacher speech must be very loud to be understood. Also, the student will have difficulty participating in group discussion and is likely to have problems with vocabulary (language usage and comprehension). Listening is hard work for such students, so they may become fatigued during activities that involve prolonged listening.
5. The teacher needs to learn how hearing aids function and how to maintain them.

Speech Impairment

Articulation disorders

Students with speech impairments cannot comprehend the spoken language of others or cannot express themselves meaningfully with spoken words. The most frequent problems that public school teachers deal with are articulation disorders. There are four common articulation disorders: omissions (*at* for *that*), substitutions (*that* for *than*), distortions (*shled* for *shed*), and additions (*puhlease* for *please*). Other problems include voice disorders (e.g., too loud, too soft, pitch too high) and stuttering.

WAYS IN WHICH THE TEACHER CAN ASSIST

1. Refer students to speech therapist for complete evaluation.
2. Help students to pronounce correct sounds.
3. Help students to *hear* their spoken errors.

4. Encourage students to use new words frequently once they can pronounce the words correctly.
5. Help students to rehearse oral skills (e.g., introducing someone) and allow them to practice the skills publicly.

Stuttering

Stuttering is still poorly understood. No one really knows what causes it, despite a variety of explanations. Thus advice on how to help students who stutter varies widely. However, the following suggestions are frequently made.

1. Cue these students before calling on them.
2. Focus on the content of what they say, not how they say it.
3. Do not label them as stutterers.
4. Do not allow them to use stuttering as a crutch (to avoid schoolwork). If the stuttering prohibits participation in an activity, be sure to have them do an additional written assignment (or some other substitute activity).
5. Many students stutter in one situation (e.g., when called on to answer) but not another (e.g., reading aloud). If so, continue to give them plenty of oral practice in those situations that do not create problems (to build confidence that may generalize to problem situations).

Mildly Mentally Handicapped

Learning disabled and mildly retarded students are the largest groups of special students with which regular classroom teachers work. Mental retardation refers to subaverage general intellectual functioning *with* accompaning deficits in adaptive behavior. To be classified as retarded, then, a child must have both a low IQ and difficulty adapting to social situations. In general, only mildly retarded children (IQ fifty to seventy) are likely to be mainstreamed, not students with more severe mental limitations.

WAYS IN WHICH THE TEACHER CAN ASSIST

1. Focus on a *few* basic skills. Be sure that assignments are highly relevant.
2. Provide concrete learning experiences as frequently as possible.
3. Present instruction in brief periods (five to ten minutes).
4. Provide frequent feedback and review.
5. Give simple, step-by-step directions.
6. Try to eliminate possible distractions.
7. Use curriculum materials that are appropriate to students' interests and reading levels.
8. Be alert to the fact that these students need more time to learn the same material.
9. After students have learned something, provide many practice/recall opportunities.
10. Do not repeatedly do for these students things that they should learn to do for themselves.

Behavior Disorders

A behaviorally disturbed student shows one or more of the following characteristics to a marked extent over time: (1) inability to learn that cannot be explained by intellectual inabilities or health problems, (2) difficulty relating to peers and teachers, (3) extreme behavioral reactions to normal events, (4) general moodiness or depression, (5) frequent physical symptoms or fear associated with school problems.

WAYS IN WHICH THE TEACHER CAN ASSIST

1. Verbalize to students the problems they present to the teacher or other students (i.e., tell them gently but honestly why others react to them negatively).
2. Help students to dispel the delusion of uniqueness (no one has problems like mine).
3. Model appropriate expression of emotions.
4. Stop misbehavior or emotionality before it becomes traumatic.
5. Develop firm behavioral expectations and clear managerial guidelines.
6. Provide praise when warranted (specify the praiseworthy behavior).
7. Set up places where these students can work alone occasionally.
8. Don't expect quick results or give up because you see little progress. These students' maladaptive behaviors were established over a long time. It takes time to resocialize inappropriate behavior.

Orthopedic Handicaps

Orthopedic handicaps include defects of structure or function of bones, joints, and muscles. Such handicaps limit movement, but in the absence of other handicapping conditions, these students can learn the same material that nonhandicapped students of similar aptitude learn.

WAYS IN WHICH THE TEACHER CAN ASSIST

1. Allow these students to do whatever they can for themselves.
2. When necessary, allow them to leave the room a couple of minutes early to avoid crowded hallways.
3. If a student is wearing orthopedic equipment, learn how it works and how to assist when simple malfunctions occur.
4. Be alert for safety problems (e.g., bad brakes on wheelchairs, worn crutch tips that will not provide stability on a slippery floor).

Learning Disabilities

The concept of learning disability is relatively new; learning-disability programs were only introduced in the late 1960s. Students with learning disabilities have learning problems (usually language usage) that do *not* involve emotional disturbance, mental retardation, or a visual or hearing impairment to a significant degree. Hence the definition is somewhat ambiguous and circular. For a learning disability to be present, there must be a serious discrepancy between potential and actual performance, and *no other* impairment substantially associated with the deficit. For an illustration of how a learning disability might be manifested, see the case study presented in Table 25.3.

TABLE 25.3 JIM AND MARK: A STUDY OF SIMILARITIES AND DIFFICULTIES

Jim	*Mark*
Age: 9 years	Age: 9 years
Grade: 3	Grade: 3
Years in school: $4\frac{1}{2}$	Years in school: $4\frac{1}{2}$
Reading achievement: 1.6 (grade equivalent)	Reading achievement: 1.6 (grade equivalent)
Group IQ score: 75	Group IQ score: 75

The preceding descriptions of Jim and Mark are obviously identical. However, their IQ scores, as indicated by an *individual* test of intelligence, are quite divergent.

Jim	Mark
Full-scale WISC IQ: 68	Full-scale WISC IQ: 102

The test indicates that Jim is very likely borderline EMR, and that Mark is probably learning disabled. Additional data are then gathered.

Jim	Mark
Arithmetic: 1.8 (grade equivalent)	Arithmetic: 3.2 (grade equivalent)

Generally, EMR students have basic skills in mathematics that are at about the same level as their reading skills, although sometimes they are higher if they mainly involve rote memory. In contrast, many learning disabled students who have severe problems in reading may do near grade-level work in mathematics as long as reading is not required. The reverse may also be true of learning disabled students; they may do satisfactory work in reading but have significant problems in mathematics. It is the inconsistency in performance among various academic areas and various types of activities that characterize learning disabled students.

Additional information about the boys' abilities in classroom interaction, apparent ability to learn from peers, and ability to conceptualize follows:

Jim	Mark
In classroom interaction regarding relationships of planets and the sun, Jim had real difficulty following the idea of relative movement. He can follow class discussion as long as concepts are simple, but has difficulty making generalizations. Jim's speaking vocabulary is better than his reading vocabulary, but is still far below the class average.	In classroom interaction regarding relationships of planets and the the sun, Mark was one of the first in the class to understand. In most topics related to science, if no classroom reading is involved, Mark does very well. On a verbal level he conceptualizes and generalizes well. Mark's reading vocabulary (words he can recognize in print) is no better than Jim's; however, his spoken vocabulary is up to the class average in all respects and is above-average in science areas.

continued

TABLE 25.3 (*continued*)

Many learning disabled students have a performance profile (in such areas as reading achievement, arithmetic achievement, vocabulary, ability to generalize, and ability to conceptualize) that is characterized by many ups and downs. They sometimes (or in some academic areas) seem average or perhaps above average, but in some areas they may be even less able than some EMR students. It is possible for a learning disabled student to be low in *all* areas of achievement and class interaction, but this is unusual. In contrast, the performance profiles of EMR students are usually relatively flat.

Source: *From B. Gearheart and M. Weishahn.* The Exceptional Student in the Regular Classroom, 3rd ed. *(St. Louis: Times Mirror/Mosby College Publishing, 1984). Copyright © 1984 Times Mirror/Mosby College Publishing. Reprinted by permission of Charles E. Merrill Publishing Company, Columbus, Ohio.*

WAYS IN WHICH THE TEACHER CAN ASSIST

1. Recognize that each student with a learning disability is likely to have unique problems.
2. Teach at the readiness level initially (not to the potential level).
3. Structure assignments that allow immediate success.
4. Make brief assignments.
5. Review work with student frequently.
6. Observe closely and attempt to determine how each student best learns. Direct experiences and manipulative materials typically work well.
7. Frequently assess students' understanding to identify inappropriate assignments as soon as possible (''What was the story about? Tell me what you've read in your own words'').
8. Give students plenty of time to respond. Processing information and searching for items in memory are usually difficult for learning disabled students. Typically, it is best to ask students a question and *wait* silently for a response. Repeating or rephrasing the question confuses such students.
9. If a student is on medication, find out the effects of the medication. If it causes excessive drowsiness or activity, see if the dosage can be adjusted.

TEACHING LEARNING-DISABLED STUDENTS IN THE SECONDARY SCHOOL

Many secondary teachers will teach students with learning disabilities. At the elementary school level, learning-disability programs focus on remediation and building basic academic skills, especially in reading and mathematics. When possible, teachers also emphasize higher-order thinking skills, especially in the upper-elementary grades.

Recommendations for working with students

This trend should continue as students with learning disabilities move into secondary programs (Gearheart & Weishahn, 1984). Although some secondary students still need basic skill instruction, many will benefit from instruction that requires them to synthesize, generalize, and apply information to everyday problems. Recognizing student differences in potential, Gearheart and Weishahn (1984) make the following recommendations for secondary teachers who work with learning-disabled students.

1. For students who can express themselves orally but are unable to prepare orderly, well-conceived written reports, a carefully taped response to an assignment might be permitted and evaluated. This avoids a situation in which inability to express oneself in writing masks significant content mastery.
2. If taped reports cannot be accepted, the teacher could agree to evaluate the content of reports without penalizing for poor mechanics. To prevent later claims that the student did not receive an effective education, however, students and their parents must understand and agree to such an arrangement and be told—preferably in writing—that the writing skills that the students do not have are deliberately not being evaluated.
3. Peer tutors can provide individualized assistance to learning-disabled students.
4. Study-skill sessions may be organized to help students explore effective ways to identify, analyze, categorize, and recall information (Sheinker & Sheinker, 1982).
5. Students can be taught to use different reading rates and study strategies for various types of materials and assignments.
6. Other skills, such as preparing for tests, taking notes, and outlining, may be emphasized (Sheinker & Sheinker, 1982). The teacher may agree to provide a student in advance with an outline of material to be learned as a framework within which to organize study.
7. The teacher can provide the student and the resource-room teacher with lists of critical new vocabulary words in advance so that the student may study them before they will be needed in class.
8. The teacher can notify the resource teacher of areas in which the student is falling behind, particularly those that will be essential in future learning.

KEEPING HANDICAPS IN PERSPECTIVE

Need for flexibility

We have listed some of the characteristics of handicapped students and the things teachers can do to help them succeed in regular classrooms. It is worth stressing, however, that one should not take these lists (or any material about handicapped students) too literally or rigidly. Neither should one apply the lists of ways that teachers can help too literally. These are just a few representative suggestions, not blueprints for solving problems. Special students probably are best served if teachers view them essentially as regular students with special needs. The following suggestions for dealing with students with visual handicaps illustrate this point (Dunn, 1973):

1. Be alert to the behavioral signs and physical symptoms of visual difficulties in *all* students. Be sure that proper referrals are made and that everything possible is done to ameliorate the problems.
2. Accept and provide for individual differences on many dimensions, of which vision is just one.
3. View visual limitation as only one difficulty, not the most important characteristic of the student. Do not (a) let handicaps become the central focus in students' lives, (b) allow handicapped students to exploit their visual limitations to get inappropriate special treatment, or (c) exploit them by ''showing them off'' to classroom visitors. As much as possible, treat them as you treat other students.
4. Make visually limited students ''your own'' as much as other students. Do not consider them as belonging to the residential school, the resource teacher, or the itinerant teacher. Get help from these resource people but do not expect them to reteach what should have been taught in the regular classroom, and do not let the student play one teacher against another.
5. When in doubt, regular classroom teachers should do what they would consider best for any student.

ACTIVE LEARNING

We stressed in Chapter 10 that students can assume more responsibility for their learning and become better at ''learning how to learn.'' This is true for all students; however, it is important to illustrate that these same instructional principles also apply to special learners.

Self-Regulated Learning

As Paris and Oka (1986) have noted, handicapped students often appear powerless, helpless, and low in motivation. This is unfortunate because it is clear that their self-views can be altered through instruction. Many poor learners simply do not understand the relation between the use of learning strategies and successful performance. Thus it is not lack of effort that depresses their performance but rather the belief that they do not have effective strategies for controlling their own learning.

Strategy training for special students

Borkowski, Johnston, and Reid (1986) used strategy training with students in grades two, three, and four who had been labeled learning disabled and hyperactive. The three training groups were (a) executive training in metacognitive skills, (b) executive training plus attribution retraining, and (c) control learning. Students who actually participated in the training (executive self-management and more positive attributions) became more able to control impulsivity and to change their attributions for success and failure in comparison to control students.

Paris and Oka argued that students need to be taught cognitive strategies and reasonable expectations for performance, with an emphasis on the fact that they can control their own learning outcomes. Students' awareness of their cognitive abilities can enable them to control their own learning, which, under certain conditions, can motivate them to seek more challenging tasks and to persist in the face of difficulty.

Metacognitive Strategy Instruction

Reciprocal teaching

The goals of metacognitive instruction are to teach students to plan, implement, and assess their strategic approaches to learning assigned material. Students need to be aware of the goals of a learning activity, obstacles that they may encounter, and how they will be asked to demonstrate mastery (e.g., preparing for an essay test differs from preparing for a multiple-choice test). Palincsar (1986) found that metacognitive strategies can enhance students' capacity for learning when teachers provide explicit instruction in efficient strategies and progressively assign more control over the application of these strategies to students, especially when students understand the purposes and consequences of using the strategies. Palincsar (1986) described a procedure called *reciprocal teaching* that she and a colleague, Ann Brown, had investigated for several years.

The cognitive strategies that students learn to use during reciprocal teaching are (1) summarizing—identifying the main idea of the text in their own words; (2) question generating—self-questioning about the information presented; (3) clarifying—assessing when comprehension is incomplete and taking necessary action to understand the material (e.g., rereading); and (4) predicting—using one's knowledge about the topic to predict what the text will say. At the beginning of each instructional period, students review the strategies they are learning and the rationale for using them. Then they read the title of the text and use background information regarding the topic to predict what they will learn in the text and to identify what they would like to learn about the topic.

After this background orientation, a "teacher" (student or adult) is appointed for the first text segment. The teacher and students read the segment (depending on the decoding skills of the students, either silently or orally) and then the teacher asks a question to which the students respond. The teacher summarizes and invites elaboration on the summary from other group members. Such procedures lead to examination and discussion of clarifications that group members want to make. At the end of the group discussion, the students make predictions regarding upcoming text, and a new teacher is appointed. During the initial days of instruction, the adult teacher initiates and sustains the dialogue, provides instruction regarding strategies, and models their appropriate application. The goal, however, is for the teacher to transfer increased responsibility to students while providing feedback and coaching them through dialogue.

Most research on reciprocal teaching has been conducted with junior high students enrolled in Chapter 1 remedial reading classes. These students usually were adequate decoders but read at least two years below grade level on standard measures of comprehension. In the initial research, adult tutors worked with students in pairs, and volunteer developmental-reading teachers supervised groups of approximately five students who read expository passages taken from basal readers written at a seventh-grade level. After reciprocal teaching was used for twenty consecutive school days, the students were retested. They were below the twentieth percentile on comprehension tests before the intervention; after the reciprocal teaching program they had moved to the fiftieth percentile and above (Brown & Palincsar, 1982; Palincsar & Brown, 1984).

Palincsar (1986) cautioned that reading material for reciprocal teaching must be selected with care. It should not present students with major decoding problems, and it should be representative of content that students will study in school. If strategy training is to transfer to school tasks, it should involve material that students will encounter in science, social studies, and other content areas.

Cognitive-instructional approach

Palincsar and Brown (1987) argued that a cognitive-instructional approach needs to be emphasized within the curriculum and that educators need to think about the content to be mastered as well as the thinking processes that promote mastery and learner self-control. Students identified as low ability or disabled tend to receive instruction that does not encourage them to think about the meaning of material that is assigned. Reading teachers, for example, have been observed encouraging good readers to evaluate critically and to think about the material that they are reading but focusing the attention of poor readers on word identification and correct pronunciation. This encourages good readers to identify the goal of reading as constructing meaning. Poor learners, however, may conclude that the purpose of reading is to pronounce words correctly and may not appreciate the need to develop strategies for comprehending text (e.g., predicting, self-questioning, rereading, and so on).

INDIVIDUAL EDUCATIONAL PROGRAMS

Public Law 94-142 requires that an Individual Educational Program (IEP) be designed to meet each handicapped student's unique needs. The IEP should describe the student's present educational performance, short-term learning goals, and annual learning goals. It also should specify the time the student will spend in the regular classroom, which teacher is responsible for which objectives, and how the student's progress will be evaluated. Once a student has been formally referred for special-education services, a placement committee is formed to write the initial IEP and to continue to supervise the student's progress for as long as the special services are provided. The core committee is likely to include the teachers who will instruct the student, the principal, the person who evaluates the student (a school psychologist or social worker), and, when feasible, a parent and the student.

Responsibility of IEP committee

The committee typically has the following responsibilities: (1) obtaining information about the student, (2) assessing the student's needs for special education, (3) developing the IEP, (4) evaluating the special services, and (5) making sure that prescribed procedures are followed to protect the rights of the student and parents. The latter includes ensuring due process with regard to keeping the parents and the student fully informed about and included in decision making, assurance of confidentiality about records, recognition of the student's right to be represented by a parent or guardian, assessment with nondiscriminatory instruments presented in the student's native language, and commitment to the principle of placing the student in the least restrictive environment feasible under the circumstances.

Assessment procedure

The assessment procedures should be complete and wide ranging, with information from several sources. This is a major departure from previous procedures in which a diagnostician administered a few tests, wrote a report, and made recommendations. Table 25.4 shows the variety of sources from which information can be drawn and the rationale for their use.

Evaluation and integration of recommendations

The placement committee is charged not merely with following recommendations but with evaluating and integrating them. Student evaluations and reports are to be judged on criteria such as the following:

TABLE 25.4 SOURCES AND USES OF INFORMATION

Source	Rationale for Use
1. Referral forms	Information contained on referral forms, if well stated, can be used to form hypotheses concerning what other kinds of information may be needed, the criteria for acceptable performance, and the perspective of the person(s) making the referral.
2. School records	Inspection of cumulative and other available records can be helpful in determining whether or not there are factors that might help to account for referral, whether or not there seem to be any trends in problem growth, and whether other areas are in need of closer evaluation.
3. Standardized tests	Standardized tests may be used to obtain information on how one child compares with other children. In many cases, standardized tests are required for determination of eligibility. These types of tests cover areas such as intelligence, achievement, and personality.
4. Developmental scales	These scales compare areas of child development within the child and as compared with other children. They are especially useful with younger or more severely handicapped children, pinpointing both strengths and weaknesses.

continued

TABLE 25.4 (*continued*)

5. Criterion-referenced tests	This type of test places the child at a certain level in some areas of skill development. It is especially helpful for planning because criterion statements can be used as goals for instruction.
6. Observation	Observational data can focus on a very specific child characteristic, such as interaction with other children, and can point out areas in need of further evaluation and confirm or disconfirm other information. Observations may be formal or informal and include things such as anecdotal records, interaction analysis, checklists, and rating scales. These observations may take place in any setting, including the home. Observational data are best obtained by those who are close to the child in his/her normal environment.
7. Interviews	Interviews with the parent, the child, and/or the teacher yield information that lends perspective to other kinds of information. They also pinpoint areas that may be priority needs or strengths.
8. Work samples	Work samples are similar to criterion-referenced testing; they provide information concerning the level of the child in some area of skill development. They are useful in planning intervention in academic areas.
9. Consultants	Consultants may provide information that is not usually available to an educational planner. This may include medical, therapeutic, and family information and may be used to plan services in related areas, define limitations on other planning, or identify areas of major need.

- Is the report written in understandable language?
- Are the tools or processes used for evaluation identified?
- Is the setting in which the evaluation occurred described?
- Does the evaluation contain concise statements of specific results?
- Are problem areas identified by the evaluation procedure specified?
- Are problem areas identified by behavioral observations specified (separately)?
- Does the report contain concise statements of strengths and weaknesses?
- Is the information relevant to educational planning?
- Does the report describe conditions that influence ability to perform tasks?

Figure 25.1 A Typical Individual Education Program

INDIVIDUAL EDUCATION PROGRAM

Child's Name Frank West

Date Referred to Committee March 2

School Crescent Point High School

SUMMARY OF PRESENT LEVELS OF PERFORMANCE

Frank wants to stay in school. He recognizes that his reading ability is low and he wants to learn to read. Teacher observations and test scores indicate that he has a basic understanding of the concepts and operations of fundamental mathematics. He has the ability to follow through on assignments which interest him. He experiences the most difficulty when he is asked to do school work which he doesn't understand or is presently incapable of doing. He is extremely unhappy in the self-contained classroom and does not associate with his classmates. He looked forward to being placed in a "regular" classroom but he has trouble controlling his anger when he can't do the required work. He does independent reading (e.g., newspapers and sports books). Teachers and school personnel often view his behavior as inappropriate for school. This has resulted in numerous suspensions.

PRIORITIZED LONG-TERM GOALS

(1) Frank will improve in his reading ability.
(2) Frank will experience success in the regular classroom.
(3) Frank will be given the opportunity to explore a range of career alternatives.
(4) Frank will develop positive relationships with peers and teachers.
(5) Frank will become more of a participant and less of a spectator in areas of interest.

continued

Figure 25.1 (continued)

Short-Term Objectives	Special Education and Related Services	Person Responsible	Beginning and Ending Dates	Review Date
(1) Design a reading program building on Frank's areas of interest:				
A. Develop sightword vocabulary builders using the newspaper and sports books.	EMR teacher/ support from remedial reading teacher/ supplemental materials	EMR teacher	March 7 June 1	May 1
OBJECTIVE: improve Frank's sight word vocabulary by 25%				
B. Using math word problems designed to incorporate new vocabulary words. Frank will improve in his ability to deal with math word problems.	EMR teacher/ supplemental materials	math teacher	March 7 June 1	May 1
C. An independent reading list based on occupational opportunities will be developed. Frank will read and discuss such materials.				
D. Frank will be encouraged to report on independent reading to his teacher–later to his peers.	EMR teacher	EMR teacher	March 15 June 1	May 15
(2) Frank will remain in the regular math class.				
A. Teacher will design sequential math materials building on Frank's strengths.	math teacher/ math supervisor	math teacher	March 7 June 1	May 15
OBJECTIVE: Frank will experience academic success.				
B. Shop teacher will design math problems in that content area. Frank will be allowed to experience finishing a project from the conceptual stage through completion.		shop teacher	March 7 June 1	May 15
C. Frank will be enrolled in an intramural or PE program.	P.E.	P.E. instructor	March 7 June 1	May 15

Figure 25.1 (continued)

(3) Frank will spend two hours per week for three weeks with the vocational counselor discussing his readings in job opportunities.	EMR teacher	vocational counselor	March 30 June 1	April 20
(4) Frank will assume increasing amounts of responsibility for his own learning as evidenced by his willingness to complete required projects and seek help from teachers.	EMR teacher	all of Frank's teachers	March 7 June 1	May 15

PLACEMENT DECISIONS

Frank will remain in EMR class for reading and language arts. He will attend a regular math class, shop class, and be enrolled in a P.E. class.

PERCENT OF TIME IN REGULAR CLASSROOM
50%

FOR THE COMMITTEE, RECOMMENDATIONS FOR SPECIFIC PROCEDURES/TECHNIQUES, MATERIALS, INFORMATION ABOUT LEARNING STYLE, ETC.

Frank's basic strength lies in the fact that he recognizes his weakness in reading and that he wants to stay in school. It is extremely important that he be allowed to experience success in an academic setting.

CRITERIA FOR EVALUATION OF ANNUAL GOALS

(1) Reading and math will be evaluated on the basis of teacher test and standardized test.
(2) Social behavior will be based on staff observations and Frank's observations as well as suspensions.
(3) Relations with teachers and peers (most likely dependent upon academic success) will be based on observations.

Committee Members Present

____
____
____
____
____

Dates of Meetings

____
____
____

Thus the committee evaluates the source and quality of available information in addition to taking the information into account in trying to decide what is best for the student. Only after assessing all of this information and integrating it with information from the participants does the committee prepare the actual IEP.

Developing a successful IEP

Figure 25.1 illustrates an IEP that follows both the spirit and the letter of the law and seems likely to organize school resources to meet the needs of the student appropriately. The program may seem deceptively simple at first, but bear in mind that the development of a successful plan involves a great deal of data gathering, resolution of differences in opinion and interpretation, compromise, and careful planning. Note the array of specific recommendations, each of which includes identification of the person responsible, specification of the time required, and provision for review and possible revision of the recommendation. This IEP shows the kind of commitment, cooperation, thoroughness, and provision for accountability that will be needed if the lofty goals of Public Law 94-142 are to be realized.

PUBLIC LAWS 99-457 AND 98-199

P.L. 99-457 amends P.L. 94-142 in important ways. It requires states to provide an appropriate public education to children ages three through five. This increases young children's access to educational programs and could improve handicapped infants' transition from home to educational settings. The law establishes a state grants program for handicapped infants from birth through two years of age. Participating states will develop educational plans that ensure children and their families an individualized family services plan.

Transition

Recent federal legislation has also focused on the transitional problems of handicapped youth when they leave secondary schools and seek employment. A major aspect of Public Law 98-199, the Education of the Handicapped Amendment, specifies funds and support for secondary education and transitional services. Ianacone and Stodden (1987) noted that increased attention to transitional services stems from the fact that unnecessarily large numbers of handicapped adults are unemployed and dependent on welfare. Between 50 and 80 percent of working-age adults who report a disability, for example, are jobless, and about 8 percent of the gross national product is spent annually on disability programs, with most of this going to programs that support dependents. Educators and policymakers now recognize important transition points for students (e.g., entering kindergarten; assuming one's first job) and conceptualize transition as a process of movement through life phases. This makes it important to identify skills that enable students to be relatively independent at various transition points.

Ianacone and Stodden noted that educators responsible for critical developmental transitions have at times been remiss in matching planning goals to instructional practices. They identified five practices that illustrate how schools have not assisted students who are mentally retarded to become independent.

Structuring Dependence

Instruction in public schools is dominated by vertical interaction between teacher and student (teacher telling the student what to do and when to do it), especially for students perceived to be mildly or severely retarded. Ianacone and Stodden suggested that this mode of communication fosters student dependence on teachers. They argued that in secondary schools it is especially depressing to see students still lining up before leaving class, being unnecessarily assisted with their coats or boots, and having extracurricular activity decisions made for them rather than with them. Such assistance reinforces dependency in students at a time when structuring independent behaviors would be valuable to them.

Decision Making

In many schools the opportunity for student decision making is limited, and students typically make decisions with only limited consequences and relevance for them. Instead, decision making should be taught in order to foster student independence and self-reliance. This can begin early with simple choices (e.g., choosing between two toys or what game to play at recess) but with emphasis on helping students to accept the consequences of their choices and on preparing them to make more mature decisions later in and out of school.

Employment Irrelevance

Ianacone and Stodden were especially disappointed that there is not more opportunity for academic content to bridge vocational- or employment-related experiences for students. This is especially a loss for secondary students in special classes, many of whom are still coloring pictures or learning to name letters when they could be focusing on vocabulary words that are functional and related to vocational training.

Self-Fulfilling Expectations

Educators often underestimate the independent functioning and employment potential of mentally retarded students. Not all individuals who are classified as moderate to severely mentally retarded are necessarily headed for sheltered employment. Because of low expectations, teachers, counselors, parents, and employers too often force these students to fit into predetermined, limited roles.

Focus on Disability

Consistent with the notion of self-fulfilling expectations, the processes associated with special education often lead to an emphasis on a student's disability rather than on what he or she can do. Teachers and counselors are forced to focus on students' disabilities to determine eligibility for services and to plan instruction. Ianacone and Stodden argued that educators often pay too much attention to a student's disability classification and act on related preconceived expectations that may prevent the problem from becoming remediated. Rather than focusing on disabilities, educators need to identify ways to help students develop independence and useful competencies.

In this chapter, we have discussed some of the handicapping conditions that students bring to the classroom and some strategies that teachers can use in responding to them. Furthermore, we have discussed Public Laws 94-142, 99-457, and 98-199, which have made regular public education more accessible to a wider range of students. Given the concerns expressed by Ianacone and Stodden, however, it is imperative that we improve education for students who have handicapping conditions. In the section that follows, we review evidence about how well the mainstreaming philosophy is working in American education.

RESEARCH ON MAINSTREAMING

Research on the effects of mainstreaming yields complex findings that are difficult to generalize from, for at least three reasons. First, most of the research has been on program "labels" and raises only mechanical questions (e.g., Does *enrollment* in special programs influence student achievement?). Too little attention has been given to the *instruction* that occurs within such programs. Second, the same program label often means different things. Mainstreaming and least restrictive environment may mean one thing in one seventh-grade class and something different in another (even one that is located across the hallway in the same building). Third, even when labels convey similar meanings, a particular philosophy may be implemented in various ways (i.e., issues of program *quality*).

Three generalizations about special education

Although the literature is complex and too few field observational studies have been completed, three generalizations can be made from research on mainstreaming. First, programs that take students with mildly handicapping conditions from regular classrooms and place them in special rooms for instruction appear to have less positive effects on achievement than approaches in which students receive instruction in regular classrooms with nonhandicapped peers. Even so, a second generalization is that the quality of instruction that mildly handicapped students receive in regular classrooms is still low in too many instances. Much of what is known about how students learn (e.g., cognitive science and child-development literature) and effective teaching (e.g., active teaching, motivational theory) is not applied to instruction of students with mildly handicapping conditions. Third, many special educators believe that educators need to reduce substantially the numbers of students who are given special-education labels and assigned to be taught in pull-out programs (Peterson, 1988; Wang, Reynolds, & Walberg, 1987). In the section that follows, we discuss some of the research evidence that leads to these generalizations.

Research Evidence

Thompson, White, and Morgan (1982) conducted an observational study of mainstreaming programs because they believed that these programs had been implemented without adequate data describing how teachers and handicapped students interact. Many special educators had predicted that students would be hurt rather than helped by mainstreaming (e.g.,

Teacher-student interaction patterns

mainstreamed students might be ignored, face more criticism, or receive less serious teaching). Thompson and associates found that although teacher-student interaction varied among certain types of students observed, there was no evidence that teachers consistently provided preferential treatment or treatment likely to result in better educational gain to any single group of students.

Much teacher time was devoted to nonacademic tasks in mainstreamed classrooms. Only about half of the teacher's time was spent on academic activities, and the rest was devoted to procedural and behavioral interactions. Behaviorally handicapped students received a larger proportion of teacher time than did other students. Thus the data from this study do not support the view that handicapped children are at a disadvantage because of preferential teacher interaction with nonhandicapped students. The investigators did conclude, however, that regular classroom teachers need to improve their management skills and teach students independent work habits so as to strike a better balance between the time spent on academic versus procedural matters. Two other recent studies have reached similar conclusions. Leinhardt (1980) compared the effects of assigning poor-prognosis first-grade students to separate transition classrooms with the effects of giving similar students instruction in regular classrooms. She also examined the effectiveness of an individualized reading program (NRS) for instructing low-performance students in beginning reading skills. Results suggested that low-performance students learned to read better in regular instructional settings and under the NRS program. Leinhardt argued that these results are most likely due to two factors. First, the individualized program provided teachers with strategies for teaching heterogeneous students. Second, students in regular classrooms received substantially *more reading instruction* than their counterparts in transition rooms.

Madden and Slavin (1983) reviewed research on the effects of placing students with mild academic handicaps in full-time special-education classrooms, part-time regular classes with resource support, or full-time regular classes. They concluded that research favors placement in regular classrooms using individualized instruction or regular instruction supplemented by well-designed resource programs to improve the achievement, self-esteem, behavior, and emotional adjustment of academically handicapped students. They found no consistent benefits of full-time special education for important outcomes.

Effects of mainstreaming

Macmillan, Keogh, and Jones (1986) reviewed the special-education research on mildly handicapped learners—those who are commonly categorized as educable mentally retarded (EMR), learning disabled (LD), behavior disordered (BD), mildly emotionally disturbed (ED), or as students with minimal brain disfunction (MBD). The authors restricted their review to mildly handicapped students largely because they are the majority of the students most affected by the current emphasis on least restrictive environment. They examined the effects of mainstreaming on EMR students in terms of the following variables: (a) the process, (b) academic achievement, and (c) social adjustment.

Concerning process, Macmillan and associates concluded that mainstreaming has not altered significantly the ethnic composition of classes in which EMR students receive instruction. A second process issue concerns the level of placement for EMR students in regular classes, that is, whether EMR students should be placed with peers of the same age (where they will likely be behind in achievement) or with younger students (where they will have a comparable achievement match). Evidence suggests that EMR students are typically placed into classes where they are one year older than classmates and where the classmates are mostly low achievers (nonhandicapped but below-average in IQ and socioeconomic status). A third process dimension is the nature of the instruction that students receive in regular and special classes. A few instructional differences between regular and special classes have been observed, but for the most part, the patterns are strikingly similar.

Results of EMR mainstreaming

According to Macmillan and associates, a major argument against segmented special EMR classes was their inability to promote good academic gains despite small class size and specially trained teachers. Some studies show achievement gains for EMR students in regular classes, but the larger conclusion is that mildly handicapped learners do poorly in all settings.

Macmillan and associates noted that the evidence on mainstreaming generally does not support the argument that mainstreaming per se improves the peer-group status of mildly handicapped learners. In fact, unless preventive steps are taken, mainstreamed students may encounter low peer acceptance. Although Gottlieb (1981) found that instruction can improve the social status of mainstreamed mildly handicapped students, many of these students have less social status than their nonhandicapped peers.

Many studies have viewed administrative arrangements as "treatments" but have not examined within-program variation in curriculum and instruction. Studies of mainstreaming suggest that schools have not been successful in teaching mildly handicapped learners, regardless of where they are placed or how they are labelled (EMR or "normal"). According to Macmillan and associates, the challenge now is to study instruction and not to continue to be preoccupied with administrative labels.

Epps and Tindal (1987) independently conducted a comprehensive review of the effects of mainstreaming on mildly handicapped students and reached conclusions similar to those of Macmillan et al. They found that the type of educational setting does not appear to be highly related to differences in how instruction is delivered, especially in terms of interactive teaching variables. This finding is seen in the research comparing Chapter 1 and non-Chapter 1 settings, as well as in research conducted in resource rooms with mildly handicapped students and in regular classrooms with nonhandicapped peers. (Although Chapter 1 is designed for a range of low-achieving and disadvantaged students—and is not a specific special-education program—Chapter 1 instruction is often included in special-education discussions because it targets special funds and program guidelines for particular students and because special-education students are often enrolled in Chapter 1 programs.)

Classroom setting

Haynes and Jenkins (1984) (reported by Epps and Tindal) observed mildly handicapped students during resource-room instruction and in their regular classes. *Comparisons of resource rooms and regular classrooms showed that more reading instruction occurred in regular classrooms.* Students averaged more time reading in regular classes than in resource rooms (seventeen minutes versus thirteen minutes) and had more indirect reading instruction (twenty-seven minues versus twelve minutes). Furthermore, despite the fact that student-teacher ratios were lower in resource rooms, students' task involvement was greater in regular classes.

There was great variability from class to class within program type, making it hard to generalize about setting (i.e., a student's experience depends on which classroom the student is in). Also, the correlation between student need and the instructional program offered was close to zero; that is, students who had a greater discrepancy between their achievement level and grade level did not receive more reading time. There was little continuity between the reading programs in the two settings.

These results, along with similar findings from other studies, led Epps and Tindal to conclude that instruction in special and regular classrooms is often indistinguishable. The years of advocacy and argument about which environment is best are ironic in that only few relatively minor differences have been noted, at least in those environments that have been studied.

Promising Mainstreaming Practices

Positive characteristics of student performance

Much remains to be learned about teaching and learning experiences that stimulate positive student attitudes and achievement in mainstreamed classrooms. Still, some leading special educators have identified tentative, but useful, findings about effective program characteristics. Reynolds and Birch (1988), for example, in reviewing extant literature, especially the work of Wang, Anderson, and Bram (1985), noted that the following program characteristics tend to be associated with positive student performance: (1) continuous assessment of student achievement, (2) alternative routes or methods of instruction, (3) variety of materials available for use in teaching, (4) explicit individualized instructional plans, (5) student self-management in parts of the school program, (6) peer assistance among students, (7) instructional teaming of teachers and other staff, and (8) use of consulting teachers.

Teacher interaction

Problems with Social Environments Some students with mildly handicapping conditions do not make progress because they are not actively taught, but others may fail because teachers do too much for them. Stipek and Sanborn (1983) observed teacher-child interactions in two preschool programs, focusing on teachers' interactions with mainstreamed handicapped children and children perceived as "high-risk" for academic problems. They found that teachers offered unrequested assistance and praise to the handicapped and high-risk children more than to nonhandicapped children and suggested that this pattern resulted from the teachers' desire to compensate for the children's handicaps. By initiating the majority of their interactions with these children, however, the teachers may have conditioned the children to play a passive role. That is, the students did not need to seek information or assistance because their teachers always offered it to them. Teachers of mainstreamed students need to guard against being overly critical and demanding of these students, but they also need to realize that they can do too much for them. Students have to initiate and learn on their own as well as respond to teacher structuring.

Low achievers may elicit more varied teacher expectations than other students. Teachers may treat mildly handicapped students and other low achievers inconsistently throughout the school year, trying one approach after another in an attempt to find something that works (i.e., teachers may give up on a strategy prematurely). Furthermore, low achievers have more teachers at a given time (regular class, resource room, classroom tutor), and these teachers may use different strategies for working with them. Some teachers minimize interactions with low achievers and are critical of them, but other teachers seek them out frequently and provide encouragement and support. Some teachers call on low achievers in an attempt to get them to participate more often, but other teachers mostly avoid them. Some teachers rarely praise lows' successes, but others praise almost everything they do, even responses that are incorrect. Student passivity is a likely outcome of such diverse treatment and expectations. Not knowing what to do, low achievers may learn to avoid initiations and wait for the teacher to structure their behavior.

According to Peterson (1988), Chapter 1 "pull-out" programs do not increase student achievement. She noted that one of the apparent problems is that these programs appear to expose students to a fragmented rather than an integrated curriculum. Furthermore, Peterson stated that pull-out programs often incorrectly label certain students, lower teacher expectations for student performance, and deny students potentially beneficial friendships with peers who differ in ability or ethnicity. Because of such data, many special educators are calling for reductions in—but not necessarily the elimination of—the number of students who are labeled as "special learners" and assigned to remedial pull-out programs (Wang, Reynolds, & Walberg, 1987).

Chapter 1 and EHA Program Services

The passage of the Elementary and Secondary Education Act of 1965 marked the beginning of the Title I program (which is now the Chapter 1 program). The purpose of this act was to provide federal support for the education of economically disadvantaged students. As Allington (1986) noted, this program has grown to the point that virtually every school district in the nation receives some federal funding under the basic act or its descendants. In 1975 the Education of All Handicapped Children Act (EHA) was passed, marking the beginning of a second federally sponsored program that was to affect educational practice in virtually every district (Singer & Butler, 1987).

Differences in orientation

These two federally initiated programs are available in most school districts, and both primarily serve students who have failed to learn to read on schedule. Each program, however, is guided by unique assumptions about the nature of reading failure (Allington & McGill-Franzen, 1989). The Chapter 1 program emphasizes the effects of environmental factors on learning to read, so economic disadvantagement is the primary criterion in establishing eligibility for services. In contrast, identification of the learning disabled under EHA focuses on assumptions about biological deficits, especially neurological impairments, which provide putative explanations for why students do not read on schedule.

Will (1986) has shown that although enrollment in both programs combined has remained nearly constant for a decade, the proportional representation of the groups has changed: the number of pupils served under Chapter 1 has declined, whereas the number served under EHA has doubled. Will argued that although a variety of social, educational, and political factors have influenced this shift, the difference in the reimbursement of educational costs by federal and state agencies typically creates a fiscal incentive for schools to serve students under EHA rather than Chapter 1. This has led to a significant increase in the number of students identified and labeled as handicapped.

Differences in amount of active reading teaching

Allington and McGill-Franzen (1989) studied the amount and type of reading instruction offered in EHA and Chapter 1 programs. Using observational records for twenty pairs of students (Chapter 1 and special education) who attended the same regular-education classrooms, these investigators found that across the school day, special-education students received not only less reading instruction but also less active teaching. Although the amount of active teaching in Chapter 1 and special-education classes did not differ, Chapter 1 students received *nearly twice as much active teaching* during regular-education reading classes as did the mainstreamed mildly handicapped students. Mainstreamed special-education students spent a larger proportion of their reading instructional time, in both regular- and special-education classes, working on seatwork activities.

These findings suggest that schools offer different instruction to students experiencing reading failure, depending on which special program the students are assigned to. It is interesting that the most striking difference reported was in the instruction in regular classrooms. The mainstreamed mildly handicapped students received *thirty-five minutes a day less reading-language arts instruction than did Chapter 1 students in regular-education classrooms*. Also, instruction offered in special-education programs involved less active teaching and more seatwork than instruction in regular-education and Chapter 1 programs.

There was important variation from school to school, so that assignment to special education did not inevitably lead to less reading instruction. Chapter 1 students tended to receive instruction in both remedial and regular settings, whereas many EHA students were denied reading instruction in regular classrooms. Perhaps the most important conclusion is that educators need to increase access to instruction in the regular-education classroom (and the *quality* of that instruction) as they attempt to solve the problems of students who have difficulty learning to read.

Myths about learning problems

Part of the problem may be that special education has created the myth that some students have learning problems that the average classroom teacher is inadequately prepared to cope with. State-certification requirements, for example, imply that most classroom teachers should not try to teach special students because they do not have the necessary specialized knowledge. In contrast, Chapter 1 guidelines may convey different expectations to teachers because they suggest that Chapter 1 students are regular students who have certain background deficiencies that are correctable with appropriate instruction. There is no connotation that Chapter 1 students have special learning problems, that they are radically different from other students, or that the regular teacher cannot help them.

Conclusions

Our review of the literature reveals that the research on mainstreaming is complex, in part because the issue itself is complex but also because too little observational research has focused on the quality and appropriateness of instruction that mildly handicapped students receive. Still, evidence leads to several broad conclusions that can guide educational practice.

1. Pull-out instruction is overused, and too many students are assigned to special programs. Although some pull-out programs are effective, they generally result in minimal achievement gains for three reasons. First, students often receive no special instruction (geared to a particular need) and sometimes receive less instruction than they do in regular classrooms. Second, students often receive a fragmented curriculum because there is little or no coordination between regular and pull-out programs. Furthermore, different teaching styles often result in varied and sometimes conflicting performance expectations for students in regular and pull-out programs. Third, the "special-education" label (perhaps especially when students are in special-education classes rather than Chapter 1 rooms) may be associated with lower student and teacher expectations for performance as well as reduced opportunity for students to interact with peers who differ in ability, learning style, or ethnicity.

2. A growing literature indicates that students who have mild handicaps learn in similar ways and generally benefit from the same type of instruction as do other students. Too often students who have mild handicaps or who are perceived as low achievers receive less reading instruction in the regular classroom or in the special program. Furthermore, the instruction that they do receive is overly focused on drill and workbook exercises.

3. When possible, students with mild handicaps usually are best instructed in regular classrooms. Many students, however, have handicapping conditions that benefit from some pull-out instruction, especially if it is coordinated with what occurs in the regular classroom and designed to remediate specific problems. Hence what happens in a program—its *quality*—is important, not its label.

TEACHING GIFTED STUDENTS

In this section we discuss the educational needs of talented students, especially those who have advanced verbal and quantitative skills (i.e., students who process information quickly and who do exceptionally well in certain curriculum areas).

The Jacob K. Javits Gifted and Talented Students Education Act of 1988 legally recognizes our educational responsibilities to talented youth. This legislation asserts that gifted students are a national resource and that elementary and secondary schools need to develop these students' talents responsibly. The purpose of the legislation is expressed in the following statement: "It is the purpose of this part to provide financial assistance to state and local educational agencies, institutions of higher education, and other public and private agencies and organizations; to initiate a coordinated program of research, demonstration projects, personnel training, and similar activities designed to build a nationwide capability in elementary and secondary schools to identify and meet the special educational needs of gifted and talented students. . . ."

Before we define gifted students and discuss their educational needs, we want to emphasize that (a) all students are unique, and (b) many students who have a handicapping condition also may be gifted in one or more areas. Still, some students clearly are sufficiently talented that teachers must find ways to accommodate their needs in the classroom.

Fenstermacher (1982) argued that the designation of giftedness is determined by how the term is defined. If one believes that every person is in some way unique, all children are gifted. If, on the other hand, one emphasizes a single attribute (such as a high score on a standardized test of verbal ability), only those who excel on this particular attribute are seen as being gifted. According to Fenstermacher, authors who argue for special instruction for gifted students often encourage freedom, support, challenging materials, and rich learning resources. Through unintentional implication, then, average and below-average learners should receive none or few of these instructional treatments. He argued, however, that all students deserve humor, support, encouragement, field trips, openness, enrichment, and other entitlements.

A focus on basic skills is devalued for gifted students because of the belief that they already know what is being taught or can learn it more quickly than other students. This implies, however, that other learners are well served by materials that are replete with minimum competencies and countless behavioral objectives: "Somehow, zealous attention to rote, low-order questions, ditto worksheets, and textbook exercises becomes appropriate for the less able in the very recognition that it is inappropriate for the more able. I know of no educational theory or philosophy of education that justifies such curricular and instructional discriminations between the gifted and the not gifted" (p. 302).

Other educators assume a different stance on this issue. They argue that all individuals are unique and merit special education and that gifted education is a right not a privilege. They believe that students who are reading four grades above grade level and who are not challenged academically will soon become disinterested and discouraged learners despite their considerable intellectual skills. Many educators argue that what they recommend for the gifted is especially appropriate for these students—not that other students should not have some of these instructional opportunities. However, it is difficult to distinguish a student right from a privilege. Meeting the special needs of all students represents an intellectual and moral challenge to teachers.

Defining Giftedness

Giftedness

Whitmore and Maker (1985) contended that four key cognitive abilities reliably differentiate gifted from nongifted individuals: (a) communication of ideas, (b) problem-solving skills, (c) creative production or thinking, and (d) retention and use of knowledge. These authors argued that students are recognized as gifted because of their fluent and advanced use of language and their ability to express themselves in clear and interesting ways. When solving problems, gifted students are analytical and can draw from a wide range of knowledge and relevant experience as they assess alternative solutions. They can also invent new ideas and think divergently.

IQ scores and standardized achievement-test scores are only two of many ways giftedness can be defined. Students may be highly skilled at processing verbal information or may have a unique capacity for expressing themselves in artistic ways. Sternberg (1986a, 1986b) noted that intelligence should not be limited to performance on academic tasks. He argued that practical intelligence (e.g., behavior in everyday settings, getting along with others at school or at work, making progress on tasks) merits additional attention. Sternberg and Wagner (1986) suggested the need to view intelligence more broadly than simply as performance on obscure academic tasks.

The seven intelligences

Gardner (1983) and Walters and Gardner (1986) suggested that it is better to view intelligence in terms of multiple intelligences because human cognitive performance is best described in terms of a set of abilities and talents. They argued that each individual has some degree of each of seven intelligences that they view as independent and of equal stature: musical, bodily-kinesthetic, logical-mathematical, linguistic, spatial, interpersonal, and intrapersonal.

One of the most widely utilized approaches for defining giftedness is Renzulli's three-ring conception of giftedness (see Figure 25.2). Renzulli argued that it is the combination of the three factors that leads to adult productivity, and he suggested that educators should focus their talent search on children who display all three characteristics. From Renzulli's viewpoint, "gifted performance" and not just gifted aptitude is required before a student is labeled as gifted. As is evident, defining the "gifted student" is not an easy task. Even educators who spend much of their professional lives trying to meet the needs of gifted students vary to some extent in how they conceptualize gifted students.

Whitmore and Maker (1985) argued that for too long intellectual giftedness was equated with a high IQ: usually students had to score over

Figure 25.2 Renzulli's Three-Ring Conception of Giftedness

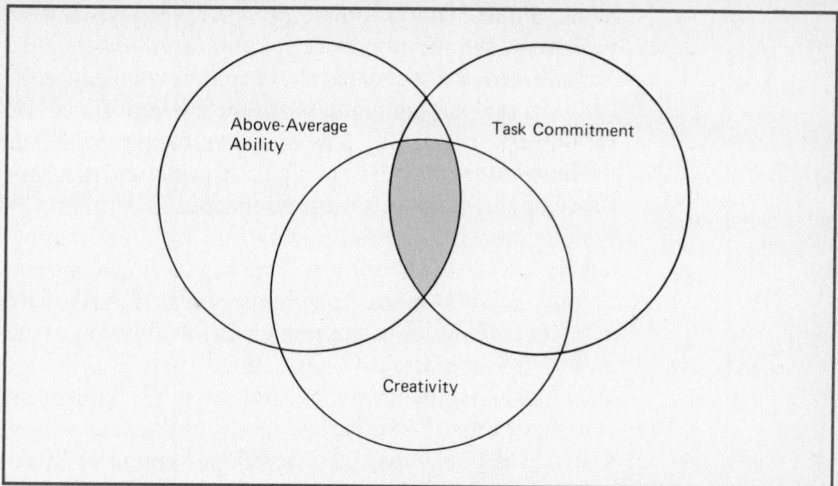

Source: J. Renzulli, *A Guidebook for Evaluating Programs for the Gifted and Talented.* (Los Angeles, National State Leadership Training Institute of the Gifted and Talented, 1979). Reprinted by permission of the National Leadership Training Institute of the Gifted and Talented, Office of the Superintendent, Ventura County Schools.

130 to be placed in a gifted program. Furthermore, students were expected to have high scores in all or most school subjects on standardized achievement tests, consistently superior grades, and recommendation from the classroom teacher. Despite a growing willingness by educators to define giftedness in more diverse ways, these methods of identification and selection for program participation still predominate. Many districts use only group-administered IQ tests because of their "cost effectiveness." This operationally defines intellectual giftedness as high academic achievement with emphasis on verbal and test-taking skills.

Expressions of giftedness

Whitmore (1982) argued that it is important for teachers not to expect outstanding performance from gifted students in all subjects but rather to recognize that there are many different ways in which students can express their giftedness. Also, it is important to recognize that all students need many of the educational features recommended for gifted students and that programs for gifted students will differ from regular education only in degree of emphasis.

Gifted Handicapped and Gifted Disadvantaged Students

Unfortunately, virtually all gifted persons with specific disabilities are first labeled and treated educationally in terms of their handicapping conditions (Whitmore & Maker, 1985). Thus many disabled students do not get the opportunity to develop their superior mental abilities in ways that would be recognized by others as giftedness. According to Whitmore and Maker, there is no accurate figure to convey the number of gifted persons with specific disabilities, but as much as 5 percent of the handicapped population may be intellectually gifted. Appropriate educational programming for these students would unleash a significant amount of creative productivity that could be of great value to society. In addition to the well-known gifted individuals who have overcome their specific disabilities (e.g., Helen Keller), many lesser-known gifted persons have also overcome potentially handicapping conditions and had productive careers. These authors lamented the unrecognized potential of many gifted handicapped persons they studied for whom successful case studies could have been written if they had received appropriate educational programs.

Creative characteristics of disadvantaged children

Many students who come from low-income or minority homes also have superior talents that go unrecognized. Torrance (1973, 1977) identified various creative characteristics that frequently appear among disadvantaged children: (1) ability to express feelings and emotions; (2) ability to improvise with commonplace materials; (3) articulateness in role playing and storytelling; (4) enjoyment of and ability in visual art; (5) enjoyment of and ability in creative movement, dance, dramatics; (6) enjoyment of and ability in music, rhythm, and so on; (7) expressive speech; (8) fluency and flexibility in nonverbal media (produces variety of ideas through drawing, dance, music, etc.); (9) enjoyment of and skills in small-group activities (tries harder in small groups or produces productive ideas in a small-group setting, skillful in group organization, etc.); (10) responsiveness to the concrete (generates ideas from concrete objects and materials); (11) responsiveness to the kinesthetic (skillful in interpreting meaning of movement); (12) expressiveness of gestures; (13) humor; (14) richness of imagery and informal language (e.g., makes people visualize when describing something in the conversation); (15) originality of ideas in problem solving; (16) problem centeredness (is hard to distract); (17) emotional responsiveness; (18) quickness of warm-up (e.g., ready to engage a task quickly; may get tired of waiting easily). Teachers should become more aware of such characteristics in disabled or economically disadvantaged students and try to help them develop beyond normal expectations in areas in which they are gifted.

Trends in Program Alternatives

Radical acceleration

Historically, one of the most common ways of responding to the needs of gifted students has been the use of acceleration programs. Acceleration activities allow gifted students to obtain educational experiences that are usually presented to older students. It may mean grade skipping, concurrent enrollment in both high school and college, early admission to college, and so on. Torrance (1986) noted that the most discussed program alternative for gifted education in recent years is *radical acceleration* (i.e., skipping several grades instead of one or two) advocated by Julian Stanley (1976, 1978). According to Torrance, there is consistent research evidence to support programs that use moderate acceleration for mature and capable students. (In a review of 200 studies conducted over a fifty-year period, Daurio [1979] found that not one study showed educational acceleration to be harmful and that two-thirds of these studies found positive effects of acceleration.) Stanley and his associates at Johns Hopkins University have experimented with radical acceleration of mathematically precocious youths and have obtained consistently good results (Stanley, 1976, 1978, 1980). This program now is national in scope and has been expanded to include students who are verbally gifted as well as other precocious groups.

IEPs for the gifted

According to Torrance (1986), for many years arguments have been made to support individual education plans for gifted students. However, it was not until IEPs were mandated for retarded and other handicapped learners that the practice became widespread. A variety of proposals have been made for implementing IEP programs, and there has been considerable experimentation with IEPs in gifted education. Most of these plans integrate several alternatives, such as regular classes with special assignments, enriched experiences, and self-directed study.

Other approaches

Other approaches to gifted education include mentoring (Boston, 1976; Lambert & Lambert, 1982; Runions, 1980); special schools (e.g., Amara & Leona, 1983); Saturday and summer school programs (Feldhusen & Sokol, 1982); special leadership training (Foster, 1981); materials in subject-matter fields (e.g., Rebbeck, 1983); and special instruction in forecasting and planning skills (Kolloff, 1983), research skills (Pellegrini, 1982), and computer skills (Beasley, 1984).

Mentoring Although it is not possible to discuss all of the trends that Torrance identified, we want to comment on mentoring because it is a popular approach that has considerable potential as a flexible program alternative. In the 1970s peer tutoring became an important part of education at all levels, and more than 10,000 programs involving the use of tutoring have been reported (Runions, 1980). All students are capable of tutoring and can benefit from it, but tutoring does not necessarily result in desirable outcomes. Certain conditions make tutoring more effective (for example, when the situation is structured in terms of task, time, materials, and procedures and when students are trained in how to perform as tutors).

Mentoring

One special type of tutoring is mentoring in which a student is tutored not by a peer but by an adult. Mentoring involves interactions between students and professional people in the community. A major difference between tutoring and mentoring is that much tutoring is compensatory-

Learning-disabled students, like their nondisabled peers, benefit from peer tutoring.

based, because some learning difficulty is being resolved (Runions, 1980). In mentoring, both tutor and tutee are extremely talented, and participants are equal partners in the learning activity. Students who are selected for mentoring have demonstrated above-average competence in an area, are committed to learning and communicating what is learned, and are ready to assume responsibility for their own learning. Mentoring is a social contract between individuals, and learners are expected to use the mentor as a source of stimulation but not to depend on the mentor for evaluation or for identification of the learning activity (i.e., to tell them what they should learn). The mentor should support self-directed trial and error and provide appropriate feedback.

Runions noted that one potential threat to mentoring is that mentors may become surrogate teachers if they are required to evaluate and record student performance in detail. More appropriate behavior would be for these individuals to maintain their roles as scientists, academics, lawyers, newspaper people, and so on, who generously provide their talents. In this sense, mentoring is not so much evaluating the student's performance as it is sharing common interests and encouraging students to think more deeply and critically about a particular area.

Curriculum Compacting Renzulli, Smith, and Reis (1982) noted that students who are academically years ahead of their peers are often frustrated because they are held accountable for classroom assignments that are repetitious, unnecessary, and hence boring. Teachers are often too busy trying to help students who are not working up to grade level and who do not understand assigned work to be able to find challenging assignments for students who understand the material and need no further review.

Curriculum streamlining

According to Renzulli and associates, providing special services for a few hours per week is one alternative, but educators are only kidding themselves if they do not also modify the regular curriculum significantly. These authors argued that teachers need to streamline the regular curriculum to (1) relieve gifted students of the boredom often associated with unchallenging work on basic skills and (2) find time for gifted students to pursue accelerated enrichment activities.

Testing students' mastery of levels

The first task is for the teacher to identify an area in the curriculum in which a student shows particular strength. If a student's reading achievement scores are three years above grade level, for example, and if this student is consistently earning A's in reading, the reading curriculum should be compacted. Also, most of the major curriculum packages have diagnostic instruments (especially in the basic skill areas of reading, language arts, and mathematics), and teachers who are interested in compacting the curriculum can use pretests and end-of-unit tests to assess students' mastery of major concepts to be presented. It makes little sense to expose students to a two-week instructional unit if they only need to learn a couple of vocabulary words or to review basic facts briefly.

If a curriculum does not include a series of preunit and postunit tests, teachers will have to review the major objectives of a unit and construct an instrument that measures most of the important content. Whether they use commercial materials or their own tests, teachers can identify students who do not need a particular unit or who can master the unit in one or two days.

Once students have demonstrated an understanding of the material in a unit, they need the opportunity to work on accelerated or enrichment activities. Renzulli and associates argued that the major consideration in making these decisions is the interests of the students. It is important, for example, not to assume that students are interested in a particular area because they happen to perform exceptionally well in the area. Thus the fact that students have earned time in mathematics class does not necessarily mean that the extra time has to be spent in mathematics. Furthermore, there is no reason that students should work on enrichment assignments alone; they can be done with other students.

Regular-Class Programs Treffinger (1982) argued that too many programs for the gifted are isolated from the regular classroom and that many educators settle for special programs that involve only a small part of the school week, few students, and have little if any relation to regular programs. According to Treffinger, no matter how good programs are, gifted students will spend most of their time in the regular classroom. Although a classroom teacher with limited resources cannot be "everything for everyone," many valuable, stimulating activities can be provided in regular classrooms.

Ideas for gifted students in regular classrooms

Treffinger offered sixty ideas for instructing gifted students in regular classrooms (although all students would benefit from many of these ideas). Ten of these ideas are described below.

1. Use pretests to enable students to "test out."
2. In a part of one lesson each day, include a discussion of questions that students did not know how to answer about the topic of study. These questions can stimulate general inquiry as well as provide a basis for independent work projects or shared group activities.
3. Have students develop a community resource file for the class. Students could interview potential resource people and characterize the various skills and insights these individuals could share with the class.
4. Provide one afternoon a week to allow students (with parents or community volunteers) seminar opportunities to explore hobbies, new topics, etc.
5. Develop a series of experimental units in which students can participate for a short time to explore new areas of interest without committing themselves to prolonged periods of study.
6. Have a "research-in-progress" corner where students can go to record information about new topics being investigated in various subjects.
7. Encourage students to write by developing a directory of publications (community, statewide, national) in which students' work can be published.

8. Encourage students to keep journals or to use pocket notebooks to record interesting ideas and to write questions that occur to them.
9. Obtain copies of textbook and curriculum materials at various grade levels to provide challenging instructional materials in a variety of subjects for advanced students.
10. Encourage students to use many senses in processing information and in expressing their ideas. Provide learning opportunities that involve observation, visualization, listening, touching, and tasting.

Clarifying Expectations for Talented Students

Coop (1982) contended that writings on the gifted tend to focus on producing "things" rather than on social processes. He advocated creating better techniques for motivating students toward positive social goals or helping them to empathize with others. The same steps that lead to the invention of products may also lead to the creation of better strategies and processes for dealing with others. Although gifted programs are paying more attention to social outcomes (e.g., leadership), we agree that these programs should focus more on social goals.

According to Coop (1982), one of the problems with recommending programs for gifted students is that there is a paucity of information linking specific programs to outcomes for students. Therefore, teachers should view the suggestions discussed here as guidelines for developing their own teaching strategies rather than rules to be followed rigidly. In this spirit, we offer some of our own observations on eight teacher expectations that cause problems for some gifted students.

Problematic Teacher Expectations for Gifted Students

Too Much Too Soon High-achieving students are often expected to do too much too soon (e.g., they must have clear career plans), and such expectations pressure these students too much. Their talent is seen by others as so "precious" that they are not allowed to make productive mistakes. The pressure also leads them to develop inappropriately premature, superficial commitments to goals. In addition to the expectation for academic success, many gifted students are also expected to be social leaders and to develop capacities in many different areas at the same time. Unfortunately, they are not encouraged to be flexible or allowed the leisure to delay important decisions as other students are often encouraged to do. (See Figure 25.3.)

Fast Curriculum Pace Gifted students are often required to cover content more quickly than other students. They get exposed to more content but often without getting enough time to think about it and consolidate their knowledge. The image is of a car going down the highway, but instead of traveling at forty or fifty miles an hour, gifted students are asked to speed along at eighty miles an hour. They seldom have the opportunity to explore interesting and productive side roads, which may be more important than simply reaching a fixed destination more quickly.

Too Few Opportunities to Reexamine and to Repeat Assignments It is critical that high-achieving students occasionally be asked to redo something—to do it better and more thoughtfully. After having completed an

Figure 25.3 No student can be at her best all the time!

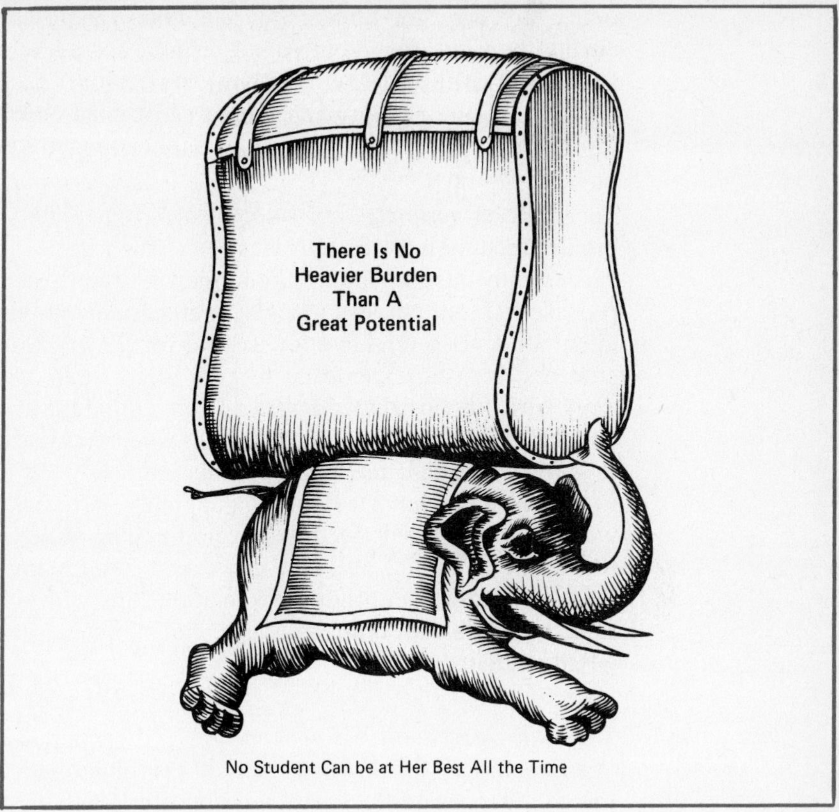

There Is No
Heavier Burden
Than A
Great Potential
No Student Can be at Her Best All the Time

Source: J. Galbraith, *The Gifted Kids' Survival Guide for Ages 11–18.* (Minneapolis, MN: Free Spirit Publishing, Inc., 1983). Reprinted by permission.

assignment, the teacher might add new dimensions for students to consider when they read the assignment or work on related activities. Gifted students often complete work and then want to know what the next task is; to them, classroom success means finishing things quickly and moving on to something else. If we want them to develop the ability to explore new topics independently, it is important to require them to revise and revisit problems or assignments.

Too Little Assimilation It is possible for a curriculum to require too little assimilation. Students, for example, can carefully outline others' views of the pros and cons of electing senators for two-year versus four-year or six-year terms, but a student's own views of this issue are most important. Many students are adept at generating lists of detailed points but have little capacity to evaluate information produced by others and develop their own beliefs. More instruction and training in this area are important.

Too Much Analysis; Too Little Synthesis In many curriculum areas, teachers spend a great deal of time helping students to be critical of and sensitive to social issues and social problems. There is too little opportunity, however, for students to follow these analyses with syntheses that enable them to offer creative suggestions for addressing problems constructively. Although the "textbook curriculum" facilitates analysis and critical thinking skills (when taught well) most curriculum materials do too little to encourage synthesis or applications of knowledge.

Too Little Opportunity to Develop Leadership Skills Considering that bright students have many ideas, can reach decisions quickly, and can successfully integrate information, they may be intolerant of students who process information less quickly or integrate it less meaningfully. Thus gifted students often have low regard for the cognitive abilities of other students. It seems important to give bright students the opportunity to work with other bright students to discover that they can learn from others and that they can develop more insight when they use others as resources. It is also vital that talented students learn how to work constructively with others who have less talent and ability. After all, in subsequent real-world jobs, they will need to develop coping strategies that allow them to use the talents of less able coworkers. Too many gifted students cut themselves off from productive relationships with other people who, although perhaps not quite as bright, can stimulate, challenge, and extend gifted students' thinking.

Too Little Opportunity to Communicate In general, gifted students learn "text material" quickly and then are presented with another text assignment that provides yet another opportunity to learn new information quickly. Thus school learning for them is a series of successes in which the key is an increase in their knowledge. These students, however, have too little opportunity to communicate what they have learned and experienced to other students or adults. A constructive use of class time would be to allow talented students to work in this area, that is, to communicate what they have learned through newspapers, critical reviews of subject matter, book reviews, or musical reviews.

Too Little Opportunity for Self-Evaluation Most talented students who go "through the curriculum" learn self-management—they learn how to set deadlines and organize their personal resources. They may be less able to enage in constructive self-evaluation, however. Too many talented students set inappropriately high expectations (Why can't I make up my mind? Why am I having difficulty with this?). They need to learn about their relative strengths and weaknesses and their emerging skills. These students need to think about their own papers, for example, and to compare them with papers that they wrote three months earlier. How have they changed their minds about earlier papers? Have the bases on which they judge their work and the criteria they use to compare their work with others' changed?

Responding to Expectation Problems

The following responses have the potential simultaneously to address several of the eight inappropriate expectations that have been outlined.

Opportunity to Learn about Careers Talented students should collect and assimilate information that enables them to consider the advantages and disadvantages of particular careers. What decisions do people have to make? What problems do they confront? Does a job call for problem finding, problem solving, or application of general knowledge to relatively straightforward issues? What are the unique challenges and satisfactions of particular careers? Having the opportunity to discuss and to compare how different types of engineers or physicians view their careers is vital. It allows students to think about jobs and how they relate to a variety of important conditions. Considering the multiple talents that these students have, getting information that helps them to consider what they want from a work situation may have long-term benefits. The issue is not what job they can perform but rather what work conditions they want.

Social Change and Implications for Individual Roles It would be constructive for gifted students to see what the world looked like in 1910, 1940, and 1960, to examine how various professions and social institutions have changed with time. What was the life of a physician like in 1910 versus 1960? How and why has the role changed? How does it compare to the role of a university professor in 1910 and in 1960? Why have some professions changed more than others? What constitutes the knowledge base of a profession? How many careers might one expect an individual to engage in in the next thirty years, given the rate at which social change is occurring? What was the role of the federal government in higher education in 1920, 1940, 1960, and 1980? Why has it changed? What are the consequences of the changes? What roles were available for women in 1900, 1940, 1990? What are the positive and negative consequences of these changes? Assignments should help talented students to see that flexibility in career planning is desirable (i.e., changing conditions must be anticipated), that it is acceptable to consider several careers, that a degree of uncertainty is expected no matter how talented one is.

Assignments That Require Problem Identification and Data Collection and Analysis Many related curriculum materials can be used in classrooms, but sometimes the best assignments involve problems and issues in the local school or community factors that are personally relevant to students. It is important that students *debate* about the best way to collect data, what the data mean, how to analyze them, and how best to present data. Debate allows constructive criticism and exchange and helps students to realize that information alone does not solve problems.

Formal Communication One frustrating issue that many talented people have to face is that others do not process information as quickly or as deeply as they do. Hence gifted students sometimes avoid communication with others and do not attempt to improve their own ability to communicate. When problems occur, they tend to blame others. Thus it is constructive to ask students to engage in activities such as (a) watching newscasts to see how newscasters face the dilemma of presenting information in a way in which the average citizen can comprehend it but also in a technically accurate fashion so as to stimulate more sophisticated viewers or (b) debating how to advertise a bond issue so that it would appeal to individuals in high-paying occupations but also to individuals who will be "hurt" economically and so that the message is ethical and fair as well as persuasive. In general, gifted students need opportunities to communicate through formal speeches, debates, radio broadcasts, book reviews, evaluations of school plays, and so on to develop their capacity to share their thinking in socially constructive ways.

Research Skills Gifted students should have opportunities to evaluate original scholarship. They might go to the library, for example, to assess alternate sources and to see how various people who were writing in 1920 viewed the coming social/economic conditions. What were the popular ways to think about the economy? What were some individual economic forecasters beginning to worry about? How did others react to their worries?

If research is done constructively in a social setting (perhaps two or three students working together), students can jointly consolidate, assimilate, synthesize, and analyze information and develop constructive leadership skills. They learn how to disagree with others yet ultimately to produce a plan or document that satisfies all of them in an intellectually honest fashion by making compromises to achieve consensus that are not expedient but represent a fair view of what they believe. Courses in history and English should stress successful library research skills, courses in biology and chemistry should help students to develop research and laboratory skills, and courses in sociology and psychology should expose students to survey and observational research and allow them to collect and analyze data and to draw meaningful conclusions about the research topic.

SUMMARY

In the past, students with special needs were placed in special institutions or classes. Data on the effectiveness of special settings and programs, however, are unimpressive, so the current trend is toward retaining special students in regular classrooms. Problems in diagnosis, the reliability and validity of classifications and their treatment implications, the negative effects of labeling, and various legal changes have all contributed to this trend. Public Law 94-142 commits the nation to a policy of mainstreaming handicapped students.

Teachers working with special students need to shed their stereotypes and recognize the many similarities of these students to their peers. Teachers should capitalize on special students' strengths, prepare other students to interact constructively with them, deal realistically and matter-of-factly with handicaps, and establish appropriate positive expectations.

Many special educators now believe that general labels are most appropriate to describe handicapping conditions because it is extremely difficult reliably to identify specific handicaps and because specific labels are often associated with narrow, rigid classroom programs that focus too much on students' disabilities rather than their abilities. Labels are still widely used, however, because educators believe that they convey some useful information, if not taken too literally, and because legislation often demands that labels be used if program funds are to be obtained. In this context, we have discussed several handicapping conditions and have presented broad classroom applications associated with these specific disabilities.

Research suggests that mildly handicapped students tend to do poorly in various educational environments in which they are placed. Instruction varies widely within general program categories (e.g., resource rooms, mainstreamed regular classrooms, etc.) as well as from classroom to classroom within a category. So far, not enough attention has been placed on the *quality* of instruction that mildly handicapped students receive in various settings. Some data suggest, however, that many programs have not been adapted to the needs of individual students.

The term *gifted* can mean many different things, but school officials place a premium on one type of giftedness—verbal facility. Although this is understandable to some extent (since success on many school tasks is highly associated with verbal ability), this is only one type of giftedness, and educators must recognize and nourish other talents that students possess, particularly in students who are seen as disadvantaged or handicapped.

Several trends in programming for gifted students are described in the chapter. Although there are many useful ideas available in the literature, few studies examine the efficacy of one model over another. Teachers need to adjust instruction to the needs of diverse learners. Although there are some distinct differences between student groups, many needs of intellectually gifted and mildly handicapped students are similar.

Questions and Problems

1. How far can ordinary public schools go in striving to meet the ideal of free public education for *all*? Specifically, what categories of students, if any, should be excluded from public schools? Why? How? Who should decide, and on what basis?
2. Considering the grade and subject you expect to teach, what special provisions will you need to make for mildly mentally handicapped students (special teaching techniques, substitute assignments, special

tests)? For blind students? Deaf students? Paraplegics? Gifted students?

3. How can conflict or disagreement among participants in an IEP meeting (principal, diagnostician, special-education teacher, classroom teacher, parents) be resolved *in the best interests of the student*? What should be done if there is no consensus?
4. What, if anything, should a teacher say about mainstreamed students to classroom visitors (parent volunteers, observers from a college of education, PTA representatives, and so on)?
5. The need for special provisions for the physically handicapped is usually obvious to everyone. But what about students with emotional or behavioral disorders? Should these students sometimes be exempted from demands or given special privileges? If so, how should this be explained to classmates?
6. What are the advantages for other students of having mainstreamed students in the classroom?
7. How can the needs of intellectually gifted students be satisfied in the classroom? In what ways do special programs for the gifted differ from regular instruction?
8. If you were speaking to a PTA meeting that included parents of both mildly handicapped and gifted students, how would you justify a special gifted program?

Case Studies

SPECIAL TEACHING TECHNIQUES. Dan Jones and Don Martin are the two most disruptive students in Joyce Putnam's class. Both are often out of their seats, are unable to concentrate on their work for long, frequently get into fights and arguments with classmates, and resist Joyce's authority. Dan has been diagnosed as hyperactive and takes Ritalin. Don does not take medication, but he has been diagnosed as emotionally disturbed, with poor impulse control and frequent inappropriate affect. How should Joyce deal with these two boys? Specifically, what special techniques or procedures should she use? Should her approach be essentially the same with both boys, or are there things she should do with one but not the other?

MOVING FORWARD. Sam had done terribly during the first two weeks of school. His work was poor, especially his seatwork. At times, it seemed as though Sam was doing an assignment other than the one that Ms. Murphy had put on the board. Yesterday Sam got into trouble several times for talking with Molly, the attractive girl seated next to him. Today he did all of his seatwork perfectly. Ms. Murphy wondered if the move (to the front of the room—near her) had helped Sam. What are possible reasons for Sam's improved performance? What should Ms. Murphy do to confirm her diagnosis?

SPECIAL INTERESTS. Tim is a talented fourth-grade student but has a club foot. He loves sports and makes constant reference to college and professional teams as well as those at the local high school. However, Tim spends recess by himself and never shoots baskets on the playground or engages in any other physical activity. In what ways might his teacher, Jeff Wilson, use Tim's interest in building classroom assignments? In what ways might Mr. Wilson help Tim become more involved in physical activities?

PART 8
MEASUREMENT AND EVALUATION

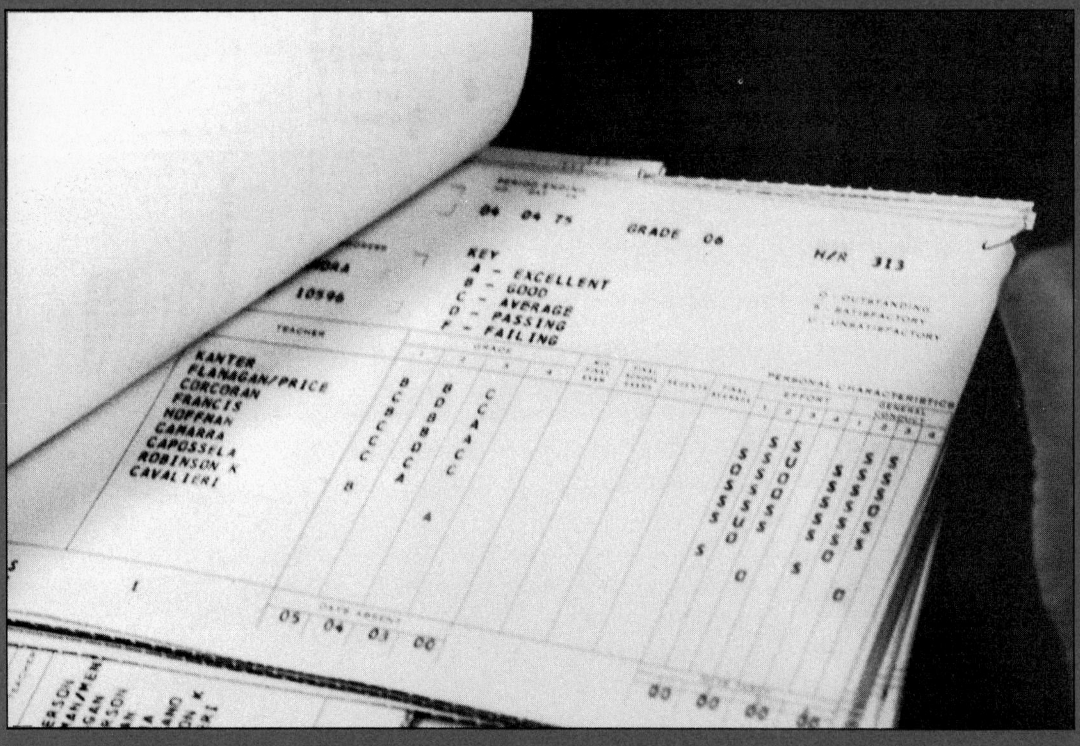

There is presently a great deal of interest in improving school and teacher performance through more testing of both teachers and students. In some states teachers must pass exams before they are certified. More and more states are requiring students at selected grade levels to pass achievement tests mandated by the state. Tests can be important indicants of performance and can be very helpful in improving the quality of instruction. Most tests (e.g., multiple-choice tests) assess knowledge that is easy to measure, however, and do not measure more complex and perhaps more important cognitive abilities. As a classroom teacher, you will likely face increasing pressure to test students in the next few years, and part of your success as a teacher will depend on your ability to determine whether or not a test is related to important instructional goals. You must not allow testing to dictate the curriculum in inappropriate ways.

Measuring and evaluating student performance are important parts of a teacher's professional responsibility. Let us assume that you are a teacher who has decided to state your grading criteria at the beginning of the school year. You pass out a sheet listing a group of tests, totaling 500 credit points. Everyone who gets 450 points (90 percent) or more will get an A, those getting between 400 and 449 points will get a B, and so on down the scale. This plan seems fair and sensible, but what if at the end of the term you find that tests scores are extremely high? If so, you face one of two possible results:

1. If you follow your plan, more than 50 percent of the students will get an A. You now realize however, that your tests were much too easy. You are sure, based on questions and comments and on class discussion, that many of the students with more than 450 points did not really learn much of the material.

2. More than 50 percent of your students should get an A. In this case students' grades match your other information. The tests were of appropriate difficulty and measured mastery of key concepts and skills. Student behavior in the classroom indicated general interest in and knowledge about the subject matter, and there was no evidence of cheating or other reasons for artificially high grades.

What might you do in these situations, and what implications might there be for you and your students? What about the opposite situation, with point totals discouragingly low, when more than 50 percent of your students will get F's?

1. You realize that your expectations were unrealistic and your test questions were too difficult or too tricky. Even your best students, who gave every evidence of interest and understanding in class discussions and activities, had difficulty with the test. You discounted student complaints that

the tests were difficult. But the tests were given, and the scores are recorded. Now what?

2. In a contrasting situation, scores are very low, but this time you have no reason to question test difficulty. The questions were drawn directly from classroom presentations and assigned readings, and there were no tricky questions. You have every reason to believe that your tests were fair and valid, but your students nevertheless did poorly. Your observations suggest that lack of motivation was the reason. Students were not studying very hard, if at all, and did not learn much. Now what?

Information that will help you to avoid such dilemmas is presented in the following chapters on basic measurement (Chapter 26), statistical concepts (Chapter 27), and sound test construction (Chapter 28). Finally, in Chapter 29 we discuss principles for grading students fairly, even when the information available is less than ideal.

CHAPTER

Principles of Educational Measurement

CHAPTER OUTLINE

OBJECTIVES

When you have mastered the material in this chapter, you will be able to

1. Explain the concept of measurement error and how the standard error of measurement can be used to interpret and accurately report test scores
2. Define *test reliability* and explain how one can use correlation coefficients or the standard error of measurement to express test reliability
3. Discuss the importance of high test reliability and the factors that can affect the reliability of a test
4. Explain content and criterion validity of tests and the factors that can decrease test validity
5. Define *norm-referenced* and *criterion-referenced tests* and explain how to distinguish them
6. Explain how questions for norm-referenced tests are selected, how such tests are "normed," and their usefulness to both teachers and students
7. State principles for the selection and effective use of standardized, norm-referenced achievement tests

Assessment and evaluation of students' progress in mastering the curriculum are basic tasks of teaching. Most teachers must collect some systematic achievement data to provide a basis for grading, but even teachers who are not required to assign formal grades still need to assess student achievement to gather feedback about the effectiveness of their own teaching, to identify topics and individual students that require additional instruction, and to provide guidance for planning new instruction.

Informal assessment

Teachers do much of this assessment informally in the process of observing students' attention to lessons and engagement in assignments, monitoring their answers to questions during class activities, and correcting their written assignments. This kind of informal assessment is very important, but it is subjective and thus open to the influence of teacher expectations and attitudes and other biasing sources. It also is usually unsystematic: teachers monitor certain students much more closely than others (e.g., see Marshall & Weinstein, 1984); some students have learned to "look good" during class activities and to get help with their written assignments, so that they appear to have mastered much more material than they really have; some will make generally good progress but consistently make certain kinds of mistakes because they do not know a key concept or lack a skill, deficiencies that are not obvious from casual daily observation. Consequently, it is important to supplement informal monitoring with formal assessment that measures student achievement under standardized conditions.

Curricula are composed of strands or sequences that build toward terminal objectives describing the knowledge or skills that students are expected to master. Occasionally, these objectives are limited and specific, as in the requirement that the student be able to name all letters of the alphabet without error or run a hundred meters within a time limit. Usually, however, objectives are more sweeping and ambitious—we want students to be able to express their thoughts in acceptable prose (spelling, grammar, and other mechanics; good paragraphing and organization generally) or to apply basic mathematical principles and facts in everyday situations (computing the best bargain, estimating how much wallpaper to purchase for a room). Here it is not feasible to test students on every possible application of what they have learned or even to test them on everything they have been taught. This is unnecessary and too time consuming in any case. Therefore, we sample students' knowledge or skills by requiring them to perform a few tasks selected from the key terminal objectives in the curriculum sequences recently taught.

ERRORS OF MEASUREMENT

Formal measurement

Formal measurement situations involve standardized conditions. Students are required to respond to the same set of questions or tasks or to equivalent forms that measure the same knowledge or skills. Ideally, all students are measured under standard conditions: They are instructed in the same ways (in general, but with individual attention as needed) and tested at the same time and under the same conditions (time limits, permission to use a book or other aids such as calculators). In general, everything is arranged to ensure that each student's score accurately represents his or her mastery.

Inaccuracy of test scores

In practice, test scores are not so accurate. First, recall that the test itself is just a sample of the full range of things that students have been taught. Any particular test favors certain students because of differences in what they learned originally or in what they emphasized in preparing for the test. Second, a great variety of situational factors affects the performance of individual students. Those who are well prepared, well rested, and able to concentrate on the test will do their best. Others, however, will lose points because of factors that may be beyond their control: they did not get a good night's sleep, they were physically ill or emotionally stressed on the day of the exam or when they were studying for it, and so on.

Because of such factors, test scores are just estimates of students' true mastery. They can be thought of as composed of two parts: true mastery and an artificial increment or decrement reflecting sampling errors (a different set of items would have yielded a different score) or situational factors (a student would have scored differently if tested at another time or under other circumstances). Along with other factors to be described later, these sampling errors and situational factors contribute to the measurement error that exists to some degree in almost any set of test scores. This is represented in the following equation:

Test score = true score plus or minus measurement error

The degree of measurement error distorting any particular student's test score cannot be determined precisely, but the measurement error associated with any particular test or measurement device can at least be estimated from information about the test's reliability (the concept of reliability is discussed below). This estimate for a specific test is called the test's standard error of measurement. The higher the standard error, the less accurate the test. The degree of error in educational measurement is usually larger than it is for measurement of height, weight, or other physical factors because educational measurement is less direct, relies on less precise instruments, and applies to knowledge and skills that are less stable than physical factors (Mehrens & Lehmann, 1978).

Standard error of measurement

For most IQ tests, the standard error is about 5 points. Therefore, if a student gets a score of 105, we can be reasonably confident that the true IQ is somewhere between 100 and 110 (assuming that there is such a thing as a true IQ score), but we cannot assume that it is exactly 105. Nor can we confidently assume that the student has more aptitude than another who scores 102 or less than one who scores 108. The test is just not that precise. Similar considerations apply to interpreting a standardized achievement score that "places" a student at a "grade level" of 6.8 or implies that the student has achieved more than precisely 63 percent of all the students at the same grade level.

Errors of measurement are assumed to be distributed randomly with

Distribution of standard error

respect to individuals' true scores, so that repeated measurements theoretically would yield a normal curve distributed on either side of the true score (the normal curve is explained in detail in the next chapter). Use of the probability statistics associated with normal curves allows us to use band interpretation of test scores when we know a test's standard error of measurement. Thus in the example above, we can state that we are 68 percent certain that the student who scored 105 has a true IQ between 100 and 110 (plus or minus one standard error from the obtained score of 105) and 95 percent certain that the true IQ is between 95 and 115 (plus or minus two standard errors).

TEST RELIABILITY

A test's standard error of measurement varies inversely with its reliability: reliable tests have low standard errors and thus allow more precise measurement and more confident interpretation. Reliability refers to the stability or consistency of test scores across repeated measurements. A reliable test should yield similar results when administered two or more times during a short period (a few weeks) to the same students. Students who obtain high scores the first time should obtain similar scores the second time, and so on.

Correlation Coefficients

Reliability is estimated using correlation methods and expressed numerically with correlation coefficients that vary from −1.00 through zero to +1.00. There are several kinds of correlation coefficients computed with various formulas that will not be reviewed here (for detailed discussions of reliability, see Cronbach et al., 1972; Kubiszyn & Borich, 1984; Mehrens & Lehmann, 1978; or Stanley, 1971). All of them, however, vary from −1.00 to +1.00 and indicate the direction and strength of the relationship, if any, between two sets of scores.

The symbol r

The symbol r stands for the correlation coefficient. When r is positive, there is a positive correlation between the two sets of scores, so individuals high on one measure are likely to be high on the other. When r is negative, there is an inverse relation (negative correlation) between the two sets of scores, and individuals high on one measure are likely to be low on the other. When r is zero, there is no correlation between the two sets of scores, so individuals' scores on the first measure give us no information at all about their probable scores on the second measure. Some typical correlations illustrating these relationships are shown below.

Measures	r
Two equivalent forms of the same test	.95
IQ subtest score and total IQ score	.70
Adult heights and weights	.60
High school and college grade point average	.50
Socioeconomic status and IQ	.35
Height and IQ	.05

Date of appearance of first tooth and college grade point average	.00
Family size and school achievement	−.30
Frequency of serious classroom disruptions and student achievement	−.40
Scores on a test of achievement and a checklist of learning deficiencies	−.80

The correlation coefficients expressing a test's reliability must be high (at least 0.70 and preferably more than 0.90) for the test to be reliable enough to be useful for confident measurement and decision making. Figure 26.1 shows scatterplots of hypothetical students' scores on two administrations of the same ten-item test. Notice that when there is a perfect positive relationship (r = 1.00), each student gets the same score on both occasions. Where r = 0.75, however, most scores vary a point or two, and many vary by three or even four points. When r = 0.50, there are more frequent and larger differences, which severely limit the usefulness of the test. Reliability is low, the standard error of measurement is high, and scores cannot be interpreted with much precision. Differences of four or five points between students are probably real, but differences of a point or two are probably just measurement error.

Importance of Reliability

Unreliable tests are not only imprecise, they are unfair to students. When scores vary like those shown in Figure 26.1, where r = 0.50, or worse yet, where r = 0.35 or zero, there is probably something wrong with most of the items, and students' answers are shaped by factors other than the knowledge or skills presumably being tested. Items probably are ambiguous, misleading, unrelated to what was taught, or otherwise inappropriate.

Item-level reliablity

A highly reliable test is reliable even at the item level, not just for total scores (see Baker, 1977, or Kubiszn & Borich, 1984, for detailed information about item analysis). Thus if John Smith got the first seven items and items nine and ten correct the first time but missed item eight and items eleven through fifteen, he should have the same or a very similar pattern of correct and incorrect answers the second time he takes the test. This assumes that John has not received any additional instruction between testings and that he has not sought answers to the questions he missed.

Reliability in the sense of consistency of scores across long periods when the same students are retested with the same test is not of particular importance in education. This is because education by its very nature involves change, specifically the attempt to increase students' knowledge and skills. Thus over a long period, we ordinarily do not expect reliability for repeated performance on the same test.

Good tests, however, should have the kind of short-term reliability that comes with well-constructed test items. Other factors that affect reliability include (Kubisyzn & Borich, 1984; Mehrens & Lehmann, 1978):

Figure 26.1 Scattergrams of Correlations of Various Sizes between Sets of Scores on the Same Ten-Item Test (N = 50 students)

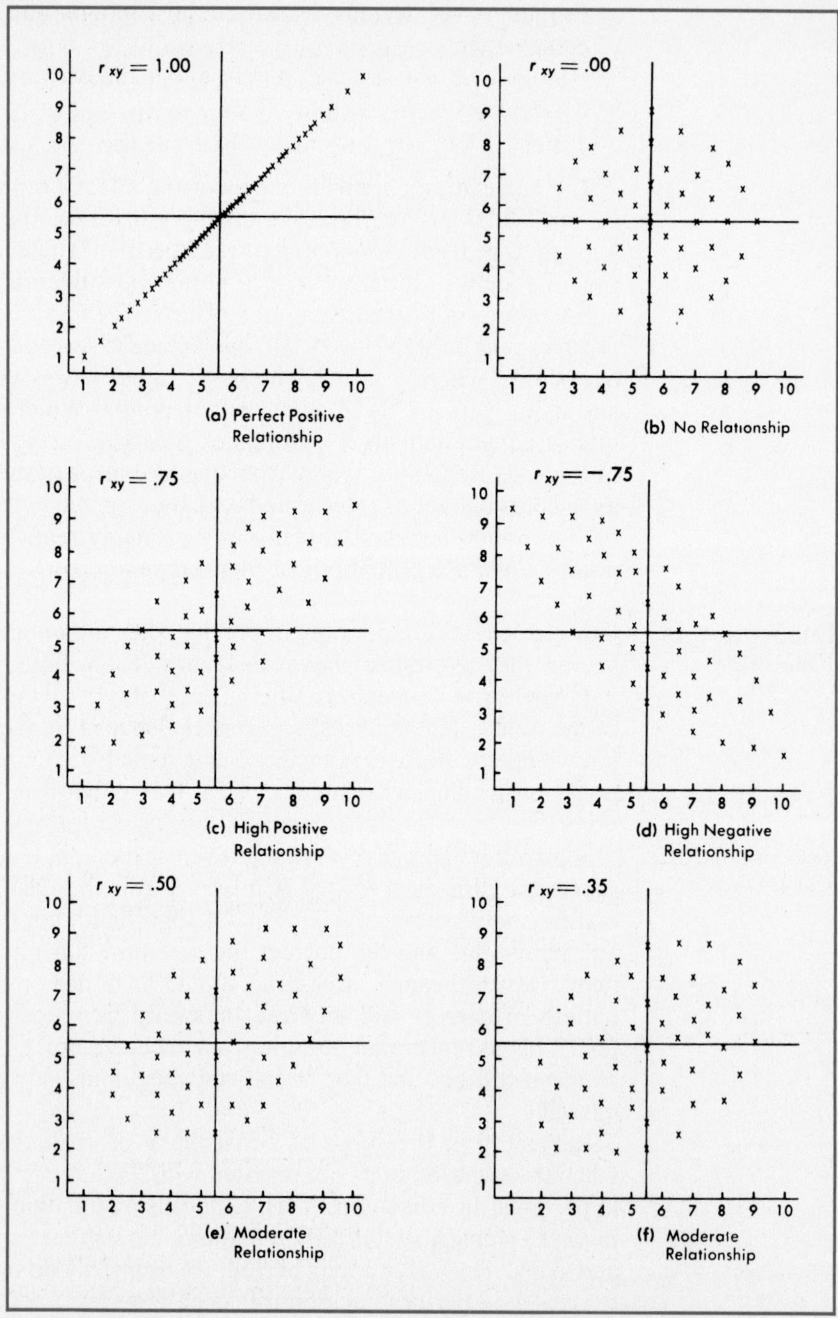

Source: From *Measurement and Evaluation in Education and Psychology*, Second Edition, William Mehrens and Irvine Lehmann, copyright © 1975 by Holt, Rinehart, and Winston, Inc., reprinted by permission of the publisher.

1. *Test length*—Other things being equal, a longer test is more reliable than a shorter one because it involves a larger sample of the knowledge or skill objectives taught.
2. *Heterogeneity of the student group*—Reliability tends to be higher when scores are spread over a large range because measurement errors are small in comparison to the range of differences between true scores.
3. *Item difficulty*—Reliability is higher when most items are of medium difficulty for the group tested because this spreads the scores over a greater range, in comparison to scores that would be obtained if most items were either too easy or too hard.
4. *Objectivity of scoring*—The reliability of tests that can be scored objectively tends to be higher because with subjective scoring, equivalent student performance might be scored differently because of differences in scorers' judgments at various times, even if the scorer is the same person.

Reliability is only one of the attributes of a good test, however. An even more basic attribute is validity. Reliability is a precondition for validity in that a test cannot be valid if it is not reliable. Validity, however, involves several considerations in addition to reliability.

TEST VALIDITY

At the most basic level, a test is said to be valid if it measures what it is supposed to measure. Some tests are not valid for anything because they are composed of items that are poorly constructed or completely inappropriate for the student population. Other tests are valid for some purposes but not for others. A very good test of mastery of the curriculum in a particular fourth-grade spelling program, for example, is less valid for measuring fourth-grade spelling mastery by students taught with a different curriculum, still less valid for measuring spelling mastery by students in adjacent grades, and invalid for measuring student mastery of curriculum areas other than spelling.

Content validity

Specialists in test construction refer to many different kinds of validity, but of them, content validity and criterion validity are the most important for teachers. *Content validity* concerns the degree to which test content is drawn from the specific curriculum being tested. Except for special situations, such as tests of creative ability or of the degree to which skills learned in a specific context will generalize, test content should be limited to knowledge and skills actually taught to students.

Tests that are valid in other ways but lack content validity usually are described as "unfair." This means that the results may be accurate—that is, the students' scores reflect their relative mastery of the content of the test—but misleading. If the test is composed of many items dealing with matters not taught in school but learned unsystematically in other experiences, it will measure neither student ability nor student achievement. Instead, it probably measures combinations of things like student socioeconomic status (SES), test-taking and guessing abilities, and differences in reading rates and preferences.

Criterion validity

Criterion validity is the degree to which scores on a test predict (correlate with) performance on other criteria, particularly behavioral ones. Criterion validity becomes more important as attention shifts from mastery of specific knowledge and skills toward attempts to measure probable success in generalizing or applying these skills. In a driver-education course, it is important that students show mastery of the knowledge taught in the course by scoring well on knowledge tests, but is even more important that they apply this knowledge when they actually drive.

Even tests that have good reliability and content validity may have poor criterion validity. In fact, this is one of the implications of recent investigations of fundamental skills in the population at large, studied in national assessment research sponsored by the government as well as in several smaller research projects. These studies indicate that many high school students cannot apply basic language arts and math skills, even though they can pass certain tests or seatwork exercises that measure knowledge of these skills in isolation from one another. Many students, for example, have difficulty communicating clearly even in short essays. Run-on sentences and spelling, capitalization, and punctuation errors are common.

Similarly, many high school students had difficulty with seemingly simple math tasks such as computing the cost of items on a grocery list, determining the amount of change that should be returned to a shopper, or converting decimals to percentages. Paragraphs explaining in simple language the gist of laws protecting consumers against impulse buying were a mystery to most readers sampled, and only a small percentage could follow the kinds of complex instructions involved in filling out income tax forms. Students do appear to be making progress in some areas, but tests show that there are still some major problems. (For an especially good review of mathematical areas where students do well and poorly, see Carpenter et al., 1984.)

Competency in basic skills

These and other data have led increasing numbers of people to conclude that schools are doing a poor job of teaching basic "life" skills. If criterion validity is given primary weight in judging education and if preparing students to perform practical, everyday tasks is a basic criterion, this negative conclusion is justified.

Threats to Validity

The validity of a test is reduced by anything that reduces the degree to which the test measures what it is supposed to measure. This is most obvious in the case of lack of content validity. Tests are unfair and inappropriate to the extent that they include material that was not taught or assigned. Even tests with content validity, however, can be invalid for other reasons.

Power test

One large category of threats to test validity includes test-taking skills, writing skills, ability to work efficiently under time pressure, and related individual differences. These skills are not specific to the subject matter, but they affect test scores. Except when speed is one criterion for success, for example, tests either should have no time limits or generous limits that will minimize the effects of ability to work under time pressure (versus degree of mastery of the material). The result will be what is called a *power test*, a test that probes students' mastery (their "power") over the material. Similarly, unless language-arts skills such as capitalization, spelling, punctuation, and writing organization are considered part of the criterion for successful performance on a test in history or science, these tests should be scored strictly for completeness and correct responses with no extra credit for good writing or deduction for poor writing.

Notice that we qualify these statements. This is because there is disagreement about the criteria for success in various subjects. Some teachers believe that speed is important for certain skills or that language-arts skills should be taken into account in grading tests in other subject areas, whereas other teachers strongly believe otherwise. There is no simple answer here. Considering the national assessment data mentioned previously, we see some merit in the argument that answers to essay questions should be written and organized coherently as well as be correct in other respects. It is not difficult to find exceptions, however. Teachers working with students who speak English as a second language, for example, may want students to develop functional competence in English as an ultimate goal, but it would be silly for them to try to assess competence in math with a word-problem test constructed in English if most of the students cannot read English functionally.

Other threats to validity concern the content of the test or types of items that compose it. Written tests are fine for assessing knowledge and comprehension, but behavioral skill objectives may require behavioral tests for valid assessment.

TEST VARIETIES

Norm-referenced tests

Tests are classified in many ways. One of the most important distinctions is between norm-referenced tests and criterion-referenced tests. *Norm-referenced tests* usually are prepared for use on a national scale by professional test developers. Standardized instructions and test items are developed in a series of pilot testings, and scoring norms are developed on the basis of responses by a large and presumably representative sample of students. These norms then are converted into standardized scores, grade-level-equivalent scores, IQ-equivalent scores, or other scores that enable test users to compare data on their students with "national norms."

Stratified random sampling

A method called stratified random sampling is used in norming these tests. It is the same method that opinion polls and television rating services use. The key to accuracy here is the identification of a representative sample. In theory, this means "representative of the nation at large," although in practice blacks and other minority groups often are excluded from such samples. Samples are stratified by making sure that certain percentages (corresponding to the percentages in the population of interest) of identifiable groups are included. Gender, SES, and geographical area are typical variables used for stratification. Within these stratification limits, sampling is supposed to be random.

If a male third grader from a middle-class background who attends an urban school in the Southeast is needed, for example, the boy selected for inclusion in the norming sample should be chosen randomly from a large list of boys who fit these classifications. Such randomizing is done partly because many of the statistics used in connection with norm-referenced tests assume random sampling and partly to guard against systematic biases that would creep in if random sampling were not used. If the sample were selected primarily from among friends of the test makers, for example, it is likely that students' motivation to do well on the test and students' rapport with the tester would be unusually high.

Appropriate stratified random sampling can produce remarkably accurate results even when the sample includes only a fraction of the total population. Television networks are able to generate precise predictions of final vote totals through computerized extrapolation from key precincts. This system has certain weaknesses, however, because the behavior of one individual in the sample is taken as representative of thousands of others in the same category. Nevertheless, the norms that come with standardized tests are usually reasonably accurate. They provide information about local performance compared to expectations or averages for the nation at large.

Criterion-referenced tests

Criterion-referenced tests are keyed to the learning objectives taught to the specific students who take the tests. The purpose is not to compare the students to other students but to determine the degree to which they have mastered these objectives. This kind of information is more useful than information from norm-referenced tests for identifying objectives that have been taught successfully or that need to be retaught. Thus criterion-referenced tests give teachers useful information for planning future teaching. Such tests, however, usually give little or no useful information for comparing local students with national norms. (For detailed information about criterion-referenced tests, see Glaser & Nitko, 1971; Gronlund, 1985; Hambleton et al., 1978; Kubiszyn & Borich, 1984; or Popham, 1972.)

Criterion-referenced versus norm-referenced tests

The different rationales and goals of criterion-referenced tests versus norm-referenced tests require that different kinds of items be included in them. Selection of items for criterion-referenced tests is straightforward. Content is confined to material actually taught to students, and the tests include either all objectives that students are supposed to have mastered or a sample of them. Samples typically stress the final or highest objectives toward which related lessons were built. Criterion-referenced tests often must be individualized, especially if they are used in programs that allow students to proceed at their own paces. Different students work on various objectives at any given time, and they will require different tests when they finish instructional sequences. Although they can be used for grading, criterion-referenced tests focus attention on the degree to which individual students have mastered specific objectives.

Norm-referenced tests, however, are concerned primarily with discriminating students from one another. This means that items are included on the basis of power to discriminate in addition to content validity. Content validity is also important, especially if the tests are intended to assess students on "universal" objectives. Norm-referenced tests do this well when curriculum content is relatively homogeneous (such as reading and math in the early grades) but are not as reliable when there is little universal content (such as social studies at any grade and most subjects at higher grades).

Regardless of the popularity or prestige of a norm-referenced test, it is a poor evaluation device if its items do not correspond well with the curriculum. Teachers may do an excellent job teaching, but student performance on a standardized test will not reflect it if the test is a poor measure of what was taught. Freeman and associates (1983) examined three widely used curricula and five standardized tests and found that some tests would be appropriate for use with a particular curriculum, but other achievement tests would seriously underestimate how much students had learned.

Discriminating among students

In addition to the problem of content validity, developers of norm-referenced tests are interested in discriminating among students. They have no interest in items that are so easy that everyone answers them correctly or so difficult that no one does, because such items contribute nothing to variance in test scores. Variance comes from items that some students pass and others fail. Theoretically, ideal items are those that half the students pass and the other half fail, because such items discriminate among similar students most clearly, producing a normal distribution of scores that also have a wide range. Because of differences in the achievement of students in the same grade, however, it is necessary to include a range of item difficulty in order to discriminate among students at different achievement levels.

The easiest items do not discriminate among high achievers and are only minimally useful for discriminating among average students. But they will discriminate the lowest 5–10 percent from the next 5–10 percent. Similarly, very difficult items do not differentiate among most students (who will fail them) but can discriminate the top 5–10 percent from the next 5–10 percent.

Combining these considerations, developers of norm-referenced tests usually first screen items for content validity, seeking items that are as universal as possible in the curricula used in schools, and then construct a test designed to discriminate as well as possible among students at each grade. This is accomplished by having the greatest number of items of moderate difficulty, with decreasing numbers of easier and harder items. Because of this distribution of the difficulty of items on norm-referenced tests, these instruments typically discriminate most reliably and meaningfully among students in the middle two-thirds or so of the distribution.

Distribution extremes

As one moves toward the extremes of the distribution, score differences are less meaningful. At the extremes (the lowest and highest 2–3 percent), even seemingly large differences may be essentially meaningless. Thus a student who scores five grades behind grade level probably is no worse off than a student who is four grades behind grade level. The same is true of IQ tests. Below about 70 or above about 130, differences in IQ scores are not useful for predicting school success, at least in most schools.

In some schools, norm-referenced tests are administered to gain information about the performances and abilities of students. To the extent that these tests measure skills and knowledge relevant to a school's instructional program, they can provide useful information about the strengths and weaknesses of the program and the progress of individual students. The norm-referenced tests of most interest to teachers are standardized tests of achievement available from commercial test publishers.

STANDARDIZED ACHIEVEMENT TESTS

Standardized achievement tests are most useful in the lower grades, because content validity is less of a problem. There is more agreement about the core curriculum for language arts and mathematics in the early grades, and the same basic skills are taught using different curriculum packages and various methods. Consequently, although they are highly correlated with IQ scores, standardized achievement tests for the early grades are relatively valid methods of assessing student progress in achieving basic skills such as letter identification and discrimination, matching, copying, spelling, knowledge of letter-sound relationships (phonics), vocabulary, reading comprehension, and basic mathematical computations.

Interpreting data correctly

Standardized test data must be interpreted carefully, however, if they are to be used appropriately. Relatively few schools have student populations comparable to the students used to develop norms for the test, so test norms are inappropriate in most cases. Schools populated by students whose home backgrounds and IQ scores are clearly higher than average can and should exceed "expectations" based on standardized tests. Depending on the nature of the school, it might be appropriate to expect 60, 80, or even 95 percent of the students to score "above grade level," even though, theoretically, many of the students should score at grade level and half of the rest should score above it and half below it. Similarly, in a school populated primarily by students from disadvantaged backgrounds who have lower than average IQs, it might be appropriate to expect that only 40, 20, or even 5 percent would score "above grade level."

Comparisons across classes should be minimized. They are most meaningful if confined to the same grade in the same school (assuming that these classes are not ability grouped or otherwise organized so that some would be expected to do better than others). Comparisons across years should be made cautiously.

Value of subtests

As with IQ test results, teachers will find feedback from standardized tests most useful if it is separated by subtests, so that they can see patterns of strengths and weaknesses. Two teachers, for example, might have similar class averages for total scores on a standardized achievement test, but one might obtain notably better results in language arts, whereas the other teacher's class might do better in math.

Norm-Referenced Tests at Higher Grades

In general, as one measures aspects of the curriculum other than basic skills and at upper grades, norm-referenced tests become less valid as measures of quality of instruction. They become more like IQ tests rather than criterion-referenced achievement tests because they contain relatively small proportions of items testing material that was specifically taught by a given teacher. Second-grade arithmetic is fairly standard around the country, for instance, but seventh-grade social studies is not. A "standardized" test of seventh-grade social studies is more likely to be a test of general knowledge than a test of specific knowledge learned in a particular seventh-grade social studies class.

Teachers attempting to interpret scores from a norm-referenced test should obtain a copy of the test and identify the degree to which it measures knowledge of the material they actually teach.

Teachers' Use of Norm-Referenced Tests

In summary, teachers are likely to find norm-referenced tests useful if they have content validity (that is, if most items measure knowledge and skills actually taught by the teacher and if they are not culturally biased) and if local students' scores can be compared meaningfully with those of the norming sample. When teachers carefully follow instructions concerning time limits, standardized directions, and other aspects of test administration and scoring, valid results can be expected.

Information about the norming sample and about testing and scoring procedures should be included in the test manual. If not, such information can be found in the various mental measurement yearbooks edited by Buros (1972, 1978). In addition, the Buros yearbooks contain detailed reviews of most standardized tests, information about their general validity and reliability and, in many cases, additional norms or other information useful for interpreting tests when they are administered to special populations. Levy and Goldstein (1984) have also prepared an extensive review of available tests. Table 26.1 summarizes the features and appli-

Students often feel pressure and even anxiety about their performance on tests.

TABLE 26.1 THE MAZE OF STANDARDIZED TESTS

Type of Test	What Is Measured	What Is Not Measured	Information Provided	Appropriate Uses	Limitations/ Abuses
INTELLIGENCE (IQ)	a sample of learning behavior; scholastic and/or academic aptitude based upon ability	personality; special aptitudes; creativity; emotional factors affecting intelligence	an indication of ability to do academic work; prognosis of individual development	classification of students according to ability to learn; diagnosis of special needs and placement decisions; counseling	weighted toward verbal competence; labeling of students could lock them in incorrect placement, such as special ed.
ACHIEVEMENT and APTITUDE	the effects of learning related to skills development in academic content areas; learning potential related to instruction in specific content areas	the ability to organize and/or analyze; the ability to use logic and critical thinking; creativity	progression of student learning; the acquisition of knowledge and skills, including discrete strengths and weaknesses; prediction of program and curriculum needs	as basis of comparision with other students and/or groups of students; provides either screening or diagnostic data related to the curriculum; program planning; curriculum modifications; guidance tools; as basis for the classification of students for special placements	when instruction is standardized in order to teach to the test and/or the test becomes the focus of the curriculum; when the individual student needs are not met through curricular and instructional modifications, thereby limiting/narrowing opportunities for students

SAT and ACT	general knowledge acquired during school years	applications and synthesis of knowledge as related to specific uses in problem-solving or critical thinking	possible success in advanced schoolwork, particularly college level	high schools communicate standing to central data collection—relative status is ranked in comparison to college-bound students	can deflate student motivation; can lead to over-zealous competition for grades; can narrow student aspirations; can over-inflate expectations
COMPETENCY (Non-Standardized)	specific content-related skills	comprehension and/or applications	mastery of given content and grade-level skills determined by a school district	to determine appropriateness of instruction for accountability; to determine grade promotion and/or student mastery	when over-emphasis on skills narrows the total learning experience; when a test becomes the focus of the curriculum
TEACHER-MADE (Non-Standardized)	the goals and objectives of instruction	standardized factors as compared with a broad and varied population	student achievement related to teaching goals and objectives	modifications for instruction and curriculum	if individual student needs are not met through instructional individualization and curricular changes

Source: *From Sandford Reichart in* Gifted and Talented Monthly, *8, No. 7 (July/August 1987), p. 8. (Sewell, NJ: Gifted and Talented Publications). Reprinted by permission of Sandford Reichart.*

cability of various types of standardized tests. The chart was developed by Dr. Sandford Reichart, professor emeritus at Case Western Reserve University and an expert in psychometrics.

DIAGNOSTIC AND PRESCRIPTIVE TESTS

IQ tests and norm-referenced achievement tests do not provide much diagnostic or prescriptive information to teachers, but certain criterion-referenced tests do. Many of them are standardized diagnostic tests developed by individuals interested in special-education students. They are designed to identify specific problems in perceiving or responding, and they can be useful for identifying the precise nature of the underlying problem when a student has persistent difficulty with particular work. They include tests of color blindness, difficulty in perceiving boundaries or in separating figure from ground, other problems in visual perception, hearing problems, difficulties in sound or sound-pattern recognition, other problems in auditory perception, physical factors that interfere with proper speech, poor motor functioning in areas such as eye-hand coordination, understanding of directional relationships, perseveration (difficulty in stopping or inhibiting a motor response once it has begun), and various coordination problems.

Tests of this sort are numerous, and they will continue to accumulate as new information about the nature and causes of learning disabilities is discovered. Teachers should keep informed of diagnostic tests of this kind in areas related to their teaching specialties. Even though the present reliability of specialists in using such tests for diagnosis and prescription is low, the tests may be used to identify specific learning disabilities and to develop treatments to help students overcome them.

SUMMARY

Informal assessment of student performance is important, but it is also subjective and thus open to bias. It is therefore important to supplement informal monitoring with formal assessment under standardized conditions. Even then, test scores are only estimates of students' true levels of mastery. The standard error of measurement provides an estimate of the degree of measurement error associated with a particular test or measurement device. It varies inversely with reliability—highly reliable tests have low standard errors and thus allow more precise estimates of student performance.

A test is said to be valid if it measures what it is supposed to measure. Content validity refers to the match between test content and curriculum content. Criterion validity refers to the degree to which scores on a test correlate with performance on criterion measures, often expressed in terms of behavioral criteria. Validity is threatened when content is inappropriate, when time plays an undue role in performance, when test-taking skills influence scores, or other extraneous factors influence test outcomes.

Tests are classified in many ways. An important distinction is between norm-referenced versus criterion-referenced tests. The former compare students with other students whereas the latter compare each student's performance with stated criteria. Norm-referenced tests are useful to teachers if they have content validity, are not culturally biased, and if students' scores can be compared meaningfully with the norming sample. Criterion-referenced tests are keyed to the learning objectives of a course and provide information about the degree to which students have mastered such objectives. Such tests can help identify specific learning disabilities and treatments that could enable students to overcome them.

Questions and Problems

1. Bear in mind that IQ tests and standardized achievement tests are carefully constructed to produce a normal distribution of scores when administered to a large and heterogeneous population. However, students in a single class are a small and often homogeneous population. What do their "standardized" test scores mean?
2. Why is high test reliability necessary but not sufficient to ensure good test validity?
3. Depending on the purpose of a test, the degree to which an item discriminates among students (about half of them pass it and about half of them fail it) might be extremely important or not important at all. When is such discrimination at the item level important, and when is it unimportant?
4. What kinds of standardized tests and statistics would you use in teaching? Why?
5. Under what circumstances, if any, is it appropriate for teachers to use anything other than pure power tests?
6. Some states are beginning to test teachers' knowledge of subject matter and their professional teaching skills. How appropriate is it to compare your knowledge and skills with those of teachers from other schools or from other states?
7. Students sometimes say, "I got an A on the test but I didn't learn anything." Can this really happen? Do tests measure learning or performance?
8. In your own words, define the term *true score*. Why do tests seldom reflect a precise, true score?

Case Studies

AN UNFAIR TEST? Carol Kewig says to her principal, "It's not fair to use that standardized achievement test as part of my evaluation. The students are learning and I am doing a better than adequate job. That test is just irrelevant. It may be useful for looking at social studies programs in some secondary schools but not in ours!''

In what ways could Carol and her principal determine whether or not the test, or part of it, could provide appropriate feedback? From your point of view, how should an elementary or secondary school teacher be evaluated?

A RESEARCH FINDING. Rapidly but with full attention, Bill Boswell read an article in the prestigious journal *Schoolhouse Research*. Later he discussed the article with Helen. ''You know, that article was very important. The authors, Akers and Silverman, contend that teachers wait less time for low achievers to respond than for high achievers. But,'' he went on excitedly, ''the important thing is that when teachers did wait for low achievers to respond, they were more likely to give an answer and to give longer answers! That's neat. Waiting behavior on the teacher's part correlates positively with the frequency and length of low achievers' answers.''

In what ways has Bill overresponded to the article he read? How would you use these results in your own teaching? What evidence would you need in order to assume a definite relationship between any teacher behavior and student behavior?

CHAPTER

Statistical Concepts

CHAPTER OUTLINE

DESCRIPTIVE STATISTICS
Central Tendency Statistics
Distribution Statistics

THE NORMAL CURVE

OBJECTIVES

When you have mastered the material in this chapter, you will be able to

1. Explain in general terms the meaning and use of descriptive statistics called central tendency and dispersion measures
2. Define and contrast the *mean*, the *median*, and the *mode*
3. Explain the meaning of skewed distributions and why it is often better to use the median rather than the mean with skewed distributions
4. Compare and explain the range and the variance/standard deviation of a distribution of scores
5. Define and discuss the uses of *percentiles* and *percentages*
6. Explain the properties of the normal distribution and its meaning for education
7. Define *standard scores* and explain how they relate to the normal distribution

When a test or other measuring device is administered to a class, each student earns a score. If the teacher's only concern is to evaluate or grade students according to absolute pass-fail criteria, each score can be considered individually. However, the teacher may want to "grade on a curve" by assigning grades that reflect students' performances relative to the rest of the class rather than relative to an absolute standard. For the teacher's own information or for school records, it may be necessary to obtain information about class performance as a group.

Descriptive statistics

Information about the performance of an entire class requires calculation of descriptive statistics. These are numerical indices indicating where on the scale of possible scores a class's actual scores are clustered (averages, or measures of central tendency) and the degree to which the class's scores are clustered closely around the average score or distributed widely along the range of possible scores (measures of range, variance, or dispersion). These statistics are described below.

Normal curve

The second part of the chapter considers statistics associated with the concept of the normal curve. These statistics are used to estimate the degree of measurement error expected in a set of test scores. They are useful in judging which test scores are essentially equivalent and which represent a genuine difference in knowledge or skill mastery (Is there a real difference between a student who scores 85 and another student who scores 78 on a test, or is this difference well within the expected measurement error and thus likely due to chance factors?).

DESCRIPTIVE STATISTICS

Measures of central tendency and dispersion

Descriptive statistics describe distributions of scores, such as the scores of a class of students on a spelling test. Typically, descriptive statistics are divided into measures of central tendency (average, mean, median, mode) and measures of dispersion (range, variance, standard deviation).

Averages

Averages, particularly means, are more familiar to most people than measures of the dispersion of scores in a distribution. In many ways, however, dispersion data provide more information than averages. This is especially true when scores are extremely variable and no score occurs frequently. In this case, the average has little meaning, even though it is possible to compute it. It makes little sense to state that the average animal weighs twenty pounds, for example, because the very concept of an "average animal" makes little sense in the first place. In discussing sizes and weights of animals, distribution statistics indicating the percentages of animals at different weights are much more informative than an average.

Score distribution

A simple score distribution and some of the statistics associated with it are shown in Table 27.1. This is a tally of student scores on a ten-item spelling test. The statistics reveal that the test was moderately difficult for the students. This may be obvious to you at a glance, but in case it is not, take a look at each of the statistics that we can compute from this score distribution and at some of the information we can infer from studying the tallies.

Grading papers provides teachers with feedback on both student performance and teacher effectiveness.

First, note that thirty students took the test, so there are thirty scores. In statistical terminology this is $N = 30$. The tallies indicate the number of students who earned each of the possible scores between zero and 10. They indicate that two students got scores of 10, three got scores of 9, three got scores of 8, and so on. This tally is called a frequency distribution. It shows the frequency with which each possible score appeared in the actual distribution. Note that no student scored zero or 2, even though these scores were possible.

This distribution provides much useful information, even without the computation of any additional statistics. For example, if we were to look only at the measures of central tendency and notice that the scores average

TABLE 27.1 FREQUENCY DISTRIBUTION OF SCORES ON A TEN-ITEM TEST TAKEN BY THIRTY STUDENTS

	Number of Students	
Score	**Tally**	**Total**
10	II	2
9	III	3
8	III	3
7	IIII III	8
6	IIII	4
5	IIII	4
4	III	3
3	II	2
2		0
1	I	1
0		0
		$N = 30$

$$\text{Mean} = \frac{\text{Sum of scores}}{\text{Number of scores}} = \frac{190}{30} = 6.33$$

Median = Middle score = 7

Mode = Most frequent score = 7

Range = 1 to 10 (possible range = 0–10)

N = Number of scores = 30

6 to 7, we might conclude that the test was too difficult, considering that 10 was perfect. The scores are spread out well, however, or to put it another way, the test discriminates between the students well. This means that the test items were at various difficulty levels. Consequently, the results can be viewed with some confidence, assuming that the test has content validity.

Contrast this with test results that have similar central tendency scores but a very narrow distribution (for example, 10 students score 7, and the other 20 score 6). This score distribution would also have an *N* of 30 and a mean of 6.33, but it might provide less information about teaching success or student learning. There probably is little meaningful difference between the students who scored 7 and those who scored 6, so the test does not discriminate among the students. Furthermore, the scores pile up in the center instead of at the bottom or top of the possible range. Unless the class is extremely homogeneous, something probably is wrong with the test.

If the scores pile up at the top, this means that the test is too easy or that the students have learned the material thoroughly. If most of the scores are at the bottom, the test is too hard or the students were not prepared for it. A concentration of scores somewhere in the middle is puzzling, however. Such a score distribution might mean that seven of the items are easy ones that most students got correct and that three items are unreasonably difficult, ambiguous in their wording, not relevant to the material the students were supposed to have mastered, or otherwise inappropriate, so few students got them correct.

Concentration of middle range scores

To investigate the problem, you would need to make a frequency distribution of scores. In this case, you would need a distribution for each item, not just for the whole test (see Table 27.2). Frequency distributions like these should be made routinely, to obtain information for interpreting averages. They also facilitate computation of central tendency measures.

Central Tendency Statistics

The most common measures of central tendency are the mean, the median, and the mode. Of them, the mean corresponds most clearly to the more familiar term *average*. The mean is computed simply by adding the scores and dividing the total by the number of scores (*N*). Thus for the distribution shown in Table 27.1, the 30 scores total 190 points. The mean is computed by dividing this 190 by 30 (the number of students) to arrive at a mean of 6.33 (rounded to two decimals).

The mean

In the distribution shown in Table 27.2, twenty students scored 6, and ten students scored 7. The score total would be 190, or $(20 \times 6) + (10 \times 7)$, so the mean would be 190 divided by 30, or 6.33.

For most statistical purposes, the mean is the preferred measure of central tendency. Many consider it to be the most representative measure because it takes into account each individual score, producing a weighted average. Students who score 10 on the test contribute 10 points to the total used in computing the mean, and students who score 1 contribute only 1 point to this total. In addition, the mean is related to several other statistics used in certain complex analyses, whereas the median and mode

TABLE 27.2 FREQUENCY DISTRIBUTION OF SCORES ON A TEN-ITEM TEST TAKEN BY THIRTY STUDENTS

Students	1	2	3	4	5	6	7	8	9	10	Total
1. Aaron	1	1	0	1	1	0	1	0	1	1	7
2. Alfred	0	1	0	1	1	0	1	0	1	1	6
3. Alice	1	1	0	1	0	0	1	0	1	1	6
4. Beth	0	1	0	1	1	0	1	0	1	1	6
5. Bonnie	1	1	0	0	1	0	1	0	1	1	6
6. Clark	1	1	0	1	1	0	1	0	1	0	6
7. Cuthbert	1	1	0	1	1	0	1	0	1	1	7
8. Dahlia	1	1	0	1	1	0	1	0	1	1	7
9. David	1	1	0	1	0	0	1	0	1	1	6
10. Douglas	1	1	0	1	1	0	1	0	1	0	6
11. Felicia	1	1	0	0	1	0	1	0	1	1	6
12. Frank	1	1	0	0	1	0	1	0	1	1	6
13. George	1	0	0	1	1	0	1	0	1	1	6
14. Helen	1	1	0	1	1	0	1	0	1	1	7
15. John L.	1	1	1	1	1	0	1	0	0	1	7
16. John R.	1	1	0	1	1	0	0	0	1	1	6
17. June	1	1	0	1	1	0	1	0	0	1	6
18. Karen	1	1	0	1	1	0	1	0	1	1	7
19. Karl	1	0	0	1	1	0	1	0	1	1	6
20. Missy	1	1	0	1	1	0	1	0	0	1	6
21. Nancy	1	1	0	1	1	0	1	0	1	1	7
22. Patricia	1	1	0	1	1	0	0	1	1	1	7
23. Raymond	1	1	0	1	1	0	1	0	1	1	7
24. Rosa	1	1	0	1	1	0	1	0	0	1	6
25. Ruby	0	1	0	1	1	0	1	0	1	1	6
26. Sam	1	1	0	0	1	0	1	0	1	1	6
27. Seth	1	1	0	1	1	0	1	0	1	1	7
28. Thomas	1	1	0	1	1	0	0	0	1	1	6
29. Vera	1	1	0	1	1	0	1	0	1	0	6
30. Walter	1	1	0	1	1	0	0	0	1	1	6
Totals	27	28	1	26	28	0	26	1	26	27	190

Scores	Tally	Total		
6	𝍸 𝍸	20	Median = 6	Possible range = 0–10
	𝍸 𝍸	10	Mode = 6	N = 30
7	𝍸 𝍸	30		

Mean = 190/30 = 6.33 Range = 6–7

are not. Statisticians prefer it because its mathematical properties allow them to do more with it than they can do with the other two measures of central tendency.

The median

The median is simply the middle score—half of the scores are above it and half are below it. In the example in Table 27.1, the median score is 7, which is the most frequent score as well. The same is true in Table 27.2, where the median is 6, and 6 is also the most frequent score. However, this was purely accidental. In a distribution in which the scores of thirty students were spread out so that three students got each of the scores betwen 1 and 10, the median would be 5.5. This is because fifteen students would have scores between 6 and 10, and fifteen would have scores between 1 and 5. In situations like this, where no score represents the median of the distribution, a common practice is to split the difference between the two scores that come closest to it. In this example, these scores are 5 and 6, so the median is 5.5.

The mode

The mode is the most frequent score. The mode is 7 in Table 27.1 and 6 in Table 27.2. The mode is less useful and meaningful than the mean or median. Sometimes it is impossible to identify, as in the distribution mentioned previously, in which exactly three students scored at each of the 10 scores possible. In this case, there is no mode. In other cases, there is more than one mode. This would happen, for example, if ten students scored 6, ten students scored 7, and the remaining ten students were dispersed over several other score categories.

Bimodal distributions

Bimodal distributions have two modes, like the distribution shown in Table 27.3. These distributions are of interest because they suggest that the scores may come from two qualitatively different groups. Bimodal distributions like those shown in Table 27.3 are found most often when the same test is given to groups of students who differ in some important way. Such a distribution, for example, might represent vocabulary scores on a test given to a combined group of second and fourth graders. Some second graders would do better than some fourth graders, but in general, the second graders would cluster around the lower mode (3), whereas the fourth graders would cluster around the higher mode (8).

The mean and median usually are equally good measures of central tendency, even though statisticians usually prefer the mean because of its mathematical relationships to other statistics. Sometimes the mean and median are considerably different, however. When this occurs, the median usually is more meaningful. The difference usually occurs because the distribution is very unusual and the effects of a few individuals with extreme scores distort the mean. The classical example of this is income distributions, where the median is much more meaningful than the mean.

TABLE 27.3 A BIMODAL DISTRIBUTION

Score	Number of Students: Tally	Number of Students: Total
10	III	3
9	III	3
8	~~IIII~~ I	6
7	III	3
6	I	1
5	II	2
4	III	3
3	~~IIII~~ I	6
2	I	1
1	I	1
0	I	1

$$\text{Mean} = \frac{\text{Sum of scores}}{\text{Number of scores}} = \frac{175}{30} = 5.83$$

Median = Middle score = 6.5

Modes(s) = Most frequent scores(s) = 3,8

Range = 0 to 10 (Same as possible range)

N = Number of scores = 30

Skewed distributions

Distributions of income by individuals or by families are seriously *skewed*. This term refers to distributions in which the scores are concentrated at one end of the possible range, so the mean has many more scores on one side of it than on the other. This can be seen in Figure 27.1, which shows a distribution of personal incomes that is fictional but typical of a distribution that might occur for a city that has about 100,000 wage earners. Note that the vast majority of wage earners are concentrated in the range between zero and $15,000 per year. These salary figures are low because part-time wage earners are also included in the distribution (i.e., teenagers who work at fast-food restaurants only in the summer). The distribution is seriously skewed: the mean is $12,800, but incomes range from zero to above $40,000 per year. In fact, this skew is even more extreme than the figures shows because the last group includes several millionaires and many others making considerably more than $40,000 a year. The incomes of these few individuals are included in the calculation of the mean, so the mean becomes an unrealistically high estimate of the average income in the community. By contrast, the median is much more realistic and meaningful.

Mean versus median

The median is more meaningful and reliable than the mean because it is not sensitive to unusually high scores at the extremes of the distribution. If the income of everyone in the community were to rise exactly one thousand dollars in the following year, for example, both the mean and the median would go up exactly one thousand dollars. Suppose however, that two millionaires moved into town. This would cause a notable increase in the mean, falsely implying that the town as a whole was improving economically. In contrast, these two individuals would have little or no effect on the median. The opposite would be the case if two or three of the town's present millionaires were to move outside its limits. Again,

Figure 27.1 Typical Distribution of Personal Income for One Year

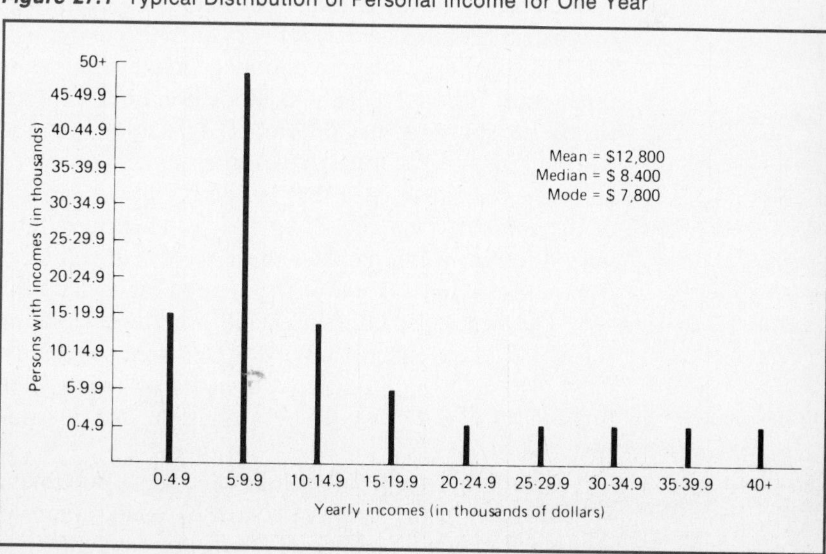

the median would be unaffected but the mean would drop notably, giving the false impression that the town was having economic difficulties. These examples show why the median is preferred over the mean as an index of average income. More generally, they illustrate how the mean is especially sensitive to extreme scores, particularly in skewed distributions. To the extent that situations like this occur in your own testing, you probably should use the median rather than the mean as an index of central tendency. This might be necessary, for example, if you were teaching in a class made up of generally low-ability students except for two or three with extremely high abilities, or vice versa.

Distribution Statistics

When feasible, often the simplest way to get information about score distributions is to tally them individually (as in Table 27.1) or in groups (as in Figure 27.1). Sometimes, however, certain statistics describing distributions are needed for other purposes. Just as several statistics describe the central tendencies of distributions, several others describe the dispersion of scores.

Range

The simplest statistic, the range, that describes the dispersion of scores has already been mentioned. The range of scores in a distribution extends from the lowest score through the highest score. Sometimes the observed range extends across the complete possible range (see Table 27.4), but not always (see Table 27.1). Taken in conjunction with a measure of central tendency, the range provides important information for interpreting descriptive statistics.

Two classes could have mean IQs of 100, for example. The classes would be very different if the first class ranged from 65 to 147, however, and the second class ranged only from 89 to 108. The latter class is homogeneous in ability compared to the former class, where the range of student ability is so great that some form of grouping or individualization seems needed.

Sometimes the range alone does not provide enough information about the distribution because it reflects only the two most extreme scores. In the heterogeneous class mentioned above, for example, we stated that the highest IQ was 147. The composition of this class and the implications for the teacher are very different if IQ scores are gradually and normally distributed between the two extremes instead of one of the extremes being

Outliers

an outlier (a single case that is notably lower or higher than all the rest of the scores). Two classes in which the highest IQs were 147 would be very different if in one class there were a dozen or so students with IQs between 110 and 147 and if the second highest IQ in the other class was 116. The first class contains many bright students, and the one with the IQ of 147 is not significantly brighter than several other students in the class. However, a student with an IQ of 147 in a class where the next highest IQ was 116 would be an outlier, considerably brighter than the rest.

Percentiles

To guard against problems like this, it is sometimes useful to go beyond specification of the range of scores by using other distribution statistics. Among the more familiar of them are percentiles. Conversion of raw

TABLE 27.4 CONVERSION OF RAW TEST SCORES TO PERCENTAGES AND RANK-ORDER SCORES IN ORDER TO COMBINE DATA INTO A SINGLE SCORE DISTRIBUTION

	Raw Scores			***Percentages*** $\left(\frac{\text{Score}}{\text{Perfect Score}}\right)$		
Students	**Test 1**	**Test 2**	**Test 3**	**Test 1**	**Test 2**	**Test 3**
1. Art	48	42	96	96	84	96
2. Bill	36	30	74	72	60	74
3. Debra	47	45	94	94	90	94
4. Fran	32	33	76	64	66	76
5. George	32	29	71	64	58	71
6. Ida	33	31	63	66	62	63
7. Jill	48	40	95	96	80	95
8. Robert	46	42	93	92	84	93
9. Sam	40	37	86	80	74	86
10. Susie	41	39	88	82	78	88
Actual range	32–48	29–45	63–96			
Perfect score	50	50	100			

Rank				
Test 1	**Test 2**	**Test 3**	**Mean %**	**Mean Rank**
1.5	2.5	1	92	1.7
7	9	8	69	8.0
3	1	3	93	2.3
9.5	7	7	69	7.8
9.5	10	9	64	9.5
8	8	10	64	8.7
1.5	4	2	90	2.5
4	2.5	4	90	3.8
6	6	6	80	6.0
5	5	5	83	5.0

scores into percentile scores involves computing the percentage of scores in the total distribution that are lower than a particular score. The fiftieth percentile, for example, is roughly equivalent to the median. Fifty percent of the scores in the distribution are higher than this score and 49 percent are below it. A score that is at the seventy-fifth percentile is lower than only 25 percent of the scores in the distribution and higher than 74 percent of the scores.

Percentages

Conversion of raw scores into percentages is useful for many purposes but especially when one wants to average scores across tests with different numbers of items and to weight the tests equally. Scores from each test can be converted into percentages of the total possible score and then averaged. Both percentiles and percentages can be used to rank students. Simple percentages are easier to compute (see Table 27.4) and thus most appropriate if they give the information needed. Percentile scores not only allow the ranking of students but also provide more specific information about the exact placement of a student relative to other students and to the range of scores as a whole.

Ranking

An even simpler way to differentiate students is to rank them. This may be all that teachers need for most purposes. However, when standardized test data are being used, simple ranking allows only comparisons within the classroom. To make comparisons with the norms that come with the test, it is necessary to transform raw scores into percentile scores or some other form of standardized score. Some tests allow only specification of quartiles (fourths), deciles (tenths), or other simplifications of percentile score conversions.

Other distribution statistics that teachers need to be familiar with, even though they are unlikely to have to compute them, are the variance and standard deviation. The two are related; the standard deviation is the square root of the variance.

Variance

The variance is the average of the squares of the differences between each individual score and the mean of the distribution. It can be computed by first computing the mean score for the distribution, then computing the difference between each individual's score and the mean, then squaring each of these difference scores, then summing these squared difference scores, and then dividing this sum by the number of scores (N). Distributions with small variances and standard deviations have many scores close to the mean (as in Table 27.2), whereas distributions with large variances and standard deviations have many scores that vary considerably from the mean (as in Table 27.1). Like the mean, the variance and standard deviation both have certain statistical properties that allow them to be used in calculations that cannot be computed otherwise.

Standard deviation

The size of the variance depends directly on the percentage of scores that differ from the mean and the size of these differences. The more such scores, and the more different from the mean they are, the larger the variance. The same is true for the standard deviation because it is simply the square root of the variance. Thus to repeat and summarize: variance and standard deviation are both measures of the degree to which scores are dispersed from the mean rather than similar to it. The larger the variance and standard deviation, the greater the dispersion of scores away from the mean.

THE NORMAL CURVE

Figure 27.2 shows two estimates of the probable results of repeated experiments designed to estimate frequencies or probabilities in a population from data on small samples. If we did not know that the probability of getting "heads" when coin tossing was 0.50, for example, we could estimate it by taking samples of ten coin tosses. The most likely result of such an experiment would be five heads and five tails. However, sometimes we would get four or six heads because of random sampling error. Less often, we would get three or seven, and still less often we would

Figure 27.2 Binomial and Normal Distributions of Ten Coin Tosses Showing Numbers of Heads Expected

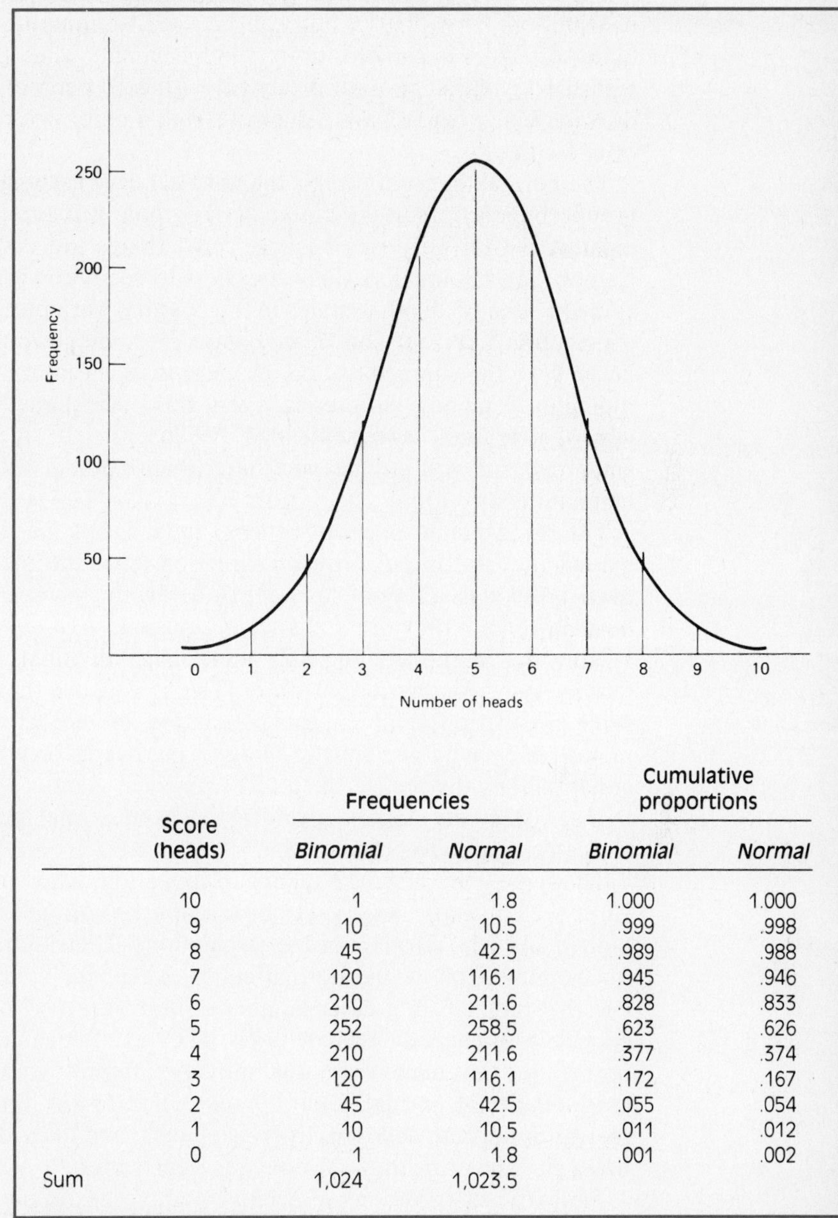

Score (heads)	Frequencies		Cumulative proportions	
	Binomial	*Normal*	*Binomial*	*Normal*
10	1	1.8	1.000	1.000
9	10	10.5	.999	.998
8	45	42.5	.989	.988
7	120	116.1	.945	.946
6	210	211.6	.828	.833
5	252	258.5	.623	.626
4	210	211.6	.377	.374
3	120	116.1	.172	.167
2	45	42.5	.055	.054
1	10	10.5	.011	.012
0	1	1.8	.001	.002
Sum	1,024	1,023.5		

Note: The binominal distribution is shown by the bar graph, the normal distribution is shown by the curve.

get either fewer or more heads. The probability is only about 0.001 that we would get either no heads or all heads in ten tosses.

These probabilities can be estimated precisely because we know in advance that the probability of heads on a random toss is 0.50. The bar graph shown in Figure 27.2 is one case of what is called the binomial distribution. This distribution can be used to compute the exact probabilties of errors in samples of ten measurements when the attribute being measured is either present or absent with a 50 percent probability, as in drawing black cards from a deck, tossing a coin, or drawing the shorter of two straws.

Normal distribution

The normal distribution and the normal curve associated with it (which is superimposed upon the binomial bar graph in Figure 27.2) are used for most statistical purposes because most things are distributed normally (rather than binomially). This is easiest to see with variables like height. If the heights of all adult males in the country were plotted in a frequency distribution like that shown in Figure 27.2, they would form a normal curve with the same statistical properties as the normal curve shown in the figure. The only difference is that this normal curve would be somewhat flatter and more extended because height is distributed more smoothly and with greater variability than bimodal variables that fit the binomial distribution.

The mean height is about seventy inches, but the range of normality extends several inches in each direction from the mean. Furthermore, even individuals a foot or so above or below the mean are still biologically normal, though they are statistically unusual.

Note that certain biologically abnormal individuals do not fit expectations based on the normal curve. This is because they are not from the same population (that is, the population of biologically normal adult males). Men who are genetic midgets or dwarfs or who have glandular abnormalities that cause them to be physical giants are qualitatively different, not merely statistically different, from normal men. They represent altogether separate populations.

The same kind of thing happens in education, where most student measures are known or assumed to be distributed normally except for certain individuals who form separate populations. Distributions of IQ scores, for example, follow the normal curve except for a "bump" at the low end that indicates a greater number of individuals with low IQs than are expected by chance (Jensen, 1969). They exist because of biological abnormalities that make them qualitatively different from the majority who are biologically normal. Low IQ scores are found, for example, among Downs Syndrome children, hydrocephalics, and individuals who suffered brain damage at birth due to oxygen deprivation.

Similarly, distributions of achievement scores in particular schools or classrooms will depart significantly from normality if "the population" really is two populations, such as in a majority speaking English as a first language and reading it with varying degrees of fluency and a minority speaking English as a second language and unable to read it functionally at all. Thus if a trait is really distributed normally in the population, repeated samples designed to estimate the mean and distribution of the trait should approximate normal curves. If more than one mode appears, or if the curve departs significantly from normality, it probably means that two qualitatively different populations are involved.

Kinds of normal curves

Any curve that fits a complex mathematical definition (that we will not explain here) is a normal curve, so there are a great many kinds of normal curves. If the attribute to be measured is constant, so that any differences in repeated samplings are due only to measurement error, and if the measurement instrument is reliable and valid, normal curves representing repeated measurements will show scores clustered at the real population mean, with little dispersion in either direction, as in Figure 27.3. This is the sort of curve that would be obtained if the height of the same individual were measured repeatedly and rounded off to the nearest quarter inch.

On the other hand, if the attribute is distributed widely in the population and does not cluster around any particular average, or if the measurement methods used in estimating it are unreliable, normal curves that look like the one in Figure 27.4 will result. Both types of curves can be used to estimate means, but estimation is much more precise in the case illustrated by Figure 27.3 because the standard deviation and variance are low. As a result, it can be stated with a high degree of confidence that the true population mean lies within a narrow range. In contrast, in situations like those illustrated in Figure 27.4, the considerable variation in repeated measurements does not allow a precise or confident estimation of the population mean.

Normal curves have many properties that make them particularly useful in education and psychology. First, if an attribute being measured is dis-

Figure 27.3 Normal Distribution of Sample Means in Situations in Which There Is Low Variance in the Population and the Measurement Is Accurate and Reliable

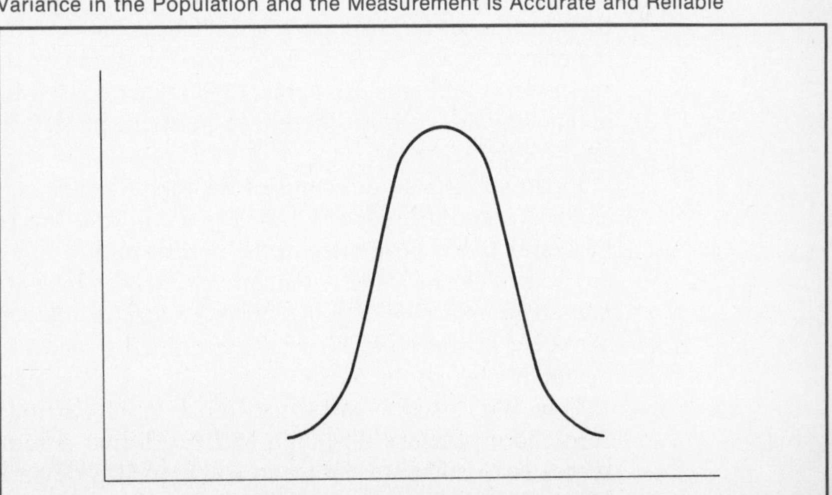

Figure 27.4 Normal Distribution of Sample Means in Situations in Which There Is High Variance in the Population and the Measurement Is Unreliable

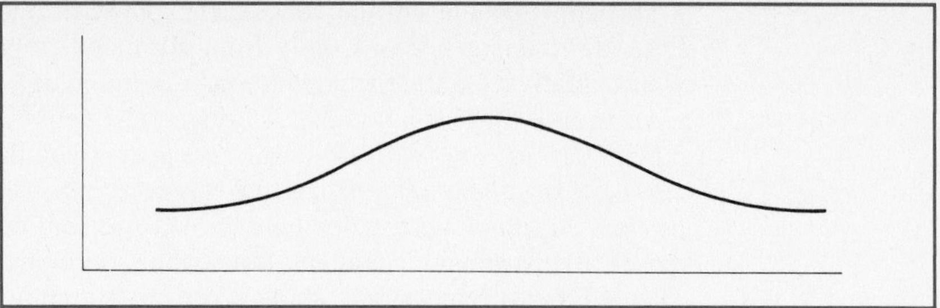

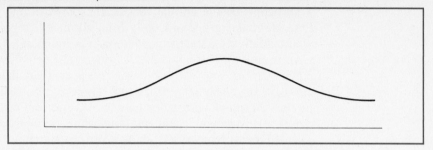

tributed normally in the population (and most are), repeated measurements from small samples will approximate the normal curve in their statistical properties. They also will approximate the real population distribution in their means and standard deviations (assuming adequate measurements). The mean, the median, and the mode will all be located at or near the real mean of the population, and errors in estimating the mean and the standard deviation can be calculated to specified probability levels. This leads to statements such as "with 95 percent confidence, the population mean is estimated to lie between 98 and 102." A statement like this might result from repeated measurements of IQ, when the mean for the population at large is 100.

The normal curve also has other useful properties. For complex statistical reasons we will not attempt to explain here, the relationships between the standard deviations of scores distributed normally and the percentage distributions of these scores are known and can be specified. About 68 percent of the scores will fall between −1 and +1 standard deviations from the mean, and about 95 percent will fall between −2 and +2 standard deviations. This is true of all normal curves, regardless of their means or standard deviations. This is illustrated in Figure 27.5. Thus the chance of a score being more than two standard deviations away from the mean is only about 5 percent. This fact is used in drawing inferences about whether or not differences between observed means are "statistically significant."

z-scores

Figure 27.5 illustrates some of the relationships between different measures of central tendency and dispersion and the relationship of these measures to the properties of the normal curve. First, it can be seen that any scores can be transformed into *z*-scores, which are standard deviation units or standard deviation scores. A score that is one standard deviation above the mean would have a *z*-score of +1.0, and a score of two standard deviations below the mean would have a *z*-score of −2.0.

Typically, *z*-scores are fitted to a normal distribution with a mean of zero and a standard deviation of 1.0. All that is required to calculate *z*-scores is to compute the mean and standard deviation of a distribution of scores, compute the differences between scores and the mean, and

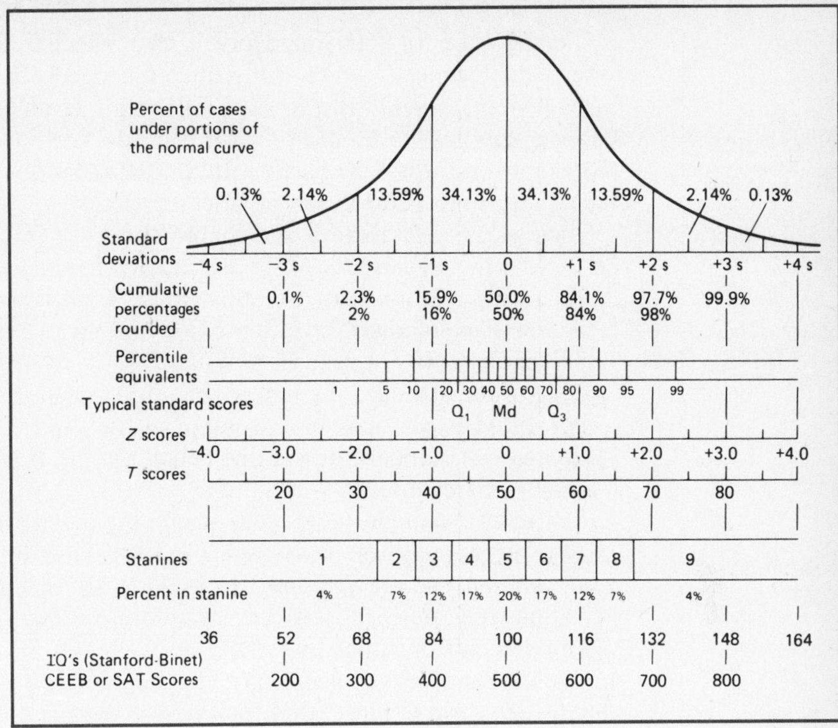

Figure 27.5 The Relationship of Several Common Scoring Scales

convert these differences into standard deviation units. If a score is 15 points above the mean and the standard deviation is 10, for example, the *z*-score would be +1.5 (15 ÷ 10 = 1.50). Transformation of raw scores into *z*-scores allows the use of the normal curve for statistical estimation and significance testing.

T-scores

Some tests provide for transformation of raw scores into standard scores, or *T*-scores. This is similar to *z*-score transformation, except that it gets rid of minus signs. Many different standard score distributions have been used, but the most common one uses a mean of 50 and a standard deviation of 10. For this type of transformation, a raw score that was at the original mean would be assigned a value of 50 and would still be at the mean of the new distribution. A raw score that was one standard deviation below the original mean would be assigned a score of 40 (one standard deviation below the new mean), and a raw score that was one and a half standard deviations above the original mean would be assigned a score of 65 (one and a half standard deviations above the new mean).

IQ scores

IQs are standard scores. In computing them, raw scores from the IQ tests are transformed into a normal distribution with a mean of 100 and a standard deviation of either 15 or 16, depending on the test. Thus students who get total raw scores equal to the mean for students their age are assigned IQs of 100, whereas students who get total raw scores two standard deviations above the mean are assigned IQs of 130 or 132, depending on the test.

The rationale for this procedure is that IQ tests measure something called "intelligence," which is distributed normally in the population. As we have seen, there is little justification for this assumption. Nevertheless, IQ tests continue to be used widely, and the method of converting raw scores into transformed scores with a normal distribution and a mean of 100 continues to be common practice.

Other useful information about normal curves is illustrated in Figure 27.5. Note that regardless of the mean and standard deviation involved, the following relationships are constant in all normal distributions:

1. Scores one standard deviation below the mean are at about the 16th percentile ($z = -1.0$, or $T = 40$).
2. Scores one standard deviation above the mean are at about the 84th percentile ($z = +1.0$, or $T = 60$).
3. Scores two standard deviations below the mean are between the 2nd and 3rd percentiles.
4. Scores two standard deviations above the mean are between the 97th and 98th percentiles.
5. In general, once raw scores are fitted to some kind of normal distribution, relationships between raw scores, standard scores, *z*-scores, and percentiles can be stated easily.
6. The farther apart two scores are, the more likely it is that the difference between them is real rather than due to chance measurement error.
7. By combining information about the differences between raw scores with information about the number of scores in the distribution and the standard deviation of the distribution, it is possible to develop precise estimates of the probability that two scores differ by chance. If this probability is low (below 0.05, for example), the difference is said to be statistically significant.

SUMMARY

To use test scores to evaluate the performance of a group of students, teachers must calculate statistics that describe the characteristics of the distributions of scores. They are usually divided into measures of central tendency (mean, median, mode) and measures of dispersion (range, variance, standard deviation). Taken together, these data reveal typical or average performance for the class as a whole and the spread of scores around that average.

The mean is found by adding all of the scores and dividing by the number of scores, the median is the middle score in any array, and the mode is the most frequently occurring score. The range is the difference between the lowest and the highest scores in an array, and the variance is found by squaring the difference between each score and the mean, adding together these squared differences, and dividing by the number of scores. The standard deviation is the square root of the variance.

The normal curve represents the distribution of many kinds of variables in a normal population. It is a useful construct in testing because it provides a basis for examining test scores or other measures in relation to each other and estimating the percentile ranks of the scores. Also, if the scores are normally distributed, it is possible to transform raw scores into standard scores such as z-scores or T-scores. This allows the use of the normal curve for statistical estimation and significance testing.

QUESTIONS AND PROBLEMS

1. Why use statistics at all? That is, why not merely report the results of tests and be done with it?
2. Transformation of raw scores into standardized scores does absolutely nothing to change the relative placement of any individual's score in comparison to those of the rest of the class. However, transformation into scores that are forced into a normal distribution *will* change the relative placement of scores with reference to one another. Do you understand this difference? What are some of its implications?
3. Ordinarily, teachers use the class mean whenever they need to express class performance on a test in a single score. Sometimes, though, the mean is misleading. When would the median be more appropriate? The mode?
4. Which indicates the best performance—a percentile equivalent score of 75, a z-score of $+1.0$, a T-score of 62 (when the mean = 50 and the standard deviation = 10)?
5. What problems would you have in trying to explain a T-score to a parent?

CASE STUDY

DIFFERENCES AMONG THREE MATH CLASSES. Ms. Lanier teaches general math to three classes of ninth graders. The classes are supposed to be formed randomly from among the ninth graders at Holt School who do not qualify for more advanced math courses. During the first week of school, Ms. Lanier gives each class the same twenty-item review/pretest. The test data are shown in the accompanying table. For each class, identify or compute the number of students and the mean, median, mode, range, and (optionally) variance and standard deviation. What do these statistics reveal about the three classes?

Score	Class 1	Class 2	Class 3
20	0	0	0
19	0	0	0
18	0	0	1
17	0	1	0
16	0	2	0
15	1	2	1
14	1	5	0
13	2	3	1
12	3	1	0
11	5	1	1
10	6	0	1
9	4	1	1
8	4	2	0
7	2	2	3
6	1	5	2
5	1	3	6
4	0	1	5
3	0	1	3
2	0	0	3
1	0	0	2
0	0	0	0

CHAPTER

Test Construction

CHAPTER OUTLINE

OBJECTIVES

When you have mastered the material in this chapter, you will be able to

1. Explain the importance of representative sampling of content and test length
2. Explain the six levels of Bloom's (1956) taxonomy of educational objectives and how the taxonomy is used in test construction
3. List the three steps involved in writing an instructional objective and discuss the advantages and disadvantages of using instructional objectives in teaching
4. Discuss the six suggestions for writing good essay questions and explain how essays should be graded to minimize teacher bias and error
5. Discuss the guidelines for writing objective test questions and contrast their advantages and disadvantages with those of essay questions
6. Define *criterion-referenced* and *norm-referenced tests*, explain how they differ, and tell when each is best used

So far, we have presented some fundamental principles of educational measurement and some of the statistics useful for describing and making decisions about the score distributions that such measurement generates. We now turn to the construction of the actual measurement devices themselves.

TEST LENGTH AND CONTENT COVERAGE

Typically, tests cover only a small sample of the content and objectives taught, and decisions have to be made about what to include. This problem is most serious for final exams given at the end of the term or school year, but is relevant to unit and weekly tests as well.

We have already mentioned one criterion—a test ordinarily should stress the terminal objectives of instruction within a content area, because they usually are the instructional objectives in the first place and because mastery of these terminal objectives usually means mastery of lower-level objectives as well. It is also helpful to sample from the full range of content taught and to include enough items to allow reliable measurement.

Sampling from content taught

Sampling from the full range of content taught will help ensure that the teacher recognizes areas of weakness, that students are accountable for learning all of the material, and that students will view the test as fair. Students may not perceive the test as fair if it emphasizes only a few areas, especially if they are areas the students thought were unimportant. A fifteen-item objective test on comparative political systems, for example, might ask several questions about evolutionary forces and key individuals who shaped the development of those systems, only a couple of questions about how the systems presently operate and about the practical implications of similarities and differences between countries, and no questions about probable future trends.

Let us examine how such a test could have biased effects. Table 28.1 shows the percentage of time that eight students of comparable ability spent studying for the test. The student victimized the most by the test is Ruth, who spent only 20 percent of her time reviewing historical development, which turned out to be 80 percent of the exam, and 60 percent of her time studying future trends, which were not included on the exam. In contrast, Judy did well on the test. She spent 75 percent of her time preparing for the first part and the remainder of her time studying material tested on the second part. Other students made different choices and scored differently on the basis of their choices.

Table 28.2 presents the distribution of scores that students might have made on such a test. It can be seen that the distribution is not directly related to the percentage of time spent studying for key parts of the exam but it does correspond closely.

In any test situation many factors operate. Bill, for example, may have scored lower than Joan because he was absent during a class discussion that dealt with material needed to answer three of the exam questions (a longer test makes such effects less likely). Joan, however, may score

TABLE 28.1 DISTRIBUTION OF TEST ITEMS AND PERCENTAGE OF TIME STUDENTS SPENT STUDYING THREE AREAS OF COMPARATIVE POLITICS

Test	Historical Development (in percent) 80 (12 Items)	Present Functioning (in percent) 20 (3 Items)	Future Trends (in percent) 0 items
Alice	33	33	33
Jane	33	33	33
Bill	25	50	25
Ted	50	25	25
Joan	50	50	0
Judy	75	25	0
Ruth	20	20	60
Tom	33	33	33

higher because she has better test-taking skills (for example, she notices subtle clues in two poorly written test questions that give the answers away). Alice may have scored lower than Jane or Tom because she spent too much time thinking about the first few questions and did not have a chance to respond to the last questions.

Measurement errors

The point is that some error of measurement will occur in any test. A test that unfairly samples content will exacerbate minor problems into major ones. As can be seen in Tables 28.1 and 28.2, the test on comparative politics is not fair. It has a systematic tendency to favor some students who guessed correctly about how to spend their study time.

Test length

Some of these problems may be connected with the length of the test. As a rule of thumb, test reliability increases with test length, so a thirty-item test is ordinarily more reliable than a fifteen-item test. This assumes that the test equally samples each of the major content areas addressed. If this is not the case, adding to the length of the test may not improve its reliability or its fairness.

If we increase our fifteen-item comparative political systems test to

TABLE 28.2 STUDENTS' SCORES ON THE CLASSROOM TEST IN COMPARATIVE POLITICS

Alice	8	Joan	12
Jane	10	Judy	14
Bill	7	Ruth	7
Ted	11	Tom	10

thirty items, for example, but ask twenty-three questions on the first part, seven questions on the second part, and none on the third part, the problems illustrated above will still exist. The test is a more reliable measure of student mastery of the first and second parts, but it still gives no information about mastery of the third part and it is still unfair to students who concentrated their study on the third part.

Even when a test does sample evenly from different aspects of the content taught, test items still might favor certain students over others. Suppose that we want to test students' abilities to read quickly and comprehend material. This requires students to read paragraphs, and these paragraphs have to be concerned with some type of content. Sally, for example, might be knowledgeable about and interested in baseball, and Ted may not. If some material on the test deals with baseball, Sally may be able to read it more quickly and remember more of it because she is more familiar with specialized terms, even though she may be no better than Ted in general reading ability and comprehension. However, if students must read several paragraphs dealing with various topics, these individual differences in knowledge and interest will balance out. This is the major reason why longer tests tend to be more reliable than shorter ones, other things being equal.

COGNITIVE LEVELS OF TEST CONTENT

Bloom's taxonomy

Besides sampling from the full range of topics covered, we might also wish to sample various levels of understanding of the material. The *Taxonomy of Educational Objectives* (Bloom et al., 1956) may be used to consider various cognitive demands that different kinds of test items make on students. The following taxonomy contains six levels, ordered from simplest to most complex (see Chapter 6 for more details about this taxonomy):

- *Knowledge*—To remember and to recall information. (Who were the first five presidents of the United States? Recite the alphabet. What author wrote *Hamlet*?)
- *Comprehension*—To understand the relations between facts or concepts. (Translate a French sentence into English. Predict the probability of rain when given key facts. Determine the relative size of a standard deviation by looking at a distribution of scores.)
- *Application*—To use information and procedures that are comprehended. (Given a set of student scores, compute the mean and standard deviation. Write sentences that are grammatically correct.)
- *Analysis*—To break down an idea into its parts. (Diagram sentences. Identify the setting, plot, and climax of a novel.)
- *Synthesis*—To rearrange parts to form a new whole. (Write a class play. Watch a film of one's teaching and plan a better strategy.)
- *Evaluation*—To know the value of methods for given purposes. (Was the play credible, well paced? Was the teaching more effective?)

To the extent that all these levels of content mastery were included as instructional goals for the curriculum sequences being tested, we might want to sample from each level. This will help yield a balanced view of each student's learning as well (some students are good at understanding and remembering discrete facts but have trouble synthesizing them, integrating them with general principles, and applying their knowledge in problem-solving situations; other students have the opposite pattern of strengths and weaknesses). Table 28.3 illustrates a plan for a test that samples both the range of topics taught and a variety of levels of cognitive demand. For simplicity, the six cognitive level categories from the taxonomy are combined to form two categories. The first (terms, facts, principles) represents the first two levels of the taxonomy (knowledge and comprehension).

Table 28.3 also summarizes the teacher's plans for three units. The first unit on weather indicates that the largest percentage of instruction will focus on application of concepts to predict weather. Hence the exam should emphasize this information, and students should know that when they prepare for the test.

The second plan indicates that understanding general facts and principles of the metric system is a key instructional goal. (Perhaps an application unit will follow this one.) Such an outline of goals helps teachers to make instructional decisions (how much time to spend in class, the type of homework to assign) and to write appropriate tests. Unfortunately,

TABLE 28.3 THREE PLANS FOR CLASSROOM TESTS WITH SPECIFICATION OF CONTENT AND COGNITIVE EMPHASIS

	Cognitive Objectives		
Content	**Terms, Facts, Principles**	**Applications**	**Total Percentage**
Unit 1: Weather			
A. Atmosphere	20	0	20
B. Air masses and fronts	15	5	20
C. Causes of precipitation	0	15	15
D. Predicting	0	40	40
E. Control	5	0	5
Unit 2: Weights and Measures			
A. Length	10	0	10
B. Weight mass	10	0	10
C. Time	10	0	10
D. Standard measures			
1. Metric system	60	0	60
2. GCS	5	0	5
3. KMS	5	0	5
Unit 3: Comparative Politics			
A. Historical development	80	0	80
B. Present function	0	20	20
C. Future trends	0	0	0

many teachers fail to provide students with this information; typically, teachers erroneously confuse general knowledge of test expectations with knowledge of specific questions.

INSTRUCTIONAL OBJECTIVES

We have discussed test construction as if all content topics and all instructional objectives included in a unit were equal. Teachers, however, often want to stress certain topics or objectives they consider to be especially important. In this case, it may make sense for the teacher not only to emphasize these key goals during instruction but to emphasize them in constructing tests and in making suggestions to students about how to allocate their preparation time.

In general, instruction is more effective to the extent that teachers have specific plans and communicate clear expectations to students about what they are to learn. These shared expectations about what course content is important and about what types of tests will be used can improve the reliability of teacher-made tests. Test construction experts contend that teachers must resolve three questions if they are to teach effectively: (1) What will I teach? (2) How will I know when students have learned it? and (3) What materials and activities will be necessary? These three questions represent the three parts that compose an instructional objective. Three steps are involved in writing these objectives (Gronlund, 1985; Mager, 1962).

1. Name the terminal behavior—what proof would you accept that the learner has achieved your goal (Must the student swim a lap or a mile, design a blueprint, or build a garage?).
2. Specify the conditions under which the behavior will be demonstrated (Will students write essay questions or deliver a speech; will answers be picked from a list or from memory; will students evaluate a live debate or analyze written material?).
3. Announce the criteria for acceptable performance (fifteen out of twenty for an A; run a mile in fewer than eight minutes for a B; write a theme with no grammatical errors to pass the grammar unit review).

In Chapter 6, we summarized the advantages and disadvantages of instructional objectives. Some of these arguments are presented below, as they apply to evaluation issues. Even before reading the list, however, it is useful to note that neither advocates of instructional objectives nor their opponents have a correct view. The value of instructional objectives depends on how teachers use them.

ADVANTAGES OF INSTRUCTIONAL OBJECTIVES

1. They increase teacher awareness of what students should be working on and lead to more optimal planning. A wider range of objectives is included.
2. They provide a basis for assessing continuous progress (allowing stu-

dents to proceed at their own rates) because instruction focuses on specific skills.
3. Students have a better blueprint for guiding their learning activity; hence, they learn more.
4. After reaching a criterion, students have more time to work on their own learning activities.

DISADVANTAGES OF INSTRUCTIONAL OBJECTIVES

1. They increase teacher control at the expense of students' control of objectives.
2. They unduly emphasize things that can be measured; only low-level objectives are likely to be measured.
3. Once established (the teacher invests the time to write objectives and set up a measurement system), the system perpetuates itself; objectives remain the same; spontaneity is reduced.
4. A great deal of instructor time is used in writing instructional objectives; such time could be better used in other ways, such as in one-to-one conferences.

Our only major concern with instructional objectives is that at times teachers apply them too specifically or apply them to content for which they are inappropriate.

Communicating Expectations to Students

It may be useful for students to know that their themes will be graded on the basis of ideas, organization, mechanics, and sentence structure. Table 28.4 shows that such knowledge has practical consequences for students. In Ms. James's class students know they should spend most of their time generating ideas; however, they also realize that they should polish their language and grammar. In contrast, students in Ms. Wilson's class should concentrate on developing major ideas. If she wishes to assess students' use of correct grammar, she will do so with separate, focused tests. Mr. Adkins's students know that they should spend about half of the time available for composition by carefully examining sentence structure, grammar, and so on. Mr. Adkins believes that the only proof of knowledge of grammar is its application in written composition. Different expectations are reflected in Ms. Stanford's objectives. She

TABLE 28.4 FOUR TEACHERS' CRITERIA FOR GRADING STUDENTS' PAPERS

Teacher	Ideas	Organization	Mechanics	Sentence Structure
Ms. James	70	10	10	10
Ms. Wilson	85	15	0	0
Mr. Adkins	50	10	25	15
Ms. Stanford	50	50	0	0*

stresses organization, especially paragraphing, more than the other teachers; however, students' grammatical mistakes do not affect their scores. In the margin, she puts an *X* by any sentence that contains a grammatical error and gives students five minutes to correct their errors. Grades are lowered slightly if students cannot find their mistakes.

Communicating teacher expectations

Teachers' performance expectations vary widely, and teachers should communicate their expectations to students before examinations. Too much information, however, may lock both teachers and students into unproductive patterns of behavior. If Mr. Adkins were to define every conceivable organizational, grammatical, and sentence-structure error and assign points in advance (minus points: 4, inappropriate use of colon or semicolon; 2, inappropriate use of comma; 5, sentence without subject; and so forth), he might inadvertently constrict student behavior. His students could learn to write three or four short paragraphs, using very simple sentences and words. If students were left at this level, it would be an unfortunate loss.

Facts versus Concepts

Test blueprints

What does a good test blueprint look like? What percentage of questions should be factual? What percentage should cover application or evaluation? There is no formula for a good plan. A plan should clarify instructional goals, assist in planning instruction, and help the teacher to prepare a test that measures intended goals. Sometimes it makes sense to have a little application and much emphasis on basic facts. At other times balance between application and facts is more appropriate, and sometimes it makes sense to stress application. The teacher should know content and cognitive goals before instruction and should match the exam to the instructional emphases. It is simply not fair to students, nor is it effective evaluation, to lead them to expect one type of test and present another.

TYPES OF TEST ITEMS

We have discussed the need for reliable tests and have noted that a test must sufficiently cover assigned content if it is to produce an interpretable score. Equally important is the need for questions that measure objectives appropriately. In this section, we describe two types of questions that teachers can use on classroom tests and we examine some of the strengths and weaknesses of these questions.

Writing Essay Questions

Teachers who use the following measurement guidelines for writing essay exams can improve their ability to measure student performance rather than teacher bias (Kubiszyn & Borich, 1984; Tenbrink, 1974; Thorndike & Hagen, 1977):

1. Know the mental processes you want students to use before writing test questions.
2. Write essay questions so that students have clear tasks. (Are students

to recognize biased presentations? Are they to distinguish verifiable from unverifiable facts?)

3. Be sure essay questions require students to do more than reproduce information.
4. Be sure that questions are not too numerous or too lengthy.
5. Include questions that vary in difficulty.
6. Provide students with clear directions for essay tests. (Students need to know if the answer is to be outlined or written out completely, the point of value of each question, and the criteria the teacher will use to evaluate their answers.)

Often teachers write essay questions that only call for factual information. To assess factual information given in response to an essay question is a waste of time. Knowledge and comprehension can be assessed more efficiently and reliably by objective tests. Teachers must decide which cognitive level they want to test before writing questions, because this decision determines the type of test they should construct. Teachers should then tell students precisely what type of response is desired.

Vague questions

Too often essay questions merely tell students to discuss an issue and they force students to guess what the teacher really wants. Imagine yourself answering the following exam question in a teacher-education course: "Discuss the factors that contribute to student learning." Does the teacher simply want a list of all factors that relate to student learning? Should you discuss the importance of each factor or the role of each factor? This question does not indicate what type of answer the teacher wants.

The question is vague in other ways as well. What is meant by the term *factors*? If you apply a literal definition, hundreds of factors are involved (quality of prenatal care, and so on). An example of a clearer question would be: "Illustrate how a teacher could hypothetically improve the performance of an anxious but capable (IQ 115) student in a speech class. Be sure that your response illustrates the use of dissonance, feedback, reward, and success in public and private classroom situations."

Essay questions, if used correctly, should require students to do more than reproduce information. Questions that ask students to predict or to write their own examples are generally better than questions that require students merely to present facts.

Problem-solving questions

Asking students to solve problems is an especially good way to use essay questions. For example: "The first paragraph that follows describes the academic problems of Ted Jenkins. The following three paragraphs describe a teacher's attempt to deal with the problems. Compare and contrast the three solutions, with special consideration to the short-term and long-term effects of the plans on Ted's general dependency, class achievement, and peer status." This question forces students to do more than simply reproduce information.

Appropriate number of questions

Some teachers, perhaps because they feel uncomfortable asking so few questions and neglecting so much content, ask too many essay questions and undermine the unique role that an essay question can play. Essay exams are useful to the extent that they provide students with an opportunity to demonstrate their ability to recall, organize, and apply facts and principles. To rush students through ten essay questions in fifty minutes, however, is self-defeating.

Arrangement by difficulty level

It is possible, though, to ask a few essay questions (four or so) in fifty minutes, and it is useful to vary the difficulty of these questions. If the questions are all simple, students with average mastery will not be differentiated from students with excellent mastery. Similarly, if all of the essay questions are very difficult, the test will not differentiate students with minimal mastery from students with average mastery. It is generally desirable to arrange test items in order of expected difficulty, to prevent some students from giving up on initially reading the most difficult or detailed questions.

Necessity for complete directions

It is also important to provide students with complete directions. Teachers may occasionally prefer, for example, that students outline their answers rather than write them out. (Teachers may not want to penalize students who write poorly, or may think that it is important to ask a few extra questions.) Such expectations should be clearly communicated to students. It is especially important to specify how many points each questions is worth. Without such knowledge, students cannot effectively plan how much time to spend on various questions.

The Essay Test Read the two answers that appear below in response to the question: "Compare the powers and organization of the central government under the Articles of Confederation with the powers and organization of our central government today." Which student deserves the higher grade? What grade should Student A receive? Student B? Which answer is better written? Which conveys more knowledge? More comprehension?

Student A

Our government today has a president, a house of representatives, and a senate. Each state has two senators, but the number of representatives is different for each state. This is because of compromise at the Constitutional Convention. The Articles of Confederation had only a Congress and each state had delegates in it and had one vote. This Congress couldn't do much of anything because all the states had to say it was alright. Back then Congress couldn't make people obey the law and there wasn't no supreme court to make people obey the law. The Articles of Confederation let Congress declare war, make treaties, and borrow money and Congress can do these things today. But Congress then really didn't have any power, it had to ask the states for everything. Today Congress can tell the states what to do and tax people to raise money they don't have to ask the states to give them money. Once each state could print its own money if it wanted to but today only the U. S. Mint can make money.

Student B

There is a very unique difference between the Central Government under the Articles of Confederation and the National Government of today. The Confederation could not tax directly where as the National Government can.The government of today has three different bodies—Legislative, Judicial, and Executive branches. The Confederation had only one branch which had limited powers. The confederate government could not tax the states directly or an individual either. The government of today, however, has the power to tax anyone directly and if they don't respond, the government has the right to put this person in jail until they are willing to pay the taxes. The confederation government was not run nearly as efficiently as the government of today. While they could pass laws (providing most of the states voted with them) the confederate government could not enforce these laws, (something which the present day can and does do) they could only hope and urge the states to enforce the laws.

How hard is it for you to *quantify* the differences between the two responses? How much better is the response you rate higher? How do you think the grades you assigned compare to those your classmates gave? We suspect that the ratings of the two responses will vary widely in your class.

Thorndike and Hagen (1969) presented these two answers (along with three others) to two groups of graduate students taking a course in tests and measurement. They asked the groups to assign a maximum of 25 points to the questions, provided them with a model answer, and stressed that the grade should be based on completeness and accuracy, not grammar or spelling. The papers received a wide variety of scores from the two groups of raters. Student A's paper received scores ranging from 5 to 25 points, and Student B's paper was scored as low as 3 and as high as 25. The ratings of the papers depended on who rated them.

These findings indicate that it is important for teachers who use essay tests to develop objective criteria for scoring such tests. Is the paper assigned a 20 or 21 really inferior to the paper assigned a 24 or 25? To put it another way, the teacher must be sure that the scores reflect demonstrated student performances, not teacher biases. Some techniques for accomplishing this follow.

Scoring Essay Exams Green (1975) noted that there are two generally acceptable techniques for grading an essay—the point-score method and the sorting method. The sorting method is easier to use than the point-score method, and, although not as reliable, it can be used fairly. The steps involved in sorting are: (1) quickly read all the papers, sort papers into piles (A, B, C, pass, fail), and place borderline papers into the higher category with a question mark on them; (2) read the responses again, paying special attention to borderline papers; (3) assign a grade to each paper on the basis of the pile it ends up in.

Sorting method

The point-score procedure calls for the following: (1) a grading key that includes features that should be present in student answers for full credit (partial credit for each part of the response should be determined in advance); (2) reading all responses to the same question consecutively and assigning the number of earned points to each question as it is read; (3)

Point-score method

reading all responses to the next question; and (4) when all questions have been read, totaling the points and assigning a grade.

Halo effect

In general, the point-score method is the best way to grade essay tests because it uses a fixed standard (an answer key) and guards against halo effects that interfere with effective grading. A halo effect refers to the tendency to rate or evaluate a person or performance on the basis of a global impression rather than according to a specific trait or performance. The sorting method also yields generally reliable scores, however, and teachers who test frequently and often use essay tests may have to rely on this technique.

Need to read papers anonymously

Both methods of grading essay questions require that teachers read papers anonymously. This can be done by telling students to put their names on the backs of their papers. It is easy to read something extra into an answer by a good student, and it is equally easy to demand more from a student we believe to be marginal (demand more proof that the student really deserves full credit). An advantage of the point-score method is that the teacher reads answers to the same question consecutively in all papers. Students who write poor responses to the first question are not as likely to be inadvertently penalized when the teacher reads answers to the second question as they would be if the teacher read responses to the two questions one after another.

If the teacher writes the point value at the bottom of the first question (where the teacher cannot avoid seeing it when he or she begins to grade the second question), however, the usefulness of this procedure is reduced somewhat. Similarly, if the teacher repeatedly grades student B's responses immediately after student A's, student B's score might be systematically influenced (Follman, Lowe & Miller, 1971; Hales & Tokar, 1975). If student A is among the best in the class, the contrast between the two papers might be sufficiently glaring for B's score to suffer. Similarly, B's score might look better than it actually is if it repeatedly follows a low scorer's paper. For this reason teachers should shuffle papers after reading all responses to a particular question.

Constructing model answers

Mehrens and Lehmann (1978) recommended that teachers construct model answers to essay questions as they write the questions, not after the test is given. This procedure calls attention to faulty wording, inadequate time allotment, inappropriate difficulty level, and similar problems early enough for teachers to correct them prior to test administration.

Writing Objective Test Items

We agree with Thorndike and Hagen (1977) and Kubiszyn and Borich (1984) who contend that multiple-choice items can measure the same aspects of an educational objective as any other pen and paper test, except written expression and originality. Analysis, synthesis, and all other levels of cognitive processing can be tested with multiple-choice items. The multiple-choice format is the most versatile form of an objective test item. The item has two parts: the *stem*, which represents the problem, and three or more possible correct answers, one of which is the correct answer and the others are *distractors*. Consider the following illustration:

A major conclusion from the Brophy and Evertson (1976) and the Good and Grouws (1975) studies is:

a. Individual learning is the most effective overall learning mode in elementary schools.

b. Varying the pace of instruction accommodates the learning needs of most elementary school pupils.

c. Different patterns of teaching behavior may be important for different types of learners.

d. Subgroup teaching is more effective than whole-class teaching.

The answer to this question is c, and choices a, b, and d are designed to be distractors—plausible alternatives for students who do not know the answer.

How can one write or recognize a good question? We know that a good test question must ask the student to respond to important content, but what other criteria are there? Thorndike and Hagen (1977) provided a number of guidelines for writing multiple-choice items:

Guidelines

1. The stem must present a problem.
2. Include most of the item in the stem and keep options short.
3. Keep the stem as short as possible.
4. Use the negative infrequently in the stem but make it noticeable by underlining the not when it is included.
5. Use new material in stem problems and attempt to measure application.
6. Include only one correct or clearly best answer.
7. Try to make all options plausible.
8. Do not cue the answer (by making it longer than the others or using predictable patterns—B, C, D, A, B, C, D, A, and so on).

The first four suggestions are all related to helping students know precisely the question they are answering. If a stem does not present a problem, the student has to spend valuable time trying to figure out what the problem is. Similarly, lengthy questions make it more difficult to identify the problem. Since the purpose of the test is to assess knowledge and not reading ability, a clear presentation of the problem is desirable. Using *not* in the stem is acceptable if the student is aware that it is there. When students read stems rapidly they may miss the word. If the word *not* is used it should be underlined.

Which of the following is not typical of successful students?

a. essentially task oriented
b. tend to be liked by peers
c. more person than task oriented
d. cooperative in class

As noted, the correct answer to this question is c. The *not* is emphasized in this question, the stem presents the problem, and both the stem and the answer choices are relatively brief.

Although it is not essential to present novel material in the stem, such material may help teachers to ask questions that require students to do more than just memorize facts. For example, rather than ask students, "Which of the following is not recommended by Thorndike and Hagen . . . ?", it is possible to present a series of ten objective questions and ask students to indicate how many test construction principles are violated in each item.

Advantage of objective test

The primary advantage of the objective test, when properly constructed, is that it provides a relatively unbiased assessment of student performance. The inclusion of partially correct answers reduces the objectivity of the test because judgments have to be made about the degree of correctness, and if answer choices are not plausible, the chances that a student will guess the answer are increased. Often test questions give away answers (the right answer is often longer, the stem provides a grammatical clue, the answer has to begin with a *not*, verb tense, or the teacher may have a habit of placing the right answer in the same position). When test answers can be guessed the test measures students' ability to take tests, not their knowledge.

Other Forms of Objective Questions

We emphasize the multiple-choice question because it is the most versatile form of objective test. There are other forms of objective tests, however, and each has advantages and limitations. Three other popular objective test formats are true–false, completion, and matching.

True-false tests

In general, true-false questions can be constructed much more quickly than multiple-choice items. Unlike multiple-choice questions, the true–false format forces students to choose between two alternatives rather than four or five. For example, true or false: assimilation occurs when the child integrates a new idea into a scheme he or she already has.

Brown (1976) noted that true–false questions can be used to good advantage with young children, especially when only a general estimate of student performance is necessary. A major problem that limits the use of true–false questions is that some content is difficult to express in true–false form. Furthermore, students will be correct 50 percent of the time by guessing; hence the diagnostic power of true–false questions is low.

Short-answer and completion tests

Short-answer and completion items require students to finish a statement from recall rather than recognition. On a multiple-choice test students select (recognize) the best answer from a series of choices. In contrast, in a short-answer format students provide their own answers. It is considerably more difficult to construct a multiple-choice item that presents four or five carefully written and plausible alternatives than it is to write a stem and to allow students to provide their own answers.

Consider this question: "Motivation can be defined as ______?" Obviously, it takes considerably more time to present this question in a multiple-choice format than to write the question in its present form. The ease of scoring multiple-choice questions, however, typically compensates for the time needed to construct the items and often yields more reliable scores than those obtained from a completion test. Indeed, some forms of completion tests possess some of the same scoring problems as essay tests. For questions like the one presented above, for example, many responses can be partially or wholly correct. Teachers must invariably use their judgment in scoring some responses to completion questions.

Short-answer and completion items are especially useful in math and science courses, where formulas or equations can be requested, and for testing spelling and language, where specific bits of information often are required. In any subject matter, they are good for testing knowledge of definitions and technical terms (Mehrens & Lehmann, 1978).

Matching exercises

Matching exercises require students to link items in one column with corresponding items in another column:

Column A	*Column B*
____ 1. Intelligence tests	A. Freud
____ 2. Cognitive development	B. Skinner
____ 3. Trust vs. mistrust	C. Erikson
____ 4. Reinforcement	D. Piaget
____ 5. Modeling	E. Kounin
____ 6. Formal operations	F. Binet
	G. None of the above

In this example, students would receive credit for answering, F, D, C, B, G, and D for items 1–6, respectively. Matching exercises are useful for testing memory of specific facts: terms, definitions, dates, events, etc. They are easy to construct and score, as long as each item has just one clearly correct answer. To avoid cuing correct answers, it is helpful to have more response alternatives (Column B in the example) than items (Column A) or to include response alternatives that may be used more than once (D in the example).

Types of Test Items: Summary

No type of test or test item is best in all circumstances. Advocates sometimes claim that essay tests are better for measuring higher-level objectives and that objective tests are better for measuring factual recall or other low-level objectives. This is not the case, however. Essay tests can be used purely to grade low-level skills (punctuation, capitalization, spelling), with no attention to the creativity of the essay, or they can be used to measure factors such as sentence structure, paragraph stucture, or story theme. Similarly, multiple-choice tests can measure learning objectives at almost any level of difficulty or sophistication. Multiple-choice tests are not necessarily restricted to low-level objectives. Thus classifications such as subjective versus objective or essay versus multiple choice are not very useful.

Other differences between test items are more a matter of teacher or student preference than of necessity. Essay tests, for example, allow students to organize their answers and to integrate material. To students with above-average writing skills, however, they provide an advantage not directly relevant to the course but relevant to success on essay tests. Essay tests are confined to a relatively small portion of the material covered, they are time-consuming to grade, and the grading is notoriously subjective.

Multiple-choice and other objective tests present different advantages and disadvantages. Advantages include speed and objectivity of scoring, sampling a much larger number of objectives in the same amount of time, quicker feedback to students, and collecting a broader-based data on how well students have mastered a wide range of course objectives. Some students, however, have test-taking skills that give them a particular advantage on this kind of test, independent of subject content. The items are structured completely by the teacher, so the test provides little opportunity for students to integrate material or to discuss it in their own words.

Using a variety of testing methods

Because there are advantages and disadvantages to different kinds of tests, perhaps the best solution is to use a variety of tests and assignments (essays or term papers, for example). This procedure enables teachers to balance differential student test-taking abilities with different kinds of tests and to achieve a balance between the kinds of learning strategies and content mastery that various tests foster.

CRITERION-REFERENCED AND NORM-REFERENCED MEASUREMENT

The distinction between criterion-referenced and norm-referenced measurement does not affect the type of item that one includes on exams but influences why a particular item is selected.

Gronlund (1985) contended that criterion-referenced tests are especially helpful in measuring the minimum knowledge or skills to be obtained from an instructional program and that norm-referenced tests are most appropriate for estimating progress toward higher-level, complex learning outcomes when continuous development is possible, as is typically the case in higher-level cognitive goals. Mastery or criterion-level measurement is not appropriate for this purpose. As Gronlund noted, however, it is possible to use criterion- and norm-referenced strategies simultaneously. For example, one could describe a student's behavior in terms of both percentage correct (Alice found ten of fourteen errors) and percentage of students surpassed (75 percent).

In both criterion-referenced and norm-referenced testing, teachers should communicate general objectives to students and use an adequate and appropriate sample of test questions. The major difference between the two types of measurement lies in the difficulty of questions.

Difficulty of questions

Again, teachers can employ both criterion- and norm-referenced techniques as the subject matter dictates. In general, if important and universal objectives can be identified, as in the early elementary grades, it appears more reasonable to stress criterion-referenced measurement and to report student progress in terms of measured objectives. In secondary settings, where goals are less clear, norm-referenced measurement (perhaps combined with minimum performance levels and criterion-referenced measurement when possible) is a viable assessment strategy.

ADDITIONAL ASSESSMENT PROCEDURES

We have discussed written tests and how they can be constructed and used appropriately. Teachers measure student learning in many other ways, however. Any assessment procedure a teacher uses must be valid and reliable if it is to be useful. We now discuss assessment procedures other than pen-and-paper tests.

Performance Tests

A performance test demands that an individual, or sometimes a group of individuals, make a decision, solve a problem, or perform some prescribed behavior like delivering a speech. Some contend that student behavior—not student knowledge as shown on pen-and-paper tests—is the critical variable in determining whether students have mastered material or developed social maturity. Indeed, many teacher-education programs use student performance as a part of assessment. Similarly, several states have now adopted beginning-teacher evaluation programs in which teachers have to demonstrate classroom competency before they are allowed to become fully certified.

Obviously, many performance measures that could be obtained are not worth the effort necessary to do so. A third-grade teacher could call students individually to the front of the class and ask them to find selected countries on the globe. The same information, however, can be obtained more reliably and quickly by asking students to write the names of a variety of countries on a dittoed, blank map.

Advantage of performance measures

Most knowledge can be assessed through pen-and-paper measures. If behaviors are critically important, however, they can be assessed with rating scales and checklists by having individuals perform. The advantage of performance measures is that they provide direct evidence that a student can perform a specific skill. The disadvantage is that the process of observing the performance of individuals is time consuming for both students and teachers.

Brown (1976) listed the following examples of skills that one might want to measure directly: painting a watercolor, typing forty words per minute, conducting an opinion poll, conducting a counseling interview, programming a computer, making a soufflé, or assembling a carburetor.

To obtain reliable scores on performance tests, as on pen-and-paper tests, students need to know precisely what they are to demonstrate and the criteria by which their performance will be judged. Similarly, teachers should prepare checklists and rating scales that adequately describe student performance.

Teachers may use performance tests or oral presentations as part of their assessment programs. The general procedure teachers follow is the same as that for construction of classroom tests: (1) identify instructional objectives (content and cognitive skills), (2) plan instructional activities, and (3) assess student learning and the instructional program.

Green (1975) noted that the content of an industrial arts course might include:

1. Common hand tools and their use
2. Common power tools and their use
3. Qualities of various types of hard and soft wood
4. Safety rules
5. Joints: butt, miter, dowel, and mortise
6. Fasteners: screws, nails, staples, corrugated fasteners, and glue
7. Finishes: oil, wax, paint, varnish, shellac, lacquer, glass and plastics
8. Project selection and construction

From this type of content list teachers make decisions about the importance of each objective (objectives 1, 2, and 3 may be 75 percent of the course) and the evidence they will accept as proof of mastery (pen-and-paper test, performance).

Immediate evaluation

In many performance-testing situations teachers must evaluate performance as it occurs (to tape speeches or to film a student cutting with a power tool is unwieldy). An example of a checklist that could be used to describe a student's observation of safety rules appears in Table 28.5. This scale allows one to mark whether or not a specific behavior occurs.

Rating Scales A rating scale does more than record the presence or absence of behavior; it forces the rater to judge the quality of the performance. An example of a rating scale appears in Table 28.6. In general, it is easier for errors to occur when using rating forms than checklists. Yet a rating is often necessary to estimate quality.

Improving reliability

Several steps can be taken to improve the reliability of ratings. The first and most important one is to obtain several ratings on different days. All of us vary from day to day and from situation to situation. The more ratings we have the more likely we will be to describe typical, not atypical, behavior. Second, make a separate rating for each performance element. Teachers using the rating scale presented in Table 28.6, for example, can note a student's inability to follow a plan without losing sight of the fact that the student used tools properly.

Too often teachers do not rate performance dimensions separately. Use of overgeneralized rating scales may result in a single behavior unduly hurting or helping a student. A speech teacher, for example, who likes an enthusiastic beginning may penalize a student too much for a slow start (unless this behavior is in a separate category), even though other parts of the speech such as eye contact, clear voice, and purpose are good.

Halo effects

Teachers must guard against halo effects when they use rating forms. It is easy for a student's previous record of performance to influence the present rating, partly because the identity of the student cannot be masked, as it can be with written papers, and because the rating must be made immediately. Thus the teacher may not rate students who typically give good speeches as critically as he or she rates other students.

Teachers sometimes use rating scales inappropriately because they divide tasks into too many small steps and fail to obtain a general rating of a project or presentation. Sometimes poor performance on one aspect

TABLE 28.5 CHECKLIST FOR EVALUATING PUPIL'S COMPLIANCE WITH SAFETY REGULATIONS IN USE OF CIRCULAR SAW

DIRECTIONS: As each pupil uses the circular saw, observe his procedure and place a check mark in the blank preceding each safety regulation with which he fails to comply.

_____ 1. He makes adjustments to the saw only when the power is turned off.
_____ 2. He uses the guard, kickback device, and spreader for all cuts except such special cuts as dadoes, etc.
_____ 3. He uses a pusher stick when ripping small pieces of stock.
_____ 4. He uses the ripping fence to guide the work when ripping stock.
_____ 5. He uses the crosscut gauge when crosscutting stock.
_____ 6. He never attempts to clear away scraps from the table top with his fingers while the saw is on.
_____ 7. He removes the ripping fence when crosscutting long pieces of stock.
_____ 8. He does not reach over and in back of the saw to pull pieces through.
_____ 9. He does not let tools and scrap stockpile up on the saw table.
_____ 10. He checks the stock before cutting to see that there are no nails, screws, or grit present in the wood.
_____ 11. He raises the saw blade no more than ½ inch above the stock being cut.
_____ 12. He asks the instructor to inspect special setups before beginning the cutting operation.

Source: *J. A. Green,* Teacher-Made Tests, *Second Edition. (New York: Harper & Row, 1975). © 1963, 1975 by John A. Green. (After "Safety Rules for the Safe Operation of Power Woodworking Tools," Frank Pexton Lumber Co., Denver, CO, pp. 8–9). Reprinted by permission of Harper & Row, Publishers, Inc.*

does not negatively affect total performance (a low score in inappropriate hand usage may not hurt the speech, while poor eye contact may make it totally ineffective). However, teachers should make considerable effort to include major criteria in the rating form itself. Green (1975) offered the following criteria for evaluating a student's oral presentation.

Criteria for evaluation

1. Rapport with audience
2. Enthusiastic presentation
3. Effective organization
4. Clarity
5. Correct grammar
6. Good word choice
7. Adequate knowledge of subject
8. Significance of material
9. Stage presence
10. Appropriate gestures

TABLE 28.6 RATING SCALE FOR PROJECTS IN INDUSTRIAL ARTS

DIRECTIONS: Rate each item in the scale on the basis of 4 points for outstanding quality of performance, 3 points for better than average, 2 points for average, 1 point for inferior, and 0 for unsatisfactory or failure. Encircle the appropriate number to indicate your rating, and enter the total of these numbers at the bottom of the sheet. If an item does not apply, draw a horizontal line through the item so that it will not be included in the total score.

Procedure Scale		Product Scale	
1. To what extent did he follow the detailed steps of his plan?	0 1 2 3 4	1. To what extent is the finished product an embodiment of the original plan?	0 1 2 3 4
2. To what extent did he avoid having to do work over because of failure to follow his plan?	0 1 2 3 4	2. Does the general appearance of the project reflect neat, orderly work?	0 1 2 3 4
3. To what extent did he refrain from spoiling materials by working accurately and carefully?	0 1 2 3 4	3. Are the dimensions of the actual project the same as those on the drawing, within reasonable tolerances?	0 1 2 3 4
4. To what extent did he follow approved procedures in performing specific operations?	0 1 2 3 4	4. How do angular measurements check with those specified?	0 1 2 3 4
5. To what extent did he exhibit skill in the use of:		5. Of what quality is the finish?	0 1 2 3 4
a. layout and measuring tools?	0 1 2 3 4	6. To what extent were materials used to advantage?	0 1 2 3 4
b. cutting edge tools?	0 1 2 3 4	7. Do all joints fit properly?	0 1 2 3 4
c. boring and drilling tools?	0 1 2 3 4	8. Are all margins uniform, curved and irregular lines properly executed, etc.?	0 1 2 3 4
6. To what extent did he show improvement in the use of tools?	0 1 2 3 4		
7. Did he select the proper tool for each operation?	0 1 2 3 4		
8. Did he use all tools properly?	0 1 2 3 4		

TABLE 28.6 (*continued*)

Procedure Scale		Product Scale
9. To what extent did he exhibit initiative in revising his plan as required by changing conditions?	0 1 2 3 4	
10. Did he practice difficult operations to minimize material spoilage and poor workmanship?	0 1 2 3 4	
11. To what extent did he keep profitably employed? Busy?	0 1 2 3 4	
12. To what extent did he maintain a fair balance between quality of work performed and time consumed?	0 1 2 3 4	
13. To what extent was he able to do his own work without assistance from instructor or other students?	0 1 2 3 4	

Source: *J. A. Green,* Teacher-Made Tests, *Second Edition. (New York: Harper & Row, 1975). © 1963, 1975 by John A. Green. (After* Measuring Educational Achievement, *by William J. Michels and R. Ray Karnes, McGraw-Hill, 1950). Reprinted by permission of Harper & Row, Publishers, Inc.*

Grading performance and progress is difficult, and errors will occur. Observation checklists and rating forms are two ways in which tests can be given more fairly. Remember that ratings are judgments, not facts. Another important factor to keep in mind is that the form used for rating will influence student behavior. If the criteria do not reward descriptive speech and penalize mispronounciation, predictable behavior will follow.

Similar concerns have been raised about the effects of scales that are used to rate teaching effectiveness or teachers' classroom behavior and decisions. Teachers may overuse items on the checklist (e.g., does the teacher use simulations, does the teacher involve students in small-group discussions).

Informal Assessment

Formal testing is only one way that teachers can obtain information, and not always the best way. In addition to using formal testing or rating, teachers can collect information by observing, by questioning, or by inspecting the work their students perform.

Oral tests

Besides this regular, informal monitoring, teachers may wish to conduct oral tests by calling on students to answer questions or recite individually. Records of this performance can be kept and used as feedback to guide instructional decisions and as information to be used in grading, just as with student performance on written assignments. Teachers who conduct oral tests should be sure to include everyone or else to randomize questions. If they only call on students who volunteer, they will overestimate student understanding, and if they only call on nonvolunteers, they will underestimate this understanding and put certain students on the spot continuously.

If everyone is to be questioned, the teacher may wish to proceed in a pattern, calling on students alphabetically or in rows. If so, the teacher probably should let the students know this, cautioning them to pay attention and think about how they would answer each question but to do so silently without calling out answers or raising their hands. This will minimize confusion and help ensure that students will get the most out of listening to exchanges between the teacher and other students.

Observing seatwork

Much useful information also can be obtained from observing and correcting students while they work on seatwork assignments. In subjects such as elementary language arts or English composition and in mathematics at almost any level, seatwork is as good or better than formal tests for monitoring progress, although teachers may wish to test for other reasons.

CLASSROOM ASSESSMENT: SOME SUMMARY SUGGESTIONS

Each teacher and testing situation is unique; however, these general guidelines can be offered:

1. If you consider testing important, it is probably a good idea for you to test frequently over short time spans, using criterion-referenced

Teachers can obtain useful feedback from in-class participation and oral tests, as well as from more formal test situations.

tests when possible so that you can use your test data for reteaching and individualized instruction, as well as for grading.

2. Be clear about learning objectives. If you are, you are unlikely to run into problems such as lack of content validity, and you will not create tests that measure content that was taught but do not measure the objectives that you want to measure.
3. Take care that you allow students ample time to finish a test unless time is a relevant factor.
4. If you intend to test over the entire course content, be sure that your test samples equally from different parts of the course.
5. On the other hand, if you wish to stress certain content, alert students to this so that they can adjust their preparation accordingly. In fact, if you are extremely clear about objectives, you can give students a number of potential test questions and inform them that the test will be composed of a subset of these questions. This will ensure that the students study all of the material that you consider important.
6. Try to maintain some balance between essay tests (or essay-type assignments) and objective tests, because certain students do notably better on one type of test than the other, independent of course content. Also, as pointed out previously, different kinds of tests promote various kinds of learning. A balance between test types is usually preferable to reliance on only one.

TEST-TAKING SKILLS

Even a carefully constructed test, under certain circumstances can yield unreliable results. One of the biggest threats to obtaining accurate information about student performance is the fact that some students can take tests better than other students. Unfortunately, some students experience debilitating anxiety during testing or evaluation situations and thus underperform. As Hill and Wigfield (1984) noted, several recent educational trends may increase this problem. Minimal competency testing, the increased use of test scores to evaluate educational programs, and greater public pressure for high skill learning and achievement in schools are some of the many reasons why some students may do poorly in evaluative situations (for a review of the effects of anxiety on student performance, see Hill & Wigfield, 1984).

Improving student skills

Hill and Wigfield argued that teachers may want to help students to understand testing and to develop more adequate skills for taking both teacher-made and standardized tests. To this end they have developed an inservice training model to help prepare students for testing situations. These authors believe that allowing students to practice with test formats, respond to difficult material, and learn good test-taking strategies will improve student effort, motivation, and performance in test situations. Evaluative data show that the inservice training program has been associated with improved student test performance, particularly in language arts. An outline of the skills and motivational dispositions follows.

EXAMPLES OF TEST-TAKING SKILLS AND MOTIVATIONAL DISPOSITIONS

1. General test skills and knowledge:
   a. Be comfortable and sit where you can write easily.
   b. Pay attention to the teacher when she or he talks.
   c. The teacher can help you understand how to work on the test but can't tell you the answer to a problem on the test.
   d. Taking tests is something we learn to do in school.
2. Positive motivation—do your best:
   a. All I ask is that you do your best. I will be really pleased if you try to do your best.
   b. If you finish a section before time is up, go back and check your answers. Don't disturb others; instead, work quietly at your desk.
   c. Before we begin, remember to listen carefully to me, be quiet, take a deep breath, and relax.
3. Positive motivation—expectancy reassurance:
   a. Some tests have some very hard problems. Don't worry if you can't do some problems.
   b. It's okay if you aren't sure what the right answer is. Choose the answer you think is best. It's okay to guess.
   c. If you work hard but don't finish a test, don't worry about it. The most important thing to me is that you try hard and do as well as you can. I know you'll do a good job if you try.
4. Test strategy and problem-solving skills:
   a. There is only *one* best answer.
   b. Do what you know first. If you can't answer a problem or it's taking a lot of time, move on to the next one. You can come back later if you have time.
   c. Don't rush. If you work *too fast*, you can make careless errors. You have to work carefully.
   d. Don't work too slowly. Do the problems at a moderate rate.
   e. Pay close attention to your work.
   f. Keep track of where you are working on the page by keeping one hand on this spot.

SUMMARY

Construction of tests involves consideration of a number of issues such as content coverage, test length, item types, weighting, and related matters. Since tests only sample mastery of content taught in a course, it is important to sample from the full range of content and to include enough items to allow reliable measurement. Otherwise, a test may yield biased results and the errors of measurement are likely to be increased. Generally, test reliability increases with test length, so errors of measurement can be reduced by adding items if content coverage and other important qualities are carefully considered.

In addition to content coverage, it is important to consider the levels of understanding involved in test items. The six levels of Bloom's taxonomy provide a convenient reference for planning test items that measure different cognitive levels. Simultaneous examination of content and level permits planning of tests that will cover the instructional objectives of a course adequately. Item type is another critical factor, since essay items can be used to assess higher levels in the cognitive domain more easily than objective items. However, it is frequently more difficult to sample a wide range of content with essay than with objective items.

Teachers can use various means of assessment other than written tests. Performance tests can be used if actual performance on a task, rather than knowledge, is the essential factor. Rating scales provide a basis for estimating the quality of performance directly. Informal assessments, perhaps based on observation supplemented by oral tests, can be used along with more formal assessments like written tests in evaluating student performance.

Students' test-taking skills can be improved by helping them to understand the reasons for testing and by helping them to develop appropriate skills for taking tests. Test-taking skill training can help to improve the reliability and validity of classroom tests.

Questions and Problems

1. What would you do if students correctly pointed out to you that your tests concentrated on only a quarter or so of the assigned material, thus benefiting those who studied this part of the material thoroughly and penalizing those who studied all of the material?
2. Some students clearly do better on objective tests than on essay tests, or vice versa. What implication, if any, does this fact have for your testing and grading practices?
3. Is it better to test frequently but briefly, or infrequently but exhaustively?
4. What types of tests do you like and dislike as a student? How might these likes and dislikes affect your behavior later as a teacher? Are your biases appropriate for the subject, grade, and types of students that you expect to teach?
5. Considering the grade and subject you expect to teach, how can you evaluate the progress of students who do not read or write English efficiently?
6. Prepare a model essay test on the functions of the Supreme Court for sixth-grade students and another for eleventh-grade students. How would the two tests vary? Compare your two essay tests with those of classmates.

Case Studies

A LESSON ON THE AMERICAN REVOLUTION. Read the following material describing the American Revolution. As you read it, identify concepts and facts that you would want students to learn. Take notes as you read in order to:

1. Write four instructional objectives that will tell students what they should learn.
2. Prepare a test blueprint.
3. Write four multiple-choice items that measure objectives in your blueprint.

THE AMERICAN REVOLUTION AND ITS MEANING. The American Revolution grew largely out of change in Britain's colonial purposes and methods.* In 1763 the American colonists seemed content with their status. If Great Britain had not attempted to tighten the loosely knit empire and to make more money out of it, the break between Britain and the colonies would probably not have come when it did or as it did.

But once the break took place changes came fast in the Americans' attitudes toward Great Britain and toward their own society. The fears, hopes, dreams, and material pressures caused by war produced some major changes in American life. Neverthless, America after the war years looked remarkably like colonial America. The conservative nature of the American Revolution was caused largely by two circumstances. The first is that the colonists began fighting in an effort to preserve what they already had rather than to create a new order. The second is that the war did little damage to agriculture, the basis of the American economy.

Reconstructing the Empire. After the French and Indian War, the British decided that they could no longer afford to neglect their American colonies. The government issued a series of laws and decrees aimed at establishing more effective control over the colonies.

With French power eliminated in America after 1763, colonists moved west and provoked a new Indian war, the Pontiac Conspiracy. To quiet the Indians and to gain time to organize the territory acquired from France, Parliament issued the Proclamation of 1753. This act forbade the colonists to settle west of the Appalachian Mountains. Then, in 1764, Parliament passed the Sugar Act. This act placed new duties on sugar, coffee, wine, and certain other imported products; reduced the tax on molasses; and provided ways to collect all duties more effectively.

There were only scattered protests to these first measures. But a major crisis over taxation quickly followed. In 1765 Parliament passed the Stamp Act. Colonial resistance took a number of forms. Colonial leaders refused to do any business requiring the use of stamps to show that the tax had been paid. Trade came to a halt, and courts of justice closed since virtually all legal papers needed stamps. Politicians organized bands of patriots, largely workingmen, who called themselves Sons of Liberty. They pressured reluctant business people to support the boycott and forced Stamp Act officials to resign by their use of threats and violence.

Even more significant was a meeting in New York of delegates from nine colonies. This Stamp Act Congress was the first really effective act of political cooperation among so many colonies. It adopted a series of

* "The American Revolution and Its Meaning" from *A New History of the United States*, Holt Social Studies, by Edwin Fenton, et al., copyright © 1969 by Holt, Rinehart and Winston, Inc., reprinted by permission of the publisher.

resolutions protesting the new tax law and other new policies, such as the trials of accused smugglers by military courts. British business people hurt by the colonial boycott persuaded Parliament to repeal the Stamp Act in 1766. At the time, Parliament restated its right to pass laws for the colonies.

Parliament continued to pass new and unpopular laws that caused the division between the colonists and Great Britain to grow larger. Occasional brawls between the colonists and the British soldiers quartered in Boston finally ended in the Boston Massacre in 1770. British soldiers shot five members of an unarmed mob. Similar brawls between soldiers and colonists occurred in New York and added to the growing dislike and fear between the colonists and the British.

The Lull and the Storm. In the spring of 1770, British-colonial relations took a marked turn for the better. The British soldiers in Boston withdrew to the fort in the harbor to prevent further incidents. A new Parliamentary ministry took office. Its leader, Lord Frederick North, had all of the Townshed duties repealed except that on tea. North allowed the Quartering Act to expire and also promised that no new taxes would be imposed on the colonies. There was rejoicing in the colonies, and for more than two years there seemed to be a real reconciliation.

Then a series of episodes produced serious conflicts that finally led to independence. The first took place in June 1772, when a group of Rhode Islanders raided and burned the *Gaspée*, a customs vessel. The British decision to try the offenders in England, assuming they could be identified, alarmed the colonists, who saw this decision as yet another blow to the right of trial by jury. The colonists organized Committees of Correspondence to keep each other informed about local conflicts between colonial and British authority and to circulate propaganda against British rule.

In 1773 the tea crisis speeded up the final break with Great Britain. The colonists saw the British East India Company's monopoly on the sale of tea as another example of colonial exploitation for British profits. The colonists prevented the sale of tea up and down the Atlantic coast. In Boston, the center of colonial protest, a band of citizens destroyed the cargo of tea ships.

Parliament responded angrily in 1774 with the Coercive Acts, labeled the Intolerable Acts by the colonists. At the same time, Parliament passed the Quebec Act, which was not intended as a colonial punishment, but which the colonists interpreted as one.

With the Intolerable Acts, Parliament showed that it intended to enforce British authority, regardless of the cost to trade and remaining colonial goodwill. All of the colonies united firmly in support of Massachusetts. The Committees of Correspondence organized a Congress, which met in Philadelphia in September 1774 to deal with the mounting crisis. The fifty-five delegates from twelve colonies (Georgia was not represented) voted to support Massachusetts, to denounce Parliament's legislation for the colonies since 1763, and to form a Continental Association to enforce a complete boycott of trade with Britain.

By the spring of 1776, it became clear to most members of the Congress that reconciliation between the colonies and Great Britain was impossible without completely surrendering the colonial position. In all thirteen colonies, the Americans had removed the royal officials. The colonists were disillusioned with the king, who had stoutly supported Parliament. And their position was strengthened by Thomas Paine's bitter attack in *Common Sense* on monarchy in general and on the king in particular. The Continental Congress responded to the events of the year by adopting the Declaration of Independence.

The War and Its Strategy. The Americans were victorious in the War of Independence for a number of reasons. First, they fought on home ground. Second, they received considerable help from France and Spain. And third, their commander, George Washington, realized that time was on the American side if he could avoid an early defeat.

The British met with serious difficulties in using their superior strength on the distant rebellion. The war against the colonies was unpopular with many merchants, some members of Parliament, and even some generals. The British did not have the manpower needed to put down the revolt so they had to hire thirty thousand mercenary soldiers from Germany. In addition, the British navy was in bad shape . . . [Material describing the war is omitted].

The Revolution at Home. After the revolution against Britain, relatively few changes occurred in American institutions. State governments were established under new constitutions, beginning in 1776, but they resembled the colonial governments they replaced. Under the new constitutions, the representative assemblies held most political power. Voters in most states elected their governors, whose power was reduced. In most of the colonies, the right to vote had depended on possession of some property. During the war, nearly all property qualifications for voting and officeholding were either lowered or dropped.

The new states guarded their powers jealously. They gave some authority to the new government of the United States formed under the Articles of Confederation in 1781. But they kept all authority relating to local government. The central government, which itself lacked an effective executive office, directed the army and conducted foreign relations. But it could not regulate commerce; nor did it have the authority to tax citizens directly. It had the right to request money from the states but could not enforce its requests.

Merchants and other creditors suffered from the interruption of commerce during the war. But farmers and debtors benefited from the demand for foodstuffs and the creation of a vast supply of paper money by the revolutionary government to pay its debts. Much property owned by Loyalists was confiscated. In most cases, it went to property holders rather than to landless people. Stimulated by war, democratic ideas affected some social relationships. Perhaps the most striking examples were the decisions of several northern states to abolish slavery. Some southern states simplified the process of freeing slaves. The numbers of freed slaves increased substantially. Most states prohibited the slave trade during the Revolution. Thus Americans emerged from their War for Independence with a working national political system and a society and economy that were not deeply divided.

TEST PLAN, AMERICAN REVOLUTION: THREE-DAY UNIT. Assume that the test plan below has been given to students to guide their study of the unit on the American Revolution. How will the plan influence student behavior? Discuss the value of this blueprint. Is it good or bad? Defend your answer.

	Cognitive Objectives		
	Terms, Facts, Principles	*Application*	*Total Percent*
A. *Causes*			
1. In England	10	0	10
2. In the colonies	10	0	10
B. *Battle Strategy*			
1. General attitude—Motivation of soldiers	20	0	20
2. Specific battles	0	0	0
C. *Consequences of the War*			
1. Relationship with England	0	5	5
2. Relationship with world	0	5	5
3. Life in the colonies	0	50	50

CHAPTER

Assigning Grades

CHAPTER OUTLINE

OBJECTIVES

When you have mastered the material in this chapter, you will be able to

1. Discuss the educational and practical purposes of grading versus evaluating students and provide reasons why strict ''grading on a curve'' is not appropriate
2. Explain how the three basic methods of grading work
3. Describe the advantages and disadvantages of fixed-standard versus norm-referenced grading systems
4. List and explain the four considerations a teacher might use in adjusting grades
5. Describe individualized contracts for grades and tell when and how contracts are appropriate to use
6. Discuss the relationship between different grading methods and student motivation and perception of success
7. Make recommendations for setting up a grading system that will minimize both teacher and student anxiety about the process

You are probably familiar with the term *grading on the curve*. Originally, this method assumed that student mastery of course material would be distributed normally, so grades would also follow a normal distribution: 2 percent A, 14 percent B, 68 percent C, 14 percent D, and 2 percent F. This notion did not last long, however, because it involves several faulty assumptions.

First, even if students' efforts were equal, the distribution of content mastery would not ordinarily be normal because the distribution of students' aptitudes is not typically normal in any classroom. Second, students' efforts usually are not equal, and many teachers want grades to reflect effort as well as objective achievement. Third, even if both effort and achievement were distributed normally, this in itself would not necessarily mean that grades should be distributed normally. The "ideal" distribution of grades varies with their intended purpose or function: to motivate/reward effort, document progress, measure achievement relative to absolute standards or individualized expectations, or qualify students for advancement or certification, among others.

Functions of grades

Grading on the curve

Most teachers intend their grades to perform several functions, typically including motivation/reward and documentation of progress. As a compromise between grading purely on the basis of effort or only according to absolute achievement, they adjust grades based on achievement to take into account effort. In addition, teachers may try to grade as highly as the facts seem to justify, believing that this will maximize the motivational value of the grades and minimize damage to students' self-concepts. The result often is a method called grading on the curve, although it does not involve using the normal curve as just described. Instead, the teacher determines in advance that the class will receive a certain percentage of each of the grades to be assigned (for example, 30 percent A, 30 percent B, 30 percent C, and 10 percent D or F). This ensures that grades will be distributed in a way that seems to make sense, assuming that differences in student performance correspond roughly to the percentages assigned.

But does it? If the class as a whole does well on the test, adhering rigidly to this grading plan means that many students who answered more than 90 percent of the items correctly will get a grade of C despite their good performance and despite the fact that the differences between them and the students who get an A are trivial. Thus grading on a curve is not always appropriate. Under what conditions would it be a fair and appropriate way to grade?

Ambiguous questions

Another point to consider is that teacher-made tests often include questions that seem straightforward to teachers but turn out to be ambiguous to students. Sometimes more than one alternative answer is correct or at least justifiable. Should you credit only the answer you considered to be correct in the first place? Should you credit only the answer you consider to be the best answer? Should you credit all answers that are justifiable? Does it make any difference? If your answer to the last question was "No," consider the probability that students who receive no credit under one procedure but would have some under another may be outraged, especially if their final grades are affected. Sometimes, due to poor phrasing or typographical omissions, none of the response alternatives is correct. What should you do about these items when you grade the test? Should you ignore them? Give everyone credit for them?

Grading versus evaluation

Thinking about these hypothetical situations probably has made you realize some of the complexities involved in grading. The simplest solution, and the one that many persons favor, is to abolish grading altogether. This is a realistic solution up to a point, but not a complete one.

It is important to make a distinction between grading and evaluation. Grading may not be necessary, but evaluation is. Teachers must evaluate both their own behavior and their students' progress regularly if they are to function efficiently. Failure to do so represents only avoidance of an uncomfortable problem, not a solution to it.

Most necessary evaluation can be accomplished without formal grading, although the complexities involved in testing apply in varying degrees to other methods as well. Student progress can be assessed through a variety of evaluation methods besides tests. Questions and comments in class, the ability to answer questions about content, performance on special assignments and projects, and written work all can help a teacher monitor student progress. When tests are used, there is no need to return them with letter grades or percentage scores. In addition, or even instead, teachers can return tests with detailed comments about the strengths and weaknesses of students' efforts, focusing on progress and on ways to improve rather than on how students did in comparison to one another.

Uses for test data

Ultimately, though, students will have to take relatively objective tests so that their performances can be compared not only with one another but with the achievement of students in the country at large. External pressures for these test data come from citizens and state educational agencies interested in school quality. Also, colleges and universities use such information to decide about admissions and course advisement.

Need for accurate assessment

Many employers require information about the basic literary and mathematical skills of prospective employees. Most desirable jobs have minimal

For tests to have value, teachers should review them in detail with students.

educational requirements. Furthermore, employers have become wary of grades because they have seen too many people with high school or college degrees who do not have the skills expected of such graduates. Consequently, in examining transcripts, many employers pay much more attention to scores on standardized tests than to grades. If no such scores are available, they are likely to test prospective employees themselves before offering to hire them. Thus due to external pressures of this sort, instructors who refuse to grade or who systematically assign very high grades to everyone regardless of performance do not do their students any favors in the long run. They are leaving to someone else the unpleasant task of making it clear to certain students that they are deficient in basic skills and will be handicapped unless they obtain remedial help.

GRADING

We have just stressed the need for accurate assessment and have noted that teachers can assess student progress through formal tests and ratings as well as informal monitoring. Ultimately, this information has to be turned into a description of student progress or a grade.

Many instructional programs, especially at the elementary school level, now stress continuous monitoring of student performance, which enables teachers to keep specific records of student progress. Often schools using such systems do not assign grades in the first few years. Instead, student progress is reported in terms of skills expected and skills mastered.

Individual-standard method

When teachers do assign grades, there are three basic methods they can use. The individual standard is based on a student's progress in relation to his or her capacity. A bright student must master more material to get an A than a slower student. Such a method demands careful testing at the beginning of the year, and students must be informed of the relative performance levels they must obtain to get specified grades. The individual-standard method is difficult to implement. If two students score 49 and 60 on a 100-item pretest, for example, how does one set fair standards for what these students must do to earn an A, B, C, or D in the course? How can effort be graded? Furthermore, most people, including employers and parents, want to know how much students learned or what they can do, not how their performance compares with their ability or potential. Some teachers, however, can and do grade on the basis of an individual standard or at least assign grades partly on the basis of such information.

Fixed-standard method

Most teachers in American classrooms use a fixed standard to assign grades—criterion-referenced tests are based on fixed standards. The teacher assigns a level of performance to correspond with different grades on the basis of how students have performed previously. Establishing a standard of performance is very difficult for the beginning teacher, who may want to obtain tests used by teachers who have taught similar students in order to begin building realistic expectations. The "fixed" standard varies from teacher to teacher. A 70 on Mr. Marx's algebra exams equals a C; in Mrs. Thomas's room it's a D. Still, when a teacher uses fixed standards, students know what performance levels correspond to different grades.

Teachers who know that some parts of a course are more difficult than others may vary their standards from exam to exam. It is best to explain the current standard to students when they are ready to take the exam: "I know this material is tough, and students in the past have had more trouble on it than any other unit. Thus on this test, any score above 80 percent will be an A." Similarly, teachers who recognize that a group of students is better or worse than the typical class they teach may alter their standards to prevent giving an excessive number of high or low marks.

Norm-referenced grading

Norm-referenced grading compares a student's achievement with the performance of the class rather than with a fixed standard of subject-matter mastery. A student's grade depends on how well other students do. If a student scores 90 on an exam, but all other students score above 90, he or she has done poorly. Conversely, if a student scores 70, but all other students score below 70, he or she has done well. Teachers who use norm-referenced grading often assign grades using the mean and standard deviation of the class. Achievement, however, is not distributed on a normal curve. Some classes, even though comparable in ability to other classes, will put out less effort, and so forth. Hence teachers who use a normal curve for grading will unfairly penalize some students. Students who perform "well" in an exceptionally capable and hard-working class, for example, would be downgraded.

A Class-Grading Example

Consider the record of student performance presented in Table 29.1. Assume that there are thirty students in the class and that each student in the table represents two other students who performed identically. We can see that Heather and Jeff have earned the most points in the course. Heather, for example, received 27 out of 30 possible points on her class presentation and was the highest performer in the class on this task (rank 1). Jeff received 26 of 30 points and tied with Sandra as the second highest scorer on this assignment (since Sandra and Jeff are tied for second and third, they receive a rank of 2.5).

How can we assign grades using the three methods just discussed? To use an individual standard we would have to have information about student ability. Assume that the students as they appear in Table 29.1 are ranked in terms of course aptitude (Heather has the most; Terrill has the least). Using such criteria, we might decide that Sandra deserves an A (she had a relatively low aptitude but high performance), and that Jeff's and Heather's performances warrant a B (high aptitude, high performance). However, Heather and Jeff have scored 90, and how high a level can we demand? In part, the criteria would be determined by the differences in students' aptitudes. If the IQ difference between Heather and Terrill was 115–108, it would be inappropriate to expect much, if any, extra performance from Heather. A difference of 140–85 would be a different case. The practical difficulties in implementing an individual stan-

TABLE 29.1 SUMMARY OF STUDENT PERFORMANCE ON FIVE COURSE ASSIGNMENTS

	Class Presentation (30%)		Assigned Paper (10%)		Exam I (25%)		Exam II (25%)		Homework (10%)			
	Raw	Rank	Raw	Rank	Raw	Rank	Raw	Rank	Raw	Rank	Total	Rank
Heather	27/30	1.0	10	1.5	20/25	5.5	24/25	1	9/10	6.5	90	1.5
James	24/30	8.5	2	8.5	19/25	8.0	12/25	8	9/10	6.5	66	10.0
Jeff	26/30	2.5	10	1.5	24/25	1.0	20/25	4	10/10	2.5	90	1.5
Jill	25/30	5.5	6	5.5	18/25	9.0	18/25	6	10/10	2.5	77	5.0
Pat	25/30	5.5	6	5.5	20/25	5.5	21/25	2	9/10	6.5	81	4.0
Peggy	24/30	8.5	3	7.0	20/25	5.5	14/25	7	8/10	9.5	69	8.0
Sam	23/30	10.0	9	3.0	16/25	10.0	10/25	10	9/10	6.5	67	9.0
Sandra	26/30	2.5	8	4.0	22/25	2.5	20/25	4	10/10	2.5	86	3.0
Skip	25/30	5.5	2	8.5	22/25	2.5	11/25	9	10/10	2.5	70	7.0
Terrill	25/30	5.5	1	10.0	20/25	5.5	20/25	4	8/10	9.5	74	6.0

dard, however, are overwhelming, and this method typically creates more misunderstanding and arbitrariness than it resolves.

A fixed standard provides a clear basis for assigning grades. It is easy to use, although it may take a great deal of time and thought to establish initial standards. Teachers using a fixed standard assign students grades on the basis of announced standards, but it is important to realize that the distribution of grades will vary as a result of the standards. Consider the three standards presented below. All would look realistic to teachers and students at the beginning of a course.

Fixed Standard A	Fixed Standard B	Fixed Standard C
A = 94% or above	A = 90% or above	A = 93% or above
B = 85–93%	B = 80–89%	B = 85–92%
C = 75–84%	C = 70–79%	C = 78–84%
D = 60–74%	D = 60–69%	D = 70–77%
F = below 60%	F = below 60%	F = below 70%

If these three standards are applied to the students in Table 29.2, however, different grades will be assigned. In general, standards A and C are higher than B, although standard A is more liberal in the D range than is standard C. Standard B establishes lower cut-off points for the assignment of A's, B's, and C's than do standards A and C.

Table 29.2 is an expanded version of Table 29.1 and represents the distribution of thirty students (assuming that the performance of each student in Table 29.1 is typical of two other students in the class). An examination of Table 29.2 and the standards proposed above indicates that no students would have received A's if fixed standards A and C were used in the course. Standard A would have resulted in the assignment of 15 D's, whereas in both standards B and C only 9 D's would have been assigned. Furthermore, standard C would have resulted in the assignment of 9 F's, but none would have been assigned using standards A or B. It should be clear that shifting standards by even small percentages can result in different distributions.

Yet another way to assign grades is by norm-referenced standards; that is, by inspecting the distribution of grades within a class and allowing natural breaks in the distribution of scores to determine the assignment of letter grades. Whenever there are no explicit standards for judging student performance, as is typically the case in secondary schools, we recommend such norm-referenced comparisons.

RECOMMENDATIONS FOR GRADING

Grading should implement the philosophy of the school and the teacher as fairly as possible. Decisions about grades have to be made on the basis of one's particular situation; you may teach in a school that has fixed grading guidelines, or you may have complete freedom to set your own

TABLE 29.2 STUDENT SCORES AND THE ASSIGNMENT OF GRADES USING THREE FIXED STANDARDS AND A NORM-REFERENCED COMPARISON

Student Score	Standard A	Standard B	Standard C	Norm-Referenced Comparisons
90	B	A	B	A
90	B	A	B	A
90	B	A	B	A
90	B	A	B	A
90	B	A	B	A
90	B	A	B	A
86	B	B	B	B
86	B	B	B	B
86	B	B	B	B
81	C	B	C	B
81	C	B	C	B
81	C	B	C	B
77	C	C	D	C
77	C	C	D	C
77	C	C	D	C
74	D	C	D	C
74	D	C	D	C
74	D	C	D	C
70	D	C	D	C−D+?
70	D	C	D	C−D+?
70	D	C	D	C−D+?
69	D	D	F	D
69	D	D	F	D
69	D	D	F	D
67	D	D	F	D
67	D	D	F	D
67	D	D	F	D
66	D	D	F	D
66	D	D	F	D
66	D	D	F	D

standards. In general, we recommend that grades not be assigned on the basis of individual standards (evaluating an individual's performance in terms of his or her ability). The establishment of individual standards makes most sense in a nongraded system characterized by continuous assessment. If individual standards are used in grading, they should be applied after the major decisions are made, when the teacher is choosing between two close alternatives (is the grade C− or D+?).

Fixed standard

Fixed standards make most sense when teachers have a firm notion of what students can do and when they can set standards based on realistic expectations (as in criterion-referenced grading). In some areas such standards are readily available (the student needs to make at least fifteen out of twenty free throws over three consecutive testings to earn an A), but in other areas it may take some time to establish realistic expectations (to earn an A should a student spell correctly, on the average, 90 or 95 percent of the assigned vocabulary?).

Dropping lowest scores

Teachers who use fixed standards must be careful that a single poor performance does not preclude a student obtaining a reasonably high mark. They can do this by allowing students to drop their lowest score, assuming that the teacher tests frequently. The procedure of allowing students to drop one of only two or three scores can cause as many problems as it solves. (Consider the situation in which Ted has a 50, 70, 90; and Jim has an 80, 70, and 70.)

Retesting

Teachers who are willing to take the extra time necessary to prepare and grade "make-up" exams can help students to continue to make an effort to learn material; that is, teachers can allow students to retake one or two exams instead of dropping their lowest test score. Retesting has the obvious disadvantage of creating more work for the teacher, but it does encourage new effort by students.

By now you realize that there is no totally fair way to grade students. Each decision is really a hypothesis about how to help students perform as well as they can. Individual students are always affected differently by "class" rules. In the example just presented, we can see that Ted will be hurt if one test score is not eliminated; however, if a test score is dropped, Jim will be hurt in comparison to Ted (in terms of total class average).

We recommend that beginning teachers use a combination of norm-referenced standards and common sense, unless they are teaching in a non-graded situation or a criterion-referenced system (most teachers from fourth grade through high school, however, do assign grades). As teachers gain more experience and have expectations about what students can do, they can shift to fixed standards.

The chief advantage of the fixed system is that it puts the control of grades in students' hands. If the standards are appropriately fixed, students who work hard can earn good grades. If the standards are too low, however, students are not challenged; if the standards are too high, students will give up.

The major disadvantage to norm-referenced comparisons is that they interpret performance not in terms of some absolute standard (fifteen out of twenty free throws) but in terms of how a student performs in comparison to other students. (If the class average is ten, fifteen may be excellent, but a fifteen may be poor if the class average is eighteen). When teachers do not have firm expectations about how students will perform, however, standards broadly imposed by the collective performance of all students will probably be fairer than fixed standards.

Adjusting Grades

Teachers do not have to rely totally on fixed standards or norm-referenced comparisons. Four possible considerations that a teacher might want to use in making grade adjustments are: (1) consistency of performance, (2) performance on major course objectives, (3) special-credit work, and (4) contract work. If teachers use any or all of these considerations, however, they should explain to students how they will be used and what influence they will have on grades early in the course.

After examining the distribution of scores in Table 29.2, we could use consistency of performance as a criterion in borderline cases. For example, Skip, a student with a 70 (see Table 29.1), falls short of the C cutoff. His grade is hurt by his score on the assigned paper and his performance on Exam II. However, his performance on Exam I is excellent. Here the criterion of consistency does not help us. If his total score was influenced by one low score, we might give him the higher grade, but his performance is inconsistent and therefore difficult to describe with a single grade.

A second criterion that might help us is the importance of particular objectives. Skip's total course performance is heavily influenced by his performance on a minor task, for example, the assigned paper. If the teacher found the paper difficult to grade or if the assignment was accompanied by consistent student complaints (e.g., not enough time to write), the teacher might assign Skip a higher grade on this basis. But Skip also did poorly on the second exam, and unless the teacher has absolutely no confidence in the grade on the assigned paper, there is no basis for giving Skip a higher mark.

Special-credit work

Although the criteria of consistency and importance of objectives may be helpful in making minor adjustments, they sometimes provide no help. For this reason teachers sometimes allow students to raise their final grades by doing special-credit work or by fulfilling contracts. Assignments that call for mastery and effort are viable ways of assessing student performance and extending teacher flexibility in grading. Credit for such assignments should be given after norm comparisons have been made. Hence a teacher might have one or two extra assignments worth a few points during a grading period. Borderline students who earn enough extra credit points would be assigned a higher grade.

Contracting for Specific Grades When individualized contracts are used, it is possible to allow students some choice concerning the degree and types of effort they will expend. This is done by explicitly promising specific grades in exchange for specific levels of accomplishment on various tasks. For example, an A might require both earning 90 percent on a test and doing a project, a B might call for only earning 90 percent on the test, a C earning 80 percent on the test, and so on. Minimal requirements can be established for those who wish to receive only a passing grade and progressively more difficult standards can be set for earning higher grades.

With this plan, students know exactly what they will need to do to get a particular grade, and they can lower their effort if they are willing to take a lower grade. In addition to providing students some choice and making a clear connection between level of effort and assigned grades, contracting allows the teacher to establish requirements that ensure that students master the objectives considered most important or essential to the course.

Keller plan

This system works very well when all students in the course are capable of achieving the highest grade, although some will require more time and effort to do so than others. Often such arrangements involve the Keller plan for personalized, self-paced instruction (Keller, 1968). In this plan, students not only can choose the effort they want to expend and the resulting grade, but they are given as much time as they need to complete their work (see Chapter 7).

This type of plan is usually not feasible in the elementary and middle-school grades, partly because relatively few students have the maturity needed to exercise choices appropriately and follow through with independent work and also because the range of individual differences is often so large that common or standard requirements for everyone in the class may not be practical. Less formalized variations of the same general ideas can be developed, however, by making agreements or contracts with individual students, adjusting the requirements so that they are matched appropriately to student abilities and present levels of achievement. Teachers must explain this process to their classes, however, because students understandably will want to know why there are different standards for different students.

GRADES AND STUDENT SUCCESS

We have argued that success is necessary if students are to maintain positive self-views and involvement in assigned schoolwork. A grading system based on absolute standards, but standards that some students cannot attain, guarantees that these students will give up and expend only minimal effort in pursuing coursework. Norm-referenced comparisons will also ensure that some students reduce their time and effort in the course, for example, those who do poorly on a first exam and have no hope of improving their relative positions in the future.

We have also argued that students do not respond to gratuitous, empty praise and that when students perceive assignments as easy they will attribute good performance not to their own efforts but instead to external causes like luck or easy assignments. Hence students' task persistence, confidence, and so on will not be maximized by easy standards.

Teachers who use grades are caught in the middle. If they assign them too leniently or too restrictively, they will not motivate students as much as they could. We encourage teachers who must use grades to set standards that allow every student to obtain at least a grade of C, or whatever grade indicates satisfactory completion of general course expectations. This does not mean that every student will achieve at least a C, but it does mean that conditions should be arranged (by offering extra work, for example) so that students who work productively can earn an acceptable mark.

GRADING: A SUMMARY

Grade inflation

We mentioned previously that grading is probably the most unpleasant aspect of teaching for most teachers but that it remains necessary despite suggestions from some persons that it be eliminated. It may be helpful to point out that much teacher concern about grading is unnecessary, because low grades are not nearly as traumatic for students as most teachers think they are. First, students are realistic about their own performances, both absolutely and in comparison to classmates, so that students' expectations concerning grades are likely to conform fairly closely to the grades they receive. Second, grades assigned are often higher than those that students expect, especially in this recent period of "grade inflation." Grade inflation is not necessarily good—in fact, it seems unlikely to motivate students positively. Also, some students are irritated when they see classmates who have accomplished much less than they have receive the same grades.

Developing and clearly communicating evaluation methods

The keys to satisfactory grading are developing clearly valid methods to assess learning (they involve measuring knowledge directly related to the content of the course, as opposed to general information, test-taking skills, or other student individual differences that are unrelated to course content) and communicating these evaluation methods and criteria precisely to students. The latter aspect is important, because many students become unnecessarily anxious if they do not know the basis on which grades will be assigned, and virtually all students want some assurance that grading will be reasonable and fair. One of the most common complaints against instructors that keeps appearing in studies of student evaluations of teaching is that they fail to specify the bases for grading or that they assign grades in an arbitrary manner or on the basis of insufficient information.

The "insufficient information" problem usually refers to grades that

Report cards let students know how they are progressing.

are assigned on the basis of a single final examination or an assignment that covers only a fraction of course content. In the case of grading on the basis of term papers rather than tests, the objection is that the grade may have little or nothing to do with the degree to which the student learned material taught in the course. Unless notified otherwise, students generally expect to be held responsible for material presented in class and in assigned readings, and they usually prefer several tests or short assignments to one or two large tests or long assignments. These preferences are understandable, and for the most part appropriate, and they seem compatible with most teaching goals, including goals involving integration of all material covered in a course. The latter objective can be accomplished by testing periodically during the course for content mastery and then giving a final exam that poses more integrative questions. For more information about marking systems (e.g., grade inflation, effects on motivating students, percentage grading, pass-fail grading, etc.), see the fifth edition of the *Encyclopedia of Educational Research* (Mitzel, 1982).

TEACHER EVALUATION STANDARDS

The reader interested in more advanced information about how teacher evaluative standards and testing practices influence student effort could profitably consult Natriello and Dornbusch (1985). These researchers hypothesize that students will respond more favorably to evaluations and to the teachers who administer them when they see those evaluations as: (1) addressed to central rather than peripheral aspects of the task at hand, (2) influential in evaluating their progress or mastery, (3) soundly based, and (4) reliable.

Natriello and Dornbusch (1985) also offer a six-stage model for evaluation designed to improve student effort and performance. Their work provides detailed information about: (1) attention to the processes of task assignment, (2) criteria setting, (3) sampling, (4) appraisal, (5) feedback, and (6) improvement. Especially interesting is their stress on the need to teach students how to interpret and evaluate data reliably. Simply put, these authors contend not only that appraisals need to be technically fair (reliable, valid), but that students need to perceive them that way.

MICROCOMPUTERS AND CLASSROOM TESTING

As Kubiszyn and Borich (1984) noted, software packages are available to help teachers with many of the technical tasks of measuring student performance that we have discussed in these four chapters. The microcomputer is a powerful clerical aid for managing classroom instruction. Teachers can use it to identify potential instructional objectives (i.e., what do other fifth-grade social studies teachers emphasize), to develop test items, to analyze the effectiveness of each test item, and to analyze grade distributions.

Statistical software programs enable teachers to keep comprehensive records of student performance over several consecutive years, thus allowing them to analyze their tests systematically without spending the considerable time now necessary to obtain information and perform calculations. Such programs could help teachers become more adept at analyzing their behavior over time. When the teacher makes a major change in the assignments in a course, for example, what effect does this have on student performance? Microcomputers thus make it possible for teachers to evaluate the effects of new instructional techniques on test performance, and make it easy to study issues like grade inflation or declines in achievement over time (Kubiszyn & Borich, 1984).

Summary

The practice of assigning grades according to a normal distribution has become less popular in recent years because it fails to take into account the fact that student aptitudes often are not normally distributed in a given classroom. Also, teachers often want grades to reflect effort as well as aptitude, since they use them for motivation/reward as well as for documentation of progress. The result is a modified system that is still called ''grading on the curve'' but does not follow the distribution of the normal curve.

Grading involves many complexities, but some form of evaluation of student performance is essential. It may involve alternatives to grading, such as progress reports or ratings, but the need for accurate and realistic information about progress is essential. When grades are used, teachers can choose the individual standard, which examines a student's progress in relation to capacity; the fixed standard, which uses established criteria; or the norm-referenced system, which compares each student's performance with the performance of the entire class. Each system has advantages and disadvantages, but in most classes there are no explicit standards and norm-referenced comparisons seem most practical.

Grading should implement the philosophy of the school and the teacher as fairly as possible. Since grades may affect motivation and general performance, it is important to examine the implications of all decisions carefully. Grade adjustments can be made on the basis of consistency, performance on major objectives, special-credit work, or contract work. Caution must be used, since grades assigned either too leniently or too restrictively will inhibit motivation and performance.

Questions and Problems

1. The assumption that grading cannot be avoided pervades this chapter. Do you agree with this assumption? If not, what would you propose as a realistic alternative?

2. It is possible to be clear and consistent in grading by announcing your intentions to students and then following through on them. But is it possible to be fair? Does the concept of fair grading make any sense at all? If so, define it. If not, why not?
3. No matter where you draw the line between grades, some students with the highest marks in a grade range will ask if they can earn extra credit or if you would extend the range down one more point so that they can get a higher grade. How will you respond to these students?
4. Some students, independent of their ability (high- and low-achievement students, male and female students, and so forth), develop what is called "fear of success." Among other things, this may include an aversion to high grades, or at least grades that are "too high." Is this their problem, or is there something that you as a teacher should try to do about it? If so, what? If you see it as "their" problem, explain your point of view.
5. How should teachers grade highly competent students who consistently do just enough to qualify for a B, even though they could do A-level work with below-average effort? Under what circumstances, if any, might it be appropriate and perhaps helpful to such students to give them less than a B?

Case Study

EVALUATING TEST RESULTS. Examine the four mathematics test scores that students have earned (each test is worth 100 points).(1) How consistent is student performance across the four tests? What problems are caused by inconsistent student performances? (2) If you were assigning grades using norm comparisons and your common sense, what would be the cut-offs for A, B, C, and D? Defend your choices for borderline students.

	Test 1 (25%)	Test 2 (25%)	Test 3 (25%)	Test 4 (25%)	Total Points
Alan	80	85	90	96	351
Candy	85	70	65	60	280
Cheri	98	92	100	90	380
Debbie	100	75	90	74	339
Ed	70	90	65	70	295
Frank	90	95	74	90	349
Gene	82	83	82	80	327
Joe	90	91	93	94	368
Karen	70	75	70	69	284
Linda	65	60	60	60	245
Owen	70	75	70	69	284
Peter	69	78	65	70	282
Ralph	60	60	70	60	250

	Test 1 (25%)	Test 2 (25%)	Test 3 (25%)	Test 4 (25%)	Total Points
Reggie	65	85	60	60	270
Renee	70	70	70	70	280
Rita	90	90	90	90	360
Sandra	93	100	85	80	358
Stan	76	72	73	71	292
Stephen	100	85	90	89	364
Warren	50	60	72	80	262

REFERENCES

Abel, R., & Kulhavey, R. (1986). Maps, mode of text presentation and children's prose learning. *American Educational Research Journal, 23*, 263–274.

Abelson, H., & diSessa, A. (1981). *Turtle geometry: The computer as a medium for exploring mathematics*. Cambridge, MA: MIT Press.

Abrami, P., Leventhal, L., & Perry, R. (1982). Educational seduction. *Review of Educational Research, 52*, 446–464.

Abramson, L., Seligman, M., & Teasdale, J. (1978). Learned helplessness in humans: Critique and reformulation. *Journal of Abnormal Psychology, 87*, 49–74.

Abramson, T., & Kagen, E. (1975). Familiarization of content and different response modes in programmed instruction. *Journal of Educational Psychology, 67*, 83–88.

Adams, G., Abraham, K., & Markstrom, C. (1987). The relations among identity development, self-consciousness, and self-focusing during middle and late adolescence. *Developmental Psychology, 23*, 292–297.

Adams, J. (1977). Motor learning and retention. In M. Marx & M. Bunch (Eds.), *Fundamentals and applications of learning*. New York: Macmillan.

Adams, R., & Biddle, B. (1970). *Realities of teaching: Explorations with videotape*. New York: Holt, Rinehart and Winston.

Ahern, F., Johnson, R., Wilson, J., McClearn, G., & Vandenberg, S. (1982). Family resemblences in personality. *Behavior Genetics, 12*, 261–280.

Alexander, L., Frankiewicz, R., & Williams, R. (1979). Facilitation of learning and retention of oral instruction using advance and post organizers. *Journal of Educational Psychology, 71*, 701–707.

Alhajri, A. (1981). Effect of seat position on school performance of Kuwaiti students. Dissertation, University of Missouri-Columbia.

Allington, R. (1983). The reading instruction provided readers of differing ability. *Elementary School Journal, 83*, 548–559.

Allington, R. (1986). Policy constraints and effective compensatory reading instruction: A review. In J. Hoffman (Ed.), *The effective teaching of reading: From research to practice*. Newark, DE: International Reading Association.

Allington, R., & McGill-Franzen, A. (1989). School response to reading failure: Instruction for Chapter I and special education students in grades 2, 4, and 8. *Elementary School Journal, 89*, 529–542.

Alschuler, A., Tabor, D., & McIntyre, J. (1971). *Teaching achievement motivation*. Middletown, CT: Educational Ventures Inc.

Amara, J., & Leona, M. (1983). Prep-tech: A vocational school for academically talented students. *Phi Delta Kappan, 64*, 372–373.

American Institutes for Research. (1976). *Impact of educational innovation on student performance: Project, methods, and findings for three cohorts*. Project LONGSTEP Final Report (Vol. 1). Palo Alto, CA: American Institutes for Research.

Ames, C. (1978). Children's achievement attributions and self-reinforcement: Effects of self-concept and competitive reward structure. *Journal of Educational Psychology, 70*, 345–355.

Ames, C., & Ames, R. (1981). Competitive

versus individualistic goal structures: The salience of past performance information for causal attributions and affect. *Journal of Educational Psychology, 73*, 411–418.

Ames, C., & Ames, R. (Eds.). (1985). *Research on motivation in education* (Vol. 2). New York: Academic Press.

Ames, C., Ames, R., & Felker, D. (1977). Effects of competitive reward structure and valence of outcome on children's achievement attributions. *Journal of Educational Psychology, 69*, 1–8.

Ames, R. (1983). Teachers' attributions for their own teaching. In J. Levine & M. Wang (Eds.), *Teacher and student perceptions: Implications for learning*. Hillsdale, NJ: Erlbaum.

Ames, R., & Ames, C. (Eds.). (1984). *Research on motivation in education* (Vol. 1). New York: Academic Press.

Anderson, C., & Smith, E. (1987). Teaching science. In V. Richardson-Koehler (Ed.), *Educators' handbook* (pp. 84–111). New York: Longman.

Anderson, J., & Bower, G. (1973). *Human associative memory*. New York: Wiley.

Anderson, L. (1984). The environment of instruction: The function of seatwork in a commercially developed curriculum. In G. Duffy, L. Roehler, & J. Mason (Eds.), *Comprehension instruction: Perspectives and suggestions*. New York: Longman.

Anderson, L., Evertson, C., & Brophy, J. (1979). An experimental study of effective teaching in first-grade reading groups. *Elementary School Journal, 79*, 193–223.

Anderson, L., Evertson, C., & Brophy, J. (1982). *Principles of small-group instruction in elementary reading*. Occasional Paper No. 58. East Lansing: Institute for Research on Teaching, Michigan State University.

Anderson, L., Stevens, D., Prawat, R., & Nickerson, J. (1988). Classroom task environments and students' task-related beliefs. *Elementary School Journal, 88*, 281–295.

Anderson, L. W. (1985). A retrospective and prospective view of Bloom's "Learning for Mastery." In M. Wang & H. Walberg (Eds.), *Adapting instruction to individual differences*. Berkeley, CA: McCutchan.

Anderson, R. (1984a). Role of the reader's schema in comprehension, learning, and memory. In R. Anderson, J. Osborn, & R. Tierney (Eds.), *Learning to read in American schools: Basal readers and content texts*. Hillsdale, NJ: Erlbaum.

Anderson, R. (1984b). Some reflections on the acquisition of knowledge. *Educational Researcher, 13*, 5–10.

Anderson, R., Hiebert, E., Scott, J., & Wilkinson, I. (1985). *Becoming a nation of readers: The Report of the Commission on Reading*. Washington, DC: National Institute of Education.

Anderson, R., Pichert, J., & Shirey, L. (1983). Effects of the reader's schema at different points in time. *Journal of Educational Psychology, 75*, 271–279.

Anderson, R., Reynolds, R., Schallert, D., & Goetz, E. (1977). Frameworks for comprehending discourse. *American Educational Research Journal, 14*, 367–381.

Anderson, T., & Armbruster, B. (1982). Reader and text studying strategies. In W. Otto & S. White (Eds.), *Reading expository material*. New York: Academic Press.

Anderson, T., & Armbruster, B. (1984). Content area textbooks. In R. Anderson, J. Osborn, & R. Tierney (Eds.), *Learning to read in American schools: Basal readers and content texts*. Hillsdale, NJ: Erlbaum.

André, M., & Anderson, T. (1978–79). The development and evaluation of a self-questioning study technique. *Reading Research Quarterly, 14*, 605–623.

Andre, T. (1987). Questions and learning from reading. *Questioning Exchange, 1*, 47–86.

Andrews, G., & Goodson, L. (1980). A comparative analysis of models of instructional design. *Journal of Instructional Development, 3*(4), 2–16.

Anshutz, R. (1975). An investigation of wait-time and questioning techniques as an instructional variable for science methods students microteaching elementary school children. (Doctoral dissertation, University of Kansas, 1973). *Dissertation Abstracts International, 35*, 5978A.

Archer, S. (1982). The lower age boundaries of identity development. *Child Development, 53*, 1551–1556.

Arehart, J. (1979). Student opportunity to learn related to student achievement of objectives in a probability unit. *Journal of Educational Research, 72*, 253–269.

Arlin, M. (1979). Teacher transitions can disrupt time flow in classrooms. *American Educational Research Journal, 16*, 42–56.

Arlin, M. (1984). Time, equality, and mastery learning. *Review of Educational Research, 54*, 65–86.

Arlin, P. (1975). Cognitive development in adulthood: A fifth stage? *Developmental Psychology, 11*, 602–606.

Arlin, P. (1981). Piagetian tasks as predictors of reading and math readiness in grades K–1. *Journal of Educational Psychology, 73*, 712–721.

Armbruster, B., & Anderson, T. (1984). Structures of explanations in history textbooks, or so what if Governor Stanford missed the spike and hit the rail? *Journal of Curriculum Studies, 16*, 181–194.

Armbruster, B., Anderson, T., & Ostertag, J. (1987). Does text structure/summarization facilitate learning from text? *Reading Research Quarterly, 22*, 331–346.

Armbruster, B., & Brown, A. (1984). Learning from reading: The role of metacognition. In R. Anderson, J. Osborn, & R. Tierney (Eds.), *Learning to read in American schools: Basal readers and content texts*. Hillsdale, NJ: Erlbaum.

Armento, B. (1977). Teacher behaviors related to student achievement on a social science concept test. *Journal of Teacher Education, 28*, 46–52.

Arons, A. (1984). Computer-based instructional dialogs in science courses. *Science, 224*, 1051–1056.

Aronson, E. (1972). *The social animal*. San Francisco: Freeman.

Aronson, E., Blaney N., Stephan, C., Sikes, J., & Snapp, M. (1978). *The jigsaw classroom*. Beverly Hills, CA: Sage.

Asher, S., & Markell, R. (1974). Sex differences in comprehension of high- and low-interest reading material. *Journal of Educational Psychology, 66*, 680–687.

Ashton, P., & Webb, R. (1986). *Making a difference: Teachers' sense of efficacy and student achievement*. New York: Longman.

Aspy, D. (1977). An interpersonal approach to humanizing education. In R. Weller (Ed.), *Humanistic education*. Berkeley, CA: McCutchan.

Atkinson, J. (1964). *An introduction to motivation*. Princeton, NJ: Van Nostrand.

Atkinson, J. W., & Litwin, G. H. (1960). Achievement motive and test anxiety as motives to approach success and avoid failure. *Journal of Abnormal and Social Psychology, 60*, 52–63.

Atkinson, R. (1975). Mnemotechnics in second-language learning. *American Psychologist, 30*, 821–828.

Atkinson, R., & Shiffrin, R. (1971). The control of short-term memory. *Scientific American, 225*, 82–90.

Ausubel, D. (1960). The use of advance organizers in the learning and retention of meaningful verbal material. *Journal of Educational Psychology, 51*, 267–272.

Ausubel, D. (1963). *The psychology of meaningful verbal learning: An introduction to school learning*. New York: Grune & Stratton.

Ausubel, D. (1978). In defense of advance organizers: A reply to the critics. *Review of Educational Research, 48*, 251–257.

Ausubel, D., Novak, J., & Hanesian, H. (1978). *Educational psychology: A cognitive view*. New York: Holt, Rinehart and Winston.

Ausubel, D., & Robinson, F. (1969). *School learning: An introduction to educational psychology*. New York: Holt, Rinehart and Winston.

Ausubel, D., & Sullivan, E. (1970). *Theory and problems of child development* (2nd ed.). New York: Grune & Stratton.

Avital, S., & Shettleworth, S. (1968). *Objectives for mathematics learning: Some ideas for the teacher*. (Bulletin No. 3). Toronto: Ontario Institute for Studies in Education.

Babad, E. (1985). Some correlates of teachers' expectancy bias. *American Educational Research Journal, 22*, 175–183.

Baddeley, A. (1976). *The psychology of memory*. New York: Basic Books.

Baddeley, A. (1986). *Working memory*. New York: Oxford University Press.

Baker, F. (1977). Advances in item analysis. *Review of Educational Research, 47*, 151–178.

Baker, F., & Brown, A. (1984). Metacognitive skills and reading. In P. Pearson, M. Camil, R. Barr, & P. Mosenthal (Eds.), *Handbook of reading research*. New York: Longman.

Bandura, A. (1977). *Social learning theory*. Englewood Cliffs, NJ: Prentice-Hall.

Bandura, A. (1982). Self-efficacy mechanism in human agency. *American Psychologist, 37*, 122–147.

Bandura, A. (1986). *Social foundations of thought and action: A social cognitive theory*. Englewood Cliffs, NJ: Prentice-Hall.

Bandura, A., & Schunk, D. (1981). Cultivating competence, self-efficacy, and intrinsic interest through proximal self-motivation. *Journal of Personality and Social Psychology, 41*, 586–598.

Bangert, R., Kulik, J., & Kulik, C. (1983). Individualized systems of instruction in secondary schools. *Review of Educational Research, 53*, 143–158.

Bank, B., Biddle, B., & Good, T. (1980). Sex roles, classrooom instruction, and reading achievement. *Journal of Educational Psychology, 72*, 119–132.

Barr, R. (1988). Conditions influencing content taught in nine fourth-grade mathematics classrooms. *Elementary School Journal, 88*(4), 413–426.

Barrett, D., Radke-Yarrow, M., & Klein, R. (1982). Chronic malnutrition and child behavior: Effects of early caloric supplementation on social and emotional functioning at school age. *Developmental Psychology, 18*, 541–556.

Barth, R. (1972). *Open education and the American school*. New York: Agathon.

Bartlett, F. (1932). *Remembering*. Cambridge: Cambridge University Press.

Baskin, E., & Hess, R. (1980). Does affective education work: A review of seven programs. *Journal of School Psychology, 18*(1), 40–50.

Baumrind, D. (1971). Current patterns of parental authority. *Developmental Psychology Monograph, 4* (No. 1, Part 2).

Bear, G., & Richards, H. (1981). Moral reasoning and conduct problems in the classroom. *Journal of Educational Psychology, 73*, 644–670.

Beasley, W. (1984). Microcomputer applications in the education of the gifted. Doctoral dissertation, University of Georgia, Athens.

Becker, H. (1982). Microcomputers: Dreams and realities. *Curriculum Review, 21*, 381–385.

Becker, H. (1988). *The impact of computer use on children's learning: What research has shown and what it has not*. Baltimore: Center for Research on Elementary and Middle Schools, Johns Hopkins University.

Becker, J. (1981). Differential teacher treatment of males and females in mathematics classes. *Journal of Research in Mathematics Education, 12*, 40–53.

Bell, R. (1971). Stimulus control of parent or caretaker behavior by offspring. *Developmental Psychology, 4*, 61–72.

Bellezza, F. (1981). Mnemonic devices: Classification, characteristics, and criteria. *Review of Educational Research, 51*, 247–275.

Benjamin, M., McKeachie, W., Lin, Y., & Holinger, D. (1981). Test anxiety: Deficits in information processing. *Journal of Educational Psychology, 73*, 816–824.

Bennett, N., & Desforges, C. (1988). Matching classroom tasks to students' attainments. *Elementary School Journal, 88*, 221–234.

Bereiter, C., & Scardamalia, M. (1986). Educational relevance of the study of expertise. *Interchange, 17*(2), 10–19.

Berk, L. (1986). Relationship of elementary school children's private speech to behavioral accompaniment to task, attention, and task performance. *Developmental Psychology, 22*, 671–680.

Berkowitz, M., & Oser, F. (Eds.). (1985). *Moral education: Theory and application*. Hillsdale, NJ: Erlbaum.

Berliner, D. (1983). The executive who manages classrooms. In B. Fraser (Ed.), *Classroom management*. Bentley, Australia: Western Australian Institute of Technology.

Berliner, D., Stein, P., Sabers, D., Clarridge, P., Cushing, K., & Pinnegar, S. (in press). Implications of research on pedagogical expertise and experience for mathematics teaching. In D. Grouws and T. Cooney (Eds.), *Perspectives on research on effective mathematics teaching*. Hillsdale, NJ: Erlbaum.

Berndt, T. (1982). The features and effects of friendship in early adolescence. *Child Development, 53*, 1447–1460.

Bettencourt, E., Gillett, M., Gall, M., & Hull, R. (1983). Effects of teacher enthusiasm training on student on-task behavior and achievement. *American Educational Research Journal, 20*, 435–450.

Biddle, B., & Anderson, D. (1986). Theory, methods, knowledge, and research on teaching. In M. Wittrock (Ed.), *Third handbook of research on teaching* (pp. 230–254). New York: Macmillan.

Bigge, M. (1982). *Learning theories for teachers* (4th ed.). New York: Harper & Row.

Biggs, J. (1978). Individual and group differences in study processes. *British Journal of Educational Psychology, 48*, 266–279.

Blank, M. (1973). *Teaching learning in the preschool: A dialogue approach*. Columbus: Merrill.

Blasi, A. (1980). Bridging moral cognition and moral action: A critical review of the literature. *Psychological Bulletin, 88*, 1–45.

Blau, Z. (1981). *Black children/white children: Competence, socialization, and social structure*. New York: Free Press.

Bleakley, M., Westerberg, V., & Hopkins, K. (1988). The effect of character sex on story interest and comprehension in children. *American Educational Research Journal, 25*, 141–155.

Block, J. (1982). Assimilation, accommodation, and the dynamics of personality development. *Child Development, 53*, 281–295.

Block, J., & Anderson, L. (1975). *Mastery learning in classroom instruction*. New York: Macmillan.

Block, J., & Burns, R. (1976). Mastery learning. In L. Shulman (Ed.), *Review of research in education* (Vol. 4). Itasca, IL: Peacock.

Block, J., Gjerde, P., & Block, J. (1986). More misgivings about the Matching Familiar Figures Test as a measure of reflection-impulsivity: Absence of construct validity in preadolescence. *Developmental Psychology, 22*, 820–831.

Bloom, B. (1964). *Stability and change in human characteristics*. New York: Wiley.

Bloom, B. (1968). Learning for mastery. (*UCLA-CSEIP*) *Evaluation Comment, 1*(2), 1–12.

Bloom, B. (1976). *Human characteristics and school learning*. New York: McGraw-Hill.

Bloom, B. (1980). *All our children learning*. Hightstown, NJ: McGraw-Hill.

Bloom, B., & Broder, L. (1950). *Problem-solving processes of college students*. Chicago: University of Chicago Press.

Bloom, B., Englehart, M., Furst, E., Hill, W., & Krathwohl, D. (1956). *Taxomony of educational objectives: The classification of educational goals. Handbook I: Cognitive domain*. New York: Longmans Green.

Blumenfeld, P., Hamilton, V., Bossert, S., Wessels, K., & Meece, J. (1983). Teacher talk and student thought: Socialization into the student role. In J. Levine & M. Wang (Eds.), *Teacher and student perceptions: Implications for learning*. Hillsdale, NJ: Erlbaum.

Blumenfeld, P., & Meece, J. (1988). Task factors, teacher behavior, and students' involvement and use of learning strategies in science. *Elementary School Journal, 88*, 234–250.

Blumenfeld, P., Mergendoller, J., & Swarthout, D. (1987). Task as a heuristic for understanding student learning and motivation. *Journal of Curriculum Studies, 19*, 135–148.

Blumenfeld, P. C., & Pintrich, P. R. (1982). Children's perceptions of school and schoolwork: Age, sex, social class, individual and classroom differences. Paper presented at the annual American Educational Research Association Meeting, New York.

Bogen, J. (1977). Some educational implications of hemispheric specialization. In M. Wittrock (Ed.), *The human brain*. Englewood Cliffs, NJ: Prentice-Hall.

Boggiano, A., & Ruble, D. (1979). Competence and the overjustification effect: A developmental study. *Journal of Personality and Social Psychology, 37*, 1462–1468.

Bogin, B., & MacVean, R. (1983). The relationship of socioeconomic status and sex to body size, skeletal maturation, and cognitive status of Guatemala City school children. *Child Development, 54*, 115–128.

Boocock, S., & Schild, E. (1968). *Simulation games in learning*. Beverly Hills, CA: Sage.

Borg, W. (1979). Teacher coverage of academic content and pupil achievement. *Journal of Educational Psychology, 71*, 635–645.

Borko, H., & Eisenhart, M. (1986). Students' conceptions of reading and their reading experiences in school. *Elementary School Journal, 86*, 589–611.

Borko, H., Shavelson, R., & Stern, P. (1981). Teachers' decisions in the planning of reading instruction. *Reading Research Quarterly, 16*, 449–466.

Borkowski, J., Johnston, M., & Reid, M. (1986). Metacognition, motivation, and the transfer of control processes. In S. Ceci (Ed.), *Handbook of cognitive, social, and neuropsychological aspects of learning disabilities*. Hillsdale, NJ: Erlbaum.

Boshier, R., & Thom, E. (1973). Do conservative parents nurture conservative children? *Social Behavior and Personality, 1*, 108–110.

Bosma, H., & Gerrits, R. (1985). Family functioning and identity status in adolescence. *Journal of Early Adolescence, 5*, 69–80.

Bossert, S. (1977). Tasks, group management, and teacher-control behavior: A study of classroom organization and teacher style. *School Review, 85*, 552–565.

Boston, B. (1976). *The sorcerer's apprentice: A case study of the role of mentoring*. Reston, VA: Council for Exceptional Children.

Botvin, G., & Murray, F. (1975). The efficacy of peer modeling and social conflict in the acquisition of conservation. *Child Development, 46*, 796–799.

Bourke, S. (1985). The study of classroom contexts and practices. *Teaching and Teacher Education, 1*, 33–50.

Bourne, L., Ekstrand, B., & Dominowski, R. (1971). *The psychology of thinking*. Englewood Cliffs, NJ: Prentice-Hall.

Bower, G. (1970). Organizational factors in

memory. *Journal of Cognitive Psychology, 1*, 18–46.

Bower, G. (1979). Analysis of a mnemonic device. *American Psychologist, 58*, 496–510.

Bower, G., & Clark, M. (1969). Narrative stories as mediators for serial learning. *Psychonomic Science, 14*, 181–182.

Bower, G., Clark, M., Lesgold, A., & Winzenz, D. (1969). Hierarchical retrieval schemes in recall of categorized word lists. *Journal of Verbal Learning and Verbal Behavior, 8*, 323–343.

Bradbard, M., & Endsley, R. (1983). The effects of sex-typed labeling on preschool children's information-seeking and retention. *Sex Roles, 9*, 247–260.

Braden, R., & Sachs, S. (1983). The most recommended books on instructional development. *Educational Technology, 23*(2), 24–28.

Brainerd, C. (1977). Feedback, rule knowledge, and conservation learning. *Child Development, 48*, 404–411.

Brandon, P., Newton, B., & Hammond, O. (1987). Children's mathematics achievement in Hawaii: Sex differences favoring girls. *American Educational Research Journal, 24*, 437–461.

Bransford, J. (1979). *Human cognition*. Belmont, CA: Wadsworth.

Bransford, J., & Franks, J. (1971). The abstraction of linguistic ideas. *Cognitive Psychology, 2*, 331–350.

Bransford, J., & McCarrell, N. (1974). A sketch of a cognitive approach to comprehension: Some thoughts about understanding what it means to comprehend. In W. Weimer & D. Palermo (Eds.), *Cognition and the symbolic processes*. Hillsdale, NJ: Erlbaum.

Bransford, J., & Stein, B. (1985). The IDEAL problem solver. San Francisco: Freeman.

Brantlinger, E., & Guskin, S. (1987). Ethnocultural social-psychological effects on learning characteristics of handicapped children. In M. Wang, M. Reynolds, and H. Walberg (Eds.), *Handbook of special education: Research in practice* (Vol. 1, pp. 7–34). Oxford: Pergamon Press.

Breaux, R. (1975). Effects of induction versus deduction and discovery versus utilization on transfer of information. *Journal of Educational Psychology, 67*, 828–832.

Briars, D., & Siegler, R. (1984). A featural analysis of preschoolers' counting knowledge. *Developmental Psychology, 20*, 607–618.

Briggs, L. (1970). *Handbook of procedures for the design of instruction*. Pittsburgh: American Institutes for Research.

Brislin, R. (1983). Cross-cultural research in psychology. In M. Rosenzweig & L. Porter (Eds.), *Annual Review of Psychology* (Vol. 34). Palo Alto, CA: Annual Reviews.

Bromage, B., & Mayer, R. (1981). Relationship between what is remembered and creative problem-solving performance in science learning. *Journal of Educational Psychology, 73*, 451–461.

Bromage, B., & Mayer, R. (1986). Quantitative and qualitative effects of repetition on learning from technical texts. *Journal of Educational Psychology, 78*, 271–278.

Bromme, R., & Brophy, J. (1986). Teachers' cognitive activity. In B. Christiansen, A. Howson, & M. Otte (Eds.), *Perspectives in mathematics education*. Boston: Reidel.

Brookover, W., Beady, C., Flood, P., Schweitzer, J., & Wisenbaker, J. (1979). *School social systems and student achievement: Schools can make a difference*. New York: Bergin.

Brooks, M., Fusco, E., & Grennon, J. (1983). Cognitive levels matching. *Educational Leadership, 40*(8), 4–8.

Brooks-Gunn, J., & Matthews, W. (1979). *He & she: How children develop their sex-role identity*. Englewood Cliffs, NJ: Prentice-Hall.

Brooks-Gunn, J., & Petersen, A. (Eds.). (1983). *Girls at puberty*. New York: Plenum.

Brooks-Gunn, J., Petersen, A., & Eichorn, D. (1985). The study of maturational timing effects in adolescence. *Journal of Youth and Adolescence, 14*, 149–161.

Brophy, J. (1977). *Child development and socialization*. Chicago: Science Research Associates.

Brophy, J. (1981). Teacher praise: A functional analysis. *Review of Educational Research, 51*, 5–32.

Brophy, J. (1983). Research on the self-fulfilling prophecy and teacher expectations. *Journal of Educational Psychology, 75*, 631–661.

Brophy, J. (1985). Interactions of male and female students with male and female teachers. In L. Wilkinson & C. Marrett (Eds.), *Gender influences in classroom interaction* (pp. 115–142). Orlando, FL: Academic Press.

Brophy, J. (1987). Synthesis of research on strategies for motivating students to learn. *Educational Leadership, 45*(2), 40–48.

Brophy, J., & Evertson, C. (1976). *Learning from teaching: A developmental perspective*. Boston: Allyn and Bacon.

Brophy, J., & Evertson, C. (1978). Context variables in teaching. *Educational Psychologist, 12*, 310–316.

Brophy, J., & Evertson, C. (1981). *Student characteristics and teaching*. New York: Longman.

Brophy, J., & Good, T. (1974). *Teacher-student relationships: Causes and consequences*. New York: Holt, Rinehart & Winston.

Brophy, J., & Good, T. (1986). Teacher effects. In M. Wittrock (Ed.), *Third handbook of research on teaching* (pp. 328–375). New York: Macmillan.

Brophy, J., & Hannon, P. (1985). The future of microcomputers in the classroom. *Journal of Mathematical Behavior, 4*, 47–67.

Brophy, J., & Putnam, J. (1979). Classroom management in the elementary grades. In D. Duke (Ed.), *Classroom management*. The seventy-eighth yearbook of the National Society for the Study of Education, Part II. Chicago: University of Chicago Press.

Brophy, J., & Rohrkemper, M. (1981). The influence of problem ownership on teachers' perceptions of and strategies for coping with problem students. *Journal of Educational Psychology, 73*, 295–311.

Brophy, J., & Rohrkemper, M. (1988). *The classroom strategy study: Summary of general findings*. Research Series Report No. 187. East Lansing: The Institute for Research on Teaching, Michigan State University.

Brown, A. (1980). Metacognitive development and reading. In R. Spiro, B. Bruce, & W. Brewer (Eds.), *Theoretical issues in reading comprehension*. Hillsdale, NJ: Erlbaum.

Brown, A., Campione, J., & Barclay, C. (1979). Training self-checking routines for estimating test readiness: Generalization from list learning to prose recall. *Child Development, 30*, 501–512.

Brown, A., Campione, J., & Day, J. (1981). Learning to learn: On training students to learn from texts. *Educational Researcher, 10*, 14–21.

Brown, A., & Day, J. (1980). Strategies and knowledge for summarizing texts: The development of expertise. Manuscript. Urbana: University of Illinois.

Brown, A., & Palincsar, A. (1982). Inducing strategic learning from texts by means of informed, self-controlled training. *Topics in learning and learning disabilities, 2*, 1–17.

Brown, A., & Smiley, S. (1978). The development of strategies for studying texts. *Child Development, 49*, 1076–1088.

Brown, F. (1976). *Principles of educational and psychological testing* (2nd ed.). New York: Holt, Rinehart and Winston.

Brown, G. (1971). *Human teaching for human learning*. New York: Viking.

Brown, J., & Burton, R. (1978). Diagnostic models for procedural bugs in basic mathematical skills. *Cognitive Science, 2*, 155–192.

Brown, M., & Precious, N. (1973). *The integrated day in the primary school.* New York: Ballantine.

Brown, R., & Kulick, J. (1977). Flashbulb memories. *Cognition, 5*, 73–99.

Brozek, J. (1978). Nutrition, malnutrition, and behavior. *Annual Review of Psychology, 29*, 157–177.

Bruner, J. (1964). The course of cognitive growth. *American Psychologist, 19*, 1–15.

Bruner, J. (1966). *Toward a theory of instruction.* Cambridge: Harvard University Press.

Bruner, J. (1971). *The relevance of education.* New York: Norton.

Bruner, J., Goodnow, J., & Austin, G. (1956). *A study of thinking.* New York: Wiley.

Bryan, J., & Walbek, N. (1970). Preaching and practicing generosity: Children's action and reactions. *Child Development, 41*, 329–353.

Bullough, V. (1981). Age at menarche: A misunderstanding. *Science, 213*, 365–366.

Burling, R. (1973). *English in black and white.* New York: Holt, Rinehart and Winston.

Buros, O. (Ed.). (1972). *The seventh mental measurements yearbook.* Highland Park, NJ: Gryphon Press.

Buros, O. (Ed.). (1978). *The eighth mental measurements yearbook.* Highland Park, NJ: Gryphon Press.

Buss, A., & Plomin, R. (1984). *Temperament: Early developing personality traits.* Hillsdale, NJ: Erlbaum.

Butkowsky, L., & Willows, D. (1980). Cognitive-motivational characteristics of children varying in reading ability: Evidence for learned helplessness in poor readers. *Journal of Educational Psychology, 72*, 408–422.

Butler, R. (1987). Task-involving and ego-involving properties of evaluation: Effects of different feedback conditions on motivational perceptions, interest, and performance. *Journal of Educational Psychology, 79*, 474–482.

Bybee, R., & Sund, R. (1982). *Piaget for educators* (2nd ed.). Columbus: Merrill.

Cahen, L., Filby, N., McCutcheon, G., & Kyle, D. (1983). *Class size and instruction.* New York: Longman.

Camp, B., & Bash, M. (1981). *Think aloud: Increasing social and cognitive skills—a problem-solving program for children, primary level.* Champaign, IL: Research Press.

Capon, N., & Kuhn, D. (1979). Logical reasoning in the supermarket: Adult females' use of a proportional reasoning strategy in an everyday context. *Developmental Psychology, 15*, 450–452.

Carey, S. (1985). *Conceptual change in childhood.* Cambridge, MA: MIT Press.

Carlson, D. (1982). "Updating" individualism and the work ethic: Corporate logic in the classroom. *Curriculum Inquiry, 12*, 125–160.

Carnine, D. (1976). Effects of two teacher presentation rates on off-task behavior, answering correctly, and participation. *Journal of Applied Behavior Analysis, 9*, 199–206.

Carpenter, T., Matthews, W., Lindquist, M., & Silver, E. (1984). Achievement in mathematics: Results from the National Assessment. *Elementary School Journal, 84*, 485–496.

Carrier, C., & Titus, A. (1981). Effects of note-taking pretraining and test mode expectations on learning from lectures. *American Educational Research Journal, 18*, 385–397.

Carroll, J. (1963). A model of school learning. *Teachers College Record, 64*, 722–733.

Carter, K., & Richardson-Koehler, V. (1989). A curriculum for an initial year of teaching program. *Elementary School Journal, 89*(4), 405–420.

Carter, R., Hohenegger, M., & Satz, P. (1982). Aphasia and speech organization in children. *Science, 218*, 797–799.

Cartledge, G., & Milburn, L. (1978). The case for teaching social skills in the classroom: A review. *Review of Educational Research, 48*, 133–156.

Casanova, U. (1987). Ethnic and cultural differences. In V. Richardson-Koehler (Ed.), *Educators' handbook* (pp. 370–393). New York: Longman.

Case, R. (1978). A developmentally based theory and technology of instruction. *Review of Educational Research, 48*, 439–463.

Case, R., & Bereiter, C. (1984). From behaviourism to cognitive behaviourism to cognitive development: Steps in the evolution of instructional design. *Instructional Science, 13*, 141–158.

Cattell, R. (1971). *Abilities: Their structure, growth, and action.* Boston: Houghton-Mifflin.

Center for Social Organization of Schools (November 1984). *School uses of microcomputers: Reports from a national survey* (Issue No. 6). Baltimore: Johns Hopkins University.

Chaffin, J. (1974). Will the real "mainstreaming" program please stand up! (or . . . should Dunn have done it?). *Focus on Exceptional Children, 6*, 1–18.

Chall, J. (1983). Literacy: Trends and explanations. *Educational Researcher, 12*, 3–8.

Champagne, A., Klopfer, L., & Anderson, J. (1980). Factors influencing the learning of classical mechanics. *American Journal of Physics, 48*, 1074–1079.

Chance, P. (1986). *Thinking in the classroom.* New York: Teachers College Press.

Chase, W., & Chi, M. (1980). Cognitive skill: Implications for spatial skill in large-scale environments. In J. Harvey (Ed.), *Cognition, social behavior, and the environment.* Hillsdale, NJ: Erlbaum.

Chazan, B. (1985). *Contemporary approaches to moral education.* New York: Teachers College Press.

Chi, M., Feltovich, P., & Glaser, R. (1981). Categorization and representation of physics problems by experts and novices. *Cognitive Science, 5*, 121–152.

Chi, M., & Glaser, R. (1982). *Final report: Knowledge and skill differences in novices and experts.* (Technical Report No. 7.) Pittsburgh: Learning Research and Development Center, University of Pittsburgh.

Chi, M., Glaser, R., & Rees, E. (1981). Expertise in problem solving. In R. Sternberg (Ed.), *Advances in the psychology of human intelligence* (Vol. 1). Hillsdale, NJ: Erlbaum.

Chomsky, N. (1965). *Aspects of the theory of syntax.* Cambridge, MA: MIT Press.

Christoplos, F., & Borden, J. (1978). Sexism in elementary school mathematics. *Elementary School Journal, 78*, 275–277.

Clarizio, H., & McCoy, G. (1976). *Behavior disorders in children* (2nd ed.). New York: Crowell.

Clark, C., Gage, N., Marx, R., Peterson, P., Stayrook, N., & Winne, P. (1979). A factorial experiment on teacher structuring, soliciting, and reacting. *Journal of Educational Psychology, 71*, 534–552.

Clark, C., & Peterson, P. (1986). Teachers' thought processes. In M. Wittrock (Ed.), *Handbook of Research on Teaching* (3rd ed.). New York: Macmillan.

Clark, C., & Yinger, R. (1979). Teachers' thinking. In P. Peterson & H. Walberg (Eds.), *Research on teaching.* Berkeley, CA: McCutchan.

Clark, D. (1971). Teaching concepts in the classroom: A set of teaching prescriptions derived from experimental research. *Journal of Educational Psychology, 62*, 253–278.

Clark, R. (1982). Antagonism between achievement and enjoyment in ATI studies. *Journal of Educational Psychology, 17*, 92–101.

Clark, R. (1983a). *Family life and school achievement: Why poor black children succeed or fail.* Chicago: University of Chicago Press.

Clark, R. (1983b). Reconsidering research on learning from media. *Review of Educational Research, 53*, 445–459.

Clarke, A., & Ruble, D. (1978). Young adolescents' beliefs concerning menstruation. *Child Development, 49*, 231–234.

Clasen, D. (1983). The effect of four different instructional strategies on the achievement of gifted seventh-grade students. Paper presented at the annual meeting of the American Educational Research Association, Montreal.

Clausen, J. (1975). The social meaning of differential physical and sexual maturation. In S. Dragastin & G. Elder (Eds.), *Adolescence in the life cycle: Psychological change and social context*. Washington, DC: Hemisphere.

Clements, D., & Nastasi, B. (1988). Social and cognitive interactions in educational computer environments. *American Educational Research Journal, 25*, 87–106.

Clifford, M. (1981). *Practicing educational psychology*, Boston: Houghton-Mifflin.

Cobb, J., & Hops, H. (1973). Effects of academic survival skill training on low achieving first graders. *Journal of Educational Research, 67*, 108–113.

Cofer, C. (1971). Properties of verbal materials and verbal learning. In J. Kling & L. Riggs (Eds.), *Woodworth and Schlosberg's experimental psychology*. New York: Holt, Rinehart and Winston.

Cohen, J., & DeYoung, H. (1973). The role of litigation in the improvement of programming for the handicapped. In L. Mann & D. Sabatino (Eds.), *A first review of special education* (Vol. 2). Philadelphia: J.S.E. Press with Buttonwood Farms.

Cohen, M. (1979). Student influence in the classroom. Doctoral dissertation, Washington University, St. Louis.

Cohen, R., & Bradley, R. (1978). Simulation games, learning, and retention. *Elementary School Journal, 78*, 247–253.

Colby, A., Kohlberg, L., Gibbs, J., & Lieberman, M. (1983). A longitudinal study of moral judgment. *Monographs of the Society for Research in Child Development, 48* (No. 1, Serial No. 200).

Cole, H., & Lacefield, W. (1980). *MACOS: Its empirical effects versus its critics*. Education Resources Information Center Document ED 194 397.

Coleman, J. (1961). *The adolescent society*. New York: Free Press.

Coleman, J., Campbell, E., Hobson, C., McPartland, J., Mood, A., Weinfield, F., & York, R. (1966). *Equality of educational opportunity*. Washington, DC: U.S. Government Printing Office.

Coleman, J., Livingston, S., Fennessey, G., Edwards, K., & Kidder, S. (1973). The Hopkins Games Program: Conclusions from seven years of research. *Educational Researcher, 2*, 3–7.

Collins, A., & Loftus, E. (1975). A spreading activation theory of sematic processing. *Psychological Review, 82*, 407–428.

Collins, A., & Stevens, A. (1983). A cognitive theory of inquiry teaching. In C. Reigeluth (Ed.), *Instructional-design theories and models: An overview of their current status*. Hillsdale, NJ: Erlbaum.

Combs, A., Blume, R., Newman, A., & Wass, H. (1974). *The professional education of teachers* (2nd ed.). Boston: Allyn and Bacon.

Coming to our senses (1977). Reports of the Arts, Education and Americans Panel, David Rockefeller, Jr., Chairman. New York: McGraw-Hill.

Commons, M., Miller, P., & Kuhn, D. (1982). The relation between formal operational reasoning and academic course selection and performance among college freshmen and sophomores. *Journal of Applied Developmental Psychology, 3*, 1–10.

Commons, M., Richards, F., & Armon, C. (Eds.). (1984). *Beyond formal operations: Late adolescent and adult cognitive development*. New York: Praeger.

Commons, M., Richards, F., & Kuhn, D. (1982). Systematic and metasystematic reasoning: A case for levels of reasoning beyond Piaget's stage of formal operations. *Child Development, 53*, 1058–1069.

Condry, J., & Chambers, J. (1978). Intrinsic motivation and the process of learning.

In M. Lepper & D. Greene (Eds.), *The hidden costs of reward: New perspectives on the psychology of human motivation* (pp. 61–84). Hillsdale, NJ: Erlbaum.

Cook, L. (1982). The effects of text structure on the comprehension of scientific prose. Doctoral dissertation, University of California, Santa Barbara.

Cooley, W., & Leinhardt, G. (1980). The Instructional Dimensions Study. *Educational Evaluation and Policy Analysis, 2*, 7–25.

Coop, R. (1982). A view of education of gifted and talented students from an educational psychologist's perspective. *Elementary School Journal, 82*, 292–297.

Cooper, H. (1979). Pgymalion grows up: A model for teacher expectation communication and performance influence. *Review of Educational Research, 49*, 389–410.

Cooper, H. (1989). *Homework*. New York: Longman.

Cooper, H., & Good, T. (1983). *Pygmalion grows up: Studies in the expectation communication process*. New York: Longman.

Coopersmith, S. (1967). *The antecedents of self-esteem*. San Francisco: Freeman.

Corno, L., & Rohrkemper, M. (1985). Self-regulated learning. In C. Ames & R. Ames (Eds.), *Research on motivation in education* (Vol. 2). Orlando, FL: Academic Press.

Cort, H., & Peskowitz, N. (1977). *A longitudinal study of Man: A course of Study. Summary Report*. Education Resource Information Center Document ED 151 275.

Cortes, J., & Gatti, F. (1965). Physique and self-description of temperament. *Journal of Consulting Psychology, 29*, 434.

Costa, A. (1984). Mediating the metacognitive. *Educational Leadership, 42*, 57–62.

Coté, J., & Levine, C. (1983). Marcia and Erikson: The relationships among ego identity status, neuroticism, dogmatism, and purpose in life. *Journal of Youth and Adolescence, 12*, 43–53.

Covington, J., & Omelich, C. (1979a). It's best to be able and virtuous too: Student and teacher evaluative responses to successful effort. *Journal of Educational Psychology, 71*, 688–700.

Covington, J., & Omelich, C. (1979b). Effort: The double-edged sword in school achievement. *Journal of Educational Psychology, 71*, 169–182.

Covington, M. (1983). Motivated cognitions. In S. Paris, G. Olson, & H. Stevenson (Eds.), *Learning and motivation in the classroom*. Hillsdale, NJ: Erlbaum.

Covington, M. (1984). Strategic thinking and the fear of failure. In J. Segal, S. Chipman, & R. Glaser (Eds.), *Thinking and learning skills: Relating instruction to basic research*. Hillsdale, NJ: Erlbaum.

Covington, M., & Beery, R. (1976). *Self-worth and school learning*. New York: Holt, Rinehart and Winston.

Covington, M., Crutchfield, R., Davies, L., & Olton, R. (1974). *The productive thinking program: A course in learning to think*. Columbus: Merrill.

Covington, M., & Omelich, C. (1981). As failures mount: Affective and cognitive consequences of ability demotion in the classroom. *Journal of Educational Psychology, 73*, 796–808.

Covington, M., Spratt, M., & Omelich, C. (1980). Is effort enough or does diligence count too? Student and teacher reactions to effort stability in failure. *Journal of Educational Psychology, 72*, 717–729.

Cox, W., & Matz, R. (1982). Comprehension of school prose as a function of reasoning level and instructional prompting. *Journal of Educational Psychology, 74*, 77–84.

Craik, F. (1979). Human memory. In M. Rosenzweig & L. Porter (Eds.), *Annual review of psychology*. Palo Alto, CA: Annual Reviews.

Craik, F., & Lockhart, R. (1972). Levels of processing: A framework for memory research. *Journal of Verbal Learning and Verbal Behavior, 11*, 671–684.

Crain, W. (1980). *Theories of development:*

Concepts and applications. Englewood Cliffs, NJ: Prentice-Hall.

Crandall, V., Katkovsky, W., & Crandall, V. (1965). Children's beliefs in their own control of reinforcement in intellectual-academic situations. *Child Development, 36*, 91–109.

Crandall, V., Katkovsky, W., & Preston, A. (1962). Motivational and ability determinants of young children's intellectual achievement behaviors. *Child Development, 33*, 643–661.

Craske, M. L. (1985). Improving persistence through observational learning and attribution retraining. *British Journal of Educational Psychology, 55*, 138–147.

Cronbach, L., Gleser, G., Nanda, H., & Rajaratnam, N. (1972). *The dependability of behavioral measurements: Multifaceted studies of generalizability*. New York: Wiley.

Cuban, L. (1983). Effective schools: A friendly but cautionary note. *Phi Delta Kappan, 64*(10), 695–696.

Cyert, R. (1980). Problem solving and educational policy. In D. Tuma & F. Reif (Eds.), *Problem solving and education: Issues in teaching and research*. Hillsdale, NJ: Erlbaum.

Damon, W., & Hart, D. (1982). The development of self-understanding from infancy through adolescence. *Child Development, 53*, 841–864.

Damon, W., & Killen, M. (1982). Peer interaction and the process of change in children's moral reasoning. *Merrill-Palmer Quarterly, 28*, 347–367.

Dansereau, D. (1983). Learning strategy research. In J. Segal, S. Chipman, & R. Glaser (Eds.), *Relating instruction to basic research*. Hillsdale, NJ: Erlbaum.

Dansereau, D., Collins, K., McDonald, B., Holley, C., Garland, J., Diekhoff, G., & Evans, S. (1979). Development and evaluation of a learning strategy training program. *Journal of Educational Psychology, 71*, 64–73.

Darch, C., Carnine, D., & Kameenui, E. (1986). The role of graphic organizers and social structure in content area instruction. *Journal of Reading Behavior, 18*, 275–295.

Dasen, P. (1972). Cross-cultural Piagetian research: A summary. *Journal of Cultural Psychology, 3*, 23–39.

Dasho, S. (1978). A communications approach to classroom socialization. Report A-78-12, Effective Teacher Education Program. San Francisco: Far West Laboratory for Educational Research and Development.

Daurio, S. (1979). Educational enrichment versus acceleration: A review of the literature. In W. George, S. Cohn, and J. Stanley (Eds.), *Educating the gifted: Acceleration and enrichment*. Baltimore: Johns Hopkins University Press.

Davis, G. (1986). *Creativity is forever* (2nd ed.). Dubuque, IA: Kendall/Hunt.

Davis, R. (1984). *Learning mathematics: A cognitive science approach to mathematics education*. London: Croom Helm.

Davis, R., & Alexander, L. (1977). *The lecture method*. East Lansing: Instructional Media Center, Michigan State University.

Davis, R., & McKnight, C. (1980). The influence of semantic content on algorithmic behavior. *Journal of Mathematical Behavior, 3*, 39–87.

Davison, M., Robbins, S., & Swanson, D. (1978). Stage structure in objective moral judgments. *Developmental Psychology, 14*, 137–146.

Deaux, K. (1985). Sex and gender. *Annual Review of Psychology, 36*, 49–82.

deBono, E. (1985). The CoRT thinking program. In J. Segal, S. Chipman, and R. Glaser (Eds.), *Thinking and learning skills, Volume 1: Relating instruction to research*. Hillsdale, NJ: Erlbaum.

deCharms, R. (1968). *Personal causation*. New York: Academic Press.

deCharms, R. (1976). *Enhancing motivation: Change in the classroom*. New York: Irvington.

deCharms, R. (1980). The origins of competence and achievement motivation in personal causation. In L. J. Fyans, Jr. (Ed.), *Achievement motivation: Recent trends in theory and research*. New York: Plenum.

deCharms, R. (1984). Motivation enhancement in educational settings. In R. Ames & C. Ames (Eds.), *Research on motivation in education* (Vol. 1). Orlando, FL: Academic Press.

Deci, E. (1975). *Intrinsic motivation*. New York: Plenum.

Deci, E., & Ryan, R. (1985). *Intrinsic motivation and self-determination in human behavior*. New York: Plenum.

Deci, E., Schwartz, A., Sheinman, L., & Ryan, R. (1981). An instrument to assess adults' orientations toward control versus autonomy with children: Reflections on intrinsic motivation and perceived competence. *Journal of Educational Psychology, 73*, 642–650.

deGroot, A. (1965). *Thought and choice in chess*. The Hague: Mouton.

DeLisi, R., & Staudt, J. (1980). Individual differences in college students' performance on formal operations tasks. *Journal of Applied Developmental Psychology, 1*, 201–208.

Dembo, M. (1988). *Applying educational psychology in the classroom* (3rd ed.). New York: Longman.

Dembo, M., & Hillman, S. (1976). An instructional model approach to educational psychology. *Contemporary Educational Psychology, 1*, 116–123.

Detterman, D., & Sternberg, R. (1982). *How and how much can intelligence be increased*? Norwood, NJ: Ablex.

DeTure, L. (1979). Relative effects of modeling on the acquisition of wait-time by preservice elementary teachers and concommitant changes in dialogue patterns. *Journal of Research in Science Teaching, 16*, 553–562.

Devine, T. (1981). *Teaching study skills: A guide for teachers*. Boston: Allyn and Bacon.

Dewey, J. (1910). *How we think*. Boston: Heath.

Dick, W. (1977). Formative evaluation. In L. Briggs (Ed.), *Instructional design: Principles and applications*. Englewood Cliffs, NJ: Educational Technology Publications.

Dick, W., & Carey, L. (1978). *The systematic design of instruction*. Glenview, IL: Scott, Foresman.

Diener, D., & Dweck, C. (1978). An analysis of learned helplessness: Continuous changes in performance, strategy, and achievement cognitions following failure. *Journal of Personality and Social Psychology, 36*, 451–462.

Dillon, J. (1979). Alternatives to questioning. *High School Journal, 62*, 217–222.

Dillon, J. (1981a). A norm against student questions. *Clearing House, 55*, 136–139.

Dillon, J. (1981b). Duration of response to teacher questions and statements. *Contemporary Educational Psychology, 6*, 1–11.

Dillon, J. (1982). Cognitive correspondence between question/statement and response. *American Educational Research Journal, 19*, 540–551.

Dillon, J. (1984). Research on questioning and discussion. *Educational Leadership, 42*(3), 50–56.

diSessa, A. (1982). Unlearning Aristotelian physics: A study of knowledge-based learning. *Cognitive Science, 6*, 37–75.

diSibio, M. (1982). Memory for connected discourse: A constructivist view. *Review of Educational Research, 52*, 149–174.

Doctorow, M., Wittrock, M., & Marks, C. (1978). Generative processes in reading comprehension. *Journal of Educational Psychology, 70*, 109–118.

Doebler, L., & Eicke, F. (1979). Effects of teacher awareness of the educational implications of field-dependent/field-independent cognitive style on selected classroom variables. *Journal of Educational Psychology, 71*, 226–232.

Dooling, D., & Lachman, R. (1971). Effects of comprehension on retention of prose.

Journal of Experimental Psychology, 88, 216–222.

Doyle, W. (1978). Task structures and student roles in classrooms. Paper presented at the annual meeting of the American Educational Research Association, Toronto.

Doyle, W. (1982). Academic work. Paper prepared for the National Commission on Excellence in Education.

Doyle, W. (1984). How order is achieved in classrooms: An interim report. *Journal of Curriculum Studies, 16*, 259–277.

Doyle, W. (1986a). Classroom organization and management. In M. Wittrock (Ed.), *Handbook of research on teaching* (3rd ed.). New York: Macmillan.

Doyle, W. (1986b). Content representation in teachers' definitions of academic work. *Journal of Curriculum Studies, 18*, 365–379.

Doyle, W. (April 1988). Curriculum in teacher education. Division K vice-presidential address presented at the annual meeting of the American Educational Research Association, New Orleans.

Dreikurs, R. (1968). *Psychology in the classroom* (2nd ed.). New York: Harper & Row.

Dubin, R., & Taveggia, T. (1968). *The teacher-learning paradox: A comparative analysis of college teaching methods*. Eugene: Center for the Advanced Study of Educational Administration, University of Oregon.

Duckworth, E. (1979). Either we're too early and they can't learn it or we're too late and they know it already: The dilemma of "applying Piaget." *Harvard Educational Review, 49*, 297–312.

Duffy, G., & Roehler, L. (1982). The illusion of instruction. *Reading Research Quarterly, 17*, 438–445.

Duffy, G., & Roehler, L. (1989). The tension between information-giving and mediation: New perspectives on instructional explanation and teacher change. In J. Brophy (Ed.), *Advances in research on teaching. Vol. I: Teaching for meaningful understanding and self-regulated learning*. Greenwich, CT: JAI Press.

Duffy, G., Roehler, L., Meloth, M., & Vavrus, L. (1986). Conceptualizing instructional explanation. *Teaching and Teacher Education, 2*, 197–214.

Duffy, G., Roehler, L., Sivan, E., Rackliffe, G., Book, C., Meloth, M., Vavrus, L., Wesselman, R., Putnam, J., & Bassiri, D. (1987). Effects of explaining reasoning associated with using reading strategies. *Reading Research Quarterly, 22*, 347–368.

Duke, P., Carlsmith, J., Jennings, D., Martin, J., Dornbusch, S., Gross, R., & Siegel-Gorelick, B. (1982). Educational correlates of early and late sexual maturation in adolescence. *Journal of Pediatrics, 100*, 633–637.

Dunkin, M., & Biddle, B. (1974). *The study of teaching*. New York: Holt, Rinehart and Winston.

Dunkin, M., & Doenau, S. (1980). A replication study of unique and joint contributions to variance in student achievement. *Journal of Educational Psychology, 72*, 394–403.

Dunn, L. (1973). *Exceptional children in the schools: Special education in transition*. New York: Holt, Rinehart and Winston.

Dunn, T. (1984). Learning hierarchies and cognitive psychology: An important link for instructional psychology. *Educational Psychologist, 19*, 75–93.

Durkin, D. (1978–79). What classroom observations reveal about reading comprehension research. *Reading Research Quarterly, 14*, 481–533.

Dusek, J. (Ed.). (1985). *Teacher expectancies*. Hillsdale, NJ: Erlbaum.

Duyme, M. (1988). School success and social class: An adoption study. *Developmental Psychology, 24*, 203–209.

Dweck, C. (1986). Motivational processes affecting learning. *American Psychologist, 41*, 1040–1048.

Dweck, C., Davidson, W., Nelson, S., & Enna, B. (1978). Sex differences in learned helplessness: II. The contingencies of evaluative feedback in the classroom and III. An experimental analysis. *Developmental Psychology, 14*, 268–276.

Dweck, C., & Elliott, E. (1983). Achievement motivation. In P. Mussen & E. Hetherington (Eds.), *Handbook of child psychology, IV: Socialization, personality and social development*. New York: Wiley.

Ebbinghaus, H. (1885). *Memory* (Translated by H. Ruger & C. Bussenius). New York: Dover, 1964 (originally published in Leipzig in 1885).

Eccles, J. (1987). Gender roles and women's achievement-related decisions. *Psychology of Women Quarterly, 11*, 135–172.

Eden, D. (1975). Intrinsic and extrinsic rewards and motives: Replication and extension with Kibbutz workers. *Journal of Applied Social Psychology, 5*, 348–361.

Eder, D. (1981). Ability grouping as a self-fulfilling prophecy: A micro-analysis of teacher-student interaction. *Sociology of Education, 54*, 151–161.

Educational Products Information Exchange (EPIE Institute). (1986). *The educational software selector (TESS)—1986/1987 edition*. New York: Teachers College Press.

Edwards, C., & Surma, M. (1980). The relationship between type of teacher reinforcement and student inquiry behavior in science. *Journal of Research in Science Teaching, 17*, 337–341.

Egan, K. (1979). *Educational development*. New York: Oxford University Press.

Ehri, L., Deffner, N., & Wilce, L. (1984). Pictorial mnemonics for phonics. *Journal of Educational Psychology, 76*, 880–893.

Eichorn, D. (1980). The school. In M. Johnson (Ed.), *Toward adolescence: The middle school years*. Chicago: National Society for the Study of Education.

Eisenberg, N., Lennon, R., & Roth, K. (1983). Prosocial development: A longitudinal study. *Developmental Psychology, 19*, 846–855.

Eisikovits, Z., & Sagi, A. (1982). Moral development and discipline encounter in delinquent and nondelinquent adolescents. *Journal of Youth and Adolescence, 11*, 217–230.

Elardo, P., & Elardo, R. (1976). A critical analysis of social development programs in elementary education. *Journal of School Psychology, 14*, 118–130.

Elawar, M. C., & Corno, L. (1985). A factorial experiment in teachers' written feedback on student homework: Changing teacher behavior a little rather than a lot. *Journal of Educational Psychology, 77*, 162–173.

Elkind, D. (1981). Child development and the social science curriculum of the elementary school. *Social Education, 45*, 435–437.

Elstein, A., Shulman, L., & Sprafka, S. (1978). *Medical problem solving: An analysis of clinical reasoning*. Cambridge, MA: Harvard University Press.

Emmer, E., Evertson, C., & Anderson, L. (1980). Effective management at the beginning of the school year. *Elementary School Journal, 80*, 219–231.

Emmer, E., Evertson, C., Sanford, J., Clements, B., & Worsham, M. (1984). *Classroom management for secondary teachers*. Englewood Cliffs, NJ: Prentice-Hall.

Engelmann, S., & Carnine, D. (1982). *Theory of instruction: Principles and applications*. New York: Irvington.

Enright, R., Lapsley, D., Harris, D., & Shawver, D. (1983). Moral development interventions in early adolescence. *Theory into Practice, 22*, 134–144.

Epps, S., & Tindal, G. (1987). The effectiveness of differential programming in serving students with mild handicaps: Placement options and instructional programming. In M. Wang, M. Reynolds, and H. Walberg (Eds.), *Handbook of special education: Research in practice, 1*, 213–248. Oxford: Pergamon Press.

Epstein, H. (1978). Growth spurts during brain development: Implications for educational policy and practice. In J. Chall and A. Mirsky (Eds.), *Education and the brain.* The seventy-seventh yearbook of the National Society for the Study of Education, Part II. Chicago: University of Chicago Press.

Erikson, E. (1968). *Identity: Youth and crisis*. New York: Norton.

Erlwanger, S. (1975). Case studies of children's conceptions of mathematics (Part I). *Journal of Children's Mathematical Behavior, 1*, 157–283.

Eshel, Y., & Klein, Z. (1981). Development of academic self-concept of lower-class and middle-class primary school children. *Journal of Educational Psychology, 73*, 287–293.

Eswara, H. (1972). Administration of reward and punishment in relation to ability, effort, and performance. *Journal of Social Psychology, 87*, 137–140.

Evans, G., & Lovell, B. (1979). Design modification in an open-plan school. *Journal of Educational Psychology, 71*, 41–49.

Everhart, R. (1983). *Reading, writing, and resistance: Adolescence and labor in a junior high school.* Boston: Routledge & Kegan Paul.

Evertson, C. (1982). Differences in instructional activities in higher- and lower-achieving junior high English and math classes. *Elementary School Journal, 82*, 329–350.

Evertson, C. (1985). Training teachers in classroom management: An experimental study in secondary school classrooms. *Journal of Educational Research, 79*, 51–58.

Evertson, C., Anderson, C., Anderson, L., & Brophy, J. (1980). Relationships between classroom behaviors and student outcomes in junior high mathematics and English classes. *American Educational Research Journal, 17*, 43–60.

Evertson, C., & Emmer, E. (1982). Effective management at the beginning of the school year in junior high classes. *Journal of Educational Psychology, 74*, 485–498.

Evertson, C., Emmer, E., Clements, B., Sanford, J., & Worsham, M. (1984). *Classroom management for elementary teachers*. Englewood Cliffs, NJ: Prentice-Hall.

Evertson, C., Emmer, E., Sanford, J., & Clements, B. (1983). Improving classroom management: An experiment in elementary school classrooms. *Elementary School Journal, 84*, 173–188.

Evertson, C., Sanford, J., & Emmer, E. (1981). Effects of class heterogeneity in junior high school. *American Educational Research Journal, 18*, 219–232.

Fagan, E., Hassler, D., & Szabo, M. (1981). Evaluation of questioning strategies in language arts instruction. *Research in Teaching of English, 15*, 267–273.

Fair, J. (1977). Skills in thinking. In D. Kurfman (Ed.), *Developing decision-making skills*. Forty-seventh NCSS yearbook (pp. 29–68). Arlington, VA: National Council for the Social Studies.

Farrar, M. (1986). Teacher questions: The complexity of the cognitively simple. *Instructional Science, 15*, 89–107.

Faust, M. (1977). Somatic development of adolescent girls. *Monographs of the Society for Research in Child Development, 42* (No. 1, Serial No. 169).

Faw, H., & Waller, T. (1976). Mathemagenic behaviors and efficiency in learning from prose. *Review of Educational Research, 46*, 691–720.

Feather, N. (Ed.). (1982). *Expectations and actions*. Hillsdale, NJ: Erlbaum.

Feiman-Nemser, S., & Floden, R. (1986). The cultures of teaching. In M. Wittrock (Ed.), *Handbook of research on teaching* (3rd ed.). New York: Macmillan.

Feingold, A. (1988). Cognitive gender differences are disappearing. *American Psychologist, 43*, 95–103.

Feldhusen, J. (1979). Problems of student behavior in secondary schools. In D. Duke (Ed.), *Classroom management*. The seventy-eighth yearbook of the National Society for the Study of Education, Part II. Chicago: University of Chicago Press.

Feldhusen, J., & Sokol, L. (1982). Extraschool programming to meet the needs of gifted youth: Super Saturday. *Gifted Child Quarterly, 21*, 450–476.

Felker, D. (1974). *Building positive self-concepts*. Minneapolis: Burgess.

Fennema, E., Carpenter, T., & Peterson, P. (1989). Learning mathematics with understanding. In J. Brophy (Ed.), *Advances in research on teaching, Volume 1: Teaching for meaningful understanding and self-regulated learning*. Greenwich, CT: JAI Press.

Fenstermacher, G. (1982). To be or not to be gifted: What is the question? *Elementary School Journal, 82*, 299–303.

Fenstermacher, G. (1983). How should implications of research on teaching be used? *Elementary School Journal, 83*, 496–499.

Ferguson, G. (1956). On transfer and the abilities of man. *Canadian Journal of Psychology, 10*, 121–131.

Ferster, C., & Skinner, B. (1957). *Schedules of reinforcement*. New York: Appleton.

Feshbach, S. (1970). Aggression. In P. Mussen (Ed.), *Carmichael's manual of child psychology* (3rd ed., Vol. 2). New York: Wiley.

Festinger, L. (1957). *A theory of cognitive dissonance*. Stanford, CA: Stanford University Press.

Feuerstein, R., Rand, Y., Hoffman, M., & Miller, R. (1980). *Instrumental enrichment: An intervention program for cognitive modifiability*. Baltimore: University Park Press.

Feuerstein, R. et al. (1985). Instrumental enrichment, an intervention program for structural cognitive modifiability: Theory and practice. In J. Segal, S. Chipman, & R. Glaser (Eds.), *Thinking and learning skills, Volume 1: Relating instruction to research*. Hillsdale, NJ: Erlbaum.

Fillmore, C. (1968). The case for case. In E. Bach & R. Harms (Eds.), *Universals of linguistic theory*. New York: Holt, Rinehart and Winston.

Finley, M. (1984). Teachers and tracking in a comprehensive high school. *Sociology of Education, 57*, 233–243.

Fish, M., & Feldman, S. (1987). Teacher and student verbal behavior in microcomputer classes: An observational study. *Journal of Classroom Interaction, 23*, 15–21.

Fisher, C., Berliner, D., Filby, N., Marliave, R., Cahen, L., & Dishaw, M. (1980). Teaching behaviors, academic learning time, and student achievement: An overview. In C. Denham & A. Lieberman (Eds.), *Time to learn*. Washington, DC: National Institute of Education.

Fitch, S., & Adams, G. (1983). Ego identity and intimacy status: Replication and extension. *Developmental Psychology, 19*, 839–845.

Flanders, N. (1970). *Analyzing teacher behavior*. Reading, MA: Addison-Wesley.

Flavell, J. (1985). *Cognitive development* (2nd ed.). Englewood Cliffs, NJ: Prentice-Hall.

Flavell, J., Beach, D., & Chinsky, J. (1966). Spontaneous verbal rehearsal in a memory task as a function of age. *Child Development, 37*, 283–299.

Flavell, J., Botkin, P., Fry, C., Wright, J., & Jarvis, P. (1968). *The development of role-taking and communication skills in children*. New York: Wiley.

Flavell, J., & Wellman, H. (1977). Metamemory. In R. Kail & J. Hagen (Eds.), *Perspectives on the development of memory and cognition*. Hillsdale, NJ: Erlbaum.

Fleetwood, R., & Parish, T. (1976). Relationship between moral development test scores of juvenile delinquents and their inclusion in a moral dilemma discussion group. *Psychological Reports, 39*, 1075–1080.

Fogarty, J., Wang, M., & Creek, R. (1983). A descriptive study of experienced and novice teachers' interactive instructional thoughts and actions. *Journal of Educational Research, 77*, 22–32.

Follman, J., Lowe, A., & Miller, W. (1971). Graphics variables and reliability and level of essay grades. *American Educational Research Journal, 8*, 365–373.

Ford, C., & Beach, F. (1951). *Patterns of sexual development*. New York: Harper & Row.

Ford, M. (1982). Social cognition and social competence in adolescence. *Developmental Psychology, 18*, 323–340.

Ford, M. (1986). A living systems conceptualization of social intelligence: Outcomes, processes, and developmental change. In R. Sternberg (Ed.), *Advances in the psychology of human intelligence*, (Vol. *3*, pp. 119–171). Hillsdale, NJ: Erlbaum.

Foster, W. (1981). Leadership: A conceptual framework for recognizing and educating. *Gifted Child Quarterly, 25*, 17–25.

Fowler, J. W., & Peterson, P. L. (1981). Increasing reading persistence and altering attributional style of learned helpless children. *Journal of Educational Psychology, 73*, 251–260.

Fox, D., & Kendall P. (1983). Thinking through academic problems: Application of cognitive-behavior therapy to learning. In T. Kratochwill (Ed.), *Advances in school psychology* (Vol. 3). Hillsdale, NJ: Erlbaum.

Francis, E. (1975). Grade level and task difficulty in learning by discovery and verbal reception methods. *Journal of Educational Psychology, 67*, 146–150.

Frank, B. (1986). Cognitive styles and teacher education: Field dependence and areas of specialization among teacher education majors. *Journal of Educational Research, 80*, 19–22.

Frank, J. (1984). A comparison between an individual and group structure contingency that differed in the behavioral contingency and performance-outcome components. Doctoral dissertation, University of Minnesota, Minneapolis.

Frauenglass, M., & Diaz, R. (1985). Self-regulatory functions of children's private speech: A critical analysis of recent challenges to Vygotsky's theory. *Developmental Psychology, 21*, 356–364.

Frederiksen, N. (1984). Implications of cognitive theory for instruction in problem solving. *Review of Educational Research, 54*, 363–407.

Freeman, D., Kuhs, T., Porter, A., Floden, R., Schmidt, W., & Schwille, J. (1983). Do textbooks and tests define a national curriculum in elementary school mathematics? *Elementary School Journal, 83*, 501–513.

Frieze, I., Francis, W., & Hanusa, B. (1983). Defining success in classroom settings. In J. Levine & M. Wang (Eds.), *Teacher and student perceptions: Implications for learning*. Hillsdale, NJ: Erlbaum.

Fuller, F. (1969). Concerns of teachers: A developmental conceptualization. *American Educational Research Journal, 6*, 207–226.

Furst, E. (1981). Bloom's taxonomy of educational objectives for the cognitive domain: Philosophical and educational issues. *Review of Educational Research, 51*, 441–453.

Fuson, K. (1982). An analysis of the counting-on solution procedure in addition. In T. Carpenter, J. Moser, & T. Romberg (Eds.), *Addition and subtraction: A cognitive perspective*. Hillsdale, NJ: Erlbaum.

Fuson, K. (1988). *Children's counting and concepts of numbers*. New York: Springer-Verlag.

Fyans, L., Salili, F., Maehr, M., & Desai,

K. (1983). A cross-cultural exploration into the meaning of achievement. *Journal of Personality and Social Psychology, 44*, 1000–1013.

Gage, N. (Ed.). (1963). *Handbook of research on teaching.* Chicago: Rand McNally.

Gage, N. (1985). *Hard gains in the soft sciences: The case of pedagogy.* Bloomington, IN: Phi Delta Kappa.

Gage, N., & Berliner, D. (1984). *Educational psychology* (3rd ed.). Boston: Houghton-Mifflin.

Gagné, E. (1985). *The cognitive psychology of school learning.* Boston: Little, Brown.

Gagné, E., & Dick, W. (1983). Instructional psychology. In M. Rosenzweig & L. Porter (Eds.), *Annual review of psychology.* Palo Alto, CA: Annual Reviews.

Gagné, R. (1970). *The conditions of learning* (2nd ed.). New York: Holt, Rinehart and Winston.

Gagné, R. (1977). *The conditions of learning* (3rd ed.). New York: Holt, Rinehart and Winston.

Gagné, R. (1984). Learning outcomes and their effects: Useful categories of human performance. *American Psychologist, 39*, 377–385.

Gagné, R., & Briggs, L. (1979). *Principles of instructional design* (2nd ed.). New York: Holt, Rinehart and Winston.

Gagné, R., Briggs, L., & Wager, W. (1988). *Principles of instructional design* (3rd ed.). New York: Holt, Rinehart and Winston.

Galbraith, J. (1983). *The gifted kids' survival guide.* Minneapolis: Free Spirit Publishing Company.

Gall, M. (1970). The uses of questions in teaching. *Review of Educational Research, 40*, 707–721.

Gall, M., Ward, B., Berliner, D., Cahen, L., Winne, P., Elashoff, J., & Stanton, G. (1978). Effects of questioning techniques and recitation on student learning. *American Educational Research Journal, 15*, 175–199.

Gardner, H. (1983). *Frames of mind: The theory of multiple intelligences.* New York: Basic Books.

Gardner, H. (1988). Beyond the IQ: Education and human development. *National Forum, 68*(2), 4–7.

Garlinger, D., & Frank, B. (1986). Teacher-student cognitive style and academic achievement: A review and mini-meta-analysis. *Journal of Classroom Interaction, 21*(2), 2–8.

Garrett-Schau, C., & Scott, K. (1984). Impact of gender characteristics of instruction materials: An integration of the research literature. *Journal of Educational Psychology, 76*, 183–193.

Gearheart, B., & Weishahn, M. (1984). *The exceptional student in the regular classroom* (3rd ed.). St. Louis: Mosby.

Geiger, K., & Turiel, E. (1983). Disruptive school behavior and concepts of social convention in early adolescence. *Journal of Educational Psychology, 75*, 677–685.

Gelman, R., & Gallistel, C. (1986). *The child's understanding of number* (2nd ed.). Cambridge: Harvard University Press.

Gesell, A., & Thompson, H. (1929). Learning and growth in identical infant twins. *Genetic Psychology Monographs, 6*, 1–24.

Getzels, J., & Csikszentmihalyi, M. (1975). From problem solving to problem finding. In I. Taylor & J. Getzels (Eds.), *Perspectives in creativity.* Chicago: Aldine.

Getzels, J., & Jackson, P. (1962). *Creativity and intelligence: Explorations with gifted students.* New York: Wiley.

Giaconia, R., & Hedges, L. (1982). Identifying features of effective open education. *Review of Educational Research, 52*, 579–602.

Gibson, S., & Dembo, M. (1984). Teacher efficacy: A construct validation. *Journal of Educational Psychology, 76*, 569–582.

Gilligan, C. (1982). *In a different voice.* Cambridge: Harvard University Press.

Gillingham, M., & Guthrie, J. (1987). Relationships between CBI and research on teaching. *Contemporary Educational Psychology, 12*, 189–199.

Ginsburg, H., & Opper, S. (1988). *Piaget's theory of intellectual development* (3rd ed.) Englewood Cliffs, NJ: Prentice-Hall.

Glaser, R. (1977). *Adaptive education: individualized diversity and learning*. New York: Holt, Rinehart, & Winston.

Glaser, R. (1984). Education and thinking: The role of knowledge. *American Psychologist, 39*, 93–104.

Glaser, R., & Nitko, A. (1971). Measurement in learning and instruction. In R. Thorndike (Ed.), *Educational measurement* (2nd ed.). Washington, DC: American Counil on Education.

Glasser, W. (1969). *Schools without failure*. New York: Harper & Row.

Glasser, W. (November–December 1977). Ten steps to good discipline. *Today's Education, 66*(4), 61–63.

Glenberg, A. (1976). Monotonic and nonmonotonic lag effects in paired-associated and recognition memory paradigms. *Journal of Verbal Learning and Verbal Behavior, 15*, 1–16.

Glover, J., & Corkill, A. (1987). Influence of paraphrased repetitions on the spacing effect. *Journal of Educational Psychology, 79*, 198–199.

Glover, J., Timme, V., Deyloff, D., & Rogers, M. (1987). Memory for student-performed tasks. *Journal of Educational Psychology, 79*, 445–452.

Glynn, E., Thomas, J., & Shee, S. (1973). Behavioral self-control of on-task behavior in an elementary classroom. *Journal of Applied Behavior Analysis, 6*, 105–113.

Goffman, E. (1959). *The presentation of self in everyday life*. Garden City, NY: Doubleday.

Golinkoff, R. (1976). A comparison of reading comprehension processes in good and poor comprehenders. *Reading Research Quarterly, 11*, 623–659.

Good, T. (1983). Classroom research: A decade of progress. *Educational Psychologist, 18*, 127–144.

Good, T., & Biddle, B. (1989). Research and the improvement of mathematics instruction: The need for observational resources. In D. Grouws & T. Cooney (Eds.), *Perspectives on research on effective mathematics teaching*. Hillsdale, NJ: Erlbaum.

Good, T., & Brophy, J. (1974). Changing teacher and student behavior: An empirical investigation. *Journal of Educational Psychology, 66*, 390–405.

Good, T., & Brophy, J. (1984). *Looking in classrooms* (3rd ed.). New York: Harper & Row.

Good, T., & Brophy, J. (1986). School effects. In M. Wittrock (Ed.), *Third handbook of research on teaching*. Chicago: Rand McNally.

Good, T., & Brophy, J. (1987). *Looking in classrooms* (4th ed.). New York: Harper & Row.

Good, T., & Brophy, J. (1988). Teaching the lesson. In R. Slavin (Ed.), *School and classroom organization*. Hillsdale, NJ: Erlbaum.

Good, T., & Grouws, D. (1975). Process-product relationships in fourth grade classes. Grant NIE-6-00-3-0123, University of Missouri, Columbia.

Good, T., & Grouws, D. (1977). Teaching effects: A Process-product study in fourth grade mathematics classrooms. *Journal of Teacher Education, 28*, 49–54.

Good, T., & Grouws, D. (1979). The Missouri Mathematics Effectiveness Project: An experimental study in fourth-grade classrooms. *Journal of Educational Psychology, 71*, 355–362.

Good, T., Grouws, D., & Beckerman, T. (1978). Curriculum pacing: Some empirical data in mathematics. *Journal of Curriculum Studies, 19*, 75–81.

Good, T., Grouws, D., & Ebmeier, H. (1983). *Active mathematics teaching*. New York: Longman.

Good, T., & Hinkel, G. (1982). Schooling in America: Some descriptive and explanatory statements. Paper prepared for the National Commission on Excellence in Education.

Good, T., & Power, C. (1976). Designing successful classroom environments for different types of students. *Journal of Curriculum Studies, 8*, 1–16.

Good, T., Slavings, R., Harel, K., & Emerson, H. (1987). Student passivity: A study of question asking in K-12 classrooms. *Sociology of Education, 60*, 181–199.

Good, T., & Stipek, D. (1984). Individual differences in the classroom: A psychological perspective. In G. Fenstermacher & J. Goodlad (Eds.), *1983 NSSE Yearbook*. Chicago: University of Chicago Press.

Good, T., & Weinstein, R. (1986). Teacher expectations: A framework for exploring classrooms. In K. Kepler-Zumwalt (Ed.), *Improving teaching*. 1986 ASCD Yearbook. Alexandria, VA: Association for Supervision and Curriculum Development.

Gordon, R., & Gross, R. (1978). An exploration of the interconnecting perspective of teaching style and teacher education. *Curriculum Studies, 10*, 151–157.

Gordon, T. (1974). *T.E.T.: Teacher effectiveness training*. New York: McKay.

Gottfredson, D. (1985). Youth employment, crime, and schooling: A longitudinal study of a national sample. *Developmental Psychology, 21*, 419–432.

Gottfried, A. (Ed.). (1984). *Home environment and early cognitive development: Longitudinal research*. New York: Academic Press.

Gottlieb, J. (1981). Mainstreaming: Fulfilling the promise? *American Journal of Mental Deficiency, 86*, 115–126.

Goulet, L., Williams, K., & Hay, C. (1974). Longitudinal changes in intellectual functioning in preschool children: Schooling- and age-related effects. *Journal of Educational Psychology, 66*, 657–662.

Grabe, M. (1985). Attributions in a Mastery instructional system: Is an emphasis on effort harmful? *Contemporary Educational Psychology, 10*, 113–126.

Grant, L. (1984). Black females' "place" in desegregated classrooms. *Sociology of Education. 57*, 98–111.

Green, J. (1975). *Teacher made tests* (2nd ed.). New York: Harper & Row.

Greenbowe, T., Herron, J., Lucas, C., Nurrenbern, S., Staver, J., & Ward, C. (1981). Teaching preadolescents to act as scientists: Replication and extension of an earlier study. *Journal of Educational Psychology, 73*, 705–711.

Greeno, J. (1980a). Some examples of cognitive task analysis with instructional implications. In R. Snow, P. Federico, & W. Montague (Eds.), *Aptitude, learning, and instruction* (Vol. 2). Hillsdale, NJ: Erlbaum.

Greeno, J. (1980b). Psychology of learning, 1960–1980: One participant's observations. *American psychologist, 35*, 713–728.

Greif, E., & Ulman, K. (1982). The psychological impact of menarche on early adolescent females: A review of the literature. *Child Development, 53*, 1413–1430.

Griffin, E. (1987). *Making friends (and making them count)*. Downers Grove, IL: InterVarsity Press.

Griffin, G., Barnes, S., Hughes, R., O'Neal, S., Defino, M., Edwards, S., & Hukill, H. (1983). *Clinical preservice teacher education: Final report of a descriptive study*. Report No. 9025. Austin, TX: Research and Development Center for Teacher Education.

Griffin, G., Barnes, S., O'Neal, S., Edwards, S., Defino, M., & Hukill, H. (1983). *Changing teacher practice: Final report of an experimental study*. R&D Report No. 9052. Austin, TX: Research and Development Center for Teacher Education, The University of Texas at Austin.

Griswold, P. (1984). Elementary students' attitudes during two years of computer-assisted instruction. *American Educational Research Journal, 21*, 737–754.

Groen, G., & Parkman, J. (1972). A chronometric analysis of simple addition. *Psychological Review, 79*, 329–343.

Groff, E., & Render, G. (1983). The effectiveness of three classroom teaching methods: Programmed instruction, simulation and guided fantasy. *Journal of the Society for Accelerative Learning and Teaching, 8*, 5–13.

Groisser, P. (1964). *How to use the fine art of questioning.* New York: Teachers' Practical Press.

Gronlund, N. (1985). *Stating objectives for classroom instruction* (3rd ed.). New York: Macmillan.

Gropper, G. (1983). A behavioral approach to instructional prescription. In C. Reigeluth (Ed.), *Instructional-design theories and models: An overview of their current status.* Hillsdale, NJ: Erlbaum.

Grusec, J., Kuczynski, L., Rushton, J., & Simutis, Z. (1978). Modeling, direct instruction, and attributions: Effects on altruism. *Development Psychology, 14*, 51–57.

Guilford, J. (1959). Three faces of intellect. *American Psychologist, 14*, 469–479.

Guilford, J. (1967). *The nature of human intelligence.* New York: McGraw-Hill.

Gump, P. (1980). The school as a social situation. In M. Rosenzweig & L. Porter (Eds.), *Annual review of psychology* (Vol. 31). Palo Alto, CA: Annual Reviews.

Gump, P., & Good, L. (1976). Environments operating in open space and traditionally designed schools. *Journal of Architectural Research, 5*, 20–27.

Guskey, T., & Gates, S. (1986). Synthesis of research on the effects of mastery learning in elementary and secondary school classrooms. *Educational Leadership, 43*(8), 73–80.

Guskin, S., & Jones, R. (1982). Attitudes toward the handicapped. In H. Mitzel (Ed.), *Encyclopedia of educational research* (5th ed., pp. 189–193). New York: Free Press.

Hains, A., & Miller, D. (1980). Moral and cognitive development in delinquent and nondelinquent children and adolescents. *Journal of Genetic Psychology, 137*, 21–35.

Haladyna, T., & Thomas, G. (1979). The attitudes of elementary school children toward school and subject matters. *Journal of Experimental Education, 48*, 18–23.

Hales, L., & Tokar, E. (1975). The effect of quality of preceding responses on the grades assigned to subsequent responses to an essay question. *Journal of Educational Measurement, 12*, 115–117.

Hall, C., & Lindzey, G. (1970). *Theories of personality* (2nd ed.). New York: Wiley.

Hall, P., & Spencer-Hall, D. (1980). *Conditions and processes of problem identification, definition, and resolution in two school systems: Toward a grounded theory.* Final report of the National Institute of Education, Grant NIE-G-78-0042.

Halpern, D. (1986). *Sex differences in cognitive abilities.* Hillsdale, NJ: Erlbaum.

Hambleton, R., Swaminathan, H., Algina, J., & Coulson, D. (1978). Criterion-referenced testing and measurement: A review of technical issues and developments. *Review of Educational Research, 48*, 1–47.

Hampden-Turner, C. (1982). *Maps of the mind.* New York: Collier.

Hannah, E., & Pilner, S. (1983). Teacher attitudes toward handicapped students: A review and synthesis. *School Psychology Review, 12*, 12–25.

Hansen, J., & Pearson, P. (1983). An instructional study: Improving the inferential comprehension of fourth-grade good and poor readers. *Journal of Educational Psychology, 75*, 821–829.

Harber, J., & Bryen, D. (1976). Black English and the task of reading. *Review of Educational Research, 46*, 387–405.

Hargreaves, D., Hester, S., & Mellor, F. (1975). *Deviance in classrooms.* London: Routledge and Kegan Paul.

Harris, A., & Kapche, R. (1978). Problems of quality control in the development and the use of behavior change techniques in public school settings. *Education and the Treatment of Children, 1*, 43–51.

Harris, B. (1979). Whatever happened to Little Albert? *American Psychologist, 34*, 151–160.

Harrow, A. (1972). *A taxonomy of the psychomotor domain*. New York: McKay.

Hart, S. (1982). Analyzing the social organization for reading in one elementary school. In G. Spindley (Ed.), *Doing the ethnography of schooling*. New York: Holt, Rinehart and Winston.

Harter, S. (1983). Developmental perspectives on the self-system. In P. Mussen (Ed.), *Handbook of child psychology* (4th ed., Vol. 4). New York: Wiley.

Hartup, W. (1970). Peer interaction and social organization. In P. Mussen (Ed.), *Carmichael's manual of child psychology* (3rd ed., Vol. 2). New York: Wiley.

Hasher, L., & Zacks, R. (1984). Automatic processing of fundamental information: The case of frequency of occurrence. *American Psychologist, 39*, 1372–1388.

Hattie, J., & Rogers, H. (1986). Factor models for assessing the relation between creativity and intelligence. *Journal of Educational Psychology, 78*, 482–485.

Hauserman, N., Miller, J., & Bond, F. (1976). A behavioral approach to changing self-concept in elementary school children. *Psychological Record, 26*, 111–116.

Havighurst, R. (1972). *Developmental tasks and education* (3rd ed.). New York: McKay.

Hayes, D., & Tierney, R. (1982). Developing readers' knowledge through analogy. *Reading Research Quarterly, 17*, 256–280.

Hayes, J. (1981). *The complete problem solver*. Philadelphia: Franklin Institute Press.

Hayes, R., & Day, B. (1980). Classroom openness and the basic skills, the self-perceptions, and the school-attendance records of third-grade pupils. *Elementary School Journal, 81*, 87–96.

Haynes, M., & Jenkins, J. (1984). Reading instruction in special education resource rooms. Manuscript. Seattle: University of Washington.

Heath, R., & Nielson, M. (1974). The research basis for performance-based teacher education. *Review of Educational Research, 44*, 463–484.

Heathers, G. (1969). Grouping. In R. Ebel (Ed.), *Encyclopedia of educational research* (4th ed.). New York: Macmillan.

Heller, J., & Reif, F. (1984). Prescribing effective human problem-solving processes: Problem description in physics. *Cognition and Instruction, 1*, 177–216.

Henderson, R. (Ed.). (1981). *Parent-child interaction: Theory, research, and prospects*. New York: Academic Press.

Henson, K. (1988). *Methods and strategies for teaching in secondary and middle schools*. New York: Longman.

Heppner, P. (1978). A review of the problem-solving literature and its relationship to the counseling process. *Journal of Counseling Psychology, 25*, 366–375.

Hermann, G. (1969). Learning by discovery: A critical review of studies. *Journal of Experimental Education, 38*, 58–71.

Hess, R. (1970). Class and ethnic influences upon socialization. In P. Mussen (Ed.), *Carmichael's manual of child psychology* (3rd ed., Vol. 2). New York: Wiley.

Hess, R., Holloway, S., Dickson, W., & Price, G. (1984). Maternal variables as predictors of children's school readiness and later achievement in vocabulary and mathematics in sixth grade. *Child Development, 55*, 1902–1912.

Hess, R., & McDevitt, T. (1984). Some cognitive consequences of maternal intervention techniques: A longitudinal study. *Child Development, 55*, 2017–3030.

Hess, R., & Shipman, V. (1965). Early experience and the socialization of cognitive modes in children. *Child Development, 34*, 869–886.

Heward, W., & Orlansky, M. (1984). *Exceptional children* (2nd ed.). Columbus: Charles E. Merrill.

Hewett, F., & Watson, P. (1979). Classroom management and the exceptional learner. In D. Duke (Ed.), *Classroom management*. The seventy-eighth yearbook of the National Society for the Study of Education, Part II. Chicago: University of Chicago Press.

Hiebert, E. (1983). An examination of ability grouping in reading instruction. *Reading Research Quarterly, 18*, 231–255.

Hill, K., & Wigfield, A. (1984). Test anxiety: A major educational problem and what can be done about it. *Elementary School Journal 85*, 105–126.

Hiller, J., Fisher, G., & Kaess, W. (1969). A computer investigation of verbal characteristics of effective classroom lecturing. *American Educational Research Journal, 6*, 661–675.

Hoetker, J., & Ahlbrand, W. (1969). The persistence of the recitation. *American Educational Research Journal, 6*, 145–167.

Hoffman, M. (1970). Moral development. In P. Mussen (Ed.), *Carmichael's manual of child psychology* (3rd ed., Vol. 2). New York: Wiley.

Hoffman, M. (1977). Personality and social development. In M. Rosenzweig & L. Porter (Eds.), *Annual review of psychology* (Vol. 28). Palo Alto, CA: Annual Reviews.

Hoffman, M. (1979). Development of moral thought, feeling, and behavior. *American Psychologist, 34*, 958–966.

Hoffman, M. (1983). Affective and cognitive processes in moral internalization. In E. Higgins, D. Ruble, & W. Hartup (Eds.), *Social cognition and social development: A sociocultural perspective* (pp. 236–274). Cambride: Cambridge University Press.

Hogrebe, M., Nist, S., & Newman, I. (1985). Are there gender differences in reading achievement? An investigation using the High School and Beyond data. *Journal of Educational Psychology, 77*, 716–724.

Holt, J. (1964). *How children fail*. New York: Pitman.

Honzik, M., McFarlane, J., & Allen, L. (1948). The stability of mental test performance between 2 and 18 years. *Journal of Experimental Psychology, 4*, 309–324.

Hooper, F., & DeFrain, J. (1980). On delineating distinctly Piagetian contributions to education. *Genetic Psychology Monographs, 101*, 151–181.

Hopkins, K., & Bracht, G. (1975). Ten-year stability of verbal and nonverbal IQ scores. *American Educational Research Journal, 12*, 469–477.

Horn, J. (1986). Intellectual ability concepts. In Sternberg, R. (Ed.), *Advances in the psychology of human intelligence* (pp. 35–77). Hillsdale, NJ: Erlbaum.

Horton, D., & Mills, C. (1984). Human learning and memory. In M. Rosenzweig & L. Porter (Eds.), *Annual review of psychology*. Palo Alto, CA: Annual Reviews.

Horwitz, R. (1979). Psychological effects of the "open classroom". *Review of Educational Research, 49*, 71–86.

Howey, K., & Zimpher, N. (1989). The role of higher education in initial year of teaching programs. *Elementary School Journal, 89*(4), 451–470.

Hudgins, E. (1979). Examining the effectiveness of affective education. *Psychology in the Schools, 16*, 581–585.

Huesmann, L., Eron, L., Lefkowitz, M., & Walder, L. (1984). Stability of aggression over time and generations. *Developmental Psychology, 20*, 1120–1134.

Hughes, D. (1973). An experimental investigation of the effects of pupil responding and teacher reacting on pupil achievement. *American Educational Research Journal, 10*, 21–37.

Hughes, J. (1988). *Cognitive behavior therapy with children in schools*. Elmsford, NJ: Pergamon.

Hunt, E., Frost, N., & Lunneborg, C. (1973). Individual differences in cognition: A new approach to intelligence. In G. Bowder (Ed.), *The psychology of learning and motivation* (Vol. 7). New York: Academic Press.

Hunter, M. (1984). Knowing, teaching and

supervising. In P. Hosford (Ed.), *Using what we know about reading*. Alexandria, VA: Association for Supervision and Curriculum Development.

Hyde, J., & Linn, M. (Eds.). (1986). *The psychology of gender: Advances through meta-analysis*. Baltimore: The Johns Hopkins University Press.

Ianacone, R., & Stodden, R. (1987). Overview: Transition issues and directions for individuals who are mentally retarded. In R. Ianacone and R. Stodden (Eds.), *Transition issues and directions*. Reston, VA: The Council for Exceptional Children.

Inhelder, B., & Piaget, J. (1958). *The growth of logical thinking from childhood to adolescence*. New York: Basic Books.

Inhelder, B., Sinclair, H., Bovet, M. (1974). *Learning and the development of cognition*. Cambridge: Harvard University Press.

Jackson, K. (1976). An assessment of long-term effects of personal causation training. Doctoral dissertation, Washington University, St. Louis.

Jackson, P. (1968). *Life in classrooms*. New York: Holt, Rinehart, and Winston.

Jackson, P. (1985). Private lessons in public schools: Remarks on the limits of adaptive instruction. In M. Wang & H. Walberg (Eds.), *Adapting instruction to individual differences*. Berkeley, CA: McCutchan.

Jamison, D., Suppes, P., & Wells, S. (1974). The effectiveness of alternative instructional media: A survey. *Review of Educational Research, 44*, 1–68.

Jantz, R., Seefeldt, C., Galper, A., & Serock, K. (1976). *Curriculum guide: Children's attitudes toward the elderly*. Department of Early Childhood/Elementary Education, College of Education, University of Maryland. Center on Aging, Division of Human & Community Resources, University of Maryland.

Jenkins, J. (1974). Remember that old theory of memory? Well, forget it! *American Psychologist, 29*, 785–795.

Jensen, A. (1969). How much can we boost IQ and scholastic achievement? *Harvard Educational Review, 39*, 1–123.

Jensen, A., & Figueroa, R. (1975). Forward and backward digit span interaction with race and IQ: Predictions from Jensen's theory. *Journal of Educational Psychology, 67*, 882–893.

Johnson, D. (1976). Crosscultural perspectives on sex differences in reading. *The Reading Teacher, 29*, 747–752.

Johnson, D., & Johnson, R. (1975). *Learning together and alone*. Englewood Cliffs, NJ: Prentice-Hall.

Johnson, D., Johnson, R., Holubec, E., & Roy, P. (1984). *Circles of learning: Cooperation in the classroom*. Alexandria, VA: Association for Supervision and Curriculum Development.

Johnson, J., & Ruskin, R. (1977). *Behavioral instruction: An evaluative review*. Washington, DC: American Psychological Association.

Johnston, P. (1984). Assessment in reading: The emperor has no clothes. In P. Pearson, M. Camil, R. Barr, & P. Mosenthal (Eds.), *Handbook of reading research*. New York: Longman.

Jones, B., Friedman, L., Tinzmann, M., & Cox, B. (1985). Guidelines for instruction-enriched mastery learning to improve comprehension. In D. Levin (Ed.), *Improving student achievement through mastery learning programs*. San Francisco: Jossey-Bass.

Jones, B., & Hall, J. (1982). School applications of the mnemonic keyword method as a study strategy by eighth graders. *Journal of Educational Psychology, 74*, 230–237.

Jones, B., & Spady, W. (1985). Enhanced mastery learning and quality of instruction. In D. Levine (Ed.), *Improving student achievement through mastery learning programs*. San Francisco: Jossey-Bass.

Jones, M. (1957). The later careers of boys who were early or late maturing. *Child Development, 28*, 113–128.

Joyce, B., & Weil, M. (1980). *Models of teaching* (2nd ed.). Englewood Cliffs, NJ: Prentice-Hall.

Kacerguis, M., & Adams, G. (1980). Erikson stage resolution: The relationship between identity and intimacy. *Journal of Youth and Adolescence, 9*, 117–126.

Kagan, J., & Kogan, N. (1970). Individual variation in cognitive processes. In P. Mussen (Ed.), *Carmichael's manual of child psychology* (3rd ed., Vol. 1). New York: Wiley.

Kagan, J., & Moss, H. (1962). *Birth to maturity: A study in psychological development*. New York: Wiley.

Kagan, J., Pearson, J., & Welch, L. (1966). Modifiability of an impulsive tempo. *Journal of Educational Psychology, 57*, 357–365.

Kagan, J., Rosman, B., Day, D., Albert, J., & Phillips, W. (1964). Information processing and the child: Significance of analytic and reflective attitudes. *Psychological Monographs, 78* (No. 1, whole number 578).

Kail, R., & Hagen, J. (1982). Memory in childhood. In B. Wolman (Ed.), *Handbook of developmental psychology*. Englewood Cliffs: NJ: Prentice-Hall.

Kamii, C., & DeClark, A. (1985). *Young children reinvent arithmetic*. New York: Teachers College Press.

Kamin, L. (1974). *The science and politics of IQ*. Potomac, MD: Erlbaum.

Keddie, N. (1971). Classroom knowledge. In F. Young (Ed.), *Knowledge and control: New directions for the sociology of education*. London: Collier-Macmillan.

Keller, F. (1968). Goodbye, teacher! *Journal of Applied Behavioral Analysis, 1*, 79–88.

Keller, F., & Sherman, J. (1982). *The PSI handbook: Essays on personalized instruction*. Lawrence, KS: TRI.

Keller, J. (1983). Motivational design of instruction. In C. Reigeluth (Ed.), *Instructional-design theories and models: An overview of their current status*. Hillsdale, NJ: Erlbaum.

Kendler, H., & Kendler, T. (1962). Vertical and horizontal processes in problem solving. *Psychological Review, 69*, 1–16.

Kepler, K., & Randall, J. (1977). Individualization: The subversion of elementary schooling. *Elementary School Journal, 77*, 358–363.

Kierwa, K. (1987). Notetaking and review: The research and its implications. *Instructional Science, 16*, 233–249.

Kierwa, K., & Benton, S. (1988). The relationship between information-processing ability and notetaking. *Contemporary Educational Psychology, 13*, 33–44.

Killian, C. (1979). Cognitive development of college freshmen. *Journal of Research in Science Teaching, 16*, 347–350.

Kinsbourne, M., & Hiscock, M. (1978). Cerebral lateralization and cognitive development. In J. Chall & A. Mirsky (Eds.), *Education and the brain*. The seventy-seventh yearbook of the National Society for the Study of Education, Part II. Chicago: University of Chicago Press.

Kintsch, W. (1974). *The representation of meaning in memory*. Hillsdale, NJ: Erlbaum.

Kintsch, W. (1977). *Memory and cognition*. New York: Wiley.

Kintsch, W., & Yarbrough, J. (1982). Role of rhetorical structure in text comprehension. *Journal of Educational Psychology, 74*, 828–834.

Klahr, D., & Wallace, J. (1976). *Cognitive development: An information-processing view*. Hillsdale, NJ: Erlbaum.

Klatzky, R. (1980). *Human memory* (2nd ed.). San Francisco: Freeman.

Klauer, K. (1984). Intentional and incidental learning with instructional texts: A meta-analysis for 1970–1980. *American Educational Research Journal, 21*, 232–339.

Klausmeier, H. (1976). Instructional design

and the teaching of concepts. In J. Levin & V. Allen (Eds.), *Cognitive learning in children: Theories and strategies*. New York: Academic Press.

Klausmeier, H., Ghatala, E., & Frayer, D. (1974). *Conceptual learning and development*. New York: Academic Press.

Kleinfeld, J. (1975). Effective teachers of Indian and Eskimo students. *School Review, 83*, 301–344.

Klinger, E., & McNelly, F. (1976). Self-states and performances of pre-adolescent boys carrying out leadership roles inconsistent with their social status. *Child Development, 47*, 126–137.

Klinzing, G., Klinzing-Eurich, G., & Tisher, R. (1985). Higher cognitive behaviours in classroom discourse: Congruencies between teachers' questions and pupils' responses. *Australian Journal of Education, 29*, 63–75.

Kohlberg, L. (1966). A cognitive-developmental analysis of children's sex-role concepts and attitudes. In E. Maccoby (Ed.), *The development of sex differences*. Stanford, CA: Stanford University Press.

Kohlberg, L. (1969). Stage and sequence: The cognitive-developmental approach to socialization. In D. Goslin (Ed.), *Handbook of socialization theory and research*. Chicago: Rand McNally.

Kohlberg, L. (1984). *Essays on moral development, Volume 2: The psychology of moral development*. New York: Harper & Row.

Kohlberg, L., Yeager, J., & Hjertholm, E. (1967). Private speech: Four studies and a review of theories. *Child Development, 39*, 691–736.

Kohlberg, L., & Zigler, E. (1967). The impact of cognitive maturity upon the development of sex-role attitudes in the years 4 to 8. *Genetic Psychology Monographs, 75*, 84–165.

Kohler, W. (1959). *The mentality of apes*. New York: Vintage.

Kolloff, P. (1983). The Center for Global Futures: Meeting the needs of gifted students in a laboratory school. *Roeper Review, 5*(3), 32–33.

Kounin, J. (1970). *Discipline and group management in classrooms*. New York: Holt, Rinehart and Winston.

Kounin, J., & Gump, P. (1974). Signal systems of lesson settings and the task-related behavior of preschool children. *Journal of Educational Psychology, 66*, 554–562.

Kounin, J., & Obradovic, S. (1968). Managing emotionally disturbed children in regular classrooms: A replication and extension. *Journal of Special Education, 2*, 129–135.

Krathwohl, D., Bloom, B., & Masia, B. (1964). *Taxonomy of educational objectives. Handbook II: Affective domain*. New York: McKay.

Krogman, W. (1953). Biological growth as it may affect pupils' success. *Merrill-Palmer Quarterly*, (1), 90–98.

Kruglanski, A. (1978). Endogenous attribution and intrinsic motivation. In M. Lepper & M. Greene (Eds.), *The hidden costs of reward: New perspectives on the psychology of human motivation* (pp. 85–107). Hillsdale, NJ: Erlbaum.

Krumboltz, J., & Krumboltz, H. (1972). *Changing children's behavior*. Englewood Cliffs, NJ: Prentice-Hall.

Kubiszyn, T., & Borich, G. (1984). *Educational testing and measurement*. Glenview, IL: Scott, Foresman.

Kuhn, D. (1974). Inducing development experimentally: Comments on a research paradigm. *Developmental Psychology, 10*, 590–600.

Kuhn, D. (1976). Short-term longitudinal evidence for the sequentiality of Kohlberg's early stages of moral judgment. *Developmental Psychology, 12*, 162–166.

Kuhn, D. (1979). The application of Piaget's theory of cognitive development to education. *Harvard Educational Reveiw, 49*, 340–360.

Kukla, A. (1978). An attributional theory of

choice. In L. Berkowitz (Ed.), *Advances in experimental social psychology* (Vol. 2). New York: Academic Press.

Kunen, S., Cohen, R., & Solman, R. (1981). A levels-of-processing analysis of Bloom's taxonomy. *Journal of Educational Psychology, 73*, 202–211.

Laboratory of Comparative Human Cognition. (1983). Culture and cognitive development. In P. Mussen (Ed.), *Handbook of child psychology* (4th ed., Vol. 4). New York: Wiley.

Laboratory of Comparative Human Cognition. (1986). Contributions of cross-cultural research to educational practice. *American Psychologist, 41*, 1049–1058.

Labov, W. (1972). *Language in the inner-city*. Philadelphia: University of Pennsylvania Press.

Ladas, H. (1980). Summarizing research: A case study. *Review of Educational Research, 50*, 597–624.

Lamb, W. (1976). Ask a higher-level question, get a higher-level answer. *Science Teacher, 43*, 22–23.

Lambert, S., & Lambert, J. (1982). Mentoring—A powerful learning device. *G/C/T*, 2, 12–13.

Laosa, L. (1982). School, occupation, culture, and family: The impact of parental schooling on the parent-child relationship. *Journal of Educational Psychology, 74*, 791–827.

Larkin, J. (1981). Cognition of learning physics. *American Journal of Physics, 49*, 534–541.

Larrivee, B. (1985). *Effective teaching for successful mainstreaming*. New York: Longman.

Lawlor, J. (1982). *Computers in composition instruction*. Los Angeles: Southwest Regional Laboratory for Educational Research and Development.

Lazar, I., & Darlington, R. (1982). Lasting effects of early education. *Monographs of the Society for Research in Child Development, 47* (Nos. 2–3, Serial No. 195).

Leacock, E. (1969). *Teaching and learning in city schools*. New York: Basic Books.

Lefcourt, H. (1966). Internal versus external control of reinforcement: A review. *Psychological Bulletin, 65*, 206–220.

Leinhardt, G. (1980). Transition rooms: Promoting maturation or reducing education? *Journal of Educational Psychology, 72*, 55–61.

Leinhardt, G. (in press). Expertise in instructional lessons: An example from fractions. In D. Grouws and T. Cooney (Eds.), *Perspectives on research on effective mathematics teaching*. Hillsdale, NJ: Erlbaum.

Leinhardt, G., & Greeno, J. (1986). The cognitive skill of teaching. *Journal of Educational Psychology, 78*, 75–95.

Leinhardt, G., Seewald, A., & Engel, M. (1979). Learning what's taught: Sex differences in instruction. *Journal of Educational Psychology, 71*, 432–439.

Leinhardt, G., & Smith, D. (April, 1984). Expertise in mathematics instruction: Subject matter knowledge. Paper presented at the annual meeting of the American Educational Research Association, New Orleans.

Lenneberg, E. H. (1967). *Biological foundations of language*. New York: Wiley.

Lepper, M. (1973). Dissonance, self-perception, and honesty in children. *Journal of Personality and Social Psychology, 25*, 65–74.

Lepper, M. (1983). Extrinsic reward and intrinsic motivation: Implications for the classroom. In J. Levine and M. Wang (Eds.), *Teacher and student perspectives: Implications for learning* (pp. 281–317). Hillsdale, NJ: Erlbaum.

Lepper, M., & Chabay, R. (1985). Intrinsic motivation and instruction: Conflicting views on the role of motivational processes in computer-based education. *Educational Psychologist, 20*(4), 217–230.

Lepper, M., & Greene, D. (1978). *The hidden costs of reward: New perspectives on the psychology of human motivation.* Hillsdale, NJ: Erlbaum.

Lerner, R., & Lerner, J. (1977). Effects of age, sex, and physical attractiveness on child-peer relations, academic performance, and elementary school adjustment. *Developmental Psychology, 13*, 585–590.

Lesgold, A. (1986). Preparing children for a computer-rich world. *Educational Leadership, 43*(6), 7–11.

Levin, J. (1981). The mnemonic '80s: Keywords in the classroom. *Educational Psychologist, 16*, 65–82.

Levin, J., Schriberg, L., Miller, C., McCormick, C., & Levin, B. (1980). The keyword method in the classroom: How to remember the states and their capitols. *Elementary School Journal, 80*, 185–191.

Levine, D. (Ed.). (1985). *Improving student achievement through mastery learning programs*. San Francisco: Jossey-Bass.

Levstik, L. (1986). Teaching history: A definitional and developmental dilemma. In V. Atwood (Ed.), *Elementary school social studies: Research as guide to practice*. NCSS Bulletin No. 79 (pp. 68–84). Washington, D.C.: National Council for the Social Studies.

Levy, P., & Goldstein, H. (1984). *Tests in education: A book of critical reviews*. London: Academic Press.

Lewin, K., Lippitt, R., & White, R. (1939). Patterns of aggressive behavior in experimentally created social climates. *Journal of Social Psychology, 10*, 271–291.

Lickona, T. (Ed.). (1975). *Morality: A handbook of moral behavior*. New York: Holt, Rinehart and Winston.

Lipman, M. (1985). Thinking skills fostered by Philosophy for Children. In J. Segal, S. Chipman, & R. Glaser (Eds.), *Thinking and learning skills, Volume 1: Relating instruction to research*. Hillsdale, NJ: Erlbaum.

Lipman, M., Sharp, A., & Oscanyan, F. (1980). *Philosophy in the classroom* (2nd ed.). Philadelphia: Temple University Press.

Lipson, J., & Fisher, K. (1983). Technology and the classroom: Promise or threat? *Theory into Practice, 22*, 253–259.

Lockwood, A. (1978). The effects of values clarification and moral development curricula on school-age subjects: A critical review of recent research. *Review of Educational Research, 48*, 325–364.

Loehlin, J., Lindzey, G., & Spuhler, J. (1975). *Race differences in intelligence*. San Francisco: Freeman.

Loftus, E., & Loftus, G. (1980). On the permanence of stored information in the human brain. *American Psychologist, 35*, 409–420.

Loftus, G., & Loftus, E. (1976). *Human memory: The processing of information*. Hillsdale, NJ: Erlbaum.

Loman, N., & Mayer, R. (1983). Signaling techniques that increase the understandability of expository prose. *Journal of Educational Psychology, 75*, 402–412.

Lorayne, H., & Lucas, J. (1974). *The memory book*. New York: Ballantine.

Loughlin, R. (1961). On questioning. *Educational Forum, 25*, 481–482.

Lucker, G., Rosenfeld, D., Sikes, J., & Aronson, E. (1976). Performance in the interdependent classroom: A field study. *American Educational Research Journal, 13*, 115–123.

Luiten, J., Ames, W., & Ackerson, G. (1980). A meta-analysis of the effects of advance organizers on learning and retention. *American Educational Research Journal, 17*, 211–218.

Lukasevich, A., & Gray, R. (1978). Open space, open education, and pupil performance. *Elementary School Journal, 79*, 108–114.

Luria, A. (1976). *Cognitive development: Its cultural and social foundations*. Cambridge, MA: Harvard University Press.

Lynch, M., Norem-Hebeisen, A., & Gergen, K. (1981). *Self-concept: Advances in theory and research.* Cambridge, MA: Ballinger.

Maccoby, E. (1980). *Social development: Psychological growth and the parent-child relationship.* New York: Harcourt, Brace, and Jovanovich.

Maccoby, E., & Jacklin, C. (1974). *The psychology of sex differences.* Stanford: Stanford University Press.

Maccoby, E., & Martin, J. (1983). Socialization in the context of the family: Parent-child interaction. In P. Mussen (Ed.), *Handbook of child psychology* (4th ed., Vol. 4). New York: Wiley.

Mackenzie, B. (1984). Explaining race differences in IQ: The logic, the methodology, and the evidence. *American Psychologist, 39*, 1214–1233.

Mackinnon, D. (1962). The nature and nurture of creative talent. *American Psychologist, 17*, 484–495.

Macmillan, D., Jones, R., & Meyers, C. (1976). Mainstreaming the mildly retarded: Some questions, cautions, and guidelines. *Mental Retardation, 14*, 3–10.

Macmillan, D., Keogh, B., & Jones, R. (1986). Special educational research on mildly handicapped learners. In M. Wittrock (Ed.), *Handbook of research on teaching* (3rd ed.). New York: Macmillan.

Madden, N., & Slavin, R. (1983). Mainstreaming students with mild handicaps: Academic and social outcomes. *Review of Educational Research, 53*, 519–569.

Maehr, M. (1983). On doing well in science: Why Johnny no longer excels; why Sarah never did. In S. Paris, G. Olson, & H. Stevenson (Eds.), *Learning and motivation in the classroom.* Hillsdale, NJ: Erlbaum.

Maehr, M. (1984). Meaning and motivation: Toward a theory of personal investment. In R. Ames & C. Ames (Eds.), *Research on motivation in education* (Vol. 1). Orlando, FL: Academic Press.

Maehr, M., & Nicholls, J. (1980). Culture and achievement motivation: A second look. In N. Warren (Ed.), *Studies in cross-cultural psychology* (Vol. 2). New York: Academic Press.

Mager, R. (1962). *Preparing instructional objectives.* Palo Alto, CA: Fearon.

Malone, T., & Lepper, M. (1987). Making learning fun: A taxonomy of intrinsic motivation for learning. In R. Snow & M. Farr (Eds.), *Aptitude, learning, and instruction, Volume 3: Conative and affective process analysis.* Hillsdale, NJ: Erlbaum.

Mansfield, R., Busse, T., & Krepelka, E. (1978). The effectiveness of creativity training. *Review of Educational Research, 48*, 517–536.

Manske, M., & Davis, G. (1968). Effects of simple instructional biases upon performance in the unusual uses test. *Journal of General Psychology, 79*, 25–33.

Marcia, J. (1980). Identity in adolescence. In J. Adelson (Ed.), *Handbook of adolescent psychology.* New York: Wiley-Interscience.

Markman, E. (1981). Comprehension monitoring. In W. Dickson (Ed.), *Children's oral communication skills.* New York: Academic Press.

Marsh, R. (1985). Phrenoblysis: Real or chimera? *Child Development, 56*, 1059–1061.

Marshall, H. (1981). Open classrooms: Has the term outlived its usefulness? *Review of Educational Research, 51*, 181–192.

Marshall, H. (1987). Motivational strategies of three fifth-grade teachers. *Elementary School Journal, 88*, 135–150.

Marshall, H., & Weinstein, R. (April 1984). Classrooms where students perceive high and low amounts of differential teacher treatment. Paper presented at the annual meeting of the American Educational Research Association, New Orleans.

Marshall, K. (1985). Social studies curriculum revision, K–8: The Boston experience. *Social Education, 49*, 314–317.

Marshall, S., & Smith, J. (1987). Sex differences in learning mathematics: A longitudinal study with item and error analyses. *Journal of Educational Psychology, 79*, 372–383.

Marten, L., & Matlin, L. (1976). Does sexism in elementary readers still exist? *The Reading Teacher, 29*, 764–767.

Martin, B. (1975). Parent-child relations. In F. Horowitz (Ed.), *Review of child development research* (Vol. 4). Chicago: University of Chicago Press.

Martin, J. (1979). Effects of teacher higher-order questions on student process and product variables in a single-classroom study. *Journal of Educational Research, 72*, 183–187.

Martin, M. (1973). *Equal opportunity in the classroom*. ESEA, Title II: Session A Report. Los Angeles: County Superintendent of Schools, Division of Compensatory and Intergroup Programs.

Martorano, S. (1977). A developmental analysis of performance on Piaget's formal operation tasks. *Developmental Psychology, 13*, 666–672.

Maslow, A. (1954). *Motivation and personality*. New York: Harper & Row.

Maslow, A. (1962). *Toward a psychology of being*. Princeton, NJ: Van Nostrand.

Masters, J., Ford, M., Arend, R., Grotevant, H., & Clark, L. (1979). Modeling and labeling as integrated determinants of children's sex-typed imitative behavior. *Child Development, 50*, 364–371.

Matz, M. (1980). Towards a computational model of algebraic competence. *Journal of Mathematical Behavior, 3*, 93–166.

Mayer, R. (1975). Different problem-solving competencies established in learning computer programming with and without meaningful models. *Journal of Educational Psychology, 67*, 725–734.

Mayer, R. (1979a). Can advance organizers influence meaningful learning? *Review of Educational Research, 49*, 371–383.

Mayer, R. (1979b). Twenty years of research on advance organizers: Assimilation theory is still the best predictor of results. *Instructional Science, 8*, 133–167.

Mayer, R. (1981). Frequency norms and structural analysis of algebraic story problems into families, categories, and templates. *Instructional Science, 10*, 135–175.

Mayer, R. (1982). Learning. In H. Mitzel (Ed.), *Encyclopedia of Educational Research* (5th ed., Vol. 2). New York: The Free Press.

Mayer, R. (1983). *Thinking, problem solving, and cognition*. San Francisco: Freeman.

Mayer, R. (1984). Aids to text comprehension. *Educational Psychologist, 19*, 30–42.

Mayer, R. (1985). Instructional design theories: Building a linking science? *Contemporary Psychology, 30*, 156–157.

Mayer, R., & Cook, L. (1981). Effects of shadowing on prose comprehension and problem solving. *Memory and Cognition, 9*, 101–109.

Mayer, R., Dyck, J., & Cook, L. (1984). Techniques that help readers build mental models from scientific text: Definitions pretraining and signaling. *Journal of Educational Psychology, 76*, 1089–1105.

McCabe, A., Siegel, L., Spence, I., & Wilkenson, A. (1982). Class-inclusion reasoning: Patterns of performance from three to eight years. *Child Development, 53*, 780–785.

McCall, R., Appelbaum, M., & Hogarty, P. (1973). Developmental changes in mental performance. *Monographs of the Society for Research in Child Development, 38* (No. 3, Serial No. 150).

McCandless, B., & Coop, R. (1979). *Adolescents: Behavior and development* (2nd ed.). New York: Holt, Rinehart and Winston.

McCandless, B., & Evans, E. (1973). *Children and youth: Psychosocial development*. Hinsdale, IL: Dryden.

McColskey, W., & Leary, M. R. (1985). Differential effects of norm-referenced and self-referenced feedback on performance expectancies, attributions, and motivation. *Contemporary Educational Psychology, 10*, 275–284.

McCombs, B. (1984). Processes and skills underlying continuing intrinsic motivation to learn: Toward a definition of motivational skills training and intervention. *Educational Psychologist, 19*, 199–218.

McConkie, G. (1977). Learning from text. In L. Shulman (Ed.), *Review of research in education* (Vol. 5). Itasca, IL: Peacock.

McCormick, C., & Levin, J. (1984). A comparison of different prose-learning variations of the mnemonic keyword method. *American Educational Research Journal, 21*, 379–398.

McDaniel, M., & Pressley, M. (1984). Putting the keyword method in context. *Journal of Educational Psychology, 76*, 598–609.

McDaniel, M., & Tillman, V. (1987). Discovering a meaning versus applying the keyword method: Effects on recall. *Contemporary Educational Psychology, 12*, 156–175.

McDonald, F. J. (1965). *Educational psychology* (2nd ed.). Belmont, CA: Wadsworth.

McDonald, F. (1977). Research on teaching: Report on Phase II of the Beginning Teacher Evaluation Study. In G. Borich & K. Fenton (Eds.), *The appraisal of teaching: Concepts and process*. Reading, MA: Addison-Wesley.

McDonnel, L. (1985). Implementing low-cost school improvement strategies. *Elementary School Journal, 85*, 423–438.

McGeoch, J., & McDonald, W. (1931). Meaningful relation and retroactive inhibition. *American Journal of Psychology, 43*, 579–588.

McGuire, K., & Weisz, J. (1982). Social cognition and behavior correlates of preadolescent chumship. *Child Development, 53*, 1478–1484.

McKay, H., Sinisterra, L., McKay, A., Gomez, H., & Lloreda, P. (1978). Improving cognitive ability in chronically deprived children. *Science, 200*, 270–278.

McKeachie, W., & Kulik, J. (1975). Effective college training. In F. Kerlinger (Ed.), *Review of Research in Education*. Itasca, IL: Peacock.

McKenzie, G. (1986). Learning and instruction. In V. Atwood (Ed.), *Elementary school social studies: Research as guide to practice*. NCSS Bulletin No. 79 (pp. 119–136). Washington, DC: National Council for the Social Studies.

McLaughlin, T. (1976). Self-control in the classroom. *Review of Educational Research, 46*, 631–663.

McLeish, J. (1976). The lecture method. In N. Gage (Ed.), *The psychology of teaching methods*. The seventy-fifth yearbook of the National Society for the Study of Education, (Part I). Chicago: University of Chicago Press.

McMann, F. (1979). In defense of lecture. *Social Studies, 70*, 270–274.

McNamee, S. (1978). Moral behavior, moral development and motivation. *Journal of Moral Education, 7*, 27–31.

Medley, D., Rosenblum, E., & Vance, N. (1989). Assessing the functional knowledge of participants in the Virginia Beginning Teacher Assistance Program. *Elementary School Journal, 89*(4), 495–510.

Medway, F. M., & Venino, G. R. (1982). The effects of effort feedback and performance patterns on children's attribution and task persistence. *Contemporary Educational Psychology, 77*, 623–630.

Meehan, A. (1984). A meta-analysis of sex differences in formal operational thought. *Child Development, 55*, 1110–1124.

Mehrens, W., & Lehmann, I. (1978). *Measurement and evaluation in education and psychology* (2nd ed.). New York: Holt, Rinehart and Winston.

Meichenbaum, D. (1977). *Cognitive-behavior modification*. New York: Plenum.

Meichenbaum, D., & Asarnow, J. (1979). Cognitive-behavioral modification and metacognitive development: Implications for the classroom. In P. Kendall & S. Hollon (Eds.), *Cognitive-behavioral intervention: Theory, research, and procedures*. New York: Academic Press.

Meichenbaum, D., & Goodman, J. (1971). Training impulsive children to talk to themselves: A means of developing self-control. *Journal of Abnormal Psychology, 77*, 115–126.

Mercer, J. (1973). *Labeling the mentally retarded*. Berkeley: University of California Press.

Merrill, M., & Tennyson, R. (1977). *Concept teaching: An instructional design guide*. Englewood Cliffs, NJ: Educational Technology.

Messer, S. (1972). The relation of internal-external control to academic performance. *Child Development, 43*, 1456–1462.

Messick, S. (1984). Assessment in context: Appraising student performance in relation to instructional quality. *Educational Researcher, 13*, 3–8.

Metz, M. (1978). *Classrooms and corridors: The crisis of authority in desegregated secondary schools*. Berkeley: University of California Press.

Meyer, B. (1977). The structure of prose: Effects on learning and memory and implications for educational practice. In R. Anderson, R. Spiro, & W. Montague (Eds.), *Schooling and the acquisition of knowledge*. Hillsdale, NJ: Erlbaum.

Meyer, B. (1981). Basic research on prose comprehension: A critical review. In D. Fisher & C. Peters (Eds.), *Comprehension and the competent reader*. New York: Praeger.

Milak, J. (1980). *A comparison of two approaches of teaching brass instruments to elementary school children*. Doctoral dissertation, Washington University, St. Louis.

Miller, G. (1956). The magical number seven, plus or minus two: Some limits on our capacity for processing information. *Psychological Review, 63*, 81–97.

Miller, L., & Bizzell, R. (1983). Long-term effects of four preschool programs: Sixth, seventh, and eighth grades. *Child Development, 54*, 727–741.

Miller, P. (1983). *Theories of developmental psychology*. San Francisco: Freeman.

Miller, R., Brickman, P., & Bolen, D. (1975). Attribution versus persuasion as a means for modifying behavior. *Journal of Personality and Social Psychology, 31*, 430–441.

Miller, S. (1986). Certainty and necessity in the understanding of Piagetian concepts. *Developmental Psychology, 22*, 3–18.

Miller, S., Brownell, C., & Zukier, H. (1977). Cognitive certainty in children: Effects of concept, developmental level, and method of assessment. *Developmental Psychology, 13*, 236–245.

Mills, S., Rice, C., Berliner, D., & Rousseau, E. (1980). The correspondence between teacher questions and student answers in classroom discourse. *Journal of Experimental Education, 48*, 194–204.

Minsky, M. (1975). A framework for representing knowledge. In P. Winston (Ed.), *The psychology of computer vision*. New York: McGraw-Hill.

Mitzel, H. (Ed.). (1982). *Encyclopedia of Educational Research*, 4 vols. (5th ed.). New York: Macmillan.

Modgil, S., & Modgil, C. (Eds.). (1982). *Jean Piaget: Consensus and controversy*. New York: Praeger.

Moessinger, P. (1978). Piaget on equilibration. *Human Development, 21*, 255–267.

Morgan, M. (1985). Self-monitoring of attained subgoals in private study. *Journal of Education Psychology, 77*, 623–630.

Morse, W. (1971). Worksheet on life space interviewing for teachers. In N. Long, W. Morse, & R. Newman (Eds.), *Conflict in the classroom: The education of children with problems* (2nd ed.). Belmont, CA: Wadsworth.

Mosher, R., (Ed.). (1980). *Moral education: A first generation of research and development*. New York: Praeger.

Moskowitz, G., & Hayman, J. (1976). Success strategies of inner-city teachers: A year-long study. *Journal of Educational Research, 69*, 283–289.

Moskowitz, J., Malvin, J., Schaeffer, G., & Schaps, E. (1985). Evaluation of Jigsaw, a cooperative learning technique. *Contemporary Educational Psychology, 10*, 104–112.

Mueller, C., & Parcel, T. (1981). Measures of socioeconomic status: Alternatives and recommendations. *Child Development, 52*, 13–30.

Murray, E. (1964). *Motivation and emotion*. New York: Prentice-Hall.

Murray, F. (1978). Teaching strategies and conservation training. In A. Lesgold, J. Pellegrino, S. Fokkema, & R. Glaser (Eds.), *Cognitive psychology and instruction*. New York: Plenum.

Murray, F., Ames, G., & Botvin, G. (1977). Acquisition of conservation through cognitive dissonance. *Journal of Educational Psychology, 69*, 519–527.

Murray, H. (1938). *Explorations in personality*. New York: Oxford University Press.

Mussen, P., & Eisenberg-Berg, N. (1977). *Roots of caring, sharing, and helping*. San Francisco: Freeman.

Mussen, P., & Jones, M. (1957). Self-conceptions, motivations, and interpersonal attitudes of late- and early-maturing boys. *Child Development, 28*, 243–256.

Myers, R., & Torrance, E. (1966). *Plots, puzzles, and ploys*. Boston: Ginn.

Nagy, P., & Griffiths, A. (1982). Limitations of recent research relating Piaget's theory to adolescent thought. *Review of Educational Research, 52*, 513–556.

Nardine, F. (1971). The development of competence. In G. S. Lesser (Ed.), *Psychology and educational practice*. Glenview, IL: Scott, Foresman.

Nash, R. (1976). Pupils' expectations of their teachers. In M. Stubbs & S. Delamont (Eds.), *Explorations in classroom observation*. New York: Wiley.

Natriello, G., & Dornbusch, S. (1985). *Teacher evaluative standard and student effort*. New York: Longman.

Neimark, E. (1979). Current status of formal operations research. *Human Development, 22*, 60–67.

Neimark, E., & Santa, J. (1975). Thinking and concept attainment. In M. Rosenzweig & L. Porter (Eds.), *Annual review of psychology* (Vol. 26). Palo Alto, CA: Annual Reviews.

Nelson, K. (1977). Facilitating children's syntax acquisition. *Developmental Psychology, 13*, 101–107.

Newell, A., & Simon, H. (1972). *Human problem solving*. Englewood Cliffs, NJ: Prentice-Hall.

Nicholls, J. (1976). Effort is virtuous, but it's better to have ability: Evaluative responses to perceptions of effort and ability. *Journal of Research in Personality, 10*, 306–315.

Nicholls, J. (1979). Quality and equality in intellectual development: The role of motivation in education. *American Psychologist, 34*, 1071–1083.

Nicholls, J. (1983). Conceptions of ability and achievement motivation: A theory and its implications for education. In S. Paris, G. Olson, & H. Stevenson (Eds.), *Learning and motivation in the classroom*. Hillsdale, NJ: Erlbaum.

Nicholls, J. (1984). Conceptions of ability and achievement motivation. In R. Ames & C. Ames (Eds.), *Research on motivation in education* (Vol. 1). Orlando, FL: Academic Press.

Nickerson, R., Perkins, D., & Smith, E. (1985). *The teaching of thinking*. Hillsdale, NJ: Erlbaum.

Ninth Annual Report to Congress on the Implementation of the Education of the Handicapped Act (1987). Prepared by the Division of Innovation and Development Office of Special Education Programs, U.S. Department of Education, Washington, D.C.

Nisan, M., & Kohlberg, L. (1982). Universality and variation in moral judgment: A longitudinal and cross-sectional study in Turkey. *Child Development, 53*, 865–876.

Norcini, J., & Snyder, S. (1983). The effects of modeling and cognitive induction on the moral reasoning of adolescents. *Journal of Youth and Adolescence, 12*, 101–115.

Novak, J., & Gowin, D. (1984). *Learning how to learn*. New York: Cambridge University Press.

Nucci, L. (1987). Synthesis of research on moral development. *Educational Leadership, 44*(5), 86–92.

Nuthall, G., & Church, J. (1973). Experimental studies of teaching behaviour. In G. Chanan (Ed.), *Toward a science of teaching*. London: National Foundation for Educational Research.

Oakland, T. (Ed.). (1977). *Psychological and educational assessment of minority children*. New York: Brunner/Mazel.

Ogbu, J. (Spring 1988). Human intelligence testing: A cultural-ecological perspective. *National Forum, 68*(2), 23–29.

Ohlsson, S. (1983). The enaction theory of thinking and its educational implications. *Scandinavian Journal of Educational Research, 27*, 73–88.

Okebukola, P. (1985). The relative effectiveness of cooperative and competitive interaction techniques in strengthening students' performance in science classes. *Science Education, 69*, 501–509.

O'Leary, K., Kaufman, K., Kass, R., & Drabman, R. (1970). The effects of loud and soft reprimands on the behavior of disruptive students. *Exceptional Children, 27*, 145–155.

O'Leary, K., & O'Leary, S. (Eds.). (1977). *Classroom management: The successful use of behavior modification* (2nd ed.). New York: Pergamon.

O'Leary, S., & Dubey, D. (1979). Applications of self-control procedures by children: A review. *Journal of Applied Behavior Analysis, 12*, 449–465.

Olejnik, A. (1980). Adults' moral reasoning with children. *Child Development, 51*, 1285–1288.

O'Neil, H. (Ed.). (1978). *Learning strategies*. New York: Academic Press.

O'Neil, H., & Spielberger, C. (Eds.). (1979). *Cognitive and affective learning strategies*. New York: Academic Press.

Orbach, E. (1977). Some theoretical considerations in the evaluation of instructional games. *Simulation and Games, 8*, 341–360.

Orlofsky, J. (1976). Intimacy status: Relationship to interpersonal perception. *Journal of Youth and Adolescence, 5*, 73–83.

Orlofsky, J., & Ginsburg, S. (1981). Intimacy status: Relationship to affect cognition. *Adolescence, 16*, 91–100.

Orlofsky, J., Marcia, J., & Lesser, I. (1973). Ego identity states and the intimacy vs. isolation crisis of young adulthood. *Journal of Youth and Adolescence, 27*, 211–219.

Osborn, J. (1984). Workbooks that accompany basal reading programs. In G. Duffy, L. Roehler, & J. Mason (Eds.), *Comprehension instruction: Perspectives and suggestions*. New York: Longman.

Osofsky, J. (1976). Neonatal characteristics and mother-infant interaction in two observational situations. *Child Development, 47*, 1138–1147.

Owen, S., Blount, H., & Moscow, H. (1978). *Educational psychology: An introduction*. Boston: Little, Brown.

Page, R. (1981). Longitudinal evidence for the sequentiality of Kohlberg's stages of moral judgment in adolescent males. *Journal of Genetic Psychology, 139*, 3–9.

Palincsar, A. (1986). Metacognitive strategy instruction. *Exceptional children, 53*(2), 118–124.

Palincsar, A., & Brown, A. (1984). Reciprocal teaching of comprehension-fostering and comprehension-monitoring activities. *Cognition and Instruction, 1*, 117–175.

Palincsar, A., & Brown, A. (1987). Advances in improving the cognitive performance of handicapped students. In M. Wang, M. Reynolds, and H. Walberg (Eds.), *Handbook of special education: Research in practice, 1*, 93–112. Oxford: Pergamon.

Palincsar, A., & Brown, A. (1989). Classroom dialogues to promote self-regulated comprehension. In J. Brophy (Ed.), *Advances in research on teaching, Volume 1:*

Teaching for meaningful understanding and self-regulated learning. Greenwich, CT: JAI Press.

Papert, S. (1980). *Mindstorms: Children, computers, and powerful ideas*. New York: Basic Books.

Parikh, B. (1980). Development of moral judgment and its relation to family environmental factors in Indian and American families. *Child Development, 51*, 1030–1039.

Paris, S., Cross, D., & Lipson, M. (1984). Informed strategies for learning: A program to improve children's reading awareness and comprehension. *Journal of Educational Psychology, 76*, 1239–1252.

Paris, S., Lipson, M., & Wixson, K. (1983). Becoming a strategic reader. *Contemporary Educational Psychology, 8*, 293–316.

Paris, S., & Myers, M. (1981). Comprehension monitoring in good and poor readers. *Journal of Reading Behavior, 13*, 5–22.

Paris, S., & Oka, E. (1986). Self-regulated learning among exceptional children. *Exceptional children, 53*, 103–108.

Parnes, S. (1967). *Creative behavior guidebook*. New York: Scribner's.

Parsons, J. (Ed.). (1980). *The psychobiology of sex differences and sex roles*. Washington, DC: Hemisphere.

Patterson, C. (1973). *Humanistic education*. Englewood Cliffs, NJ: Prentice-Hall.

Patterson, G., & Stouthamer-Loeber, M. (1984). The correlation of family management practices and delinquency. *Child Development, 55*, 1299–1307.

Pavlov, I. (1927). *Conditional reflexes*. London: Oxford University Press.

Pearson, P., & Dole, J. A. (1987). Explicit comprehension instruction: A review of research and a new conceptualization of instruction. *Elementary School Journal, 88*, 151–165.

Pearson, P., & Gallagher, M. (1983). The instruction of reading comprehension. *Contemporary Educational Psychology, 8*, 317–344.

Pearson, P., & Johnson, D. (1978). *Teaching reading comprehension*. New York: Holt, Rinehart and Winston.

Pellegrini, A. (1982). The effects of exploration training on young children's associative fluency. *Creative Child and Adult Quarterly, 7*, 226–233.

Perlmuter, L., & Monty, R. (1979). *Choice and perceived control*. Hillsdale, NJ: Erlbaum.

Perrott, E. (1982). *Effective teaching: A practical guide to improving your teaching*. New York: Longman.

Perry, M. (1988). Problem assignment and learning outcomes in nine fourth-grade mathematics classes. *Elementary School Journal, 88*(4), 413–426.

Peskin, J. (1980). Female performance and Inhelder and Piaget's tests of formal operations. *Genetic Psychology Monographs, 101*, 245–256.

Peters, R. (1988). Working smarter: The business of practical intelligence. *National Forum*, Spring, *68*(2), 12–14.

Petersen, A., & Taylor, B. (1980). Puberty: Biological change and psychological adaptation. In J. Adelson (Ed.), *Handbook of adolescent psychology*. New York: Wiley.

Peterson, P. (1979). Direct instruction reconsidered. In P. Peterson and H. Walberg (Eds.), *Research on teaching: Concepts, findings and implications*. Berkeley, CA: McCutchan.

Peterson, P. (1988). Selecting students and services for compensatory education: Lessons from aptitude-treatment interaction research. *Educational Psychologist, 23*, 313–352.

Peterson, P., & Comeaux, M. (1987). Teachers' schemata for classroom events: The mental scaffolding of teachers' thinking during classroom instruction. *Teaching and Teacher Education, 3*, 319–331.

Petty, O., & Jansson, L. (1987). Sequencing examples and nonexamples to facilitate concept attainment. *Journal for Research in Mathematics Education, 18*, 112–125.

Pflaum, S., Pascarella, E., Boswick, M., &

Auer, C. (1980). The influence of pupil behaviors and pupil status factors on teacher behaviors during oral reading lessons. *Journal of Educational Research, 74*, 99–105.

Piaget, J. (1932). *The moral judgment of the child* (Translated by M. Worden). New York: Harcourt, Brace, and World.

Piaget, J. (1970). *Science of education and the psychology of the child*. New York: Orion.

Piaget, J. (1983). Piaget's theory. In P. Mussen (Ed.), *Handbook of child psychology* (4th ed., Vol. 1). New York: Wiley.

Piaget, J., & Inhelder, B. (1964). *The early growth of logic in the child* (Translated by L. Lunzer & D. Papert). London: Routledge & Kegan Paul.

Piattelli-Palmarini, M. (Ed.). (1980). *Language and learning: The debate between Jean Piaget and Noam Chomsky*. Cambridge: Harvard University Press.

Pichert, J., & Anderson, R. (1977). Taking different perspectives on a story. *Journal of Educational Psychology, 69*, 309–315.

Plass, J. A., & Hill, K. T. (1986). Children's achievement strategies and performance: The role of time pressure, evaluation anxiety, and sex. *Developmental Psychology, 22*, 31–36.

Plomin, R., & Foch, T. (1981). Sex differences and individual differences. *Child Development, 52*, 383–385.

Policastro, M. (1975). Notetaking: The key to college success. *Journal of Reading, 18*, 372–375.

Polya, G. (1957). *How to solve it* (2nd ed.). Princeton, NJ: Princeton University Press.

Popham, W. (1972). *Criterion-referenced measurement*. Englewood Cliffs, NJ: Educational Technology Publications.

Porter, A., Floden, R., Freeman, D., Schmidt, W., & Schwille, J. (1988). Content determinants in elementary school mathematics. In D. Grouws and T. Cooney (Eds.), *Perspectives on research on effective mathematics teaching* (Vol. 1, pp. 96–113). Reston, VA: Lawrence Erlbaum and National Council of Teachers of Mathematics.

Posner, G., & Rudnitsky, A. (1986). *Course design: A guide to curriculum development for teachers* (3rd ed.). New York: Longman.

Pozner, J., & Saltz, E. (1974). Social class, conditional communication, and egocentric speech. *Developmental Psychology, 10*, 764–771.

Pratt, M., Golding, G., & Hunter, W. (1984). Does morality have a gender? Sex, sex role, and moral judgment relationships across the adult lifespan. *Merrill-Palmer Quarterly, 30*, 321–340.

Prawat, R., & Nickerson, J. (1985). Relationship between teacher thought and action and student affective outcomes. *Elementary School Journal, 85*, 529–540.

Premack, D. (1965). Reinforcement theory. In D. Levine (Ed.), *Nebraska Symposium on Motivation* (Vol. 13). Lincoln, NE: University of Nebraska Press.

Pressey, S. (1932). A third and fourth contribution toward the coming "industrial revolution" in education. *School and Society, 36*, 668–672.

Pressley, M. (1979). Increasing children's self-control through cognitive interventions. *Review of Educational Research, 49*, 319–370.

Pressley, M., & Dennis-Rounds, J. (1980). Transfer of a mnemonic keyword strategy at two age levels. *Journal of Educational Psychology, 72*, 575–582.

Pressley, M., Levin, J., Kuiper, N., Bryant, S., & Michener, S. (1982). Mnemonic versus nonmnemonic vocabulary-learning strategies: Additional comparisons. *Journal of Educational Psychology, 74*, 693–707.

Pressley, M., Levin, J., & Miller, G. (1982). The keyword method compared to alternative vocabulary-learning strategies. *Contemporary Educational Psychology, 7*, 50–60.

Pressley, M., Reynolds, W., Stark, K., & Gettinger, M. (1983). Cognitive strategy training and children's self-control. In M. Pressley & J. Levin (Eds.), *Cognitive strategy research: Psychological foundations*. New York: Springer-Verlag.

Preston, R. (1962). Reading achievement of German and American children. *School and Society, 90*, 350–354.

Purkey, S. C., & Smith, M. S. (1985). School reform: The district policy implications of effective school literature. *Elementary School Journal, 85*, 353–389.

Purkey, W. (1970). *Self-concept and school achievement*. Englewood Cliffs, NJ: Prentice-Hall.

Purpel, D., & Ryan, K. (Eds.). (1976). *Moral education . . . it comes with the territory*. Berkeley, CA: McCutchan.

Raphael, T. (1984). Teaching learners about sources of information for answering comprehension questions. *Journal of Reading, 27*, 303–311.

Raths, L., Harmin, M., & Simon, S. (1966). *Values in teaching*. Columbus: Merrill.

Rebbeck, B. J. (1983). Foreign language techniques for the gifted or watch your blooming language! *Roeper Review, 5*(4), 136–139.

Redfield, D., & Rousseau, E. (1981). A meta-analysis of experimental research on teacher questioning behavior. *Review of Educational Research, 51*, 237–245.

Redl, F. (1966). *When we deal with children*. New York: Free Press.

Redl, F., & Wineman, D. (1951). *Children who hate*. New York: Free Press.

Reigeluth, C. (Ed.). (1983). *Instructional-design theories and models: An overview of their current status*. Hillsdale, NJ: Erlbaum.

Renner, J., Stafford, D., Lawson, A., McKinnon, J., Friot, E., & Kellogg, D. (1976). *Research on teaching and learning with the Piaget model*. Norman: University of Oklahoma Press.

Renzulli, J., Smith, L., & Reis, S. (1982). Curriculum compacting: An essential strategy for working with gifted students. *Elementary School Journal, 82*, 185–194.

Rescorla, R. (1988). Pavlovian conditioning: It's not what you think it is. *American Psychologist, 43*, 151–160.

Rest, J. (1974). Developmental psychology as a guide to value education: A review of "Kohlbergian" programs. *Review of Educational Research, 44*, 241–259.

Rest, J., Davison, M., & Robbins, S. (1978). Age trends in judging moral issues: A review of cross-sectional, longitudinal, and sequential studies of the Defining Issues Test. *Child Development, 49*, 263–279.

Reynolds, M. (1978). Some final notes. In J. Grosenick & M. Reynolds (Eds.), *Teacher education: Renegotiating roles for mainstreaming*. Reston, VA: Council for Exceptional Children.

Reynolds, M. (1984). Classification of students with handicaps. In E. W. Gord (Ed.), *Review of research in education* (Vol. 2, pp. 63–92). Washington, DC: American Educational Research Association.

Reynolds, M., & Birch, J. (1988). *Adaptive mainstreaming: A primer for teachers and principals* (3rd ed.). White Plains, NY: Longman.

Reynolds, R., & Anderson, R. (1982). Influence of questions on the allocation of attention during reading. *Journal of Educational Psychology, 74*, 623–632.

Rice, D. (1977). The effect of question-asking instruction on preservice elementary science teachers. *Journal of Research in Science Teaching, 14*, 353–359.

Rickards, J. (1979). Adjunct postquestions in text: A critical review of methods and processes. *Review of Educational Research, 49*, 181–196.

Rickards, J. (1982). Homework. In H. Mitzel (Ed.), *Encyclopedia of Educational Research* (5th ed.). New York: The Free Press.

Rickards, J., & August, G. (1975). Generative underlining strategies in prose recall. *Journal of Educational Psychology, 67*, 860–865.

Reynolds, M. (1987). Introduction to section 3. In M. Wang, M. Reynolds, & H. Waberg. *Handbook of special education: Research and practice.* Vol. I, pp. 251–252. Oxford: Pergamon Press.

Riegel, K. (1973). Dialectic operations: The final period of cognitive development. *Human Development, 16*, 346–370.

Riley, J. (1980). The effects of teachers' wait-time and cognitive questioning level on pupil science achievement. Paper presented at the annual meeting of the National Association for Research in Science Teaching, Boston.

Riley, M., Greeno, J., & Heller, J. (1982). The development of children's problem solving ability in arithmetic. In H. Ginsberg (Ed.), *The development of mathematical thinking*. New York: Academic Press.

Ringness, T. (1975). *The affective domain in education*. Boston: Little, Brown.

Rippey, R. (1975). Speech compressors for lecture review. *Educational Technology, 15* (November), 58–59.

Robin, A. (1976). Behavioral instruction in the college classroom. *Review of Educational Research, 46*, 313–354.

Robin, A., Schneider, M., & Dolnick, M. (1976). The turtle technique: An extended case study of self-control in the classroom. *Psychology in the Schools, 13*, 449–453.

Robinson, F. (1970). *Effective study* (4th ed.). New York: Harper & Row.

Rogers, C. (1983). *Freedom to learn: For the 80s*. Columbus: Merrill.

Rogers, C., Smith, M., & Coleman, J. (1978). Social comparison in the classroom: The relationship between academic achievement and self-concept. *Journal of Educational Psychology, 70*, 50–57.

Rogoff, B. (1981). Schooling and the development of cognitive skills. In H. Triandis & A. Heron (Eds.), *Handbook of cross-cultural psychology: Developmental psychology* (Vol. 4). Boston: Allyn and Bacon.

Rogoff, B., & Wertsch, J. (Eds.). (1984). *Children's learning in the "zone" of proximal development*. San Francisco: Jossey-Bass.

Rohner, R., & Nielsen, C. (1978). *Parental acceptance and rejection: A review and annotated bibliography of research and theory*. New Haven: HRAF Press.

Rohrkemper, M., & Brophy, J. (1983). Teachers' thinking about problem students. In J. Levine & M. Wang (Eds.), *Teacher and student perceptions: Implications for learning*. Hillsdale, NJ: Erlbaum.

Rohrkemper, M., & Corno, L. (1988). Success and failure on classroom tasks: Adaptive learning and classroom teaching. *Elementary School Journal, 88*, 297–312.

Rollins, H., & Genser, L. (1977). Role of cognitive style in a cognitive task: A case favoring the impulsive approach to problem solving. *Journal of Educational Psychology, 69*, 281–287.

Rosch, E. (1978). Principles of categorization. In E. Rosch & B. Lloyd (Eds.), *Cognition and categorization*. Hillsdale, NJ: Erlbaum.

Rosch, E., & Lloyd, B. (Eds.). (1978). *Cognition and categorization*. Hillsdale, NJ: Erlbaum.

Rosch, E., & Mervis, C. (1975). Family resemblances: Studies in the internal structure of categories. *Cognitive Psychology, 7*, 573–605.

Rosch, E., Mervis, C., Gray, W., Johnson, D., & Boyes-Braem, P. (1976). Basic objects in natural categories. *Cognitive Psychology, 8*, 382–439.

Rosenbaum, J. (1976). *Making inequality*. New York: Wiley-Interscience.

Rosenbaum, M., & Drabman, R. (1979). Self-control training in the classroom: A review and critique. *Journal of Applied Behavior Analysis, 12*, 467–485.

Rosenfield, P., Lambert, N., & Black, A. (1985). Desk arrangement effects on pupil classroom behavior. *Journal of Educational Psychology, 77*(1), 101–108.

Rosenholtz, S. (1989). *Teachers' workplace:*

The social organization of work. New York: Longman.

Rosenholtz, S., & Rosenholtz, S. (1981). Classroom organization and the perception of ability. *Sociology of Education, 54*, 132–140.

Rosenholtz, S., & Smylie, M. (1984). Teacher compensation and career ladders. *Elementary School Journal, 85*, 149–166.

Rosenshine, B. (1970). Enthusiastic teaching: A research review. *School Review, 78*, 499–514.

Rosenshine, B. (1983). Teaching functions in instructional programs. *Elementary School Journal, 83*, 335–351.

Rosenshine, R. (1968). To explain: A review of research. *Educational Leadership, 26*, 275–280.

Rosenthal, R., & Jacobson, L. (1968). *Pygmalion in the classroom: Teacher expectation and pupil's intellectual development.* New York: Holt, Rinehart & Winston.

Ross, R. (1984). Classroom segments: The structuring of school time. In L. Anderson (Ed.), *Time and school learning: Theory research and practice.* London: Croom Helm.

Rosswork, F. (1977). Goal setting: The effects on an academic task with varying magnitudes of incentive. *Journal of Educational Psychology, 69*, 710–715.

Rothkopf, E. (1970). The concept of mathemagenic activities. *Review of Educational Research, 40*, 325–336.

Rotter, J. (1966). Generalized expectancies for internal versus external control of reinforcement. *Psychological Monographs, 80*, 1–28.

Rotter, J. (1980). Interpersonal trust, trustworthiness, and gullibility. *American Psychologist, 35*, 1–7.

Rowe, M. (1974). Wait-time and rewards as instructional variables, their influence on language, logic and fate control: Part I. Wait-time. *Journal of Research in Science Teaching, 11*, 81–94.

Rowe, M. (1986). Wait time: Slowing down may be a way of speeding up! *Journal of Teacher Education, 37*, 43–50.

Royer, J., & Cable, G. (1975). Facilitated learning in connected discourse. *Journal of Educational Psychology, 67*, 116–123.

Rozin, P., Fallon, A., & Mandell, R. (1984). Family resemblence in attitudes to foods. *Developmental Psychology, 20*, 309–314.

Rubenstein, N. (1975). *Patterns of problem solving.* Englewood Cliffs, NJ: Prentice-Hall.

Rubin, A. (1982). The computer confronts language arts: Cans and shoulds for education. In A. Wilkinson (Ed.), *Classroom computers and cognitive science.* New York: Academic Press.

Ruble, D., & Brooks-Gunn, J. (1982). The experience of menarche. *Child Development, 53*, 1557–1566.

Ruble, D., & Flett, G. (1988). Conflicting goals in self-evaluative information seeking: Developmental and ability level analysis. *Child Development, 59*, 97–106.

Rumelhart, D. (1975). Notes on a schema for stories. In D. Bobrow & A. Collins (Eds.), *Representation and understanding.* New York: Academic Press.

Rumelhart, D., Lindsay, P., & Norman, D. (1972). A process model for long-term memory. In E. Tulving & W. Donaldson (Eds.), *Organization of memory.* New York: Academic Press.

Rumelhart, D., & Norman, D. (1978). Accretion, tuning, and restructuring: Three modes of learning. In J. Cotton & R. Klatzky (Eds.), *Semantic factors in cognition.* Hillsdale, NJ: Erlbaum.

Runions, T. (1980). The mentor academy program: Educating the gifted/talented for the 80's. *Gifted Child Quarterly, 24*(4), 152–157.

Rushton, J., & Sorrentino, R. (Eds.). (1981). *Altruism and helping behavior: Social, personality, and developmental perspectives.* Hillsdale, NJ: Erlbaum.

Russell, J. (1982). Cognitive conflict, transmission, and justification: Conservation attainment through dyadic interaction.

Journal of Genetic Psychology, 140, 283–297.

Russell, P. (1979). *The Brain Book*. New York: Dutton.

Rutter, M. (1983). School effects on pupil progress: Research findings and policy implications. In L. Shulman & G. Sykes (Eds.), *Handbook of teaching and policy*. New York: Longman.

Ryan, E. (1981). Identifying and remediating failure in reading comprehension: Toward an instructional approach for poor comprehenders. In T. Waller & G. MacKinnon (Eds.), *Advances in reading research*. New York: Academic Press.

Ryan, F. (1973). Differentiated effects of levels of questioning on student achievement. *Elementary School Journal, 41*, 63–67.

Ryan, F. (1974). The effects on social studies achievement of multiple student responding to different levels of questioning. *Journal of Experimental Education, 42*, 71–75.

Ryan, R. (1982). Control and information in the intrapersonal sphere: An extension of cognitive evaluation theory. *Journal of Personality and Social Psychology, 43*, 450–461.

Sachs, J. (1967). Recognition memory for syntactic and semantic aspects of connected discourse. *Perception and Psychophysics, 2*, 437–442.

Sadker, M., & Sadker, D. (1986). Sexism in the classroom: From grade school to graduate school. *Phi Delta Kappan, 67*, 512–515.

Safer, D., & Allen, R. (1976). *Hyperactive children: Diagnosis and management*. Baltimore: University Park Press.

Safford, P. (1978). *Teaching young children with special needs*. St. Louis: Mosby.

Sagaria, S., & DiVesta, F. (1978). Learner expectations induced by adjunct questions and the retrieval of intentional and incidental information. *Journal of Educational Psychology, 17*, 280–288.

Sagerman, N., & Mayer, R. (1987). Forward transfer of different reading strategies evoked by adjunct questions in science text. *Journal of Educational Psychology, 79*, 189–191.

Sagotsky, G., Patterson, C., & Lepper, M. (1978). Training children's self-control: A field experiment in self-monitoring and goal-setting in the classroom. *Journal of Experimental Child Psychology, 25*, 242–253.

Samelson, F. (1980). J. B. Watson's Little Albert, Cyril Burt's twins, and the need for a critical science. *American Psychologist, 35*, 619–625.

Samson, G., Strykowski, B., Weinstein, T., & Walberg, H. (1987). The effects of teacher questioning levels on student achievement: A quantitative synthesis. *Journal of Educational Research, 80*, 290–295.

Samuel, W. (1977). Observed IQ as a function of test atmosphere, tester expectation, and race of tester: A replication for female subjects. *Journal of Educational Psychology, 69*, 593–604.

Sandoval, J., & Irwin, M. (1988). Review of the Stanford-Binet Intelligence Scale: Fourth edition. *Professional School Psychology, 3*(2), 157–161.

Sarason, I., & Sarason, B. (1981). Teaching cognitive and social skills to high school students. *Journal of Consulting and Clinical Psychology, 49*, 908–918.

Satterly, D. (1976). Cognitive styles, spatial ability, and school achievement. *Journal of Educational Psychology, 68*, 36–42.

Savin-Williams, R. (1979). Dominance hierarchies in groups of early adolescents. *Child Development, 50*, 923–935.

Scarr-Salapatek, S. (1975). Genetics and the development of intelligence. In F. Horowitz (Ed.), *Review of research in child development* (Vol. 4). Chicago: University of Chicago Press.

Schaffer, R. (1977). *Mothering*. Cambridge: Cambridge University Press.

Schank, R., & Abelson, R. (1977). *Scripts, plans, goals, and understanding*. Hillsdale, NJ: Erlbaum.

Schiedel, D., & Marcia, J. (1985). Ego identity, intimacy, sex role orientation, and gender. *Developmental Psychology, 21*, 149–160.

Schiff, M., Duyme, M., Dumaret, A., & Tomkiewicz, S. (1982). How much *could* we boost scholastic achievement and IQ scores? A direct answer from a French adoption agency. *Cognition, 12*, 165–192.

Schoenfeld, A. (1979). Explicitly heuristic training as a variable in problem solving performance. *Journal for Research in Mathematics Education, 10*, 173–187.

Schoenfeld, A., & Hermann, D. (1982). Problem perception and knowledge structure in expert and novice mathematical problem solvers. *Journal of Experimental Psychology, 8*, 484–494.

Schofield, H. (1981). Teacher effects on cognitive and affective pupil outcomes in elementary school mathematics. *Journal of Educational Psychology, 73*, 462–471.

Schriberg, L., Levin, J., McCormick, C., & Pressley, M. (1982). Learning about "famous" people via the keyword method. *Journal of Educational Psychology, 74*, 238–247.

Schuck, R. (1981). The impact of set induction on student achievement and retention. *Journal of Educational Research, 74*, 227–232.

Schulman, M., & Mekler, E. (1985). *Bringing up a moral child: A new approach for teaching your child to be kind, just, and responsible*. Reading, MA: Addison-Wesley.

Schunk, D. H. (1985). Self-efficacy and classroom learning. *Psychology in the Schools, 22*, 208–223.

Schunk, D. H., & Hanson, A. R. (1985). Peer models: Influence on children's self-efficacy and achievement. *Journal of Educational Psychology, 77*, 313–322.

Schwille, J., Porter, A., Belli, G., Floden, R., Freeman, D., Knappen, L., Kuhs, T., & Schmidt, W. (1983). Teachers as policy brokers in the content of elementary school mathematics. In L. Shulman & G. Sykes (Eds.), *Handbook of teaching and policy*. New York: Longman.

Seddon, G. (1978). The properties of Bloom's taxonomy of educational objectives for the cognitive domain. *Review of Educational Research, 48*, 303–323.

Sedlak, M., Wheeler, C., Pullin, D., & Cusick, P. (1985). High school reform and the "bargain" to learn. *Education and Urban Society, 17*, 204–214.

Sharan, S. et al. (1984). *Cooperative learning in the classroom: Research in desegregated schools*. Hillsdale, NJ: Erlbaum.

Shavelson, R. (March 1978). A model of teacher decision making. Paper presented at the annual meeting of the American Educational Research Association, Toronto.

Shavelson, R. (1983). Review of research on teachers' pedagogical judgments, plans, and decisions. *Elementary School Journal, 83*, 392–413.

Shavelson, R., & Stern, P. (1981). Research on teachers' pedagogical thoughts, judgments, decisions, and behavior. *Review of Educational Research, 51*(4), 455–498.

Sheinker, J., & Sheinker, A. (1982). *Study strategies: A metacognitive approach: Skimming, note taking, summarizing, outlining* (four handbooks). Rock Springs, WY: White Mountain Publishing Co.

Sheldon, W. (with the collaboration of S. Stevens). (1942). *The varieties of temperament: A psychology of constitutional differences*. New York: Harper.

Shepard, J. (May 1973). Lost at C. *Playboy*, 143–144; 192–196.

Shimmerlick, S., & Nolan, J. (1976). Organization and the recall of prose. *Journal of Educational Psychology, 68*, 779–786.

Shulman, L. (1983). Autonomy and obligation: The remote control of teaching. In L. Shulman and G. Sykes (Eds.), *Handbook of teaching and policy*. New York: Longman.

Shulman, L. (1986). Paradigms and research programs in the study of teaching: A contemporary perspective. In M. Wittrock (Ed.), *Third handbook of research on teaching* (pp. 3–36). New York: Macmillan.

Shulman, L., & Elstein, A. (1975). Studies of problem solving, judgment, and decision making: Implications for educational research. In F. Kerlinger (Ed.), *Review of research in education* (No. 3). Itasca, IL: Peacock.

Shulman, L., & Keislar, E. (Eds.). (1966). *Learning by discovery*. Chicago: Rand McNally.

Shulman, L., & Sykes, G. (Eds.). (1983). *Handbook of teaching and policy*. New York: Longman.

Shulman, L., & Sykes, G. (January 1986). A national board for teaching? In search for a bold standard. Paper presented for the Task Force on Teaching as a Profession, Carnegie Forum on Education and the Economy.

Sieber, R. (1979). Classmates as workmates: Informal peer activity in the elementary school. *Anthropology and Education Quarterly, 10*, 207–235.

Siegler, R. (1986). *Children's thinking*. Englewood Cliffs, NJ: Prentice-Hall.

Sigel, I. (1984). A constructivist perspective for teaching and thinking. *Educational Leadership, 42*, 18–21.

Sigel, I. (Ed.). (1985). *Parental belief systems: The psychological consequences for children*. Hillsdale, NJ: Erlbaum.

Sigel, I., Brodzinsky, D., & Golinkoff, R. (Eds.). (1981). *New directions in Piagetian theory and practice*. Hillsdale, NJ: Erlbaum.

Sigel, I., & Coop, R. (1974). Cognitive style and classroom practice. In R. Coop and K. White (Eds.), *Psychological concepts in the classroom*. New York: Harper & Row.

Silberman, C. (Ed.). (1973). *The open classroom reader*. New York: Vintage.

Silver, E. (1979). Student perceptions of relatedness among mathematical verbal problems. *Journal for Research in Mathematics Education, 10*, 195–210.

Simon, H. (1979). Information processing models of cognition. In M. Rosenzweig & L. Porter (Eds.), *Annual review of psychology*. Palo Alto, CA: Annual Reviews.

Simon, H. (1980). Problem solving and education. In D. Tuma & R. Reif (Eds.), *Problem solving and education: Issues in teaching and research*. Hillsdale, NJ: Erlbaum.

Simon, H. (1981). *The sciences of the artificial* (2nd ed.). Cambridge, MA: MIT Press.

Simon, S., Howe, L., & Kirschenbaum, H. (1972). *Values clarification: A handbook of practical strategies for teachers and students*. New York: Hart.

Simpson, E., & Gray, M. (1976). *Humanistic education: An interpretation*. Cambridge, MA: Ballenger.

Singer, H., & Donlan, D. (1982). Active comprehension: Problem solving schema with question generation for comprehension of complex short stories. *Reading Research Quarterly, 5*, 228–240.

Singer, J., & Butler, J. (1987). The Education for All Handicapped Children Act: Schools as agents of social reform. *Harvard Educational Review, 57*, 125–152.

Sirotnik, K. (1983). What you see is what you get—consistency, persistency, and mediocrity in classrooms. *Harvard Educational Review, 53*, 16–31.

Skinner, B. (1948). *Walden two*. New York: Macmillan.

Skinner, B. (1954). The science of learning and the art of teaching. *Harvard Educational Review, 24*, 86–97.

Skinner, B. (1958). Teaching machines. *Science, 128*, 969–977.

Skinner, B. (1968). *The technology of teaching*. New York: Appleton-Century-Crofts.

Skinner, B. (1971). *Beyond freedom and dignity*. New York: Knopf.

Skinner, B. (1974). *About behaviorism*. New York: Knopf.

Skinner, B. (1986). Programmed instruction revisited. *Phi Delta Kappan, 68*, 103–110.

Slavin, R. (1983). *Cooperative learning*. New York: Longman.

Slavin, R. (1984). Students motivating students to excel: Cooperative incentives, cooperative tasks, and student achievement. *Elementary School Journal, 85*, 53–64.

Slavin, R. (1985). Team-assisted individualization: A cooperative learning solution for adaptive instruction in mathematics. In M. Wang & H. Walberg (Eds.), *Adapting instruction to individual differences*. Berkeley, CA: McCutchan.

Slavin, R., & Karweit, N. (1984). Mastery learning and student teams: A factorial experiment in urban general mathematics classes. *American Educational Research Journal, 21*, 725–736.

Slavin, R., Sharan, S., Kagan, S., Lazarowitz, R., Webb, C., & Schmuck, R. (Eds.). (1985). *Learning to cooperate, cooperating to learn*. New York: Plenum.

Sloan, D. (Ed.). (1985). *The computer in education: A critical perspective*. New York: Teachers College Press.

Smith, B. (1980). Influence of solicitation pattern, type of practice example, and student response on pupil behavior, commitment to discussion and concept attainment. *Theory and Research in Social Education, 7*, 1–17.

Smith, C. (1982). *Promoting the social development of young children: Strategies and activities*. Palo Alto, CA: Mayfield.

Smith, L. (1979). Task-oriented lessons and student achievement. *Journal of Educational Research, 73*, 16–19.

Smith, L. (1985). Presentational behaviors and student achievement in mathematics. *Journal of Educational Research, 78*, 292–298.

Smith, L., & Land, M. (1981). Low-inference verbal behaviors related to teacher clarity. *Journal of Classroom Interaction, 17*, 37–42.

Smith, L., & Sanders, K. (1981). The effects on student achievement and student perception of varying structure in social studies content. *Journal of Educational Research, 74*, 333–336.

Smith, S., & Rothkopf, E. (1984). Contextual enrichment and distribution of practice in the classroom. *Cognition and Instruction, 1*, 341–358.

Snarey, J., Reimer, J., & Kohlberg, L. (1985). Development of social-moral reasoning among kibbutz adolescents: A longitudinal cross-cultural study. *Developmental Psychology, 21*, 3–17.

Snow, R. (1984). Placing children in special education: Some comments. *Educational Researcher, 13*, 12–14.

Snyder, M., Stephan, W., & Rosenfield, D. (1978). Attributional egotism. In J. Harvey, W. Ickes, & R. Kidd (Eds.), *New directions in attribution research* (Vol. 2). New York: Wiley.

Soar, R., & Soar, R. (1979). Emotional climate and management. In P. Peterson & H. Walberg (Eds.), *Research on teaching: Concepts, findings, and implications*. Berkeley, CA: McCutchan.

Solomon, D., & Kendall, A. (1979). *Children in classrooms: An investigation of person-environment interaction*. New York: Praeger.

Soule, C. (April, 1988). Collaborative intervention research: An array of findings. Paper presented at the annual meeting of the American Educational Research Association. New Orleans.

Spearman, C. (1927). *The abilities of man*. New York: Macmillan.

Spencer-Hall, D. (1976). A grounded theory of aligning actions in an elementary classroom. Doctoral dissertation, University of Missouri-Columbia.

Spiro, R. (1977). Remembering information from text: Theoretical and empirical issues concerning the "State of Schema" reconstruction hypothesis. In R. Anderson, R. Spiro, & W. Montague (Eds.), *Schooling and the acquisition of knowledge*. Hillsdale, NJ: Erlbaum.

St. John, N. (1971). Thirty-six teachers:

Their characteristics and outcomes for black and white pupils. *American Educational Research Journal, 8*, 635–648.

Staffieri, J. (1967). A study of social stereotypes of body image in children. *Journal of Personality and Social Psychology, 7*, 101–104.

Stallings, J. (1975). Implementation and child effects of teaching practices in Follow-Through classrooms. *Monographs of the Society for Research in Child Development, 40* (Nos. 7–8, Serial No. 163).

Stallings, J. (1980). Allocated academic learning time revisited, or beyond time on task. *Educational Researcher, 9*(11), 11–16.

Stallings, J., Cory, R., Fairweather, J., & Needels, M. (1977). *Early childhood education classroom evaluation*. Menlo Park, CA: SRI International.

Stallings, J., Cory, R., Fairweather, J., & Needels, M. (1978). *A study of basic reading skills taught in secondary schools*. Menlo Park, CA: SRI International.

Stanford, G. (1977). *Developing effective classroom groups: A practical guide for teachers*. New York: Hart.

Stanley, J. (1971). Reliability. In R. Thorndike (Ed.), *Educational measurement* (2nd ed.). Washington, DC: American Council on Education.

Stanley, J. (1976). The case for extreme educational acceleration of intellectually brilliant youths. *Gifted Child Quarterly, 20*, 66–75.

Stanley, J. (1978). Radical acceleration: Recent educational innovation at Johns Hopkins University. *Gifted Child Quarterly, 22*, 62–67.

Stanley, J. (1980). On educating the gifted. *Educational Researcher, 9*, 8–12.

Staub, E. (1979). *Positive social behavior and morality: Socialization and development*. New York: Academic Press.

Stein, B., & Bransford, J. (1979). Constraints on effective elaboration: Effects of precision and subject generation. *Journal of Verbal Learning and Verbal Behavior, 18*, 769–777.

Steinberg, L. (1987). Impact of puberty on family relations: Effects of pubertal status and pubertal timing. *Developmental Psychology, 23*, 451–460.

Steinmetz, S. (1977). *The cycle of violence: Assertive, aggressive, and abusive family interaction*. New York: Praeger.

Sternberg, R. (1977). *Intelligence, information processing, and analogical reasoning: The componential analysis of human abilities*. Hillsdale, NJ: Erlbaum.

Sternberg, R. (1984). What should intelligence tests test? Implications of a triarchic theory of intelligence for intelligence testing. *Educational Researcher, 13*, 5–15.

Sternberg, R. (1985). *Beyond IQ: A triarchic theory of human intelligence*. New York: Cambridge University Press.

Sternberg, R. (Ed.) (1986a). *Advances in the psychology of human intelligence* (Vol. 3). Hillsdale, NJ: Erlbaum.

Sternberg, R. (1986b). Intelligence, wisdom, and creativity: Three is better than one. *Educational Psychologist, 21*, 175–190.

Sternberg, R. (1987). Questions and answers about the nature and teaching of thinking skills. In J. Baron & R. Sternberg (Eds.), *Teaching thinking skills: Theory and practice*. New York: Freeman.

Sternberg, R. (1988). Beyond IQ testing. *National Forum, 68*(2), 8–11.

Sternberg, R., & Bhana, K. (1986). Synthesis of research on the effectiveness of intellectual skills programs: Snake-oil remedies or miracle cures? *Educational Leadership, 44*(2), 60–67.

Sternberg, R., & Wagner, R. (1986a). *Practical intelligence: Nature and origins of competence in the everyday world*. Cambridge: Cambridge University Press.

Sternberg, R., & Wagner, R. (1986b). Introduction: The nature and scope of practical intelligence. In R. Sternberg and R. Wagner (Eds.), *Practical intelligence* (pp.

1–10). Cambridge: Cambridge University Press.

Stevenson, H. (1970). Learning in children. In P. Mussen (Ed.), *Carmichael's manual of child psychology* (3rd ed., Vol. 1). New York: Wiley.

Stevenson, H., Parker, T., Wilkenson, A., Bonnevaux, B., & Gonzalez, M. (1978). Schooling, environment, and cognitive development: A cross-cultural study. *Monographs of the Society for Research in Child Development, 43* (No. 3, Serial No. 175).

Stewig, J., & Knipfel, M. (1975). Sexism in picture books: What progress? *Elementary School Journal, 75*, 151–155.

Stipek, D. (1984a). The development of achievement motivation. In R. Ames & C. Ames (Eds.), *Research on motivation in education* (Vol. 1). Orlando, FL: Academic Press.

Stipek, D. (1984b). Young children's performance expectations: Logical analysis of wishful thinking? In J. G. Nicholls (Ed.), *The development of achievement motivation*. Greenwich, CT: JAI Press.

Stipek, D. (1988). *Motivation to learn: From theory to practice*. Englewood Cliffs, NJ: Prentice-Hall.

Stipek, D., & Hoffman, J. (1980). Development of children's performance-related judgments. *Child Development, 51*, 912–914.

Stipek, D., & Sanborn, M. (1983). Preschool teachers' task-related interactions with handicapped and nonhandicapped boys and girls. A paper presented at the American Educational Research Association, Montreal, Canada.

Stipek, D., & Tannatt, L. (1984). Children's judgments of their own and their peers' academic competence. *Journal of Educational Psychology, 76*, 75–84.

Stodolsky, S., Ferguson, T., & Wimpelberg, K. (1981). The recitation persists, but what does it look like? *Journal of Curriculum Studies, 13*, 121–130.

Stout, C. (1989). Teachers' views of the emphasis on reflective teaching skills during their student teaching. *Elementary School Journal, 89*(4), 511–527.

Strike, K. (1975). The logic of discovery. *Review of Educational Research, 45*, 461–483.

Strother, D. (1984). Homework: Too much, just right, or not enough? *Phi Delta Kappan, 65*, 423–426.

Suchman, R. (1966). *Inquiry development program: Developing inquiry*. Chicago: Science Research Associates.

Sullivan, H. (1953). *The interpersonal theory of psychiatry*. New York: Norton.

Swift, J., & Gooding, C. (1983). Interaction of wait time feedback and questioning instruction on middle school science teaching. *Journal of Research in Science Teaching, 20*, 721–730.

Tadlock, D. (1978). SQ3R—why it works, based on information processing theory. *Journal of Reading, 22*, 110–112.

Tanner, J. (1970). Physical growth. In P. Mussen (Ed.), *Carmichael's manual of child psychology* (3rd ed., Vol. 1). New York: Wiley.

Tanner, J. (1973). Growing up. *Scientific American, 229*(3), 35–43.

Tanner, L. (1978). *Classroom discipline for effective teaching and learning*. New York: Holt, Rinehart and Winston.

Taylor, B. (1982). Text structure and children's comprehension and memory for expository material. *Journal of Educational Psychology, 70*, 323–340.

Taylor, R. (1980). *The computer in the school: Tutor, tool, tutee*. New York: Teachers College Press.

Tenbrink, T. (1974). *Evaluation: A practical guide for teachers*. New York: McGraw-Hill.

Tennyson, R., & Park, O. (1980). The teaching of concepts: A review of instructional design research literature. *Review of Educational Research, 50*, 55–70.

Thomas, J. (1970). *Tutoring strategies and effectiveness: A comparison of elementary age tutors and college tutors*. Doctoral dissertation, University of Texas at Austin.

Thompson, M., Brassell, W., Persons, S., Tucker, R., & Rollins, H. (1974). Contingency management in the schools: How often and how well does it work? *American Educational Research Journal, 11*, 19–28.

Thompson, R., White, K., & Morgan, D. (1982). Teacher-student interaction patterns in classrooms with mainstreamed mildly handicapped students. *American Educational Research Journal, 19*, 220–236.

Thornburg, H. (1982). *Development in adolescence* (2nd ed.). Monterey: Brooks/Cole.

Thorndike, E. (1913). *The psychology of learning: Educational psychology* (Vol. 2). New York: Teachers College Press.

Thorndike, E. (1924). Mental discipline in high school studies. *Journal of Educational Psychology, 15*, 1–22, 83–98.

Thorndike, R., & Hagen, E. (1969). *Measurement and evaluation in psychology and education* (3rd ed.). New York: Wiley.

Thorndike, R., & Hagen, E. (1977). *Measurement and evaluation in psychology and education* (4th ed.). New York: Wiley.

Thorndyke, P. (1977). Cognitive structures in comprehension and memory of narrative discourse. *Cognitive Psychology, 9*, 77–110.

Thurstone, L. (1938). *Primary mental abilities*. Chicago: University of Chicago Press.

Tierney, R., & Cunningham, J. (1984). Research on teaching reading comprehension. In P. Pearson, M. Camil, R. Barr, & P. Mosenthal (Eds.), *Handbook of Reading Research*. New York: Longman.

Tikunoff, W., Berliner, D., & Rist, R. (1975). An ethnographic study of the forty classrooms of the Beginning Teacher Evaluation Study known sample. Technical Report No. 75-10-5. San Francisco: Far West Laboratory.

Tobias, S., & Ingber, T. (1976). Achievement-treatment interactions in programmed instruction. *Journal of Educational Psychology, 68*, 43–47.

Tobin, K. (1980). The effect of an extended teacher wait-time on science achievement. *Journal of Research in Science Teaching, 17*, 469–475.

Tobin, K. (1987). The role of wait time in higher cognitive level learning. *Review of Educational Research, 57*, 69–95.

Tobin, K., & Capie, W. (1982). Relationships between classroom process variables and middle-school science achievement. *Journal of Educational Psychology, 74*, 441–454.

Tollefson, N., Tracy, D., Johnsen, E., Farmer, W., & Buenning, M. (1984). Goal setting and personal responsibility for LD adolescents. *Psychology in the Schools, 21*, 224–233.

Tom, D., Cooper, H., & McGraw, M. (1984). Influences of student background and teacher authoritarianism on teacher expectation. *Journal of Educational Psychology, 76*, 259–265.

Torrance, E. (1962). *Guiding creative talent*. Englewood Cliffs, NJ: Prentice-Hall.

Torrance, E. (1966). *Torrance Tests of Creative Thinking: Norms-technical manual.* Princeton, NJ: Personnel Press.

Torrance, E. (1972). Predictive validity of the Torrance Tests of Creative Thinking. *Journal of Creative Behavior, 6*, 236–252.

Torrance, E. (1973). Non-test indicates of creative talent among disadvantaged children. *Gifted Child Quarterly,17*(1), 3–9.

Torrance, E. (1975). Creativity research in education: Still alive. In I. Taylor & J. Getzels (Eds.), *Perspectives in creativity*. Chicago: Aldine.

Torrance, E. (1977). Discovery and nurturance of giftedness in the culturally different. Reston, VA: Council for Exceptional Children.

Torrance, E. (1986). Teaching creative and gifted learners. In M. Wittrock (Ed.), *Handbook of research on teaching* (3rd ed.). New York: Macmillan.

Torrance, E., Tan, C., & Allman, T. (1970).

Verbal originality and teacher behavior: A predictive validity study. *Journal of Teacher Education, 21*, 335–341.

Towler, J., & Wheatley, G. (1971). Conservation concepts in college students: A replication and critique. *Journal of Genetic Psychology, 118*, 265–270.

Trabasso, T., & Bower, G. (1968). *Attention in learning*. New York: Wiley.

Trachtenberg, D. (1974). Student tasks in text material: What cognitive skills do they tap? *Peabody Journal of Education, 52*, 54–57.

Treffinger, D. (1982). Gifted students, regular classrooms: Sixty ingredients for a better blend. *Elementary School Journal, 82*, 267–283.

Tudor, I. (1986). Advance organizers as adjuncts to L2 reading comprehension. *Journal of Research in Reading, 9*, 103–115.

Tulving, E. (1985). How many memory systems are there? *American Psychologist, 40*, 385–398.

Tulving, E., & Thomson, D. (1973). Encoding specificity and retrieval processes in episodic memory. *Psychological Review, 80*, 352–373.

Tuma, D., & Reif, R. (Eds.). (1980). *Problem solving and education: Issues in teaching and research*. Hillsdale, NJ: Erlbaum.

Tversky, A., & Kahneman, D. (1974). Judgment under uncertainty, heuristics and biases. *Science, 195*, 1124–1134.

Tversky, B. (1973). Encoding processes in recognition and recall. *Cognitive Psychology, 5*, 275–287.

Tyler, L. (1965). *The psychology of human differences* (3rd ed.). New York: Appleton.

Underwood, B. (1961). Ten years of massed practice on distributed practice. *Psychological Review, 68*, 229–247.

Underwood, B. (1983). *Attributes of memory*. Glenview, IL: Scott, Foresman.

Underwood, B., Kapelak, S., & Malmi, R. (1976). The spacing effect: Additions to the theoretical and empirical puzzles. *Memory and Cognition, 4*, 391–400.

Van Patten, J., Chao, C., & Reigeluth, C. (1986). A review of strategies for sequencing and synthesizing instruction. *Review of Educational Research, 56*, 437–471.

Van Rossum, E., & Schenk, S. (1984). The relationship between learning conception, study strategy and learning outcome. *British Journal of Educational Psychology, 54*, 73–83.

Vernon, P. (1981). Level I and Level II: A review. *Educational Psychologist, 16*, 45–64.

Vinsonhaler, J., Weinshank, A., Wagner, C., & Polin, R. (1983). Diagnosing children with educational problems: Characteristics of reading and learning disabilities specialists, and classroom teachers. *Reading Research Quarterly, 18*, 134–164.

Vosniadou, S., & Brewer, W. (1987). Theories of knowledge restructuring in development. *Review of Educational Research, 57*, 51–67.

Voss, J., & Bisanz, G. (1982). Models and methods used in the study of prose comprehension and learning. In S. Black & B. Britton (Eds.), *Expository text*. Hillsdale, NJ: Erlbaum.

Voth, R. (1975). On lecturing. *Social Studies, 66*, 247–248.

Voyat, G. (1982). *Piaget systematized*. Hillsdale, NJ: Erlbaum.

Vygotsky, L. (1962). *Thought and language*. Cambridge, MA: MIT Press.

Vygotsky, L. (1978). *Mind in society: The development of higher psychological processes* (Edited by M. Cole, V. John-Steiner, S. Scribner, & E. Souberman). Cambridge: Harvard University Press.

Waber, D., Carlson, D., Mann, M., Merola, J., & Moylan, P. (1984). SES-related aspects of neuropsychological performance. *Child Development, 55*, 1878–1886.

Wadsworth, B. (1978). *Piaget for the classroom teacher*. New York: Longman.

Walberg, H. (1985). Instructional theories

and research evidence. In M. Wang & H. Walberg (Eds.), *Adapting instruction to individual differences*. Berkeley, CA: McCutchan.

Walberg, H., Schiller, D., & Haertel, G. (1979). The quiet revolution in educational research. *Phi Delta Kappan, 61*, 179–183.

Waldrop, M. (1984). The necessity of knowledge. *Science, 223*, 1279–1282.

Walker, L. (1980). Cognitive and perspective-taking prerequisites for moral development. *Child Development, 51*, 131–139.

Walker, L. (1982). The sequentiality of Kohlberg's stages of moral development. *Child Development, 53*, 1330–1336.

Walker, L. (1983). Sources of cognitive conflict for stage transition in moral development. *Developmental Psychology, 19*, 103–110.

Walker, L., De Vries, B., & Trevethan, S. (1987). Moral stages and moral orientations in real-life and hypothetical dilemmas. *Child Development, 58*, 842–858.

Wallach, M. (1970). Creativity. In P. Mussen (Ed.), *Carmichael's manual of child psychology* (3rd ed., Vol. 1). New York: Wiley.

Wallach, M., & Kogan, N. (1965). *Modes of thinking in young children*. New York: Holt, Rinehart and Winston.

Wallas, G. (1921). *The art of thought*. New York: Harcourt, Brace, and World.

Walters, J., & Gardner, H. (1986). The theory of multiple intelligence: Some issues and answers. In R. Sternberg and R. Wagner (Eds.) *Practical intelligence* (pp. 163–182). Cambridge: Cambridge University Press.

Wang, M. (1973). *Teacher's manual for the exploratory learning component of the LRDC individualized instructional program for the early learning grades*. Pittsburgh: University of Pittsburgh Learning Research and Development Center.

Wang, M., Anderson, K., & Bram, P. (1985). *Toward an empirical data base on mainstreaming: A research synthesis of program implementation and effects*. Pittsburgh: Learning Research and Development Center, University of Pittsburgh.

Wang, M., & Lindvall, C. (1984). Individual differences in school learning environments: Theory, research, and design. In E. Gordon (Ed.), *Review of research in education* (Vol. 11). Washington, D.C.: American Educational Research Association.

Wang, M., Reynolds, M., & Walberg, H. (1987). *Handbook of special education: Research in practice* (Vol. 1). Oxford: Pergamon Press.

Wang, M., & Walberg, H. (Eds.). (1985). *Adapting instruction to individual differences*. Berkeley, CA: McCutchan.

Wapner, J., & Conner, K. (1986). The role of defensiveness in cognitive impulsivity. *Child Development, 57*, 1370–1374.

Ware, B. (1978). What rewards do students want? *Phi Delta Kappan, 59*, 355–356.

Waterman, A. (1982). Identity development from adolescence to adulthood: An extension of theory and a review of research. *Developmental Psychology, 18*, 341–358.

Watson, J. (1914). *Behavior*. New York: Holt.

Watson, J. (1925). *Behaviorism*. Chicago: University of Chicago Press.

Watson, J., & Rayner, R. (1920). Conditioned emotional reactions. *Journal of Experimental Psychology, 3*, 1–14.

Webb, N. (1984). Microcomputer learning in small groups: Cognitive requirements and group processes. *Journal of Educational Psychology, 76*, 1076–1088.

Weil, M., & Joyce, B. (1978). *Information processing models of teaching*.. Englewood Cliffs, NJ: Prentice-Hall.

Weiner, B. (1966). The role of success and failure in the learning of easy and complex tasks. *Journal of Personality and Social Psychology, 3*, 339–343.

Weiner, B. (1972). *Theories of motivation: From mechanism to cognition*. Chicago: Rand McNally.

Weiner, B. (1984). Principles for a theory

of student motivation and their application within an attributional framework. In R. Ames & C. Ames (Ed.), *Research on motivation in education* (Vol. 1). Orlando, FL: Academic Press.

Weiner, B. (1986). *An attributional theory of motivation and emotion.* New York: Springer-Verlag.

Weiner, B., Anderson, A., & Prawat, R. (1982). Affective experience in the classroom. Manuscript. University of California, Los Angeles.

Weinshank, A. (1978). *The relationship between diagnosis and remediation in reading: A pilot study*. Research Series No. 37. East Lansing: Institute for Research on Teaching, College of Education, Michigan State University.

Weinshank, A. (1982). The reliability of diagnostic and remedial decisions of reading specialists. *Journal of Reading Behavior, 14*, 33–50.

Weinstein, C. (1977). Modifying student behavior in an open classroom through changes in the physical design. *American Educational Research Journal, 14*, 249–262.

Weinstein, C. (1979). The physical environment of the school: A review of the research. *Review of Educational Research, 49*, 577–610.

Weinstein, C. (1982). Training students to use elaboration learning strategies. *Contemporary Educational Psychology, 7*, 301–311.

Weinstein, C., & Mayer, R. (1986). The teaching of learning strategies. In M. Wittrock (Ed.) *Handbook of research on teaching* (3rd ed., pp. 315–327). New York: Macmillan.

Weinstein, C., & Underwood, V. (1983). Learning strategies: The *how* of learning. In J. Segal, S. Chipman, & R. Glaser (Eds.). *Relating instruction to basic research*. Hillsdale, NJ: Erlbaum.

Weinstein, R. (1976). Reading group membership in first grade: Teacher behaviors and pupil experience over time. *Journal of Educational Psychology, 68*, 103–116.

Weinstein, R. (April 1988). An expectancy model for improving the motivational climate of classrooms and schools. Paper presented at the annual meeting of the American Educational Research Association, New Orleans.

Weisz, J., & Cameron, A. (1985). Individual differences in students' sense of control. In C. Ames & R. Ames (Eds.), *Research on motivation in education, Volume 2: The classroom milieu* (pp. 93–140). Orlando, FL: Academic Press.

Wertsch, J. (1985). *Vygotsky and the social formation of mind.* Cambridge: Harvard University Press.

White, B. (1975). *The first three years of life*. Englewood Cliffs, NJ: Prentice-Hall.

White, B., & Watts, J. (1973). *Experience and environment: Major influences on the development of the young child.* Englewood Cliffs, NJ: Prentice-Hall.

White, C., Bushnell, N., & Regnemer, J. (1978). Moral development in Bahamian school children: A 3-year examination of Kohlberg's stages of moral development. *Developmental Psychology, 14*, 58–65.

White, R., & Tisher, R. (1986). Research on natural sciences. In M. Wittrock (Ed.), *Handbook of research on teaching* (3rd ed.). New York: Macmillan.

Whitehurst, G. (1977). Comprehension, selective imitation, and the CIP hypothesis. *Journal of Experimental Child Psychology, 23*, 23–38.

Whitley, B. E., & Frieze, I. H. (1985). Children's causal attributions for success and failure in achievement settings: A meta-analysis. *Journal of Educational Psychology, 77*, 608–616.

Whitmore, J. (1982). Recognizing and developing hidden giftedness. *Elementary School Journal, 82*, 274–283.

Whitmore, J., & Maker, C. (1985). *Intellectual giftedness in disabled persons*. Rockville, MD: Aspen Systems Corporation.

Whorf, B. (1956). *Language, thought, and reality: Selected writings*. Cambridge, MA: Technology Press.

Wickelgren, W. (1981). Human learning and memory. In M. Rosenzweig & L. Porter (Eds.), *Annual review of psychology*. Palo Alto, CA: Annual Reviews.

Wilen, W., & Clegg, A. (1986). Effective questions and questioning: A research review. *Theory and Research in Social Education, 14*, 153–161.

Wilhite, S. (1983). Prepassage questions: The influence of structural importance. *Journal of Educational Psychology, 75*, 234–244.

Wilkinson, L., & Marrett, C. (Eds.). (1985). *Gender influences in classroom interaction*. Orlando, FL: Academic Press.

Will, M. (1986). *Educating students with learning problems: A shared responsibility*. Washington, DC: Office of Special Education and Rehabilitation Services, U.S. Department of Education.

Willerman, L. (1979). *The psychology of individual and group differences*. San Francisco: Freeman.

Willis, S. (1972). Formation of teachers' expectations of students' academic performance. Doctoral dissertation, Department of Educational Psychology, University of Texas at Austin.

Wineburg, S. (1988). The self-fulfillment of the self-fulfilling prophecy: A critical appraisal. *Educational Researcher, 16*(9), 28–37.

Winne, P. (1979). Experiments relating teachers' use of higher cognitive questions to student achievement. *Review of Educational Research, 49*, 13–50.

Winograd, T. (1975). Frame representations and the declarative/procedural controversy. In B. Bobrow & A. Collins (Eds.), *Representation and understanding*. New York: Academic Press.

Witkin, H., Dyk, R., Faterson, H., Goodenough, D., & Karp, S. (1962). *Psychological differentiation*. New York: Wiley.

Witkin, H., Moore, C., Goodenough, D., & Cox, P. (1977). Field-dependent and field-independent cognitive styles and their educational implications. *Review of Educational Research, 47*, 1–64.

Wittig, M., & Petersen, A. (Eds.). (1979). *Sex-related differences in cognitive functioning: Developmental issues*. New York: Academic Press.

Wittrock, M. (1974). Learning as a generative process. *Educational Psychologist, 11*, 87–95.

Wittrock, M. (Ed.). (1977). *Learning and instruction*. Berkeley, CA: McCutchan.

Wittrock, M. (1978). Education and the cognitive processes of the brain. In J. Chall & A. Mirsky (Eds.), *Education and the brain*. The seventy-seventh yearbook of the National Society for the Study of Education, Part II. Chicago: University of Chicago Press.

Wittrock, M. (1986). Students' thought processes. In M. Wittrock (Ed.), *Third handbook of research on teaching* (pp. 297–314). New York: Macmillan.

Wittrock, M., Marks, C., & Doctorow, M. (1975). Reading as a generative process. *Journal of Educational Psychology, 67*, 484–489.

Wixson, K. (1984). Level of importance of postquestions and children's learning from text. *American Educational Research Journal, 21*, 419–433.

Wixson, K., Bosky, A., Yochum, M., & Alvermann, D. (1984). An interview for assessing student's perceptions of classroom reading tasks. *Reading Teacher, 37*, 346–352.

Wong, B., & Jones, W. (1982). Increasing metacomprehension in learning disabled and normally achieving students through self-questioning training. *Learning Disability Quarterly, 5*, 228–240.

Woodson, M. (1974). Seven aspects of teaching concepts. *Journal of Educational Psychology, 66*, 184–188.

Wright, C., & Nuthall, G. (1970). Relationships between teacher behaviors and pupil achievement in three experimental elementary science lessons. *American Educational Research Journal, 7*, 477–491.

Wright, I. (1978). Moral reasoning and conduct of selected elementary school students. *Journal of Moral Education, 7*, 199–205.

Wyckoff, W. (1973). The effect of stimulus variation on learning from lecture. *Journal of Experimental Education, 41*, 85–90.

Yando, R., Seitz, V., & Zigler, E. (1979). *Intellectual and personality characteristics of children: Social-class and ethnic-group differences*. Hillsdale, NJ: Erlbaum.

Yinger, R. (1977). A study of teacher planning: Description and theory development using ethnographies and information processing methods. Dissertation, Michigan State University, East Lansing.

Yoshida, R., Fenton, K., Maxwell, J., & Kaufman, M. (1978). Group decision making in the planning team process: Myth or reality? *Journal of School Psychology, 16*, 237–244.

Ysseldyke, J. (1987). Classification of handicapped students. In M. Wang, M. Reynolds, & H. Walberg (Eds.), *Handbook of special education: Research in practice* (Vol. 1, pp. 253–271). Oxford; Pergamon Press.

Ysseldyke, J., Algozzine, B., & Allen, D. (1981). Participation of regular education teachers in special education team decision making. A naturalistic investigation. *Elementary School Journal, 82*, 160–165.

Zigler, E., & Valentine, J. (Eds.). (1979). *Project Head Start: A legacy of the war on poverty*. New York: Free Press.

Zivin, G. (1979). *The development of self-regulation through private speech*. New York: Wiley.

Zumwalt, K. (Ed.). (1986). *Improving teaching*. (1986 ASCD Yearbook). Alexandria, VA: Association for Supervision and Curriculum Development.

INDEX